WEST ACADEMIC PUBLISHING'S EMERITUS ADVISORY BOARD

JESSE H. CHOPER
Professor of Law and Dean Emeritus
University of California, Berkeley

YALE KAMISAR
Professor of Law Emeritus, University of San Diego
Professor of Law Emeritus, University of Michigan

MARY KAY KANE
Professor of Law, Chancellor and Dean Emeritus
University of California, Hastings College of the Law

LARRY D. KRAMER
President, William and Flora Hewlett Foundation

JAMES J. WHITE
Robert A. Sullivan Emeritus Professor of Law
University of Michigan

WEST ACADEMIC PUBLISHING'S LAW SCHOOL ADVISORY BOARD

JOSHUA DRESSLER
Distinguished University Professor Emeritus
Michael E. Moritz College of Law, The Ohio State University

MEREDITH J. DUNCAN
Professor of Law
University of Houston Law Center

RENÉE McDONALD HUTCHINS
Dean and Joseph L. Rauh, Jr. Chair of Public Interest Law
University of the District of Columbia David A. Clarke School of Law

RENEE KNAKE JEFFERSON
Joanne and Larry Doherty Chair in Legal Ethics &
Professor of Law, University of Houston Law Center

ORIN S. KERR
Professor of Law
University of California, Berkeley

JONATHAN R. MACEY
Professor of Law,
Yale Law School

DEBORAH JONES MERRITT
Distinguished University Professor,
John Deaver Drinko/Baker & Hostetler Chair in Law
Michael E. Moritz College of Law, The Ohio State University

ARTHUR R. MILLER
University Professor, New York University
Formerly Bruce Bromley Professor of Law, Harvard University

GRANT S. NELSON
Professor of Law Emeritus, Pepperdine University
Professor of Law Emeritus, University of California, Los Angeles

A. BENJAMIN SPENCER
Dean & Chancellor Professor of Law
William & Mary Law School

CRITICAL JUSTICE
SYSTEMIC ADVOCACY IN LAW AND SOCIETY

■ ■ ■

Francisco Valdes
University of Miami School of Law

Steven W. Bender
Seattle University School of Law

Jennifer J. Hill

AMERICAN CASEBOOK SERIES®

The publisher is not engaged in rendering legal or other professional advice, and this publication is not a substitute for the advice of an attorney. If you require legal or other expert advice, you should seek the services of a competent attorney or other professional.

American Casebook Series is a trademark registered in the U.S. Patent and Trademark Office.

© 2021 LEG, Inc. d/b/a West Academic
    444 Cedar Street, Suite 700
    St. Paul, MN 55101
    1-877-888-1330

West, West Academic Publishing, and West Academic are trademarks of West Publishing Corporation, used under license.

Printed in the United States of America

ISBN: 978-1-62810-204-8

ACKNOWLEDGMENTS

First and foremost I thank my co-editors, Steve Bender and Jennifer Hill, for nursing this book to completion with joy and diligence, and equally so the many contributors who worked actively and so creatively on this project, as a team, during varied times in the ten-plus years of its development, including: Sumi Cho, Christine Zuni-Cruz, Margaret Montoya, Athena Mutua, Ibrahim Gassama, Carmen Gonzalez, Marc Tizoc-González, Gil Gott, Tayyab Mahmud, Ileana Porras, Charles Pouncy, and Sheila Vélez Martínez. I thank also the many thoughtful participants at workshops and other presentations over the years, and the careful readers who provided rigorous feedback along the way, each helping enormously to shape and sharpen the book, including, among others too numerous to name here, Natsu Saito, Aníbal Rosario-Lebrón, Bill Quigley, and Brenda Williams. In addition, I thank deeply the many scholars and activists whose labors pioneered and informed this book, whether or not we were able to include them in it, and to the LatCrit Board and community for their steady commitment to this project over the years. I extend a special thanks to Marysabel Merino, my assistant, for years of generous help and attention to detail, and to Anthony Varona for his substantive feedback over the years as a friend and colleague, and, more recently, for his enthusiastic support as Dean of Miami Law. And finally I thank many friends around the country, colleagues at Miami, and especially my family—Joe, Ceci, and Juan—for their unbounded kindness, love, care, and support during the difficult times that I had to confront as we worked to complete this book with integrity and quality. Despite our earnest efforts, any remaining shortcomings or errors I share with Steve and Jennifer.

Francisco Valdes, Miami FL, November 2020

My gratitude is especially for co-editors Frank and Jennifer, who taught me more than I expected I needed to learn. My research assistant Angel Ramirez worked diligently on permissions, and Ariana Headrick on a variety of other projects, and my dean, Annette Clark, supported the book throughout. My librarian Kerry Fitz-Gerald was consistently and constantly on-the-job, cheerfully running down sources. Our editors at West, starting with Junior Torres and finishing years later with Megan Putler, were supportive and patient through the many twists and turns of developing this innovative and important text. It's been a long journey to get to this point, and I look forward to sharing the text with students in the critical classrooms that will bring theory to life.

Steven Bender, Seattle WA, November 2020

ACKNOWLEDGMENTS

Heartfelt thanks to co-editors Steve and Frank, who have been generous spirits and daring partners throughout. Many individuals have shared insights through conversations, workshops, and the inspiring example of their work, including but not limited to Charu Al-Sahli, Fran Ansley, Ana Avendaño, Carrie Bettinger López, Nejla Calvo, Ken Casebeer, Natalie Castellanos, Donna Coker, Gracia Cuzzi, Evian White de Leon, Dorcas Gilmore, Juan Gomez, Mary Gundrum, Miriam Harmatz, Ellen Hemley, A.J. Hernandez, Jon Hiatt, Chaumtoli Huq, Meena Jagannath, Allison Kent, Mark Kessler, Romy Lerner, Oscar Londoño, Viviana Bonilla López, Marnie Mahoney, Peggy Maisel, Liam McGivern, Roseanne Murphy, Charlotte Noss, Liz O'Connor, Aidil Oscariz, Spring Miller, Nneoma Nwogu, Melba Pearson, Anne Recinos, Kelly Fay Rodríguez, J.J. Rosenbaum, Kathleen Rubenstein, Rebecca Sharpless, Andrew Stanton, Kele Stewart, Lane Windham, and Mary Yanik. University of Miami research librarian Robin Schard shared resources endlessly, and Marysabel Merino coordinated our efforts with patience and skill. Special thanks—forever—to Susan Butler Plum, guiding light of the Skadden Fellowship Foundation; Mia Sussman, who welcomed and connected us to the vibrant network at Equal Justice Works; and Sarah Zearfoss, extraordinary friend, attorney, and Michigan Law School leader. New friends in the LatCrit circle have shared wisdom and laughs to move this project to completion, and old friends from the worlds of labor and community organizing have made it infinitely stronger. Deepest thanks for the boundless support of family—Kate, Jeff, Michele, Jeffrey, Joan, Tom, Margaret, Bill, Andy, Elisa, Evie, Paul, and Billie Joan.

Jennifer Hill, Miami FL, November 2020

COPYRIGHT ACKNOWLEDGMENTS

List of Sources Used with Permission

Sparky Abraham, How Student Debt Is Worsening Gender and Racial Injustice, Current Affairs (June 26, 2018)—Reprinted with permission

Muneer I. Ahmad, Resisting Guantánamo: Rights at the Brink of Dehumanization, 103 Nw. U. L. Rev. 1683 (2009)—Reprinted with permission

Muneer I. Ahmad, The Ethics of Narrative, 11 Am. U. J. Gender Soc. Pol'y & L. 117 (2002)—Reprinted with permission

Raquel Aldana, The Indispensable Ones: A Story of Mining Resistance from La Puya, adapted from the volume From Extraction to Emancipation: Development Reimagined (Raquel Aldana and Steven W. Bender eds. 2018)—Reprinted with permission

Deleso Alford, Critical Race Feminist Bioethics: Telling Stories in Law School and Medical School in Pursuit of "Cultural Competency," 72 Alb. L. Rev. 961 (2009)—Reprinted with permission

Alicia Alvarez, Lawyers, Organizers, and Workers: Collaboration and Conflict in Worker Cooperative Development, 24 Geo. J. on Poverty L. & Pol'y 353 (2017)—Reprinted with permission

Kate Andrias, Confronting Power in Public Law, 130 Harv. L. Rev. Forum 1 (2016)—Reprinted with permission

Antony Anghie, LatCrit and TWAIL, 42 Cal. W. Int'l L.J. 311 (2012)—Reprinted with permission

Frances Ansley, Doing Policy from Below: Worker Solidarity and the Prospects for Immigration Reform, 41 Cornell Int'l L.J. 101 (2008)—Reprinted with permission

Fran Ansley and Anne Lewis, Going South, Coming North: Migrant and Union Organizing in Morristown, Tennessee, Southern Spaces (May 19, 2011)—Reprinted with permission

Sameer M. Ashar, Deep Critique and Democratic Lawyering in Clinical Practice, 104 Cal. L. Rev. 201 (2016)—Reprinted with permission

Ian Ayres, Fair Driving: Gender and Race Discrimination in Retail Car Negotiations, 104 Harv. L. Rev. 817 (1991)—Reprinted with permission

Shalanda H. Baker, Adaptive Law in the Anthropocene, 90 Chi.-Kent L. Rev. 563 (2015)—Reprinted with permission

Rev. Dr. William J. Barber II, Research is Vital to the Moral Integrity of Social Movements, Economic Policy Institute, Working Economics Blog (Apr. 4, 2019)—Reprinted with permission

Derrick A. Bell, Jr., Brown v. Board of Education and the Interest-Convergence Dilemma, 93 Harv. L. Rev. 518 (1980)—Reprinted with permission

Derrick A. Bell, Jr., Serving Two Masters: Integration Ideals and Client Interests in School Desegregation Litigation, 85 Yale L.J. 470 (1976)—Reprinted with permission

Gary Bellow, Steady Work: A Practitioner's Reflections on Political Lawyering, 31 Harv. C.R.-C.L. L. Rev. 297 (1996)—Reprinted with permission

Rabia Belt, "And Then Comes Life": The Intersection of Race, Poverty, and Disability in HBO's The Wire, 13 Rutgers Race & L. Rev. 1 (2012)—Reprinted with permission

Rabia Belt, Disability: The Last Marriage Equality Frontier, Stanford Public Law Working Paper No. 2653117 (Aug. 29, 2015)—Reprinted with permission

Elizabeth Berenguer, Lucy Jewel & Teri A. McMurtry-Chubb, Gut Renovations: Using Critical and Comparative Rhetoric to Remodel How the Law Addresses Privilege and Power, 23 Harv. Lat. L. Rev. 205 (2020)—Reprinted with permission

Caroline Bettinger-Lopez, Davida Finger, Meetali Jain, JoNel Newman, Sarah Paoletti & Deborah M. Weissman, Redefining Human Rights Lawyering Through the Lens of Critical Theory: Lessons for Pedagogy and Practice, 18 Geo. J. on Poverty L. & Pol'y 337 (2011).

Gary Blasi, Framing Access to Justice: Beyond Perceived Justice for Individuals, 42 Loy. L.A. L. Rev. 913 (2009)—Reprinted with permission

Michael Boucai, Glorious Precedents: When Gay Marriage Was Radical, 27 Yale J. of L. & Human. 1 (2015)—Reprinted with permission

Maurice BP-Weeks and Liz Perlman, Bargaining for the Common Good as Racial Justice, The Forge: Organizing Strategy and Practice (Mar. 31, 2020)—Reprinted with permission

Cheryl Bratt, Top-Down or From the Ground?: A Practical Perspective on Reforming the Field of Children and the Law, 127 Yale L.J. Forum 917 (2018)—Reprinted with permission

Kitty Calavita, Collisions at the Intersection of Gender, Race, and Class: Enforcing the Chinese Exclusion Laws, 40 Law & Soc'y Rev. 249 (2006)—Reprinted with permission

COPYRIGHT ACKNOWLEDGMENTS

John O. Calmore, A Call to Context: The Professional Challenges of Cause Lawyering at the Intersection of Race, Space, and Poverty, 67 Fordham L. Rev. 1927 (1999)—Reprinted with permission

Nejla Calvo, Fellowship Application, University of Miami School of Law—Reprinted with permission

Devon W. Carbado, Straight Out of the Closet, 15 Berkeley Women's L.J. 76 (2000)—Reprinted with permission

Susan D. Carle, Re-Valuing Lawyering for Middle-Income Clients, 70 Fordham L. Rev. 719 (2001)—Reprinted with permission

Kristen A. Carpenter & Eli Wald, Lawyering for Groups: The Case of American Indian Tribal Attorneys, 81 Fordham L. Rev. 3085 (2013)—Reprinted with permission

Robert S. Chang, The End of Innocence or Politics After the Fall of the Essential Subject, 45 Am. U.L. Rev. 687 (1996)—Reprinted with permission

Robert S. Chang and Jerome M. Culp, Jr. Business as Usual? *Brown* and the Continuing Conundrum of Race in America, 2004 U. Ill. L. Rev. 1181 (2004)—Reprinted with permission

Anthony R. Chase, Race, Culture, and Contract Law: From the Cottonfield to the Courtroom, 28 Conn. L. Rev. 1 (1995)—Reprinted with permission

Erwin Chemerinsky, The Segregation and Resegregation of American Public Education: The Courts' Role, 81 N.C. L. Rev. 1597 (2003)—Reprinted with permission

B. S. Chimni, International Institutions Today: An Imperial Global State in the Making, 15 Eur. J. Int'l L. 1 (2004)—Reprinted with permission

Luke W. Cole and Caroline Farrell, Structural Racism, Structural Pollution and the Need for a New Paradigm, 20 Wash. U. J.L. & Pol'y 265 (2006)—Reprinted with permission

Ruth Colker, Anti-Subordination Above All: Sex, Race, and Equal Protection, 61 N.Y.U. L. Rev. 1003 (1986)—Reprinted with permission

Marion Crain, The Transformation of the Professional Workforce, 79 Chi.-Kent L. Rev. 543 (2004)—Reprinted with permission

Charlie Cray, The Lewis Powell Memo: Corporate Blueprint to Dominate Democracy, Greenpeace Blog (Aug. 23, 2011)—Reprinted with permission

Kimberlé Williams Crenshaw, Race, Reform, and Retrenchment: Transformation and Legitimation in Antidiscrimination Law, 101 Harv. L. Rev. 1331 (1988)—Reprinted with permission

Scott L. Cummings, How Lawyers Manage Intragroup Dissent, 89 Chi.-Kent L. Rev. 547 (2014)—Reprinted with permission

Scott L. Cummings, Law in the Labor Movement's Challenge to Wal-Mart: A Case Study of the Inglewood Site Fight, 95 Cal. L. Rev. 1927 (2007)—Reprinted with permission

Nazly Sobhi Damasio, Global Labor Justice/International Labor Rights Forum, Photo—Used with permission

Adrienne D. Davis, The Private Law of Race and Sex: An Antebellum Perspective, 51 Stan. L. Rev. 221 (1999)—Reprinted with permission

Peggy C. Davis, Law as Microaggressions, 98 Yale L.J. 1559 (1989)—Reprinted with permission

Richard Delgado and Jean Stefancic, Images of the Outsider in American Law and Culture: Can Free Expression Remedy Systemic Social Ills?, 77 Cornell L. Rev. 1258 (1992)—Reprinted with permission

Nancy Ehrenreich, The Colonization of the Womb, 43 Duke L.J. 492 (1993)—Reprinted with permission

Nancy Ehrenreich and Beth Lyon, The Global Politics Of Food: A Critical Overview, 43 U. Miami Inter-Am. L. Rev. 1 (2011)—Reprinted with permission

Antonia Eliason, With No Deliberate Speed: The Segregation of Roma Children in Europe, 27 Duke J. Comp. & Int'l L. 191 (2017)—Reprinted with permission

Sally Engle Merry, Law and Colonialism, 25 Law & Soc'y Rev. 889 (1991)—Reprinted with permission

Ruth Fassinger and Susan Morrow, Toward Best Practices in Quantitative, Qualitative, and Mixed-Method Research: A Social Justice Perspective, 5 J. for Soc. Action in Counseling and Psych. 69, https://openjournals.bsu.edu (2013)—Reprinted with permission

Mary Anne Franks, Where the Law Lies: Constitutional Fictions and Their Discontents, in Law and Lies: Deceptions and Truth-Telling in the American Legal System (Austin Sarat ed. 2015)—Reprinted with permission

Marc Galanter, Why the "Haves" Come Out Ahead: Speculations on the Limits of Legal Change, 9 Law & Soc'y Rev. 95 (1974)—Reprinted with permission

César Cuauhtémoc García Hernández, Naturalizing Immigration Imprisonment, 103 Cal. L. Rev. 1449 (2015)—Reprinted with permission

Heather Gehlert, Ending The School-To-Prison Pipeline: A Case Study of Community-Led Disciplinary Reform in Kern County, Berkeley Media Studies Group (June 2018)—Reprinted with permission

Martin Gilens and Benjamin I. Page, Testing Theories of American Politics: Elites, Interest Groups, and Average Citizens, 12 Perspectives on Politics 564 (Sept. 2014)—Reprinted with permission

Carmen Gonzalez, Bridging the North-South Divide: International Environmental Law in the Anthropocene, 32 Pace Envtl. L. Rev. 407 (2015)—Reprinted with permission

Thalia González, A Quiet Revolution: Mindfulness, Rebellious Lawyering, and Community Practice, 53 Cal. W. L. Rev. 49 (2016)—Reprinted with permission

Jennifer Gordon, Law, Lawyers, and Labor: The United Farm Workers' Legal Strategy in the 1960s and 1970s and the Role of Law in Union Organizing Today, 8 U. Pa. J. Lab. & Emp. L. 1 (2005)—Reprinted with permission

Jennifer Gordon, We Make the Road by Walking: Immigrant Workers, the Workplace Project, and the Struggle for Social Change, 28 Harv. C.R.-C.L. L. Rev. 407 (1995)—Reprinted with permission

Gil Gott, The Devil We Know: Racial Subordination and National Security Law, 50 Vill. L. Rev. 1073 (2005)—Reprinted with permission

Marie Gottschalk, Bring It On: The Future of Penal Reform, the Carceral State, and American Politics, 12 Ohio St. J. Crim. L. 559 (2015)—Reprinted with permission

Trina Grillo, Anti-Essentialism and Intersectionality: Tools To Dismantle the Master's House, 10 Berkeley Women's L.J. 16 (1995)—Reprinted with permission

Michael Grinthal, Power With: Practice Models for Social Justice Lawyering, 15 U. Pa. J. L. & Soc. Change 25 (2011)—Reprinted with permission

Lani Guinier and Gerald Torres, Changing The Wind: Notes Toward A Demosprudence of Law and Social Movements, 123 Yale L.J. 2740 (2014)—Reprinted with permission

Jon D. Hanson and Kathleen Hanson, The Blame Frame: Justifying (Racial) Injustice in America, 41 Harv. C.R.-C.L. L. Rev. 413 (2006)—Reprinted with permission

Alycia Harr & Ellie Robertson, Photo—Used with permission

Angela P. Harris, Heteropatriarchy Kills: Challenging Gender Violence in a Prison Nation, 37 Wash. U. J.L. & Pol'y 13 (2011)—Reprinted with permission

Cheryl I. Harris, Whiteness As Property, 106 Harv. L. Rev. 1709 (1993)—Reprinted with permission

Danielle Kie Hart, Contract Law Now—Reality Meets Legal Fictions, 41 U. Balt. L. Rev. 1 (2011)—Reprinted with permission

Berta Esperanza Hernández-Truyol, The Rule of Law and Human Rights, 16 Fla. J. Int'l L. 167 (2004)—Reprinted with permission

Mónica Hernández with Francisco Argüelles, Building Immigrant Leaders in the South: INDELI 2004-06—Reprinted with permission

Luke Herrine, The Law and Political Economy of A Student Debt Jubilee, 68 Buff. L. Rev. 281 (2020)—Reprinted with permission

Bill Ong Hing, Coolies, James Yen, and Rebellious Advocacy, 14 Asian Am. L.J. 1 (2007)—Reprinted with permission

Benjamin Hoffman and Marissa Vahlsing, Collaborative Lawyering in Transnational Human Rights Advocacy, 21 Clinical L. Rev. 255 (2014)—Reprinted with permission

Emily M.S. Houh and Kristin Kalsem, It's Critical: Legal Participatory Action Research, 19 Mich. J. Race & L. 287 (2014)—Reprinted with permission

Carmen Huertas-Noble, Worker-Owned and Unionized Worker-Owned Cooperatives: Two Tools to Address Income Inequality, 22 Clinical L. Rev. 325 (2016)—Reprinted with permission

Betty Hung, Letter to a Young Public Interest Attorney, 1 L.A. Pub. Int. L.J. 319 (2009)—Reprinted with permission

Nan D. Hunter, Varieties of Constitutional Experience: Democracy and the Marriage Equality Campaign, 64 UCLA L. Rev. 1662 (2017)—Reprinted with permission

Ann Kennedy, Chronic Harm, 25 Wm. & Mary J. Race, Gender & Soc. Just. 131 (2018)—Reprinted with permission

Michele Johnson, Tennessee Justice Center, Photo—Used with permission

Duncan Kennedy, Legal Education and the Reproduction of Hierarchy, 32 J. Legal Educ. 591 (1982)—Reprinted with permission

Nina A. Kohn, The Lawyer's Role in Fostering an Elder Rights Movement, 37 Wm. Mitchell L. Rev. 49 (2010)—Reprinted with permission

Charles R. Lawrence III, "Justice" or "Just Us": Racism and the Role of Ideology, 35. Stan. L. Rev. 831 (1983)—Reprinted with permission

Daryl Levinson, Forward: Looking for Power in Public Law, 130 Harv. L. Rev. 31 (2016)—Reprinted with permission

Oscar Londoño, WeCount!, Photo—Used with permission

Gerald P. López, Changing Systems, Changing Ourselves, 12 Harv. Latino L. Rev. 15 (2009)—Reprinted with permission

Lynn M. LoPucki, The Systems Approach to Law, 82 Cornell L. Rev. 479 (1997)—Reprinted with permission

David Luban, Taking Out the Adversary: The Assault on Progressive Public-Interest Lawyers, 91 Cal. L. Rev. 209 (2003)—Reprinted with permission

Elizabeth L. MacDowell, Reimagining Access to Justice in the Poor People's Courts, 22 Geo. J. on Poverty L. & Pol'y 473 (2015)—Reprinted with permission

Tayyab Mahmud, Colonialism and Modern Constructions of Race: A Preliminary Inquiry, 53 U. Miami L. Rev. 1219 (1999)—Reprinted with permission

Martha R. Mahoney, Constructing Solidarity: Interest and White Workers, 2 U. Pa. J. Lab. & Emp. L. 747 (2000)—Reprinted with permission

Thurgood Marshall, Reflections on the Bicentennial of the United States Constitution, 101 Harv. L. Rev. 1 (1987)—Reprinted with permission

George A. Martinez, Legal Indeterminacy, Judicial Discretion and The Mexican-American Litigation Experience: 1930–1980, 27 U.C. Davis L. Rev. 555 (1994)—Reprinted with permission

Mari J. Matsuda, Beside My Sister, Facing the Enemy: Legal Theory Out of Coalition, 43 Stan. L. Rev. 1183 (1991)—Reprinted with permission

Mari J. Matsuda, Beyond, And Not Beyond, Black And White: Deconstruction Has a Politics, in Crossroads, Directions, and a New Critical Race Theory (Francisco Valdes, Jerome McCristal Culp & Angela P. Harris eds. 2002)—Used by permission of Temple University Press. ©2002 Temple University. All Rights Reserved.

Mari J. Matsuda, Foreword: McCarthyism, the Internment and the Contradictions of Power, 40 B.C. L. Rev. 9 (1998)—Reprinted with permission

Mari J. Matsuda, Looking to the Bottom: Critical Legal Studies and Reparations, 22 Harv. C.R.-C.L. L. Rev. 323 (1987)—Reprinted with permission

Dayna Bowen Matthew, Structural Inequality: The Real COVID-19 Threat to America's Health and How Strengthening the Affordable Care Act Can Help, 108 Geo. L.J. 1679 (2020)—Reprinted with permission

Serena Mayeri, Marital Supremacy and the Constitution of the Nonmarital Family, 103 Cal. L. Rev. 1277 (2015)—Reprinted with permission

Teri McMurtry-Chubb, Still Writing At The Master's Table: Decolonizing Rhetoric in Legal Writing for a "Woke" Legal Academy, 21 Scholar: St. Mary's L. Rev. & Soc. Just. 255 (2019)—Reprinted with permission

Shannon Price Minter, "Déjà Vu All Over Again": The Recourse to Biology by Opponents of Transgender Equality, 95 N.C. L. Rev. 1161 (2017)—Reprinted with permission

Margaret E. Montoya, Mascaras, Trenzas, y Greñas: Un/Masking the Self While Un/Braiding Latina Stories and Legal Discourse, 17 Harv. Women's L.J. 185, 15 Chicano-Latino L. Rev. 1 (1994)—Reprinted with permission

Sagit Mor, With Access and Justice For All, 39 Cardozo L. Rev. 611 (2017)—Reprinted with permission

Jill C. Morrison, Resuscitating the Black Body: Reproductive Justice as Resistance to the State's Property Interest in Black Women's Reproductive Capacity, 31 Yale J.L. & Feminism 35 (2019)—Reprinted with permission

Stephen R. Munzer, Dam(n) Displacement: Compensation, Resettlement, and Indigeneity, 51 Cornell Int'l L.J. 823 (2019)—Reprinted with permission

Athena D. Mutua, Framing The Elite Consensus, Ideology and Theory & A ClassCrit Response, 44 Sw. L. Rev. 635 (2015)—Reprinted with permission

Athena D. Mutua, Shifting Bottoms and Rotating Centers: Reflections on LatCrit III and the Black/White Paradigm, 53 U. Miami L. Rev. 1177 (1999)—Reprinted with permission

Makua Mutua, Terrorism and Human Rights: Power, Culture, and Subordination, 8 Buff. Hum. Rts. L. Rev. 1 (2002)—Reprinted with permission

Douglas NeJaime, Winning Through Losing, 96 Iowa L. Rev. 941 (2011)—Reprinted with permission

Julie A. Nice, The Gendered Jurisprudence of the Fourteenth Amendment, in Research Handbook on Feminist Jurisprudence (Robin West & Cynthia Grant Bowman eds. 2019)—Reprinted with permission

Ellen J. Pader, Space of Hate: Ethnicity, Architecture, and Housing Discrimination, 54 Rutgers L. Rev. 881 (2002)—Reprinted with permission

Russell G. Pearce, White Lawyering: Rethinking Race, Lawyer Identity, and Rule of Law, 73 Fordham L. Rev. 2081 (2005)—Reprinted with permission

Juan F. Perea, *Hernandez v. New York*: Courts, Prosecutors, and the Fear of Spanish, 21 Hofstra L. Rev. 1 (1992)—Reprinted with permission

Ileana M. Porras, European Origins, The Doctrine of the Providential Function of Commerce, and International Law's Embrace of Economic Growth, 107 Am. Soc'y Int'l L. Proc. 374 (2014)—Reprinted with permission

Catherine Powell and Camille Gear Rich, The "Welfare Queen" Goes to the Polls: Race-Based Fractures in Gender Politics and Opportunities for Intersectional Coalitions, Geo. L.J. 19th Amend. Special Ed. 105 (2020)—Reprinted with permission

john a. powell, Disrupting Individualism and Distributive Remedies with Intersubjectivity and Empowerment: An Approach to Justice and Discourse, 1 Margins 1 (2001)—Reprinted with permission

Theodore Quant, Photo—Used with permission

William P. Quigley, Letter to a Law Student Interested in Social Justice, 1 DePaul J. for Soc. Just. 7 (2007)—Reprinted with permission

Deborah L. Rhode and Scott L. Cummings, Access to Justice: Looking Back, Thinking Ahead, 30 Geo. J. Legal Ethics 485 (2017)—Reprinted with permission

Willmai Rivera-Perez and Juan C. Garcia-Ellin, Flexible Accumulation: Changes in the Legal Profession and Their Effects in Legal Education, 49 Rev. Jur. U. Inter. P.R. 629 (2015)—Reprinted with permission

Russell K. Robinson and David M. Frost, "Playing it Safe" With Empirical Evidence: Selective Use of Social Science in Supreme Court Cases About Racial Justice and Marriage Equality, 112 Nw. U.L. Rev. 1565 (2018)—Reprinted with permission

Daria Roithmayr, Deconstructing the Distinction Between Bias and Merit, 85 Cal. L. Rev. 1449 (1997); 10 La Raza L.J. 363 (1998)—Reprinted with permission

Tom I. Romero, II, The Color of Water: Observations of a Brown Buffalo on Water Law and Policy in Ten Stanzas, 15 U. Denv. Water L. Rev. 329 (2012); 1 U. Miami Race & Soc. Just. L. Rev. 107 (2011)—Reprinted with permission

Aníbal Rosario-Lebrón, If These Blackboards Could Talk: The Crit Classroom, A Battlefield, 9 Charleston L. Rev. 305 (2015)—Reprinted with permission

Natsu Taylor Saito, Tales of Color and Colonialism: Racial Realism and Settler Colonial Theory, 10 Fla. A&M U.L. Rev. 1 (2014)—Reprinted with permission

Antoinette Sedillo Lopez, Ethnocentrism and Feminism: Using a Contextual Methodology in International Women's Rights Advocacy and Education, 28 So. U.L. Rev. 279 (2001)—Reprinted with permission

SEIU 32BJ, Photo—Used with permission

Susan K. Serrano, Dual Consciousness About Law and Justice: Puerto Ricans' Battle for U.S. Citizenship in Hawai'i, 29 Centro J. 164 (2017)—Reprinted with permission

Purvi Shah, Rebuilding the Ethical Compass of Law, 47 Hofstra L. Rev. 11 (2018)—Reprinted with permission

Reva B. Siegel, "The Rule of Love": Wife Beating as Prerogative and Privacy, 105 Yale L.J. 2117 (1996)—Reprinted with permission

Tyler Kasperek Somes, The Legal Services NYC Strike: Neoliberalism, Austerity and Resistance, 71 Nat'l Law. Guild Rev. 8 (2014)—Reprinted with permission

Hon. Sonia Sotomayor, A Latina Judge's Voice, 13 Berkeley La Raza L.J. 87 (2002)—Reprinted with permission

Dean Spade, For Those Considering Law School, 6 Unbound: Harv. J. Legal Left 111 (2010)—Reprinted with permission

Kapu'ala Sproat, Wai Through Kānāwai: Water for Hawai'i's Streams and Justice for Hawaiian Communities, 95 Marq. L. Rev. 127 (2011)—Reprinted with permission

Robert J. Steinfeld, Property and Suffrage in the Early American Republic, 41 Stan. L. Rev. 335 (1989)—Reprinted with permission

Nicholas F. Stump, Following New Lights: Critical Legal Research Strategies as a Spark for Law Reform in Appalachia, 23 Am. U. J. Gender Soc. Pol'y & L. 573 (2014)—Reprinted with permission

Julie A. Su and Eric K. Yamamoto, Critical Coalitions: Theory and Praxis, in Crossroads, Directions, and a New Critical Race Theory (Francisco Valdes, Jerome McCristal Culp & Angela P. Harris eds. 2002)—Used by permission of Temple University Press. ©2002 Temple University. All Rights Reserved.

Allison Anna Tait, The Law Of High-Wealth Exceptionalism, 71 Ala. L. Rev. 981 (2020)—Reprinted with permission

Carl Takei, From Mass Incarceration to Mass Control, and Back Again: How Bipartisan Criminal Justice Reform May Lead to a For-Profit Nightmare, 20 U. Pa. J.L. & Soc. Change 125 (2017)—Reprinted with permission

John Tehranian, Selective Racialization: Middle-Eastern American Identity and the Faustian Pact with Whiteness, 40 Conn. L. Rev. 1201 (2008)—Reprinted with permission

Chantal Thomas, Globalization or Global Subordination?: How LatCrit Links the Local to Global and the Global to the Local: Globalization and the Reproduction of Hierarchy, 33 U.C. Davis L. Rev. 1451 (2000)—Reprinted with permission

Gerald Torres, Synecdoche, 14 Harv. Latino. L Rev. 263 (2011)—Reprinted with permission

Rebecca Tsosie, Indigenous Peoples and Epistemic Injustice: Science, Ethics, and Human Rights, 87 Wash. L. Rev. 1133 (2012)—Reprinted with permission

Amelia J. Uelmen, "Millenial Momentum" for Revising the Rhetoric of Lawyer's Relationships and Roles, 9 U. St. Thomas L.J. 446 (2011)—Reprinted with permission

Francisco Valdes, Race, Ethnicity, and Hispanismo in a Triangular Perspective: The "Essential Latina/o" and LatCrit Theory, 48 UCLA L. Rev. 305 (2000)—Reprinted with permission

Francisco Valdes and Sumi Cho, Critical Race Materialism: Theorizing Justice in the Wake of Global Neoliberalism, 43 Conn. L. Rev. 1513 (2011)—Reprinted with permission

Leti Volpp, American Mestizo: Filipinos and Antimiscegnation Laws in California, 33 U.C. Davis L. Rev. 795 (2000).

Janet Weinstein, Linda Morton, Howard Taras & Vivian Reznik, Teaching Teamwork to Law Students, 63 J. Legal Educ. 36 (2013)—Reprinted with permission

Cornel West, The Role of Law in Progressive Politics, 43 Vand. L. Rev. 1797 (1990)—Reprinted with permission

Laura Westhoff, Citizenship Schools and the Civil Rights Movement, National Council for History Education, 26 History Matters Archive (Feb. 2014)—Reprinted with permission

Lucie E. White, To Learn and Teach: Lessons From Driefontein on Lawyering and Power, 1988 Wis. L. Rev. 699 (1988)—Reprinted with permission

Mary Margaret White, Mississippi Today, Marhsall Ramsey df—Reprinted with permission

Robert A. Williams, Jr., Vampires Anonymous and Critical Race Practice, 95 Mich. L. Rev. 741 (1997)—Reprinted with permission

Lane Windham, Knocking on Labor's Door: Union Organizing in the 1970s and the Roots of a New Economic Divide, 190–91 (2017)—Copyright © 2017 by Lane Windham. Used by permission of the University of North Carolina Press. www.uncpress.org

Tryon P. Woods, The Implicit Bias of Implicit Bias Theory, 10 Drexel L. Rev. 631 (2018)—Reprinted with permission

Eric K. Yamamoto, Rethinking Alliances: Agency, Responsibility, and Interracial Justice, 3 Asian Pac. Am. L.J. 33 (Fall 1995)—Reprinted with permission

Christine Zuni Cruz, [On The] Road Back In: Community Lawyering in Indigenous Communities, 5 Clinical L. Rev. 557 (1999); 24 Am. Indian L. Rev. 229 (2000)—Reprinted with permission

Summary of Contents

Acknowledgments III
Copyright Acknowledgments V
Table of Cases XXXVII
Table of Authorities XXXIX

Editors' Introduction 1

PART I. INTRODUCING THE CRITICAL CHALLENGE OF USING LAW FOR EQUAL JUSTICE

Chapter 1. Looking to the Bottom Is Step One in Systemic Advocacy 5
1.1 Law Isn't Always What It Seems to Be—If You Look at It from the Bottom 10
1.2 Collective Knowledge "From the Bottom" Anchors Advocacy in Group Struggles 14
1.3 Depending on Circumstance and Context, Bottoms (and Tops) Can Shift—So Must Advocates and Advocacy 35
1.4 Critical "Schools" and Advocacy "Approaches" Provide Wells of Knowledge for "Different" Groups and Their Advocates 42
1.5 Deconstruction and Dual Consciousness Empower Subordinated Groups 66
1.6 Systemic Injustice Is Epistemic Injustice 76

Chapter 2. Framing the Dimensions and Dynamics of the Critical Challenge 81
2.1 Reflections and Lessons on the Critical Challenge of Using Law for Equal Justice—Adjudication, Lawyering, and Formal Equality 87
2.2 Does Formal Legal Equality Deliver Actual Social Change and Progress? 107
2.3 Legal Indeterminacy Magnifies Complexity and Discretion—Make Them Windows of Opportunity 113
2.4 Beyond Formal Equality—Identities and Groups, Interests and Power (IGIP) 118
2.5 Democracy's Role in Making the Critical Challenge Stick—While Hiding Systemic Inequalities in Plain Sight 130
2.6 Legalized Violence Enforces the Critical Challenge—Militarized Policing, Mass Incarceration, and Crimmigration 142
2.7 Fighting Back Smartly—Using Amelioration for Transformation 159
2.8 Chronic Injustice Is Systemic Violence 175

PART II. UNDERSTANDING THE SYSTEMIC POWER OF SOCIAL IDENTITIES AND ORGANIZED GROUPS

Chapter 3. Unlearning and Relearning Systems, Social Identities, and Castes 181
3.1 Systems Are Judged on Actual Outputs and Recurrent Results 183
3.2 The "Rule of Law" System: Originating in Europe, Transplanted Through Colonialism, and Failing by Design 189
3.3 Systemic or Not?—Public Health, Global Pandemics, and Social Problems 201
3.4 Critical History and Other Disciplines Help Advocates Challenge Systemic Outputs 206
3.5 Social Identities (Still) Matter in Legal Decision Making 229
3.6 Law Dispenses and Normalizes Private-Public Privilege and Subordination 255

Chapter 4. Unlearning and Relearning Winning, Losing, and Progress over—and Using—Time 279
4.1 Elites Manipulate Law, Time, and Change to Preserve Identity Castes 281
4.2 Reproductive Liberty and Justice—Preservation Through Transformation Today? 302
4.3 Long-Term Struggles Need Contextual Metrics for Winning, Losing, and Progress 314
4.4 Managing Risk, Privilege, and Time in Organized Long-Term Struggles 341

Chapter 5. Roadtest: Reclaiming Group Identities for Antisubordination Insight, Consciousness, and Solidarity 351
5.1 Colorblindness Is a Racist Fiction and Top-Down Myth 353
5.2 Critical Self-Reflection Unmasks and Redefines Social Realities; "Asking Other Questions" Uncovers Systemic Patterns 363
5.3 Flipping Systemic Scripts—Social Identities as Group Assets for Long-Term Struggles 377
5.4 Antisubordination Solidarity Builds Power Across Multiple Kinds of Difference 397
5.5 Transforming Advocacy Helps to Transform Society—Bit by Bit, Year by Year 412

Chapter 6. Organizing Bottom-Up Groups to Contest Top-Down Power and Rewrite "Ground Rules" 423
6.1 Elites Structured Society to Be Collectively on Top Always 427
6.2 Public Enforcement of "Private" Property and Contracts Is Central to Identity Castes 438
6.3 Elites Orchestrate Power, Privilege, and Profit Continuously for Local-Global Rule 456

6.4	Elites Use Neoliberal Ideology as Law to Magnify and Concentrate the Public Power of Private Wealth	476
6.5	Elites (Still) Suppress Voting to Manipulate Democracy and Control Outcomes	489
6.6	Advocates Support Organized Groups as "Repeat Players" to Contest Background Premises, Ground Rules, and Foundational Concepts	495
6.7	Seeding, Sparking, and Supporting Long-Term Coalitions: A Tennessee Case Study	505

PART III. LEARNING TO WORK WITH DIVERSE TEAMS ON SYSTEMIC PROJECTS

Chapter 7. Road Test: Collaborating to Connect Experience and Knowledge for Teamwork and Coalitions ... 531

7.1	Recognizing Failure by Design to Overcome It	535
7.2	Crafting Analytical Narratives for Advocacy Projects	543
7.3	Teams and Teamwork Expand the Capacity of Systemic Advocates	554
7.4	Collaborative Professionalism and Critical Coalitions Empower Advocacy	565

Chapter 8. Road Test: Designing a Systemic Advocacy Project Around Social Problems and Three-Layered Goals ... 583

8.1	Mapping the Process and Components of Project Development	584
8.2	Rights Are Important for Resistance but Insufficient for Transformative Projects	595
8.3	Situating International Human Rights in Local Systemic Advocacy	605
8.4	Three-Layered Goals Must Be Integral to Project Design	612
8.5	The Politics of Funding Require Multiple Ways and Means	620
8.6	Advocates Act Despite Risks of Retaliation, Cooptation, and Tokenism	634
8.7	Restrategizing Solutions for Transformative Access to Justice Projects	646
8.8	Environmental Justice, Private Profit, and Climate Change	659

PART IV. TRANSCENDING THE LEGAL INDUSTRY TO PURSUE THREE-LAYERED GOALS

Chapter 9. Exposing the Values, Handcuffs, Blindfolds, and Hierarchies of Law as an Industry ... 675

9.1	Law as an Industry Pursues Profits over Justice	678
9.2	Elites Designed Law as an Industry for Group Power and Privilege and to "Take out" Dissent or Competition	701
9.3	Legal Education Handcuffs the Industry to Instill Top-Down Conformity	730

SUMMARY OF CONTENTS

9.4 Legal Formalism Blindfolds Analysis Selectively to Obscure Systemic Injustice at Work 740
9.5 Legal Individualism—a Key Formalism—Atomizes Law to Mismatch Problems and Solutions 764
9.6 Elites Use Public Power to Hide Private Power in Law and Society 768
9.7 Legal Ethics Teach and Enforce Industry Handcuffs, Blindfolds, and Hierarchies 775

Chapter 10. Advancing and Defending Three-Layered Goals in Systemic Contexts 787
10.1 Systemic Advocacy Centers Persistent Social Problems in Complex Contexts 791
10.2 Three-Layered Goals Are Geared to Three Recurrent Advocacy Scenarios 804
10.3 Second-Layer Goals Combine Persuasion and Pressure to Build and Exercise Power 833
10.4 Third-Layer Goals Connect Micro-Macro Facts to Shift Consciousness and Cultures 840
10.5 Systemic Advocates Combine Traditional and Critical Tools for Three-Layered Progress 851

PART V. OUTLINING THE STAGES OF SYSTEMIC ADVOCACY FOR CRITICAL JUSTICE

Chapter 11. Stage One—Diagnosing Problems in Context Through Critical Research & Analysis to Prepare for Complex Actions 857
11.1 Knowledge Always Has a Politics, Which Can Bias Analysis and Action 860
11.2 Advocates Diagnose Problems and Strategize Solutions in Two Recurring Stages 874
11.3 Three Bottom-Up Methods of Critical Research for Three-Layered Progress 894
11.4 Three Norms Help Expand and Deepen the Impact of Critical Research and Analysis 934
11.5 Four "Mapping" Techniques Help Tailor and Implement Contextual Action Plans 943

Chapter 12. Stage Two—Building Campaigns and Institutions as Complex Actions for Three-Layered Progress 957
12.1 Complex Actions Combine Pressure and Persuasion in Stage Two of Systemic Advocacy 960
12.2 Supporting Complex Actions by Organized Groups: Finding Your Role 1021
12.3 Collaboration and Conflict Coexist in Complex Actions 1032

PART VI. MAPPING THE HISTORICAL ROOTS AND IDEOLOGICAL DESIGN OF LAW AS A SYSTEM

Chapter 13. Situating the Critical Challenge in the "Rule of Law" as Systemic Ideology 1055
13.1 Colonial Settlers Came for Conquest, Not as Immigrants, and Created Identity Castes for Racial States 1056
13.2 Racial States in Historical and International Context—an Admiring Perspective 1086
13.3 Imperialism and Globalization Entrenched and Expanded White Supremacy (and Related Identity Ideologies) by Force and Law 1088
13.4 Law-as-Identity Still Creates, Expands, and Perpetuates Colonial Castes and Ideologies 1113

Chapter 14. Road Test: Dismantling "Ideological Illusions of Equality" to Resist Hegemony 1131
14.1 Social Ills—like Sexism, Racism, and Homophobia—Prop up "Ideological Illusions of Equality" to Justify Persistent Group Inequalities 1135
14.2 Over Time, Internalized Ideologies Shape People, Choices, and Castes 1149
14.3 The Social Hegemony of Identity-as-Ideology Kills Bottoms 1159

PART VII. CLOSING REFLECTIONS ON CRITICAL JUSTICE AND SYSTEMIC ADVOCACY

Chapter 15. Running the Critical Justice Marathon—*Brown*, Formal Equality, and Beyond in Public Education 1171
15.1 Unpacking Persistent Educational Inequality and Material Injustice 1174
15.2 Upholding by Law the Systemic Linkage of Property to Identity for Unequal Education 1184
15.3 Designing Student Debt in Higher Education as New Professional Handcuffs 1191
15.4 Countering Systemic Violence in the Structuring of Public Education Today 1200
15.5 Cross-Cultural Comparisons—and Their Limits 1211

Chapter 16. Road Test: Crafting Long-Term Pathways Toward Critical Justice 1219
16.1 Every Advocate Must Unlearn and Relearn Problem Solving to Craft Their Own Lifelong "Road" to Critical Justice 1221
16.2 Pathways Change Along the Way—So Must Groups, Advocates, and Advocacy 1247
16.3 Deep Critique and Systemic Advocacy for the Long Haul 1268

Editors' Closing Reflections 1277
INDEX 1279

TABLE OF CONTENTS

Acknowledgments III
Copyright Acknowledgments V
Table of Cases XXXVII
Table of Authorities... XXXIX

Editors' Introduction 1

PART I. INTRODUCING THE CRITICAL CHALLENGE OF USING LAW FOR EQUAL JUSTICE

Chapter 1. Looking to the Bottom Is Step One in Systemic Advocacy 5
1.1 Law Isn't Always What It Seems to Be—If You Look at It from the Bottom 10
    Reflections on the Bicentennial of the United States Constitution 11
1.2 Collective Knowledge "From the Bottom" Anchors Advocacy in Group Struggles 14
    Looking to the Bottom: Critical Legal Studies and Reparations 15
    Changing the Wind: Notes Toward a Demosprudence of Law and Social Movements 23
    Notes and Questions 34
1.3 Depending on Circumstance and Context, Bottoms (and Tops) Can Shift—So Must Advocates and Advocacy 35
    Shifting Bottoms and Rotating Centers: Reflections on LatCrit III and the Black/White Paradigm 35
    Notes and Questions 41
1.4 Critical "Schools" and Advocacy "Approaches" Provide Wells of Knowledge for "Different" Groups and Their Advocates 42
    LatCrit and TWAIL 47
    Steady Work: A Practitioner's Reflections on Political Lawyering 52
    Changing Systems, Changing Ourselves 56
    Notes and Questions 65
1.5 Deconstruction and Dual Consciousness Empower Subordinated Groups 66
    Dual Consciousness About Law and Justice: Puerto Ricans' Battle for U.S. Citizenship in Hawai'i 67
1.6 Systemic Injustice Is Epistemic Injustice 76
    Indigenous Peoples and Epistemic Injustice: Science, Ethics, and Human Rights 77

xxiii

Chapter 2. Framing the Dimensions and Dynamics of the Critical Challenge 81

2.1 Reflections and Lessons on the Critical Challenge of Using Law for Equal Justice—Adjudication, Lawyering, and Formal Equality 87
   Brown v. Board of Education 87
   Brown v. Board of Education (II) 90
   The Segregation and Resegregation of American Public Education: The Courts' Role 92
   Serving Two Masters: Integration Ideals and Client Interests in School Desegregation Litigation 99
   Notes and Questions 106

2.2 Does Formal Legal Equality Deliver Actual Social Change and Progress? 107
   Race, Reform, and Retrenchment: Transformation and Legitimation in Antidiscrimination Law 108
   Notes and Questions 112

2.3 Legal Indeterminacy Magnifies Complexity and Discretion—Make Them Windows of Opportunity 113
   Legal Indeterminacy, Judicial Discretion and the Mexican-American Litigation Experience: 1930–1980 114
   Notes and Questions 117

2.4 Beyond Formal Equality—Identities and Groups, Interests and Power (IGIP) 118
   Brown v. Board of Education and the Interest-Convergence Dilemma 119
   Foreword: McCarthyism, the Internment and the Contradictions of Power 121
   Notes and Questions 130

2.5 Democracy's Role in Making the Critical Challenge Stick—While Hiding Systemic Inequalities in Plain Sight 130
   Testing Theories of American Politics: Elites, Interest Groups, and Average Citizens 132
   Notes and Questions 141

2.6 Legalized Violence Enforces the Critical Challenge—Militarized Policing, Mass Incarceration, and Crimmigration 142
   From Mass Incarceration to Mass Control, and Back Again: How Bipartisan Criminal Justice Reform May Lead to a For-Profit Nightmare 145
   Naturalizing Immigration Imprisonment 152
   Bring It on: The Future of Penal Reform, the Carceral State, and American Politics 155
   Notes and Questions 158

2.7 Fighting Back Smartly—Using Amelioration for Transformation 159
   The Color of Water: Observations of a Brown Buffalo on Water Law and Policy in Ten Stanzas 163
   The Indispensable Ones: A Story of Mining Resistance from La Puya 166

Notes and Questions 173
2.8 Chronic Injustice Is Systemic Violence 175
Notes and Questions 176

PART II. UNDERSTANDING THE SYSTEMIC POWER OF SOCIAL IDENTITIES AND ORGANIZED GROUPS

Chapter 3. Unlearning and Relearning Systems, Social Identities, and Castes 181
3.1 Systems Are Judged on Actual Outputs and Recurrent Results 183
The Systems Approach to Law 185
3.2 The "Rule of Law" System: Originating in Europe, Transplanted Through Colonialism, and Failing by Design 189
The Rule of Law and Human Rights 191
European Origins, the Doctrine of the Providential Function of Commerce, and International Law's Embrace of Economic Growth 196
Notes and Questions 200
3.3 Systemic or Not?—Public Health, Global Pandemics, and Social Problems 201
Structural Inequality: The Real COVID-19 Threat to America's Health and How Strengthening the Affordable Care Act Can Help 202
Notes and Questions 206
3.4 Critical History and Other Disciplines Help Advocates Challenge Systemic Outputs 206
Collisions at the Intersection of Gender, Race, and Class: Enforcing the Chinese Exclusion Laws 210
Marital Supremacy and the Constitution of the Nonmarital Family 216
Glorious Precedents: When Gay Marriage Was Radical 221
Notes and Questions 228
3.5 Social Identities (Still) Matter in Legal Decision Making 229
Johnson and Graham's Lessee v. M'Intosh 230
Dred Scott v. Sandford 233
Bradwell v. State 237
Downes v. Bidwell 239
Buck v. Bell 241
Korematsu v. United States 242
Bowers v. Hardwick 244
A Latina Judge's Voice 246
Trump v. Hawaii 249
Our Lady Of Guadalupe School v. Morrissey-Berru 253
Notes and Questions 254
3.6 Law Dispenses and Normalizes Private-Public Privilege and Subordination 255
Straight out of the Closet 258

Law as Microaggressions 266
Space of Hate: Ethnicity, Architecture and Housing
    Discrimination 271
Notes and Questions.. 274

Chapter 4. Unlearning and Relearning Winning, Losing, and Progress over—and Using—Time 279

4.1   Elites Manipulate Law, Time, and Change to Preserve Identity
      Castes 281
      "The Rule of Love": Wife Beating as Prerogative and Privacy 281
      "Playing It Safe" with Empirical Evidence: Selective Use of Social
          Science in Supreme Court Cases About Racial Justice and
          Marriage Equality.. 291
      "Déjà Vu All over Again": The Recourse to Biology by Opponents of
          Transgender Equality.. 294
      Notes and Questions.. 300

4.2   Reproductive Liberty and Justice—Preservation Through
      Transformation Today? 302
      Resuscitating the Black Body: Reproductive Justice as Resistance
          to the State's Property Interest in Black Women's
          Reproductive Capacity 303
      Chronic Harm 306
      Notes and Questions 310

4.3   Long-Term Struggles Need Contextual Metrics for Winning,
      Losing, and Progress 314
      Varieties of Constitutional Experience: Democracy and the
          Marriage Equality Campaign 316
      Winning Through Losing 329
      Disability: The Last Marriage Equality Frontier 337
      Notes and Questions 339

4.4   Managing Risk, Privilege, and Time in Organized Long-Term
      Struggles 341
      The Role of Law in Progressive Politics 343
      Notes and Questions 349

Chapter 5. Roadtest: Reclaiming Group Identities for Antisubordination Insight, Consciousness, and Solidarity 351

5.1   Colorblindness Is a Racist Fiction and Top-Down Myth.................... 353
      White Lawyering: Rethinking Race, Lawyer Identity, and Rule of
          Law 357
      Notes and Questions 362

5.2   Critical Self-Reflection Unmasks and Redefines Social Realities;
      "Asking Other Questions" Uncovers Systemic Patterns 363
      Mascaras, Trenzas, y Greñas: Un/Masking the Self While
          Un/Braiding Latina Stories and Legal Discourse 365
      Beside My Sister, Facing the Enemy: Legal Theory out of
          Coalition 371

	"And Then Comes Life": The Intersection of Race, Poverty, and Disability in HBO's The Wire 375
	Notes and Questions 377
5.3	Flipping Systemic Scripts—Social Identities as Group Assets for Long-Term Struggles 377
	The Devil We Know: Racial Subordination and National Security Law 378
	The End of Innocence or Politics After the Fall of the Essential Subject 383
	American Mestizo: Filipinos and Antimiscegenation Laws in California 386
	Anti-Essentialism and Intersectionality: Tools to Dismantle the Master's House 390
	Notes and Questions 395
5.4	Antisubordination Solidarity Builds Power Across Multiple Kinds of Difference 397
	Anti-Subordination Above All: Sex, Race, and Equal Protection 399
	Constructing Solidarity: Interest and White Workers 403
	Notes and Questions 410
5.5	Transforming Advocacy Helps to Transform Society—Bit by Bit, Year by Year 412
	Coolies, James Yen, and Rebellious Advocacy 412

Chapter 6. Organizing Bottom-Up Groups to Contest Top-Down Power and Rewrite "Ground Rules" 423

6.1	Elites Structured Society to Be Collectively on Top Always 427
	Where the Law Lies: Constitutional Fictions and Their Discontents 430
	Property and Suffrage in the Early American Republic 434
6.2	Public Enforcement of "Private" Property and Contracts Is Central to Identity Castes 438
	Race, Culture, and Contract Law: From the Cottonfield to the Courtroom 439
	The Private Law of Race and Sex: An Antebellum Perspective 444
	Whiteness as Property 447
	Contract Law Now—Reality Meets Legal Fictions 454
	Notes and Questions 455
6.3	Elites Orchestrate Power, Privilege, and Profit Continuously for Local-Global Rule 456
	The Lewis Powell Memo: Corporate Blueprint to Dominate Democracy 460
	International Institutions Today: An Imperial Global State in the Making 468
	Notes and Questions 473

6.4	Elites Use Neoliberal Ideology as Law to Magnify and Concentrate the Public Power of Private Wealth	476
	Framing the Elite Consensus, Ideology and Theory & a ClassCrit Response	478
	The Global Politics of Food: A Critical Overview	480
	Notes and Questions	489
6.5	Elites (Still) Suppress Voting to Manipulate Democracy and Control Outcomes	489
	The "Welfare Queen" Goes to the Polls: Race-Based Fractures in Gender Politics and Opportunities for Intersectional Coalitions	493
	Notes and Questions	494
6.6	Advocates Support Organized Groups as "Repeat Players" to Contest Background Premises, Ground Rules, and Foundational Concepts	495
	Re-Valuing Lawyering for Middle-Income Clients	496
	Why the "Haves" Come out Ahead: Speculations on the Limits of Legal Change	502
6.7	Seeding, Sparking, and Supporting Long-Term Coalitions: A Tennessee Case Study	505
	Going South, Coming North: Migrant and Union Organizing in Morristown, Tennessee	508
	Two Months After the Raid: An Update from Morristown Tennessee Immigrant and Refugee Rights Coalition	515
	Tennessee OSHA Slams Meatpacking Plant Where Massive ICE Raid Took Place with 27 Violations and $41,775 in Penalties	516
	Doing Policy from Below: Worker Solidarity and the Prospects for Immigration Reform	518
	Notes and Questions	524

PART III. LEARNING TO WORK WITH DIVERSE TEAMS ON SYSTEMIC PROJECTS

Chapter 7. Road Test: Collaborating to Connect Experience and Knowledge for Teamwork and Coalitions 531

7.1	Recognizing Failure by Design to Overcome It	535
	Structural Racism, Structural Pollution and the Need for a New Paradigm	536
7.2	Crafting Analytical Narratives for Advocacy Projects	543
	Vampires Anonymous and Critical Race Practice	545
7.3	Teams and Teamwork Expand the Capacity of Systemic Advocates	554
	Teaching Teamwork to Law Students	559
	Notes and Questions	564

7.4	Collaborative Professionalism and Critical Coalitions Empower Advocacy	565
	Collaborative Lawyering in Transnational Human Rights Advocacy	566
	Critical Coalitions: Theory and Praxis	577
	Notes and Questions	578

Chapter 8. Road Test: Designing a Systemic Advocacy Project Around Social Problems and Three-Layered Goals ... 583

8.1	Mapping the Process and Components of Project Development	584
	Notes and Questions	594
8.2	Rights Are Important for Resistance but Insufficient for Transformative Projects	595
	Resisting Guantánamo: Rights at the Brink of Dehumanization	597
8.3	Situating International Human Rights in Local Systemic Advocacy	605
	Redefining Human Rights Lawyering Through the Lens of Critical Theory: Lessons for Pedagogy and Practice	606
	Notes and Questions	610
8.4	Three-Layered Goals Must Be Integral to Project Design	612
8.5	The Politics of Funding Require Multiple Ways and Means	620
	Notes and Questions	632
8.6	Advocates Act Despite Risks of Retaliation, Cooptation, and Tokenism	634
	Synecdoche	638
	Notes and Questions	646
8.7	Restrategizing Solutions for Transformative Access to Justice Projects	646
	Access to Justice: Looking Back, Thinking Ahead	650
	Framing Access to Justice: Beyond Perceived Justice for Individuals	651
	With Access and Justice for All	653
	Notes and Questions	656
8.8	Environmental Justice, Private Profit, and Climate Change	659
	Adaptive Law in the Anthropocene	661
	Bridging the North-South Divide: International Environmental Law in the Anthropocene	666
	Notes and Questions	670

PART IV. TRANSCENDING THE LEGAL INDUSTRY TO PURSUE THREE-LAYERED GOALS

Chapter 9. Exposing the Values, Handcuffs, Blindfolds, and Hierarchies of Law as an Industry ... 675

9.1	Law as an Industry Pursues Profits over Justice	678
	The Transformation of the Professional Workforce	679

	The Legal Services NYC Strike: Neoliberalism, Austerity and Resistance	689
	Flexible Accumulation: Changes in the Legal Profession and Their Effects in Legal Education	695
	Notes and Questions	700
9.2	Elites Designed Law as an Industry for Group Power and Privilege and to "Take out" Dissent or Competition	701
	The Law of High-Wealth Exceptionalism	703
	Taking out the Adversary: The Assault on Progressive Public-Interest Lawyers	712
	Deconstructing the Distinction Between Bias and Merit	722
	Notes and Questions	728
9.3	Legal Education Handcuffs the Industry to Instill Top-Down Conformity	730
	Legal Education and the Reproduction of Hierarchy	731
	Notes and Questions	740
9.4	Legal Formalism Blindfolds Analysis Selectively to Obscure Systemic Injustice at Work	740
	Geduldig v. Aiello	743
	General Electric Company v. Gilbert	745
	Hernandez v. New York	747
	Rice v. Cayetano	750
	Hernandez v. New York: Courts, Prosecutors, and the Fear of Spanish	754
	Wai Through Kānāwai: Water for Hawai'i's Streams and Justice for Hawaiian Communities	757
	Still Writing at the Master's Table: Decolonizing Rhetoric in Legal Writing for a "Woke" Legal Academy	760
	Notes and Questions	762
9.5	Legal Individualism—a Key Formalism—Atomizes Law to Mismatch Problems and Solutions	764
	Disrupting Individualism and Distributive Remedies with Intersubjectivity and Empowerment: An Approach to Justice and Discourse	766
9.6	Elites Use Public Power to Hide Private Power in Law and Society	768
	Foreword: Looking for Power in Public Law	769
	Confronting Power in Public Law	773
	Notes and Questions	775
9.7	Legal Ethics Teach and Enforce Industry Handcuffs, Blindfolds, and Hierarchies	775
	Rebuilding the Ethical Compass of Law	779
	Notes and Questions	782

Chapter 10. Advancing and Defending Three-Layered Goals in Systemic Contexts 787

10.1 Systemic Advocacy Centers Persistent Social Problems in Complex Contexts.. 791
   A Call to Context: The Professional Challenges of Cause Lawyering at the Intersection of Race, Space, and Poverty 793
   Notes and Questions.. 802
10.2 Three-Layered Goals Are Geared to Three Recurrent Advocacy Scenarios 804
   To Learn and Teach: Lessons from Driefontein on Lawyering and Power 806
   Notes and Questions.. 830
10.3 Second-Layer Goals Combine Persuasion and Pressure to Build and Exercise Power 833
   Notes and Questions.. 839
10.4 Third-Layer Goals Connect Micro-Macro Facts to Shift Consciousness and Cultures 840
   The Blame Frame: Justifying (Racial) Injustice in America 841
   Notes and Questions.. 848
10.5 Systemic Advocates Combine Traditional and Critical Tools for Three-Layered Progress 851
   Notes and Questions.. 853

PART V. OUTLINING THE STAGES OF SYSTEMIC ADVOCACY FOR CRITICAL JUSTICE

Chapter 11. Stage One—Diagnosing Problems in Context Through Critical Research & Analysis to Prepare for Complex Actions 857

11.1 Knowledge Always Has a Politics, Which Can Bias Analysis and Action.. 860
   Beyond, and Not Beyond, Black and White: Deconstruction Has a Politics 862
   The Ethics of Narrative.. 866
   Notes and Questions.. 872
11.2 Advocates Diagnose Problems and Strategize Solutions in Two Recurring Stages.. 874
   Following New Lights: Critical Legal Research Strategies as a Spark for Law Reform in Appalachia 879
11.3 Three Bottom-Up Methods of Critical Research for Three-Layered Progress.. 894
   A. Participatory Action Research 895
      It's Critical: Legal Participatory Action Research 897
   B. Critical Empiricism 908
      Fair Driving: Gender and Race Discrimination in Retail Car Negotiations 909

		C.	Analytical Narrative 918

            Critical Race Feminist Bioethics: Telling Stories in Law School and Medical School in Pursuit of "Cultural Competency" 922

            Notes and Questions 929

11.4 Three Norms Help Expand and Deepen the Impact of Critical Research and Analysis 934
    A. Counterdisciplinarity 935
    B. Critical Comparativism 935
    C. Social Analytics and Social Media 937
       Notes and Questions 943

11.5 Four "Mapping" Techniques Help Tailor and Implement Contextual Action Plans 943
    A. Concept or Problem Mapping 944
    B. Asset Mapping 946
    C. Stakeholder Mapping 947
    D. Power Mapping 949
       Notes and Questions 952

Chapter 12. Stage Two—Building Campaigns and Institutions as Complex Actions for Three-Layered Progress 957

12.1 Complex Actions Combine Pressure and Persuasion in Stage Two of Systemic Advocacy 960

      Law in the Labor Movement's Challenge to Wal-Mart: A Case Study of the Inglewood Site Fight 968

      Worker-Owned and Unionized Worker-Owned Cooperatives: Two Tools to Address Income Inequality 987

      We Make the Road by Walking: Immigrant Workers, the Workplace Project, and the Struggle for Social Change 999

      Notes and Questions 1017

12.2 Supporting Complex Actions by Organized Groups: Finding Your Role 1021

      Power with: Practice Models for Social Justice Lawyering 1024

      Notes and Questions 1032

12.3 Collaboration and Conflict Coexist in Complex Actions 1032

      Lawyers, Organizers, and Workers: Collaboration and Conflict in Worker Cooperative Development 1036

      How Lawyers Manage Intragroup Dissent 1048

      Notes and Questions 1051

PART VI. MAPPING THE HISTORICAL ROOTS AND IDEOLOGICAL DESIGN OF LAW AS A SYSTEM

Chapter 13. Situating the Critical Challenge in the "Rule of Law" as Systemic Ideology 1055

13.1 Colonial Settlers Came for Conquest, Not as Immigrants, and Created Identity Castes for Racial States 1056

Law and Colonialism 1057
Tales of Color and Colonialism: Racial Realism and Settler
    Colonial Theory 1062
Colonialism and Modern Constructions of Race: A Preliminary
    Inquiry 1078
Notes and Questions 1085

13.2 Racial States in Historical and International Context—an
    Admiring Perspective 1086
13.3 Imperialism and Globalization Entrenched and Expanded White
    Supremacy (and Related Identity Ideologies) by Force and Law 1088
Critical Race Materialism: Theorizing Justice in the Wake of
    Global Neoliberalism 1095
Globalization or Global Subordination?: How LatCrit Links the
    Local to Global and the Global to the Local: Globalization
    and the Reproduction of Hierarchy 1104
Notes and Questions 1109
13.4 Law-as-Identity Still Creates, Expands, and Perpetuates Colonial
    Castes and Ideologies 1113
The Gendered Jurisprudence of the Fourteenth Amendment 1114
Selective Racialization: Middle-Eastern American Identity and
    the Faustian Pact with Whiteness 1117
Terrorism and Human Rights: Power, Culture, and
    Subordination 1121
Notes and Questions 1129

**Chapter 14. Road Test: Dismantling "Ideological Illusions of
Equality" to Resist Hegemony** 1131
14.1 Social Ills—like Sexism, Racism, and Homophobia—Prop up
    "Ideological Illusions of Equality" to Justify Persistent Group
    Inequalities 1135
"Justice" or "Just Us": Racism and the Role of Ideology 1135
Images of the Outsider in American Law and Culture: Can Free
    Expression Remedy Systemic Social Ills? 1143
Notes and Questions 1147
14.2 Over Time, Internalized Ideologies Shape People, Choices, and
    Castes 1149
The Colonization of the Womb 1151
Race, Ethnicity, and Hispanismo in a Triangular Perspective:
    The "Essential Latina/o" and LatCrit Theory 1153
14.3 The Social Hegemony of Identity-as-Ideology Kills Bottoms 1159
Heteropatriarchy Kills: Challenging Gender Violence in a Prison
    Nation 1159
Notes and Questions 1166

PART VII. CLOSING REFLECTIONS ON CRITICAL JUSTICE AND SYSTEMIC ADVOCACY

Chapter 15. Running the Critical Justice Marathon—*Brown*, Formal Equality, and Beyond in Public Education 1171

15.1 Unpacking Persistent Educational Inequality and Material Injury 1174
    Business as Usual? *Brown* and the Continuing Conundrum of Race in America 1175
    Notes and Questions 1182

15.2 Upholding by Law the Systemic Linkage of Property to Identity for Unequal Education 1184
    San Antonio Independent School District v. Rodriguez 1184
    Notes and Questions 1190

15.3 Designing Student Debt in Higher Education as New Professional Handcuffs 1191
    The Law and Political Economy of a Student Debt Jubilee 1191
    Notes and Questions 1197

15.4 Countering Systemic Violence in the Structuring of Public Education Today 1200
    Ending the School-to-Prison Pipeline: A Case Study of Community-Led Disciplinary Reform in Kern County 1201
    Notes and Questions 1210

15.5 Cross-Cultural Comparisons—and Their Limits 1211
    Ethnocentrism and Feminism: Using a Contextual Methodology in International Women's Rights Advocacy and Education 1212
    With No Deliberate Speed: The Segregation of Roma Children in Europe 1214
    Notes and Questions 1217

Chapter 16. Road Test: Crafting Long-Term Pathways Toward Critical Justice 1219

16.1 Every Advocate Must Unlearn and Relearn Problem Solving to Craft Their Own Lifelong "Road" to Critical Justice 1221
    [On The] Road Back in: Community Lawyering in Indigenous Communities 1222
    Letter to a Young Public Interest Attorney 1229
    Letter to a Law Student Interested in Social Justice 1233
    For Those Considering Law School 1242
    Notes and Questions 1246

16.2 Pathways Change Along the Way—So Must Groups, Advocates, and Advocacy 1247
    Law, Lawyers, and Labor: The United Farm Workers' Legal Strategy in the 1960s and 1970s and the Role of Law in Union Organizing Today 1248
    Notes and Questions 1267

16.3 Deep Critique and Systemic Advocacy for the Long Haul 1268
     Deep Critique and Democratic Lawyering in Clinical Practice 1269
     Notes and Questions 1274

Editors' Closing Reflections 1277

INDEX 1279

TABLE OF CASES

The principal cases are in bold type.

American Express Co. v. Italian Colors Restaurant, 464
AT&T Mobility LLC v. Concepcion, 464
Batson v. Kentucky, 749
Bowers v. Hardwick, 244
Bradwell v. State, 65, 237
Brown v. Board of Education, 87, 92, 93
Brown v. Board of Education (II), 90
Buck v. Bell, 241
Burwell v. Hobby Lobby Stores, Inc., 310
Bush v. Gore, 491
Chae Chan Ping v. United States, 209
Citizens United v. FEC, 458
Davis, et al. v. Cox, et al., 720
Deposit Guar. Nat'l Bank v. Roper, 463
Dodge v. Ford Motor Co., 458, 1018
Doe v. University of Michigan, 1148
Downes v. Bidwell, 239, 1073, 1074
Dred Scott v. Sandford, 233
Employment Division v. Smith, 301
Epic Systems Corp. v. Lewis, 464
Gayle v. Browder, 34
Geduldig v. Aiello, 743
General Electric Company v. Gilbert, 745
Gonzales v. Carhart, 312
Gratz v. Bollinger, 933
Grutter v. Bollinger, 933
Hernandez v. New York, 747
Hoffman Plastic Compounds, Inc. v. National Labor Relations Board, 1003
Johnson and Graham's Lessee v. M'Intosh, 230
Korematsu v. United States, 242
Lawrence v. Texas, 244
Lindsey v. Normet, 1187
Lochner v. New York, 65
Masterpiece Cakeshop, Ltd. v. Colorado Civil Rights Comm'n, 252
Muller v. Oregon, 43
Obergefell v. Hodges, 314, 316
Offutt v. United States, 754
Our Lady Of Guadalupe School v. Morrissey-Berru, 253

Parents Involved in Community Schools v. Seattle School District No. 1, 107
Plessy v. Ferguson, 88, 89, 209
Rice v. Cayetano, 86, 750
Roe v. Wade, 302, 312, 313
San Antonio Independent School District v. Rodriguez, 1184
Shack, State v., 762
Stanley v. Georgia, 245
Trump v. Hawaii, 249
UWM Post, Inc. v. Board of Regents, 1148
Wal-Mart Stores, Inc. v. Dukes, 464

TABLE OF AUTHORITIES

3 Ways to Meet the "Staggering" Amount of Unmet Legal Needs, YourABA (July 2018), 728

Abel, Richard L., American Lawyers (1989), 778

Abel, Richard L., The Globalization of Public Interest Law, 13 UCLA J. Int'l L. & Foreign Aff. 295 (2008), 961, 1021

Abichandani, Dimple, Pandemic Philanthropy: Moving from Relief to Power, Inside Philanthropy (May 7, 2020), 622

Abraham, Sparky, How Student Debt Is Worsening Gender and Racial Injustice, Current Affairs (June 26, 2018), 1199

Adams, Frank and Myles Horton, Unearthing Seeds of Fire: The Idea of Highlander (1975), 499

Ahmad, Muneer I., Resisting Guantánamo: Rights at the Brink of Dehumanization, 103 Nw. U.L. Rev. 1683 (2009), 597

Ahmad, Muneer I., The Ethics of Narrative, 11 Am. U. J. Gender Soc. Pol'y & L. 117 (2002), 866

Aiken, Jane H. and Stephen Wizner, Measuring Justice, 2013 Wis. L. Rev. 79 (2013), 328

Aiken, Jane H., Provocateurs for Justice, 7 Clinical L. Rev. 287 (2001), 365

Albelda, Randy, Robert W. Drago & Steven Shulman, Unlevel Playing Fields: Understanding Wage Inequality and Discrimination 121 (2d ed. 2004), 208

Albiston, Catherine R. and Laura Beth Nielsen, Funding the Cause: How Public Interest Law Organizations Fund Their Activities and Why It Matters for Social Change, 39 Law & Soc. Inquiry 62 (2014), 625

Aldana, Raquel, The Challenge and Potential for a Universal Human Rights Regime to Manage Migration in the Americas, in Compassionate Migration and Regional Policy in the Americas 113 (Steven W. Bender and William F. Arrocha eds. 2017), 611

Aldana, Raquel, The Indispensable Ones: A Story of Mining Resistance from La Puya, 166

Alexander, Michelle, Go to Trial: Crash the Justice System, N.Y. Times (Mar. 10, 2012), 525

Alexander, Michelle, The New Jim Crow: Mass Incarceration in the Age of Colorblindness (2010), 144, 175

Alexandre, Michéle, The New Frontiers of Civil Rights Litigation xxv–xxviii (2019), 113

Alfieri, Anthony V., The Antinomies of Poverty Law and a Theory of Dialogic Empowerment, 16 N.Y.U. Rev. L. & Soc. Change 659 (1988), 1131

Alford, Deleso, Critical Race Feminist Bioethics: Telling Stories in Law School and Medical School in Pursuit of, 922

Alinsky, Saul D., Reveille for Radicals 12–14 (1945), 499

Alinsky, Saul, Rules for Radicals: A Practical Primer for Realistic Radicals (1971), 499

Allinder, Sara M. and Janet Fleischman, The World's Largest HIV Epidemic in Crisis: HIV in South Africa, Center for Strategic and International Studies: Commentary (Apr. 2, 2019), 831

Alvarez, Alicia, Lawyers, Organizers, and Workers: Collaboration and Conflict in Worker Cooperative Development, 24 Geo. J. on Poverty L. & Pol'y 353 (2017), 1036

American Association of University Women, Deeper in Debt: Women and Student Loans (2020), 1199

American Association of University Women, The Simple Truth about the Gender Pay Gap, 1182

American Bar Association Task Force on Access to Civil Justice Et Al., Report to the House of Delegates (2006), 649

American Bar Found., Access Across America: First Report of the Civil Justice Infrastructure Mapping Project v (2011), 647

American Public Transportation Association, Who Rides Public Transportation (Jan. 2017), 34

Ancheta, Angelo N., Community Lawyering, 81 Cal. L. Rev. 1363 (1993), 56

Andrias, Kate, Confronting Power in Public Law, 130 Harv. L. Rev. Forum 1 (2016), 773

Anghie, Antony, LatCrit and TWAIL, 42 Cal. W. Int'l L.J. 311 (2012), 47

Ansley, Fran and Anne Lewis, Going South, Coming North: Migrant and Union Organizing in Morristown, Tennessee, Southern Spaces (May 19, 2011), 508

Ansley, Fran and John Gaventa, Researching for Democracy and Democratizing Research, 29 Change 46 (Jan.–Feb. 1997), 896

Ansley, Fran, Inclusive Boundaries and Other (Im)possible Paths Toward Community Development in a Global World, 150 U. Pa. L. Rev. 353 (2001), 1134

Ansley, Frances, Doing Policy from Below: Worker Solidarity and the Prospects for Immigration Reform, 41 Cornell Int'l L.J. 101 (2008), 518

Anzilotti, Eillie, More U.S. Businesses Are Becoming Worker Co-Ops: Here's Why, 1018

Archer, Deborah N., The New Housing Segregation: The Jim Crow Effects of Crime-Free Housing Ordinances, 118 Mich. L. Rev. 173 (2019), 1183

Armstrong, Margalynne J. and Stephanie M. Wildman, Teaching Race/Teaching Whiteness: Transforming Colorblindness to Color Insight, 86 N.C. L. Rev. 635 (2008), 355

Arriola, Elvia R., Staying Empowered by Recognizing Common Grounds, . . ., 71 UMKC L. Rev. 447 (2002), 958

Arriola, Elvia, Remarks Upon Receiving the Critical Pioneer Award at Latina/o Critical Legal Theory Conference (Oct. 2017), 1220

Arriola, Elvia, Symposium, Difference, Solidarity and Law: Building Latina/o Communities Through LatCrit Theory, Foreword—MARCH!, 19 Chicano-Latino L. Rev. 1 (1998), 181

Arthur, Andrew, A Good Rule, Poorly Written: How the Financial Crisis Highlighted the Inadequacy of IOLTA Rate Rules, 64 Cath. U. L. Rev. 729 (2015), 627

Article 19, The Right to Protest Background Paper (2016), 468

Asbed, Greg and Sean Sellers, The Fair Food Program: Comprehensive, Verifiable, and Sustainable Change for Farmworkers, 16 U. Pa. J. L. & Soc. Change 39 (2013), 1019

Ashar, Sameer M., Deep Critique and Democratic Lawyering in Clinical Practice, 104 Cal. L. Rev. 201 (2016), 1269

Ashar, Sameer M., Law Clinics and Collective Mobilization, 14 Clin. L. Rev. 355 (2008), 500, 1023

Ashar, Sameer, Public Interest Lawyers and Resistance Movements, 95 Cal. L. Rev. 1879 (2007), 1045

Auerbach, Jerold S., Unequal Justice: Lawyers and Social Change in Modern America (1976), 724, 778

Ayres, Ian, Fair Driving: Gender and Race Discrimination in Retail Car Negotiations, 104 Harv. L. Rev. 817 (1991), 909

Aziz, Sahar F., Identity Politics is Failing Women in Legal Academia, 69 J. Leg. Ed. (forthcoming 2021), 636

Bagust, Joanne, The Legal Profession and the Business of Law, 35 Syd. L. Rev. 27 (2013), 688

Baker, Shalanda H., Adaptive Law in the Anthropocene, 90 Chi.-Kent L. Rev. 563 (2015), 661

Bali, Asli U. and Aziz Rana, Pax Arabica?: Provisional Sovereignty and Intervention in the Arab Uprisings, 42 Cal. W. Int'l. L.J. 321 (2012), 939

Bandes, Susan, Empathy, Narrative, and Victim Impact Statements, 63 U. Chi. L. Rev. 361 (1996), 920

Bannai, Lorraine K., Enduring Conviction: Fred Korematsu and His Quest for Justice (2015), 243

Bannon, Alicia, Cathleen Lisk, and Peter Hardin, Who Pays for Judicial Races, Brennan Center for Justice (2019), 621

Bannon, Alicia, The Rise of Dark Money is a Threat to Judicial Independence, ABA J. (July 5, 2018), 621

Barber, Rev. Dr. William J., II, Research is Vital to the Moral Integrity of Social Movements, Economic Policy Institute, Working Economics Blog (Apr. 4, 2019), 411

Barkan, Steven M., Deconstructing Legal Research: A Law Librarian's Commentary on Critical Legal Studies, 79 L. Libr. J. 617 (1987), 185

Barnes, Mario, Black Women's Stories and the Criminal Law: Restating the Power of Narrative, 39 U.C. Davis L. Rev. 941 (2006), 919

Barry, Bruce, As Governor, Phil Bredesen Got Absurdly High Marks for C-Grade Work, The Nashville Scene (Jan. 6, 2011), 627

Barton, Ben, A Comparison Between the American Markets for Medical and Legal Services, 67 Hastings L.J. 1331 (2016), 729

Bascuas, Ricardo J., The American Inquisition: Sentencing After the Federal Guidelines, 45 Wake Forest L. Rev. 1 (2010), 155, 648

Baskaran, Priya, Introduction to Worker Cooperatives and their Role in the Changing Economy, 24 J. of Affordable Housing 355 (2015), 987

Bell, Derrick A., Jr., Brown v. Board of Education and the Interest-Convergence Dilemma, 93 Harv. L. Rev. 518 (1980), 119

Bell, Derrick A., Jr., Serving Two Masters: Integration Ideals and Client Interests in School Desegregation Litigation, 85 Yale L.J. 470 (1976), 99, 1173

Bell, Derrick, The Civil Rights Chronicles, 99 Harv. L. Rev. 4 (1985), 189

Bellow, Gary, Steady Work: A Practitioner's Reflections on Political Lawyering, 31 Harv. C.R.-C.L. L. Rev. 297 (1996), 52, 342, 495

Belt, Rabia, "And Then Comes Life": The Intersection of Race, Poverty, and Disability in HBO's The Wire, 13 Rutgers Race & L. Rev. 1 (2012), 375

Belt, Rabia, Disability: The Last Marriage Equality Frontier, Stanford Public Law Working Paper No. 2653117 (Aug. 29, 2015), 337

Bender, Steven W., From Sandoval to Subprime: Excluding Latinos from Property Ownership and Property Casebooks, in Vulnerable Populations and Transformative Law Teaching: A Critical Reader (2011), 762

Bender, Steven W., How the West Was Juan: Reimagining the U.S.-Mexico Border (2017), 1090

Bender, Steven W., Mea Culpa: Lessons on Law and Regret From U.S. History 8–9 (2015), 597

Bender, Steven W., Tierra y Libertad: Land, Liberty, and Latino Housing ch. 2 (2010), 1090

Benfer, Emily A., Contaminated Childhood: The Chronic Lead Poisoning of Low-Income Children and Communities of Color in the United States (Aug. 8, 2017), 161

Bennett, Michael and Cruz Reynoso, California Rural Legal Assistance (CRLA): Survival of a Poverty Law Practice, 1 Chicano L. Rev. 1 (1972), 777

Bennett, Susan D., Little Engines That Could: Community Clients, Their Lawyers, and Training in the Arts of Democracy, 2002 Wis. L. Rev. 469 (2002), 556

Bennett, Susan, On Long-Haul Lawyering, 25 Fordham Urb. L.J. 771 (1998), 1219

Berenguer, Elizabeth, Lucy Jewel & Teri A. McMurtry-Chubb, Gut Renovations: Using Critical and Comparative Rhetoric to Remodel How the Law Addresses Privilege and Power, 23 Harv. Lat. L. Rev. 205 (2020), 785

Bernal, Vanessa Gómez and Beltrán Roca, Disability, Social Movements and Radical Theory: An Anthropological Approach, 22 Anthropological Notebooks 79 (2016), 377

Bettinger-Lopez, Caroline, Davida Finger, Meetali Jain, JoNel Newman, Sarah Paoletti & Deborah M. Weissman, Redefining Human Rights Lawyering Through the Lens of Critical Theory: Lessons for Pedagogy and Practice, 18 Geo. J. on Poverty L. & Pol'y 337 (2011), 606, 961

Bezdek, Barbara L., Alinsky's Prescription: Democracy Alongside Law, 42 John Marshall L. Rev. 723 (2009), 499

Bezdek, Barbara, Digging into Democracy: Reflections on CED and Social Change Lawyering after #OWS, 77 Md. L. Rev. Endnotes 16 (2018), 423

Bhatti, Saqib and Stephen Lerner, Labor Must Take on Capital (Aug. 9, 2016), 1019

Bhutto, Fatima, Caste by Isabel Wilkerson Review—A Dark Study of Violence and Power, The Guardian (July 30, 2020), 84

Birgden, Astrid, Maximizing Desistance: Adding Therapeutic Jurisprudence and Human Rights to the Mix, 24 Crim. Just. & Behav. 19 (2015), 784

Biu, Ofronama, Race to Lead: Women of Color in the Nonprofit Sector, Building Movement Project (2019), 624

Blasi, Gary, Framing Access to Justice: Beyond Perceived Justice for Individuals, 42 Loy. L.A. L. Rev. 913 (2009), 648, 651

Blasi, Gary, What's a Theory For?: Notes on Reconstructing Poverty Law Scholarship, 48 U. Miami L. Rev. 1063 (1994), 876

Bobo, Kim, Jackie Kendall & Steve Max, Organizing for Social Change, Midwest Academy Manual for Activists 11–13 (2001), 499, 962

Bonilla, Daniel, Legal Clinics in the Global North and South: Between Equality and Subordination—An Essay, 16 Yale Hum. Rts. & Dev. L.J. 1 (2013), 961

Bonilla-López, Viviana, Beyond Medical Legal Partnerships: Addressing Recovery-Harming Social Conditions through Clubhouse-Legal Partnerships, 43 N.Y.U. Rev. of L. & Soc. Change 429 (2019), 653

Borrego, Susan E., Understanding My Privilege, TEDx Talks (Dec. 9, 2016), 256

Bosman, Julie, Kate Taylor & Tim Arango, A Common Trait Among Mass Killers: Hatred Toward Women, N.Y. Times (Aug. 10, 2019), 1165

Boucai, Michael, Glorious Precedents: When Gay Marriage Was Radical, 27 Yale J. of L. & Human. 1 (2015), 221

Bourdieu, Pierre, Social Space and Symbolic Power, 7 Soc. Theory 14 (1989), 738

Bourdieu, Pierre, Utopia of Endless Exploitation: The Essence of Neoliberalism, Le Monde Diplomatique (Dec. 1998), 477

Bowman, Lorenzo, Tonette Rocco & Elizabeth Peterson, The Exclusion of Race from Mandated Continuing Legal Education Requirements: A Critical Race Theory Analysis, 8 Seattle J. Soc. Just. 229 (2009), 730

Bown, Stephen R., Merchant Kings: When Companies Ruled the World, 1600–1900 (2010), 198, 1095

BP-Weeks, Maurice and Liz Perlman, Bargaining for the Common Good as Racial Justice, The Forge: Organizing Strategy and Practice (Mar. 31, 2020), 1211

Braley, Mark D., Legal Aid, Facing State Cuts, Remains Crucial During Pandemic, Va. Mercury (Apr. 22, 2020), 628

Brandeis, Louis D., The Opportunity in the Law, in Business—A Profession 321 (1914), 675

Bratt, Cheryl, Top-Down or from the Ground?: A Practical Perspective on Reforming the Field of Children and the Law, 127 Yale L.J. Forum 917 (2018), 847

Brewer, Adam, The Coronavirus Was an Emergency Until Trump Found Out Who was Dying, The Atlantic (May 8, 2020), 1085

Brothers, John, Report: LGBT Nonprofits See Increase in Philanthropic Funding, Nonprofit Quarterly (Jan. 6, 2015), 621

Brown, Emma, On the Anniversary of Brown v. Board, New Evidence that U.S. Schools Are Resegregating, Wash. Post (May 17, 2016), 1173

Browne, Simone, Dark Matters: On the Surveillance of Blackness (2015), 943

Browning, Gary and Andrew Kilmister, Critical and Post-Critical Political Economy (2006), 208

Brown-Nagin, Tomiko, Courage to Dissent: Atlanta and the Long History of the Civil Rights Movement (2011), 1173

Bruno, Kenny, Joshua Karlina & China Brotsky, Greenhouse Gangsters vs. Climate Justice, Transnational Resource and Action Center (Nov. 1999), 660

Bryant, Susan, Collaboration in Law Practice: A Satisfying and Productive Process for a Diverse Profession, 17 Vt. L. Rev. 459 (1993), 531, 1044

Burden-Stelly, Charisse, Caste Does Not Explain Race, Bost. Rev. (Dec. 15, 2020), 85

Burke, Marion C., Lessons from Labor Feminists: Using Collective Action to Improve Conditions for Women Lawyers, 26 Am. U. J. Gender Soc. Pol'y & L. 559 (2017), 686

Burke, Mary C. and Mary Bernstein, How the Right Usurped the Queer Agenda: Frame Co-optation in Political Discourse, 29 Sociological Forum 830 (2014), 635

Butler, Paul, Let's Get Free: A Hip-Hop Theory of Justice (2010), 143, 159

Cain, Patricia A., Lesbian Perspective, Lesbian Experience, and the Risk of Essentialism, 2 Va. J. Soc. Pol'y & L. 43 (1994), 389

Calavita, Kitty, Collisions at the Intersection of Gender, Race, and Class: Enforcing the Chinese Exclusion Laws, 40 Law & Soc'y Rev. 249 (2006), 210

Callahan, David, Felicia Wong on Challenging Neoliberalism and Reimagining Capitalism, Blue Tent (Feb. 12, 2021), 953

Callahan, David, Systemic Failure: Four Reasons Philanthropy Keeps Losing the Battle Against Inequality, Inside Philanthropy, (Jan. 10, 2018), 633

Calmore, John O., A Call to Context: The Professional Challenges of Cause Lawyering at the Intersection of Race, Space, and Poverty, 67 Fordham L. Rev. 1927 (1999), 176, 793

Campney, Brent M.S., Brown, Black, and White in Texas, Southern Spaces (Mar. 13, 2012), 873

Capulong, Eduardo R.C., Client Activism in Progressive Lawyering Theory, 16 Clinical L. Rev. 109 (2009), 1273

Carbado, Devon W., Predatory Policing, 85 UMKC L. Rev. 545 (2016), 143

Carbado, Devon W., Straight out of the Closet, 15 Berkeley Women's L.J. 76 (2000), 258

Cardozo, Benjamin, The Nature of the Judicial Process (1921), 42

Carle, Susan D., How Should We Theorize Class Interests in Thinking About Professional Regulation: The Early NAACP as a Case Example, 12 Cornell J.L. & Pub. Pol'y 571 (2003), 777

Carle, Susan D., Re-Valuing Lawyering for Middle-Income Clients, 70 Fordham L. Rev. 719 (2001), 496

Carmody, Tim, How the Flint River Got So Toxic (Feb. 26, 2016), 159

Carpenter, Kristen A. and Eli Wald, Lawyering for Groups: The Case of American Indian Tribal Attorneys, 81 Fordham L. Rev. 3085 (2013), 783

Carter, President Jimmy, Remarks at the 100th Anniversary Luncheon of the Los Angeles County Bar Association, in 64 A.B.A. J. 840 (1978), 646

Casebeer, Kenneth M., Community Syndicalism for the United States: Democratic Production in Resisting Hegemonic Globalization and Law, 17 Employee Rts. & Emp. Pol'y J. 237 (2013), 987

Casebeer, Kenneth, Aliquippa: The Company Town and Contested Power in the Construction of Law, 43 Buff. L. Rev. 617 (1995), 423

CBO Report: Rich Get Richer, Poor Get Poorer (Aug. 18, 2016), 1182

Center for American Progress, Aisha C. Moodie-Mills, Jumping Beyond the Broom: Why Black Gay and Transgender Americans Need More Than Marriage Equality, 301

Chacón, Jennifer M., Privatized Immigration Enforcement, 52 Harv. C.R.-C.L. L. Rev. 1 (2017), 143

Chanbonpin, Kim David, How the Border Crossed Us: Filling the Gap between Plume v. Seward and the Dispossession of Mexican Landowners in California after 1848, 52 Clev. St. L. Rev. 297 (2005), 1090

Chang, Robert S. and Jerome M. Culp, Jr., Business as Usual? Brown and the Continuing Conundrum of Race in America, 2004 U. Ill. L. Rev. 1181 (2004), 1175

Chang, Robert S. and Keith Aoki, Centering the Immigrant in the Inter/National Imagination, 10 La Raza L.J. 309 (1997), 846

Chang, Robert S. and Keith Aoki, Centering the Immigrant in the Inter/National Imagination, 85 Cal. L. Rev. 1395, 846

Chang, Robert S., The End of Innocence or Politics After the Fall of the Essential Subject, 45 Am. U.L. Rev. 687 (1996), 383

Chapman, Peter, Bananas: How the United Fruit Company Shaped the World 197 (2007), 1094

Charlie Cray, The Lewis Powell Memo: Corporate Blueprint to Dominate Democracy, Greenpeace Blog (Aug. 23, 2011), 460

Chase, Anthony R., Race, Culture, and Contract Law: From the Cottonfield to the Courtroom, 28 Conn. L. Rev. 1 (1995), 439

Cházaro, Angélica, The End of Deportation, 67 UCLA L. Rev. (forthcoming 2021), 228

Chemerinsky, Erwin, The Segregation and Resegregation of American Public Education: The Courts' Role, 81 N.C. L. Rev. 1597 (2003), 92

Chess, Simon, Alison Kafer, Jessi Quizar & Mattie Udora Richardson, Calling All Restroom Revolutionaries 217, in That's Revolting!: Queer Strategies for Resisting Assimilation (Mattilda Sycamore ed. 2008), 580

Chimni, B. S., International Institutions Today: An Imperial Global State in the Making, 15 Eur. J. Int'l L. 1 (2004), 468

Chin, Gabriel J. and Randy Wagner, The Tyranny of the Minority: Jim Crow and the Counter-Majoritarian Difficulty, 43 Harv. C.R.-C.L. L. Rev. 65 (2008), 131

Ching, Jennifer, Thomas B. Harvey, Meena Jagannath, Purvi Shah & Blake Strode, A Few Interventions and Offerings from Five Movement Lawyers to the Access to Justice Movement, 87 Fordham L. Rev. Online (2018), 653

Cho, Sumi K., Essential Politics, Essential Politics, 2 Harv. Latino L. Rev. 433 (1997), 5

Chu, David, Setting a Research Agenda: Knowledge Is Power . . . If You Know What to Do With It, 12 Labor Res. Rev. 41 (1993), 859

Chuang, Janie A., Using Global Migration Law to Prevent Human Trafficking, 111 AJIL Unbound 147 (2017), 671

Chun, Jennifer Jihye, George Lipsitz & Young Shin, Intersectionality as a Social Movement Strategy: Asian Immigrant Women Advocates, 38 Signs: J. of Women in Culture and Soc. 917 (2013), 394

Churchill by Himself: The Definitive Collection of Quotations vii (2008), 131

Clarke, Jessica A., They, Them, and Theirs, 132 Harv. L. Rev. 894 (2019), 395

Climate Justice Youth Summit, Climate Justice Alliance (Oct. 3, 2019), 660

Clulow, Adam and Tristan Mostert, The Dutch and English East India Companies: Diplomacy, Trade and Violence in Early Modern Asia (2019), 1095

Coker, Donna, Shifting Power for Battered Women: Law, Material Resources and Poor Women of Color, 33 U.C. Davis L. Rev. 1009 (2000), 918

Cole, David, Turning the Corner on Mass Incarceration?, 9 Ohio St. J. Crim. L. 27 (2011), 143

Cole, Luke W. and Caroline Farrell, Structural Racism, Structural Pollution and the Need for a New Paradigm, 20 Wash. U. J.L. & Pol'y 265 (2006), 536

Colker, Ruth, Anti-subordination Above All: A Disability Perspective, 82 Notre Dame L. Rev. 1415 (2007), 1218

Colker, Ruth, Anti-Subordination Above All: Sex, Race, and Equal Protection, 61 N.Y.U. L. Rev. 1003 (1986), 399

Collective Impact Forum, 10 Lessons Learned from Engaging the Business Community in Collective Impact (July 14, 2015), 593

Conger, Kate and Noam Scheiber, Employee Activism is Alive in Tech. It Stops Short of Organizing Unions, N.Y. Times (July 8, 2019), 701

Constitutional Law 558 (Geoffrey R. Stone, Louis M. Seidman, Cass R. Sunstein, Mark V. Tushnet & Pamela S. Karlan eds. 8th ed. 2017), 754

Cook, Anthony E., The Spiritual Movement Towards Justice, 1992 U. Ill. L. Rev. 1007 (1992), 443

Cook, Daniella Ann and Adrienne D. Dixson, Writing Critical Race Theory and Method: A Composite Counterstory on the Experiences of Black Teachers in New Orleans

Post-Katrina, 26 Int'l J. of Qualitative Studies in Educ. 1238 (2013), 920

Cook, Nancy L., Outside the Tradition: Literature as Legal Scholarship, 63 U. Cin. L. Rev. 95 (1994), 920

Cooper, Elizabeth B., The Appearance of Professionalism, 71 Fla. L. Rev. 1 (2019), 729

Cooper, Michael, Caught in the Middle of #MeToo: Unions that Represent Accusers and Accused, N.Y. Times (May 17, 2019), 839

Cover, Robert, Violence and the Word, 95 Yale L.J. 1601 (1986), 176

Cox, Oliver Cromwell, Caste, Class, and Race: A Study in Social Dynamics (1948), 85

Crain, Marion, Colorblind Unionism, 49 UCLA L. Rev. 1313 (2002), 686

Crain, Marion, The Transformation of the Professional Workforce, 79 Chi.-Kent L. Rev. 543 (2004), 679

Crenshaw, Kimberlé W., From Private Violence to Mass Incarceration: Thinking Intersectionally About Women, Race, and Social Control, 59 UCLA L. Rev. 1418 (2012), 143

Crenshaw, Kimberlé Williams, Race, Reform, and Retrenchment: Transformation and Legitimation in Antidiscrimination Law, 101 Harv. L. Rev. 1331 (1988), 108

Crenshaw, Kimberlé, Demarginalizing the Intersection of Race and Sex: A Black Feminist Critique of Antidiscrimination Doctrine, Feminist Theory and Antiracist Politics, 1989 U. Chi. Legal F. 139 (1989), 388

Crenshaw, Kimberlé, Mapping the Margins: Intersectionality, Identity Politics, and Violence Against Women of Color, 43 Stan. L. Rev. 1241 (1991), 388

Cruz, Christine Zuni, [On The] Road Back in: Community Lawyering in Indigenous Communities, 24 Am. Indian L. Rev. 229 (2000), 1021, 1222

Cruz, Christine Zuni, [On The] Road Back in: Community Lawyering in Indigenous Communities, 5 Clinical L. Rev. 557 (1999), 1222

Culp, Jerome M., Jr., Angela P. Harris & Francisco Valdes, Subject Unrest, 55 Stan. L. Rev. 2435 (2003), 399

Culp, Jerome M., Jr., Latinos, Blacks, Others, and the New Legal Narrative, 2 Harv. Latino L. Rev. 479 (1997), 517

Cummings, Scott I., How Lawyers Manage Intragroup Dissent, 89 Chi.-Kent L. Rev. 547 (2014), 556

Cummings, Scott L. and Alan K. Chen, Public Interest Lawyering (2013), 778

Cummings, Scott L. and Douglas NeJaime, Lawyering for Marriage Equality, 57 UCLA L. Rev. 1235 (2010), 315

Cummings, Scott L., Community Economic Development as Progressive Politics: Toward a Grassroots Movement for Economic Justice, 54 Stan. L. Rev. 399 (2001), 963

Cummings, Scott L., Developing Cooperatives as a Job Creation Strategy for Low-Income Workers, 25 N.Y.U. Rev. L. & Soc. Change 181 (1999), 987

Cummings, Scott L., How Lawyers Manage Intragroup Dissent, 89 Chi.-Kent L. Rev. 547 (2014), 1048

Cummings, Scott L., Law in the Labor Movement's Challenge to Wal-Mart: A Case Study of the Inglewood Site Fight, 95 Cal. L. Rev. 1927 (2007), 968

Cummings, Scott L., Rethinking Foundational Critiques of Lawyers in Social Movements, 85 Fordham L. Rev. 1987 (2017), 1172

Cummings, Scott, Critical Legal Consciousness in Action, 120 Harv. L. Rev. F. 62 (2007), 1172

Cummins, Eleanor, Michigan is Practically Giving Away Clean Water—But Not To Flint (Apr. 13, 2018), 160

da Silva, Denise Ferreira, An Outline of a Global Political Subject: Reading Evo Morales's Election as a (Post-) Colonial Event, 8 Seattle J. Soc. Just 25 (2009), 82

Dalrymple, William, The Anarchy: The East India Company, Corporate Violence, and the Pillage of an Empire (2019), 1095

Dansinger, Larry, Class Diversity Improves Your Nonprofit Board, Class Action (Sept. 21, 2017), 623

Dastin, Jeffrey, Amazon Scraps Secret AI Recruiting Tool That Showed Bias Against Women (Oct. 9, 2018), 363

Davis, Adrienne D., The Private Law of Race and Sex: An Antebellum Perspective, 51 Stan. L. Rev. 221 (1999), 444

Davis, Angela J., Policing the Black Man: Arrest, Prosecution, and Imprisonment (Angela J. Davis ed. 2017), 175

Davis, Angela Y., Women, Culture, and Politics 14 (1989), 206

Davis, Peggy C., Law as Microaggression, 98 Yale L.J. 1559 (1989), 264, 266

Dawson, Andrew B., Labor Activism in Bankruptcy, 89 Am. Bankr. L.J. 97 (2015), 504

de Castro, Douglas, The Colonial Aspects of the International Environmental Law—Treaties as Promoters of Continuous Structural Violence, 5 Groningen J. of Int'l L. 168 (2017), 860

Dearden, Nick, Generating Terror: The Role of International Financial Institutions in Sustaining Guatemala's Genocidal Regimes, Jubilee Debt Campaign 3–4 (Dec. 2012), 1111

Delgado, Richard and David Yen, "The Speech We Hate": First Amendment Totalism, the ACLU, and the Principle of Dialogic Politics, 27 Ariz. St. L.J. 1281, 1148

Delgado, Richard and Jean Stefancic, California's Racial History and Constitutional Rationales for Race-Conscious Decision Making in Higher Education, 47 UCLA L. Rev. 1521 (2000), 933

Delgado, Richard and Jean Stefancic, Home-Grown Racism: Colorado's Historic Embrace—And Denial—Of Equal Opportunity in Higher Education, 70 U. Colo. L. Rev. 703 (1999), 933

Delgado, Richard and Jean Stefancic, Images of the Outsider in American Law and Culture: Can Free Expression Remedy Systemic Social Ills?, 77 Cornell L. Rev. 1258 (1992), 1143

Delgado, Richard and Jean Stefancic, Why Do We Ask the Same Questions? The Triple Helix Dilemma Revisited, 99 Law Libr. J. 307 (2007), 879

Delgado, Richard and Jean Stefancic, Why Do We Tell the Same Stories? Law Reform, Critical Librarianship, and the Triple Helix Dilemma, 42 Stan. L. Rev. 207 (1989), 895

Delgado, Richard, Law's Violence: Derrick Bell's Next Article, 75 U. Pitt. L. Rev. 435 (2014), 675

Delgado, Richard, Storytelling for Oppositionists and Others: A Plea for Narrative, 87 Mich. L. Rev. 2411 (1988), 921

Dennis, Andrea L., Black Contemporary Social Movements, Resource Mobilization, and Black Musical Activism, 79 Law & Contemp. Probs. 29 (2016), 474

Derocher, Robert J., The IOLTA Crash: Fallout for Foundations, 37 ABA Bar Leader (Sept.–Oct. 2012), 627

Diamond, Michael and Aaron O'Toole, Leaders, Followers, and Free Riders: The Community Lawyer's Dilemma When Representing Non-Democratic Client Organizations, 31 Fordham Urb. L.J. 481 (2004), 556, 778

Dias-Abey, Manoj, Justice in Our Fields: Can "Alt-Labor" Organizations Improve Migrant Farm Workers' Conditions, 53 Harv. C.R.-C.L. L. Rev. 167 (2018), 1019

Disability in Philanthropy and Nonprofits: A Study on Inclusion and Exclusion of the 1-in-5 People Who Live with a Disability and What You Can Do to Make Things Better, Respectability 2 (2019), 624

Dolloff, Ross and Luke Hill, Collaboration with Broad-Based Organizing Projects—The Legal Services Staffer and Organizer Perspectives, Mgmt. Info. Exchange J. 3 (Fall 2000), 499

Domhoff, G. William et al., Studying the Power Elite: Fifty Years of Who Rules America? (2018), 427

Dorsey, Cheryl, Jeff Bradach, and Peter Kim, Racial Equity and Philanthropy: Disparities in Funding for Leaders of Color Leave Impact on the Table, Echoing Green and The Bridgespan Group 3 (2020), 622

Dudziak, Mary L., Cold War, Civil Rights: Race and the Image of American Democracy 13 (2000), 130

Dunbar-Ortiz, Roxanne, Stop Saying This is a Nation of Immigrants!, Resisting Colonialism, Colours of Resistance Archive, 1057

Dyrness, Andrea, Research for Change versus Research as Change: Lessons from a Mujerista Participatory Research Team, 39 Anthro. & Educ. Q. 23 (2008), 857

Eagly, Ingrid V., Community Education: Creating a New Vision of Legal Services Practice, 4 Clin. L. Rev. 433 (1998), 958

Eastman, Herbert A., Speaking Truth to Power: The Language of Civil Rights Litigators, 104 Yale L.J. 763 (1995), 43

Edwards, Linda H., Telling Stories in the Supreme Court: Voices Briefs and the Role of Democracy in Constitutional Deliberation, 29 Yale J. of L. and Feminism 29 (2017), 43

Edwards, Linda H., Where Do the Prophets Stand? Hamdi, Myth, and the Master's Tools, 13 Conn. Pub. Int. L.J. 43 (2013), 742, 929

Ehrenreich, Nancy and Beth Lyon, The Global Politics of Food: A Critical Overview, 43 U. Miami Inter-Am. L. Rev. 1 (2011), 480

Ehrenreich, Nancy, The Colonization of the Womb, 43 Duke L.J. 492 (1993), 1151

Eisenberg, Pablo, Foundation Boards Shouldn't Be Filled with Just Wealthy People, The Chronicle of Philanthropy (June 1, 2011), 623

Elias, Marilyn, The School-to-Prison Pipeline, Teaching Tolerance (Spring 2013), 142

Eliason, Antonia, With No Deliberate Speed: The Segregation of Roma Children in Europe, 27 Duke J. Comp. & Int'l L. 191 (2017), 1214

Ellinger-Locke, Maggie, Anti-Protest Legislation is Threatening our Climate, Greenpeace (May 3, 2019), 467

Elsesser, Charles, Community Lawyering—the Role of Lawyers in the Social Justice Movement, 14 Loy. J. Pub. Int. L. 375 (2013), 365, 500, 957

Engler, Russell, Connecting Self-Representation to Civil Gideon: What Existing Data Reveal About When Counsel is Most Needed, 37 Fordham Urb. L.J. 37 (2010), 647

Equal Access to Justice: Ensuring Meaningful Access to Counsel in Civil Cases, Including Immigration Proceedings (July 2014), 647

Equal Education For All, Wash. Post (May 19, 1954), 87

Erickson, Erick-Woods, What Trump Got Wrong on Charlottesville, N.Y. Times (Aug. 13, 2017), 1129

Essed, Philomena and Sara Louise Muhr, Entitlement Racism and Its Intersections: An Interview with Philomena Essed, Social Justice Scholar, 18 Ephemera: Theory and Politics in Organization 183 (2018), 1133

Fact Sheet, How to Promote Gender Equity in Career and Technical Education: A Primer for Schools, National Women's Law Center (2007), 1174

Farbenblum, Bassina and Justine Nolan, The Business of Migrant Worker Recruitment: Who Has the Responsibility and Leverage to Protect Rights?, 52 Tex. Int'l L.J. 1 (2017), 941

Farber, Daniel A. and Suzanna Sherry, Beyond All Reason: The Radical Assault on Truth in American Law 78 (1997), 921, 930

Farley, Anthony P., Perfecting Slavery, 36 Loy. U. Chi. L.J. 225 (2004), 280

Fassinger, Ruth and Susan Morrow, Toward Best Practices in Quantitative, Qualitative, and Mixed-Method Research: A Social Justice Perspective, 5 J. for Soc. Action in Counseling and Psych. 69 (2013), 865

Fay-Ramirez, Suzanna, Therapeutic Jurisprudence in Practice: Changes in Family Treatment Court Norms over Time, 40 L. & Soc. Inquiry 205 (2015), 784

Feagin, Joe R. and Kimberley Ducey, Elite White Men Ruling: Who, What, When, Where, and How (2017), 427, 1166

Feldman, S. M., The Transformation of An Academic Discipline, 54 J. Legal Ed. 206 (2004), 741

Ferguson, Sian, Privilege 101: A Quick and Dirty Guide, Everyday Feminism (Sept. 29, 2014), 257

Ferree, Myra Max and Silke Roth, Gender, Class, and the Interaction Between Social Movements: A Strike of West Berlin Day Care Workers, 12 Gender & Soc'y 626 (1998), 1047

Ferree, Myra Max, The Discursive Politics of Feminist Intersectionality, in Framing Intersectionality: Debates on a Multi-faceted Concept in Gender Studies 58 (Helma Lutz, Maria Teresa Herrera Vivar & Linda Supik eds. 2011), 741

Fine, Janice, Worker Centers: Organizing Communities at the Edge of the Dream, 50 N.Y. L. Sch. L. Rev. 417 (2005–2006), 499

Fineman, Martha Albertson, Vulnerability and Social Justice, 53 Val. U.L. Rev. 341 (2019), 768

Fiss, Owen, Groups and the Equal Protection Clause, in Equality and Preferential Treatment: A Philosophy and Public Affairs Reader 84, 106 (Marshall Cohen, Thomas Nagel & Thomas Scanlon eds. 1977), 398

Flagg, Barbara J., Was Blind But Now I See (1997), 255

Fletcher, Bill, Jr., Race Is About More Than Discrimination: Racial Capitalism, the Settler State, and the Challenges Facing Organized Labor in the United States, Monthly Rev. (July 1, 2020), 839

Flores, Claudia, Beyond the Bad Apple—Transforming the American Workplace for Women After #MeToo, 2019 U. Chi. Legal F. 85 (2019), 1019

Frank, Jerome, Law and the Modern Mind (1930), 742

Frank, Jerome, What Courts Do In Fact, 26 Ill. L. Rev. 645 (1932), 42

Franks, Mary Anne, Where the Law Lies: Constitutional Fictions and Their Discontents, In Law and Lies: Deceptions and Truth-Telling in the American Legal System (Austin Sarat ed. 2015), 430

Frazwlle, Brian R., A Banner Year for Business as the Supreme Court's Conservative Majority is Restored, 2017–2018 Term, Constitutional Accountability Center (July 17, 2018), 459

Freeman, Andrea, You Better Work: Unconstitutional Work Requirements, 53 U.C. Davis L. Rev. 1531 (2020), 303

Freeman, Jim, Supporting Social Movements: A Brief Guide for Lawyers and Law Students, 12 Hastings Race & Poverty L.J. 191 (2015), 500, 958

Freire, Paulo, Pedagogy of the Oppressed (1970), 499

From Extraction to Emancipation: Development Reimagined (Raquel Aldana and Steven W. Bender eds. 2018), 166

Galanter, Marc, Why the "Haves" Come out Ahead: Speculations on the Limits of Legal Change, 9 Law & Soc'y Rev. 95 (1974), 502

Gamble, Barbara, Putting Civil Rights to a Popular Vote, 41 Am. J. of Pol. Science 245 (Jan. 1997), 131

Ganz, Marshall, Organizing: People, Power, Change, Week 1: What is Organizing? (Sept. 2006), 501

Ganz, Marshall, Why David Sometimes Wins: Leadership, Organization and Strategy in the California Farm Worker Movement (2009), 499

Ganzi, John, Frances Seymour, Sandy Buffett & Navroz Dubash, Leverage for the Environment: A Guide to the Private Financial Services Industry (1998), 951

García Hernández, César Cuauhtémoc, Naturalizing Immigration Imprisonment, 103 Cal. L. Rev. 1449 (2015), 152

Gehlert, Heather, Ending the School-to-Prison Pipeline: A Case Study of Community-Led Disciplinary Reform in Kern County, 1201

George, Marie-Amélie, Queering Reproductive Justice, 54 U. Rich. L. Rev. 671 (2020), 313

Gerstein, Josh, Alito's Politically Charged Address Draws Heat, Politico (Nov. 13, 2020), 253

Gilbertsen, Beth and Vijit Ramchandani, Developing Effective Teams: Proven Methods for Smoother and More Productive Teamwork 1–2 (Wilder Foundation, Sept. 2003), 555

Gilens, Martin and Benjamin I. Page, Testing Theories of American Politics: Elites, Interest Groups, and Average Citizens, 12 Perspectives on Politics 564 (Sept. 2014), 132

Gilman, Michele E., En-Gendering Economic Inequality, 32 Colum. J. Gender & L. 1 (2016), 310

Gilman, Sander I., Are Jews White: Theories of Race and Racism: A

Reader, 294–302 (John Solomos and Les Back eds. 2009), 396

Giridharadas, Arnand, Winners Take All: The Elite Charade of Changing the World (2018), 628

Giving By and For Women, IUPUI Women's Philanthropy Institute 6 (2018), 622

Glendon, Mary Ann, A World Made New (2001), 605

Glick, Brian, Two, Three, Many Rosas! Rebellious Lawyers and Progressive Activist Organizations, 23 Clinical L. Rev. 611 (2017), 649, 1023, 1266

Global Gender Based Violence in the Walmart Garment Supply Chain, Workers Voices from the Global Supply Chain: A Report to the ILO 2018, Asia Floor Wage Alliance, CENTRAL Cambodia, & Global Labor Justice (May 2018), 803

Globalization from Below: Toward a Cosmopolitan Legality (Boaventura de Sousa Santos and César Rodriguez-Garavito eds. 2006), 961

Glover, J. Maria, "Encroachments and Oppressions": The Corporatization of Procedure and the Decline of Rule of Law, 86 Fordham L. Rev. 2113 (2018), 462

Goldberg, David Theo, The Racial State 112 (2002), 1062

Gómez, Laura E., Trump's White House Says Critical Race Theory is Anti-American. Here's the Truth (Sept. 11, 2020), 66

Gonzalez, Carmen G., Bridging the North-South Divide: International Environmental Law in the Anthropocene, 32 Pace Envtl. L. Rev. 407 (2015), 666

Gonzalez, Jacinta and Jennifer J. Rosenbaum, Deporting the Evidence: Migrant Workers in the South Expose How U.S. Immigration Enforcement Against Human Rights Defenders Violates the International Covenant on Civil and Political Rights (2013), 648

González, Marc-Tizoc, Critical Ethnic Legal Histories: Unearthing the Interracial Justice of Filipino American Agricultural Labor Organizing, 3 U.C. Irvine L. Rev. 991 (2013), 207, 921

González, Thalia, A Quiet Revolution: Mindfulness, Rebellious Lawyering, and Community Practice, 53 Cal. W.L. Rev. 49 (2016), 658

Goodman, Peter S., End of Apartheid in South Africa? Not in Economic Terms, N.Y. Times (Oct. 24, 2017), 831

Gordon, Jennifer, Law, Lawyers, and Labor: The United Farm Workers' Legal Strategy in the 1960s and 1970s and the Role of Law in Union Organizing Today, 8 U. Pa. J. Lab. & Emp. L. 1 (2005), 1248

Gordon, Jennifer, Suburban Sweatshops: The Fight for Immigrant Rights (2009), 998

Gordon, Jennifer, The Lawyer is not the Protagonist, 95 Cal. L. Rev. 2133 (2007), 500

Gordon, Jennifer, We Make the Road by Walking: Immigrant Workers, the Workplace Project, and the Struggle for Social Change, 30 Harv. C.R.-C.L. L. Rev. 407 (1995), 999

Gordon, Robert W., The Struggle Over the Past, 44 Cleve. St. L. Rev. 123 (1996), 207

Gorn, Elliott J., Mother Jones: The Most Dangerous Woman in America 99 (2001), 706

Gott, Gil, The Devil We Know: Racial Subordination and National Security Law, 50 Vill. L. Rev. 1073 (2005), 378

Gottschalk, Marie, Bring It on: The Future of Penal Reform, the Carceral State, and American Politics, 12 Ohio St. J. Crim. L. 559 (2015), 155

Gottschalk, Marie, Caught: The Prison State and the Lockdown of American Politics 2 (2015), 143

Government Accountability Office, Department of Labor: Wage and Hour Division's Complaint Intake and Investigative Processes Leave Low Wage Workers Vulnerable to Wage Theft, GAO-09-458T (Mar. 25, 2009), 647

Grassroots Policy Project, Race, Power and Policy: Dismantling Structural Racism (2010), 208

Grewal, David Singh, Amy Kapczynski, and Jedediah Purdy, Law and Political Economy: Toward a Manifesto (Nov. 6, 2017), 207

Grillo, Trina, Anti-Essentialism and Intersectionality: Tools to Dismantle the Master's House, 10 Berkeley Women's L.J. 16 (1995), 390

Grinthal, Michael, Power with: Practice Models for Social Justice Lawyering, 15 U. Pa. J. L. & Soc. Change 25 (2011), 1024

Gruber, Aya, Navigating Diverse Identities: Building Coalitions Through Redistribution of Academic Capital—An Exercise in Praxis, 35 Seton Hall L. Rev. 1201 (2005), 635

Guinier, Lani and Gerald Torres, Changing the Wind: Notes Toward a Demosprudence of Law and Social Movements, 123 Yale L.J. 2740 (2014), 23

Guinier, Lani, Michelle Fine, Jane Balin, Ann Bartow & Deborah Lee Stachel, Becoming Gentlemen: Women's Experiences at One Ivy League Law School, 143 U. Pa. L. Rev. 1 (1994), 738

Guinier, Lani, The Tyranny of the Majority 107–08 (1994), 770

Gustafson, Kaaryn, More Work Needs to be Done to Prevent Exclusion of the Disabled, N.Y. Times (July 26, 2015), 580

Guyette, Curt, Schuette, Orr, Obstruct Scrutiny of PA 436, Detroit Metro Times (May 5, 2014), 174

Hair, Penda D., Louder than Words: Lawyers, Communities and the Struggle for Justice (2001), 576

Hallett, Nicole, From the Picket Line to the Courtroom: A Labor Organizing Privilege to Protect Workers, 39 N.Y.U. Rev. L. & Soc. Change 475 (2015), 720

Hanauer, Nick, Better Schools Won't Fix America, The Atlantic (July 2019), 1174

Haney López, Ian F., Dog Whistle Politics: How Coded Racial Appeals Have Reinvented Racism and Wrecked the Middle Class (2015), 495

Haney López, Ian F., Post-Racial Racism: Racial Stratification and Mass Incarceration in the Age of Obama, 98 Cal. L. Rev. 1023 (2010), 143

Haney-López, Ian F., The Social Construction of Race: Some Observations on Illusion, Fabrication, and Choice, 29 Harv. C.R.-C.L. Rev. 1 (1994), 385

Hansford, Justin, Cause Judging, 27 Geo. J. Legal Ethics 1 (2014), 1023

Hanson, Jon D. & Kathleen Hanson, The Blame Frame: Justifying (Racial) Injustice in America, 41 Harv. C.R.-C.L. L. Rev. 413 (2006), 534, 841

Hao, Karen, This is How AI Bias Really Happens—And Why It's So Hard to Fix (Feb. 4, 2019), 363

Happel, Robin, The Next Generation of Southern Organization, The Nation (Aug. 17, 2018), 517

Harding, Sandra, The Feminist Standpoint Theory Reader: Intellectual and Political Controversies (2004), 860

Harding, Sandra, The Science Question in Feminism (1986), 860

Harrington, Brooke, Capital Without Borders: Wealth Managers and the One Percent 232 (2016), 701

Harris, Angela and Leslie Espinoza, Afterword—Embracing the Tar-Baby: LatCrit Theory and the Sticky Mess of Race, 10 La Raza L.J. 499 (1998), 858

Harris, Angela and Leslie Espinoza, Afterword—Embracing the Tar-Baby: LatCrit Theory and the Sticky Mess of Race, 85 Cal. L. Rev. 1585 (1997), 857

Harris, Angela P., From Stonewall to the Suburbs? Toward a Political Economy of Sexuality, 14 Wm. & Mary Bill Rts. J. 1539 (2006), 280

Harris, Angela P., Heteropatriarchy Kills: Challenging Gender Violence in a Prison Nation, 37 Wash. U. J.L. & Pol'y 13 (2011), 1159

Harris, Angela P., Race and Essentialism in Feminist Legal Theory, 42 Stan. L. Rev. 581 (1990), 389

Harris, Angela, Margaretta Lin & Jeff Selbin, From "The Art of War" to "Being Peace:" Mindfulness and Community Lawyering in a Neoliberal Age, 95 Cal. L. Rev. 2073 (2007), 365

Harris, Cheryl I., Whiteness as Property, 106 Harv. L. Rev. 1709 (1993), 447

Harris, Jasmine E., The Frailty of Disability Rights, 169 U. Pa. L. Rev. Online 29 (2020), 205

Hart, Danielle Kie, Contract Law Now—Reality Meets Legal Fictions, 41 U. Balt. L. Rev. 1 (2011), 454

Harvey, David, A Brief History of Neoliberalism 2 (2005), 768

Hawthorne, Sydney L., Do Desperate Times Call for Desperate Measures in the Context of Democracy? Michigan's Emergency Manager Law & The Voting Rights Act, 41 N.Y.U. Rev. L. & Soc. Change 181 (2017), 174

Hayman, Robert L., Jr., Presumptions of Justice: Law, Politics, and the Mentally Retarded Parent, 103 Harv. L. Rev. 1201 (1990), 241

Hedgepapers No. 26, Puerto Rico: Pain and Profit (Mar. 21, 2017), 489

Hegel, Georg Wilhelm Friedrich, Phenomenology of Spirit (A.V. Miller trans. 1977) (1807), 860

Hernández Escontrías, Pilar Margarita, Setting the Bar: The Sordid Past of Legal Ethics (unpublished manuscript on file with editors), 776

Hernández, Mónica with Francisco Argüelles, Building Immigrant Leaders in the South: INDELI 2004–06, 515

Hernández-Truyol, Berta Esperanza, The Rule of Law and Human Rights, 16 Fla. J. Int'l L. 167 (2004), 182, 190, 191

Hernandez-Truyol, Berta, Angela P. Harris & Francisco Valdes, Afterword—Beyond the First Decade: A Forward-Looking History of LatCrit Theory, Community and Praxis, 26 Chicano-Latino L. Rev. 237 (2006), 787

Herrera, Luz, Reflections of a Community Lawyer, 3 Mod. Am. 39 (2007), 778

Herrine, Luke, The Law and Political Economy of a Student Debt Jubilee, 68 Buff. L. Rev. 281 (2020), 1191

Hess, Wendy N., Slut Shaming in the Workplace: Sexual Rumors & Hostile Work Environment Claims, 40 N.Y.U. Rev. L. & Soc. Change 581 (2016), 848

Hill, Jaribu, In Praise of Hope Lewis—Thank You, 10 N.E. U.L. Rev. 473 (2018), 762

Hill, Jennifer, Wage Theft: Low-Income Workers and Community Centers, in American Labor Struggles and Law Histories 591 (Kenneth M. Casebeer ed. 2017), 647

Hill, Julianne, For More Good: Law Firms Find Other Ways to Provide Service to Society, ABA J. (Feb. 2017), 585

Hing, Bill Ong, Coolies, James Yen, and Rebellious Advocacy, 14 Asian Am. L.J. 1 (2007), 412

Ho, Jeremiah A., Queer Sacrifice in Masterpiece Cakeshop, 31 Yale J.L. & Feminism 249 (2020), 279

Hoffman, Benjamin and Marissa Vahlsing, Collaborative Lawyering in Transnational Human Rights Advocacy, 21 Clinical L. Rev. 255 (2014), 565

Holmes, Janerick, How Advocates in the Deep South Are Putting Race Front and Center of Anti-Poverty Advocacy, The Shriver Brief (Nov. 7, 2017), 1086

Holmes, Oliver Wendell, Jr., The Path of the Law, 10 Harv. L. Rev. 457 (1897), 43

Horton, Myles and Paulo Freire, We Make the Road by Walking (1990), 499

Houh, Emily M.S. and Kristin Kalsem, It's Critical: Legal Participatory Action Research, 19 Mich. J. Race & L. 287 (2014), 897

Houh, Emily M.S., Critical Interventions: Toward an Expansive Equality Approach to the Doctrine of Good Faith in Contract Law, 88 Cornell L. Rev. 1025 (2003), 42

Houseman, Alan and Linda E. Perle, Securing Equal Justice for All: A Brief History of Civil Legal Assistance in the United States 40, 50–51 (2018), 719

Hoyer, Mary, The Power of Collaboration, Grassroots Economic Organizing (July 9, 2015), 1020

Huber, Lindsay, Beautifully Powerful: A LatCrit Reflection on Coming to an Epistemological Consciousness and the Power of Testimonio, 18 Am. U. J. Gender Soc. Pol'y & L. 839 (2010), 920

Huertas-Noble, Carmen, Worker-Owned and Unionized Worker-Owned Cooperatives: Two Tools to Address Income Inequality, 22 Clinical L. Rev. 325 (2016), 987

Hung, Betty, Letter to a Young Public Interest Attorney, 1 L. A. Pub. Int. L.J. 319 (2009), 1229

Hunter, Daniel, Building a Movement to End the New Jim Crow: An Organizing Guide (2015), 499

Hunter, Nan D., Varieties of Constitutional Experience: Democracy and the Marriage

Equality Campaign, 64 UCLA L. Rev. 1662 (2017), 316

Huq, Chaumtoli, (inter)Generation Movement Lawyer 2.0, Law at the Margins (2014), 5, 456

Hutcheson, Joseph C., Jr., Judgment Intuitive: The Function of the Hunch in Judicial Decision, 14 Cornell L. Rev. 274 (1929), 742

International Labour Conference, Convention 190, Convention Concerning the Elimination of Violence and Harassment in the World of Work (June 21, 2019), 1052

Jacobs, Michelle S., Pro Bono Work and Access to Justice for the Poor: Real Change or Imagined Change?, 48 Fla. L. Rev. 509 (1996), 648

Jenkins, Steve, Organizing, Advocacy, and Member Power: A Critical Reflection, 6 WorkingUSA 56 (2002), 835

Jewel, Lucille A., Bourdieu and American Legal Education: How Law Schools Reproduce Social Stratification and Class Hierarchy, 56 Buff. L. Rev. 1155 (2008), 737

Johnson, Allan G., The Blackwell Dictionary of Sociology: A User's Guide to Sociological Language 293 (2d ed. 2000), 257

Johnson, Douglas A. and Nancy L. Pearson, Tactical Mapping: How Nonprofits Can Identify the Levers of Change, Nonprofit Q. 92 (2009), 950

Johnson, Kevin R., How Racial Profiling in America Became the Law of the Land: United States v. Brignoni-Ponce and Whren v. United States and the Need for Truly Rebellious Lawyering, 98 Geo. L.J. 105 (2010), 143

Jolls, Christine, The Role and Functioning of Public-Interest Legal Organizations in the Enforcement of Employment Laws, in Emerging Labor Market Institutions for the Twenty-First Century 144 (Richard B. Freeman, Joni Hersch & Lawrence Mishel eds. 2004), 647

Jones, Trina, Race, Economic Class, and Employment Opportunity, 72 Law & Contemp. Probs. 57 (2009), 1129

Jones, Trina, Shades of Brown: The Law of Skin Color, 49 Duke L.J. 1487 (2000), 943

Jordan, Miriam, ICE Came for a Tennessee Town's Immigrants. The Town Fought Back, N.Y. Times (June 8, 2018), 506

Judging in a Therapeutic Key: Therapeutic Jurisprudence and the Courts (Bruce J. Winick and David B. Wexler eds. 2003), 784

Juravich, Tom, Beating Global Capital: A Framework and Method for Union Strategic Corporate Research and Campaigns, in Global Unions: Challenging Transnational Capital through Cross-Border Campaigns (Kate Bronfenbrenner ed. 2007), 950, 962

Kaijser, Anna and Annica Kronsell, Climate Change through the Lens of Intersectionality, 23 Environ. Politics 417 (2014), 389

Kairys, David, The Politics of Law: A Progressive Critique 140, 160–61 (1982), 185

Karakatsanis, Alec, The Punishment Bureaucracy: How to Think About "Criminal Justice Reform," 128 Yale L.J. Forum 848 (Mar. 28, 2019), 349, 636

Karp, Jack, "Not Our Best Days": The Fiscal Crisis Coming for Legal Aid, Law360 (Apr. 12, 2020), 628

Katzenbach, Jon R. and Douglas K. Smith, The Discipline of Teams, 71 Harvard Bus. Rev. 111 (1993), 555

Kaufman, Alexander C., States Have Put 54 New Restrictions on Peaceful Protest Since Ferguson (June 5, 2020), 476

Kennedy, Ann, Chronic Harm, 25 Wm. & Mary J. Race, Gender & Soc. Just. 131 (2018), 306

Kennedy, Duncan, Form and Substance in Private Law Adjudication, 89 Harv. L. Rev. 1685 (1976), 185

Kennedy, Duncan, Legal Education and the Reproduction of Hierarchy, 32 J. Legal Educ. 591 (1982), 731

Killelea, Amy, Collaborative Lawyering Meets Collaborative Doctoring: How a Multidisciplinary Partnership for HIV/AIDS Services Can Improve Outcomes for the Marginalized Sick, 16 Geo. J. on Poverty L. & Pol'y 413 (2010), 653

Kim, Tammy, Lawyers as Resources in Struggles for Social Change, 13 N.Y. City L. Rev. 213 (2009), 1023

King, Tiffany Lethabo and Ewuare Osayande, The Filth on Philanthropy: Progressive Philanthropy's Agenda to Misdirect Social Justice Movements, in The Revolution Will Not Be Funded: Beyond the Non-Profit Industrial Complex 80–81 (INCITE!, ed. 2007), 629

Kivel, Paul, Social Service or Social Change?, in The Revolution Will Not Be Funded: Beyond the Non-Profit Industrial Complex 129, 137–38 (INCITE! ed. 2007), 628

Klare, Karl E., Labor Law as Ideology: Toward a New Historiography of Collective Bargaining Law, 4 Indus. Relations L.J. 450 (1981), 1150

Klarman, Michael J., Brown, Racial Change, and the Civil Rights Movement, 80 Va. L. Rev. 7 (1994), 1173

Klas, Mary Ellen, Florida Leads Nation in Disenfranchising Former Felons, Miami Herald (Aug. 12, 2016), 143

Klein, Jessie, Sexuality and School Shootings: What Role Does Teasing Play in School Massacres?, 51 J. of Homosexuality 39 (2006), 1165

Klonoff, Robert, The Decline of Class Actions, 90 Wash. U. L. Rev. 729 (2013), 464

Kohl-Arenas, Erica, Will the Revolution be Funded? Resource Mobilization and the California Farm Worker Movement, 13 Soc. Movement Stud. 482 (2014), 632

Kohn, Nina A., The Lawyer's Role in Fostering an Elder Rights Movement, 37 Wm. Mitchell L. Rev. 49 (2010), 524

Kourany, Janet, The Place of Standpoint Theory in Feminist Science Studies, 24 Hypatia 209 (2009), 860

Kretzmann, John P. et al., Discovering Community Power: A Guide to Mobilizing Local Assets and Your Organization's Capacity (2005), 946

Krieger, Lawrence S. with Kennon M. Sheldon, What Makes Lawyers Happy?: A Data-Driven Prescription to Redefining Professional Success, 83 Geo. Wash. L. Rev. 554 (2015), 558

Krishna, Gowri J., Worker Cooperative Creation as Progressive Lawyering? Moving Beyond the One-Person, One-Vote Floor, 34 Berkeley J. Emp. & Lab. L. 65 (2013), 987

Kuehn, Robert R. and Bridget M. McCormack, Lessons from Forty Years of Interference in Law School Clinics, 24 Geo. J. Leg. Ethics 59 (2011), 721

Kuehn, Robert R. and Peter A. Joy, An Ethics Critique of Interference in Law School Clinics, 71 Fordham L. Rev. 1971 (2003), 721

Kupenda, Angela Mae, Will the South Rise Again and, If So, in What Form? Lessons from LatCrit About Resisting Fear of Cultural Understanding, 47 J. Marshall L. Rev. 1211 (2014), 200

Laffey, Allison E. and Allison Ng, Diversity and Inclusion in the Law: Challenges and Initiatives, ABA (May 2, 2018), 729

LatCrit Symposium, Countering Kulturkampf Politics through Critique and Justice Pedagogy, 35 Seton Hall L. Rev. 1155 (2005), 1113

LatCrit Symposium, Countering Kulturkampf Politics through Critique and Justice Pedagogy, 50 Vill. L. Rev. 749 (2005), 1113

Law Firm Associates Should Unionize, Prawfsblawg (Feb. 28, 2008), 686

Lawrence, Charles R., III, "Justice" or "Just Us": Racism and the Role of Ideology, 35 Stan. L. Rev. 831 (1983), 1135

Lawyers' Ethics and the Pursuit of Social Justice: A Critical Reader (Susan D. Carle and Robert W. Gordon eds. 2007), 778

Lee, Stephen, The Food We Eat and the People Who Feed Us, 94 Wash. U.L. Rev. 1249 (2017), 1019

Legal Professions: The Status of Women and Men, Center for Research on Gender in the Professions, University of California-San Diego (2013), 624

Legal Servs. Corp., Documenting the Justice Gap in America: The Current Unmet Civil Needs of Low-Income Americans 1 (2009), 647

Lerner, Stephen, Breaking Laws to Change Laws, 25 New Labor Forum 17 (2015), 838

Levi, Lili, Social Media and the Press, 90 N. Car. L. Rev. 1531 (2012), 939

Levin, Benjamin, American Gangsters: RICO, Criminal

Syndicates and Conspiracy Law as Market Control, 48 Harv. C.R.-C.L. L. Rev. 105 (2013), 466

Levin, Rachel N., The Problem with Pronouns, Inside Higher Ed (Sept. 19, 2018), 395

Levinson, Ariana R., Union Co-ops and the Revival of Labor Law, 19 Cardozo J. Conflict Resol. 453 (2018), 987

Levinson, Ariana, Founding Worker Cooperatives: Social Movement Theory and the Law, 14 Nev. L.J. 322 (2014), 987

Levinson, Daryl, Foreword: Looking for Power in Public Law, 130 Harv. L. Rev. 31 (2016), 769

Levit, Nancy, Reshaping the Narrative Debate, 34 Seattle U.L. Rev. 751 (2011), 920

Levit, Nancy, Theorizing the Connections Among Systems of Subordination, 71 U. Mo-K.C. L. Rev. 227 (2002), 390

Lindo, Edwin, Brenda Williams, and Marc-Tizoc González, Uncompromising Hunger for Justice: Resistance, Sacrifice, and LatCrit Theory, 16 Seattle J. Soc. Just. 727 (2018), 352, 531

Llewellyn, Karl, The Common Law Tradition: Deciding Appeals (1960), 42

Lobel, Orly, The Paradox of Extralegal Activism: Critical Legal Consciousness and Transformative Politics, 120 Harv. L. Rev. 937 (2007), 636, 1172

London, Sarah, Reproductive Justice: Developing a Lawyering Model, 13 Berkeley J. Afr.-Am. L. & Pol'y 71 (2011), 791

Lopez, Antoinette Sedillo, Ethnocentrism and Feminism: Using a Contextual Methodology in International Women's Rights Advocacy and Education, 28 So. U.L. Rev. 279 (2001), 1212

López, Gerald P., Changing Systems, Changing Ourselves, 12 Harv. Latino L. Rev. 15 (2009), 56

López, Gerald P., Rebellious Lawyering: One Chicano's Vision of Progressive Law Practice (1992), 10

LoPucki, Lynn M., The Systems Approach to Law, 82 Cornell L. Rev. 479 (1997), 184, 185

Losen, Daniel J. and Paul Martinez, Lost Opportunities: How Disparate School Discipline Continues to Drive Differences in the Opportunity to Learn (Oct. 2020, updated Jan. 2021), 1200

Luban, David, Lawyers and Justice: An Ethical Study 319 (1988), 556

Luban, David, Taking out the Adversary: The Assault on Progressive Public-Interest Lawyers, 91 Cal. L. Rev. 209 (2003), 647, 712

Lubin, Judy, Fred Clavel & Elise Goldstein, Talent Justice Report: Investing in Equity in the Nonprofit Workforce, Fund the People and Center for Urban and Racial Equity 7 (2019), 623

Luchisi, Annita, Violence Against Native Women and Girls, 946

MacDowell, Elizabeth L., Reimagining Access to Justice in the Poor People's Courts, 22 Geo. J. on Poverty L. & Pol'y 473 (2015), 658

MacNamara, Jessica, Sarah Glann, and Paul Durlak, Experiencing Misgendered Pronouns: A Classroom Activity to Encourage Empathy, 45 Teaching Sociology 269 (July 2017), 395

Mahmud, Tayyab, Colonialism and Modern Constructions of Race: A Preliminary Inquiry, 53 U. Miami L. Rev. 1219 (1999), 1078

Mahmud, Tayyab, What's Next? Counter-Stories and Theorizing Resistance, 16 Seattle J. for Soc. Just. 607 (2018), 921

Mahoney, Martha R., Constructing Solidarity: Interest and White Workers, 2 U. Pa. J. Lab. & Emp. L. 747 (2000), 403

Mahoney, Martha R., What's Left of Solidarity: Reflections on Law, Race, and Labor History, 57 Buff. L. Rev. 1515 (2009), 878

Malin, Martin H., Alt Labor? Why We Still Need Traditional Labor, 95 Chi.-Kent L. Rev. 157 (2020), 1019

Maltz, Earl M., Slavery and the Supreme Court, 1825–1861 (2009), 233

Mananzala, Rickke and Dean Spade, The Nonprofit Industrial Complex and Trans Resistance, 5 Sexuality Research & Social Pol'y 53 (Mar. 2008), 628

Manian, Maya, Side Effects of the Abortion Wars, 38 Women's Rts. L. Rep. 362 (2017), 313

Marcantonio, Richard A. and Samuel P. Tepperman-Gelfant, Seizing the Power of Political Participation, Clearinghouse 2, 964

Marcos, Subcomandante Insurgente, Conversations with Durito: Stories of Zapatistas and Neoliberalism (2005), 1171

Marshall, Shauna I., Mission Impossible?: Ethical Community Lawyering, 7 Clinical L. Rev. 147 (2000), 556

Marshall, Thurgood, Reflections on the Bicentennial of the United States Constitution, 101 Harv. L. Rev. 1 (1987), 11, 245

Martin, Nick, The Radical Possibilities of Not Paying Your Student Loans, New Republic (Feb. 7, 2020), 1197

Martinez, George A., Legal Indeterminacy, Judicial Discretion and the Mexican-American Litigation Experience: 1930–1980, 27 U.C. Davis L. Rev. 555 (1994), 114, 185

Martínez, George, Philosophical Considerations and the Use of Narrative in Law, 30 Rutgers L.J. 683 (1999), 920

Matache, Margareta and Cornel West, Roma and African Americans Share a Common Struggle, The Guardian (Feb. 20, 2018), 1217

Matambanadzo, Saru M., Jorge R. Roig and Sheila I. Vélez Martínez, Foreword to LatCrit 2017 Symposium: What's Next? Resistance Resilience and Community in the Trump Era, 9 U. Miami Race & Soc. Just. L. Rev. 1 (2019), 1219

Matsuda, Mari J., Beside My Sister, Facing the Enemy: Legal Theory out of Coalition, 43 Stan. L. Rev. 1183 (1991), 371

Matsuda, Mari J., Foreword: McCarthyism, the Internment and the Contradictions of Power, 40 B.C. L. Rev. 9 (1998), 121

Matsuda, Mari J., Looking to the Bottom: Critical Legal Studies and Reparations, 22 Harv. C.R.-C.L. L. Rev. 323 (1987), 15, 185

Matsuda, Mari, Beyond, and Not Beyond, Black and White: Deconstruction Has a Politics in Crossroads, Directions, and a New Critical Race Theory (Francisco Valdes, Jerome McCristal Culp & Angela P. Harris eds. 2002), 862

Matsuda, Mari, Dissent in a Crowded Theater, 72 SMU L. Rev. 441 (2019), 661

Matsuda, Mari, Looking to the Bottom: Critical Legal Studies and Reparations, 22 Harv. C.R.-C.L. L. Rev. 323 (1987), 860

Matsui, Sarah, Learning from Counternarratives in Teach for America: Moving from Idealism Towards Hope 3–17 (2015), 118

Matthew, Dayna Bowen, Structural Inequality: The Real COVID-19 Threat to America's Health and How Strengthening the Affordable Care Act Can Help, 108 Geo. L.J. 1679 (2020), 202

Mauer, Marc, Race to Incarcerate (2006), 175

Maya Angelou, I Know Why the Caged Bird Sings (1969), 787

Mayeri, Serena, Marital Supremacy and the Constitution of the Nonmarital Family, 103 Cal. L. Rev. 1277 (2015), 216

McCambridge, Ruth, The Philanthropy We Need: Ford Foundation President Calls for Transformation (Jan. 10, 2019), 633

McFarlane, Audrey, Race, Space and Place: The Geography of Economic Development, 36 San Diego L. Rev. 295 (1999), 964

McIntosh, Peggy, White Privilege: Unpacking the Invisible Knapsack first appeared in Peace and Freedom Magazine 10–12 (July/Aug. 1989), 255

McMurtry-Chubb, Teri, Still Writing at the Master's Table: Decolonizing Rhetoric in Legal Writing for a "Woke" Legal Academy, 21 Scholar: St. Mary's L. Rev. & Soc. Just. 255 (2019), 760

Meadows, Donella H., Thinking in Systems: A Primer 2 (2008), 184

Memorandum from Lewis F. Powell to Eugene Sydnor, Attack on American Free Enterprise System (Aug. 23, 1971), 457

Mendez v. Westminster: For All the Children/Para Todos los Niños (2003 documentary), 1182

Merry, Sally Engle, Law and Colonialism, 25 Law & Soc'y Rev. 889 (1991), 1057

Mettler, Katie, "Permanently Disabled" Baton Rouge Officer Sues Black Lives Matter for 2016 Ambush Shooting, Wash. Post (July 10, 2017), 474

Miller, Arthur R., Of Frankenstein Monsters and Shining Knights: Myth, Reality, and the "Class Action Problem," 92 Harv. L. Rev. 664 (1979), 463

Miller, Carina J., Protecting the Argentine Jewish Community and Jewish Identity in Times of Crisis: Local Efforts, Global Community, and Foreign Support, 16 Fla. J. Int'l L. 677 (2004), 351

Mills, C. Wright, The Power Elite, 269–278 (1956), 427

Mills, Charles W., The Racial Contract (1997), 1084

Minter, Shannon Price, "Déjà Vu All over Again": The Recourse to Biology by Opponents of Transgender Equality, 95 N.C. L. Rev. 1161 (2017), 294

Mishel, Lawrence and Julia Wolfe, CEO Compensation Has Grown 940% Since 1978: Typical Worker Compensation Has Risen Only 12% During That Time, Economic Policy Institute (Aug. 14, 2019), 1018

Missing and Murdered Indigenous Women & Girls, Urban Indian Health Institute (2016), 945

Mitchell, Corey, In Flint, Schools Overwhelmed by Special Ed. Needs in Aftermath of Lead Crisis, Education Week (Aug. 26, 2019), 173

Molinari, Carmen, Lexi Owens, & Robert Fontana, You Can't Win Without a Fight: Why Worker Cooperatives Are a Bad Strategy, Organizing Work (Jan. 29, 2021), 1020

Montez, Jennifer Karas, Policy Polarization and Death in the United States, 92 Temp. L. Rev. 889 (2020), 473

Montoya, Margaret E., Foreword, in Francisco Valdes and Steven W. Bender, LatCrit: From Critical Legal Theory to Academic Activism (2021), 377

Montoya, Margaret E., Mascaras, Trenzas, y Greñas: Un/Masking the Self While Un/Braiding Latina Stories and Legal Discourse, 15 Chicano-Latino L. Rev. 1 (1994), 365

Montoya, Margaret E., Mascaras, Trenzas, y Greñas: Un/Masking the Self While Un/Braiding Latina Stories and Legal Discourse, 17 Harv. Women's L.J. 185 (1994), 365

Montoya, Margaret E., Religious Rituals and LatCrit Theorizing, 19 Chicana/o-Latina/o L. Rev. 417 (1998), 1132

Mor, Sagit, With Access and Justice for All, 39 Cardozo L. Rev. 611 (2017), 653

Moran, Beverly I., Disappearing Act: The Lack of Values Training in Legal Education, 38 S.U. L. Rev. 1 (2010), 778

Moreno, Sarah and Enrique Flor, They Have Fixed Up Their Homes and Paid Them Off. Now, They May Wind Up on the Street, Miami Herald (Apr. 19, 2018), 614

Morrison, Jill C., Resuscitating the Black Body: Reproductive Justice as Resistance to the State's Property Interest in Black Women's Reproductive Capacity, 31 Yale J.L. & Feminism 35 (2019), 303

Munger, Frank W., Scott L. Cummings & Louise G. Trubek, Mobilizing Law for Justice in Asia: A Comparative Approach, 31 Wis. Int'l L.J. 353 (2013), 645

Munzer, Stephen R., Dam(n) Displacement: Compensation, Resettlement, and Indigeneity, 51 Cornell Int'l L.J. 823 (2019), 1111

Murray, Yxta Maya, "FEMA Has Been a Nightmare:" Epistemic Injustice in Puerto Rico, 55 Willamette L. Rev. 321 (2019), 848

Mutua, Athena D., Framing the Elite Consensus, Ideology and Theory & a ClassCrit Response, 44 Sw. L. Rev. 635 (2015), 478

Mutua, Athena D., Shifting Bottoms and Rotating Centers: Reflections on LatCrit III and the Black/White Paradigm, 53 U. Miami L. Rev. 1177 (1999), 35

Mutua, Makau, Terrorism and Human Rights: Power, Culture, and Subordination, 8 Buff. Hum. Rts. L. Rev. 1 (2002), 1121

Nadal, Kevin L. et al., Religious Microaggressions in the United States in Microaggressions and Marginality: Manifestation, Dynamics, and Impact (Derald Wing Sue ed. 2010), 265

NALP Foundation for Law Career Research and Education and The Center for Women in Law, Women of Color: A Study of Law School Experiences (2020), 739

National Immigration Law Center, Tennessee OSHA Slams Meatpacking Plant Where Massive ICE Raid Took Place with 27 Violations and $41,775 in Penalties, 516

Native American Protester Calls for Dismissal of Vengeful Dakota Access Pipeline Lawsuit, Center for Constitutional Rights (Jan. 28, 2019), 467

Nearing, Scott and Joseph Freeman, Dollar Diplomacy 261–62 (1925), 1091

Nedelsky, Jennifer, Private Property and the Limits of American Constitutionalism: The Madisonian Framework and Its Legacy 1–3 (1990), 438

NeJaime, Douglas, Cause Lawyers Inside the State, 81 Fordham L. Rev. 649 (2012), 1023

NeJaime, Douglas, Winning Through Losing, 96 Iowa L. Rev. 941 (2011), 329

Nembhard, Jessica Gordon, Principles and Strategies for Reconstruction: Models of African American Community-Based Economic Development, 12 Harv. J. Afr. Am. Pub. Pol'y 39 (2006), 965

New Law and Political Economy Project Launched, Yale Law School (Apr. 29, 2019), 271

New Orleans Worker Center for Racial Justice, Legal Department Overview, 7

Newmark, Jesse, Legal Aid Affairs: Collaborating with Local Governments on the Side, 21 B.U. Pub. Int. L.J. 195 (2012), 579

Nice, Julie A., The Gendered Jurisprudence of the Fourteenth Amendment in Research Handbook on Feminist Jurisprudence (Robin West and Cynthia Grant Bowman eds. 2019), 1114

No New Jails NYC: Ford Foundation President, Darren Walker Requests a Meeting (Sept. 27, 2019), 625

Obasogie, Osagie K., Can the Blind Lead the Blind? Rethinking Equal Protection Jurisprudence through an Empirical Examination of Blind People's Understanding of Race, 15 U. Pa. J. Const. L. 705 (2013), 356

Obasogie, Osagie K., Do Blind People See Race? Social, Legal, and Theoretical Considerations, 44 Law & Soc'y Rev. 585 (2010), 356

Ohio Juvenile Justice System: Perspectives from the Field— Summary of Stakeholder's Priorities 1 (2010), 948

Oko, Okechukwu, The Problems and Challenges of Lawyering in Developing Societies, 35 Rutgers L.J. 569 (2004), 961

Olderman, Justine and Runa Rajagopal, A National Movement for Access to Justice Must Be Holistic, 87 Fordham L. Rev. Online (2018), 656

Olsen, Frances, The Family and the Market: A Study of Ideology and Legal Reform, 96 Harv. L. Rev. 1497 (1983), 271

Osoria, José Atiles, The State of Exception and the Puerto Rican Financial Crisis, 25 Tex. Hisp. J. L. & Pol'y 91 (2019), 488

Pacheco, Denise and Veronica Nelly Velez, Maps, Mapmaking, and Critical Pedagogy: Exploring GIS and Maps as a Teaching Tool for Social Change, 8 Seattle J. Soc. Just. 273 (2009), 583

Pader, Ellen J., Space of Hate: Ethnicity, Architecture and Housing Discrimination, 54 Rutgers L. Rev. 881 (2002), 271

Palestinian Human Rights Advocacy in the U.S., Palestine Solidarity Legal Support and Center for Constitutional Rights (2013), 720

Paulas, Rick, A New Kind of Labor Movement in Silicon Valley, Atlantic (Sept. 4, 2018), 701

Payne, Charles, I've Got the Light of Freedom: The Organizing Tradition and the Mississippi Freedom Struggle (1995), 499

Pearce, Russell G., White Lawyering: Rethinking Race, Lawyer Identity, and Rule of Law, 73 Fordham L. Rev. 2081 (2005), 357

Perea, Juan F., Hernandez v. New York: Courts, Prosecutors, and the Fear of Spanish, 21 Hofstra L. Rev. 1 (1992), 754

Perelman, Jeremy and Lucie E. White, Introduction to Stones of Hope: How African Activists Reclaim Human

Rights to Challenge Global Poverty 1, 2 (Lucie E. White and Jeremy Perelman eds. 2011), 961

Perelman, Jeremy, Transnational Human Rights Advocacy, Clinical Collaborations, and the Political Economics of Accountability: Mapping the Middle, 16 Yale Hum. Rts. & Dev. L.J. 89 (2013), 961

Peters, Jean Koh and Susan Bryant, Teaching About Race, in Transforming the Education of Lawyers: The Theory and Practice of Clinical Pedagogy 375, 376 (Susan Bryant, Elliott S. Milstein & Ann C. Shalleck eds. 2014), 362

Petrella, Christopher, The Resegregation of America (Dec. 3, 2017), 107

Pew Research Center, America's Incarceration Rate Is At a Two-Decade Low (May 2, 2018), 143

Picard, Ann, Women's Rights are Human Rights Redux: Ain't I a Human?, 26 J. Civ. Rts. & Econ. Dev. 753 (2012), 389

Piomelli, Ascanio, The Challenge of Democratic Lawyering, 77 Fordham L. Rev. 1383 (2009), 1271

Piomelli, Ascanio, The Democratic Roots of Collaborative Lawyering, 12 Clinical L. Rev. 541 (2006), 533

Plater, Zygmunt J.B., Dealing with Dumb and Dumber: The Continuing Mission of Citizen Environmentalism, 20 J. Envtl. L. & Litig. 9 (2006), 457

Plum, Susan Butler, Skadden Fellows Share the Impact of the Program After 30 Years, 534, 585

Polikoff, Nancy D., Am I My Client? The Role Confusion of a Lawyer-Activist, 31 Harv. C.R.-C.L. L. Rev. 443 (1996), 1021

Polletta, Francesca and Pang Ching Bobby Chen, Narrative and Social Movements, in The Oxford Handbook of Cultural Sociology 487, 487–88 (Jeffrey C. Alexander et al. eds. 2012), 930

Polletta, Francesca, Three Mechanisms by Which Culture Shapes Movement Strategy: Repertoires, Institutional Norms, and Metonymy, in Strategies for Social Change 43, 54 (Gregory M. Maney et al. eds. 2012), 942

Pope, James Gray, Mass Incarceration, Convict Leasing, and the Thirteenth Amendment: A Revisionist Account, 94 N.Y.U. L. Rev. 1465 (2019), 175

Porras, Ileana M., European Origins, the Doctrine of the Providential Function of Commerce, and International Law's Embrace of Economic Growth, 107 Am. Soc'y Int'l L. Proc. 374 (2014), 196

Pouncy, Charles R., Recovery from the Recovery: Law and Contemporary Processes of Accumulation by Dispossession, 26 J. of Civ. Rts. and Eco. Dev. 107 (2010), 476

Pouncy, Charles R.P., Institutional Economics and Critical Race/LatCrit Theory: The Need for a Critical "Raced" Economics, 54 Rutgers L. Rev. 841 (2002), 208, 424, 455

Pound, Roscoe, The Scope and Purpose of Sociological Jurisprudence, 23 Harv. L. Rev. 591 (1911), 43

Powell, Catherine and Camille Gear Rich, The "Welfare Queen" Goes to the Polls: Race-Based Fractures in Gender Politics and Opportunities for Intersectional Coalitions, Geo. L.J. 19th Amend. Special Ed. 105 (2020), 492, 493

powell, john a., Disrupting Individualism and Distributive Remedies with Intersubjectivity and Empowerment: An Approach to Justice and Discourse, 1 Margins 1 (2001), 766

Powell, Robyn M., Safeguarding the Rights of Parents with Intellectual Disabilities in Child Welfare Cases: The Convergence of Social Science and Law, 20 CUNY L. Rev. 127 (2016), 241

Professionals as New Workers, in Professionals as Workers: Mental Labor in Advanced Capitalism 15–16 (Charles Derber ed. 1982), 686

"Protect the Protest" Coalition Launched to Fight Back Against SLAPPs, Center for Constitutional Rights, 468

Quigley, William P., Letter to a Law Student Interested in Social Justice, 1 DePaul J. for Soc. Just. 7 (2007), 534, 1233

Quigley, William P., Reflections of Community Organizers: Lawyering for Empowerment of Community Organizations, 21 Ohio N.U. L. Rev. 455 (1994), 500

Quigley, William P., Revolutionary Lawyering: Addressing the Root Causes of Poverty and Wealth, 20 Wash. U. J.L. & Pol'y 101 (2006), 189, 583

Ranghelli, Lisa, Leveraging Limited Dollars: How Grantmakers Achieve Tangible Results by Funding Policy and Community Engagement 1, The National Committee for Responsive Philanthropy (2012), 622

Rankin, Sara K., Punishing Homelessness, 22 New Crim. L. Rev. 99 (2019), 848

Ratifications of C190—Violence and Harassment Convention, 2019 (No. 190), 1052

Recommendation 206, Recommendation Concerning the Elimination of Violence and Harassment in the World of Work (June 21, 2019), 1052

Reforms Introduced to Protect the Freedom of Assembly, International Center for Not-for-Profit Law (July 2020), 476

Reich, Rob, Just Giving: Why Philanthropy is Failing Democracy and How It Can Do Better (2018), 628

Rendon, Jim, Nonprofits Led by People of Color Win Less Grant Money with More Strings, The Chronicle of Philanthropy (May 7, 2020), 623

Reynoso, Julissa, The Impact of Identity Politics and Public Sector Reform on Organizing and the Practice of Democracy, 37 Colum. Hum. Rts. L. Rev. 149 (2005), 499

Rhode, Deborah L. and Scott L. Cummings, Access to Justice: Looking Back, Thinking Ahead, 30 Geo. J. Legal Ethics 485 (2017), 650

Rhode, Deborah L., Leadership in Law, 69 Stan. L. Rev. 1603 (2017), 729

Rhode, Deborah, Access to Justice: Connecting Principles to Practice, 17 Geo. J. Legal Ethics, 369 (2004), 728

Right to Protest, Article 19: Defending Freedom of Expression, Brutal Repression of Protests Continues in Brazil, 468

Riley, John, Trump Administration Poised to Rewrite Obamacare, Without LGBTQ Protections, Metro Weekly (Apr. 27, 2020), 301

Ristroph, Alice, An Intellectual History of Mass Incarceration, 60 B.C. L. Rev. 1949 (2019), 143

Ritvo, Elizabeth A. and Joel B. Sherman, Grantmaking in a Down Economy: Thoughts from the Boston Bar Foundation, Boston B.J. 7 (Winter 2012), 627

Rivera-Perez, Willmai and Juan C. Garcia-Ellin, Flexible Accumulation: Changes in the Legal Profession and Their Effects in Legal Education, 49 Rev. Jur. U. Inter. P.R. 629 (2015), 695

Roberts, Dorothy E., Constructing a Criminal Justice System Free of Racial Bias: An Abolitionist Framework, 39 Colum. Hum. Rts. L. Rev. 261 (2007), 181

Roberts, Dorothy E., Foreword: Abolition Constitutionalism, 133 Harv. L. Rev. 1 (2019), 175

Roberts, Dorothy E., The Social and Moral Costs of Mass Incarceration in African American Communities, 56 Stan. L. Rev. 1271 (2004), 143

Roberts, Molly, Stop Blaming White Supremacy on "Identity Politics," Wash. Post (Aug. 14, 2017), 1130

Robins, Nick, The Corporation that Changed the World: How the East India Company Shaped the Modern Multinational (2012), 198, 1095

Robinson, Russell K. and David M. Frost, "Playing It Safe" with Empirical Evidence: Selective Use of Social Science in Supreme Court Cases About Racial Justice and Marriage Equality, 112 Nw. U.L. Rev. 1565 (2018), 291

Rochmes, Daniel M. and G.A. Elmer Griffin, The Cactus That Must Not be Mistaken for a Pillow: White Racial Formation Among Latinos, 197, 200, in Racializing Justice, Disenfranchising Lives: The Racism, Criminal Justice, and Law Reader (Manning Marable, Ian Steinberg & Keesha Middlemass eds. 2007), 873

Rodriguez, Dylan, remarks at The Revolution Will Not Be Funded: Beyond the Non-Profit Industrial Complex Conference (2004), 628

Roig, Jorge R., The First Thing We Do, 47 J. Marshall L. Rev. 1275 (2014), 182

Roithmayr, Daria, Deconstructing the Distinction Between Bias and Merit, 10 La Raza L.J. 363 (1998), 722

Roithmayr, Daria, Deconstructing the Distinction Between Bias and Merit, 85 Cal. L. Rev. 1449 (1997), 722

Rojas-Páez, Gustavo, Whose Nature? Whose Rights? Criminalization of Social Protest in a Globalizing World, 4 Oñati Socio-Legal Series 1 (2014), 672

Romero, Mary, Historicizing and Symbolizing a Racial Ethnic Identity: Lessons for Coalition Building with a Social Justice Agenda, 33 U.C. Davis L. Rev. 1599 (2000), 395

Romero, Tom I., II, The Color of Water: Observations of a Brown Buffalo on Water Law and Policy in Ten Stanzas, 1 U. Miami Race & Soc. Just. L. Rev. 107 (2011), 163

Romero, Tom I., II, The Color of Water: Observations of a Brown Buffalo on Water Law and Policy in Ten Stanzas, 15 U. Denv. Water L. Rev. 329 (2012), 163

Rosario-Lebrón, Aníbal, If These Blackboards Could Talk: The Crit Classroom, A Battlefield, 9 Charleston L. Rev. 305 (2015), 764

Roseberry, William, Anthropologies and Histories, 49 (1990), 208

Rosenbaum, Carrie L., Crimmigration—Structural Tools of Settler Colonialism, 16 Ohio St. J. Crim. L. 9 (2018), 144

Rosenberg, Eli, Workers Are Forming Unions at Nonprofits and Think Tanks. Their Bosses Aren't Always Happy, Wash. Post (Feb. 4, 2020), 625

Rosenberg, Gerald N., The Hollow Hope: Can Courts Bring About Social Change? (1991), 1173

Ross, Loretta, SisterSong Women of Color Reproductive Health Collective, What is Reproductive Justice, in Berkeley Law Reproductive Justice Briefing Book: A Primer on Reproductive Justice and Social Change, 791

Rothstein, Richard, Brown v. Board at 60: Why Have We Been So Disappointed? What Have We Learned?, Economic Pol'y Inst. Report (Apr. 17, 2014), 1190

Rubenstein, William B., In Communities Begin Responsibilities: Obligations at the Gay Bar, 48 Hastings L.J. 1101 (1997), 778

Ruiz Cameron, Christopher David, One Hundred Fifty Years of Solitude: Reflections on the End of the History Academy's Dominance of Scholarship on the Treaty of Guadalupe Hidalgo, 5 Sw. J.L. & Trade in the Americas 83 (1998), 1091

Russel, Dominic, Carrie Sloan, and Alan Smith, The Financialization of Higher Education: What Swaps Cost Our Schools and Students (June 2016), 953

Ryan, Tim, Trump Budget Seeks to Cut Off Legal Aid Group, Courthouse News Service (Mar. 18, 2019), 719

Saito, Natsu Taylor, For "Our" Security: Who Is An "American" and What is Protected by Enhanced Law Enforcement and Intelligence Powers, 2 Seattle J. Soc. Just. 23 (2003), 874

Saito, Natsu Taylor, Tales of Color and Colonialism: Racial Realism and Settler Colonial Theory, 10 Fla. A&M U.L. Rev. 1 (2014), 1062

Saito, Natsu Taylor, Whose Liberty? Whose Security? The USA PATRIOT Act in the Context of COINTELPRO and the Unlawful Repression of Political Dissent, 81 Or. L. Rev. 1051 (2002), 874

Sandefur, Rebecca L. et al., Accessing Justice in the Contemporary USA: Findings from the Community Needs and Services Study 3 (2014), 647

Sarat, Austin and Stuart A. Scheingold, State Transformation, Globalization, and the Possibilities of Cause Lawyering in Cause Lawyering and the State in the Global Era (Austin Sarat and Stuart Scheingold eds. 2001), 961

Sarat, Austin and Stuart Scheingold, Something to Believe In: Politics, Professionalism, and Cause Lawyering (2004), 961

Sarat, Austin and Stuart Scheingold, What Cause Lawyers Do For, and To, Social Movements: An Introduction, in Cause Lawyers and Social Movements 1 (Austin Sarat and Stuart A. Scheingold eds. 2006), 1172

Sato, Grace and Seema Shah, Latino Leadership: Foundation Boards, The Foundation Center in

Collaboration with Hispanics in Philanthropy (2015), 623

Schlanger, Margo, Offices of Goodness: Influence Without Authority in Federal Agencies, 36 Cardozo L. Rev. 53 (2014), 1023

Schlesinger, Stephen and Stephen Kinzer, Bitter Fruit: The Story of the American Coup in Guatemala (rev. ed. 2005), 1109

Scrubb, Victoria, Political Systems and Health Inequity: Connecting the Apartheid Policies to the HIV/AIDS Epidemic in South Africa, J. of Global Health (Apr. 1, 2011), 831

Sen, Rinku and Kim Klein, Stir It Up: Lessons in Community Organizing and Advocacy (2003), 499

Sen, Rinku and Lori Villarosa, Grantmaking with a Racial Justice Lens: A Practical Guide, Philanthropic Initiative for Racial Equity (2018), 621

Serrano, Susan K., Dual Consciousness About Law and Justice: Puerto Ricans' Battle for U.S. Citizenship in Hawai'i, 29 Centro J. 164 (2017), 67

Shah, Daniel S., Lawyering for Empowerment: Community Development and Social Change, 6 Clinical L. Rev. 217 (1999), 964, 1022

Shah, Hina, Notes from the Field: The Role of the Lawyer in Grassroots Policy Advocacy, 21 Clinical L. Rev. 393 (2015), 1022

Shah, Purvi, Rebuilding the Ethical Compass of Law, 47 Hofstra L. Rev. 11 (2018), 779

Shah, Seema, Kavitha Mediratta, and Sara McAlister, Securing a College Prep Curriculum for All Students (June 2009), 1174

Shah, Seema, Reina Mukai & Grace McAlister, Foundation Funding for Hispanics/Latinos in the United States and for Latin America, The Foundation Center in collaboration with Hispanics in Philanthropy (2011), 621

Shapiro, Fred, The First WASPs?, N.Y. Times (Mar. 14, 2012), 737

Sharpless, Rebecca, More Than One Lane Wide: Against Hierarchies of Helping in Progressive Legal Advocacy, 19 Clinical L. Rev. 347 (2012), 56, 631, 1022

Shek, Dina, Centering Race at the Medical-Legal Partnership in Hawai'i, 10 U. Miami Race & Soc. Just. L. Rev. 109 (2019), 653

Siegel, Reva B., "The Rule of Love": Wife Beating as Prerogative and Privacy, 105 Yale L.J. 2117 (1996), 281

Simon, William, The Community Economic Development Movement, 2002 Wis. L. Rev. 377 (2002), 963

Simonson, Jocelyn, Democratizing Criminal Justice Through Contestation and Resistance, 111 Nw. U.L. Rev. 1609 (2017), 526

Singh, Anneliese A., Kate Richmond & Theodore R. Burnes, Feminist Participatory Action Research with Transgender Communities: Fostering the Practice of Ethical and Empowering Research Designs, 14 Int'l J. of Transgenderism 93 (2013), 934

Sinha, Anita, Arbitrary Detention? The Immigration Detention Bed Quota, 12 Duke J. Const. L. & Pub. Pol'y 77 (2017), 143

Sirriyeh, Ala, "Felons Are Also Our Family": Citizenship and Solidarity in the Undocumented Youth Movement in the United States, 45 J. of Ethnic and Migration Studies 133 (2018), 401

Smith, Lance C. and Richard Q. Shin, Queer Blindfolding: A Case Study on Difference "Blindness" Towards Persons Who Identify as Lesbian, Gay, Bisexual, and Transgender, 61 J. of Homosexuality 940 (2014), 355

Smith, Peggie R., Organizing the Unorganizable: Private Paid Household Workers and Approaches to Employee Representation, 79 N.C. L. Rev. 45 (2000), 1022

Smith, Priscilla J., Comstockery: Reasoning from Immorality to Illness in the Twenty-First Century, 47 Conn. L. Rev. 971 (2015), 312

Smith, Rebecca, Engaging in Direct Action Campaigns Without Getting SLAPP'ed: Take Action Against Wage Theft!, National Employment Law Project (2007), 523, 719

Smith, Ryan, Advancing Racial Equity In Career and Technical Education, Center for American Progress (Aug. 28, 2019), 1174

Smith, Terry, Race and Money in Politics, 79 N.C. L. Rev. 1469 (2001), 141

Solis, Jorge A., Detained Without Relief, 10 Ala. C.R. & C.L. L. Rev. 357 (2019), 143

Solórzano, Daniel G. and Lindsay Pérez Huber, Racial Microaggressions: Using Critical Race Theory to Respond to Everyday Racism (2020), 264

Somes, Tyler Kasperek, The Legal Services NYC Strike: Neoliberalism, Austerity and Resistance, 71 Nat'l Law. Guild Rev. 8 (2014), 689

Sotomayor, Hon. Sonia, A Latina Judge's Voice, 13 Berkeley La Raza L.J. 87 (2002), 246

Southern Poverty Law Center, Unlocking Your Community's Hidden Strengths: A Guidebook to Community Asset Mapping (2012), 947

Spade, Dean, For Those Considering Law School, 6 Unbound: Harv. J. Legal Left 111 (2010), 1242

Sproat, Kapua'ala, Wai Through Kānāwai: Water for Hawai'i's Streams and Justice for Hawaiian Communities, 95 Marq. L. Rev. 127 (2011), 757

Srikantiah, Jayashri and Janet Martinez, Applying Negotiations Pedagogy to Clinical Teaching: Tools for Institutional Client Representation in Law School Clinics, 21 Clinical L. Rev. 283 (2014), 556, 949

Srikantiah, Jayashri and Jennifer Lee Koh, Teaching Individual Representation Alongside Institutional Advocacy: Pedagogical Implications of a Combined Advocacy Clinic, 16 Clinical L. Rev. 451 (2010), 1023

St. Pierre, Pascale Cornut, Investigating Legal Consciousness through the Technical Work of Elite Lawyers: A Case Study in Tax Avoidance, 53 Law & Soc'y Rev. 323 (2019), 1150

Staples, Lee, Roots to Power: A Manual for Grassroots Organizers (2d ed. 2004), 499

Stefancic, Jean and Richard Delgado, How Lawyers Lose Their Way: A Profession Fails Its Creative Minds xi (2005), 742

Steinfeld, Robert J., Property and Suffrage in the Early American Republic, 41 Stan. L. Rev. 335 (1989), 434

Stevenson, Bryan, Confronting Mass Imprisonment and Restoring Fairness to Collateral Review of Criminal Cases, 41 Harv. C.R.-C.L. L. Rev. 339 (2006), 143

Stewart-Winter, Timothy, After Marriage Equality, What? (Fall 2015), 340

Striedinger, Angelika, How Organizational Research Can Avoid the Pitfalls of a Co-optation Perspective: Analyzing Gender Equality Work in Austrian Universities with Organizational Institutionalism, 19 Int'l Feminist J. of Politics 201 (2017), 635

Stump, Nicholas F., Following New Lights: Critical Legal Research Strategies as a Spark for Law Reform in Appalachia, 23 Am. U. J. Gender Soc. Pol'y & L. 573 (2014), 879

Su, Julie A. and Eric K. Yamamoto, Critical Coalitions: Theory and Praxis in Crossroads, Directions, and a New Critical Race Theory (Francisco Valdes, Jerome McCristal Culp & Angela P. Harris eds. 2002), 577

Su, Julie A., Making The Invisible Visible: The Garment Industry's Dirty Laundry, 1 J. Gender, Race and Just. 405 (1998), 575

Sundquist, Christian, Critical Praxis, Spirit Healing, and Community Activism: Preserving a Subversive Dialogue on Reparations, 58 N.Y.U. Ann. Surv. Am. L. 659 (2003), 768

Sunstein, Cass R., Must Formalism Be Defended Empirically?, 66 U. Chi. L. Rev. 636 (1999), 677

Tai, Steph, Food Sustainability in the Age of Complex, Global Supply Chains, 71 Ark. L. Rev. 465 (2018), 1019

Tait, Allison Anna, The Law of High-Wealth Exceptionalism, 71 Ala. L. Rev. 981 (2020), 703

Takei, Carl, From Mass Incarceration to Mass Control, and Back Again: How Bipartisan Criminal Justice Reform May Lead to a For-Profit Nightmare, 20 U. Pa. J. L. & Soc. Change 125 (2017), 145

Taylor, Keeanga Yamahtta, Five Years Ahead, Do Black Lives Matter?, The Wire (Oct. 6, 2019), 625

Teach for America Counter-Narratives: Alumni Speak Up and Speak Out (T. Jameson Brewer and Kathleen deMarrais ed. 2015), 118

Tehranian, John, Selective Racialization: Middle-Eastern American Identity and the Faustian Pact with Whiteness, 40 Conn. L. Rev. 1201 (2008), 1117

The Dutch and English East India Companies: Diplomacy, Trade, and Violence in Early Modern Asia (Adam Clulow & Tristan Mostert eds. 2018), 198

The Flint Water Crisis: Systemic Racism Through the Lens of Flint, A Report of the Michigan Civil Rights Commission (Feb. 17, 2017), 162

The Justice Gap: Measuring the Unmet Civil Legal Needs of Low-income Americans, Legal Services Corporation (June 2017), 728

The Shriver Center on Poverty Law, Advocates Are Building a Model to Disrupt the School-to-Prison Pipeline in Mississippi—and Beyond, 142

Thomas, Chantal, Globalization and the Reproduction of Hierarchy, 33 U.C. Davis L. Rev. 1451 (2000), 1055

Thomas, Chantal, Globalization or Global Subordination?: How LatCrit Links the Local to Global and the Global to the Local: Globalization and the Reproduction of Hierarchy, 33 U.C. Davis L. Rev. 1451 (2000), 1104

Thompson, Matt, The Hoods Are Off (Aug. 12, 2017), 1129

Thorne, Nicholas, Missing and Murdered Indigenous Women and Girls and Pipelines, ArcGIS Story Maps (May 7, 2020), 946

Thuku, Muthee, Mapping for Human Rights, Amnesty International 1 (2017), 945

Thyfault, Roberta K. and Kathryn Fehrman, Interactive Group Learning in the Legal Writing Classroom: An International Primer on Student Collaboration and Cooperation in Large Classrooms, 3 J. Marshall L.J. 135 (2009), 555

Tonneson, Sara, Stronger Together: Worker Cooperatives as a Community Economic Development Strategy, 20 Geo. J. on Poverty L. & Pol'y 187 (2012), 987

Top Trends: COVID-19 and Civic Space, International Center for Not-for-Profit Law (July 2020), 475

Torres, Edén E., Power, Politics, and Pleasure: Class Differences and the Law, 54 Rutgers L. Rev. 853 (2002), 208

Torres, Gerald, Synecdoche, 14 Harv. Latino L. Rev. 263 (2011), 638

Transgender People and Marriage Laws, Chapter XIII, Trans Toolkit, 341

Tremblay, Paul R., Counseling Community Groups, 17 Clinical L. Rev. 389 (2010), 556

Tremblay, Paul R., Critical Legal Ethics Review of Lawyers Ethics and the Pursuit of Social Justice: A Critical Reader, Susan D. Carle, ed., 20 Geo. J. Legal Ethics 133 (2007), 54

Tremblay, Paul R., Transactional Legal Services, Triage, and Access to Justice, 48 Wash. U. J.L. & Pol'y 11 (2015), 1035

Trubek, Louise G., Critical Lawyering: Toward a New Public Interest Practice, 1 B.U. Pub. Int. L.J. 49 (1991), 279, 567

Trubek, Louise G., On Long Haul Lawyering, 25 Fordham Urb. L.J. 801 (1998), 280, 1267

Tsosie, Rebecca, Indigenous Peoples and Epistemic Injustice: Science, Ethics, and Human Rights, 87 Wash. L. Rev. 1133 (2012), 77

Turner, Ronald, The Dangers of Misappropriation: Misusing Martin Luther King Jr.'s Legacy to Prove the Colorblind Thesis, 2 Mich. J. Race and Law 101 (1996), 354

Tushnet, Mark V., Following the Rules Laid Down: A Critique of Interpretivism and Neutral Principles, 96 Harv. L. Rev. 781 (1983), 185

Tushnet, Mark V., The NAACP's Legal Strategy Against Segregated Education, 1925–1950 (1987), 1173

Understanding Antisemitism: An Offering to Our Movement, Jews for Racial & Economic Justice (2017), 397

Valdes, Francisco and Sumi Cho, Critical Race Materialism: Theorizing Justice in the Wake of Global Neoliberalism, 43 Conn. L. Rev. 1513 (2011), 1095

Valdes, Francisco, Culture, "Kulturkampf" and Beyond: The Antidiscrimination Principle under the Jurisprudence of Backlash, in The Blackwell Companion to Law and Society (Austin Sarat ed. 2003), 1113

Valdes, Francisco, Race, Ethnicity, and Hispanismo in a Triangular Perspective: The "Essential Latina/o" and LatCrit Theory, 48 UCLA L. Rev. 305 (2000), 1153

Van Dam, Andrew, What Southern Dynasties' Post-Civil War Resurgence Tells Us About How Wealth is Really Handed Down, Wash. Post (Apr. 4, 2019), 300

Vargas-Vargas, Geiza, The Investment Opportunity in Mass Incarceration: A Black (Corrections) or Brown (Immigration) Play, 48 Cal. W. L. Rev. 351 (2012), 175

Vázquez, Yolanda, Crimmigration: The Missing Piece of Criminal Justice Reform, 51 U. Rich. L. Rev. 1093 (2017), 143

Vega, Tanzina, Students See Many Slights as Racial "Microaggressions," N.Y. Times (Mar. 21, 2014), 274

Vélez Martínez, Sheila I., Towards an Outcrit Pedagogy of Anti-Subordination in the Classroom, 90 Chi.-Kent L. Rev. 585 (2015), 676

Venator Santiago, Charles R., From the Insular Cases to Camp X-Ray, 39 Studies in Law, Politics and Society 15 (2006), 1092

Verza, Sofia, SLAPP: The Background of Strategic Lawsuits Against Public Participation, Resource Centre: European Centre for Press & Media Freedom (July 12, 2018), 713

Villanueva, Edgar, Decolonizing Wealth: Indigenous Wisdom to Heal Divides and Restore Balance (2018), 628

Volpp, Leti, "Obnoxious to Their Very Nature:" Asian Americans and Constitutional Citizenship, 5 Citizenship Studies 57 (2001), 209

Volpp, Leti, American Mestizo: Filipinos and Antimiscegenation Laws in California, 33 U.C. Davis L. Rev. 795 (2000), 386

Vought, Russell, Memorandum for the Heads of Executive Branch Departments and Agencies (Sept. 4, 2020), 65

Waggoner, David, The Jurisprudence of White Supremacy: Inter Caetara, Johnson v. M'Intosh and San Antonio Independent School District v. Rodriguez, 44 Sw. L. Rev. 749 (2015), 1184

Wallerstein, Immanuel, World-Systems Analysis: An Introduction 98 (2004), 184

Warren, Mark, Parents Must Shut Down the School-to-Prison Pipeline (Jan. 22, 2019), 142

Watkins, Dawn and Laura Guihen, Using Narrative and Metaphor in Formative Feedback: Exploring Students' Responses, 68 J. Legal Ed. 154, 156 (2018), 364

We Need to Change How We Think: Perspectives on Philanthropy's Underfunding of Native Communities and Causes, First Nations Development Institute (2018), 621

Weathering the Storms: Building Social Justice Resilience Against Opposition Attacks (2015), RoadMap Consulting, 861

Weinstein, Janet et al., Teaching Teamwork to Law Students, 63 J. Legal Educ. 36 (2013), 555

Weinstein, Janet, Linda Morton, Howard Taras & Vivian Reznik, Teaching Teamwork to Law Students, 63 J. Legal Educ. 36 (2013), 558

Weiss, Marley S., Human Trafficking and Forced Labor: A Primer, 31 ABA J. of Lab. & Empl. L. 1 (2015), 941

West, Cornel, The Role of Law in Progressive Politics, 43 Vand. L. Rev. 1797 (1990), 343, 364

Westhoff, Laura, Citizenship Schools and the Civil Rights Movement, National Council for History Education, 26 History Matters Archive (Feb. 2014), 507

Weston, Rubin Francis, Racism in U.S. Imperialism 6–7 (1972), 1091

What's Up, Map the Power: Research for the Resistance, LittleSis, a project of the Public Accountability Initiative, 952

White, Lucie E., To Learn and Teach: Lessons from Driefontein on Lawyering and Power, 1988 Wis. L. Rev. 699 (1988), 806

White, Lucie, Collaborative Lawyering in the Field? On Mapping Paths from Rhetoric to Practice, 1 Clinical L. Rev. 157 (1994), 534

Whitford, William C., Critical Empiricism: A Comment on David M. Trubek & John Esser, Gerd Winter & Volkmar Gessner, 12 German L.J. 179 (2011), 908

Whitman, James Q., Hitler's American Model: The United States and the Making of Nazi Race Law (2017), 1086, 1111

Wilkerson, Isabel, Caste: The Origin of Our Discontents ch. 4 (2020), 85

Wilkins, David B., Class Not Race in Legal Ethics: Or Why Hierarchy Makes Strange Bedfellows, 20 L. & Hist. Rev. 147 (2002), 777

Williams, Patricia J., Alchemical Notes: Reconstructing Ideals from Deconstructed Rights, 22 Harv. C.R.-C.L. L. Rev. 401 (1987), 596

Williams, Robert A., Jr., Vampires Anonymous and Critical Race Practice, 95 Mich. L. Rev. 741 (1997), 545

Williams, Susan H., Legal Education, Feminist Epistemology, and the Socratic Method, 45 Stan. L. Rev. 1571 (1993), 860

Wilson, Amanda, Putting Therapeutic Jurisprudence on Edge: A Gendered Engagement, 47 U. B.C. L. Rev. 1185 (2014), 784

Windham, Lane, Knocking on Labor's Door: Union Organizing in the 1970s and the Roots of a New Economic Divide 190–91 (2017), 837

Wing, Adrien Katherine, Brief Reflections Toward a Multiplicative Theory and Praxis of Being, 6 Berkeley Women's L.J. 181 (1991), 389

Wing, Adrien Katherine, Critical Race Feminism and International Human Rights, 28 U. Miami Inter-Am. L. Rev. 337 (1997), 81, 787

Winter, Caroline, Nestlé Makes Billions Bottling Water It Pays Nearly Nothing For, Bloomberg Businessweek (Sept. 21, 2017), 161

Winton, Jenna, Rebranding Valentine's Day for Honoring Murdered and Missing Indigenous Women, Cultural Survival (Feb. 19, 2014), 946

Women of Color Pursue Change Strategies with Limited Resources, Candid: Philanthropy News Digest (July 2, 2020), 621

Wong, Alia and Adrienne Green, Campus Politics: A Cheat Sheet, The Atlantic 15 (Apr. 4, 2016), 274

Wood, Gordon S., The Creation of the American Republic 410–11 (1969), 439

Woods, Tryon P., The Implicit Bias of Implicit Bias Theory, 10 Drexel L. Rev. 631 (2018), 275

Working toward Equity and Excellence for All, What We Do, Teach for America, 117

Yamamoto, Eric K., Conflict and Complicity: Justice Among Communities of Color, 2 Harv. Latino L. Rev. 495 (1997), 1033

Yamamoto, Eric K., Critical Procedure: ADR and the Justices' "Second Wave" Constriction of Court Access and Claim Development, 70 SMU L. Rev. 765 (2017), 465

Yamamoto, Eric K., Critical Race Praxis: Race Theory and Political Lawyering Practice in Post-Civil Rights America, 95 Mich. L. Rev. 821 (1997), 555, 1033

Yamamoto, Eric K., Rethinking Alliances: Agency, Responsibility and Interracial Justice, 3 Asian Pac. Am. L.J. 33 (1995), 850, 1033

Yang, Andrea C., Re-considering Progressive Lawyering: The Theory and a Growing Practice in Asian Immigrant Communities, 16 Asian Pac. Am. L.J. 100 (2010–11), 787

Yeazell, Stephen C., From Group Litigation to Class Action, Part I: The Industrialization of Group Litigation, 27 UCLA L. Rev. 514 (1979–80), 463

Yeazell, Stephen C., From Group Litigation to Class Action, Part II: Interest, Class, and Representation, 27 UCLA L, Rev. 1067 (1979–80), 463

Yeazell, Stephen C., Group Litigation and Social Context: Toward a History of the Class Action, 77 Colum. L. Rev. 866 (1977), 463

Zweigenhaft, Richard L. and G. William Domhoff, Diversity in the Power Elite: Ironies and Unfulfilled Promises (2018), 427

CRITICAL JUSTICE
SYSTEMIC ADVOCACY IN LAW AND SOCIETY

EDITORS' INTRODUCTION

■ ■ ■

After more than a decade working on this book, how can we settle on expressing a single purpose? We can't, really; but if we could, it might go something like this: to provide a reliable, accessible, diverse, and adaptable resource for all kinds of justice-seeking users—teachers, students, practitioners, organizers, activists, and posterity. This book aims to interweave knowledge and experience in practical, thematic terms for today's increasingly complex, dangerous, and challenging contexts.

The daily news makes the urgency of systemic analysis and solutions ever clearer. No social problem is just personal, local, idiosyncratic, or atomized. From climate change to extreme poverty and COVID-19, humanity's problems are undeniably collective—interlinked, both locally and globally. In this state of affairs, individuals frequently feel overwhelmed and disempowered. The first cognitive step in understanding this daunting reality is developing knowledge, awareness, and consciousness. This first critical step, as Joe Biden pointed out in his 2021 presidential inauguration, is knowing that "what just is, is not justice."

The advocates and activists whose work is presented in this book—in articles, notes, questions, footnotes, and charts—offer hard-won insights drawn directly from the front lines of ongoing group struggle against systemic injustice. These reflections and bottom lines honor the contributions made by valiant persons and groups. Despite fear and loss, many have sought and continue to seek greater lived justice in a complex, selectively indifferent, and often hostile world. These reflections honor the gains of past labors and the lessons to be drawn going forward to do better in the next round of urgent struggles.

We aim to do the same, and in the same spirit. Recognizing the generations of diverse histories of advocacy, struggle, and fragile progress for equal justice, we dedicate this book to them and to future generations of systemic advocates prepared to pick up where they left off. As we note in the book's concluding part, historical and contemporary struggles to overcome inequality in law and society are a critical marathon, an inter-generational process to which we hope this book contributes in practical and conceptual ways.

As one whole, this book sets out a comprehensible, actionable story of systemic injustice and advocacy. It is equally designed as a practical manual, a theory primer, a reference guide, a critical reader, and a community tool. Using your own knowledge and the book's offerings, you can begin a course of reading, reflection, and discussion with others. Now or later, perhaps this resource can help you and others to organize actions together. These steps may lead to something or to nothing. It's okay. We can always try again tomorrow. All of us can act in small—and large—ways as individuals and as professionals to continually help to lessen systemic injustice. Even simple but intentional adjustments in our choices can help set the stage for transformative change down the road.

The notorious RBG—Ruth Bader Ginsburg—put it most simply: lean and act on principle, but always in ways that lead others to join you. Appreciate, as Abraham Lincoln forewarned us in 1866, that we cannot escape history and its legacies; we have the power and responsibility to do justice and make progress. Therefore, to paraphrase John F. Kennedy nearly a century later, we are here not only cursing the darkness but also lighting and stringing the candles. As U.S. poet and National Youth Poet Laureate Amanda Gorman urged during the 2021 Presidential Inaugural, we recognize that even in the most tumultuous of systemic conditions, "There is light if we are only brave enough to see it, brave enough to be it." And, remembering always Act-Up's bottom line of the 1990s—Silence=Death—we point anyone who still doubts the human toll and planetary devastation of systemic inequities toward Pope Paul VI's pithy teaching: if you want peace, work for justice. We hope this book helps us all to be "brave enough"—personally and collectively—to make Critical Justice and social peace a systemic reality for all.

We have no way around it: changing systems requires systemic change, which depends on personal and collective action. So, take your time; absorb and reflect. Then, collaborate, act, and repeat. Yes, this book *does* present a lot to take in—a lot. But in the end, it's not rocket science. Chapter by chapter, section by section, we hope this handy compendium for systemic advocacy improves your work and life, and that of those around you, daily. When you look back, we trust and hope you'll see the difference you helped to make.

Note on Footnotes and Format: Footnotes are numbered consecutively throughout and we did not retain the original numbering of any footnotes found in excerpted sources. Sometimes the content of those original source footnotes has been shortened to cite only a key source mentioned in the main text excerpt, and modified to use the citation style consistently used in this book.

PART I

INTRODUCING THE CRITICAL CHALLENGE OF USING LAW FOR EQUAL JUSTICE

...

CHAPTER 1

LOOKING TO THE BOTTOM IS STEP ONE IN SYSTEMIC ADVOCACY

■ ■ ■

Table of Sections

1.1 Law Isn't Always What It Seems to Be—If You Look at It from the Bottom
1.2 Collective Knowledge "From the Bottom" Anchors Advocacy in Group Struggles
1.3 Depending on Circumstance and Context, Bottoms (and Tops) Can Shift—So Must Advocates and Advocacy
1.4 Critical "Schools" and Advocacy "Approaches" Provide Wells of Knowledge for "Different" Groups and Their Advocates
1.5 Deconstruction and Dual Consciousness Empower Subordinated Groups
1.6 Systemic Injustice Is Epistemic Injustice

OPENING THOUGHTS

Practice needs theory and theory needs practice just like fish need clean water.

—Paulo Freire

We saying that theory's cool, but theory with no practice ain't shit.

—Fred Hampton

Critical Legal Theory . . . allows the student to better understand how laws have operated historically and what ideologies were employed to maintain certain narratives that denied rights to people and communities.

—Chaumtoli Huq, (inter)Generation Movement Lawyer 2.0, Law at the Margins (2014)

I have a vision of a very strong, vocal and articulate critical movement that forwards a theory and a practice that challenges the judiciary's departure from good faith reasoning and its cynical instrumentalization of racial egalitarianism in the maintenance of sheer white supremacy.

—Sumi K. Cho, Essential Politics, 2 Harv. Latino L. Rev. 433, 435–36 (1997)

INTRODUCTION

Despite a century or more of legal reforms and social changes, everyday headlines make plain that the U.S. constitutional commitment to "Equal Justice Under Law" remains illusory for many individuals and for some entire communities. Today's front-burner legal and social issues and targets of group struggle range from equal pay for equal work to mass incarceration and police violence, voter suppression, student debt, climate adaptation, marriage equality, immigration justice, healthcare access, and many more topical controversies. Some are new, while most connect to injustices, struggles, and aspirations of past generations. The same is true globally.

Advocacy groups around the world use the term "systemic injustice" to identify injustice perpetrated systematically, almost automatically, because it has been ingrained and institutionalized by law. In response, advocates and activists have begun to develop myriad approaches to "systemic advocacy." Systemic advocacy aims to counter systemic injustice in a collective way that achieves systemic justice. In this work, law is central—both to systemic injustice and to systemic advocacy. Law permits collective inequality to persist. And law is an essential part of the solution. Advocates, activists, and others thus face the pressing Critical Challenge this book details:

How does one help translate law's noble promises into lived social realities for all?

Or, to put it simply, how does one use law for equal justice and social equity in material, practical, and ethical terms?

A common thread binds global efforts to oppose injustice and advance justice systemically: a focus on groups, legal systems, persistent inequalities, and on developing multidisciplinary tools to both critically diagnose and strategically address systemic injustice. Such work prioritizes collaboration based on views of those living the injustice—views from "the bottom" of a persistent, systemic problem.

Reflecting these common themes and aspirations, the mission statement of the Systemic Justice Project at Harvard Law School describes itself as confronting entrenched sources of persistent injustice:

> [SJP] is a policy innovation collaboration, organized and catalyzed by Harvard Law School students devoted to identifying injustice, designing solutions, promoting awareness, and advocating reforms to policymakers, opinion leaders, and the public. While targeting specific policy challenges, SJP is devoted to understanding common and systemic sources of injustice by analyzing the historical, cultural, political, economic, and psychological context of particular problems. Toward that end,

> SJP is committed to collaborating with scholars, lawyers, lawmakers, and citizens and to working with existing institutions in promoting attainable, pragmatic, and lasting policy solutions.[1]

This mission statement makes clear that traditional notions of legal "relevance" and analysis are insufficient for systemic justice. Not only is the conceptual framework for understanding problems transformed in the context of systemic advocacy, so are traditional notions of typical legal action as discrete, individualized dispute resolution and of typical relationships among advocates, clients, and communities. The Legal Department of the New Orleans Worker Center for Racial Justice, for example, described its work with an emphasis on collaboration that aims to address social problems, build power accountable to "the bottom," and shift legal and cultural understandings of foundational notions like equality and justice:

> NOWCRJ's five attorneys work closely in integrated campaign teams with organizers, advocates, and communications staff to build collective leadership by affected workers and communities, use litigation to document and legitimize their experience, change the terms of the public debate, and build transformative coalitions. Our campaigns have transformed allies and opponents, won innovative legislative and regulatory changes at the federal and local level, and developed innovative opportunities for workers and communities to bargain with the state and with their "real boss" on complex global supply chains. [Our work] supports grassroots leaders in developing demands rooted in a transformative vision of freedom and equality, develops the policy proposals and community-based enforcement system to make policy real, and delivers the power for these vibrant, transformative campaigns to win and to develop long term organizational forms.[2]

As these examples—and many others you will see throughout this book—jointly make plain, a focus on systemic injustice and systemic advocacy employs and expands the conventions and resources of legal analysis and problem solving to reach the root causes of familiar, entrenched, collectivized inequalities. This expansion focuses on identities, groups, interests, and power as crucial elements of the Critical Challenge facing advocates around the world today.

Systemic advocacy consequently is not limited to the United States or to any other country or region. For example, in Canada, The Representative for Children and Youth of Nunavut (a Canadian territory

---

[1] https://systemicjustice.law.harvard.edu.

[2] New Orleans Worker Center for Racial Justice, Legal Department Overview (not available online).

populated mostly by indigenous Inuit residents) ascribes four elements to their understanding of systemic advocacy. By their definition, a "systemic" issue:

1. Affects many children or youth;
2. Often happens when government policies and practices are not working;
3. If left alone will probably happen again; and
4. May require an organization to change its policies, practices or even legislation.[3]

In Australia, the Family Advocacy organization explains that, "[s]ystemic advocacy is not individual, though it can be undertaken by just one person advocating on behalf of a group. The aim of systemic advocacy is to make positive change for a whole group of people. While this kind of advocacy takes time, strategy, and resources, in the medium or long term it is more effective than negotiating [the same] systemic barrier person by person, over and over again."[4] This work prioritizes collaboration based on the views of those living the situation or the injustice—that is, views from "the bottom" of the systemic problem. Clearly, then, neither systemic advocacy nor the Critical Challenge is confined by geography or locale. As a practical matter, systemic advocacy must be collaborative and coalitional, as well as local and global, because systemic injustice is collective, entrenched, and globalized.

As indicated by these examples, the systemic nature of a persistent social problem may be evidenced by its continuing recurrence in many "individual" instances, which cumulatively establish patterns of outputs upon which systems are judged. These examples explain why systemic advocacy must connect particularities to reveal, and change, patterns—why advocacy must account for both the micro and the macro. These individualized outputs, and their patterns, reflect the ways in which law interlocks with other systems (social, political, economic) based on social, group identities. In response, activists, organizers, groups, and advocates long have collaborated for bottom-up progress, as they still do.

To support this ongoing, transgenerational work, this chapter (and the book as a whole) inter-connect key concepts and core skillsets for systemic advocacy, beginning below with:

- anchoring advocacy in knowledge drawn from "the bottom"—those who experience social problems directly and who engage in social struggle to advance equal justice;

---

[3] www.rcynu.ca/families-public/our-work/what-we-do/systemic-advocacy.
[4] www.family-advocacy.com/what-we-do/systemic-advocacy/.

- using criticality—critical and self-critical reflection—to center knowledge from the bottom and to expose the interplay of identities, groups, interests, and power in law and social struggle;
- learning from the realist and critical Schools of legal analysis and the field-based advocacy Approaches that deepen understanding of systemic behaviors and outputs and provide advocacy strategies to counter them in favor of justice;
- developing a dual consciousness to both operate effectively as a legal insider deploying legal tools and to maintain a critical outsider perspective on law's limits and intentional systemic failures;
- collaborating across many disciplines and many sorts of social differences in teams and coalitions to build shared values, principles, goals, and movements; and
- managing time with conscious strategic intent to impede opposition or advance progress toward equal justice.

As the first two points explicitly state, systemic advocacy reflects and applies the insights of "critical" knowledge produced "from the bottom" through collective struggle and self-critical reflection. This kind of experiential knowledge and self-critical reflection is personal as well as systemic. This critical, bottom-up knowledge must be sourced in varied contexts through research and analysis using both traditional *and* nontraditional methods of learning and fact-finding. Experience—personal and professional, individual and collective—and its lessons always can (and often does) provide a starting point for critical understandings of problems and bottom-up solutions to them.

The critical Schools and the advocacy Approaches outlined in this chapter spotlight from the get-go that knowledge is power when made actionable—*and* when action is organized for the long haul and held accountable to those at the social bottom. These various bottom-up bodies of critical knowledge produced by successive generations of scholars, practitioners, organizers, and activists—in law and other disciplines—teach the same lessons that activists like Georgia's Stacey Abrams of Fair Fight preach and practice daily: systemic advocates must acknowledge the context, center the bottom, build sustainable groups, and act on bottom-up knowledge diligently, innovatively, and courageously. Youthful organizers of March for Our Lives aimed to "get ready and stay steady" in their own work after the 2018 mass shooting at their Florida high school in Parkland.

But there are no panaceas. We have no silver bullets for systemic injustice. Instead, we have ourselves, each other, what we collectively know, and what we can learn as we build systemic advocacy projects and engage in social movement activism. Gerald López, a pioneer of the rebellious lawyering approach to systemic advocacy, explained the challenge for advocates this way:

> None of these people has thoroughly worked out the answers to all the questions they confront. None of them has entirely escaped the inconsistencies and contradictions. None is immune from frustrations and failures. What each does understand, however, is that there's no self-executing blueprint for changing law practice any more than there is a magic plan for changing the world. Their work reflects . . . a profound appreciation that lawyering, no less than other activist vocations, must itself reflect and occasionally even usher in the world we hope to create.[5]

Evolving U.S.-centric and law-centric bodies of knowledge are not the only sources of critical knowledge from the bottom important to systemic advocacy, but they do reflect how law, as a system, is central both to persistent patterns of injustice and to effective solutions. Historically and presently, these (and associated) bodies of critical knowledge are an intellectual and practical response to the persistence of identity-based group inequalities within and beyond the United States.

1.1 LAW ISN'T ALWAYS WHAT IT SEEMS TO BE— IF YOU LOOK AT IT FROM THE BOTTOM

The opening excerpt below presents a prominent example of a core practice in contemporary approaches to systemic advocacy: reflection that is critical, as well as self-critical, to help us better understand persistent "gaps" between law and justice. At the time of this reflection, U.S. elites had organized an extravagant, coast-to-coast campaign of self-congratulation to mark the 200th anniversary of the constitution, drafted in 1787 and adopted in 1789. But to Justice Thurgood Marshall—the first non-white U.S. Supreme Court Justice, confirmed in 1964—the occasion commemorated events, choices, and actions not worthy of celebration. The difference was in perspective. Justice Marshall's perspective reflected the history of collective experience with law of those at "the bottom" of the system erected by that document, while the celebrants reflected the perspective from above—those who collectively had benefitted at the expense of those below. Marshall's reflection supplies our point of departure for proficiency in systemic advocacy today: law isn't always what it seems, or purports, to be if you take time to look at it from the bottom in critical and self-critical ways.

---

[5] Gerald P. López, Rebellious Lawyering: One Chicano's Vision of Progressive Law Practice (1992).

REFLECTIONS ON THE BICENTENNIAL OF THE UNITED STATES CONSTITUTION

Thurgood Marshall
101 Harv. L. Rev. 1 (1987)

The year 1987 marks the 200th anniversary of the United States Constitution. A Commission has been established to coordinate the celebration. The official meetings, essay contests, and festivities have begun.

The planned commemoration will span three years, and I am told 1987 is "dedicated to the memory of the Founders and the document they drafted in Philadelphia." We are to "recall the achievements of our Founders and the knowledge and experience that inspired them, the nature of the government they established, its origins, its character, and its ends, and the rights and privileges of citizenship, as well as its attendant responsibilities."

Like many anniversary celebrations, the plan for 1987 takes particular events and holds them up as the source of all the very best that has followed. Patriotic feelings will surely swell, prompting proud proclamations of the wisdom, foresight, and sense of justice shared by the framers and reflected in a written document now yellowed with age. This is unfortunate—not the patriotism itself, but the tendency for the celebration to oversimplify, and overlook the many other events that have been instrumental to our achievements as a nation. The focus of this celebration invites a complacent belief that the vision of those who debated and compromised in Philadelphia yielded the "more perfect Union" it is said we now enjoy.

I cannot accept this invitation, for I do not believe that the meaning of the Constitution was forever "fixed" at the Philadelphia Convention. Nor do I find the wisdom, foresight, and sense of justice exhibited by the framers particularly profound. To the contrary, the government they devised was defective from the start, requiring several amendments, a civil war, and momentous social transformation to attain the system of constitutional government, and its respect for the individual freedoms and human rights, that we hold as fundamental today. When contemporary Americans cite "The Constitution," they invoke a concept that is vastly different from what the framers barely began to construct two centuries ago.

For a sense of the evolving nature of the Constitution we need look no further than the first three words of the document's preamble: "We the People." When the Founding Fathers used this phrase in 1787, they did not have in mind the majority of America's citizens. "We the People" included, in the words of the framers, "the whole Number of free Persons." On a matter so basic as the right to vote, for example, Negro slaves were excluded, although they were counted for representational purposes—at three-fifths each. Women did not gain the right to vote for over a hundred and thirty years.

These omissions were intentional. The record of the framers' debates on the slave question is especially clear: the Southern states acceded to the demands of the New England states for giving Congress broad power to regulate commerce, in exchange for the right to continue the slave trade. The economic interests of the regions coalesced: New Englanders engaged in the "carrying trade" would profit from transporting slaves from Africa as well as goods produced in America by slave labor. The perpetuation of slavery ensured the primary source of wealth in the Southern states.

Despite this clear understanding of the role slavery would play in the new republic, use of the words "slaves" and "slavery" was carefully avoided in the original document. Political representation in the lower House of Congress was to be based on the population of "free Persons" in each state, plus three-fifths of all "other Persons." Moral principles against slavery, for those who had them, were compromised, with no explanation of the conflicting principles for which the American Revolutionary War had ostensibly been fought: the self-evident truths "that all men are created equal, that they are endowed by their Creator with certain unalienable Rights, that among these are Life, Liberty and the pursuit of Happiness."

. . .

As a result of compromise, the right of the Southern states to continue importing slaves was extended, officially, at least until 1808. We know that it actually lasted a good deal longer, as the framers possessed no monopoly on the ability to trade moral principles for self-interest. But they nevertheless set an unfortunate example. Slaves could be imported, if the commercial interests of the North were protected. . . .

No doubt it will be said, when the unpleasant truth of the history of slavery in America is mentioned during this bicentennial year, that the Constitution was a product of its times, and embodied a compromise which, under other circumstances, would not have been made. But the effects of the framers' compromise have remained for generations. They arose from the contradiction between guaranteeing liberty and justice to all, and denying both to Negroes.

The original intent of the phrase, "We the People," was far too clear for any ameliorating construction. Writing for the Supreme Court in 1857, Chief Justice Taney penned the following passage in the *Dred Scott* case, on the issue of whether, in the eyes of the framers, slaves were "constituent members of the sovereignty," and were to be included among "We the People":

> We think they are not, and that they are not included, and were not intended to be included. . . . [T]hey had no rights which the

white man was bound to respect.... [A]ccordingly, a negro of the African race was regarded ... as an article of property, and held, and bought and sold as such.... [N]o one seems to have doubted the correctness of the prevailing opinion of the time.

And so, nearly seven decades after the Constitutional Convention, the Supreme Court reaffirmed the prevailing opinion of the framers regarding the rights of Negroes in America. It took a bloody civil war before the thirteenth amendment could be adopted to abolish slavery, though not the consequences slavery would have for future Americans.

While the Union survived the civil war, the Constitution did not. In its place arose a new, more promising basis for justice and equality, the fourteenth amendment, ensuring protection of the life, liberty, and property of *all* persons against deprivations without due process, and guaranteeing equal protection of the laws. And yet almost another century would pass before any significant recognition was obtained of the rights of black Americans to share equally even in such basic opportunities as education, housing, and employment, and to have their votes counted, and counted equally. In the meantime, blacks joined America's military to fight its wars and invested untold hours working in its factories and on its farms, contributing to the development of this country's magnificent wealth and waiting to share in its prosperity.

What is striking is the role legal principles have played throughout America's history in determining the condition of Negroes. They were enslaved by law, emancipated by law, disenfranchised and segregated by law; and, finally, they have begun to win equality by law. Along the way, new constitutional principles have emerged to meet the challenges of a changing society. The progress has been dramatic, and it will continue.

The men who gathered in Philadelphia in 1787 could not have envisioned these changes. They could not have imagined, nor would they have accepted, that the document they were drafting would one day be construed by a Supreme Court to which had been appointed a woman and the descendent of an African slave. "We the People" no longer enslave, but the credit does not belong to the framers. It belongs to those who refused to acquiesce in outdated notions of "liberty," "justice," and "equality," and who strived to better them.

And so we must be careful, when focusing on the events which took place in Philadelphia two centuries ago, that we not overlook the momentous events which followed, and thereby lose our proper sense of perspective. Otherwise, the odds are that for many Americans the bicentennial celebration will be little more than a blind pilgrimage to the shrine of the original document now stored in a vault in the National Archives....

Thus, in this bicentennial year, we may not all participate in the festivities with flag-waving fervor. Some may more quietly commemorate the suffering, struggle, and sacrifice that has triumphed over much of what was wrong with the original document, and observe the anniversary with hopes not realized and promises not fulfilled. I plan to celebrate the bicentennial of the Constitution as a living document, including the Bill of Rights and the other amendments protecting individual freedoms and human rights.

This opening reflection highlights the "omissions" and "contradictions" that have generated entrenched patterns of collectivized injustice in the 200-plus years since the U.S. system's establishment. These intentional omissions and contradictions occurred because elite groups used their power to further their group interests over general principles of liberty, equality, and freedom that they simultaneously professed. This use—or abuse—of power violated the egalitarian principles that elites proclaimed were their reasons for revolting against British rule, the lawful system then in place. These privileged elites defined themselves, as well as those targeted for exclusion or subordination, on the basis of social identities (like race and sex) and on the basis of belief systems based on those social identities (like white supremacy and patriarchy). Privileged elites were quite overt about the whole thing. Charting today's systemic advocacy agendas begins with understanding these now-entrenched patterns of collectivized injustice. Changing these patterns has become the Critical Challenge for advocates: the challenge of using law for equal justice.

1.2 COLLECTIVE KNOWLEDGE "FROM THE BOTTOM" ANCHORS ADVOCACY IN GROUP STRUGGLES

Marshall's bicentennial reflection illustrates that critical forms of knowledge are indispensable in understanding legalized injustice and that critical forms of knowledge must emanate from the bottom to inform advocacy. This method has become central to groups and advocates aiming to expose law's original omissions and continuing contradictions. Those calculated omissions and contradictions create a design—a systemic architecture—that ensures collectivized inequalities from generation to generation. Over time, the Critical Challenge of using law for equal justice begins to appear—on purpose—as normal and insurmountable. But this appearance too is false.

Groups originally excluded and subordinated in the delivery of justice, joined by others, have sustained struggles for equality that demand the system deliver on its promises and principles. Those difficult struggles, and the critical, bottom-up knowledge they have produced, have prevented the systemic consolidation of this Critical Challenge and its biases as a "hegemony"—an unquestioned and unquestionable status quo maintained by top-down power and (at least by some) bottom-up acquiescence, as we explore more fully in Part VI.

Supplementing Marshall's bottom-up perspective, critical legal scholar Mari Matsuda describes and considers "looking to the bottom" as critical method. Matsuda also explains how knowledge from the bottom helps groups and advocates to dissect—or "deconstruct"—root causes of persistent collectivized inequalities. This excerpt illustrates how critical, bottom-up knowledge is actionable—or practical—knowledge, and underscores the centrality of *self*-criticality to all critical analyses of group hierarchies.

LOOKING TO THE BOTTOM: CRITICAL LEGAL STUDIES AND REPARATIONS

Mari J. Matsuda
22 Harv. C.R.-C.L. L. Rev. 323 (1987)

Introduction

When you are on trial for conspiracy to overthrow the government for teaching the deconstruction of law, your lawyer will want black people on your jury. Why? Because black jurors are more likely to understand what your lawyer will argue: that people in power sometimes abuse law to achieve their own ends, and that the prosecution's claim to neutral application of legal principles is false. This article discusses the similar perspectives and goals of people of color and critical legal scholars. It also suggests that the failure of the two groups to develop an alliance is tied to weaknesses of the Critical Legal Studies (CLS) movement.

... This article suggests that those who have experienced discrimination speak with a special voice to which we should listen. Looking to the bottom—adopting the perspective of those who have seen and felt the falsity of the liberal promise—can assist critical scholars in the task of fathoming the phenomenology of law and defining the elements of justice. . . .

... The method of looking to the bottom can lead to concepts of law radically different from those generated at the top. Reparations is suggested ... as a "critical legalism," a legal norm suggested by the experience of people of color. . . .

Critical Legal Studies and the Minority Scholar

The movement known as Critical Legal Studies [CLS] is characterized by skepticism toward the liberal vision of the rule of law, by a focus on the role of legal ideas in capturing human consciousness, by agreement that fundamental change is required to attain a just society, and by a utopian conception of a world more communal and less hierarchical than the one we know now.

This movement is attractive to minority scholars, because its central descriptive message—that legal ideals are manipulable and that law serves to legitimate existing maldistributions of wealth and power—rings true for anyone who has experienced life in non-white America. . . .

. . . [W]hat is needed now is an expanded method of inquiry, akin to feminist consciousness-raising.

Looking to the bottom can help. . . .

The dissonance of combining deep criticism of law with an aspirational vision of law is part of the experience of people of color. . . . Applying the double consciousness concept to rights rhetoric allows us to see that the victim of racism can have a mainstream consciousness of the Bill of Rights, as well as a victim's consciousness. These two viewpoints can combine powerfully to create a radical constitutionalism that is true to the radical roots of this country. . . .

. . . Consciousness-raising in the feminist context is the collective discussion and consideration of the concrete, felt experience of gender in order to identify commonalities and build a theory of the cause, effect and means of eradication of sexist oppression. Consciousness-raising deliberately examines the detail of life in a gender-biased society. As method, it differs from the typical top-down, abstract method of male-dominated jurisprudential inquiry. The method can, however, respond to the same inquiries: what is law, how does it work, what can it be, what should it be?

. . . To the question "How can one know that a rule or principle is just?" the CLS scholar could reply, "Ask someone who has suffered and fought against oppression, study their experience, and understand their world vision. They will help you find the right answer." . . .

Reparations as a Critical Legalism: An Example of Law Derived From the Bottom

. . . Reparations is a legal concept generated from the bottom. It arises not from abstraction but from experience. . . .

The Native Hawaiian Claim for Reparations

Native Hawaiians are . . . seeking reparations from the United States for the overthrow of native Hawaiian rule and loss of native lands. Native Hawaiians are unique among indigenous Americans in that they lived prior to annexation under a western-style constitutional government, whose sovereignty was recognized internationally as well as by the United States. That sovereignty ceased, however, upon the overthrow of the Hawaiian monarchy—an overthrow in which the United States participated. The Hawaiians' claim for loss of their government as well as their land forms a unique basis for reparations.

The Hawaiians descended from Polynesian voyagers who settled in the Hawaiian Islands, establishing a communal, agrarian society governed by a regime of custom and ruled by hierarchical leadership. The Hawaiian leaders, who governed the islands for over a thousand years before the arrival of Captain Cook, proved adept at responding to the influx of outside influence during the nineteenth-century period of Pacific exploration and trade. King Kamehameha used Western military devices to consolidate control of the islands, and his royal descendants instituted a Western-style constitutional monarchy in order to establish Hawaiian sovereignty in Western eyes. The major international powers, including the United States, formally recognized Hawaiian sovereignty.

The Hawaiian monarchy quickly adopted Western laws and acquired Western tastes in royal accoutrements. . . .

White Americans, a growing economic presence in the islands, resented the Hawaiian leadership. These planters, merchants and traders desired annexation by the United States. They accused the Hawaiian monarchy of incompetence, waste and anti-democratic rule. Dissatisfaction came to a head in 1893, when a handful of foreigners and white subjects of the Kingdom carried out a revolution.

Native Hawaiians, the overwhelming majority of the population, together with white loyalists, opposed the quest for annexation. U.S. government representatives, however, saw the threatened revolution as an opportunity to wrest the islands from indigenous control. United States Minister for Hawaii John L. Stevens had written earlier to the State Department, "The Hawaiian pear is now fully ripe, and this is the golden hour for the United States to pluck it."

The self-appointed revolutionaries were a small band of poorly-armed merchants and planters. Alone, they were no match for Queen Liliuokalani's military forces. However, Stevens landed U.S. troops on the islands to secure the Queen's surrender. The Queen, desiring to avoid bloodshed and trusting that the United States government would adhere to its treaties respecting Hawaiian sovereignty, temporarily surrendered and appealed to the President to restore her to the throne. . . .

Newly-installed President Grover Cleveland dispatched an emissary to investigate the U.S. involvement. He determined that the takeover was indeed a result of American military intervention against the will of the majority of Hawaiian citizens, a violation of international law as well as American foreign policy. The government's commitment to legality, however, faltered in the face of powerful political considerations, including strategic and economic benefits, that favored annexation. The Hawaiian government was never restored to power, and after a five-year congressional stand-off between anti-imperialists and annexationists, Hawaii became a [U.S.] territory in 1898.

Native Hawaiians never voted in any plebiscite on either the overthrow or annexation. In fact, the highly literate and politically astute Hawaiians overwhelmingly supported their native government and mourned the U.S. takeover.

In the process of the takeover, the United States obtained vast acreages of land that had belonged to the Kingdom and had been held in trust for the Hawaiian people. Some of this land remains in federal hands today, as vast military bases, national parks and open spaces. The remainder was returned to the State of Hawaii, which agreed to hold the land in trust for the native Hawaiian people. The State, however, has never complied with the trust mandate. Proceeds from trust land are commingled with other revenue and are not targeted to benefit the indigenous Hawaiian community. . . .

Native Hawaiians seek reparations for the overthrow of the Hawaiian government and loss of land. They request a formal recognition of the illegal destruction of Hawaiian sovereignty and an apology from the United States. They also seek resumption of Hawaiian rule, return of at least part of the lands presently held by the federal and state governments, and monetary compensation. . . .

Reparations Claims Within the Context of Liberal-Legalism

This section considers standard objections to reparations and suggests critical responses that can be strengthened by looking to the bottom.

Standard Doctrinal Objections to Reparations

The standard doctrinal objections to reparations claims fall under four general categories:

1. factual objections and excuse or justification for illegal acts;
2. difficult identification of perpetrator and victim groups;
3. lack of sufficient connection between past wrong and present claim;
4. difficulty of calculation of damages.

. . . [T]he preliminary question presented here is whether, assuming the fact of past illegal and unjustified acts directed against particular ethnic groups, reparations makes sense to the legal mind. . . .

Identification of Victims and Perpetrators

The problem of specific identification of wrongdoers and victims is a common objection to reparations. This reservation reflects a penchant for horizontal and vertical logic in legal doctrine. Privity, standing, and nexus are typical conceptual expressions of this compulsion for close and ordered relations between individual disputants. Reparations challenges this rigid order by suggesting new connections between victims and perpetrators.

The standard legal claim resembles:

Plaintiff A (individual victim)

v.

Defendant B (perpetrator of recent wrong-doing)

A claim in reparations looks like this:

Plaintiff Class A (victim group members)

v.

Defendant Class B (perpetrator descendants and current beneficiaries of past injustice)

... Looking to the bottom helps refute the standard objections to reparations. In response to the problem of horizontal connection among victims and perpetrators, a victim would note that as the experience of discrimination against the group is real, the connections must exist. The hierarchical relationship that places white people over people of color was promoted by the specific wrongs of the past. The destruction of Hawaiian sovereignty ... [is] tied to the idea of white dominance and non-white difference. Each specific act of oppression against a minority group reinforces, entrenches, and promotes the assumption that non-whites are different and appropriately treated as different.

... The continuing group damage engendered by past wrongs ties victim group members together, satisfying the horizontal unity sought by the legal mind. Indigenous Hawaiians, for example, are on the bottom of every demographic indicator of social survival: they have lower birth weights, higher infant mortality, and, if they survive, higher rates of disease, illiteracy, imprisonment, alcoholism, suicide and homelessness. Hawaiians realize their forgotten status in their own land. Poor and rich, Democrat and Republican, commoner and royalty—native Hawaiians largely agree that they have been robbed. ...

A horizontal connection exists as well within the perpetrator group. Members of the dominant class continue to benefit from the wrongs of the past and the presumptions of inferiority imposed upon victims. They may decry this legacy, and harbor no racist thoughts of their own, but they cannot avoid their privileged status.

Any non-native resident of Hawaii, for example, benefits from the loss of Hawaiian sovereignty and the demise of the Hawaiian land ownership. If Hawaiians had not lost their land, others would not be living on it. If the

Hawaiians had not been pushed to the bottom of the socioeconomic pile, non-natives would not hold as many positions of power and influence.... Beneficiaries not required to prove their intelligence, responsibility, and worth to the same extent as victim group members are protected by a subtle magic they may not notice because they have never had the experience of life without it. In addition, the abundance of material comforts in this nation results in part from the labor of the non-white workers who have been relegated to some of the hardest, most dangerous, and least compensated work. This list includes black slaves, Chinese railroad workers, Chicano miners, and legions of today's undocumented toilers in factory and field. One cannot be detached from privilege while enjoying the benefits of this country's high standard of living; in that sense, we are all part of the beneficiary class. Victims and perpetrators belong to groups that, as a matter of history, are logically treated in the collective sense of reparations rather than the individual sense of the typical legal claim. Looking to the bottom, we can expand our narrow vision of what a legal relationship should look like, addressing the historical reality before us.

Linkage Between Act and Present Claim

The linkage of victims and perpetrators for acts occurring in the immediate past is another trait of standard legal claims. Concepts such as the time-bar, proximate cause, and laches ensure that claims are fresh, capable of factual determination, and reasonably connected in time and space to the act of an individual wrongdoer. These rules promote efficiency by allowing people to go about their business without waiting for the ax of the long-gone past to fall. They also satisfy a sense of fairness: the sins of the past should not forever burden the innocent generations of the future, nor should the consequences of one false step create disproportionate fault into eternity.

... Traditional discourse limits these doctrines through standard exceptions. Plaintiffs operating under a disability are not required to press their claims until the disability is removed; a continuing wrong does not start the clock running under a statute of limitation until the wrong culminates in an act of finality; fraud in concealing the availability of or grounds for an action is another standard exception. All of these exceptions apply to claims for reparations. Indeed, the need for reparations arises precisely because it takes a nation so long to recognize historical wrongs against those on the bottom....

Reparations claims are based on continuing stigma and economic harm. The wounds are fresh and the action timely given ongoing discrimination. Furthermore, the injuries suffered—deprivation of land, resources, educational opportunity, person-hood, and political recognition—are disabilities that have precluded successful presentation of the claim at an earlier time. Outright fraud and factual misrepresentation have also delayed presentation of claims....

... It would have required no clairvoyant skill to predict the harm that would befall Hawaiians from the loss of their nation and land.... What a reasonable person would have predicted would occur, did in fact occur, thus satisfying one classic test for proximate causal connection....

The reparations concept also serves the goal of retribution. The decision to award reparations is an act of contrition and humility that can ease victims' bitterness and alienation. A classic legal justification for imposing public liability—avoiding the chaos of individual, private revenge-seeking—is advanced, thereby strengthening the social order.

Relief

Finally, the impossibility of a fair damage assessment is a standard doctrinal objection to reparations. How can we attach a monetary figure to the loss of a right? Amorphous ideas such as sovereignty, dignity, personhood and liberty are incapable of uniform valuation. We risk undervaluing the right to avoid bankrupting the government, or, conversely, over-valuing it in relation to actual economic losses.

This objection should carry little weight. Judges and juries calculate non-quantifiable damages all the time. As Richard Delgado points out, the refusal to formulate compensation for racial hate messages is in itself racist, given a tort law system that calculates damages for loss of such intangibles as privacy, reputation and mental tranquility. Similarly, the selective choice to refuse to quantify damages for reparations claimants is suspect....

... Given the doctrinal basis for reparations thus revealed, the question becomes one of whether, given our conception of justice and our social goals, we wish to exercise that doctrinal option....

The Refrain of Reparations Within the Victims' Constitution

In interpreting the Constitution and distilling its values, those on the bottom have found the inspiration for a new order....

For those Americans, the constitutional promise of liberty holds special meaning. Liberty, viewed from the bottom, has encompassed physical liberty from constraint of the person. It has encompassed life itself—freedom from life-threatening abuse as well as the right to seek the nurturance and livelihood human beings need for survival. Liberty has meant personhood and participation—the recognition of one's existence as a human being, free and equal, with power and control over the political processes that govern one's life. The promise of liberty, for those on the bottom, has meant freedom from public and private racism, freedom from inequalities of wealth distribution, and freedom from domination by dynasties. This interpretation of liberty, implicit in the founding document of this nation, is the interpretation that has convinced so many on the bottom to work for, rather than against, the Constitution. That so many have believed in this version of the Constitution, and fought to establish and preserve the union on the basis of that belief, lends historical support to the victim's interpretation.

This interpretation supports a doctrine of reparations. Reparations recognizes the personhood of victims. Lack of legal redress for racist acts is an injury often more serious than the acts themselves, because it signifies the political non-personhood of victims. The grant of reparations declares, "You exist. Your experience of deprivation is real. You are entitled to compensation for that deprivation. This nation and its laws acknowledge you." . . .

Conclusion: "The Pen is Ours to Wield"

Critical legal scholars have much to offer people of color. They also have much to learn from them. Looking to the bottom will expand the critical scholar's ability to work toward positive change. . . .

Matsuda demonstrates how principled applications of conventional legal doctrines should produce remedies for systemic injustice—but don't because the view (and dominant interests) from the top disallow it. Conventional appeals that simply ask for accepted principles to be applied consistently are necessary and yet insufficient. Using reparations to illustrate bottom-up methodology and knowledge production, Matsuda also emphasizes a recurring theme throughout this book: the materiality—the tangibility—of collective inequality and systemic injustice. The next excerpt amplifies these points with an added emphasis on democracy, rather than adjudication, as a venue of organized group struggles for equal justice. Both examples demonstrate how looking to the bottom can make a difference in strategy and in outcome.

Critical race scholars Lani Guinier and Gerald Torres turn our attention to advocacy that is not court or litigation-centric. Guinier and Torres call upon advocates to learn not only the lessons of group struggle in judicial venues—the "jurisprudence" or doctrine resulting from litigation and its limits—but also the lessons of "demosprudence" derived from direct group struggles over law and policymaking in the trenches of group struggle. Guinier and Torres thus help bring into focus another recurring theme of this book: building strong organizations capable of direct collective action.

CHANGING THE WIND: NOTES TOWARD A DEMOSPRUDENCE OF LAW AND SOCIAL MOVEMENTS
Lani Guinier and Gerald Torres
123 Yale L.J. 2740 (2014)

Introduction

I say here's how you recognize a member of Congress. They're the ones walking around with their fingers up in the air. And then they lick their finger and they put it back up and they see which way the wind is blowing.

You can't change a nation by replacing one wet-fingered politician with another. You change a nation when you change the wind. . . . [W]e've got to now be wind-changers. Not lobbyists, but wind-changers. How do we—by our service, by our doing in our lives—how do we then join together and knit together a movement that holds politics accountable?

—Reverend Jim Wallis

. . . We believe that the role played by social movement activism is as much a source of law as are statutes and judicial decisions. Our goal, therefore, is to create analytic space to enable a greater understanding of lawmaking as the work of mobilized citizens in conjunction with, not separate from, legal professionals. Our aim is to better understand and recognize the important roles played by ordinary people who succeed in challenging unfair laws through the sounds and determination of their marching feet. The role played by legal professionals—from judges to legislators to lawyers—is essential. Yet the civil rights movement grew in its efficacy in the 1950s and 1960s—helping to expand the "constitutional canon"—by putting its boots on the ground. It was the mobilization of ordinary people willing to play a significant role in shifting the law both locally and nationally that had a decisive effect.

Thus, this essay argues that social movements have played key roles in redefining the meaning of our democracy by creating the necessary conditions for a genuine "community of consent." . . .

Like Martin Luther King, Jr., we believe that it is often by the thick action of concerted social movement through which "we the people"—meaning, in our view, the people who reflect a genuine community of consent—discover and legitimize the principles on which our democracy presumably rests. We use the "wind changers" metaphor to test the following four-part hypothesis:

1. For those interested in social change, it is useful to view lawmaking from the perspective of popular mobilizations, such as social movements and other sustained forms of contentious politics and collective action that serve to make formal institutions, including those that regulate legal culture, more democratic.

2. One of the important functions of law resides in its power to translate lived experience into a series of stories about individual and social fairness and justice. Although courts and lawyers are important participants in the creation of these narratives through the shaping of the discourse of law, social movements and organized constituencies of non-expert participants also play an important role in the creation of authoritative interpretative communities.

3. A fundamental claim of legal liberalism is that social movements achieve their goals when they translate their claims into law. The most efficient way of achieving social change, therefore, is directly through litigation and legislative actions. A commitment to legal liberalism drives the litigation and policy focus that is the priority of conventional cause lawyering. We posit almost the reverse: for legal change to reflect real social change it must take account of, and engage with, alternative or contending sources of power. Such change must also, in some measure, transform the culture.

4. We do not want to minimize the importance of legislative change, especially legislation of constitutional dimension. Our main point is that such legislative change—and to a large extent judicially driven change—gets its enduring force from "We, the People."

... We seek in this essay to ... propose a new paradigm that we call demosprudence. Demosprudence is the study of the dynamic equilibrium of power between lawmaking and social movements. Demosprudence focuses on the legitimating effects of democratic action to produce social, legal, and cultural change. Although democratic accountability as a normative matter includes citizen mobilizations organized to influence a single election, a discrete piece of legislation, or a judicial victory, we focus on the interaction between lawmaking and popular, purposive mobilizations that seek significant, sustainable social, economic, and/or political change. Put differently, we seek to understand, analyze, and document those social movements that increase the extant democratic potential in our polity, and which do so in a way that produces durable social and legal change. Whereas jurisprudence examines the extent to which the rights of "discrete and insular" minorities are protected by judges interpreting ordinary legal and constitutional doctrine, demosprudence explores the ways that political, economic, or social minorities cannot simply rely on judicial decisions as the solution to their problems. Rather than turning over their agency to lawyers, they must find a way to integrate lawyers not as leaders but as fellow advocates. Borrowing a phrase from social theory, proponents of progressive social change must be advocates in themselves and for themselves and others. Understanding the roles played by social movements in producing durable social and legal change is central to our inquiry.

Introducing Demosprudence

As a method, demosprudence requires us to ask two overarching questions: (1) How and when do disadvantaged or weak minorities (whether political, economic, or identitarian) mobilize to protect their own rights in a majoritarian democracy?; and (2) Does the mobilization of these constituencies have a democracy-enhancing effect? By democracy enhancing, we mean that the mobilization opens up space to those previously excluded or marginalized and enables them to participate more fully in helping to make decisions that affect their lives. Demosprudence, therefore, is the study of the relationship between social movements and law in the creation of authoritative meaning within a democratic polity. . . .

Scholars of demosprudence . . . draw attention to the "dynamic constituencies" who call power to account through their participation in "contentious" politics and other forms of legal meaning making that also call democracy to account. Constituencies refer to those actors who make up the body of support for leaders and elites in the process of governing or policy change. We use the term "constituencies of accountability" to refer to those groups who are not committed primarily to any particular person or leader, but rather to a particular vision of change against which they measure the effectiveness of those using state power. . . .

As a practice, demosprudence trains its sights on the lawyer or public citizen who functions as a crucial source of moral authority and democratic legitimacy in facilitating the interaction between social movements and formal lawmaking. Demosprudence is a way to examine how lawyers and other public citizens represent social movements to make law. . . .

The demos in demosprudence are those people who are collectively mobilized both to make change and to create constituencies of accountability to which their representatives (including non-elected elite decision makers) must answer. . . . They succeed when they (1) shift the rules that govern social institutions, (2) transform the culture that controls the meaning of legal changes, and (3) affect the interpretation of those legal changes by providing the foundation for naturalizing those changes into the doctrinal structure of law and legal analysis. . . .

Nomos and Narrative: All of Us is Tired

"We didn't come all this way for no two seats . . . all of us is tired."

In August 1964, the Mississippi Freedom Democratic Party [MFDP] challenged the right of the all-white segregationist Mississippi Democratic Party to represent Mississippi at the Democratic National Convention. The Freedom Democratic Party, an insurgent organization open to all Mississippians, arrived in Atlantic City poised to make a public stand against segregation. Its delegation, including Fannie Lou Hamer, Victoria Jackson Gray, and Annie Devine, was composed of ministers, farmers, sharecroppers, domestics, and the unemployed. Activists spanned the Mississippi black community, and they demanded to be seated at the convention as official Mississippi delegates.

The party was founded in the spring of 1964 after unsuccessful attempts to secure black participation in the local branches of the Democratic Party and in the midst of a violent backlash in Mississippi against the gains that were being made nationally, such as the civil rights bill of 1963 (signed into law as the Civil Rights Act in 1964). Telling the Credentials Committee at the Democratic National Convention why they created the MFDP, Hamer explained:

> We formed our own party because the whites wouldn't even let us register [to vote].... We followed all the laws that the white people themselves made. We tried to attend the precinct meetings and they locked the doors on us or moved the meetings and that's against the laws they made for their ownselves. So we were the ones that held the real precinct meetings. At all these meetings across the state we elected our representatives, to go to the National Democratic Convention in Atlantic City. But we learned the hard way that even though we had all the law and all the righteousness on our side—that white man is not going to give up his power to us.

... Hamer mesmerized a national television audience at the 1964 Democratic National Convention with her stark but riveting description of the struggle to register to vote. However, Hamer's physical sacrifice and spellbinding performance were not enough to convince either Lyndon Johnson, the Democratic Party's presidential candidate, or Hubert Humphrey, its eventual vice-presidential candidate, to take on the state segregationists in a face-off with the Freedom Democrats. Instead, the Democratic national party leaders cobbled together a compromise: they would pledge to ban segregation at future conventions, but for now, the MFDP would have to settle for two seats as at-large delegates.

... [T]he Freedom Democratic Party refused to be placated: Hamer said simply, but firmly, "We didn't come all this way for no two seats, 'cause all of us is tired."

Fannie Lou Hamer's convention speech was political theater in service of a profound challenge to both the national and the local party's understandings of democracy....

Hamer spoke to the nation on behalf of an organized and mobilized constituency that reimagined the structure of democratic representation. The MFDP didn't travel from Mississippi just to play normal politics. The MFDP came to Atlantic City to contest the way in which representation was understood. They were not just there to be able to get a seat on the floor, but to dispute the legitimacy by which the seats were allocated.

Hamer and the other MFDP delegates were clear. Their role in democratic life should be taken seriously. For the MFDP, this was a moral not just a political struggle. . . .

For Joe Rauh, MFDP's attorney, it was a different matter. He knew the game of politics. He arrived at the Democratic National Convention as an insider. . . .

His MFDP clients had charged him to bargain for nothing less than what other challengers had gotten: shared seats with the regulars. Yet, Rauh expressed enthusiasm for the two-seat compromise, focusing on the practicalities of negotiation and bargaining rather than justice, law, and the rights of black Mississippians to participate. In an interview at the Convention, shortly after the announcement of the compromise, a self-satisfied Rauh declared:

> We've got an offer to our people, we've got a great deal out of this. I think to call this a loss is a bad . . . mistake. I think we've made a terrific gain. You always talk "no compromise" in a Convention until you get the best you can then you quit.

. . . [D]espite his genuine commitment to the MFDP cause, Rauh misunderstood the power of the MFDP, which he tried to channel into conventional deal-making. The MFDP power came from the evident justice of their claim that the Mississippi delegation was patently illegitimate. Their position was not about accommodating two reasonable sides to a political contest. They saw this as a right side and a wrong side. The meaning of democratic participation meant seating the truly legitimate party, the one party that offered to represent everyone. The challenge was not about getting the best deal; the challenge was not to abandon fundamental values. . . .

What Rauh did not grasp is that Hamer . . . had a vision of democracy that did not begin and end with "politics" or with "put[ting] a point over." Moreover, the MFDP did more than represent a broader and more participatory view of democracy. As an uneducated though eloquent sharecropper, Hamer's mere presence—televised to the nation—put conventional ideas about leadership in jeopardy, as well. Hamer and the other delegates of the MFDP sought to expand the democratic potential in Mississippi and in Atlantic City by saying that the right to participate belonged to all, not just to those deemed qualified by elites, whether black or white. Merely securing the right to vote, or gaining access to a convention seat for two "representatives," was not the same as "freedom." "By representing the poorest of Mississippi's residents, people without the 'qualifications' that accompanied middle-class status, the MFDP repudiated traditional criteria of leadership."

This fight was not about abstract rights for invisible people. Voting rights were a precondition to mobilization, not its end. The goal was to organize, to develop the power of the local people to change their own circumstances. As Mississippi activist Lawrence Guyot explained, voting rights assure the right to begin to fight "in the way we want to fight." And the way they wanted to fight involved ordinary people speaking for themselves. . . .

The dominance of elite thought reveals a tension in the ways even the most sympathetic elites "represent" non-elites at the moment of action. For example, Martin Luther King, Jr. lobbied for the compromise and against it simultaneously. . . . [I]n trying to balance the competing pressures, King equivocated. "So, being a Negro leader, I want you to take this, but if I were a Mississippi Negro, I would vote against it." . . .

[In this context, Hamer] was clear where her power and authority came from. She was speaking for, to, and with every Mississippi Negro who took the promise of democracy seriously.

. . . Hamer's stand made the national leadership aware of a constituency that would try to hold them accountable to a larger vision of justice. Hamer's stand was an exhortation as well as an implicit critique of King's conception of representation and leadership. The role that Hamer played was exemplary of the capacity for members of a mobilized constituency to change the rules of the game and to hold those who would claim the mantle of leadership accountable. . . .

In juxtaposing King's ambivalence with Hamer's . . . steadfastness, we see how social movement actors can tell a competing story of democracy that reframes the idea of participation, the meaning of representation, and the sources of democratic authority. Hamer and the other MFDP delegates changed the idea of participation from an obligation to obey to an obligation to speak out. They were no longer content to be the passive objects of power; they became active subjects of legitimate authority. Hamer also embodied a different meaning of representation. Unlike King's fundamental confusion as to the source of his power and to whom he was obligated, Hamer rejected the offer of representation when it was presented as a bribe of individual access dressed up as power. Hamer's conception of representation bound her to the community, which was a reservoir of their power, not hers. She knew that the source of her authority came from the struggle of the activists in Mississippi, rather than the boardrooms of Washington or any other polished corridor of power from which those activists, to be sure, would have been excluded. . . .

. . . The stories of [MFDP] members also play an important role in understanding the wellspring of movement "successes." They illustrate the vital role of the MFDP as an alternative interpretative community that helped drive rule shifts and changes in law. The MFDP—here exemplified by the person of Fannie Lou Hamer but also embodied in the actions of many of her cohorts—helped create obligations, not just new incentives for those with formal power to change the rules.... [T]he formal rules of the Democratic Party ultimately changed because they excluded large numbers of the Democratic Party base.

The MFDP, as an alternative interpretative community and a constituency of accountability, ... forced two issues to the fore: (1) whether they would be granted a role in the national party that claimed to represent their interest, and (2) whether they would even be allowed to vote as full citizens. ...

Fannie Lou Hamer and her MFDP associates exemplify an alternative but important source of lawmaking power that is not controlled entirely by elections, legislatures, executives, or courts. ...

We now turn to the Montgomery Bus Boycott to further examine some of the same issues—considering again the perspective and practice of lawyers who "represent" a dynamic constituency.

The Montgomery Bus Boycott

On the night of December 5, 1955, Dr. King put succinctly the relationship between law on the books and law as experienced. Well before King became a "national" leader, he delivered his very first speech as head of the Montgomery Improvement Association (MIA). Earlier that day, Rosa Parks had been convicted of disorderly conduct for refusing to acquiesce to the Jim Crow laws of the segregated bus system. ... At the mass meeting celebrating the first day of the bus boycott, King asserted: "We are here because of our love for democracy, because of our deep-seated belief that democracy transformed from thin paper to thick action is the greatest form of government on earth." ...

... [F]ifty thousand black people in a single city refused to ride the segregated buses for more than a year.

At the time, black Montgomery attorney Fred Gray was bright, aggressive, and a year out of law school. Gray, who moonlighted on weekends as a preacher, wanted to challenge the city's segregation laws even before Rosa Parks was arrested for refusing to obey them on a city bus. Yet Gray waited to file his case until the MIA leadership voted to grant him that authority. More significant than Gray's apparent self-restraint were the institutional restraints imposed on him by the MIA, whose executive board and strategy committee rendered Gray unable to dominate their broader extra-legal strategies. ...

Gray supported rather than led the boycott organized by the MIA, whose key resources grew out of grassroots mobilization and mass action. Moreover, the deliberately non-bureaucratic structure of the MIA, an "organization of organizations," extended to, and endured because of, the MIA's grassroots fundraising. The MIA's carpool and other capital-dependent activities were initially supported by collections at the mass meetings, which literally "refueled" the boycott. Although money soon flowed from outside, these funds were raised in large part by black churches, organizations (including NAACP branches), and individuals, as well as some northern white individuals and organizations. . . .

The MIA was a constituency of accountability, capable of holding lawyers like Gray to the discipline of shared power. . . . Although it was the intervention of the Supreme Court, ruling on the case Fred Gray brought in federal court, that ultimately declared the segregated buses unconstitutional, it was the social movement activism embedded in a biblical belief in justice that shortened the distance between our democracy's reality and its potential to be the "greatest form of government on earth." Story-making by community members became mantras of the movement. One memorable mantra was Mother Pollard reassuring MLK that: "My feets is tired, but my soul is rested." Told in their own words, these narratives of justice repositioned blacks in Montgomery from victims with a grievance to citizens with a cause. They captured the dignity of the community's effort, inspired protests in other cities, built other insurgent organizations such as SCLC [Southern Christian Leadership Conference], and ultimately influenced blacks North and South to believe in their own agency to transform our democracy from "thin paper to thick action." . . .

As a result of the supportive and influential role of Fred Gray, and the community-driven power of the MIA, the boycott's successes went beyond the litigation victory that decisively desegregated the buses. . . .

The bus boycott involved a theory of popular mobilization and a theory of representative democracy. . . . By interrogating their collective discourse in the same ways lawyers and scholars carefully analyze Supreme Court oral arguments and the resulting decisions, we can begin to understand the way social movement actors author legal meaning.

The mass mobilization created a shared purpose and was symbolized by the middle class black community committing its private automobiles to the creation of an alternative public transportation system. . . . This was vital to the cross-class integrity of the protest that led to its success and power. It could not have lasted as long as it did without this crucial contribution. . . . The community was able to leverage its resources that would individually be relatively meager but in combination provided the critical capacity to resist.

. . . [We see] at least two independently important results of the local, regional, and national coverage of the events in Montgomery. First, it validated a new model of protest and created a place where what black people knew to be the truth could be validated without the mediation of institutions that were controlled by others. . . . [T]he perspectives of black people [were] given a central place. The concrete meaning of inequality could be exposed in the disparate distribution of both public and private wealth. Also, the minor indignities and multitudinous microaggressions could be understood as part of the system of white racial supremacy. This may have had an effect on local federal judges that encouraged or enabled them to act more quickly to do justice despite the wrath of their peers: keep it in the courts and not on the streets. Second, it mobilized a local black community—tempered through the months of struggle—that was able to pressure the city into complying with the Supreme Court's order because noncompliance put too much at risk for the city.

Of longer term significance was the formation of new organizations, both the MIA and the SCLC. These organizations helped institutionalize the idea of mass mobilization and hastened the transformation of the church by centering it on the social gospel and locating its claims in politics and morality. The success helped launch a national movement and created a new cadre of young leadership. Equally important is that it gave agency and dignity to participants. It validated their experience in a way that others had to credit. The national publicity educated whites and others outside of the South, and in this way would help transform the national debate about race. . . .

Conclusion: Democracy at Its Best is a Social Movement

The point of the stories we have told, which are only exemplary, is that the courts alone are not the voice of change. At best, the courts ratify change. The social movement activists—through their political mobilization and their transformation of the culture—made the actions of the Supreme Court seem appropriate and long overdue.

In the case of both the Mississippi Freedom Democratic Party and the Montgomery Bus Boycott, black activists did not just want a chance to compete for a seat at a convention or on a bus. To allow two individuals to represent the whole, as Joseph Rauh and Martin Luther King, Jr. did in the MFDP conflict, takes the power away from the community they claim to represent. In Montgomery, the MIA did not want just more seats, or even the mere desegregation of the buses; they wanted to eliminate the private enforcement of Jim Crow laws by the bus drivers. Thus activists in both Mississippi and Montgomery claimed an alternative source of power, one that took the promise of democracy seriously. They restructured the meaning of opportunity at the same time that they restructured the meaning of representation. . . .

. . . [L]egal advocates and cause lawyers also often lose perspective when they move to study and learn from the places where lawyers are most in control during these public conflicts. The conflict may be translated into the legal documents they study, but they often forget that it is a translation for a specialized audience using a rarefied way of talking about and understanding the world. It is not that the legal elites are wrong; it is just that their representation is only a partial view of the cathedral. They zoom in on the brief Rauh wrote [to the Credentials Committee at the Democratic National Convention] citing the relevant statutes, organizational rules, and court decisions. They may even parse the legal documents and subsequent case law in search of the conflict's enduring meaning. For these inquisitors, what matters over time is the way elite actors ultimately give meaning to the actions of non-elite activists. We are arguing that the reverse is often closer to the truth. The elite actors often derive the social meaning of their actions from the efforts of non-elite activists like Fanny Lou Hamer and all of the others standing behind and beside her.

The boycotters in Montgomery and the activists of the MFDP moved from marginal characters to members of authoritative interpretative communities. What they were reinterpreting was the meaning of American constitutional justice. They ultimately restructured the politics of the possible. They gave their actions a plausible explanation, one that formed the basis for shared understanding. That understanding initially grew from an internal explanation that allowed a sense of community to exist. But it ultimately had to persuade external actors, as well. These two communities became authoritative because other members of the polity found themselves having to come to terms with their interpretations. In a heroic version of the actions of the Montgomery boycotters and the MFDP activists, they demonstrated that institutional change was necessary in order to validate the rhetoric of democracy and equality. These two movements illustrate . . . [that] rule shifting without culture shifting is not enough to produce real and sustained change.

While the black people in Montgomery and the MFDP activists wanted seats, the metaphor should not be lost. Their stories are "texts" in what we have come to call demosprudence. Defying the rules for seating on a bus or at a national political convention both implicated and challenged the private use of state power. The Mississippi and Alabama activists were not, however, merely confronting the authority of the state. They were also confronting the claims of what constituted justice. They removed the mantle of authority from what claimed to be authoritative but which was shown to be false. They challenged the "is" with a vision of the "ought" and pushed the larger society to contemplate "what might be" if justice would be made real. Most importantly, they helped shift the cultural norms, not just the rules. They enacted a "normative" or "motivating" vision of a just society that was both remedial and aspirational. It was through their actions that dramatic interventions in the status quo were enacted rather than merely contemplated. . . .

. . . By expressing what the law means to those subject to it, activists create new grounds on which to interpret the law and make it harder for elites to say it means something other than what those on the street thought it should mean if it were talking to their experience. Any substantial disjunction is felt as injustice. It is through this potential feedback effect that those who sing the music of law can have a role in composing its logic.

By defining winning in its narrowest possible terms, as Joe Rauh did with the MFDP, lawyers may prompt litigants to celebrate important tactical victories. At the same time, the strategic vision essential to sustainable long-term change can be lost. . . . Because lawyers occupy both an elite and expert position and often do not reflect on the impact of their expertise on their imagination, their role in social movements deserves more attention.

. . . Lawyers, in particular, too often assume that their maximum opportunity to influence the law is through formal argument in judicial settings. . . .

By contrast, we contend that democratic societies are organized to produce a variety of authoritative interpretive communities. . . .

Hamer and the other MFDP delegates were exemplary "wind changers." Their goal was to widen the scope of meaningful participation in decision-making. They questioned the limited definition of what is legitimate representation; they redefined meaningful participation; and they insisted on a wider scope for who should be included in decision-making. By contrast, the politicians and the national leaders, as members of the state apparatus, stood with their wet fingers in the wind without noticing that the weather was changing.

The roles played by Fred Gray and other lawyers in the Montgomery Bus Boycott, the story that law ultimately tells, the driving ideal of equality, the assumption about the source of power to make change, and the definition of success all reflect the distinctive interpretive communities to which the lawyers felt they were accountable. In the case of the bus boycott, law is practiced tactically. It retains its link to a mobilized community that is seeking change to produce justice. . . . Through their collective struggle and communal resourcefulness they gain a sense of agency and create a constituency of resistance that builds a new organization and inspires a series of national movements.

The texts of their stories were written with the ink of consummate courage by a mobilized community that actively represented itself. These social movement actors changed the background against which questions of legality and justice were understood. They marched. They sang. They declaimed in their unschooled voices. They changed the wind. And in the process, they transformed the "thin paper" of democracy to the "thick action" of government of, by, and for the people.

As Guinier and Torres show, knowledge from the bottom affects goals as well as tactics and strategies. Insights from the bottom produce different calculations of both risk and benefit that can substantially affect advocacy plans and outcomes. We thus see that critical knowledge from the bottom is actionable, both as jurisprudence and as demosprudence, and that it can determine both means and ends. As we explore further in Part II, critical knowledge of jurisprudence and of demosprudence is actionable knowledge largely because it helps advocates to "unlearn and relearn"—or to pierce through—the many myths of the legal system instilled in and internalized by individuals and groups across the social order from cradle to grave, and thus to chart and navigate toward more effective systemic solutions for persistent group injustice.

NOTES AND QUESTIONS

1. *Sites of Advocacy and Struggle.* After the Supreme Court's iconic ruling in *Brown v. Board of Education* (excerpted in Chapter 2), the battle in the courts over schools racially segregated by law shifted to school busing. Pursuant to court orders, students were transported over long distances to or from racially isolated neighborhoods. Busing may have aimed to ensure public schools were more integrated, but it did nothing to address the segregation of U.S. neighborhoods that continues today. The Montgomery Bus Boycott arose in the related but different context of public transportation. A 2017 national study found that transit riders (bus, subways, and the like) most often are traveling to and from work, and 40 percent of riders say they lack money or a vehicle to travel by other means. Most transit riders are people of color, and more women than men use public transportation.[6] Thus, public transportation is a context laden with social identity, such as race, gender, class, and disability. In 1956, the Supreme Court summarily affirmed a lower court's order under the U.S. Constitution requiring that the city of Montgomery and the state of Alabama desegregate public buses, *Gayle v. Browder*, 352 U.S. 903 (1956). The Court supplied the same formal legal equality in public transportation that it had dictated two years earlier in *Brown* for public schools. But did these formal rights, obtained through adjudication and hard-fought struggles to ensure equality in bus and classroom "seats," prove transformative—did they fundamentally change the lived realities of those at the bottom of societal castes? How can an understanding of demosprudence help explain these struggles and their outcomes?

---

[6] American Public Transportation Association, Who Rides Public Transportation (Jan. 2017), https://www.apta.com/wp-content/uploads/Resources/resources/reportsandpublications/Documents/APTA-Who-Rides-Public-Transportation-2017.pdf.

1.3 DEPENDING ON CIRCUMSTANCE AND CONTEXT, BOTTOMS (AND TOPS) CAN SHIFT— SO MUST ADVOCATES AND ADVOCACY

Advocates are tasked with learning from the bottom to make progress under a system designed both to promise and deny justice. But details of systemic injustice vary from context to context. Although the four key elements of the Critical Challenge are always present—identities, groups, interests, and power—they combine in various ways to produce similar results across diverse times, places, and circumstances. For this reason, advocates must understand that bottoms of legal and societal hierarchies—and tops—can vary according to context and can shift over time and due to circumstance. Systemic advocates concern themselves both with the particularities of their context *and* with the patterns that recur or persist across contexts.

In the following excerpt, critical race feminist Athena Mutua examines this complex reality, comparing groups and contexts. She asks, "What group should be at the center" of a project or agenda? Mutua notes that histories of identities, groups, interests, and power are necessary to a critical understanding of context. She introduces a prominent theme throughout this book: the importance of context. To appreciate how systemic injustice works, notice the patterns already emerging from "different" contexts; can you see correlations between tops or bottoms as social groups and specific social identities, like race, ethnicity, or sex?

SHIFTING BOTTOMS AND ROTATING CENTERS: REFLECTIONS ON LATCRIT III AND THE BLACK/WHITE PARADIGM
Athena D. Mutua
53 U. Miami L. Rev. 1177 (1999)

... "What group should be at the center of a given study or enterprise? Whose "faces are at the bottom of the well;" and, what model shall we use to analyze a given situation?"

At first glance, the questions seem simple and the answers self-evident: everybody should be the center of attention sometime—many of the groups are at the bottom together, or at one point or another; and the model you use depends on what it is you are trying to analyze. Actually, the questions are complex, and the answers unclear because limited resources of time, space, money and energy often pit group against group when priorities must be set. More significantly, the problems of building coalitions and developing political agendas bring us face-to-face with the reality that different racial and ethnic groups have distinct histories and interests, some of which collide. . . .

Historical Context: [Defining "Bottoms"]

The history of the United States is complex and anything but linear. However, a cursory look reveals that the United States was a de jure racial dictatorship from its founding until the Voting Rights Act was passed in 1965. The white American dictatorship went far beyond the mere failure to extend the [right to vote]. It exterminated Indians and appropriated their land; enslaved blacks and appropriated their labor; excluded and oppressed Chinese and other Asians; conquered and annexed the land of Mexicans; interred the Japanese, and, employed Jim Crow, immigration, citizenship and property laws, among other tools, to maintain this racial dictatorship. The theory was Anglicized white supremacy; the goal, a White nation. However, the nation moved from one ruled through brutal dictatorship to one ruled through hegemony after the 1960's. Today, it is hegemony informed by Anglicized white supremacy and privilege. It is also hegemony influenced by the struggles and survival of the [subordinated] other, as well as new constituent groups.

In this process of constructing a nation, American race, races, racism, and racialism were born. So too were white power's obsessions. These obsessions are many, varied and changing, but even today are ultimately informed by the same Anglicized, White, upper-class male perspectives that ruled the historical dictatorship. This perspective reflects the "core culture" of U.S. society, which is "white, Protestant, English-speaking, Anglo-Saxon," and, one might add, heterosexual. Moreover, this perspective views itself as being superior to others, having dominated the country since its inception. Consistent with its dominant position, this perspective has projected its own reflection onto the nation, all too often defining itself as the only legitimate America. The social goals envisioned by this perspective include ideas of liberty and equality. Yet, these ideas are organized around its core culture and are limited by its values as well as one of its primary goals—maintaining itself in Power. At the same time, this perspective defines, and is defined by, aspects of others' group identities, usually those aspects that most challenge white power's conception of itself and its social vision. In the assertion of these aspects of group identity, an assertion that often embodies meanings and visions contrary to those imposed by white power, people bearing these aspects of identity will be bitterly opposed. This is particularly so when the bearers are significant in number. The opposition will manifest itself in many kinds of institutional and societal oppression, despite opportunities for society to do otherwise. This oppression calls forth resistance, which further fuels the obsession, unless the resistance is crushed or is successful in altering power relations. It is these factors which constitute the "bottom."

Although there is a danger in imposing upon contextualized histories a universalized American construct about how white power maintains itself, thinking about our varied oppressions in this way provides some intellectual insight and clears the path for our coalition efforts.

The Mark of Blackness: [Color and Culture]

It is often said that blacks are at the "bottom" of the American racial hierarchy. Is this true? And if so, what does it mean? The statement is correct to the extent we are talking about a colorized racial hierarchy and noting the tremendous influence that this colorized racial system has had in the United States. As to its meaning, most obviously it suggests when the races are ranked from most degraded to most exalted, blacks are in the lowest rank and whites in the highest. Let us, however, parse this a bit more. I wish to posit equivalence between these two propositions: blacks, as a race, are at the "bottom;" and, one of white power's greatest racial obsessions has been with "blackness" and the black body. In fact, I would assert that the black body consistently has been the primary symbol of "race." From this perspective, it is the intensity of white obsession marked by conceptual opposition (or "otherness") and continuous oppression despite societal changes that determine the "bottom." Furthermore, in the context of colorized racial categories, blackness has had no close competition for at least the past four hundred years.

. . . [T]he long history of white oppression of blacks and blackness will demonstrate why . . . [b]lack people represent the metaphorical bottom of a colorized racial hierarchy . . . people marked by blackness have . . . posed the most direct challenge to white Power's conceptualization of itself and its social vision as white and consequently privileged; . . . and, black people have resisted this oppression, thereby reinforcing White Power's obsession with blackness.

White Power's obsession with blackness begins with slavery. White power created blackness, parasitically defining itself in opposition to it and seeking to oppress and suppress it in order to maintain the power it derived from blackness, in both tangible and psychological terms. White power, wealth, and privilege required both blackness as subjugation and black people as slaves; and therefore, black humanity could not be tolerated.

Conceptually, whiteness as the polar opposite of blackness had meaning in European history long before slavery. Whiteness was a symbol of cleanliness, purity, virtue, godliness, etc., and was in stark contrast to blackness. Blackness, on the other hand, signified the devil, evil, dirtiness. These notions undoubtedly influenced Europeans during their initial contact with Africans, their most salient feature in European eyes being blackness. . . . In slavery the conceptual opposition between blackness and whiteness would be experienced. . . .

In . . . white minds, slavery, a system of labor coercion, combined with color-delineated races, reinforce[ed] both. This fusion between slavery and color-delineated "races" was partly a result of how slavery came to function in America[,] a function White Power consolidated and encoded into law. Slavery operated primarily along differences in skin color, embracing descent. It thereby created the color line where "white" came to mean free and "black" came to mean slave. Cheryl Harris, explains:

> "Black" racial identity marked who was subject to enslavement, whereas "white" racial identity marked who was "free" or, at a minimum, not a slave.... Because the "presumption of freedom [arose] from color [white]" and the "black color of the race [raised] the presumption of slavery,['] whiteness became a shield from slavery, a highly volatile and unstable form of property.... Because Whites could not be enslaved or held as slaves, the racial line between white and black was extremely critical.

The color line, therefore, functioned not only to define people marked by black skin as presumptive slaves, but it also defined white people as privileged. This "privileging" of white people started the process of whites consolidating themselves as a racial group. Poor whites aligned themselves with upper class whites in opposition to, and parasitic upon, people marked by black skin. For example, ... in Virginia, Bacon's Rebellion, a lower class white rebellion, was resolved in part by expanding the African slave trade.... This resolution united lower and upper class whites against blacks in a way that slavery alone might not have accomplished. Thus, racial [black] slavery provided the glue for white racial solidarity vertically aligning white interests across class lines. As a result of this merger of slavery with race, or rather slavery with the color line that delineated the races, White Power was enriched, white people privileged, and white racial identity coalesced.

In this context, whiteness became more than just a concept, it became a valuable commodity. Cheryl Harris has argued persuasively that whiteness became a property interest, shielding people defined as white from slavery and privileging them during slavery and thereafter. Blackness, on the other hand, came to mean everything that whiteness was not. Whiteness was free, powerful, superior, privileged, civilized, industrious, intelligent, and beautiful, while blackness was slave, subjugation, inferior, savage, lazy, dumb, and ugly. In other words, while slavery functioned to enrich White Power, blackness functioned to further define and privilege it.

Ultimately, White Power came to view those who possessed whiteness as human while those marked by blackness were viewed as subhuman, three-fifths human, chattel. The color line separated people of African descent from their humanity. And, White Power, defining itself in opposition to blackness, denied humanity and human treatment, particularly the freedom desired by the human spirit, to the people marked by blackness. Consequently, what emerged from slavery was not the

Asante, Yoruba, Bakongo, and other [African] groups that initially entered slavery, but rather, a race of people. These people, marked by blackness as subjugated and inferior, were organized in solidarity around the black body. Their culture was a mixture of various African cultures and the emerging "American" culture, which was heavily influenced by the experience of slavery and resistance. They were identified as, and identified themselves as, Coloreds, Negroes, Blacks, and African-Americans in a century-long contest over the meaning of blackness. . . .

. . . As the number of African slaves grew, so did the apparatus to control Blacks. The laws however, made clear that the threat of insurrection was one of White Power's overriding concerns. Insurrection, humanity asserting itself in a black face and possibly resulting in black freedom, increased White Power's obsession with blackness because insurrection not only threatened the wealth of some Whites, but it also undermined the concept of white as free, privileged and in control. In order to prevent rebellion and to reassert this conception, White Power had to codify law and exercise violence that severely regulated all black life. Consequently, no detail of black life was too petty to note and White Power obsessively regulated every aspect of life for those marked as black. The more numerous the slaves, the harsher the codes, even in areas with sizable free black populations. What emerged therefore, was a particular kind of slave law, namely race control laws. . . . [L]abor extraction, the goal of slavery, was privatized, meaning the owner himself had to coerce labor from slaves, while race control, managing the movements and activities of blacks in society generally, became a matter of public concern and legislation. Ostensibly, the public control of black lives facilitated the extraction of labor by keeping slaves in their place in white homes and plantations. But ultimately all black life, both slaves lives, and the lives of free Blacks had to be regulated and denigrated. What lingered after slavery's demise was the concept and practice of race control meant to devalue black humanity and to maintain blackness as subjugation and inferiority.

Black freedom posed innumerable challenges to White Power's conception of itself and its social order on the eve of Reconstruction. . . . The Civil War, Emancipation, Reconstruction, and the passage of the Thirteenth and Fourteenth Amendments, all of which embroiled the nation into considerations of what slavery and blackness meant, marked instances where White Power could have reconstructed whiteness and blackness as something other than in opposition. But it did not. These efforts only appear to have hardened the color-line and increased the obsession. . . . White Power invented new and different institutional and systematic oppressions to maintain blackness as subjugated and black people as oppressed. These new institutional mechanisms were evidenced by legal segregation, new forms of labor exploitation, excessive legal violence and discrimination. At the same time, people marked by blackness and organized around blackness resisted oppression. However, such resistance, in the form of establishing functioning and prosperous black towns, was often met with fire and destruction; independence was met with lynching; and defiance was met with violence. Resistance seemed to fuel the obsession and rebound with additional violence despite the altered conditions.

Similarly, the civil rights movement asserted black power; pronounced black as beautiful, and demanded just and human treatment for black people. It therefore presented White Power with another lost opportunity to re-create itself as something other than in opposition to blackness and to provide blackness with alternative meanings in white minds. Although the Civil Rights movement brought about some progress, many have noted the progress was limited. It appears the claims of the movement proved too contradictory to both the practice and concept of black as subjugated and inferior.

The endurance of the obsession and oppression of blackness and blacks, despite the tremendous opportunities for change, has led some to believe the position of blacks on the colorized racial bottom is permanent.... [T]he seeming permanence of these relations and meanings, is a crucial insight of the "bottom" metaphor....

Shifting Bottoms: A Language Hierarchy and Multiple Racial Systems

Nonetheless, Blacks likely are not on the "bottom" with regard to language oppression within the United States, as the "Black over White" paradigm might suggest. Instead, it appears Latinos/as are on the "bottom" because they embody, so to speak, a shared language uniting them that is the object of White Power's obsession. While the suppression of language might be characterized as a form of either ethnic or racial oppression, both characterizations implicate White Power's obsessions, and neither the "White Over Black" paradigm nor the notion of Blacks as the colorized racial "bottom" contributes much illumination. Here, White Power's obsession is either with brown bodies or the Spanish language; black bodies have little to do with it as a distraction or fundamental point. In this country, Spanish translates to a central site or category of oppression, thereby relegating its speakers to the metaphorical "bottom" of this society in those specific terms.

Many writers have noted that language is an aspect of ethnic identity. Language is central to culture and fundamental to ethnicity. We not only communicate through language, but language structures how we think.

The Spanish language, having been spoken by Latinos three centuries before Anglo expansion and up to the present day, is central to the Latino identity. It is a basis for cohesion in the community, and historically, has been a basis upon which they have been discriminated. . . .

. . . Spanish spoken in the United States challenges White Power's conception of itself and its social goals in two significant ways. First, the increasing numbers of Latinos/as portend significant political power for a group that speaks a language other than English. This threatens White Power's mythical vision of a solitary nation united around one language, occupied by one people descended from the same ancestor. Second, Spanish is associated with a racialized group and culture.

. . . [T]he "English Only" movement is linked to efforts to dismantle bilingual education, toughen immigration laws, and to deny social welfare benefits to immigrants. In trying to eliminate Spanish as a basis of cohesion for the Latino/a community, while simultaneously limiting their participation in American society, White Power is reinforced and its cultural hegemony left firmly intact.

[In sum,] the "bottom" metaphor leads us to the idea that the groups represented at the "bottom" shift, depending on the issue and circumstance. The shifting "bottom" directs us to shift our focus, shift our thinking, and perhaps shift our analytical tools when we are trying to understand the experiences of different groups. It instructs us to look specifically at how different groups and issues are constructed and experienced both in similar and dissimilar ways. This essay suggests that although Blacks are at the bottom of a colorized racial hierarchy, Latino/as are at the bottom of a racialized language hierarchy, at a minimum, and perhaps at the bottom of a racial system marked by the Spanish language, among other things. The "bottom" has indeed shifted.

. . . Only through [a] commitment to cross-racial knowledge production can we hope collectively to overcome the legacies of White Supremacy that still deny equal justice to *all*.

Group hierarchies can and do shift from one context to another, although all may still be interconnected by design. One response to this complexity that Mutua suggests is to "map out our similarities and differences while building the theory and coalitions necessary to articulate a different, fairer future." She thus emphasizes another recurrent theme and core practice of systemic advocacy: the need to collaborate contextually across multiple kinds of difference based on shared values, principles, and goals.

NOTES AND QUESTIONS

1. *Complexity of Hierarchical Tops and Bottoms.* Although the Latinx group may be at the "bottom" when language oppression is centered, Blacks do not necessarily become the "top." Moreover, some contexts and issues reveal

multiple bottoms, or tops. For example, in thinking about the experience of police violence, which group or groups constitute the bottom? Equally important, what opportunities (and problems) for coalition-building do Mutua's insights reveal?

1.4 CRITICAL "SCHOOLS" AND ADVOCACY "APPROACHES" PROVIDE WELLS OF KNOWLEDGE FOR "DIFFERENT" GROUPS AND THEIR ADVOCATES

Law is a continually contested system—in complicated ways, law remains part of the systemic justice problem and of potential solutions to it. Nonetheless, "formalism" has dominated law—and still dominates legal culture—even while challenged by the realist and critical Schools of legal knowledge and field-based advocacy Approaches. In the traditional formalist school of legal knowledge, as we will see more fully in Part IV, legal decisions are made by applying legal principles to legally cognizable and relevant facts to reach conclusions insulated from actual outcomes in individual lives and communities. Below, we survey how sustained resistance to formalism within the legal profession gave rise to the Schools (of realist and critical theory) and advocacy Approaches (to the use of law for justice) as distinct yet overlapping formations within legal culture, whose decades of insight inform this book.

"Legal realists" in the late 19th and early 20th century began to criticize the legal fictions that justified persistently unequal outcomes and introduced a less "mechanical" approach to legal analysis and problem solving. To emphasize their more sociological approach, realists called for advocates and courts to align doctrine with reality. Legal realists asserted that formalist approaches to law "created an illusion of certainty that masked the unspoken social and political assumptions guiding much judicial decision making. The exposure of this illusion of certainty led to Realist pronouncements of the indeterminate nature of the law."[7]

Realists insisted that both the actual operations of legal processes and their concrete outcomes should be studied to improve legal problem solving in complex societies.[8] Realists like Oliver Wendell Holmes, Karl Llewellyn, Jerome Frank, Felix Cohen, and others argued that law could not be understood as a disembodied, acontextual process of deducing legal outcomes from principles. Holmes, for instance, cautioned in 1897 that "law" is what lawyers and judges actually do and that no one should believe

---

[7] Emily M.S. Houh, Critical Interventions: Toward an Expansive Equality Approach to the Doctrine of Good Faith in Contract Law, 88 Cornell L. Rev. 1025, 1055–56 (2003).

[8] See Benjamin Cardozo, The Nature of the Judicial Process (1921); Jerome Frank, What Courts Do In Fact, 26 Ill. L. Rev. 645 (1932); Karl Llewellyn, The Common Law Tradition: Deciding Appeals (1960).

that law is "a system of reason that is a deduction from principles of ethics or admitted axioms or what not, which may or may not coincide with the decisions."[9] From this sociological perspective, the problem with the entrenched legalisms of the mechanical or formalistic approach to law was that social facts, processes, and outcomes were ignored: "Justice in concrete cases ceases to be their aim. Instead, [judges] aim at thorough development of the logical content of established principles through rigid deduction."[10] Realists thus advocated for law to incorporate social fact-finding. Advocates put the insights of Holmes, Roscoe Pound, and other realists to practical use by expanding the techniques of legal research and writing to incorporate the gathering and use of sociological data. The now-famous "Brandeis brief"—in which the lawyer peppers the legal brief with social facts—illustrates this legal turn toward society. Legal culture, as a whole, became consciously more guided by documented social facts.

The Brandeis brief became a mechanism for introducing sociological information and analysis into legal proceedings. The first such brief was filed in *Muller v. Oregon* in 1908, a case considering whether the state had authority to restrict working hours for women to protect their health.[11] Statements from experts and workers and sociological data were presented to elaborate on the effects of overwork on women. More recently, "thick pleadings" and "voices briefs" have been used as mechanisms for incorporating socially-grounded and diverse facts, stories, and analysis into briefs.[12] These developments increasingly questioned the narrow version of legal "relevance" that formalism had established for analysis and action.

Legal realists and others continued to deepen their critiques of formalism over the decades. According to critics, the dominant framework fails in part because formalism ignores interests, power, and experience. Benjamin Cardozo criticized formalism in 1921:

> My analysis of the judicial process comes then to this, and little more: logic, and history, and custom, and utility, and the accepted standards of right conduct, are the forces which singly or in combination shape the progress of the law. Which of these forces dominate depends largely upon the comparative importance or value of the social interests that will be thereby promoted or

---

[9] Oliver Wendell Holmes, Jr., The Path of the Law, 10 Harv. L. Rev. 457 (1897).

[10] Roscoe Pound, The Scope and Purpose of Sociological Jurisprudence, 23 Harv. L. Rev. 591, 596 (1911).

[11] *Muller v. Oregon*, 208 U.S. 412 (1908).

[12] See Herbert A. Eastman, Speaking Truth to Power: The Language of Civil Rights Litigators, 104 Yale L.J. 763, 789 (1995); Linda H. Edwards, Telling Stories in the Supreme Court: Voices Briefs and the Role of Democracy in Constitutional Deliberation, 29 Yale J. of L. and Feminism 29 (2017) (describing the "daring" amicus brief including stories about abortions from more than 100 women lawyers, law professors, and former judges submitted in *Whole Women's Health v. Hellerstedt*).

impaired.... The most fundamental social interest is that law shall be uniform and impartial.... Uniformity ceases to be a good when it becomes uniformity of oppression.[13]

The realist cure was the production of more social facts—the critical incorporation of more cross-disciplinary knowledge—that would always be external to law in origin but employed internally in legal venues to guide legal actions. The turn to realism spread across legal culture, from education to adjudication to practice. Social statistics, empirical methods, and cross-disciplinary knowledge increasingly informed legal choices and constructions. In this way, notions of legal relevance slowly and reluctantly began to expand.

Realist sensibilities set the stage for introducing cross-disciplinary and transnational knowledge in U.S. legal culture, as well as for "critical" challenges to formalism. Legal realism gradually opened the door to critically-minded "schools" or efforts focused on identity. These schools all seek, in varied ways, to make law more socially just as applied. These schools of legal criticality thus follow from realist insights, intuitions, and initiatives. Although each may use a "different" social identity, like race or sex, as a point of entry, they all investigate wider patterns of systemic injustice based on the interplay—or intersection—of varied identities in concrete settings.

Starting in the 1970s, for instance, the Law and Society Association (LSA) and Clinical Legal Scholarship emerged as two key developments in this historical process of knowledge production. As its name suggests, LSA scholarship devotes itself to understanding and reforming law as applied, as empirically experienced, and as informed by disciplines beyond law. Likewise, Clinical Legal Scholarship focuses on, and is rooted in, applications of law in socially sensitive settings. Often, but not primarily, these bodies of scholarship focus on social group identities, especially in class-conscious frameworks designed to attack persistent patterns of poverty.

In the 1980s, two other key movements emerged as pioneers of the critical Schools from which today's systemic advocates draw. Critical Legal Studies (CLS) questioned the claimed legitimacy of law as a principled system, focusing chiefly on class hierarchies and obfuscating legalisms. CLS highlighted law's many inexplicable inconsistencies and showed how the manipulation of legal indeterminacy obscures discretionary uses of power to protect group privilege and justify patterns of subordination. Focusing on gender as its point of critical inquiry, Feminist Legal Theory (FLT) mounted the same challenges to systemic legalisms that helped to normalize patriarchal hierarchies. During this decade, these two

---

[13] Cardozo, Nature of the Judicial Process, at 112.

movements effectively linked "critical" studies with "identity" analysis to question the legitimacy and utility of law as a guarantor of equal justice.

Taking the next step, Critical Race Theory (CRT) and Critical Race Feminism (CRF) in the late 1980s and early 1990s then centered social identity, in the form of race and gender and their interplay, alongside CLS and FLT. Similarly, other genres of identity-sensitive scholarship soon developed, helping to further chart and connect "different" identities and systems to the same unjust patterns. By the mid-1990s, the critical Schools of legal knowledge were coalescing into overlapping networks of critical studies (known collectively as Critical Outsider Jurisprudence). Critical Outsider Jurisprudence focused on varied, overlapping "outsider" social identities, based on ethnicity, nationality, indigeneity, sexuality, disability, class, and religion. These critical and outsider—or OutCrit—networks launched and nurtured QueerCrit, LatCrit (Latina and Latino Critical Legal Theory), ClassCrit, DisCrit (Dis/ability Critical Race Studies), and similar schools to better connect law with justice and reality across "different" identity groups in increasingly multicultural, globalized contexts.

During these same decades, scholarly movements focused on Law and Social Change and on Therapeutic Jurisprudence aimed to make law and its remedies more socially holistic and principled in relation to its equal justice promise. Other initiatives, like the various "Law-and" schools of inquiry, sought to introduce insights of other disciplines including, notably, critical approaches to the social sciences and humanities. Other fields like subaltern studies, political economy, and critical ethnic studies are expanding the critical edge of actionable knowledge.

Likeminded bodies of scholarship furthermore have connected these efforts across the borders of cultures and nation-states. New Approaches to International Law and Third World Approaches to International Law (NAIL/TWAIL) developed in similar ways across various legal systems shaping transnational legal (and social) realities. From the 1970s to this day, the creation of this deep well of post-realist knowledge—and the ongoing development of critical lessons drawn from advocacy Approaches below—have sharpened the tools of systemic advocacy (despite the top-down perspectives and interests advanced during this same period by schools of legal knowledge like "law and economics" or "public choice" theory).

We know the bottom-up Schools and Approaches provide potent resources for effective advocacy and organized struggle because of the collective fear, anxiety, and retaliation that they provoke from the most traditional elite quarters. In the 1990s, high-profile institutions organized purges of "critical" legal scholars associated with these Schools and Approaches. Continuing direct attacks on Critical Race Theory—one of the bottom-up Schools—attests to the fundamental power of critical knowledge as actionable knowledge. The most recent attack, coming in August 2020 at the direction of then-President Trump, was the Director of the Office Management and Budget banning any federal government training related to Critical Race Theory, labeling it "anti-American propaganda." Swift responses defending the contributions of CRT included one from the five law deans of the University of California:

> The OMB memorandum equates Critical Race Theory to two inaccurate and wildly oversimplified tenets: (1) that the United States is "an inherently racist or evil country" and (2) that white people are "inherently racist or evil." This characterization reduces a sophisticated, dynamic field, interdisciplinary and global in scope, to two simplistic absurdities. In fact, a central principle of Critical Race Theory is that there is nothing "inherent" about race. Rather, CRT invites us to confront with unflinching honesty how race has operated in our history and our present, and to recognize the deep and ongoing operation of "structural racism," through which racial inequality is reproduced within our economic, political, and educational systems even without individual racist intent.[14]

The collective, cumulative wells of critical knowledge provide actionable tools and insights in varied contexts, but they also record and remember potent bottom-up truths—both historical and current. These critical truths are put at a premium whenever a society is subjected systematically to escalating top-down campaigns of deception or disinformation, as appeared to be occurring in the United States by the early 1990s, and as confirmed particularly by the intensified campaigns of increasingly bald deception surrounding (and in between) recent presidential elections. Only two decades into a new millennium, systemic and social realities increasingly were morphing as George Orwell had imagined in his famed novel, *1984*. During the past quarter of a century, the Big Lie in the United States has mushroomed into a big systemic problem—for law and society at large, and for systemic justice and advocacy in particular.

In this state of affairs, the constant manufacture and delivery of misinformation, including outright falsehoods, become official, daily policy. In this systemic scheme, the "Big Lie" perhaps is the single most powerful weapon in elites' knowledge-control arsenal: as pioneered in the 1930s, this "Big Lie" strategy describes a top-down approach to controlling the public premised on the theory that the biggest lies are the most believable simply because "reasonable" people will tend to disbelieve that a lie so big could be told so openly, so repeatedly, so authoritatively, so audaciously—even if

---

[14] www.taxprof.typepad.com/taxprof_blog/2020/09/deans-of-all-five-university-of-california-law-schools-defend-critical-race-theory-against-trumps-at.html.

easily disproved. And so public opinion (and compliance) are shaped and reshaped, from top to bottom. When Big Lies proliferate, systemic advocates must understand how they work, and how to work against them. The Schools and Approaches provide key starting points for current analysis *and* follow-up action.

As we will see repeatedly throughout this volume, critical knowledge is not "merely" a bunch of academic theories that complicate the urge to act quickly. On the contrary, it helps advocates to unlearn and relearn advocacy before wading into systemic problem-solving, just like knowledge of swimming helps swimmers to swim better before jumping into the water and splashing about. Systemic advocacy draws from previous experience, knowledge, and action to develop "theory" for future analyses and actions in never-ending cycles that fuse theory with practice.

Illustrating how critical scholars invoke, apply, and contribute to the Schools—and how the Schools themselves, as evolving bodies of knowledge, overlap and reinforce each other—TWAIL scholar Antony Anghie examines below the origins of international law from the bottom. In particular, Anghie unpacks the top-down legal conception of sovereignty—and international law as a system—as a legal invention used to justify the domination of those placed at the top and the subjugation of those pushed to the bottom. Sovereignty specifically, and international law generally, became (and remain) legal levers for collectivized privilege and collectivized subordination based on the key elements of identities, groups, interests, and power.

LATCRIT AND TWAIL

Antony Anghie
42 Cal. W. Int'l L.J. 311 (2012)

... Sovereignty is the foundation of the discipline of international law. Indeed, international law is commonly understood as the law that governs relations between sovereign states. My interest lies in understanding what historical narratives support conventional approaches to international law and in trying to recover other histories in order to suggest a new analytical framework—a set of ideas that might make us better appreciate and illuminate the ways in which these ostensibly neutral doctrines have affected (and continue to affect) the lives of the people who are often the victims of these processes.

... [T]he conventional history of international law is based on three fundamental premises. The first premise is that international law is created through the history and experience of the West or, even more particularly, Europe. This idea is powerfully reinforced by the notion that sovereignty itself, the very foundation of the discipline, was created in Europe....

The second closely-related premise is that the non-European world is peripheral to the making of international law. That is, doctrines such as sovereignty were created in the European world and then extended out to encompass the non-European world.... This is what basically occurred in the latter half of the nineteenth century....

The third related premise is the notion that the major issue confronting the discipline of international law is how law can be created among equal and sovereign states. Put differently, is international law really "law" when the international system lacks an overarching sovereign that can legislate and enforce the law? Specifically, how can international law be created in a system of horizontal authority in which all sovereign states are equal, at least juridically?...

By contrast, I suggest that each of these premises or structuring principles is either wrong or seriously inadequate in terms of its characterization—both in the role of non-European peoples in the making of international law, and in terms of appreciating the effects of international law on non-European peoples.

... [I]nternational law was not created in Europe and then transferred to the non-European world. Rather, international law was created out of the imperial encounter. That is, sovereignty was structured in such a way as to empower one side, the West, and disempower the other side, the non-West. The conventional argument suggests that the non-European world was somehow lacking sovereignty and this sovereignty had to be gradually bestowed upon them by Europe. But how was it decided that non-European peoples were lacking in sovereignty in the first place?... [T]he sovereignty doctrine, as it emerged from the imperial encounter, plays the crucial role of stripping non-European peoples of their sovereignty. Once this is done, these people, dispossessed of the legal personality that would enable them to participate in the international system and claim rights within it, can be the object of conquest and violence by imperial European states. While this conventional approach to sovereignty presents it as a benevolent process that extends out to empower the marginalized and disempowered, I would argue that the sovereignty doctrine has mechanisms of exclusion built within it that are continuously developed, refined, and adapted by encounters with the new "others." These "others" are the new challengers to the ever-expanding reach of international law and the powers it represents. This process of empowerment/disempowerment is an enduring one.

[Dominant legal] doctrines such as the sovereignty doctrine, the foundation of international law, are based on particular identities, which is not a great revelation for international lawyers, who insist—and in some cases celebrate—the fact that international law was very explicitly based on European values. International law was based on the *jus publicum*

Europaeum, the public law of Europe. However, this European identity did not emerge in splendid isolation. Imperialism, far from being peripheral to the discipline, is central to its very existence and character. It could not be otherwise. Historically, it was only through the process of imperialism that non-European states were incorporated into a system of law that was essentially European. Equally important, in the violence of this encounter, European international law devised doctrines that would diminish and delegitimize non-European peoples. Further, it was vital for these European states to formulate the doctrines and principles that would enable them to take control of the resources of those people and would justify colonial governance over them. It is from these colonial origins that international economic law and arguably, international human rights law emerged. . . .

But how do we write a history that is adequate for the purposes of telling the story of the relationship between European and non-European peoples? What are the themes and principles that emerge if we use that history as exemplary and formative to the source of the doctrines and principles of international law? As I have argued above, such a history, if approached critically might indicate that sovereignty should be seen not as a doctrine of empowerment, but of exclusion. . . .

Anghie traces the origins of international law to identity-based hierarchies meant to further elite interests, confirming that systemic injustice is embedded in all forms of law, whether deemed domestic or international. As a set, Anghie and the preceding excerpts demonstrate how the critical Schools of legal knowledge comprise overlapping networks or scholars and activists. Recognizing and working with the promises and limits of law, these overlapping Schools highlight the missing elements in traditional legal analysis central to this book—identities, groups, interests, and power—to go beyond the blindfolds of legal formalism and to push for equal justice. Both the Schools (listed only partially in Chart A) and the Approaches (outlined only partially in Chart B) sometimes originate with activists and scholars situated within or employed by prestigious universities and institutions, but their principal purpose is to produce critical knowledge from those privileged perches to support bottom-up group struggles. As we will see further below, advocates (if lawyers) generally share similar credentials, training, and privileges, and similarly will be called upon to deploy their professional privileges as system "insiders" on behalf of bottom-up, outsider groups. Even though these Schools and Approaches may have different points of emphasis, their common purpose is to make law more principled and accountable as equal justice for all.

Chart A: Critical "Schools" of Legal Knowledge

Asian American Scholarship: Centers the Asian and Pacific Islander experience with law. Shows how Asian Americans are considered "perpetual foreigners" even if U.S. born. Connects nationality and ethnicity to race.

ClassCrits Theory: Critiques neoliberalism and classical economics to uncover their fallacies. Targets root sources of material inequality. Relates class to other social identities, like sex and race.

Clinical Legal Scholarship: Promotes experiential legal training. Spearheads legal clinics based in law schools and related teaching techniques. Aims to provide legal services to poor or vulnerable populations.

Critical Legal Studies: Focuses on class and hierarchy by law. Exposes legal indeterminacy and discretion in decision making. Situates law as raw power.

Critical Race Theory/Critical Race Feminism: Use race as a principal lens of study. Aims to dismantle white supremacy and privilege. Also developed intersectionality.

Disability Legal Studies (and DisCrit (Dis/ability Critical Race Studies)): Places disability alongside other identity-focused Schools. Deconstructs legal notions of ability and disability. Concerned with accessibility of social and legal aspects of life.

Environmental Justice: Maps relationship between social identities and environmental risks. Strives to stop environmental degradation. Transnational.

Feminism: Examines gender relations socially and legally. Questions dominant notions of sameness and difference, especially between men and women. Confronts patriarchy in law and society.

Indigenous/Indian Scholarship: Studies indigeneity in the U.S. and globally as distinct from race, ethnicity, or nationality. Examines colonialism and its legacies for native peoples. Key concerns include land, resources, identity, culture, and self-determination.

LatCrit Theory: Focuses on Latinx populations. Links the local to the global. Prioritizes praxis and community-building.

Law and Society: Analyzes "law in action"—as applied—rather than as written. Emphasizes empirical and transnational approaches to law. Employs interdisciplinary studies to understand law.

> **NAIL/TWAIL: "New Approaches"/"Third World Approaches" to International Law**: Focuses on the international legal system and present-day effects of colonialism. Associated with subaltern studies.
>
> **Queer Theory/Trans Studies**: Employs sex, sexual orientation, and gender identity to combat the legal subordination of sexual minorities, both cis and trans. Challenges homophobia, transphobia, and heterosexism socially and legally. Seeks formal equality as well as social liberation.
>
> **Realism**: Responds to the "mechanical" jurisprudence of legal formalism. Shifts attention from abstract logic to social facts. Sometimes called "sociological" jurisprudence.
>
> **Therapeutic Jurisprudence**: Centers individual and social wellbeing as a key purpose of the legal system. Chronic legal distress contradicts equal justice. Legal remedies should promote social healing and wellness.

It is no coincidence that these Schools reflect the collective concerns of groups based on social identities ranging from class, race, and ethnicity to sex, sexuality, and disability. These are among the identity-based groups pushed to the bottom of the social and economic order by law as a system. This Chart therefore provides an overview of the social identities used by dominant groups during or since colonial times, as well as the responses from legal scholars attempting to produce knowledge relevant to bottom-up solutions to injustice.

Similarly, an array of advocacy Approaches also emerged in recent decades to center the critical insights of group experience with struggles against systemic injustice. These bottom-up Approaches developed "in the field" both independently and in dynamic interaction with the realist and critical Schools (and vice versa); these two historical developments—the Schools and Approaches—were mutually reinforcing in ways both intentional and inadvertent. Not surprisingly, then, these Schools and Approaches share common ideas, projects, actors, and aspirations. Like the Schools, these advocacy Approaches provide key lessons, insights, concepts, terms, and techniques for systemic advocates.

Today, then, the Schools and Approaches *jointly* are the wells from which systemic activists and advocates draw critical knowledge based on experience from the bottom both with injustice and with struggles against it. That cumulative experience includes struggling together with community groups to address persistent social problems systemically, struggling within the profession to sustain sites and resources for systemic advocacy, and struggling with oneself to change personal and professional practices that impede progress. Built on the shoulders and lessons of advocates who fought before, the Schools and Approaches are, themselves, products of historical struggle and continuing perseverance and continue to thrive despite systemic efforts from above to shut them down. Both the Schools and Approaches are venues and instruments of ongoing struggles against the Critical Challenge.

In the excerpt below, longtime advocate Gary Bellow describes one Approach, which he denominates "political lawyering" to underscore that law is always "political" because "the practice of law always involves exercising power." Bellow founded Harvard Law School's clinical program after working with such diverse clients as the United Farm Workers and the Black Panther Party. In this "self-conscious" law practice, as Bellow explains, "social vision is part of the operating ethos." Note the importance of critical and self-critical analysis in "vision-making" as a foundational aspect of this Approach.

STEADY WORK: A PRACTITIONER'S REFLECTIONS ON POLITICAL LAWYERING
Gary Bellow
31 Harv. C.R.-C.L. L. Rev. 297 (1996)

... In some of the efforts, we sought rule changes or injunctive relief against a particular practice on behalf of an identified class. In other situations, we pursued aggregate results by filing large numbers of individual cases. Some strategies were carried out in the courts. At other times we ignored litigation entirely in favor of bureaucratic maneuvering and community and union organizing. Even when pursuing litigation, we often placed far greater emphasis on mobilizing and educating clients, or strengthening the entities and organizations that represented them, than on judicial outcomes. And always, we employed the lawsuit, whether pushed to conclusion or not, as a vehicle for gathering information, positioning adversaries, asserting bargaining leverage, and adding to the continuing process of definition and designation that occurs in any conflict. Like politics itself, it is doubtful that political lawyering can be defined easily by the means it employs. Rather, what the examples seem to have in common is a particular, "politicized" orientation to the goals, commitments, and relationships reflected in the following strands of a practitioner's approach to legal work.

In each of these efforts, the legal work was done in service to both individuals and larger, more collectively oriented goals. We were not detached professionals offering advice and representation regardless of consequences; we saw ourselves responsible for, and committed to, shaping those consequences. Indeed, we made each move and maneuver with an eye to its impact on adversaries, decision makers, various parties concerned with the particular dispute, and our own clients. Moreover, the visions we embraced, particularly those that sought radical extensions of democracy, equality, and racial justice, were focused on deep-seated, structural, and cultural change.... Experienced in this way, it is virtually impossible to have been involved in any of the examples I have set out and not have thought of our law work as politics.

Inevitably, there were many more contradictions, hierarchies, and hypocrisies in our hopes than any of us recognized. And, more often than I wish were the case, our vision, or more particularly, the policies, practices, and programs that we believed our vision entailed, was flawed or shortsighted. Even when such policies, principles, and programs made sense, we compromised and adapted them to new circumstances less often than we might have—but such are always the pitfalls of passionate politics.

What has always puzzled me in my efforts to teach and recruit other lawyers to this perspective is the often made claim, and related unease in less articulated reactions, that there was some deep impropriety connected with our view of how and to what ends our legal skills should be employed. Law should not be practiced, used, or instrumentalized in how and to what ends our legal skills should be employed. Law should not be practiced, used, or instrumentalized in this way, it was said.

Yet, the practice of law always involves exercising power. Exercising power always involves systemic consequences, even if the systemic impact is a product of what appear to be unrelated cases pursued individually overtime. Lawyers influence and shape the practices and institutions in which they work, if only to reinforce and legitimate them. Clients, similarly, bring to their legal advisers and representatives claims and concerns that arise from and are examples of underlying institutional arrangements and culturally created controls. It would be a poor corporate lawyer who did his or her work without regard to the long-term systemic and aggregate effects on clients and others of any particular course of action or strategy. In many ways, we did no more than that, and we argued with those of our contemporaries who shared our politics and our commitments that they should do no less.

Social vision is part of the operating ethos of self-conscious law practice. The fact that most law practice is not done self-consciously is simply a function of the degree to which most law practice serves the status quo. Self-conscious practice appears to be less important, and is always less destabilizing, when it serves what is, rather than what ought to be. The kind of political lawyering embedded in the foregoing examples is distinguishable from general law work by the degree to which it was fueled by a more dissatisfied and change-oriented self-consciousness than the law practice of most of our contemporaries.... It surely requires a new generation to define an adequate social vision and self-consciousness for today's complicated times. It seems enough here to say that "vision-making" work is fundamental to the activist strategies political lawyering inevitably embodies.

The advocacy Approaches, in Bellow's words, are "self consciously" rooted in field-based experiences and add to the body of practical and theoretical knowledge in law. These overlapping Approaches—variously called "public interest" lawyering, "community" lawyering, "rebellious" lawyering, "third dimensional" lawyering, "cause" or "movement" lawyering, and so forth—are not mutually exclusive. Rather, like the Schools, they share a sense of vision and mission and can be mined for insights and used in action in creative combinations.

These Approaches do not represent a consensus on "best" practices in every circumstance but a dynamic, exploratory, self-critical, and ongoing dialogue to sharpen all advocacy for social justice. The Approaches, focused as they are on producing and testing theory in practice, are useful across identity groups and issue areas, such as health, environmental justice, labor, immigration, gender justice, disability, housing, civil rights, economic development, LGBTQ anti-discrimination, and indigenous rights. These "newer developing wisdoms are tentative, and the explorations continue apace. It is therefore a great time to be a progressive lawyer, even if the role may not be an entirely comfortable one."[15] These Approaches—together with the Schools—provide a platform for competence in bottom-up research, analysis, and action toward equal justice.

Importantly, the names for these Approaches (like the Schools above) were developed primarily by practitioners and academics embedded in U.S. and Western institutions and culture, although drawing often on work with marginalized communities locally and globally. Because developed primarily with this Western bent, the principles or practices have been used, modified, and rejected in other contexts, and this process of local-global development continues from generation to generation. With these caveats, Chart B provides a partial snapshot of advocacy Approaches, describing the concerns on which they are most focused.

Chart B: "Approaches" to Systemic Advocacy

Approaches	**Key Problem-Solving Concerns**
Cause lawyering, Community lawyering, Integrative lawyering, Guerrilla lawyering, Law and organizing, Movement or mobilization lawyering, Revolutionary lawyering	Relationships of advocates to groups, organizing strategies, sites of practice, and social movements

---

[15] Paul R. Tremblay, Critical Legal Ethics Review of Lawyers Ethics and the Pursuit of Social Justice: A Critical Reader, Susan D. Carle ed., 20 Geo. J. Legal Ethics 133, 134 (2007).

Client-centered lawyering, Collaborative lawyering, Critical lawyering, Facilitative lawyering, Rebellious lawyering, Reconstructive poverty lawyering, Therapeutic lawyering	Relationships, voice, decision making, and empowerment among clients, advocates, and other team members
Democratic lawyering, Political lawyering, Legislative lawyering, Poverty lawyering, Public interest lawyering, Third dimensional lawyering, Civil rights lawyering, Legal pragmatism, People's lawyering, Progressive lawyering, Social justice lawyering	Professional and social decision-making processes, roles, public resistance, and material outcomes for subordinated groups

By distinguishing the Schools and Approaches in these charts, we do not recycle the division between theory and practice that is so characteristic of formalism. Instead, we aim to appreciate how both the Schools and the Approaches create theory, and how both help to craft actions, albeit perhaps in different sites of practice and by sometimes-different methods. And we emphasize that mutual cross-pollination is the norm, not the exception. Critical knowledge and theory have developed from both academy-based and field-based experiences—a historical process that continues to this day, as this book itself demonstrates. By exploring Approaches and Schools as wells of actionable knowledge, advocates garner ever-greater insights to sharpen continually their capacity for systemic advocacy.

This fusion of action based on theory and theory based on practice allows advocates to create a "praxis" that maximizes their effectiveness and integrity. Oversimplified, praxis amounts to applied theory—the active, self-critical use of knowledge from previous experience to future plans and actions. As we see throughout this text, the concept of praxis describes systemic advocacy for systemic justice.

Our concluding excerpt on the Schools and Approaches also begins our study of "narratives and experiences" as tools of bottom-up advocacy. Gerald López, who sparked a critical interrogation among advocates when he introduced "rebellious lawyering" in the early 1990s,[16] reflects on, and recounts, his own upbringing, training, and advocacy. Showing how personal experience and reflection can provide a starting point for systemic

---

[16] López, Rebellious Lawyering.

analysis and advocacy, López agrees with the basics of Bellow's "political" Approach. Connecting the micro to the macro, the "rebellious" Approach López pioneered asks advocates to change themselves in order to change systems and "bring about positive changes that improve our collective existence"[17] from the bottom up.

CHANGING SYSTEMS, CHANGING OURSELVES
Gerald P. López
12 Harv. Latino L. Rev. 15 (2009)

... In thinking about transforming systems, I find myself returning to events earlier in my life.... I want to highlight certain ideas and attitudes that came to feel central to a rebellious vision: the inevitable intermingling and mutually defining character of obedience and rebellion, of lay and professional problem solving, of the way we work and the way we live.

Let me share three experiences that, together, suggest why I believe changing systems inevitably entails changing ourselves.

Three Formative Experiences

In one, I am about eight years old. I already felt bewildered and infuriated by the overlapping systems that all too powerfully and, thankfully, all too imperfectly limited the lives of those of us who called East Los Angeles home. I'm talking about the educational system. The health care system. The criminal justice system. The electoral system. I'm also talking about the racial and cultural and class systems that shaped and reflected housing and labor markets and public and private and civic relations. How did such systems (from gargantuan institutions to personal interactions) come into being and maintain themselves?

I realized that systems of every sort knew both how to target and how to neglect residents of East L.A. They seemingly tracked our every move through law enforcement practices and truancy policies and immigration laws, for example. And they apparently never cared about our lack of access to quality health care, K–12 public education, and financial services, to name only some obviously important means of everyday survival and social mobility. If the systems in L.A. appeared at times to carry forward robotically or naturally, their patterns revealed human bias in operation.

These biased systems traced their origins—as do all systems—to a mix of deliberate design, capricious choice, and accidental rites. To target us

---

[17] Angelo N. Ancheta, Community Lawyering, 81 Cal. L. Rev. 1363, 1367 (1993). Ancheta is a proponent of "community lawyering," another advocacy Approach, which shares the rebellious emphasis on bottom-up leadership from affected communities. Like the Schools, and like advocacy in general, the Approaches draw controversy and self-critical analysis. See, e.g., Rebecca Sharpless, More Than One Lane Wide: Against Hierarchies of Helping in Progressive Legal Advocacy, 19 Clinical L. Rev. 347 (2012) (critiquing the seeming disregard in rebellious lawyering literature for direct service providers that diminishes the contributions particularly of women of color to public interest advocacy).

and to neglect us reflected and reinforced accepted wisdom about how you get the most out of, and maintain control over, a people with an especially limited capacity to contribute. The stock stories and arguments that shaped law and life in the 1950s defined Mexicans (Mexican-Americans, Mexicanos, Chicanos) as genetically and culturally inferior. Regarded as unworthy of the fully equal citizenship that in principle defined membership in the national community, we Mexicans instead got what we merited, what a mixed-race mongrel breed deserved. No more and no less.

Not everyone bought into these stereotypes, of course. Mexicanos and Mexican-Americans I knew challenged them. So did Blacks and Asians in other parts of L.A., and so did Natives who had worked alongside my grandparents in Arizona mining towns. So did White teachers and merchants and nuns and priests and coaches. . . .

Surrounded by such staunch oppositionists, I found it all the more confusing that the diverse systems that considered Mexicans everlastingly inferior appeared to engender remarkably broad allegiance. I saw pronounced loyalty in those contentedly benefiting all the way to those painfully subordinated. Some formally defended the status quo; others would not openly confront systems that they perceived as so deeply ingrained as to be virtually unchangeable; others still seemed to smilingly stomach dreadful disrespect. I witnessed many who combined these behaviors, accustomed, if not attached, to the way things were.

Fortunately for me, my parents raged against degrading stereotypes. They understood the connection between these stereotypes and the systems that at once unfairly targeted and neglected those of us who lived in places like East L.A. My Dad and Mom raged . . . [t]hrough their active political involvement, helping to mobilize registration and get-out-the-vote campaigns for state and national elections, and leading efforts to incorporate East Los Angeles.

My Mom and Dad proudly celebrated the defiant—the mundane and not-so-mundane efforts on the part of others to stand up to systems that denied in practice the very principle of democratic equality central to our country's professed convictions. At their best, my Mom and Dad treated each moment as a potential opportunity to live out a largely counterfactual world, one they could now and then glimpse, but only by behaving as if the world they imagined were already in place.

Every bit as fortunately for me, my parents raged while struggling to get by day-to-day. They coped with those jobs they could get, without the health insurance we needed, and with the many individuals and institutions refusing to afford them the basic decency and honor that lies at the heart of justice. . . .

... I started to appreciate that the very people who with all their hearts hope to change a system simultaneously live within its jurisdiction. ...

I began to practice seeing in others, and all around me, the rebelliousness that otherwise might escape my notice. ...

... In another experience, I'm twenty-one, a few months into the first year of law school. A brute fact is dawning on me for the first time: legal education has incredibly little to do with lawyering—the dynamic problem solving dwelling within what every lawyer does. Instead, the focus of law school is law or, more particularly, a stylized parsing of edited appellate judicial opinions. When legal educators do talk about lawyering, they talk typically in terms of "doing legal analysis," "reasoning legally," "thinking like a lawyer." And when they use these terms they refer to an elusive and perhaps even indescribable way of thinking, apparently different from and superior to how humans otherwise think, certainly fundamentally different from and superior to how people who hail from places like East L.A. think.

... I had expected law school to introduce me to and provide the means for me to advance toward a deep understanding of what lawyers do, of what lawyers do when they do it well, and of what lawyers do to improve over the course of a career. ...

While studying law principally through edited appellate judicial opinions seemed like an extremely limited way of studying lawyering, talking about how lawyers think as something discontinuous from how humans otherwise think was perplexing. Initially I found the incomplete explanation of and enigmatic aura surrounding "thinking like a lawyer" outrageous, pompous, and silly. Who regards themselves that way? ...

... [But to] regard thinking like a lawyer as special, ineffable, even unique, made a certain symmetrical sense. An entirely separate way of thinking would account for what we could not initially fathom and what we might someday master as insiders.

That reconciliation proved powerfully seductive for many. I watched as some students embraced this notion. I realized many faculty members and practicing lawyers did too. The test seemed obvious: If you are willing to put to the side who and what you are, including how you think and feel, you can perhaps enter the ranks of those who can operate comfortably within and even command what otherwise cannot be fully described and yet informs so much of those very systems that together rule our lives. You too can become influential clergy.

The closer I looked, however, the more I doubted this story. More than anything else, the cultivated foreignness of the legal culture seemed to reflect certain historical arcs, institutional efficiencies, and profession-protecting aims. ...

What bothered me most, however, was that the exaggerated mysteriousness of the legal culture tended to obscure the connections between professional law practice and everyday problem solving.... I believed we should begin by understanding how we all solve problems and then understand professional lawyering as a variation on shared cognitive and cultural mechanics.

In any event, beginning to see the relationship between legal and everyday problem solving made me examine afresh my interpretation of the approach to law practice I already had found dismaying among the first wave of activist lawyers to hit East L.A. In my limited experience, these lawyers too rarely worked with us—with individual clients, with families, with extended networks of diverse people, organizations, coalitions, and communities. They often appeared unable or unwilling to imagine how our knowledge of the problems we faced and the strategies we already employed might mesh well, enhance, or even potentially revolutionize what they did as professionals. I concluded that these activists, having explored a range of explicit options, consciously chose to practice the way they did.

I likely had figured wrong, however.... Even the best activist lawyer would seem to have been immersed in training that typically treated how lawyers think as different than—and superior to—how everyone else thinks. Such training made robust teamwork appear unrelated and perhaps antithetic to productive practice....

Instead, the habits of mind and heart inculcated by law schools cast grave doubt on the very idea of systematic collaboration.... And legal education made deeply inconceivable (or at least absurdly utopian) the idea of regularly joining forces as equals with others, especially with those who live in places like East L.A. No matter how well-intentioned, the first wave of activist lawyers I had observed would have had to overcome legal education—on top of and mixed in with every other operable stereotype—if they were to team up as equals with us and with others like us.

I found myself at twenty-one beginning what would be a lifetime exercise—an exercise that worked from different directions toward the same aim. I tried to make the habitual unfamiliar again: to see what I could not typically see in our everyday problem solving by excavating and making explicit what we've made so routine that we no longer remain mindful of what we're doing. At the same time, I tried to decode the law: to identify in what felt foreign about professional legal culture all that seemed rooted in ordinary life....

This new exercise was not an attempt to prove that professional lawyering was a fiction or that everyday people I knew in places like East L.A. were superhuman. I did not believe either was true then, and I do not believe either is true today. I simply had not found persuasive the standard account of how lawyers think in ways disconnected from how everyone else thinks. And I needed to develop my own view of expertise, one that sorted through both my own experiences and other available evidence of how humans think and behave. To do so, I wanted to see as far as I could through the sumptuous trappings and cultivated awe that make the work of lawyers feel nearly beyond description to large numbers of law school teachers, students, and graduates. And I wanted to see as far as I could through the plainclothes wrap and nurtured dullness that make the problem solving ordinary people pursue appear to many (including most scholars) utterly unworthy of sustained study.

Searching for continuities helped me begin to appreciate—and strive to explicitly describe—both what we all do in solving problems and what lawyers (and other professionals) do in helping others solve problems. . . .

In the final experience, I'm now twenty-four. After taking time off, I chose to return to my third year.

. . . I understood [now] more explicitly than when I began law school that what lawyers do well is an extension of, and should be connected to, what everyone does when trying to cope and thrive within overlapping systems they at once accept and challenge. . . . I pledged to see each case and every discussion as an opportunity to examine what lawyers did with others in addressing particular problems within systems that could indeed declare truths and yet not entirely control perceptions, plans, and trajectories.

. . . In trying to see law school through lawyering eyes, at least now and then I understood a bit differently than before what I already had experienced in my first two years. I knew legal education mainly encouraged lawyers to believe they did not need to know much at all about the client communities and larger systems with which they dealt. But in my third year, I sensed law school training instilled in future lawyers the belief that what lawyers do does not typically require understanding how a wide variety of others frame problems, how to design and implement strategies, or how to monitor and evaluate feedback. How could such training promote respect for what others know, for making the most of limited resources, or for enabling collective growth about solving problems more effectively? . . .

. . . [Eventually I] could detect, I think, a partially articulated idea of how lawyers might work as equals with people historically regarded as inferior. Certainly, there was a shared sense that something much different from what dominated our training and our experiences could express how we just might team up. In circulation was a powerfully attractive and evocative image: lawyers within networks of collaborating problem solvers, learning from one another, taking on "all-powerful" systems, sorting through and naming what together they found themselves doing. . . .

Rebellious Vision Briefly Sketched

In several years time, the expanse between my performance and my aspirations had shrunk some. And, with the help of many, I already had begun to see two significant ways of living—the reigning vision and the rebellious vision. Within each way of living, I saw a corresponding idea of problem solving. And as one instance and one part of each respective way of problem solving, I pictured a corresponding vision of progressive law practice.

Consider only some questions to which regnant and rebellious visions offer opposing answers: Who qualifies as an expert? What counts as valuable knowledge? With whom do experts collaborate in framing problems and vetting strategies? Monitoring and evaluating interventions? In what ways do problem-solving and living practices define one another? On close inspection, these two ways of living and problem solving reveal conflicting empirical assumptions about human behavior and contrasting normative aspirations about future communal trajectories. Perhaps miniature sketches will stir up the contrasts that mold these two visions and our experiences.

Experts rule in the reigning vision. They behave—and others come to rely upon them—as if they can see panoramically. In framing problems and choices, identifying and implementing worthy strategies, and deciding how much and whose feedback qualifies as necessary for effective monitoring and evaluation, these experts collaborate principally and often exclusively with one another. They issue mandates. Through diverse intermediaries, subordinates typically comply in order to be regarded as doing their jobs as workers and as citizens.

The reigning vision pervades most systems in which we work and live—across public, private, and civic realms. Through these systems, we learn and teach which people should be regarded as experts and which people should be regarded as worthy collaborators. Who gets classified as an expert and as a worthy collaborator can vary from context to context. But, across contexts, in the reigning approach we typically pick ahead of time those worth listening to and learning from. And in most systems, we pick elites.

It's not just elites selecting and defending the selection of elites. The reigning vision inclines us all to think and feel we should pick elites to collaborate with one another and to govern our lives. . . .

In mounting a challenge to the reigning vision, the rebellious rival unites key fundamentals in pursuit of radical democracy, where equal citizenship is a concrete everyday reality and not just a vague promise. In the rebellious vision, everyone collaborates in problem solving, seeking out and sharing knowledge about existing problems, available resources, and useful strategies. Varied problem solvers connect those who face problems with those in public, private, and civic realms who help address them, building networks of valuable know-how among diverse problem solvers and helping shape and meet common goals.

Whenever problems remain unaddressed even after making such connections, problem solvers attempt to fill voids by scavenging around for resources, leveraging what is available with what may never have been tried, and assembling, as needed, one-time trouble-shooting squads or more permanent full-fledged partnerships. Committed routinely to monitoring and evaluating strategies, rebellious practitioners aim always to enhance problem-solving capacity. Problem solving rebelliously pursued melds street savvy, technical sophistication, and collective ingenuity into a compelling practical force.

Working in this way aims to produce, and depends upon, networks of co-eminent institutions and individuals collaborating with one another. Such collaborators consistently engage and learn from one another, neither bottom-up nor top-down, but every which way at once. . . .

This way of problem solving aims to support and reinforce—and, now and then, take the lead in demonstrating—how we might live together in a fully robust democracy. That goal cannot be achieved easily, much less automatically. Ideology does not work in this way. But rebellious variations of problem solving (lawyering, prominent among them) and radical democracy parallel and enrich one another. Trying collectively to secure cooperation in the midst of unavoidable complexity, difference, and vulnerability—a synonym for rebellious problem solving—takes as its point of departure and declares as its goal engaging equals in understanding and enhancing life.

Some Thoughts You Almost Certainly Have Anticipated

In thinking and speaking about transforming the world, Latinas and Latinos too often focus on the need to change people other than ourselves and practices other than our own. In this sense, as in others, we are like everyone else. "If we could only get rid of them." "If we could only alter their ways of doing things." "If we could only," we'd be on our way to better days. . . .

But it's a decisive mistake to think we can change systems without changing ourselves. We're implicated in everything we may aim to alter. . . . And, even without knowing the word hegemony, many in kitchens and factories and fields have pointed out our collective acquiescence in, and defense of, systems we otherwise claim to regard as deeply antihuman.

But we're all better at acknowledging our collusion than embracing the implications of this admission. . . . Our stock of stories and arguments blame "them" and immunize "us" more than they do anything else. We emotionally distance ourselves from the involvement we formally acknowledge.

It's not that we're incapable of reflection. We know how to critique. We may even call into question our own decisions. The trouble is, we too often critique and then do nothing more. Like witnesses to the Holocaust, like the children of the witnesses, we seem unable or at least unwilling to face in a sustained way what we might have done differently. Familiar critiques serve as just another available rationalization of our own collusion. Through them, we anesthetize ourselves—and perhaps wish to immunize ourselves....

... What we face is the need for a concerted effort to work with one another to learn how better to avoid reinforcing what we claim to want to transform. By vowing to meet this challenge, we would call ourselves to account in the way the best among us already do. And, in coming clean about our own mix of obedience and rebellion, we just might enable ourselves to be more fully human.

Effectively changing ourselves as part of changing systems turns out to be as gruelingly difficult as it is joyously rewarding. We take our stands, like everyone else, from within the very blend of forces that makes opposition uncertain and perilous. Deep biases pervade systems of every sort. Think only of how class, gender, and sexuality historically have altered interactions between individuals, groups, and neighborhoods.... Race and racism remain central. Some will regard me as unable to let go of the past. But I am talking about right now. The truth today about race and racism is both less sweet and more complicated than "colorblind" advocates acknowledge.

I profoundly appreciate the great contrast between how race and racism work today and how race and racism worked in the mid-1950s. When I was eight, people all over L.A. regarded as justified the subordination of those of us who lived in places like East L.A., Watts, Pacoima, San Pedro, Gardena. When I was in my early twenties, a surprising number had absorbed the anger and passion and justice of the modern Civil Rights Movement, had downsized considerably (at least in mixed company) their racist name-calling, and considered remedying institutional discrimination against various targeted and neglected groups. Today, in 2009, the sophisticated stock account proclaims that race does not much matter and probably should not matter at all. Racism, in this popular portrayal, has diminished greatly and perhaps even vanished in everyday life, except of course for vulgar holdouts whose numbers are typically trivial and whose presence should not trouble us much.

If, like me, you find today's sophisticated stock account inconsistent with experience, you should know that modern science sides with us. A wide range of scholars have gathered evidence that reveals potent bias towards people of color and other outgroups.... Today, bias and discrimination and subordination sculpt the very same world in which so many insist "we're over all that."...

Neither my own work, nor the experiences of others, nor the very best ideas offered by talented scholars amount to a proven "de-biasing" game plan. But not knowing exactly what to do about our current condition hardly argues for silence or denial or both. We can and should talk about race and racism—especially when others would have us regard them both as irrelevant. And we should consciously probe for ways in which we can not only formally condemn racism's presence but clean up its pernicious consequences.

Already, though, we can see how the pervasiveness of human bias—perhaps particularly racism—might explain our limited inclination toward the collaboration presupposed by and sought through the rebellious vision. How can we find compelling a vision of problem solving that insists we must team up with others we believe to be less than equal? ... We would be sacrificing expertise, and our own collective health, to quixotic aims.

Roughly at this point in the debate about collaboration, those of us who espouse the rebellious vision often get turned into cartoon figures. Others accuse us of wanting to substitute street wisdom for elite knowledge—as if turning the hierarchy upside down is what we are really about....

... To acknowledge that anyone might teach you, might even turn your ideas inside out, frightens those whose rule—whose identity—centers around supposedly knowing lots about what others supposedly know far less.

In the rebellious vision, even the best among us, especially the best among us, should want to learn from anyone.... If someone proves us wrong, if anyone proves us wrong, we should shout, "Hallelujah!" If we cannot be wrong, we cannot learn. And if we cannot learn, we have renounced a central part of what it should mean to be human....

None of us can plausibly speak of "changing the system" as if systems are somehow out there, unrelated to us and what we know and what we do. None of us should desire to be so disentangled, so above it all, so panoramically positioned.

Some people mock the label "rebellious." They insist the last thing we need in problem solving, or in living, is the experimentation of those who have yet to outgrow their dreams. I dissent. In fact, to borrow from my wonderful friend Tom Elke, I understand working to make dreams come true "as a job fit for grown-ups." If young folks want to join us, great. But do not expect me to believe that adulthood requires abandoning or even limiting our imagination. I do not agree. In fact, I will rebel. And I hope you will with me. Time and again.

López reflects on the mutually reinforcing connections between systems and selves from the perspective of a "rebellious vision" that looks at law critically, and from the bottom up. He not only illustrates how scholars and advocates contribute to the development of advocacy Approaches but also how systemic injustice connects individuals to systems—how systems impose macro scripts that then govern life at the micro, or individual, level—both in professional and in personal situations. This excerpt thus emphasizes another recurrent theme of this book: the top-down connection of micro and macro injustice and, hence, its importance to bottom-up struggles for equal justice.

NOTES AND QUESTIONS

1. *Is Realism Transformative?* As detailed above, the "Brandeis brief" was first used in the *Muller* case, with over 100 pages of interdisciplinary information that supported the Supreme Court's eventual ruling to uphold Oregon law restricting a woman's workday in a factory or laundry to 10 hours. Relying on a perceived difference between the sexes, the Court found it essential "to preserve the strength and vigor of the race" by protecting women from long workdays that could endanger their motherhood. 208 U.S. 412 (1908). This perceived identity difference "allowed" the Court to distinguish precedent, just three years before, in *Lochner v. New York*, 198 U.S. 45 (1905), striking down state law limiting the workday and workweek of bakery employees without regard to gender. Earlier, in 1872, the Supreme Court had let stand a state's refusal to issue a married woman a license to practice law. See *Bradwell v. State*, 83 U.S. 130 (1873), with a concurring Justice writing that "[t]he natural and proper timidity and delicacy which belongs to the female sex evidently unfits it for many of the occupations of civil life." At the time of the Oregon legislation and the Court's decision, all the legislative and judicial actors were male. Does knowing that fact affect your view of those decisions? What/who was "the bottom" in that time and context? Did the outcomes improve their lives? Is that context of long workdays in potentially hazardous workplaces a relic of the past? Which group(s) experience them today, and why? Can legal reform ameliorate the problem as it seemingly did in Oregon for one identity group?

2. *Elites Respond to the Schools and Approaches.* As noted above, in September 2020, President Trump ordered the Director of the Office of Management and Budget to issue a memo defining cross-cultural sensitivity and skills training based on critical race theory as "anti-American propaganda." The memo directed federal agencies and bureaus to identify any trainings that use terms like "white privilege" or "critical race theory" so that contracts can be severed with those training providers.[18] Under that order, for

---

[18] See Russell Vought, Memorandum for the Heads of Executive Branch Departments and Agencies (Sept. 4, 2020) (stating that critical theory-inspired trainings "not only run counter to the fundamental beliefs for which our Nation has stood since its inception, but they also engender

example, this book could never be used among lawyers and others in federal agencies. In addition to the law deans' response noted above, Laura E. Gómez, director of UCLA's Critical Race Studies Program, replied to these top-down attacks, noting that: "Far from being anti-American, as Trump's administration alleges, critical race theory aspires to the ideal of equality represented in our post-Civil War Constitution, an ideal we are far from achieving even 150 years later."[19] Any thoughts or reactions?

3. *Reflection Exercise.* Reflect on your education thus far. Does your experience mirror that of López or differ? In your view, what might or should be better?

1.5 DECONSTRUCTION AND DUAL CONSCIOUSNESS EMPOWER SUBORDINATED GROUPS

The collective, transgenerational process that produced the Schools and Approaches remains vibrant despite pushback from above. Critical scholars, activists, and advocates continue to expand and adapt their work to promote equal justice. They continue drawing and innovating from these wells of critical knowledge precisely because they represent the cumulative critical lessons of group experience with collaboration and reflection as part of long-term struggle. Deepening these points and themes, critical race scholar Susan Serrano applies two key concepts/practices: deconstruction and dual consciousness. Deconstruction is the first step toward a critical understanding of subordination, and dual consciousness allows advocates to stay realistic about law's perils and limits. In turn, deconstruction and dual consciousness jointly provide the platform for critical analysis and knowledge, as Serrano shows so clearly. Using these analytical tools, Serrano documents how Puerto Ricans' struggles in Hawai'i a century or more ago confirm three corresponding bottom lines for today: (1) how and why critical and self-critical reflections from the bottom yield insights that lead to collective action; (2) how and why collaboration that is multidisciplinary, multicultural, and accountable to the bottom sparks and sustains organized long-term struggles; and (3) how and why systemic advocates draw on the Schools and Approaches to guide their advocacy. As the following chapters elaborate, these and similar insights are key parts of the critical "toolkit" for systemic advocacy.

---

division and resentment within the Federal workforce" and demanding that executive branch offices "cease and desist from using taxpayer dollars to fund these divisive, un-American propaganda training sessions"), www.whitehouse.gov/wp-content/uploads/2020/09/M-20-34.pdf.

[19] Laura E. Gómez, Trump's White House Says Critical Race Theory is Anti-American. Here's the Truth (Sept. 11, 2020), www.nbcnews.com/think/opinion/trump-s-white-house-says-critical-race-theory-anti-american-ncna1239825.

DUAL CONSCIOUSNESS ABOUT LAW AND JUSTICE: PUERTO RICANS' BATTLE FOR U.S. CITIZENSHIP IN HAWAI'I

Susan K. Serrano
29 Centro J. 164 (2017)

Introduction

Only weeks after the passage of the Jones Act—which in 1917 collectively naturalized "citizens of Puerto Rico" as U.S. citizens—Manuel Olivieri Sánchez, a Puerto Rican residing in the Territory of Hawai'i, travelled to the Honolulu county clerk's office to register to vote in the upcoming Hawai'i elections. David Kalauokalani, the county clerk, refused to place Olivieri Sánchez's name on the great register of voters. . . . Across the territory, Puerto Ricans who attempted to register to vote were turned away.

Olivieri Sánchez fought back. He filed a writ of mandamus to compel the clerk to register him and other Puerto Rican residents. In the first and only case to rule upon the citizenship of Puerto Ricans in Hawai'i following the Jones Act, the lower court ruled that Olivieri Sánchez did not become a U.S. citizen upon the Act's passage. According to the court, Congress intended to make Puerto Ricans U.S. citizens only if they "remained inhabitants of Porto [sic] Rico, giving them thereby a citizenship anal[o]gous to State citizenship . . . which would be lost by removal from Porto Rico." Puerto Ricans in Hawai'i were declared a people "without a country."

Six months later, the Supreme Court of the Territory of Hawai'i reversed. In *Sanchez v. Kalauokalani*, the court held that Olivieri Sánchez became a U.S. citizen pursuant to the Jones Act even though he had moved to Hawai'i in 1901. According to the court, under the Jones Act, all "citizens of Porto Rico" (as defined by the 1900 Foraker Act) acquired U.S. citizenship. Nothing in the Act, it found, evinced Congress' intent "to exclude . . . citizens of Porto Rico, . . . who were at the date of the act of March 2, 1917, absent from Porto Rico." . . . Hawai'i's Puerto Ricans celebrated this hard-fought legal victory. As newly recognized U.S. citizens—and because of Olivieri Sánchez's advocacy and the community's solidarity—Puerto Ricans in Hawai'i attained the right to vote in the Territory and a measure of economic mobility.

At the same time, U.S. citizenship changed little about the legal and social climate for Puerto Rican laborers in Hawai'i. They were still cast as "vagrants" and "lawbreakers," rounded up and imprisoned based on actions of a few, forced to live in some of the worst plantation housing, and marginalized based on the fear that they—as U.S. citizens—would gain increased political power. Puerto Ricans therefore continued to protest laws that governed the territory, both on and off of the sugar plantations. They sent petitions to newspapers in Puerto Rico and to the federal and local governments asserting that they were denied basic rights, treated inhumanely on the plantations, arrested and punished without cause, and left without recourse. . . .

Sanchez v. Kalauokalani—decided amidst harsh plantation practices and vagrancy laws deployed to subjugate Puerto Ricans and other workers of color—sheds light on Puerto Ricans' experiences with law and legal process in Hawai'i. Rather than rejecting the law as a tool only of the powerful, or blindly embracing the law as a silver bullet, I contend that Hawai'i's Puerto Ricans embraced what W.E.B. Du Bois termed a "double consciousness" about their experience with law and rights assertion. Puerto Ricans held both a deep criticism of the ways in which laws were used to benefit those in power as well as an aspirational and transformative vision of law as a vehicle to validate their place in the U.S. polity. They knew the value of rights under law—and fought for them—but at the same time were aware that legal recognition as U.S. citizens would not mean freedom from discriminatory treatment through policy and by the populace. This duality served as a source of resilience in the face of injustice.

As critical theorists recognize, the double consciousness of those at the bottom "accommodates both the idea of legal indeterminacy as well as the core belief in a liberating law that transcends indeterminacy." Indeed, outsiders have intimate knowledge of the legal system's injustice against subordinated others, and acknowledge that aspects of that subordination would continue even if they achieve "legal rights." But these outsiders also have "passionately invoked legal doctrine, legal ideals, and liberal theory in the struggle" against injustice and have succeeded in part because of the "passionate response that conventional legalism can at times elicit." For this reason, critical race theorists underscore the importance of rights assertion for oppressed peoples and communities of color as a vehicle to compel powerful actors and institutions to recognize disempowered people's dignity and humanity.

Drawing on realist and critical theory insights, and through archival research, this article explores how Puerto Ricans in Hawai'i, despite their small numbers and lack of political clout, asserted their claims to U.S. citizenship in the same courts and political climate that regularly contributed to their subjugation. They did so knowing that it would be difficult to achieve judicial recognition of new legal rights and that, even if so recognized, mere possession of those rights would not necessarily transform their treatment or status in society. By simultaneously being "aware of the historical abuse of law" while embracing "law as a tool of necessity," they made "legal consciousness their own in order to attack injustice." Indeed, although the sugar oligarchy controlled the legal system, Puerto Ricans perceived the distinct value of rights and fought for and attained U.S. citizenship in *Sanchez*. While recognizing that formal U.S.

citizenship would not automatically confer "first class" citizenship, they saw the need to push for the attendant rights of that citizenship as well as against cultural vilification and inferior treatment in their daily lives. . . .

Puerto Ricans In Hawai'i: A Brief Overview

When the first group of Puerto Ricans arrived in Hawai'i in 1900, Westerners controlled nearly all aspects of Hawai'i's economic and political life. In the mid-1800s, Europeans and Americans acquired vast tracts of land when Native Hawaiian communal land tenure was converted into a Western private property system. Native Hawaiian lands were divided, confiscated, sold away. Plantations diverted water from agrarian Hawaiian communities. Native Hawaiians were separated from the land, thereby severing cultural and spiritual connections.

Private land ownership and the Reciprocity Treaty of 1875—which lifted tariffs on Hawai'i-grown sugar exported to the United States—paved the way for massive sugar plantations and impending U.S. control. Following the illegal overthrow of the Hawaiian nation in 1893, American military and plantation owners lobbied hard for Hawai'i's annexation to the United States. With a military base at Pearl Harbor and sugar at stake, the United States annexed Hawai'i in 1898 and took control of the provisional government as well as all former Hawaiian government and royal lands.

Desperate for cheap labor to support large-scale sugar production, planters began importing "plodding Chinese coolie[s]" under low-wage contracts. To induce competition and racial divisions between workers, the sugar planters shipped in laborers from Japan and Portugal, and later, from Korea, Puerto Rico, the Philippines, and even the U.S. South. Important to this enterprise was the Westerners' belief in their racial superiority and "the notion that the white race could not perform labor under the difficult conditions of tropical and subtropical plantations." Plantation owners used physical force and tight economic control to dominate these workers of color. The stage was set for what would become a highly racially stratified plantation system throughout the 1900s.

At the same time, debates swirled over the United States' new "imperial" role and how to handle the "racially inferior people inhabiting the conquered areas." Decision-makers warned against bestowing constitutional guarantees upon the "ignorant" and "half-civilized" peoples of Puerto Rico and the Philippines. Even those who supported "an honorable and fruitful association" with Puerto Rico "accept[ed] the proposition that the United States could not and would not 'incorporate the alien races, [or the] civilized, semi-civilized, barbarous, and savage peoples of [the] islands into [the U.S.] body politic.' " In the infamous *Insular Cases*, the U.S. Supreme Court worried that Puerto Rico's "racially different others" threatened the very heart of white Anglo-Saxon dominance: Justice

Brown's opinion in *Downes v. Bidwell* warned that the offspring of the colonies' inhabitants, "whether savages or civilized," would be "entitled to all the rights, privileges and immunities of citizens."

Race was also key in legitimizing the Hawai'i sugar oligarchy's confiscation of land and exploitation of laborers of color from around the globe. While the sugar planters "used race to legitimize conquest, denigrating, in racial terms, those colonized," they also sought to civilize those colonial people "through the acquisition of [W]estern values and work discipline." At that time, cheap labor was in desperate demand: Hawai'i's annexation to the United States halted the importation of Chinese and alien contract laborers, and Japanese were considered overly "demanding." The planters thus found a solution in "Porto Ricans and . . . Negroes from the Southern States." With false promises of high wages, plantation owners recruited Puerto Ricans to work as cheap labor and strikebreakers. About 5,000 Puerto Ricans arrived in Hawai'i between 1900 and 1901.

The powerful white plantation oligarchy easily exploited Puerto Rican laborers because of their ambiguous citizenship status. The Treaty of Paris between the United States and Spain, which ended the Spanish-American War in 1898, did not confer citizenship on the "native inhabitants" of Puerto Rico, and the 1900 Foraker Act establishing a civil government for Puerto Rico described them as "citizens of Porto Rico"—not citizens of the United States. In 1904, the United States Supreme Court ruled that Puerto Ricans were not "alien immigrants" and could not be barred from entering the United States, but they were not U.S. citizens, either. . . .

Hawai'i's sugar planters . . . sought to ensure that Puerto Ricans did not have the same rights as U.S. citizens. In 1902, only two years after the first group arrived, sixty Puerto Rican laborers sent a petition to the *San Juan News* chronicling widespread mistreatment by sugar planters and police in the Territory of Hawai'i. The Hawai'i Republican Territorial Committee immediately asked the Territory Attorney General to determine whether Puerto Ricans were U.S. citizens entitled to vote. The Committee was alarmed that "if [Puerto Ricans] were allowed to vote it would . . . introduce[ ] a new element into the political situation of the Hawaiian Islands of a rather uncertain quality." The Attorney General, of course, determined that Puerto Ricans were not U.S. citizens and thus had no right to vote in Hawai'i Territory. Because citizenship was an "indispensable qualification for the suffrage in [Hawai'i] Territory," the Attorney General wrote, "[i]t follows that Porto Ricans cannot vote here without being first naturalized."

To justify its treatment of Puerto Ricans as unworthy of participating in the polity, Hawai'i's sugar oligarchy strategically characterized them as uncivilized and inferior. . . . U.S. decision-makers had already deployed some of these depictions to bolster the United States' conquest of Puerto

Rico, and U.S. agribusiness and Hawai'i's government spread these images to destabilize and dehumanize Puerto Ricans as a means of controlling and suppressing labor.

Puerto Ricans in Hawai'i were thus acutely aware from the start that Hawai'i's legal system reflected the interests and values of those most powerful. But, as discussed below, they invoked legal doctrine and the language of "rights" to pursue their justice claims to citizenship, and later their claims to the rights attendant to that citizenship—because those claims held transformative potential. The law, for them, could both sanction oppression and also provide openings to liberation.

"Double Consciousness" About Law and Legal Process

The awareness of this tension between the law's ability to oppress and liberate developed partially as critical race theory's response to critical legal studies. Critical legal studies scholars in the 1970s and 1980s deconstructed formalist methods of legal analysis and understandings of law as inherently neutral and objective. Taking their cue from the legal realist movement as well as poststructuralism and postmodernism, critical legal scholars demonstrated that the law is indeterminate, contradictory and politically charged; and that legal decision-making is deeply influenced by judges' ideological views, history, and political conditions.

... [C]ritical legal scholars exposed how the law maintains hierarchies, particularly those regarding class. They contended that legal language tends to mask politics and reflect the interests of those in power, and that the law's images and technical language operate to convince people that legal arrangements are natural and inevitable.

Critical legal scholars also maintained that the rhetoric of liberalism and the seductiveness of "rights" deceives oppressed groups, resulting in a "false consciousness" about the fairness of the legal system. According to Marxist thought, members of subordinate classes suffer from false consciousness—they are unable to see the ways in which surrounding social relations of production conceal the realities of exploitation and domination embodied in those social relations. In the legal setting, critical legal studies scholars employed the concept of false consciousness to mean that liberalism's claims of equality and fairness have duped subordinated groups into blindly accepting an oppressive legal system.

Thus, many critical legal scholars "trashed" rights-based approaches to equality. They argued that rights are malleable, offer artificial hope, and alienate people from each other. As a result, critical legal scholars claimed that individuals and groups "should abandon a rights-centered approach to social justice, replacing it with more informal, often undefined, mechanisms for the attainment of justice."

Despite its pathbreaking insights, critical legal studies was challenged as elitist, overwhelmingly white, and disconnected from the concrete struggles of ordinary communities. It also failed to fully resonate with marginalized groups who were acutely aware of the law's ability to subordinate, but who also refused to wholly abandon the legal system because of its potential to uplift and liberate in certain contexts.

Critical race theorists in the 1980s embraced many of the methodologies and insights of critical legal studies.... But for critical race theorists, critical legal studies lacked an understanding of the role of race and racism in both the U.S. legal system and in society itself....

... [C]ritical race theorists exposed the "legal manifestations of white supremacy and the perpetuation of the subordination of people of color." ... Critical race theorists therefore offered scholarship and discourse that "looks to the bottom"—to the experiences of the most oppressed—to contextualize and give meaning to their theory.

Drawing from complex litigation experiences, critical race theorists also embraced W.E.B. Du Bois' concept of "double consciousness," which describes the way in which African Americans held two perspectives at once—the majority perspective (which demonized and despised them) as well as their own....

... For critical race theorists, this duality laid a foundation for understanding oppressed groups' limited but compelling legal and political challenges to existing social arrangements....

Critical race theorists therefore maintain that oppressed groups can have a profound cynicism about law and legal process while acknowledging the historical and social role that rights have played in both liberating (even if imperfectly) and elevating the psyche of subordinated groups. Rather than a mere "false consciousness," critical race scholars contend that marginalized groups possess a "critical consciousness": the subordinated can both "understand subordination and derive means of liberation from it."...

For these reasons, critical race theorists underscore the importance of rights assertion for oppressed peoples and communities of color.... Critical race theorists thus viewed critical legal studies' "rights trashing" as divorced from communities' complex experiences with law and legal process.

... This double consciousness—the simultaneous acknowledgment of the oppressive effect of differential power in the enforcement of law, and the value in rights discourse and legal claims even if they may fail—is, therefore, a source of strength.

As described below, Hawai'i's Puerto Ricans also possessed a critical consciousness: they both comprehended subordination and derived methods of liberation from it. They possessed a deep distrust of law and legal process, stemming from their lived experience on Hawai'i's sugar plantations. At the same time, they saw the important role that the fight for U.S. citizenship—and the rights attendant to that citizenship—played to compel powerful actors and institutions to recognize their humanity and dignity.

Puerto Ricans' Dual Consciousness

Hawai'i's Puerto Ricans were uniquely situated among the racial groups on Hawai'i's sugar plantations. While they experienced oppression in common with other racial communities, they also faced particular hardships because they inhabited an undefined space between citizen and alien. From this vantage point, they grappled with the subordinating effects of law, but they also embraced the American promises of "rights" and "justice." And, as discussed below, the *Sanchez* case provided an opening for Puerto Ricans to compel enforcement of their rights and secure a measure of legal equality. Even after obtaining U.S. citizenship, however, Puerto Ricans knew that freedom from discriminatory treatment would not come easily.

Life on the Sugar Plantation: The Subordinating Effects of Law

Puerto Ricans in Hawai'i learned very early that the white plantation oligarchy wielded inordinate power over Hawai'i's legal, political and economic systems. Five former missionary families-turned-multinational corporations, known as "The Big Five," spun their "web of control" over nearly every facet of life, from banking and shipping to the courts and governmental decision-making. The Hawaii Sugar Planters' Association (HSPA), controlled by the Big Five, exerted considerable direct influence over the growth of agribusiness in the United States, helping to transform agriculture from small farms into multi-national corporate-controlled "big business."

To further Hawai'i's agribusiness trade, plantation owners had to exert control over recalcitrant workers. Working in conjunction with local authorities, sugar planters used vagrancy laws to maintain order on the plantations and to capture and selectively criminalize "deserters." When Puerto Ricans left their assigned plantations because of maltreatment or lack of services, the sugar planters and territorial authorities characterized Puerto Ricans as lazy "vagrants" and began rounding them up for that reason. . . .

Employing the language of rights, Puerto Ricans resisted in ways big and small. In 1904, Puerto Rican laborers sent a petition to the Territorial Governor calling for an investigation into their inhumane treatment on a plantation on the island of Kaua'i. They contended, among other things, that other racial groups' rights were valued, but that they were "unprotected" in their American "home."

... Puerto Ricans were acutely aware of the law's ability to subordinate. They were jailed at a disproportionate rate, offered "nothing more than ... small and poor habitations," and had no representative to "fight[ ] for their rights." At the same time, they refused to wholly abandon the legal system because of its potential to uplift and liberate in certain contexts. For them, the American promise of rights under law was a "guaranty of [their] future." The *Sanchez v. Kalauokalani* case, discussed below, and its affirmation of U.S. citizenship for Hawai'i's Puerto Ricans reflects Puerto Ricans' understanding that even though the law could often be subordinating, it could at times provide small openings toward justice.

Sanchez v. Kalauokalani and U.S. Citizenship: A Transformative View of Law

Indeed, in 1917, Hawai'i's Puerto Ricans turned to the same courts that had historically denied their rights to full participation. In Hawai'i, as elsewhere, their turn to the courts can be explained in part by their desire for the full participatory selfhood that rights elicit; they, like others, while recognizing the sharp limits of the law, embraced a transformative vision of law as a vehicle to validate their place in the U.S. polity. Their fight for U.S. citizenship in *Sanchez v. Kalauokalani* offered that transformative potential.

In April 1917, about one month after the enactment of the Jones Act, Manuel Olivieri Sánchez, a Puerto Rican former plantation laborer-turned-court reporter residing in the Territory of Hawai'i, attempted to register to vote in the local Hawai'i elections. The clerk of the city and county of Honolulu, David Kalauokalani, refused to register Olivieri Sánchez, "claiming that [Sánchez] was not and is not a citizen of the United States and therefore not entitled to register as a voter."

Olivieri Sánchez took the case to court. Represented by a small law office, he filed a petition for writ of mandamus to direct the clerk to place his name on the voting register. At the same time, he rallied other fellow Puerto Ricans to refuse the draft—to which they had recently become eligible as U.S. citizens—if they were not allowed to vote....

In October 1917, the Supreme Court of the Territory of Hawai'i ... unanimously held that Olivieri Sánchez became a U.S. citizen pursuant to the Jones Act even though he had moved to Hawai'i in 1901....

Thus, while often questioning law's efficacy to remedy the "inhuman[e]" treatment on the plantations, Hawai'i's Puerto Ricans "passionately invoke[d] legal doctrine [and] legal ideals" in their quest for U.S. citizenship. Indeed, *Sanchez* represents their fight for formal recognition as members of the U.S. polity—their quest for a sense of definition, a marker of their "participatoriness." At the same time, as discussed below, they pursued their claims knowing that the plantation laws still controlled much of their daily lives and that mere possession of formal U.S. citizenship would not automatically transform their treatment or status in society. They continued to protest laws that governed the territory for that reason.

Sanchez's Aftermath: The Law's Conflicting Capacity Simultaneously to Oppress and Open Paths Toward Liberation

As newly recognized U.S. citizens, Hawai'i's Puerto Ricans obtained the right to vote in Hawai'i elections, but because of their numbers, still held little political clout. They also experienced some economic benefit, such as eligibility for defense industry jobs (particularly at Pearl Harbor) and increased job opportunity and mobility. And for some, U.S. citizenship also contributed to a sense that, notwithstanding the challenges, Hawai'i would become their permanent home.

For many, however, the acquisition of U.S. citizenship changed little about their treatment. In many instances, Puerto Ricans were pitted against other racial groups on the plantations, were targeted by plantation and governmental authorities, and faced discrimination in broader Hawai'i society.

For this reason, as illustrated below, Puerto Ricans in Hawai'i possessed a critical consciousness—they understood oppression and "derive[d] means of liberation from it." In the face of ongoing derogatory treatment, even as U.S. citizens, "[t]heir consciousness . . . of the ultimate legitimacy of their fight" permitted them to hold "unpopular and ultimately transformative opinions with confidence, and to risk retribution from powerful opponents." Through grassroots and media advocacy, they called on authorities to remedy deprivations of their liberty and to extend basic human rights on the plantations, all while acknowledging that they would not easily escape unjust treatment or damaging characterizations as "lawbreakers" and "illiterates." . . .

Thus, rather than rejecting the law and rights assertion as futile, or blindly embracing the law as a cure-all, Hawai'i's Puerto Ricans, like Olivieri Sánchez, embraced a complex "double consciousness" about their experience with law and legal process. As shown by their acts of protest, Puerto Ricans were deeply critical of the ways in which laws were used to benefit the powerful. At the same time, they held an aspirational vision of law as a vehicle to validate their place in the U.S. polity, and fought for and attained U.S. citizenship in *Sanchez*.

They realized, however, that mere legal recognition as U.S. citizens would not mean true equality on the plantation and in society. But they had an "unalterable conviction that something must be done, that action must be taken" within the law and beyond; that they needed to take the fight simultaneously to judges, policymakers, bureaucrats and the general populace. Indeed, they continued to fight for both the rights attendant to citizenship and against continued cultural oppression and unequal treatment, all while acknowledging the law's dual power to oppress and open small paths toward liberation. As critical race theorists recognize, their double consciousness embraced the concept of legal indeterminacy alongside "the core belief in a liberating law that transcends indeterminacy." . . .

Serrano shows why and how systemic advocacy is stronger when advocates engage in the core practices of (1) rooting advocacy in knowledge from the bottom, including history, (2) working in collaboration across disciplinary and identity-group divisions, and (3) drawing on the critical Schools and Approaches to develop and deploy dual consciousness. These three points depend on a critical and self-critical awareness that simultaneously recognizes the potential of law for justice, as well as its systemic complicity in persistent injustice. These points thus depend also on critical histories of "knowledge" (or epistemology) itself, as the concluding section next illustrates.

1.6 SYSTEMIC INJUSTICE IS EPISTEMIC INJUSTICE

Fundamentally, the Schools and Approaches represent intergenerational collective efforts in bottom-up knowledge production to counter the imposition of power from above through and since settler colonialism. For five centuries or more, this top-down process entailed not only physical, material, actual conquest but also cultural, intellectual, and symbolic domination. Experience from below was trivialized or suppressed to privilege interests and perspectives from above—an incremental, long-term process that suppresses native knowledge and enforces European preferences. This material and epistemic process attributed an intrinsic inferiority to people, groups, nations, and cultures targeted for subordination, and helps explain the importance of the Schools and Approaches as a bottom-up response to that violence and its legacies.

To elaborate, indigenous peoples scholar Rebecca Tsosie outlines the relationship between Western and indigenous conceptions and uses of "knowledge" to illustrate how they affect justice. She argues that Western conceptions of "science" are used to displace native understandings of reality in material and symbolic terms. This displacement produces an epistemic kind of injustice that subordinates the viewpoints of those already at the bottom *as part of* their subordination. By looking to the bottom, systemic advocacy flips this framework locally and globally.

INDIGENOUS PEOPLES AND EPISTEMIC INJUSTICE: SCIENCE, ETHICS, AND HUMAN RIGHTS

Rebecca Tsosie
87 Wash. L. Rev. 1133 (2012)

... Native Nations and The Jurisprudence Of "Discovery": Indigenous Peoples and Nineteenth Century Science

... *The Differences Between Western and Indigenous Thought*

... [C]onflicts between Western scientists and indigenous peoples typically arise because indigenous peoples are treated as the "objects" of Western scientific discovery rather than as equal participants in the creation of knowledge or public policy (as a shared endeavor). This is not the fault of science or scientists. It is largely the fault of a public policy discourse that uses terms such as "knowledge" and "benefit" as though they are neutral and fully capable of intercultural exchange. In fact, the terms are often used as political devices to advance or suppress particular interests and values.

The Impact of Nineteenth Century Science Policy upon Indigenous Peoples

... [T]he genesis of American science as a public policy tool in the nineteenth century ... had the most enduring impact on the rights of indigenous peoples in the United States....

The nineteenth century was America's enlightenment era, and the scientific quest for "new knowledge and understanding" was pivotal to the formation of a new nation.... Discovery has remained a dominant theme of scientific inquiry and one that is protected by the United States Constitution, which is the foundation for property rights in technology and innovation. Thus, for indigenous peoples, "discovery" is a theme that has operated continuously within American policy to impair their rights to land and cultural heritage....

The European Doctrine of Discovery only pertained to "civilized nations" that could acquire "title" to newly discovered lands merely by virtue of being the first to "discover" the lands and establish a minimal settlement upon them.

The Doctrine of Discovery may have originated in the international law authorizing European colonialism, but it was ultimately incorporated into domestic law. In the 1823 case *Johnson v. M'Intosh*, Chief Justice John Marshall held that the United States acquired the title by discovery as the successor to Great Britain, and that the Indian Nations had only a "title of occupancy," which could be extinguished by the United States through "purchase or by conquest." At the material level, the Lewis and Clark Expedition [starting in 1803] gave the United States the information it needed to extinguish Native land titles and promote westward expansion by white settlers—the only group entitled to U.S. citizenship at the time....

... Native American peoples inhabiting these lands were involuntarily incorporated into the United States not as citizens, but as "wards" of the federal government.

This "guardian/ward" relationship is a cornerstone of federal Indian law ... [as] represented in the *Cherokee Cases*, which, like *Johnson v. M'Intosh*, are also authored by Chief Justice John Marshall. The *Cherokee Cases* stated that as the "guardian," the United States had the power to coerce Native peoples into accepting the "arts of civilization." ... The United States carefully employed a combined policy of war and peace to coerce the tribes' submission as "dependents" of the United States....

Contemporary Science Policy and the Legacy of the Past

... [T]he political status of Indians as "wards" and their exclusion from U.S. constitutional citizenship (though the 1924 Indian Citizenship Act naturalized Indians to citizenship by virtue of federal law) has complicated the notion of equal citizenship for Native peoples....

Science and Ethics: The Problem of Epistemic Injustice

... *Understanding Epistemic Injustice*

As demonstrated above, many of the conflicts between indigenous peoples and scientists revolve around fundamental differences in their respective systems of thought, particularly as these concern the categories of experience that are relevant to understanding the natural world. These epistemological differences, in turn, heavily influence the formation of public policy and can operate to cause forms of "epistemic injustice" for the affected groups.

... [I]ndigenous peoples have been excluded from full participation in shaping domestic law and public policy....

Testimonial Injustice

... [T]estimonial injustice commonly arises from a dysfunction in a testimonial practice that is related to identity. For example, listeners may evaluate some speakers as more credible due to the speaker's gender, age, class, income, accent, or appearance. Conversely, others will experience a "credibility deficit" due to the same factors.

Many of these practices exist at the level of informal social interaction, but others are formalized into our legal, social or political structures, which leads to "systemic testimonial injustice."...

Courts are unlikely to recognize tribal members as having the same credibility as an "expert witness," although certain tribal cultural practitioners, including tribal historians and traditional healers, may have recognized cultural expertise in specific areas. . . .

In *Tee-Hit-Ton Indians v. United States*, the tribe brought a Fifth Amendment takings claim against the United States in connection with the government's decision to authorize timber harvesting from the tribe's traditional lands in Alaska. . . . The Tee-Hit-Ton Indians maintained that they were the rightful owners of these lands and thus had a property interest in the timber that sustained their takings claim. The Supreme Court disagreed, noting that the testimony offered by the tribal member selected to be the group's expert witness merely proved the tribe's "group" claim to the area in accordance with the tribe's "hunting and fishing stage of civilization." The Court saw this "primitive" form of land use as merely establishing the group's claim to "aboriginal title" on the same level as other Indians but not establishing a true "property interest" within the meaning of the U.S. Constitution. . . .

The Supreme Court's interpretation of the testimony provided by the tribal [expert] witness was based on a shared social experience of "property rights" informed by Western thought, and it had no resonance with the experience of the Native claimants. . . . Not surprisingly, the dominant society's interpretive norms routinely exclude indigenous categories of experience.

Hermeneutical Injustice

. . . [H]ermeneutical injustice is "the injustice of having some significant area of one's social experience obscured from collective understanding" because the group . . . cannot participate on an equal basis in creating a shared meaning for the social experience. . . .

Hermeneutical injustice is what occurs with many Native American claims to protect aspects of their cultural identity from harms that are not recognized standard categories of law. . . .

. . . The Native Village of Kivilina is losing its entire land base as a result of global climate change and sea level rise. Thus far, the Native Village of Kivilina has not prevailed in its attempt to sue several oil companies for the harm of public nuisance. This is because the courts have been unable to find any particular liability given the multiple interactions that are responsible for rising levels of greenhouse gas emissions. Indeed, no cause of action currently exists for the loss of an entire nation . . . [due to] a "natural" phenomenon like flooding, as opposed to military conquest.

[In this case and others,] the harms asserted include cultural and spiritual claims that do not fall within an available category of experience or thought within the Western legal system. However, the harms are felt by indigenous peoples. This is their experience, and it is shared among many different indigenous groups because they possess a different understanding of the world.... In each case, Western science's limited framework is used to justify the exclusion of Native experience for purposes of establishing a legal cause of action.

Structural Forms of Epistemic Injustice Impair Equal Citizenship

Why should American society care about these structural deficiencies within its pluralistic democracy? [Because] the capacity to give knowledge is a fundamental capacity of human beings. When a society treats some groups as incapable of giving knowledge on an equal basis, it treats those groups as less than fully human, an intrinsic harm. Society also hinders the groups' further development by discounting their intellectual abilities, an epistemic harm. As illustrated by the Doctrine of Discovery and its incorporation into U.S. law, American legal and educational institutions have historically treated Western knowledge as a privileged form of knowledge, discounting the ability of indigenous peoples to generate knowledge or convey it in ... public policy discourse. In the process, American society has prevented indigenous peoples from articulating their own social experience, including the harms they have experienced as a result of the dominant society's public policies....

As Tsosie shows, systemic injustice often tracks specific social identities and includes epistemic injustice—the dismissal and suppression of knowledge from below to justify the violence of collectivized injustice from above. This epistemic subordination historically and presently declares bottoms incapable of knowing social realities or contributing to knowledge about them. Rejecting this dehumanizing hierarchy, systemic advocacy relies affirmatively yet critically on knowledge from the bottom to navigate the complexities of systemic injustice.

CHAPTER RECAP

This chapter introduced the Critical Challenge of using law for systemic justice, including how advocates use knowledge from the bottom to ground analysis and action. In addition to personal experience, the Schools and Approaches—and other disciplines, like history—offer relevant, actionable knowledge. This critical and self-critical advocacy depends on actionable insights from all these sources, including "deconstruction" and "dual consciousness"—a critical unpacking of complex problems that appreciates both the potential and the perils of trying to use law for justice.

Chapter 2

Framing the Dimensions and Dynamics of the Critical Challenge

■ ■ ■

Table of Sections

2.1 Reflections and Lessons on the Critical Challenge of Using Law for Equal Justice—Adjudication, Lawyering, and Formal Equality
2.2 Does Formal Legal Equality Deliver Actual Social Change and Progress?
2.3 Legal Indeterminacy Magnifies Complexity and Discretion—Make Them Windows of Opportunity
2.4 Beyond Formal Equality—Identities and Groups, Interests and Power (IGIP)
2.5 Democracy's Role in Making the Critical Challenge Stick—While Hiding Systemic Inequalities in Plain Sight
2.6 Legalized Violence Enforces the Critical Challenge—Militarized Policing, Mass Incarceration, and Crimmigration
2.7 Fighting Back Smartly—Using Amelioration for Transformation
2.8 Chronic Injustice Is Systemic Violence

OPENING THOUGHTS

All we say to America is, "Be true to what you said on paper."

  —**Dr. Martin Luther King Jr.,** Memphis speech the day before he was assassinated

Equality between men and women cannot remain a paper right found only in the constitution.

  —**Adrien Katherine Wing**, Critical Race Feminism and International Human Rights, 28 U. Miami Inter-Am. L. Rev. 337, 358 (1997)

You have to act as if it were possible to radically transform the world. And you have to do it all the time.

  —**Angela Davis**

Dispossession is a name for . . . Europeans' expropriation of land, labor, and resources. Dispossession refers to the outcomes of the relationship between dislocation, destitution, and decimation; that is, removal from territory (death, reservations, boarding schools), appropriation of resources, and subjugation to another (colonial or national) political entity. Not much conceptual work is required to see that these ... terms refer back to one crucial signifier—violence.

> —**Denise Ferreira da Silva**, An Outline of a Global Political Subject: Reading Evo Morales's Election as a (Post-) Colonial Event, 8 Seattle J. Soc. Just 25 (2009)

INTRODUCTION

Persistent social problems seem intractable—poverty, lack of healthcare, inadequate education, violence, tainted food and water, low incomes, harassment, mass incarceration—and the list goes on. Systemic injustice persists when rights, power, resources, and security are distributed unevenly among members of different social groups in systematic ways, ensuring that group-wide social problems rooted in these inequalities continue over long, indefinite periods of time. Systematic thus means by design. Over time, systemic outputs reproduce "social problems" and their identity-based group inequalities, becoming simply "business as usual." These unjust (but made to appear justified) outcomes gradually fade into the background, becoming so normalized that they almost are invisible "officially." Elites use systems to establish hegemonies, but recurrent unjust outcomes are never quite accepted by all groups without objection and resistance. Advocates and activists struggle together to combat systemic injustice, and the Schools and Approaches mentioned in Chapter 1 gather insights from this experience to inform future action.

The Schools and Approaches make clear that law plays a key role in both systemic injustice and struggles against it. After all, law is the system humans designed ostensibly to resolve social problems and to deliver equal justice, *for all*. Equal justice is the solemn promise the legal system makes to produce accountable and principled decision making through democracy and adjudication. Fulfilling this promise is a core source of law's practical utility and moral legitimacy. Advocates, and people in general, expect "Equal Justice under Law" because it is the promise literally etched onto the marble portico of the U.S. Supreme Court and written into other foundational documents. "Establish[ing] Justice" is second among the systemic purposes of law expressed explicitly in the Preamble of the U.S. Constitution:

> We the People of the United States, in Order to form a more perfect Union, establish Justice, insure domestic Tranquility, provide for the common defense, promote the general Welfare, and secure the Blessings of Liberty to ourselves and our Posterity, do ordain and establish this Constitution for the United States of America.

This purpose and promise are foundational to law not only in the United States but in other legal systems, including the system of international law. But unequal justice remains a reality for entire social groups because the commitment to equal justice has been trumped by something else. That something else has been a volatile combination of four elements sketched immediately below and developed throughout the book: identities, groups, interests, and power:

1. By social *identities,* we refer to markers such as gender, race, ethnicity, sexual orientation, and others. Social identities are not natural or immutable but socially constructed to serve interests—usually to elevate those with certain markers and subordinate those who are "different." The traits or experiences associated with individuals who share an identity are not the same for all group members; identities thus are not "essentialist." Identities do not operate in isolation but are multiple and "intersectional" both at the individual and the social levels.

2. Social identities define membership in social *groups.* Social identities are given meaning, organized hierarchically, and used to classify individuals into social groups. For example, cis male and cis female are two of many gender identities; if you are determined by society to be cis male, you are put into the group cis "men." Similarly, identities are used to create social groups identified as women, black, white, old, young, and so on. In this process, "elite" groups are dominant and privileged, receiving identity-based advantages; "other" social groups are subordinated and disadvantaged. Among racialized and gendered elites, some have great wealth and power, while others may have fewer material resources; like bottoms, tops too are intersectional and not essentialist. In addition to identity-based social groups, advocates also work with varied kinds of groups, most notably organized collectives that are actors in social struggles. In systemic advocacy, important groups include many kinds of intentional communities, like congregations, community groups, unions and cooperatives, or any number of advocacy organizations, whether highly organized or relatively inchoate.

3. Because inequalities track broad identity-based social groups in consistent ways, groups have collective *interests.* Group interests may converge or diverge, and can include anything valued by the group, whether tangible or intangible. Some indicators reflecting various potential interests span income, wealth, infant mortality, and educational access, for example. Because these markers vary by social identity, bottoms generally have an interest in change and progress and tops, conversely, have an interest in preserving the status quo that privileges them. Both tops *and* bottoms organize groups to advance their personal and collective interests.

4. *Power* is, in simple terms, the ability to obtain desired outcomes. Power comes and is deployed in varied ways and forms that morph and adapt all the time. Groups aim to build and exercise collective power in all

its forms to achieve specific and general objectives, whether in the short or long term. Ruling elites and their allies use power to win discrete battles from day to day and generation to generation, to build their own power along the way, and to suppress the capacity for organized action by bottom groups. Subordinated groups and their advocates also aim to win discrete amelioration while building bottom-up power for transformative aims.

However, the interactive roles of identities, groups, interests, and power in law are routinely denied, ignored, or cabined because ruling elites aim to convince others that their wins were achieved fairly—in accord with fair rules established by a principled and accountable legal system, not through exercises of unjust privilege or raw power. To fashion and maintain this Critical Challenge, the legal system both establishes the "rules of the game" for democratic and adjudicative decision making *and* creates the justifications that disguise manipulations that favor elites. In this way, patterns of systemic injustice become entrenched, normalized, and inculcated.

As we survey throughout this book, today's entrenched castes result from centuries of top-down manipulation, using these four elements within and as law to produce, enforce, and obscure the Critical Challenge under inspection here. A caste system of group hierarchies "elevates and empowers members of a 'dominant caste' at the perpetual expense of a 'subordinate caste.' "[1] As Black journalist and Pulitzer Prize winner Isabel Wilkerson details the origins, interests, and evolution of U.S. caste:

> The creation of a caste system was a process of testing the bounds of human categories and not the result of a single edict. It was a decades-long sharpening of lines whenever the colonists had a decision to make. When Africans began converting to Christianity, they posed a challenge to religious-based hierarchy [until race superseded it to keep blacks on the bottom]. Their efforts to claim full participation in the colonies was in direct opposition to the European hunger for the cheapest, most pliant labor to extract the most wealth from the New World. . . .
>
> The colonists had been unable to enslave the native population on its own turf and believed themselves to have solved the labor problem with the Africans they imported. With little use for the [indigenous] inhabitants, the colonists began to exile them from their ancestral lands and from the emerging caste system.
>
> This left Africans firmly at the bottom [during and after slavery]. . . .

---

[1] Fatima Bhutto, Caste by Isabel Wilkerson Review—A Dark Study of Violence and Power, The Guardian (July 30, 2020), www.theguardian.com/books/2020/jul/30/caste-the-lies-that-divide-us-by-isabel-wilkerson-review.

> The dominant caste system [later] devised a labyrinth of laws to hold the newly freed people on the bottom rung ever more tightly, while a popular new pseudoscience called eugenics worked to justify the renewed debasement. People on the bottom rung could be beaten or killed with impunity for any breach of the caste system, like not stepping off the sidewalk fast enough [for a white person] or trying to vote. . . .
>
> Thus, each new immigrant—the ancestors of most current-day Americans—walked into a preexisting hierarchy, bipolar in construction, arising from slavery and pitting the extremes in human pigmentation at opposite ends. . . .
>
> To gain acceptance, each fresh infusion of immigrants had to enter into a silent, unspoken pact of separating and distancing themselves from the established lowest caste. Becoming white meant defining themselves as furthest from its opposite—black. They could establish their new status . . . by joining in on violence against [blacks] to prove themselves worthy of admittance to the dominant caste.[2]

England-based Indian journalist Fatima Bhutto adds:

> *Caste* is a dark history of the inexhaustible scope of human violence.
>
> . . . Caste is why Robert E Lee, the Confederate general who went to war against his own country for the right to enslave other humans can be honoured by 230 memorials across the land. It is why Alabama was the last state in the union to throw out its law banning interracial marriage, which it did in 2000, 36 years after the Civil Rights Act ended segregation. And it is why Lyndon B Johnson, who signed that act into law, was the last Democrat ever to win the presidency with the majority of the white electorate.[3]

As these excerpts indicate, in the United States (and other places or systems), castes are group hierarchies characterized by their deep rootedness in supremacist ideologies that grip both law and society—that permeate life both as culture and as force. Caste systems aim for complete, absolute, totalizing top-down domination and bottom-up obedience. This

---

[2] Isabel Wilkerson, Caste: The Origin of Our Discontents ch. 4 (2020). Throughout this book we emphasize that bottom-up struggle rooted in bottom-up knowledge and leadership is the foundation of resistance to systems of caste, including U.S. and other colonial identity castes. For a critique of Wilkerson's framing of caste and her top-down approach to its dismantling see Charisse Burden-Stelly, Caste Does Not Explain Race, Bost. Rev. (Dec. 15, 2020), http://boston review.net/race/charisse-burden-stelly-caste-does-not-explain-race (contesting Wilkerson's view that perception and attitudes among elites sustain structural inequality and relying on Oliver Cromwell Cox, Caste, Class, and Race: A Study in Social Dynamics (1948), who documented how the U.S. racial order is rooted instead in political economy and, as top-down material exploitation, can be dismantled only from the bottom).

[3] Bhutto, Caste.

elite aspiration amounts to, as we see and explain further below, a hegemony—that is, an unquestioned and unquestionable status quo that (at least some of) the bottoms willingly and earnestly support, thus participating in the perpetuation of their own (and others') subordination, both personally and collectively.

But systemic injustice has never been accepted by majorities in groups most affected by it. Consequently, resistance and social struggle are hallmarks of modern societies. Just as systemic injustice and social problems are ongoing, so are resistance and struggle against it. Law inevitably plays a pivotal role in this ongoing contestation. Against this backdrop, what we call Critical Justice is gauged by lived social realities, not simply by the "glittering generalities"[4] of legal doctrine and procedure as words on paper. In accordance with basic principles of systemic analysis we review below in Part II, Critical Justice extends beyond the symbolic attainments of rights and encompasses materiality—equality judged by actual outcomes at both the micro (individualized) and macro (group-wide and systemic) levels of human relations.

In this chapter, we survey the Critical Challenge of using law for equal justice, faced today by countless advocates worldwide in all kinds of settings established historically by law. We use a commonly-known example of law understood as (much-delayed) justice: the 1954 and 1955 unanimous U.S. Supreme Court opinions in *Brown v. Board of Education,* which reversed decades of rulings declaring that "separate but equal" facilities in education and elsewhere satisfied the legal promise of equality for all. In known fact, the segregated facilities were manifestly not "equal" although they were brutally kept separate. Until 1954, generations of judges (and advocates) propagated, upheld, and enforced the fictions that this segregationist judicial doctrine obscured. Politicians—policymakers— did the same. Law, both as doctrine and as legislation, mandated widespread group-based inequalities tied to social identities and interests while proclaiming the opposite.

This status quo is known as formal equality because it is characterized by lofty formal declarations of equality with contrary social and economic facts on the ground. By committing itself to its twin ideals of accountable democracy and principled adjudication, law as a system presents itself formally as a tool for impartial justice in "public" (democracy) and "private" (adjudication) disputes. But, by making group inequalities seem normal, inevitable, and even deserved, law also is, in practice, a tool for legalizing collectivized injustice—systems of caste that trump the rule of law itself. Today's resulting status quo *is* the Critical Challenge for systemic advocates, both in the United States and elsewhere.

---

[4] *Rice v. Cayetano,* 528 U.S. 495, 527 (2000) (J. Stevens dissent).

2.1 REFLECTIONS AND LESSONS ON THE CRITICAL CHALLENGE OF USING LAW FOR EQUAL JUSTICE—ADJUDICATION, LAWYERING, AND FORMAL EQUALITY

Most U.S. students are exposed to *Brown v. Board of Education*, the case declaring separate but ostensibly equal public schools inherently unequal and therefore unconstitutional because they stigmatize the group subordinated by the segregation. The NAACP Legal Defense and Educational Fund calls *Brown* "the most celebrated victory in its storied history."[5] It easily makes the list of what *USA Today* in 2015 called the 21 most famous Supreme Court decisions,[6] joining many "famous" cases we will consider in this text—some "infamous" such as *Dred Scott*, *Plessy*, and *Korematsu*, and others celebrated as victories against identity-based subordination, such as *Roe v. Wade* and *Obergefell v. Hodges*. As we see throughout history, the legacies of each remains contested.

But, back in the 1950s, *Brown* prompted the *Washington Post* to conflate the abstract "equality of opportunity" of this judicial outcome on paper with the lived facts on the ground for groups at the bottom by proclaiming: "Now, at last, the equality of opportunity which is a fundamental premise of the American society is to become a fact in regard to education—which is, after all, the key to opportunity."[7] Did that aspirational prediction come to pass? We begin with the Court's 1954 unanimous opinion.

BROWN V. BOARD OF EDUCATION
347 U.S. 483 (1954)

MR. CHIEF JUSTICE WARREN delivered the opinion of the Court.

These cases come to us from the States of Kansas, South Carolina, Virginia, and Delaware. They are premised on different facts and different local conditions, but a common legal question justifies their consideration together in this consolidated opinion.

In each of the cases, minors of the Negro race, through their legal representatives, seek the aid of the courts in obtaining admission to the public schools of their community on a nonsegregated basis. In each instance, they have been denied admission to schools attended by white children under laws requiring or permitting segregation according to race.

---

[5] www.naacpldf.org/case/brown-v-board-education.

[6] www.usatoday.com/story/news/politics/2015/06/26/supreme-court-cases-history/29185891/.

[7] Equal Education For All, Wash. Post (May 19, 1954), www.washingtonpost.com/news/post-nation/wp/2014/05/16/how-the-washington-post-covered-brown-v-board-of-education-in-1954/?noredirect=on&utm_term=.898f7dc7976a.

This segregation was alleged to deprive the plaintiffs of the equal protection of the laws under the Fourteenth Amendment. In each of the cases other than the Delaware case, a three-judge federal district court denied relief to the plaintiffs on the so-called "separate but equal" doctrine announced by this Court in *Plessy v. Ferguson*, 163 U.S. 537 [1896]. Under that doctrine, equality of treatment is accorded when the races are provided substantially equal facilities, even though these facilities be separate. In the Delaware case, the Supreme Court of Delaware adhered to that doctrine, but ordered that the plaintiffs be admitted to the white schools because of their superiority to the Negro schools.

The plaintiffs contend that segregated public schools are not "equal" and cannot be made "equal," and that hence they are deprived of the equal protection of the laws.... Reargument was largely devoted to the circumstances surrounding the adoption of the Fourteenth Amendment in 1868. It covered exhaustively consideration of the Amendment in Congress, ratification by the states, then existing practices in racial segregation, and the views of proponents and opponents of the Amendment. This discussion and our own investigation convince us that, although these sources cast some light, it is not enough to resolve the problem with which we are faced. At best, they are inconclusive. The most avid proponents of the post-War Amendments undoubtedly intended them to remove all legal distinctions among "all persons born or naturalized in the United States." Their opponents, just as certainly, were antagonistic to both the letter and the spirit of the Amendments and wished them to have the most limited effect. What others in Congress and the state legislatures had in mind cannot be determined with any degree of certainty.

... [Here] there are findings below that the Negro and white schools involved have been equalized, or are being equalized, with respect to buildings, curricula, qualifications and salaries of teachers, and other "tangible" factors. Our decision, therefore, cannot turn on merely a comparison of these tangible factors in the Negro and white schools involved in each of the cases. We must look instead to the effect of segregation itself on public education.

... In approaching this problem, we cannot turn the clock back to 1868 when the Amendment was adopted, or even to 1896 when *Plessy v. Ferguson* was written. We must consider public education in the light of its full development and its present place in American life throughout the Nation. Only in this way can it be determined if segregation in public schools deprives these plaintiffs of the equal protection of the laws.

Today, education is perhaps the most important function of state and local governments. Compulsory school attendance laws and the great expenditures for education both demonstrate our recognition of the importance of education to our democratic society. It is required in the performance of our most basic public responsibilities, even service in the armed forces. It is the very foundation of good citizenship. Today it is a principal instrument in awakening the child to cultural values, in preparing him for later professional training, and in helping him to adjust normally to his environment. In these days, it is doubtful that any child may reasonably be expected to succeed in life if he is denied the opportunity of an education. Such an opportunity, where the state has undertaken to provide it, is a right which must be made available to all on equal terms.

We come then to the question presented: Does segregation of children in public schools solely on the basis of race, even though the physical facilities and other "tangible" factors may be equal, deprive the children of the minority group of equal educational opportunities? We believe that it does.

. . . To separate [children] from others of similar age and qualifications solely because of their race generates a feeling of inferiority as to their status in the community that may affect their hearts and minds in a way unlikely ever to be undone. The effect of this separation on their educational opportunities was well stated by a finding in the Kansas case by a court which nevertheless felt compelled to rule against the Negro plaintiffs:

> Segregation of white and colored children in public schools has a detrimental effect upon the colored children. The impact is greater when it has the sanction of the law; for the policy of separating the races is usually interpreted as denoting the inferiority of the negro group. A sense of inferiority affects the motivation of a child to learn. Segregation with the sanction of law, therefore, has a tendency to (retard) the educational and mental development of Negro children and to deprive them of some of the benefits they would receive in a racial(ly) integrated school system.

Whatever may have been the extent of psychological knowledge at the time of *Plessy v. Ferguson*, this finding is amply supported by modern authority. Any language in *Plessy v. Ferguson* contrary to this finding is rejected.

We conclude that in the field of public education the doctrine of "separate but equal" has no place. Separate educational facilities are inherently unequal. Therefore, we hold that the plaintiffs and others similarly situated for whom the actions have been brought are, by reason of the segregation complained of, deprived of the equal protection of the laws guaranteed by the Fourteenth Amendment. . . .

Addressing segregation in Kansas schools, the Supreme Court ruling in *Brown* also encompassed similar cases in Delaware, South Carolina, and Virginia. Although the Kansas litigation had determined that teachers, buildings, and other aspects of the separate Black schools were equal to those for whites, lower courts in the other three states ruled the Black schools in fact were inferior to the white schools. This background helps explain why the Court in *Brown* focused on racial separation—common to all the cases before the Court—rather than the equality of the schools in terms of teachers, infrastructure, funding, and curriculum. All nine Supreme Court justices acknowledge in the opinion the symbolic as well as material aspects of group-wide inequalities to conclude that either, alone, is insufficient: equal justice requires the combination of symbolic and material equality. The disjunction between the symbolic *and* the material that "separate but equal" upheld was set aside unequivocally. Yet, somehow, the new legal regime of *Brown*—formal equality—nonetheless replicated the disjunction between symbolic and material equality. How?

One reason, as we see next below, is sheer systemic complexity. Another is the power of top-down obstruction, which generates ever-more baroque complexities in conceptual and material ways. After centuries of de jure discrimination conferring privilege and advantage on white residents, legalized inequality was deeply embedded everywhere. Group-wide inequalities were entrenched nationally as well as locally. The legalized supremacy of the white identity groups was a matter of consistent systemic enforcement and fierce local politics. Deferring to systemic complexity and local flexibility, the Supreme Court a year after *Brown I* issued the following opinion (*Brown II*) concerning its implementation.

BROWN V. BOARD OF EDUCATION (II)
349 U.S. 294 (1955)

MR. CHIEF JUSTICE WARREN delivered the opinion of the Court.

... The opinions of [May 17, 1954], declaring the fundamental principle that racial discrimination in public education is unconstitutional, are incorporated herein by reference.... There remains for consideration the manner in which relief is to be accorded....

Full implementation of these constitutional principles may require solution of varied local school problems. School authorities have the primary responsibility for elucidating, assessing, and solving these problems; courts will have to consider whether the action of school authorities constitutes good faith implementation of the governing constitutional principles. Because of their proximity to local conditions and the possible need for further hearings, the courts which originally heard these cases can best perform this judicial appraisal. Accordingly, we believe it appropriate to remand the cases to those courts.

In fashioning and effectuating the decrees, the courts will be guided by equitable principles. Traditionally, equity has been characterized by a practical flexibility in shaping its remedies and by a facility for adjusting and reconciling public and private needs. These cases call for the exercise of these traditional attributes of equity power. At stake is the personal interest of the plaintiffs in admission to public schools as soon as practicable on a nondiscriminatory basis.... To effectuate this interest may call for elimination of a variety of obstacles in making the transition to school systems operated in accordance with the constitutional principles set forth in our May 17, 1954, decision. Courts of equity may properly take into account the public interest in the elimination of such obstacles in a systematic and effective manner....

While giving weight to these public and private considerations, the courts will require that the defendants make a prompt and reasonable start toward full compliance with our May 17, 1954, ruling. Once such a start has been made, the courts may find that additional time is necessary to carry out the ruling in an effective manner. The burden rests upon the defendants to establish that such time is necessary in the public interest and is consistent with good faith compliance at the earliest practicable date.... [T]he cases are remanded to the District Courts to take such proceedings and enter such orders and decrees consistent with this opinion as are necessary and proper to admit to public schools on a racially nondiscriminatory basis with all deliberate speed the parties to these cases....

To handle the complex task of dismantling white supremacy in both symbolic and material terms, the Supreme Court invoked the inherent equity powers of courts to fashion effective remedies as needed by local circumstances. But this complex task would also take time. It had taken much time to entrench and normalize race-based supremacy as being consistent with equal justice, and it would take time to disentangle supremacy from equality. It would take time, to use the Court's language, to manage the complexities needed for "elimination" of racist symbolic *and* material injustice in public education. In effect, *Brown* handed the solution back to the wrongdoers for its implementation; however well intentioned, the unanimous Court placed the fox back in the henhouse, where it stayed for the years to come.

Identities and groups—and their interests and power—have played a key role in this U.S. story of race and legalized injustice. To illustrate, constitutional law scholar Erwin Chemerinsky provides an account of *Brown's* aftermath, and how judicial "sabotage" helps perpetuate the Critical Challenge. The decades since *Brown* testify to the power of elites and kindred groups accustomed to controlling law and dominating society, as well as to the commitment of subordinated groups to personal struggles for collective equality.

THE SEGREGATION AND RESEGREGATION OF AMERICAN PUBLIC EDUCATION: THE COURTS' ROLE

Erwin Chemerinsky
81 N.C. L. Rev. 1597 (2003)

Schools in the South and throughout the country are resegregating. Why is this occurring, and why were desegregation efforts limited in their success? This Essay argues that the Supreme Court is largely to blame. In a series of decisions in the 1970s, the Court ensured separate and unequal schools by preventing interdistrict remedies, refusing to find that inequities in school funding are unconstitutional, and making it difficult to prove a constitutional violation in northern de facto segregated school systems. In a series of decisions in the 1990s, the Court ordered an end to effective desegregation orders. Lower federal courts have followed these rulings and, in many areas, have ended remedies despite the likelihood that resegregation will follow. As *Brown v. Board of Education* nears its fiftieth anniversary, American public schools are increasingly separate and unequal. The institution that provided the impetus for desegregation and offered so much hope—the courts—is responsible for this failure.

Introduction

A half century of efforts to end school desegregation have largely failed. Gary Orfield's powerful recent study, Schools More Separate: Consequences of a Decade of Resegregation, carefully documents that, during the 1990s, America's public schools have become substantially more segregated. . . .

. . . From 1964 to 1988, there was significant progress. . . . But since 1988, the percentage of African-American students attending majority white schools has declined. . . .

Quite significantly, Professor Orfield's study shows that the same pattern of resegregation is true for Latino students. The historic focus for desegregation efforts has been to integrate African-American and white students. The burgeoning Latino population requires that desegregation focus on this racial minority too. The percentage of Latino students attending schools where the majority of students are of minority races, or almost exclusively of minority races, increased steadily over the 1990s. Professor Orfield notes that "[Latinos] have been more segregated than blacks now for a number of years, not only by race and ethnicity but also by poverty."

The simple and tragic reality is that American schools are separate and unequal. As Professor Orfield documents, to a very large degree, education in the United States is racially segregated. By any measure, predominately minority schools are not equal in their resources or their quality. Wealthy suburban school districts are almost exclusively white; poor inner city schools are often exclusively comprised of African-American and Hispanic students. The year 2004 will be the fiftieth anniversary of *Brown v. Board of Education*, and American schools will mark that occasion with increasing racial segregation and gross inequality.

There are many causes for the failure of school desegregation. None of the recent Presidents—neither Reagan, nor either Bush, nor even Clinton—have done anything to advance desegregation. None have used the powerful resources of the federal government, including the dependence of every school district on federal funds, to further desegregation. "Benign neglect" would be a charitable way of describing the attitude of recent Presidents to the problem of segregated and unequal education; the issue has been neglected, but there has been nothing benign about this neglect. A serious social problem that affects millions of children has simply been ignored.

Nor has the federal government, or for that matter have state or local governments, acted to solve the problem of housing segregation. In a country deeply committed to the ideal of the neighborhood school, residential segregation often produces school segregation. But decades have passed since the enactment of the last law to deal with housing discrimination, and efforts to enhance residential integration seem to have vanished.

There is not a simple explanation for the alarming trend toward resegregation. In this Essay, I argue that the courts must share the blame; courts could have done much more to bring about desegregation, and instead, the judiciary has created substantial obstacles to remedying the legacy of racial segregation in schools. . . .

Desegregation will not occur without judicial action; desegregation lacks sufficient national and local political support for elected officials to remedy the problem. Specifically, African Americans and Latinos lack adequate political power to achieve desegregation through the political process. This relative political powerlessness was true when *Brown* was decided and remains true today. The courts are indispensable to effective desegregation, and over the last thirty years the courts, especially the Supreme Court, have failed. . . .

. . . The judiciary's failure lies in its actions, not in inherent limits to its power. Had the Supreme Court decided key cases differently, the nature of public education today would be very different. Although there are many causes for segregated schools, the overarching explanation for the Court's rulings is simple: Justices appointed by Republican presidents have undermined desegregation. Four Justices appointed by President Richard Nixon are largely to blame for the decisions of the 1970s; the cases were 5–4 decisions, with those four Justices helping to make up the majority. Five Justices appointed by Presidents Ronald Reagan and George H.W. Bush are responsible for the decisions of the 1990s that have contributed substantially to resegregation of schools. The resegregation of schools is largely a result of the Court's decisions, not of the inherent limits in the judicial process....

The Decisions of the 1970s: The Supreme Court Contributes to the Resegregation of American Public Education

The 1970s were a particularly critical time in the battle to desegregate American schools. From *Plessy v. Ferguson* in 1896 until Brown in 1954, government-mandated segregation existed in every southern state and many northern states.... After *Brown*, southern states used every imaginable technique to obstruct desegregation. Some school systems attempted to close public schools rather than desegregate. Some school boards adopted so-called "freedom of choice" plans which allowed students to choose the school where they would enroll and resulted in continued segregation. In some places, school systems outright disobeyed desegregation orders. The phrase "massive resistance" appropriately describes what occurred during the decade after Brown.

... For a decade after *Brown*, the Court largely stayed out of the desegregation effort. It was not until 1964 that the Court lamented that "[t]here has been entirely too much deliberation and not enough speed" in achieving desegregation.

Too few scholars have focused their attention on whether the Court could have done more in the decade after *Brown* to hasten desegregation. The conventional wisdom seems to be that the resistance was so great and the techniques of obstruction so varied as to require years of conquering opposition to achieve desegregation. While this view is worthy of merit, it may be too generous to the Supreme Court....

Had the Court dictated timetables, outlined remedies, and been more actively involved from 1954 to 1964, results might well have been different, at least in some places.

By the 1970s, as described above, the nation finally saw substantial progress towards desegregation. But ... crucial problems emerged [in response to that progress]: white flight to suburbs threatened school integration efforts ... and pervasive inequalities existed in funding, especially between city and suburban schools. The Court's handling of these issues was critical in achieving desegregation. In each instance, the Court, with four Nixon appointees in the majority, ruled against the civil rights plaintiffs and dramatically limited the effectiveness of efforts at desegregation and equal educational opportunity.

White Flight

By the 1970s, a crucial problem had emerged: white flight to suburban areas. White flight came about, in part, to avoid school desegregation and, in part, as a result of a larger demographic phenomenon, namely endangered successful desegregation. White families moved to suburban areas to avoid being part of desegregation orders affecting cities. In virtually every urban area, the inner city was increasingly comprised of racial minorities. By contrast, the surrounding suburbs were almost exclusively white and what little minority population did reside in suburbs was concentrated in towns that were almost exclusively African-American. School district lines parallel town borders, meaning that racial separation of cities and suburbs results in segregated school systems. . . .

Thus, by the 1970s, effective school desegregation required interdistrict remedies. . . . As Professor Smedley explains:

> Regardless of the cause, the result of this movement [of whites to suburban areas] is that the remaining city public school population becomes predominately black. When this process has occurred, no amount of attendance zone revision, pairing and clustering of schools, and busing of students within the city school district could achieve substantially integrated student bodies in the schools, because there simply are not enough white students left in the city system.

. . . In 1974, the Supreme Court started to take a different turn in its jurisprudence of granting broad powers to federal courts in desegregation cases. In *Milliken v. Bradley*, the Court imposed a substantial limit on the courts' remedial powers in desegregation cases. *Milliken* involved the Detroit-area schools and the reality that, like so many areas of the country, Detroit was a mostly African-American city surrounded by predominately white suburbs. A federal district court imposed a multi-district remedy to end de jure segregation in one of the districts. The Supreme Court ruled that this desegregation technique is impermissible:

> Before the boundaries of separate and autonomous school districts may be set aside by consolidating the separate units for remedial purposes or by imposing a cross-district remedy, it must first be shown that there has been a constitutional violation within one district that produces a significant segregative effect in another district.

Thus, the Court concluded that "without an interdistrict violation and interdistrict effect, there is no constitutional wrong calling for an interdistrict remedy."

Milliken has a devastating effect on the ability to achieve desegregation in many areas. In a number of major cities, inner-city school systems are substantially African-American and are surrounded by almost all-white suburbs. Desegregation requires the ability to transfer students between the city and suburban schools. There simply are not enough white students in the city, or enough African-American students in the suburbs, to achieve desegregation without an interdistrict remedy. Yet, *Milliken* precludes an interdistrict remedy unless plaintiffs offer proof of an interdistrict violation. In other words, a multidistrict remedy can only be formulated for those districts whose own policies fostered discrimination or if a state law caused the interdistrict segregation. Otherwise, the remedy can include only those districts found to violate the Constitution. While such proof is often unavailable, plaintiffs in relatively rare cases have met *Milliken's* requirements.

. . . The segregated pattern in major metropolitan areas—African Americans in the city and whites in the suburbs—did not occur by accident, but rather was the product of myriad government policies. Moreover, *Milliken* has the effect of encouraging white flight. Whites who wish to avoid desegregation can do so by moving to the suburbs. If *Milliken* had been decided differently, one of the incentives for such moves would be eliminated. The reality is that in many areas the *Milliken* holding makes desegregation impossible. . . .

Inequality in School Funding

By the 1970s, substantial disparities existed in school funding. In 1972, education expert Christopher Jencks estimated that, on average, the government spent 15% to 20% more on each white student's education than on each African-American child's schooling. This disparity existed throughout the country. For example, the Chicago public schools spent $5,265 for each student's education; but the Niles school system, just north of the city, spent $9,371 on each student's schooling. The disparity also corresponded to race: in Chicago, 45.4% of the students were white and 39.1% were African-American; in Niles Township, the schools were 91.6% white and 0.4% African-American. . . . There is a simple explanation for the disparities in school funding. In most states, education is substantially funded by local property taxes. Wealthier suburbs have significantly larger tax bases than poor inner cities. The result is that suburbs can tax at a lower rate and still have a great deal to spend on education. Cities must tax at a higher rate and nonetheless have less to spend on education.

The Court had the opportunity to remedy this inequality in education in *San Antonio Independent School District v. Rodriguez*. The Court, however, profoundly failed and concluded that the inequalities in funding did not deny equal protection. *Rodriguez* involved a challenge to the Texas system of funding public schools largely through local property taxes. Texas's financing system meant that poor areas had to tax at a high rate, but had little to spend on education; wealthier areas could tax at low rates, but still had much more to spend on education. One poorer district, for example, spent $356 per pupil, while a wealthier district spent $594 per student.

The plaintiffs challenged this system on two grounds: it violated equal protection as impermissible wealth discrimination and it denied children in the poorer districts the fundamental right to education. The Court rejected the former argument by holding that poverty is not a suspect classification and thus discrimination against the poor need meet only rational basis review. The Court explained that where wealth is involved, the Equal Protection Clause does not require absolute equality or precisely equal advantages. In thoroughly viewing the Texas system for funding schools, the Court determined that the system met the rational basis test.

Moreover, the Court rejected the claim that education is a fundamental right:

> It is not the province of this Court to create substantive constitutional rights in the name of guaranteeing equal protection of the laws. Thus, the key to discovering whether education is "fundamental" is not to be found in comparisons of the relative societal significance of education as opposed to subsistence or housing. Nor is it to be found by weighing whether education is as important as the right to travel. Rather, the answer lies in assessing whether there is a right to education explicitly or implicitly guaranteed by the Constitution.

Justice Powell, writing for the majority, then concluded that "[e]ducation, of course, is not among the rights afforded explicit protection under our Federal Constitution. Nor do we find any basis for saying it is implicitly so protected." ... The Court also noted that the Texas government did not completely deny an education to students; the challenge was to inequities in funding. In concluding, the Court found that strict scrutiny was inappropriate because neither discrimination based on a suspect classification nor infringement of a fundamental right occurred. The Court found that the Texas system for funding schools met the rational basis test.

... Education is essential for the exercise of constitutional rights, for economic opportunity, and, ultimately, for achieving equality. Chief Justice Warren eloquently expressed this view in *Brown*:

> ... In these days, it is doubtful that any child may reasonably be expected to succeed in life if he is denied the opportunity of an education.

... Education is so basic to the exercise of other constitutional rights, and so basic for success in society, that the Court should have found a fundamental right to a quality education.

The combined effect of *Milliken* and *Rodriguez* cannot be overstated. *Milliken* helped to ensure racially separate schools and *Rodriguez* ensured that the schools would be unequal. American public education is characterized by wealthy white suburban schools spending a great deal on education surrounding much poorer African-American city schools that spend much less on education.

Why Have Courts Failed?

... Desegregation likely would have been more successful, and resegregation less likely to occur, if the Supreme Court had made different choices.

... What, then, explains the Court's choices? The answer is obvious: its decisions result from the conservative ideology of the majority of the Justices who sat on the Court when these cases were decided. *Milliken* and *Rodriguez* were both 5–4 decisions, and the majority included the four Nixon appointees who joined the Court in the few years before those rulings. . . .

The cause for the judicial failure could not be clearer: conservative Justices have effectively sabotaged desegregation. . . .

Conclusion

... The Supreme Court seems intent on declaring victory over the problem of school segregation and withdrawing the judiciary from solving the problem. But as Professor Orfield demonstrates, the problem has gotten worse, not better. The years ahead look even bleaker as courts end successful desegregation orders.

People can devise rationalizations to make this desegregation failure seem acceptable: that courts could not really succeed; that desegregation does not matter; that parents of minority students do not really care about desegregation. But none of these rationalizations are true. *Brown v. Board of Education* stated the truth: separate schools can never be equal. Tragically today, America has schools that are increasingly separate and unequal.

Chemerinsky tracks how top-down reaction and opposition to equal justice coopted *Brown* as law and progress within a few decades. Continued inequality in education is, in great measure, the deliberate consequence of "opinions" by successive generations of elite judges—virtually all of them white men. The "cause for the judicial failure could not be clearer: conservative Justices have effectively sabotaged desegregation." This sabotage is a collective act carried out by decision makers over decades—generations—of time.

Below, Derrick Bell grounds analysis of *Brown's* consequences in the lives of those most affected by segregation, desegregation, and resegregation. Bell was a founder of critical race theory—a key School of knowledge informing systemic advocacy—and worked as a lawyer on cases implementing *Brown*. Here, he reflects on uses of litigation to "win" desegregation victories, asking self-critically whether those "victories" solved the persistent social problem of unequal education from the point of view of the relevant bottom—the NAACP's actual clients (parents and communities). Concluding they did not, he sharply questions the role of lawyers and lawyering, asking which master, or interests, those civil rights advocates were serving in fact.

Those masters included the lawyers' own well-intentioned ideals that prioritized symbolic subordination and sidetracked client priorities on material remedies—prioritizing formal equality over material equality. Bell shows how lawyers—not just judges—can be part of the problem that sustains the Critical Challenge. This retrospective testimonial on advocates, advocacy, progress, and justice raises serious, complicated questions about client-attorney relationships, and underscores the importance of critical and self-critical reflection in principled and accountable advocacy. Notably, Bell's suggestion that civil rights lawyers may have elevated their own ideals above the interests of their clients led, in time, to today's "client-centered" approach in U.S. legal clinics and law schools. From your current perspective, what might systemic advocates learn—or unlearn—about law, equal justice, and advocacy from Bell's account today—nearly half a century later?

SERVING TWO MASTERS: INTEGRATION IDEALS AND CLIENT INTERESTS IN SCHOOL DESEGREGATION LITIGATION

Derrick A. Bell, Jr.
85 Yale L.J. 470 (1976)

In the name of equity, we ... seek dramatic improvement in the quality of the education available to our children. Any steps to achieve desegregation must be reviewed in light of the black community's interest in improved pupil performance as the primary characteristic of educational equity. We define educational equity as the absence of discriminatory pupil placement and improved performance for all children who have been the objects of discrimination. We think it neither necessary, nor proper to endure the dislocations of desegregation without reasonable assurances that our children will instructionally profit.

—Coalition of black community groups in Boston

... How should the term "client" be defined in school desegregation cases that are litigated for decades, determine critically important constitutional rights for thousands of minority children, and usually involve major restructuring of a public school system? How should civil rights attorneys represent the often diverse interests of clients and class in school suits? Do they owe any special obligation to class members who emphasize educational quality and who probably cannot obtain counsel to advocate their divergent views? Do the political, organizational, and even philosophical complexities of school desegregation litigation justify a higher standard of professional responsibility on the part of civil rights lawyers to their clients, or more diligent oversight of the lawyer-client relationship by the bench and bar? . . .

Civil rights lawyers[,] . . . [h]aving achieved so much by courageous persistence, . . . have not wavered in their determination to implement *Brown* using racial balance measures developed in the hard-fought legal battles of [previous] decades. This stance involves great risk for clients whose educational interests may no longer accord with the integration ideals of their attorneys. . . .

School Litigation: A Behind-the-Scenes View

The Strategy

Although *Brown* was not a test case with a result determined in advance, the legal decisions that undermined and finally swept away the "separate but equal" doctrine of *Plessy v. Ferguson* were far from fortuitous. Their genesis can be found in the volumes of reported cases stretching back to the mid-19th century, cases in which every conceivable aspect of segregated schools was challenged. By the early 1930's, the NAACP, with the support of a foundation grant, had organized a concerted program of legal attacks on racial segregation. . . . According to the NAACP Annual Report for 1934, "the campaign [was] a carefully planned one to secure decisions, rulings and public opinion on the broad principle instead of being devoted to merely miscellaneous cases." These strategies were intended to eliminate racial segregation, not merely in the public schools, but throughout the society. The public schools were chosen because they presented a far more compelling symbol of the evils of segregation and a far more vulnerable target than segregated railroad cars, restaurants, or restrooms. . . .

Thurgood Marshall . . . became Director-Counsel of the NAACP Legal Defense and Educational Fund (LDF) when it became a separate entity in 1939. Jack Greenberg, who succeeded Marshall in 1961, recalled that the legal program "built precedent," treating each case in a context of jurisprudential development rather than as an isolated private lawsuit. Of course, it was not possible to plan the program with precision: "How and when plaintiffs sought relief and the often unpredictable course of litigation were frequently as influential as any blueprint in determining the sequence of cases, the precise issues they posed, and their outcome." But as lawyer-publisher Loren Miller observed of *Brown* and the four other school cases decided with it, "There was more to this carefully stage-managed selection of cases for review than meets the naked eye."

In 1955, the Supreme Court rejected the NAACP request for a general order requiring desegregation in all school districts, issued the famous "all deliberate speed" mandate, and returned the matter to the district courts. It quickly became apparent that most school districts would not comply with *Brown* voluntarily. Rather, they retained counsel and determined to resist compliance as long as possible.

By the late 1950's, the realization by black parents and local branches of the NAACP that litigation would be required, together with the snail's pace at which most of the school cases progressed, brought about a steady growth in the size of school desegregation dockets. Because of their limited resources, the NAACP and LDF adopted the following general pattern for initiating school suits. A local attorney would respond to the request of a NAACP branch to address its members concerning their rights under the *Brown* decision. Those interested in joining a suit as named plaintiffs would sign retainers authorizing the local attorney and members of the NAACP staff to represent them in a school desegregation class action. Subsequently, depending on the facts of the case and the availability of counsel to prepare the papers, a suit would be filed. In most instances, the actual complaint was drafted or at least approved by a member of the national legal staff. With few exceptions, local attorneys were not considered expert in school desegregation litigation and served mainly as a liaison between the national staff lawyers and the local community.

Named plaintiffs, of course, retained the right to drop out of the case at any time. They did not seek to exercise "control" over the litigation, and during the early years there was no reason for them to do so. Suits were filed, school boards resisted the suits, and civil rights attorneys tried to overcome the resistance. Obtaining compliance with *Brown* as soon as possible was the goal of both clients and attorneys. But in most cases, that goal would not be realized before the named plaintiffs had graduated or left the school system.

The civil rights lawyers would not settle for anything less than a desegregated system. While the situation did not arise in the early years, it was generally made clear to potential plaintiffs that the NAACP was not interested in settling the litigation in return for school board promises to provide better segregated schools. . . .

The Theory

The rights vindicated in school litigation literally did not exist prior to 1954. Despite hundreds of judicial opinions, these rights have yet to be clearly defined. This is not surprising. Desegregation efforts aimed at lunchrooms, beaches, transportation, and other public facilities were designed merely to gain access to those facilities. Any actual racial "mixing" has been essentially fortuitous; it was hardly part of the rights protected (to eat, travel, or swim on a nonracial basis). The strategy of school desegregation is much different. The actual presence of white children is said to be essential to the right in both its philosophical and pragmatic dimensions. In essence the arguments are that blacks must gain access to white schools because "equal educational opportunity" means integrated schools, and because only school integration will make certain that black children will receive the same education as white children. This theory of school desegregation, however, fails to encompass the complexity of achieving equal educational opportunity for children to whom it so long has been denied.

The NAACP and the LDF, responsible for virtually all school desegregation suits, usually seek to establish a racial population at each school that (within a range of 10 to 15 percent) reflects the percentage of whites and blacks in the district. But in a growing number of the largest urban districts, the school system is predominantly black. The resistance of most white parents to sending their children to a predominantly black school and the accessibility of a suburban residence or a private school to all but the poorest renders implementation of such plans extremely difficult. . . . All too little attention has been given to making black schools educationally effective. . . .

The basic civil rights position that *Brown* requires maximum feasible desegregation has been accepted by the courts and successfully implemented in smaller school districts throughout the country. The major resistance to further progress has occurred in the large urban areas of both South and North where racially isolated neighborhoods make school integration impossible without major commitments to the transportation of students, often over long distances. The use of the school bus is not a new phenomenon in American education, but the transportation of students over long distances to schools where their parents do not believe they will receive a good education has predictably created strong opposition in white and even black communities. . . .

Lawyer-Client Conflicts: Sources and Rationale

Civil Rights Rigidity Surveyed

Having convinced themselves that *Brown* stands for desegregation and not education, the established civil rights organizations steadfastly refuse to recognize reverses in the school desegregation campaign—reverses which, to some extent, have been precipitated by their rigidity. . . .

The Boston Case

The Boston school litigation provides an instructive example of what, I fear, is a widespread situation. Early in 1975, . . . black representatives [of Boston's black community groups] were ambivalent about the busing plans. They did not wish to back away after years of effort to desegregate Boston's schools, but they wished to place greater emphasis on upgrading the schools' educational quality, to maintain existing assignments at schools which were already integrated, and to minimize busing to the poorest and most violent white districts. . . .

At the meeting I attended, black representatives hoped to convince the lawyers to incorporate their educational priorities into the plaintiffs' Phase II desegregation plan. The lawyers assigned to the Boston case by the NAACP listened respectfully to the views of the black community group, but made clear that a long line of court decisions would limit the degree to which those educational priorities could be incorporated into the desegregation plan the lawyers were preparing to file.... [Ultimately the judge] adopted several provisions designed to improve the quality of the notoriously poor Boston schools. But as in ... Atlanta ... these provisions were more the product of judicial initiative than of civil rights advocacy....

The Atlanta Case

... [T]he most open confrontation between NAACP views of school integration and those of local blacks who favored plans oriented toward improving educational quality occurred in Atlanta. There, a group of plaintiffs became discouraged by the difficulty of achieving meaningful desegregation in a district which had gone from 32 percent black in 1952 to 82 percent black in 1974. Lawyers for the local NAACP branch, who had gained control of the litigation, worked out a compromise plan with the Atlanta School Board that called for full faculty and employee desegregation but for only limited pupil desegregation. In exchange, the school board promised to hire a number of blacks in top administrative positions, including a black superintendent of schools.

The federal court approved the plan. The court's approval was apparently influenced by petitions favoring the plan's adoption signed by several thousand members of the plaintiffs' class. Nevertheless the national NAACP office and LDF lawyers were horrified by the compromise....

... NAACP opposition to the Atlanta Compromise Plan was not deterred by the fact that local leaders, including black school board members, supported the settlement. Defending the Compromise Plan, Dr. Benjamin E. Mays, one of the most respected black educators in the country, stated:

> We have never argued that the Atlanta Compromise Plan is the best plan, nor have we encouraged any other school system to adopt it. This plan is the most viable plan for Atlanta—a city school system that is 82 percent Black and 18 percent white and is continuing to lose whites each year to five counties that are more than 90 percent white.

... Alternatives to the Rigidity of Racial Balance

Dr. May's thoughtful statement belies the claim that *Brown* can be implemented only by the immediate racial balancing of school populations. But civil rights groups refuse to recognize what courts in Boston ... and

Atlanta have now made obvious: where racial balance is not feasible because of population concentrations, political boundaries, or even educational considerations, there is adequate legal precedent for court-ordered remedies that emphasize educational improvement rather than racial balance.

The plans adopted in these cases were formulated without the support and often over the objection of the NAACP and other civil rights groups. They are intended to upgrade educational quality, and like racial balance, they may have that effect. But neither the NAACP nor the court-fashioned remedies are sufficiently directed at the real evil of pre *Brown* public schools: the state-supported subordination of blacks in every aspect of the educational process. Racial separation is only the most obvious manifestation of this subordination. Providing unequal and inadequate school resources and excluding black parents from meaningful participation in school policymaking are at least as damaging to black children as enforced separation.

... [R]emedies that fail to attack all policies of racial subordination almost guarantee that the basic evil of segregated schools will survive and flourish, even in those systems where racially balanced schools can be achieved. Low academic performance and large numbers of disciplinary and expulsion cases are only two of the predictable outcomes in integrated schools where the racial subordination of blacks is reasserted in, if anything, a more damaging form.

... Much more effective remedies for racial subordination in the schools could be obtained if the creative energies of the civil rights litigation groups could be brought into line with the needs and desires of their clients....

The Resolution of Lawyer-Client Conflicts

... It is essential that lawyers "lawyer" and not attempt to lead clients and class. Commitment renders restraint more, not less, difficult, and the inability of black clients to pay handsome fees for legal services can cause their lawyers, unconsciously perhaps, to adopt an attitude of "we know what's best" in determining legal strategy. Unfortunately, clients are all too willing to turn everything over to the lawyers. In school cases, perhaps more than in any other civil rights field, the attorney must be more than a litigator. The willingness to innovate, organize, and negotiate—and the ability to perform each with skill and persistence—are of crucial importance. In this process of overall representation, the apparent—and sometimes real—conflicts of interest between lawyer and client can be resolved....

... Lacking more viable alternatives, the black community has turned to the courts. After several decades of frustration, the legal system, for a number of complex reasons, responded. Law and lawyers have received perhaps too much credit for that response. The quest for symbolic manifestations of new rights and the search for new legal theories have too often failed to prompt an assessment of the economic and political condition that so influence the progress and outcome of any social reform improvement.

In school desegregation blacks have a just cause, but that cause can be undermined as well as furthered by litigation. A test case can be an important means of calling attention to perceived injustice; more important, school litigation presents opportunities for improving the weak economic and political position which renders the black community vulnerable to the specific injustices the litigation is intended to correct. Litigation can and should serve lawyer and client as a community-organizing tool, an educational forum, a means of obtaining data, a method of exercising political leverage, and a rallying point for public support.

But even when directed by the most resourceful attorneys, civil rights litigation remains an unpredictable vehicle for gaining benefits, such as quality schooling, which a great many whites do not enjoy. The risks involved in such efforts increase dramatically when civil rights attorneys, for idealistic or other reasons, fail to consider continually the limits imposed by the social and political circumstances under which clients must function even if the case is won. . . .

. . . For reasons quite similar to those which enabled blacks to win in *Brown* in 1954 and caused them to lose in *Plessy* in 1896, even successful school litigation will bring little meaningful change unless there is continuing pressure for implementation from the black community. The problem of unjust laws, as Professor Gary Bellow has noted, is almost invariably a problem of distribution of political and economic power. The rules merely reflect a series of choices by the society made in response to these distributions. " '[R]ule' change, without a political base to support it, just doesn't produce any substantial result because rules are not self executing: they require an enforcement mechanism."

In the last analysis, blacks must provide an enforcement mechanism that will give educational content to the constitutional right recognized in *Brown*. Simply placing black children in "white" schools will seldom suffice. Lawyers in school cases who fail to obtain judicial relief that reasonably promises to improve the education of black children serve poorly both their clients and their cause. . . .

In 1935, W. E. B. DuBois [wrote]:

[T]he Negro needs neither segregated schools nor mixed schools. What he needs is Education. What he must remember is that there is no magic, either in mixed schools or in segregated schools. . . .

DuBois spoke neither for the integrationist nor the separatist, but for poor black parents unable to choose, as can the well-to-do of both races, which schools will educate their children. Effective representation of these parents and their children presents a still unmet challenge for all lawyers committed to civil rights.

Conclusion

The tactics that worked for civil rights lawyers in the first decade of school desegregation—the careful selection and filing of class action suits seeking standardized relief in accordance with set, uncompromising national goals—are no longer unfailingly effective. In recent years, the relief sought and obtained in these suits has helped to precipitate a rise in militant white opposition and has seriously eroded carefully cultivated judicial support. Opposition to any civil rights program can be expected, but the hoped-for improvement in schooling for black children that might have justified the sacrifice and risk has proven minimal at best. It has been virtually nonexistent for the great mass of urban black children locked in all-black schools, many of which are today as separate and unequal as they were before 1954.

Political, economic, and social conditions have contributed to the loss of school desegregation momentum; but to the extent that civil rights lawyers have not recognized the shift of black parental priorities, they have sacrificed opportunities to negotiate with school boards and petition courts for the judicially enforceable educational improvements which all parents seek. . . .

Chemerinsky's account focused on the ways in which one set of actors—judges—are willfully complicit in the persistence of caste systems privileging an identity group or groups over others. Bell's reflection questions the effectiveness of a different set of actors—civil rights lawyers. Specifically, Bell explores how lawyerly neglect of parent groups as clients and of their individual interests as an intergenerational collective, can undermine civil rights progress. Both reflections question the effectiveness and accountability of lawyers, judges, and other legal decision makers to individual and organizational clients. Do these reflections affect your understanding of *Brown* as a "successful" example of advocacy for equal justice? Why and how—or why not?

NOTES AND QUESTIONS

1. *Identities, Groups, Interests, and Power (IGIP).* How did identities, groups, interests, and power appear in Bell's school desegregation reflection? For example, what were the interests of the relevant parent/child groups before the *Brown* desegregation decision? Did the outcome of *Brown* change those

interests? In light of these interests, do you see *Brown* as shifting power away from the dominant group? If not, did it at least ameliorate the suffering of the disadvantaged social group? As a lawyer, how would you discern your client's interests? What if those interests fail to connect to recognized legal theories and remedies?

2. *More Sabotage?* Decided four years after Chemerinsky's reflection, the Court in *Parents Involved in Community Schools v. Seattle School District No. 1*, 551 U.S. 701 (2007) refused to uphold a Seattle school district policy meant to help ensure that longstanding neighborhood segregation was not fully replicated in the local schools. A group of five justices appointed to the Court by Presidents Ronald Reagan, George H.W. Bush, and George W. Bush joined to find the policy unconstitutional. Does this outcome bolster Chemerinsky's conclusions? How about Bell's conclusions?

3. *Class and/or Race?* In the wake of the *Seattle* litigation, schools seeking integration shifted their models to ones based on class rather than race to avoid strict scrutiny. For example, schools in Jefferson County, Kentucky, adopted voluntary neighborhood-level plans to assign children to achieve diversity in schools, taking into account socioeconomic factors like family income and educational attainment. Is this shift to class a "better" remedy for systemic racism in public education? Why, or why not?

4. *All Deliberate Speed?* In reviewing the post-*Brown* legacy of resegregation, one commentator referred to the "arsenal of tools" that white communities deployed to resist the mandate of *Brown*.[8] Elites, as we have seen and noted, rely on a variety of tools, including control of the legal system itself, to maintain racial and other hierarchies of privilege and subordination. Systemic advocates have discovered that some of these elite tools and techniques can be appropriated and deployed in the struggle for transformative social change. Can you think of any based on your readings and reflections thus far?

2.2 DOES FORMAL LEGAL EQUALITY DELIVER ACTUAL SOCIAL CHANGE AND PROGRESS?

Legal reform and social progress are not one and the same—just as law and justice are not one and the same. Experience teaches that even well-seeming legal reforms might fail to redress systemic injustice, and sometimes actually entrench it further. Formal equality in the post-*Brown* era is an apt example.

To explain further, critical race scholar Kimberlé Crenshaw connects the dots leading up to the resegregation of public schooling that Chemerinsky noted and revisits the continuity of group-wide systemic subordination that Bell documented above. These dots include the complex—important yet insufficient—role of formal legal "rights" as

---

[8] Christopher Petrella, The Resegregation of America (Dec. 3, 2017), www.nbcnews.com/think/opinion/resegregation-america-ncna801446.

remedies in struggles for equal justice that include material and symbolic aspects of subordination. What lessons does Crenshaw add to Chemerinsky's and Bell's?

RACE, REFORM, AND RETRENCHMENT: TRANSFORMATION AND LEGITIMATION IN ANTIDISCRIMINATION LAW

Kimberlé Williams Crenshaw
101 Harv. L. Rev. 1331 (1988)

. . . The Role of Race Consciousness in a System of Formal Equality

Prior to the civil rights reforms, Blacks were formally subordinated by the state. Blacks experienced being the "other" in two aspects of oppression, which I shall designate as symbolic and material. Symbolic subordination refers to the formal denial of social and political equality to all Blacks, regardless of their accomplishments. Segregation and other forms of social exclusion—separate restrooms, drinking fountains, entrances, parks, cemeteries, and dining facilities—reinforced a racist ideology that Blacks were simply inferior to whites and were therefore not included in the vision of America as a community of equals.

Material subordination, on the other hand, refers to the ways that discrimination and exclusion economically subordinated Blacks to whites and subordinated the life chances of Blacks to those of whites on almost every level. This subordination occurs when Blacks are paid less for the same work, when segregation limits access to decent housing, and where poverty, anxiety, poor health care, and crime create a life expectancy for Blacks that is five to six years shorter than for whites.

Symbolic subordination often created material disadvantage by reinforcing race consciousness in everything from employment to education. In fact, the two are generally not thought of separately: separate facilities were usually inferior facilities, and limited job categorization virtually always brought lower pay and harder work. Despite the pervasiveness of racism, however, there existed even before the civil rights movement a class of Blacks who were educationally, economically, and professionally equal—if not superior—to many whites, and yet these Blacks suffered social and political exclusion as well.

It is also significant that not all separation resulted in inferior institutions. School segregation—although often presented as the epitome of symbolic and material subordination—did not always result in inferior education. It is not separation *per se* that made segregation subordinating, but the fact that it was enforced and supported by state power, and accompanied by the explicit belief in African-American inferiority.

The response to the civil rights movement was the removal of most formal barriers and symbolic manifestations of subordination. . . . These legal reforms and the formal extension of "citizenship" were large achievements precisely because much of what characterized Black oppression was symbolic and formal.

Yet the attainment of formal equality is not the end of the story. Racial hierarchy cannot be cured by the move to facial race-neutrality in the laws that structure the economic, political, and social lives of Black people. White race consciousness, in a new form but still virulent, plays an important, perhaps crucial, role in the new regime that has legitimated the deteriorating day-to-day material conditions of the majority of Blacks.

The end of Jim Crow has been accompanied by the demise of an explicit ideology of white supremacy. The white norm, however, has not disappeared; it has only been submerged in popular consciousness. It continues in an unspoken form as a statement of the positive social norm, legitimating the continuing domination of those who do not meet it. Nor have the negative stereotypes associated with Blacks been eradicated. The rationalizations once used to legitimate Black subordination based on a belief in racial inferiority have now been reemployed to legitimate the domination of Blacks through reference to an assumed cultural inferiority.

... White race consciousness, which includes the modern belief in cultural inferiority, acts to further Black subordination by justifying all the forms of unofficial racial discrimination, injury, and neglect that flourish in a society that is only formally dedicated to equality. In more subtle ways, moreover, white race consciousness reinforces and is reinforced by the myth of equal opportunity that explains and justifies broader class hierarchies.

Race consciousness also reinforces whites' sense that American society is really meritocratic and thus helps prevent them from questioning the basic legitimacy of the free market. Believing both that Blacks are inferior and that the economy impartially rewards the superior over the inferior, whites see that most Blacks are indeed worse off than whites are, which reinforces their sense that the market is operating "fairly and impartially;" those who should logically be on the bottom are on the bottom. This strengthening of whites' belief in the system in turn reinforces their beliefs that Blacks are *indeed* inferior. After all, equal opportunity *is* the rule, and the market *is* an impartial judge; if Blacks are on the bottom, it must reflect their relative inferiority. Racist ideology thus operates in conjunction with the class components of legal ideology to reinforce the status quo, both in terms of class and race.

... Like legal consciousness, race consciousness makes it difficult—at least for whites—to imagine the world differently....

Rights Discourse as a Challenge to the Oppositional Dynamic

... Casting racial issues in the moral and legal rights rhetoric of the prevailing ideology helped create the political controversy without which the state's coercive function would not have been enlisted to aid Blacks.

... Blacks gained by using a powerful combination of direct action, mass protest, and individual acts of resistance, along with appeals to public opinion and the court couched in the language of the prevailing legal consciousness. The result was a series of ideological and political crises. In these crises, civil rights activists and lawyers induced the federal government to aid Blacks and triggered efforts to legitimate and reinforce the authority of the law in ways that benefited Blacks. Simply insisting that Blacks be integrated or speaking in the language of "needs" would have endangered the lives of those who were already taking risks—and with no reasonable chance of success. President Eisenhower, for example, would not have sent federal troops to Little Rock simply at the behest of protesters demanding that Black schoolchildren receive an equal education. Instead, the successful manipulation of legal rhetoric led to a crisis of federal power that ultimately benefited Blacks.

... In the context of white supremacy, engaging in rights discourse should be seen as an act of self-defense. This was particularly true because the state could not assume a position of neutrality regarding Black people once the movement had mobilized people to challenge the system of oppression: either the coercive mechanism of the state had to be used to support white supremacy, or it had to be used to dismantle it. We know now, with hindsight, that it did both.

... The eradication of barriers has created a new dilemma for those victims of racial oppression who are not in a position to benefit from the move to formal equality. The race neutrality of the legal system creates the illusion that racism is no longer the primary factor responsible for the condition of the Black underclass; instead, as we have seen, class disparities appear to be the consequence of individual and group merit within a supposed system of equal opportunity. Moreover, the fact that there are Blacks who are economically successful gives credence both to the assertion that opportunities exist, and to the backlash attitude that Blacks have "gotten too far." Psychologically, for Blacks who have not made it, the lack of an explanation for their underclass status may result in self-blame and other self-destructive attitudes.

Another consequence of the formal reforms may be the loss of collectivity among Blacks. The removal of formal barriers created new opportunities for some Blacks that were not shared by various other classes of African-Americans. As Blacks moved into different spheres, the experience of being Black in America became fragmented and multifaceted, and the different contexts presented opportunities to experience racism in different ways. The social, economic, and even residential distance between the various classes may complicate efforts to unite behind issues as a racial group. Although "White Only" signs may have been crude and debilitating, they at least presented a readily discernible target around which to organize. Now, the targets are obscure and diffuse, and this difference may create doubt among some Blacks whether there is enough similarity between their life experiences and those of other Blacks to warrant collective political action.

Formal equality significantly transformed the Black experience in America. With society's embrace of formal equality came the eradication of symbolic domination and the suppression of white supremacy as the norm of society. Future generations of Black Americans would no longer be explicitly regarded as America's second-class citizens. Yet the transformation of the oppositional dynamic—achieved through the suppression of racial norms and stereotypes, and the recasting of racial inferiority into assumptions of cultural inferiority—creates several difficulties for the civil rights constituency. The removal of formal barriers, although symbolically significant to all and materially significant to some, will do little to alter the hierarchical relationship between Blacks and whites until the way in which white race consciousness perpetuates norms that legitimate Black subordination is revealed. This is not to say that white norms alone account for the conditions of the Black underclass. It is instead an acknowledgment that, until the distinct racial nature of class ideology is itself revealed and debunked, nothing can be done about the underlying structural problems that account for the disparities. The narrow focus of racial exclusion—that is, the belief that racial exclusion is illegitimate only where the "White Only" signs are explicit—coupled with strong assumptions about equal opportunity, makes it difficult to move the discussion of racism beyond the societal self-satisfaction engendered by the appearance of neutral norms and formal inclusion.

Crenshaw's account of retrenchment under formal equality makes clear that systemic justice depends on actual social change measurable in material metrics of progress. Formal legal reforms and formal declarations of formal rights play a complex role: rights allow subordinated groups to assert individual and collective claims for their enforcement, but formal rights also enable elites to argue that the systemic problem is solved even though few material improvements actually have taken place. In this latter scenario, rights are both part of the solution and part of the problem—a mirage (and substitute) for progress rather than a platform for it. Using a dual consciousness of law's double edges, systemic advocacy emphasizes material change on the ground as a key measure of Critical Justice.

NOTES AND QUESTIONS

1. *The Power of Judicial Opinions.* Perhaps the most acclaimed Supreme Court opinion did not produce change in its specific context—segregated public schools—much less improve the lived material realities of Black students, their parents, and communities. If so, what does this say about the power of judicial decisions? Having seen how a seemingly transformative judicial opinion can be undercut by subsequent decisions, as an advocate what might you do differently now?

2. *Unlearning and Relearning.* Do you remember first learning about *Brown v. Board of Education*? At which stage(s) of your education? How did those discussions of *Brown* differ from the critical insights on the case and its legacy presented above? What do these self-critical accounts of *Brown* beckon you to unlearn and relearn today about law as a system, and about justice as its aim?

3. *The Salience of History and Time.* In our study of *Brown*, we have seen two elements in the background—the passage of time and the salience of history—that help expose the Critical Challenge advocates face. The passage of time can help entrench a problem and suppress the odds of progress later. But systemic advocates learn to use time as a resource. Reflecting more than 50 years after the *Brown* decision, legal scholar Michéle Alexandre notes the importance of looking back while thinking and acting ahead to improve systemic advocacy:

> Lessons and deconstruction of twentieth century civil rights laws deepen understanding of the contributions of this prior movement. For example, the famed scholar, Derrick Bell, ... [showed that], sometimes, the desire to achieve integration might have caused attorneys to evaluate proposed integration models inadequately, instead of making quality education for the plaintiffs the sole priority. Indubitably, it is easier 50 years after *Brown* to see the danger of an exclusive focus on integration. At the time, the emergency and the dire conditions of segregation often blurred the lines. As a result, Bell's observation or discussion of the twentieth century's shortcomings should not be viewed as an indictment of the civil rights attorneys then. Instead, Bell simply reminds us all with these words of the importance of critical analysis in every stage of a movement. Critical evaluation is crucial to tweaking and improving models inherited from prior generations. . . . How should we fulfill the promise inherited from twentieth century civil rights activists and scholars? To fully grapple with these issues, one must engage constantly with the foundational doctrines and structure of civil rights jurisprudence. . . .
>
> For example, our discrimination laws ... are based on harm done to others based on race, sex, religion, etc. While these protections provide a good starting point ... [h]ow much more powerful would it be if, instead of more routine single cause and identity movements, more models designed to serve multiple

intersecting interests were crafted? What effects could that coalition building and merging of interests have on civil rights movements' lasting success?[9]

This passage puts on display how critical scholars and activists learn from critical reflection on ongoing experience, producing new theories from past experience to plan future actions in endless cycles of contestation—a theme that will recur throughout this book. This process takes time, and uses time, to absorb the lessons of time—the lessons of history and struggle. Take note also of Alexandre's concluding queries, which point to another set of recurrent themes, including the indispensability of collaborations and coalitions for bottom-up progress toward Critical Justice. What does Alexandre add to, or change about, your understanding of systemic injustice and advocacy in light of Chemerinsky, Bell, and Crenshaw?

2.3 LEGAL INDETERMINACY MAGNIFIES COMPLEXITY AND DISCRETION—MAKE THEM WINDOWS OF OPPORTUNITY

We know the world and its systems are complex. Partly for this reason, law is indeterminate—uncertain. Therefore, judges can justify a multitude of outcomes—even when they or other legal actors deny that they are exercising any discretion. In practice, indeterminacy and complexity are systemically interrelated: law is inherently indeterminate because legal rules cannot anticipate and account for every possible set of facts. Top-down uses of complexity can and do compound inequality, but bottom-up advocacy also can and should exploit indeterminacy. Often, it is in these spaces of uncertainty or indeterminacy that compelling, innovative advocacy can make a systemic difference.

Below, legal scholar and philosopher George Martinez reviews court decisions on access to education for another group, Mexican-Americans. He finds that courts over decades repeatedly used their discretion in the face of indeterminacy to resist integration and limit more far-reaching interpretations of *Brown*. The following excerpt urges advocates to identify and fill spaces of indeterminacy with rigorous arguments rooted in critical knowledge that can pierce through normalized, top-down complexities.

---

[9] Michéle Alexandre, The New Frontiers of Civil Rights Litigation xxv–xxviii (2019).

Legal Indeterminacy, Judicial Discretion and the Mexican-American Litigation Experience: 1930–1980

George A. Martinez
27 U.C. Davis L. Rev. 555 (1994)

Introduction

... Traditional legal theory has recognized that legal doctrine is sometimes indeterminate in that it does not always dictate results.... [P]ragmatists, critical legal scholars, and others have argued that law is indeterminate in the sense that legal materials—statutes and court decisions—often permit a judge to justify multiple outcomes to lawsuits.

In light of this open texture in the law, legal theorists have argued that judicial decisions are often not logically compelled and are instead the result of conscious or unconscious discretionary policy choices[,] ... [which] is important for two principal reasons. At one level, exposing the exercise of judicial discretion is significant because it helps reveal the extent to which the courts have helped or failed to help establish the rights of Mexican-Americans. At another level, exposing false necessity in judicial decision-making by explaining how the decision might have gone another way—i.e., offering a counterstory—is important because it may help break down barriers to racial reform.... [P]roviding judges with counterstories or alternative perspectives on civil rights issues is one way to help them overcome the "unthinking conviction that their way of seeing the world is the only one—that the way things are is inevitable, natural, just, and best." By acknowledging their limited perspective, judges can avoid serious moral error and promote justice in civil rights cases....

Litigation to Desegregate Public Schools, 1930–1969

Segregation Not Authorized by Statute

In this era, all courts took the position, for various reasons, that segregation of Mexican-Americans in public schools was permissible. The cases indicate that this position was not inevitable. One of the key areas of legal indeterminacy in these early cases centers on the question whether segregation of Mexican-Americans was permissible where it was not authorized by statute....

The first case to litigate this issue appears to be *Independent School District v. Salvatierra*. The city of Del Rio, Texas operated a "Mexican" elementary school, that the city used exclusively for teaching children of Mexican descent. No Texas statute expressly authorized the segregation of Mexican-Americans. Mexican-Americans sought to enjoin this segregation. The Texas Court of Civil Appeals held that the school authorities could not arbitrarily segregate Mexican-American children solely because of ethnic background. The court, however, ruled that Del Rio was not arbitrarily segregating these Mexican-American children. The court found that the reasons the district gave for segregating the children—linguistic difficulties and starting school late because of migrant farm working—were sound if impartially applied to all children alike.

... Because only Mexican-Americans were segregated for linguistic difficulties and migrant farm-working patterns, the court might have found that, in effect, such segregation was race-based and therefore illegal. Alternatively, the court might have followed the reasoning of courts in other jurisdictions which had held that, in the absence of express legislation, segregation was illegal. As no legislation expressly authorized the specific segregation at issue in *Salvatierra*, the court could have held that segregation—even for linguistic or migrant farm worker reasons—was illegal. ...

Brown v. Board of Education

The first case to be decided on the merits after *Brown* was *Hernandez v. Driscoll Consolidated Independent School District*. Mexican-Americans claimed that the defendant school district violated their constitutional rights by maintaining separate classrooms for children of Mexican descent in the first and second grades and by requiring a majority of the children to spend three years in the first grade before promotion to the second grade. Following *Salvatierra*. . ., the court held that segregation of Mexican-Americans was permissible so long as the classification was not arbitrary. Specifically, the court held that language handicaps could justify segregation into separate classrooms, but only after a credible examination of each child by the appropriate school official. The district had failed to administer language tests, thus the court determined that the segregation constituted arbitrary and unreasonable race discrimination.

The decision could have gone another way. First, the court might have read *Brown* to prohibit the segregation of Mexican-American children even for language difficulties.... Second, there was expert testimony that the best way to address the language difficulties was to group all children together regardless of their language ability. The court, nonetheless, chose to permit linguistic problems to justify segregation. It took this position despite clear evidence that school officials used the linguistic rationale as a pretext for segregating Mexican-Americans from Anglos. If the district was truly concerned about the language difficulties of its Mexican-American students, it would have administered language tests to assess the students' levels of English proficiency. Most telling, however, is the district's refusal to admit a Mexican student to the Anglo school even though she spoke no Spanish. . . .

Litigation to Desegregate Public Schools, 1970–1980: Legal Indeterminacy and De Facto Versus De Jure Segregation

In the 1970's Mexican-Americans again took to the courts attempting to fulfill the promise of *Brown* by putting an end to the segregation of

Mexican-American children.... From 1970–1980, courts found a new way to uphold the segregation of Mexican-Americans. In many cases, courts took the position that the Federal Constitution prohibited only de jure (intentionally caused) segregation as opposed to de facto segregation....

... The courts in this generation rejected [earlier] "benign" reasons for segregation, but developed a more sophisticated doctrine to permit segregation: the de jure/de facto distinction. Thus, most courts took the position that de facto segregation of Mexican-Americans did not violate the Federal Constitution. The cases indicate that the decision to prohibit only de jure segregation was not logically compelled [and therefore a product of indeterminacy]....

Bilingual Education

... Mexican-Americans have brought lawsuits under Title VI of the 1964 Civil Rights Act in order to compel school authorities to provide bilingual/bicultural education. In this area as well, Mexican-Americans felt the effect of legal indeterminacy—in particular, indeterminacy resulting from the manipulation of precedent to generate conflicting results....

The Mexican-American's struggle for bilingual and bicultural education began on a promising note.... However, other courts so severely limited [an earlier opinion] that Mexican-Americans would not be able to compel a school district to provide them with bilingual/bicultural education so long as the district had taken some steps to remedy language difficulties. Thus, Mexican-Americans sustained a significant defeat in this area.

Summary and an Alternative Vision

... [In sum,] most courts exercised their discretion to permit the segregation of Mexican-Americans for "benign" reasons—e.g., linguistic difficulties—or because the segregation was "merely" de facto. Finally, with respect to bilingual education, courts generally exercised discretion to limit access to bilingual and bicultural education.

... [E]xposing the lack of inevitability in civil rights decision-making may help break down barriers to racial reform ... such as the majoritarian mindset. Richard Delgado has described this mindset as "the bundle of presuppositions, received wisdom, and shared understandings against a background of which legal decision-making takes place."

The view that judicial decision-making is highly influenced by the perspective and preconceptions of the judge, and that the perspective of the dominant group may present a barrier to racial reform, finds substantial support in the recent revival of pragmatism in legal philosophy. Pragmatists treat "thinking as contextual and situated." Thinking is "always embodied in practices—habits and patterns of perceiving and conceiving." ... [But] the dominant perspective or mindset makes current social and legal arrangements seem fair and natural. Bringing this mindset to the bench, judges may commit moral error in civil rights cases because narrow habits of perceiving lead them to believe that the way things are is inevitable or just.

One way to help judges break down mindset, broaden their perspectives, and promote justice in civil rights cases, is to provide counterstories—i.e., explain how decisions were not inevitable. Through this process judges can "overcome ethnocentrism and the unthinking conviction that their way of seeing the world is the only one—that the way things are is inevitable, natural, just, and best" ... [S]ome pragmatists have urged judges to try to grasp the world from the perspective of the dominated or the oppressed. As Martha Minow has explained, the effort to take the perspective of another may help us see that our perspective is limited and that the status quo is not inevitable or fair. This article has sought, in part, to break down narrow habits of perceiving that stand in the way of racial reform, by offering alternative perspectives or counterstories that explain how decisions were not inevitable. . . .

Martinez emphasizes that complexity and indeterminacy are double-edged. Just as elites can exploit them to their benefit, so can subordinated groups and their advocates. Expanding our earlier note about narrative as critical method, Martinez calls for advocacy based on "counterstories that explain how [those] decisions were not inevitable."

NOTES AND QUESTIONS

1. *Dominant Stories and Bottom-Up Counterstories.* Counterstorytelling is a mechanism for psychic preservation and challenging the normative reality imposed by elites by listening to those affected. Using counterstories helps advocates diagnose causes of social problems and strategize about their solutions. Consider, for example, dominant narratives advanced about the role of Teach for America (TFA). TFA is an organization established ostensibly to address educational inequality. On its website, TFA describes itself as "a diverse network of leaders who confront educational inequity by teaching for at least two years and then working with unwavering commitment from every sector of society to create a nation free from this injustice."[10] Counterstories emerged that question the TFA narrative about its effectiveness in advancing equity, with one describing the TFA narrative as creating "cognitive dissonance" and disguising realities experienced by the "corps members":

> Many of TFA's narratives about both students and teachers emphasize the singular power of hard work to overcome injustice—a

---

[10] Working toward Equity and Excellence for All, What We Do, Teach for America, www.teachforamerica.org/what-we-do.

simple equation founded on principles of meritocracy and idealism. . . .

> . . . One of the central limits of [the TFA narrative of] idealism is that it treats structural inequity as a result of individual failure that can be wholly overcome by individual heroic effort. Idealism decontextualizes educational inequity from its relationship to historical and present power structures; this narrative presents the euphemized problem of "the achievement gap" without questioning how this gap was created[,] . . . [which] encourages blaming students for their disenfranchisement or scapegoating structural inequity on individual educators.[11]

What is your reaction?

2.4 BEYOND FORMAL EQUALITY—IDENTITIES AND GROUPS, INTERESTS AND POWER (IGIP)

Above, Derrick Bell questioned the decision of advocates to prioritize integration over pursuing equality of all public schools, segregated or not. Four years later, in a follow-up reflection on *Brown's* lessons, Bell also questioned the timing of its decision to reject de jure segregation. The issue, after all, had been programmatically litigated by NAACP and other advocates since at least the 1930s, with no similar breakthrough. Why did nine white, male elite judges unanimously choose to change positions in 1954? Below, Bell suggests the explanation might be, in part, an "interest convergence" during the Cold War between those at the top and those at the bottom of the U.S. racial caste system. During that time, Communist nations transmitted worldwide the vivid images of (white) U.S. policemen beating, clubbing, and water-hosing (nonwhite) demonstrators demanding civil rights. These images allowed Communist powers to argue with increasing success to the "non-aligned" leaders and populations of Africa, Asia, South America, the Middle East, and elsewhere that they could expect little from the United States in the way of dignity, equality, and justice. In that tricky foreign relations context, the interests of white elites in the U.S. North in charge of national affairs differed—collectively—from those of Southern-based white elites and working whites generally. At that historical moment in the aftermath of World War II, both white national elites and Black local communities became similarly interested in ending de jure racial discrimination: for the white elites, this step would remove a key argument from the Communist arsenal, while for local Black communities this step would give them a formal symbolic right to assert for further material progress. However, this convergence was temporary— a historical anomaly. Enforcement was not a high-profile point; after all,

---

[11] Sarah Matsui, Learning from Counternarratives in Teach for America: Moving from Idealism Towards Hope 3–17 (2015). See also Teach for America Counter-Narratives: Alumni Speak Up and Speak Out (T. Jameson Brewer and Kathleen deMarrais ed. 2015).

everyone acknowledged progress would take time. By the 1970s, "détente" waned the Cold War, and elite interests began shifting back to historical patterns. *Brown's* fate is but one example of the complexities, or dilemmas, that inhere in the construction of interests. As you read, note how interests can be personal and collective, tangible and intangible, "real" and (only) perceived—susceptible to shifts and realignments, both intentional and not. Observe that interests (and power), in addition to or instead of principles, can account for social and legal change.

BROWN V. BOARD OF EDUCATION AND THE INTEREST-CONVERGENCE DILEMMA

Derrick A. Bell, Jr.
93 Harv. L. Rev. 518 (1980)

... [I]t is necessary to remember that the issue of school segregation and the harm it inflicted on black children did not first come to the Court's attention in the *Brown* litigation: blacks had been attacking the validity of these policies for 100 years.... What accounted, then, for the sudden shift in 1954 away from the separate but equal doctrine and towards a commitment to desegregation?

... [T]he decision in *Brown* to break with the Court's long-held position on these issues cannot be understood without some consideration of the decision's value to whites, not simply those concerned about the immorality of racial inequality, but also those whites in policymaking positions able to see the economic and political advances at home and abroad that would follow abandonment of segregation. First, the decision helped to provide immediate credibility to America's struggle with Communist countries to win the hearts and minds of emerging third world peoples. At least this argument was advanced by lawyers for both the NAACP and the federal government. And the point was not lost on the news media. *Time* magazine, for example, predicted that the international impact of *Brown* would be scarcely less important than its effect on the education of black children: "In many countries, where U.S. prestige and leadership have been damaged by the fact of U.S. segregation, it will come as a timely reassertion of the basic American principle that 'all men are created equal.'"

Second, *Brown* offered much needed reassurance to American blacks that the precepts of equality and freedom so heralded during World War II might yet be given meaning at home. Returning black veterans faced not only continuing discrimination, but also violent attacks in the South which rivaled those that took place at the conclusion of World War I. Their disillusionment and anger were poignantly expressed by the black actor, Paul Robeson, who in 1949 declared: "It is unthinkable ... that American Negroes would go to war on behalf of those who have oppressed us for generations ... against a country the Soviet Union which in one generation has raised our people to the full human dignity of mankind." It is not impossible to imagine that fear of the spread of such sentiment influenced subsequent racial decisions made by the courts.

Finally, there were whites who realized that the South could make the transition from a rural, plantation society to the sunbelt with all its potential and profit only when it ended its struggle to remain divided by state-sponsored segregation. Thus, segregation was viewed as a barrier to further industrialization in the South.

These points may seem insufficient proof of self-interest leverage to produce a decision as important as *Brown*. They are cited, however, to help assess and not to diminish the Supreme Court's most important statement on the principle of racial equality. Here, as in the abolition of slavery, there were whites for whom recognition of the racial equality principle was sufficient motivation. But, as with abolition, the number who would act on morality alone was insufficient to bring about the desired racial reform.

Thus, for those whites who sought an end to desegregation on moral grounds or for the pragmatic reasons outlined above, *Brown* appeared to be a welcome break with the past. When segregation was finally condemned by the Supreme Court, however, the outcry was nevertheless great, especially among poorer whites who feared loss of control over their public schools and other facilities. Their fear of loss was intensified by the sense that they had been betrayed. They relied, as had generations before them, on the expectation that white elites would maintain lower class whites in a societal status superior to that designated for blacks.... Today, little has changed. Many poorer whites oppose social reform as "welfare programs for blacks" although, ironically, they have employment, education, and social service needs that differ from those of poor blacks by a margin that, without a racial scorecard, is difficult to measure.

Unfortunately, ... recent decisions, most notably by the Supreme Court, indicate that the convergence of black and white interests that led to *Brown* in 1954 and influenced the character of its enforcement has begun to fade....

... [T]he Court has increasingly erected barriers to achieving the forms of racial balance relief it earlier had approved. Plaintiffs must now prove that the complained-of segregation was the result of discriminatory actions intentionally and invidiously conducted or authorized by school officials. It is not enough that segregation was the "natural and foreseeable" consequence of their policies. And even when this difficult standard of proof is met, courts must carefully limit the relief granted to the harm actually proved....

At the very least, these decisions reflect a substantial and growing divergence in the interests of whites and blacks....

As we saw above in *Brown* itself, identities and groups are central to systemic injustice and remedies for it. Bell's excerpt here shows that interests related to those groups and identities are equally important. But identity groups need power to advance their interests. Armed with this insight, systemic advocates can use interests—and reckon with power—to supplement appeals to principle that otherwise might fail.

The next excerpt emphasizes the final of the four elements—power: "naked power which grabs and smashes without need for denial or justification." In this instance, the dominant racial group targets a "different" non-white identity, and the tools of elite supremacy also differ. But the internment of Japanese-Americans and the segregation of African-Americans were occurring simultaneously for the consistent and *collective* benefit of the group at the top of the caste system. To underscore this last point, critical race scholar Mari Matsuda provides a deeper review of *Brown's* segregation system in relationship to the internment system. In this excerpt, Matsuda details the collectivized internment of Japanese Americans during World War II as a legalized abuse of power to incarcerate entire communities indefinitely, and to confiscate their properties, based on a shared social identity. This account confirms how and why persistent social problems typically have material as well as symbolic dimensions and inter-connections.

FOREWORD: MCCARTHYISM, THE INTERNMENT AND THE CONTRADICTIONS OF POWER

Mari J. Matsuda
40 B.C. L. Rev. 9 (1998)

Introduction

There is naked power, which grabs and smashes without need for denial or justification. There is legitimized power, which justifies without denying. There is masked power, which never justifies, because the denial of its own existence is complete. . . .

Using the internment [of Japanese Americans by the United States during World War II] as a locus of analysis expands our understanding of the history of power. That understanding is critical in confronting a significant violation of civil liberties that occurred immediately in the wake of the internment. The massive repression known as McCarthyism, like the internment, was a repudiation of Constitutional values in the name of preserving the republic. This was at once an old story and a new one, for the repression of the McCarthy period occurred while a newly acknowledged commitment to racial equality was gaining ascendancy. The internment was becoming a wrong in the normative Constitutional mind at the moment when a huge, enforced silence made condemnation of red-baiting a normative impossibility. The internment story both presages and diverges from the Cold War story, making way for our contemporary map of power: racism and class privilege dancing unscathed behind the curtains marked "formal equality" and "free market." Understanding the changing rhetorical response to the internment is part of understanding how the present state of masked power came about.

In addition to analyzing the operation of repressive power in both the internment and McCarthyism, I make an explicit, value-laden claim: There is a Constitutional promise of liberty and equality, violated in both instances, which we have yet to uphold. . . . I ask for repair of the damage of McCarthyism and call for both reparations to the domestic Cold War victims and an end to continued red-baiting. The closing prescription of this introduction asks what our inquiry and our activism might look like without the legacy of red-baiting. What could we say about class, distributive fairness, illegitimate power, and the need for revolutionary change, if our voices were not stilled by a collective memory of people dragged from their beds at night because they believed in economic justice? . . .

The Internment as a Lens Through Which We See Power

. . . Using the internment as our departure point is a way to make the camp names more than a private [Japanese-American] catechism. It makes the recitation American, taking the center to the margin to ask: What do we know about our nation when we consider what it did in imprisoning its own? Some see this methodology, like the move to multiculturalism, as balkanizing. The introduction of ethnic studies was violently opposed by those who felt American knowledge should remain centered on European culture. This resistance to the integration of knowledge is driven by a need to keep power where it is, but it also represents a confusion that one could have in good faith: By parceling out knowledge into discrete identity packages, don't we end up knowing less rather than more? This question suggests that separating women's history, Black history, indigenous history, working class history, and gay/lesbian history destroys the ability to know and understand history as a synthesized and overarching thing of importance.

. . . [T]he opposite is true. The lens of the internment is exactly what we need to illuminate grand themes, connections, and a deep understanding of American consciousness. How do we understand the modern conception of the state if we leave out one of the key instances of a democratic government trampling on citizens' rights in order to protect something called the state? . . .

Unjustified Power and Justified Power

When the Europeans first swept over the world in what they came to call the Age of Discovery, or the Age of First Contact, known to native people as the Age of Genocide, they felt no particular compunction to justify. . . . [T]his was still in the time of kings, and the notion that anyone on the losing end of a power grab was entitled to explanation was not well-entrenched in the worldview of elites.

The legacy of the Enlightenment, as codified in the American legal system, is the need for power to justify itself. A naked grab, justified only by superior force, posed a problem for a nation founded on the revolutionary idea of the inherent rights of human beings to autonomy and self-governance. . . . Power, justified, is sold to the people as in their interest, rather than taken from the people because it is takable.

. . . [T]he internment was justified by widely believed lies. First was the lie of inherent racial being, part of the lie of race. The Japanese Americans were a distinct species, marked by the inability to Americanize. Second was the lie of military necessity. The Japanese Americans were part of a secret fifth column situated to destroy America from within, such that there was neither time nor ability to discern individual loyalty. As with the threat of terrorism today, as with the mysterious Communists that McCarthy searched for, the lack of evidence against the accused Japanese Americans became an additional, solipsistic reason to violate their rights: there was no other way to fight such a hidden threat. Third was the lie concealing true purpose. Military necessity masked the real impetus of lust for Japanese-American land holdings and fear of Japanese-American competition in the highly profitable West Coast farming industry.

The justification for internment, as weak on the evidence then as it is now, was not believed by many of the people who implemented it. Nonetheless, it was offered as a rationale both at the time of the internment and in subsequent court challenges to the internment. A few lonely voices rose up to challenge the justification, but their challenge was repudiated by a perceived threat to survival that required suspension of rights. Pearl Harbor had been bombed and the nation faced a real war. . . .

Japanese Americans were rhetorically transformed into a monolithic, fearsome, inhuman enemy. Japanese Americans were called "mad dogs," "yellow vermin," "treacherous," "warlike," "fifth column," and the ubiquitous "J__p." Like the Communists, who were frequently prosecuted on laughable evidence, the fact that Japanese Americans were never found to participate in espionage was used as evidence against them:

> [M]any of our people in other parts of the country are of the opinion that because we have had no sabotage and no fifth column activities in this State [California] since the beginning of the war,

that means that none have been planned for us. But I take the view that that is the most ominous sign in our whole situation. It convinces me more than perhaps any other factor that the sabotage that we are to get, the fifth column activities that we are to get, are timed just like Pearl Harbor was timed....

... Red-baiting was justified with the same dehumanizing, paranoid language. In testimony before the House Committee on Un-American Activities (HUAC), Communists were referred to as part of a "worldwide organization of gangsters," "disease spreading," and "a worldwide conspiratorial movement."...

Additionally, any organization that advocated progressive causes was quickly labeled a "Communist front" and targeted by HUAC....

Just as Congress in the 1950s exposed progressive organizations as Communist fronts, the California state legislature, in 1943, branded as "subversive" organizations that advocated for the rights of Japanese Americans during the war....

In the case of both HUAC and the internment, class interests were at once obvious and denied. Evicting Japanese Americans from their communities and denying Japanese Americans equal participation in California's economy advantaged white growers and land speculators. Fueling racial hatred kept working class whites pitted against Japanese Americans, continuing a nineteenth century anti-Asian populist tradition that had long made a coalition of white and Asian workers against ruling economic elites unthinkable. A multiracial coalition of workers demanding state concessions to their class interests was a real possibility in the wake of Depression-era worker militancy. Asian Americans marched on Washington with Black and white and Latino unemployed at the height of this period, and the implementation of the New Deal was, in part, a concession to this militancy. To keep the coalition in check, it was useful to keep the myth of the Yellow Peril alive.

Similarly, the lasting legacy of McCarthyism was the purging of Communists, who were often tireless and effective organizers, from factory and field, from intellectual life and cultural production, from government and education; in short, from every place where incisive criticism of capitalism could prove effective. This gift to the capitalist class—the emaciation of the labor movement and the chilling of public criticism, accompanied by the legitimization of greed and of the income gap—was not a mere by-product of anti-Communist witch-hunting. It was the goal, albeit never the acknowledged one.

In addition to this legitimization of capitalism, the domestic Cold War was part of the justification for the actual Cold War and the military/industrial complex that went along with it. If there was a Communist under every bed, eager to betray us to the powerful Soviet

Union, then the largest peacetime military expenditure in world history, and the fortunes made therefrom, were justified. The threat of the outside invader was used to mask class interests in the cases of McCarthyism and the internment. In both of these instances, thin rhetorical tricks trumped Constitutional values, and few spoke up to challenge the weakness of the rhetorical structure.

A key question of legitimacy for the Constitutional order is why its champions are historically so selective in their timing. The silence of good liberals during the internment silently echoed a decade later when the McCarthy purges began. This time, however, race played a different role.

The Changing Face of Power: How We Became Members of the Human Race in Exchange for Silence on the Question of Class

The internment created a contradiction between the democratic commitment to racial equality and the racist doctrine of military necessity that would not go away.... A deliberate practice of leaders from A. Philip Randolph during the war, and Dr. King after it, was to leverage the contradiction by heightening it and embarrassing the nation. The leaders of the free world were hard-pressed to claim moral superiority when they upheld Jim Crow laws, sent attack dogs after school children, or sent ministers to jail for seeking voting rights.

Just at the moment when overt racism—and anti-Semitism—was becoming publicly illegitimate, anti-Communism was becoming patriotic....

We had fought a war against Hitler and denounced the master race theory. This was clear in the public consciousness. We could not uphold racial supremacy after going to war to end it. It was less clear why Communists should have the right to speak and organize, given effective propaganda teaching that Communists *were* Hitler, intent on world domination and military destruction of the United States....

Public racism and anti-Semitism were replaced with public anti-Communism, putting the old fear and hatred in a new, more comfortable place....

In a remarkable feat of inversion, [President] Hoover further alleged that Communists were propagating the racism and anti-Semitism that the nation now condemned. He claimed that, "Historically, the [Communist] party has exploited minority groups. It hypocritically clamors for an end to discrimination while, at the very same time, it shamelessly practices racial discrimination within its own ranks." In contravention of the fact that Communists espoused racial equality, the state asserted itself as the protector of minorities in comparison with alleged Communist exploitation and discrimination.

This conversion from race-baiting to red-baiting explains in part why President Reagan, at the height of Reaganomics and in contravention of his promise of less government and fewer social programs, signed the Redress bill into law [granting modest reparations to those interned]. We were the country of anti-racism, the one that recognized and redressed its human rights errors. The story of our gradual progress toward racial equality was part of our greatness, part of the justification for our military adventurism abroad and for the continuation of the Cold War.

... The end result of red-baiting replacing race-baiting in elite discourse was the elimination of a progressive social agenda with economic justice at its core. Eric Foner describes this effect in the immediate postwar period. President Truman's proposals for national health insurance and construction of public housing were rejected as "socialized." Civil rights organizations that pushed to end poverty and empower workers were destroyed by red-baiting, and, in Foner's assessment, "[t]heir demise left a gaping hole that the NAACP, with its narrowly legalistic strategy, was ill-prepared to fill."

For critical race theorists, the jurisprudential legacy of this period is one that we have spent our intellectual lives describing, deconstructing, and struggling against. Once the demand for jobs, housing, healthcare, and workplace dignity were excised from the civil rights movement, the quest for formal, legal equality was the paltry remains. The great leaders of the civil rights movement, and the legions who participated in it, never separated the quest for economic parity from the fight to end segregation. No one who listened to A. Philip Randolph, to Dr. King, to Fanny Lou Hamer, to Septima Clark understood them to separate the need for a decent standard of living from the need for racial equality. Their words were edited through the politics of the red scare, and the most radical elements of their claims were repressed. The war on poverty started and stopped, leaving us with the inadequate modern-day civil rights acts, which are narrowly directed at ending explicit, formal, and intentional instances of racial discrimination. Formal racial discrimination, perpetuated by a few bad actors, became the social ill that good Americans would condemn. . . .

Defining equality narrowly, as critical race theorists have explained, is exactly what was needed to deny responsibility for institutional racism, unconscious racism, and continuing racist social practices. Thus, we ended "whites only" public schools, but we deny responsibility for widespread educational segregation that occurs because of white flight to the suburbs, or because of economic privilege that gives preference in college admissions to children of alumni and big donors. We ended "help wanted, male" ads in the newspapers, but we allow extreme gender segregation in the highest paying jobs because the market, rather than any identifiable sexist bigot, created that situation. The struggle over affirmative action reveals this result most clearly. If racism is personified in the self-aware bigot who deliberately denies access to education or jobs, then affirmative action makes no sense. We should simply find the bigot and make him stop discriminating. We do not need to institutionalize inclusion based on race or gender. In the worldview of formal equality, affirmative action results in undeserved preferences for individuals who have suffered no proven harm. Affirmative action only makes sense if a history of institutional discrimination, promoted by unconscious acts and normalized white/male preferring social practices, constructs present opportunity.

The social criticism and activist practice required to keep a structural analysis of privilege at the forefront became unthinkable in the wake of McCarthyism. I do not fault the civil rights movement for the loss of its most radical insights. It is not that people stopped seeing or saying that a narrow elite was using race and class privilege to run this country in an oligarchic, anti-democratic way. Indeed, the HUAC transcripts themselves are full of moments of high drama in which the accused Communists and alleged fellow travelers attempted to make that critique in a public forum....

... Paul Robeson was taunted by the Committee as he invoked the Fifth Amendment. He told them:

> I am being tried for fighting for the rights of my people, who are still second-class citizens in this United States of America.... And they are not. They are not in Mississippi. And they are not in Montgomery, Alabama. And they are not in Washington. They are nowhere, and that is why I am here today. You want to shut up every Negro who has the courage to stand up and fight for the rights of his people, for the rights of workers, and I have been on many a picket line for the steelworkers too. And that is why I am here today.

... There, in the HUAC transcripts, lies the record of the state's suppression of the voice linking racial justice to workers' rights.

... Fighting the Power that Denies Its Power

... How do we understand the internment as part of a larger struggle between the forces of repression and the forces of liberty, and how do we prevent the victory of redress for the internment from being another part of the late twentieth century form of power denial?

... [Robeson] linked labor rights, domestic civil rights, and international liberation struggles in every public appearance he made. HUAC was no exception. As he maneuvered to insert his views before the hostile Committee, he included references to the history of slavery, the struggles of steel workers, and his allegiance to independence movements in Africa, India, and Indonesia....

As Robeson and W.E.B. DuBois were sent into exile, so was their analysis linking racism to political economy and colonialism. . . .

. . . The internment gave us the beginning of modern equal protection doctrine. In the *Korematsu* case, the court declared racism an illegitimate reason for government action and simultaneously refused to acknowledge that racial vilification of the Japanese Americans permeated government decision-making at the time. This stance—"Racism is bad, and if it is proven to motivate government action to our satisfaction, we will declare a Constitutional violation"—leaves significant space for continued, legally sanctioned racial subordination. It also leaves room for anti-racist struggle, because the proof is sometimes available to force public condemnation of racist government action. Thus, subsequent criticism of *Korematsu*, and the putative discovery that it was based on erroneous assumptions, led to redress and reparations for Japanese Americans. We are not a country that officially tolerates government racism. In the meantime, McCarthyism erased the linkage between racism and class oppression and stifled structural critiques of power distributions.

Seeing the internment and McCarthyism as the intellectual funnel through which contemporary equal protection doctrine squeezes, illuminates the ongoing project of critical race theory. It is that funnel that reduces, for example, the feminization of poverty to a bad hair day: If she is living on the street and has no place to shower, that is about individual choices, not about collective responsibilities. There is nothing in contemporary equal protection doctrine that says otherwise. . . .

At the end of the day, or at the end of the century, if there are still those for whom the Bill of Rights is an illusion, and if there is no specific moment at which an official government actor decided to deny that individual's rights, then there is no claim. Harm, maybe, but no foul. No one need even say, "sometimes the people at the bottom just belong there." The beauty of the state action requirement combined with the formal equality requirement is that those in power can remain agnostic about whether the degradation of any particular group or individual is a good thing. Whether it is or not, no one in power is responsible for correcting it. Each relatively privileged citizen is then left to private, lonely conscience in deciding whether or not to undertake a rescue mission.

This is not where we were, conceptually or morally, before McCarthyism. When Roosevelt spoke of freedom from want, he spoke a language of substantive equality and can-do optimism that resonated with Americans. His policies called for worker empowerment and restraints on the excesses of corporate greed. For this, his administration became the first target of McCarthyism. The goal of the original HUAC was to discredit the New Deal by exposing so-called Communist infiltrators.

While programs such as social security maintain great citizen loyalty, the New Deal notions of citizen entitlement and collective responsibility are largely dormant. To raise them once again means learning to talk like New Deal democrats and their Communist allies, to demand that all who work share fairly in the benefit of their toil, and that all who are unable to care for themselves find a place of care. This is the kind of talk that will make the story of the internment a progressive story, revealing the cause of the incarceration of Japanese Americans as both racism and class oppression, and making the promise of redress part of an ongoing obligation to confront and repair all injustice.

In summary, *Korematsu* plus HUAC equals an impoverished liberalism that destroys any visionary notion of substantive justice. The longing for the Constitution to mean more than that is alive in the history of abolition and of the civil rights and labor movements. A challenge for the Japanese-American community is to make the victory of redress part of a progressive Constitutional vision. This is our obligation, for the courage to stand up for redress was inspired by our brothers and sisters in the African-American civil rights movement. They sought a Constitution that would feed the children, and so should we.

Conclusion: Reparation is a Process

The HUAC tried to teach that there are things we cannot say or think. Things such as "the rich did not earn their wealth" or "all citizens are entitled to, and the state must provide, a job, a house, health care, quality education, and leisure." The HUAC tried to teach that there are things we cannot do, such as organizing the poorest workers or traveling to assist anti-colonial struggles abroad. [Today is marked by] the unprecedented drive to imprison all able-bodied Black men in America.... With one in three Black men captured by the law enforcement/prison/industrial complex, they would have called it genocide, and certainly called it capitalism, in the time of Robeson and DuBois. Their words were unlearned in the crucible of the Cold War....

Apologies are not clear victories.... Whether they are isolated moments of sweet victory or parts of broader movements for human rights is determined by larger forces....

... Justice requires apology and monetary payment to all victims of red-baiting. And even if we do apologize, and do pay, it will not be enough.

Reparation is a process, not an end....

There is no neat ending to this story....

Matsuda's excerpt builds on the initial consideration of the *Brown* decision and its connections to identities, groups, interests, and power. As Matsuda emphasizes, remediation of systemic injustice always requires a material component. But power gives up nothing. On the contrary, the history and record of power is expansion, acquisition, and accumulation. For this reason, the complex story that Matsuda elaborates above, together with Bell, has "no neat ending"—every generation inherits the system and its legacies.

NOTES AND QUESTIONS

1. *Interest Convergence.* Legal scholar Mary Dudziak later detailed Bell's connection of *Brown* to the Cold War, showing how elites created a favorable civil rights narrative to protect cherished U.S. systems from revolution and replacement:

> [T]he federal government engaged in a sustained effort to tell a particular story about race and American democracy: a story of progress, a story of the triumph of good over evil, a story of U.S. moral superiority. The lesson of this story was always that American democracy was a form of government that made the achievement of social justice possible, and that democratic change, however slow and gradual, was superior to dictatorial imposition. The story of race [and racial reform] in America, used to compare democracy and communism, became an important Cold War narrative.

Mary L. Dudziak, Cold War, Civil Rights: Race and the Image of American Democracy 13 (2000). In your view, was *Brown* more a product of principle or of self-interest? What does this experience suggest about the limits (or benefits) of interest convergence as a tool for systemic advocacy? In light of the above materials, how might you learn about the interests of clients and adversaries to incorporate them effectively into your analyses and action plans?

2.5 DEMOCRACY'S ROLE IN MAKING THE CRITICAL CHALLENGE STICK—WHILE HIDING SYSTEMIC INEQUALITIES IN PLAIN SIGHT

In *Brown*, the U.S. Supreme Court invalidated public school segregation laws from coast to coast. Those laws had been enacted and enforced by state legislatures, governors, city and county commissions, mayors, school boards, zoning councils, and other "democratically" elected public officials. This arrangement was blessed by federal law. For decades, both state and federal judges upheld these laws in part because they were said to represent "the will of the people." This assertion may have applied to places like Kansas, where whites were a majority, but not to others where black or brown majorities existed. Even in these areas, white elites devised poll taxes, literacy tests, domestic terrorism, and other means to nullify the right to vote guaranteed on paper by the Fifteenth Amendment since the 1870s. These apartheid laws illustrate both the tyranny of the majority as well as the tyranny of the minority, and they show the key systemic role of formal democracy—in tandem with judicial review—in creating and maintaining the Critical Challenge of using law for equal justice.[12]

In the view of many, democracy is a sentinel achievement of modern times. As Winston Churchill famously said, repeating an unsourced aphorism, democracy is "the worst form of Government, except for all those other forms that have been tried from time to time."[13] Typically, modern legal systems rely on democracy and adjudication as their principal problem-solving mechanisms. Generally, the promise of democracy is to ensure that policy making and legislation serve the will of the people by actually solving social problems. And in case democracy somehow fails its role, adjudication professes to hold democracy accountable to principle (which includes the promise of equal justice for all). And vice versa: when relief is sought unsuccessfully from the courts, democracy is alerted to an unresolved social problem and acts to remedy what the judiciary has failed to redress. Over time, then, democracy and adjudication profess in tandem and separately to deliver principled, accountable, and effective problem solving. How, then, do schools stay segregated and unequal for generations along identity lines encompassing race, class, and other groups?

The answer is that democracy is not an antidote to inequality. In theory, democracy is a level playing field on which self-interested factions pursue their self-interest. In practice, however, democracy has functioned as an unlevel playing field in which already-dominant and already-subordinated groups largely reenact the relations of caste. And we have seen how elites consistently use adjudication both to justify the status quo and to control any "democratic" changes to it. Here, then, is another key and recurring point: democracy and adjudication can be mixed and matched in varied combinations to make progress or to block it. As the following extensive study of democracy in action documents, it still is decidedly a top-down production.

Below, political scientists Martin Gilens and Benjamin Page describe their comprehensive research covering 1,779 policy choices between 1981 and 2002 to assess which theory of democracy accurately corresponds to law's actual, systemic outputs. Their empirical findings show how democracy operates as an instrument of organized economic elites and their collectivized power despite popular sentiments—and actual majorities—to the contrary. Economic elites, moreover, correspond to racial and gender elites, connecting class to other social identities. Gilens and

---

[12] For an illuminating review, see Gabriel J. Chin and Randy Wagner, The Tyranny of the Minority: Jim Crow and the Counter-Majoritarian Difficulty, 43 Harv. C.R.-C.L. L. Rev. 65 (2008). In the United States, formal democracy has frequently been used directly by dominant groups to deny or "take back" minority rights. For a good sampling, see Barbara Gamble, Putting Civil Rights to a Popular Vote, 41 Am. J. of Pol. Science 245 (Jan. 1997).

[13] Churchill statement, House of Commons, Nov. 11, 1947, quoting an unknown earlier speaker. Churchill by Himself: The Definitive Collection of Quotations vii (2008).

Page found the only force capable of stopping economic elites was collective action by organized groups: "average" individuals can, and do, advance their interests, but only when they collaborate coalitionally. If so, democracy is a daily, year-round process of policy making punctuated by periodic electoral spectacles that make little difference in policy choices, which must be coupled with year-round bottom-up organizing and action to help make a difference both daily and during formal elections. Formal democracy, too, is part of the Critical Challenge, and of struggles against it. As you read, recall the lessons of demosprudence from Chapter 1.

TESTING THEORIES OF AMERICAN POLITICS: ELITES, INTEREST GROUPS, AND AVERAGE CITIZENS

Martin Gilens and Benjamin I. Page
12 Perspectives on Politics 564 (Sept. 2014)

... Who governs? Who really rules? To what extent is the broad body of U.S. citizens sovereign, semi-sovereign, or largely powerless? These questions have animated much important work in the study of American politics.

While this body of research is rich and variegated, it can loosely be divided into four families of theories: *Majoritarian Electoral Democracy*, *Economic-Elite Domination*, and two types of interest-group pluralism—*Majoritarian Pluralism*, in which the interests of all citizens are more or less equally represented, and *Biased Pluralism*, in which corporations, business associations, and professional groups predominate. Each of these perspectives makes different predictions about the independent influence upon U.S. policy making of four sets of actors: the *Average Citizen* or "median voter," *Economic Elites*, and *Mass-based* or *Business-oriented Interest Groups* or industries.

... The central point that emerges from our research is that economic elites and organized groups representing business interests have substantial independent impacts on U.S. government policy, while mass-based interest groups and average citizens have little or no independent influence. Our results provide substantial support for theories of Economic-Elite Domination and for theories of Biased Pluralism, but not for theories of Majoritarian Electoral Democracy or Majoritarian Pluralism. ...

Four Theoretical Traditions

... Given the nature of our data, we focus on the societal *sources* of influence that these theories posit, rather than on the *mechanisms* of influence that they discuss.

Majoritarian Electoral Democracy

Theories of majoritarian electoral democracy, as positive or empirical theories, attribute U.S. government policies chiefly to the collective will of average citizens, who are seen as empowered by democratic elections. . . .

Economic-Elite Domination

A quite different theoretical tradition argues that U.S. policy making is dominated by individuals who have substantial economic resources, i.e., high levels of income or wealth—including, but not limited to, ownership of business firms.

Not all "elite theories" share this focus. Some emphasize social status or institutional position—such as the occupancy of key managerial roles in corporations, or top-level positions in political parties, in the executive, legislative, or judicial branches of government, or in the highest ranks of the military. Some elite theories postulate an amalgam of elites, defined by combinations of social status, economic resources, and institutional positions, who achieve a degree of unity through common backgrounds, coinciding interests, and social interactions.

For example, C. Wright Mills' important book, *The Power Elite*, offers a rather nuanced account of how U.S. social, economic, political, and military elites have historically alternated in different configurations of dominance. Mills noted that his elites derived in substantial proportions from the upper classes, including the very rich and corporate executives, but their elite status was not defined by their wealth. Our focus here is on theories that emphasize the policy-making importance of *economic* elites.

Analyses of U.S. politics centered on economic elites go back at least to Charles Beard, who maintained that a chief aim of the framers of the U.S. Constitution was to protect private property, favoring the economic interests of wealthy merchants and plantation owners rather than the interests of the then-majority small farmers, laborers, and craft workers. A landmark work in this tradition is G. William Domhoff's detailed account of how elites (working through foundations, think-thanks, and an "opinion-shaping apparatus," as well as through the lobbyists and politicians they finance) may dominate key issues in U.S. policy making despite the existence of democratic elections. . . .

Our third and fourth theoretical traditions posit that public policy generally reflects the outcome of struggle among organized interest groups and business firms.

Majoritarian Pluralism

The roots of what we can characterize as theories of "majoritarian" interest-group pluralism go back to James Madison's *Federalist Paper* No. 10, which analyzed politics in terms of "factions"—a somewhat fuzzy concept that apparently encompassed political parties and even popular majorities, as well as what we would today consider organized interest groups, business firms, and industrial sectors. Madison argued that struggles among the diverse factions that would found in an extensive republic would lead to policies more or less representative of the needs and interests of the citizenry as a whole—or at least would tend to defeat "tyrannical" policies, including the much-feared issuance of inflationary paper money that might cater to local majority factions of farmer-debtors but would be costly to merchant creditors. . . .

Biased Pluralism

. . . Theories of biased pluralism generally argue that both the thrust of interest-group conflict and the public policies that result tend to tilt toward the wishes of corporations and business and professional associations.

. . . Charles Lindblom outlined a number of ways—including the "privileged position" of business—in which business firms and their associations influence public policy. Thomas Ferguson has posited an "investment theory" of politics in which "major investors"—especially representatives of particular industrial sectors—fund political parties in order to get policies that suit their economic interests. . . . Jacob Hacker and Paul Pierson's analysis of "winner-take-all-politics," which emphasizes the power of the finance industry, can be seen as a recent contribution to the literature of biased pluralism.

Marxist and neo-Marxist theories of the capitalist state hold that economic *classes*—and particularly the bourgeoisie, the owners of the means of production—dominate policy making and cause the state to serve their material interests. As the *Communist Manifesto* put it, "The bourgeoisie has . . . conquered for itself, in the modern representative State, exclusive political sway." . . .

As to empirical evidence concerning interest groups, it is well established that organized groups regularly lobby and fraternize with public officials, move through revolving doors between public and private employment, provide self-serving information to officials, draft legislation, and spend a great deal of money on election campaigns. Moreover, in harmony with theories of biased pluralism, the evidence clearly indicates that most interest groups and lobbyists represent business firms or professionals. Relatively few represent the poor or even the economic interests of ordinary workers, particularly now that the U.S. labor movement has become so weak.

But do interest groups actually influence policy? . . .

Very few studies have offered quantitative evidence concerning the impact of interest groups based on a number of different public policies. . . .

Testing Theoretical Predictions

Prior to the availability of the data set that we analyze here, no one we are aware of has succeeded at assessing interest-group influence over a comprehensive set of issues, while taking into account the impact of either the public at large or economic elites—let alone analyzing all three types of potential influences simultaneously.

Testing Theoretical Predictions

What makes possible an empirical effort of this sort is the existence of a unique data set, compiled over many years by one of us (Gilens) for a different but related purpose: for estimating the influence upon public policy of "affluent" citizens, poor citizens, and those in the middle of the income distribution.

Gilens and a small army of research assistants gathered data on a large, diverse set of policy cases: 1,779 instances between 1981 and 2002 in which a national survey of the general public asked a favor/oppose question about a proposed policy change.... The included policies ... tend to concern matters of relatively high salience, about which it is plausible that average citizens may have real opinions and may exert some political influence....

Our dependent variable is a measure of whether or not the policy change proposed in each survey question was actually adopted within four years after the question was asked....

Influence Upon Policy of Average Citizens, Economic Elites, and Interest Groups

Before we proceed further, it is important to note that ... [p]olicy making is not necessarily a zero-sum game among these actors. When one set of actors wins, others may win as well, if their preferences are positively correlated with each other....

But net interest-group stands are *not* substantially correlated with the preferences of average citizens. Taking all interest groups together, the index of net interest-group alignment correlates only a non-significant .04 with average citizens' preferences! ... Indeed, ... even the net alignments of the groups we have categorized as "mass-based" correlate with average citizens' preferences only at the very modest (though statistically significant) level of .12.

Some particular U.S. membership organizations—especially the AARP and labor unions—do tend to favor the same policies as average citizens. But other membership groups take stands that are unrelated (pro-life and pro-choice groups) or negatively related (gun owners) to what the average American wants. Some membership groups may reflect the views of corporate backers or their most affluent constituents. Others focus on issues on which the public is fairly evenly divided. Whatever the reasons, all mass-based groups taken together simply do not add up, in aggregate, to good representatives of the citizenry as a whole. Business-oriented groups do even worse, with a modest *negative* over-all correlation of -.10.

Nor do we find an association between the preferences of economic elites and the alignments of either mass-based or business-oriented groups. The latter finding, which surprised us, may reflect profit-making motives among businesses as contrasted with broader ideological views among elite individuals. For example, economic elites tend to prefer lower levels of government spending on practically everything, while business groups and specific industries frequently lobby for spending in areas from which they stand to gain. Thus pharmaceutical, hospital, insurance, and medical organizations have lobbied for more spending on health care; defense contractors for weapons systems; the American Farm Bureau for agricultural subsidies, and so on.

Initial Tests of Influences on Policy Making

... Clearly the median citizen or "median voter" at the heart of theories of Majoritarian Electoral Democracy does not do well when put up against economic elites and organized interest groups.... Not only do ordinary citizens not have *uniquely* substantial power over policy decisions; they have little or no independent influence on policy at all.

By contrast, economic elites are estimated to have a quite substantial, highly significant, independent impact on policy. This does not mean that theories of Economic-Elite Domination are wholly upheld, since our results indicate that individual elites must share their policy influence with organized interest groups. Still, economic elites stand out as quite influential—more so than any other set of actors studied here—in the making of U.S. public policy.

Similarly, organized interest groups (all taken together, for now) are found to have substantial independent influence on policy. Again, the predictions of pure theories of interest-group pluralism are not wholly upheld, since organized interest groups must share influence with economically-elite individuals. But interest-group alignments are estimated to have a large, positive, highly significant impact upon public policy.

These results suggest that reality is best captured by mixed theories in which both individual economic elites and organized interest groups (including corporations, largely owned and controlled by wealthy elites) play a substantial part in affecting public policy, but the general public has little or no independent influence....

When both interest groups and affluent Americans oppose a policy it has an even lower likelihood of being adopted (these proposed policies consist primarily of tax increases). At the other extreme, high levels of support among both interest groups and affluent Americans increases the probability adopting a policy change, but a strong status quo bias remains evident. Policies with strong support (as defined above) among both groups are only adopted about 56 percent of the time (strongly favored policies in our data set that failed include proposed cuts in taxes, increases in tax exemptions, increased educational spending for K–12, college support, and proposals during the Clinton administration to add a prescription drug benefit to Medicare).

Majoritarian Electoral Democracy

. . . [O]ur evidence indicates that the responsiveness of the U.S. political system when the general public wants government *action* is severely limited. Because of the impediments to majority rule that were deliberately built into the U.S. political system—federalism, separation of powers, bicameralism—together with further impediments due to anti-majoritarian congressional rules and procedures, the system has a substantial status quo bias. Thus when popular majorities favor the status quo, opposing a given policy change, they are likely to get their way; but when a majority—even a very large majority—of the public favors change, it is not likely to get what it wants. In our 1,779 policy cases, narrow pro-change majorities of the public got the policy changes they wanted only about 30 percent of the time. More strikingly, even overwhelmingly large pro-change majorities, with 80 percent of the public favoring a policy change, got that change only 43 percent of the time.

. . . [O]rdinary citizens get what they want from government only when they happen to agree with elites or interest groups that are really calling the shots. When push comes to shove, actual influence matters.

Economic Elites

Economic-Elite Domination theories do rather well in our analysis, even though our findings probably understate the political influence of elites. . . . The real-world impact of elites upon public policy may be still greater.

. . . [W]e need to reiterate that our data concern *economic* elites. Income and wealth tend to be positively correlated with other dimensions of elite status, such as high social standing and the occupancy of high-level institutional positions, but they are not the same thing. We cannot say anything directly about the non-economic aspects of certain elite theories, especially those that emphasize actors who may not be highly paid, such as public officials and political party activists.

Organized Interest Groups

Our findings of substantial influence by interest groups is particularly striking because little or no previous research has been able to estimate the extent of group influence while controlling for the preferences of other key non-governmental actors. Our evidence clearly indicates that— controlling for the influence of both the average citizen and economic elites—organized interest groups have a very substantial independent impact upon public policy. Theories of interest-group pluralism gain a strong measure of empirical support. . . .

Distinguishing between Majoritarian Pluralism and Biased Pluralism

. . . We have already reported several findings that cast serious doubt upon Majoritarian Pluralism. . . . We also know that the composition of the U.S. interest-group universe is heavily tilted toward corporations and business and professional associations. . . .

. . . It is simply not the case that a host of diverse, broadly-based interest groups take policy stands—and bring about actual policies—that reflect what the general public wants. Interest groups as a whole do not seek the same policies as average citizens do. "Potential groups" do not fill the gap. Relatively few mass-based interest groups are active, they do not (in the aggregate) represent the public very well, and they have less collective impact on policy than do business-oriented groups—whose stands tend to be *negatively* related to the preferences of average citizens. These business groups are far more numerous and active; they spend much more money; and they tend to get their way.

. . . When the alignments of business-oriented and mass-based interest groups are included . . . average citizens' preferences continue to have essentially zero estimated impact upon policy change, while economic elites are still estimated to have a very large, positive, independent impact.

American Democracy?

. . . Overall, net interest-group alignments are not significantly related to the preferences of average citizens. The net alignments of the most influential, business-oriented groups are *negatively* related to the average citizen's wishes. So existing interest groups do not serve effectively as transmission belts for the wishes of the populace as a whole. . . .

Furthermore, the preferences of economic elites (as measured by our proxy, the preferences of "affluent" citizens) have far more independent impact upon policy change than the preferences of average citizens do. . . .

Of course our findings speak most directly to the "first face" of power: the ability of actors to shape policy outcomes on contested issues. But they also reflect—to some degree, at least—the "second face" of power: the ability to shape the agenda of issues that policy makers consider. . . . Our results speak less clearly to the "third face" of power: the ability of elites to shape the public's preferences. We know that interest groups and policy makers themselves often devote considerable effort to shaping opinion. If they are successful, this might help explain the high correlation we find between elite and mass preferences. But it cannot have greatly inflated our estimate of average citizens' influence on policy making, which is near zero.

What do our findings say about democracy in America? They certainly constitute troubling news for advocates of "populistic" democracy, who want governments to respond primarily or exclusively to the policy preferences of their citizens. In the United States, our findings indicate, the majority does *not* rule—at least not in the causal sense of actually determining policy outcomes. When a majority of citizens disagrees with economic elites or with organized interests, they generally lose. Moreover, because of the strong status quo bias built into the U.S. political system, even when fairly large majorities of Americans favor policy change, they generally do not get it.

. . . Perhaps economic elites and interest-group leaders enjoy greater policy expertise than the average citizen does. Perhaps they know better which policies will benefit everyone, and perhaps they seek the common good, rather than selfish ends, when deciding which policies to support.

But we tend to doubt it. We believe instead that—collectively—ordinary citizens generally know their own values and interests pretty well, and that their expressed policy preferences are worthy of respect. Moreover, we are not so sure about the informational advantages of elites. Yes, detailed policy knowledge tends to rise with income and status. Surely wealthy Americans and corporate executives tend to know a lot about tax and regulatory policies that directly affect them. But how much do they know about the human impact of Social Security, Medicare, food stamps or unemployment insurance, none of which is likely to be crucial to their own well-being? Most important, we see no reason to think that informational expertise is always accompanied by an inclination to transcend one's own interests or a determination to work for the common good.

All in all, we believe that the public is likely to be a more certain guardian of its own interests than any feasible alternative. . . .

. . . [O]ur analysis suggests that majorities of the American public actually have little influence over the policies our government adopts. Americans do enjoy many features central to democratic governance, such as regular elections, freedom of speech and association, and a widespread (if still contested) franchise. But we believe that if policymaking is dominated by powerful business organizations and a small number of affluent Americans, then America's claims to being a democratic society are seriously threatened.

As noted by Gilens and Page, "democratic" decision making in the contemporary U.S. is systemically skewed to defeat democracy itself. Wealthy individuals and corporations act in organized ways to use the collective leverage of their concentrated material power to advance group interests even further. Elites also ensure that "average" folks lack the same—organization, resources, and power.

Consequently, actual, documented majorities of diverse yet average citizens routinely do *not* affect policy outcomes when their interests or preferences differ from the priorities of (mostly white and cis male) economic elites. On issue after issue—1,779 examined in this empirical study—elite interests dictated policy, and that policy tended to increase the already-concentrated power of elites for future rounds of contestation. Unless checked by systemic advocacy, every such round follows the same script to entrench the Critical Challenge further.

This history has reduced formal democracy in the United States over time to periodic public rituals (elections) in which typically fewer than half of eligible voters bother to participate. However, according to regular surveys, these formally absent voters *have* registered their views of the system and of the "choices" it allows to the people—they have effectively voted their sense of estrangement and futility with their individual and collective feet. By design, this reduction of democracy to public rituals is thoroughly racialized and gendered.

To amplify, legal scholar Terry Smith explains how moneyed, racialized elites use their control of adjudication to ensure their control of democracy—and vice versa. The entire arrangement hinges on enough voters trained to act enough of the time as members of "racial blocs" in periodic electoral clashes. As Smith explains:

> If I am a wealthy individual (and correlatively a white individual), I can contribute up to $[2,800] per election cycle ... to the candidate of my choice. I may contribute [additional] "hard money" [within specified limits and] ... an unlimited amount of "soft money" [to a political party or political action committee for "party-building" activities]. ... All of these contributions and expenditures can be made with a subordinating intent or effect— that is, they can be used to mobilize majorities of voters against outsider groups.... [But] when it comes to money, the Constitution, at least as interpreted by the Court and opponents of reform, permits private resources a liberal (some would say virtually unchecked) influence on the public sphere.
>
> Now assume that I am a black (and correlatively poorer) voter.... I want to run for Congress ... I, along with a group of other like-minded black voters, lobby members of our black state legislative caucus, who in turn put pressure on their white party cohorts, to create a majority-minority district.... We are successful....
>
> [Such] districts are held unconstitutional on Fourteenth Amendment grounds, however[:] ... "When the State assigns

voters on the basis of race, it engages in the offensive and demeaning assumption that voters of a particular race, because of their race, 'think alike, share the same political interests, and will prefer the same candidates at the polls.' " The short answer to the Court's concern is that blacks either do or do not prefer candidates of their same race; if they do, why is this expression not as protected as the expenditure of money under the First Amendment? Why, in short, is the Supreme Court soft on money but hard on race?[14]

Smith shows how elite-appointed judges equate money with speech by fiat. This equation is asserted judicially as law precisely because it can exempt those who wield power in the form of "big" and "dark" money from virtually all public disclosure or legal regulation—even though nothing in the First Amendment compels this anti-democratic choice. Simultaneously, those same appointees constrict the capacity of subordinated groups (like U.S. Blacks) to organize for democratic action around shared racial grievances, equating those efforts with "suspect" choices subjected to "strict scrutiny." This prohibition is imposed judicially precisely because those grievances represent already-racialized systemic injuries—even though nothing in the Fourteenth Amendment warrants or compels this dual scheme. Indeed, a principled legal regime based on these two Amendments might instead be seen to compel the exact opposite of this status quo.

Racialized and gendered economic elites collectively use their accumulated money and power to manipulate adjudication in combination with democracy. In this way, they maximize their continuous, collective control both of law and society. These and similar historical or current experiences have led to the elite playbook outlined in Part II and to the critical lessons and bottom-up calls of demosprudence that Guinier and Torres urged in Chapter 1.

NOTES AND QUESTIONS

1. *Formal Democracy as Top-Down Democracy.* Given findings like those of Gilens and Page above, how might systemic advocates "work" formal democracy to advance bottom-up priorities?

2. *Interest Convergence in Top-Down Democracy.* What do the empirically-based insights of Gilens and Page add to your understanding of interest convergence, and its limitations for progress through formal democracy?

---

[14] Terry Smith, Race and Money in Politics, 79 N.C. L. Rev. 1469, 1496–1500 (2001).

2.6 LEGALIZED VIOLENCE ENFORCES THE CRITICAL CHALLENGE—MILITARIZED POLICING, MASS INCARCERATION, AND CRIMMIGRATION

Systems of public education—and the racialized parallel systems of private and parochial education—dispense privilege and subordination day by day based on the power of training and knowledge. The public educational system is funded in starkly unequal terms that correlate with race, ethnicity, class, sex, and other social identities, and that facilitate a massive transfer of public resources to largely-white private schools—all largely structured by the legal system.[15] With vastly unequal resources and skewed teaching, some groups are systematically validated for "personal" success while others are pushed toward collective failure due purportedly to personal faults.

All the time, this systemic inequality is presented and defended as fair, normal, legitimate. In this way, education—both public and private—systematically trains members of all groups to accept their place in the identity caste systems protected by the Critical Challenge. Education as a system generally instills and normalizes a top-down consciousness of docility and culture of obedience, as we will examine in Part IV in the context of legal education. The social structure of legalized inequality is internalized, entrenched, and preserved. Unless disrupted, systems routinely reproduce themselves and their outputs to uphold the status quo of entrenched castes.

Bottom-up disruptions, usually organized by students, parents, and teachers, might focus on disparate funding sourced in property taxes, on efforts to divert resources away from majority-minority school districts, or on administrative and disciplinary practices that reinforce systemic inequalities—such as the "school to prison pipeline" or unequal access to special education programs.[16] Disruptions may interfere with the function of education as training for the acceptance and reproduction of inequality. If or when education fails to keep the masses tranquilized, law maintains

---

[15] See Part VII for discussion of this lawful inequality of educational funding.

[16] Education-focused advocacy has both a long history and an ongoing vitality. Grassroots membership groups, unions, and legal advocacy organizations all are active. See, for example, The Shriver Center on Poverty Law, Advocates Are Building a Model to Disrupt the School-to-Prison Pipeline in Mississippi—and Beyond (describing joint work between the Mississippi Center for Justice and the American Civil Liberties Union), www.theshriverbrief.org/advocates-are-building-a-model-to-disrupt-the-school-to-prison-pipeline-in-mississippi-and-beyond-863095053779; Marilyn Elias, The School-to-Prison Pipeline, Teaching Tolerance (Spring 2013) (explaining that racial disparities are stark, especially for racial minorities with disabilities and describing advocacy work by the Southern Poverty Law Center, the NAACP, and Dignity in Schools), www.tolerance.org/magazine/spring-2013/the-school-to-prison-pipeline; and Mark Warren, Parents Must Shut Down the School-to-Prison Pipeline (Jan. 22, 2019) (reviewing local parent organizing by Racial Justice NOW! in Ohio and CADRE in South Los Angeles in collaboration with national advocacy groups).

other systemic ways and means ready to enforce the Critical Challenge by raw might and brute force.

Militarized policing, mass incarceration, and crimmigration provide three inter-related examples. The first two work in synergy—militarized policing leads to mass incarceration, and mass incarceration beckons evermore policing.[17] The third—crimmigration—describes the extension and fusion of this complex maintenance of caste in the field of immigration.[18] The violence of this trio tracks social identities and their caste systems, both symbolically and materially. These systems of physical violence make the United States the number one "carceral state" on the planet,[19] with per capita incarceration rates exceeding North Korea, China, Iran, Cuba, and others that U.S. elites condemn as repressive.[20]

In addition, most of the imprisoned masses in this carceral state are Black, brown, and poor. Often, after they have completed their sentences, they remain barred from voting, thereby suppressing their capacity to participate in democratic policy making even after serving their time. This extended, collectivized disenfranchisement can decide future elections for years, making formal U.S. democracy ever-more unrepresentative of "the people"[21] and, ironically, more like those countries that U.S. elites denounce as dictatorships.

---

[17] For descriptions of policing practices and incarceration working in tandem and with legal justification, see Paul Butler, Let's Get Free: A Hip-Hop Theory of Justice (2010); Devon W. Carbado, Predatory Policing, 85 UMKC L. Rev. 545 (2016); Dorothy E. Roberts, The Social and Moral Costs of Mass Incarceration in African American Communities, 56 Stan. L. Rev. 1271 (2004); David Cole, Turning the Corner on Mass Incarceration?, 9 Ohio St. J. Crim. L. 27 (2011); Alice Ristroph, An Intellectual History of Mass Incarceration, 60 B.C. L. Rev. 1949 (2019); Kevin R. Johnson, How Racial Profiling in America Became the Law of the Land: *United States v. Brignoni-Ponce* and *Whren v. United States* and the Need for Truly Rebellious Lawyering, 98 Geo. L.J. 105 (2010); Bryan Stevenson, Confronting Mass Imprisonment and Restoring Fairness to Collateral Review of Criminal Cases, 41 Harv. C.R.-C.L. L. Rev. 339 (2006); Ian F. Haney López, Post-Racial Racism: Racial Stratification and Mass Incarceration in the Age of Obama, 98 Cal. L. Rev. 1023 (2010); Kimberlé W. Crenshaw, From Private Violence to Mass Incarceration: Thinking Intersectionally About Women, Race, and Social Control, 59 UCLA L. Rev. 1418 (2012).

[18] César Cuauhtémoc García Hernández, Migrating to Prison: America's Obsession with Locking Up Immigrants (2019); Anita Sinha, Arbitrary Detention? The Immigration Detention Bed Quota, 12 Duke J. Const. L. & Pub. Pol'y 77 (2017); Jennifer M. Chacón, Privatized Immigration Enforcement, 52 Harv. C.R.-C.L. L. Rev. 1 (2017); Jorge A. Solis, Detained Without Relief, 10 Ala. C.R. & C.L. L. Rev. 357 (2019); Yolanda Vázquez, Crimmigration: The Missing Piece of Criminal Justice Reform, 51 U. Rich. L. Rev. 1093 (2017).

[19] Marie Gottschalk, Caught: The Prison State and the Lockdown of American Politics 2 (2015).

[20] Pew Research Center, America's Incarceration Rate Is At a Two-Decade Low (May 2, 2018), www.pewresearch.org/fact-tank/2018/05/02/americas-incarceration-rate-is-at-a-two-decade-low/.

[21] Florida provides a good example: in the 2000 presidential election, the margin of victory for Republican George W. Bush in that decisive state for electoral college purposes was a mere 537 votes. Had the state's former felons, many of them racial minorities, been allowed to vote rather than being disenfranchised, even at a very low turnout rate of 13 percent, they would have cast 13,000 votes and likely changed the outcome. Mary Ellen Klas, Florida Leads Nation in Disenfranchising Former Felons, Miami Herald (Aug. 12, 2016), www.miamiherald.com/news/politics-government/election/article95076927.html. A similar scenario plays out in other states,

This sprawl of systems—law, education, police, prisons, immigration, and others—ensures the impoverishment and disempowerment of Black and brown lives, as well as the enrichment and empowerment of ruling elites. Criminal law scholar Carrie Rosenbaum explains that the carceral state is a continuation of U.S. settler colonial history (detailed in Part VI of this book):

> There remains a divide in United States civil society, where people racialized as nonwhite do not have the same lived experience as people racialized as white.... [B]eing poor increases the chances of being incarcerated, while being a person racialized as nonwhite is part of the equation in socio-economic standing and the likelihood of experiencing incarceration....
>
> These problems are replicated in and by the crimmigration system. Just as people racialized as nonwhite are more likely to be relatively socio-economically poor and more likely to have contact with the criminal justice system, immigrants racialized as nonwhite face these same challenges. The effects of racialization are significant, and the mechanisms purportedly designed to reverse, erase, or change these dynamics have failed immigrants and citizens racialized as nonwhite.
>
> ... Settler colonialism is a continuing form of nation building, whereby settlers fortify the dominant culture, removing and replacing communities with constructed ones.... These methodologies also help explain why and how crimmigration is an extension of settler colonialism and is responsible for reinforcing racialized differences.[22]

The policies and practices of the carceral state keep the Critical Challenge in place, day by day and decade by decade. These interlocking systems have been described as the "new" Jim Crow because they resurrect the systemic mechanisms of top-down control that prevailed before *Brown*.[23] Sketching how force (police) kicks in when training (education) falls short, the excerpts below also show how bottom-up actions are used by activists and advocates to confront the carceral state. The first excerpt, from an ACLU staff attorney who spent much of his career focused on immigration detention and the private prison industry, illustrates how top-down systems of raw power back up systems of cultural control to enforce the Critical Challenge of using law for equal justice.

---

ensuring that formal democracy in the U.S. remains a top-down system that elites can control most of the time.

[22] Carrie L. Rosenbaum, Crimmigration—Structural Tools of Settler Colonialism, 16 Ohio St. J. Crim. L. 9, 10–11 (2018).

[23] Michelle Alexander, The New Jim Crow: Mass Incarceration in an Age of Colorblindness (2010).

From Mass Incarceration to Mass Control, and Back Again: How Bipartisan Criminal Justice Reform May Lead to a For-Profit Nightmare

Carl Takei

20 U. Pa. J. L. & Soc. Change 125 (2017)

Introduction

It is now widely acknowledged that the United States incarcerates far too many people. Though the country has less than 5% of the world's population, it houses nearly 25% of the world's prisoners. And despite fierce partisanship on most issues, major actors across the political spectrum agree that something needs to be done about this mass incarceration epidemic.

Every major civil rights organization involved in criminal justice issues . . . and major progressive-aligned think tanks like the Sentencing Project, the Center for American Progress and the Brennan Center for Justice have called for an end to mass incarceration.

On the right, think tanks . . . and conservative thought leaders . . . have all called for criminal justice reform. . . . Even the Koch brothers—perhaps the most infamous financial supporters of ultraconservative causes—are now publicly supporting and funding efforts at criminal justice reform. . . .

The left and the right, however, each come to this alliance with distinct and, ultimately, incompatible interests. . . .

Mass Incarceration And The Carceral State

In this article, I use Marie Gottschalk's term "carceral state" to refer to the full range of penal punishments and controls, from secure confinement in prisons and jails to various forms of supervision and governmental control. I reserve the narrower term "mass incarceration" for the use of secure confinement. Although mass incarceration is the most visible and inhumane component of the carceral state, it is part of a larger system, and . . . criminal justice reform efforts that focus only on the mass incarceration component of the carceral state are unlikely to actually end either the carceral state or mass incarceration in the long term. . . .

Birth of a Carceral Nation

From 1925 (when the Bureau of Justice Statistics first began collecting nationwide data) to 1972, the U.S. per-capita incarceration rate remained relatively stable, with prison and jail populations rising in tandem with the overall population. But starting in 1972, the United States embarked on an historically unprecedented prison boom that grew unabated for nearly three decades. . . . As President Barack Obama stated in a July 2015 speech, "For what we spend to keep everyone locked up for one year, we could eliminate tuition at every single one of our public colleges and universities."

Since 2009, there has been some progress in reducing the incarcerated population.... [But] claims that mass incarceration is clearly or inevitably on its way out have been greatly exaggerated....

Why Did Mass Incarceration Happen?

... The consensus explanation points to changes in law enforcement priorities and sentencing policy that resulted in state and federal authorities putting more people in prison for more reasons and for longer periods of time than at any prior time in U.S. history.... [T]hese changes in policy and practice were largely a response to racist fear mongering ... and the perceived urgency of the War on Drugs.... Both liberals and conservatives supported many of these changes—including the shift from indeterminate sentencing to the use of sentencing guidelines, which liberals incorrectly believed would reduce racial disparities and biases in sentencing.

... [Currently, the] carceral state functions as a "racial caste system ... a set of structural arrangements that locks a racially distinct group into a subordinate political, social, and economic position." ...

The Modern Carceral State ...

Mass Incarceration in Prisons and Jails

... Prisons are the primary focus of most efforts at decarceration, both because the absolute number of people in prison are larger than the number of people in jail and because prisons are operated by the state and federal governments rather than local jurisdictions—which makes it easier to reduce prison populations through a combination of changes to state and federal criminal statutes and changes to the policies of state executive agencies and the federal government.

In contrast, the 728,000 people incarcerated in local jails are scattered across some 2,850 jurisdictions nationwide. These jurisdictions are typically city or county entities, run by locally-elected officials—most often sheriffs. Nationwide, more than 60% of the people in jail are being detained pretrial and have not actually been convicted of a crime; the remainder are typically serving sentences too short to justify transfer to a prison—usually one year or less. This represents a mass sorting of rich defendants from poor defendants, as the vast majority of those detained pretrial are held simply because they cannot afford to pay bail. Those who cannot make bail feel increased pressure to plead guilty because each successive day in jail means lost liberty, lost income, and separation from family. Continued pretrial detention may also mean denial of necessary medical care or even death....

... Jails are also where people targeted by aggressive policing policies are most likely to be incarcerated. "Broken Windows" policing strategies—which target minor public order offenses such as vandalism, panhandling, and public drinking—are a prime example. The chief impact of such strategies is to create a steady number of arrests of poor people of color. Additionally, aggressive efforts to collect criminal justice fines and fees create another source of unnecessary arrests. . . .

Community Corrections Facilities and Supervision

The reach of the carceral state extends far beyond prisons and jails. On any given day, there are an unknown number of people in residential community corrections facilities and nearly 4.7 million people on some form of community supervision, such as probation or parole.

Community Corrections Facilities

There is no concise, generally agreed-upon definition of a community corrections facility. Generally speaking, they are residential facilities in or near population centers where prisoners are assigned either to serve a sentence in lieu of prison or to serve the final portions of their sentence. . . .

Unlike prisons, community corrections facilities are usually not directly operated by the government. Instead, they are operated by nongovernmental entities—sometimes non-profit, sometimes for-profit—that contract with correctional agencies. . . .

Supervision

Supervision can be imposed at three different stages of the criminal justice process: pretrial supervision for people released pending trial, a sentence of probation imposed in lieu of some or all of a prison or jail term, and parole supervision following release from prison or jail.

Pretrial supervision is often the fate of the people "lucky" enough to avoid pretrial detention. . . . Electronic monitoring—chiefly tracking people with GPS monitors—has become especially common. . . .

Probation generally involves severe limitations on a supervisee's Fourth Amendment rights; the U.S. Supreme Court has held that probation conditions may authorize warrantless searches of a supervisee's home and person without probable cause, and any law enforcement officer (not just probation officers) may freely take advantage of this warrantless search authority. Additionally, a sentence of probation typically involves numerous behavioral requirements. Within the federal system, for example, all probation supervisees must submit to periodic drug tests regardless of whether or not their crime was drug-related, and standard conditions of probation include not traveling outside a specific geographic area, avoiding places where drugs are illegally sold or used, avoiding associating with "any persons engaged in criminal activity," avoiding associating with anyone else with a felony record without the probation officer's permission, and permitting the probation officer to "visit the defendant at any time at home or elsewhere" to observe and seize "contraband." . . . When a person violates any of these conditions, his or her probation officer has discretion to decide whether to bring the violation to the court's attention and, if so, what sanctions to recommend to the court . . . [including] continuing or extending probation, modifying the terms of probation, or revoking probation and immediately imposing the original suspended prison sentence. . . .

Parole enables prisoners to complete their sentences under supervision rather than serving their entire sentences in prison. . . . Like probation, release on parole involves restrictions on liberty and onerous supervision requirements. . . and punish[es] for failing to meet all required conditions.

How Community Corrections and Supervision Feed Back into Mass Incarceration

According to the Bureau of Justice Statistics, reincarcerations accounted for one-fifth of all exits from probation and more than a quarter of all exits from parole in 2015, most of which occurred because the supervisee had violated one or more probation or parole conditions. . . . A study of courts in Wisconsin found that defendants sentenced to community supervision were subject to an average of thirty conditions per person. The more stringent the conditions, the higher the risk that the supervisee will be unable to successfully exit supervision. Additionally, supervisees who are offered rehabilitative interventions, such as counseling or drug treatment, are often more likely to end up having probation or parole revoked than those who are not offered treatment services. This makes intuitive sense—the more frequently a person must travel to check in with a probation or parole officer, go to court (which often involves long waits before one's case is called), and attend required programming, the more difficult it is for that person to maintain a job and keep strong family connections. Yet maintaining employment and supporting one's family are often themselves set as conditions of supervision—leaving the supervisee caught between the Scylla of failure to check in and the Charybdis of unemployment. . . .

Criminal Justice Debt as a Further Path into Incarceration

In many places, defendants who cannot afford to pay fines and fees imposed on conviction—which frequently add up to thousands of dollars, and can even accumulate interest while the person is incarcerated—end up being placed on supervision to pay these debts, and then being arrested and re-jailed solely for failing to pay them off. This phenomenon—dubbed "modern-day debtors' prisons" in 2010 by the ACLU and the Brennan Center for Justice—violates the Equal Protection Clause of the Fourteenth Amendment.

Nevertheless, modern-day debtors' prisons remain widespread. . . .

Immigration Detention

Immigration detention is another component of mass incarceration. It is carried out under the authority of the Immigration and Customs Enforcement ("ICE"), the interior enforcement agency of the U.S. Department of Homeland Security ("DHS"). Its purpose is not to punish, but to hold people while their civil immigration proceedings are pending. In practice, however, immigrants are detained in jails and jail-like facilities.

ICE detention is far smaller than the criminal justice system as a whole . . . [but] has been a vanguard of both privatized, for-profit incarceration and privatized, for-profit supervision. It is estimated that more than 60% of immigration detention beds are run by private prison companies. These privately run beds are located both in private prisons dedicated to immigration detention and in privatized county jails that contract out some or all of their beds to ICE. (Just 11.8% of ICE beds are actually operated by the agency itself.) Additionally, since 2004, ICE has entirely contracted out the function of supervising immigrants on release—both the contract for intensive supervision ("ISAP") and a recent family supervision contract have been awarded to subsidiaries of GEO Group, a private prison company. . . .

. . . Significant concerns have been raised about over-use of GPS tracking by the GEO Group subsidiary that ICE relies on for ISAP. Such over-use appears to be incentivized by the contract, which both allows the contractor to select the level of supervision for each individual and compensates the contractor more generously when it puts a person on GPS tracking instead of less-intrusive telephone check-ins. . . .

The Role of Private Prisons in the Carceral State

Nationwide, about 7% of state prisoners and 18% of federal prisoners are held in private prisons run by for-profit companies. However, there are major variations from state to state. . . . Additionally, the private prison industry is increasingly diversifying into for-profit community corrections facilities and for-profit post-release supervision, as well as supervised release for non-citizens awaiting outcomes in their immigration cases.

While it has historical antecedents in both the Eighteenth-century English "keeper" system and the post-Civil War practice of "convict leasing," the modern private prison industry did not begin until 1983, with the founding of Corrections Corporation of America ("CCA/CoreCivic"). In the ensuing decades, private prisons grew rapidly—from a population of approximately 7,000 prisoners in 1990, to 87,000 in 2000, to more than 126,000 in 2015—because mass incarceration enabled them to make alluring offers to both their host communities and state correctional officials. To struggling rural towns with few opportunities for economic growth, the private prisons offered the prospect of desperately-needed new jobs—and, with the seemingly limitless growth of the prison population, these jobs seemed like they would be secure for many years to come. In exchange, the host communities eagerly provided generous development subsidies, including tax-free construction bonds, property tax abatements, and subsidized road and sewer connections. To state correctional officials, the private prisons offered new prison space that could rapidly be brought online, did not require the state to commit to funding construction or being responsible for the entire multi-decade lifecycle of the physical plant (that risk was, instead, borne by the host community), and would use the magic of the free market to increase efficiency and decrease costs to the state.

Yet neither promise was fully realized. For host communities, recent research has concluded that building new private prisons is actually associated with negative local job growth and depressed wages. . . .

As more and more prisoners are housed in private prisons, the early promises of flexibility and freedom give way to vendor lock-in: once a state houses a substantial number of people in private prisons, officials no longer have the ability to quickly cancel contracts and relocate prisoners if they become dissatisfied. . . .

Additionally, correctional officials and the public slowly realized that handing control of prisons over to for-profit companies has profound human consequences. In slightly more than thirty years of operation, the private prison industry has racked up a long and disturbing record of abuse, neglect and misconduct. . . .

Despite this record, private prisons have grown into a multibillion-dollar industry. The two largest private prison companies—Corrections Corporation of America/CoreCivic and GEO Group—are both publicly traded, with annual revenues of, respectively, $1.79 billion and $1.84 billion in 2015. They have developed into a potent lobbying force in both state and federal arenas, with their lobbying and campaign contributions targeted at particular states and particular congressional committees. . . .

The private prison industry depends on the expansion of the carceral state for its continued profitability. . . .

The "User-Funded" Criminal Justice System

. . . [F]or-profit companies have taken over key supervision functions like GPS monitoring—and bill criminal defendants for the costs of their own monitoring. These costs can be cripplingly high; for example, one private, for-profit GPS monitoring company reportedly charges supervisees $300 per month, plus a $179.50 setup fee, for their court-ordered GPS monitoring. Supervisees who fail to pay the fees are sent back to jail.

... [T]he more that government agencies hand off these functions to private entities, the more these profiteers will be able to block supervisees from exiting the criminal justice system.

Reform Efforts

... *Voices in the Wilderness*

In the early years of the War on Drugs, liberal leaders—including many Black leaders—initially responded by lining up in support of harsher sentencing and heavier police presences in Black neighborhoods. For example, thirteen of the twenty voting members of the Congressional Black Caucus ("CBC") supported the Anti-Drug Abuse Act of 1986—including the now-infamous 100:1 sentencing disparity between crack and powder cocaine that this bill created.

... Although members of the CBC eventually reversed positions and called for an end to the sentencing disparities between crack sales and powder cocaine sales, a moral panic over drugs and urban crime continued to dominate the mainstream liberal discourse. In 1992, then-Governor Bill Clinton ran for president on an explicitly "tough on crime" platform. After Clinton's election, Sen. Joe Biden (D-DE) and Rep. Charles Schumer (D-NY) spearheaded an effort to develop and pass the 1994 Crime Bill, which—among other things—dramatically ratcheted up mandatory minimum sentences, expanded the federal death penalty, and authorized billions of dollars in funding for new prisons. . . .

... Meanwhile, mainstream civil rights organizations often decried individual instances of unfairness, but did not attack the larger system. . . .

... Rather than focusing narrowly on the goal of decarceration and shifting people from prisons to punitive forms of supervision, we can chart out an alternative future that shrinks the entire carceral state. We can radically rethink who should be incarcerated, for how long, in what kind of environment, and for what purposes. We can develop non-punitive alternatives to incarceration, and develop strategies for addressing root causes such as poverty, substance abuse, and mental illness, and other root causes. We can prioritize racial justice, community participation, and human value. Indeed, these ideas are already circulating in Black Lives Matter and elsewhere in the grassroots left. Those of us in mainstream progressive organizations ought to listen carefully to what they are saying.

The United States is in a rare political moment where we may be able to begin a real, fundamental shift away from the carceral paradigm. We should not squander the opportunity by narrowing our horizons in a way that locks us into an even more nightmarish future.

Takei's overview of the carceral state describes the intertwining of mass incarceration and mass control, as well as links to immigration detention and removal. Below, legal scholar César Cuauhtémoc García Hernández offers reflections on the intersection of criminal and immigration law—crimmigration. Crimmigration—and the carceral state generally, as Takei notes—morph over time as elite institutions and individuals maneuver to benefit from coercive state power.

NATURALIZING IMMIGRATION IMPRISONMENT
César Cuauhtémoc García Hernández
103 Cal. L. Rev. 1449 (2015)

... Immigration law enforcement is a feature of both the civil administrative law process and the criminal justice system. On the civil side, federal immigration officials in the Department of Homeland Security (DHS) use an array of initiatives, tens of thousands of personnel, and billions of dollars to enforce civil immigration law, which governs who can be admitted into the United States and what conditions they must meet to stay here. In the criminal justice system, the same federal agencies that investigate and enforce all types of federal criminal laws also police suspected violations of federal immigration crimes, such as unauthorized entry and unauthorized reentry into the United States. State and local counterparts often engage in similar activities, having vigorously turned to their traditional police powers to regulate unwanted activity related to migrant status.

Whether characterized as a matter of civil or criminal law, and whether carried out by federal, state, or local officials, every type of immigration law enforcement shares a common central feature: imprisonment. While differences exist, the government subjects all immigration prisoners to its coercive powers through forcible confinement in secure facilities where detainees are closely watched and access is limited. The vast majority of people detained due to immigration law violations are held in jails, prisons, or other secure facilities that are modeled on those designed for prisoners awaiting criminal proceedings or serving sentences. Not surprisingly, all of the criminal detainees are kept in jails and prisons. Roughly half of the approximately 250 facilities where DHS holds civil immigration detainees function as jails and prisons that do not purport to be anything but penal institutions. Most of DHS's remaining civil immigration detainees are confined in secure structures designed to include many of the hallmarks of prisons and jails: involuntary confinement, strictly controlled access, barbed wire, steel doors, closely watched movements, and more.

Every year, these facilities house vast numbers of people.... Though several immigration-related crimes exist, the most commonly prosecuted include unauthorized entry (a federal misdemeanor) and unauthorized reentry (a federal felony).

. . . Alongside criminal incarceration, DHS used its civil immigration detention authority to confine . . . individuals for alleged violations of civil immigration law provisions (e.g., being physically present in the United States without authorization). In total, hundreds of thousands of people are incarcerated each year for allegedly engaging in nonviolent immigration activity prohibited by state or federal civil or criminal law—or, in some instances, both. These violations range from entering the United States without the federal government's permission to using an invented social security number to gain employment.

Evidence shows that migrants suffer unthinkable harms while imprisoned. At the same time, policies regulating migration have not only remained indifferent to these realities, but have become increasingly punitive over the last thirty years.

Imprisonment, then, befalls people who engage in prohibited immigration-related conduct through both criminal- and civil-law processes. Because confinement in these instances turns on migrant status or on activity inextricably tied to being a migrant (e.g., hiring someone to transport you clandestinely into the United States), viewing the practice of locking up migrants as a single, multi-stranded phenomenon of immigration imprisonment better reflects the reality of immigration law enforcement today than demarcating distinctions based on criminal- or civil-law powers. As former immigration detainee Malik Ndaula put it, to those locked up—the nation's immigration prisoners—"prison is prison no matter what label you use." . . .

[I]mprisonment has become a normal, routine, and self-replicating feature of immigration policing—that is, . . . immigration imprisonment has naturalized. . . .

. . . [I]mmigration imprisonment falls most heavily on people of color, especially migrants from Mexico and other Latin American countries. . . .

Such racially skewed enforcement may lead to the perception that immigration law enforcement targets people of color generally and Latinos specifically. This can lead to a delegitimation of immigration law enforcement in the eyes of Latino migrants, their friends, and their families. Law enforcement processes perceived as racially skewed threaten to delegitimize immigration law. If migrants come to think that legal proceedings are stacked against them, they are less likely to abide by the rules of the proceedings. This is an obviously undesirable outcome.

Moreover, immigration imprisonment's broad reach means that many people may view it as indiscriminate. Given that only a small percentage of people incarcerated for immigration law violations have committed a violent act, sympathetic commentators frequently claim that migrants have done nothing worthy of detention. Indeed, a common refrain among immigrants' rights advocates is that migrants are not criminals and thus should not be treated as such. Former Florida Governor Jeb Bush illustrated a variation of this framing recently, commenting that unauthorized migrants "crossed the border because they had no other means to work to be able to provide for their family—yes, they broke the law, but it's not a felony...—it's an act of love." A law enforcement regime that is perceived as punishing good-hearted people who seek only to provide for their families risks losing moral credibility.

Finally, detention adversely affects rule-of-law norms. Since detention severely impacts a migrant's ability to access counsel, it is impossible to know whether pro se migrants are removed because the law mandated that outcome or simply because no one was available to make the migrant's case. Detention, therefore, indirectly diminishes the legitimacy of the outcome....

García Hernández sketches the expansion of mass detention and deportation: public agencies (like the Department of Homeland Security) and private institutions (like for-profit corrections companies) have grown stronger and richer in the process. Keeping with established patterns of identity hierarchy, this coercive use of state power has depended on and fed heightened anti-immigrant and racist political rhetoric. The damage has degraded Black and brown lives, while further enriching and elevating ruling elites.

The damage also has undermined the system's capacity to actually litigate and adjudicate cases, including criminal prosecutions that can lead to incarceration and, after that, disenfranchisement. Focusing on the creation of the federal Sentencing Commission and Guidelines in 1984 and its systemic effects since then, criminal law scholar Ricardo Bascuas documents and explains:

> In a regime of fixed, harsh sentences, exclusive executive control over mitigation greatly facilitates prosecutions. Defendants whose only hope for a less-than-Draconian sentence lies with the prosecutor can be made to plead guilty and to provide helpful information and testimony against others. To achieve that, [the Department of Justice] has continually pressed to keep Guidelines sentences high and to prevent judges from departing downward without the prosecution's acquiescence. The Department has even managed to have sentencing reductions for guilty pleas partially depend on whether the prosecutor is satisfied that the defendant has confessed fully.

> ... [T]he Guidelines impose[ ] real costs on the right to trial. ... The data show that ... [in] 2008, federal prosecutors tried fewer than half as many cases [in court] as they did in 1980 despite a two-and-a-half-fold increase in the number of cases. The reason for the overwhelming increase in guilty pleas is that the Guidelines force defendants to opt for the sentence imposed for "accepting responsibility" or risk a drastically higher sentence for the chance of an acquittal.[24]

The modern-day systemic disappearance of the criminal jury trial was carried out in plain sight by top-down "reforms" that made access to jury verdicts increasingly risky and difficult. As a practical matter, making access to a trial unreachable for most defendants undercuts the purposes given for the constitutional right to counsel: to ensure a fair hearing before an impartial jury of peers. But instead, this systemic restructuring ensures that fewer advocates (and judges) have the experience, capacity, or expectation to ensure "fair" procedures under a purportedly adversarial system; over time, trials fade "naturally" as institutional memory forgets how to conduct them. This intentional "gap" and its elite cultivation thus help to explain the system-wide persistence of "access" problems despite repeated top-down expressions of fidelity to equal justice under law: by design, this systemic redrawing of ground rules and foundational concepts makes mass incarceration easier, quicker, and cheaper for elites. Over time, the disappearance of trials and the pressure to "plead out" keep the carceral state humming.

Below, Marie Gottschalk, an early critic of the expanding carceral state who also coined the term, deepens the themes laid out by Takei, García Hernández, and Bascuas. She points out that neither "politics as usual" nor "economics as usual" can adequately take on interests invested in the carceral state. Rather, organized struggle is required to change "ground rules" of the legal-political-economic "game."

BRING IT ON: THE FUTURE OF PENAL REFORM, THE CARCERAL STATE, AND AMERICAN POLITICS

Marie Gottschalk
12 Ohio St. J. Crim. L. 559 (2015)

... The incipient movements to challenge the carceral state and other inequalities in the United States ... cannot bet their future on politicians and the two main political parties. Establishing vibrant and independent institutions and organizations such as unions, women's groups, community and immigrant centers, and an alternative press was key to mounting

---

[24] Ricardo J. Bascuas, The American Inquisition: Sentencing After the Federal Guidelines, 45 Wake Forest L. Rev. 1 (2010).

successful challenges to gaping political and economic inequalities in the past and will continue to be key in the future.

The sobering reality is that "true criminal justice ultimately awaits true social justice." . . . Vast and growing economic inequalities rooted in vast and growing political inequalities are the preeminent problem facing the United States today. They are the touchstone of many of the major issues that vex the country—from mass incarceration to mass unemployment to climate change to the economic recovery of Wall Street but not Main Street and Martin Luther King Street. In the face of the enormous political chasm between the 99 percent and the 1 percent, a strategy of elite-led, bipartisan deal cutting premised on calls for "shared sacrifice" leaves this grossly inequitable economic and political fabric intact. As such, the 99 percent are caught in the vise of small-bore policies from their supposed friends and allies while their opponents encircle them with scorched-earth politics.

Faced with an economic meltdown widely understood to be the result of breathtaking malfeasance by the financial sector and its political patrons, President Obama and his key advisers first singled out health care costs and the deficit as the leading threats to the country's long-term economic health. Characterizing the country's economic problems this way was politically costly. It fostered an exaggerated faith in the possibilities to forge productive coalitions with elite political and economic interests. At the same time, it diminished interest in cultivating a wider political and social movement to press for far-reaching changes in issues ranging from mass unemployment to mass incarceration.

. . . President Franklin D. Roosevelt [FDR] came into office at an exceptional moment in 1933. Four years into the Depression, the Hoover administration was thoroughly discredited, as was the business sector. FDR recognized that the country was ready for a clean break with the past as he symbolically and substantively cultivated that sentiment. The break did not come from FDR alone. Massive numbers of Americans mobilized in unions, women's organizations, veterans' groups, senior citizen associations, and civil right organizations to ensure that the country changed course.

During the Depression, President Roosevelt was forced to broaden the public understanding of crime to include corporate crime. The Senate's riveting Pecora hearings during the waning days of the Hoover administration and the opening months of the Roosevelt presidency turned a scorching public spotlight on the malfeasance of the corporate sector and its complicity in sparking the Depression. As he put the House of Morgan and other bankers on trial, Ferdinand Pecora, chief counsel of the Senate Banking Committee, helped popularize during the age of Al Capone a term no longer heard today—the "bankster." These hearings compelled

Roosevelt to support stricter regulation of the financial sector that he might not have otherwise.

One cannot talk about crime in the streets today without talking about crime in the suites. Over the past four decades, the growing public obsession with getting tougher on street crime has coincided with the retreat of the state in regulating corporate malfeasance—everything from hedge funds to credit default swaps to workplace safety. Keeping the focus on street crime was a convenient strategy to shift public attention and resources from crime in the suites to crime in the streets.

As billionaire financier Warren Buffet quipped in 2006 shortly before the Great Recession descended, "There's class warfare, all right, but it's my class, the rich class, that's making war, and we're winning." The signs of victory are everywhere. Income inequality rivals the Gilded Age.... The United States today has the largest proportion of low-wage workers of any advanced industrialized country. In 2011, the official poverty rate was 15 percent, a steep increase from 12 percent a decade ago.

President Obama's persistent calls during his first term for a politics that rises above politics, premised on "shared sacrifice," denied this reality and was politically demobilizing. It thwarted the emergence of a compelling alternative political vision on which new coalitions and movements could be forged to challenge fundamental inequities, including mass imprisonment and the growing tentacles of the carceral state. As political scientist E. E. Schattschneider once said, "The definition of the alternatives is the supreme instrument of power." If the political and economic agenda needs to be fundamentally changed and not just tinkered with, we should expect more "bring it on" politics, not less.

... For all the bluster about political polarization, the debate over what to do about the economy, the social safety net, and the regulation of the financial sector—like the elite discussions over what to do about mass incarceration—oscillate within a very narrow range defined by neoliberalism and austerity policies....

... Buying into austerity politics means buying into the false idea that profligate spending by states and municipalities was at the root of the budget crises for state and local governments. The primary cause was actually a perilous drop in the main sources of revenue for local and state governments—property, income, and sales taxes—as the housing bubble burst and the economy contracted thanks to Wall Street's malfeasance. These budgetary shortfalls have been used as a pretext to dismantle key government functions and services or to hive them off to the private sector—everything from schools to health care to prisons.... [P]rogressives have generally been slow to mount an aggressive defense of expanding fiscal policy at a time when the private sector lacks the will or the capacity to invest in ways that reduce mass employment and that foster enlightened social and economic policies.

. . . This may be a winning political strategy for the short term. It is wholly inadequate, however, to address the enormous problems that the country faces. It is incapable of galvanizing wide swaths of the public to participate in convulsive politics from below to force the dismantling of the carceral state . . . and the amelioration of other gaping inequalities.

As these excerpts show, top-down politics and policies have reversed policies that promote broad economic and social well-being to instead fund a police state. This redistribution of resources has allowed inter-group inequalities to increase, exacerbating the violence of systemic injustice. When education fails to produce sufficient conformity with top-down imperatives, the militarized police forces of the carceral state stand ready to enforce them with raw might, mass incarcerations, and other coercive instruments.

NOTES AND QUESTIONS

1. *Interest Convergence.* Reflecting on the above materials, how might you describe the converging and diverging interests that help to maintain the carceral state? How do identities, groups, and power affect your understanding of those interests?

2. *Can "Good People" Become Prosecutors?* Criminal law scholar and former federal prosecutor Paul Butler provocatively asked whether lawyers could create change by working from the "inside" as sympathetic prosecutors:

> The adversarial nature of the justice system, the culture of the prosecutor's office, and the politics of crime pose insurmountable obstacles for prosecutors who are concerned with economic and racial justice. . . . [P]rosecutors spend too much of their time making arguments in favor of police power. They ask judges to adopt pinched interpretations of the Constitution and individual rights. . . . Becoming a prosecutor to help resolve unfairness in the criminal justice system is like enlisting in the army because you are opposed to the current war. It's like working for an oil refinery because you want to help the environment. . . .
>
> In the state system, where 90 percent of criminal cases are brought, the head prosecutor is a politician who in most cases was elected pursuant to the dysfunctional politics of criminal justice in which people get votes to put more people in cages. . . .
>
> [In sum,] does working within the system contribute to the problem? [Yes.] . . . Second, is it possible to make a real difference from the inside? If mere "reform" is required, working within the

system might accomplish that change. If, on the other hand, a more substantial transformation is necessary, it becomes more evident that the change must come from without. Those who work inside can tinker with the punishment regime, but they probably cannot overhaul it.[25]

Butler concludes that prosecutors "are more part of the problem than the solution." What is your response?

2.7 FIGHTING BACK SMARTLY—USING AMELIORATION FOR TRANSFORMATION

Above, we surveyed how legal and social changes associated with *Brown* present a more complicated portrait of "progress" under and by law. Formal reforms, or even social changes, are never secure—and never, by themselves, can produce equal justice. Moreover, *Brown's* complexity is paradigmatic, not anomalous, when it comes to law, justice, and progress. These complexities are not limited to any particular issue, place, group, or time.

With these points in mind, now think about Flint. In Flint, Michigan, officials of a predominantly Black community with the nation's highest poverty rate switched the drinking water supply to the heavily polluted Flint River as a cost-saving measure during a municipal financial emergency. This change poisoned community members when that corrosive water interacted with Flint's aging lead pipe infrastructure.[26]

A traditional remedy to this problem might aim to ameliorate the effects of the poisoned water. For example, the crisis prompted the Nestlé corporation to donate more than a million plastic water bottles since 2015 to Flint residents.[27] This gave residents clean drinking water for a time. This act is ameliorative, in line with the saying, "Give a man a fish, and you feed him for a day." That's not a bad thing—providing clean water to those who need it. That adage goes on to say, "Teach a man to fish, and you feed him for a lifetime." In the Flint case, officials worked with local community partners to help individuals get water filters and learn how to install them, encouraged efforts to make sure Flint residents got water bills reduced so they were not having to pay for contaminated water, and

---

[25] Paul Butler, Let's Get Free: A Hip-Hop Theory of Justice 101–02, 108–09, 120 (2010).

[26] See generally Tim Carmody, How the Flint River Got So Toxic (Feb. 26, 2016), www.theverge.com/2016/2/26/11117022/flint-michigan-water-crisis-lead-pollution-history (discussing the structural problems behind the crisis that are replicated across the U.S.).

[27] See How Much Water has Nestlé Donated to the Flint Michigan Relief Efforts?, www.nestle-watersna.com/en/who-we-are/frequently-asked-questions/how-much-water-has-nestle-donated-to-the-flint-michigan-relief-efforts.

supported residents in becoming "citizen-scientists" capable of understanding the quality of their water system.[28] That is all important.

But is it transformative? Do these solutions, in isolation, make it less likely that the residents of Flint will have poisoned water now or more likely they will maintain access to clean water over time? Do these measures ensure that decision making will be accountable to residents' priorities and responsive to their needs? In the case of Flint, receiving free bottles of water or even learning to filter and monitor their own water is not enough—it partially ameliorates the effects of the immediate problem. But it does not transform systems to make such pollution in low-income communities of color (so common that it has a name—environmental racism) unthinkable. Amelioration alone fails to build power to ensure residents can exercise more influence over decision making that affects their health and prosperity.

In fact, the gesture of help from Nestlé suggests why deeper systemic solutions are needed. At about the same time that Nestlé was providing free bottled water to Flint residents, the company also secured rights to extract clean water from Michigan natural springs at a bargain price and sell it elsewhere for considerable profit. The company's annual access fee for pumping 250 gallons a minute from Michigan's White Pine Springs was only $200, lower than the annual water bill of many homeowners. The state Department of Environmental Quality approved this extraction despite 80,945 letters of protest from residents compared to only 75 in favor.[29] This is part of a corporate plan:

> Nestlé has come to dominate a controversial industry, spring by spring, often going into economically depressed municipalities with the promise of jobs and new infrastructure in exchange for tax breaks and access to a resource that's scarce for millions. Where Nestlé encounters grass-roots resistance against its industrial-strength guzzling, it deploys lawyers; where it's welcome, it can push the limits of that hospitality, sometimes with the acquiescence of state and local governments that are too cash-strapped or inept to say no. There are the usual costs of doing business, including transportation, infrastructure, and salaries. But Nestlé pays little for the product it bottles—sometimes a

---

[28] www.huffingtonpost.com/entry/how-to-help-flint-water-crisis_us_569e8e78e4b0cd99679b9541.

[29] See Eleanor Cummins, Michigan is Practically Giving Away Clean Water—But Not To Flint (Apr. 13, 2018), www.popsci.com/flint-michigan-nestle-bottled-water (discussing the privatization of the public resource of clean water).

municipal rate and other times just a nominal extraction fee. In Michigan, it's $200.[30]

Over time, the privatization of water supplies shifts control away from government decision making and into the hands of corporations. This continual transference steadily reduces community control over, and diminishes, public resources. Decision making thereby is fundamentally altered—moved even further away from even the formal semblance of democratic accountability. So, the failures of accountable democracy and principled oversight that allowed Flint officials to poison the water are made more deeply entrenched and likely to recur by privatized water deals. Even as the Flint crisis is "fixed," the next failures are made more likely.

This pattern of decision making, which systemically places some groups in peril while protecting or advantaging other groups, is not new—in Flint or elsewhere.[31] As the Report of the Michigan Civil Rights Commission on the Flint crisis notes, this local crisis builds on intentional, legally-authorized exclusions and material deprivations of earlier eras:

> [T]o properly and completely assess the causes of the Flint water crisis, we must look back much further. We believe the underlying issue is historical and systemic, dates back nearly a century, and has at its foundation race and segregation of the Flint community. These historical policies, practices, laws and norms fostered and perpetuated separation of race, wealth and opportunity.
>
> We are not suggesting that those making decisions related to this crisis were racists, or meant to treat Flint any differently because it is a community primarily made up by people of color. Rather, the disparate response is the result of systemic racism that was built into the foundation and growth of Flint, its industry and the suburban area surrounding it. This is revealed through the story of housing, employment, tax base and regionalization which are interconnected in creating the legacy of Flint.
>
> . . . [The long history of segregation] was a result of both private discrimination (restrictive covenants) and government policies (mortgage requirements, school district lines, etc.) Of course, much of this was possible because American jurisprudence at the time [these practices were established] was largely based

---

[30] Caroline Winter, Nestlé Makes Billions Bottling Water It Pays Nearly Nothing For, Bloomberg Businessweek (Sept. 21, 2017), www.bloomberg.com/news/features/2017-09-21/nestl-makes-billions-bottling-water-it-pays-nearly-nothing-for.

[31] For example, the poisoned water in Flint connects to a legacy of lead poisoning through other delivery modes—such as lead-based paint in older, deteriorating housing—that disproportionately impacts children and communities on the basis of economic class and color. See Emily A. Benfer, Contaminated Childhood: The Chronic Lead Poisoning of Low-Income Children and Communities of Color in the United States (Aug. 8, 2017), www.healthaffairs.org/do/10.1377/hblog20170808.061398/full/.

on the U.S. Supreme Court's adoption of the "separate but equal" doctrine in *Plessy v. Ferguson*.

. . . [But even more recently] the legacy of discrimination remained. It has brought the city of Flint to where it now finds itself—with a majority of its residents being people of color, and their complaints, along with those of their white neighbors, largely ignored.

This brings us to the question: Would the Flint water crisis have been allowed to happen in [92% white] Birmingham, [73% white] Ann Arbor or [95% white] East Grand Rapids? We believe the answer is no.[32]

A bedrock lesson of Flint and countless similar examples is that even urgent ameliorative solutions—residents getting free bottles of water or learning to filter and monitor water themselves—are just not enough. Those measures do not account for the long history of communities excluded or marginalized on the basis of social identity. For this key reason, systemic advocacy employs amelioration as scaffolding for transformation.

Recall the adage: Getting fish, learning to fish. But they are functionally the same if all the healthy fish are behind a dam in a pond owned by elites who dump poison down where the "average people" live. This illustrates concretely the importance of seeing law and being able to discuss in community and other settings the complex operations of law as a system. Even when the system is seeming to fail, it is doing so by design. What must be gained are the analytical skills to see and communicate that systemic failure—and the practical skills to dismantle the dam and stop the poisoning so that average people are not disadvantaged while elites prosper.

Flint effectively illustrates the importance of both amelioration and transformation in crafting solutions for systemic injustice. Part of the Critical Challenge is that elites may tolerate ameliorative solutions to derail transformation. The critical question that the Flint crisis raises for systemic advocates is whether and how advocates can fight for ameliorative solutions and also build into that fight the sorts of changes that might transform future decision-making and outputs. The ongoing challenge that this book details is whether activists and advocates can "fix" problems while also transforming cultural understandings and shifting power to "average" people.

But, as Flint also illustrates, even ameliorative solutions are hard-won. They require numerous individuals to mobilize and collaborate as a group for justice. In fact, no one really "gave" Flint residents anything.

---

[32] The Flint Water Crisis: Systemic Racism Through the Lens of Flint, A Report of the Michigan Civil Rights Commission (Feb. 17, 2017), www.michigan.gov/documents/mdcr/VFlint CrisisRep-F-Edited3-13-17_554317_7.pdf.

Flint residents struggled to bring attention to the problem, and they organized to demand solutions. Residents became activists, and activists worked with allies, including professionals—lawyers and scientists and physicians and others—to bring to light the poisoned water and its effects on children and families in Flint. They worked in creative, collaborative ways against organized opposition to win recognition and (some) redress. With Flint's lessons in mind, this chapter's final two excerpts delve deeper into amelioration and transformation in systemic problem solving.

In the first excerpt, legal historian Tom Romero examines water inequalities in the western U.S., noting the centrality of race and of elite interests in controlling and monetizing this natural resource. Romero shows how law accepts and enforces "gross disparities" in access, quality, and consumption that correlate to social identities. This analysis shows how a seemingly colorless "natural" element that is essential for all life is commodified by law to reflect and reinforce social inequalities also erected and enforced by law.

THE COLOR OF WATER: OBSERVATIONS OF A BROWN BUFFALO ON WATER LAW AND POLICY IN TEN STANZAS
Tom I. Romero, II
15 U. Denv. Water L. Rev. 329 (2012); 1 U. Miami Race & Soc. Just. L. Rev. 107 (2011)

...Law is everywhere when it comes to water. From the very nascent stages of civilization, humans have developed a complex body of rules, rights, and procedures governing the capture, use, and distribution of water....

... After the gold rush and homesteading radically altered the demographic composition of the western half of the United States, litigants, lawyers, judges, and legislators . . . [applied] the principle of "first in time, first in right," [and the resulting] doctrine of prior appropriation protects the first person to use the water against all subsequent takers. . . . In many cases, this leaves no water for the second person or any other subsequent users.

In Colorado, which "pioneered" prior appropriation law, the legal regime of Mexican water law co-existed in relative tension with the emerging priority scheme. "Under Mexican law, for instance, all users, whatever their priority, would find themselves included in structure of access to a state-owned patrimony that looked to principles of equitable sharing and necessity to allocate water among all users." . . . [S]oon after statehood and the adoption of Article XIV to the Colorado Constitution providing for the right of prior appropriation, the first priority right in the state was granted in the Spanish-speaking San Luis Valley. The consequence was to overlay and thereby eradicate the communal rights of Hispano residents in the state. . . .

The doctrine of prior appropriation, and the principles of property and private enterprise that it represented, became the basis by which those in the United States seized the great watercourses of the American West and deployed them in the service of suburbanization and metropolitan fragmentation....

Along the border of the United States and Mexico [today], a true "borderlands" of water law and policy exists. In this space over half-a-million poor Latinos live in so-called Colonia communities....

At the most basic level, Colonias are unregulated subdivisions that have emerged as unincorporated municipalities ... [with no] basic powers of zoning, taxing, and eminent domain. As a result, Colonias lack basic infrastructure ... [including] water or sewage lines....

... [Colonias are created when landowners] in unincorporated rural areas subdivide pieces of agriculturally worthless land that often lies in low-lying flood plains. The landowning developer then sells, with a Contract for Deed, plots to prospective low-income Latinos who seek affordable housing. Though the developer would make vague promises about future development, the land was almost always unimproved and did not have piping for the delivery of potable water or any capability for wastewater disposal. Nor did the developers make provisions for adequate drainage. Thus, when it rains, Colonia residents find themselves subject to significant property damage and contamination by human waste....

... Health care advocates blamed the lack of safe drinking water and wastewater disposal as the primary culprit for increased rates of hepatitis, anencephaly, cholera, tuberculosis, encephalitis, and diarrhea in Colonia communities.

Law ... has played a primary role in the racial inequity of Colonia communities.... [B]oth county governments and state legislatures choose to ignore or only partially address the problems. It was not until the late 1980s and early 1990s ... [that some state governments] created the Economically Distressed Area Program ("EDAP").... The EDAP provided funding for water and sewer services to economically distressed areas ... [but] it exempted many Colonia communities, contained various loopholes, and was grossly underfunded.

Additionally, ... the EDAP fails to account for the municipal underbounding problem, by which municipalities refuse to annex [and strengthen infrastructure in] impoverished, minority, fringe communities....

... Colonias are internal racialized colonies structured by American law and policy that epitomize racialized water law and policy problems in the developed world [and mirror those around the world]....

> [T]here has been massive private investment in water over the last two decades. Motivated initially by the so-called "Washington Consensus," the World Bank, the International Monetary Fund, and regional development banks encouraged the privatization of water systems around the world....
>
> ... [T]he privatization of public water services has proven to be a mixed bag at best, and tremendously unequal at worst. Huge profits, higher water prices, cutoffs to customers, reduced water quality, shoddy maintenance, and even greater levels of public debt represent the legacy of privatization from Atlanta, Georgia to Cochabamba, Bolivia.
>
> Privatization also aggregates control of water in the hands of a few private companies or individuals, who are outside the bounds of either public scrutiny or accountability....
>
> The commodification of water ... ensures that "decisions regarding the allocation of water center on commercial, not environmental or social justice considerations...."
>
> Water [thus] contributes to the creation of distinct color lines, marking the type of home one owns or occupies; it helps to identify the way government comes to interact with distinct neighborhoods and communities; it determines whether children are healthy enough to attend school and receive an equal education. In the end, the racialized inequities of the contemporary world come to light in the troubled rivers, lakes, ponds, aquifers, septic tanks, and reservoirs....

As Romero shows with the commodification of water in the United States, critical analysis of persistent social problems can expose their deep roots in identity-based groups, interests, and power. These deep roots make amelioration infinitely easier than transformation—even though amelioration also requires long and hard battles. But advocacy satisfied with just amelioration will never change systems. One of the most creative, continuing, and challenging tasks of advocacy is building into actions for amelioration the steps or paths necessary for transformation.

In the excerpt below, Central American-born legal scholar Raquel Aldana develops these points in a contemporary context outside of the United States: indigenous peoples in Guatemala resisting the extraction and pollution of their environment by foreign-based multi-national corporations. Aldana underscores the complexity both of systemic injustice *and* of group struggles against it. She illustrates the materiality and economics of oppression, which extend from the micro, individual level to group-wide or even global macro effects. As you read, consider Aldana's account from the perspective of amelioration and then from the perspective of transformation. Compare her account of Guatemala to Romero's account of the colonias along the U.S.-Mexico border. Do you see any patterns across time, place, and group?

THE INDISPENSABLE ONES: A STORY OF MINING RESISTANCE FROM LA PUYA
Raquel Aldana[33]

There are those who fight one day and they are good. Others fight a year and they are better. There are those who fight many years, and they are very good. But those who fight a lifetime: they are the indispensable ones.[34]

The rapid growth in consumption and production around the world in recent decades has escalated the need for energy and raw materials. As the world's economy uses more materials and energy, conflicts over resource extraction have increased. The rise in conflict is also explained by the displacement of extractive projects from the Global North toward the Global South.

Extractive industries generate significant negative environmental and social impacts including deforestation, biodiversity loss, high water consumption, groundwater contamination, and forced displacement. Yet, due to corruption and failed democracies, the distribution of burdens and benefits is terribly uneven among stakeholders. While investors and consumers of energy or raw materials reap the immediate benefits of increased profits and consumption, the local communities most directly affected by the mining activity in their territory suffer gravely and must live with the scientific uncertainty of unknown risks in the future. Sadly, extractive projects in the Global South almost always occur without the participation of local communities in any of the decision-making.

This chapter tells the story of a mining conflict in one community in Guatemala: the Peaceful Resistance Movement of La Puya. La Puya describes the site of extraction of tons of gold since 2014 by Kappes, Cassiday & Associates (Kappes), a U.S.-based mining company. To write this story, I interviewed twenty activists, mostly women, at two sites of permanent peaceful resistance. I relied on the blessing of Dr. Yuri Melini, Founding Director of the Center for Legal-Environmental and Social Action of Guatemala (CALAS)) to gain the access and trust of the community. The community entrusted me with telling its story so that other movements across the globe could be inspired and learn from the story of La Puya. The community also wanted U.S. lawyers, law students, and the U.S. public to know its plight and understand that its struggle is not just for them but for

---

[33] Adapted by the author from her chapter in From Extraction to Emancipation: Development Reimagined (Raquel Aldana and Steven W. Bender eds. 2018) (the volume arose out of the LatCrit Guatemala Study Space in 2015).

[34] Quote from Bertolt Brecht, a German poet; also known to be the lines of a famous song by Cuban singer Silvio Rodriguez, titled *Los Imprescindibles*.

all of us. The stories I heard were interwoven in themes that transcended the narration of a single story to reveal the intimate and spiritual web that created the collective. The presence of lawyers and legal institutions make up an essential thread in the story, both as facilitators of extraction and as protectors of communities and the environment.

Contextualizing La Puya

Guatemala has been the site of six mining conflicts in recent decades. La Puya's movement stands out among these conflicts for several reasons. Foremost, the resolve and persistence of members of the community literally to use their physical bodies twenty-four hours a day, seven days a week, for more than five years and counting, to create a permanent and visible fixture of resistance, is nothing short of incredible. Also, La Puya would become among the first movements to win important partial legal victories in Guatemala's courts to shut down a mine.

La Puya shares commonalities with other anti-mining resistance movements. By 2010, La Puya's peaceful resistance movement was already underway and significant questions had surfaced publicly about the legal validity of the exploitation license. Community resistance had two principal complaints: the lack of a legally valid consultation process conducted by the government with local communities and the very flawed and compromised Environmental Impact Assessment (EIA) that should have never been approved. By the time of my visit, five years after the mine's operation, the community in resistance lamented the loss of the forest, the lack of water or its contamination, and the inability to grow food on its land.

Another of La Puya's shared reality with other mining conflicts is having to endure harassment, social and familial alienation, physical attacks, and deprivation of liberty as a result of their activism. Every year in Guatemala, hundreds of environmental activists are targeted with physical attacks, threats, and criminalization. Hundreds have been killed and nearly all of these murders remain unpunished. In La Puya, hostility toward the movement in the form of physical attempts to dismantle it or campaigns to tarnish the movement's reputation came early and involved police, the military, and citizens who sympathized and profited from the mine.

Another common characteristic of La Puya with other mining conflicts is the contestation and redefinition of ethnic identity as part of the resistance. Most discussions of Guatemala's mining conflicts by international organizations are quick to label the affected communities as indigenous. Legally, the label has mattered in order to trigger the protections of the International Labor Organization's Indigenous and Tribal People's Convention 169, including the local community's right to prior consultation for any development project in its territory. However, ethnic identity in a postcolonized Guatemala, where racism has shaped identity, is complex. In La Puya, indigenous identity has become integral to the public face of the mining conflict and accompanying legal strategies to stop its operation, despite the reality that its presence is more elusive in the movement.

Gender roles have also been reshaped in La Puya. Overall, there are fewer men in the movement than women. I observed a total of about one hundred people during my time at La Puya, of which nearly two-thirds were women. The women have challenged patriarchal structures in favor of collective governance and have also largely influenced the nonviolence that is a characteristic of the movement.

Finally, La Puya is also emblematic of Latin America's rejection since the 1990s of neoliberal values imposed in the region by countries in the North since the 1970s. In turn, these conflicts are also a reclamation of values seeking the preservation of the planet, respect for mother earth, and the reallocation of resource control in local communities. As such, these mining conflicts are the site of the clash in values where the participants reject globalization and consumerism in favor of a more minimalist way of life and the centralization of power in favor of local government. In this space, communities are favored over the individual as are local over the national or global communities.

In Their Own Words: The Story of La Puya Resistance as a Way of Life

The model of resistance has been simultaneously intuitive and strategic, organic and planned. Some members of the resistance talk about an intuition that is both physical and spiritual from deep in their DNA to defend their land. Initially at La Puya, the model was peaceful physical obstruction to prevent the mining company from entering. When that failed, the idea emerged that their permanent physical presence in front of the mine would build a moral wall that would ultimately stop the mine.

For some, resistance reveals itself in a defiance of *Ladinization*, a term Guatemalans use to describe the assimilation of indigenous and mixed peoples into a socially constructed "whiteness." Disturbingly, Ladinization is now employed by those who oppose the movement, in order to undermine the community's assertion of the sacredness of Mother Earth. Some within the resistance resent the strategic efforts of the opposition to describe the movement as indigenous because most members of the movement have had their indigeneity muddled as a by-product of colonization. Thus, part of the resistance reveals itself in two seemingly conflicting ways: First, there is a reclaiming among some of their Xinca identity, as best as it can be known, through stories and readings. "Our ancestors are the Xinca," they say. "They came from Peru to Guatemala about 1,500 years ago and they were fierce in defending their territory against the Spaniards. They lost because they were few. Today, we are Xinca, and we renew their fight." Hence, amidst worship in traditionally Catholic or Evangelical ways, Mayan sacred rituals have also been incorporated. Second, there is an effort to defy the notion that only those recognizable today in Guatemala as indigenous—like the K'akchikel who are also in the territory of the mining site—should be the only ones with rights to protect their land and way of life. "We are tribal," they say, "in the way the meaning is expressed in the ILO Convention 169 [the Indigenous and Tribal Peoples Convention of the UN agency International Labour Organization]. We have cultivated this land for the past 400 years. We too, have a right to be consulted before they destroy our land and leave us nothing."

For others, resistance is also a rejection of individuality and patriarchy. Their way of governance and reaching decisions is through consensus in general assembly. They reject the label of leader, though there are clearly persons who guide. Many are women, though their voices became louder while in the movement: "they stopped being silent and submissive." Most participate as nuclear families. Men support the women and view them as pillars of the movement. The women feed the men, both literally and figuratively.

For others, resistance is also against the materialism and greed that the mine represents. Their struggle surpasses the mine: their lives, even for those who live in the city, are daily commitments to simplify. It is a conscious choice to reject excess. One mother said, "Our resistance and that of our children began when they were still in my womb." Their resistance is also against the apathy and selfishness of all of us who consume and ignore too much. . . . Despite the resistance community's commitment to religion, they do not find support in the local churches. Local mayors are accused of corruption and of supporting the mine for the meager royalties they get from Kappes' underreporting of the gold they take. As for the rest of their country people, the indifference and sometimes outright hostility of Guatemalans pain the resistance community. To the international community, the resistors' message is their story. Their collective agreement to permit us to tell their story is to raise consciousness about the environment, corporate greed, and injustice in the degree of natural resource consumption and its impact on mother earth. Their message is simple: conserve, recycle, simplify your lives, and educate yourselves. "Water is sacred and it will not be around forever. Treasure it as if your life depended on it, because it does."

Toxic Opposition

Members of the resistance use terms such as *humiliating, debasing, defaming,* and *cruel* to describe the way retired military colonels and a few recruits waged their campaign to remove them from La Puya. The opposition formed a group called Retired Military Mining Services of

Central America (Ex Militares Servicios Mineros de Centro América). Their strategy seemed to be to run the resistance out through sheer insults delivered face-to-face or through defamatory rumors and wait it out. They specifically targeted women, knowing their leadership was vital within the movement. Their methods sought to tarnish the women's reputations: spreading rumors of infidelity, publishing nude pictures of one resistance member, and calling them whores. Children of the resistance were also bullied at school, which was particularly hard. Then, the opposition resorted to criminalization. Kappes and their supporters leveled criminal accusations against several members of the resistance for alleged kidnapping, obstruction of judicial orders, or destruction of private property. Three were convicted before the movement sought legal representation from CALAS. The three remain condemned today although out on bail and for time served.

Mayday: The Day the Resistance Died and Was Born Again

With the resistance holding steady to shut down the entrance to the mine, counter-resistance would soon turn forceful and violent. Hundreds of armed anti-riot police waged a few violent encounters leading up to the fateful two days and nights in May 2014. The attack on the camp started after midnight on May 23. Members of the resistance not at the camp were awakened by the sounds of bells or ring tones calling for help and ran to their aid in their sleepwear, some with mismatched shoes. All of them mention the rocks, tear gas, and pepper bombs hurled at them in the form of hundreds of little bottles from the pockets of the police: "We could drink nothing; even the water tasted like pepper and bitterness." People hid in the camps, ready to die. Some fought back, hurling insults and rocks, wishing to be armed. The anti-riot police destroyed the camp, the kitchen, everything.

Kappes machinery entered the mine on May 25, 2014. For a moment, the shattered movement considered what would come next. Leaving was not an option. So, they decided to stay, no longer blocking the site but nonetheless visibly present right outside. Kappes had won, at least momentarily.

Ojalá que remonte su vuelo, más que el condor y el águila real (May He Retake his Flight, Higher Than the Condor and the Golden Eagle)

The movement was no longer the same. The camp had to learn to live with the noise, the dust, and the knowledge that right next to them a mine was taking their water and gold, and only spewing out contamination. The fight had to continue, although this time it would continue freshly armed with political and legal advocacy while still surrounded by hundreds of supporters nationally and internationally.

Legally, the movement sought help from CALAS and the Human Rights Law Firm (Bufete Jurídico de Derechos Humanos). There, they found two fierce human rights and environmental lawyers, Rafael Maldonado and Edgar Pérez Archila, who together provided effective defense for the remaining half dozen members of the resistance facing criminal charges. In addition, CALAS challenged the very legality of the mining license. CALAS would ultimately succeed in securing provisional measures from the Guatemalan Supreme Court to stop the mine from noncompliance with the mandated requirement of prior, free, and informed consent found in ILO Convention 169.

La Puya Wounded

The mine's closure, whether temporary or permanent, cannot undo the harm caused. La Puya is a term that speaks of trees with spikes that would prick people as they passed by. There were large trees there, some nearly 400 years old. Now, those trees are gone. Some of the women of the resistance still cry over the trees that were chopped down to build the mine. "The elders of the community especially cried rivers that day," they say. La Puya leaders are especially worried about water either drying up or being contaminated. They are aware that the drought aggravates their meager water supplies. However, they insist that the mine's water waste in its nearly two years of operation, consuming in an hour what a family would in 20 years, is primarily responsible. La Puya leaders speak of four deposits of toxic waste, much bigger than authorized by the environmental impact report, sitting on top of a highly seismic area, ready to burst. La Puya leaders insist that the water that residents drink is already contaminated by arsenic. The digging of the mine and the additional arsenic added in the process have turned the water into poison but no one is documenting the problem. People speak of strange illnesses, of sores on peoples' bodies, but no one has any proof yet and the MEM [Guatemala Ministry of Energy and Mines] is not seeking it. It is, thus, much too easy to ignore the crisis; meanwhile, people drink the water out of necessity, despite warnings that their skin could scale up like fish over time.

Doomed Eureka: No Compromise

At this juncture, it is impossible for resistance members to conceive any circumstance under which they could accept mining in their territory. There are roughly one hundred deeply committed members of the resistance who show up regularly in protest at the sites. Among those interviewed, they estimate that in the towns another 5,000 to 6,000 persons are reliably against the mine and would participate if called to speak against it. Those interviewed do not believe that their land could ever be paid in gold. They also do not believe that the cost of gold could be anything less than the sacrifice of their land and their way of life.

The Legal Battle

Neither the resistance nor the lawyers could have stopped the mine alone. The resistance needed the lawyers to take their stories to the courts framed in legal arguments; the lawyers needed the resistance to cloak the legalese with moral weight and public scrutiny. Since May 2014, while the movement kept watch over the mine's daily operations right outside its doors, it mobilized a multifaceted strategy in alliance with several local and international nonprofits to wage an advocacy campaign and a legal battle to stop the mine. The first legal victory came in July 2015 when an appellate judge in Guatemala issued a preliminary injunction ordering the suspension of the mine based on deficiencies in the EIA and the failure to consult with the affected communities. Kappes, however, refused to stop its mining operations, prompting several members of the U.S. Congress to write a letter to Guatemala's then President, Alejandro Maldonado Aguirre, urging him to ensure that Kappes complied with the Court's ruling (Congress of the United States 2015). Then, in February 2016, CALAS procured a preliminary injunction in Guatemala's Supreme Court to void El Tambor's mining license based on the lack of consultation with the local community as required by ILO Convention 169. Compliance with the Court's judgment would require significant and sustained political pressure. It would take the establishment of a second mining resistance site called La Puyita outside the MEM, significant transitions of power in Guatemala including the resignation of the head of MEM, and a political climate of significant international oversight for the MEM, for the MEM to agree to comply with the Supreme Court.

On May 5, 2016, Guatemala's Supreme Court made the preliminary injunction permanent and suspended Kappes' mining license. By this time, the mine had already ceased operations. To the community, however, its victory was bittersweet. It does not know if there is anything left to rescue from the mine. More importantly, Kappes is gone and no one is left to restore the mountain, decontaminate the water that remains, or plant the trees. Kappes could even return; their original mining license was after all, for twenty years. If that were to happen, the community prepares for the arduous task of convincing deeply divided towns to reject the mine.

For now, the mining license is suspended and the mining operation stalled. La Puya leaders do not think this is the end: there is still too much gold in there, they say, for Kappes to simply walk away. They expect a fight. In fact, in 2017, the Constitutional Court received an *amparo* [a writ seeking recourse for a violation of fundamental rights] from the mine's owners alleging that the community's protests and efforts to block entry into the mine violated their liberty rights to act, to move, and to do business. They sought to order the President of Guatemala and relevant officials to protect their rights. The Constitutional Court held that because the prior ruling suspended operation of the mine, the complainants had no claim of imminent injury.

Legally, if the MEM takes seriously Guatemala's Constitutional Court's ruling, then what must happen is the execution of prior, informed, and free consent. Unfortunately, the legal uncertainty of this process and the political pro-mining stance by the Guatemalan national government raises significant skepticism that it could be done right. Meanwhile, the resistance seeks time, hopefully two years, to have an opportunity to educate people. Some fear that if a consultation occurred today, they risk losing. They fear people will be bought off easily by Kappes through similar types of meager donations as in the past. They worry about the lack of support from the mayors and local priests, in addition to other forms of local corruption. Still, people have faith in a grass-roots movement of educating the public and there are already ongoing efforts. I met a young resistance member who is working with youth. Young people have always been involved with raising consciousness; since the beginning of the movement, they would travel to Guatemala City to become informed and then educate their community. Even now, they hold workshops and have young resistance members speak about mines and their own motivation for resisting. So far, the groups are small and these workshops must occur outside of schools and churches that do not support these educational campaigns.

As Aldana shows, formal legal rights, in this case the right to be consulted as a community over a proposed mining operation, can be overcome by powerful interests and actors. Compare this account from Guatemala to Crenshaw's overview of formal equality in the United States. Think back to Flint. What lessons do you draw about "rights," identity, and justice in relationship to amelioration and transformation?

NOTES AND QUESTIONS

1. *Questioning Amelioration and Transformation.* Mindful of the excerpts and examples above, how might advocates in the borderlands colonias or in Guatemala combine amelioration with transformation for problem-solving synergies with longer-term impacts?

2. *Connecting Flint to* Brown. With the Flint water crisis came a dramatic boost in the number of special needs students in public schools, prompting a lawsuit by Flint families against the school district and others alleging the "systemic failure to meet the needs of special education students."[35] Can you connect the dots between *Brown*, the Flint water crisis, and now the special

---

[35] See Corey Mitchell, In Flint, Schools Overwhelmed by Special Ed. Needs in Aftermath of Lead Crisis, Education Week (Aug. 26, 2019), www.edweek.org/ew/articles/2019/08/28/special-ed-concerns-loom-large-after-flint.html?cmp=eml-contshr-shr.

education crisis? If so, how do these connections affect what you deem necessary to ameliorate the damage? What about to transform the system and its outputs? What role can courts play as a means of securing meaningful access to such basic human needs as clean water, food for survival, and shelter? What role should legislatures play? Where else might people seek protection from systemic violence?

3. *Accountable Democracy and Flint.* The Flint crisis itself arose from failures of accountable democracy and principled oversight, allowing a government cost-saving response to a financial crisis to cause a public health crisis along identity lines. During Michigan's financial crisis, more than half of Michigan's Black residents, including residents of Detroit, were subject to local rule by governor-appointed emergency managers who displaced their elected local leaders and, in the case of Flint, green-lighted the switch to toxic drinking water; at that same time, only two percent of the state's white population was so governed.[36] Michigan's state attorney defended this wholesale displacement of local officials in Black communities under the state's emergency manager law, saying simply that "a unique time . . . requires unique solutions."[37] But the United States has a long history of regrettable top-down decision making in times of crisis—whether fiscal, national security, or otherwise. Can you think of any examples of crisis lawmaking in U.S. history that reinforced or accelerated known identity hierarchies?

4. *Connecting Flint to (Legal v. Systemic) Justice.* In January 2021—seven years after Flint's poisoning—Michigan's Attorney General charged ex-Governor Rick Snyder and eight others with crimes ranging from perjury to misconduct in office to involuntary manslaughter.[38] Thinking of both individuals and groups—and of amelioration and transformation—what is the significance of an indictment? Of a conviction? How is criminal prosecution related to "fixing" the problem—remedying past harms, stopping continuing water troubles, or ensuring no future recurrence? Would convictions constitute justice delayed or justice denied?

5. *Shifting Bottoms (and Tops).* In Chapter 1, we saw in the Mutua excerpt how the bottom and top of an identity-based caste may shift depending on the issue or context. Reflecting on Aldana's account, how would you describe the tops and bottoms in that context? If the top includes U.S.-based actors, how does their power and influence extend across borders to reach into remote locations like La Puya? Under these transnational circumstances, how might bottom-up advocacy also cross borders to overcome the Critical Challenge?

---

[36] See Sydney L. Hawthorne, Do Desperate Times Call for Desperate Measures in the Context of Democracy? Michigan's Emergency Manager Law & The Voting Rights Act, 41 N.Y.U. Rev. L. & Soc. Change 181 (2017).

[37] Curt Guyette, Schuette, Orr, Obstruct Scrutiny of PA 436, Detroit Metro Times (May 5, 2014), www.metrotimes.com/detroit/schuette-orr-obstruct-scrutiny-of-pa-436/Content?oid=2202131.

[38] https://www.nytimes.com/2021/01/14/us/rick-snyder-flint-water-charges.html; https://www.theguardian.com/us-news/2021/jan/14/flint-water-crisis-charges-rick-snyder-nick-lyon-eden-wells.

6. *Systemic Advocacy*. Aldana describes the symbiotic relationship of lawyers and clients in the mining struggle: "The resistance needed the lawyers to take their stories to the courts framed in legal arguments; the lawyers needed the resistance to cloak the legalese with moral weight and public scrutiny." Mindful of this mutuality, what knowledges, values, skills, and attitudes might systemic advocates wish to develop professionally to better serve clients, communities, and causes? What knowledges, values, skills, and attitudes do these excerpts indicate that systemic advocates should cultivate to achieve amelioration *plus* transformation?

2.8 CHRONIC INJUSTICE IS SYSTEMIC VIOLENCE

We use "systemic injustice" interchangeably with "systemic violence" because the two terms are, in effect, synonymous. Systemic injustice (or systemic violence) is thus the routine production and redistribution of disadvantages to subordinated social groups (accompanied, simultaneously, by the corollary advantages to privileged ones). The always-accumulating toll creates persistent and chronic stress, suffering, deprivation, worry, illness, and isolation for members of subordinated groups—an enormous assault on dignity, safety, prosperity, and security. Day by day, decade by decade, humiliation and risk are normalized. In its cumulative effects, systemic injustice becomes recognizable as systemic violence.

Unsurprisingly, systemic violence does not always shock the contemporary conscience, even though systemic violence frequently is shocking in retrospect. Many of the routinized, at times bureaucratized, instances of systemic violence in history are recognized—now—as horrific. For instance, South African apartheid, the German Holocaust, and Jim Crow lynchings in the U.S. South are seen today as extreme examples of systemic violence, but were endorsed by many when occurring. Those examples apparently did not seem horrific to many of those who engineered or served as frontline soldiers in the institutions meting out punishments or enforcing rules of identity-based caste. The growing literature on "The New Jim Crow" of mass incarceration illustrates how current patterns of systemic violence connect to eras now widely recognized as brutal and oppressive—the "old" Jim Crow and pre-Civil War days of racialized enslavement.[39] While it's happening, systemic injustice is "just" a daily routine that, over time, numbs the conscience.

---

[39] See generally Michelle Alexander, The New Jim Crow: Mass Incarceration in the Age of Colorblindness (2012); Marc Mauer, Race to Incarcerate (2006); Dorothy E. Roberts, Foreword: Abolition Constitutionalism, 133 Harv. L. Rev. 1 (2019); James Gray Pope, Mass Incarceration, Convict Leasing, and the Thirteenth Amendment: A Revisionist Account, 94 N.Y.U. L. Rev. 1465 (2019); Angela J. Davis, Policing the Black Man: Arrest, Prosecution, and Imprisonment (Angela J. Davis ed. 2017); Geiza Vargas-Vargas, The Investment Opportunity in Mass Incarceration: A Black (Corrections) or Brown (Immigration) Play, 48 Cal. W. L. Rev. 351 (2012).

Every generation hopes that nothing like that exists today. Yet myriad legal actors play key roles in the mechanisms that inflict continuing systemic violence. For example, the criminal justice system routinely prosecutes, convicts, incarcerates, and kills people of color at a higher rate than white people, and poor people more often than wealthy people. This routine *is* systemic violence, which can take many forms.[40] Consider each category presented in the (abbreviated) list below. Can you think of examples for each?

- Dehumanization, devaluation, and denials of human dignity;
- Murder, mass killings, and genocide;
- Cultural erasure and epistemic injustice;
- Criminalization and physical or violent control of bodies, reproduction, and communities;
- Exclusion from civic life and voice;
- Marginalization in living standards;
- Exploitation and precarity in work;
- Dispossession of territory and extraction of resources; and
- Fomenting division and alienation among peoples and groups.[41]

Systemic injustice may not appear—in real time—as starkly wrong because the very nature of systemic violence is routine, quiet, bureaucratic. Systemic violence occurs daily as part of the "normal" operations of society. As we have seen time and again, law is the grease that keeps this top-down machine humming—but that also can help bottom-up struggles against its violence.

NOTES AND QUESTIONS

1. *Unlearning and Relearning.* Advocates regularly undertake exercises in unlearning what was previously believed to be "true" and relearning a more complex and critical understanding of problems, patterns, and solutions. Reflect now on what you previously thought "violence" to mean or entail. Did you understand earlier that substandard housing, for example, is a type of violence? What about tainted drinking water? What other social problems might be examples of routinized systemic violence that you have experienced, witnessed, or studied?

2. *How Could They/We?* Legal actors, educators, public officials, and private individuals all routinely helped enforce imperatives of racial (and other types

---

[40] Robert Cover, Violence and the Word, 95 Yale L.J. 1601, 1611, 1627 (1986).

[41] See John O. Calmore, A Call to Context: The Professional Challenges of Cause Lawyering at the Intersection of Race, Space, and Poverty, 67 Fordham L. Rev. 1927, 1937 (1999).

of) segregation or hierarchy in schools and elsewhere in U.S. society. See generally Steven W. Bender, Mea Culpa: Lessons on Law and Regret From U.S. History (2015); Martin Luther King, Jr., Letter from Birmingham Jail (Apr. 16, 1963). As King noted, struggle often is identified in negative terms—as creating undue tension, precipitating violence, or rushing change. But tension and violence already exist in the "normal" experiences of those affected by systemic violence. Bottom-up struggles do not create tensions, but they do surface the tensions that pervade life at the bottom. How might individuals today discern which routinized policies and practices will someday be seen widely as unjust? How might systemic advocates identify and reveal such legal and policy "blind-spots" to help prevent or end violence and suffering?

CHAPTER RECAP

This chapter surveyed the Critical Challenge in and since *Brown*—during the civil rights movement that represents perhaps the most famous U.S. example of collectivized subordination and collective struggle for equal justice. This Challenge spans democracy and adjudication and requires responses that combine amelioration with transformation, in both symbolic and in material terms. Durable lived progress depends on it.

Part II

Understanding the Systemic Power of Social Identities and Organized Groups

∎ ∎ ∎

CHAPTER 3

UNLEARNING AND RELEARNING SYSTEMS, SOCIAL IDENTITIES, AND CASTES

■ ■ ■

Table of Sections

3.1 Systems are Judged on Actual Outputs and Recurrent Results
3.2 The "Rule of Law" System: Originating in Europe, Transplanted Through Colonialism, and Failing by Design
3.3 Systemic or Not?—Public Health, Global Pandemics, and Social Problems
3.4 Critical History and Other Disciplines Help Advocates Challenge Systemic Outputs
3.5 Social Identities (Still) Matter in Legal Decision Making
3.6 Law Dispenses and Normalizes Private-Public Privilege and Subordination

---

OPENING THOUGHTS

The most important lessons lay not in what I needed to learn, but in what I first needed to unlearn.

—**Jim Collins,** author

A system cannot fail those it was never designed to protect.

—**W.E.B. Du Bois**

How do we rectify a system that so brilliantly serves its intended purpose?

—**Dorothy E. Roberts,** Constructing a Criminal Justice System Free of Racial Bias: An Abolitionist Framework, 39 Colum. Hum. Rts. L. Rev. 261 (2007)

[I]t takes systematic work on ourselves and on the oppressor that lives inside of us to learn how to confront the elements of racist, homophobic, classist, and sexist societies.

—**Elvia Arriola,** Symposium, Difference, Solidarity and Law: Building Latina/o Communities Through LatCrit Theory, Foreword—MARCH!, 19 Chicano-Latino L. Rev. 1, 14 (1998)

INTRODUCTION

In Part I, we surveyed the Critical Challenge of using law for equal justice and the role of organized action in combatting systemic injustice. In this chapter, we examine how systemic analysis functions, how critical history illuminates this analysis, and how social identities are used to maintain castes not despite change but through change and over time. Identity, recall, is one of the four "missing" elements excluded from traditional legal analysis, along with groups, interests, and power.

Unlearning and relearning how identities function socially and legally is foundational to equal justice: "The first thing we do when we are born is learn.... We immediately engage in a conversation with our surroundings.... Education is the first thing we do."[1] And then, unlearning and relearning is the second—and forever—thing we do. Otherwise, Critical Justice is impossible, as we remain perpetually caged by the legacies of the past. This lifelong process of questioning all received wisdoms is personal and professional, practical and conceptual, individual and collective, and critical and self-critical.

Unlearning and relearning, together, make up a fundamental method of systemic advocacy to help advocates pierce systemic disguises, distractions, and denials. Advocates unlearn and relearn so that they can act—differently, more strategically, more thoughtfully, and more effectively. Advocates unlearn myths about social identities and relearn how to see identities as complex, socially constructed, and intersectional—ideas we explore in this chapter. Unlearning and relearning as critical method helps advocates see how law distributes privilege and subordination at both micro and macro levels. Unlearning and relearning helps advocates to think and act outside of, as well as within, systemic boxes. The materials below present opportunities for unlearning and relearning in a variety of settings to sharpen analysis involving diverse groups.

Before turning to identities within law as a system, we look at the meaning and relevance of systemic analysis to equal justice and social equity under the rule of law. Put simply, the Western origins of law start from conflicts among European elites. Its development followed from the spread of European colonialism and its legacies. This now-globalized system, often called "the rule of law," is the principal focus of our studies. The rule of law systems we study here signify elastic sets of interrelated notions, practices, and institutions developed to ensure "procedural fairness, honesty, and consistency," as opposed to "rule by men [which] 'has the connotation of arbitrariness, corruption, and instability.' "[2] The results

---

[1] Jorge R. Roig, The First Thing We Do, 47 J. Marshall L. Rev. 1275, 1275 (2014).

[2] Berta Esperanza Hernández-Truyol, The Rule of Law and Human Rights, 16 Fla. J. Int'l L. 167, 175 (2004).

of law should be deemed fair and legitimate and not appear to be the whimsical or biased commands of the powerful. In short, this system was supposed to replace the capricious rule of power with the principled and accountable rule of law.

In historical terms, this turn to law as a justice system describes a collectivized response to unprincipled, unaccountable, tyrannical, self-interested, or otherwise unjust ruling elites. These origins explain the central commitment to justice over power: the rule of law is supposed to guarantee *equal* justice in problem solving, both through democratic policymaking and the adjudication of disputes. In substantive terms, this system relies on this lofty rationale to justify its existence and design; critical scholars use this same rationale to question its performance as reflected in its actual outputs. In geographic terms, rule of law systems are now local, national, regional, and international.

Today, law is a uniquely crucial system because it regulates and governs so many other law-related systems—economic, political, and more. As you read, consider whether and how a systemic perspective might alter your evaluation of law, as well as your own work toward Critical Justice.

3.1 SYSTEMS ARE JUDGED ON ACTUAL OUTPUTS AND RECURRENT RESULTS

Social, cultural, political, economic, and legal landscapes are engineered through systems. Every historical moment reflects the status of ongoing struggles between top-down engineering and bottom-up fight back. Systems matter, both to individuals and to groups. They matter in material as well as symbolic terms. Systems script and embed micro relations as part of macro arrangements; everyone is taught to play their "part" by following "the rules." The "rule of law" is a system that, like all social systems, has been devised and maintained by its creators and controllers for purposes that may be explicit or not.

Generally speaking, "systems" are flexibly interrelated constellations of individuals, institutions, ideas, and interests that affect individuals and groups in many ways, ranging from the cultural and symbolic to the economic and material. Social systems exist in all societies, and all individuals are born into them. The purpose of a social system is measured by its regular outputs, even if those outputs differ partly or fully from the system's stated goals. Like ecosystems, social systems are dynamic yet continuous.

In both natural and social systems, as environmental scientist and systems theorist Donella Meadows has noted, the connected elements "are coherently organized in a way that achieves something." Systems link a characteristic set of behaviors that effectively define the system's purpose or "a set of things—people, cells, molecules, or whatever—interconnected in such a way that they produce their own patterns of behavior over time."[3] Immanuel Wallerstein, who famously developed a world-systems analysis, similarly defines a system as "some kind of connected whole, with internal rules of organization and some kind of continuity."[4] Systems can be conceptual—a constellation of ideas—as well as concrete—manifested in material terms, including institutions and other instrumentalities to accomplish the system's purposes.

The ecology of social systems, like that of natural systems, tends to be complex and fluid. Social systems constantly overlap, interact with, and learn from each other—economic, legal, and political systems, for example. Systems also encompass, and are constituted by, subsystems that share characteristics with the larger system. Within this web of systems, the borders or margins of any given system may shift, but the system itself continues.

In systems analysis, the key to understanding a social system and its effectiveness is to determine its purpose. Rather than relying on stated goals or rhetoric, systems theory determines systemic purpose and efficacy from systemic behavior—choices and effects. As Meadows reminds advocates, "When a systems thinker encounters a problem, the first thing he or she does is look for data, time graphs, the history of the system. That's because long-term behavior provides clues to the underlying system structure. And structure is the key to understanding not just *what* is happening but *why*."[5] Rather than viewing social conditions as the result of mere "events" like stock market booms or entrenched poverty, systems analysis requires a deeper understanding, which is obtained by situating events in a historical and contemporary context.

Often, when people create systems, the process includes expressions of the concerns and goals behind the system—its purposes. But sometimes people create systems with mixed purposes—both overt and covert, direct and indirect. Therefore, all systems are complex—even more so with the passage of time. Systems legal scholar Lynn LoPucki explains, "Systems analysis is a methodology specifically directed at the management of complexity."[6] Complexity, as noted in Part I, is inherent to human society and, therefore, also to law. However, complexity in law results in part from the forced disjunction between law and equal justice and from the need to explain or cover up that disjunction. Judges, elected officials, and other elite actors spin fictions, which make the already-existing complexity even

---

[3] Donella H. Meadows, Thinking in Systems: A Primer 2 (2008).

[4] Immanuel Wallerstein, World-Systems Analysis: An Introduction 98 (2004) (recognizing a tension in social science among some scholars who believe social systems are not the primary explanation of historical reality and others who see social actions as resulting from individual action, so that the "system" is just the sum of these individual actions).

[5] Meadows, Thinking in Systems, at 89 (emphasis in original).

[6] Lynn LoPucki, The Systems Approach to Law, 82 Cornell L. Rev. 479, 522 (1997).

more difficult to understand. In that way, elite manipulations of law "thicken" complexity but don't add up to equal justice.

As we saw in Part I, law also is complex because of general "indeterminacy"—"that which is uncertain, or not particularly designated"[7]—in the interactions of law with society. Legal rules and activities are inherently indeterminate because the variety and complexity of the world cannot be anticipated completely and written into a comprehensive, and thus determinate, set of specific rules. Legal rules are necessarily flexible enough to "permit a judge to justify multiple outcomes to lawsuits."[8] So, one set of facts could be "controlled" by many different concepts and contradictory precedent.[9]

Despite the inevitability of complexity and indeterminacy, systems analysis judges *all* systems, including law, on results—not on promises. Systemic advocates keep their eyes on the prize: upending actual systemic outputs over time and across place or circumstance. The following excerpt, by legal scholar Lynn LoPucki, elaborates on "the systems approach to law."

THE SYSTEMS APPROACH TO LAW
Lynn M. LoPucki
82 Cornell L. Rev. 479 (1997)

Introduction

. . . Restricting one's attention to particular aspects of reality reduces complexity, making it possible to solve problems that otherwise would boggle the mind. The disadvantage in restricting one's attention, however, is that it often screens out important aspects and leads the analyst to the wrong conclusion. . . .

"Systems analysis" is a methodology developed in the fields of engineering, business information systems, and computer programming specifically to manage complexity. Instead of screening complexity out, the systems analyst attempts to accommodate as much complexity as possible.

---

[7] Black's Law Dictionary, 2d ed. See also Mari J. Matsuda, Looking to the Bottom: Critical Legal Studies and Reparations, 22 Harv. C.R.-C.L. L. Rev. 323, 328 (1987) (arguing that legal indeterminacy works in different ways in different contexts, sometimes against the interests of subordinated groups); David Kairys, The Politics of Law: A Progressive Critique 140, 160–61 (1982); Mark V. Tushnet, Following the Rules Laid Down: A Critique of Interpretivism and Neutral Principles, 96 Harv. L. Rev. 781, 819 (1983); Duncan Kennedy, Form and Substance in Private Law Adjudication, 89 Harv. L. Rev. 1685 (1976) (describing how law is infused with irreconcilably opposed principles and ideals).

[8] Kairys, The Politics of Law, at 160–61 (1982). See also George A. Martinez, Legal Indeterminacy, Judicial Discretion and the Mexican-American Litigation Experience: 1930–1980, 27 U.C. Davis L. Rev. 555 (1994).

[9] Steven M. Barkan, Deconstructing Legal Research: A Law Librarian's Commentary on Critical Legal Studies, 79 L. Libr. J. 617, 629 (1987).

A comprehensive description of the system's functioning is a precondition to the analysis. Abstraction is employed sparingly....

Systems analysis proceeds by identifying systems, discovering their goals or attributing goals to them, mapping their subsystems and the functions each performs, determining their internal structures, depicting them with attention paid to efficiency of presentation, and searching for internal inconsistencies. These methods generate analytical power by increasing the number of goals, elements, and circumstances that the analyst can take into account simultaneously. These methods also provide a language by which to express the kinds of relationships that are commonly encountered.

This Article describes the methods of systems analysis and how they are being applied in the field of law....

What Is Systems Analysis?

A "system" is "a regularly interacting or interdependent group of items forming a unified whole." The "items" might be the atoms that interact to form a molecule; the bones, organs, and tissues that constitute the human body; the sun and planets that together form the solar system; or the police, lawyers, judges, courts, prisons, and computer programs that together make up the "criminal justice system." To "analyze" a system is to break it down into its constituent parts, to determine the nature and identity of its subsystems, and to explain the relationships among them.

The idea that a molecule and a judicial system have enough in common to make it profitable to study both using the same basic methodology may at first seem odd. In fact, the theory that links them—called "general systems theory"—is less than three decades old. "General systems theory" postulates that "systemness" is a characteristic of the organization of the universe; for reasons not yet unexplained, phenomena order themselves largely as discrete systems....

Systems analysis regards systems as goal-seeking. That is, systems analysis regards each system as having one or more purposes or functions. With biological systems, the idea seems intuitive. A rabbit, for example, is a system. Most observers would not be troubled by the notion of attributing to the rabbit the goals of finding food, surviving, and reproducing. But with physical systems—an atom, for example—the approach is counter-intuitive. An atom does not seem to have a goal, and its "function" seems to be attributed to it by people who themselves have goals. Nevertheless, many of the best metaphors for explaining scientific phenomena depend on anthropomorphism. Computers "search" for the right data, positive and negative electrical charges "attract" one another, and a mixture of chemicals "seeks" equilibrium.

Most legal scholars, judges, and legislators regard law-related systems as purposeful, and they do not hesitate to attribute to laws goals or purposes....

When regarding a social system as goal-seeking, it is important to distinguish the goals of the system from the goals of participants in the system. The participants may have a variety of conflicting goals. The prosecutor may seek to lock up as many people as possible for as long as possible. The crusading public defender may seek only to frustrate the prosecutor, or may even seek to "bring down the system." The parole officer may want nothing more from the system than to hang onto her job and minimize the number of hours she must work. The purpose of the system—to protect society and its members from criminal activity—may enter none of their minds.

... Systems "shake into place" as their components and environment interact. Numerous changes—some intended and some not—contribute to the whole. Changes that are successful from the standpoint of the system survive; unsuccessful ones are overwritten. The system evolves toward a state in which no one who has the power to impose changes on the system would choose to do so. Presumably, the system will then serve its constituency reasonably well.

Systems are composed of subsystems. Subsystems are themselves systems, which in turn have their own subsystems. For example, a house typically includes at least the following subsystems: foundation, structure (walls), roof, electrical system, plumbing system, and heating and air conditioning system. The concrete foundation is itself a system, one of the components of which is concrete. The crystalline structure of concrete has as a subsystem, the molecules of its components. Those molecules have atoms as their subsystems.

To analyze a system is to break it down into its component parts, and to examine how those parts relate to one another and contribute to the functioning of the whole. The emphasis in systems analysis is on relationships rather than on the component parts themselves.

When analyzing social systems, analysts often seek to improve the system's functioning. When they do, consistency and efficiency in achieving the system's goals are the criteria for quality. The analyst wants the system to work, or to work better. That is, however, not always the case. Social groups often choose to employ systems that contain inconsistencies or that work inefficiently....

In any event, ... [t]he "systems approach" is a method for understanding systems. An analyst can seek to understand a system for the purpose of rendering it inefficient, disrupting its functioning, or destroying it.

Law-Related Systems

... The systems approach to comparison is most powerful when the analyst has direct empirical evidence of how each system functions. In the absence of direct empirical evidence, the analyst can derive useful information from judicial opinions, legislative history, the language of statutes, interviews with participants in the system, and other descriptions that link the facts of cases with legal outcomes. But these kinds of materials must be used cautiously, because they may reflect what the system purports to be doing, rather than what it actually does. ...

Conclusion

A complex, modern society is composed of law-related systems that perform a variety of functions. Among other things, these systems process litigation, produce goods and services, provide financing for entrepreneurs, gather and publish information, and control behavior in public places. The control necessary for the proper functioning of these systems is provided through physical systems, social norms, and formal law. ...

The systems approach provides a way for legal scholars to get in touch with reality, to discover how law-related systems work through empiricism, and to discover how they can be improved through modeling. The method is analogous to the kind of systems analysis used to manage complexity in the creation of business information systems and other complex computer programs[:] ... systems analysis [is] "the investigation of a system to decide what needs to be done to make it more efficient and effective." ...

The first step ... is to figure out ... the purposes of the system. To do that, the analyst examines the existing system to see how it works and interviews people [with knowledge] to find out how the system presently serves them and how it could serve them better in the future. The second step is to generate a system design, a sort of "blueprint" for the system. This blueprint "identif[ies] the components of a system and specif[ies] their operation and interaction."

... To analyze a law-related system, the analyst must take account of the complex interrelationships among its parts. The limit on what the analyst can accomplish in that regard is the limit on what the human mind—with whatever external aids are available—can comprehend. Systems analysis is a methodology specifically directed at the management of complexity. The analytical power of the methodology is a function of the number of goals, elements, and circumstances that the methodology can take into account simultaneously.

... Systems analysis identifies [key] questions for empirical research and thereby provides the theoretical framework for empirical inquiry. ... By making the putative goals and system functions explicit, systems analysis facilitates normative debate. In the process, it offers humanity the opportunity to take conscious control of the systems by which we live.

In this excerpt, LoPucki provides a working familiarity with systems for use in advocacy. Systems analysis looks primarily at empirical systemic outcomes—and patterns of outcomes—to ascertain the purpose(s) behind a system, despite the uncertainties of complexity. Advocates identify patterns of unequal outcomes in contemporary terms, while appreciating the system's history, its proclaimed justice purposes, and its resulting interests in appearing to be principled and accountable. Poking through false systemic appearances to spotlight contradictions of equal justice puts pressure on the system to change or justify its outcomes and its self. Over time and using time, this continual poking helps educate the public at large on systemic realities versus appearances. Awareness and use of systemic analysis sharpens systemic advocacy for systemic solutions.

3.2 THE "RULE OF LAW" SYSTEM: ORIGINATING IN EUROPE, TRANSPLANTED THROUGH COLONIALISM, AND FAILING BY DESIGN

The "rule of law" offers an origin myth that purports to explain its social purpose. Under that top-down account, the legal system evolved over the centuries to restrain abuse—unprincipled or unaccountable power—as then being exercised by European royals, nobles, and warlords. Centuries later, the system's promise is to produce equal justice using principled adjudication and accountable democracy. But the tension lies between story and reality. The rule of law system is characterized by an ongoing "tragic divide between what is legal and what is just."[10]

The modern, Western version of the rule of law has emerged and expanded from 16th century Europe. In England, the rule of law is associated with the Magna Carta. In the United States, it is associated with the original Constitution of 1789 and the reconstructed Constitution of 1868. More recently, the ban on group genocide and the Universal Declaration of Human Rights in the wake of World War II are sometimes said to establish the rule of law internationally. During the past two or so centuries, the rule of law has become the dominant problem-solving instrument throughout the world.

---

[10] William P. Quigley, Revolutionary Lawyering: Addressing the Root Causes of Poverty and Wealth, 20 Wash. U. J.L. & Pol'y 101, 112 (2006). See also Derrick Bell, The Civil Rights Chronicles, 99 Harv. L. Rev. 4 (1985) (discussing specifically the "American contradiction" in which the constitution's "framers made a conscious, though unspoken, sacrifice of the rights of some in the belief that this forfeiture was necessary to secure the rights of others in a society embracing, as its fundamental principle, the equality of all").

Many variations now exist internationally. These interrelated rule of law systems share the notion that law *must* derive from an accountable democracy (free and fair elections) and an independent judiciary (principled adjudication). In this scheme, adjudication (in the form of legal doctrine and the related dispute resolution processes) and democracy (in the form of political and policy making processes) jointly promise equal justice under the rule of law.[11] These two features are today said to distinguish legitimate legal systems that must be obeyed from those that "the people" might properly overthrow as unjust.

As noted above, the rule of law signifies an elastic set of interrelated notions, practices, and institutions developed to ensure greater procedural fairness and consistency than that produced under "rule by men [which] 'has the connotation of arbitrariness, corruption, and instability.'"[12] The promise of equal justice is a very powerful motivator—both for the system and for those it oppresses. When the system fails to adequately explain persistent failure, the system loses legitimacy. The promise motivates the system to cover up failure by design; otherwise, it must concede failure or fix it. Simultaneously, the promise motivates group struggle to attain the promise. Over time, unrest may grow in the face of persistent injustice as increasing numbers of persons and groups resist, disobey, withdraw, and struggle with increasing intensity.

The excerpt below, by international law scholar Berta Hernández-Truyol, sketches a history of the rule of law, its promises, and some standing critiques that question whether the rule of law ensures that "no one is above the law." Hernández-Truyol situates this system specifically within its own promise of "human rights" embraced formally in international law during the 20th century. On paper, these formal rights of international law reflect, and expand, the promise of equality. Hernández-Truyol thus reminds us that the commitment to equal justice under law now is embedded within both domestic "civil rights" *and* international human rights.

---

[11] Many of these notions are valorized in non-Western legal traditions, as well, but may have different meanings, nuances, and implications. Here, we are focused on the characteristics of systems that have grown out of or been affected by Western colonialization and globalization. For discussions of alternative concepts related to justice and law, see Amartya Sen, The Idea of Justice (2009).

[12] Berta Esperanza Hernández-Truyol, The Rule of Law and Human Rights, 16 Fla. J. Int'l L. 167, 175 (2004).

THE RULE OF LAW AND HUMAN RIGHTS
Berta Esperanza Hernández-Truyol
16 Fla. J. Int'l L. 167 (2004)

The Rule of Law [as] Idea

Defining the rule of law is a difficult undertaking.... The definitional challenge derives from the reality that the rule of law is a contested concept. With the passing of time, different conceptions have evolved. Moreover, different legal traditions have divergent understandings of what the rule of law idea is or should be.

The modern idea of the rule of law has been traced as far back as Aristotle for whom the rule of law was tantamount to the rule of reason. Others have identified the rule of law with natural law or respect for transcendent rights. The term itself, however, at least in its contemporary usage, is more directly traced to the British jurist Albert Venn Dicey, who articulated it as follows:

> We mean, in the first place, that no man is punishable or can be lawfully made to suffer in body or goods except for a distinct breach of law established in the ordinary legal manner before the ordinary Courts of the land.... We mean in the second place, ... not only that with us no man is above the law, but (what is a different thing) that here every man, whatever be his rank or condition, is subject to the ordinary law of the realm and amenable to the jurisdiction of the ordinary tribunals.

... Modern theorists have observed that three characteristics are central to a cogent notion of the rule of law: (1) absence of arbitrary power on the part of the government; (2) administration of ordinary law by ordinary tribunals; and (3) existence of general rules of constitutional equality resulting from the ordinary law of the land. With these characteristics, the rule of law serves three purposes: (1) it protects against anarchy; (2) it allows persons to rely on laws and plan their lives in a way in which they can predict what consequences will flow from their actions; and (3) it protects against arbitrary and capricious action of the government.

... [More recently,] [i]n its Rule of Law Project, the International Commission [of Jurists] defined the rule of law in a manner that fits a diverse global world:

> The principles, institutions and procedures, not always identical but broadly similar, which the experience and traditions of lawyers in different countries of the world, often having themselves varying political structures and economic backgrounds, have shown to be important to protect the individual from arbitrary government and to enable him to enjoy the dignity of man.

Like Dicey's definition, the Commission's version addresses the three concerns regarding arbitrary government power: basic laws, implementation, and a higher authority. In domestic contexts, the higher authority is constitutional norms; in the international realm, the higher authority is . . . human rights. . . .

[In sum,] rule of law provides that no one is above the law, not even the government, which itself is subject to norms and normative standards. . . .

The Rule of Law and Culture

The idea of just laws is a difficult and complex one. For example, the rule of law in the [W]estern tradition emphasizes individual rights. Other philosophical foundations emphasize communitarian duties and responsibilities. The [W]estern vision does not, however, reject the communitarian ideals. . . .

Significantly, the notion of the rule of law, as it has evolved in the dominant Anglo-American experience and in the formulation that has been exported wholesale, is rooted in the Judeo-Christian ethic which . . . is grounded on the liberal tradition that focuses on the individual. Such a notion of the rule of law is inextricably intertwined with the dual [W]estern goals of democratization and capitalism. In this vein, the rule of law discourse emphasizes the notion of individual rights, which can be juxtaposed to other traditions and cultures with an emphasis on communitarianism such as Greek and various Asian ones.

For example, a rule of law founded in ancient Greek philosophies would center on the idea of a "polis" which seeks order that is attainable through social or political structures. Chinese scholars have cited Aristotle's notion that the rule of law encompasses two ideas: one, that there needs to be compliance with established norms; and two, that the law's content is a good one. Other contemporary Chinese scholars note that Confucianism advocates a rule of law by virtue and ethics rather than by norms. . . .

Indeed, while some [W]estern critics equate a rule of law under socialism with the possibility of arbitrary and unfettered government action, Chinese scholars argue that the rule of law under socialism is at a higher level of evolution than the rule of law under capitalism. They explain that the driving force of socialism is one of human emancipation because it enables human beings to completely develop the full extent of their capacities. . . .

The rule of law idea [nevertheless] "requires a system of accountability of government and its actors which includes a check against the bias, irrationality, corruption, or abuse of those in power—be it the lawmakers, the executive, the judges, or some outlaw group that nonetheless is in control of the state or some part thereof"—whose time might be occupied by matters other than justice and just governance. It is inherent in the rule of law ideal that government action has limitations. . . .

Moreover, . . . the rule of law must mean something more than blind adherence to written laws; it must mean pursuit of justice. Martin Luther King poignantly articulated this sentiment when, quoting St. Augustine, he said "An unjust law is no law at all." This is indeed a key principle of the rule of law vis-a-vis human right norms: unconditional or unqualified obedience to unjust laws is not a requirement. . . .

Beyond governments at one end of the spectrum of the rule of law and the individual at the other, civil society—the collective of institutions, groups, and individuals who create and express social values and morality—has a role in ensuring the attainment of justice. Civil society and government need to work congruently, with one checking the other's jurisdiction so that neither has nor exercises unbridled power to oppress individuals and suppress individual autonomy and freedoms. They also must work coherently to request and guide necessary changes in the legal structures when moral, social, and civil transformations so require.

Critiques of the Rule of Law

As this [outline] has shown, there are different conceptualizations of the rule of law in different cultures. However, the ideal of a global rule of law is captured by the International Commission of Jurists' definition in its Rule of Law Project. . . .

Notwithstanding this ideal, the varied cultural settings in which the rule of law applies has resulted in powerful critiques of the concept. Some view the rule of law as nothing other than a tool of the powerful to maintain the status quo in the legal system. The general consensus is that the status quo, far from being neutral, serves to protect the powerful at the expense of the disempowered. This lack of neutrality in the rule of law runs contrary to the ideal, traced to Aristotle, that in light of the law every person should be equal; that it is one's humanity, not one's status in society, that requires that laws be justly applied. As one commentator has stated[:]

> . . . [W]e cannot be a nation of equal citizens under a Rule of Equal Laws if only half of us have control over our bodies and our lives, while the other half remain subject to the ultimate control of the state. . . . [A]ll can at least share . . . the desire to incorporate basic notions of decency and compassion into a strong and principled Rule of Law.

. . . Indeed some writers even have argued that a rule of law may be, at times, nothing more than a post hoc rationalization or attempted legitimization of results that may be better explained by extralegal (including, but not necessarily limited to, emotional) responses to the facts, the litigants, or the litigants' lawyers, all of which may go unstated. . . .

Another challenge to the neutrality of the rule of law is the perceived attempt to universalize a [W]estern vision. [S]ome argue that the exportation of the [W]estern rule of law effectively is but a rhetorical trope to legitimize global power differentials. The patterns of the exportation of the rule of law are viewed as fitting neatly into imperialistic practices—some more subtle than others. Sometimes the rule of law is imposed on states overtly; sometimes in a way that is masked by contract and made to appear to be voluntary—evoking the label of "subtle blackmail." . . . [R]egardless of form, . . . economically deprived and less powerful states must [often] accept the [W]estern rule of law in order to have access to the global market and to engage in economic activity necessary for the states' survival.

The doctrine of the rule of law [therefore] is also critiqued as . . . capitalistic ideology . . . [as well as] a cultural [form of domination]. For example, Asian scholars have three main criticisms of the [W]estern rule of law that is being exported wholesale. One is that its virtues are overstated—a criticism that dovetails with the critiques about the [contradiction] between the notion of the rule of law and [systemic] justice. A second criticism, which also parallels other critiques discussed above, is that it is a thinly veiled attempt to impose the economic market goals of the United States on the world. The third criticism is an interesting twist on the cultural critiques as it posits that the rule of law is simply a proxy for establishing a global system that reflects the U.S. legal culture of "legalism and litigiousness." . . .

Yet other critics reject the formalistic notions of the rule of law in favor of a goal of justice. Examples of laws that are anathema to notions of justice are "laws that enshrine irrational prejudice, such as the miscegenation laws . . . or the racial bias . . . or the irrational animus toward gay[s]. . . . [These] are not laws at all." . . . [S]uch laws could be deemed to be illegitimate laws and the rule of law idea would warrant that they not be followed. . . .

. . . [In sum, while] the law "restrains power . . . it also prevents power's benevolent exercise. It creates formal equality—a not inconsiderable virtue—but it promotes substantive inequality by creating a consciousness that radically separates law from politics, means from ends, process from outcomes." The goal of the rule of law ought to be to enable full personhood, human flourishing. Any law that does not do so cannot be part of the rule of law. . . .

[Finally,] if one looks at the origins of the formal development of trade law, and of human rights law, one sees a virtually identical cast of characters—the same players on the world stage having conversations about developing norms for interaction. These same players were the architects of robust systems of norms that have developed along parallel tracks ... —worlds apart while occurring in the same small world, occluding their interconnectivity and interdependence....

[Thus, b]oth human rights and trade depend on the notion of the rule of law....

Conclusion

The rule of law is an idea about law, justice, and morality. It considers what laws, norms, rules, procedures, systems, and structures should be and what they should not be. Norms should be proclaimed publicly by the peoples and/or their appropriate representatives. All the people who will be bound by the norm, and not just an elite group, must have a voice in norm creation. The public nature of the process informs those who are bound by the law as to what the rules are. The idea also suggests that laws, norms, and regulations need to be clear so that people understand what rules are to be followed, and they need to be predictable in their application so that persons know what behavior is appropriate.

Inherent in this formulation are three realities. One is that the law governs people as well as the government itself. Next, persons should obey the law. Third is that the norms we call law need to be obeyable—not only in the sense of being known, knowable and predictable, but in the deepest sense of being just.

Therefore, to be just and justly applied, predictable, understandable, and obeyable, laws need to be both universal and culturally contingent. We do not have, nor do I think want, a homogenized world; we do want an ordered and peaceful world in which there is human progress, thriving of peoples and cultures, and economic development. The limitations on the rule of law are not universality or cultural contingency although there may be cultural parameters within which a rule of law paradigm may be deployed. The universal should not be used as pretext to decimate just and viable local norms and the local should not be used as pretext to impose a reign of corrupt, irrational, arbitrary, abusive, and discriminatory power. So while law should be congruent with social values, neither social values nor law can violate a higher order of justice either locally or internationally.

Central to the rule of law idea[l] is that we, as humans, should be able to conduct our lives without surprises, without governmental interference that we cannot calculate because of its unpredictability or arbitrariness, and with dignity. Key to this observation is the recognition of individuals' existence within society as both autonomous individuals and community members, free beings with dignitary rights because of their humanness.

As Hernández-Truyol notes, the rule of law, though dominant, has been subject to critique and skepticism from many. In the next excerpt, international legal scholar Ileana Porras focuses on a doctrine of international law—the "providential function of commerce"—to demonstrate the material, or economic, priorities of the then-emergent system. Law played a key role in the creation of colonial empires and was shaped, by design, for the pursuit of colonial power *and* imperial profit. Profit from commerce was as much a driving force for colonization as anything else; it is not until the mid-20th century, in the aftermath of World War II, that international human rights are allowed to enter this system.

EUROPEAN ORIGINS, THE DOCTRINE OF THE PROVIDENTIAL FUNCTION OF COMMERCE, AND INTERNATIONAL LAW'S EMBRACE OF ECONOMIC GROWTH
Ileana M. Porras
107 Am. Soc'y Int'l L. Proc. 374 (2014)

. . . Properly understood, the claim that international law finds its origin in Europe is not controversial. In the first place, origination describes not an event, but a process that unfolded over hundreds of years, culminating in what today we call international law. Furthermore, it is clear that despite its origin, international law has borrowed from and been influenced by ideas and practices from elsewhere. Indeed, international law's foundational conceptions evolved in response to the European encounter with the New World and in an ongoing effort to delineate and manage difference within a universal frame. Thus, far from evolving in splendid isolation within Europe, international law is the result of multiple engagements with the rest of the world. Moreover, international law has gone through many stages or epochs; its substantive content—how it is theorized and practiced—has changed. Furthermore, at no time has there been a single uncontested version of international law or agreement as to its proper direction. In this regard, from at least the mid-nineteenth century some of the most radical contestation arose from the periphery.

Nonetheless, the claim of European origination is important because it serves to emphasize that at its heart international law was and, in some respects, remains a European project. One of the effects of this origination is that to the extent that international law has a very specific geographic, cultural, political, and philosophical center of gravity, we would expect that it would tend to reflect and serve the concerns and interests of its originators. At the very least, the fact that international law has a European origin supports the suspicion that international law is in some way always already biased. Given that one of the deep-seated internal (European-origined) claims about international law is that it must by definition be universal in reach or at least universally valid, this inherent parochial bias may seem to run counter to the deep promise of international law—a promise that encompasses something like community, equality, and justice.

. . . [T]he European origin of international law has left its imprint on the present moment. In particular, I [below] trace the ways in which the set of ideas and attitudes towards commerce, encapsulated by the term "the providential function of commerce," became an integral component of international law. . . . [T]hat the providential function of commerce was embedded in international law from the beginning and has contributed in no small way to the conviction, now seemingly unassailable, that the ultimate objective of international law should be to support international trade and national economic development. Without elaborating the point in these brief remarks, I posit that the strength of this conviction, built into the very fabric of international law, renders the possibility of shifting gears and pursuing sustainable development almost impossible.

International law in Europe was born in the midst of three distinct, and each in its way novel, conditions: First, it responded to the shock of the European encounter with the New World (and the need to justify the ensuing exploitation and conquest); second, it responded to the clash among Europeans competing for economic opportunities in the distant seas of the East Indies (and the ensuing struggle for influence, land, and access to resources); and third, it responded to the devastating and intractable inter- and intra-European conflicts that characterized the period between the sixteenth and the eighteenth centuries, conflicts by and large colored by inter-denominational religious differences. In other words, international law evolved in an attempt to manage three sets of relationships: intra-European relationships in Europe; inter-European relationships in distant places; and European-to-non-European relationships abroad. The doctrine of the providential function of commerce, I would argue, provided international law with a way of framing these competitive relationships in a positive way—a way that could be imagined as mutually beneficial, in diametric opposition to the way of war with its winners and losers.

According to the doctrine of the providential function of commerce . . . trace[d] back to the fourth century A.D., international commerce was not simply a human activity among others. Instead, international commerce was to be understood as a divinely inspired post-Babel mechanism, designed by God as a means of bringing separated humanity back into friendship. To engage in international commerce was, in other words, to do God's work. . . .

. . . [In historical practice, however, Europeans used] the doctrine of the providential function of commerce to discover a right to hospitality: a right to hospitality that must be protected because it is the necessary condition to enable God's design—international commerce—and the concomitant friendship among the Earth's separated nations to flourish. [This] privilege to engage in commerce is subsumed under the right to hospitality. As a counterpart, interference with the privilege to engage in commerce is a violation of the right to hospitality and therefore an injury. Since those seeking to engage in commerce are by providential design seeking to meet the needs or lacks of their own nation, the violation obstructs God's design and inflicts an actual harm to the well-being of the people whose lack cannot be fulfilled.

. . . Simply put, [Europeans] . . . discovered a right, whose inevitable violation provided a cause for just war. Thus, while the right of hospitality was identified as a precondition for the possibility of trade and international friendship, in practice it served to justify war.

Despite this obvious paradox, and despite the fact that the international seaborne trade was known to be marred by violence, conquest, and exploitation, the doctrine of the providential function of commerce continued to play an important function in subsequent developments in international law. It influenced not only the specific doctrines favoring international commerce but, I would argue, it structured the very way in which Europeans imagined international relations. . . .

Porras highlights colonial attention to law as an instrument of conquest, occupation, and extraction for elite profit, power, and dominance, which characterizes the entire "rule of law" system more generally, as Hernández-Truyol sketched previously. While this design for international relations was labeled providential, it required specific human machinery—institutions, ground rules, and systems—to materialize God's will. Consequently, to set up and help administer their competing transnational empires, colonizing public-private elites chartered the earliest multinational corporations. Granting them monopolies and privileges over vast resources, peoples, and territories, while simultaneously restricting the colonies' "trade" only with or through them, this one-way system of colonial mercantilism stripped everything deemed of value from colonized areas worldwide—ranging from India to Cuba—and then shipped it all to Dutch, Spanish, British, French and other European "merchant kings" and/or crowns.[13] By law, this arrangement dispossessed many peoples and continents for many centuries in order to accumulate and concentrate the world's wealth (and its power) in perpetuity among the very, very few.

---

[13] For background, see Stephen R. Bown, Merchant Kings: When Companies Ruled the World, 1600–1900 (2010); Nick Robins, The Corporation that Changed the World: How the East India Company Shaped the Modern Multinational (2012); The Dutch and English East India Companies: Diplomacy, Trade, and Violence in Early Modern Asia (Adam Clulow & Tristan Mostert eds. 2018).

Historically, perhaps the most notable of these public-private collusions for "accumulation through dispossession" have been the Dutch and British East India companies, as well as the Dutch West India Company. But, over time, networking elites also fashioned other similar entities around the globe, and also for quite specific public-private purposes—such as the Russian American Company, the Hudson Bay Company, the British South Africa Company, and (in the Western Hemisphere especially) the United Fruit Company. Using law and corporations as key tools of continual expansion and enrichment, European (and later U.S.) elites—the ruling classes in charge of both government *and* corporations—directly fused public power to private profit for self gain: that is, they transplanted the rule of law, and invented international law, chiefly to promote and protect their personal and group interests (over all else). As we examine more fully in Part VI, the providential nature of commerce—and of international law as a system—commingled the rise of the "rule of law" globally with the rise of big corporations (and their collective, now-globalized dominance) in mutually destructive ways, and particularly at the expense of equal justice for all.

The excerpts reviewed thus far—from Marshall in Part I to Porras in this chapter—provide critical snapshots of a morphing system in the continual process of re/making itself. The system exalts justice as a chief purpose, but many centuries of systemic outputs across many locales have shown otherwise, as the United States itself admitted recently. In September 2020, FBI Director Christopher Wray was openly describing "white supremacy" as the biggest U.S. domestic terror problem. Wray noted that, of all "domestic violence extremism," the "biggest bucket" was "racially motivated" extremism—and that, of all racially or ethnically motivated kinds of extremism, "white supremacist ideology is certainly the biggest chunk."[14] The FBI's very plainspoken assessment was both an echo and a forecast.

Dozens of investigations echoed this assessment following the January 6, 2021, storming of the U.S. Capitol by a mob laden with white supremacist emblems, slogans, costumes, and banners. On January 20, 2021, shortly after that attempted insurrection, President Joseph Biden spoke aloud the words "white supremacy" for the first time ever during a presidential inauguration address, acknowledging (finally) a fundamental point: that "the sting of systemic racism" had rendered the United States a "broken land" over the five-plus centuries since its colonial roots were designed and put in place by European settlers.[15]

---

[14] https://www.fbi.gov/news/testimony/worldwide-threats-to-the-homeland-091720; https://www.facebook.com/TheHill/posts/within-the-domestic-terrorism-bucket-the-category-as-a-whole-racially-motivated-/10158810007549087/.

[15] https://www.whitehouse.gov/briefing-room/speeches-remarks/2021/01/20/inaugural-address-by-president-joseph-r-biden-jr/.

Legal scholar Angela Mae Kupenda and others have similarly (and critically) observed:

> Our casebooks and historical texts speak volumes of the efforts of those widely recognized as the founding fathers to implement and maintain a White culture and to diminish all of the other rich cultures that existed prior to the arrival of Whites on this continent and those from nonwhite cultures who arrived on this continent later, even some by force ... through separation and denigration, and at times, economic exploitation.[16]

The rule of law, a multifaceted and multilayered blueprint for social formation and group dominion, emanated from Europe as a conceptual and a concrete system to envelop the entire globe. Inexorably, this continuing historical process links domestic legal systems to equivalent international systems. International law thus fails by design as well: systems are designed to interlock in justifying and entrenching identity castes. To advance equality in the face of this longstanding scheme, advocates use critical understandings of the system's design, history, and outputs to overcome the Critical Challenge in local *and* global settings.

NOTES AND QUESTIONS

1. *The ABA World Justice Project.* In 2007, the American Bar Association established the World Justice Project, in part to develop a globally accepted definition of the amorphous and contested term, rule of law, that in turn could be used as an index to measure local adherence to that standard. The resulting definition included these four principles:

> A system of self-government in which all persons, including the government, are accountable under the law;
>
> A system based on fair, publicized, broadly understood and stable laws;
>
> A fair, robust, and accessible legal process in which rights and responsibilities based in law are evenly enforced; and
>
> Diverse, competent, and independent lawyers and judges.[17]

Taken from the teaching materials developed by the ABA to engage its rule of law definition, consider these questions:

> The World Justice Project asserts that "the rule of law is the platform for communities of opportunity and equity and is essential to addressing the world's most persistent and harmful ills." Do you agree with this statement? Why or why not?

---

[16] Angela Mae Kupenda, Will the South Rise Again and, If So, in What Form? Lessons from LatCrit About Resisting Fear of Cultural Understanding, 47 J. Marshall L. Rev. 1211, 1221 (2014).

[17] https://www.americanbar.org/advocacy/rule_of_law/what-is-the-rule-of-law/.

Think about your own experiences or familiarity with the law in the United States. To what extent do you think the Rule of Law in the United States adheres to the World Justice Project's definition of the Rule of Law? To what extent do you think that the United States fails to live up to this definition?

The World Justice Project suggests that the four principles it has used to define the Rule of Law are universal principles. Do you think that these principles would be universally accepted by nations around the world? Why or why not? Do you think these principles *should* be universally accepted? If not, how would you modify this definition to reflect what you think are universal principles of the Rule of Law?[18]

Compare the World Justice Project definition to the description in the Hernández-Truyol excerpt, written before the Project's work, and the other rule of law descriptions we have supplied. In each instance, the law proclaims itself devoted to justice. How do the conceptions vary? How are they similar?

3.3 SYSTEMIC OR NOT?—PUBLIC HEALTH, GLOBAL PANDEMICS, AND SOCIAL PROBLEMS

In Part I we reviewed some examples from the United States and elsewhere describing advocates' understandings of, and approaches to, problems they deem systemic. Some problems, then, are systemic and some are not. Like those mentioned in Part I, advocates for *systemic* justice must understand what makes a problem (and a solution) systemic in nature.

Generally speaking, systemic problems are by definition both historical and contemporary, which thus requires familiarity with both the past and present in order to design and fight for a more equitable future. Moreover, identity-based systemic problems are simultaneously personal as well as communal—micro as well as macro. They are cultural, political, and material problems all at once—in addition to being legal problems. For these interlocking reasons, systemic problem solving must design solutions that include law but go beyond it—that bring amelioration for individuals as well as transformation for systems, groups, and societies.

As a U.S. example, remember Hurricane Katrina in 2005? Remember Maria in 2017? Both Katrina and Maria were relatively short natural events followed by enduring social catastrophes. As documented repeatedly, the social aftermath of both natural events exacerbated and accelerated existing systemic inequities. And, in turn, those same inequities (still) flow from the systemic interplay of identities, groups, interests, and power—IGIP. Are the familiar historical skews of these present-day, still-reverberating social results coincidence or design?

---

[18] *Id.*

Consider, in this critical vein, the systemic outputs of law in other extended social catastrophes, which also followed in the wake of natural events. For instance, consider public health settings that include, most notably, out-of-control global pandemics. Within weeks of its advent in early 2020, COVID-19 was transforming human life around the globe. Societies and localities were closing, and economies were shuttering. Within months, millions were infected and deaths exceeded 500,000 within one year just in the United States: to grasp the breathtaking scale of the catastrophe, this twelve-month death toll matched the total U.S. casualties during its two-plus years of global warfare against Germany, Japan and other "Axis" powers during the 1940s. This new global pandemic was not entirely unanticipated—nor are more like it. Nevertheless, as widely documented during its first full year, the pandemic bared and sharpened deep inequities among identity groups and their health consequences in the United States (and around the world).

In the following excerpt, legal scholar Dayna Bowen Matthew describes these inequalities in public health as systemic problems abetted by law. COVID-19 certainly presented many "private" problems (including death) for millions of individuals and their loved ones, but did this global pandemic (and elite reactions to it) also present social, public, systemic problems tied to group inequalities? What makes a problem systemic, and thus of public concern? Recall (or go back and review) the definitions of systemic advocacy presented in Part I from advocates and activists based in the U.S., Canada, Australia and elsewhere. As you read, also keep LoPucki's bottom line in mind: systems and their purposes are measured by their outputs, not their claims or promises.

STRUCTURAL INEQUALITY: THE REAL COVID-19 THREAT TO AMERICA'S HEALTH AND HOW STRENGTHENING THE AFFORDABLE CARE ACT CAN HELP

Dayna Bowen Matthew
108 Geo. L.J. 1679 (2020)

Introduction

... Gradually, healthcare providers, ranging from individual clinicians to the largest hospitals and integrated healthcare systems, have recognized that it is pervasive social inequality, which denies marginalized populations equal access to the social determinants of health—housing, employment, education, food security, and the environment, for example—that drives disparate health outcomes.

... The empirical evidence of growing structural inequalities is compelling. By all measures, inequalities that separate the advantaged from the disadvantaged in America are severe and worsening to levels not seen since the Great Depression. The top one percent of earners take home twenty percent of the nation's income, while the bottom fifty percent of the population earns less than thirteen percent of national income. Wealth inequity is even more concentrated; the top one percent of households hold nearly forty percent of all wealth, while the bottom ninety percent share less than a quarter of the nation's wealth. . . .

Structural inequality is directly associated with poor health in the United States and globally. . . . [I]n the United States, research shows that widening gaps in income inequality predict increasing differences in life expectancy; and differences in life expectancy are directly related to gaps in educational attainment. However, these vast social inequities are well beyond the capacity of the healthcare industry to address on its own.

The global COVID-19 pandemic provides the most recent and disturbing proof that structural inequality is a causal factor in producing deadly health disparities, and that a massive legal intervention will be required to correct it. . . . In the United States, the earliest data showed that African-Americans contracted and died from COVID-19 at disproportionately high rates. In "hotspot" areas . . . black and Latinx populations were [and] are over-exposed to several structural risk factors for COVID-19. They are overrepresented among low-wage workers whose jobs do not allow them to stay home and shelter in place to avoid exposure . . . [and] are more likely to live in densely populated urban neighborhoods and communities traumatized by violence and poverty. African-American and Latinx neighborhoods typically have inferior access to quality healthcare; are more likely located proximate to environmental pollution hazards; and are less likely to contain ample green and recreational spaces. . . . [T]hese populations have inferior access to early diagnostic and aggressive therapeutic care. . . . The temptation is to cast these disproportionalities as individual-level failings of health behavior or heredity. Although individual factors are not irrelevant, the most powerful explanation for minority populations' susceptibility to the COVID-19 disease and its devastation is the structural inequality that characterizes their lives and historic experiences in this country. . . . [I]nequitable societies are the most vulnerable, least safe, and least healthy in the world.

. . . That is why healthcare providers, public health professionals, and sociologists [have begun] addressing structural inequality. . . .

. . . [H]ealthcare innovations . . . adopt a public-health approach to improving population health rather than simply delivering care to individuals . . . [to] address the underlying social causes of disease rather than just the diseases themselves. . . . Inequitable access to decent, affordable housing; inequitable distribution of healthy food; education disparities; and disproportionate exposure to violence and childhood trauma are four examples of the inequalities that these health providers have confronted in order to promote good health. . . . [T]he aggregate effect of inequity in each of these social domains combines so that adversity becomes cumulative and structural. Sociologists have defined structural inequality as "an inequality in the distribution of a valued resource, such as wealth, information, or technology, that brings social power." Structural inequality delivers cumulative advantage to the affluent—and cumulative disadvantage to others—by disparately allocating access to education, employment, housing, food, healthcare, political power, and legal representation.

How Legal Inequality Affects Health Inequity

... [R]acial inequality thrives when laws designed to limit it are not enforced. The resulting freedom to discriminate in housing, education, employment, civil, and criminal justice systems is the essence of structural racism and affects population health in three ways. First, ... access to the basic building blocks of a healthy life. It is estimated that only ten to fifteen percent of health outcomes are determined by access to healthcare and genetic make-up of individuals respectively. In contrast, social determinants—the environments in which people live, work, and play—are estimated to represent forty percent of the influences that determine health outcomes. Another forty percent of health outcomes are related to health behaviors that occur within a social context and are therefore also susceptible to environmental influences. To the extent that racial discrimination affects access to, and the quality of these social determinants, health outcomes for blacks relative to whites are disproportionately and adversely impacted. Second, uncontrolled discrimination not only leads to systemic and structural inequalities; these burdens disproportionately increase exposure to social stressors that produce anxiety, depression, suicide, and unhealthy behaviors. Without question, increased exposure to racial discrimination has a profoundly adverse impact on minorities' mental health. Taken together, these first two health-harming effects comprise what has been termed "structural" or "institutionalized racism."

The third harm caused by the systemic inequality associated with unchecked discrimination defies the prevailing fallacy that discrimination is only a problem for those who are discriminated against. Data and experience tell us this one-sided account is untrue. . . .

. . . Discrimination in housing, education, environmental pollution, and law enforcement cumulatively erect structural barriers to an equal opportunity to achieve good health. . . . [W]henever constitutional prohibitions against discrimination are ignored, structural inequities are institutionalized and result in unequal health outcomes. In contrast, whenever our legal institutions strengthen constitutional protections of equality, specifically within the social determinants, health disparities decrease. . . .

The Affordable Care Act and Equality

On March 30, 2010, the Affordable Care Act (ACA) was signed into law. Despite seventy-one attempts at legislative repeal, and numerous constitutional threats, the ACA continues to endure. Furthermore, the evidence suggests the law has had a modestly positive impact on reducing inequality. . . .

. . . All racial groups showed gains in health-insurance coverage after the passage of the ACA, but gains were especially strong for minority groups and low-income groups below 200% of the federal poverty level. . . . The COVID-19 crisis hit hardest in states where the ACA did not expand insurance coverage—states that rejected the Medicaid expansion. In these states, low-income populations lacked access to preventive care, heightening their risk of contracting and dying from the virus. . . .

Conclusion

. . . Social determinants of health are the conditions in which Americans live, work, and play; these are the societal causes behind the causes of health inequity. . . . [T]o the extent that racial discrimination affects access to and the quality of these social determinants, health outcomes . . . are disproportionately and adversely impacted. . . .

Matthew depicts public health issues illustrated most recently by COVID-19 as systemic and revolving around identities, groups, interests, and power. Legal scholar Jasmine Harris similarly asserts that pandemics and other natural events or systemic disasters may offer condensed examples of elites protecting their collectivized interests by means of manipulating social change and denying the systemic nature of persistent social problems:

> Whoever said pandemics were equalizers doesn't know a thing about disability legal history. It does not take much of a pretext to rollback disability rights. This is because disability rights laws, despite enumerated principles of equal opportunity and civil rights, have always been viewed as "nice to do" and not "must do."
> . . . These problems are compounded when medical supplies, personnel, and time are limited.[19]

Compounding the impacts Harris describes of state ventilator and ICU-bed rationing plans that disfavored or excluded disabled persons, vaccination distribution patterns eventually followed the same identity-based skews that had tilted infection rates based on pre-existing systemic conditions. Consider also how government vaccine websites often lacked accessibility

---

[19] Jasmine E. Harris, The Frailty of Disability Rights, 169 U. Pa. L. Rev. Online 29, 30, 33 (2020).

features for millions of U.S. residents with a visual disability—who also may have difficulty in ensuring social distancing in public. What, if anything, makes the problem(s) related to COVID-19 *systemic* in nature? How might advocates craft strategies and actions that similarly are systemic? How do notions of public and private affect the problem(s) and solution(s)?

NOTES AND QUESTIONS

1. *Defining "Systemic" Advocacy.* Compare the definitions and examples of "systemic" advocacy from Part I to Matthew's analysis here. Now search "systemic advocacy" on the Internet and reflect on the results. Combining all these sources, write out your understanding, or definition, of systemic problems and advocacy. How does your definition of systemic advocacy compare to "law practice" as you understand it? What insights, if any, does this comparison add to your understanding of systemic advocacy? Of law practice?

2. *Systems, Histories, and Failure by Design.* Assessment of a system is based on its outputs, which requires knowing the system's articulated purpose, its historical record, and its current outcomes. Recall the discussion of militarized policing, mass incarceration, and crimmigration from Part I. Look at the recurring outcomes of the U.S. criminal justice system along racial, class, and other identity-lines. What might you articulate as the systemic purpose(s) of "criminal justice" today? What purposes are offered to justify the system's record—its outputs—from critical questioning? Has this system "failed," or does it function as designed? We will address these questions further in Part III.

3.4 CRITICAL HISTORY AND OTHER DISCIPLINES HELP ADVOCATES CHALLENGE SYSTEMIC OUTPUTS

Every system has a design and a history. The work of exploring the design and history of a status quo often is relegated to secondary priority in a world crying out for relief *now*. Historical knowledge sometimes is deemed to be "just" background information. But when advocates ignore systemic design and history, their advocacy may not alter systemic outputs and deliver needed relief—they may fail to get at the roots of injustice. As Angela Davis observed, being radical "simply means 'grasping things at the root,' "[20] and, as with weeds, one must uncover the root before doing the pulling.

Advocates engage in cross-disciplinary research, build multidisciplinary teams, and engage in complex actions to understand social problems and devise effective solutions. Principal among these are history, economics, political economy, sociology, and various sorts of

---

[20] Angela Y. Davis, Women, Culture, and Politics 14 (1989).

interdisciplinary studies. Both critical history and political economy, in particular, excavate connections between past and present and local and global relevant to systemic problem solving.

In general terms, critical history is a bottom-up examination of the past to better understand the present, and to plan for a better future. For instance, LatCrit scholar Marc-Tizoc González emphasizes that, "Scholars who identify with multiply diverse, yet racialized ethnic groups . . . collaborate in the cultivation of critical ethnic legal histories—stories about our communities' centurial, complexly interwoven, and transnational pasts—from which we may distill socio-legal insights for today's social justice struggles."[21] Critical legal scholar Robert Gordon similarly explains that, "The history of law has come to be a vital contested ground . . . [because] [h]istory supplies . . . a legal system structured to preserve . . . formally equal rights . . . which supposedly will operate so as to reward every individual precisely in proportion to his or her merit. . . . The importance of history . . . is chiefly in the way it reveals [the] rule of law as a utopian fantasy."[22] Appreciating these points, systemic advocates research bottom-up histories to craft critical solutions for present-day injustices.

In similarly general terms, political economy is a field of analysis connecting materiality—economic realities—with political decision making and legal doctrines that reproduce systemic inequalities based on social identities, especially class, race, and sex.[23] Political economy as a discipline emerges from basic facts about life: "From the moment you are born, you enter an unlevel playing field. Each of us may have the opportunity to try hard . . . but overall, [persons and groups] do not have equal resources and the rules of the game favor some over others. . . . [Therefore] political economists view society [through] the 'Four C's' of political economy—context, collective behavior, conflicting interests, and change . . . to inform their analyses of almost any economic issue, whether it is air pollution,

---

[21] Marc-Tizoc González, Critical Ethnic Legal Histories: Unearthing the Interracial Justice of Filipino American Agricultural Labor Organizing, 3 U.C. Irvine L. Rev. 991 (2013).

[22] Robert W. Gordon, The Struggle Over the Past, 44 Cleve. St. L. Rev. 123 (1996).

[23] For example, the Law and Political Economy Project (LPE) is a new collaboration at Yale Law School that "seeks to offer an alternative vision for law and legal scholarship that starts from the premise that politics and the economy cannot be separated and that both are undergirded in essential respects by law." www.law.yale.edu/yls-today/news/new-law-and-political-economy-project-launched. This project is part of an emerging "law and political economy" movement in legal scholarship. See David Singh Grewal, Amy Kapczynski, and Jedediah Purdy, Law and Political Economy: Toward a Manifesto (Nov. 6, 2017) (highlighting the "artificial division between the economy and politics has worked its way into law, in part through legal scholarship and law school pedagogy" and "challeng[ing] these divisions . . . to excavate the implications of inequality for the political order"), www.lpeblog.org/2017/11/06/law-and-political-economy-toward-a-manifesto/.

economic development, raising children, or . . . discrimination and wage inequality."[24] Understood critically, political economy is:

> [t]he attempt to constantly place culture in time, to see a constant interplay between experience and meaning in a context in which both experience and meaning are shaped by inequality and domination [and the] attempt to understand the emergence of particular peoples at the conjunction of local and global histories, to place local populations in the larger currents of world history. This way of viewing political economy allows for a situating of human experience within a historical moment, and also requires a reading of particular experiences under a framework that acknowledges power and powerlessness.[25]

As a critical approach to research and analysis, political economy makes clear that identities, groups, interests, and power are missing as much from traditional economic theory as from traditional legal theory—with the same consequence of obscuring systemic violence.[26] For example, as the Grassroots Policy Project notes, political economy unmasks systemic patterns:

> [R]acialization impacts economic arrangements. Its cumulative and structural effects, or structural racism, are manifest in ways that perpetuate race-based economic inequities. Racialization and the political economy continually interact, from who controls sources of wealth in society, such as land, labor and capital, to where people live, go to school, get access to transportation and healthcare, and so much more. . . . This history shapes the political economy much more so than notions of free markets and the invisible hand.[27]

We examine in Part VI the history of the rule of law system's development through key economic eras—from colonization to imperialism to globalization. These eras show changing but persistent processes that maintain identity-based castes, a continuing social reality made clear by critical history and political economy.

Below, law and society scholar Kitty Calavita tracks how the U.S. Congress explicitly incorporated social identities into statutory law to exclude persons from Asia, as a group, from entry. This effort lasted decades after the Civil War and the Fourteenth Amendment and was

---

[24] Randy Albelda, Robert W. Drago & Steven Shulman, Unlevel Playing Fields: Understanding Wage Inequality and Discrimination 121 (2d ed. 2004).

[25] See William Roseberry, Anthropologies and Histories, 49 (1990).

[26] Charles R.P. Pouncy, Institutional Economics and Critical Race/LatCrit Theory: The Need for a Critical "Raced" Economics, 54 Rutgers L. Rev. 841 (2002); Gary Browning and Andrew Kilmister, Critical and Post-Critical Political Economy (2006); Edén E. Torres, Power, Politics, and Pleasure: Class Differences and the Law, 54 Rutgers L. Rev. 853 (2002).

[27] Grassroots Policy Project, Race, Power and Policy: Dismantling Structural Racism (2010).

carried out through the 1882 (and subsequent) "Chinese Exclusion Laws," which the Supreme Court upheld in 1889 as legitimate exercises of legislative power.[28] To detail behind-the-scene "collisions" of those laws' enforcement, Calavita examines internal administrative memos exchanged between federal agents across the country. This critical history shows how legislation, administration, and adjudication mutually uphold and reinforce systemic inequality.

As perceived by the Court, Chinese people are incapable, as a group, to become a part of "the People" in this country. According to U.S. Supreme Court Justice John Marshall Harlan, the Chinese race "was so different from our own that we do not permit those belonging to it to become citizens of the United States."[29] Chinese people were subject to U.S. legal "walls" against their entry until wartime 1943, when legal barriers were reduced through an interest convergence after Japan tried to use anti-Asian prejudice to divide the United States from its important wartime ally—China.

As critical feminist scholar Leti Volpp explains, this "American Orientalism" describes "how the national identity of the United States has been constructed in opposition to Asians and Asian-Americans—who are characterized as 'foreigners' in contrast to 'citizens' . . . [causing] the fitness of Asian Americans for integration into our national body [to become] suspect." During this period of imperialism, as Part VI explains further, the "American Empire"—so named by Supreme Court opinions since Marshall's in *M'Intosh*, as we see below in this chapter—grew exponentially, stretching from Cuba and Puerto Rico to Guam and the Philippines. In each instance, U.S. elites (and their judges) invoked "scientific" rationales (as with eugenics) to determine whether each of the peoples in the newly acquired lands were, collectively, "obnoxious to their very nature" and, therefore, to be excluded by law from physical entry and/or formal U.S. citizenship. Within this imperial U.S. framework, elites deemed both Asian and Latinx populations obnoxious to their very nature when compared (by elites) to their "ability to perform the characteristics [that elites] associated with whiteness."[30] This critical history helps to explain why some conquests—like the entire southwestern U.S. and Hawai'i—were officially annexed as states (albeit after a long delay in places like New Mexico until whites moved there in sufficient numbers), while other places within the empire—like Cuba, Puerto Rico, and the Philippines—were not.

Set against this systemic backdrop, Calavita exposes how identities and ideologies related to race, gender, and class were deployed for

---

[28] *Chae Chan Ping v. United States*, 130 U.S. 581 (1889).

[29] *Plessy v. Ferguson*, 163 U.S. 537, 561 (1896) (dissenting opinion).

[30] Leti Volpp, "Obnoxious to Their Very Nature:" Asian Americans and Constitutional Citizenship, 5 Citizenship Studies 57 (2001).

collectivized exclusion by law. She shows how enforcement of those dictates produced endless contradictions and systemic incoherence. And, while this historical account critically examines top-down decision making, these moments also set the stage for organized bottom-up challenges to systemic injustice, as we see throughout this book.

COLLISIONS AT THE INTERSECTION OF GENDER, RACE, AND CLASS: ENFORCING THE CHINESE EXCLUSION LAWS

Kitty Calavita
40 Law & Soc'y Rev. 249 (2006)

... President Chester Arthur signed the Chinese Exclusion Act in 1882 suspending the entry of Chinese laborers into the United States, thereby barring immigrants on the basis of their nationality for the first time in American history. . . .

. . . [C]lass ideologies permeated and spiked the racist rhetoric [surrounding passage of this law]. For example, Chinese merchants and others "not in the laboring classes" were exempt from the exclusion. While the exemption for merchants was in part carved out so as not to interfere with the lucrative trade with China, it was justified on the grounds that "[t]he Chinese mercantile class is entirely different from the working class."

Still less visible in these [congressional] debates were the gender ideologies that nonetheless shaped the legislation and that ultimately caused considerable confusion and turmoil among enforcement officials. This invisibility was related to gendered assumptions about Chinese women—that they were neither laborers nor merchants and thus irrelevant to the matter at hand. . . . Congress's omission meant that enforcement officials had to determine for themselves, for example, whether a woman could ever be considered a "laborer."

Conceptualizations of gender, race, and class were so entangled during discussions of Chinese exclusion that they often stood in for each other, or bled into and defined each other. . . .

This article explores the ramifications of these ideological intersections for the enforcement of the Chinese Exclusion Laws. . . .

. . . This is fundamentally a study of what law-in-action—and the unexpected social realities it encountered and the unresolvable dilemmas it confronted—can tell us about the hidden assumptions of the lawmakers' hegemonic worldview and the tangled logics that permeated those assumptions. . . . I focus here on what these challenges and these collisions at the intersection of race(ism), class(ism), and gender(ism)—and at least as important, how they were dealt with on the ground—can tell us about the essential arbitrariness of those ideological constructions, their incoherence and their malleability.... I argue here that the self-contradictions into which immigration officials and jurists were forced when interpreting and applying the exclusion laws exposed the incoherencies within and among the *ideologies* associated with such identity categories....

Descriptive Background

Approximately 110,000 Chinese entered the United States between 1850 and 1882, most coming through the port of San Francisco. By 1882, one-third of the workforce in San Francisco comprised Chinese immigrants or their children. The vast majority of these immigrants were men; according to the 1890 census, 102,620 men and just 3,868 women of Chinese origin lived in the United States. Most Chinese men worked in mining, railroad construction, and agriculture and were welcomed by employers as a plentiful source of cheap labor. By the time the Central Pacific Railroad was completed in the 1870s, however, the men who had been so central to its construction were increasingly being disdained as "coolie labor." And Chinese women—many of whom worked as domestic servants, seamstresses, or gardeners, or in laundries—were almost universally associated with prostitution.

Responding to and fueling the anti-Chinese fervor in California, Congress passed the Page Act in 1875 barring the entry of involuntary "Oriental" labor, prostitutes, and others coming for "lewd and immoral purposes." In 1876, the California Senate established a committee to research the impact of Chinese immigration and sent its report, "An Address to the People of the United States upon the Evils of Chinese Immigration," to Congress...."

... In addition to barring the entry of Chinese laborers for 10 years, [in 1882 Congress] reiterated the ineligibility of Chinese to naturalization as "nonwhite" persons that had been affirmed in a San Francisco circuit court decision in 1878.

... Administration of the laws was initially delegated to the Treasury Department, where it was enforced by customs collectors and their staffs of "Chinese inspectors" at every port of entry, with the vast majority of Chinese inspectors stationed at the busy port of San Francisco. When the Bureau of Immigration was established in the Treasury Department in 1891, the exclusion laws remained under the jurisdiction of customs officials, underscoring their distinction from other immigration laws. Administrative supervision of Chinese exclusion was moved to the Immigration Bureau in 1900, but even then customs collectors retained control of its actual enforcement at the ports. Not until 1903, when the Immigration Bureau was transferred to the newly created Department of Commerce and Labor, did the Chinese Exclusion Laws come under the full purview of the regular immigration bureaucracy.

Of Axioms and Axes: Congress Speaks of Gender, Race, and Class

... Metaphors abounded, with Congress likening Chinese immigrants to an "indigestible mass," "herds," "leeches," "floods," "an exhaustless human hive," "hordes of ... rats," "locusts," and "flies on a bee-gum on a summer's day." A few themes were repeated over and over in this race narrative. Among the most ironic, given the exploitation of Chinese workers by employers who paid them less than the prevailing wage, was the claim that Chinese workers had the biological capacity to subsist on below-subsistence wages and were thus unfair competitors to American workingmen and workingwomen. ...

Another recurring theme was the deceitful nature of the Chinese. Time and again it was contended [in Congressional documents] that the Chinese were natural liars. ... The Chinese were denounced as "pagan in religion, inferior in mental and moral qualities," and "cruel and indifferent to their sick" and there was little doubt that "the[se] features of his character are ingrained in his being." ...

Repeated references to African Americans, the experience of slavery, and lingering hostilities less than 30 years after the Civil War, confirmed that Chinese exclusion was being framed first and foremost as a race issue. ...

... At the same time that Congress depicted the Chinese as a distinct race with biologically ingrained character flaws, they lauded the superior nature of the "merchant class," a discursive move no doubt predicated on the need to exempt merchants, with their lucrative trade potential, from the exclusion. ...

... Women were rarely mentioned in the debates, and nothing in the 1882 law applied specifically to them. When the subject of women did come up, it was in the context of making the case for Chinese racial and moral inferiority. In the House of Representatives, it was proclaimed, "There are from 1,200 to 2,000 [Chinese women] in the city [of San Francisco], and they are all prostitutes or concubines, or second wives." ...

Gender, race, and class thinking intersected ... as the moral mandates implicit in them collided in the enforcement process. ... [T]he dilemmas that officials faced in dealing with the Chinese women who desired entry to the United States, and the practical solutions these officials devised, underscored not just the fragility and vulnerability of the operative conceptual categories but the instability of the ideological imperatives those categories implied.

Law-in-Action: Administrative Struggles, Judicial Juggling, and Ideological Triage

The Chinese Exclusion Act was signed on May 6, 1882. It did not take long before letters and memos began arriving at the Office of the Treasury in

Washington, D.C., from San Francisco and other ports requesting information on how to enforce this law that was so far-reaching yet left so much unsaid. Among the most immediate questions posed by customs officials who had overnight become "Chinese Inspectors" was how the 1882 exclusion law was to be applied to women. A long, handwritten letter from San Francisco Customs Collector E. W. Sullivan to his superiors in Washington soon after the law passed listed seven questions, one of which was "Does this term <u>laborer</u> apply to females, servants, or married women?" Treasury Secretary Charles Folger replied succinctly to his query the following month: "A woman may be a laborer. A wife takes the condition of her husband." The secretary's decision set the stage for much that was to follow and was misleading in its apparent simplicity. In fact, there are really two decisions expressed here, and they are of interest for two reasons.

First, the question of whether a woman could be a laborer forced Secretary Folger to make a decision that coincided with the reality that some arriving Chinese women were in fact "laborers" according to most straightforward definitions of that term. But the decision contradicted patriarchal ideals of dependent womanhood—ideals echoed in the secretary's second statement that "a wife takes the condition of her husband." Thus, the decision that a woman was an independent being (who could be excluded as a laborer) was uneasily coupled with the notion of women's derivative status. . . .

Second, while the Treasury Secretary temporarily resolved the questions of whether Chinese women could be laborers and how to consider Chinese wives, the practical question of what documents to require of these women was left unanswered. The issue became particularly troublesome in the case of wives of Chinese laborers who were returning from a visit abroad. Until 1888, Chinese laborers already in the United States at the time of the signing of the exclusion law were allowed to make visits to China (and elsewhere) and reenter upon presentation of a certificate given them at their port of departure from the United States. Many Chinese men in the United States returned to China specifically to marry, and the question of whether and how their wives might be admitted was a pressing one. The Treasury Secretary's decision that a wife took on the status of her husband meant that wives of returning laborers were themselves defined as laborers who, if they had not been in the United States at the time of the exclusion law's passage and thus had no "return certificate," were to be excluded. Wives of returning Chinese laborers thus experienced the worst of both worlds—their derivative status was dependent on that of their laborer husbands, yet they were treated as legally separate persons when it came to the issue of certificates. . . .

. . . Policy decisions relating to the wives of merchants were even more tortured than those applying to the wives of returning laborers, and they continued to confound the enforcement bureaucracy for decades.... [F]ormal and informal policies relating to the admission of merchants' wives were modified almost annually in the early years, with each change pivoting on the crucial questions of whether wives of merchants were distinct persons or appendages of their husbands, and what intrinsic rights the husbands had to their company.

In the first years after the 1882 exclusion law was passed, customs collectors appeared to use their discretion in admitting wives of Chinese merchants. While they were usually required to have their own Section 6 certificates attesting to their honorary "merchant" status, the requirement was not always strictly enforced. A note dispatched from Treasury Secretary Folger in response to a query in 1883 thus referred to a broad policy of requiring [certificates] but concluded with an unceremonious (and unelaborated) nod to administrative discretion; in some cases, the secretary wrote, the wives and minor children of merchants "may land in the U.S. without the statutory certificates, *if it should be impracticable to obtain them.*" ...

... But the following year, the circuit court in Oregon ruled against the Treasury's policy of requiring [certificates for merchant wives], claiming that it violated the Angell Treaty with China, was inconsistent with statutory intent, and contradicted the "natural right" of a man to the company of his wife....

Declaring that "the manifest purpose of this legislation is to exclude Chinese laborers," Justice Matthew Deady reasoned that requiring certificates of merchants and their wives was not intended to limit their entry, but simply to guard against laborers gaining admission disguised as merchants. Thus, all that should be required was any good evidence that they were actually members of "these favored classes." ...

... According to Justice Deady, the reason Congress never mentioned merchants' wives as admissible under the exclusion law was because it was so taken for granted that "the domicile of the wife and children is that of the husband and father." ...

Conclusion

... While Congress could deploy its ticklish logic in the service of important interests—such as the political advantage secured by restricting Chinese immigration and the economic benefits of exempting merchants with their lucrative trade potential—and dodge any fallout from that logic, those on the frontlines of enforcement had no such luxury....

Some of the most enduring dilemmas pitted the contradictory moral imperatives of patriarchy, racism, and classism against each other in an intricate pas de trois that played out daily at major ports of entry, in the courts, and in administrative appeals. In the process, enforcement officials were repeatedly put in the unenviable position of having to sacrifice one or more ideological principles for the sake of another. . . .

If ideology is not a fixed thing, neither is it composed only of beliefs; rather, it entails the activation of those beliefs in practice. . . . Much as racism is clearly both an attitude and a subordinating practice, all [identity] ideologies are simultaneously thought and action. . . .

Calavita's critical history of enforcement in the years following passage of the Exclusion Laws shows how law works as a system *in action*—engaging with multiple identities at once, sometimes in contradiction, to pursue a consistent purpose: to promote white superiority. This enforcement of practical and conceptual contradictions brings into view how intersecting social identities reflect and project supremacist beliefs about identity groups. Calavita concludes by emphasizing that ideology as law is neither abstract nor ephemeral: enforcement of ideology as law, or of law as ideology, "entails the activation of those beliefs in practice" to shape social and economic realities—if necessary, by top-down force.

Calavita's critical history of the Exclusion Laws' enforcement also confirms that even elites cannot manage all the internal contradictions *and* external social realities that limit identity ideologies as law. These limitations are the proverbial "cracks" or "weak links" that advocates target: identity ideologies, like other instruments of control, are sites of struggle. Every instance of top-down subordination provides also an opportunity for bottom-up resistance. Challenges to identity-based castes are continually raised, spurring changes in law and society and preventing the top-down consolidation of the status quo as absolute or hegemonic.

Calavita thus highlights another two key themes recurrent throughout this book. One is the importance of critical history to understanding (and solving) contemporary, persistent social problems. The other is how law functions as identity-based ideology to fail justice deliberately, or by design. Developing these two themes further, the following pair of excerpts offers critical histories related to law and marriage that amplify Calavita's account.

First, legal historian Serena Mayeri describes how "marital supremacy" is etched in U.S. society. She outlines key cases in the 1960s and 1970s that challenged legal definitions of illegitimacy and legitimacy and their linkage to systemic gender, race, and class castes. These challenges exposed—and incrementally changed—harms caused by marital supremacy as designed and enforced by elites. But both political constraints and advocates' own strategic choices limited the transformative potential of these cases. Keep the two themes noted above in mind as you read this pair of excerpts.

MARITAL SUPREMACY AND THE CONSTITUTION OF THE NONMARITAL FAMILY

Serena Mayeri
103 Cal. L. Rev. 1277 (2015)

... Marital supremacy—the legal privileging of marriage—endures, despite soaring rates of nonmarital childbearing and a widening "marriage gap" that divides Americans by race, wealth, and education. The stakes of marital supremacy are higher than ever as marriage becomes the province of the privileged.

Yet marital supremacy has a contested history. . . .

The history recounted here has been almost entirely forgotten. . . .

Illegitimacy penalties occupied a peculiar position in midcentury law and public policy. Progressive reformers had long lamented the stigma and material disadvantages imposed upon nonmarital children as cruel and anachronistic relics. . . . Nevertheless, [by the 1960s,] reforms were uneven and incomplete: illegitimate children often could not inherit from their biological fathers or paternal relatives, receive government benefits to which legitimate children were entitled, sue for their parents' wrongful death or workers' compensation, or effectively enforce nonmarital fathers' child support obligations. . . .

Illegitimacy litigation did not proceed from a carefully planned, incremental constitutional strategy. Cases cropped up organically, without the handpicked plaintiffs favored by the NAACP Legal Defense Fund (LDF) in earlier campaigns against de jure racial segregation, and later, by Ruth Bader Ginsburg's American Civil Liberties Union (ACLU) Women's Rights Project in pursuit of sex equality. But the LDF and the ACLU did enter the fray, injecting broader concerns about race and poverty into their constitutional challenges to illegitimacy-based classifications. . . .

In 1960, Louisiana's "suitable home" law, which withheld public assistance from mothers who had given birth outside of marriage, sparked a national outcry. The legislation, a direct response to racial desegregation efforts, purged tens of thousands of impoverished African American families from the state's welfare rolls. By this time, the success of constitutional challenges to racial segregation provided the legal tools to question illegitimacy penalties on equal protection grounds. On behalf of the ACLU, a young lawyer named Melvin Wulf wrote a brief to the Department of Health, Education, and Welfare (HEW) attacking Louisiana's policy.

. . . Just as *Brown v. Board of Education* held that "the classification of Negroes qua Negroes was baseless," the "differential treatment accorded a class of citizens designated as 'illegitimate' is equally baseless." Need, not status, was the appropriate criterion by which to determine welfare eligibility. . . .

Wulf's memo contained seeds of the constitutional arguments that litigators would later raise in court, including the illegitimacy penalties' racially discriminatory intent and effect; the idea that illegitimacy-based distinctions were invidious discrimination rather than justifiable privileging of normative marital families; a reluctance to directly challenge the state interests in deterring nonmarital childbearing and regulating sexual morality; and skepticism about the state's true motives, nurtured by the attenuated relationship between the means employed by the state and the ends purportedly sought.

. . . In *Equal Protection for the Illegitimate*, published in 1967, [Illinois law professor Harry] Krause framed the stakes as "a *child's* right to a familial relationship *with his father*," which he argued was "more akin to a 'fundamental right and liberty' or a 'basic civil right of man' than to a mere economic interest" entitled to a presumption of constitutionality. He depicted illegitimacy as a "second-class status," calling its impact "a psychic catastrophe." . . .

Krause deliberately emphasized the child's plight, rather than that of his parents, and the *paternal* bond as the crucial loss suffered by nonmarital children. . . .

. . . Krause was careful not to question all laws privileging marriage and traditional family relationships—only those that punished children, who had no control over their parents' marital status.

Nor did Krause contest the government's ability to regulate sexual activity. . . . Krause did not question the validity of the *government interest* in combating illegitimacy. Rather, he argued that the *fit between means and ends* could not withstand constitutional scrutiny. . . .

. . . [But by] the early 1970s, with new constitutional weapons in hand, some feminists and anti-poverty lawyers challenged the child-centered focus of illegitimacy litigation. . . .

. . . The "legal literature," [feminist advocates] wrote in 1974, was "replete with expressions of concern for the 'innocent' child," ignoring the impact of illegitimacy penalties on women and on "the family unit as a whole." This approach ignored "an independent justification for abolition of illegitimacy: the right of women to self-determination requires that they be free from all forms of male domination." . . .

. . . Patriarchy and poverty were the true culprits. . . .

. . . Like feminists of earlier eras who decried sexual double standards, advocates also highlighted how illegitimacy classifications shamed and penalized sexually active unmarried women while allowing men to engage in nonmarital sex and procreation with impunity. . . .

The most sophisticated version of this argument appeared in Katie Mae Andrews's attack on a Mississippi school district's ban on hiring unwed parents, filed in 1973. In *Andrews v. Drew Municipal Separate School District*,[31] social psychologist Kenneth Clark (author of the "doll studies" cited in *Brown*) testified that the challenged rule was part of "a long history of discrimination against females on matters of sex and sexual behavior . . . designed to subordinate females to an essentially inferior role. . . .

Depriving women of any claim on fathers' resources also infringed upon their reproductive freedom, advocates contended. For many women, the ability to exercise control over reproduction meant more than the right to use contraception or to terminate a pregnancy. Poor women, especially unmarried women of color, faced involuntary sterilization at the hands of doctors who took it upon themselves—often with explicit or tacit encouragement from government officials—to curb the fertility of populations considered burdens on the public fisc. For these women, some of whom had religious or moral objections to abortion, the private relationship between woman and physician elevated by Blackmun's opinion in *Roe v. Wade* was often a site of coercion rather than cooperative counsel. . . .

. . . Race played an especially prominent role in *Andrews*, the Mississippi teachers' case. All five applicants denied jobs were African American women, and as many as 40 percent of the Drew school district's African American students were born to unmarried parents. Superintendent George F. Pettey presided over a school district that had mightily resisted desegregation; after most whites decamped to "segregation academies," Drew's student population was 80 percent black, but the number of white teachers and administrators rose. . . . Andrews's attorney, twenty-four-year-old Charles Victor McTeer, an African American [attorney,] . . . secured the testimony of civil rights paragons Kenneth Clark and Fannie Lou Hamer. . . .

. . . Hamer's and Carter's testimony valorized the plaintiffs' efforts to lift themselves out of poverty and support their children on their own as evidence of strong character rather than moral delinquency. Hamer highlighted the catch-22 imposed by powerful whites on black families generally and black women in particular: single mothers were damned if they relied on stingy and stigmatized public assistance, and damned if they sought a decent living through employment in the public school system. . . .

---

[31] The hiring ban ultimately was struck down by the lower courts on constitutional grounds, and the Supreme Court never weighed in.—Eds.

By the mid-1970s, advocates could rely upon a growing complement of constitutional sex equality precedents to support their case against the sex discriminatory effects of illegitimacy penalties. To the extent that illegitimacy penalties could be framed as sex-based classifications, advocates [could] . . . invoke heightened scrutiny of the relationship between means and ends. And the disparate impact on women of restricting the employment of parents of nonmarital children called such policies into question under both statutory and constitutional precedents. . . .

The illegitimacy cases changed the law in important ways. [Courtroom and legislative victories] . . . striking down most distinctions between "legitimate" and "illegitimate" children meant that many nonmarital families enjoyed greater protection from legal disabilities such as children's inability to inherit or obtain child support from fathers, and that nonmarital children received government benefits from which they had long been excluded. By extension, these rule changes benefited (some) parents of nonmarital children and made the world safer for nonmarital sex and childbearing, even if their underlying rhetoric and rationale were less progressive than they might have been.

. . . [But] advocates did not deploy the full arsenal of feminist challenges to illegitimacy penalties in court. They did not, for instance, directly question the privatization of dependency within the nuclear family. Even *Andrews*, which celebrated women's economic autonomy from men, depicted the plaintiffs as engaged in an admirable quest for independence from public assistance, for self-sufficiency through market work. . . .

It is also true that no feminist organization prioritized the illegitimacy cases or launched a concerted campaign on behalf of unmarried mothers in particular. . . . Attacking male supremacy within marriage—which loomed large on the agenda of leading feminist legal advocates—posed a fairly radical challenge to American law and social life. Challenging marital supremacy in a political environment where feminists stood accused . . . of assaulting traditional marriage and family relationships likely seemed impolitic. . . .

Communities in which nonmarital childbearing was prevalent were themselves divided over the wisdom of fighting for "unwed mothers'" rights: Katie Mae Andrews's lawyer, Charles Victor McTeer, for instance, recalls sharp divisions within Drew, Mississippi's, African American community over her case. . . .

Notwithstanding these limitations, imposed under considerable political constraints, courtroom advocates advanced a much more capacious account of what was wrong with illegitimacy penalties than judicial opinions ever made visible.

Despite their efforts, by the end of the 1970s, the child-focused view of illegitimacy's harm had prevailed.... Further, illegitimacy jurisprudence conveyed the impression that sex, race, and illegitimacy were separate, non-overlapping categories—suitable for purposes of (often unfavorable) comparison but not for illuminating their mutually reinforcing and deeply intertwined character....

... Failing to question the legal privileging of marriage as an instance of race-, gender-, and class-salient harm obscured the pernicious effects of marital supremacy on the very groups that could least afford to lose access to the benefits that accompany marriage....

... [A]s a primary vehicle for managing and privatizing dependency in the absence of a robust welfare state or other social supports for families, marriage remains central to American political economy as well as a unique source of legal and cultural legitimacy. Threatening marital supremacy was and is therefore perceived by many as an assault on the very foundation of society. Progressives, then and now, often join conservatives and traditionalists in policing the boundaries between marriage and non-marriage, even if they disagree about who should be able to marry and what roles husbands and wives should assume.

... [T]he history of the illegitimacy cases suggests that focusing on the harm to (presumptively innocent) children while downgrading or penalizing their parents' nonmarital (and presumptively not so innocent) relationships has destructive symbolic and material consequences for nonmarital families. Plaintiffs attacking illegitimacy penalties won significant victories, to be sure, and they made understandable strategic decisions along the way. The story told here makes clear, though, that winning is not everything: the terms [determine whether a legal victory] is the latest chapter in the history of marital supremacy or the opening salvo in a renewed battle for racial, sexual, and economic justice.

This excerpt shows how "marital supremacy" is a legal regime that connects inequality based on illegitimacy to inequality based on gender, race, class, and other social identities—even though it may appear otherwise at first blush. Marital supremacy, like the Asian exclusion laws, reflects and projects notions and beliefs—supremacist ideologies—attempting to justify persistent group-wide inequalities despite the equal justice promise. Although unfolding in different moments and contexts, the critical histories of these two top-down legal regimes—Asian exclusion and marital supremacy—show the centrality of identities, groups, interests, and power in systemic, collective, persistent inequalities.

Expanding on this complex history and its legacies, legal scholar Michael Boucai examines foundational litigation by same-sex couples to have their right to marry recognized by the state. LGBTQ marriage litigation, as it emerged in the 1970s, aimed for "gay liberation" from, not assimilation into, heteronormativity as a way of life. Gay liberationists sought not only formal recognition of their right to marry but also to challenge by their example the supremacy of patriarchal marriage itself.

Litigants first sought court approval to marry after the 1969 Stonewall riots in New York City. At Stonewall, drag queens of color led a gay insurrection against police and Mafia abuses. That insurrection unleashed LGBTQ community activism on a scale never seen before in the United States. Marriage litigation arose in the context of that emerging insurrection—part direct action, part law reform. Advocates and activists faced intense opposition for the next five decades, as the bottom-up campaign became gradually more sophisticated and narrower in its focus on "marriage equality." Boucai argues that the early cases, as a "political act," constitute the "radical heritage of a now-mainstream movement" that shifted directions from liberation to assimilation.

Both Mayeri and Boucai describe how the transformative potential of these efforts was blunted or displaced by top-down opposition as well as by strategic choices of advocates, litigants, and activists themselves. But radical roots remain embedded in the DNA, as it were, of challenges to marital supremacy as an institution. As you read, consider what lessons for systemic advocacy you can draw from the critical histories presented by Mayeri and Boucai.

GLORIOUS PRECEDENTS: WHEN GAY MARRIAGE WAS RADICAL

Michael Boucai
27 Yale J. of L. & Human. 1 (2015)

Introduction

"There are some glorious precedents for thinking of homosexuality as truly disruptive. . . ."

"Since when is marriage a path to liberation?"

In the years immediately following the Stonewall riots of June 1969, a period when "gay liberation" rather than "gay rights" described the ambitions of a movement, at least ten same-sex couples across the United States applied or attempted to apply for marriage licenses. All were refused except for two men in Texas, one of whom apparently looked convincing in a miniskirt, a wig, and false eyelashes. Lawsuits ensued in five states, and four made their way to and beyond trial. The three that produced written judicial opinions—*Baker v. Nelson* in Minnesota, *Jones v. Hallahan* in Kentucky, and *Singer v. Hara* in Washington State—have endured for decades as precedents supporting a heterosexual definition of marriage. . . .

To speak of *Baker*, *Jones*, and *Singer* as "the first same-sex marriage cases" is therefore to notice something other than the novelty of the basic question they raised about who may and may not marry. These lawsuits were firsts because they framed that question not defensively but offensively, in constitutional terms, just as gay rights advocates would do with greater success in such landmark cases as *Baehr v. Lewin*, *Goodridge v. Department of Public Health*, and *United States v. Windsor*.

Yet *Baker*, *Jones*, and *Singer* were more than mere precursors to *Baehr*, *Goodridge*, and *Windsor*. . . .

. . . [T]he first gay marriage cases were deliberately "failed performances," clearly unable to achieve the legal goal they ostensibly sought. . . .

. . . About a month before Jack Baker and Michael McConnell "donned their best suits" and appeared in the Hennepin County Clerk's office, John Howard, a sociology professor at Rutgers University, reported to colleagues in his field on the recent emergence of gay liberation. His lecture emphasized two "turning points": the founding in April 1969 of Homosexuals Intransigent at City College of New York; and, of course, the Stonewall riots of June 1969 in New York's Greenwich Village. According to Howard, both events were representative of the "essential elements differentiating . . . gay liberation" from the homophile movement of prior decades—namely, "open declaration of identity and tactical militance [sic]." . . .

Advocating the liberation of homosexuality, even as distinct from the liberation of homosexuals, was one way for gay liberationists to "Fight Repression of Erotic Expression," the declared goal of the University of Minnesota student group—FREE—that marriage plaintiff Jack Baker led in his first year of law school. But it was hardly the only way. In *Sexual Politics* (1969), a work widely celebrated and deeply influential among gay liberationists Kate Millet described the range of battles that a true "sexual revolution" would have to win: A sexual revolution would require, perhaps first of all, an end of traditional sexual inhibitions and taboos, particularly those that most threaten patriarchal monogamous marriage: homosexuality, "illegitimacy," adolescent, [and] pre- and extra-marital sexuality. . . . The goal . . . would be a permissive single standard of sexual freedom, and one uncorrupted by the crass and exploitative economic bases of traditional sexual alliances. Primarily, however, a sexual revolution would bring the institution of patriarchy to an end, abolishing the ideology of male supremacy and the traditional socialization by which it is upheld in matters of status, role, and temperament. . . . A related event here would be the re-examination of the traits categorized as "masculine" and "feminine," with a reassessment of their human desirability. . . .

Millett's linkage of homophobia and patriarchy was a central premise of gay liberationist thought. . . . Asked to state in a single sentence what gay liberation was "trying to do," the group's leaders declared: "Smash cultural and institutional sexism."

Many gay liberationists sought alliance not only with feminism but with the full range of causes associated with the New Left of the late sixties and early seventies. Whereas homophile activists of previous decades had quietly sought tolerance for a narrow and largely invisible constituency, the Stonewall generation's demands for "freedom" and "acceptance" purported to target the same "politico-economic system" challenged by "black panthers, student militants, women's liberationists and others seeking a dramatic restructuring of the society." . . .

Nowhere did feminist and anticapitalist critique combine so forcefully as in gay liberation's attacks on the "patriarchal capitalist family." . . . Premised on "inflexible" gender roles, it was assigned special responsibility for producing the "artificial categories" of masculinity and femininity and, in turn, the equally "false categories of homosexuality and heterosexuality." . . .

Unsurprisingly, the gay liberation movement's ambitions far outstripped its capacity to implement them. . . .

When it came to political engagement outside the gay community, the movement's "special sphere of opportunity" was "to raise questions by confrontation, to force the straight majority to acknowledge the homosexuals in [its] midst and consider what to do about them." . . .

Minneapolis: Jack Baker and Michael McConnell

. . . Jack Baker and Michael McConnell [ ] lived in Minneapolis in a "stable" and "long-lasting" relationship. . . . Baker was a second-year law school student at the University of Minnesota and [ ] McConnell was pursuing a master's degree in library science. . . . Baker began "socializing and going to gay bars" at age twenty. Six years later, on Thanksgiving Day, 1969, he came out to his siblings. "My eldest brother took it badly," Baker recalled. "He said he never wanted me in his house again." McConnell's family in Norman, Oklahoma, was more supportive. They progressed quickly from advocating conversion therapy to offering Baker and McConnell matching, homemade bathrobes for Christmas: "My parents couldn't care less what I am. . . . They kiss and hug Jack like they do me."

. . . Baker proposed on New Year's Eve, 1969. From the start of their engagement, the couple aspired to be not only spiritually but legally married, but they deferred their plan until they were out of Oklahoma. "We decided," said Baker in 1971, "that when I got to law school I would get into the movement full force." . . .

... FREE, the first gay liberation group in the upper Midwest ... was founded, surprisingly, in May 1969—one month before the Stonewall riots.... FREE received official recognition as a student organization, apparently without controversy, the same semester that Baker began law school....

[Within FREE,] Baker and McConnell fell somewhere in the "militant middle." ... [B]oth men were ... vocal feminists, and both eagerly anticipated a "tremendous" (if non-violent) "socio-sexual revolution." Baker and McConnell sought gay people's "integration" into straight society, but on their own terms; assimilation for those who "look like heterosexuals and behave nicely" was not their idea of progress.... Baker and McConnell vocally rejected both "male-female role playing" and conformity to a "heterosexual standard" of sexual monogamy that, said Baker, "doesn't fit in the gay world."...

Thus it was quite an unconventional pair who, accompanied by other FREE members, appeared at the Hennepin County Clerk's office on May 18, 1970.... By a letter dated May 22, 1970, the County Clerk informed Baker and McConnell that he was "unable to issue the marriage license" because Minnesota law "prohibit[s] the marriage of two male persons."...

Each of the most prominent arguments in today's gay marriage arsenal was presented in these first cases. Plaintiffs leaned heavily on the theory that state law did not explicitly ban same-sex marriages and so did not prohibit them at all, an argument that gay rights advocates have sometimes pressed (though not so strenuously) in more recent litigation. Relying on then-recent Supreme Court precedents like *Loving v. Virginia* and *Griswold v. Connecticut*, [early same-sex marriage] couples claimed that their exclusion from civil marriage violated a fundamental right to marry and intruded on constitutionally protected privacy interests. They argued that same-sex marriage bans invidiously discriminated on the basis of sex, and so violated their right to equal protection of the laws....

Judges rebuffed the plaintiffs' claims at every turn. The U.S. Supreme Court's dismissal of *Baker* "for want of a substantial federal question" captures the perfunctory reaction of nearly all the benches that heard these first cases.... When the case reached the Minnesota Supreme Court for oral argument, "none of the seven justices asked a single question" and one of them, Justice Fallon Kelly, is said (perhaps apocryphally) to have swiveled in his seat, "literally turning his back" on attorney Mike Wetherbee. The court's short and unanimous opinion "dismiss[ed] without discussion" plaintiffs' arguments under the First and Eighth Amendments, and it disposed cursorily of their equality and right-to-marry claims on the ground that marriage, an institution "as old as the book of Genesis," "uniquely involv[es] the procreation and rearing of children."

... What enabled such dismissive responses ... was an understanding of marriage so intuitive, so "fundamental," as to render sustained legal analysis superfluous. ...

Perhaps all gay marriage plaintiffs, at all times, are courageous simply by virtue of their willingness to tolerate public scrutiny. But it was gutsier to bring a marriage case in the early 1970s. The probability of drastic consequences was not just higher then; it was huge. ... Mike McConnell, who came to Minneapolis with an offer in hand to work in the University of Minnesota library, likewise found himself suing the state Board of Regents; his appointment was revoked when the Board determined that his marriage "stunt" would "subject the University to ridicule, embarrassment, and criticism." ...

... [B]oth men considered marriage "a horseshit institution" that, in McConnell's words, was "definitely on its way out." [But] the couple's "secret plan" to obtain a license by fraud was evidence, said Baker, of "how much Mike and I want to be married." ...

[Nevertheless, legal] matrimony was, at most, an ostensible goal of the first gay marriage cases. ... McConnell frankly acknowledged that his and Baker's lawsuit was "a political act with political implications." ...

But why this act specifically? Why marriage litigation? ...

First, marriage litigation was a forceful assertion of gay equality. This proposition may sound innocuous to many twenty-first century liberals and (no doubt for other reasons) it might have seemed bland to many gay liberationists in the early 1970s. But "fighting to establish equal rights for homosexuals" was an important project even then. For Jack Baker, a marriage case was simply the most noted accomplishment in an activist career whose "emphasis all the time," he said, "was equal rights, equal rights in all areas of society!" ...

Second, these cases protested the gendered nature of marriage, the vastly different expectations of husbands and wives and, in turn, of men and women. These roles continue to define the lives of millions of Americans, but in the early 1970s, before the great feminist law reforms of that decade, they defined what it meant to be legally married. ... The Minnesota couple's expectation that their case would "help women's liberation ... by calling into question laws that treat wives and husbands differently" goes far in explaining Baker and McConnell's intention to "cause a re-examination and re-evaluation of the institution of marriage," as well as their notion that gay marriage could "turn the whole institution ... upside down." ...

Third ... these lawsuits were opportunities to posit visions and critiques of marriage beyond the specific issue of traditional gender roles. A "companionate" as opposed to "conjugal" view of the marital relationship, arguably implicit in the very notion of gay marriage, was made explicit in the plaintiffs' legal arguments.... "Procreation cannot be the only standard used to legally recognize a significant love relationship.... We feel it's the relationship, i.e., love and concern, that is important—not procreation...."

Fourth, marriage litigation was a sure way to bring intense publicity to a movement that ... was doing whatever it could just to "get people to say the word 'gay'" [and] ... "to show that we were organizing."...

In Minneapolis, ... opposition to the lawsuits came not from the gay liberationist circles in which the plaintiffs themselves moved, but from the old-fashioned, cautious, and largely closeted homosexuals whom liberationists defined themselves against....

... [And] there was room on the gay left to reconcile agitation around marriage with a staunchly radical agenda. One reason why gay liberationists could rally around the call for gay marriage is that, as Michael Warner observes, the demand was "contextualized ... in more sweeping changes designed to ensure that single people and non-standard households, not just same-sex couples, would benefit from it."...

Most importantly, the first marriage cases' sheer audacity "won support from emerging gay liberation groups," which appreciated their " 'in your face' political style." In pursuing marriage licenses, same-sex couples showed "guts and dedication to each other and to the Gay Liberation cause."...

Defying the conventional distinction between confrontational tactics like "direct action, protest, and disruption" and institutional tactics like litigation, the first gay marriage cases attest to law's multifaceted role in the strategic repertoires of social movements. They confirm that even " 'losing' litigation can achieve limited success in stimulating ... meaningful social change." Ostentatiously useless as instruments of legal redress, these constitutional challenges to the heterosexual definition of marriage were used instead to communicate some of gay liberation's central messages. The *Baker* [and other] cases broadcast the movement's demand for legal equality between gays and straights, and its assertion of moral equality between heterosexuality and homosexuality. They raised implicit and explicit objections to the gender roles embedded in heterosexual marriage, to governmental favoritism of (and coercion toward) particular family forms, and to the marital norm of monogamy. Lastly, they garnered visibility, both as a means (in Jack Baker's words) of forcing straight society to "take notice of the gay movement" and as a revelation to other gay people of the shameless lifestyles to be enjoyed in a burgeoning, politicized subculture.

... Then as now, the idea of gay marriage served as a synecdoche for perfect state neutrality as between hetero- and homosexuality. But the cause of equality, symbolized by the claim to marriage, has changed in at least two crucial respects. First, Stonewall-era protests against discrimination between different-sex and same-sex couples complemented concurrent objections to discrimination between married people and everyone else—single individuals, unwed cohabitants, hippie communes. Contemporary marriage advocacy, by contrast, tends to reify rather than dismantle marital privilege; indeed it has positively alienated other groups that are marginalized by marriage's supremacy....

... Where the claim to marriage was once a device for disputing homosexuality's supposed wickedness, marriage itself increasingly serves as the measure of gay people's virtue. Where the [early] plaintiffs used marriage's privileged relationship to sex and romantic love to underscore the shocking notion that "gay is good," more recent marriage equality campaigns insinuate that goodness is not intrinsic to gayness but is instead established by various indicia of bourgeois respectability—most importantly gay relationships' conformity to marital convention, gay couples' yearning for the dignity of matrimony, and gay people's subscription to the sentimental ideology of marriage....

Gone, then, are the days when gay marriage advocacy was a platform for critiquing the institution or for offering, as Baker put it, "an alternative to the nuclear family." Gone, too, are the days when marriage litigation waged an unambiguous attack on gender roles. On this last score, the gay rights movement is only partly to blame. With the demise of legal distinctions between husband and wife, and with different-sex couples' increasing embrace of egalitarianism, "same-sex marriage" has ceased to be the contradiction-in-terms it once was.... Many contemporary gay rights advocates have deep feminist commitments and surely some believe that legalizing gay marriage weakens traditional gender roles even when those roles are no longer written into marriage law. If so, however, they are far less determined than their predecessors to communicate that message.

Still, one might protest, the fight for gay marriage continues to advance that most important of Stonewall-era goals: visibility.... Yet something important has changed since the early 1970s. That something is not whether the marriage debate promotes gay visibility, but rather which gay people, which gay relationships, and which gay politics are rendered visible. Plaintiffs in the marriage cases engineered by major gay rights litigation firms are "chosen for their suitability," their ambassadorial value as "stable, appealing, and upstanding members of the community."...

The *Baker* [and other early] cases remind us what the signal gay rights issue of our time once represented, and they reveal what it may come to represent once more. These "glorious precedents" illuminate some of gay marriage's obscured and perhaps latent possibilities, whose fulfillment in future decades could depend less on any traceable descendant of gay liberation—which, after all, aspired ultimately to human liberation—than on new and unanticipated constituencies for sexual freedom, gender dissent, and alternative family forms. Those ideals, no less than equality, constitute the radical heritage of a now-mainstream movement. Let us not forget them.

Many activists and advocates aiming for gay liberation since the 1960s, as Boucai describes, sought to bring into accepted practice the ideals of "sexual freedom, gender dissent, and alternative family forms." Not everyone agreed with those goals, even within the LGBTQ movement and among allies. Disputing views arose. What was the "cause"—access to marriage (and for whom?) or the restructuring of marriage as a legally enforced and culturally preferred family form? Who benefited from and who was left out of legal victories—or even hurt by those victories? What, then, are the best strategies to advance the cause, however defined, and who should be "at the table" making decisions about priorities, tactics, and strategy?

Despite the narrowed and assimilationist aims of the marriage equality campaign, top-down opposition remains entrenched and proactive, with calls to reverse equality and reinstate exclusion. As with *Brown*, even modest progress meets adamant, unrelenting opposition—including widely-reported refusals to do business with same-sex couples. These critical histories and their legacies thus demonstrate that every gain must be protected vigilantly and *proactively*: advocate always anticipate "the next round" precisely because the struggle over law as justice is perpetual—always contested and always contingent.

NOTES AND QUESTIONS

1. *Calavita and Critical Histories of Immigration Policy.* What forms of systemic violence do you recognize in the enactment and enforcement of the Chinese Exclusion Laws? Can you point to examples of systemic violence in today's immigration system rife with family separation and immigrant detention in prisons or prison-like conditions? What justifications does the system offer for today's immigration practices and policies that systemic advocates and those at the bottom might properly characterize as systemic violence? Do any of those justifications connect to notions of sovereignty introduced in Part I's excerpt from Antony Anghie?[32] Do you consider these legitimate justifications for what is felt by the bottom as systemic violence?

---

[32] See Angélica Cházaro, The End of Deportation, 67 UCLA L. Rev. (forthcoming 2021) (drawing on indigenous studies and international law scholarship to contest the notions of sovereignty that underlie justifications for U.S. deportation of migrants).

Historically, the intersection of U.S. citizenship status (or lack thereof) and other disfavored social identities has resulted in exclusions based solely on identity categories. For example, both U.S. federal and state law banned the entry of poor migrants considered likely to be reliant on government services. Reflecting prevailing prejudices against gay people, the exclusion of migrants of "psychopathic inferiority," as mandated under the federal Immigration Act of 1917, was intended by Congress to bar "homosexuals and sex perverts" from entry and U.S. citizenship. Although Congress finally removed the bar in 1990, same-sex partners were nonetheless excluded from participating in family reunification allowances under immigration law until 2013 when the Supreme Court invalidated the Defense of Marriage Act, by which Congress had refused to recognize the legitimacy of gay marriage or unions. Religious prejudice led to a discriminatory national origin structure in a 1924 U.S. immigration law that survived until 1965 and helped exclude European Jews from entry. Can you think of examples of current immigration policy or rhetoric that rely on social identities to subordinate (or elevate) groups?

3.5 SOCIAL IDENTITIES (STILL) MATTER IN LEGAL DECISION MAKING

Critical history shows that social identities and ideologies have mattered to law as a system from inception. Although white supremacy may serve as an apt exemplar, identity groups and supremacist ideologies do differ or shift in different places and times. But identity castes still matter in law and across society.

Law as a system incorporated social identities into its very fabric—its defining texts and "rules of the game" for both democracy and adjudication. Social identities were used to assign groups into individual and collective "winners" and "losers." In the following excerpts from both well-known and new U.S. Supreme Court cases, we see how social groups based on identity have been at the center of legal decision making from colonial times until now. We are not focusing here on *how* identity groups are constructed—that follows next—but simply noting that groups, defined in terms of different identities, repeatedly are at the core of legal decision making. Identity-based groups are targets for subordination and domination in society and law. Each case below is an output of law and shows law as a system in action. As systemic analysis explains, each is an indicator of the legal system's priorities and purposes.

These cases simultaneously record imposition of and resistance to identity-based systemic injustice. Each case points to larger group struggles to change laws through policymaking and to change social outcomes directly. Often these group struggles are not seen as relevant to legal decision making and thus not explicitly discussed in judicial opinions. But these cases illustrate in multiple contexts that law is an instrument of oppression *and* of struggle—both at once. And identities, groups, interests, and power can be seen in each case as central to the system and to claims for justice.

In the first excerpt, from *Johnson v. M'Intosh*, the Supreme Court justified U.S. appropriation of Native land by force as a lawful title by conquest. Backed by the judiciary, the federal government eventually turned desirable indigenous land over to white "homesteaders," putting in place identity-grounded control over indigenous lands that remains enforced to this day.

JOHNSON AND GRAHAM'S LESSEE V. M'INTOSH
21 U.S. 543 (1823)

MR. CHIEF JUSTICE MARSHALL delivered the opinion of the Court.

The plaintiffs in this cause claim the land, in their declaration mentioned, under two grants, [from] the chiefs of certain Indian tribes, constituting the Illinois and the Piankeshaw nations; and the question is, whether this title can be recognised in the Courts of the United States?

The facts ... show the authority of the chiefs who executed this conveyance, so far as it could be given by their own people; and likewise show, that the particular tribes for whom these chiefs acted were in rightful possession of the land they sold. The inquiry, therefore, is, in a great measure, confined to the power of Indians to give, and of private individuals to receive, a title which can be sustained in the Courts of this country. . . .

On the discovery of this immense continent, the great nations of Europe were eager to appropriate to themselves so much of it as they could respectively acquire. Its vast extent offered an ample field to the ambition and enterprise of all; and the character and religion of its inhabitants afforded an apology for considering them as a people over whom the superior genius of Europe might claim an ascendency. The potentates of the old world found no difficulty in convincing themselves that they made ample compensation to the inhabitants of the new, by bestowing on them civilization and Christianity, in exchange for unlimited independence. But, as they were all in pursuit of nearly the same object, it was necessary, in order to avoid conflicting settlements, and consequent war with each other, to establish a principle, which all should acknowledge as the law by which the right of acquisition, which they all asserted, should be regulated as between themselves. This principle was, that discovery gave title to the government by whose subjects, or by whose authority, it was made, against all other European governments, which title might be consummated by possession.

The exclusion of all other Europeans, necessarily gave to the nation making the discovery the sole right of acquiring the soil from the natives, and establishing settlements upon it. . . .

. . . In the establishment of these relations, the rights of the original inhabitants were, in no instance, entirely disregarded; but were necessarily, to a considerable extent, impaired. They were admitted to be the rightful occupants of the soil, with a legal as well as just claim to retain possession of it, and to use it according to their own discretion; but their rights to complete sovereignty, as independent nations, were necessarily diminished, and their power to dispose of the soil at their own will, to whomsoever they pleased, was denied by the original fundamental principle, that discovery gave exclusive title to those who made it.

While the different nations of Europe respected the right of the natives, as occupants, they asserted the ultimate dominion to be in themselves; and claimed and exercised, as a consequence of this ultimate dominion, a power to grant the soil, while yet in possession of the natives. These grants have been understood by all, to convey a title to the grantees, subject only to the Indian right of occupancy.

The history of America, from its discovery to the present day, proves, we think, the universal recognition of these principles.

Spain did not rest her title solely on the grant of the Pope. Her discussions respecting boundary, with France, with Great Britain, and with the United States, all show that she placed it on the rights given by discovery. Portugal sustained her claim to the Brazils by the same title. France, also, founded her title to the vast territories she claimed in America on discovery. . . .

No one of the powers of Europe gave its full assent to this principle, more unequivocally than England. . . . [E]arly as the year 1496, her monarch granted a commission to the Cabots, to discover countries then unknown to *Christian people*, and to take possession of them in the name of the king of England. Two years afterwards, Cabot proceeded on this voyage, and discovered the continent of North America, along which he sailed as far south as Virginia. To this discovery the English trace their title.

. . . The right of discovery given by this commission, is confined to countries "then unknown to all Christian people;" and of these countries Cabot was empowered to take possession in the name of the king of England. Thus asserting a right to take possession, notwithstanding the occupancy of the natives, who were heathens, and, at the same time, admitting the prior title of any Christian people who may have made a previous discovery. . . .

Thus has our whole country been granted by the crown while in the occupation of the Indians. These grants purport to convey the soil as well as the right of dominion to the grantees. In those governments which were denominated royal, where the right to the soil was not vested in individuals, but remained in the crown, or was vested in the colonial government, the king claimed and exercised the right of granting lands, and of dismembering the government at his will. The grants made out of the two original colonies, after the resumption of their charters by the crown, are examples of this. The governments of New England, New York, New Jersey, Pennsylvania, Maryland, and a part of Carolina, were thus created. In all of them, the soil, at the time the grants were made, was occupied by the Indians. . . .

. . . Thus, all the nations of Europe, who have acquired territory on this continent, have asserted in themselves, and have recognised in others, the exclusive right of the discoverer to appropriate the lands occupied by the Indians. . . .

By the treaty which concluded the war of our revolution, . . . the powers of government, and the right to soil, which had previously been in Great Britain, passed definitively to these States. . . .

The United States, then, have unequivocally acceded to that great and broad rule by which its civilized inhabitants now hold this country. . . . They maintain . . . that discovery gave an exclusive right to extinguish the Indian title of occupancy, either by purchase or by conquest. . . .

. . . The title by conquest is acquired and maintained by force. The conqueror prescribes its limits. . . .

. . . [T]he tribes of Indians inhabiting this country were fierce savages, whose occupation was war, and whose subsistence was drawn chiefly from the forest. To leave them in possession of their country, was to leave the country a wilderness; to govern them as a distinct people, was impossible, because they were as brave and as high spirited as they were fierce, and were ready to repel by arms every attempt on their independence.

What was the inevitable consequence of this state of things? The Europeans were under the necessity either of abandoning the country, and relinquishing their pompous claims to it, or of enforcing those claims by the sword, and by the adoption of principles adapted to the condition of a people with whom it was impossible to mix, and who could not be governed as a distinct society, or of remaining in their neighbourhood, and exposing themselves and their families to the perpetual hazard of being massacred.

Frequent and bloody wars, in which the whites were not always the aggressors, unavoidably ensued. European policy, numbers, and skill, prevailed. As the white population advanced, that of the Indians necessarily receded. The country in the immediate neighbourhood of agriculturists became unfit for them. The game fled into thicker and more unbroken forests, and the Indians followed. The soil, to which the crown originally claimed title, being no longer occupied by its ancient inhabitants, was parceled out according to the will of the sovereign power, and taken possession of by persons who claimed immediately from the crown, or mediately, through its grantees or deputies.

. . . [T]he Court is decidedly of the opinion, that the plaintiffs [who received title from tribal chiefs rather than from the conqueror] do not exhibit a title which can be sustained in the Courts of the United States. . . .

Now consider the notorious 1857 case of *Dred Scott v. Sandford* as a complement to the appropriation of real property. There, judges appointed by settler elites upheld the institution of identity-based slavery and the legal rights of slave owners over slaves, specifically Black slaves, as their personal property. The Supreme Court concluded that, as a matter of law, a Black slave like Scott could not be deemed a Missouri citizen under the U.S. Constitution because it had been universally understood that Black people never were part of "We, the People" as those words were used in the original Constitution. Therefore, as a technical matter, Blacks like Scott could not properly invoke the diversity jurisdiction of federal courts.[33] The outcome denied freedom to a Black slave despite being taken by his owner, a U.S. army surgeon, from a slave-holding state into U.S. regions where slavery was outlawed.

DRED SCOTT V. SANDFORD
60 U.S. 393 (1857)[34]

MR. CHIEF JUSTICE TANEY delivered the opinion of the court.

. . . The question is simply this: Can a negro, whose ancestors were imported into this country, and sold as slaves, become a member of the political community formed and brought into existence by the Constitution of the United States, and as such become entitled to all the rights, and privileges, and immunities, guaranteed by that instrument to the citizen? One of which rights is the privilege of suing in a court of the United States in the cases specified in the Constitution.

. . . The words "people of the United States" and "citizens" are synonymous terms, and mean the same thing. They both describe the political body who, according to our republican institutions, form the sovereignty, and who hold the power and conduct the Government through

---

[33] Moreover, in a part of the opinion not excerpted here, a Congressional law prohibiting slavery in certain U.S. regions, known as the Missouri Compromise, was deemed void.

[34] For additional background on the decision, see Earl M. Maltz, Slavery and the Supreme Court, 1825–1861 (2009).

their representatives. They are what we familiarly call the "sovereign people," and every citizen is one of this people, and a constituent member of this sovereignty. The question before us is, whether the class of persons described in the plea in abatement compose a portion of this people, and are constituent members of this sovereignty? We think they are not, and that they are not included, and were not intended to be included, under the word "citizens" in the Constitution, and can therefore claim none of the rights and privileges which that instrument provides for and secures to citizens of the United States. On the contrary, they were at that time considered as a subordinate and inferior class of beings, who had been subjugated by the dominant race, and, whether emancipated or not, yet remained subject to their authority, and had no rights or privileges but such as those who held the power and the Government might choose to grant them.

It is not the province of the court to decide upon the justice or injustice, the policy or impolicy, of these laws. The decision of that question belonged to the political or law-making power; to those who formed the sovereignty and framed the Constitution. The duty of the court is, to interpret the instrument they have framed, with the best lights we can obtain on the subject, and to administer it as we find it, according to its true intent and meaning when it was adopted.

. . . In the opinion of the court, the legislation and histories of the times, and the language used in the Declaration of Independence, show, that neither the class of persons who had been imported as slaves, nor their descendants, whether they had become free or not, were then acknowledged as a part of the people, nor intended to be included in the general words used in that memorable instrument.

It is difficult at this day to realize the state of public opinion in relation to that unfortunate race, which prevailed . . . [when the Constitution was adopted, but] the public history of every European nation displays it in a manner too plain to be mistaken.

They had for more than a century before been regarded as beings of an inferior order, and altogether unfit to associate with the white race, either in social or political relations; and so far inferior, that they had no rights which the white man was bound to respect; and that the negro might justly and lawfully be reduced to slavery for his benefit. He was bought and sold, and treated as an ordinary article of merchandise and traffic, whenever a profit could be made by it. This opinion was at that time fixed and universal in the civilized portion of the white race. . . .

And in no nation was this opinion more firmly fixed or more uniformly acted upon than by the English Government and English people. They not only seized them on the coast of Africa, and sold them or held them in slavery for their own use; but they took them as ordinary articles of merchandise to every country where they could make a profit on them, and were far more extensively engaged in this commerce than any other nation in the world.

The opinion thus entertained and acted upon in England was naturally impressed upon the colonies they founded on this side of the Atlantic. And, accordingly, a negro of the African race was regarded by them as an article of property, and held, and bought and sold as such, in every one of the thirteen colonies which united in the Declaration of Independence, and afterwards formed the Constitution of the United States. . . .

. . . [State laws] show that a perpetual and impassable barrier was intended to be erected between the white race and the one which they had reduced to slavery, and governed as subjects with absolute and despotic power, and which they then looked upon as so far below them in the scale of created beings, that intermarriages between white persons and negroes or mulattoes were regarded as unnatural and immoral, and punished as crimes, not only in the parties, but in the person who joined them in marriage. And no distinction in this respect was made between the free negro or mulatto and the slave, but this stigma, of the deepest degradation, was fixed upon the whole race.

. . . The language of the Declaration of Independence is equally conclusive:

It [states,] . . . "We hold these truths to be self-evident: that all men are created equal; that they are endowed by their Creator with certain unalienable rights; that among them is life, liberty, and the pursuit of happiness; that to secure these rights, Governments are instituted, deriving their just powers from the consent of the governed."

The general words above quoted would seem to embrace the whole human family, and if they were used in a similar instrument at this day would be so understood. But it is too clear for dispute, that the enslaved African race were not intended to be included, and formed no part of the people who framed and adopted this declaration; for if the language, as understood in that day, would embrace them, the conduct of the distinguished men who framed the Declaration of Independence would have been utterly and flagrantly inconsistent with the principles they asserted; and instead of the sympathy of mankind, to which they so confidently appealed, they would have deserved and received universal rebuke and reprobation.

Yet the men who framed this declaration were great men—high in literary acquirements—high in their sense of honor, and incapable of asserting principles inconsistent with those on which they were acting. They perfectly understood the meaning of the language they used, and how it would be understood by others; and they knew that it would not in any part of the civilized world be supposed to embrace the negro race, which, by common consent, had been excluded from civilized Governments and the family of nations, and doomed to slavery....

... The brief preamble [to the Constitution] sets forth by whom it was formed, for what purposes, and for whose benefit and protection. It declares that it is formed by the *people* of the United States; that is to say, by those who were members of the different political communities in the several States; and its great object is declared to be to secure the blessings of liberty to themselves and their posterity. It speaks in general terms of the *people* of the United States, and of *citizens* of the several States, when it is providing for the exercise of the powers granted or the privileges secured to the citizen. It does not define what description of persons are intended to be included under these terms, or who shall be regarded as a citizen and one of the people. It uses them as terms so well understood, that no further description or definition was necessary.

... More especially, it cannot be believed that the large slaveholding States regarded them as included in the word citizens, or would have consented to a Constitution which might compel them to receive them in that character from another State. For if they were so received, and entitled to the privileges and immunities of citizens, it would exempt them from the operation of the special laws and from the police regulations which they considered to be necessary for their own safety. It would give to persons of the negro race, who were recognized as citizens in any one State of the Union, the right to enter every other State whenever they pleased, singly or in companies, without pass or passport, and without obstruction, to sojourn there as long as they pleased, to go where they pleased at every hour of the day or night without molestation, unless they committed some violation of law for which a white man would be punished; and it would give them the full liberty of speech in public and in private upon all subjects upon which its own citizens might speak; to hold public meetings upon political affairs, and to keep and carry arms wherever they went. And all of this would be done in the face of the subject race of the same color, both free and slaves, and inevitably producing discontent and insubordination among them, and endangering the peace and safety of the State.

... No one, we presume, supposes that any change in public opinion or feeling, in relation to this unfortunate race, in the civilized nations of Europe or in this country, should induce the court to give to the words of the Constitution a more liberal construction in their favor than they were intended to bear when the instrument was framed and adopted.... [A]s long as it continues to exist in its present form, it speaks not only in the same words, but with the same meaning and intent with which it spoke when it came from the hands of its framers, and was voted on and adopted by the people of the United States. Any other rule of construction would abrogate the judicial character of this court, and make it the mere reflex of the popular opinion or passion of the day. This court was not created by the Constitution for such purposes. Higher and graver trusts have been confided to it, and it must not falter in the path of duty.

What the construction was at that time, we think can hardly admit of doubt.... And if anything in relation to the construction of the Constitution can be regarded as settled, it is that which we now give to the word "citizen" and the word "people."

Women also have been routinely subordinated as a group. Importing the British common law tradition of marriage, many U.S. states once prohibited women from entering into contracts without their husband's consent or from owning property independently. Husbands controlled any wages their wives earned. Married women gained the right to contract and to own property only with the passage by U.S. states of Married Women's Property Acts in the late 19th century, but wider progress was slow. Thus, women were still broadly prohibited from employment in lucrative or prestigious occupations—including law itself. In *Bradwell v. State*, the Court targets women as a group to uphold the denial of their right to practice law.

BRADWELL V. STATE
83 U.S. 130 (1873)

MR. JUSTICE MILLER delivered the opinion of the court.

... We agree ... there are privileges and immunities belonging to citizens of the United States, in that relation and character, and that it is these and these alone which a State is forbidden to abridge. But the right to admission to practice [law] in the courts of a State is not one of them. This right in no sense depends on citizenship of the United States. ...

MR. JUSTICE BRADLEY:

I concur....

The claim of the plaintiff, who is a married woman, to be admitted to practice as an attorney and counselor-at-law, is based upon the supposed right of every person, man or woman, to engage in any lawful employment for a livelihood. The Supreme Court of Illinois denied the application on the ground that, by the common law, which is the basis of the laws of Illinois, only men were admitted to the bar, and the legislature had not made any change in this respect....

... [T]he court felt compelled to deny the application of females to be admitted as members of the bar. Being contrary to the rules of the common law and the usages of Westminster Hall from time immemorial, it could not be supposed that the legislature had intended to adopt any different rule.

The claim that, under the fourteenth amendment of the Constitution, which declares that no State shall make or enforce any law which shall abridge the privileges and immunities of citizens of the United States, the statute law of Illinois, or the common law prevailing in that State, can no longer be set up as a barrier against the right of females to pursue any lawful employment for a livelihood (the practice of law included), assumes that it is one of the privileges and immunities of women as citizens to engage in any and every profession, occupation, or employment in civil life.

It certainly cannot be affirmed, as an historical fact, that this has ever been established as one of the fundamental privileges and immunities of the sex. On the contrary, the civil law, as well as nature herself, has always recognized a wide difference in the respective spheres and destinies of man and woman. Man is, or should be, woman's protector and defender. The natural and proper timidity and delicacy which belongs to the female sex evidently unfits it for many of the occupations of civil life. The constitution of the family organization, which is founded in the divine ordinance, as well as in the nature of things, indicates the domestic sphere as that which properly belongs to the domain and functions of womanhood. The harmony, not to say identity, of interest and views which belong, or should belong, to the family institution is repugnant to the idea of a woman adopting a distinct and independent career from that of her husband. So firmly fixed was this sentiment in the founders of the common law that it became a maxim of that system of jurisprudence that a woman had no legal existence separate from her husband, who was regarded as her head and representative in the social state; and, notwithstanding some recent modifications of this civil status, many of the special rules of law flowing from and dependent upon this cardinal principle still exist in full force in most States. One of these is, that a married woman is incapable, without her husband's consent, of making contracts which shall be binding on her or him. This very incapacity was one circumstance which the Supreme Court of Illinois deemed important in rendering a married woman incompetent fully to perform the duties and trusts that belong to the office of an attorney and counselor.

It is true that many women are unmarried and not affected by any of the duties, complications, and incapacities arising out of the married state, but these are exceptions to the general rule. The paramount destiny and mission of woman are to fulfil the noble and benign offices of wife and mother. This is the law of the Creator. And the rules of civil society must be adapted to the general constitution of things, and cannot be based upon exceptional cases.

The humane movements of modern society, which have for their object the multiplication of avenues for woman's advancement, and of occupations adapted to her condition and sex, have my heartiest concurrence. But I am not prepared to say that it is one of her fundamental rights and privileges to be admitted into every office and position, including those which require highly special qualifications and demanding special responsibilities.... It is the prerogative of the legislator to prescribe regulations founded on nature, reason, and experience for the due admission of qualified persons to professions and callings demanding special skill and confidence. This fairly belongs to the police power of the State; and, in my opinion, in view of the peculiar characteristics, destiny, and mission of woman, it is within the province of the legislature to ordain what offices, positions, and callings shall be filled and discharged by men, and shall receive the benefit of those energies and responsibilities, and that decision and firmness which are presumed to predominate in the sterner sex.

... MR. JUSTICE SWAYNE and MR. JUSTICE FIELD concurred in the foregoing opinion of MR. JUSTICE BRADLEY.

As *M'Intosh, Scott,* and *Bradwell* illustrate, Native American, Black, and female individuals suffered because judicial decision making targeted the identity-based groups to which they belonged for subordination. Group targeting also operated against identities that emerged as "new" areas of struggle took place. In *Downes v. Bidwell,* the Court decided that some groups are unfit to become part of the United States on the basis of identities that make them "different." The Court declared in this and the other *Insular Cases*[35] that the Constitution does not control law at all in some places, at some times, and for some people—a conclusion necessary, the justices assert, to uphold the "American empire" that law—as a system—is designed to protect.

DOWNES V. BIDWELL
182 U.S. 244 (1901)

... MR. JUSTICE BROWN announced the conclusion and judgment of the court:

This case involves the question whether merchandise brought into the port of New York from Porto [sic] Rico since the passage of the Foraker act is exempt from duty....

---

[35] The Insular Cases encompass several rulings, including this one, determining whether the "Constitution follows the flag" when the United States expands territory and population through imperial conquest and occupation.

The case also involves the broader question whether the revenue clauses of the Constitution extend of their own force to our newly acquired territories. The Constitution itself does not answer the question. . . .

. . . [A]s we observed in *De Lima* v. *Bidwell*, the power to establish territorial governments has been too long exercised by Congress and acquiesced in by this court to be deemed an unsettled question. Indeed, in the *Dred Scott Case* it was admitted to be the inevitable consequence of the right to acquire territory.

. . . [T]he practical interpretation put by Congress upon the Constitution has been long continued and uniform to the effect that the Constitution is applicable to territories acquired by purchase or conquest, only when and so far as Congress shall so direct.

We are also of opinion that the power to acquire territory by treaty implies, not only the power to govern such territory, but to prescribe upon what terms the United States will receive its inhabitants, and what their status shall be in what Chief Justice Marshall termed the "American empire." . . .

. . . It is obvious that in the annexation of outlying and distant possessions grave questions will arise from differences of race, habits, laws, and customs of the people, and from differences of soil, climate, and production, which may require action on the part of Congress that would be quite unnecessary in the annexation of contiguous territory inhabited only by people of the same race, or by scattered bodies of native Indians.

. . . A false step at this time might be fatal to the development of . . . the American empire. . . . [P]ossessions [may be] inhabited by alien races, differing from us in religion, customs, laws, methods of taxation, and modes of thought, [and] the administration of government and justice, according to Anglo-Saxon principles, may for a time be impossible. . . . We decline to hold that there is anything in the Constitution to forbid such action.

We are therefore of opinion that the island of Porto [sic] Rico is a territory appurtenant and belonging to the United States, but not a part of the United States within the revenue clauses of the Constitution; that the Foraker act is constitutional, so far as it imposes duties upon imports from such island, and that the plaintiff cannot recover back the duties exacted in this case.

In 1927, the U.S. Supreme Court addressed the constitutionality of a Virginia program in which a woman with perceived intellectual impairments, who had been committed to a state-supported institution, was sterilized without her consent. The assumption that individuals with intellectual disabilities are unfit to raise children has a long history.[36] *Buck v. Bell* arose in the heyday of the eugenics movement, which aimed to prevent "unfit" parents from reproducing. Carrie Buck was 17 years old and pregnant, having been raped, when she came to the state institution. After she gave birth, the institution's superintendent ordered her sterilized, an authority granted under Virginia's sterilization statute. In *Buck*, the justices upheld the statute and stated that "three generations of imbeciles are enough"—referring to Carrie's mother, Carrie, and her infant daughter. The Court's justification rested on the notion that "the best interest of patients and of society" was served by sterilizing intellectually impaired women, considered "unfit" as a group.

BUCK V. BELL
274 U.S. 200 (1927)

MR. JUSTICE HOLMES delivered the opinion of the Court.

This is a writ of error to review a judgment . . . by which the defendant in error, the superintendent of the State Colony for Epileptics and Feeble Minded, was ordered to perform the operation of salpingectomy upon Carrie Buck, the plaintiff in error, for the purpose of making her sterile. . . . The case comes here upon the contention that the statute authorizing the judgment is void under the Fourteenth Amendment as denying to the plaintiff in error due process of law and the equal protection of the laws.

Carrie Buck is a feeble-minded white woman who was committed to the State Colony. . . . She is the daughter of a feeble-minded mother in the same institution, and the mother of an illegitimate feeble-minded child. She was eighteen years old at the time of the trial of her case in the Circuit Court in the latter part of 1924. An Act of Virginia approved March 20, 1924 . . . recites that the health of the patient and the welfare of society may be promoted in certain cases by the sterilization of mental defectives, under careful safeguard, etc.; that the sterilization may be effected in males by vasectomy and in females by salpingectomy, without serious pain or substantial danger to life; that the Commonwealth is supporting in various institutions many defective persons who if now discharged would become a menace but if incapable of procreating might be discharged with safety and become self-supporting with benefit to themselves and to society; and that experience has shown that heredity plays an important part in the transmission of insanity, imbecility, etc. The statute then enacts that whenever the superintendent of certain institutions including the abovenamed State Colony shall be of opinion that it is for the best interest

---

[36] Robert L. Hayman, Jr., Presumptions of Justice: Law, Politics, and the Mentally Retarded Parent, 103 Harv. L. Rev. 1201 (1990); Robyn M. Powell, Safeguarding the Rights of Parents with Intellectual Disabilities in Child Welfare Cases: The Convergence of Social Science and Law, 20 CUNY L. Rev. 127 (2016).

of the patients and of society that an inmate under his care should be sexually sterilized, he may have the operation performed. . . .

The attack is not upon the procedure but upon the substantive law. . . .

The judgment finds the facts that have been recited and that Carrie Buck "is the probable potential parent of socially inadequate offspring, likewise afflicted, that she may be sexually sterilized without detriment to her general health and that her welfare and that of society will be promoted by her sterilization," and thereupon makes the order. In view of the general declarations of the Legislature and the specific findings of the Court obviously we cannot say as matter of law that the grounds do not exist, and if they exist they justify the result. We have seen more than once that the public welfare may call upon the best citizens for their lives. It would be strange if it could not call upon those who already sap the strength of the State for these lesser sacrifices, often not felt to be such by those concerned, in order to prevent our being swamped with incompetence. It is better for all the world, if instead of waiting to execute degenerate offspring for crime, or to let them starve for their imbecility, society can prevent those who are manifestly unfit from continuing their kind. The principle that sustains compulsory vaccination is broad enough to cover cutting the Fallopian tubes. . . . Three generations of imbeciles are enough. . . .

In the following case, the Court blessed the collective internment and confiscation of property based on identity group membership. Those of Japanese descent residing in the United States during the wartime 1940s were considered a threat to national security. By this time, the Equal Protection Clause of the Fourteenth Amendment had been a formal part of the Constitution for nearly a century, but its promise of equality was still unrealized.

KOREMATSU V. UNITED STATES
323 U.S. 214 (1944)

MR. JUSTICE BLACK delivered the opinion of the Court.

The petitioner, an American citizen of Japanese descent, was convicted in a federal district court for remaining in San Leandro, California, a "Military Area," contrary to Civilian Exclusion Order No. 34 of the Commanding General of the Western Command, U.S. Army, which directed that after May 9, 1942, all persons of Japanese ancestry should be excluded from that area. No question was raised as to petitioner's loyalty to the United States. . . .

It should be noted, to begin with, that all legal restrictions which curtail the civil rights of a single racial group are immediately suspect.

That is not to say that all such restrictions are unconstitutional. It is to say that courts must subject them to the most rigid scrutiny. Pressing public necessity may sometimes justify the existence of such restrictions; racial antagonism never can. . . .

We uphold the exclusion order as of the time it was made and when the petitioner violated it. In doing so, we are not unmindful of the hardships imposed by it upon a large group of American citizens. But hardships are part of war, and war is an aggregation of hardships. . . . Compulsory exclusion of large groups of citizens from their homes, except under circumstances of direst emergency and peril, is inconsistent with our basic governmental institutions. But when under conditions of modern warfare our shores are threatened by hostile forces, the power to protect must be commensurate with the threatened danger. . . .

It is said that we are dealing here with the case of imprisonment of a citizen in a concentration camp solely because of his ancestry, without evidence or inquiry concerning his loyalty and good disposition towards the United States. Our task would be simple, our duty clear, were this a case involving the imprisonment of a loyal citizen in a concentration camp because of racial prejudice. . . . Korematsu was not excluded from the Military Area because of hostility to him or his race. He was excluded because we are at war with the Japanese Empire, because the properly constituted military authorities feared an invasion of our West Coast and felt constrained to take proper security measures, because they decided that the military urgency of the situation demanded that all citizens of Japanese ancestry be segregated from the West Coast temporarily, and finally, because Congress, reposing its confidence in this time of war in our military leaders—as inevitably it must—determined that they should have the power to do just this. There was evidence of disloyalty on the part of some, the military authorities considered that the need for action was great, and time was short. We cannot—by availing ourselves of the calm perspective of hindsight—now say that at that time these actions were unjustified.

Affirmed.

While purporting to be vigilant against the uses of identities to legalize collective inequality, the Court in *Korematsu* did just that. The Court allowed the indefinite detention of an entire group solely on the basis of identity-related fears—fears of disloyalty later revealed not only to have been false, but known by the government to be false at the time of the detentions.[37]

---

[37] See Lorraine K. Bannai, Enduring Conviction: Fred Korematsu and His Quest for Justice (2015).

Separate from (but often related to) gender-based oppressions, sexual identity also is used to target disfavored groups. The Supreme Court sanctioned the oppressive control of sexuality through the criminal justice system as recently as 1986. Before reversing course in 2003 in *Lawrence v. Texas*, 539 U.S. 558, the Court upheld the discriminatory application of criminal sodomy laws to homosexual partners. Concurring in that 1986 result, Chief Justice Warren Burger cited customs and beliefs branding same-sex intimacies a "deeper malignity" than rape and a "disgrace to human nature." As with other identities, *Bowers* bootstraps colonial beliefs about identities and social groups to justify legalized subordination of entire populations.

BOWERS V. HARDWICK
478 U.S. 186 (1986)

JUSTICE WHITE delivered the opinion of the Court.

In August 1982, respondent Hardwick ... was charged with violating the Georgia statute criminalizing sodomy by committing that act with another adult male in the bedroom of respondent's home. . . .

This case does not require a judgment on whether laws against sodomy between consenting adults in general, or between homosexuals in particular, are wise or desirable. . . . The issue presented is whether the Federal Constitution confers a fundamental right upon homosexuals to engage in sodomy and hence invalidates the laws of the many States that still make such conduct illegal and have done so for a very long time. The case also calls for some judgment about the limits of the Court's role in carrying out its constitutional mandate.

. . . [R]espondent would have us announce, as the Court of Appeals did, a fundamental right to engage in homosexual sodomy. This we are quite unwilling to do. . . .

Proscriptions against [consensual sodomy] have ancient roots. . . . Sodomy was a criminal offense at common law and was forbidden by the laws of the original thirteen States when they ratified the Bill of Rights. In 1868, when the Fourteenth Amendment was ratified, all but 5 of the 37 States in the Union had criminal sodomy laws. In fact, until 1961, all 50 States outlawed sodomy, and today, 24 States and the District of Columbia continue to provide criminal penalties for sodomy performed in private and between consenting adults. Against this background, to claim that a right to engage in such conduct is "deeply rooted in this Nation's history and tradition" or "implicit in the concept of ordered liberty" is, at best, facetious. . . .

Respondent, however, asserts that the result should be different where the homosexual conduct occurs in the privacy of the home. He relies on

Stanley v. Georgia, 394 U.S. 557 (1969), where the Court held that the First Amendment prevents conviction for possessing and reading obscene material in the privacy of one's home. . . .

Stanley did protect conduct that would not have been protected outside the home, and it partially prevented the enforcement of state obscenity laws; but the decision was firmly grounded in the First Amendment. The right pressed upon us here has no similar support in the text of the Constitution, and it does not qualify for recognition under the prevailing principles for construing the Fourteenth Amendment. Its limits are also difficult to discern. Plainly enough, otherwise illegal conduct is not always immunized whenever it occurs in the home.

Victimless crimes, such as the possession and use of illegal drugs, do not escape the law where they are committed at home. . . . And if respondent's submission is limited to the voluntary sexual conduct between consenting adults, it would be difficult, except by fiat, to limit the claimed right to homosexual conduct while leaving exposed to prosecution adultery, incest, and other sexual crimes even though they are committed in the home. We are unwilling to start down that road.

Even if the conduct at issue here is not a fundamental right, respondent asserts that there must be a rational basis for the law and that there is none in this case other than the presumed belief of a majority of the electorate in Georgia that homosexual sodomy is immoral and unacceptable. This is said to be an inadequate rationale to support the law. The law, however, is constantly based on notions of morality, and if all laws representing essentially moral choices are to be invalidated under the Due Process Clause, the courts will be very busy indeed. Even respondent makes no such claim, but insists that majority sentiments about the morality of homosexuality should be declared inadequate. We do not agree, and are unpersuaded that the sodomy laws of some 25 States should be invalidated on this basis. . . .

The above Supreme Court opinions demonstrate the targeting of groups for advantages and disadvantages across identities and time. The cases range from *M'Intosh* in 1823, *Scott* in 1857, *Bradwell* in 1872, *Downes* in 1901, *Buck* in 1927, *Korematsu* in 1944, to *Bowers* in 1986. These cases illustrate that identities are used to justify systemic injustice—the legal system's actual outputs over the past two centuries—as a purposeful feature of law as a system. Law functions to maintain inequality as much as to advance equality. To help elucidate this basic point, we began Chapter 1 with reflections from Justice Thurgood Marshall.[38] Marshall pointed to

---

[38] Thurgood Marshall, Reflections on the Bicentennial of the United States Constitution, 101 Harv. L. Rev. 1 (1987).

"intentional" identity-based "omissions" that rendered the original Constitution "defective from the start, requiring several amendments, a civil war, and momentous social transformation to attain the system . . . we hold as fundamental today."

Marshall wrote his bicentennial reflections as the first non-white person appointed to the Supreme Court—in the 1960s, and after decades of experience in the trenches of advocacy. A few decades later in 2009, the first woman of color was appointed to that same bench. Justice Sonia Sotomayor similarly has reflected publicly on the role of identity in the legal system and society. In the excerpt below, Sotomayor attests to the connections that bind the present to past. This connection links the role of identity in the micro (her story) with the macro (the larger systemic story) levels of law and society. She sketches how law, culture, identity, and society are interlocking legacies of group marginalization and subordination. Sotomayor also reflects on how identity can, and should, inform a more realistic and just approach to adjudication.

A LATINA JUDGE'S VOICE
Hon. Sonia Sotomayor
13 Berkeley La Raza L.J. 87 (2002)

. . . I intend . . . to talk to you about my Latina identity, where it came from, and the influence I perceive it has on my presence on the bench.

Who am I? I am a "Newyorkrican." For those of you on the West Coast who do not know what that term means: I am a born and bred New Yorker of Puerto Rican-born parents who came to the states during World War II.

. . . [M]y parents came because of poverty and to attempt to find and secure a better life for themselves and the family that they hoped to have. They largely succeeded. . . . The story of that success is what made me and what makes me the Latina that I am. The Latina side of my identity was forged and closely nurtured by my family through our shared experiences and traditions.

. . . Now, do any one of these things make me a Latina? Obviously not, because each of our Caribbean and Latin American communities has their own unique food and different traditions at the holidays. I only learned about tacos in college from my Mexican-American roommate. Being a Latina in America also does not mean speaking Spanish. I happen to speak it fairly well. But my brother, only three years younger, like too many of us educated here, barely speaks it. . . .

. . . We are a nation that takes pride in our ethnic diversity, recognizing its importance in shaping our society and in adding richness to its existence. Yet, we simultaneously insist that we can and must function and live in a race and color-blind way that ignores these very differences that in other contexts we laud. That tension between "the melting pot and the salad bowl"—a recently popular metaphor used to describe New York's diversity—is being hotly debated today in national discussions about affirmative action. Many of us struggle with this tension and attempt to maintain and promote our cultural and ethnic identities in a society that is often ambivalent about how to deal with its differences. . . .

I was born in the year 1954. That year was the fateful year in which *Brown v. Board of Education* was decided. . . .

As of September 1, 2001, the federal judiciary consisting of Supreme, Circuit and District Court Judges was about 22% women. In 1992, nearly ten years ago, when I was first appointed a District Court Judge, the percentage of women in the total federal judiciary was only 13%. Now, the growth of Latino representation is somewhat less favorable. As of [2002] we have . . . no Supreme Court justices, and we have only 10 out of 147 active Circuit Court judges and 30 out of 587 active district court judges. Those numbers are grossly below our proportion of the population. As recently as 1965, however, the federal bench had only three women serving and only one Latino judge. So changes are happening, although in some areas, very slowly. . . .

Let us not forget that between the appointments of Justice Sandra Day O'Connor in 1981 and Justice Ginsburg in 1992, eleven years passed. . . . For women of color the statistics are more sobering. As of September 20, 1998, of the then 195 circuit court judges, only two were African-American women and two Hispanic women. Of the 641 district court judges, only twelve were African-American women and eleven Hispanic women. African-American women comprise only 1.56% of the federal judiciary and Hispanic-American women comprise only 1%. . . .

Sort of shocking, isn't it? This is the year 2002. We have a long way to go. . . .

. . . I accept . . . that in any group of human beings there is a diversity of opinion because there is both a diversity of experiences and of thought. . . . [So] there is not a single voice of feminism, not a feminist approach but many who are exploring the possible ways of being that are distinct from those structured in a world dominated by the power and words of men. Thus, feminist theories of judging are in the midst of creation and are not and perhaps will never aspire to be as solidified as the established legal doctrines of judging can sometimes appear to be.

That same point can be made with respect to people of color. No one person, judge or nominee will speak in a female or people of color voice. I need not remind you that Justice Clarence Thomas represents a part but not the whole of African-American thought on many subjects. Yet, because I accept the proposition [of legal scholar Judith Resnik] that, . . . "to judge is an exercise of power" and because [as legal scholar Martha Minow put it] . . . "there is no objective stance but only a series of perspectives—no neutrality, no escape from choice in judging"—I further accept that our experiences as women and people of color affect our decisions. The aspiration to impartiality is just that—it's an aspiration because it denies the fact that we are by our experiences making different choices than others. Not all women or people of color, in all or some circumstances or indeed in any particular case or circumstance but enough people of color in enough cases, will make a difference in the process of judging. . . .

. . . Justice O'Connor has often been cited as saying that a wise old man and wise old woman will reach the same conclusion in deciding cases. I am not so sure. . . . First, . . . there can never be a universal definition of wise. Second, I would hope that a wise Latina woman with the richness of her experiences would more often than not reach a better conclusion than a white male who hasn't lived that life.

Let us not forget that wise men like Oliver Wendell Holmes and Justice Cardozo voted on cases which upheld both sex and race discrimination in our society. Until 1972, no Supreme Court case ever upheld the claim of a woman in a gender discrimination case. . . .

. . . For people of color and women lawyers, what does and should being an ethnic minority mean in your lawyering? For men lawyers, what areas in your experiences and attitudes do you need to work on to make you capable of reaching those great moments of enlightenment which other men in different circumstances have been able to reach? For all of us, how do we change the fact that in every task force study of gender and race bias in the courts, women and people of color, lawyers and judges alike, report in significantly higher percentages than white men that their gender and race has shaped their careers, from hiring, retention to promotion and that a statistically significant number of women and *minority* lawyers and judges, both alike, have experienced bias in the courtroom?

Each day on the bench I learn something new about the judicial process and about being a professional Latina woman in a world that sometimes looks at me with suspicion. I am reminded each day that I render decisions that affect people concretely and that I owe them constant and complete vigilance in checking my assumptions, presumptions and perspectives and ensuring that to the extent that my limited abilities and capabilities permit me, that I reevaluate them and change as circumstances and cases before me requires. I can and do aspire to be greater than the sum total of my experiences but I accept my limitations. I willingly accept that we who judge must not deny the differences resulting from experience and heritage but attempt, as the Supreme Court suggests, continuously to judge when those opinions, sympathies and prejudices are appropriate. . . .

Sotomayor's testimonial, like Marshall's, reminds us that group exclusion from the Supreme Court has been a systemic identity-based pattern spanning multiple identities and generations. Her testimonial puts on display the central role of identities in relationship to groups, interests, and power in creating law and organizing society. These cases and testimonials show *why* systemic advocates must learn how to incorporate identities, groups, interests, and power proactively (and as assets) into legal problem solving.

Consider now a recent Supreme Court case in which the justices disagreed about the roles of identity in the facts and analysis of the case. In basic terms, this 2018 case is a continuation of the entire line of cases reviewed above—together demonstrating that identity (still) matters in law. In the majority opinion below, the Supreme Court countenanced the exclusion of individuals arriving to the United States from seven countries despite factual details presented in the spirited dissent. Five of these countries are majority-Muslim, and the ban was put in place by the president after his repeated statements connecting the ban (and its prior versions) to Muslim religious identity. In *Trump v. Hawaii*, the justices in the majority assert that the "Muslim ban" has nothing to do with Muslims and is "rational" as an exercise of law. What does this case suggest about the continuing salience of identity to judicial and legal decision-making?

TRUMP V. HAWAII
138 S.Ct. 2392 (2018)

CHIEF JUSTICE ROBERTS delivered the opinion of the Court.

... [T]he President concluded that it was necessary to impose entry restrictions on nationals of countries that do not share adequate information for an informed entry determination, or that otherwise present national security risks. The plaintiffs in this litigation, respondents here, challenged the application of those entry restrictions to certain aliens abroad. We now decide whether the President had authority under the [federal Immigration and Nationality] Act to issue the Proclamation, and whether the entry policy violates the Establishment Clause of the First Amendment.

... Plaintiffs believe that the Proclamation violates this prohibition by singling out Muslims for disfavored treatment. The entry suspension, they contend, operates as a "religious gerrymander," in part because most of the countries covered by the Proclamation have Muslim-majority populations.... Relying on Establishment Clause precedents concerning laws and policies applied domestically, plaintiffs allege that the primary purpose of the Proclamation was religious animus and that the President's stated concerns about vetting protocols and national security were but pretexts for discriminating against Muslims. ...

At the heart of plaintiffs' case is a series of statements by the President and his advisers casting doubt on the official objective of the Proclamation. For example, while a candidate on the campaign trail, the President published a "Statement on Preventing Muslim Immigration" that called for a "total and complete shutdown of Muslims entering the United States until our country's representatives can figure out what is going on." . . . Then-candidate Trump also stated that "Islam hates us" and asserted that the United States was "having problems with Muslims coming into the country." Shortly after being elected, when asked whether violence in Europe had affected his plans to "ban Muslim immigration," the President replied, "You know my plans. All along, I've been proven to be right." . . .

Plaintiffs also note that . . . the President expressed regret that his prior order had been "watered down" and called for a "much tougher version" of his "Travel Ban." Shortly before the release of the Proclamation, he stated that the "travel ban . . . should be far larger, tougher, and more specific," but "stupidly that would not be politically correct." More recently, on November 29, 2017, the President retweeted links to three anti-Muslim propaganda videos. . . .

. . . But the issue before us is not whether to denounce the statements. It is instead the significance of those statements in reviewing a Presidential directive, neutral on its face, addressing a matter within the core of executive responsibility. In doing so, we must consider not only the statements of a particular President, but also the authority of the Presidency itself.

. . . The upshot of our cases in this context is clear: "Any rule of constitutional law that would inhibit the flexibility" of the President "to respond to changing world conditions should be adopted only with the greatest caution," and our inquiry into matters of entry and national security is highly constrained. . . . For our purposes today, we assume that we may look behind the face of the Proclamation to the extent of applying rational basis review. That standard of review considers whether the entry policy is plausibly related to the Government's stated objective to protect the country and improve vetting processes. . . .

Given the standard of review, it should come as no surprise that the Court hardly ever strikes down a policy as illegitimate under rational basis scrutiny. On the few occasions where we have done so, a common thread has been that the laws at issue lack any purpose other than a "bare . . . desire to harm a politically unpopular group."

The Proclamation does not fit this pattern. . . . [B]ecause there is persuasive evidence that the entry suspension has a legitimate grounding in national security concerns, quite apart from any religious hostility, we must accept that independent justification. The Proclamation is expressly premised on legitimate purposes: preventing entry of nationals who cannot be adequately vetted and inducing other nations to improve their practices. The text says nothing about religion. . . .

Finally, the dissent invokes *Korematsu v. United States* . . . (1944). Whatever rhetorical advantage the dissent may see in doing so, *Korematsu* has nothing to do with this case. The forcible relocation of U.S. citizens to concentration camps, solely and explicitly on the basis of race, is objectively unlawful and outside the scope of Presidential authority. But it is wholly inapt to liken that morally repugnant order to a facially neutral policy denying certain foreign nationals the privilege of admission. The entry suspension is an act that is well within executive authority. . . .

JUSTICE SOTOMAYOR, with whom JUSTICE GINSBURG joins, dissenting.

. . . "When the government acts with the ostensible and predominant purpose" of disfavoring a particular religion, "it violates that central Establishment Clause value of official religious neutrality, there being no neutrality when the government's ostensible object is to take sides." . . . To determine whether plaintiffs have proved an Establishment Clause violation, the Court asks whether a reasonable observer would view the government action as enacted for the purpose of disfavoring a religion. . . .

In answering that question, this Court has generally considered the text of the government policy, its operation, and any available evidence regarding "the historical background of the decision under challenge, the specific series of events leading to the enactment or official policy in question, and the legislative or administrative history, including contemporaneous statements made by" the decisionmaker. . . . At the same time, however, courts must take care not to engage in "any judicial psychoanalysis of a drafter's heart of hearts." . . .

Although the majority briefly recounts a few of the statements and background events that form the basis of plaintiffs' constitutional challenge, that highly abridged account does not tell even half of the story. The full record paints a far more harrowing picture, from which a reasonable observer would readily conclude that the Proclamation was motivated by hostility and animus toward the Muslim faith.

During his Presidential campaign, then-candidate Donald Trump pledged that, if elected, he would ban Muslims from entering the United States. . . . Trump justified his proposal during a television interview by noting that President Franklin D. Roosevelt "did the same thing" with respect to the internment of Japanese Americans during World War II. . . . In March 2016, he expressed his belief that "Islam hates us. . . . [W]e can't allow people coming into this country who have this hatred of the United States . . . [a]nd of people that are not Muslim." . . . [The President] called for surveillance of mosques in the United States, blaming terrorist attacks on Muslims' lack of "assimilation" and their commitment to "sharia law."

. . .

As Trump's presidential campaign progressed, he began to describe his policy proposal in slightly different terms. In June 2016, for instance, he characterized the policy proposal as a suspension of immigration from countries "where there's a proven history of terrorism." He also described the proposal as rooted in the need to stop "importing radical Islamic terrorism to the West through a failed immigration system." . . . He then explained that he used different terminology because "[p]eople were so upset when [he] used the word Muslim." . . .

As the majority correctly notes, "the issue before us is not whether to denounce" these offensive statements. Rather, the dispositive and narrow question here is whether a reasonable observer, presented with all "openly available data," the text and "historical context" of the Proclamation, and the "specific sequence of events" leading to it, would conclude that the primary purpose of the Proclamation is to disfavor Islam and its adherents by excluding them from the country. The answer is unquestionably yes.

Taking all the relevant evidence together, a reasonable observer would conclude that the Proclamation was driven primarily by anti-Muslim animus, rather than by the Government's asserted national-security justifications. . . .

Moreover, despite several opportunities to do so, President Trump has never disavowed any of his prior statements about Islam. . . . [I]t is unsurprising that the President's lawyers have, at every step in the lower courts, failed in their attempts to launder the Proclamation of its discriminatory taint. Notably, the Court recently found less pervasive official expressions of hostility and the failure to disavow them to be constitutionally significant. Cf. *Masterpiece Cakeshop, Ltd. v. Colorado Civil Rights Comm'n,* 138 S.Ct. 1719, 1732 (2018) ("The official expressions of hostility to religion in some of the commissioners' comments—comments that were not disavowed at the Commission or by the State at any point in the proceedings that led to the affirmance of the order—were inconsistent with what the Free Exercise Clause requires"). It should find the same here.

Ultimately, what began as a policy explicitly "calling for a total and complete shutdown of Muslims entering the United States" has since morphed into a "Proclamation" putatively based on national-security concerns. But this new window dressing cannot conceal an unassailable fact: the words of the President and his advisers create the strong perception that the Proclamation is contaminated by impermissible discriminatory animus against Islam and its followers.

Rather than defend the President's problematic statements, the Government urges this Court to set them aside and defer to the President on issues related to immigration and national security. The majority accepts that invitation and incorrectly applies a watered-down legal standard in an effort to short circuit plaintiffs' Establishment Clause claim. . . .

"Religious liberty" has emerged as a new "right" to divert progress toward marriage equality and other LGBTQ protections, marked by Justice Alito's claim of reverse discrimination in a 2020 Federalist Society speech: "For many today, religious liberty is not a cherished freedom. . . . The question we face is whether our society will be inclusive enough to tolerate people with unpopular religious beliefs."[39] In a similar vein, religious liberty has been invoked of late to suppress the gains of broad statutory antidiscrimination mandates encompassing many subordinated groups—in the Court's 2020 opinion briefly excerpted below, protections against disability and age discrimination in the workplace. Note how, in contrast to *Trump* where the Court ignored discrimination against a religious group, the case below protects the right of a religious school in turn to lawfully discriminate against other groups, even when serving non-religious interests, such as financial ones, or expressing invidious animus toward groups. As this final example in our historical outline of social identities in U.S. law confirms, social identities—*and their denial*—still matter greatly.

OUR LADY OF GUADALUPE SCHOOL V. MORRISSEY-BERRU
140 S.Ct. 2049 (2020)

JUSTICE SOTOMAYOR, with whom JUSTICE GINSBURG joins, dissenting.

Two employers fired their employees allegedly because one had breast cancer and the other was elderly. . . . [T]he majority shields those employers from [statutory] disability and age-discrimination claims. In the Court's view, because the employees taught short religion modules at Catholic elementary schools, they were "ministers" of the Catholic faith and thus could be fired for any reason, whether religious or nonreligious, benign or bigoted, without legal recourse. The Court reaches this result even though the teachers taught primarily secular subjects, lacked substantial religious titles and training, and were not even required to be Catholic. In foreclosing the teachers' claims, the Court skews the facts [and] ignores the applicable standard of review. . . .

The "ministerial exception" . . . is a judge-made doctrine . . . [that] gives an employer free rein to discriminate because of race, sex, pregnancy, age, disability, or other traits protected by law when selecting or firing their "ministers". . . .

---

[39] Josh Gerstein, Alito's Politically Charged Address Draws Heat, Politico (Nov. 13, 2020), www.politico.com/news/2020/11/13/alito-speech-religious-freedom-436412.

... [T]he Court's apparent deference [in the case at hand] threatens to make nearly anyone whom the [religious] schools might hire "ministers" unprotected from discrimination in the hiring process. That cannot be right. Although certain religious functions may be important to a church, a person's performance of some of those functions does not mechanically trigger a categorical exemption from generally applicable antidiscrimination laws.

... So long as the employer determines that an employee's "duties" are "vital" to "carrying out the mission of the church," then today's laissez-faire analysis appears to allow that employer to make employment decisions because of a person's skin color, age, disability, sex, or any other protected trait for reasons having nothing to do with religion. This sweeping result is profoundly unfair. The Court is not only wrong on the facts, but [it] also risks upending antidiscrimination protections for many employees of religious entities. Recently, this Court has lamented a perceived "discrimination against religion." Yet here it swings the pendulum in the extreme opposite direction, permitting religious entities to discriminate widely and with impunity for reasons wholly divorced from religious beliefs. The inherent injustice in the Court's conclusion will be impossible to ignore for long, particularly in a pluralistic society like ours. . . .

This closing case excerpt displays the legal salience of social identities in yet more group contexts, specifically involving religion, identity, and discrimination. This excerpt also illustrates another key theme of critical systemic analysis: how private preferences are enforced by (or as) public power. As amplified by the following section, these patterns in legal decisions matter greatly in social and economic relations, both "micro" and "macro."

NOTES AND QUESTIONS

1. *Reflection Exercise.* Reflect on the excerpted Court opinions as a line of systemic outputs. Do you observe any patterns? Can you discern which group (or groups) remains always in the background under the cover of "neutral" legal doctrines—never making an explicit appearance—and yet remains the object of constant systemic protection? How was time evident in some of the opinions as a justification for continuing subordinations along identity group lines? How did religion function as an elite tool in some of the opinions? Particularly for those opinions from decades past, are there social problems today you can connect to those subordinating rulings?

3.6 LAW DISPENSES AND NORMALIZES PRIVATE-PUBLIC PRIVILEGE AND SUBORDINATION

Identities matter to law and injustice specifically because dominant systems use them to funnel both privilege and subordination, simultaneously, to individuals and groups. Systems misuse social identities to create and preserve collectivized benefits—privilege—bestowed individually based on group identities. Simultaneously, systems abuse social identities to create and preserve collectivized burdens—subordination—bestowed individually based likewise on group identities. This systemic and simultaneous lifting up of some and pushing down of others creates the hierarchies of the resulting caste system. Over time, the opportunities, trajectories, and destinies of "different" people are shaped—both personally and collectively—by the entrenchment of this consistent tipping of systemic scales based on social identities.

Generally, then, systemic privilege refers to unearned advantages, rewards, or opportunities reserved for favored identities that benefit from the status quo, and systemic subordination refers to unearned burdens, exclusions, and degradations imposed on disfavored identities that bear the brunt of systemic injustice or violence. Privilege and subordination appear in tangible and intangible forms—such as prestige and wealth to some, devaluation and poverty to others. Privilege and subordination—both symbolic and material—are tied to social group identities to suit dominant, or elite, interests.

Consequently, examination of both sides of the inequality coin—of subordination as well as of privilege—is essential to a functional understanding of any caste system. For those with substantial privilege, the latter often is more difficult than the former—like "unpacking the invisible knapsack" of unearned benefits.[40] Feminist legal scholar Barbara Flagg (who is white) calls this top-end obliviousness to race-based privilege the "transparency" phenomenon—the invisibility of whiteness (and its structural privileges) to many (most?) white people.[41] As Flagg shows, elites and systems are "blind" not to race, but to (white) privilege.

Elaborating, Peggy McIntosh, a scholar and activist in Women's Studies, similarly scrutinized identity-based privilege and subordination based both on race and gender. Outlining how individuals from privileged groups are taught to recognize others' subordination while denying their

---

[40] Peggy McIntosh's article White Privilege: Unpacking the Invisible Knapsack first appeared in Peace and Freedom Magazine 10–12 (July/Aug. 1989), a publication of the Women's International League for Peace and Freedom, Philadelphia, PA, www.nationalseedproject.org/white-privilege-unpacking-the-invisible-knapsack.

[41] Barbara J. Flagg, Was Blind But Now I See (1997).

own privilege, and the symbiotic relationship between the two, McIntosh explains:

> Through work to bring materials from Women's Studies into the rest of the curriculum, I have often noticed men's unwillingness to grant that they are over-privileged, even though they may grant that women are disadvantaged. They may say they will work to improve women's status, in the society, the university, or the curriculum, but they can't or won't support the idea of lessening men's. . . .
>
> [I realized that] there was likely a phenomenon of white privilege that was similarly denied and protected. As a white person, I realized I had been taught about racism as something that puts others at a disadvantage, but had been taught not to see one of its corollary aspects, white privilege, which puts me at an advantage.
>
> . . . I have come to see white privilege as an invisible package of unearned assets that I can count on cashing in each day, but about which I was "meant" to remain oblivious. White privilege is like an invisible weightless knapsack of special provisions, maps, passports, codebooks, visas, clothes, tools and blank checks.[42]

Some persons and groups clearly benefit from the maintenance of identity-based hierarchies, and others clearly suffer for it. However, *all* individuals share in the responsibility to counter them, whether from positions of relative privilege or relative subordination. Indeed, for most individuals—although not for all—relative combinations of the two may be highly situational.

Expanding awareness of privilege and subordination—in relative and shifting situations—can be emotionally and intellectually difficult. Journalist Sian Ferguson reflects in the blog Everyday Feminism on the lifelong project of understanding privilege and subordination:

> Think of privilege not as a single lesson, but as a field of study. To truly understand privilege, we must keep reading, learning, and thinking critically. . . .
>
> Guilt is an unhelpful feeling: It makes us feel ashamed, which prevents us from speaking out and bringing about change. . . .
>
> You don't need to feel guilty for having privilege because having privilege is not your fault. It's not something you chose. But what you can choose is to push back against your privilege

---

[42] McIntosh, White Privilege, at 10. See also Susan E. Borrego, Understanding My Privilege, TEDx Talks (Dec. 9, 2016), www.youtube.com/watch?v=XlRxqC0Sze4 (describing how a white woman who grew up poor struggled to understand the nature of white privilege despite having suffered deprivations due to her class position).

and to use it in a way that challenges oppressive systems instead of perpetuating them....

But merely understanding privilege is not enough. We need to take action. Listen to people who experience oppression. Learn about how you can work in solidarity with oppressed groups.[43]

Unequal distributions of privilege and subordination are so embedded in day-to-day life that injustice may have become normalized. Ingrained routines of institutionalized injustice are not always easy to identify. Yet individuals know themselves and others to be members of social groups, each with a place in the caste system. As The Blackwell Dictionary of Sociology notes:

> A white man may not himself actively participate in oppressive behavior directed at blacks or women, for example, but he nonetheless benefits from the general oppression of blacks and women simply because he is a white man. In this sense, all members of dominant and subordinate categories participate in social oppression regardless of their individual attitudes or behavior.
>
> Social oppression becomes institutionalized when its enforcement is so embedded in the everyday workings of social life that it is not easily identified as oppression and does not require conscious prejudice or overt acts of discrimination.[44]

Systemic advocates "map" specific unearned benefits and burdens of "different" identities in symbolic and material terms. Advocates understand that identities both funnel privilege and subordination and organize the resulting sense of collectivized group interests based on that linkage of identities to castes. Below, critical race scholar Devon Carbado provides an example by deconstructing aspects of his daily living. He offers an unlearning-relearning exercise in assessing privilege and subordination in personal and professional life. As he explains, subordination imposes a "negative identity signification" to convey inferiority, while privilege bestows superiority through a positive identity signification. Carbado also points out that identities are social constructions—inventions of particular cultures. Thus, social identities do not identify natural or universal traits regardless of context. The meaning of "woman" and "man" or "Black" and "white" can and does shift depending on circumstance, time, and culture. Social identities are complex and contextual, rather than fixed or essential. Similarly, Carbado recognizes that social identities combine in many

---

[43] Sian Ferguson, Privilege 101: A Quick and Dirty Guide, Everyday Feminism (Sept. 29, 2014), www.everydayfeminism.com/2014/09/what-is-privilege/.

[44] Allan G. Johnson, The Blackwell Dictionary of Sociology: A User's Guide to Sociological Language 293 (2d ed. 2000) (defining oppression and describing the bail bond system as a U.S. example of race and class prejudice).

variations. These complexities create shifting tops and bottoms—adjustments in the allocation of privilege and subordination. Carbado's autobiographical accounting connects the daily, practical, "micro" mechanics of *intersectional* social identities to the historical, big-picture, "macro" scripts of systemic privilege. What would result if you carried out the same exercise, deconstructing aspects of your daily life or of those in close social or economic proximity?

STRAIGHT OUT OF THE CLOSET
Devon W. Carbado
15 Berkeley Women's L.J. 76 (2000)

... All of us enjoy at least some privilege. Are all of us perpetrators of discrimination? Perhaps. The answer may depend on what we do with, and to, our privileges. All of us, through the ways in which we negotiate our identities, play a role in entrenching a variety of social practices, institutional arrangements, and laws which disadvantage other(ed) people. All of us make choices every day that legitimize certain discriminatory practices. I came to work at UCLA Law School even as [California's anti-affirmative action law] has drastically reduced the number of certain students of color, and especially Black students, at the law school. Many of us get married and/or attend weddings, even as lesbian and gay marriages are not legally recognized. Others of us have racially monolithic social encounters, live in de facto white only (or predominantly white) neighborhoods, or send our kids to white only (or predominantly white) schools. Still others of us have "straight only" associations—that is, our friends are all heterosexuals and our children's friends all have mommies and daddies. These choices are not just personal; they are political. And the cumulative effect of these micro-political choices is the entrenchment of the very social practices—racism, sexism, classism, and homophobia—we profess to abhor.

In other words, there is a link between privilege and discrimination. Our identities are both reflective and constitutive of certain systems of oppression. Racism requires white privilege. Sexism requires male privilege. Homophobia requires heterosexual privilege. Thus, all of us have an obligation to expose and to challenge our privileges. We have to remake ourselves—our identities—if we are to remake our institutions. We cannot hope to institutionalize our political commitments unless we personalize our politics. Resistance to identity privileges may be futile, we cannot know for sure. But, to the extent that we do nothing, this much is clear: we perpetuate the systems of discrimination that our identities reflect.

But precisely what constitutes a privilege? How do we identify our privileges? And what acts are sufficiently disruptive of our privileges to amount to resistance? Focusing on male and heterosexual privileges, this

Article addresses the foregoing questions ... to identify and resist male and heterosexual privileges....

A Male Feminist Method: Identifying Everyday Privilege

... Broadly speaking, there are two categories of privileges.... The first category can be described as "an invisible package of unearned assets that [men] can count on cashing in each day." The second category includes a series of disadvantages that men do not experience precisely because they are men. The following list presents examples from both categories.

Gender Privileges: A List [edited for space]

1. I can walk in public, alone, without fear of being sexually violated.
2. Prospective employers will never ask me if I plan on having children.
3. I can be confident that my career path will never be tainted by accusations that I "slept my way to the top" (though it might be "tainted" by the perception that [as a person of color] I am a beneficiary of affirmative action).
4. I don't have to worry about whether I am being paid less than my female colleagues (though I might worry about whether I'm being paid less than my white male colleagues).
5. When I get dressed in the morning, I do not worry about whether my clothing "invites" sexual harassment.
7. My career opportunities are not dependent on the extent to which I am perceived to be as good as a man (though they may be dependent upon the extent to which I am perceived to be "a good black"—i.e., racially assimilable).
8. I do not have to choose between having a family or having a career.
9. I do not have to worry about being called selfish for having a career instead of having a family.
10. It will almost always be the case that my supervisor will be a man (though rarely will my supervisor be Black).
11. I can express outrage without being perceived as irrational, emotional, or too sensitive (except if I am expressing outrage about race).
12. I can fight for my country without controversy.
13. No one will qualify my intellectual or technical ability with the phrase "for a man" (though they may qualify my ability with the phrase "for a Black man").
14. I can be outspoken without being called a "bitch" (though I might be referred to as uppity).

15. I do not have to concern myself with finding the line between being assertive and aggressive (except with respect to conversations about race).

16. I do not have to think about whether my race comes before my gender, about whether I am Black first and a man second.

17. The politics of dress—to wear or not to wear make-up, high heels, or trousers, to straighten or not to straighten, to braid or not to braid my hair—affect me less than they do women.

19. I was not "supposed" to change my name upon getting married.

20. I am rewarded for vigorously and aggressively pursuing my career.

21. I do not have to worry about opposite-sex strangers or close acquaintances committing gender violence against me (though I do have to worry about racial violence).

23. My reputation does not diminish with each additional person with whom I have sexual relations.

26. I am praised for spending time with my children, cooking, cleaning, or doing other household chores.

29. The responsibility for birth control is not placed on men's shoulders and men are not accused of getting pregnant.

This list does not reflect the male privileges of all men. It is both under and over inclusive. Class, race, and sexual orientation impact male identities, shaping the various dimensions of male privilege. For example, the list does not include as a privilege the fact that men are automatically perceived as authority figures. While this may be true of white men, it has not been my experience as a Black man. Moreover, my list clearly reveals my class privilege. My relationship to patriarchy is thus not the same as that of a working class Black male. In constructing a list of male privilege, then, one has to be careful not to universalize manhood, not to present it as a "cohesive identity" in ways that deny, obscure, or threaten the recognition of male multiplicity....

Negative Identity Signification

... Those of us on the "other" side of race, gender, or sexual orientation have to contend with and respond to negative identity signification. That is to say, we live with (even as we fight against) the reality that our identities are not normative. We are "different." Thus, our identities have negative social meanings. Some of these meanings are more entrenched in the American psyche than others. Race, gender, and sexually oriented assumptions about personhood are especially difficult to dismantle.

For example, when I walk into a department store, my identity signifies not only that I am Black and male but also that I am a potential criminal. My individual identity is lost in the social construction of Black manhood. I can try to adopt race-negating strategies to challenge this dignity-destroying social meaning. I can work my identity (to attempt) to repudiate the stereotype. I might, for example, dress "respectable" when I go shopping. There is, after all, something to the politics of dress, particularly in social contexts in which race matters—that is to say, in every American social context. . . .

White people do not have to worry about employing these strategies. White people do not have to work their identities to respond to these racial concerns. Nor should they have to—no one should. However, white people should recognize and grapple with the fact that they do not have to employ or think about employing these strategies. White people should recognize that they do not have to perform this work. This is a necessary first step for white people to come to terms with white privilege. . . .

According to Barbara Flagg, "[t]here is a profound cognitive dimension to the material and social privilege that attaches to whiteness in this society, in that the white person has an everyday option not to think of herself in racial terms at all." This, reasons Flagg, is indeed what defines whiteness: "to be white is not to think about it." Flagg refers to the propensity of whites not to think in racial terms as the "transparency phenomenon."

Importantly, Flagg does not suggest that white people are unmindful of the racial identities of other whites or the racial "difference" of nonwhites. . . . Rather, her point is that because whiteness operates as the racial norm, whites are able "to relegate their own racial specificity to the realm of the subconscious." As a result, racial distinctiveness is Black, is Asian, is Latina/o, is Native American, but it is not white. . . .

Peggy McIntosh's work provides a specific indication of some of the every day "distributive effects" of white racial privilege. . . . McIntosh exposes the "unearned" advantages that she accrues on a daily basis because she is white. For example, precisely because she is white, McIntosh did not have to educate her children to be aware of systemic racism for their own daily physical protection. . . .

McIntosh is careful to point out that the term "privilege" is something of a misnomer: "The word 'privilege' carries the connotation of being something everyone must want. Yet some of the conditions . . . work to systematically overempower certain groups." Accordingly, McIntosh distinguishes between "positive advantages that we can work to spread . . . and negative types of advantage that unless rejected will always reinforce our present hierarchies."

Heterosexual Privilege (and Race)

... Like whiteness, heterosexuality should be critically examined. Like whiteness, heterosexuality operates as an identity norm. Heterosexuality functions as the "what is" or "what is supposed to be" of sexuality. ... Like non-whiteness, then, homosexuality signifies "difference"—more specifically, sexual identity distinctiveness.... Heterosexuality is always already presumed.

... [Here, then,] I hope to challenge the pervasive tendency of heterosexuals to see homophobia as something that [only] puts others at a disadvantage and not something that [also] actually advantages them.

Heterosexual Privileges: A List [edited for space]

1. Whether on television or in the movies, (white) heterosexuality is always affirmed as healthy and/or normal (Black heterosexuality and family arrangements are still, to some degree, perceived to be deviant).

3. A husband and wife can comfortably express affection in any social setting, even a predominantly gay one.

4. The children of a heterosexual couple will not have to explain why their parents have different genders—why they have a mummy and a daddy.

5. (White) Heterosexuals are not blamed for creating and spreading the AIDS virus (though Africans—as a collective group—are blamed).

6. Heterosexuals do not have to worry about people trying to "cure" their sexual orientation (though Black people have to worry about people trying to "cure" Black "racial pathologies").

10. Friends of heterosexuals generally do not refer to heterosexuals as their "straight friends" (though non-Black people often to refer to Black people as their "Black friends").

12. White heterosexuals do not have to worry about whether a fictional film villain who is heterosexual will reflect negatively on their heterosexuality (though Blacks may always have to worry about their racial representation in films).

13. Heterosexuals are entitled to legal recognition of their marriages throughout the United States and the world.

15. Heterosexuals can take jobs with most companies without worrying about whether their spouses will be included in the benefits package.

23. Heterosexuals are not denied custody or visitation rights of their children because they are heterosexuals.

24. Heterosexual men are welcomed as leaders of Boy Scout troops.

25. Heterosexuals can visit their parents and family as who they are, and take their spouses, partners, or dates with them to family functions.

28. Heterosexual couples do not have to worry about whether kissing each other in public or holding hands in public will render them vulnerable to violence.

29. Heterosexuals do not have to struggle with "coming out" or worry about being "outed."

30. The parents of heterosexuals do not love them "in spite of" their sexual orientation, and parents do not blame themselves for their children's heterosexuality.

31. Heterosexuality is affirmed in most religious traditions.

32. Heterosexuals can introduce their spouses to colleagues and not worry about whether the decision will have a detrimental impact on their careers.

Conclusion: Resisting Privileges

... The lists ... are politically valuable. For one thing, the items on the lists reveal that men enforce and maintain their gender privileges through the personal actions they take and do not take every day. For another, to the extent that the lists focus our attention on privileges, they invite men to think about the extent to which they are unjustly enriched because of certain aspects of their identities....

None of this is to say that awareness and acknowledgement of privilege is enough. Resistance is needed as well. But how does one resist? And what counts as resistance? With respect to marriage, for example, does resistance to heterosexual privilege require heterosexuals to refrain from getting married and/or attending weddings? It might mean both of those things. At the very least, resistance to identity privilege would seem to require "critical acquiescence": criticizing, if not rejecting, aspects of our life that are directly linked to our privilege. A heterosexual who gets married and/or attends weddings but who also openly challenges the idea that marriage is a heterosexual entitlement is engaging in critical acquiescence.

In the end, critical acquiescence might not go far enough. It might even be a cop out. Still, it is a useful and politically manageable place to begin.

Carbado concludes this unlearning-relearning exercise with the notion of "resisting privilege"—even when all we can do amounts to "critical acquiescence" in some everyday personal or professional contexts. Critical acquiescence entails at a minimum "criticizing"—registering vocally or otherwise a critique of the immediate situation, even if powerless in the moment to change it. Critical acquiescence is a temporary, practical, and affirmative response to a situation beyond immediate repair, based on the recognition that "resistance is needed" even in limiting circumstances. Otherwise, acquiescence becomes *uncritical* and functions like "a cop out." Critical acquiescence is useful because it acknowledges a key hard fact with integrity: sometimes routines of systemic injustice are so ingrained that we can do little in the here and now to disrupt them. Sometimes, situations are so rigidly regimented that acquiescing critically and temporarily to their dominance is both sensible and principled. This key fact is especially true when we (need to) act spontaneously and individually rather than strategically and collectively.

Many people have turned to this tactic of last resort: Blacks in everyday life, women in marriages, Latinx migrants in the fields, gays in every aspect of family life. As they have shown, biting your lip and biding your time are both affirmative uses of time—if conceived like this. This critical concept provides a useful—a pragmatic yet principled—handle for temporary moments of acquiescence, coupled with a reminder that organized collective action from below is the hallmark of enduring social progress against systemic social problems.

Carbado's review of identity in micro—everyday, interpersonal—life focused on the omnipresent benefits of privilege. Another prerogative of privilege is committing "microaggressions" with little likelihood of repercussions. Microaggressions are personal, individual, situational exercises of identity-based group privilege, typically directed against persons associated with subordinated groups or identities. Microaggressions are "subtle, stunning, often automatic, and [sometimes] non-verbal[,] exchanges which are 'put downs' of [subordinate group members] by offenders."[45] They are top-down personal exercises of group privileges that enforce systemic subordination in everyday life.

While microaggressions certainly qualify as instances of rudeness, they are more. Unlike examples of generalized social coarseness, microaggressions are individualized re-enactments of larger systemic castes. Whether or not they "intend" it, individuals committing microaggressions are reenacting cultural practices and hegemonic scripts that help to validate inherited legacies of systemic injustice. These micro-interactions tend to flourish in everyday situations and personal relationships, continuing the ideological linkage of macro to micro both in law and in society.

Hate crimes, non-violent discrimination, and microaggressions exist at different points along a range of choices or actions motivated by prejudice.

---

[45] Peggy Davis, Law as Microaggression, 98 Yale L.J. 1559, 1565 (1989). See also Daniel G. Solórzano and Lindsay Pérez Huber, Racial Microaggressions: Using Critical Race Theory to Respond to Everyday Racism (2020).

One type of prevalent microaggression is religious microaggression.[46] As with all acts, microaggressions arise in particular situations. So, for example, in the United States, where both Jews and Muslims are minority groups, these religious groups have been targets of microaggression. In Asia and Africa, where Christians are minorities and tend to live in poverty, anti-Christian microaggressions are common.[47] All over the world, religious microaggression can target atheists and agnostics as well. Scholars have categorized religious microaggressions to include the following:

> Category 1, endorsing religious stereotypes, involves a perpetrator stereotyping victims through religiously biased statements and behaviors. By endorsing a stereotype about a religious or nonreligious group, it is implied that the group is inferior and does not deserve to be learned about. . . .
>
> Category 2, exoticization, . . . transpire[s] when an individual holds views of other religious groups as "foreign" or "bizarre" and acts accordingly. . . .
>
> Category 3, pathology of different religious groups, refers to the conscious (and sometimes unconscious) belief that there is something wrong or abnormal with someone of a different religion. This may lead to behaviors in which individuals may be punished, judged, or mistreated.[48]

Other categories of religious microaggressions include "pathologizing different groups' values," assuming religious homogeneity, and denial of religious prejudices.[49] Microaggressions therefore also can take the form of insult, invalidation, dismissal, appropriation, and devaluation. The results of these microaggressions are micro-harms, but repeated experiences cause much social damage. Microaggressions wear away at relationships and energy, with physical and emotional harm accumulating over time to reinforce already-entrenched inequalities. Recalling Tsosie from Part I, they are, in the end, another form of epistemic violence.

To develop these points further, legal scholar Peggy Davis next analyzes the appearance and significance of microaggressions specifically in legal venues or contexts. Davis centers perspectives from the bottom to consider how spatial and cultural backgrounds help to script interpersonal relations today among individuals in both public and private realms of social life. She shows how "macro" conditions of law and society—material and symbolic—drive and shape micro situations of everyday life,

---

[46] Kevin L. Nadal et al., Religious Microaggressions in the United States in Microaggressions and Marginality: Manifestation, Dynamics, and Impact (Derald Wing Sue ed. 2010).

[47] Id. at 290.

[48] Id. at 300–01.

[49] Id. at 301–04.

demonstrating the importance of challenging dehumanizing interactions in routine interactions in social and in legal settings.

LAW AS MICROAGGRESSIONS
Peggy C. Davis
98 Yale L.J. 1559 (1989)

... With striking regularity minority people, in New York and elsewhere in the United States, report [their belief] that the law will work to their disadvantage....

... The causes are not easily established. Those who perceive the courts as biased admit that incidents of alleged bias are usually ambiguous; that systematic evidence of bias is difficult to compile; and that evidence of bias in some aspects of the justice system is balanced by evidence that the system acts to correct or to punish bias in other sectors of the society.

This essay places the perceptions of one minority group, black Americans, in a context that explains the source and the strength of minority conviction that courts (as well as other non-minority social institutions) are capable of bias.... [The closing section considers] ways in which minorities are perceived within the legal system and the relationship between those modes of perception and the minority view that the legal system is an agent of bias.

The Lens Through Which Blacks Are Perceived

... The claim of pervasive, unconscious racism... is examined here in the context of a small incident. The incident, reported below, will be analyzed first from the point of view of a white participant and as an instance of stereotyping. [Subsequently,] it will be analyzed from the point of view of a black participant and as an instance of the "incessant, often gratuitous and subtle offenses" defined by black mental health professionals as "microaggressions."

The scene is a courthouse in Bronx, New York, A white assistant city attorney takes the court elevator up to the ninth floor. At the fifth floor, the doors open. A black woman asks: "Going down?" "Up," says [the city attorney]. And then, the doors close: "You see? They can't even tell up from down. I'm sorry, but it's true."

The black woman's words are subject to a variety of interpretations. She may have thought it efficient, appropriate, or congenial to ask the direction of the elevator rather than to search for the indicator. The indicator may have been broken. Or, the woman may have been incapable of competent elevator travel. The city attorney is led, by cognitive habit and by personal and cultural history, to seize upon the pejorative interpretation.

The city attorney lives in a society in which blacks are commonly regarded as incompetent. The traditional stereotype of blacks includes inferior mentality, primitive morality, emotional instability, laziness, boisterousness, closeness to anthropoid ancestors, occupational instability, superstition, care-free attitude, and ignorance. Common culture reinforces the belief in black incompetence. . . .

It is likely that the city attorney assimilated negative stereotypes about blacks before she reached the age of judgment. She will, therefore, have accepted them as truth rather than opinion. Having assimilated the stereotypes, the city attorney will have developed a pattern of interpreting and remembering ambiguous events in ways that confirm, rather than unsettle, her stereotyped beliefs. If she sees or hears of two people on a subway, one white, one black, and one holding a knife, she is predisposed to form an impression that the black person held the knife, regardless of the truth of the matter. She will remember examples of black incompetence and may fail to remember examples of black competence. . . .

Historians tell us of the rootedness of the city attorney's views. During the early seventeenth century, the circumstances of blacks living in what was to become the United States were consistent with principles of open, although not equal, opportunity. African-Americans lived both as indentured servants and as free people. This early potential for egalitarianism was destroyed by the creation of a color-caste system. Colonial legislatures enacted slavery laws that transformed black servitude from a temporary status, under which both blacks and whites labored, to a lifelong status that was hereditary and racially defined. Slavery required a system of beliefs that would rationalize white domination, and laws and customs that would assure control of the slave population. . . .

The laws and customs that assured control of the slave population reinforced the image of blacks as incompetent and in need of white governance. The master was afforded ownership, the right to command labor, and the virtually absolute right of discipline. Social controls extending beyond the master-slave relationship served to exclude the slave—and in some respects to exclude free blacks—from independent, self-defining activity. . . . Breaches of the social order, such as "insolence" of a slave towards a white person, were criminally punishable.

This history is part of the cultural heritage of the city attorney. The system of legal segregation, which maintained caste distinctions after abolition, is part of her life experience. . . .

The civil rights movement and post-1954 desegregation efforts are also part of the city attorney's cultural heritage. As an educated woman in the 1980s, she understands racial prejudice to be socially and morally unacceptable. Psychological research that targets her contemporaries reveals an expressed commitment to egalitarian ideals along with lingering negative beliefs and aversive feelings about blacks. "Prejudiced thinking and discrimination still exist, but the contemporary forms are more subtle, more indirect, and less overtly negative than are more traditional forms."

Recent research also suggests that the city attorney can be expected to conceal her anti-black feelings except in private, homoracial settings. . . . Americans of the city attorney's generation live under the combined influence of egalitarian ideology and "cultural forces and cognitive processes that . . . promote prejudice and racism." Anti-black attitudes persist in a climate of denial. . . .

The View from the Other Side of the Lens: Microaggressions

Return to the fifth floor and to the moment at which the elevator door opened. The black women sees two white passengers. She inquires and perceives the response to her inquiry. She sees and hears, or thinks she sees and hears, condescension. It is in the tone and body language that surround the word, "Up." Perhaps the tone is flat, the head turns slowly in the direction of the second passenger and the eyes roll upward in apparent exasperation. Perhaps the head remains lowered, and the word is uttered as the eyes are raised to a stare that suggests mock disbelief. The woman does not hear the words spoken behind the closed elevator doors. Yet she feels that she has been branded incompetent, even for elevator travel. This feeling produces anger, frustration, and a need to be hypervigilant against subsequent, similar brandings.

The elevator encounter is a microaggression. "These are subtle, stunning, often automatic, and non-verbal exchanges which are 'put downs' of blacks by offenders." Psychiatrists who have studied black populations view them as "incessant and cumulative" assaults on black self-esteem.

> Microaggressions simultaneously sustain [ ] defensive-deferential thinking and erode [ ] self confidence in Blacks. . . . [B]y monopolizing . . . perception and action through regularly irregular disruptions, they contribute [ ] to relative paralysis of action, planning and self-esteem. They seem to be the principal foundation for the verification of Black inferiority for both whites and Blacks.

The management of these assaults is a preoccupying activity, simultaneously necessary to and disruptive of black adaptation. . . .

Vigilance and psychic energy are required not only to marshal adaptational techniques, but also to distinguish microaggressions from differently motivated actions and to determine "which of many daily microaggressions one must undercut."

The microaggressive acts that characterize interracial encounters are carried out in "automatic, preconscious, or unconscious fashion" and "stem from the mental attitude of presumed superiority." ... A fictitious continuation of the elevator incident illustrates microaggressions that are ... complete in their achievement of subordination:

> *The city attorney decides to leave the elevator. She is standing at the right side of the car—directly opposite, but several feet away from, the black woman. Although she might easily exit by walking a path angled toward the center of the car, she takes a step directly forward. After a moment's hesitation, the black woman steps aside.*

This is microaggression in its most potent form. It is the direct descendent of an aspect of color-caste behavior described fifty years ago as "deference":

> The most striking form of ... "caste behavior" is deference, the respectful yielding exhibited by the Negroes in their contacts with whites.... [I]n places of business the Negro should stand back and wait until the white has been served before receiving any attention, and in entering or leaving he should not precede a white but should stand back and hold the door for him. On the streets and sidewalks the Negro should "give way" to the white person.

... "Both races have come to expect and accept as unremarkable that the blacks' time, energy, space, and mobility will be at the service of the white." The inferiority of the black is more than an implicit assertion; it is a background assumption that supports the seizure of a prerogative.

The Legal System Perceived by Victims of Microaggression

We do not know what business the black elevator traveler has in the courthouse. Whether she is a judge, a litigant, a court officer, or a vagrant, it is likely that her view of the legal system is affected by her status as a regular target of microaggressions. If she has a role in the system, she will be concerned about the ways in which she is heard and regarded. When a court decides matters of fact, she will wonder whether the judgment has been particularized or based upon generalizations from immutable irrelevancies. When a court decides matters of law, she will wonder whether it considers and speaks to a community in which she is included....

Davis illustrates how centering perspectives from the bottom can reveal that law isn't always what it seems, or claims, to be. Both Carbado and Davis show how systemic and social privilege combines with subordination, and vice versa, to script daily, individual life for *everyone* in systemic terms. They show how the micro and the macro continuously reinforce each other—unless disrupted.

As a final examination of law's micro-macro connections, consider urban planning scholar Ellen Pader's review of modern living arrangements, illustrating how even mundane spaces are racialized and gendered. The terms of "domestic spatial organization" at the micro level are set by land use and housing codes at the macro level, which are "profoundly political." The legal regulation of supposedly consensual living arrangements "selectively use[s] occupancy standards and concepts of proper family formations as proxies for racism ... to keep people from unwanted ethnic groups out of sight and out of their neighborhoods." Since colonialism, the social as well as the material architecture of life has been arranged legally by identities and ideologies. Using critical history, political economy, community-based research, and other sources of knowledge, advocates look for such tangible but disguised linkages and bring them to light.

Pader also provides another example of the deceptive separation of so-called private and public spheres. As we see below, "private" living arrangements are not exempt from but constructed in part by "public" decision making through democracy and adjudication. The formal distinction between public and private spheres, in fact, often serves to normalize enrichment of elites and material deprivation of subordinated groups.

Critical advocates and activists repeatedly have exposed and acted against the premises of this illusory distinction. Using the quintessential example of the "home" and the "market" as separate private and public "spheres," feminist legal scholar Fran Olsen deconstructed this private-public distinction to bare its ideological, identity-inflected, top-down functions both as law and in society:

> The vision of the market and the family as a dichotomy—the perception that social life comprises two separate though interdependent spheres—can be described as a structure of consciousness[,] ... a shared vision of the social universe that underlies a society's culture and also shapes the society's view of what social relationships are "natural'" and, therefore, what social reforms are possible.
>
> The separate and unequal spheres constituted for men and women had two opposite effects on women: the woman's sphere both constrained women and provided them with valuable opportunities. In the early nineteenth century, as men's work was largely removed to the factory while women's work remained primarily in the home, there came to be a sharp dichotomy between "the home'" and "the [workaday] world." ... The home was said to provide a haven from the anxieties of modern life—"a shelter for those moral and spiritual values which the commercial spirit and the critical spirit were threatening to destroy.'"

... [S]o-called "private law'" [is] a state grant of partial sovereignty to one of the economic actors. Thus, contract law does not simply put into effect the agreement of the parties; rather, the mechanisms for enforcing contract put " 'the sovereign power of the state at the disposal of one party to be exercised over the other party.' " Similarly, private property is seen to confer on its owner the "sovereign power [of] compelling service and obedience' " from those who need access to the property. This vision of property and contract law undermines the notion that the state can be a noncoercive, neutral arbiter in the market.[50]

Similar to Olsen's deconstruction, legal scholar Jeremiah Purdy notes, "[We need] to move beyond conventional divisions between 'public' and 'private' law, and between 'economic' and 'social' issues."[51] These scholars thus highlight another recurring point in this book: the private-public distinction and its top-down identity politics.

Mindful of Olsen and Purdy, while recalling Calavita and other previous excerpts, track how this formalistic legal distinction functions as identity-based ideology to justify and maintain entrenched group hierarchies. Recall also Romero and Aldana from Part I; here, again, we encounter a context seemingly free of identity and ideology: architecture and construction under local zoning laws. As you read Pader's excerpt below, consider the kinds of "private" houses and households privileged or restricted by "public" law in concrete and intrusive terms—and why some are restricted while others are privileged.

SPACE OF HATE: ETHNICITY, ARCHITECTURE AND HOUSING DISCRIMINATION
Ellen J. Pader
54 Rutgers L. Rev. 881 (2002)

Introduction

Embedded within the most everyday, trivial facets of daily life lie the secrets for understanding how and why popular culture, politicians, policymakers, and judges turn their own truths into determinations of what is reasonable to the "ordinary" person. . . . [Consider these everyday facts:]

1. Do you share the place you live with anyone?
2. If so, what is the relationship of the people in the home?
3. Where in your home do you sleep?

---

[50] Frances Olsen, The Family and the Market: A Study of Ideology and Legal Reform, 96 Harv. L. Rev. 1497, 1498–99, 1508–09 (1983).

[51] New Law and Political Economy Project Launched, Yale Law School (Apr. 29, 2019), www.law.yale.edu/yls-today/news/new-law-and-political-economy-project-launched.

4. With whom, if anyone, do you share the place in which you sleep?

5. What do you call the space in which you sleep?

6. How do you determine if a room is a bedroom or a living room or a hallway or kitchen?

7. How do you decide that a bed should or should not appropriately be put in a particular named space?

8. Are, or should, these questions be the business of anyone other than the residents of a home?

9. And finally, where do architecture, ethnicity, politics, and discrimination coincide in these questions?

... [T]hese questions and others like them influence how houses are designed, based on what seems the most appropriate use of space to the designer, but how space is set up has a cognitive affect on how the inhabitants learn to think about themselves and their relations with others.... Domestic spatial organization is also a profoundly political experience.

The more rigidly one adheres to a universal set of right answers to questions about such mundane everyday activities as where and how one should sleep and with whom one lives, the more cultural and political house design and household composition become.... [Zoning and housing laws enable ruling local elites] to rid a town of ethnic populations that the dominant power structure does not like, on the grounds of house design and household composition and size....

... [I]f concepts of appropriate use of domestic space are culturally specific, do current occupancy standards and family definitions discriminate ... on the basis of national origin[?] ...

Historical Context of Current Occupancy Standards

... Starting with some history of occupancy standards: as the nineteenth century turned into the twentieth, scientific wisdom held that a person could literally drown in his or her own impure breath if there were insufficient circulation of air in a room. Miasma, as this impure air was called, helped usher in particular occupancy standards that are at the base of today's standards....

Simultaneously, urban life was undergoing many new pressures, including a large influx of non-English-speaking moneyless immigrants. The primarily upper-class establishment of Northern European background considered these not-yet-white immigrant populations, such as Eastern European Jews, Irish, and Italians, to be intellectually and morally inferior to the policy-making, established population. This belief was legitimized by the then dominant scientific belief of eugenics, or the hereditary transmission of behavioral characteristics.

... In a 1950 publication, Planning the Home for Occupancy, the American Public Health Association was very explicit that the minimum occupancy standards they deemed necessary to attain the goal of healthful housing "closely approximate actual practice in the high-income groups." This statement makes explicit that one sector of society, the high-income, primarily White Northern European Protestant, had become the social, cultural, and political model of American normalcy. This ratio of people to bedrooms combined a particular morality with a particular sociopolitical stance.

... The foundations of the now-accepted standards have been long forgotten, yet they remain implicitly with us, having become part of our common-sense, everyday, unquestioned reality of what is reasonable.

... In countries as different as Japan and Mexico, household members commonly choose to share bedrooms while leaving others unused; it is not just an economic issue. Sharing sleeping and other spaces is often part of a cultural emphasis on interdependency as a personal and political goal, while sleeping alone, and other emphases on physically bounded private domestic space, help enculturate a greater emphasis on individualism. This point was not missed by the housing reformers of the turn of the twentieth century.

This century-old lesson of correlating physical privacy, individualism, and capitalism has been well learned....

Naming

So, why do we still call the place where we sleep a bedroom rather than a playroom, for instance? The naming of appropriate activities that should occur in a particular bounded and named space imbues that space with meaning and gives it some sort of moral, emotional, physical, and practical imperative, even if it is not how it is used in reality. It allows a town to dictate the maximum number of people who may share a bedroom or the relationship of the people in a house, and call it a moral and health issue....

... [F]or how long will we continue to allow culturally-determined domestic spatial relations to be a conduit for discriminatory practices against non-dominant ethnic groups?

If the fundamental base of the standards cannot hold up ... they discriminate not only against people on account of their national origin, but against other protected (and unprotected) categories of people who are hurt by them as well.

[W]hile the occupancy standards might be facially neutral, their effect certainly is not, and their intent often is not either. . . .

Conclusion

. . . [W]hen you decide where to put your bed, and with whom to share your bed or home, realize that you are not just making a personal decision, but also a social and political one. . . . [I]magine being told that the way you have chosen to organize your domestic space is wrong and that you can be evicted for health, safety, or even moral reasons. And by extension, you and your family are—what, immoral, ignorant? . . . While we are happy to depend on their work to maintain our standards of living, many communities nonetheless selectively use occupancy standards and concepts of proper family formations as proxies for racism and as a convenient resource to keep people from unwanted ethnic groups out of sight and out of their neighborhoods.

Buildings—residential and commercial—seem identity-neutral: a "common-sense, everyday, unquestioned reality of what is reasonable" in fact. Still, the spatial configuration of the material world was codified more than a century ago by multiple laws to enforce the "actual practice in the high-income group" of that time. Pader, like Carbado and Davis, shows how systemic scripts channel personal, private "choices" and how these micro-macro connections are identity-based and mutually reinforcing.

NOTES AND QUESTIONS

1. *Reflection on Life and Identity.* Reflect on the Carbado piece and on at least one aspect of your identity that is privileged in relation to other groups—whether based in gender, sexuality, dis/ability, race, citizenship, class, or other identity lines. Think about the content of the "knapsack" of unearned benefits that you carry and how critical acquiescence might function for you.

2. *Reflection Exercise on Microaggressions on Campus.* Particularly in recent years, racial incidents at universities, as well as the racism embedded in names of buildings and athletic teams, prompted protests across the United States.[52] As one example, someone defaced the hallway portraits of African American law professors at Harvard with black tape. Have you experienced or witnessed microaggression(s) on campus? How did the university respond, if at all? Has a professor ever mispronounced your name repeatedly? Misjudged your gender? For a photo list of various microaggressions experienced by Fordham

---

[52] See generally Tanzina Vega, Students See Many Slights as Racial "Microaggressions," N.Y. Times (Mar. 21, 2014), www.nytimes.com/2014/03/22/us/as-diversity-increases-slights-get-subtler-but-still-sting.html; Alia Wong and Adrienne Green, Campus Politics: A Cheat Sheet, The Atlantic 15 (Apr. 4, 2016), www.theatlantic.com/education/archive/2016/04/campus-protest-roundup/417570/ (discussing that the U.S. Education Department's Office for Civil Rights received more than 1,000 complaints of campus racial harassment during a seven-year period).

University students, see www.buzzfeed.com/hnigatu/racial-microagressions-you-hear-on-a-daily-basis?utm_term=.bsNjn65rK#.ac3dMX345.

3. *Reflection Exercise on Living Arrangements*. Take a look around your living space. Consider how rooms are laid out and designated. Reflect on your daily routines. Do you use the rooms of your living space according to their designation? All the time, some of the time, or not at all? Why? Did the COVID-19 pandemic change your living arrangement—how so? How does this exercise affect your sense of your own living arrangements, if at all?

4. *The Implicit Bias Feel-Good*. Implicit bias theory receives a lot of attention from scholars, activists, and funders. This may be because the findings help individuals understand the persistence of racism, sexism, and other social ills. It may be, however, because much implicit bias theory sanitizes analysis of social ills as causing systemic violence. That is, one might learn about implicit bias and react by thinking, "Oh, well, now that I am aware that I have some biases, I can watch out for them." Another reaction might be to think, "Well, I can't be aware of these biases—they are implicit and unconscious—so I can't do anything about them." One either does nothing because, after all, unconscious biases are the way the brain works so one can't be held responsible or perhaps one applauds oneself for having become more aware and "tries hard" to keep on that path. These reactions are too easy.

For the notion of implicit bias to advance systemic advocacy, micro-level instances must be exposed so that patterns can be seen. For example, research shows that applicants with "black-sounding" or "female" names are less likely to be asked to a job interview than those with "white-sounding" or "male" names. Advocates could investigate and expose this pattern in their own workplaces—collecting and analyzing data. And they could change systems so that names are eliminated from resumes before review—akin to anonymous grading on law school exams. That is a salutary step, suggested by many employment lawyers and human resources managers.

But that step reinforces rather than disrupts the assumption that biased outcomes are the result of errors rather than systemic design—unconscious shortcuts that wrongly associate black with criminal and white with professional or male with logic and tech work and female with emotions and caring work, for example. Unless implicit bias theory is deployed in connection with structural analyses that includes attention to identities, groups, interests, and power, then that theory enhances the status quo. It becomes a way to help whites, men, and others to feel less threatened by the exposure of systemic social ills and separates individual/cultural consciousness-raising from collective power-building.

Legal scholar Tryon Woods notes that implicit bias theory "is truly double-edged, both highlighting unconscious racism and downgrading racism from violence to a natural neurobiological phenomenon."[53] It is no surprise, then, to learn implicit bias research is well-funded. As you read, consider when and

---

[53] Tryon P. Woods, The Implicit Bias of Implicit Bias Theory, 10 Drexel L. Rev. 631 (2018).

how you first learned about implicit bias—if you have been introduced before now. Consider also when—or whether—you learned about Black Power or other liberation movement theories—theories that focus less on the attitudes of privileged groups and more on bottom-up knowledge and power.

> [A key implication] of the relation between power and knowledge signified by implicit bias theory points to the role of philanthropic foundations in forwarding political agendas through specific knowledge formation, while crowding out others. Large, wealthy foundations seem comfortable investing a lot of money into researching implicit bias and disseminating the findings. . . . Phillip Atiba Goff—one of the main figures in the study of implicit bias and the President of the Center for Policing Equity—has received funding from the National Science Foundation, Russell Sage Foundation, W.K. Kellogg Foundation, Open Society Foundations, Open Society Institute-Baltimore, Atlantic Philanthropies, William T. Grant Foundation, the Community Oriented Policing Services (COPS) Office of the Department of Justice, the Major Cities Chiefs Association, the NAACP LDF, National Institutes of Mental Health, the Woodrow Wilson Foundation, the Ford Foundation, the Mellon Foundation, and Google, among others. He was a witness for the President's Task Force on 21st Century Policing and has presented before congressional panels, Senate press briefings, and White House Advisory Councils. This impressive institutional support and consuming audience for implicit bias research is revealing. During the Black Power era of the late 1960s to early 1970s, when students were shutting down historically white universities around the nation to demand the creation of Black Studies programs, philanthropies were at the forefront of the effort to control the movement's impact on the production of knowledge.
>
> The Ford Foundation, in particular, was a pioneer in shaping Black Studies by diverting funds away from program applications evincing a Black Power sensibility and directing support to applicants who proposed curricula based on integrationism. The Foundation favored educational designs that promoted making white students comfortable with the topic of race and racism, while it disfavored programs that prioritized black empowerment through black history, community accountability, and a critical engagement with Western civilization.[54]

Given the double-edged complexities of implicit bias, how might systemic advocates use critical knowledge of it for principled and accountable progress?

---

[54] *Id.* at 652–54.

CHAPTER RECAP

This chapter introduced systemic analysis as an outcome-focused framework for advocates to understand systemic designs and purposes—regardless of top-down proclamations to the contrary that distract attention and dissipate work. We also examined how critical history helps advocates to unlearn and relearn top-down denials and disguises that justify or prolong historical castes—disguises like the private-public distinction and the phenomenon of preservation through transformation addressed in the next chapter. Critical histories of law display that social identities (still) matter under the rule of law, both to systemic injustice and to systemic advocacy; systems channel micro-macro privilege and subordination using social identities, overtly and covertly. In this process of continuous struggle, advocates also must learn to use time proactively and strategically to confront the ongoing opposition of elites; in the following chapter we tackle key mechanisms for making and assessing "progress" over—and using—time.

CHAPTER 4

UNLEARNING AND RELEARNING WINNING, LOSING, AND PROGRESS OVER—AND USING—TIME

■ ■ ■

Table of Sections

4.1　Elites Manipulate Law, Time, and Change to Preserve Identity Castes
4.2　Reproductive Liberty and Justice—Preservation Through Transformation Today?
4.3　Long-Term Struggles Need Contextual Metrics for Winning, Losing, and Progress
4.4　Managing Risk, Privilege, and Time in Organized Long-Term Struggles

OPENING THOUGHTS

We as critical lawyers must also learn how to live in the contradiction . . .: helping bring about basic change and social mobilization while working within a legal system rooted in the status quo. . . . It requires recognition that advocates for subordinated groups will win few easy victories. It forces us to insist that all our actions foster empowerment.

—**Louise G. Trubek**, Critical Lawyering: Toward a New Public Interest Practice, 1 B.U. Pub. Int. L. J. 49, 56 (1991)

[S]o long as the kind of sexual minorities seeking remedial protection under antidiscrimination laws seem to pose a threat to the status quo, the interest to protect them is less aligned than when the litigants seemed more assimilated and respectable. As a result, the status quo will be preserved if a solution to do so exists.

—**Jeremiah A. Ho**, Queer Sacrifice in *Masterpiece Cakeshop*, 31 Yale J.L. & Feminism 249 (2020)

Law by its nature is conservative, and when calls for change that threaten to destabilize existing distributions of material and symbolic power are made, change through law will occur in ways that preserve existing distributions to the greatest extent possible.

> —**Angela P. Harris**, From Stonewall to the Suburbs? Toward a Political Economy of Sexuality, 14 Wm. & Mary Bill Rts. J. 1539, 1542 (2006)

The movement from slavery to segregation to neosegregation is the movement of slavery perfecting itself. . . . All of it is white-over-black, only white-over-black, and that continually. The story of progress up from slavery is a lie, the longest lie.

> —**Anthony P. Farley**, Perfecting Slavery, 36 Loy. U. Chi. L.J. 225, 226 (2004)

INTRODUCTION

In Part I of this book, we learned how, despite the seeming gains of formal equality delivered by the *Brown* decision, the everyday lives of black families were not systemically bettered, nor was the longstanding segregation of schools undone. Many white families and their money moved to new schools in enclaves, or they stayed put and enrolled children in private schools. Despite the seeming upheaval of *Brown* and the civil rights laws that followed, the racial order returned to its systemic equilibrium in short order.

This process of resetting the systemic equilibrium for continued inequality after seemingly equality-enhancing gains is not confined to education. Elites regularly deploy shifting tactics or rhetoric to preserve the status quo. This phenomenon has a name—"preservation through transformation." Preservation through transformation describes how elites maintain the status quo of identity-based castes undergirded by law despite formal reforms and social changes. Note that inequality is preserved not *despite* transformation but *by means of* elite manipulation of change over time. Elites proactively and strategically work to generate the image of progress in law and society, while blocking meaningful improvements in the lived realities of subordinated groups.

Unlearning and relearning helps prepare advocates for the long-haul struggle required to address the machinations of preservation through transformation.[1] Advocates unlearn the notion that progress is either inevitable or complete. Progress is incremental and contested, and opposition is never-ending. The reassuring but false notions of progress must be abandoned so advocates can root their *critical* assessments of "winning" and "losing" in bottom-up perspectives.

Advocates who unlearn disabling myths about progress can then learn to use time proactively as a strategic resource for sustaining bottom-up

---

[1] See Louise G. Trubek, On Long Haul Lawyering, 25 Fordham Urb. L.J. 801 (1998) (describing why "multiple organizational structures, expanded lawyering skills, and intensive collaborative relationships" are necessary for overcoming challenges to innovative, progressive lawyering that is sustainable over time).

struggles. Advocates develop strategies to make change incrementally over time. Advocates defend prior gains and look for new opportunities to move the legal system toward more principled and accountable decision making. Over time and using time, advocates think and act strategically for the long haul.

4.1 ELITES MANIPULATE LAW, TIME, AND CHANGE TO PRESERVE IDENTITY CASTES

Law's design includes ways and means of adaptation that allow the system to reproduce its intended outputs over time and through change. Key aspects of this complex phenomenon have been called "preservation through transformation"—a recognition of a paradox. Law is a living example of the adage that "the more things change, the more they stay the same."

In the excerpt below, feminist legal scholar Reva Siegel traces the same sort of adaptation-for-continued-dominance of legal rules, in this case those designed to give men, as a group, control of women, as a group. This domination has been preserved despite—or, more accurately, by means of—manipulating time and change. Judges, policymakers, agency officials, and other legal actors discard, modify, or invent rules to respond to social change. While claiming "progress," they aim to preserve patriarchy despite, or through, unavoidable change. Law accommodates inevitable social change in order to absorb it. Observe the private-public distinction at work. Note Siegel's concluding analogy to civil rights reforms, emphasizing that preservation through transformation is neither rare nor random—nor cabined to a single social struggle. By design, this systemic dynamic of adaptation (and cooptation) perpetuates the Critical Challenge across a variety of social groups and legal fields.

"THE RULE OF LOVE": WIFE BEATING AS PREROGATIVE AND PRIVACY
Reva B. Siegel
105 Yale L.J. 2117 (1996)

Introduction

The Anglo-American common law originally provided that a husband, as master of his household, could subject his wife to corporal punishment or "chastisement" so long as he did not inflict permanent injury upon her. During the nineteenth century, an era of feminist agitation for reform of marriage law, authorities in England and the United States declared that a husband no longer had the right to chastise his wife. Yet, for a century after courts repudiated the right of chastisement, the American legal system continued to treat wife beating differently from other cases of assault and battery. While authorities denied that a husband had the right to beat his wife, they intervened only intermittently in cases of marital violence: Men who assaulted their wives were often granted formal and informal immunities from prosecution, in order to protect the privacy of the family and to promote "domestic harmony." In the late 1970s, the feminist movement began to challenge the concept of family privacy that shielded wife abuse, and since then, it has secured many reforms designed to protect women from marital violence. Yet violence in the household persists. The U.S. Surgeon General recently found that "battering of women by husbands, ex-husbands or lovers '[is] the single largest cause of injury to women in the United States.'" "[T]hirty-one percent of all women murdered in America are killed by their husbands, ex-husbands, or lovers."

The persistence of domestic violence raises important questions about the nature of the legal reforms that abrogated the chastisement prerogative. By examining how regulation of marital violence evolved after the state denied men the privilege of beating their wives, we can learn much about the ways in which civil rights reform changes a body of status law. In the nineteenth century, and again in the twentieth century, the American feminist movement has attempted to reform the law of marriage to secure for wives equality with their husbands. Its efforts in each century have produced significant changes in the law of marriage. The status of married women has improved, but wives still have not attained equality with their husbands—if we measure equality as the dignitary and material "goods" associated with the wealth wives control, or the kinds of work they perform, or the degree of physical security they enjoy. Despite the efforts of the feminist movement, the legal system continues to play an important role in perpetuating these status differences, although, over time, the role law plays in enforcing status relations has become increasingly less visible.

As this Article will show, efforts to reform a status regime do bring about change—but not always the kind of change advocates seek. When the legitimacy of a status regime is successfully contested, lawmakers and jurists will both cede and defend status privileges—gradually relinquishing the original rules and justificatory rhetoric of the contested regime and finding new rules and reasons to protect such status privileges as they choose to defend.... I call this kind of change in the rules and rhetoric of a status regime "preservation through transformation," and illustrate this modernization dynamic in a case study of domestic assault law as it evolved in rule structure and rationale from a law of marital prerogative to a law of marital privacy.

... A survey of criminal and tort law regulating marital violence during the Reconstruction Era reveals that ... chastisement law was supplanted by a new body of marital violence policies that were premised on a variety of gender-, race-, and class-based assumptions. This new body of common law differed from chastisement doctrine, both in rule structure and rhetoric. Judges no longer insisted that a husband had the legal prerogative to beat his wife; instead, they often asserted that the legal system should not interfere in cases of wife beating, in order to protect the privacy of the marriage relationship and to promote domestic harmony. Judges most often invoked considerations of marital privacy when contemplating the prosecution of middle- and upper-class men for wife beating. Thus, as I show, the body of formal and informal immunity rules that sprang up in criminal and tort law during the Reconstruction Era was both gender- and class-salient: It functioned to preserve authority relations between husband and wife, and among men of different social classes as well....

... Examined from this perspective, the reform of chastisement doctrine can teach us much about the dilemmas confronting movements for social justice in America today....

The Right of Chastisement and Its Critics

Until the late nineteenth century, Anglo-American common law structured marriage to give a husband superiority over his wife in most aspects of the relationship. By law, a husband acquired rights to his wife's person, the value of her paid and unpaid labor, and most property she brought into the marriage. A wife was obliged to obey and serve her husband, and the husband was subject to a reciprocal duty to support his wife and represent her within the legal system. According to the doctrine of marital unity, a wife's legal identity "merged" into her husband's, so that she was unable to file suit without his participation, whether to enforce contracts or to seek damages in tort. The husband was in turn responsible for his wife's conduct—liable, under certain circumstances, for her contracts, torts, and even some crimes.

As master of the household, a husband could command his wife's obedience, and subject her to corporal punishment or "chastisement" if she defied his authority....

... [C]ases in a number of [U.S.] states, particularly in the southern and mid-Atlantic regions, recognized a husband's prerogative to chastise his wife....

... Woman's rights advocates protested the hierarchical structure of marriage; and, as they did so, they attacked the chastisement prerogative as a practical and symbolic embodiment of the husband's authority over his wife....

For woman's rights advocates, a structural diagnosis of male violence against women dictated a structural remedy. Beginning in the 1850s, ... [advocates] were united in the view that state-sanctioned violence in the marriage relationship evidenced fundamental defects in its structure and proved the justice of women's demand to participate in the enactment and enforcement of the laws. They pointed to the chastisement prerogative and to gruesome reports of wife beating in the tabloid press as proof that women needed the vote and did not in fact receive "virtual representation" through male suffrage....

Formal Repudiation of the Right of Chastisement

Over time, the American legal system did respond to these criticisms of wife beating. Decades of protest by temperance [advocating alcohol Prohibition] and woman's rights advocates, combined with shifting attitudes toward corporal punishment and changing gender mores, together worked to discredit the law of marital chastisement. By the 1870s, there was no judge or treatise writer in the United States who recognized a husband's prerogative to chastise his wife.... In several states, legislatures enacted statutes specifically prohibiting wife beating; three states even revived corporal punishment for the crime, providing that wife beaters could be sentenced to the whipping post.

But it would be misleading to look to the repudiation of chastisement doctrine as an indicator of how the legal system responded to marital violence.... [D]uring the Reconstruction Era, jurists and lawmakers vehemently condemned chastisement doctrine, yet routinely condoned violence in marriage....

Relief for Battered Wives: Separation and Divorce

... [N]ineteenth-century judges developed a body of divorce law premised on the assumption that a wife was obliged to endure various kinds of violence as a normal—and sometimes deserved—part of married life. Furthermore, ... judges reasoned ... that the evidence required to prove "extreme cruelty" varied by class, on the doctrinally explicit assumption that violence was a common part of life among the married poor.

The class-based assumptions about marital violence that shaped divorce law in this era also shaped the criminal law, but with very different regulatory consequences. While courts pointed to the prevalence of domestic violence among the "coarser" classes as a reason for restricting poor women's access to divorce, during the Reconstruction Era this same belief was offered as a reason for intensifying the criminal prosecution of poor men who beat their wives.

Race and Class Bias in the Criminal Prosecution of Wife Beaters

... During the Reconstruction Era, public interest in marital violence rose as wife beating began to shift in political complexion from a "woman's" issue to a "law and order" issue. Wife beating now attracted the interest of groups not known for their commitment to temperance or woman's rights causes. During this period, the Ku Klux Klan took an interest in punishing wife beaters (both white and black), and began to invoke wife beating as an excuse for assaults on black men.... By the 1880s, prominent members of the American Bar Association advocated punishing wife beaters at the whipping post, and campaigned vigorously for legislation authorizing the penalty. Between 1876 and 1906, twelve states and the District of Columbia considered enacting legislation that provided for the punishment of wife beaters at the whipping post. The bills were enacted in Maryland (1882), Delaware (1901), and Oregon (1906).

With this surge of interest in wife beating, the wife beater was demonized as a deviant character, whose criminal or licentious propensities authorities needed to control in order to secure social stability. . . .

Thus, as the American legal system repudiated the husband's prerogative to chastise his wife, it did begin to respond differently to wife beating—yet did not adopt policies calculated to provide married women much relief from family violence. Women of the social elite might escape husbands who beat them by obtaining a divorce, if they were not deemed blameworthy, and if they were willing to subject themselves and their children to the economic perils and social stigma associated with single motherhood. Women of poorer families might have a husband fined, incarcerated, or perhaps even flogged, if they were willing to turn him over to a racially hostile criminal justice system. The law thus provided relief to some battered wives, but the majority had little recourse against abusive husbands.

We are left with a striking portrait of legal change. Jurists and lawmakers emphatically repudiated the doctrine of marital chastisement, yet responded to marital violence erratically—often condoning it, and condemning it in circumstances suggesting little interest in the plight of battered wives. Given this record, how are we to make sense of chastisement's demise? . . .

Regulating Marital Violence in an Era of Companionate Marriage

. . . [By the mid-1800s,] . . . [companionate] conceptions of marriage [emerged] . . . By the 1840s, the woman's rights movement was protesting the husband's prerogative to chastise his wife, along with many other hierarchical features of marital status law. Because chastisement so powerfully contradicted norms of companionate marriage, it provided an easy target for feminists interested in demonstrating the injustice of the common law. . . .

. . . If a judge believed that marriage ought be a relation of love, not force, he could denounce chastisement as a relic of a barbaric past—without endorsing the equality norms and associated reform demands of the woman's rights movement. . . .

The Discourse of Affective Privacy in Domestic Assault Law: But She Yields—Not Through Authority, But Love.

... The rise of companionate marriage discredited marital chastisement. And the cases do supply evidence supporting this view ... that "the rule of love has superseded the rule of force." ...

A key concept in the doctrinal regime that emerged from chastisement's demise was the notion of marital privacy....

As courts addressed the regulation of marital violence in the wake of chastisement's demise, judges raised concerns about invading the privacy of the marriage relationship—most often, it would appear, when they contemplated the prospect of sanctioning wife beating in households of the middle and upper classes.

... [P]rivacy talk was deployed in the domestic violence context to enforce and preserve authority relations between man and wife....

Affective Privacy in the Emerging Law of Interspousal Tort Immunity

While it was clear by the second half of the nineteenth century that wife beating was a crime, it was not at all clear that this same conduct constituted a tort. A criminal prosecution for wife beating was brought against a husband by the state, while a tort claim was prosecuted by the married woman herself. Could a battered wife bring suit against her husband in order to vindicate her own injuries without depending upon the state to intervene and protect her? The question was startling.... Interspousal litigation violated fundamental precepts of the doctrine of marital unity....

... "Privacy" supplied grounds on which to justify interspousal tort immunity—grounds that were seemingly independent of the increasingly discredited language of marital hierarchy. And so the discourse of marital status began to shift from the rhetoric of "marital unity" to the rhetoric of "privacy" and "domestic harmony." By 1914 the Supreme Court of Oklahoma ... noted that ... [to hear tort claims between spouses] "would tend to invade the holy sanctity of the home and shatter the sacred relations between husband and wife." ...

... It was not until the late 1970s that the contemporary women's rights movement mounted an effective challenge to this regime. Today, after numerous protest activities and law suits, there are shelters for battered women and their children, new arrest procedures for police departments across the country, and even federal legislation making gender-motivated assaults a civil rights violation. Yet, as this Article opens by observing, battering of women by husbands, ex-husbands, and lovers remains the single largest cause of injury to women in the United States today....

Historical Perspectives

Status regimes [such as male over female or white over black] are not static, but dynamic—revitalized from time to time as they are reshaped by diverse political forces and draw on evolving social mores....

Modernization of a status regime occurs when a legal system enforces social stratification by means that change over time. [For example,] [o]ne commonly recognized way that law enforces social stratification is by according groups hierarchically differentiated entitlements and obligations. In antebellum America, the law of slavery and marriage enforced race and gender hierarchy by such overt means. But by the Reconstruction Era, the law of race and gender status had begun, slowly, to evolve, in diverse ways eschewing the overtly hierarchical forms of the antebellum period. In this era, the legal system continued to draw distinctions on the basis of race and gender, but it now began to emphasize formal equality of entitlements in relationships once explicitly organized as relationships of mastery and subordination, and to repudiate openly caste-based justifications for such group-based distinctions as the law continued to enforce. While the American legal system continued to distribute social goods and privileges in ways that favored whites and males, it now began self-consciously to disavow its role in doing so....

Civil rights agitation plays a significant role in precipitating the modernization of status regimes. Abolitionist protest (and a civil war) contributed to the modernization of racial status law during the Reconstruction Era, just as woman's rights protest contributed to the modernization of gender status law during this same period. If successful, protest of this sort will draw the legitimacy of a status regime into question, and so bring pressure to bear on lawmakers and other legal elites to cede status privileges. In such circumstances, legal elites may begin to cede status privileges, but they will also defend them. They will initially defend privileges within the traditional rhetoric of the status regime—but because the traditional rhetoric of the status regime is now socially contested, they will begin to search for "new reasons" to justify such status privileges as they choose to defend. As reform of the common law marital status rules illustrates, this process of ceding and defending status privileges will result in changes in the constitutive rules of the regime and in its justificatory rhetoric—with the result that, over time, status relationships will be translated from an older, socially contested idiom into a newer, more socially acceptable idiom. In short, civil rights reform is an important engine of social change. Yet civil rights reform does not simply abolish a status regime; in important respects, it modernizes the rules and rhetoric through which status relations are enforced and justified.

Considered from this vantage point, status law has no "essential" or transhistorical form. Instead, the manner in which a legal system enforces social stratification will evolve over time, changing shape as it is contested. Attempts to dismantle a status regime, if successful, will discredit the rules and reasons employed to enforce status relations at a particular juncture in history, and create pressure for elites to reform the contested body of law sufficiently so that the regime that emerges from reform can be differentiated from its contested predecessor. Assuming that something of value is at stake in such a struggle, it is highly unlikely that the regime that emerges from reform will redistribute material and dignitary "goods" in a manner that significantly disadvantages groups that were the beneficiaries of the prior, contested regime. But for the regime that emerges from reform to reestablish its legitimacy, it must distribute social goods in a manner that can be differentiated from the prior, contested regime. The dynamic of negation and differentiation precipitated by the quest to reestablish legitimacy produces constant mutation in the properties of a body of status law. Social struggle over the legitimacy of a status regime will produce changes in its formal structure until such a point as its legitimacy can be reestablished and the reformed body of law can once again be justified as "reasonable." At this point, the legal system may still be enforcing social stratification, but by new means: Especially under changing social conditions, it is possible to modify the rules and reasons by which the legal system distributes social goods so as to produce a new regime, formally distinguishable from its predecessor, that will protect the privileges of heretofore dominant groups, although not necessarily to the same degree.

The dynamic of preservation-through-transformation that I am describing need not arise through the conspiratorial or malevolent motivations of the legal elites directing reform. Indeed, we can posit for purposes of argument that the legal elites who implement these changes in the constitutive rules and rhetoric of a status regime are acting in "good faith." For example, I assume that the judges who repudiated marital chastisement, yet developed the interspousal tort immunity doctrine to constrain interpretation of the married women's property acts, did not snicker in the robing room in gleeful appreciation of their interpretive sophistry. They could well have harbored the good faith conviction that privacy and domestic harmony were important social values that required protection as they superintended the marriage relation through a period of turbulent legal transformation. Thus, as judges contemplated the question of whether the reform statutes granting married women a tort claim for injury to their persons and property should be construed to enable wives to sue their husbands, judges could well have decided, in all sincerity, that considerations of "public policy" warranted interpreting the statutes to bar the claim.

Yet it also seems clear that, as educated, propertied men, judges reasoned about this question within certain legal traditions and from a certain social position that predisposed them to certain legal conclusions. Judges who initially adopted the tort immunity rule openly embraced it as preserving elements of the doctrine of marital unity; only as the doctrine of marital unity was progressively discredited did courts come to rely exclusively on justifications couched in the discourse of affective privacy. Moreover, given the social position from which judges reasoned about "public policy," they were far more likely to appreciate the benefits of the tort immunity rule (to propertied husbands) than to register its costs (to battered wives)—a phenomenon Paul Brest has elegantly dubbed "selective sympathy and indifference." Of course, we can assume that at least some of these judges had the critical faculties to discern, and thus to correct for, the biases to which their deliberative processes were subject. Sometimes, however, critical oblivion is bliss, especially when it is interest-convergent.

... [I]t thus seems useful to consider just how large a role the legal system played in constructing the aspects of society to which it claimed to defer.... Specifically, the aspiration to govern by "rule of law" creates a need for principled reasons to account for particular decisions—particularly those decisions involved in the partial disestablishment of a socially contested status regime.... [P]roducing principled reasons to account for a partial reform of a status regime formally satisfies the requirements of justice. At one and the same time, the process of rationalizing partial reform modernizes the rhetoric in which privilege is justified. Considered from this standpoint, law would appear to be a double-edged weapon of social change, repeatedly demonstrating the capacity to legitimate privileges it seems at first to challenge.

... A status regime is modernized (or deformalized) when, despite changes in its rules and rhetoric, it continues to distribute material and dignitary privileges ... in relatively continuous terms. But modernization of a status regime may still bring about perceptible, even significant, changes in status relations. We can posit that African-Americans were "better off" under a regime of Jim Crow than a regime of chattel slavery, certainly in terms of dignitary values, and possibly in terms of their material welfare as well. Similarly, we can posit that married women were "better off" under a regime of formal and informal immunities for wife beating, certainly in terms of dignitary values, and, possibly, in terms of their material welfare as well.

There is, however, one way in which members of each group were indisputably worse off: in their capacity to achieve further, welfare-enhancing reform of the status regime in which they were subordinated. By the mid-nineteenth century, slavery and marital status law (chastisement, in particular) were socially contested and substantially discredited practices. They lacked legitimacy in the eyes of many. But once racial status law and marital status law were reformed in the Reconstruction Era, each status regime gained substantially in legitimacy.

As each regime was translated from contested rules and rhetorics into more contemporary rules and rhetorics, each was again "naturalized" as just and reasonable, in significant part because each was now formally and substantively distinguishable from its contested predecessor: Each could be justified in terms of social values that were distinct from the orthodox, hierarchy-based norms that characterized its predecessor (slavery, marriage) as a regime of mastery. Considered from this perspective, we can see that civil rights reform may alleviate certain dignitary or material aspects of the inequalities that subordinated groups suffer; but we can also see that civil rights reform may enhance the legal system's capacity to legitimate residual social inequalities among status-differentiated groups.

Of course, struggle persists . . . As the recent life of the colorblindness trope illustrates, civil rights rhetoric can supply "legitimate," "nondiscriminatory" reasons for opposition to affirmative action and other reforms intended to break down remaining racial and gender inequalities. . . .

In offering these reflections on civil rights reform, I . . . intend my comments to extend beyond the story of marital chastisement alone. I have explored . . . and discern some frequently recurring, if not absolutely regular, features of civil rights reform that are worthy of consideration. These reform dynamics deserve consideration because they are recurring today in the wake of the civil rights revolutions of the 1960s and 1970s, and because there is little in the current Court's understanding of equal protection that conduces to their public discussion. . . .

Siegel concludes by analogizing reforms against patriarchy to civil rights reforms based on race. Given these experiences and their lessons, how must notions of "progress" be unlearned and relearned to manage this paradox in the real world? Consider questions like these as you read the next excerpt, extending Siegel's closing analogy of sex and race to include sexual orientation.

Below, we see through a critical "triangulation of affirmative action, criminal justice, and marriage equality" how the equilibrium of the status quo is preserved despite legal reforms and social change. Does this systemic triangulation suggest transformation, preservation, or both? Legal scholar Russell Robinson and social psychologist David Frost argue that a key lesson from struggles against the Critical Challenge in varied contexts is that the Supreme Court "carefully cabins its opinions to preserve the social hierarchy" because the justices and other social-legal elites carry a "fear of too much justice." Is this, too, part of preservation through transformation?

"PLAYING IT SAFE" WITH EMPIRICAL EVIDENCE: SELECTIVE USE OF SOCIAL SCIENCE IN SUPREME COURT CASES ABOUT RACIAL JUSTICE AND MARRIAGE EQUALITY

Russell K. Robinson and David M. Frost
112 Nw. U.L. Rev. 1565 (2018)

The last five years have seen historic shifts in social justice movements that focus on race and sexual orientation. In 2013, a jury acquitted George Zimmerman of charges related to the shooting of Trayvon Martin, an unarmed African-American teenager whom he wrongly suspected to be criminal. Three black women activists responded with a social media-fueled movement called #BlackLivesMatter. Additional tragic deaths of unarmed African-Americans in 2014 and 2015 galvanized unrest in African-American communities (and beyond) and activism contesting police tactics such as racial profiling and excessive force. At the same time, marriage equality activists and lawyers were building the cases that they hoped would secure a nationwide constitutional right to marry a partner of the same sex. In 2013, they persuaded the Court to invalidate part of the Defense of Marriage Act, a federal law refusing to recognize same-sex marriages. Two years later, the Court, in *Obergefell v. Hodges*, announced that every state had to license same-sex marriages, a decision viewed by many as the capstone of decades of lesbian, gay, bisexual, and transgender (LGBT) legal advocacy....

The battery of Supreme Court cases that rebuff the overwhelming majority of legal challenges to police misconduct remains very much intact. This disparity might lead a casual observer to think that LGBT people secured full legal equality in recent years, while African-Americans and other people of color continue to lose at the Supreme Court.

... We argue that a "fear of too much justice" connects race and sexual orientation cases. Even when LGBT people win in cases like *Obergefell*, or underrepresented racial minorities win in affirmative action cases like *Fisher v. University of Texas*, the Court carefully cabins its opinions to preserve the social hierarchy with only incremental changes....

Marriage equality lawyers played this game by presenting predominantly white, middle-class, and "all-American" plaintiffs—people who were ultimately depicted by Justice [Anthony] Kennedy as "needing" to assimilate into marital norms rather than desiring to change them.... By sketching the road not taken—an intersectional, more inclusive, and more LGBT-affirming marriage equality claim—our analysis suggests that the actual claim in *Obergefell* mainly mirrored the interests of the most privileged members of the class.

... Our triangulation of affirmative action, criminal justice, and marriage equality suggests the Court's preference for affirming civil rights only when doing so will not dismantle entrenched social hierarchies.

Our analysis builds on some first principles. First, science has sometimes been used to perpetuate the subordination of people of color, women, LGBT people, and many others. Second, courts sometimes invoke science in order to conceal their value choices in "objective" garb. For both of these reasons, scholars should subject scientific findings, and legal claims utilizing such findings, to critical analysis. A close examination of the Court's treatment of social science in certain leading equal protection cases also undercuts any assumption that the Court treats social science in a uniform manner. We suggest that the Court's openness to social science in such litigation will depend on the extent to which its presentation threatens to unleash what the Court regards as "too much justice." When faced with competing bodies of social scientific discourse, we can expect the Court to emphasize the strand that minimally disrupts the status quo.

... The core of the Supreme Court's analysis in *Obergefell* asked whether the reasons why marriage is essential for heterosexuals also apply to same-sex couples. This framing basically inquired whether same-sex couples are similarly situated to heterosexuals with respect to marriage. By evaluating four benefits of marriage, the majority concluded that "the reasons marriage is fundamental under the Constitution apply with equal force to same-sex couples." These four benefits are the following: (1) marriage as an expression of personal autonomy, (2) marriage as a unique opportunity, (3) marriage as a means of protecting children and family, and (4) marriage as a central social institution. ...

... Marriage has been—and remains—a divisive issue among LGBT people.... [Some] view marriage, or at least the marriage equality movement, as an attempt to assimilate into mainstream society, which they consider a betrayal of "queer" values. From this vantage point, LGBT people should be focused on disrupting dominant norms, not blending into them. ...

The discomfort that a significant number of LGBT people have about marriage's prominence overlaps with racial and socioeconomic disparities. Studies suggest that middle-class and affluent people, whether heterosexual or LGBT, are more likely to take advantage of the right to marry or seek a civil union or domestic partnership. Low-income people of color, especially African-Americans, are potentially less likely to benefit from the efforts of the marriage equality movement as much as affluent white people in part because people of color are underrepresented in the population of LGBT people in same-sex partnerships. ...

Marriage equality is a deeply important step toward eliminating discriminatory social policies and structural stigma in LGBT lives. ...

... [But t]he marriage equality movement ... largely framed denial of access to marriage as a unique harm rather than sufficiently connecting it to overlapping structural forms of subordination, which cannot be eradicated simply by granting marriage licenses. The movement's narrow focus seems most beneficial for the most affluent members of the class, those who managed to obtain stable, satisfying, and exemplary relationships and, in some cases, to raise healthy children, despite significant exposure to minority stress. . . .

Many sexual minorities are not prepared to take advantage of marriage equality because they are struggling with basic needs, such as access to stable housing, or because they are incarcerated. LGBT people are disproportionately likely to be homeless and to be incarcerated. Even in the marriage equality era, LGBT sexuality remains highly stigmatized. As a result, many sexual minorities continue to hide their identities and to conduct any sexual or romantic relationships in secret. Many sexual minorities' attempts to form enduring romantic relationships are hindered by discrimination at work, at school, in public, and from parents and other family members.

Conclusion

. . . The connecting thread in these cases is the judicial struggle to enforce equal protection while minimally disrupting the status quo and extricating the courts from extended structural reform. Although many lawyers have catered to this judicial instinct, we want to highlight those who have pressed the Court to think bigger. . . . We encourage scholars and lawyers similarly to resist the "fear of too much justice."

The two excerpts above illustrate how elites deploy different tactics or shifting rhetoric to preserve the past while appearing to transform law for justice. Siegel's sex-gender example showcased judicial manipulation of formal concepts and vocabularies to produce outcomes that change law on its face but preserve the status quo in society, concluding with an analogy to race and retrenchment. Robinson and Frost's race-sexual orientation example showcased a different tactic for this top-down strategy, pointing out how judges and other elites chip away at—and "take back"—previous formal "reforms" for one identity group (racial minorities) while simultaneously acquiescing to formal reforms for another identity group (sexual minorities). This contra-positioning of legal regression on race against legal "reform" on orientation preserves the Critical Challenge of using law for justice.

Moreover, as Robinson and Frost (and others) argue, lawyers (and legal scholars) sometimes facilitate this top-down strategy, whether wittingly or not. Though their clients are at the bottom, lawyers sometimes bend over backwards to reassure elites that granting the requested relief won't really change anything in fact, and, if so, only cosmetically. Sometimes, and perhaps too frequently, as Derrick Bell's excerpt in Part I noted, advocates serve more than one master. When they do, they participate in social preservation through legal transformation.

Consider in this same vein a final and contemporary example involving a different identity group. The following excerpt puts front and center a third tactic in the elite strategy of preservation through transformation: recycling and repackaging old (and discredited) arguments or concepts based on supposedly "neutral" reasons for preserving group castes justified by history, custom, morality, nature, biology, or religion. These arguments and concepts were also used against racial or ethnic minorities, women generally, and lesbians and gays (and ultimately rejected). Below, Shannon Price Minter, a leading U.S. transgender attorney and activist, reviews new, yet old, rationales for group inequality that preserve the status quo despite legal change.

"DÉJÀ VU ALL OVER AGAIN": THE RECOURSE TO BIOLOGY BY OPPONENTS OF TRANSGENDER EQUALITY
Shannon Price Minter
95 N.C. L. Rev. 1161 (2017)

Introduction

Historically, biological arguments have been used to justify many different types of discrimination, from slavery to coverture to the forced sterilization of people with disabilities. In recent years, those seeking to exclude same-sex couples from marriage also invoked biological arguments. In cases challenging state marriage bans, state officials and others argued that the bans did not discriminate against same-sex couples, but rather simply reflected their inability to procreate biologically. Ultimately, such arguments failed. In 2015, the U.S. Supreme Court . . . rejected the notion that biology was a sufficient justification for the harms imposed on same-sex couples and their children by discriminatory marriage laws.

Today, those who oppose transgender equality are once again appealing to biology to support exclusionary laws and policies—in this case, laws and policies that isolate transgender people and treat them differently than others. . . . On this view, restricting access to restrooms based on a person's "biological sex" is warranted by the physiological differences between men and women. . . .

. . . Like the biology-based claims previously used by marriage equality opponents, these arguments seek to insulate discrimination against transgender people from meaningful scrutiny by claiming that any such discrimination merely reflects neutral biological differences between men and women. . . .

. . . [M]uch of the current focus on transgender issues centers on restrooms. Indeed, just as the freedom to marry became the public focus of equality for lesbian, gay, and bisexual people, the freedom to use restrooms based on one's gender identity has now become the public focus of equality for transgender persons. Unlike the focus on marriage, however, which was driven in significant part by the choice of LGBT advocates to prioritize the issue, the current centrality of restrooms in the battle for transgender equality has been the result of a concerted effort by conservative public officials and groups, who have forced this issue to the forefront through aggressive legislation and litigation. . . .

Why Biology-Based Arguments Played a Central Role In the Marriage Equality Debate

The Supreme Court's 2015 *Obergefell* decision, which struck down state laws barring same-sex couples from marriage, was the culmination of an extraordinary shift in the legal and social position of gay people in the United States. . . . [Previously], those defending the bans sought to portray them as a mere reflection of the biological, sex-based differences involved in procreation, rather than as measures intentionally designed to exclude same-sex couples. Initially, some courts accepted those arguments. In the long run, however, most courts—including the Supreme Court—rejected biology-based rationales as circular and required states to justify their discriminatory treatment of same-sex couples, which they were unable to do. . . .

The Shift to Biology-Based Arguments and Why It Failed

Because defenders of state marriage bans could [no longer] credibly appeal to overt gender stereotypes or to the immorality or pathology of same-sex relationships, they looked elsewhere to justify the exclusion of same-sex couples from marriage. . . .

. . . [S]tate officials and others defending state marriage bans . . . argued that the purpose of marriage is to channel biological procreation and encourage couples that have children together to enter into a stable family relationship. In effect, they reverse engineered a vision of marriage that focused on the one characteristic that distinguishes same-sex couples from many opposite-sex couples: their inability to procreate. . . .

The tactical benefits of this argument were clear. By contending that marriage is defined by its link to heterosexual procreation, defenders of state marriage bans could argue that the restriction of marriage to opposite-sex couples simply reflects a biological reality, not animus or bias toward same-sex couples. . . .

. . . While some courts initially accepted arguments based on procreation as a sufficient justification for state marriage bans, over time, courts increasingly rejected them as fatally under-inclusive both of the purposes of marriage (which include protecting couples who do not have children) and the range of families (including same-sex parents) who would benefit from the stability and protections of marriage. In *Obergefell*, . . . the Court held that excluding same-sex couples from marriage undermined, rather than furthered, the state's interest in responsible procreation. . . .

The Revival of Biology-Based Arguments in the Debate Over Transgender Equality

The movement to achieve transgender equality has, in many ways, paralleled the legal battle for marriage equality. After years of judicial losses, the last decade has brought about a sea change in the courts, with more and more decisions protecting the right of transgender persons to equal treatment under the law. At the same time, medical science has recognized that being transgender is a normal variation of human experience and that, with the proper support, transgender people can be healthy, productive members of society. In response to these changes, those who oppose transgender equality have found themselves in a dilemma similar to that previously confronting those who opposed marriage equality for same-sex couples—namely, wishing to defend laws and policies that treat transgender persons differently than others, but unable to credibly do so based either on overt appeals to gender stereotypes or to arguments based on the immorality or pathology of transgender identity. . . .

"The Transgender Tipping Point"

Just as the push for marriage equality gained unprecedented traction in the 1990s and escalated rapidly in the years before *Obergefell*, the movement to gain equality for transgender people has hit a critical tipping point in the last decade. . . .

. . . [J]ust as medical science rejected older models of gay identity as pathological, medical experts increasingly have recognized that being transgender is not a disorder. In the most recent edition of the American Psychiatric Association's Diagnostic and Statistical Manual of Mental Disorders ("DSM"), the diagnosis given to facilitate medical treatment for transgender people was changed from "gender identity disorder" to "gender dysphoria," to better reflect that simply being transgender is not in itself a mental disorder. . . . Transgender people have gained tremendous visibility in popular culture as well, including positive depictions of transgender characters in television shows and of transgender public figures in mainstream media publications.

Backlash: Mounting Opposition to Transgender Equality

In response to this unprecedented progress, state officials and conservative groups have launched an equally unprecedented counterattack. Across the country, those who oppose transgender equality are bringing lawsuits challenging nondiscrimination policies, sponsoring legislation to restrict the rights of transgender people, boycotting businesses that have pledged not to discriminate against transgender people, and mounting public campaigns depicting the transgender equality movement as misguided and dangerous. . . . [A]s happened in the marriage equality battles, those who oppose the rapid progress of transgender equality are once again invoking biology-based arguments—this time, in an attempt to justify the exclusion of transgender people from restrooms.

The Focus on Restrooms

As a strategic matter, it is no accident that opponents of transgender equality have focused so intently on restrooms—one of the few places where gender segregation is still permitted. By sponsoring legislation and bringing cases that focus on restrooms, opponents have forced transgender advocates onto vulnerable terrain, compelling them to defend antidiscrimination policies for transgender people in a context that triggers many people's deep-seated anxieties and fears about sexuality and gender. In addition, being forced to devote time and resources to defending equal treatment in restrooms diverts transgender advocates from other goals. Certainly, being able to use restrooms based on one's gender identity is important and often is a prerequisite to other more important rights, such as being able to attend school or work without fear of discrimination. For example, a transgender student who is constantly "outed" as such by being forced to use a separate bathroom is likely to be targeted for harassment, and, at a minimum, will be negatively affected by the constant stigma of being treated differently than other students.

Nonetheless, if transgender advocates were able to choose their own priorities, equal treatment in restrooms, in and of itself, would likely fall lower on the scale than ensuring that transgender people are able to work, attend school, be free from hate violence, have access to homeless shelters and medically necessary care, secure accurate state-issued identification, raise children, obtain asylum, and be protected from violence and abuse in prisons, jails, and detention facilities. Rather than focusing on any of these other equality issues, where seeking to justify discrimination would be more challenging, the opponents of transgender equality have made a strategic choice to make restrooms the centerpiece of their opposition. In so doing, they have identified the one context where, on its face, biological differences between men and women are likely to seem most important, just as focusing on the role of procreation in marriage highlighted the one aspect of marriage where biological differences were likely to be seen as highly relevant.

For opponents of transgender equality, this narrow focus on restrooms serves many of the same strategic purposes as the narrow focus on procreation served for the opponents of marriage equality. First, it allows them to tell a story about the origins and purposes of sex-separated restrooms that resonates with popular understandings about "biological sex" and the importance of anatomical differences between men and women. Second, by highlighting those biological differences, it provides a ready way to deny that policies barring transgender people from shared restrooms are based on animus or bias and to depict such policies as a benign reflection of natural reality. Finally, it allows those defending such exclusionary policies to exploit fears about the vulnerability of women and children—themes with a long history among those opposing both gender equality and equality for LGBT people.

Appeals to the "Traditional" Definition of Sex

Just as marriage equality opponents sought to defend a "traditional" view of marriage, defined by biological procreation, so transgender equality opponents are now seeking to defend a "traditional" view of sex, defined by the "physiological differences between men and women, rather than differences in gender identity." . . .

Claims That Exclusionary Policies Reflect Biology, Not Bias

As the marriage cases show, biological arguments provide a way to gloss over the complex histories that have shaped institutions such as marriage and gender-segregated restrooms. Acknowledging those histories would require equality opponents to concede that those institutions did not simply fall from the skies, but rather have been shaped by changing cultural and legal norms. In turn, such a concession would require them to defend their normative vision of how those institutions should be structured—and in particular, to explain why the exclusion of same-sex couples or transgender people is justified. Instead, equality opponents invoke biology in order to bypass the need for such explanations. Rather than offering substantive justifications for limiting marriage only to male-female couples or for requiring transgender people to use separate restrooms, they tell a timeless "origin story" that—no matter how dubious as a historical matter—resonates with deeply held popular beliefs about purportedly "natural" differences between men and women.

Biological Justifications for State Marriage Bans

For supporters of state marriage bans, that origin story was simple: marriage exists because "sex between men and women makes babies." According to this view, laws barring same-sex couples from marriage merely reflected the biological reality that men impregnate women through sexual intercourse. . . .

. . . In *Obergefell*, the Supreme Court addressed this issue directly, noting that marriage "has not stood in isolation from developments in law and society," but "has evolved over time." . . . Such a view is far removed from attempts to portray marriage as a timeless, cross-cultural vehicle for channeling biological procreation.

Biological Justifications for Laws and Policies Barring Transgender Persons from Shared Restrooms

Today, transgender equality opponents seek to rely on a similarly timeless and universal tale about the supposedly biological origins of gender-separated restrooms. In this account, gender-separated bathrooms are simply the natural reflection of the physiological differences between men and women. Because men and women have different bodies, this story goes, they require different restrooms. . . .

In fact, as scholars from a variety of disciplines have documented, this ahistorical narrative ignores the evolving legal and cultural norms that have shaped the modern conception of public restrooms. Gender-separated restrooms have not been a universal feature either of all other cultures across time or of our own culture. In this country, Massachusetts passed the first law mandating gender-segregated restrooms in 1887. . . . Like regulations limiting the hours that women could work and the types of jobs they could hold, laws mandating separate restrooms reflected widespread cultural anxieties about the entry of women into public workplaces. Far from simply reflecting biological differences between the sexes, these laws were "deeply bound up with early nineteenth century moral ideology concerning the appropriate role and place for women in society." . . .

Claims That Exclusionary Policies Protect Women

Proponents of biology-based arguments about marriage and gender-segregated restrooms also frequently argue that maintaining a discriminatory exclusion is justified by the gender-based vulnerability of women and girls. . . .

Proponents of this view claim that permitting transgender people to use restrooms based on their gender identity will render women and girls more vulnerable to sexualized, gender-based violence. Generally, they do not contend that transgender women pose a threat to others. Rather, the argument is that permitting transgender people to use shared restrooms is such a radical alteration of current biology-based norms that it effectively destroys the very institution of gender-segregated restrooms, opening the door to men masquerading as women (or falsely claiming a transgender identity) in order to gain access to women's restrooms for improper purposes. . . .

Conclusion

. . . [S]chool districts and those challenging equal restroom policies argue that they should be permitted to provide transgender students with separate facilities and that doing so is sufficient to meet the requirement of equal protection. The arguments against such an approach are similar to those against [racial equality,] civil unions and domestic partnerships: such a "solution" imposes inequality and stigma by singling out transgender students for disparate treatment based on a characteristic that has no relevance to their ability to use the same restrooms as others, or more broadly, to participate in public life on equal terms....

Minter illustrates how even seemingly neutral, small or mundane aspects of everyday life—like buying wedding cakes and using public restrooms—are turned into mutually-reinforcing flashpoints, which fuel privilege for some and subordination for others. These flashpoints are selected to demean and disempower the targeted group(s), enforcing larger or interlocking systems of stratification depicted as "natural" and therefore just. All are designed to prey on public ignorance, fear, or prejudice to preserve existing group inequalities. This excerpt shows how flashpoints are chosen *intentionally* to preserve the past in the face of the social or legal present; equally important, it shows the still-unfolding struggle of trans persons to overcome the Critical Challenge of using law for equal justice.

NOTES AND QUESTIONS

1. *Preserving Economic Gains Through Time.* Formal equality, as measured from the bottom, has little effect on the lived material reality of disfavored groups. Siegel explains that privileged groups ensure the preservation of inferior status despite the sheen of formal gains in legal status. Presumably, then, even legal change dismantling structures of oppression, such as slavery, will give rise to new public and private tools to preserve the continuity of (in this case, racial) control. But what about the other side of the coin? Dismantling the institution of slavery, even if it did not transform the lived experience of the subordinated group, must have hurt the material standing of the former slave owners, right? Yet a new study suggests that less than two decades after the Civil War, former Southern slave-owner dynasties had restored their place at the top of the economic pyramid.[2]

2. *Asserting Biology and Religion to Legitimate Illegal Discrimination.* Since the achievement of formal marriage equality, opponents have turned to other concepts or arguments to trump it. Religious liberty is among the most common of these, although no one has yet pointed to a religious tenet prohibiting trade and commerce between sexual minorities and sexual majorities in common everyday interactions (like selling breads, cakes, and other baked goods). Extremely loose assertions of this "right" in secular or economic contexts show why equality advocates must be prepared to defend as well as to make progress. Recent examples come from top-down attacks on the Affordable Care Act (ACA), attacks occurring through executive agencies and governmental support for litigation challenges to undo it, including two 2018 rules exempting

---

[2] Andrew Van Dam, What Southern Dynasties' Post-Civil War Resurgence Tells Us About How Wealth is Really Handed Down, Wash. Post (Apr. 4, 2019) (discussing a study showing that by 1880, the sons of slave owners were better off financially than sons of Southern whites who had equal wealth but weren't as invested in slavery).

employers from covering contraceptive services on the basis of "sincerely held religious beliefs." Another proposed rule restricts gender identity protection to instances of discrimination based on the individual's gender assigned at birth and rolls back broader LGBTQ protections.[3] Although some religions do condemn women's use of birth control, does a corporate insurance policy for employees that includes contraception violate any bona fide religious tenet? Does commerce between people with different sexual orientations violate any genuine religious belief? Which religion(s)? Which tenet(s)? And how, specifically, do these corporate policies interfere with any religious belief(s)? In other words, where is it written?

3. *"Religious" Liberty—a Special (Christian) Right to Discriminate?* Should any group be exempt from enforcement of a "generally applicable" law based on their claimed or authentic religious beliefs? In *Employment Division v. Smith*, 494 U.S. 872 (1990), the Supreme Court said no (confirming that ritualistic uses of peyote in native religions could be punished under a general anti-drug law). Is the current Christian claim of religious liberty any different from that of the native tribes rejected in *Smith* decades ago? How? What qualifies identity-based discrimination in commerce or employment as a *religious* practice? Might identities, groups, interests, and power have anything to do with either or both of these examples?

4. *Transgender Identity and Struggle Across Borders and Cultures.* Transgender individuals face violence and threats to their physical safety as well as discrimination in health care and other everyday settings in law and society. These risks, and legal impediments to their personhood, travel across borders, as does struggle. An example of ongoing contestation is the efforts of United Caribbean Trans Network (UCTRANS), a regional network that highlights the need for legal reform to ensure legal gender identity recognition:

> Trans rights are human rights, trans people do exist in the Caribbean, and we are entitled to get our gender identity recognized. It's time for our governments to take a step forward to equality. UCTRANS urges our governments to fulfill the international human rights obligations and honour the diversity that characterizes the Caribbean region, joining efforts to protect and recognize the rights of trans persons and to grant gender identity recognition through expedited administrative procedures.[4]

---

[3] John Riley, Trump Administration Poised to Rewrite Obamacare, Without LGBTQ Protections, Metro Weekly (Apr. 27, 2020), www.metroweekly.com/2020/04/trump-administration-poised-to-rewrite-obamacare-without-lgbtq-protections/. Update: The rule was issued in June 2020, but the subsequent Supreme Court decision in *Bostock v. Clayton County, GA*, led a court to issue a preliminary injunction against the rule.

[4] Center for American Progress, Aisha C. Moodie-Mills, Jumping Beyond the Broom: Why Black Gay and Transgender Americans Need More Than Marriage Equality, www.outrightinternational.org/content/united-caribbean-trans-network-launches-first-regional-network-promote-human-rights-trans.

As the examples in this section show, preservation through transformation is always a possibility. Systemic advocates anticipate, plan for, and contain that possibility across identities, groups, and contexts. Consider another contemporary example.

4.2 REPRODUCTIVE LIBERTY AND JUSTICE—PRESERVATION THROUGH TRANSFORMATION TODAY?

As Siegel showed above, generations of women lived under their husbands' right of chastisement. The right to get an education, to vote, to own property, to enter contracts, to serve on juries, to become licensed attorneys and doctors, and to own businesses all came belatedly and over constant opposition. In fact, patriarchy has made the meaning of equality, liberty, and justice for women a social fantasy under the rule of law. The liberty of women to make reproductive choices freely is part of this big picture—a formally recognized liberty that amounts to a social fantasy. This section sketches the role of law in maintaining reproductive oppression. This section also illustrates how advocates and activists unraveled legal fictions and confronted social manipulations based on collectivized identities in the struggle for reproductive justice.

In 1972, the Supreme Court recognized in *Roe v. Wade*[5] the "fundamental" right of women to make reproductive choices freely as part of their due process "liberty." *Roe*, however, did not establish this right as an independent dimension of women's equality, but rather coupled a woman's decision making with the free exercise of medical judgment by her physician. As Supreme Court Justice Ruth Bader Ginsburg said during her 1993 Senate confirmation hearing, "This is something central to a woman's life, to her dignity. It's a decision that she must make for herself. And when government controls that decision for her, she's being treated as less than a fully adult human responsible for her own choices."[6]

Since then, campaigns of unrelenting resistance have followed, characterized by top-down reactions to family law reforms, civil rights gains, and recognition of marriage equality. Anti-abortion forces have assassinated doctors, vandalized clinics, intimidated workers and clients, invented new definitions of ("potential") life and other fictions to legalize control of women's bodies—and engaged generally in tactics of preservation through transformation. They agitate for restrictive laws designed to impose tangible and intangible costs on providers and women. The formal legal right on paper looks very different from the right in practice.

---

[5] *Roe v. Wade*, 410 U.S. 113 (1973).

[6] Hearings Before the Committee on the Judiciary (July 20, 21, 22, & 23, 1993), www.loc.gov/law/find/nominations/ginsburg/hearing.pdf.

The concept of reproductive justice was defined in 1994 by a group of Black women, later organizing as the SisterSong collective, as "the human right to maintain personal bodily autonomy, have children, not have children, and parent the children we have in safe and sustainable communities."[7] These are the kinds of choices formally protected by "liberty"—but as reclaimed from the bottom.

Below, two excerpts show how current restrictions mimic colonial castes with modern legal justifications. These excerpts also outline work of advocates and activists to pierce those top-down myths through consciousness-raising, analytical narratives, critical histories, collective action, and coalitional solidarity—all of which we review in this part and deepen in subsequent chapters. First, Jill Morrison, director of the Women's Law and Public Policy fellowship program at Georgetown University, illustrates how rhetoric opposing reproductive justice has been deployed to deny Black women's agency and suppress feminist social struggle. Next, gender studies scholar Ann Kennedy describes how law—through both policy making and adjudication—has limited women's control over childbearing and manipulated care work to serve elite interests and diminish women's autonomy. Law has structured who may or may not have babies, who may or may not keep their babies, and who may care for their own babies, with state support, versus those who must care for others' babies, sometimes by state mandate. Over time, state regulation of reproductive rights and care work has functioned to maintain identity castes based on gender, class, race, and, more recently, immigration status. Consider, as you read, how elites have used time and change to preserve castes in reproductive (and other) justice contexts.

RESUSCITATING THE BLACK BODY: REPRODUCTIVE JUSTICE AS RESISTANCE TO THE STATE'S PROPERTY INTEREST IN BLACK WOMEN'S REPRODUCTIVE CAPACITY

Jill C. Morrison
31 Yale J.L. & Feminism 35 (2019)

. . . [P]resent-day reproductive oppression reflects an attempt by the State to retain a property interest in Black women's bodies once held by their owners during the time of enslavement. . . . The Reproductive Justice [RJ] framework seeks to remove these property interests in Black women's bodies and return them to their rightful "owners." . . .

Abortion rates have declined significantly for all groups since the early 1980s, but the rate for Black women remains at almost three times the rate

---

[7] See Reproductive Justice, SisterSong: Women of Color Reproductive Justice Collective, www.sistersong.net/reproductive-justice. Reproductive autonomy, a linked notion, "includes contraception, sterilization, and abortion, [and] extends to breastfeeding, a reproductive bodily function." Andrea Freeman, You Better Work: Unconstitutional Work Requirements, 53 U.C. Davis L. Rev. 1531, 1603 (2020).

as for White women. . . . Despite the well-documented and complex factors causing the high abortion rate among Black women, this fact is often used as "evidence" that abortion is a racist plot to diminish the Black population. . . .

. . . [Earlier activists] were justified in their suspicion of State-supported family planning. Birth control was the government's preferred panacea to poverty, promoting contraception, abortion, and sterilization rather than actually responding to poverty's root causes . . .

. . . [But it is easy] to distinguish government-imposed population control from individually-chosen family planning, yet this rhetoric was reinvigorated in 2009 by the documentary *Maafa 21: Black Genocide in 21st Century America*, made by a white antiabortion activist. . . .

Planned Parenthood is the primary focus of those claiming that abortion constitutes Black genocide, with its founder Margaret Sanger receiving much of the criticism. It is well-documented that Margaret Sanger believed in eugenics—limiting reproduction to the mentally and physically fit. Yet Sanger still rejected the idea of State control of women's reproductive choices that was at the heart of eugenic ideology. Planned Parenthood has addressed and denounced this and other troubling actions and beliefs held by Sanger. Furthermore, there is no evidence that Sanger coerced women of color into using family planning. It is also well-documented that Sanger was invited to work in partnership with Black leaders, organizations, and healthcare providers to increase access to contraception in Black communities. . . .

There is also a claim that Planned Parenthood situates its facilities in predominately Black areas, with the implication being that Black women terminate their pregnancies at higher rates simply because abortion services are conveniently available. Aside from this argument being incredibly simplistic and insulting, it is also false. Less than ten percent of abortion facilities are located in neighborhoods with a majority Black population. . . .

The most prominent campaign in recent memory arose from the Radiance Foundation . . . These and other "pro-life" supporters asserting an interest in the disproportionate rate of abortions among Black women have otherwise shown no commitment to the well-being of mothers, infants, or children of any race. . . .

The Co-opting of Black Lives Matter

The most recent racialized anti-abortion rhetoric grows out of the Black Lives Matter (BLM) movement. BLM, started by Black women in 2013, has an explicitly anti-patriarchal frame. . . .

Attempting to draw attention away from BLM and redirect to their antiabortion campaign, the Radiance Foundation's most recent poster reads: *Black Lives Matter In and Out of the Womb*. The founder of the Radiance Foundation has also decried the "hypocrisy" of the [BLM-RJ organizations'] partnership, noting that Planned Parenthood "kills more unarmed black lives in one day than police are accused of killing in one entire year." Again, this statement presumes that Black women have no agency in determining whether or not to continue a pregnancy....

The first Crisis Pregnancy Center (CPC) was established in 1967 in Hawaii, with the express purpose of dissuading women from having abortions through false information.... CPCs are organizations that advertise pregnancy testing and options, leading women to think that they provide abortion services. Once in the door, staff use a variety of methods to convince women to continue their pregnancies....

... Citing the high rates of abortion in communities of color, CPCs have explicitly targeted what they call "underserved" communities....

... CPCs are largely funded by conservative, evangelical Christian organizations, and most have white, male leadership. Another significant portion of their funding comes from governments ...

CPCs view women of color as passive victims of abortion.... This reproductive paternalism, and presumption that Black women are not competent decisionmakers regarding their own reproduction, reflects the most abhorrent and stereotyped notions about Black women's humanity and competency. This harks back to enslavement, which "marked Black women . . . as objects whose decisions about reproduction should be subject to social regulation rather than to their own will." ...

Building on the argument that the higher abortion rate among Black women is some sort of evidence of a genocidal conspiracy, legislation has been proposed to ban abortion based on race.... [P]roponents claim that the disproportionate rate of abortions among Black women is driven by some animus that these women have against their fetuses based on its race....

... The Supreme Court recently denied Indiana's request for review of the provisions related to race and sex-selective abortions on the ground that the issue had not been presented in any other Court of Appeals. Justice Clarence Thomas wrote a dissent that attempted to draw a connection between the disproportionate abortion rate among Black women and eugenic motives, while devoting nary a word to Black women's capacity for decision-making....

The racialized rhetoric . . . characterizes Black women as objects, and not actors. This particular form of objectifying Black women was also an integral part of how they were controlled during enslavement. As property, they were merely to be acted upon, with their owners holding all rights over them.

Property theory posits that there are two primary property rights: use and exclusion. For the purposes of this analysis, the right of use of one's reproductive capacity and sexuality includes all of the benefits that one could draw from her own sexual decision-making and reproductive labors. With regard to the right of exclusion, this means one's right to determine who has sexual access to her body, whether that body will be used for reproduction, and whether that body will be subjected to restrictions based on one's reproductive status (for example, the state of being pregnant). The RJ framework considers these rights as encompassing the right to decide whether or not to have children, the right to raise children with adequate supports, and the right to express one's sexuality free from violence or coercion. . . .

. . . Current methods of reproductive oppression, in which the State holds property rights over Black women's bodies through restrictive laws and policies, replicate what was once owners' private property interest in their female slaves. . . .

. . . Reproductive Justice organizations led by Black women and based in the communities they serve have been responding to these current attempts to render Black women objects without agency, and centered the time- and place-specific needs of Black women. . . . These organizations have led local and national fights to decriminalize sex work, expand birthing options for women on Medicaid, and destigmatize abortion.

. . . [T]he regulation of Black women's sexuality and reproduction must be treated as a matter of racial justice. . . . Current attempts to marginalize and objectify Black women vis-à-vis their reproductive capacities reflect this centuries-long history of oppression and must be explicitly rejected on this basis.

CHRONIC HARM
Ann Kennedy
25 Wm. & Mary J. Race, Gender & Soc. Just. 131 (2018)

. . . Reproductive Justice and the Anti-Archive

. . . The reproductive justice framework developed from the activism of women of color in the 1990s, although its roots are in earlier women of color and socialist feminisms in the 1970s, such as the Committee to End Sterilization Abuse, the National Welfare Rights Organization, Women of All Red Nations (WARN), and Chicana activists who helped fight the sterilization of predominantly Chicana women in California in the case of *Madrigal v. Quillen*, the Indian Health Services record of coerced sterilizations, and eventually change [in] the sterilization consent standards at [the federal Department of Health, Education, and Welfare]. . . .

One of the methods utilized to organize the reproductive justice movement is storytelling. . . . [C]ounter-narratives are not merely stories, but stories that challenge the hegemonic logic that structures public policy and legal decision-making. . . .

The counter-narratives of critical race feminism are power analytics and cannot be separated from the explicit desire to transform the legal system. . . .

Over the course of the last two decades, Carrie Buck has emerged as an important historical figure because she was chosen as a constitutional test case [in *Buck v. Bell* in 1927] for eugenicist Harry Laughlin's model sterilization law. . . . Buck was a young white woman living with a foster family, the Dodds, who was raped by one of the family members; when they discovered her pregnancy the Dodds had her admitted to the Virginia asylum where her mother [Emma] was already institutionalized and where Carrie gave birth to a daughter, Vivian. Medical historians have spent many years "proving" that Carrie's diagnosis as "feebleminded" in 1924 was a fabrication, relying on the very records used to sanction her sterilization.

The medical-legal and welfare archives leave a rich accounting of her case. . . . Carrie is named and renamed, in the medical records as "feebleminded;" by Justice Holmes as an "imbecile;" in the words of Albert Priddy, the superintendent of the Virginia State Colony for Epileptics and Feebleminded, where Carrie was an inmate; Carrie is of the type of "the shiftless, ignorant, and worthless class of antisocial whites of the South."

. . . In Carrie's case, we can see . . . that the archive is a site for the regulation of difference as hierarchy. . . .

In the twenty-first century, Carrie became a figure of interest to historians of the eugenic project, but also to feminists, particularly those invested in reproductive justice. . . .

Queer, disabled artist Eli Clare titles their piece "Yearning Toward Carrie Buck." . . .

Clare addresses Carrie through identification with the ableist narration of Carrie's story by historians and feminists. Clare tells Carrie, "recent historians seem to think the court case and your sterilization might have been less a travesty if you had been intellectually disabled. . . ." . . . [W]hy, asks Clare, is it important to proclaim Emma, Carrie, and Vivian as *not* imbeciles? What would have been justified if they were found to have intellectual disabilities? . . . Clare asks: when we strike down the facts of the archives, in our zeal do we leave intact its premises? . . .

... The meaning of *Buck* for contemporary reproductive justice is also a record of institutional violence against the female body. ... [T]he family, the school, the state institution, and the courts deny Carrie her parental rights in incorporating her daughter back into the same family that victimized her. ...

The categorization of Carrie['s] ... placement as "care" is shown to be a systemic investment in providing the domestic labor of poor girls to middle-class families. In fact, ... Carrie was expected and did return to the domestic work that she had been doing before her institutionalization. ...

... Clare brings her address to Carrie to a close by addressing herself to contemporary feminists, stating:

> [b]eyond the histories, I imagine a congress of sterilized women and men—raging, fierce, grief filled. Puerto Rican women sit with Appalachian men. First Nations teenagers sit with self-described mad women. Disabled folks who have lived their entire lives locked away in state-run hospitals sit with southern Black women who know all too well the words *Mississippi appendectomy*, the meaning behind them. Women of color ordered by judges or paid to take Norplant sit with women tricked into signing tubal ligation consent forms. They won't be asking for apologies nor giving absolution, but rather holding remembrance, demanding reparation, planning revolution.

Clare's ending points us toward a future that imagines reproductive justice out of the revolutionary demands of communities in coalition, that recognizes sterilization as a collective harm to communities as well as a violation of bodily integrity and personhood of those already made vulnerable by a racist patriarchal state. This vision recognizes difference and signifies coalition in the struggle for reparations. ...

Chronic Harm: Reproductive Justice and the Exploitation of Care Labor

... [More recently, in the 2014 Supreme Court case *Harris v. Quinn*,] Pamela Harris, the caregiver for her disabled son, received a Medicaid subsidy from the state so that she could take care of him in her home. However, Harris objected to paying union dues to the Service Employees International Union (SEIU), which represented health care workers in Illinois who were paid by the state to act as personal attendants in the home. Although Harris was not required to join the union, she was required to pay union dues, according to the "fair share" law designed to prevent workers from accepting the benefits of the union's collective bargaining without contributing to its financial support. The Supreme Court ... concluded that caregivers supported by Medicaid funds could not be compelled to pay union dues because the client [and not the state] was the "true" employer.

As a jointly authored piece in *The Nation* pointed out, the majority opinion threatened state employee unionism but was also aligned with a racist patriarchal tradition of excluding care work from labor protections:

> [the majority opinion in] *Harris* is an extension of a different tradition in American labor law, the denial of rights to workers in industries dominated by female and non-white workers. Far from universal, the major New Deal labor laws—the National Labor Relations Act, the Social Security Act and the Fair Labor Standards Act—explicitly excluded particular occupations, including farm work and domestic labor, which had large numbers of female, African-American and Mexican-American workers. While some racially and sexually biased exclusions were later eliminated, *Harris* effectively extends this history of discrimination.

In direct contrast to the undervaluation of this labor, Justice Kagan argued in her *Harris* dissent that "[s]uch a ruling subverts the state's determination of these labors as being of the utmost public interest." . . .

> . . . [This case is an elite] strategic move to resist organizers' attempts to bring together care and labor, to bringing home and work together in a way that frames low-income and no-income women's role as caregivers as central to the state. If we return to the archives that focus on the exploitive use of the "feeble-minded" as domestic workers, then we see the relationship between eugenic sterilization and the logics of the majority in *Harris*: of utmost interest is the *lesser cost to the state* through exploitation of women's labor, even if it leaves those who do paid care work in poverty and without the ability to exercise the kind of "ideal motherhood" represented by Pamela Harris.

> . . . [Unlike Harris,] most workfare placements for recipients of Temporary Assistance to Needy Families "designated home care, like home-based child care, an appropriate workfare placement only if performed for individuals other than [their own] family." Thus, the split between care and work is implicit in the treatment of mothers based on their social class, because mothers of children with disabilities are considered deserving of a subsidy to prevent the institutionalized care of their loved ones and mothers receiving Temporary Assistance for Needy Families are not. . . .

> . . . Harris is rewarded for her marital status, her class status, and her symbolic representation of "ideal motherhood" but only so far as her interests align with the interests of the state and her work can be defined in relation to her son's disability—perhaps if institutionalization were cheaper or more convenient for the state, then Harris, too, might find herself excluded from the public interest. . . .

In this case, the state makes invisible the racist patriarchal assumptions of the structure of labor and public policy, denying that the state benefits from the care work of low-income women—indeed, as we learned from the eugenic archives, the state has systemically exploited that work. . . .

Journalist Liza Featherstone puts it this way: feminism needs to be concerned with those "whose bodies prevent them from creating profits for capital" because the contempt with which they are treated shows us that we are all disposable. This requires struggling against feminist historical collusion with capitalist eugenic framing of the body, including forced sterilization, and the use of state systems to exploit the care of women of color.

In the excerpts above, Morrison and Kennedy ask who—in terms of group identities—suffers because of continuing reproductive injustices, as well as who benefits and who makes key decisions regarding the regulation of children, families, and care work. Both find that colonial identity-based castes have been preserved despite seemingly remarkable change in the home and work lives of women. Both examples demonstrate how bottom-up knowledge, consciousness-raising, and critical history can help expose patterns of collective injustice and inform the work of those aiming to improve the lived realities of childbearing and caregiving.

NOTES AND QUESTIONS

1. Hobby Lobby *and the Economics of Reproductive Justice.* As Morrison and Kennedy point out, reproductive justice includes abortion and contraception and extends to broader decisions about family and health. In *Burwell v. Hobby Lobby Stores, Inc.*, 573 U.S. 682 (2014), the Supreme Court allowed corporations—as "persons" engaging in the "exercise of religion"—to be exempted from the requirement of covering contraception costs as part of "minimum essential coverage" under the Affordable Care Act (ACA). The Court "overturned a legislative solution intended to correct for a market imperfection that resulted from sex discrimination, i.e., a lack of accessible preventive care for all female employees," according to feminist legal scholar and clinician Michele Gilman.[8] In its majority opinion, the Court recounted the "family" nature of the corporations involved, founded by patriarchs and managed by sons who expressed the belief that human life begins at conception. The majority paid little attention to the views of employees and their dependents, who might desire to make their own contraception choices. The Court's understanding of the market, Gilman notes, obscures its role in promoting gender inequality. Gilman suggests that legal actors should adopt feminist economic theory:

---

[8] Michele E. Gilman, En-Gendering Economic Inequality, 32 Colum. J. Gender & L. 1 (2016).

> First, feminist economists include domestic and care work within the study of economic systems.... [T]raditional economics excludes care work from its analysis, as well as from standard measures of productivity, such as the Gross National Product....
>
> Second, feminist economists maintain that economic success should be measured in terms of human well-being—or the "ability to lead a life one values"—and not simply by efficiency or profit-maximization norms....
>
> A third feminist economic principle is that human agency is essential to assessing economic events. Accordingly, "questions of power, and unequal access to power, are part of the analysis from the beginning" ... within the household, within the workplace, and within the public sphere.
>
> Fourth, ... economic analysis should include intersectional understandings of how class, race, ethnicity, gender, sexual orientation, and other identities interact.... This also means that feminist theorists need to be aware of their own privilege and to interrogate their own values and ideology.[9]

According to Gilman, the *Hobby Lobby* decision allowed corporations a personhood that reinforced gender inequality "based on male norms of health needs." In contrast, Justice Ginsburg's dissent regarded the market as imperfect and thus needing the ACA's legislative fix to meet women's needs. How would *Hobby Lobby* or other decisions be different if childbearing, childrearing, and care work were considered through the lens of feminist economic theory?

2. *Abortion, Contraception, and the "Protection" of Women by Law.* Nineteenth and early twentieth century opponents of contraception argued that non-procreative sex was immoral and harmed women. That argument was sufficient to win passage in 1873 of the federal Comstock Act and mini-Comstock state laws prohibiting the distribution of contraception. More recently, opponents of contraception have used similar "woman-protective health arguments" purportedly based on science. This pattern mimics anti-abortion arguments, which also moved from morality-based rationales to supposedly-scientific arguments that women need protection *from* abortion. As legal scholar Priscilla Smith notes, the aim is to imbed arguments in law that restrict women's sexual freedom, particularly low-income women and women of color:

> If successful, this ... could undermine, or at the least prevent the expansion of, government programs that provide contraceptives or [insurance] coverage of contraceptives.... As importantly, the attempt to clothe opposition to contraceptives in a benevolent concern for women's welfare is revealed here as a pretext for promoting a familiar, if outmoded, moral view that sexual intercourse is immoral

---

[9] *Id.* at 18–21.

if undertaken for pleasure alone, without the risk of pregnancy. Sex for pleasure, at least for women, is rejected....

... This opposition to non-procreative sex is remarkably regressive, extends to sex for pleasure within marriage, and unites the opposition against reproductive rights and same-sex marriage.[10]

3. *The Collateral Health Consequences of Chipping Away at* Roe. Constitutional law scholar Maya Manian has studied efforts to reverse *Roe v. Wade*, 410 U.S. 113 (1973). Abortion opponents have framed abortion as a threat to women's health, as noted above. This has led not only to increasing post-*Roe* restrictions but to collateral damage to women's health. For example, the "partial birth" abortion ban upheld in *Gonzales v. Carhart*, 550 U.S. 124 (2007), purports to prohibit abortion procedures late in pregnancy; in fact, physicians' fear of prosecution has changed the way women are treated when miscarrying, resulting in limited care. Similarly, "conscience clauses" allow individuals and institutions to refuse to provide abortion care without liability—even when abortion is an accepted medical treatment to reduce health risks in emergency situations. Manian describes how anti-abortion restrictions limit implementation of women's end-of-life care decisions:

> While men can plan in advance to refuse life-sustaining treatment, women of reproductive age cannot because of pregnancy exclusions from laws otherwise respecting advance health care directives. These laws are clearly a part of the anti-abortion movement's push to treat fetuses as separate persons and patients under the law....
>
> Marlise Munoz was only thirty-three years old when she collapsed in November 2013 from a pulmonary embolism (a blood clot in the lungs). She was eventually pronounced brain dead. Brain death—in both medicine and law—is death.... Marlise had discussed her end-of-life wishes with her family and made it clear she would never want to be kept artificially alive with no hope of recovery.... However, Marlise was fourteen weeks pregnant at the time of her death. The treating hospital argued that a Texas law forbade withdrawal of medical support from pregnant women, regardless of their wishes for end of life care, and that the law applied to Marlise even though she was dead. Although . . . fetal health was highly uncertain, Texas officials argued that the state could use her body as an incubator against her and her family's wishes.... The Munoz family had to watch Marlise's body slowly decompose through two months of court battles before they were finally allowed to bury her.
>
> The Texas court ultimately decided that the statute did not apply to brain dead pregnant women, but it did not reach the larger

---

[10] Priscilla J. Smith, Constitutional Comstockery: Reasoning from Immorality to Illness in the Twenty-First Century, 47 Conn. L. Rev. 971 (2015).

question whether limiting end of life decision making for pregnant women in other circumstances is constitutional.[11]

Given the one-step-forward, two-steps-back nature of abortion-related advocacy in recent years, has *Roe's* promise been fulfilled? What was won? What subsequently was lost? For whom and in what ways was progress achieved?

4. *Queering Reproductive Justice.* According to Marie-Amélie George, an historian and legal scholar, advocates have "tended to ignore the queer community's specific reproductive issues."[12] Issues include insurance coverage, assisted reproductive technologies, family law issues, and inclusive sex education. These issues are related to legal principles such as autonomy, privacy, and equality. LGBTQ cases implicating these fundamental rights have had greater success in recent years than has litigation over abortion and other reproductive rights issues. So, George asks, could focusing on queer reproductive issues allow advocates to make gains for all?

> In *Roe v. Wade*, the Supreme Court recognized the right to personal privacy as an inherent part of individuals' liberty interests.... Recently, however, the Court has moved away from this conception of abortion and its role in promoting fundamental constitutional values....
>
> ... [But] the Court has repeatedly underscored equality in LGBTQ rights decisions, framing equality as a matter of dignity, autonomy, privacy, and liberty. Even [when, in *Masterpiece Cakeshop, Ltd. v. Colo. Civil Rights Comm'n*,] the Court ruled in favor of a baker who objected to same-sex marriage on religious grounds, the decision emphasized that "gay persons and gay couples cannot be treated as social outcasts or as inferior in dignity and worth." ... LGBTQ issues are currently a more robust area for rights recognition and preservation than abortion or contraception....
>
> ... Sex education tends to exclude, and sometimes discriminates against, queer youth. Challenging the curricula's antiqueer formulation may provide an avenue for changing the materials more generally. As for medical decisionmaking, [important issues include] ... intersex infant normalization surgery, insurance coverage for transition-related care, and religious refusals to provide gender transition treatment. All of these tie directly to concerns about abortion and contraception access....
>
> By focusing on queer reproductive rights, the reproductive justice movement may invert the typical social movement framework, whereby advocates tend to prioritize the needs of more privileged group members. Rather than tackling abortion and contraception

---

[11] Maya Manian, Side Effects of the Abortion Wars, 38 Women's Rts. L. Rep. 362, 367–69 (2017).

[12] Marie-Amélie George, Queering Reproductive Justice, 54 U. Rich. L. Rev. 671, 672 (2020).

rights, and then having those principles trickle down to LGBTQ reproductive justice issues, queer rights advances would trickle up to nonqueer issues. Given that the reproductive justice movement formed to address the needs of marginalized women, families, and communities, this new strategy would promote the movement's goals *and* principles. For that reason, the reproductive justice movement would not just win specific rights battles—it would secure victories in ways that also further its fundamental values.[13]

As these examples show, contestation related to reproductive justice issues has crossed generations and connected issues from childbearing and childrearing to care work. Systemic advocates aim always to contain the possibility of preservation through transformation, even when deceptive appearances make it difficult to distinguish change from progress. In response, systemic advocates design action and define progress—winning and losing—using clear, contextual, long-term goals and metrics.

4.3 LONG-TERM STRUGGLES NEED CONTEXTUAL METRICS FOR WINNING, LOSING, AND PROGRESS

As Boucai noted above in this chapter, many activists and advocates since the 1960s have aimed for gay "liberation"—that is, "sexual freedom, gender dissent, and alternative family forms." This array of goals targets broad, systemic changes in law and society. Not everyone agreed with those goals, even within the LGBTQ movement and among allies.

In the marriage equality campaign, many internal debates focused on how to use adjudication *and* democracy to advance sexual minority access to formal marriage. As we will see in Part V, campaigns often include litigation in conjunction with other methods and techniques of bottom-up struggle. Litigation can be vital, as can other legal tools of adjudication and democracy, as well as tools derived from fields such as organizing, communications, fundraising, and research. But focusing on litigation in isolation from other aspects of struggle leads to a misunderstanding of strategic and tactical choices that advocates and activists make to win transformative progress incrementally.

Legal scholars Scott Cummings and Douglas NeJaime, writing about marriage equality before the Supreme Court recognized a constitutional right to same-sex marriage in *Obergefell v. Hodges,* 576 U.S. 644 (2015), noted the importance of understanding advocacy as a complex endeavor in the fluid, dynamic contexts of systemic injustice:

---

[13] *Id.* at 673–74, 677, 702–03.

Movement advocacy around marriage equality is multidimensional, contextual, and unpredictable. Litigation plays an important, but not decisive, strategic role: It is part of an overall arsenal that includes legislative advocacy and public education, and it is always undertaken in the context of a careful analysis of the likely political consequences and how they might be addressed. Opposition is constant and sophisticated, so that there is never a clear "win," only moves that are certain to be countered. In this sense, the model of lawyering in the marriage equality context is not one of avoiding backlash, but managing its inevitable onset by influencing its form and intensity.

... [Advocates are] sophisticated political agents within a complex field characterized by: (1) multiple actors, including allies and opponents, as well as political decisionmakers and the general public, whom lawyers seek to persuade to support their goals; (2) a range of tactical choices to advance policy ends in which litigation is an important option, but not preordained, and one that is complemented by legislative advocacy, public education, and grassroots organizing; and (3) multiple and overlapping institutional domains within which policy ends may be advanced, including courts, legislatures, administrative agencies, the ballot initiative system, extralegal channels (public pressure, boycotts), and private bargaining processes, all of which operate at different scales—local, state, federal, and international—that present distinct opportunities and challenges for advocates seeking reform.[14]

Legal scholar and marriage equality advocate Nan Hunter hones these points below, considering actual choices made in the long marriage equality campaign, specific concerns and compromises raised, significant advances achieved, and continued exclusions still blocking the path to Critical Justice. She also addresses—and largely accepts—one of Boucai's main points: that the deeper structural changes sought in the 1970s by early same-sex marriage litigants were abandoned as explicit goals by the 1990s. With the strategy changing from "liberation" to "assimilation"—and with decision making shifting from local grassroots to experts in a centralized war room—Hunter relates how the litigation victory in *Obergefell* was won. She also shows who made decisions and who thereby benefited more (and less) from those decisions—with lasting legacies in law and society.

---

[14] Scott L. Cummings and Douglas NeJaime, Lawyering for Marriage Equality, 57 UCLA L. Rev. 1235, 1329–30 (2010).

VARIETIES OF CONSTITUTIONAL EXPERIENCE: DEMOCRACY AND THE MARRIAGE EQUALITY CAMPAIGN
Nan D. Hunter
64 UCLA L. Rev. 1662 (2017)

. . . No contemporary issue has elevated questions of law and politics quite like the question of whether same-sex couples have a constitutional right to marriage. The U.S. Supreme Court's decision in *Obergefell v. Hodges* was preceded by massive social contestation outside of courts and legislatures, almost all of it involving social movements. The content of the arguments centered on moral and political questions that were frequently debated in electoral arenas, but were often framed in constitutional terms.

The story of the LGBT rights campaign illustrates that the influence of elections on minority rights is not limited to the direct substantive effect of changes in law nor to the results of litigation. To a greater extent than is known or understood, the campaign for marriage equality was shaped most powerfully by electoral politics, rather than by litigation or legislative battles. Most accounts begin with a mid-1990s court decision in Hawaii that provided the rationale for Republicans to force enactment of the Defense of Marriage Act (DoMA), under which the federal government refused to recognize same-sex marriages as valid under state law. The end came with two Supreme Court decisions: the first in 2013 ruling that DoMA was unconstitutional and the second, two years later, mandating that same-sex couples be allowed to marry in every state. In many ways, however, ballot questions had a greater influence on the campaign. What constitutes ordinary politics may not have a precise definition, but it surely includes election campaigns. Ballot questions, which are distinctive only in that the contestants are proposals to amend statutory or constitutional text rather than candidates, powerfully merge law and politics. At least as much as through legislative representation, direct democracy mechanisms profoundly influence the framing and social meaning of such concepts as rights, equality and fairness.

What was unique about the LGBT rights/marriage equality movement was that a definitive Supreme Court victory resulted from a campaign that de-emphasized litigation for most of its duration and was dominated until the final two years by ballot questions, most of which were forced by opponents. . . .

The marriage equality debate began as a struggle between two identity groups: lesbians and gay men on one side and religious conservatives on the other, both supported by their strongest allies. Each side began with a core cluster of arguments which it later modified. In the 1990s, conservatives supplemented their original morality-based claims with their own version of a secular rights argument based on the "no special rights" trope, which handily mapped onto white backlash against civil rights protections for persons of color. Roughly a dozen years later, LGBT rights lawyers moved in the opposite direction and systematically de-emphasized rights claims in favor of emotive appeals wrapped in narrative.

Based on their experience in ballot question elections, marriage equality advocates built a new model for law-oriented social movements. The new strategy combined universalizing, rather than minoritizing, rhetoric with the technology and knowledges of national political campaigns. In the process, these advocates invented a form of public policy marketing that is poised to recur across the ideological spectrum and with regard to many different issues. The rhetorical foundation for the new organizational model was a legal and cultural argument built on sameness, positioning same-sex couples in ways that sought respect based on respectability.

The discursive strategy became assimilation in and through law, based on the convergence of cultural interests. . . .

What began as a conflict within the terms of identity group politics evolved and expanded beyond the two minorities. A new cultural détente on accommodating homosexuality emerged with seemingly little disruption of heteronormativity, though perhaps with significant diminishment in the authority of organized religion to enforce traditional beliefs regarding sexuality. The legal precedent that was established ended an exclusion, but it may provide little if any support for future claims that would require denaturalizing gender and disrupting patterns of sexualized racial oppression—two names for continuing hierarchies of subordination that marriage equality advocates dared not speak.

In addition, the marriage equality campaign developed a new model for social movements in several respects. Structurally, the new model produced a hybrid organization geared to winning elections as well as law reform; strategically, its primary investment was in communications research and social marketing techniques; and politically, its discursive priority was in emphasizing how a minority group's norms and values were the same as those of the majority. . . .

. . . [I]t is true and deeply ironic that without the interplay between law and politics—between elite and popular interpretations of the Constitution which characterize ballot question debates and bedevil LGBT advocates—marriage equality likely would have taken far longer to secure. . . .

Popular Constitutionalism and LGBT Rights

. . . At least in the abstract, ballot questions are "as near to a democracy as you can get.". . .

... On the marriage issue alone, citizens in thirty-six states have voted, sometimes more than once, on whether the law of marriage should exclude same-sex couples.

For almost all of this nearly fifty-year period, anti-equality forces won the great majority of gay-related ballot contests. ... [T]o win at the ballot box became the priority not just for LGBT groups generally, but for LGBT litigation and lobbying organizations as well.

The Role of Direct Democracy in the LGBT Rights Movement

... [T]he tactic of using methods of direct democracy to constrain advances in equality became a favored device for conservatives [in response to civil rights gains in the 1950s]. The questions most often put before voters during that time first appeared in 1959 with "a wave of ballot box assaults in the area of fair housing and public accommodation laws." ...

The data on ballot questions closely tracks the history of the LGBT rights movement. Starting in the mid-1970s, local elected bodies adopted or added antidiscrimination protections for sexual orientation to municipal codes, a development that spread to state legislatures in the 1980s. LGBT rights advocates deployed arguments based on the themes of civil rights, equality, and privacy to secure these laws, and generally used conventional organizing and lobbying methods. ...

... [In 1992,] social conservatives in Colorado ... secured a place on the ballot for Amendment 2, a proposal to amend the state constitution that deployed both aspects of the strategy developed in the earlier campaigns against racial equality: Amendment 2 not only repealed local ordinances providing civil rights protections for lesbians and gay men, but also forbade adoption of any state or local law according rights to homosexuals except by further amending the state constitution, a far more burdensome process than legislative enactment. ...

... When *Romer v. Evans* reached the U.S. Supreme Court, that Court ... struck [Amendment 2] down. ...

Direct Democracy and Marriage

Within a few months of *Romer v. Evans*, ... Congress enacted the Defense of Marriage Act (DoMA), signaling that LGBT rights debates had moved to a new level. On the issue of same-sex marriage, politics quickly swallowed law in at least three dimensions: partisan mobilization, advocacy technologies, and strategic prioritization.

Partisan Mobilization

The partisanship was not subtle. DoMA emerged from a Republican-controlled Congress just prior to the 1996 election, thereby forcing President Clinton and every Democratic member of Congress either to anger the pro-LGBT segment of the party's base by supporting it, or to alienate the middle-of-the-road voters who objected to same-sex marriage by opposing it. . . .

. . . With each state that adopted or more deeply inscribed its ban on same-sex marriage, the sense deepened that Americans intended marriage to exist as a naturalized institution, grounded in religion, and functioning as a natural right a priori to the state.

Technologies of Advocacy

During the same period, pro-equality groups led the increasing use of election-campaign-oriented tools of advocacy in litigation, the second bleed from politics into law. . . .

GLAD's challenges to marriage exclusions in Vermont and Massachusetts pioneered the use of the technologies of electoral politics, especially polling and voter canvassing, as central components of marriage-equality litigation. . . . In both states, activities included training volunteers for public speaking in favor of marriage equality, designation of a media team, and town halls and open meetings to test the level of support for litigation and to build infrastructure for broader public education efforts once it was filed. . . .

Strategic Prioritization

The importance of ballot questions in antidiscrimination and marriage equality efforts shaped the internal dynamics of the movement as well as the broader legal and political landscape. The dominance of electoral politics effectively resolved internal disputes over movement directions and tactics. . . .

. . . [T]ension grew out of the ideological paradox of same-sex marriage: It simultaneously embodies conservative norms and radical change. To traditionalists, especially those with a strong affiliation to a conservative religious faith, the idea of two men or two women marrying seemed an extremist, liberal, secular travesty, a violation of natural law. To some progressives, especially feminists and sex-radical gay men, the idea of expanding the scope of an institution steeped in gendered practices and linked to the legitimation of some forms of consensual sex but not others seemed misguided at best and retrogressive at worst. . . .

. . . Increased professionalization of campaign methods made success in elections more likely, but its assimilationist message contributed to the impression that gay translated into white and middle-class. Internal debates proliferated over "evasive messaging." . . . These internal conflicts persisted, but were increasingly sidelined as the stakes in the marriage debate heightened. . . .

. . . Operating in this dense legal and cultural ecosystem, social movements contribute directly to the construction of constitutional meaning.... A particular form of lawmaking—direct democracy—drove the creation of a new model of social movement.

Structure: A New Social Movement Model

During 2004, a quarter of the states banned same-sex marriage. In response, ten leaders of LGBT rights organizations gathered for a two-day strategy summit in a Jersey City airport hotel in May 2005. Almost all were lawyers, most from litigation organizations; participation was by invitation only. The meeting arose from a decision by LGBT rights advocates and the leading funders for the movement to rethink the marriage strategy, with the understanding that a number of funders would work collaboratively to support an effort that was more cooperative among the advocacy groups. By the time the meeting ended, the participants had adopted a new strategy to achieve same-sex marriage. The agreement was embodied in *Winning Marriage: What We Need to Do* (hereafter *Winning Marriage I*), which was modified at a meeting five years later by a slightly larger set of organizational representatives in *Winning Marriage: The Path Forward* (hereafter, *Winning Marriage II*).

The goal of the new phase of the marriage equality movement that *Winning Marriage I* called for was to create the social conditions under which institutions with Supremacy Clause power could be persuaded to act. The strategy of both *Winning Marriage* documents was derived from a particular historical understanding of why certain civil rights movements had succeeded: that the Supreme Court and Congress function as consolidators, rather than creators, of new social norms, "[d]espite widespread beliefs to the contrary." Based on that understanding, Matt Coles of the ACLU and the other authors expected federal law to "foster[ ] the eventual national resolution" to allow same-sex marriage, but only after it became socially acceptable and legally valid in many states.

Winning Marriage I: A Movement/Campaign Hybrid

Winning Marriage I called for a coordinating organization, separate from all existing groups, to execute state-specific plans and strategies, "[m]uch like a national candidate campaign." Although *Winning Marriage I* acknowledged important roles for legislatures and, to a lesser degree, courts, it argued that the essential goal was "winning the public." ... Strikingly, litigation was de-emphasized, contradicting the conventional wisdom of much law and society scholarship that litigation will play a central role in any social movement. Also striking was the group adoption of an election campaign as its core, primary strategy.

Winning Marriage I sought to create a tipping point specifically for the Supreme Court, where final and complete success would be achieved. The authors proposed a state-by-state approach in which advocates would seek to shift states into greater levels of legal recognition for same-sex couples....

The Winning Marriage project ... built on two earlier versions of an incrementalist concept for law reform. The NAACP Legal Defense Fund achieved fame for the systematic march-to-Georgia-style approach to test litigation in its desegregation campaign, winning a series of Supreme Court decisions that culminated in *Brown v. Board of Education*. More recently, it has become commonplace for public interest organizations to eschew litigation-only strategies and instead deploy multiple modes of advocacy that integrate lobbying and public education. With this newer approach, different zones of law can form the cutting edge at different times and in different jurisdictions, allowing for versatility in identifying the most receptive institutions for new interpretations of law.

Winning Marriage I took the multi-modal strategy for legal change to a third stage. Although the ultimate goal was highly specific and quite narrow—to end an exclusion through identified specific intermediate legal achievements, the method behind the strategy was to give muscle and meaning to clichés about the power of "the court of public opinion" in ways that could be elaborated both discursively and organizationally. *Winning Marriage I* incorporated election campaigns focused on issues rather than candidates into the menu of venues that the movement would prioritize, and it baked election victories into its core metric of success. This step had cascading effects. Central to the Winning Marriage effort was using multiple substantive and emotional messages (not just legal or quasi-legal arguments), which could be micro-targeted to specific audiences, and using metrics of success—such as opinion poll numbers, interactions with voters, and get-out-the-vote results—that were drawn from the operations of a political campaign.

... What was different in *Winning Marriage I* was the combination of placing "the primary goal of changing the way people think ... at the forefront" of a "national campaign to win marriage" with elections as the central barometer of success.

... Patterns began to emerge....

... [In 2008] California's Proposition 8, which [amended] the state constitution to specify that marriage could exist only between a man and a woman, ... provided an acid test of the electoral politics model. ...

Winning Marriage II: Regrouping After Armageddon

Advocates responded to Proposition 8 by doubling down on their efforts to develop a strategy that would succeed in electoral arenas. The same group of strategists as in 2005 was joined by representatives of four foundations and convened again in late March 2010 to revise their strategy. Again, while the new strategy agreement, *Winning Marriage II*, addressed multiple venues for advocacy, elections loomed largest....

The advocates gathered for the *Winning Marriage II* summit revisited the tipping point metaphor from *Winning Marriage I*, understood as the key to "get[ting] the Court ready for marriage." . . .

. . . Advocates began framing the tipping point to be when major opinion polls repeatedly found that a majority of the population agreed with marriage equality for same-sex couples.

The group entered what turned out to be the final phase of the Winning Marriage campaign with a recommitment to developing "deeper strategies aimed at ultimate persuasion" and to working even more collaboratively. . . .

. . . What emerged was a network architecture that linked research, testing, state affiliates, litigators, lobbyists, and media, with [the advocacy group] Freedom to Marry at the hub. The different organizations involved in the effort, although often rivals, agreed to share the results of opinion polls and surveys. . . .

The long-sought breakthrough in an electoral arena came in the fall 2012 election, when marriage equality advocates surprised even themselves by winning all four marriage questions on the November ballot in Maine, Maryland, Minnesota, and Washington. Expertise, technology, and resources gelled to create sophisticated campaigns in each state. . . . [S]trategists switched from using canvassers primarily to identify supporters for later get-out-vote-efforts to a model of "conversation canvassing" in which hundreds of paid and volunteer staff members went door-to-door seeking to explain to voters why same-sex couples wanted and needed marriage. . . . Equality supporters spent an estimated $42 million on the campaigns in the four jurisdictions.

Seven months after the 2012 election, the judicial breakthrough came. In *United States v. Windsor*, the Supreme Court ruled that DoMA was unconstitutional. After *Windsor*, the movement changed its focus from winning elections to litigation. Lawsuits were filed in every state that barred same-sex marriage. The Civil Marriage Collaborative directed a greater portion of financial support to financing the litigation. . . .

In many ways, *Windsor* itself was the tipping point, at least for lower court judges who read the opinion as a clear signal that marriage equality was rapidly approaching. . . .

Movements, Campaigns, and Metrics

. . . There is no magic definition for the distinction between a social movement and a campaign. A reasonable distillation of several versions in the sociological literature would define a social movement as a broad, long-range effort to change fundamental aspects of social relations, whereas a campaign generally targets a more specific goal to be achieved in a shorter time of intense activity. Consistent with that definition, I use "movement" in reference to the effort to win legal and social equality for LGBT Americans. . . .

Lawyers as Leaders

In the literature about accountability in social movements, social scientists have argued that efforts aimed primarily at changes in law, led by lawyers, suffer from a kind of gravitational pull that produces agendas that favor the concerns of elites, strategies constrained by legal doctrines, and outcomes that bear little resemblance to the ambitious visions of those in the movement whose involvement tends toward protest and direct action. . . . It is not difficult, nor would it be entirely wrong, to critique the marriage equality campaign as merely an example that illustrates the harshest of these observations . . . [particularly as] related to accountability (or its lack) in some aspect of goal definition: in selecting which issues to focus on, in defining the scope and depth of what would constitute success, and in portraying the movement's constituency through the prism of particular goals. . . .

Assessing Law-Oriented Cause Efforts

Regardless of category or nomenclature, I offer the following set of queries as a metric for assessing strengths and weaknesses in outcomes for a law-oriented cause effort:

1. Did the movement or campaign achieve the material or tangible changes in law that were its primary goal and then follow up with steps to implement and embed those changes to protect them from countermovement responses?

2. In the internal dynamics of the movement or campaign, were there mechanisms for accountability and deliberation to create broad and diverse support within the relevant constituency or political group for its goals and strategies?

3. Did the work of the movement or campaign enhance the power and voice of those within its constituency?

4. Did the strategies of the movement or campaign include mechanisms to maintain mobilization and momentum for future efforts, including responses to possible backlash?

5. Did the overall effect of the work of the movement or campaign change the surrounding social culture as well as the law?

. . . The question of whether *Obergefell* survives in robust or only formalistic terms will probably turn on whether conservative religious groups can successfully draw on a sufficient institutional base for resistance, in a way comparable to how the public school administrative structure created the infrastructure that supported the efforts of Southern school officials to undercut desegregation plans. . . .

Looking to the Future

What the future holds for the structure of legal and political initiatives is unclear. The most difficult challenges for a social movement involve policy changes that would benefit persons perceived as most different from the white middle-class norm and that would entail redistribution of resources from those with more to those with less. The marriage equality campaign succeeded in surmounting the first of these barriers by renorming the LGB constituency to fit a conventional model of couples, and it did not confront redistribution questions.

In its structure, the marriage equality campaign may come to be seen as an early example of a particular type of social change effort: a methodologically versatile, professionally managed, expertise-rich, and well-funded public policy campaign with limited, measurable goals for change. . . .

As with the marriage campaign, the structures to which such efforts will be held accountable likely will not take the form of mass organizations with active memberships, but instead will consist of those with the resources to invest in the particular project. This continues a trend in which civil society organizations increasingly depend on professional staff with the diminishment of meaningful member involvement. Resource providers will include individual donors, charitable foundations, and other political actors of all ideological stripes—a sector of the public interest law world that likely will continue to accrue greater power and influence. Management of donors may become a standard part of a cause lawyer's job description. . . .

Social Meanings: The Battle for Discursive Space

. . . The process that emerged from ballot question elections related to LGBT rights provides a granular account of meaning construction. Elections became a laboratory for testing legal arguments, and, to a limited but noticeable extent, litigation strategy took on attributes of a political campaign.

. . . As we have seen, after the main focus of ballot questions turned to marriage, equality advocates shifted emphasis away from the rights arguments. . . . [T]hey constructed ads using a narrative structure that responded to emotions as much as ideas, using elements of narrativity—the creation of characters, the construction of a storytelling arc and the depiction of conflict being resolved.

The single most important communication change was the adoption of the "journey story," which became known as "J stories." J story ads featured family members and other non-gay messengers telling the story of how they changed their minds about same-sex marriage. The focus was less on the arguments and more on the process of changing one's mind. The speakers identified themselves with demographic groups not usually associated with predictably liberal positions: clergy members, Republicans, grandparents, elder veterans. J story ads became marriage equality's not so secret weapon.

. . . No recommendation from the communications research was more important to claims made either in litigation or popular discourse than the emphasis on the desire of same-sex couples to "join" marriage rather than alter it. . . . The primary brief in *Obergefell v. Hodges*, after arguing based on the experience of Massachusetts that "same-sex couples are strengthening marriage, not harming it," concludes with these words:

> [E]nding the exclusion of same-sex couples from the freedom to marry no more changes the nature of marriage than *Loving* did, and it no more changes the nature of marriage than women's suffrage changed voting or the end of segregation at lunch counters changed eating in public. . . .

Cultural Interest Convergence

Derrick Bell's insight that social and political gains for disadvantaged minorities are unlikely to occur unless the dominant majority perceives those gains to be in their self-interest has become one of the most powerful precepts in critical race theory. . . . With regard to marriage equality, the dominant interests being served are not necessarily material or political in the traditional sense. . . . Rather, the convergence is primarily cultural and discursive.

The processes for changing law and changing culture both involve the construction of meanings and of forging new conceptual paths for understanding our society, our places in it, and the consequences of our normative commitments. Interactions between law and culture prod us to generate new versions of "the stories we tell ourselves about who we are."

. . . What was at stake for the movable middle was the preservation of cultural norms and traditional practices, even as the institution of marriage was being democratized around them. In response, the Winning Marriage collaborators devised a strategy, based on cultural rather than logical principles of persuasion, that was designed to reassure moderate voters that these norms and practices were not being threatened. . . .

In their reconstruction of difference and sameness arguments, marriage equality advocates . . . enlisted in, or were swept into, a broader respectability politics, a term coined by historian Evelyn Higginbotham in describing the efforts of African American churchwomen roughly a hundred years ago. . . . [R]espectability is marked by the vision of households characterized by economic self-sufficiency and marital procreation, with an absence of other socially visible sexuality. . . .

. . . Same-sex marriage remained both radical and conservative to the end.

Conclusion

. . . The paradox of popular constitutionalism is that its grassroots, bottom-up focus . . . may drive a movement or campaign to adopt a safer, more conservative discursive strategy than [progressives] would wish.

The Supreme Court's decision in *Obergefell v. Hodges* did not change the legal meaning of marriage, but it did signal that a change had occurred in its social meaning. . . .

. . . Doctrinally, if not politically, securing access for same-sex couples to marriage was a modest step, the extension of what has long been recognized as a fundamental right. That it was modest does not mean that it was easy. What remains unsettling about the constitutional import of *Obergefell* is its . . . jurisprudence of sameness. This, perhaps, is what passes for civil rights in a post-civil rights world.

In this excerpt, Hunter recounts the difficult circumstances and choices that advocates and activists necessarily confronted in the campaign for marriage equality as the mechanisms and outputs of democracy and adjudication—both federal and state—shifted circumstances and possibilities. These hard choices are made more complex when decisional accountability to marginalized communities becomes attenuated. In an era of declining membership groups, professionalized decision making, and large-scale foundation funding, "respectability politics" designed for assimilation effectively determined tactics, strategies, and outcomes. These factors combined to ensure that "winning" marriage equality "remained both radical and conservative."

As Hunter makes clear, no easy or clear answers exist. Instead, collaborative, self-critical, give-and-take discussion is the best way to hash out the answers most conducive to solidarity and justice. These complex decisions include setting priorities, raising resources, and assembling organizational structures. Hard choices are rendered even more complex by the need for accountability, plus the inevitability of opposition and conflict that inhere in any collective struggle against normalized systems of injustice. Looking forward, do any linkages or patterns connect the marriage equality litigation "victory" to the historical experience with formal legal reform and preservation through transformation?

As we asked above: Who decided? Who benefitted? Who lost? Consider, in this vein, the Center for American Progress report by Aisha C. Moodie-

Mills. Published in 2012 while the campaign for marriage equality was at the center of sexual minority activism, this report examined "Why Black Gay and Transgender Americans Need More Than Marriage Equality:"

> [Many remaining questions] regarding black gay and transgender Americans . . . cannot be answered without robust data that highlight the intersections of race, economics, sexual orientation, and gender identity, and fully reflect what marginalized populations experience. . . .
>
> In short, black gay and transgender people fall through the cracks when lumped under either a gay or black umbrella. Such categorical thinking ignores the fact that black gay and transgender people are at once both gay and transgender and black. As a result they experience complex vulnerabilities that stem from the combination of racial bias and discrimination due to their sexual orientation and/ or gender identity. So advocacy agendas that prioritize the eradication of one bias over the other do not fully respond to the needs of the population—nor will they eliminate the inequities [of systemic injustice]. . . .
>
> By almost every measure, studies report that black gay and transgender Americans fare worse than their straight black and white gay and transgender counterparts when looking at indicators such as poverty rates, health care access, incidence of certain physical diseases and mental illnesses, and hate-crime rates. . . .
>
> . . . [R]ace, ethnicity, gender, poverty, and other characteristics marked by discrimination also matter, and must be addressed simultaneously [with tackling sexual orientation and gender identity discrimination] in order to achieve full equality for marginalized populations like black gay and transgender people who are impacted by multiple forms of oppression. . . .[15]

These findings show that marriage equality, by itself, does not relieve all the material, systemic problems that Black gay and trans people face every day. Not everyone is similarly situated with respect to the benefits and burdens of marriage equality. For many, other group priorities—including housing, employment, nutrition, and health came first, yet remain unfulfilled. So the questions persist: what was the point of achieving marriage equality? Was it an end in itself? Or was it also a means to something else? If so, what is that something else? In your view, is this "something else" being accomplished?

---

[15] https://cdn.americanprogress.org/wp-content/uploads/issues/2012/01/pdf/black_lgbt.pdf?_ga=2.67213714.2099831776.1613840323-554840379.1613840323.

In the legal industry, "success" generally is evaluated according to the volume of cases and win rates. But traditional quantitative measures of legal services programs may have dual outcomes: such measures may justify more investments in direct legal services for the poor but less investment in hard-to-measure, cause-related advocacy. Legal scholars Jane Aiken and Stephen Wizner explain why evaluating effectiveness requires nuanced metrics—and evaluating progress is even more challenging:

> [Q]uantifying the work of a lawyer is not easy. How do we ensure that any measure of justice captures outcomes for both trial-based advocacy and non-trial-based advocacy on behalf of clients, including negotiated outcomes? How do we quantify the role lawyers play in listening to our clients, explaining the systems in which they operate, and supporting them through often very difficult times in their lives? How do we ensure that any measure of justice includes a client's sense of the process as well as the outcome? . . .
>
> . . . [Lawyers for the poor] see beyond win/loss records to questions about whether the overall system ought to be improved to meet the needs of their clients. . . . Winning, in some cases, may meet the needs of the current client but not the needs of society as a whole. Measuring justice, therefore, becomes part of a larger question about structures themselves—changing the rules altogether. . . .
>
> . . . Most legal problems are not resolved on a binary, win-lose basis but rather through legal advice and counseling, negotiating agreements and settlements, and helping clients make difficult choices about what may or may not be achievable through formal legal actions. Constructing studies that capture this kind of legal assistance in human terms is both important and difficult. However, it is critical that we not embrace a methodology that flattens this rich, contextual understanding of justice. Using a win-loss methodology looks at legal services largely from the point of view of the lawyer. While legal services providers ought not be immune from evaluation of the success of their work, methods need to be employed that capture the experience from the client's perspective.[16]

This sketch only begins to show the complexity of bottom-up "progress" as social change: over time and using time, today's struggles (and their mixed results) are the basis for tomorrow's.

---

[16] Jane H. Aiken and Stephen Wizner, Measuring Justice, 2013 Wis. L. Rev. 79, 79–80, 82 (2013).

The following excerpt, by gay legal scholar Douglas NeJaime, adds to Hunter's account and Moodie-Mills' report. NeJaime further describes the marriage equality campaign and related struggles, and questions critically the meanings of "winning" and "losing"—and the relationship between the two—in social progress. If winning and losing are related to progress, then the meaning and metrics of progress must be tailored to the complexities of the context, action, and goals. To measure the "net" progress of groups at the bottom, how might advocates (and others) identify the best metrics to use?

WINNING THROUGH LOSING
Douglas NeJaime
96 Iowa L. Rev. 941 (2011)

Introduction

We live in a culture that prioritizes winning. We declare winners and losers, and we deem it fair and reasonable to distribute benefits based on that distinction: To the victor go the spoils. Perhaps nowhere is the continued articulation of the winner-loser distinction more apparent than in law. Litigation, every day, produces winners and losers—often in very public ways. Some parties prevail, and some do not. To the prevailing parties go a host of remedies, including money, injunctions, and declarations of rights. The losers, of course, submit to the winners, paying damages or ceasing some action.

In our winning-obsessed culture, it is not surprising that conventional legal analysis relies on a storyboard narrative in which a harmed party seeks and obtains judicial redress. The court, in this account, remedies the harm. Sociolegal scholars, however, have questioned whether events unfold this neatly in practice. Instead, litigation victories might be illusory. The win in court might fail to produce an adequate remedy. The remedy might never be effectively implemented or enforced, and the aggrieved party, who prevailed in court, might continue to suffer harm. Many scholars have observed favorable judicial decisions without similarly favorable outcomes on the ground. One might win in court and still lose in life.

But, claim some of these scholars, winning is still desirable. Even if the change promised by the court never materializes, multiple benefits—both tangible and intangible—might nonetheless accrue to the winners.... Court victories may lend legitimacy to a cause, mobilize constituents, and provide much-needed publicity. Litigation wins may also generate elite support, pressure adversaries, and increase a social movement's bargaining power.

... Our preoccupation with winning and our assumption that the winner-loser divide governs the distribution of tangible and intangible assets blind us to the function of loss....

Litigation loss may, counterintuitively, produce winners. When savvy advocates lose in court, they may nonetheless configure the loss in ways that result in productive social movement effects and lead to more effective reform strategies. Loss may yield many of the indirect effects that scholars have identified in the context of litigation victory and litigation process, but it may do so in ways that are uniquely tied to loss itself. A range of social movement tactics, aimed at a variety of audiences, may draw strength from litigation loss precisely because such loss demonstrates and documents the limitations of court-centered change. . . .

The Limitations and Possibilities of Court-Centered Strategies

. . . [A] central question revolves around whether—and if so, how—court-centered strategies can in fact bring about such change. . . . While many scholars agree on the limited ability of courts themselves to produce significant reform, the question of productive indirect effects splits sociolegal scholars along not just empirical, but also theoretical and methodological, lines. . . .

Constrained Courts and the Empty Promise of Litigation

Scholars who argue that litigation is an ineffective vehicle for social reform point to several constraints that courts (and strategies reliant on courts) face. As . . . part of a dominant legal culture with an interest in maintaining the status quo, judges understand the political and professional risks of departing from accepted norms. More concretely, the ability of judges to break new ground is constrained by precedent and (for all but Supreme Court Justices) the prospect of reversal.

In addition . . . [c]ourts may be reluctant to contravene perceived community and legislative preferences. . . .

Even where courts manage to overcome key constraints and order significant social reform, they often lack adequate independent power to ensure that such reform materializes. Courts may need help from other actors, particularly ground-level administrators, to implement and enforce their decisions. Through tactics ranging from stalling and withholding necessary funds to overt opposition and defiance, those resistant to the decision can make realization of the court's ordered reform exceedingly difficult.

Scholars who adhere to this pessimistic view of courts point to the Supreme Court's *Brown v. Board of Education* decision as a paradigmatic example of litigation's failed promise. Even though this decision followed in a line of desegregation and racial-equality decisions, it met with intense resistance from both elites and ordinary citizens. . . .

The Positive Indirect Effects of Litigation

Many sociolegal scholars, particularly in the legal mobilization and cause lawyering fields, offer a compelling counternarrative to the pessimistic account of court-centered change. Although they identify tangible benefits that courts often bestow on subordinated groups, to a certain extent these scholars agree with the claim that courts themselves often fail to directly produce significant social reform. That is, scholars who redeem the power of litigation recognize the limitations of courts and acknowledge the constraints courts face in attempting to directly bring about social change but focus on the positive indirect benefits that movements gain from court-centered strategies....

... For instance, while *Brown* may not have produced the desired remedial action, scholars who stress the indirect benefits of litigation credit *Brown* with fueling a powerful social movement by raising consciousness, driving fundraising, legitimizing a cause, and influencing other state actors. This competing account of *Brown* turns away from the "myth of rights," in which lawyers naïvely rely on courts to bring about social reform, and instead turns toward ... the "politics of rights," in which lawyers seize on the political nature of rights. This approach decouples success from the implementation and enforcement of judicial orders and focuses on the discursive and political power of courts' pronouncements.

... [There are] a variety of important benefits that litigation—from the mere act of litigating to a favorable judicial decision—produces. I characterize these benefits as internal (those relating to the movement itself) and external (those relating to the movement's interactions with outside actors)....

Building a Theoretical Framework for an Analysis of Litigation Loss

The dispute over the effects of social-change litigation is more than just an empirical one.

Turning Courts' Constraints on Their Head

... Litigation loss shapes advocates' strategies. Advocates do not simply turn away from courts and erase what happened there; instead, they cultivate the loss to advance the complex process of reform....

... [A]dvocates use the limits of court-based strategies to advance their social movement agenda. Both the inherent constraints of courts and the limitations of court-based strategies may actually become part of an optimistic account of litigation for social change....

Contextualizing Litigation Loss in the Legal Mobilization Framework

... Social movement lawyers recognize the process of law and social change as complex, dynamic, and interactive. Accordingly, they [engage in] "multidimensional advocacy"—advocacy that relies on a variety of tactics deployed in multiple institutional domains across all levels of government.... [C]ontemporary social movement lawyers do not trust that courts, on their own, will bring about reform. They ... appreciate the importance of policy formation emanating from nonjudicial channels. These advocates cultivate the political potential of rights-claiming tactics by seizing on moments across the full spectrum of litigation—from filing to process to outcome, including both victory and defeat.

The multidimensional-advocacy framework is central to an appreciation of the function of litigation loss. Rather than invest all hope and resources in litigation, social movement advocates treat litigation loss as a routine part of their social-change campaigns. They plan for wins and losses and use losses to shape strategies in other venues. Significantly, ... they continue to view litigation as an essential, but partial, strategy....

The Productive Potential of Litigation Loss

... It is important to note that I address the mobilization of loss as a strategy of necessity. Advocates may take cases they suspect they might lose, but they nonetheless hope (and attempt) to win. These advocates then react to the loss by reconfiguring the result in productive ways and by drawing lessons from the failed litigation. In this sense, strategies developed in the wake of loss operate as second-best alternatives—as responses to the failure of the initial tactic....

Internal Effects

Constructing Organizational Identity

... [L]itigation loss may be constitutive of organizational identity and may, counterintuitively, contribute to an organization's stature and longevity within a movement.... [O]rganizational representatives may use loss, at least in the early years of the organization's life, to stake out a position in a competitive social movement....

Contextualizing Organizational Identity

... A concerted Christian Right litigation campaign emerged from the larger political and cultural movement in the 1990s.... [A] handful or organizations ... command the bulk of financial resources, lead most high-profile litigation, and pride themselves on their courtroom victories....

Many smaller legal organizations are still staking out their identities in this broader movement. TMLC [The Thomas More Law Center], founded in 1999, is a prime example.... The organization was founded by a

Catholic donor, Tom Monaghan, whereas most other prominent Christian Right legal organizations have been directed by evangelical Protestant groups. And with its base in Ann Arbor, Michigan, TMLC finds itself removed geographically from traditional (coastal) centers of power.... [But] TMLC's willingness to take on hot-button issues that go to the core of constituents' worldviews, and to do so despite relatively slim odds of success, has been key to forming its identity.

Loss in Court

TMLC loses at a higher rate than other significant Christian Right legal organizations and demonstrates a willingness to address and embrace litigation loss, rather than to sweep it under the rug and move on.... [From data on court results,] TMLC had a success rate of 35%....

While TMLC certainly hopes and attempts to win, it has a tendency to take on relatively weak cases that other firms might decline.... In representing conservative Christian parents in the school-programming domain, TMLC most often challenges school districts that implement progressive programming relating to sex, sexuality, sexual orientation, gender identity, and non-Western religions. In representing school districts, TMLC often defends implementation of science programming that challenges the primacy of evolution. Given the relatively settled legal principles governing both sets of cases, it becomes clear that TMLC represents parties (whether parents or school districts) in disputes where those parties have a relatively minor chance of success. But with these cases, TMLC has staked out a specialty among Christian Right legal organizations, and it has done so on a hot-button issue—school programming—that strikes at the core of movement constituents' beliefs and concerns....

In soliciting donations for his organization, Thompson situated TMLC's litigation efforts within broader cultural struggles. His fundraising pitch at the end of 2008 depicted Christians at war with "non-believers" (both secularists and Muslims)....

... Thompson relies on an image of the judiciary as an elitist and politically unaccountable institution out of touch with mainstream American values.

Yet he paints continued litigation as necessary, even if it does not produce social change in the near future.... In taking on school-curriculum challenges, and often losing, TMLC lawyers portray themselves as the lone defenders of religious parents—warriors committed to a long-term battle....

Mobilizing Constituents, Building Resolve, and Fundraising

... When a court validates a claim, the group's claim enjoys the legitimacy that comes with the state's approval. When a court rejects the group's claim, however, the demand that the legal claim embodies might be made more pressing and the deprivation more acute. That is, denial of the claim might serve to highlight more intensely the injustice suffered by the group. While victory might signal that continued or increased activism is no longer necessary, loss might incentivize more aggressive organization and advocacy....

... [T]his phenomenon emerged in the wake of marriage-equality losses in state supreme courts. For example, after the Washington Supreme Court overturned two lower-court decisions recognizing same-sex couples' right to marry, Lambda Legal lawyers framed the defeat in a way that contextualized it historically to both reassure and motivate constituents. Jennifer Pizer, now Director of Lambda Legal's Marriage Project, explained that her firm was "disappointed but not discouraged" and declared that "time is on our side." Relying on a model of "prophetic litigation," Pizer announced that "[h]istory has shown that in cases of this magnitude the opinions of the dissenting justices later become the law of the land."

Loss, rather than the litigation itself, crystallizes the deprivation of rights and the unequal treatment that the movement is fighting....

... [In this way,] movement leaders may use an official, published, and publicized instantiation of unfair treatment to raise consciousness and mobilize constituents.... Defeat announces that the fight must go on, that more resources are necessary, more citizens are required, and more time is needed. Advocates tap into a historical narrative of "prophetic litigation," but they do so for immediate social movement purposes.

External Effects

Appealing to Other State Actors

In the wake of a litigation loss, advocates might shift venues at the same time that they use the loss to render more compelling the appeal to decision makers in these new venues.... [T]wo significant shifts [are]: (1) shifts across levels of government, e.g., from federal to state-based activism and (2) shifts across branches of government, e.g., from courts to legislative and executive officials.

Shifts Across Levels of Government

Loss in the U.S. Supreme Court, or more generally in the federal courts, might prompt a reworked strategy that focuses on state-based venues. In this sense, litigation loss might lead to a critical rethinking of tactics that may ultimately yield a more robust and effective movement. More significantly, though, advocates may use the federal litigation loss to encourage players at the state level to act. The loss itself may specifically aid the appeal to the targets of the new tactics.... In this sense, a two-way street exists between the federal and state levels of government. The LGBT-rights movement again provides relevant examples.

. . . The decades-long fight against Florida's blanket ban on adoption by lesbians and gay men provides a more recent illustration of the shift from federal to state venues and the use of federal litigation loss to advocate in these new venues. In the early 1990s, LGBT-rights advocates pursued state litigation aimed at invalidating the Florida law. While they experienced mixed results at the trial-court level, the Florida Supreme Court ultimately refused to overturn the ban. But after the larger movement's success in *Lawrence* [*v. Texas*], Florida advocates had new and compelling federal case law on which to build a federal challenge to the ban. To these advocates' dismay, the Eleventh Circuit Court of Appeals, in *Lofton v. Secretary of the Department of Children & Family Services*, rejected the challenge and held that the ban was rationally related to legitimate governmental interests. The U.S. Supreme Court denied certiorari. Advocates then faced the prospect of returning to state venues in an attempt to overturn the law.

During the [federal] *Lofton* litigation, advocates did not pursue state legislative efforts to repeal the adoption ban. Lawyers leading the federal-court challenge advised against such activism, instead seeking to preserve their argument that the ban represented a 1970s-era law that garnered little modern support. In this sense, advocates sought to deliberately isolate courts based on their understanding of courts' relationship to other lawmaking institutions. . . . [M]ovement advocates seized on this [judicial loss] to demand legislative reform. In the wake of *Lofton*, Equality Florida, a state-based LGBT-rights legislative-advocacy organization, urged legislators to act and eventually obtained its first legislative hearing on repealing the adoption ban. . . .

. . . While legislative work failed to achieve repeal of the adoption ban, activism in the state courts continued to work in conjunction with state legislative efforts. . . . LGBT-rights lawyers in Florida turned to state-court judges, urging them to use state-law grounds, some of which the Florida Supreme Court had not considered, to remedy the injustice perpetrated by *Lofton*.

In 2008, two trial-court judges invalidated the ban, and the Florida Court of Appeal recently affirmed one of those decisions. At the trial-court level, Judge Cindy Lederman relied on novel state-law grounds, finding that the law violated children's right to permanency as expressed in Florida's statutory regulations on adoption. Then, in accepting the equal-protection claim, Judge Lederman situated *Lofton* as out of date, given the volume of intervening studies on the effects of sexual orientation on parenting. Rather than view *Lofton* as controlling on the equal-protection analysis, Judge Lederman explained that the issue of whether Florida's adoption ban violates equal-protection guarantees, whether under the state or federal constitution, "is again ripe for consideration." The state court staked out an independent role, at the urging of social movement lawyers, in the ongoing interpretation and articulation of general constitutional guarantees, and offered a compelling counternarrative to the federal court's earlier reasoning.

In affirming Judge Lederman's ruling, the Florida District Court of Appeal relied exclusively on state equal-protection grounds. After explaining that the Florida Supreme Court left open the equal-protection issue in its 1995 decision, the court found no rational basis for the discriminatory treatment of lesbians and gay men in the adoption context. Florida Governor Charlie Crist responded to the appellate court ruling by announcing that the state would stop enforcing the discriminatory law, and the Florida Department of Children and Families made clear that it would not appeal the ruling. . . . LGBT-rights advocates hailed the end of the adoption ban.

Shifts Across Branches of Government

In addition to shifts across levels of government, advocates use litigation loss to shape shifts across branches of government. . . .

The women's-rights movement, in which legal defeats have spurred legislative reform, provides a useful starting point. Elizabeth Schneider shows how after women's-rights advocates failed to convince the Supreme Court to treat pregnancy discrimination as a sex-equality issue, Congress passed the Pregnancy Discrimination Act, which adopted the exact legal arguments advocates had made in court. In her work on demosprudence, Guinier documents the pay-equity issue as a more recent example from the women's-rights movement. After *Ledbetter v. Goodyear Tire & Rubber Co.*, in which the Supreme Court rejected an equal-pay claim under Title VII based on a constrained reading of filing deadlines, Congress and the President acted quickly to remedy the issue. Movement advocates successfully demonstrated that the Court's failure to recognize the employment-based injustice necessitated legislative and executive action. . . . While in both of these instances advocates would have preferred to prevail in court, they were able to positively use the litigation losses to achieve the movement's goals by other means. . . .

Appealing to the Public

Just as litigation victory may help a movement sell its cause to the public, litigation loss may ironically have a similar effect. . . . This tactic has been especially effective when advocates urge the public to use the initiative process to overturn a judicial decision. . . .

Conclusion

This Article . . . attests to the ways in which social movement advocates use litigation to mobilize constituents, influence decision makers, and convince the public to support their cause. . . .

Operating across a range of institutional settings, systemic advocates deploy litigation as merely one of several available tactics. In this mix, litigation can help publicize and mobilize organized resistance to systemic injustice. And, as NeJaime emphasizes, *even a loss* in adjudication can become the springboard for collective action that can generate desired wins through democracy. This approach to advocacy expands not only the meaning, but also the metrics, of progress; these metrics must be measured contextually from the bottom. NeJaime's analysis compels critical, contextual reconsideration of winning and losing in all advocacy.

Moreover, developments in one context may affect developments in other contexts, whether for better or worse. Even when "rights" are recognized, their very recognition raises new issues; rights on paper, as we have seen, can be gutted or taken back. NeJaime's excerpt thus underscores how every gain—or loss—necessarily sets the stage for a next round of struggle.

Set against this backdrop, legal historian Rabia Belt lays down a challenge in next-generation marriage equality advocacy: marriage equality for disabled individuals. As in other identity contexts, marriage law in this context enforces exclusion, disempowerment, and stigmatization. This group, Belt argues, personifies "the last marriage equality frontier." As you read, can you think of other groups or frontiers relevant to equal justice for *all* in family and marriage law?

DISABILITY: THE LAST MARRIAGE EQUALITY FRONTIER
Rabia Belt
Stanford Public Law Working Paper No. 2653117 (Aug. 29, 2015)

Introduction

Jim Obergefell and John Arthur never expected to become gay activists. Yet the case that bears their name has dramatically advanced the marriage equality movement for gay couples. What has drawn less attention is the fact that *Obergefell* is also a case about disability: Arthur's struggle with Lou Gehrig's disease triggered their marriage and subsequent discrimination. Turning our attention about marriage equality from sexual orientation to disability, we find a landscape rife with discrimination: federal and state law continues to rest upon a longstanding foundation of cultural stereotypes and animus. Marriage for people with disabilities remains the last marriage equality frontier.

Eugenic Origins

Discouraging the marriages of people with disabilities is longstanding and stretches before the federal statutory system penalizing marriage. Historically, cultural stereotypes [have] either desexualized people with disabilities or deemed their sexuality as dangerous. The legal system has followed these social edicts.

As far back as 1846, "no insane person or idiot" was allowed to marry. Over 30 states passed legislation that called for involuntary sterilization of people with disabilities. This practice was enshrined and endorsed in the notorious 1927 Supreme Court decision of *Buck v. Bell*. Over 65,000 people with disabilities were involuntarily sterilized. Some states still have not removed their laws disallowing marriage and reproduction among people with disabilities from the books.

... [Moreover, c]urrently, there are no group homes designed to support married couples with developmental disabilities. ...

Parenting

Over 4 million parents of children under the age of 18 have disabilities. Parents and aspiring parents with disabilities face numerous barriers in the legal system, from disproportionate loss of custody, difficulty adopting children, disparate impact of the Adoption and Safe Families Act of 1997 (ASFA), and lack of use of the Americans with Disabilities Act [ADA].

In 37 states and the District of Columbia, parents with disabilities can have their custodial rights terminated on the mere basis of having a disability. Additionally, 32 states (30 by statute and 2 by case law) and the District of Columbia consider disability as a factor in a custody determination. Only Maine, South Dakota, and Vermont do not consider disability as a factor for both custody determinations and termination of parental rights. The removal rates for parents with a psychiatric disability can reach as high as 70 to 80 percent. Removal rates for parents with intellectual disabilities range from 40 to 80 percent. Thirteen percent of parents with physical disabilities also report discriminatory treatment.

In a custody termination or determination proceeding, the best interests of the child comprise the ultimate criterion. ... A divorce or post-divorce action or a referral from the police, a social services agency, or a mandatory reporter may bring before a judge the question who has the right to have what sort of custody of a child.

... Every state allows the consideration of disability for determining the best interests of a child and nearly every state includes disability as a ground for terminating parental rights. Most states follow the Uniform

Marriage and Divorce Act, which uses "the mental and physical health of all individuals involved" as a determining factor.

Disability can bear on this process in any of at least three stages. First, a judge may find a parent unfit because the parent has a disability. Second, the judge may find a parent unfit for an independent reason but restrict the parent's custody because the parent has a disability. Third, the judge may order that the parent take some rehabilitative action (*e.g.*, take a parenting class) which the parent cannot take because of her disability. . . .

Courts rarely use the ADA when determining the parental rights of people with disabilities, despite the ADA mandate requiring that public entities make reasonable accommodations for people with disabilities. . . . Agencies lack training and procedures for dealing with parents with disabilities. . . . Rather than utilizing the ADA to enable help for parents with disabilities, instead, disabilities are used against these parents to remove their children. Due to stigma, discrimination, and the lack of training for agency contacts, parents . . . fear losing their children because of their disability if they get divorced, [and] they will stay in problematic or abusive marriages. . . .

Conclusion

Justice Kennedy, in writing the *Obergefell* opinion for the majority, said of marriage that, "Its dynamic allows two people to find a life that could not be found alone, for a marriage becomes greater than just the two persons. Rising from the most basic human needs, marriage is essential to our most profound hopes and aspirations." The lack of protection for and facilitation of marriages for people with disability causes dignitary and financial harm. Marriage and sex provide positive health benefits. Marriage in particular is protective of mental and physical health. *Obergefell* emphasizes the importance of marriage for dignity and emotional well-being as well as recognizing all the economic and legal benefits that accrue to marriage. Families with disabilities should also [be equally protected in marriage and family relations].

Belt makes clear that disabled persons as a group, including members of sexual minorities, have received little attention in marriage equality struggles. Formal marriage equality is a significant achievement for any group—and yet not enough to satisfy the standards of equal justice for *all*. Does formal marriage equality replicate the pros and cons of formal equality more generally?

NOTES AND QUESTIONS

1. *Formal Legal Equality—Cross-Race and Same-Sex Marriages.* In 1967, *Loving v. Virginia* recognized the equality of cross-race unions. Over four

decades later, *Obergefell* did the same for same-sex unions. In light of the race experience since *Loving*, what do you expect formal legal equality to mean for LGBTQ communities? How does formal marriage equality make a difference (or not) for the lived material reality of identity-based communities? What are the lessons from the post-*Brown* experience we reviewed earlier? Do any apply here? Why and how—or why not?

2. *Seizing the Critical Challenge.* Although NeJaime writes before *Obergefell*, how would you describe the principal takeaways for advocates from NeJaime's discussion of winning, losing, and progress in light of *Obergefell*? Based on your readings thus far, is NeJaime's "multidimensional" framework unique to bottom-up advocacy for systemic justice, or have those same insights and tactics been used—top-down—to preserve identity caste systems? What metrics should advocates adopt now for measuring social progress (or regress) post-*Obergefell*?

3. *The Next Frontier.* Belt described disability as the last marriage equality frontier. If so, what "next steps" should the LGBTQ "movement" prioritize? Who should determine those priorities? What are the challenges in developing organized group representation for disabled individuals or others who make up part of any "new frontier"? What levels of activism and advocacy—local, state, national, international—might be targeted for action, and what forums—courts, legislatures, "public opinion," or other—might prove important? How can advocates anticipate and prepare for opposition? See generally Timothy Stewart-Winter, After Marriage Equality, What? (Fall 2015), www.dissentmagazine.org/article/lgbt-politics-marriage-equality-what-next.

4. *Losing Wins.* Hunter's excerpt above describes two strategy documents that "won" the litigation outcome in *Obergefell*. Immediately after that outcome, the campaign coalition announced its disbanding and shutdown. Even then, the religious liberty claim was poised to invalidate that win and to repeat (in this context) the historical process of preservation through transformation. Keeping NeJaime's account also in mind, jump to now, several years later: if the same organizations and funders that created Winning Marriage I and Winning Marriage II were reconvened, what should they do proactively to avoid the loose claims of religious liberty that render formal marriage equality hollow?

5. *Progress for Transgender Families in Law and Society.* The *Obergefell* decision did not, in itself, achieve actual marriage equality. To illustrate further, Lambda Legal's Transgender Rights Toolkit lays out examples of ongoing problems affecting transgender families:

> Some courts will continue to challenge certain parent-child relationships.
>
> Not all state or local officials provide a marriage license that reflects a person's gender identity.

> Many states only have marriage licenses and certificates with "bride" and "groom" language, which may not be relevant for all couples.
>
> Some officials may insist that a person's name and gender be registered according to what is listed on identity documents, even when the information is no longer accurate.
>
> None of these scenarios affect the validity of a marriage, but some may have the effect of outing people, and parenting disputes often have serious repercussions.[17]

Sometimes, the ongoing, somewhat plodding work of turning high-profile wins into real-world change is dismissed as "routine" and unimportant. So advocates affirmatively must prioritize the follow-up work necessary to implement and protect big victories—work which often is left undone or is underfunded and patchy in nature. This continuing need to monitor, defend, and advance formal legal wins is both practical and fundamental, prompting, for example, advocates around the country to establish local funds that turn frontline activists and community groups into human or labor "rights monitors." This example is just that: can you identify other ways of implementing equality in marriage-related contexts for all groups?

4.4 MANAGING RISK, PRIVILEGE, AND TIME IN ORGANIZED LONG-TERM STRUGGLES

As the next chapter details further, systemic advocates learn to convert identities into antisubordination assets to help diminish preservation through transformation, and as seen above they craft metrics to measure progress. In doing so, advocates navigate multiple risks and tensions, including those arising from the privileged (yet limited) status of lawyers. Advocates find themselves being "insiders" in the legal system—where existing rules operate—and "outsiders" disrupting and reshaping those rules. This duality creates an inherently ambiguous position for law-trained advocates—aiming both for effectiveness and for deep alliance with subordinated groups. This duality requires lawyer-advocates to check customary professional privileges and to practice solidarity as guided from the bottom. Gary Bellow, a longtime advocate and legal scholar, reflected on these tensions as part of "political lawyering," an advocacy Approach informed by an "oppositionist" vision:

> [A] word needs to be said about a surprisingly neglected aspect of political work in law: relations with power holders. Power holders include a wide array of individuals—judges, legislators, city council members, opposing counsel, contending parties, colleagues, and allies. What makes these relationships so central

---

[17] Transgender People and Marriage Laws, Chapter XIII, Trans Toolkit, www.lambdalegal.org/sites/default/files/transgender_booklet_-_marriage.pdf.

to what I understand as political lawyering is the change-oriented focus of the enterprise. . . . [T]here were times when we bargained and argued only for marginal positional gains, increased negotiating leverage, or some public relations advantage. . . . But we were always pursuing larger aims: a genuine changing of minds or an enduring alteration of the circumstances in which the conflicts arose. Whatever else the enterprise embodied, the social goals we were seeking reached not only across large numbers of people, but from their present into some altered version of the future.

Relations with power holders are surely the source of many of the most complex tensions in this kind of work. Lawyers engaged in politicized efforts spend a great deal of time with adversaries and, if they do their job well, even more time talking and trying to understand them. We "work" the systems in which we lobby and litigate. We nurture relationships, search for coalitions, and worry about polarization and retaliation against ourselves and our clients.

. . . Sometimes, such efforts are the beginning of a seductive process that turns us into political power brokers, rather than loyal allies, in the struggles that we joined. Nowhere are the ambiguous roles lawyers play in the "fights of others" more sharply focused than when they work in the worlds of their adversaries and the power holders to whom they, as legal strategists, must often appeal. . . .

Faced with the dilemma of outsider ineffectiveness and insider ambivalence, the best of us have become less impatient with ambiguity, more realistic about the disrepair and disarray likely to be found on any road to change, and much more appreciative of what knowledge and influence within the status quo offers to outsiders if it can be genuinely shared with and used by them.[18]

Bellow highlights "the relations of power"—the systemic politics—that legal advocacy for transformation faces. These relations afford privileges and impose risks. They create "complex tensions" advocates must navigate.

Like Bellow, philosopher Cornel West calls upon lawyers to situate themselves critically as both systemic insiders *and* outsiders. West urges legal professionals to take calculated risks to use their insider power to make space for outsider agendas. Although advocates often use their systemic power in "defensive" work, West notes this work must be designed simultaneously to propel "social motion"—organized group struggles that

---

[18] Gary Bellow, Steady Work: A Practitioner's Reflections on Political Lawyering, 31 Harv. C.R.-C.L. L. Rev. 297 (1996).

THE ROLE OF LAW IN PROGRESSIVE POLITICS
Cornel West
43 Vand. L. Rev. 1797 (1990)

What is the role and function of the law in contemporary progressive politics? Do legal institutions represent crucial terrain on which significant social change can take place? If so, how? . . .

. . . My argument rests upon three basic claims. First, the fundamental forms of social misery in American society neither can be adequately addressed nor substantially transformed within the context of existing legal apparatus structures. Serious and committed work within this circumscribed context, however, remains indispensable if progressive politics is to have any future at all. Second, this crucial work will be primarily defensive unless significant extraparliamentary social motion brings power and pressure to bear on the prevailing status quo. Social motion and movements presuppose either grass roots citizen participation in credible progressive projects or rebellious acts of desperation that threaten the social order. Third, progressive legal practitioners confront the difficult task of linking their defensive work within the legal system to possible social motion and movements that attempt fundamentally to transform American society.

Any argument regarding the role of law in progressive politics must begin with two sobering facts about past and present American history. First, American society is disproportionately shaped by the outlooks, interests, and aims of the business community, especially corporate America. The extraordinary influence of corporate capital on our government and its legal institutions makes it difficult even to imagine a free and democratic society with publicly accountable mechanisms that alleviate the vast disparities in resources, wealth, and income. Those who focus on forms of social misery—like hunger, poverty, and homelessness—must think in epochal, not apocalyptic, terms.

The second brute fact about the American past and present is its chronically racist, sexist, homophobic, and jingoistic nature. The complex and tortuous quest for American identity from 1776 to the present has produced a culture in which people primarily define themselves in terms of race, gender, sexual orientation, and political activities. America's uniqueness among other modern nations—with the exceptions of South Africa and Hitler's Germany—is that race has served as the linchpin in regulating its quest for identity. . . . The historical articulation and impact of African slavery and Jim Crowism on forms of American patriarchy, homophobia, and anti-American (usually communist and socialist) repression and surveillance yield a profoundly conservative culture.

The irony of this cultural conservatism is that it tries to preserve a highly dynamic, corporate-driven economy; a stable, election-centered democracy; and a precious liberties-guarding rule of law....

My first point is that the extension of American liberalism in response to racial, class, and sexual equality is desirable but insufficient. It is insufficient because the extension of American liberalism leaves relatively untouched the fundamental cause of social misery—the maldistribution of resources, wealth, and power in American society. Yet the extension of American liberalism with regard to race, labor, gender, and homosexuality appears to be radical on the American ideological spectrum principally because it challenges America's deeply entrenched cultural conservatism. In fact, this extension, as seen for example in the 1930s [New Deal programs] and 1960s [civil right laws], occurs through insurgent social motion and movements that convince political and legal elites to enact legislation or judicial decrees against the will of the majority of the population.

The law has played a crucial role in those periods in which liberalism has been extended. It has done so precisely because of the power of judicial review and an elected body of officials responding to social movements—not because cultural conservatism had diminished significantly....

If the extension of American liberalism is the only feasible radical option within American political culture, then the defensive role of progressive lawyers becomes even more important. Their work constitutes one of the few buffers against cultural conservatism that recasts the law in its own racist, sexist, antilabor, and homophobic image. Furthermore, defensive work within the existing legal system helps keep alive memory traces left by past progressive movements of resistance—memory traces requisite for future movements. This defensive work, though possibly radical in intent, is liberal in practice in that it proceeds from within the legal system in order to preserve the effects of former victories threatened by the conservative offensive. This same defensive work has tremendous radical potential, especially within the context of vital oppositional activity against the status quo. Thus, the distinction between liberal and radical legal practice is not sharp and rigid; rather, it is fluid and contingent on the ever-changing, larger social situation. Clearly, the crucial role of this kind of legal practice, be it to defend the rights of activists, secure permits to march, or dramatize an injustice with a class action suit, is indispensable for progressive politics. In "cold" moments of American history, however, when cultural conservatism and big business fuse with power and potency, radical lawyers have little option other than defensive work. This work, although often demoralizing, serves as an important link to past victories and as a basis for the next wave of radical action.

... Can progressive legal practice be anything more than defensive? My second point holds that there are but two ways out of this labyrinth. In situations of sparse resources, degraded self-images, and depoliticized sensibilities, one avenue for poor people is rebellion and anarchic expression. The capacity to produce social chaos is the last resort of desperate people. It results from a tragic quest for recognition and survival. The civil terrorism and criminality that haunt our city streets partly are poor people's response to political neglect and social invisibility. Like most behavior in American society, this anarchic expression is linked directly to market activity—the sale and purchase of commodities. The commodities tend to be drugs, alcohol, and the human body itself. These tragic forms of expression have yet to take on an explicitly political character, yet they may in the near future. If and when the situation becomes political, the prevailing powers will be forced to make political responses—not simply legal ones that lead to prison overcrowding.

One major challenge for progressive politics is to find a way of channeling the poor's talent and energy into forms of social motion that can have impact on the ruling powers. This second way out of the impasse is the promotion of citizens' organized participation in credible progressive projects. Yet, the American political culture militates against this. The status quo lives and thrives on the perennial radical dilemma of disbelief: ordinary citizens find it hard to believe that their actions can make a difference when resources, wealth, and power disproportionately are held by the corporate community....

There can be no substantive progressive politics beyond the extension of American liberalism without social motion or movements. Moreover, despite the symbolic and cathartic electoral victories of liberal women and people of color, all remain thoroughly shackled by corporate economic priorities and debt-ridden administrations. Under such conditions, the plight of the ill-fed, ill-clad, and ill-housed only can worsen.

Given the lethargic electoral system—nearly exhausted of progressive potential, though never to be ignored as possible conservative politicians lust for more power—we must look toward civil society, especially to the mass media, universities, religious and political groupings, and trade unions, for social motion. Despite the decline of popular mobilization, political participation, and unionization, there still exists a vital and vibrant culture industry, religious life, student community, and labor movement. In the midst of a market-driven culture of consumption—with its spectators passivity, evasive banality, and modes of therapeutic release—there is an increasing sense of social concern and political engagement. These inchoate progressive sentiments search for an effective mode of organized expression. Until channels are created for these inchoate sentiments legal progressive practice will remain primarily defensive.

How do we create these channels of resistance and contestation to corporate power? What positive messages can we offer? What programs can we put forward? These questions lead to my third point regarding the lawyer's role in progressive politics. In a society that suffers increasingly from historical amnesia—principally because of the dynamic past-effacing activities of market forces—lawyers have close contact with the concrete traces and residues of past progressive struggles. . . .

The role of progressive lawyers not only is to engage in crucial defensive practices—a liberal practice within the court system—but also to preserve, recast, and build on the traces and residues of past conflicts. This latter activity is guided by a deep historical sensibility. This sensibility not only deconstructs the contradictory character of past and present legal decisions (or demystifies the power relations operative in such decisions), but also concocts powerful and enabling narratives that demonstrate how these decisions constitute the kind of society in which we live and how people resist and try to transform it. Progressive lawyers can become politically engaged narrativists who tell analytically illuminating stories of how the law has impeded or impelled struggles for justice and freedom. Like the best rap artists, progressive lawyers can energize a demoralized citizenry with insights on the historical origins and present causes of social misery. Lawyers can perform this role more easily than others because of their prestige and authority in American society. Progressive lawyers can seize this opportunity to highlight the legal system's internal contradictions and blatant hypocrisy, using the very ideals—fairness, protection, formal equality—it heralds. This kind of progressive legal practice, narrative in character and radical in content, can give visibility and legitimacy to issues neglected by and embarrassing to conservative administrations and can educate citizens on the operations of economic and political powers in the courts. . . .

Without this kind of historical consciousness and analytical storytelling, it is difficult to create channels for resistance and challenge to corporate power. In addition, those who challenge that power must emphasize the moral character of past and present leaders and followers who cared, sacrificed, and risked their lives and reputations for the struggle of justice and freedom. Progressive lawyers must reveal the ethical motivations of those who initiated and promoted the legal victories that furthered the struggles for racial, sexual, and class equality within the limiting parameters of American law.

The Critical Legal Studies [CLS] movement is significant primarily because it introduces for the first time in legal discourse a profoundly historical approach and theoretical orientation that outlines simultaneously the brutal realities of class exploitation, racial subordination, patriarchal domination, homophobic marginalization, and ecological abuse in American history....

Legal formalism, legal positivism, and even legal realism have remained relatively silent about the brutal realities of the American past and present. This silence has forced American liberalism for the most part to remain captive to cultural conservatism. It also has limited radical alternatives in legal studies to extensions of American liberalism. The grand breakthrough of the CLS movement is to expose the intellectual blinders of American liberal legal scholarship and to link these blinders to the actual blood that has flowed because of the hidden realities. CLS calls attention to the human costs paid by those who suffer under the institutional arrangements sanctioned by liberal law in the name of formal equality and liberty.

Yet CLS cannot be more than a progressive movement within a slice of the professional managerial stratum without connections to other social motions....

... To avoid illusions one must sustain hope for social change by keeping alive the memory of past and present efforts and victories and remaining engaged in such efforts ... for the wretched of the earth and those who fight to enhance their plight. In America, this memory and morality consists of recurring cycles of collective insurgency and violent repression, social upsurge and establishmentarian containment. Because of the powers of big business and cultural conservatism, the American left is weak and feeble during periods of social stability. Usually led by charismatic spokespersons, American radicalism surfaces in the form of social movements contesting this stability with a moral message that borrows from the Nation's collective self-definition (as democratic and free). These social movements change the prevailing status quo, but rarely rearrange fundamentally the corporate priorities of American society ... because of repression and incorporation. After such social movements, American radicalism is relegated to a defensive posture, trying to preserve its victories by defending extensions of American liberalism.

... [T]he major role of the law in progressive politics is threefold. First, past victories encoded in the law must be preserved in order to keep alive the memory of the past, the struggle in the present, and the hope for the future. Second, this preservation, though liberal in practice, is radical in purpose. It yearns for new social motion and movements that can enact and enforce more progressive laws before repression and incorporation solidify.... Third, the new memories and victories inscribed in new laws are kept alive by the defensive work of progressive lawyers to help lay the groundwork for the next upsurge of social motion and movements....

. . . Progressive legal practice must put forward interpretations of the precious ideal of democracy that call into question the unregulated and unaccountable power of corporate America. It also must set forth notions of the precious ideal of liberty that expose the authoritarian attitudes of cultural conservatism. This two-pronged ideological strategy should consist of an unrelenting defense of substantive democracy (in a decentralized, nonstatist fashion) and all-inclusive liberty (as best articulated in the Bill of Rights). This defense is utopian in that it strives to further the possibility of social movements. It is realistic in that it acknowledges the necessity of liberal legal practices for radical lawyers to preserve the gains after social movements have been crushed or absorbed. . . .

. . . What is needed is neither a vanguard party nor purist ideology, but rather the common pursuit of the overlapping goals. . . . The profits and investments of corporate America should be scrutinized and questioned for public accountability and civil responsibility. The xenophobia and jingoism of cultural conservatives has to be morally rejected and has to be judicially checked. A new world is in the making. Let us not allow the lethargy of American politics, the predominance of corporate power, and the pervasiveness of cultural conservatism to blunt the contributions we can make—especially if some of us choose the law as the vocational terrain for progressive politics.

West invokes insights drawn from the critical Schools and advocacy Approaches to map interconnections among law, power, injustice, and identity over time. Systemic advocates use history and narratives to unlearn—and to help others unlearn—disabling top-down myths. Systemic advocates "play" both defense and offense in social struggles. Advocates and activists build solidarity and collective action, while navigating the dangers of cooptation and repression.

And they do this over and over—across time. The rule of law was designed to last forever. Inevitably, then, time matters in law, society, and struggle. Elites have done "whatever it takes" to secure profit and maintain domination. Entrenched elites never relinquish even a sliver of privilege without deploying defensive, offensive, and cooptive strategies. Elites engage in long-term organized actions, and so must systemic advocates and activists.

Using time strategically as a resource is a key operational bottom line for systemic advocacy. Plainly put, time never stands still. Time is always someone's friend. Time thus becomes part of a calculated strategy that includes periods of action and periods of "biding time." Neither of these periods is passive, however. Even "waiting" is an intentional use of time.

On a personal level, systemic advocates steel themselves for the endurance and resilience that traditional lawyers often do not require—for struggle that may outlast the current client base and the systemic advocate. Using time and timing, then, is a professional skill to be honed. Sometimes, as the saying goes, timing *is* everything. Long-term outcomes often depend on time and timing. Sharpen your timing skills by paying daily attention to time and your affirmative uses of it.

NOTES AND QUESTIONS

1. *Does Reform Change Anything?* Even transformative change is incremental, partial, and continually contested, making any "reform" an elite opportunity for preservation through transformation. Consider, in closing, another example: the scathing critique of "reform" initiatives in criminal justice from legal scholar Alec Karakatsanis and many others. Is this another case in which elites manipulate and "manage" reform to serve as an effective, if disguised, tool for preservation through transformation?

> The emerging "criminal justice reform" consensus is superficial and deceptive. . . . These "reform"-advancing punishment bureaucrats are co-opting a movement toward profound change by convincing the public that the "law enforcement" system as we know it can operate in an objective, effective, and fair way based on "the rule of law." These punishment bureaucrats are dangerous because, in order to preserve the human caging apparatus that they control, they must disguise at the deepest level its core functions. As a result, they focus public conversation on the margins of the problem without confronting the structural issues at its heart.[19]

Looking ahead, how should advocates distinguish formal reforms that function as preservation-through-transformation from bottom-up efforts for Critical Justice? Think of another legal context in which you have heard the mantra of "legal reform." Does "reform" in that context amount to preservation through transformation, or to bottom-up progress?

2. *"Storytelling" as Knowledge Production and Critical Analysis.* West emphasizes above a technique he calls analytical narrative or storytelling, a knowledge-producing tool to illuminate the past, explain the present, and envision the future. In particular, West (and others) explain that, "Without this kind of historical consciousness and analytical storytelling, it is difficult to create channels for resistance and challenge to corporate power." Analytical narration is a radical use of a venerable technique, reflecting the same purpose as Biblical parables, Viking sagas, or Greek myths. Analytical narration also represents the critical use of a mainstream lawyering technique—legal storytelling, which law students usually are taught with the goal of better conveying the "story" of the case from their client's viewpoint. This potent tool

---

[19] Alec Karakatsanis, The Punishment Bureaucracy: How to Think About "Criminal Justice Reform," 128 Yale L.J. Forum 848 (Mar. 28, 2019).

often serves as a steppingstone to begin designing systemic advocacy projects, as well as an ongoing tool of bottom-up advocacy. Used strategically, analytical stories can move minds, hearts, and systems.

CHAPTER RECAP

We have focused on how advocates use time and other resources consciously and strategically to counter preservation through transformation and to make progress toward equal justice. Elites always use time strategically to preserve identity-based castes; with every step that seems to advance equal justice come often-disguised but unceasing elite efforts to move law and society two steps backward. Advocates unlearn and relearn notions of winning, losing, and progress, and they develop contextual, specific, and practical metrics to measure progress.

In this process, advocates navigate insider-outsider tensions and ambiguities. As "insiders" in the legal system, they work within existing rules to advance the interests and goals of client-groups. As outsiders in alliance with subordinated communities, advocates simultaneously aim to disrupt and rewrite the system's rules. Advocates take calculated risks to use time and change for progress.

In particular, advocates constantly defend prior gains while also supporting organized group struggles positioned for future breakthroughs. Systemic advocates and activists design and carry out long-term organized actions for progress, just as elites carry out long-term organized actions to block or co-opt progress. Using time and timing, then, is a key aspect of systemic advocacy and a professional skill to be developed. To build on these points, the next chapter focuses on how advocates design their work to support organized bottom-up action over time, using critical consciousness and methods based on antisubordination.

CHAPTER 5

ROADTEST: RECLAIMING GROUP IDENTITIES FOR ANTISUBORDINATION INSIGHT, CONSCIOUSNESS, AND SOLIDARITY

■ ■ ■

Table of Sections

5.1 Colorblindness Is a Racist Fiction and Top-Down Myth
5.2 Critical Self-Reflection Unmasks and Redefines Social Realities; "Asking Other Questions" Uncovers Systemic Patterns
5.3 Flipping Systemic Scripts—Social Identities as Group Assets for Long-Term Struggles
5.4 Antisubordination Solidarity Builds Power Across Multiple Kinds of Difference
5.5 Transforming Advocacy Helps to Transform Society—Bit by Bit, Year by Year

---

OPENING THOUGHTS

Walls turned sideways are bridges.

> **—Angela Davis**

Trans-border bonds stemming from a common national, ethnic, or religious identity can be a very valuable resource—whether for Palestinians gathering diplomatic support, Salvadoran victims of a devastating earthquake seeking aid to rebuild their lives, or Argentine Jews trying to cope with a pernicious economic crisis and a judicial investigation gone awry.

> **—Carina J. Miller,** Protecting the Argentine Jewish Community and Jewish Identity in Times of Crisis: Local Efforts, Global Community, and Foreign Support, 16 Fla. J. Int'l L. 677, 694 (2004)

[T]o be identity-blind is to be reality blind. Identities map realities.

> **—Margaret Montoya with Angela Harris,** "Who is a LatCrit?," Jerome Culp and Angela Harris Provide Answers and Ways of Being, 16 Seattle J. for Soc. Just. 701, 706 (2018)

Let us continue to struggle together, especially with those closest to the issues, because this praxis and struggle brings us closer to justice.

> —**Edwin Lindo**, reflecting in Uncompromising Hunger for Justice: Resistance, Sacrifice, and LatCrit Theory, 16 Seattle J. Soc. Just. 727, 817 (2018) (with Brenda Williams and Marc-Tizoc González)

INTRODUCTION

We saw earlier that the rule of law (still) uses identities to construct groups, assign individuals to them, and arrange them hierarchically to channel outcomes and shape society as a whole. In the United States and many other former European colonies, social identities were at the core of law from its inception. They have remained there since, overtly or covertly, in micro-macro and material-symbolic terms. Systemic advocates must understand identities and their complex, intersecting effects in law and society, for two primary reasons:

- To make headway toward Critical Justice, advocates navigate through conflicts, contests, or other obstacles based on social identities and help chart a pathway to group cohesion and action despite multiple types of fear, disaffection, or difference.

- To mobilize collective action against a common injury based on shared social identity, advocates use social identities as *assets* to raise consciousness and rally organization.

Systemic advocates must come to terms with social identities because the social order and legal system remain organized around them. This roadtest chapter is designed to help you develop actionable understandings of the roles that social identities can—or should—play in critical analysis and systemic advocacy. The goal of this roadtest is to help you develop the knowledge and skills to convert social identities from top-down instruments of systemic injustice to group assets for long-term, bottom-up struggles. This unlearning-relearning process marshals the histories and facts of shared grievances to help organize groups that can struggle for justice more effectively. The objective is to build critical consciousness of systemic privilege and subordination based on social identities to cultivate a coalitional sense of antisubordination solidarity across multiple kinds of difference.

We begin below with critical inspections of "colorblindness" as a keystone legal conception. In the United States, judges and lawmakers have equated colorblindness to equal justice. Under this "formal equality" approach, as we saw in Part I, decision makers are not supposed to "notice" race. But they do, and judges and lawmakers know this, too. Colorblindness as legal ideology is one of their biggest fictions—a fiction that matches the social effects of the predecessor "separate but equal" fiction: preservation of entrenched identity castes.

This fiction, in fact, is impossible for humans to make real; even people who are literally blind perceive social identities like race. Despite the claims or aspirations of colorblindness, this fiction amounts to blindfolding. This fiction blindfolds law to the many ways in which social identities saturate law and society. This fiction blindfolds law to social reality. Though it claims to be a "neutral" principle, in practical effect, colorblindness operates as a "new" kind of racism.

In response, critical advocates and activists deconstruct their environments using a combination of experience, "book" knowledge drawn from the Schools and Approaches, and field research. Anyone can use critical sources of actionable knowledge: stories, histories, empirical investigation, asking "other" questions when confronted with a particular injustice, followed by reflection, discussion, action, and more reflection. These practices can be incorporated into the advocate's toolkit. This process helps to convert diverse subordinated identities into sources of empowerment and to develop intentional groups for organized action.

The Schools and Approaches offer concepts like social construction, intersectionality, and antiessentialism, illustrated below, to help advocates navigate collectivized similarities and differences in the course of collective action. The Schools and Approaches also offer antisubordination values as bedrocks of inter- and intra-group solidarity. Antisubordination values stand for a clear proposition: we all stand against all forms of subordination. This proposition provides the measure of choices and actions. Bridging multiple kinds of difference, these values guide principled, accountable advocacy. This chapter's critical concepts provide practical tools to help advocates use social identities affirmatively as antisubordination assets.

5.1 COLORBLINDNESS IS A RACIST FICTION AND TOP-DOWN MYTH

One common myth in law and society is the notion that colorblindness and other identity blindnesses are neutral, effective corrections to centuries of white supremacy and heteropatriarchy. Elites rely on selective systemic blindfolding to defeat equality-enhancing initiatives, including affirmative action programs, reparations proposals, or other initiatives seeking economic (or symbolic) equality. Ronald Reagan, while President, often invoked Martin Luther King, Jr. while at the same time dismantling equality programs of all sorts, contending:

> We are committed to a society in which all men and women have equal opportunities to succeed, and so we oppose the use of [affirmative action] quotas. We want a color-blind society. A

society, that in the words of Dr. King, judges people not by the color of their skin, but by the content of their character.[1]

This cooptation from above uses colorblinding in a formalistic way that denies social and economic differences between groups today and denies to identity groups at the bottom adequate remedies for injuries framed systemically around those same identities. Formalistic deployments of colorblindness sever injury from remedy, inverting the well-established legal principle that remedies should mirror injuries. This identity blindfolding is a "new" kind of racism.

As used in law, colorblinding amounts to "selective blindfolding," where the use of identities to justify oppression is seen as a relic of the past, the continued identity-based patterns of oppression are denied, and the uses of identities by subordinated groups to motivate struggle in contemporary times are decried as illegitimate. Selective blindfolding sets up the background for top-down accusations that someone is "playing the race card" or engaging in "identity politics"—terms that somehow never are directed at uses of identity for social and legal subordination. Dominant accusations of "identity politics" always aim to delegitimize struggles against continued patterns of subordination.[2] This one-sided notion of identity politics attempts to suppress the capacity of advocates and groups to use shared identity-based grievances as points of coalescence and organization to support bottom-up group struggles. As Lance Smith and Richard Shin, scholars in counseling and education, respectively, note, systemic blindfolding that ignores relevant differences reinforces the status quo across identity castes:

> Because the term *blindness*, when used in a pejorative sense, is inherently oppressive to those who thrive without being sighted, we choose the less offensive term *blindfolding*. We also prefer the verb *blindfolding* as a subtle indication that this discursive position is in some sense a choice; either consciously or subconsciously, subjects adopt this particular narrative strategy over others that are available.
>
> ... [C]ritical scholars agree that in the post-civil rights era, ... color-blindness renders systemic racism invisible.... We suggest that queer blindfolding operates in a similar manner:
>
> • Positioning subjects to minimize heterosexual privilege

---

[1] Ronald Turner, The Dangers of Misappropriation: Misusing Martin Luther King Jr.'s Legacy to Prove the Colorblind Thesis, 2 Mich. J. Race and Law 101, 124, 130 (1996) ("Any such misuse of King as a symbol for colorblindness must be recognized for what it is: a deception (knowing or unknowing) built on misleading sound-bites, ahistorical and acontextual 'analysis' and other fundamentally flawed premises;" instead King was color-aware and supported affirmative action and other redress for centuries of injustice against African Americans).

[2] Colonial elites in the U.S. and elsewhere initiated the template for identity politics, which still reproduces colonial identity-based castes. See Part VI.

- Eschewing the egregious negative effects of heteronormativity
- Buttressing the invisibility of queer identities.[3]

Colorblinding, and difference blindfolding more generally, "disappear" the operations of privilege and subordination in law and society. Colorblinding is a systemic lie that serves collectivized injustice. Nevertheless, this phenomenon occurs in rule of law societies around the world, where overt expressions of bias are seen to constitute unacceptable discrimination—but formally identity-neutral practices and sentiments that reinforce existing inequalities are just fine.

In response, critical scholars Margalynne Armstrong and Stephanie Wildman urge unlearning the dominant social norms of top-down blindfolding. Armstrong and Wildman suggest replacing that notion with a critical awareness of color (and difference), called color insight or color awareness, which involves cultivating color consciousness without supremacist designs:

> The hegemony of colorblindness suggests that by noticing race, one is undermining equality itself. Any conversation about race, or about whiteness in particular, must work against that dominant social norm.
>
> ... An aspiration to color insight would serve society as a better value than colorblindness. Color insight would encourage noticing race in each context in which it arises, including the operation of white privilege and any other advantaging or disadvantaging function of race. . . .
>
> Color insight would serve to promote equality and to emphasize non-discrimination among races. Color insight would admit that most of us do see race and underline the need to understand what that racial awareness [or identity awareness] might mean. Color insight [or identity insight] would not assume that people or groups have any specific traits or propensities. Teaching to develop color insight, rather than colorblindness, would better prepare students for the heterogeneous, democratic society that American ideals embrace.[4]

The effects of identity blindness in legal analysis separate law from justice and from social reality. To illustrate, interdisciplinary scholar Osagie

---

[3] Lance C. Smith and Richard Q. Shin, Queer Blindfolding: A Case Study on Difference "Blindness" Towards Persons Who Identify as Lesbian, Gay, Bisexual, and Transgender, 61 J. of Homosexuality 940, 940–42 (2014).

[4] Margalynne J. Armstrong and Stephanie M. Wildman, Teaching Race/Teaching Whiteness: Transforming Colorblindness to Color Insight, 86 N.C. L. Rev. 635 (2008). See also Ruth Frankenberg, White Women, Race Matters 14–15 (1993) (describing "race cognizance" as an awareness of difference that is purposefully anti-racist).

Obasogie explores "whether the absence of vision affects individuals' perceptions of race" and demonstrates through empirical research how blind persons "see" race in similar ways as sighted persons. In other words, not even the literally blind are actually colorblind:

> [B]lind and sighted people understand and experience race in a similar fashion: visually. The data overwhelmingly show that, contrary to beliefs within the sighted community, race is not only significant to blind people, but is visually salient as a marker of visually distinguishable physical traits such as skin color and facial features....
>
> ... [R]ace becomes visually salient to blind (and sighted) individuals through social practices that train people to perceive human differences in particular ways. For sighted people this socialization process is entwined with their visual engagement with the world, making it difficult to disentangle what is obvious and what is produced. Blind people, on the other hand, are subject to the same social practices without the confounding visual stimuli and can thus detail the ways in which their visual understanding of race develops....
>
> ... [T]his data suggests that it may be time to rethink the assumption embedded throughout equal protection jurisprudence that the salience of race stems from its visual obviousness. In short, the empirical evidence suggests that "seeing race" has less to do with anything visually obvious about human bodies and more about the social practices that train us to look a certain way at them. This suggests that the "race" ipsa loquitur trope that orients the scrutiny inquiry, colorblindness, and the intent doctrine may not only be misinformed, but may also fundamentally warp the [Supreme] Court's understanding of how race becomes salient in a manner that can lead to remarkable injustices.[5]

Obasogie concludes that "Put bluntly, race has less to do with what one sees than how one is socialized to see, regardless of whether one can see or not."[6] Below, he elaborates on how blind persons are uniquely able to "see" race and to appreciate this socialization process that everyone (still) undergoes despite the illusion of societal colorblindness:

> Blind and sighted are part of the same social milieu that directs individuals to pay inordinate attention to visual cues denoting

---

[5] Osagie K. Obasogie, Can the Blind Lead the Blind? Rethinking Equal Protection Jurisprudence through an Empirical Examination of Blind People's Understanding of Race, 15 U. Pa. J. Const. L. 705, 748, 751, 755 (2013).

[6] See Osagie K. Obasogie, Do Blind People See Race? Social, Legal, and Theoretical Considerations, 44 Law & Soc'y Rev. 585, 609 (2010).

> race through which people organize their lives. This process is effortlessly transparent for sighted people, whereby racial knowledge is thought to be visually obvious. But the process takes a bit more work for blind people, who are detached from vision's ability to seduce them into uncritically reducing race to what is seen. Blind people are uniquely capable of discussing the social practices that give the visual cues associated with race an obvious feel. To the extent that blind and sighted people occupy the same social environment, the social forces that give visual understandings of race their coherency to blind people are likely to be similarly influential for those who are sighted. The irony ... is that sighted people are, in a sense, blinded by their sight; their vision prevents them from "seeing" or appreciating the social factors that make their visual understandings of race seem obvious, tangible, and coherent.[7]

Obasogie reveals that colorblindness is an incoherent metaphor—a legal fiction with vicious social consequences. He empirically demonstrates the general social impossibility of colorblindness, exposing the legal fiction as false. This fiction distorts equality doctrine in anti-equality ways. Similar myths surrounding "difference" also distort the culture, practice, and profession of law.

To amplify, legal ethics scholar Russell Pearce examines below norms and habits of the legal profession to expose how they discourage white lawyers from acknowledging the salience of their own race and exploring the role of their white identity in the work setting. White lawyers simultaneously perform and uphold practices slanted toward whiteness in law practice, which undermines their work. Pearce's analysis of the "symbiosis" of whiteness and professionalism is a key point of unlearning and relearning for effective systemic advocacy: color insight is important in all settings of law *and* society, including the legal profession, and for white lawyers as well as those of color.

WHITE LAWYERING: RETHINKING RACE, LAWYER IDENTITY, AND RULE OF LAW

Russell G. Pearce
73 Fordham L. Rev. 2081 (2005)

... The Symbiosis of Whiteness and Professionalism Undermines White Lawyers' Work

... [W]hite lawyers tend to deny the influence of their racial identity group on their work as lawyers. When professionalism's ideological commitment to color blindness reinforces this tendency, the resulting symbiosis

---

[7] *Id.* at 602.

undermines the capacity of white lawyers to represent clients to the best of their ability.

The Symbiosis of Whiteness and Professionalism

A dominant value common to the organizational identity of lawyers is professionalism's commitment to the color blindness of lawyers' conduct. In Sandy Levinson's famous formulation, professional socialization "bleaches out" racial differences among lawyers, as well as other individual characteristics. Under this view, all lawyers should be—and in most instances are—fungible. Not only should race play no role in how a lawyer approaches her work, but with few exceptions it will play no role. White lawyers who follow the dominant approach will actually believe that this is an accurate account and that they themselves are neutral as to race. Accordingly, they will reject the notion that they should examine the influence of their white identity on their lawyering. . . .

Some whites with this perspective will view law practice, like society, as essentially color-blind. In this world, racial influence is rare, generally extending only to those few whites who are openly racist. Accordingly, when people of color raise issues of race, they "play the race card" and create phony issues to promote their own interests.

Other whites with a similar understanding of racial dynamics may reach an opposite conclusion. They believe that white racism is a significant societal problem. White people, lacking a proper claim to racial identity and colluding in white racial dominance, have little to offer on racial issues. Under this view, people of color have—and whites lack—the ability to understand, or to engage in productive discussions regarding, race. White people should defer to people of color who are experts on race.

Professionalism's "bleaching out" approach and these tendencies of white people mutually reinforce certain conduct. They discourage white lawyers from acknowledging that their race is an influence and from exploring the extent to which their white identity plays a role in their work settings. They further discourage white lawyers from engaging in dialogue regarding issues of race with each other, as well as with people of color. In a diverse legal system, where white lawyers work with colleagues, adversaries, judges, clients, and witnesses of color, the potential negative impact of these practices on a lawyer's work is quite significant.

How the Symbiosis Undermines Lawyer's Work: An Illustration

White law professor Clark Cunningham has provided an extraordinarily thoughtful and nuanced analysis of the representation he and two white students provided an African-American man facing a misdemeanor charge of disturbing the peace arising from a traffic stop. The police officer had described the African-American client as having told the police he had been stopped "because he was black" and the Judge "described [the] client as 'hollering racism.'" Nonetheless, even though Cunningham suspected that "what happened . . . was a 'racial incident,' . . . as a lawyer [he] did not talk about 'the case' that way, and therefore [he] ceased to think in terms of racial issues. . . ." Accordingly, Cunningham and the students did not discuss with their client, or argue to the court, that the treatment of their client had a racial dimension. After the prosecution dismissed the case, the client angrily assailed Cunningham and the students for patronizing him and treating him the same way that other white authority figures did.

Cunningham attributes the failure to address the racial aspects of the case to two factors. First, the client never raised the claim with his white lawyers. Cunningham suggests that his African-American client might not have believed he could share with his white lawyers the view he expressed after the completion of the case—that the white lawyers would have been just as skeptical as other white authority figures were. Second, Cunningham and his students did not reach the racial issue because as lawyers they turned first to readily available "race neutral" defenses.

What Cunningham does not explore is the possibility that race influenced his own conduct and that of his students. Perhaps as whites and lawyers, they began assuming the norm that race is not a factor. Therefore, they would not on their own initiative raise the possibility that race played a role either in the matter or in their relationship with their client. . . .

The lawyers' white identity could also have attributed to their failure to follow up on specific evidence indicating that they should explore how racial identities influenced the case. Here, the police report revealed that the African-American client had suggested that his race was a factor in his stop. When the white judge described the charge against the African-American defendant as an "attitude" charge, he may very well have been signaling that the charge resulted from the defendant's inappropriate and racially based response to the police officers. Even though Cunningham as a progressive white person had an "impression" that the incident was racial, he may not have pursued this intuition because the embeddedness of the authority relationship with his client was consistent with that of the white police officer and judge. After the case ended, the African-American client certainly noted that this was his perception—that the white lawyers had treated him in the same paternalistic way as the other white authority figures.

Last, Cunningham's explanation that the white lawyers naturally turned to a race-neutral strategy represents a symbiosis of whiteness and of professional values. The professional ideal that lawyers and law should be neutral provides support for preferring a race-neutral strategy if readily available, as in this case. It also supports the tendency of whites to avoid confronting racial issues. In this way, whiteness and professional values are mutually reinforcing. . . .

Rethinking the Construction of Professional Identity and Rule of Law

... The legal profession should discard the bleaching out assumption in favor of an integration-and-learning perspective that acknowledges the influence of identity group affiliations on lawyers' work.

The Integration-and-Learning Approach Works Better Than a Color-Blind Model

In two recent studies, leading organizational scholars Robin Ely and David Thomas have demonstrated that the "integration-and-learning" paradigm is more effective in achieving organizational goals than the "discrimination-and-fairness" model currently dominant in the legal profession. In the integration-and-learning approach, members of a work force "are receptive to the notion that racial differences may underlie team members' expectations, norms, and assumptions about work and that these differences are worth exploring as a source of insights into how the group might improve its effectiveness." Co-workers "openly acknowledge and negotiate their differences in service of their goals."

In contrast, in the discrimination-and-fairness approach, such as the "bleaching out" paradigm dominant in the legal profession, "cultural diversity is a mechanism for eliminating racial injustice, and ... is of no use in furthering the group's work." Under this paradigm, "group members aspire to be color blind" and confine "discourse about race ... to the possibility of racial biases in the group." ...

Applying the Integration-and-Learning Model to Legal Practice

... **Integration-and-Learning in Client Representation**

The integration-and-learning approach requires reflection and discussion in all aspects of client representation. As lawyers increase their "competence [in] dealing with racial matters," they should consider how their identity group, as well as the identity groups of others with whom they are working, influences their relationships with colleagues, clients, adversaries, and court personnel. Lawyers should then, with their colleagues and clients, make explicit that issues of race are open for discussion and "speak openly, frankly, and professionally about relations." With this framework, lawyers will learn much more from their colleagues and clients, who in turn will learn much more from them. As Ely and Thomas demonstrate, this framework will result in lawyers treating—and being perceived as treating—each other and their clients with more respect, moving beyond erroneous assumptions to more accurate analysis and more effective strategies, and working more successfully as a team with colleagues.

Ely and Thomas remind us that these strategies do not avoid conflict. Rather, they offer a more effective way to manage conflicts that are likely to occur or to exist even without open acknowledgement. . . .

If the white lawyers had applied this approach in the case study described above, they would have acted quite differently. First, they would have asked themselves whether their white identity influenced how they perceived and were perceived by their African-American client, the white police officer, and the white judge. Second, from the beginning of the relationship and continuing throughout, they would have invited their client to engage with them openly on issues of race. Had they done so, they might have recognized the racial issues in the case themselves, have learned of those implications from their client, and have examined those issues in cooperation with their client. . . .

While resembling some of the approaches in the literature on "cross-cultural lawyering," this approach has a different emphasis. . . .

. . . [Whereas] cross-cultural lawyering seeks a "non-judgmental approach towards yourself and client," the integration-and-learning approach rejects this goal as a form of unrealistic and counterproductive color blindness or culture-blindness. It instead requires informed judgments, together with "open[ ], frank[ ], and professional[ ]" exchanges regarding those judgments. . . .

Rethinking Rule of Law

. . . The dominant conception of rule of law makes the command of role morality even stronger for lawyers than for other professionals. Under this view, "[r]ule of law implies that the quality of lawyering and of justice an individual receives does not depend on the group identity of the lawyer or judge." This conception "posits that the clash of opposing views before a neutral fact finder is the best way to ascertain truth and justice." For the system to work properly, "all parties [must] receive equal representation" and for that to happen, lawyers must "function as extreme partisans who should not bring their own [identity] to bear on their representation."

. . . If our organizational goal is equal justice under law, an integration-and-learning approach will more likely have greater success than the dominant "bleaching out" paradigm. As Martha Minow has observed, in a world where differences matter, "a commitment to equality—to treating like[ ] [cases alike under the rule of law,]—will be caught in a contradiction." She, like Ely and Thomas, argues that "you cannot avoid trouble through ignoring difference; you cannot find a solution in neutrality." The task for the legal profession is to promote equal justice in the best way in light of the persistence of group identities. . . .

The call to blindness serves as cover for an "unfortunate symbiosis" with costs both to the profession and to the larger legal system as a whole, not to mention the affected clients. As legal clinicians Jean Koh Peters and Susan Bryant note, disrupting this symbiosis requires both the will and the skills to change patterns in classrooms, firms, courtrooms, and other sites of legal formation and decision making:

> [U]nless we talk about race [as professors and students] in the clinic and speak explicitly with our students about how to talk about race, we will not have prepared them for important work in their future workplaces. We are sending students a message from our failure to talk about issues of implicit bias, structural inequalities based on race, or racial tension in interpersonal relationships. Students who experience race-based microaggressions towards themselves and their clients may have no framework to talk about these acts and how to respond. Lawyers who do not consider how they might help both their own client and others by taking race into account fail to analyze the context within which their client's case occurs.[8]

Obasogie and Pearce, augmented by Koh Peters and Bryant, among others, thus expand our critical understanding of the complex ways—overt and covert—that social identities still matter today despite blindfolding myths to the contrary.

NOTES AND QUESTIONS

1. *Color Insightful Self-Reflection.* In their quoted article, Armstrong and Wildman ask the reader to reflect on these questions: What is your race? How do you know? What is your first memory of race? Obasogie also has suggested additional queries: How do you define race? If you dated or married outside of your race, how did/would your family respond? Is knowing someone's race useful to you? Why do you think some people find race to be important?[9] As an exercise in color insight, engage in self-reflection on these questions.

Expanding these queries beyond race and color, reflect on the same questions, but this time with regard to a different identity-marker typically used by society to distribute privilege and subordination—one salient in your life. For example, reflect on these same questions using your gender, sexuality, religion, dis/ability, indigeneity, age, or economic class.

2. *Artificial Intelligence and Caste.* Having learned how blind persons "see" race in similar ways as sighted persons, thus debunking the notion that we can readily "unsee" color, consider how artificial intelligence "sees" race. At least a robot or similar applications of artificial intelligence can be taught to act in a

---

[8] Jean Koh Peters and Susan Bryant, Teaching About Race, in Transforming the Education of Lawyers: The Theory and Practice of Clinical Pedagogy 375, 376 (Susan Bryant, Elliott S. Milstein & Ann C. Shalleck eds. 2014).

[9] Obasogie, Do Blind People See Race?, at 591.

colorblind manner, right? But researchers in a variety of settings have demonstrated, thus far, that artificial intelligence is bounded by the same limitations and race socialization as its programmers. Whether the context is self-driving vehicles failing to recognize darker-skinned pedestrians or software predicting the likelihood of black and white convicted criminals to reoffend, artificial intelligence may replicate human bias, particularly the biases of software developers.[10] The equality disconnect in technology may stem from societal systemic injustice, among other causes. For example, the technology industry preferred hiring men when humans did the hiring based on their evaluation and "hunches." When software was designed to evaluate job candidates, that software "learned" its evaluation technique from reviewing the company's history of applicant resumes and hiring. That software system likely taught itself to prefer male candidates. Amazon allegedly discovered this flaw in its own recruiting engine and scrapped it.[11] Technology at this critical juncture might help solve social problems, or it might remain mired in the same ruts of societal caste.

3. *Invisible Identity*. Not all identities are necessarily or always conveyed through visual cues. For example, some physical disabilities are visually apparent. Society teaches us to view those in wheelchairs or carrying a white cane as disabled. But many physical and mental disabilities are debilitating but not visibly apparent, such as Crohn's disease, dyslexia, autism, or autoimmune diseases. Those afflicted may "pass" on some or most days, in contexts that range from public interactions to employment interviews. Might society (such as in the context of handicapped parking) or employers (when asked to make reasonable accommodation) fail to give credence to identities they cannot visualize? How might a learning-and-integration approach, as Pearce describes, change organizational discourse and decision making around such identities?

5.2 CRITICAL SELF-REFLECTION UNMASKS AND REDEFINES SOCIAL REALITIES; "ASKING OTHER QUESTIONS" UNCOVERS SYSTEMIC PATTERNS

Advocates frequently encounter discomfort as they unlearn and relearn the sources of the Critical Challenge. Exploring more deeply how law isn't always what it pretends to be can be disorienting. Counteracting systemic injustice *is* daunting. And yet, the commitment to criticality requires the courage and resilience to ask questions and pursue answers even when—or especially when—they disturb settled dogmas.

---

[10] Karen Hao, This is How AI Bias Really Happens—And Why It's So Hard to Fix (Feb. 4, 2019), www.technologyreview.com/s/612876/this-is-how-ai-bias-really-happensand-why-its-so-hard-to-fix/.

[11] Jeffrey Dastin, Amazon Scraps Secret AI Recruiting Tool That Showed Bias Against Women (Oct. 9, 2018), www.reuters.com/article/us-amazon-com-jobs-automation-insight/amazon-scraps-secret-ai-recruiting-tool-that-showed-bias-against-women-idUSKCN1MK08G.

Advocates therefore ask questions—critical, uncomfortable questions about "others" excluded, marginalized, or subordinated. Asking "other" questions to produce identity-related insights is a ready means of unlearning and relearning across multiple contexts. This process of critical and self-critical inquiry "unmasks" social realities in micro-macro terms, and leads to new knowledge that helps make more possible the multiple collaborations and coalitions necessary for organized group struggles.

Below, legal scholar Margaret Montoya, the first Latina admitted to Harvard Law School, describes how her *personal* background informed her *professional* advocacy work over the long course of her career. Like West in the previous chapter, Montoya shows and explains how critical "storytelling" functions as "personal and collective reflection" as well as a "challenge to traditional legal discourse." Montoya's excerpt illustrates how reflection often will be expressed, at least initially, through a particular kind of narrative—an analytical narrative. This kind of narration is only one among many kinds of "legal storytelling." As we explore more fully in Part V, this kind of narrative also is one among many knowledge-producing methods available to systemic advocates.

In general, narratives are a venerable and common means of transmitting knowledge across ages and cultures:

> The word "narrative" derives from the Latin *narrow* which means "to tell" and from *gnarus*, meaning "knowing;" and these two facets of the word explain the significance of narrative or storytelling as "a universal tool for knowing as well as telling, for absorbing information as well as expressing it." Stories ... are a vehicle through which we, as human beings, make sense of ourselves and our lived experiences. Narratives help to shape our identities, our relationships, and our behaviors; "For we dream in narrative, daydream in narrative, remember, anticipate, hope, despair, believe, doubt, plan, revise, criticize, construct, gossip, learn, hate, and love by narrative."[12]

Analytical narratives are a critically purposeful kind of narration, which recount "how the law has impeded or impelled struggles for justice and freedom" geared to bottom-up progress:

> Like the best rap artists, progressive lawyers can energize a demoralized citizenry with insights on the historical origins and present causes of social misery ... [to] educate citizens on the operations of economic and political powers in the courts ... [and] empower society's victims to transform society.[13]

---

[12] Dawn Watkins and Laura Guihen, Using Narrative and Metaphor in Formative Feedback: Exploring Students' Responses, 68 J. Legal Ed. 154, 156 (2018).

[13] Cornel West, The Role of Law in Progressive Politics, 43 Vand. L. Rev. 1797, 1802 (1990).

As you read the narrative below, consider yourself in the same knowledge-producing position: if you were to write about your experiences in childhood, school, community life, and work settings, what interests would surface, what ideas and hopes might emerge, and what scars might be present? How might that guide your decisions as you imagine contributions you would like to make through advocacy? Remember that your self-reflection is not meant to be self-congratulatory or isolated from communities and groups in need. What kind of story would emerge? What would your analytical narrative help to unmask in personal (or micro) yet systemic (or macro) terms? How might this unlearning/relearning reflection process provide a starting point for your advocacy work?[14]

MASCARAS, TRENZAS, Y GREÑAS: UN/MASKING THE SELF WHILE UN/BRAIDING LATINA STORIES AND LEGAL DISCOURSE

Margaret E. Montoya
17 Harv. Women's L.J. 185 (1994); 15 Chicano-Latino L. Rev. 1 (1994)

Mascaras: Un/Masking the Self

... *My Story*

One of the earliest memories from my school years is of my mother braiding my hair, making my *trenzas* [braids]. In 1955, I was seven years old. I was in second grade at the Immaculate Conception School in Las Vegas, New Mexico. Our family home with its outdoor toilet was on an unpaved street, one house from the railroad track. . . .

She would begin at the top of my head pressing down as she drew the comb down to the nape of my neck. . . . "I don't want you to look *greñudas*," my mother would say. ["I don't want you to look uncombed."]

Hearing my mother use both English and Spanish gave emphasis to what she was saying. She used Spanish to talk about what was really important: her feelings, her doubts, her worries.

. . . The real message of "*greñudas*" was conveyed through the use of the Spanish word—it was unspoken and subtextual. She was teaching us that our world was divided, that They-Who-Don't-Speak-Spanish would see us as different, would judge us, would find us lacking. Her lessons about combing, washing and doing homework frequently relayed a deeper message: be prepared, because you will be judged by your skin color, your names, your accents. They will see you as ugly, lazy, dumb and dirty.

---

[14] For descriptions of the role and examples of critical reflection and self-reflection in lawyering see also Charles Elsesser, Community Lawyering—The Role of Lawyers in the Social Justice Movement, 14 Loy. J. Pub. Int. L. 375 (2013); Jane H. Aiken, Provocateurs for Justice, 7 Clinical L. Rev. 287 (2001); Angela Harris, Margaretta Lin & Jeff Selbin, From "The Art of War" to "Being Peace:" Mindfulness and Community Lawyering in a Neoliberal Age, 95 Cal. L. Rev. 2073 (2007).

As I put on my uniform and as my mother braided my hair, I changed; I became my public self. My *trenzas* announced that I was clean and well-cared-for at home. My *trenzas* and school uniform blurred the differences between my family's economic and cultural circumstances and those of the more economically comfortable Anglo students. I welcomed the braids and uniform as a disguise which concealed my minimal wardrobe and the relative poverty in which my family lived....

By the age of seven, I was keenly aware that I lived in a society that had little room for those who were poor, brown, or female. I was all three. I moved between dualized worlds: private/public, Catholic/secular, poverty/privilege, Latina/Anglo. I moved between these worlds. My *trenzas* and school uniform were a cultural disguise. They were also a precursor for the more elaborate mask I would later develop.

Presenting an acceptable face, speaking without a Spanish accent, hiding what we really felt—masking our inner selves—were defenses against racism passed on to us by our parents to help us get along in school and in society....

Mine is the first generation of Latinas to be represented in colleges and universities in anything approaching significant numbers. We are now represented in virtually every college and university. But, for the most part, we find ourselves isolated. Rarely has another Latina gone before us. Rarely is there another Latina whom we can watch to try and figure out all the little questions about subtextual meaning, about how dress or speech or makeup are interpreted in this particular environment....

When I arrived as a student at Harvard Law School, I dressed so as to proclaim my politics. During my first day of orientation, I wore a Mexican peasant blouse and cutoff jeans on which I had embroidered the Chicano symbol of the *águila* (a stylized eagle) on one seat pocket and the woman symbol on the other. The *águila* reminded me of the red and black flags of the United Farm Worker rallies; it reminded me that I had links to a particular community. I was never to finish the fill-in stitches in the woman symbol. My symbols, like my struggles, were ambiguous....

As time went on, my clothes lost their political distinctiveness. My clothes signified my ambivalence: perhaps if I dressed like a lawyer, eventually I would acquire more conventional ideas and ideals and fit in with my peers. Or perhaps if I dressed like a lawyer, I could harbor for some future use the disruptive and, at times, unwelcome thoughts that entered my head. My clothing would become protective coloration. Chameleon-like, I would dress to fade into the ideological, political and cultural background rather than proclaim my differences.

Máscaras and Latina Assimilation

Academic success traditionally has required that one exhibit the linguistic and cognitive characteristics of the dominant culture....

To support their academic progress, Latinos have encouraged their children to speak English well and have tolerated other aspects of acculturation, such as changes in friends, clothes and recreational preferences. As they undertake the daily interactions involved in socialization, students adopt masks of the dominant culture which manifest the negative values ascribed to traditional Latina/o culture....

... Assimilation has become yet another mask for the Latina/o to hide behind....

Belonging to a higher economic class than that of one's family or community and affecting the mannerisms, clothing styles or speech patterns that typify the privileged classes can strain familial and ethnic bonds. Families, even those who have supported the education and advancement of their children, can end up feeling estranged from their children and resentful of the cultural costs involved in their academic and economic success. Accusations of *vendida,* "selling-out," forgetting the ethnic community, and abandoning the family can accompany academic success.

... Resolution of these issues need not be an isolating, individualistic or secretive process, alienating us from our families or our communities....

My Story Continues

My memories from law school begin with the first case I ever read in Criminal Law. I was assigned to seat number one in a room that held some 175 students.

The case was entitled *The People of the State of California v. Josefina Chavez.* It was the only case in which I remember encountering a Latina, and she was the defendant in a manslaughter prosecution. The facts, as I think back and before I have searched out the casebook, involved a young woman giving birth one night over the toilet in her mother's home without waking her child, brothers, sisters, or mother. The baby dropped into the toilet. Josefina cut the umbilical cord with a razor blade. She recovered the body of the baby, wrapped it in newspaper and hid it under the bathtub. She ran away, but later she turned herself in to her probation officer.

The legal issue was whether the baby had been born alive for purposes of the California manslaughter statute: whether the baby had been born alive and was therefore subject to being killed. The class wrestled with what it meant to be alive in legal terms. Had the lungs filled with air? Had the heart pumped blood?

For two days I sat mute, transfixed while the professor and the students debated the issue. Finally, on the third day, I timidly raised my hand. I heard myself blurt out: What about the other facts? What about her youth, her poverty, her fear over the pregnancy, her delivery in silence? I spoke for perhaps two minutes, and when I finished, my voice was high-pitched and anxious.

An African American student in the back of the room punctuated my comments with "Hear! Hear!" Later other students thanked me for speaking up and in other ways showed their support.

I sat there after class had ended, in seat number one on day number three, wondering why it had been so hard to speak. Only later would I begin to wonder whether I would ever develop the mental acuity, the logical clarity to be able to sort out the legally relevant facts from what others deemed sociological factoids. Why *did* the facts relating to the girl-woman's reality go unvoiced? Why were her life, her anguish, her fears rendered irrelevant? Engaging in analyses about The Law, her behavior and her guilt demanded that I disembody Josefina, that I silence her reality which screamed in my head.

Perhaps my memory has played tricks with me. I decide to look for the casebook and reread the *Chavez* case. I am surprised, after years of thinking about the case, to learn that her name was Josephine and not Josefina. My memory distorted her name, exaggerating her ethnicity, her differences. The facts in the opinion are even more tragic than I remembered....

... The appellate court affirmed the judgment of the lower court, concluding that a criminal act had been committed because of the mother's "complete failure ... to use any of the care towards the infant which was necessary for its welfare and which was naturally required of her."

The appellate opinion focused on the legal personhood of the dead baby, but questions of criminal intent, mens rea and diminished capacity thread through the case. Contextualization of the facts through the use of gender-linked and cultural information would inform our understanding of the latter legal issues....

A discussion raising questions about the gender-, class-, and ethnicity-based interpretations in the opinion, however, would have run counter to traditional legal discourse. Interjecting information about the material realities and cultural context of a poor Latina woman's life introduces taboo information into the classroom. Such information would transgress the prevalent ideological discourse.... [It would] admit knowing about the details of pregnancies and self abortions, or the hidden motivations of a *pachuca* (or a *chola,* a "homegirl" in today's Latino gang parlance). By overtly linking oneself to the life experiences of poor women, especially *pachucas,* one would emphasize one's differences from those who seemed to have been admitted to law school by right.

Information about the cultural context of Josephine Chavez's life would also transgress the linguistic discourse within the classroom. One would find it useful, and perhaps necessary, to use Spanish words and concepts to describe accurately and to contextualize Josephine Chavez's experience. In the 1970s, however, Spanish was still the language of Speedy Gonzales, José Jimenez and other racist parodies....

I recall that my Criminal Law professor ... though his own Socratic dialogue had neither invited such remarks nor presented Josephine Chavez as a complex person worthy of our attention....

Over time, I figured out that my interpretations of the facts in legal opinions were at odds with the prevailing discourse in the classroom, regardless of the subject matter. Much of the discussion assumed that we all shared common life experiences....

For multiple and overlapping reasons I felt excluded from the experiences of others, experiences that provided them with knowledge that better equipped them, indeed privileged them, in the study of The Law, especially within the upper class domain that is Harvard....

... As time went on, I felt diminished and irrelevant. It wasn't any one discussion, any one class or any one professor. The pervasiveness of the ideology marginalized me, and others; its efficacy depended upon its subtextual nature, and this masked quality made it difficult to pinpoint.

Issues of race or gender are never trivial or banal from my perspective. Knowing how or when to assert them effectively as others react with hostility, boredom or weariness can be a "crazy-making" endeavor....

Speaking out assumes prerogative. Speaking out is an exercise of privilege. Speaking out takes practice.

Silence ensures invisibility. Silence provides protection. Silence masks.

... Storytelling as Personal and Collective Redefinition

In deciding to use an autobiographical narrative format, I am seizing literary space that has rarely been occupied by Latinas in either Spanish or English....

That I am writing autobiographically as a Latina is unusual; that I choose to do so in the context of legal scholarship is more unusual yet. My purposes resemble some of the goals ascribed to African American autobiography. Autobiographical writing by African Americans has been described as serving descriptive and persuasive functions that are distinct from White autobiography. African American autobiography "looks not backward over a completed career, but forward to what the black writer is doing and intends to do in the future."

Feminist method has been inextricably linked to consciousness-raising and the primacy of women's experience.... Language, images and masks are key factors.... Writing about my experiences, as a child and as a law student, will hopefully contribute to a new critical understanding of what it means to be a Latina and increase the discursive space for the telling of stories from the Latina perspective. Telling my stories about my everyday experiences and capturing those experiences through two languages challenges the societal indifference that has isolated and marginalized Latinas....

Storytelling as a Challenge to Traditional Legal Discourse

The law and the practice of law are grounded in the telling of stories. Pleadings and judicial orders can be characterized as stylized stories. Legal persuasion in the form of opening statements and closing arguments is routinely taught as an exercise in storytelling. Client interviews are storytelling and story-listening events. Traditionally, legal culture within law firms, law schools and courthouses has been transmitted through the "war stories" told by seasoned attorneys. Narrative laces through all aspects of legal education, legal practice and legal culture. In these various ways the use of narrative is not new to the legal academy.

Only recently however, has storytelling begun to play a significant role in academic legal writing. In the hands of Outsiders, storytelling seeks to subvert the dominant ideology. Stories told by those on the bottom ... challenge and expose the hierarchical and patriarchal order that exists within the legal academy and pervades the larger society. Narrative that focuses on the experiences of Outsiders thus empowers both the storyteller and the story-listener by virtue of its opposition to the traditional forms of discourse....

Conclusion

New discursive formats, including the use of Latina autobiography in legal scholarship, enable us to reinvent ourselves. We can reject the dualistic patriarchal masks that we shrank behind and seize instead our multiple, contradictory and ambiguous identities ... [using] our histories, our ancestries and our past experiences [to] give us renewed appreciation for who we are as well as a clearer sense of who we can become.

Our conceptual *trenzas,* our rebraided ideas, even though they may appear unneat or *greñudas* to others, suggest new opportunities for unmasking the subordinating effects of legal discourse. Our rebraided ideas, the *trenzas* of our multicultural lives, offer personally validating interpretations for the *máscaras* [masks] we choose to wear. My masks are what they are....

Montoya explains not only her own professional pathways but also how "masking" and "unmasking"—like unlearning and relearning—are central in the process of personal and collective reflection, development, and grounding. This process helps individuals and groups redefine themselves and their environments. Sometimes this process starts with shared stories based on personal experiences; other times, it begins with the stories of others.

Next, Mari Matsuda recounts the work of women of color who struggled against collectivized injustice for decades as activist-scholars. Like all advocates, they navigate an always-complex combination of difference and similarity. Matsuda outlines the sometimes-painful task of "asking questions" to unmask systemic patterns that can lead to coalitional knowledge and action grounded in solidarity. Notice that this excerpt, too, relies on and practices analytical narration.

BESIDE MY SISTER, FACING THE ENEMY: LEGAL THEORY OUT OF COALITION

Mari J. Matsuda
43 Stan. L. Rev. 1183 (1991)

Introduction

... "Is it worth it?" is the question every person who works in coalition confronts. ...

This essay ... [suggests] the instrumental use of coalition-building to achieve certain political goals is merely the beginning of the worth of this method. The deeper worth of coalition is the way in which it constructs us as ethical beings and knowers of our world. ...

Three Women Working

Daughter of Pi'ilani

Haunani-Kay Trask ... writes of working in coalition with environmentalists who, in her community of Hawai'i, are often white in-migrants. Expressing bitterness and frustration, ... Trask speaks of the haole (Caucasian) colonizers who removed the Hawaiian government by force, leaving wounds in the native population that have never healed. ... [Yet she also] works with whites in coalition on a variety of issues. ...

I have heard people say of Professor Trask, "She would be much more effective if she weren't so angry" ... There is a politics of anger: who is allowed to get angry, whose anger goes unseen, and who seems angry when they are not.

Once, when I intended to compliment an African-American woman on a powerful speech she had made, I said: "I admire your ability to express anger." She looked at me coolly and replied, "I was not angry. If I were angry I would not be speaking here." . . .

I remember this exchange because it was an uncomfortable one for me, and because it was a moment of learning. . . . [I]f she were hatefully angry, beyond hope of coalition, she would not talk. In this light, Professor Trask's strong words are acts of engagement, not estrangement.

. . . There is a cost to speaking without anger. . . . [F]ailure to express the pain . . . discounts the subordination experienced by one's community . . . [and] is a betrayal of the self.

. . . I could shelter myself from conflict by leaving the conversation, but I have come to believe that the comfort we feel when we avoid hard conversations is a dangerous comfort, one that seduces us into ignorance about the experiences of others and about the full meaning of our own lives.

Women of Color and Public Policy

. . . June Inuzuka writes of coalition as strategy. Her concept of coalition is grounded in the world of practical politics and in the recognition that women of color are a numerical minority in the arena of policy formation. In order to meet the immediate and material need for access to government largess, Inuzuka and others like her have worked within organizations dominated by white, middle-class women. . . .

There is a realpolitik awareness in the way Inuzuka . . . has chosen to de-emphasize the separate and sometimes conflicting categorizations of "white feminist" and "women of color" in coalition-building. . . .

. . . Inuzuka is an example of an activist who recognizes differences and who chooses, nonetheless, to work with groups formed around the category of "women."

The Multi-Cultural Feminist

. . . Unlike June Inuzuka, who operates in the world of practical politics, Sharon Parker chooses to complexify the notion of "women of color." She identifies herself as a "multi-ethnic" woman and includes "white" as one of the racial identities she claims. . . .

What does it mean to claim white, African, and Native ancestry? . . . Implicit in Parker's statement of her ancestry is her commitment to the cultures represented by that ancestry, as well as her refusal to fit neatly into a single racial category. . . .

These three writers—Parker, Inuzuka, and Trask—have found work in coalition painful. Each describes the racism and condescension they have experienced. . . . Each suggests that coalition has limits of both tolerance and utility.

Why, then, given the frustration of coalition, do these women not retreat into racial separatism? . . .

My answer is that we cannot, at this point in history, engage fruitfully in jurisprudence without engaging in coalition. . . .

Theory Out of Coalition

Through our sometimes painful work in coalition we are beginning to form a theory of subordination; a theory that describes it, explains it, and gives us the tools to end it. As lawyers working in coalition, we are developing a theory of law taking sides, rather than law as value-neutral. We imagine law to uplift and protect the sixteen-year-old single mother on crack rather than law to criminalize her. We imagine law to celebrate and protect women's bodies; law to sanctify love between human beings—whether women to women, men to men, or women to men, as lovers may choose to love; law to respect the bones of our ancestors; law to feed the children; law to shut down the sweatshops; law to save the planet.

This is the revolutionary theory of law that . . . we can only develop in coalition. . . .

Ask the Other Question: The Interconnection of All Forms of Subordination

The way I try to understand the interconnection of all forms of subordination is through a method I call "ask the other question." When I see something that looks racist, I ask, "Where is the patriarchy in this?" When I see something that looks sexist, I ask, "Where is the heterosexism in this?" When I see something that looks homophobic, I ask, "Where are the class interests in this?" Working in coalition forces us to look for both the obvious and non-obvious relationships of domination, helping us to realize that no form of subordination ever stands alone. . . .

In trying to explain this to my own community, I sometimes try to shake people up by suggesting that patriarchy killed Vincent Chin. Most people think racism killed Vincent Chin. When white men with baseball bats, hurling racist hate speech, beat a man to death, it is obvious that racism is a cause. It is only slightly less obvious, however, when you walk down the aisles of Toys R Us, that little boys grow up in this culture with toys that teach dominance and aggression, while little girls grow up with toys that teach about being pretty, baking, and changing a diaper. And the little boy who is interested in learning how to nurture and play house is called a "sissy." When he is a little older he is called a "f—g." He learns that acceptance for men in this society is premised on rejecting the girl culture and taking on the boy culture, and I believe that this, as much as racism, killed Vincent Chin. I have come to see that homophobia is the disciplinary system that teaches men . . . [and that] this homophobia is a cause of rape and violence against women. I have come to see how that same homophobia makes women afraid to choose women, sending them instead into the arms of men who beat them. I have come to see how class oppression creates the same effect, cutting off the chance of economic independence that could free women from dependency upon abusive men.

I have come to see all of this from working in coalition. . . .

The women of color movement has, of necessity, been a movement about intersecting structures of subordination. This movement suggests that anti-patriarchal struggle is linked to struggle against all forms of subordination. It has challenged communities of color to move beyond race alone in the quest for social justice. . . .

. . . [First,] and most obviously, in unity there is strength. No subordinated group is strong enough to fight the power alone, thus coalitions are formed out of necessity.

Second, some of us have overlapping identities. Separating out and ranking oppression denies and excludes these identities. . . .

Finally, perhaps the most progressive reason for moving beyond race alone is that racism is best understood and fought with knowledge gained from the broader anti-subordination struggle. . . .

. . . Moving beyond race to include discussion of other forms of subordination risks breaking coalition. Because I believe that the most progressive elements of any liberation movement are those who see the intersections (and the most regressive are those who insist on only one axis), I am willing to risk breaking coalition by pushing intersectional analysis.

. . . Adding on gender must involve active feminists, just as adding on considerations of indigenous peoples must include activists from native communities. Coalition is the way to achieve this inclusion.

. . . In raising this I do not mean that we cannot speak of subordination second-hand. Rather, I wish to encourage us to do this, and to suggest that we can do this most intelligently in coalition, listening with special care to those who are actively involved in knowing and ending the systems of domination that touch their lives.

Conclusion

. . . The false efficiencies of law schools, where we edit facts out of cases and cabin concepts such as "crime" and "property" into semester-sized courses, ill-prepare us for the long, slow, open-ended efficiencies of coalition . . . but coalition at its best never works that way. The slow and difficult early work [of discussion and even conflict] gives us efficiencies when we need them: when the real challenges come, when justice requires action, when there is no time to argue over how to proceed. . . . When called upon they will answer with a courage and wisdom born in their place of coalition.

Matsuda urges advocates to "ask the other question" to see how "different" systems of subordination are interconnected and mutually reinforcing. Although simple as method, asking other questions can unmask social realities and their mutually reinforcing linkages. Consider these points in another context. Below, legal scholar Rabia Belt demonstrates how even a "kaleidoscopic" and "complex" view of social problems can be enriched when one raises "other" questions. Belt asks another question—the disability question—as reflected in the early 2000s television series, *The Wire*, a fictional world aiming to capture the "real" world, and widely celebrated for doing so. In your view, do Belt's analytical narration and asking of other questions reveal or clarify systemic inter-connections that otherwise might escape notice or nuance?

"AND THEN COMES LIFE": THE INTERSECTION OF RACE, POVERTY, AND DISABILITY IN HBO'S THE WIRE

Rabia Belt
13 Rutgers Race & L. Rev. 1 (2012)

Introduction

... The Wire has caught and kept the attention of critics, academics, and others interested in the urban landscape.... The brainchild of David Simon, a former journalist at the Baltimore Sun and ... Ed Burns, a former Baltimore police detective and Baltimore city public school teacher, The Wire gave viewers a kaleidoscopic view of Baltimore....

... Injury abounds in The Wire. Police officers are shot, suspects are beaten, drug addicts overdose. Despite the onslaught of injury, disability is an underdeveloped part of the world of The Wire....

Disability among minorities

... The disability rights movement began in the 1970s with an explicitly civil rights-oriented framework that attacked the old paternalist, medical-focused model of disability....

... Disability studies has certainly had its successes in altering this landscape, most notably, the American Disabilities Act of 1990 (ADA).... [But] disability studies lacks sustained attention to the interlocking problems of racism, poverty, and disability.

... [D]isability and poverty issues are both interrelated and ... flow and compound each other.

... [O]f the thirteen million adults who received means-tested cash, food, or rent assistance in the mid 1990s, ... half of them had a severe disability....

. . . Currently, people with disabilities are three times more likely to live in poverty than a person without a disability. . . .

And significantly, the relationship between poverty and disability is amplified by racism. Even controlling for socioeconomic status, race is correlated with an increased risk for ill-health and disability. . . .

Where can information about poverty, disability, and race be found on The Wire? In a word, nowhere. . . . Of course, like any text, The Wire's silences and whispers about disability speak volumes. . . .

The first, and only, explicit mention of disability on the show comes early, on the fourth episode of the first season. Lieutenant Cedric Daniels is attempting to construct an elite force to investigate the gang controlling the inner-city drug trade. . . . [O]ther police leaders see the task force as an opportunity to shed themselves of the dregs of their units. Two such rejects, the alcoholic white police officers Polk and Mahone, are the focus. . . . [Mahone is injured in a] botched raid. . . . [Later,] Mahone points out the "injury" on the x-ray and triumphantly announces that it is his ticket off the force with a disability pension. . . .

Unlike the predominantly minority and predominantly poor cast of The Wire and the recipients of government disability resources more generally, in this scene, the beneficiaries of disability largesse are older, middle-class white men. . . .

[After Officer Kima Gregg is shot,] the viewer is provided only glimpses of Greggs's injury and convalescence: Greggs in a coma, looking out the window of her hospital room, speaking to the officers about the shooting, using a walker, and then later, completely healed with the exception of a neck scar. . . .

Kima's shooting is indicative of a larger trend within the show: the display of injury with an absence of rehabilitation or healing. . . .

. . . [P]eople with disabilities are placed in the "stigmatophobic" areas of the show where their sole function is to repel other characters who are not disabled, instead of demonstrating their own lived experiences. . . . People with disabilities are a pointed exception to the "forms of complex personhood" reflected through other characters in The Wire. . . .

. . . [D]isability, like other topics such as caretaking and parenting, are erroneously relegated to [a] "private" sphere as cultural motifs that have little to do with policy. Significantly, the absence of these "private" activities serves to minimize the burdens on poor women. . . .

Advocates notice "areas of emphasis and inattention" that frame our understandings of reality, as Belt and Matsuda point out. One asks about individuals or groups omitted and also about relations of privilege and subordination unexplored—making "a shift from speaking about *disabled persons* to *disabling societies*," for example.[15] The insights gained position advocates to envision more clearly how social identities might be marshaled as assets in bottom-up struggles.

NOTES AND QUESTIONS

1. *Asking Other Questions.* In a subsequent reflection, Margaret Montoya relates a conversation with her daughter in spring 2020 that bears on her antisubordination work:

> I was conversing with my younger daughter Alejandra about the current protests; she had joined the BLM protests in the streets of Washington, D.C., in the days following the George Floyd atrocity. She asked me what steps I was taking to center Blackness in my work and activism. I began by saying that the COVID-19 infection statistics for Latinx were as bad as those for Black people and in some cases worse. "Stop," she said to me, "that's whataboutism. Listen to yourself; we, non-Black People of Color, non-Black Latinxs, are being asked to quiet those impulses; to hear the demands in Black terms. What will YOU do differently?"[16]

Can you reconcile this call for centering Black experience and struggle with Matsuda's entreaty "to ask the other question" in coalitional, antisubordination struggle? How should advocates combine and balance the twin needs to understand particularities (differences) as well as patterns (similarities)? How might timing help advocates accomplish both—over time and using time?

5.3 FLIPPING SYSTEMIC SCRIPTS—SOCIAL IDENTITIES AS GROUP ASSETS FOR LONG-TERM STRUGGLES

We have seen how systems effectively script daily life and society at large. Systems set the terms of, and stage for, human relations and activities. The systemic uses of social identities have produced *political* identities—that is, politicized identities rooted in shared or similar experiences with systemic injustice and, perhaps, with social struggle. Recognizing shared grievances and aspirations helps advocates convert those identities into assets that help create and sustain a collective consciousness for longer-term group struggle. It effectively flips the script on top-down uses of identity to preserve colonial hierarchies so that advocates can use social identities as assets.

---

[15] Vanessa Gómez Bernal and Beltrán Roca, Disability, Social Movements and Radical Theory: An Anthropological Approach, 22 Anthropological Notebooks 79, 86 (2016).

[16] Margaret E. Montoya, Foreword, in Francisco Valdes and Steven W. Bender, LatCrit: From Critical Legal Theory to Academic Activism (2021).

The example below draws from the U.S. Muslim experience since 2011. After the terrorist attacks in September of that year, Muslims across the United States (and beyond) were subjected to special scrutiny based on that shared identity. Many were mistreated. Some were detained without cause. Others were imprisoned and disappeared. These experiences of systemic injustice helped to politicize Muslims as Muslims, allowing Muslim advocates to unite collectively. Below, political scientist Gil Gott explains the historical process and contemporary injustices that allow advocates to use Muslim identity as an asset for organizing and action. As you read, think of similar instances from earlier reading and personal or professional experience. These examples can inform your advocacy work with various groups.

THE DEVIL WE KNOW: RACIAL SUBORDINATION AND NATIONAL SECURITY LAW
Gil Gott
50 Vill. L. Rev. 1073 (2005)

Since September 11, Muslims, Arabs and South Asians in the United States have had to contend with disparate and abusive treatment, both within civil society and at the hands of state actors including security, law enforcement and prison officials. . . .

Racialization of Muslims, Arabs and South Asians Before September 11

. . . As early as 1909, a federal judge declared that a Syrian/Arab applicant met the statutory requirement of whiteness for [U.S.] naturalization eligibility [at a time when nonwhites were ineligible]. . . .

. . . [However,] not all judges agreed that Muslims, Arabs and South Asians should be classified as white, and some judges refused them access to citizenship through naturalization. . . . In addition, in 1987, the Supreme Court held that ethnic groups, such as Arabs, could bring section 1981 civil actions for discrimination. . . . Scholars familiar with . . . mixed signals sent from U.S. society to Muslims, Arabs and South Asians adopted the term "invisible minority" to capture the groups' unique status.

Ambiguity of racial status, resulting from some degree of mixed classification under the law, has been reinforced by the different waves of immigration from the Middle East. Prior to World War II, for example, Arab immigrants to the United States were mostly Christians from Syria and Lebanon. Thereafter, immigrants came from North Africa and elsewhere in the Arab World, and many were Muslim, a racialized religion. Moreover, "external" politics have had a unique impact on the status of Arabs and Muslims in the United States. Fallout from the 1967 Arab-Israeli War was an early watershed. This led to ostracism of Arabs and Muslims in the United States but also provided the impetus toward those groups' formation of a sense of collective identity. Michael Suleiman traces the rise of "Arab-American pride" to the consequences of post-1967 Middle East politics and U.S. foreign policy in the region. He notes that many Arabs in the United States felt humiliated by the quick defeat of Arab armies and resentful of the partiality that the U.S. government and its people showed toward Israel. Arab-Americans responded by organizing to fight the negative stereotypes of Arabs that increasingly permeated U.S. media and to make U.S. foreign policy more balanced in the Middle East.

Thus, 1967 saw the creation of the Association of Arab-American University Graduates (AAUG), the first Arab American organization with "political-scholarly goals." This signaled the beginning of a new era of pan-Arab organizing in the United States. Other groups followed, including the National Association of Arab American and the American-Arab Anti-Discrimination Committee. Despite the creation of such advocacy organizations, negative images of Arabs and Muslims continued to dominate media representations. . . . Between forty and fifty-one percent of the respondents in a survey in 1981 agreed that Arabs were barbaric, cruel (44%), treacherous, cunning (49%), warlike, bloodthirsty (50%), mostly anti-Christian (40%) and/or anti-Semitic (40%), and that Arabs mistreated women (51%). . . .

. . . The first Gulf War in 1991 only added to the dehumanization of Arabs and Muslims, as reflected in the comments of General Norman Schwarzkopf when he referred to Iraqis in Kuwait as not being part of the "same human race we are." Racial epithets were used to goad U.S. troops forward in Iraq, and racist depictions of Iraqis appeared in U.S. newspapers. Mosques were bombed and Muslim schools, organizations and businesses were vandalized. Hate crimes again surged against Arabs, and the FBI engaged in intimidating interviews of Arabs in the United States. Sudden, event-related surges in hate crimes and anti-Arab and anti-Muslim media representations became a recurring theme in the 1990s. This theme repeated itself after the 1993 World Trade Center bombing and the 1995 Oklahoma City bombings. Thus, U.S. Arab and Muslim communities' well-being became closely linked to events and forces beyond their control. . . .

The result has been the formation within U.S. society of a racialized and subordinated sub-group that has moved toward forming a non-assimilated cultural and political identity in response to state and societal othering processes. . .:

> The racial transformation of Arab identity within [the United States] has been influenced in large part by a second wave of [pan-Arab oriented] Arab-American immigration, by the formation of Arab-American political organizations beginning in the 1960s, and by a growing resistance among these groups to U.S. foreign

policy in the Middle East. In the wake of the Persian Gulf War, Arab-Americans emerged as a semi-legitimate minority group.

In ways that parallel the experiences of the "unmeltable" peoples of color in the United States, Muslims and Arabs do not have the same choices that are available to whites to opt in or out of ethnic identities. The boundary-marking differences that set these groups apart from whites evince an immutability that has been the hallmark of enduring forms of racialized group-based subordination. . . .

State Action in the Racialization of Muslims, Arabs and South Asians After September 11

Abundant evidence of post-September 11 racialization and abuse of Muslims, Arabs and South Asians exists. . . . Generally, the record shows that the government quickly extended its pre-September 11 discrimination of Muslims, Arabs and South Asians through the most vulgar forms of racial profiling. Law enforcement officials immediately began apprehending racially profiled Muslim and Arabs. . . . Given that these detentions resulted from racial profiling and programs like the selectively-targeted (anti-Arab and anti-Muslim) Absconder Apprehension Initiative and the National Security Entry-Exit Registration System ("NSEERS"), we may assume that nearly all of the detained persons have been Arabs, Muslims or South Asians living in the United States[,] . . . [leading a scholar to conclude:]

> Instead of helping to weave Muslims into the fabric of the nation and garner their support in anti-terrorism efforts, recent government policies [such as NSEERS] have singled them out as a group that is dangerous and suspect, as potential subversives. By requiring Muslim community organizations to use their resources on self-defense—resources that have been substantially depleted by government closures of charitable institutions and community fears—programs focused on community building must be cut-back or sacrificed. (Not unlike the resource drain caused by the federal government's targeting of civil rights activists in the 1960's).

. . . Racialization of Muslims, Arabs and South Asians in Post-September 11 Society and Culture

The American-Arab Anti-Discrimination Committee reported some 700 violent incidents directed at "Arab Americans or those perceived to be Arab Americans," occurring in the first nine weeks after September 11. . . .

Hate crimes against Arabs, Muslims and South Asians did not, unfortunately, disappear after the immediate aftermath of September 11. . . . Again, cultural (religious), racial (foreign-ness) and foreign policy (anti-war, pro-Palestinian) determinants combine in the construction of

Arabs and Muslims as demonized and dehumanized outsiders, available to a hateful and fearful public as literal and figurative punching bags.

Employment and other forms of economic discrimination also increased sharply after September 11 . . . against individuals who are or are perceived to be Muslim, Arab, Afghani, Middle Eastern or South Asian. . . .

Political Identity and Racialization

The race-based civil rights movements of the mid-twentieth century brought about a "great transformation" in U.S. political culture. . . . Importantly, the transformation entailed the articulation of collective, race-based political identities that proved resilient enough to survive the demise of the civil rights movement and many of the policies that movement shaped. . . . [T]he notion of "interests" in politics expanded to include not just economic but also social and cultural dimensions. . . . [T]he civil rights movement's most permanent success lay in creating new racial subjects; race-based political identities that formed around the practices and possibilities of "collective opposition."

. . . Racialized collective identities [consequently] are pragmatic in that they allow for effective group mobilization, but differ from more conventional interest-group formations in projecting a desire to confront the deeper social structures of racial subordination. In modern United States history, racialized and collectively conscious political subjects stand as an unmistakable challenge to the equality claims of liberal democracy. The consolidation of such identities has corresponded with the great fault lines of social, political and legal closures that characterize the United States as a settler-colony. Typically, such identities move collectivities beyond political advocacy of narrow material interests or attempts to reshape United States foreign policy in support of national causes abroad.

Racialization of political identities in the United States has entailed the bridging of national or ethnic differences through "pan-ethnic" formations. Evidence of such a trend among Muslims and Arabs existed well before September 11. . . . The result was the creation of a number of professional national Muslim political advocacy groups in the late 1980s and early 1990s that sought to politicize Muslims in the United States.

The American Muslim political organizations acted as lobbyists for Muslim interests and as recruitment vehicles to encourage Muslims to run for office. Just before the elections in 2000, a merger of organizations occurred that indicated the further consolidation of Muslim political organizations. Moreover, in the same year, a historic meeting brought together the four major Arab and five major Muslim organizations. This pan-ethnic group agreed to a common agenda involving the "future of Jerusalem, civil and human rights, participation in the electoral process, and inclusion in political structures," thus entailing a mix of foreign policy and domestic civil rights and political empowerment issues. . . .

In the post-September 11 context, several important shifts have occurred that may augur in the direction of an even more sustained civil rights-based political identity for Muslims, Arabs and South Asians. . . .

Studies have shown a marked increase in both religiosity and political ambition among Muslims since September 11. Researchers draw a connection between the strengthening of Islamic ties among Muslims and an increased desire to participate in United States politics. Amaney Jamal shows such a correlation in her study of mosques attendance and political participation. Interestingly, Jamal's work drew inspiration from the role played by Black churches in the creation of politicized group consciousness among African Americans. Jamal found that for Arab Muslims, "mosques are directly linked to political activity, civic participation and group consciousness." A sense of "common fate," a characteristic of the group consciousness for which Jamal tested, brings Arab Muslims to see "the injustice that occurs to one Muslim" as "an injustice that has befallen the entire Muslim community." . . .

Equally as impressive is the sustained . . . [effort in] fielding candidates in local, state and national elections. . . . These electoral trends are paralleled by an active Muslim and Arab civil society. . . . [O]ppositional politics emanating from such groups in the post-September 11 context evinces a pronounced reliance on identity as a basis for gathering support. . . .

The evidence presented here reveals that the status of Muslims, Arabs and South Asians in the United States society has been, and continues to be, shaped by forces . . . operating at the levels of the state, society and market. . . . Hostility and conflict, evincing cultural and racial but also ideological forms of animus, have been met with responses indicating the formation of racialized, group-based political identities. . . .

Gott shows, in this contemporary setting, that preexisting social identities can be weaponized from above. In turn, the resulting injustices can help foster group consciousness from below. This heightened consciousness brings into focus identity-framed grievances around which people, entities, and movements can coalesce for organized action.

Below, critical race scholar Robert Chang analyzes group experiences with "identity politics" for equal justice. Like Gott, he shows how identity-related experience can generate personal yet collective consciousness. Instead of Muslims, he focuses on "people of color" as a group. In both instances, as in others (like Latinx groups) these categories signify "pan identities" that include varied racial, ethnic, nationality, gender, and other kinds of identity groups. As sources of *critical* consciousness based on experience, subordinated social identities can become a means of developing action-oriented groups—rather than of dividing them—and thus are key to social justice struggle. As you read, keep in mind Gott's analysis of Muslim identity as an asset for organized struggle. Drawing on both excerpts, what do you see as the means and significance of identity consciousness for bottom-up advocacy?

THE END OF INNOCENCE OR POLITICS AFTER THE FALL OF THE ESSENTIAL SUBJECT
Robert S. Chang
45 Am. U.L. Rev. 687 (1996)

. . . As each oppressed group struggles to assert its place in the national polity, it is necessary to recuperate it from its marginal position. This process is often accomplished through an embrace of a new, positively formulated identity. In the context of persons of Asian descent, there was a moment in history when some student activists at UCLA in 1968 held an Are You Yellow? conference. After protests by Filipino Americans who did not consider themselves "Yellow," and after a brief flirtation with "Oriental," activists settled on "Asian American." This new Asian American consciousness was accompanied by a struggle to regain history, a struggle to tell our own stories, and to articulate our claim to rights in American society. Through this process we have become, and are becoming, Asian American. This process is ongoing.

. . . [In this ongoing collective process, a necessary step] is to explore how to account for differences while at the same time allowing us to participate in each others' struggles.

Coalition building has been put forward as one strategy to achieve this goal. The need for coalitions is an acknowledgment of the democratic process. It is also an acknowledgment that minorities have been unable to gain any real political voice, despite such legislation as the Voting Rights Act. In this sense, coalition building can be seen as a strategy of resistance.

Coalition building has gained a new importance as demographic projections now make it possible to imagine a majority of color. This news has generated mixed reactions. In some communities, the coming majority of color exists as a specter, the new bogeyman that strikes fear into the hearts of whites afraid of no longer being the majority. For many people of color, it has engendered new hope. . . .

Coalitional politics, growing out of identity-based, interest-group politics, is an expansive form of identity politics. Insofar as you can articulate a common identity, which results in common interests (or common interests that result in a common identity), coalitions are strong. But with strength comes weakness—coalitions form and dissipate depending on specific political exigencies. For example, with English-Only or immigration restrictions, Asian Americans and Latinos sometimes finds themselves in coalition against whites and blacks. With affirmative action, Latinos and Blacks sometimes find themselves in opposition to whites and Asian Americans. I have grossly overgeneralized, but my point about the difficulties of coalitional politics holds true.

. . . [T]his overgeneralization reveals a question we must ask of identity politics. How effective are politics that use identity as a central organizing principle? To what extent is identity coextensive with common interests? . . . [I]dentity [can be] a poor proxy for common interests. Identity [can be] both overinclusive and underinclusive as an organizing principle for [coalitional] politics. . . .

[Therefore] we must take seriously the insights of anti-essentialists/constructionists. Identity, with its essential moorings, is inadequate for the task at hand. . . .

Angela Harris reminds us of the work to be done:

> There are no "people of color" waiting to be found; we must give up our romance with racial community. . . . If any lesson of the politics of difference can yet be identified, it is that solidarity is the product of struggle, not wishful thinking; and struggle means not only political struggle, but moral and ethical struggle as well.

It will be a struggle to establish a "people of color" solidarity in the service of a progressive agenda. . . .

[To establish and maintain successful coalitions,] we must develop a greater appreciation of the interconnectedness of different forms of oppression. For "people of color," we can begin with the ideology of white supremacy, which permitted the genocide of Native Americans, the enslavement of Africans, the conquest and dispossession of Mexicans, and the exclusion of Asians. But we must not stop there if we are to deepen the democratic chain of equivalences. How are race and gender connected? Sexual orientation? Class? A progressive agenda that does not take these connections seriously will fail along all three dimensions. It will fail politically, morally, and ethically. . . .

. . . [History] teaches us that the color line is not something that exists in nature to be discovered. The color line is something that is created by human actors; it is a site of contestation. I would draw the color line differently to establish a chain of equivalences that would deepen our identification with each other, strengthen our solidarity. I see this as the challenge of radical democracy—to redraw the color line, understanding identity as political, and not essential. . . .

Chang explains that social identities such as "people of color" are created by people themselves—both from above and from below. Social identities are political because dominant systems have made them so from above to justify caste systems. But they are political also in part because people can reclaim and redeploy them from below to undo them. They have been invented—engineered and administered—by people to reflect (and reinforce) a hierarchical sense of group commonality and/or difference determined, in fact, by group interests and power.

Learning that social identities are socially engineered—purposefully constructed—entails understanding, for example, that all girls are not born with an essential inclination for pink nor boys for blue. This critical understanding further entails an appreciation that the categories of "girl" and "boy" are themselves social constructions. Social identities are much like another invented currency: money. Both identity and money are significant in everyday life, even though money and identity are widely understood to be just human fictions (which is why the currency of one country is just paper in the next). That is, everyone understands that the coins or paper called "money" can have value in one place—and no value elsewhere—because those items can be given or denied value. None of us is puzzled by the fact that coins have no intrinsic, fixed, universal value. The same understanding applies to whiteness, Blackness, and other kinds of social identity, which similarly can be given or denied social value in a given place or time. Race, for example, is a category that reflects primarily top-down social agendas:

> "[R]ace" [signifies] a vast group of people loosely bound together by historically contingent, socially significant elements of their morphology and/or ancestry. . . . In other words, social meanings connect our faces to our souls. Race is neither an essence nor an illusion, but rather an ongoing, contradictory, self-reinforcing process subject to the macro forces of social and political struggle and the micro effects of daily decisions. . . . [T]he referents of terms like Black, White, Asian, and Latino are social groups, not genetically distinct branches of humankind.[17]

Social construction is a critical concept underlining a systemic fact: no single identity trait carries with it a fixed social meaning across space and

---

[17] Ian F. Haney-López, The Social Construction of Race: Some Observations on Illusion, Fabrication, and Choice, 29 Harv. C.R.-C.L. Rev. 1, 7 (1994). See also Audrey Smedley, Social Origins of the Idea of Race, Race in 21st Century America, 3–23 (Curtis Stokes, Theresa Meléndez & Genice Rhodes Reed eds. 2001) ("From their inception, racial categories have been arbitrary and subjective, and racial ideology itself is capable of being molded to fit the exigencies of any social or political situation. . . . 'Race' became a way of looking at the world's peoples, dividing them into separate, discrete, and exclusive populations, arbitrarily linking each with distinct physical and behavioral (and moral and intellectual) features conceived as inherited and unalterable, and socially ranking each grouping so that they have unequal access to society's resources and rewards.").

time. No identity possesses an "essential" quality. Like money, the meaning of any identity varies depending on context and circumstance.

To illustrate further, critical feminist scholar Leti Volpp examines the social construction of Filipinx identities within the United States by law—in her words, how "race is made" in this context.

AMERICAN MESTIZO: FILIPINOS AND ANTIMISCEGENATION LAWS IN CALIFORNIA
Leti Volpp
33 U.C. Davis L. Rev. 795 (2000)

... The first antimiscegenation statute affecting marriage was enacted in 1661 in Maryland. The statute did not prohibit marriage between whites and blacks but it enslaved white women that married black men, as well as the couple's children. By the time the Supreme Court finally declared antimiscegenation laws unconstitutional in *Loving v. Virginia*, thirty-nine states had enacted antimiscegenation laws. . . . While the original focus of these laws was primarily on relationships between blacks and whites, also prohibited were marriages between whites and "Indians" (meaning Native Americans), "Hindus" (South Asians), "Mongolians" (into which were generally lumped Chinese, Japanese, and Koreans), and "Malays" (Filipinos). . . . The statutes varied in their enforcement mechanisms: some simply declared miscegenous marriages void; others punished them as felonies. . . .

What questions does this history raise? . . .

. . . Miscegenation laws directed against excludable "racial aliens"—whether Chinese, Japanese, or Filipino—were sharply linked to both sex specific patterns of migration and calls for expulsion. Where racialization of Chinese and Japanese may have diverged from Filipinos is in the history of U.S. colonization. The colonization of Filipinos, accompanied by Americanization projects, may have facilitated a racialization that differentiated Filipinos from Chinese and Japanese through the perception of Filipinos as less foreign. . . .

. . . The history of Filipinos in California makes vivid the gendered relationship between racial identity and the marriage contract. In addition to cases in which Filipino/white couples sought to marry and who therefore asserted that Filipinos were not "Mongolians," the racial classification of Filipinos was put at issue in the case of a mother seeking to stop her daughter's marriage, in two cases where annulment of marriage was sought, one by a white woman, the other by a Filipino man, and in one case in which a prosecutor sought to void a marriage so a white wife could testify against her Filipino husband. These parties all argued that Filipinos fell under the jurisdiction of the antimiscegenation statute, because they sought a basis on which to alter legal entitlements and to shape behavior.

... [G]ender has historically been bound up with race through the linkages of manhood, citizenship, and whiteness. The history of antimiscegenation laws targeting Filipinos in California reveals a complicated desire to protect white women from "brown men." This desire must be understood as being shaped by class. White women that associated with Filipino men appear to have been largely working class women—and not women considered deserving of greater protection because of middle class status. ...

... The concern to protect "women" was of course also racialized. ...

... In 1907, Congress passed the Expatriation Act, which provided that any American woman who married a foreigner was automatically denaturalized. Congress partially repealed the law in 1922, but continued to require that any woman who married a man ineligible to naturalize—in other words, one racially barred from doing so—would lose her citizenship. This provision remained law until 1931. ...

Considering the relationship of gender to miscegenation law requires a recognition of the manner in which the control of women and their sexuality is understood as necessary to maintaining and reproducing the identity of communities and nations. Women are thought to guard the purity and honor of communities. Nationalism entwines with race so that women are subjected to control in order to achieve the aim of a national racial purity. This is visible in the history described here. Filipino male sexual engagement with white women was considered a national threat, requiring the literal expulsion of Filipino men from the body politic, accomplished through the simultaneous granting of independence to the Philippines, and the revocation of "national" status which had formerly allowed Filipinos to freely travel to the United States. ...

Filipina/o Identities

... Specifically, this history raises the question of the relationship of Filipinas/os to the Asian American identity category. We have here a very real rupture of Mongolian with Malay, of East Asian with Filipino, made manifest in legal history. Does this mean anything more than antiquated notions of ethnology? Well, yes—this rupture is something that is continually perpetuated. One critic has called the continued inclusion of Filipinas/os within the term "Asian American" a form of semiotic violence inflicted on Filipinas/os, when Asian American is translated as Chinese or Japanese American by Asian American activists or legal scholars. ...

... As important as Spanish colonialism to the Filipino experience may be the experience of U.S. colonialism [which reflects] ... the general failure to focus on the history of U.S. imperialism and the role of the United States as a colonial power.

Conclusion

. . . Identity is central to the writing of history—communities are named and name themselves within the narratives of the past. The positioning of Filipinos as "Mongolian," or the positioning of Filipinos in opposition to Mongolians, as the ethnologically different "Malay," provides a narrative within which the contemporary identity of Filipinos is created. The historical question of whether to group Filipinos with Chinese and Japanese as "Mongolian" for purposes of miscegenation laws is echoed in the contemporary quandary about positioning Filipinas/os as Asian American, when the center of that identity category is clearly occupied by Chinese and Japanese Americans.

. . . This history demonstrates the manner in which racial identity is created. There is nothing natural or preordained about the classification of Filipinos as "Malay" or as "Mongolian"—or as any other identity. Racial identity is shaped in relation to other forces. Here, such forces include assumptions about racialized sexuality, colonial relations between the United States and the Philippines, the importation of exploitable laborers without political rights, and the intertwining of gender and nationalism. The legal history of the shifts in racial classification of Filipinos in California, between "Mongolian" and "Malay," underlines the manner in which race is made.

Like with previous examinations of other identity groups, Filipinx identities are shaped by supremacist ideologies that equate top-down notions of sameness and difference with top-down notions of superiority and inferiority. These insights—the social construction of identities—point advocates to the reasons why social identities—or, more precisely, their social effects—are intersectional. And, hence, why no group identity should be mistaken as monolithic, or "essentialized" as a collective. All social identities are not only socially constructed, but also intersectional, calling for antiessentialist analyses of identity groups. As a set, this trio of concepts provides conceptual tools for analysis and advocacy designed to promote critical understanding of identity-based hierarchies in relation to each other.[18] These conceptual tools are designed to be used in support of group struggles against systemic injustice through collaborations and coalitions.

These tools enhance advocates' capacity to recognize how every individual occupies positions in multiple categories at once: "every human

---

[18] See Kimberlé Crenshaw, Demarginalizing the Intersection of Race and Sex: A Black Feminist Critique of Antidiscrimination Doctrine, Feminist Theory and Antiracist Politics, 1989 U. Chi. Legal F. 139 (1989); Kimberlé Crenshaw, Mapping the Margins: Intersectionality, Identity Politics, and Violence Against Women of Color, 43 Stan. L. Rev. 1241 (1991).

has multiple identities to be acknowledged, honored, and celebrated,"[19] such that the character of a person or population cannot be reduced to any single identity trait.[20] Even individuals who share a particular identity do not necessarily share the same experiences of life; all groups are internally diverse, no matter how they are socially constructed, and therefore every group may differ internally on interests and priorities. Identity categories are overlapping, in flux, and complex. Assuming that *any* identity category carries an "essential" or universally fixed viewpoint or social significance with corresponding interests is an analytical error of the first order for politicians, scholars, and advocates, among others. Even though social identities define personal experience in collectivized terms, that process is infinitely varied and intersectional across systemic contexts.[21]

As individual lives and social conditions vary, so do the salience and meaning of any shared identity. For example, a woman victim of domestic violence who is an undocumented immigrant might decide not to report an assault to police, thinking that being vulnerable to deportation as an undocumented immigrant is more salient in the situation than is being a victim of domestic violence. Her calculation is different than a person of the same race, gender, class, and age who is a documented immigrant or citizen. As critical legal scholar Kimberlé Crenshaw explains, "intersectional subordination . . . is frequently the consequence of the imposition of one burden that interacts with preexisting vulnerabilities to create yet another dimension of disempowerment."[22] "Essentializing" either "women" or "immigrants" would distort analysis because it would obscure relevant complexities. Legal scholar Nancy Levit adds that, by thinking in intersectional and antiessentialist terms, activists and advocates come to understand problems and solutions differently:

> On an experiential level, one person might belong to several identity groups.... Discrimination on the basis of one identity characteristic could be compounded by discrimination based on another aspect of identity. A black woman, for instance, experiences not just racism and sexism, but the greater-than-double burden of intertwined racism and sexism, which is its own unique (and perhaps particularly virulent) form of discrimination. On a class level, discrimination manifests against groups along multiple, intersecting axes. For example, minority race males,

---

[19] Ann Picard, Women's Rights are Human Rights Redux: Ain't I a Human?, 26 J. Civ. Rts. & Econ. Dev. 753, 786 (2012).

[20] Patricia A. Cain, Lesbian Perspective, Lesbian Experience, and the Risk of Essentialism, 2 Va. J. Soc. Pol'y & L. 43 (1994); Adrien Katherine Wing, Brief Reflections Toward a Multiplicative Theory and Praxis of Being, 6 Berkeley Women's L.J. 181 (1991); Angela P. Harris, Race and Essentialism in Feminist Legal Theory, 42 Stan. L. Rev. 581 (1990).

[21] Anna Kaijser and Annica Kronsell, Climate Change through the Lens of Intersectionality, 23 Environ. Politics 417, 423 (2014).

[22] Crenshaw, Mapping the Margins, at 1249.

especially those who are economically deprived, may be particularly vulnerable to selective criminal prosecution, incarceration, higher sentences, and imposition of the death penalty.[23]

Connecting these concepts and points as analytical tools, critical feminist scholar Trina Grillo discusses intersectionality and antiessentialism jointly as bottom-up concepts that follow from the recognition that social identities are social constructions. Drawn from the Schools and Approaches, these and similar concepts help us make sense of and navigate identity-based realities, assumptions, and contradictions that can affect advocacy and may inhibit progress. These critical concepts and practices help advocates convert subordinated identities into assets for group organization and action while avoiding analytical or strategic errors.

ANTI-ESSENTIALISM AND INTERSECTIONALITY: TOOLS TO DISMANTLE THE MASTER'S HOUSE

Trina Grillo
10 Berkeley Women's L.J. 16 (1995)

... [Let's] begin ... with a quote from the late poet Audre Lorde: "The master's tools will never dismantle the master's house." ... [A]nti-essentialism and intersectionality ... are indispensable tools for dismantling the master's house.

... I believe these two concepts embody what is essentially the same critique, but made from two different starting points. For simplicity's sake, as I continue I am often going to talk about them together.

Intersectionality

... In every set of categories there is not only subordination, but also its counterpart, privilege.

The most vivid description of this interrelationship ... [is as] a "double-headed hydra": you cannot get rid of the subordination without eliminating the privilege as well.

To look at white, middle-class women as subordinated as women is accurate as far as it goes, but their experience of oppression is not interchangeable with the oppression of non-white, non-middle-class women. The whiteness and middle-class status supply privilege even as the femaleness conveys oppression.

Anti-Essentialism

Essentialism is the notion that there is a single woman's, or Black person's, or any other group's, experience that can be described independently from

---

[23] Nancy Levit, Theorizing the Connections Among Systems of Subordination, 71 U. Mo-K.C. L. Rev. 227, 228 (2002).

other aspects of the person—that there is an "essence" to that experience. An essentialist outlook assumes that the experience of being a member of the group under discussion is a stable one, one with a clear meaning, a meaning constant through time, space, and different historical, social, political, and personal contexts.

The perceived need to define what "women's" experience is and what oppression "as women" means has prompted some feminists to analyze the situation of woman by stripping away race and class. To be able to separate out the oppressions of race and class (as well as sexual orientation and other bases of oppressions), the theory goes, we must look at someone who is not experiencing those oppressions and then we will see what oppression on the basis of gender alone looks like. This approach, however, assumes that the strands of identity are separable. . . . But as the intersectionality critique has taught us, they are different and not just [additive].

Race and class can never be just "subtracted" because they are in ways inextricable from gender. The attempt to subtract race and class elevates white, middle-class experience into the norm, making it the prototypical experience. . . . [S]uch essentialism "makes the participation of other women inessential to the production of the story. How lovely: the many turn out to be one, and the one that they are is me." . . .

But remember, we speak with multiple voices only because we have categories that describe these voices as separate from one another. . . .

Some have described the anti-essentialism and intersectionality critiques as dangerous in that, if carried to their furthest conclusions, they make it impossible to talk of any oppression. If each woman, if each Black, has a different experience, how can one say that women as women, or Blacks as Blacks, are oppressed? How can we use the feminist method of paying attention to our experience, without being essentialist ourselves? Elizabeth Spelman asks whether it is "possible to give the things women have in common their full significance without thereby implying that the differences among us are less important." If we emphasize our differences, then do we not risk losing all credence as women? . . .

[In response,] it is important to emphasize that essentialism is not always a bad thing; however, unconscious, self-protective, self-advancing essentialism is. The question is whether the essentialism, which is sometimes unavoidable, is explicit, is considered temporary, and is contingent. . . .

In the end, the anti-essentialism and intersectionality critiques ask only this: that we define complex experiences as closely to their full complexity as possible and that we not ignore voices at the margin. The fact is, the choice with which we seem to be presented is either to accept a white, middle-class woman's view of the world or to talk explicitly about different types of women.... Essentialist feminist theory [thus far] has picked one pebble and asked it to represent all.

Lessons to Be Learned From the Anti-Essentialism and Intersectionality Critiques...

Lesson One

The anti-essentialism and intersectionality critiques teach us to look carefully at what is in front of our faces. When things are being described in ways contrary to our sensory experiences, we must pay particular attention. We must look at the evidence of our bodies, and we must believe what our bodies tell us. They teach us to check for the deep, internal discomfort we feel when something is being stated as gospel but does not match our truth. Then they teach us how to spin that feeling out, to analyze it, to accept that it is true but to be able to show why that is so. They also teach us to be brave.

... If we accept the definition of Black which we have been given—a definition which historically defined anyone with "one drop of Black blood" as Black—we ignore the existence of multiracial people. We ignore people whose experiences may be different from those experiences which have been defined as constituting the Black experience—that is, the "essentialized" Black experience. By so essentializing, we assume that the taxonomy of race proposed by nineteenth-century white supremacists—that human beings can be classified into four races and everyone fits neatly into one slot—is a valid one. On the other hand, if we do classify multiracial people as Black, the potential for group solidarity is much greater. "We are all Black," we say. "You cannot divide us."

... What does anti-essentialism teach about this situation? ... The confusion that a biracial child feels does not derive from being classified as Black, but from essentialist notions that being Black is one particular experience, and that this experience is not hers or his....

Lesson Two

Another way that anti-essentialism and intersectionality critiques help us is by keeping us from being diverted by ... "the oppression sweepstakes."

Oppression based on my race has always seemed closer to my rage and has reached a place more central to my being than oppression based on my gender or on other aspects of my self.... But now I understand a little better the anti-essentialist lesson which says I should not permit myself to be pressed, to be made to choose which part of myself is most important to me. The lessons of anti-essentialism and intersectionality are that the oppressions cannot be dismantled separately because they mutually reinforce each other. Racism uses sexism as its enforcer. Homophobia enforces sexism by making people pay a heavy price for departing from socialized gender roles. And those of us who are middle-class, or members of otherwise privileged elites, can be used as unwitting perpetuators of the subordination of others.

We have spent a lot of time arguing over whose pain is greater. That time would be better used trying to understand the complex ways that race, gender, sexual orientation, and class (among other things) are related.

A note: To say that the oppressions are related does not mean that they are the same. It is dangerous at the least to expect that experiencing one oppression means that one understands the others. In fact, to expect so is disrespectful in that it wipes out the true, lived experience of that group in exchange for one's own, self-serving fantasy.

Lesson Three

We all have the impulse to essentialize. It is built into our brains. This means it is important to remember who we are. Even though we may be "underrepresented" persons in many ways, many of us are living in this very master's house that we are hoping to help dismantle. We may be living in the basement, and the others in the house are not always particularly nice to us, but our view is still shaped by where we are situated.

. . . What this means is that although our own experience is our touchstone, we must be careful about generalizing from that experience. In other words, we must be careful about essentializing the experiences of persons in the group to which we belong. I certainly cannot speak for all Black persons, Latinas, or women. What I can do is to pay careful attention to the lives and material conditions of women who are underrepresented in the law and to believe that their struggles have meaning and have much to teach me and the world. What I can also do is help their voices be heard, not by presuming to speak for them, but rather by doing what I can to put a microphone in front of them. What I can do is to work where I am today to make these changes. . . .

For example, wherever I work, I can begin to struggle against the tyranny we have permitted the Educational Testing Service, the Bar Examiners, and other such organizations—for the most part private, power-mad, and secret—over decisions about who gets into school, who gets a job, who is thought of as smart, and who thinks well of herself once having arrived.

. . . Anti-essentialism and intersectionality are checks on us; they help us make sure that we do not speak for those we cannot speak for or ask others to share our agenda while they patiently wait for their own. . . .

. . . Of course, it is easy to romanticize the vision of the outsiders. Some acts labelled resistant actually reproduce and support the status quo. Still, I think it is important to accept what I view as fact: That each of us has a limited view of the world, that we have a better chance of forming a vision of a post-patriarchal, post-racist society both by trusting in our own experiences and by seeking out voices that are drowned out by essentialism in all its forms.

As this discussion of social construction, antiessentialism, and intersectionality makes clear, social group identities are important in systemic advocacy because they are important in law and thus in modern-day societies. Jennifer Jihye Chun, George Lipsitz, and Young Shin expand on these points in practical, actionable terms. They worked as organizers and advocates with Asian Immigrant Women Advocates (AIWA), a California-based immigrant justice group, and they describe the practical importance of understanding social identities contextually for transformative advocacy:

> AIWA does not embrace intersectionality simply because its members have been wounded by racism, sexism, imperialism, class exploitation, and language discrimination, but because each realm of these experiences has helped the organization to see how power works and how new identities are needed to combat its intersectional reach and scope. . . .
>
> . . . Hate crimes and housing discrimination alike evidence "racial lumping" through which hostility to particular Asian nationalities is generalized to all. . . .
>
> . . . [I]f used correctly, delineations of difference can well become sources of social empowerment and reconstruction under some circumstances. . . . All politics are identity politics. All struggles over power concern the social meanings applied to constructed identities and identifications to some degree. . . .
>
> Gender- and race-based movements like AIWA seek to give identity a political definition, to unite groups around common beliefs and experiences rather than common phenotypes or biological characteristics. . . . Positions and politics belittled as identity politics actually entail necessary efforts by aggrieved groups to turn negative ascription into positive affirmation. Identity-based mobilizations are tactical moves that draw their determinate logic and social force from the utility of emphasizing the things that unite a group rather than the things that divide it. They invite constituencies to inhabit the identities that have been imposed upon them in order to work through them. . . .[24]

As Gott, Chang, Volpp, Grillo, and the AIWA advocates show, critical insights like social construction, antiessentialism, and intersectionality are

---

[24] Jennifer Jihye Chun, George Lipsitz & Young Shin, Intersectionality as a Social Movement Strategy: Asian Immigrant Women Advocates, 38 Signs: J. of Women in Culture and Soc. 917, 918, 936–38 (2013).

not idle concepts. They are designed for real-world applications—to analyze contexts and organize actions despite systemic blindfolding and legal fictions. They help advocates understand how to convert identities into assets for action while avoiding common errors. These critical tools have been used in varied contexts to support organized group struggle.

Sociologist Mary Romero similarly has explained that:

> The ways in which race-based movements and racialized communities construct their identities ha[ve] enormous implications for setting justice agendas and for coalition building. Racialized ethnicities were forged out of centuries of colonialism, conquest, slavery, capitalism, racism, sexism, classism, and the politics of appropriation and co-optation. Consequently, all forms of resistance and struggle pose extremely complex questions. In order to resist effectively, we must constantly reconsider and reconstruct identity [as an asset for bottom-up progress].[25]

Echoing Calavita's analysis of identity collisions in Chapter 3, Romero concludes that, "Although the social constructions of race in the U.S. present identity as fixed and stagnant, ideologies of race are anything but consistent." Using identities as assets, organized group struggles pursue antisubordination values and aims that cross multiple kinds of identity difference, as laid out in the next section.

NOTES AND QUESTIONS

1. *Reflection Exercise.* Back in the heyday of overt de jure discrimination by law, states aiming to discriminate against Black residents by legislation had trouble figuring out just who was "Black" for such purposes. Virginia, for example, adhered to the so-called one-drop rule in preventing interracial marriage, reserving the white race only for those "entirely white, having no known, demonstrable or ascertainable admixture of the blood of another race." Despite the advent of formal equality of the races under *Brown* and subsequent civil rights laws, the issue of racial identification remains relevant today in official settings that range from the national census to affirmative action. Consider how you would self-identify within some or all of the various socially constructed categories of identity raised in this book. Should these identities matter to employers or clients? Why or why not?[26]

---

[25] Mary Romero, Historicizing and Symbolizing a Racial Ethnic Identity: Lessons for Coalition Building with a Social Justice Agenda, 33 U.C. Davis L. Rev. 1599 (2000).

[26] See generally Jessica A. Clarke, They, Them, and Theirs, 132 Harv. L. Rev. 894 (2019); Yale University, A Guide to Gender Identity and Affirmation in the Workplace (2016), https://lgbtq.yale.edu/sites/default/files/guide_to_gender_identity_and_affirmation_in_the_worlkplace_at_yale_2016_0.pdf. Greater consideration has been paid to inclusive language in classrooms, as well. See generally Jessica MacNamara, Sarah Glann, and Paul Durlak, Experiencing Misgendered Pronouns: A Classroom Activity to Encourage Empathy, 45 Teaching Sociology 269 (July 2017). But see Rachel N. Levin, The Problem with Pronouns, Inside Higher Ed (Sept. 19, 2018) (arguing that asking individuals to disclose their preferred pronouns may have unintended

2. *The "Definitional Instability" of Jewish Identity.* Jewish identity—like that of other groups in various ways—demonstrates "definitional instability," according to cultural and literary historian Sander Gilman. Noting that race "is a constructed category of social organization," Gilman points to 18th and 19th century racial definitions in which "the 'blackness' of the Jew was not only a mark of racial inferiority, but also an indicator of the diseased nature of the Jew." Physical differences—"the appearance, the skin color, the external manifestation of the Jew"—led to a "general consensus of the ethnological literature of the late nineteenth century . . . that Jews were 'black' or, at least, swarthy," which in turn was associated with "the group's general infirmity."[27] The racial definition of Jews has morphed. In different eras and places, Jews have been considered variously as Black, white, a distinct racial group neither Black nor white, and not one racial group at all. Because racial identity is both a tool for channeling subordination and privilege and an asset for mobilization around shared experiences, this definitional instability has significant social consequences. The advocacy group Jews for Racial and Economic Justice describes some of the complexities of Jewish identity and consequences:

> In the United States, Jews were certainly *not* Black, but were not considered to be quite white either. This distinction was further entrenched by the advent of "scientific" racism. Jews faced some legal barriers before and after the American Revolution and were later subjected to immigration restrictions and discrimination via housing covenants as well as quotas and bans at educational institutions. However, those oppressions were nothing like those faced by African-Americans, Native Americans and many other immigrant groups. Like the Irish and Italians, light-skinned Jews of European descent once faced pervasive, racialized bigotry. Today they primarily identify as white and are read as white, benefit from white privilege, and participate in upholding the system of white supremacy. However, this whiteness is contextual and conditional. While white supremacy may have embraced Jews of European descent in the last century, white supremacists have never considered any Jews to be white, as was abundantly clear watching the neo-Nazi rallies in Charlottesville, VA in the summer of 2017. . . . [A]ntisemitic beliefs predate modern white supremacy ideology. But white supremacy has since been incorporated into antisemitism, creating a shifting, slippery mixture of religious intolerance, mythology and racism. This means that Jews [of European descent] can sometimes be racialized as white, but antisemitism persists. . . . As a community, we have the critical job of agitating many of our people around white privilege while also taking very seriously the impact that antisemitism has on us. We don't see that work as contradictory. . . . [B]eing targeted by

---

consequences that diminish inclusivity and safety in classrooms), www.insidehighered.com/views/2018/09/19/why-asking-students-their-preferred-pronoun-not-good-idea-opinion.

[27] Sander I. Gilman, Are Jews White: Theories of Race and Racism: A Reader, 294–302 (John Solomos and Les Back eds. 2009).

one oppression doesn't negate being privileged by, complicit in, or acting as a perpetrator of another. . . .

    Meanwhile, like all other People of Color, Jews of Color are the targets of racism and white supremacy, while as Jews they are also targeted by antisemitism.[28]

Jewish identity thus has been continuously racialized in the United States (and elsewhere), but the precise nature of that racialization has shifted across time and geography. This definitional instability highlights the social construction of race, as Gilman notes. Are all categories to some extent similarly unstable in definitions and boundaries—and their meanings—simply because they are defined by humans? Are some categories more subject to instability across time and place to serve the interests of elites? How might this affect advocates' and activists' ability to affirmatively use social identities to mobilize and to build coalitions?

3. *Identity, Complexity, and Indeterminacy.* Recall the Martinez excerpt from Part I outlining litigation to determine whether Mexican-American groups are white or Black, and his discussion of ambiguity, discretion, and opportunity resulting from the social complexity and legal indeterminacy of that context. How do the materials and excerpts above amplify your understanding of these points? Do these concepts and tools help you understand why and how social identities can and must be converted from top-down tools of oppression to bottom-up assets for equal justice?

5.4 ANTISUBORDINATION SOLIDARITY BUILDS POWER ACROSS MULTIPLE KINDS OF DIFFERENCE

Judicial conceptions of antidiscrimination delineate the law of formal equality and its accommodation of inequalities. In the United States, the "antidiscrimination principle" dominates equality law. As interpreted judicially, this antidiscrimination framework looks only to whether a plaintiff can produce "smoking gun" evidence showing that the defendant individually, consciously, and overtly "intended" to discriminate against the individual plaintiff. This narrow approach ignores known problems of pretextual discrimination and the use of proxies to disguise intentional discrimination. This doctrine also declares evident discriminatory *effects* to be mostly irrelevant; legally, only manifest "purpose" matters. This judicial framing creates evidentiary hurdles that exculpate discrimination and reinforce inequality.

    A key aspect of antidiscrimination as an approach to equal justice is its design to protect individualism, which distorts the entire system to

---

[28] Understanding Antisemitism: An Offering to Our Movement, Jews for Racial & Economic Justice (2017), www.jfrej.org/assets/uploads/JFREJ-Understanding-Antisemitism-November-2017-v1-3-2.pdf.

justify injustice. The idealized "appeal of the antidiscrimination principle may be nothing more than an illusion"[29] because persistent social problems are in fact collective, not individual. They require collective remedies, as well as individual ones. Judicial doctrines that unduly demand individualized claims and remedies perpetuate a mismatch between actual problems and potential solutions; these doctrines demand abstracted, decontextualized claims, doctrines, and outputs. This mismatch ensures that remedies never match the injury, continuing the injustice of entrenched caste systems.

This doctrinal regime also disregards social positions and asymmetries of "different" actors. It equates whites with Blacks and men with women, as if persons in each group shared a similar history and position of equality already. Antidiscrimination doctrine blindfolds law to the difference between systemic privilege and systemic subordination. As a result, the antidiscrimination principle fails, by judicial design, to distinguish between *remedial* and *invidious* forms of "discrimination." This failure enabled judicial notions of "reverse discrimination" to halt race-conscious remedies for invidious discrimination, such as affirmative action programs enacted by democratic means. Under the antidiscrimination principle, remedies to discrimination were transmuted into a new kind of discrimination; the democratic remedy became the new judicial problem. Nevertheless, the systemic problem was and is subordination. Any good faith cure must serve antisubordination ends, or systemic inequality will continue to fester despite professed commitments to equal justice.

In fact, whites and men *as groups* have never encountered systemic blocks against their right to vote, to education, to property ownership, to jury service, or to any other social good. Meanwhile, due to invidious discrimination, women and Blacks have been subjected to systemic exclusion and disempowerment; they have been denied all of the above rights for decades, if not centuries. The two groups in each pair obviously are not on equal terms even today (and, of course, these binary "pairs" are themselves an oversimplification of racial and gender identity categories).

The ultimate difference in systemic uses of social identity to maintain colonial caste systems from above and critical counter-uses of identity to dismantle them from below is in the social ends, or values, that those respective uses pursue. From below, those values reflect a commitment to the "antisubordination" principle—a critical conception of equal justice designed in the 1970s and since to transcend formal equality and its "antidiscrimination" approach. Antisubordination is geared to be anticaste; antidiscrimination as judicially crafted is not.

---

[29] Owen Fiss, Groups and the Equal Protection Clause, in Equality and Preferential Treatment: A Philosophy and Public Affairs Reader 84, 106 (Marshall Cohen, Thomas Nagel & Thomas Scanlon eds. 1977).

The antisubordination principle emphasizes a twin focus: first, a focus on caste systems, and, second, a focus on the groups actually involved in them. This approach aims to displace legal formalism with social reality. The antidiscrimination approach focuses on individuals as social atoms and declares the group nature of systemic injustice to be anomalous or "irrelevant," whereas antisubordination puts identity castes at the center of collective injustice and social struggle. As critical legal scholars Jerome Culp, Jr., Angela Harris, and Francisco Valdes note:

> Critical race theorists therefore start with . . . what it is like to have as part of one's everyday experience the possibility that one is the target of discrimination—the possibility, that is, of becoming without warning the victim of "spirit murder." . . . To be part of a pattern of discrimination that we can "prove" at the aggregate level but never at the individual level is to be a subject the truth of whose experience is always in doubt. For critical race theory, this analytical structure is the Catch-22 of prevalent forms of antidiscrimination discourse.[30]

The antidiscrimination approach expresses the perspective and collectivized interests from above; antisubordination expresses the view and interests from below. Antisubordination values help to anchor critical decisions about advocacy. Feminist legal scholar Ruth Colker explains next how judicial crafting of antidiscrimination fails by design to remedy the problem of ongoing systemic discrimination. Colker sketches how antisubordination values can and should guide advocates—and decision makers—through social complexity, including distortions created by the antidiscrimination (or, as she calls it, the "anti-differentiation") approach itself.

ANTI-SUBORDINATION ABOVE ALL: SEX, RACE, AND EQUAL PROTECTION
Ruth Colker
61 N.Y.U. L. Rev. 1003 (1986)

. . . [T]he anti-differentiation perspective . . . is an individual rights perspective in two respects. First, it focuses on the motivation of the individual institution that has allegedly discriminated, without attention to the larger societal context in which the institution operates. Second, the anti-differentiation perspective focuses on the specific effect of the alleged discrimination on discrete individuals, rather than on groups. Race-and sex-specific policies or actions are invalid under this perspective because they reflect invidious motivation and result in dissimilar treatment for similarly situated individuals. It is equally invidious for white men to be

---

[30] Jerome M. Culp, Jr., Angela P. Harris & Francisco Valdes, Subject Unrest, 55 Stan. L. Rev. 2435, 2442–44 (2003).

treated differently from black women as for black women to be treated differently from white men under this perspective, because both situations violate the preeminent norm of equal treatment. Anti-differentiation advocates therefore argue for "color-blindness" or "sex-blindness" in the development and analysis of legislative and institutional policies, and frequently criticize affirmative action as violating that principle. . . .

In contrast to the anti-differentiation approach, the anti-subordination perspective is a group-based perspective, in two ways. First, it focuses on society's role in creating subordination. Second, it focuses on the way in which this subordination affects, or has affected, groups of people. It is more invidious for women or blacks to be treated worse than white men than for men or whites to be treated worse than black women under this perspective, because of the differing histories and contexts of subordination faced by these groups. Anti-subordination proponents therefore advocate the use of race- or sex-specific policies, such as affirmative action, when those policies redress the subordination of racial minorities or women. . . .

. . . Historically, the equal protection principle developed to remedy a history of subordination against a particular group in society, blacks. Aspirationally, it reminds us that no group should remain subordinated in our society and that we should therefore take seriously the claims of women and of other discrete minorities that they have been subjected to pervasive discrimination in our society.

The anti-differentiation principle, in contrast, does a disservice to this history and fundamental aspiration by asserting that discrimination against whites is as problematic as discrimination against blacks. We have not decided, as a nation, that all distinctions are invidious. We permit distinctions on the basis of intelligence or ability. We only prohibit distinctions that we have good reason to believe are biased or irrational, and it is group-based experiences that primarily inform us as to which kinds of distinctions are biased or irrational. Thus, the anti-subordination principle, by recognizing and drawing on the historical subordination of blacks and women, offers a substantive explanation for why certain distinctions are subjected to closer scrutiny. . . .

Bringing the Principle of Anti-Subordination to the Forefront

. . . The proposed [anti-subordination] framework has two key advantages. First, it would allow institutions to implement and defend remedial race- and sex-specific policies and actions without having to rely on stereotypes about minorities or women. A defendant would be able . . . to show that its policy would help eliminate subordination. Second, the framework would ensconce the normative values of anti-subordination within the entire equal protection analysis and thereby make that analysis more [legally principled and socially] meaningful. . . . This framework would provide the analytic process of equal protection with a consistent theoretical base [for principled outcomes]. . . .

Colker outlines above basic distinctions between antidiscrimination (or anti-differentiation) versions of equality doctrine and antisubordination alternatives. When antidiscrimination approaches prevail, as now, formal equality blesses actual and systemic inequalities. When antisubordination approaches guide law, not only are groups central, but group interests also are key. As we see next, building a shared consciousness of "different" group interests within and among identity-based groups is part of building solidarity.

The shifts in advocacy and activism surrounding "Dreamers" provide an apt example in an immigration context. Dreamers are undocumented young adults who, starting around 2001, campaigned for the federal Development, Relief and Education for Alien Minors (DREAM) Act to create a pathway to citizenship for many who came to the United States as children. The Act never passed, but Dreamers achieved gains when President Barack Obama signed an administrative order staying deportation and granting work authorization to some young undocumented individuals. As sociologist Ala Sirriyeh notes, in early stages, Dreamers argued they deserved citizenship because they were "innocent, assimilated, the brightest and the best." That argument was criticized as excluding many undocumented youth and separating Dreamers from others who struggled for full citizenship:

> [N]eoliberal governance has profoundly altered the nature of citizenship . . . [by] guarding the divide between "deserving" productive citizens and "undeserving" "failed citizens." This transformation of citizenship hits hard at already marginalized populations. . . . [A]ttention rests on individual choices rather than structural causes; the aim being to produce citizens who make the "right choices."[31]

Over time, however, Dreamers rejected the idea that citizenship should be accorded to just those with "merit" and denied those without "merit," when notions of merit were created to exclude many groups based on social identities like indigeneity, class, race, religion, dis/ability, and sexual orientation. Rather, Dreamers chose a path of building solidarity. This shift involved asserting the right to political inclusion even before attaining citizenship and making connections to historical and contemporary struggles of other marginalized groups:

---

[31] Ala Sirriyeh, "Felons Are Also Our Family": Citizenship and Solidarity in the Undocumented Youth Movement in the United States, 45 J. of Ethnic and Migration Studies 133 (2018).

> [T]here are useful examples of solidarities expressed in the undocumented youth movement's messaging and actions around race, particularly in recent campaigns critiquing criminalization and the immigrant industrial complex. . . .
>
> . . . In questioning which "America" they claimed membership of and under what terms, [these youth] presented a different narrative of US citizenship and history. This was not the celebratory "nation of immigrants" where hardworking immigrants could achieve the American Dream. Instead, the United States was narrated as a site of struggle and suffering. Through storytelling and direct actions drawing on histories of resistance by oppressed peoples in the United States, undocumented youth narrated themselves into the chronology of this alternative US story of protest and struggle against injustice. In doing so they widened the constituency they addressed, looking beyond the white neoliberal subject and identifying common ground with marginalised citizens. . . .
>
> [For example, an undocumented advocate] . . . campaigned against the detention of undocumented people, but also for US citizens and immigrants caught up in the criminal justice system . . . [using] a narrative of resistance to the systemic race and class oppression which excluded both undocumented people and US legal citizens from citizenship rights and entitlements in practice.[32]

In shifting their advocacy framework, the Dreamers built solidarity within and across "different" immigrants, a stepping-stone toward coalitional actions, as the following excerpt emphasizes.

Below, legal scholar Martha Mahoney shows the centrality of groups *and* their interests in constructing coalitional solidarity. Sustained collaboration between Blacks and whites empowered both groups as workers, while judicial interventions aimed to fragment them. This crisp example shows workers cultivating antisubordination solidarity across multiple kinds of difference despite the top-down pressures or barriers of law. Recall, as you read, the key points on interest convergence (and divergence) presented by Bell and others in Part I.

---

[32] *Id.*

CONSTRUCTING SOLIDARITY: INTEREST AND WHITE WORKERS

Martha R. Mahoney
2 U. Pa. J. Lab. & Emp. L. 747 (2000)

... Solidarity is work. During the 1990s, social and legal theory explored race as a social construction and whiteness as a racial construction. Legal theory, however, paid very little attention to the intersection of class and whiteness. This Comment treats both class and whiteness as social constructions that affect each other rather than developing in isolation from each other, focusing on the example of the interest in solidarity among white workers at the Kmart Distribution Center in Greensboro, North Carolina. Black employees led the organizing drive and black ministers led community support, but white workers joined in, expressing solidarity in a number of ways. Law and legal theory need to recognize solidaristic interest in white workers and support it on terms that strengthen minorities, both in politics and in labor law.

White workers made up about one third of the work force at Kmart. North Carolina has a long history of racism that helped keep workers unorganized. As a result of a series of cases on voting rights, Greensboro was moved from a mostly-black congressional district, represented in Congress by a black Democrat, to a mostly-white district represented by a white Republican. ... [T]he interests of the white working class people of Greensboro are not represented better under the new political system; rather, if they had retained minority political leadership, their chances for representation of their labor interests and for transformation of their class and race consciousness would have improved.

The Greensboro Distribution Center was the only Kmart distribution center with a mostly-African-American work force. Workers at the Greensboro Distribution Center were paid an average of $5.10 per hour less than workers in identical jobs at other centers. Therefore, all the workers, including approximately one-third who were white, suffered financial losses because of racism.

The drive to organize a union at the distribution center began with the leadership of black workers and support from the black community. Black ministers voluntarily were arrested in support of the organizing drive, and they organized community support when the company refused to negotiate with the union. When the workers demonstrated at Kmart, blacks met first at the church and whites met first at the union hall. The union was literally the base from which whites entered shared organization with African-Americans. When Kmart sued black workers and black ministers, white workers held a press conference and demanded to know why they too had not been sued. Black community support was crucial in mobilizing community support in general in Greensboro. White workers therefore gained directly from the strength of black community figures during the several years of struggle.

The success of the drive eventually brought union benefits to white workers as well as to blacks. When the union won a contract, it marked the first time in the history of the Kmart corporation that a distribution center had been organized. Although whites were a minority of the union, they had gained considerably from the leadership of black employees and black community figures. Reverend Nelson Johnson and the other black ministers had carefully described their campaign as one for "sustainable community" in part to avoid a double trap: when the struggle was described as a fight for racial justice, white workers did not see it as their problem; and when the struggle was defined in purely economic terms, blacks felt the campaign ignored its racial dimension.

Race is a social construction in which whiteness is a distinct socially constructed identity. Both class and race are socially constructed categories, and the meanings of these categories are forged through human relationships and historical and social processes. The interaction of the material world and the ways we explain and understand it generate "experience" and, therefore, the "experience" of lived whiteness is something continuously constructed, reconstructed, and transformed for white people. Although privileged identity requires reinforcement and maintenance, protection against seeing the mechanisms that maintain privilege is an important component of the privilege itself.... Whiteness facilitates achievement, diminishes conflict, and grants access, while simultaneously diminishing white awareness of white racial identity. Whites therefore see themselves as acting as individuals, rather than as members of a culture.

Most whites understand racism as something that a second party (the racist actor) does to a third party (the subordinated person of a minority race); racism appears to be a phenomenon distinct from themselves. Because whites do not see the dominant norm of whiteness and the mechanisms of its reproduction, bigotry and prejudice—individualized and intentional harms—become the focus of inquiry for whites.... For white Americans above the working class—those who write the books and do most social analysis—racism often appears to be something that working class whites (particularly Southerners) do to African-Americans and other people of color. In the absence of any widely agreed upon concept of class interest, wealthier and more educated whites perceive working class whites only as racists....

Because law and legal theory have difficulty recognizing class interest and are relatively new at recognizing whiteness, the interest of whites in solidarity can be especially difficult to explore. Focusing on status rather than class as an analytical category leads to the belief that white interest in retaining privilege is natural and essential for all whites, regardless of economic class. Without a vision of solidaristic interest, the elimination of white privilege is treated theoretically as depending on persuading whites to reject inauthentic privilege rather than on mobilizing some aspects of white self-interest, as well as moral persuasion, against race privilege. . . .

Class, Status, and the Construction of Whiteness

. . . Sociologists and historians have labored to articulate the relationship between economic and social structures and consciousness, ideology, and struggle. Structural relations are experienced in the lives of people, both individually and socially, no matter how we describe them. Collective action and the sorting of possibility and decision also happen through experience of real people. . . .

White privilege is therefore vital to an understanding of "class" in America. Once "class" is understood as a social process, it is easy to see that race plays an important role in making class and consciousness. In the field of law, however, a general focus on status and distribution rather than on class and production tends to naturalize the existing distribution of power and privilege.

. . . The satisfaction of shared struggle and the development of solidaristic identity, exemplified by the assertion made at the press conference that white workers must be counted as part of the lawsuit, has no place in a vulgar status regime. Therefore, part of protecting solidarity in law is to increase the exploration of class issues in legal theory along with the critique of whiteness and to avoid naturalizing the concept of white privilege by focusing only on status.

Subordination and Solidarity

Consciousness and action for white working class people are a contest of identification: How much will they wind up being white in ways that make it harder to "do class," and when will they "do class" in ways that lead to new or solidaristic behaviors and beliefs? Change may begin with behavior modification. Given the history of racial exclusion in the Southern workplace, this means increasing willingness to work with people of color at all ("we are all in this together"). Change may include a commitment to egalitarianism, ("we all deserve good treatment") or it may involve the rejection of white supremacy as destructive and inauthentic—in other words, actively taking positions against racism. Because consciousness and action are interrelated, the fight to name interests is therefore part of the construction of class itself. . . .

. . . The Kmart organizers purposely avoided characterizing their struggle as concerned solely with racial or economic justice, to avoid alienating either whites or blacks.

... The Kmart situation provides a good example of ... [a social or systemic] "borderland" within which identity can change through mutual interaction. ...

Race and Power, Class and Interest

... There is an interactive relationship between low levels of union organization and class consciousness in American society. The legal conditions necessary for labor to organize are eroded or lost in part because of the lack of labor's political power. As labor's presence in national politics diminishes, challenging legal rules that protect employers becomes more difficult. Low levels of union organization decrease the capacity of workers to pursue their interests as a class and make them increasingly dependent on the state for protection. ... Working people become disproportionately dependent on the general attentiveness—or lack of it—of their political representatives, who may not be directly responsive to labor at all.

Low levels of labor organization also lead white workers to interact less with leaders who have an investment in building antiracist solidarity. As a result of pervasive residential segregation, working class whites often do not live near working class people of color. Since class formation happens outside the workplace as well as within it, and given the history and persistence of racism in America, promoting antiracist class-based mobilization is a practical challenge as well as a theoretical one. Political leaders in mostly-white districts often consolidate voting bases that do not require interracial solidarity. The loss of organized labor's political leadership and the transition to less organized participation within broader civic processes both tend to diminish the total amount of antiracist messages that white workers hear.

... In the absence of political representation for labor, representational appeals to white working class people are often pitched overtly or covertly to whiteness and threats to whiteness. In the infamous political advertisement during Jesse Helms's senatorial campaign against African-American Harvey Gantt, a pair of white hands crumpled a slip of paper while the narrator said, "You really needed that job, but it went to a minority because of a quota." These types of messages tell white workers that people of color are their real problem, inflicted on them by the intervention of powerful outsiders into the natural state of affairs where white people had access based on their own individual merit. Since neither Democrats nor Republicans are pursuing labor-protective legislation to protect these voters as workers, however, nobody claims to speak directly to their self-interest except those who speak to them as white workers, as did the "white hands" commercial. ... It is particularly important, then, to examine the redistricting struggles in North Carolina in the district within which the Kmart struggle was located.

In the early 1990s, to comply with the Voting Rights Act, North Carolina created a mostly-black district that spanned much of [Interstate]-85 through the industrial centers of the Piedmont district, which at the time included Greensboro. The district was challenged by white plaintiffs, who complained that they had been placed in a mostly-black district on the basis of their race. The Court held that the "bizarre" shape of the district and the fact that it created a black majority district juxtaposed to areas of white majority created the appearance of "racial gerrymander." Justice O'Connor's majority opinion held that the act of classifying by race is itself "odious," without regard to whether the classification creates privilege, subordination, harm, or deprivation.

The underlying logic of [the opinion in *Shaw v. Reno*] depends on the white discursive strategies of power evasion and color evasion. The opinion is color evasive. As many scholars have pointed out, mostly-white districts are not suspicious in the midst of whites, no matter how oddly they are shaped. Only proximity to the "Other" triggers suspicion. To Justice O'Connor, noticing race is "odious" because she and other whites believe race itself is bad; race became bad because it was firmly linked to concepts of subordination and inferiority. Because color evasion includes avoiding seeing whiteness, whites will never notice color in all-white areas. *Shaw* is also power evasive: The Constitution is offended not by the exercise of power resulting in racial subordination, but by the very act of classification by race. . . .

Finally, Justice O'Connor's assertion that majority-minority districts may "pull us apart" reflects the positioned white belief that there exists a social "we" who are not currently "apart." . . .

. . . [Thus, the] invisible dominant norms of whiteness and status combine to make it easy for judges to conceive of voting cases as "race" cases when they concern minority voting rights and "political power" cases when they appear to concern whites.

But the political economy of District Twelve was less mysterious than the Court insisted, and its organization seems to have favored the labor interests of white workers who lived within it. The interstate highway through the Piedmont tracks much of the history of labor struggle in North Carolina because it linked the mills and factories. Greensboro was home to the corporate headquarters of Burlington Mills, Cone Mills, and other textile companies; there, paternalism as a labor system disintegrated into labor struggles by the time of the Depression. Further down the highway, in Kannapolis, home of the giant Cannon Mills, the needle trades union UNITE won a National Labor Relations Board (NLRB) election in June 1999 after twenty-five years of organizing.

The placement of highways through the Piedmont is not arbitrary. Roads track the organization of production, as materials and people must be moved from place to place. Along those routes, black and white working people came to work in mills, factories, and the businesses that developed around them. As the textile industry grew through the late nineteenth and twentieth centuries, mill villages became close-knit white working-class communities. Blacks were excluded from all but the heaviest jobs and lived outside the mill villages. Blacks were only able to obtain industry jobs in large numbers after the federal government brought pressure for desegregation of the textile mills. The presence of black workers brought both segmentation of the labor market and a militancy that had been forged from collective action and the civil rights movement into struggles of textile workers. Black support proved fundamental to union successes after 1970. But racism continued to be used as an anti-union strategy in fighting organizing drives, and many textile companies continued to reserve supervisory positions and better jobs for whites. . . .

If the goal of legislative districting in North Carolina were to increase the political strength of working class people, and particularly of organized labor, the Piedmont would need a district through the textile and furniture belt along the interstate. However, North Carolina has never sought to maximize working class strength. Quite the opposite. . . . [Elites] mobilize[d] racism in opposition to class solidarity through racist rhetoric and inflammatory denunciation of African-Americans. . . . Violence and terror against both blacks and whites, including whippings and killings, was part of the repression of biracial political alliances. . . .

Therefore, "traditional" districting practices in North Carolina could never unite working class districts to gain electoral power. . . .

The *Shaw* cases disrupted a district well suited to developing class-based politics that linked industrial locations along an interstate highway while creating a black-majority voting district. . . . By moving Greensboro out of District Twelve, the *Shaw* Court made it improbable that white workers would continue to have minority leadership that would help protect their interests. The Court therefore constructed a political theater in which "class," meaning combined mobilization and consciousness, is less likely to "happen" at all. . . .

. . . [T]he decisions on the Voting Rights Act and District Twelve have not been aimed at labor but at questions of minority power in America. As has happened before in North Carolina, however, some white workers will suffer losses as well.

Working class interest in the voting rights cases would favor strong representation for labor and an end to the myth that black domination is dangerous for white workers. When a white worker desires to pursue class-conscious interests in America today, he or she may be best represented in a minority district. Minority-concentrated districts may serve the class needs of white workers far better than cross-class white majority political districts. White working class people in wealthier suburban districts may discover that their elected leadership consistently opposes their class interest. Because consciousness and organization interact in making class, and because Americans possess little social awareness of class, placing white working class people in wealthy districts may result in their identification with people of "middle class" status. This diminishes class consciousness and opportunities for class mobilization.

The interest of whites in black leadership is seldom explored in law. When racial classification is defined as a harm in itself, or intentional placement in a mostly-minority district is defined as a harm to whites, exploration into the nature of subordination disappears. The reasoning of *Shaw* makes it impossible to hold the searching inquiry into the real nature of harm and interest that is fundamental to increasing class consciousness today. When either whiteness or class is ignored, white workers are placed in an inherently more reactionary position than when they are considered together. If we notice only whiteness, then working class whites only identify with those aspects of themselves which they share with whites of other classes and fail to identify those aspects of self which they share with people of color. If we emphasize only class, race does not disappear from American society. Rather, because whites do not perceive white privilege and norms as a matter of course, demands for inclusion from people of color are experienced by white workers as disruptive of the natural state of affairs.

Formalism on race (the *Shaw* approach) combined with the invisibility of class places white workers in the most reactionary position of all. Transformative work requires both the recognition of structures of power and of mutual need. Eventually this includes developing an understanding of the limits that racism places on class advancement. For whites, therefore, transformative identity does not lie in separate organization on the basis of their whiteness, nor in emphasizing only privilege and not class solidarity, but rather in the recognition of shared goals on the basis of equality and strength for minorities.

Elites used labor, election, zoning, and equal protection law to preserve power, as Mahoney shows. But group struggle can shift consciousness through joint action, and that shifted consciousness in turn helps shape new solidaristic forms of action. Antiracist solidarity requires white people both to *see* they share a working-class identity with Blacks and other people of color and to *see through* the color evasion that makes white privilege within the working class invisible to many whites. Solidarity then becomes a creative force that unites interest, identity, and antisubordination for collectivized group struggle.

NOTES AND QUESTIONS

1. *A Grown-Up Conversation About Race and Class.* The Rev. William Barber, II initiated Moral Monday demonstrations at the General Assembly in North Carolina in 2013, roughly 20 years after the events Mahoney analyzed above. During the next several years, tens of thousands of people participated in protests, aiming to prevent the legislature's conservative majority from enacting policies to suppress voting, reduce access to healthcare, eliminate wage protections, and otherwise reinforce elite power. In 2017, Rev. Barber was appointed to lead Repairers of the Breach, a national coalition of faith-based social justice organizations operating with an intentionally class-conscious and intersectional identity framework. Repairers of the Breach and the Kairos Center for Religions, Rights, and Social Justice[33] started a modern-day "Poor People's Campaign,"[34] modeled after the economic justice work of the Rev. Martin Luther King, Jr. and others in the 1960s. Among other principles, the Poor People's Campaign is dedicated to the notion that "equal protection under the law is non-negotiable."[35]

In the context of that work, Rev. Barber has called for a "grown-up conversation about race" that addresses racial subordination and class interests to advance solidarity, recognizing that "poverty and economic equality cannot be understood apart from a society built on white supremacy." Barber also calls upon advocates and activists to use critical research methods that draw on history and "see race" in the way that Obasogie, Armstrong, and Wildman highlighted above. Information derived from such research helps to "construct solidarity," as Mahoney describes, by framing intersections of collective group interests based on social identities. Barber suggests that bottom-up research should highlight the short-sightedness of working "in silos with black folk on one end fighting against voter suppression and then white folk on the other end fighting [economic] neo-liberalism." We will talk more about critical research methods in Part V. Consider here how Rev. Barber connects research, collective interests, and identity-based solidarity to effective advocacy addressing the five "fatal diseases" of democracy and society:

> Right now in the Poor People's Campaign, we are saying that there are five potentially fatal diseases that are impacting this democracy: systemic racism, systemic poverty, ecological devastation, the war economy, and the false distorted moral narrative of religious nationalism that gives cover for the four other social diseases.
>
> ... [W]e have to have researchers that can connect all five of them and help people to understand that you cannot talk about

---

[33] See Kairos Center, Who We Are, www.kairoscenter.org/who-we-are/ (defining the Center's work as "drawing on the power of religions and human rights" to build a movement of poor people working in solidarity in a "broad transformative movement to end poverty").

[34] See Poor People's Campaign (stating that organizing and advocacy "to transform the political, economic and moral structures of our society" comes "not from above but from below"), www.poorpeoplescampaign.org.

[35] See Fundamental Principles, Poor People's Campaign, www.poorpeoplescampaign.org/about/our-principles/.

economic advancement, living wages, and lifting the poor if you don't deal with the systemic racism, for instance, of voter suppression. . . .

Research and revolutions go hand in hand. . . . Revolutionaries have to be re-educated by the research because that's what helps them think beyond the predominant mindset of the larger society.

For example, most people don't realize that voter suppression in this moment is more of a white issue than a black issue. The research shows that the states that have participated in racialized voter suppression are among the poorest states in the nation. So the people that get elected through racialized voter suppression pass policies that hurt mostly white people because they are still the majority of the population in those states. We're losing too often on these issues because we work in silos with black folk on one end fighting against voter suppression and then white folk on the other end fighting neoliberalism. We work in silos because we've been conditioned to think they are separate issues when in fact they're all connected.

People are ready for a grown-up, researched movement that can handle dealing with race and poverty, and ecological devastation, and the war economy all in the same space, and can use that kind of power and research to build out a long-term strategy. . . . So, where do we start?

. . . [We start] by building the coalitions of white and black and brown and Latino and Asian and poor folk in the South to raise up this movement and to vote. That's what it's going to take to shift the political calculus in this country. . . . [W]e cannot wait until election season to do the work. It has to be done year round and every year.[36]

The Moral Mondays policy protests and Poor People's Campaign aim to map a path toward principled and accountable decision making under law—toward equal justice. This ongoing organizing and advocacy, springing up in the same region as the Kmart campaign, draws on critical understandings of social identities, collective interests, solidarity, and social progress to guide systemic advocacy. How do the goals and methods of Moral Mondays and the Poor People's Campaign reflect an understanding of collective social identities and related interests as socially constructed, antiessentialist, and intersectional? What seeds were planted by the work of community-labor coalitions supporting the Kmart campaign and other garment and textile workers decades earlier? Do you believe that a critical understanding of that civil and labor rights history informs recent organizing and advocacy work, and, if so, how? And why does Barber say that "research and revolutions go hand in hand"? How might critical research promote the sorts of unlearning and relearning needed to go

---

[36] Rev. Dr. William J. Barber II, Research is Vital to the Moral Integrity of Social Movements, Economic Policy Institute, Working Economics Blog (Apr. 4, 2019), www.epi.org/blog/research-is-vital-to-the-moral-integrity-of-social-movements/.

"beyond the predominant mindset of the larger society" to support systemic advocacy and social progress?

5.5 TRANSFORMING ADVOCACY HELPS TO TRANSFORM SOCIETY—BIT BY BIT, YEAR BY YEAR

Confronting law-as-usual to advance advocacy rooted in antisubordination is risky work. But the antisubordination value—and collaborative solidarity that grows out of that value—can guide everyday action to help transform advocacy and society. Unlearning and relearning advocacy itself is a means toward the broader transformation of systems and societies.

Below, Asian American law scholar Bill Ong Hing describes how James Yen created meaningful changes in society through transformative advocacy. Yen designed a public education project starting with "what the people know" and building on what they have. These two points endure today as cornerstones of systemic advocacy. They illustrate how advocates can launch and sustain a project: start with what the bottoms already have, including their knowledge, and build on it. As Hing explains, Yen's work illustrates concretely many elements of systemic advocacy, including antisubordination consciousness, collaboration, and action. Hing concludes with seven practical pointers for advocates that flow from his analysis of Yen's work and that connect to modern advocacy Approaches, such as community lawyering, rebellious lawyering, third dimensional lawyering, and political lawyering. Note the common emphasis on collaboration with clients and communities based on shared identities, grievances, values, and interests. How might these pointers figure in your potential uses of group identities for antisubordination consciousness, collective power, and action planning? Does Yen's example help clarify the relationship of broad transformative change to everyday, incremental yet long-term practice? What connections do you see between transforming your advocacy and transforming society?

COOLIES, JAMES YEN, AND REBELLIOUS ADVOCACY
Bill Ong Hing
14 Asian Am. L.J. 1 (2007)

Go to the people
Live among them
Learn from them
Love them
Serve them
Plan with them
Start with what they know

> *Build on what they have*
> —Y.C. James Yen

Introduction

Those of us who engage in progressive legal work need to be constantly reminded that we do not know everything—that we are not knights in shining armor swooping in to save subordinated communities. We should be collaborators: working with rather than simply on behalf of clients and allies from whom we have much to learn. Though lawyering for social change is arduous work, there is much to gain in these battles against subordination, not simply from the potential outcome but from the collaborative process itself: as our clients gain strength and confidence, we too are renewed. Thus invigorated by the talent, spirit, and innovation that our clients and allies bring to the table, we aspire to bring that same sense of renewal to those with whom we work.

... I have drawn the invaluable lesson that the fight against discrimination—in essence, the fight against subordination—is one that community lawyers wage most effectively with allies and clients. In their work, these allies demonstrate that the struggle requires skills, techniques, and approaches that, unfortunately, conventional law school classrooms neglect in their curriculum.

If we seek to become more effective collaborative lawyers, then we should keep our eyes open for individuals from whom we can learn. Long before I became a lawyer, I met such a person named Y.C. James Yen. . . . Yen's work has merited accolades all over the world, as well as broadened and enriched my own perspective of progressive lawyering. . . .

The Formative Years

When Yen graduated [form Yale] in 1918, he began work for the War Work Council of the Young Men's Christian Association (YMCA). For his first assignment, Yen was to provide services for 5,000 Chinese laborers—coolies—who were working in France for the Allied forces during the war. Yen's challenging experiences in France would change the course of his life.

Literacy for Chinese Laborers in France

During World War I, the British and U.S. governments recruited 200,000 Chinese laborers to work behind the front lines in France, namely to repair roads, transport food, and dig trenches. The British had enlisted most of these laborers from northern China with the permission of the Chinese government. The men were predominantly poor peasants. . . .

. . . The men were desperately homesick but unable to write letters to their families in China because they were illiterate. Yen discovered that the men had never had educational opportunities because they belonged to the laborer class in China.

Several of the men approached Yen one night, asking him to write home for them, and Yen gladly complied.... The plight of these men—unable to understand the languages spoken around them, unable to read books or newspapers—opened Yen's eyes to the greatest need of the Chinese people: the need to be literate and informed. The more Yen taught them, the more convinced he became that their illiteracy was a deep injustice. Yen realized that what he wanted to do, above all else, was educate the common people of China.

Yen's contact with coolies in France helped mold his belief that a principal reason for the turmoil, tyranny, and corruption in China was that most of the people were docile due to illiteracy and lack of information. He felt that if the foundation of a country was weak, the nation could never become strong....

Yen refused to write any more letters for the Chinese laborers in France and determined that, instead, he would teach them to read and write for themselves. Yen announced his plans to the entire camp and was met with disbelief. For 4,000 years the craft of writing Chinese characters had been reserved for scholars. The peasants, long accustomed to the idea that they were incapable of being educated, could only laugh at Yen's intentions.

Yet Yen proceeded to recruit volunteers, and the work of undoing centuries of subordination began. That first day, forty of the 5,000 men agreed to receive lessons in reading and writing....

Yen recognized early on that he could not personally teach every student, but he knew he could give his students the tools with which to teach each other. Thus, by making each pupil a teacher as well, Yen was able to extend the literacy training to countless others.

Once armistice was reached in November of 1918, Yen extended the literacy movement into other camps of Chinese laborers throughout France.... Yen decided to write, publish, and circulate a newspaper in vernacular Chinese. Yen's paper, The Chinese Laborer's Weekly, not only provided reading material but served a political purpose as well, through its coverage of current events and inclusion of editorials....

Yen's Return to China

Within two years, Yen was in China trying to spread literacy across the entire nation....

[As the program grew, Yen began enrolling girls.] For most Chinese, the idea that females could be educated was a revolutionary notion. For thousands of years, education was an honor reserved strictly for men. Historically, Chinese women had been treated as chattel with their feet being bound and when they married they became the property of their husband's family. Now, however, Yen's campaign was instrumental in the liberation of these women....

... Through the efforts of Yen and thousands of recruited volunteers, China's mass education movement flourished, enrolling approximately 5 million students, ranging in age from 10 to 60, in mass education schools by 1929.

The Village of Dingxian

Although the literacy movement made progress in cities throughout China, Yen was concerned that the movement was not reaching the rural areas that needed education most.... Based on survey results, Yen proposed to use the xian (county), the basic governmental unit in China, as a laboratory for experimental research. China was divided into 1,900 xian in which about eighty-five percent of China's population of 400 million people lived.... By selecting one xian for experimental research, he believed that the results would be applicable to other xian as well.

... Yen determined that the most effective way to use the xian for educational research purposes was to know the xian. His strategy entailed mobilizing intellectuals to live and work with the peasants. In the fall of 1929, Yen moved his entire family from Beijing to [the xian of] Dingxian. Under Yen's influence and example, many intellectuals, including university professors and presidents, as well as individuals with specialized training in foreign affairs and policy, gave up their comfortable lives in the cities and moved to the villages. He insisted that the intellectuals first learn from the peasants to change their perspective before they did any teaching. For Yen, only after the intellectuals learned how to see things from the peasants' perspective could they begin to analyze and solve the problems endemic to the villages.

The Dingxian experiment was probably the first time in China's history that scholars and modern scientists actually went to the people instead of simply romanticizing about them.... In Dingxian, Yen's team did not go and build a separate "little Beijing" to live in. Instead, they actually approached farmers and asked to live in spare rooms. All of the teachers were housed through the farmers' generosity and hospitality....

... Village projects had to be developed with little funds and complete simplicity. Thus, an agricultural expert from Cornell University struggled for weeks to perfect a chicken brooder that could be replicated by the villagers. Doctors from Johns Hopkins had to be re-educated in practical "public health" methods by peasants who had never even heard of the term. Health workers were taught how to maintain sanitary wells, build latrines, and administer vaccinations. Eventually, volunteers from the farming villages were trained as health workers and proudly staffed free clinics.

While Yen and his staff organized literacy efforts, residents followed through with implementing the campaign. Yen's team conducted weeks of "social calls" and group meetings with various residents to explain the goals of the literacy campaign. At a large town meeting, the residents elected a council to take charge. . . .

As the process repeated itself from village to village, Yen's team would set up three or four demonstration schools in centrally located villages. . . . These schools, taught and supported by the people themselves, were referred to as the "People's Schools." . . .

Through his many projects, Yen and his team demystified the process of education and raised the farmers' consciousness of their power over subordination. . . . Learning how to read kindled an awareness of the larger community and a desire to become more informed and involved. Increased literacy led to the creation of The Farmer, the first daily newspaper published for Chinese farmers. A radio station was installed for daily broadcasts of useful information about farming techniques, home improvements, child care, cooperatives, and health. Communities developed self-help cooperatives as an alternative to getting loans from local "bankers" who charged high interest rates. Given "fatter pigs, better seeds, [pollution] control, more eggs per hen, cooperatives for credit, marketing and purchasing," the income of Dingxian farmers skyrocketed. . . .

The Path to a Correlated, Collaborative Approach

Based on their experiences from living among the peasants, Yen and his team revised their intellectual, book-based theories about rural reform. Yen realized that illiteracy was only one piece of the puzzle; "once a man starts to read, his mind begins to grow and he wants to learn how to live. When he has won the fight against illiteracy, he wants to carry on the battle against his other foes—poverty, disease, and misgovernment." Thus, the mass education movement was premised on four new principles: education to combat illiteracy; livelihood to combat poverty; health to combat disease; and self-government to combat civic inertia. . . .

The Dingxian Model in the Philippines

Yen's work in Dingxian and other parts of China became a model for rural reconstruction movements throughout the world. The Philippines, Thailand, India, Ghana, Guatemala, and Colombia adopted the Dingxian model of reconstruction to reform rural societies and bring literacy to undeveloped nations. . . .

The [International Institute of Rural Reconstruction] IIRR adopted Yen's credos: "The village is important but the villagers are more important" and "Start with what the people know. Build on what the people have." . . .

Today at the IIRR, Yen's overarching principles remain the driving force. The IIRR continues to develop strategies that release the powers of the rural poor to transform their lives. The Institute works with the people, rather than for them. IIRR's strategy recognizes that the poor face multiple problems: lack of education, inadequate income opportunities, poor health, a degraded environment, and political oppression. The IIRR uses bottom-up, participatory, integrated strategies to address the complex nature of rural poverty. . . .

The Relevance of Yen's Work to Collaborative and Rebellious Lawyering Scholarship

In reflecting on the accomplishments of Y.C. James Yen in helping peasants, laborers, and farmers in Europe, China, and the Philippines, the similarities to the theoretical lawyering framework advanced by Jerry López, Lucie White, and, most recently, Ascanio Piomelli, become clear. . . . Yen's efforts advance their framework by providing an important example of working for social change on the ground . . . [that yields seven pointers for advocates:]

- Educating clients and communities to support resistance;
- Opening ourselves to being educated by clients, communities, and allies;
- Recognizing that there is no need to romanticize the client's knowledge or vision;
- Highlighting the importance of collaboration;
- Respecting clients instead of repeating a subordinating experience;
- Taking on the extremely challenging battles that collaborative advocacy leads to, despite the odds;
- Integrating and navigating many worlds. . . .

Educate clients and communities to support resistance

Community legal services offices commonly engage in community education . . . to demystify the law . . . [and] to nurture and further their resistance to social, political, and economic subordination by "train[ing] groups of subordinated people to represent themselves and others." . . .

Be open to being educated by clients, communities, and allies

. . . Rebellious lawyers "must open themselves up to being educated by all those with whom they come into contact, particularly about the traditions and experiences of life on the bottom and at the margins." . . .

Eliminate needless romanticization of clients

... [S]ubordinated people's knowledge and stories are not necessarily better than those of lawyers—both groups are essential to the struggle "to fundamentally transform the world." To make such change, López explains, subordinated groups and their attorneys do not want simply to add to each other's knowledge—a bit of this and a bit of that coexisting easily. Instead, they desire to challenge what each knows—how each gained it, what each believes about it, how each shares and uses it." As an alternative to emphasizing lower-income clients' fragility or placing them on a pedestal, López urges lawyers to engage their clients as true equals, worthy not only of respect but also of caring confrontation.

... [While Yen] had the utmost respect and admiration for the peasants with whom he worked and from whom he learned, he also challenged their views, as they challenged his....

Collaborate, collaborate, collaborate

... In what White labels the "third dimension" of lawyering for social change, lawyering is no longer a "unidirectional professional service." It should become a collaborative and communicative practice, demanding strategic innovation, and requiring critical reflection on the forces conditioning the subordination of the poor, as well as the ways the poor might resist and redirect those forces to achieve justice. Through such action and reflection, the poor and their lawyer-allies voice aspirations, identify concrete action strategies, and discover grounds for political unity.

... Instead of describing their objective simply as lawyering for social change or lawyering in the public interest, Piomelli argues, collaborative lawyering theorists take as their goal "lawyering against subordination"—making clearer their commitment to joining with others to eradicate relationships based on domination and subservience.... This "people's movement" for which Yen's approach was responsible is a perfect example of Piomelli's true participatory democracy that can result from meaningful collaboration.

Respect clients

Rebellious lawyers, in their collaborative efforts to avoid subordination, must avoid subordinating their own clients....

Piomelli recognizes that the "problem [for underprivileged clients] is not being represented, but always being represented—never being actively involved in speaking or acting directly on one's behalf or with others." Collaborative lawyers ought to be striving to implement a "collective, cooperative approach to problem-solving [that] treats clients and communities as fully human partners."

... Yen's refusal to subordinate his students was demonstrated time and again through his actions, from the first time he informed his first group of students in France that they would have to write their own letters, to his encouragement of subsequent generations of farmer-scholars and the transformation of countless numbers of peasants from students to teachers.... Leadership development, an offshoot of respect for students, was itself an integral part of the strategy; the result was that both teachers and students emerged with elevated spirit and an increased sense of worth.

Take on the battles that collaborative advocacy leads to, even if the odds seem insurmountable

White, in particular, warns the rebellious lawyer that in collaborating with others and in reconceptualizing her role, the battles may become extremely challenging. Why engage in these impossible battles? ... First of all, a "loss" is only a "loss" depending on who is defining its parameters. Much can still be gained from the effort. The gain may come from the unity of the effort, from the camaraderie, and from the sense of worth or even pride in fighting the battle. A sense of empowerment can be derived from the process as well as from being heard, or even from the freedom of expression. Secondly, who knows? You may actually accomplish the impossible! ...

Yen took on these seemingly insurmountable odds, and perhaps this is his most important lesson for rebellious advocates. It should not be surprising that collaborative work can lead to difficult challenges. After all, this is about listening and learning from the community. This is a fight against subordination, against traditions, against the toughest borders. Yen was willing to fight for the education of 180,000 coolies in Europe, 400,000 peasants in Dingxian, and hundreds of villages, in addition to combating the effects of poverty and illiteracy on health, economics, and citizenship.... He advanced the revolutionary notion of opening schools to women. He also recognized that this was not simply about China:

> [W]e must not think of nations as units—we must think really internationally of peoples. The world is the unit—any other planning is futile. Educating one people is so useless unless all are educated for a better life....

... Integrate and navigate many worlds

In López's vision, lawyers must be skilled legal technicians and engaged public citizens and activists. They must expertly navigate and integrate many worlds: the legal, the interpersonal, the social, and the political. White also notes the importance for "political lawyers to leave the shelter of their offices and give up the false sense of control that goes with one-to-one client representation."

Much of Yen's success was due to his well-honed ability to navigate and integrate many different worlds. He was at home with peasants, school teachers, intellectuals, college presidents, public officials, political leaders, entrepreneurs, and the wealthy. He created new curricula by working with farmers and by integrating these disparate parties.... He convinced Henry Ford and the Rockefeller family to fund his efforts.... Indeed, Yen became a master in many different worlds as he combated subordination.

Conclusion

... As rebellious, collaborative lawyers carrying on Yen's legacy today, we must reflect conscientiously on what it means to be community lawyers—on whether our work is effective, on whether we ought to consider other collaborative strategies, on what events around us affect our clients and our work. Our work certainly involves the daily representation of clients, impact litigation, social mobilization, economic development, and community education; but it also entails stepping back and looking at the bigger picture. It is about recognizing the roots of subordination and finding creative ways to address it. It is about relating our local struggles to broader movements beyond our neighborhoods. At whichever level we engage—local, national, or international—we must maintain our belief that our day-in, day-out efforts can have lasting impacts.

Yen's example is one for the ages of rebellious, collaborative advocates. His example was a model of dedication and hard work, humility, collaboration, respect for laborers and peasants and appreciation of their work, broadening of support networks, strategic innovation and flexibility, and courage in the face of immense challenges. His example inspires us to get back to the streets, roll up our sleeves, be creative, and fully engage in our community work.

This excerpt illustrates how one advocate, in collaboration with many others, was able to transform his work in order to transform social conditions. As Hing describes, Yen started simply but concretely, based on personal experience, observation, and reflection. From that critical perspective, he was better able to appreciate "what the people know" and, with that bottom-up knowledge, to form collaborative initiatives to "build on what the people have." Can you envision situations in which you might do the same?

CHAPTER RECAP

This chapter surveyed concepts and tools that advocates use to convert subordinated group identities into assets for organized struggle. These critical concepts and tools—like social construction, intersectionality, antiessentialism, antisubordination values, solidarity, and collaboration—are derived from collective experience with identities as instruments of caste and as assets in collective struggle. In this process of unlearning and relearning, advocates see the falsehoods of colorblindness and legal blindfolding. They cultivate critical self-reflection to unmask micro-macro social realities and expansively ask other questions to uncover patterns that interlock "different" identity castes. This chapter highlighted the connection of these group identities with collective interests and the challenge and importance for systemic advocacy of intentionally constructing intergroup solidarity and collaborative practice. Amplifying these points, the next chapter focuses on the collective power of identity groups and their capacity to contest ground rules as similarly important determinants of progress.

CHAPTER 6

ORGANIZING BOTTOM-UP GROUPS TO CONTEST TOP-DOWN POWER AND REWRITE "GROUND RULES"

■ ■ ■

Table of Sections

6.1 Elites Structured Society to Be Collectively on Top Always
6.2 Public Enforcement of "Private" Property and Contracts Is Central to Identity Castes
6.3 Elites Orchestrate Power, Privilege, and Profit Continuously for Local-Global Rule
6.4 Elites Use Neoliberal Ideology as Law to Magnify and Concentrate the Public Power of Private Wealth
6.5 Elites (Still) Suppress Voting to Manipulate Democracy and Control Outcomes
6.6 Advocates Support Organized Groups as "Repeat Players" to Contest Background Premises, Ground Rules, and Foundational Concepts
6.7 Seeding, Sparking, and Supporting Long-Term Coalitions: A Tennessee Case Study

---

OPENING THOUGHTS

Power is what people actually experience as their law.

—**Kenneth Casebeer,** Aliquippa: The Company Town and Contested Power in the Construction of Law, 43 Buff. L. Rev. 617, 620 (1995)

Power never takes a step back, except in the face of more power.

—**Malcolm X**

My clients, my city, our nation, the world—all face mounting social, economic, and ecological predicaments. The world we have is the product of hoarding, by a very few, of the vastly disproportionate share of wealth, power, and privilege. . . . [T]he imperative question: How can people build enough collective power to not only demand a better world, but to create one?

—**Barbara Bezdek,** Digging into Democracy: Reflections on CED and Social Change Lawyering after #OWS, 77 Md. L. Rev. Endnotes 16, 39 (2018)

Economics and economic concerns have so thoroughly infiltrated the law that it is difficult to discuss any topic of law without a concomitant descent into considerations of efficiency, utility and rationality, goals, values, processes keyed to the conservation of the present [unequal] allocation of assets, resources, and opportunities.

> —**Charles R.P. Pouncy,** Institutional Economics and Critical Race/LatCrit Theory: The Need for Critical "Raced" Economics, 54 Rutgers L. Rev. 841, 843 (2002)

INTRODUCTION

As we have seen in public education, water quality, abortion, and other contexts, individuals and groups struggle from below in the face of opposition from elite adversaries. When they do, they immediately, inevitably, and constantly confront questions of power and its uses or abuses. Under the rule of law, power from the top is used to support elite interests—anything that elites value and wish to preserve, including "staying on top." Elites acquire, concentrate, and transfer material wealth across generations. In this way, dominant groups entrench castes materially and legally. They pass on privilege to heirs or, if not literal descendants, to "successors in interest"—that is, to those who have stepped into their systemic shoes. Without successors in interest, the colonial pyramid scheme would have ended long ago.

Over time—and using time—ruling elites have created a top-down playbook of sorts—a set of recurring tactics and strategies that systemic advocates can recognize and counteract. To help you do so, this chapter sketches some of the keystones upon which elites rely. The top-down playbook of elites—based on IGIP—now is matched by the bottom-up toolkit based on critical knowledge recorded in the Schools, Approaches, and other sources of knowledge (including your own critical research using methods like those presented in Parts III and V).

Bottom-up power is developed and used by marginalized groups to challenge the status quo, including the power to redefine foundational concepts and rewrite "ground rules" that influence systemic outcomes. Ground rules are especially important for long-term struggles because they set the terms for all other engagements and their consequences. In effect, these terms often are skewed, setting the stage for particular outcomes. Operationally, ground rules craft the incentive (and disincentive) structure for the choices and actions of all participants—all players. Repeat players have the upper hand because they have insider experience, tools, roles, and contacts, which add up to power—the power to understand contexts, seize opportunities, head off adversaries, realign interests, reshape incentives, and thereby to steer systemic decisions.

Bottom-up power, by contrast, draws on the antisubordination principle in developing organizations and "critical coalitions." Bottom-up groups aim to be capable of challenging foundational terms, cultivating long-term solidarity, and influencing systemic outcomes. Struggle builds not only progress toward equal justice but also relationships of mutual familiarity, trust, and cooperation—which, in turn, help to strengthen groups for future rounds of struggle. Every round of struggle aims to preserve achieved gains *and* to expand upon them.

In general, the Critical Challenge exists because cumulative and collective power abuses have trumped law's professed commitment to equal justice, while denying it. In the resulting conflicts, all groups aim to build power—both tops and bottoms. Importantly, groups build power to use power; power is both a means and an end. As with other muscles, you use power or you lose it. Building and using power are mutually reinforcing. For this reason, dominant groups have organized themselves for the long run. Although not monolithic, they used their collective power to subordinate "other" groups while simultaneously strengthening their position, or power, to consolidate their dominance for future rounds of struggle.

Although organized elites usually win the outcomes they desire, pervasive inequalities of power are neither fixed nor absolute—not (yet) a hegemony—due to the histories of bottom-up resistance chronicled in this book. Those critical histories make plain that power affects all relationships and decisions, both at the micro and macro levels of life and law. Relations of power are relevant to advocacy in both the public or governmental arena and in the so-called private decision making of employers and workers, or among family members, and in other arenas. Organized power, in relation to group identities and interests, shapes both systemic injustice and systemic advocacy.[1]

Challenging systemic power innovatively and collaboratively is the daily bread-and-butter of long-term social struggle for steady, enduring progress. These tasks, as we explore throughout the book, track three "layers" of goals, both long and short term. These goals are designed to ameliorate immediate injustices while also helping to transform the social and legal landscape going forward; this approach uses amelioration as scaffolding for transformation, as noted in Part I. These layered goals prompt advocates to craft solutions that look equally to the past, the present, and the future to open windows of opportunity for progress.

As Part IV elaborates more fully, when focusing on the first layer, advocates and activists aim to win "technical fixes"—substantive outcomes that materially improve the lives (or at least limit the damage) for members

---

[1] Ongoing experiments in power building create tensions that call into question learned ways of understanding power. Advocates can best grapple with the tensions if they start by imagining power as a creative, changing, and limiting force operating through discursive practices at both interpersonal and social levels. Power constructs, channels, and limits—and power does all of that through ongoing practices.

of subordinate groups but that do not "shake up" the system. Therefore, this ameliorative layer is supplemented in systemic advocacy with two others designed to reframe approaches to amelioration for longer-term progress: building power and shifting cultural or mainstream understanding of "the" problem and, hence, of best solutions.

Not coincidentally, this three-layered framework mirrors organized elite actions to maintain top-down control and trickle-down justice. Elites write and rewrite the premises, foundational concepts, and ground rules of "the system" to preserve identity-based hierarchies, as Siegel, Minter, and others illustrated above. As a result, group-based inequalities in power already are "baked into" the mechanisms of decision-making, including democracy and adjudication. Organized elites consequently win—over and over across issues and generations.

Systemic advocates must understand—and can learn valuable lessons from—the manner in which elites operate to empower themselves collectively. Systemic advocates adapt these means to counter systemic injustice and to help groups empower themselves. Applying these lessons allows advocates to open windows of opportunity to flip systemic scripts.

Converting these insights into actionable knowledge, systemic advocates build power for and with subordinated groups in three primary ways:

- by unlearning myths about decision making through democracy and adjudication and relearning—and sharing—critical, complex views of how elites use adjudication and democracy in tandem to block progress;
- by strengthening power in specific, measurable, concrete ways in organized groups of subordinated communities as a routine part of advocacy; and
- by challenging the background premises, foundational concepts, and "rules of the game" of democracy and adjudication to create a level playing field for decision making, and thus overcome elite blocks to progress.

Advocates do this work within and beyond the confines set by the rule of law as a system. Putting these three points into practice is not simple, as we see throughout this book, but understanding how elites "do it" is a first step toward undoing it. This chapter unpacks the elite "toolkit" for perpetual rule (as demonstrated by history, experience, and outputs) to help bottom-up groups and their advocates fight back and push forward more effectively. As this introduction already indicates, raw might or "naked power" plays a big role in this top-down arsenal. We begin with a brief review of elites as complex (and "different") groups or networks that organize themselves continually to be on top in law and society collectively, personally, and perpetually.

6.1 ELITES STRUCTURED SOCIETY TO BE COLLECTIVELY ON TOP ALWAYS

European settlers established themselves as identifiable elites, first in the colonies and, later, in the settler states they controlled. Throughout this process, described in more detail in Part VI, elites organized peers into networks and groups. Elites used their collectivized power to create institutions and systems to maintain their personal and shared interests despite time and change. This "power elite"—or network of elites—consists of interlocking persons, groups, and interests organized around legal, political, economic, social, and cultural systems of society. Collectively, over time, elites organized society itself to perpetuate their dominance.

U.S. elites originated among "men of affairs" from wealthy families who settled during the colonial era. They gradually created established networks across law, politics, the economy, and the military. Those original "men of affairs" from Europe who colonized indigenous lands set into motion a process of system-building that coincided with the consolidation, collectively, of this group as the ruling class. This continuing process shows that elites are complex, but that—over time—they maintain one purpose: to remain the ruling class with its material gains.

This enduring status quo is the legacy of a complex historical process summarized by sociologist C. Wright Mills in 1956 in *The Power Elite*, a work that spawned greater scrutiny of U.S. elites. The "power elite" originated in the United States with colonialism and unfolded in four (or more) periods.[2] During the first epoch of elite formation, under the original Constitution of 1789, "the social and economic, the political and military institutions were more or less unified in a simple and direct way: the individual men of these several elites moved easily from one role to another at the top of each of the major institutional orders." A majority of the population at that time, of course, was excluded by law from leadership or even participation in "social life, economic institutions, military establishment, and political order." As a result, original colonial elites from Europe ensconced themselves as local settler elites as they founded the new settler state under the rule of law.

During the second stage, leading up to the Civil War, these "economic and political and military orders" became more consolidated and

---

[2] The following sketch draws and quotes from C. Wright Mills, The Power Elite, 269–278 (1956). See also G. William Domhoff et al., Studying the Power Elite: Fifty Years of Who Rules America? (2018); Richard L. Zweigenhaft and G. William Domhoff, Diversity in the Power Elite: Ironies and Unfulfilled Promises (2018); Joe R. Feagin and Kimberley Ducey, Elite White Men Ruling: Who, What, When, Where, and How (2017).

interlocking: "In this society, the 'elite' became a plurality of top groups, each in turn loosely made up." Elites expanded the nation's territorial reach through additional military conquest and settlement, even as they feuded with each other about racial policy and related identity politics. In earlier decades of this period, "the elite was at most a loose coalition" of powerful persons and groups with complex but frequently coinciding interests. Over time, those "loose" cliques "tightened up."

The third phase, after the Civil War and through the First World War, established "the supremacy of corporate economic power," abetted by the U.S. Supreme Court declaring in 1886 that the Fourteenth Amendment protected corporations. Consequently, "[t]hat period witnessed the transfer of initiative from government to corporation" and ushered in "an age of raids on government by the economic elite, and a time of simple corruption, when Senators and judges were simply bought up" by "moneyed interests." The result was that "the economic elite overshadowed the political" elite. Many believe this era was the "golden era" of the U.S. ruling class. Established settler elites became more integrated at the national level to pursue their self-styled sense of "Manifest Destiny," conquering more peoples and colonizing more lands.

The fourth stage, resulting from a Great Depression and, later, a Second World War, produced the New Deal, which "did *not* reverse the political and economic relations of the third era, but did create . . . competing centers of power that challenged those of corporate directors." Early in this era, "the economic elite, which in the third period had fought against the growth of 'government' while raiding it for crafty privileges, belatedly attempted to join [the New Deal] on the higher levels." Eventually, "they did come to control and to use for their own purposes the New Deal institutions whose creation they had so bitterly denounced." These identity-based elites began to internationalize in earnest. They produced the globalized institutions that now dominate law and other systems as one transnational whole. New identities, interests, and groups were drawn into the power equation to maintain the continuity of systemic outputs.

This sketch, recall, was put forth in 1956. In each step of this complex and extended process, elites and systems reproduce themselves according to original templates laid down with and by the rule of law. Maintaining identity-based hierarchies served the consistent purpose of elite personal and collective enrichment. The 1956 analysis concluded with the following prognostications on a "fifth epoch" in this process, which emerged after World War II. This fifth epoch led to today's form of corporate globalization in which the intertwining of business and government "reached a new point of explicitness" that "accelerated the long-term relegation of the professional politicians in the Congress to middle levels of power." This economic ascendancy relies on a related "military ascendancy" in which a "seemingly permanent military threat places a premium on the military and upon their control of men, material, money, and power; [hence] virtually all political and military actions are now judged in terms of military definitions of reality." The dual ascendancy of economic and military orders produces a permanent war economy and a private corporate economy through which each sector feeds the other at society's overall expense. Corporate globalization thus is dominant under the rule of law.

The result, as predicted by Mills in 1956, is that U.S. capitalism is "in considerable part a military capitalism, and the most important relation of the big corporation to the state rests on a coincidence of interests between military and corporate needs, as defined by warlords and [the] corporate rich." This new elite ordering subordinates the role of "the merely political men. Not politicians, but corporate executives, sit with the military and plan" humanity's future.

The "power elite" therefore consists of dominant and frequently coinciding interests across four "major institutional orders"—"social life, economic institutions, military establishment, and political order"—that have been established under the auspices of law and use law to enforce mutually reinforcing orders. This complex historical process has been shaped—distorted—by the forcible absence of most of the population using group exclusions based on race, sex, and class, also enforced by law. Consequently, resulting systems omit perspectives of the excluded groups and erase or subordinate their interests to those of identity groups represented among elites.

The Constitution and other core documents of U.S. law and politics are described below as foundational "lies"—interlocking developments of elites and the systems designed to serve their interests. The assertion that "We the People" formed the new system is a bedrock element of law-as-ideology. This assertion gave the new system an aura of legitimacy as a choice ratified by a majority of "the people" in 1789. Feminist legal scholar Mary Anne Franks examines below the hard-wired interconnections of identity, law, property, and democracy in the moment of formal conception as a system. As Justice Marshall noted in the opening reflection in Part 1, this assertion masks the exclusion of a majority of the actual people from self-governance. These foundational fictions and deceptions literally constitute the system and direct its social ramifications, and Frank's account below captures the moment when the Critical Challenge of using law for justice became systemic in the United States.

WHERE THE LAW LIES: CONSTITUTIONAL FICTIONS AND THEIR DISCONTENTS

Mary Anne Franks
In Law and Lies: Deceptions and Truth-Telling in the American Legal System
(Austin Sarat ed. 2015)

The Constitutional Lie

America is built on a lie. That lie inheres in its foundational text, the Constitution of the United States, which begins in the false claim to speak of and for "we the people" even as the majority of its population—in particular black men and all women—were denied access to the most basic forms of political participation. This simultaneous act of symbolic inclusion and material exclusion has never been fully acknowledged or confronted, which is another way of saying that it has never really ended. As many lies are, America's constitutional lie is generative: it produces other, secondary, mutually reinforcing legal fictions that obscure the deception buried deep in the social and political structure. These fictions serve multiple purposes, including providing reassurance to those holding abstract commitments to equality as well as seducing and subduing excluded groups that might otherwise demand recognition and reparation for injustices done to them. As long as these constitutional fictions persist, the political existence of women and black men remains fundamentally unstable.

To understand these claims, we must first clearly define what is meant by a "lie." . . . I will use a Kantian definition: *"the making of an untruthful statement with the intention that the statement be believed to be true."* . . . A lie is an affirmative statement by an entity that knows the statement to be false and who intends to mislead others into believing that it is true. This Kantian conception of lying is usefully supplemented by Freudian insight: the audience we intend to mislead often includes ourselves.

. . . Here, I take aim at lies embedded in law itself, which as a category tend to be harmful, portentous, and obscure. This is especially true of lies that are "constitutional" in a dual sense, that is, laws that are both foundational to a society and embedded in a society's actual founding documents. Constitutional lies undermine the intelligibility of the state itself, and the submerged nature of such lies makes challenging them difficult. . . .

The Constitution is America's binding document; its foundational text; the "supreme law of the land." . . . It is meant to be and believed to be a promise between the governed and the governing. It begins with these famous words:

> We the People of the United States, in Order to form a more perfect Union, establish Justice, insure domestic Tranquility, provide for the common defence, promote the general Welfare, and secure the Blessings of Liberty to ourselves and our Posterity, do

ordain and establish this Constitution for the United States of America.

But "the people" did not in fact ordain and establish the Constitution.... In 1787, a small group of white, property-owning men declared foundational rules that were to govern the entire population. The signatories to the Constitution included not a single representative of women or black people of either gender....

The authors of the Declaration of Independence expressed the lie even more boldly, claiming that governments are established "deriving their just powers from the consent of the governed." The authors were fully aware that they had obtained no such consent from large segments of the population or from their representatives.

... "We the People" is perhaps the oldest and most well-known "legal fiction" in American history....

One may object that to call these assertions "lies" is inaccurate. The authors of America's foundational texts may have sincerely believed, this argument goes, that they did represent the interests of the entire population, even those that were fully excluded from political participation. That is, that the interests of slaves and women were naturally folded into the declarations made by their masters and husbands, and that it would have simply been beyond comprehension at this point in history to have contemplated either black individuals or women as having separate political interests. This reading is contradicted by many documents written by the Founders themselves, most notably John Adams. Abigail Adams' famous plea to her husband to "remember the ladies" was an eloquent and clear-eyed assessment of the injustice of forming a nation without any form of participation from women: "Remember, all men would be tyrants if they could. If particular care and attention is not paid to the ladies, we are determined to foment a rebellion, and will not hold ourselves bound by any laws in which we have no voice or representation." John Adams' response was both crude and belittling:

> As to your extraordinary code of laws, I cannot but laugh. We have been told that our struggle has loosened the bonds of government everywhere; that children and apprentices were disobedient; that schools and colleges were grown turbulent; that Indians slighted their guardians, and negroes grew insolent to their masters. But your letter was the first intimation that another tribe, more numerous and powerful than all the rest, were grown discontented.

Adams clearly found the possibility of women's political rights even more ludicrous than the idea of political rights for Native Americans or black individuals, all of which he found fit to compare to the idea of political rights for children....

John Adams responded far more earnestly to a question about the consent of the governed when it was posed by fellow statesman James Sullivan. In response to Sullivan's suggestion that the voting franchise be extended to white men who did not own property, Adams reflected, "It is certain, in theory, that the only moral foundation of government is, the consent of the people. But to what an extent shall we carry this principle?" . . .

> Depend upon it, Sir, it is dangerous to open so fruitful a source of controversy and altercation as would be opened by attempting to alter the qualifications of voters; there will be no end of it. New claims will arise; women will demand a vote . . . and every man who has not a farthing, will demand a voice equal with any other, in all acts of state. It tends to confound and destroy all distinctions; and prostrate all ranks to one common level.

Thus it is clear that Adams, like many of the Founders, had certainly contemplated the possibility of political rights for groups such as women and slaves, and resoundingly rejected it. Those who proclaimed the principles of equality and freedom in the name of "We the People" were well aware that they were lying. . . .

We return, then, to the question of why the Founders lied. . . .

. . . To establish the legitimacy of the great American project, the Framers had to convince themselves that they were acting in the best interests of the excluded. The lie served to protect their self-perception, to reassure them of the justice of their ambition, and to quell attempts by subordinated populations to demand their rights.

. . . [T]he Framers believed on some level that the people they were binding without consultation were not fully "people," and that their humanity, such that it was, was adequately represented by Convention delegates. . . .

The lie served the additional purpose of appeasing the vast populations excluded from representation by presenting them with the attractive fiction that they were in fact included. As long as women and black people were kept under strict physical and political control (women by domestic servitude, black men and women by slavery, both groups by a complex political and cultural networks of subordination), this abstract rhetoric likely sufficed to keep dissent at bay. Whether either population truly embraced the idea of consent by proxy was likely a moot point, as their options for disagreement were severely limited. . . . However, it would be another forty years—after the Civil War had been fought, the Emancipation Proclamation had been issued, and the Thirteenth Amendment had been ratified—before the Fifteenth Amendment, establishing black male suffrage, would be passed in 1870. It would be another fifty years before the Nineteenth Amendment would grant women this most basic right of participation in society.

. . . Following the concession of basic rights to more than half the population, it remains a lie: the enfranchisement of black men and women, granted 83 and 133 years, respectively, after the establishment of the Constitution cannot retroactively render the foundational claim to consent of the governed any more true. These belated, formal, and incomplete gestures towards equal citizenship for black men and women are no more than the least the state could have done. . . .

But what of all the laws created, enforced, or revised in the 83 years before a significant minority was allowed to vote, and 133 years before half the population received even the most basic political right? What of the legal, social, and political institutions that were built up over years without contribution from women or African-Americans? Their power to bind the populations that had no say in their creation is not questioned. . . .

. . . Our fundamental legal prohibitions and expectations were shaped long before either black men or women got the vote; the concept of *stare decisis* compels us to honor and defer to what has come before except in extreme circumstances. Openly recognizing the long-held lie would not only create administrative and organizational problems, but also psychological ones. Humans are not well-suited to radical change; inertia is one of the most difficult forces to overcome. It requires far less legal, cognitive, and psychological energy to participate in the legal fiction of constitutional truth than to try to expose and battle its comprehensive reach.

Is it so bad to embrace the legal fiction[?] . . . The failure to recognize and denounce the constitutional lie means that constitutional existence of the excluded will always be precarious. Put another way, the lie of abstract equality serves to obscure the reality of lived inequality. This obscurity is compounded by the tendency of constitutional lies to proliferate: they produce smaller lies that reinforce and disguise the larger, structural lies.

The repressed truth—that women and black men were treated fundamentally as objects and not subjects of the law—resurfaces in . . . lies that structure law enforcement abuses, which disproportionately burden black men, and the lies that structure law enforcement passivity, which disproportionately burden women. These deceptive and repressive practices have common origins in the lies that structure the concept of consent. . . .

. . . We must reject the legal fiction that our Framers believed that all men are created equal and that "men" signified the family of humankind, including women. They did not believe either of these things. Women and black men were excluded from the start, and their full subjecthood remains an ongoing project. Decades of injustice and inequality cannot be undone by formal declarations of universality, and the implied promise that the

Constitution makes with the American people—now all American people—can only be delivered by recognizing that the past leaves its marks. Neither the Founding Fathers nor any of the successive leaders of this country have "given" rights to women and men; they have only belatedly acknowledged what should have been recognized from the beginning. . . .

Franks outlines the collective deceptions that form the foundations of U.S. law as a system. Over time, "the lie of abstract equality serves to obscure the reality of lived inequality" maintained by voter exclusion, suppression, and manipulation.

Below, legal scholar Robert Steinfeld deepens these points, describing how colonial elites developed legal constructions of "property" and solvency that enabled the wealthy (elites) to control the propertyless or indebted (masses) economically and politically. Like Marshall and Franks, Steinfeld tracks how early elites invented rules to exclude most people from governance, including denying the right to vote and thus access to democratic lawmaking.

PROPERTY AND SUFFRAGE IN THE EARLY AMERICAN REPUBLIC
Robert J. Steinfeld
41 Stan. L. Rev. 335 (1989)

Introduction

. . . By the end of the nineteenth century, fourteen states had excluded either "paupers" generally or inmates of poorhouses from the suffrage. As late as 1934, all of these states continued to do so. The term "pauper" in these clauses ordinarily referred to persons in receipt of poor relief.

. . . Most commonly, pauper exclusions were adopted as states replaced property qualifications with taxpaying qualifications. . . .

Why should Americans have been moved in the decades after the Revolution to deprive recipients of poor relief of the vote? And why should they have done so just at the time they were otherwise broadening the suffrage?

. . . Far from being anachronisms, pauper exclusions were integral to a new, nineteenth century way of defining full membership in a republican polity. This new set of conceptions was much more than a temporary weigh station on the road to universal suffrage. It was a self-contained scheme of understandings about the proper order of the polity which developed at a particular moment in American history, in . . . the decades after the Revolution. And it was a set of basic conceptions which endured. . . .

The Contradictory Legacy of the American Revolution

... By the middle of the eighteenth century, all the American colonies save one had adopted property qualifications for the suffrage. Colonists explained the disfranchisement of the propertyless in their midst in part by observing that such people "had no wills of their own." Under colonial restrictions all the propertyless, regardless of whether they were wage earners or recipients of poor relief, occupied the same political status. After the Revolution, as many states began to enfranchise some of those who owned no property, mainly wage earners and leaseholders, under taxpaying or manhood suffrage provisions, they began simultaneously to disfranchise others such as paupers. In such states, the undifferentiated propertyless of the colonial era were being separated into two distinct categories.

Some of the propertyless would henceforth be qualified to vote, some would not. . . . [A]s some of the propertyless were enfranchised and others were explicitly disfranchised, it became necessary to redefine not only the former but also the latter. Much more was involved than the simple persistence of traditional attitudes in the new era.

As the traditional undifferentiated propertyless were divided into two groups, the new political-cultural categories of independent wage earner and dependent pauper emerged together, defining each other by mutual contrast. Whatever qualities now seemed to define paupers as dependent, it was the absence of those qualities which made it seem possible to view propertyless wage earners as independent.

It was no accident that this division of the traditional world of the propertyless began to occur at this particular moment in American history. The movement toward distinguishing among the traditional propertyless developed as one response to the contradictory legacy of the American Revolution. That legacy had left American political culture embracing fundamentally inconsistent premises. To state the dilemma in its simplest terms: On the one hand, Americans continued to adhere to the classical republican notion that only property ownership conferred independence on a man. On the other hand, they had also come to believe that "*all men* were by nature *equally free and independent* and had certain inherent and unalienable rights." . . .

As Americans struggled over the question of broadening the suffrage in the decades after the Revolution, they simultaneously struggled with these deeply inconsistent premises. The division of the traditionally undifferentiated propertyless into two new categories defined as binary opposites of one another represented an accommodation of these fundamental, yet inconsistent, premises of America life. . . .

Property and Self-Government: Relationships of Dependence in the Early Modern Period

Economic/Social Relationships of Dependence and Governance

When eighteenth century writers of practically all political hues insisted that the propertyless should not vote because they were governed by other men, we must understand that their views were based squarely on their experience of life in their world.... The inhabitants of that world frankly acknowledged and openly exercised the power over others which property ownership conferred.

In the early modern period, a wide range of adult relationships of dependence were considered normal. Hardly anyone questioned the right of persons who controlled resources to use those resources to create relationships of dependence. Such relationships were grounded in the notion that those who controlled resources might extend their protection and care to those who did not. The latter, in return, would owe loyalty and obedience. They were expected to serve their protectors and do their bidding. Those who controlled no resources had little choice about the matter. They frequently had to enter one of these relationships and submit to the government of others, simply in order to survive.

Explicit relationships of dependence were a common feature of social life at all levels, both in Europe and America. In late colonial New York City, for example, a system of personal loyalty and "economic clientage" was well established. "Numerous artisans were beholden to merchants, lawyers, and urban landholders who controlled their rents, job opportunities, credit, and even personal affairs...."

... In this world, social deference and material necessity converged to place some men explicitly under the control of other men....

Legal Relationships of Dependence and Governance

For the very poor in this period (and for women and children), the situation was even worse. They frequently found themselves in a form of dependence relationship that was even more rigorous. For if social convention dictated that property owners were entitled to command the loyalty of those to whom they extended care and protection, it was a matter of legal doctrine that heads of household were entitled to command the loyalty and services of those for whom *they* provided. Household dependents not only included wives and children, but also propertyless wage earners who lived with the master. Before the nineteenth century in the colonies, most propertyless people were dependents in a propertied household—wives, children, slaves, servants, apprentices, journeyman, hired laborers. Apart from these groups, a smaller number of tenant farmers, common seamen and casual laborers set up independent households without a property owner as the head. But for the most part, inequality between the property owners and the propertyless was a domestic affair.

In the legal relationship of dependence (master and servant, husband and wife, parent and child) of this period, the head of household was responsible for the maintenance, care and protection of all his dependents. They could bring a variety of legal actions to enforce the duty of support which he owed them. But in return, he was given, in varying degrees, legal jurisdiction or control over them. This jurisdiction included rights to their services, and even, in certain cases, rights to chastise or confine them. . . .

One of the crucial points to understand about the propertyless who became recipients of poor relief in this period is that when they accepted [government] assistance, they too entered this kind of legal relationship of dependence. The relationship of towns to their "paupers," was structured in exactly the same way as the relationship of heads of household to their dependents. Both were reciprocal relationships in which one party owed a duty of support and the other owed a duty of loyalty and service in return. . . .

In this period, relationships of dependence, whether formalized in law or only a matter of social convention, were essentially based on a similar idea. Persons who controlled resources might extend their protection and care to others. In return, these others would incur obligations to serve and obey their protectors and providers. But in the legal relationships of dependence, these obligations of service and obedience assumed a more stringent form. The power over persons stemming from control over resources took the form of legal jurisdiction. We might almost say that in these relationships the power of property was "established."

Steinfeld argues that the "power of property was established" in the decades following the Constitution's adoption. Elites specifically denied access to property to a majority of the population based on social identities, like race and sex. Then, they bootstrapped property to put those without it among the groups excluded from democracy. In time, property qualification was converted into a solvency—or anti-pauperism—qualification, making those deemed paupers legally incapable of participating in governance. Today's economic elites control law and society as successors in interest to the colonial settlers who set up this scheme as law. Like colonial elites, modern day elites control founding concepts and rules of the system and thus effectively control the system's outcomes. Below, we examine how first colonial and now modern elites maintain their dominance.

6.2 PUBLIC ENFORCEMENT OF "PRIVATE" PROPERTY AND CONTRACTS IS CENTRAL TO IDENTITY CASTES

The regulation of property and contract is fundamental to U.S. society and law and deeply-embedded systemic injustice based on identity castes. Legal scholar Jennifer Nedelsky notes:

> Private property has shaped the structure of the American political system. The framework of [U.S.] political institutions and the categories through which [its residents] understand politics developed around the problems of making popular government compatible with the security of private property. This focus on property has been the source of the greatest strengths of American democracy, of its greatest weaknesses, and the distorted quality even of its strengths.[3]

Nedelsky explains the systemic centrality of property "has its roots in the Framers' concern with protecting property from democratic incursion."[4] This original U.S. "preoccupation with property generated a shallow conception of democracy and a system of institutions that allocates political power unequally and fails to foster political participation."[5] Thus, "inequality [is] at the center of American constitutionalism."[6]

The first U.S. Constitution—drafted in Philadelphia during the summer of 1787—illustrates how private property became the object of legal protection. The drafters asserted a fear of majoritarian tyranny. As a result, they created only two core "rights" with a striking commonality: protecting property. First, they declared that contracts could not be "impaired." By design, this "right" only protects creditors (the few tops) from debtors (the many bottoms). The second prohibited the "taking" of property without "just compensation." This provision, similar to the first, was designed to protect land barons (the few tops) from local majorities (the many bottoms). Tellingly, these two are the only individual rights expressed textually in that document.

Acknowledging the centrality of property in law as a system, James Madison, principal framer of the original constitution, declared in Federalist No. 10 that "the most common and durable source of factions has been the various and unequal distribution of property. Those who hold and those who are without property have ever formed distinct interests in

---

[3] Jennifer Nedelsky, Private Property and the Limits of American Constitutionalism: The Madisonian Framework and Its Legacy 1–3 (1990).
[4] *Id.* at 1.
[5] *Id.*
[6] *Id.* at 2.

society."[7] These "rights of property originate . . . from the diversity in the faculties of *men*" (emphasis added).[8] The skewed distributions of property, in Madison's view, were due to individual merit—"the faculties of men"—not systemic design. And exclusions from the right to property, formally tied to identities like sex and race, favored a meritorious minority: "Only a minority, said Madison, 'can be interested in preserving the rights of property.' "[9] If so, that result is engineered through elite uses of identity to define property and access to its power.

The excerpts below show how the U.S. legal system was designed to enable elites to accumulate wealth exponentially and in perpetuity. They also show that public enforcement of "private" law is a core feature of the legal system even though, as we have seen previously, elites assert there is a formal "distinction" between public and private spheres in law and society. First, legal scholar Anthony Chase describes the enduring, racialized paradigm of U.S. contract law—an area of law that purports to be identity-neutral but isn't. Notice again the revelatory power of critical histories—in this case, those behind the top-down ground rules of U.S. contract law—that take account of identities, groups, interests, and power in the making and application of those (and other) ground rules.

RACE, CULTURE, AND CONTRACT LAW: FROM THE COTTONFIELD TO THE COURTROOM
Anthony R. Chase
28 Conn. L. Rev. 1 (1995)

. . . The Interaction of American Contract Law and Slavery

The history of American contract law and issues of race and culture are inextricably intertwined. The corresponding failure to acknowledge racial and cultural issues in contemporary discourse implicitly ratifies the historical legal paradigm and dooms us to repeat its failings. . . .

History of American Contract Law and Theory

American contract law is based on English contract law. . . .

By the mid-eighteenth century, Great Britain emerged as "the greatest trading nation" in the world and was the first nation to enter the Industrial Revolution. The concept of freedom of contract mirrored developments in theories of political and economic freedom. The Social Contract theory of government and the development of the contractual theory of freedom of contract share the same roots: philosophers such as Thomas Hobbes and John Locke theorized that man owns his own body and his own labor and

---

[7] www.billofrightsinstitute.org/founding-documents/primary-source-documents/the-federalist-papers/federalist-papers-no-10/.
[8] *Id.*
[9] Gordon S. Wood, The Creation of the American Republic 410–11 (1969).

is free to contract for the use of his labor, which is his property. Both believed that the individual is free to enter into relationships with others and that the role of government is to protect the rights of property. Adam Smith, a classical or political economist and author of The Wealth of Nations, represented man as a rational being who seeks to maximize his pleasure and to minimize his pain. According to Smith, . . . [i]nterference with the workings of the free market stems from a desire to further the self-interest of a particular group at the expense of the public.

By the early nineteenth century, political economy had become a guiding philosophy in Great Britain and the United States. . . . The will theory of contracts developed in both Great Britain and the United States and viewed contracts "as mutual obligations voluntarily created by the parties and . . . expressed in the form of an offer and acceptance." It became the duty of the court to discover and enforce the concurring intentions of the parties. . . .

. . . [T]he law of contracts created the illusion that all men were free to enter or not enter into contracts as they chose. However, the reality was that the law of contracts during the Industrial Revolution enabled the industrialists to control the working class, who either accepted the wages offered and hours demanded or starved.

This illusion was repeated in American courts during the post-slavery era . . . Newly freed African-Americans who came to the courts seeking dignity, mutual respect, and justice (i.e., "the American Dream"), found instead a legal system which resonated with the racism of mainstream society in its application of contract law, thereby validating and necessarily valorizing the social, economic, and political systems in operation. . . .

African-Americans as Subjects of Contracts . . .

The Institutionalization of Slavery

. . . Originally there were no laws establishing slavery. Such laws came into existence as the institution of slavery became more entrenched in the American colonies. These laws did not create slavery, but rather acknowledged the institution of slavery. The first statute to impose the condition of slavery was passed in Maryland in 1664 and provided that all blacks then living in the colony or later imported into the colony, regardless of their present conditions of servitude, were to be slaves for life and that the condition of slavery was hereditary for all blacks as well. . . . African-Americans ceased to exist as human beings "endowed by their Creator with certain unalienable Rights" and became, simply, property.

Slaves as Human Property

Slaves were assets in the hands of their masters and were variously deemed as both real and personal property. When declared by statute as real estate, slaves descended in the same manner as land to heirs at law;

if not devised specifically, they passed to the personal representatives. Absent such a statute, however, slaves were considered personal property for purposes of descent and dower.... Further, slaves were viewed as personal possessions in all statutes or contracts involving chattels that did not specifically exclude them. Consequently, as chattel, slaves were liable to attachment in satisfaction of an owner's debt....

In the laws and cases regarding the sale, transfer, and inheritance of slaves, we ... see the contradiction between the liberal ideology that man has natural rights, liberty, and is free to contract for his own labor, and the institution of slavery.... The judicial system, rather than addressing this incongruity, focused on enforcing contract law for the controlling white culture, despite its condemning effects on African-Americans....

African-Americans as Parties to Contracts

Apart from criminal law, a slave held no legal status and virtually no rights....

The list of things that slaves legally were prohibited from doing was a long one. A slave could not prosecute or defend a suit, be a witness in a lawsuit, or obtain citizenship. Slaves were also incapable of owning either real or personal property; any extra earnings or gifts that a slave might acquire legally belonged to the master although the slave might be permitted to possess the items at the master's discretion. Additionally, a slave who was given a choice under the terms of his master's will between freedom or selecting a home on the plantation was considered incapable of making such a choice and legally could not claim his freedom....

Slaves legally could not enter into contracts, not even contracts of matrimony.... Rather than being void, slave marriages were voidable. Just as the voidable marriage of a minor can be valid if recognized after the removal of the disability (i.e., minority), so a slave marriage could become valid with the removal of the "disability" of slavery and its concomitant inability to contract. Freedom gained by manumission of both parties or by emancipation transformed the voidable marriage contract into a valid one.

With the exception of marriage contracts, all contracts with slaves were void and illegal unless made with the consent of the master....

The Post-Slavery Era

Conditions after the abolition of slavery were different only with regard to freedom from de jure slavery.... At first the former slave owners used intimidation and violence to keep former slaves in a condition that was essentially slavery. Soon, however, the need to guarantee cheap labor prompted the Southern states to enact the Black Codes. The Codes prohibited free movement of African-Americans and detailed appropriate behavior towards whites. The Codes were violated if African-Americans left their jobs or were considered vagrants, thereby assuring that the former slaves were required to work....

... Even when a state's Black Codes apparently granted freedom of contract to African-Americans, in practice, white employers simply refused to contract with the former slaves except on the employers' terms. Furthermore, white employers frequently paid their African-American laborers any amount that the employer deemed fit, regardless of any bargained-for wage. The judicial system, society's primary means of redressing contract disputes, was completely controlled by and sympathetic to white parties, thereby providing no forum for African-Americans to redress their grievances....

Nationwide, the concept of judicial non-interference with the right to contract gripped the country in the laissez-faire economic milieu following the Civil War.... In *Lochner v. New York*, the U.S. Supreme Court extended the definition of liberty to include freedom of contract, giving close scrutiny to any government regulation of that freedom. Finally, in *Coppage v. Kansas*, freedom of contract expanded to include contracts which required the worker to agree not to become a union member as a condition of employment ("yellow-dog" contracts). The ideological basis for such cases was that inhibiting the employer's freedom to contract impinged on his liberty interest. Indeed, it impinged on the worker's freedom as well since, theoretically, each individual was able to bargain equally for the best deal he was able to obtain.

Such discrimination in the contracting process had long lasting, harmful effects on both African-Americans and the nation.... As a result of the Black Codes, subsequent discriminatory practices in the South, and the U.S. Supreme Court's alignment with the capitalist/employer segment of society, the newly freed slaves who started their lives of freedom with no property, no money, no education, and usually no vocation other than farming were unable to use the one thing they did possess, their labor, in a manner consistent with capitalism. In other words, they were unable to use market functions to bargain for higher wages and better living and working conditions. As a consequence, the originally freed slaves remained economically deprived and their descendants reaped "a disproportionately small share of society's bounty as each successive generation passe[d] along its inherited economic disadvantage to the next." Equally important, such post-freedom discrimination exacerbated the feelings of dehumanization and low self-esteem already inflicted on African-Americans during the slavery era. Finally, the entire nation, besides suffering from problems associated with the economic deprivation of a significant portion of the population, revealed itself as a hypocritical nation—one that verbally espoused the high ideals of equality, liberty, and justice, but in reality practiced apartheid....

... The fashioning of racial hegemony could hardly foster trust and confidence in the legal system. ... The message to African-Americans, and whites as well, is that African-Americans are not, and have never been, a recognized part of the "system" or power structure of the nation. ...

For the most part, both African-Americans and whites are ashamed of the role that race has played in our history. Because Americans are not proud of that role, they prefer not to discuss it. ... The modern solution has been to remove the issue from the table of discussion, resulting in silence. Silence removes the issue from the realism of social and critical discourse.

... [But] [t]he problem with this thinking is that, in order to be fixed, the problem must first be identified. If one cannot discuss the issue, then it is impossible to ascertain the root, scope, and depth of the problem. ...

In our silence, the realities of a race-oriented society remain unremedied. ...

As Chase notes, contract rights were designed to function as protectors of collectivized privilege and became normalized as such. Next, critical race scholar Adrienne Davis extends Chase's analysis to reveal how property and contract jointly extend the past into tomorrow as bulwarks of systemic inequalities related to identity ideologies and hierarchies. Focusing on "testamentary freedom," Davis similarly shows how "private" law manufactures and manipulates social and material realities tied frequently to identities, groups, interests, and power. Davis deepens and extends critical understanding of property as "private" power enforced by—yet simultaneously distinguished from—"public" action and law.

This pervasive public-private distinction, as we have seen in other contexts, collapses under critical analysis in this context, too: as scholars have long noted, "the logically fastidious lines dividing the public from the private ... are blurred as one discovers that ... private property, independent of a public sphere that defines and enforces property rights, is incomprehensible, and ... the influence of private concentrations of property on public space seems incontrovertible.[10] Consider the Davis excerpt with these thoughts in mind.

---

[10] Anthony E. Cook, The Spiritual Movement Towards Justice, 1992 U. Ill. L. Rev. 1007, 1011 (1992).

The Private Law of Race and Sex:
An Antebellum Perspective
Adrienne D. Davis
51 Stan. L. Rev. 221 (1999)

... Private Law and the Dead

This is an article about private law, race, and sex. . . .

Material Effects and Ideological Tensions

. . . As these [testamentary transfer] case studies will emphasize, sexual bonds often generate economic relationships. It is the task of private law to determine which relationships will give rise to enforceable (or permissible) obligations, and which ones will not. Succession law sorts and ranks relationships that stem from sexual or companionate bonds between men and women, or biological ones between generations. . . . By investigating efforts of the formerly enslaved to establish intestacy chains on behalf of their families, this article illustrates how the legal assignment of economic abilities and disabilities to sexual relationships distributed wealth not only between men and women, but also between whites and blacks. It also gives close attention to the ideological productions that accompanied the articulation of the rules of law. . . .

. . . Southern antebellum culture is typically represented as strongly committed to both racial hierarchy and private property. Usually, support for property rights strengthened racial hierarchies. But as these wills show, interracial liaisons in a racialist system raised the possibility of wealth transfers from whites to blacks. Such diversions of wealth would appear to threaten antebellum economic and social hierarchies predicated on race, gender, and (enslaved) status. Investigating how law managed the testamentary transgressions by elite white men of the very social norms and hierarchies that benefited their class yields greater understanding of the relationship of property to race, gender, and sex. . . .

Terminology

. . . It is difficult to find terms in twentieth-century vocabulary to describe the relationships of the antebellum period. In discussing the relationships between the enslaved, I hesitate to use the term "marriage," as that term designates a series of legal relationships that were denied to the enslaved. Instead, I use the terms "companionate relationships" and "sexual family" interchangeably.

More troubling has been the inability to find satisfactory terms to refer to the black women I will discuss or to describe their relationships with the elite white men who enslaved them. . . . The absence of language is itself suggestive of the unsatisfactory nature of the existing conversations on this topic. . . . Moreover, most of these terms cannot account for the complexity of nineteenth-century male sexual power combined with race and status differences....

The Racial Economics of Sex

In every society, the schemes governing transmission of "wealth" (scarce resources) from one generation to the next speak volumes about the political economy and its ideology....

Inheritance in America

At the time of the American Revolution, the English law of estate disposition still expressed a strong preference for the lineal, intergenerational transfer of wealth. Doctrinal rules endorsed this mode over intragenerational transfers to conjugal partners or collateral kin, and also imposed severe limitations on transfers of wealth outside of kinship lines....

Inheritance is fundamentally an economic process in which sexual relationships become dispositive.... In Anglo-American law, legitimacy has been a determinant factor in directing succession; some sexual relationships yield economic entitlements to conjugal partners and their children.... Absent a will, succession doctrine assigns and prioritizes rights to an estate, therefore establishing initial "bargaining positions" in the language of law and economics.

The basic elements of the property regime in the United States adhere to English common law....

Post-Revolutionary America saw a marked growth in testamentary freedom in tandem with the abolition of primogeniture, entail, and other common law devices that restricted the ability to make individual dispositions of property....

In the southern states, these redefinitions of inheritance practices incorporated specific rules to deal with the political economy of slavery. Balancing testamentary freedom versus lineal descent of wealth and redefining chains of succession were complicated by slavery's peculiar treatment of race and sexuality, as suggested by the following case.

The Southern Dimension of Inheritance

In 1808, the estate of Charles F. Bates, an attorney and planter in Virginia, became the subject of a complicated probate. The conflict arose from the existence of two testamentary documents, one dated 1799 and the other dated 1803. Both of these documents had been executed prior to Bates' marriage to Mary Heath Bates in 1806....

... [T]he Supreme Court of Appeals of Virginia concluded that both wills had been canceled. Thus, Bates was declared an intestate, entitling his widow to the majority of his estate. As is typical in probates and challenges to wills, the holding of the court turned on its assessment of

Bates' intent. They determined that he had planned to author a third will to govern the disposition of his estate, and in the interim had revoked both of the previous documents.

There was an intriguing revelation in Bates' second will of a daughter born prior to his marriage to Mary Heath Bates. Bates had written:

> I have a daughter called Clemensa, at Walter Keeble's, in Cumberland, I declare her to be free to every right and privilege which she can enjoy by the laws of Virginia. I most particularly direct, that she be educated in the best manner that ladies are educated in Virginia. I give her my lot in the town of Cartersville, and three hundred dollars, to be laid out at interest, renewed yearly, and paid when she marry or come of age.

Bates introduced his only child into antebellum Virginia society as illegitimate, black, and enslaved. Her presence in certain aspects of the case and her marked absence in others illustrate how slavery added a racial dimension to postmortem wealth transfers.

Sexual Relationships and Material Commitments

Bates' mother and widow, the parties to the case, struggled over whether Bates' probate would be governed by a will or the law of intestacy. Testamentary transfer and intestate succession are the two mechanisms through which Anglo-American law disposes of estates. Testamentary transfers are essentially wealth transactions after death, which are not enforceable until death, while intestate succession governs the default, dictating distribution of the estate in the absence of a will. Wills might then be thought of as privately directed transfers, which probate courts must decide whether to implement or invalidate. In the absence of a will, or in the case of its invalidation, intestate succession emerges as the state's fixed preference for the descent of estates. Thus, the conflict in *Bates v. Holman* implicated both of the doctrinal mechanisms that govern postmortem wealth transfers.

Per succession law, neither widows nor parents were entitled to full inheritance. Intestacy law directed the lineal transmission of estates, with a life interest in a conjugal partner. Why then was Bates' daughter, Clemensa, not permitted to revel in "lineal glory?"

None of the several opinions issued by the court noted where Clemensa stood within the line of intestate succession. Her potential status as an "heir," who might exercise her own claim to the estate, thereby altering the distribution of the estate between Bates' widow and mother, was completely overlooked. In fact, one of the opinions says, "[T]he law makes ample provision for the widow: but far different is the case respecting his natural daughter, who, together with her future offspring, the law has doomed to perpetual slavery, to her nearest blood relations, unless emancipated by their clemency...." A similar expression of sentiments is as follows:

> As to Clemensa, it is, perhaps, her misfortune that the testator died intestate: I say, perhaps, for circumstances might have happened to change his opinion on that subject. Her's [sic] is, at most, the common case of a party's failing to provide by will for those who have strong claims upon him.

It appears clear that any rights, whether to emancipation or wealth, inuring to Clemensa would stem from Bates' own testamentary authority, and not from her own rights of inheritance. Hers is a missing link in the chain of estate succession for reasons the court does not feel compelled to explain, but only to lament. . . .

Focusing on wills and estates, Davis traces how legal notions of property and contract were created to give advantages to the propertied, based on group identity, and maintained across generations. The architecture of caste established in early property and contract law continues to be enforced. Critical race scholar Cheryl Harris explains below in her analysis of "whiteness as property" how elites use group identities to create and recreate private-public hierarchies by force of law to control society.

WHITENESS AS PROPERTY
Cheryl I. Harris
106 Harv. L. Rev. 1709 (1993)

... Introduction

In the 1930s, some years after my mother's family became part of the great river of Black migration that flowed north, my Mississippi-born grandmother was confronted with the harsh matter of economic survival for herself and her two daughters. Having separated from my grandfather, who himself was trapped on the fringes of economic marginality, she took one long hard look at her choices and presented herself for employment at a major retail store in Chicago's central business district. This decision would have been unremarkable for a white woman in similar circumstances, but for my grandmother, it was an act of both great daring and self-denial, for in so doing she was presenting herself as a white woman. In the parlance of racist America, she was "passing."

Her fair skin, straight hair, and aquiline features had not spared her from the life of sharecropping into which she had been born in anywhere/nowhere, Mississippi—the outskirts of Yazoo City. But in the burgeoning landscape of urban America, anonymity was possible for a Black person with "white" features. She was transgressing boundaries, crossing borders, spinning on margins.... [S]he could thus enter the white world, albeit on a false passport, not merely passing, but *tres*passing....

... Day in and day out, she made herself invisible, then visible again, for a price too inconsequential to do more than barely sustain her family and at a cost too precious to conceive. She left the job some years later, finding the strain too much to bear.

From time to time, as I later sat with her, she would recollect that period, and the cloud of some painful memory would pass across her face.... On rare occasions she would wince, recalling some particularly racist comment made in her presence because of her presumed, shared group affiliation. Whatever retort might have been called for had been suppressed long before it reached her lips, for the price of her family's well-being was her silence. Accepting the risk of self-annihilation was the only way to survive.

... The fact that self-denial had been a logical choice and had made her complicit in her own oppression at times fed the fire in her eyes when she confronted some daily outrage inflicted on Black people. Later, these painful memories forged her total identification with the civil rights movement. Learning about the world at her knee as I did, these experiences also came to inform my outlook and my understanding of the world.

My grandmother's story is far from unique.... Passing is well-known among Black people in the United States and is a feature of race subordination in all societies structured on white supremacy....

The persistence of passing is related to the historical and continuing pattern of white racial domination and economic exploitation that has given passing a certain economic logic. It was a given to my grandmother that being white automatically ensured higher economic returns in the short term, as well as greater economic, political, and social security in the long run. Becoming white meant gaining access to a whole set of public and private privileges that materially and permanently guaranteed basic subsistence needs and, therefore, survival. Becoming white increased the possibility of controlling critical aspects of one's life rather than being the object of others' domination.

My grandmother's story illustrates the valorization of whiteness as treasured property in a society structured on racial caste. In ways so embedded that it is rarely apparent, the set of assumptions, privileges, and benefits that accompany the status of being white have become a valuable asset that whites sought to protect and that those who passed sought to attain—by fraud if necessary. Whites have come to expect and rely on these benefits, and over time these expectations have been affirmed, legitimated, and protected by the law. Even though the law is neither uniform nor explicit in all instances, in protecting settled expectations based on white privilege, American law has recognized a property interest in whiteness that, although unacknowledged, now forms the background against which legal disputes are framed, argued, and adjudicated. . . .

The Construction of Race and the Emergence of Whiteness as Property

. . . [U]ndergirding both [the subordination of African Americans and Native Americans] was a racialized conception of property implemented by force and ratified by law.

. . . These distinct forms of exploitation each contributed in varying ways to the construction of whiteness as property.

Forms of Racialized Property: Relationships Between Slavery, Race, and Property

The Convergence of Racial and Legal Status. Although the early colonists were cognizant of race, racial lines were neither consistently nor sharply delineated among or within all social groups. . . . The distinction between African and white indentured labor grew, however, as decreasing terms of service were introduced for white bond servants. . . .

By the 1660s, the especially degraded status of Blacks as chattel slaves was recognized by law. Between 1680 and 1682, the first slave codes appeared. . . . Racial identity was further merged with stratified social and legal status: "Black" racial identity marked who was subject to enslavement; "white" racial identity marked who was "free" or, at minimum, not a slave. The ideological and rhetorical move from "slave" and "free" to "Black" and "white" as polar constructs marked an important step in the social construction of race.

Implications for Property. . . . Through slavery, race and economic domination were fused.

Slavery produced a peculiar, mixed category of property and humanity—a hybrid possessing inherent instabilities that were reflected in its treatment and ratification by the law. The dual and contradictory character of slaves as property and persons was exemplified in the Representation Clause of the Constitution. Representation in the House of Representatives was apportioned on the basis of population computed by counting all persons and "three-fifths of all other persons"—slaves. Gouveneur Morris's remarks before the Constitutional Convention posed the essential question: "Upon what principle is it that slaves shall be computed in the representation? Are they men? Then make them Citizens & let them vote? Are they property? Why then is no other property included?"

The cruel tension between property and humanity was also reflected in the law's legitimation of the use of Blackwomen's bodies as a means of increasing property. In 1662, the Virginia colonial assembly provided that "children got by an Englishman upon a Negro woman shall be bond or free according to the condition of the mother...." In reversing the usual common law presumption that the status of the child was determined by the father, the rule facilitated the reproduction of one's own labor force. Because the children of Blackwomen assumed the status of their mother, slaves were bred through Blackwomen's bodies. The economic significance of this form of exploitation of female slaves should not be underestimated. Despite Thomas Jefferson's belief that slavery should be abolished, like other slaveholders, he viewed slaves as economic assets, noting that their value could be realized more efficiently from breeding than from labor. A letter he wrote in 1805 stated: "I consider the labor of a breeding woman as no object, and that a child raised every 2 years is of more profit than the crop of the best laboring man."

Even though there was some unease in slave law, reflective of the mixed status of slaves as humans and property, the critical nature of social relations under slavery was the commodification of human beings....

... Because whites could not be enslaved or held as slaves, the racial line between white and Black was extremely critical; it became a line of protection and demarcation from the potential threat of commodification.... White identity and whiteness were sources of privilege and protection; their absence meant being the object of property.

Slavery as a system of property facilitated the merger of white identity and property.... Whiteness was the characteristic, the attribute, the property of free human beings.

Forms of Racialized Property: Relationships Between Native American Land Seizure, Race, and Property

... [T]he settlement and seizure of Native American land supported white privilege through a system of property rights in land in which the "race" of the Native Americans rendered their first possession rights invisible and justified conquest....

Although the Indians were the first occupants and possessors of the land of the New World, their racial and cultural otherness allowed this fact to be reinterpreted and ultimately erased as a basis for asserting rights in land. Because the land had been left in its natural state, untilled and unmarked by human hands, it was "waste" and, therefore, the appropriate object of settlement and appropriation.... Only particular forms of possession—those that were characteristic of white settlement—would be recognized and legitimated. Indian forms of possession were perceived to be too ambiguous and unclear.

... Not all first possession or labor gave rise to property rights; rather, the rules of first possession and labor as a basis for property rights were qualified by race. This fact infused whiteness with significance and value because it was solely through being white that property could be acquired and secured under law. Only whites possessed whiteness, a highly valued and exclusive form of property.

Critical Characteristics of Property and Whiteness

The legal legacy of slavery and of the seizure of land from Native American peoples is not merely a regime of property law that is (mis)informed by racist and ethnocentric themes. Rather, the law has established and protected an actual property interest in whiteness itself. . . .

. . . [P]roperty may "consist of rights in 'things' that are intangible, or whose existence is a matter of legal definition." Property is thus said to be a right, not a thing, characterized as metaphysical, not physical. . . .

Whiteness is not simply and solely a legally recognized property interest. It is simultaneously an aspect of self-identity and of personhood, and its relation to the law of property is complex. . . . According whiteness actual legal status converted an aspect of identity into an external object of property, moving whiteness from privileged identity to a vested interest. The law's construction of whiteness defined and affirmed critical aspects of identity (who is white); of privilege (what benefits accrue to that status); and, of property (what *legal* entitlements arise from that status). Whiteness at various times signifies and is deployed as identity, status, and property, sometimes singularly, sometimes in tandem.

Whiteness as a Traditional Form of Property. Whiteness fits the broad historical concept of property described by classical theorists. In James Madison's view, for example, property "embraces every thing to which a man may attach a value and have a right," referring to all of a person's legal rights. Property as conceived in the founding era included not only external objects and people's relationships to them, but also all of those human rights, liberties, powers, and immunities that are important for human well-being, including: freedom of expression, freedom of conscience, freedom from bodily harm, and free and equal opportunities to use personal faculties.

Whiteness defined the legal status of a person as slave or free. White identity conferred tangible and economically valuable benefits and was jealously guarded as a valued possession, allowed only to those who met a strict standard of proof. Whiteness—the right to white identity as embraced by the law—is property if by property one means all of a person's legal rights. . . .

Because the law recognized and protected expectations grounded in white privilege (albeit not explicitly in all instances), these expectations became tantamount to property that could not permissibly be intruded upon without consent. . . . When the law recognizes, either implicitly or explicitly, the settled expectations of whites built on the privileges and benefits produced by white supremacy, it acknowledges and reinforces a property interest in whiteness that reproduces Black subordination. . . .

De-Legitimating The Property Interest In Whiteness Through Affirmative Action

. . . The property interest in whiteness has proven to be resilient and adaptive to new conditions. Over time it has changed in form, but it has retained its essential exclusionary character and continued to distort outcomes of legal disputes by favoring and protecting settled expectations of white privilege. The law expresses the dominant conception of "rights," "equality," "property," "neutrality," and "power": rights mean shields from interference; equality means formal equality; property means the settled expectations that are to be protected; neutrality means the existing distribution, which is natural; and, power is the mechanism for guarding all of this.

One reason then for the court's hostility toward affirmative action is that it seeks to de-legitimate the assumptions surrounding existing inequality. It exposes the illusion that the original or current distribution of power, property, and resources is the result of "right" and "merit." It places in tension the settled expectations of whites, based on both the ideology of white supremacy and the structure of the U.S. economy, that have operated to subordinate and hyper-exploit groups identified as the "other." It opens to critique the idea that individualized and discrete claims to remedy identified discrimination will achieve the promise of equality contained in the Fourteenth Amendment. It conceives of equality in transgenerational terms, and demands a new and different sense of social responsibility in a society that defines individualism as the highest good, and the "market value" of the individual as the just and true assessment. It unmasks the limited character of rights granted by those who dominate. In a word, it is destabilizing.

Affirmative action begins the essential work of rethinking rights, power, equality, race, and property from the perspective of those whose access to each of these has been limited by their oppression. This approach follows Mari Matsuda's suggestion of "looking to the bottom" for a more humane and liberating view. From this perspective, affirmative action is required on both moral and legal grounds to de-legitimate the property interest in whiteness—to dismantle the actual and expected privilege that has attended "white" skin since the founding of the country. Like "passing," affirmative action undermines the property interest in whiteness. Unlike passing, which seeks the shelter of an assumed whiteness as a means of extending protection at the margins of racial boundaries, affirmative action de-privileges whiteness and seeks to remove the legal protections of the existing hierarchy spawned by race oppression. What passing attempts to circumvent, affirmative action moves to challenge. . . .

Fundamentally, affirmative action does not reestablish a property interest in Blackness because Black identity is not the functional opposite of whiteness.... Acknowledging Black identity does not involve the systematic subordination of whites, nor does it even set up a danger of doing so. Affirmative action is based on principles of antisubordination, not principles of Black superiority.

The removal of white privilege pursuant to a program of affirmative action ... is thus not a matter of implementing systematic disadvantage to whites or installing mechanisms of group exploitation. Whites are not an oppressed people and are not at risk of becoming so. Those whites that are disadvantaged in society suffer not because of their race, but in spite of it. Refusing to implement affirmative action as a remedy for racial subordination will not alleviate the class oppression of poor whites. Indeed, failing to do so will reinforce the existing regime of race and class domination that leaves lower class whites more vulnerable to class exploitation. Affirmative action does not institute a regime of racialized hierarchy in which all whites, because they are white, are deprived of economic, social, and political benefits. It does not reverse the hierarchy, but levels the racial privilege.

However, affirmative action is more than a program: it is a principle, internationally recognized, based on a theory of rights and equality. Formal equality overlooks structural disadvantage and requires mere nondiscrimination or "equal treatment;" by contrast, affirmative action calls for *equalizing treatment* by redistributing power and resources in order to rectify inequities and to achieve real equality.... [If affirmative action] were conceptualized from the perspective of those on the bottom, it might assist in moving away from a vision of affirmative action as an uncompensated taking and inspire a new perspective on identity as well. The fundamental precept of whiteness—the core of its value—is its exclusivity. But exclusivity is predicated not on any intrinsic characteristic, but on the existence of the symbolic "other," which functions to "create an illusion of unity" among whites. Affirmative action might challenge the notion of property and identity as the unrestricted right to exclude. In challenging the property interest in whiteness, affirmative action could facilitate the destruction of the false premises of legitimacy and exclusivity inherent in whiteness and break the distorting link between white identity and property....

Conclusion

Whiteness as property has carried and produced a heavy legacy. It is a ghost that has haunted the political and legal domains in which claims for justice have been inadequately addressed for far too long.... It is long past time to put the property interest in whiteness to rest. Affirmative action can assist in that task. Affirmative action, if properly conceived and implemented, is not only consistent with norms of equality, but is essential to shedding the legacy of oppression.

———

Harris shows how property rights and white identities continue *today* to be socially and systemically bundled to channel privilege and power, both public and private. ClassCrits scholar Danielle Hart adds another apt example, showing how disclosure statutes—mandating that one party to a private contract disclose certain pieces of information to the other party—channel advantages to parties with greater bargaining power in contract law *today* while foreclosing inquiry into the sources, nature, and effects of that unequal power. Legal "doctrine" thus helps keep property and contract as twin pillars of a status quo made unjust by top-down power, both private and public.

CONTRACT LAW NOW—REALITY MEETS LEGAL FICTIONS
Danielle Kie Hart
41 U. Balt. L. Rev. 1 (2011)

[Compliance with disclosure statutes] will likely eliminate several contract policing doctrines that would otherwise be available to challenge the presumption of contract validity. For example, a claim that the implied obligation of good faith was breached would probably fail because the term was disclosed up front.... [A] claim or defense based on fraud or misrepresentation, including misrepresentation in the form of a material non-disclosure, would also likely fail because there would arguably be no fraudulent or material misrepresentation.

In all likelihood, an unconscionability claim or defense would probably fail, again because of the disclosure of the term. Under these circumstances, there is no "unfair surprise" and, therefore, arguably, no procedural unconscionability....

In short, compliance with disclosure statutes only serves to strengthen the presumption of contract validity by making it appear that the quality of the weaker party's mutual assent has increased and by ruling out the application of several contract policing doctrines. By strengthening the presumption of contract validity, these outcomes (1) simultaneously create systemic incentives for the party with more bargaining power to impose even more onerous or one-sided terms during contract formation; and (2) increase the power of that stronger contracting party by effectively immunizing the exercise of that bargaining power during contract formation from subsequent challenge....

Power is ubiquitous; it exists everywhere. This is not an original conclusion. The Legal Realists, Critical Legal Studies, feminism, and more "other-oriented" social justice theories such as Critical Race Theory and

Queer Legal Theory exposed it. Thus, it is not at all surprising that power is also present in modern contract law. What is surprising is that the systemic and structural role state power plays in contract law is not acknowledged or discussed. This omission is especially surprising given that the modern contract law system adopts the premise that contracts are made binding as a cardinal principal, continues to adhere to a framework that is constructed on assumptions that cannot be sustained, and institutionalizes unequal bargaining power. Constructing the system in this fashion comes with unacknowledged costs. Specifically, such a system not only reifies pre-existing distributions and power imbalances, but also exacerbates and ultimately obscures them to the ultimate detriment of parties with less bargaining power. Modern contract's formation rules and disclosure statutes play an important role in this obfuscatory process. . . .

Hart's examples show (again) that contracts, although pretending to be "private" agreements, have value only if enforced as law by public power. All contracts reflect the shadow of public regulation and enforcement—a legal shadow that ignores glaring disparities of power between contracting parties that track identity-based skews.[11] As Franks and Steinfeld spelled out above, women, people of color, and other identity groups were excluded by law from the private-public opportunities of property and contracts for this very calculated reason. Making explicit the root tensions, hidden connections, and mutually reinforcing contradictions of this system is integral to exposing and confronting the Critical Challenge, and to achieving material and social equality for all.

NOTES AND QUESTIONS

1. *Critical History and the Private-Public Distinction.* The preceding excerpts and passages demonstrate how critical history and analysis can pierce formal legal illusions, like this private-public distinction, in varied contexts. Clinical legal scholar Chaumtoli Huq puts it this way:

> Making explicit the internal tensions, contradictions within the doctrine are helpful to demystify the law. . . . Simply by asking, for example, what are the policy imperatives for certain rulings to

---

[11] Charles R.P. Pouncy, Institutional Economics and Critical Race/LatCrit Theory: The Need for a Critical "Raced" Economics, 54 Rutgers L. Rev. 841, 842 (2002) (explaining that "the processes by which [unequal] distributions are maintained will become the battle lines and boundaries that circumscribe and limit our ability to achieve praxis—for those boundaries protect the financial claims that flow to people with white skin as a consequence of the ideologies and white privilege and white superiority").

enforce private contracts—who benefits, what interests are served . . . [will generate] a robust conversation on law and economics.[12]

In effect, Huq urges critical analysis from the bottom to reveal the system's fault lines. As Matsuda urged in Part II, "simply by asking" critical questions advocates can help deconstruct fallacies that prop up the Critical Challenge. Is Huq's urging an example of this critical method? If so, is it helpful? How?

6.3 ELITES ORCHESTRATE POWER, PRIVILEGE, AND PROFIT CONTINUOUSLY FOR LOCAL-GLOBAL RULE

Elites have stayed on top because they have networked, organizing themselves continuously for collective plans and actions with strategic endgames. From generation to generation, elites have built networks to help them pursue common interests, and these networks created institutions that constitute today's systems. Elites' efforts include highly personal choices related to marriage and family formation, as well as controlling the succession of wealth and knowledge intergenerationally. Elite dominance depends on this collectivized capacity to leverage material advantage for strategic actions that span generations.

In this process, elites continually focus on foundational concepts and ground rules. These foundational concepts include legal ideas like justice, equality, due process, sovereignty, conquest, property, contract, the public-private distinction, antidiscrimination (as opposed to antisubordination), and others. Ground rules determine the terms and means of access to adjudicative and democratic decision-making. These rules in the arena of adjudication define jurisdiction, atomize claims, structure procedure, regulate the timing, limit what counts as evidence, determine allowable remedies, and generally facilitate the exploitation of advantage by the already advantaged. In democratic decision making, ground rules establish voting rights, election methods, electoral campaign funding, and structure policymaking procedures, rules, and access to legislators and legislative processes. Foundational concepts and ground rules define, and redefine, the terrain on which systemic advocates work. They generate immediate and long-term effects. When left to elites, these concepts and rules serve only elite interests.

A relatively recent and clear-cut example of this long haul planning for systemic control comes from 1971, when future Supreme Court Justice Lewis Powell (serving from 1972–1987) wrote a memorandum

---

[12] Chaumtoli Huq, (inter)Generation Movement Lawyer 2.0, Law at the Margins (2014), https://billquigley.wordpress.com/2013/09/21/intergeneration-movement-lawyering-by-chaumtoli-huq/.

commissioned by the U.S. Chamber of Commerce.[13] His memo begins, "No thoughtful person can question that the American economic system is under broad attack." The memo also includes a footnote, "The American political system of democracy under the rule of law is also under attack, often by the same individuals and organizations who seek to undermine the enterprise system." From Powell's elite perspective as a corporate and tobacco industry lawyer, those adversaries are "socialistic" movements seeking "civil rights, environmental regulation, labor rights, consumer protection, and attempts to roll back the military-industrial complex."[14] Powell's list of targets identifies organized groups pressing collectivized claims for equal justice from below and shows how elites orchestrate adjudication, democracy, and wealth to rule, and profit from, society.

Powell outlined "possible avenues of action" for the Chamber and its corporate members to enact. After critiquing corporations for "appeasement, ineptitude, and ignoring the problem," Powell suggested actions to retake control of U.S. educational systems because "there is reason to believe that the campus is the single most dynamic source" of resistance to corporate agendas. Powell acknowledged that elites see knowledge as a concomitant to power—particularly critical knowledge like that reflected in the critical Schools and advocacy Approaches. Powell outlined a long-term corporate agenda for control of adjudication and democracy designed to concentrate corporate power and profits. The decades long "sabotage" of *Brown* that Chemerinsky outlined in Part I is a partial demonstration of this agenda.

Written a few months before President Nixon appointed Powell to the U.S. Supreme Court, the Powell memo urged major corporations and their supporters to invest substantial resources in a collective campaign for greater power and profits. This plan laid out long-term, coordinated actions relying on joint financing and guidance through both the U.S. Chamber of Commerce and the National Association of Manufacturers. Powell proposed that corporations create and fund a plethora of pro-corporate institutions (e.g., "public interest" law firms, think tanks, speakers bureaus, lobbying arms, and foundations) to reverse the strength of liberal and left-of-liberal ideas and policy. From the start, this campaign led to the creation of new entities, designed to carry out various ongoing activities—including, perhaps, other campaigns.

This top-down framing purposefully centered big corporations and their interests, both in democratic and adjudicatory systems that make and remake law. It made corporations ever more political in self-interested

---

[13] Memorandum from Lewis F. Powell to Eugene Sydnor, Attack on American Free Enterprise System (Aug. 23, 1971), www.law.wlu.edu/deptimages/Powell%20Archives/PowellMemorandumTypescript.pdf.

[14] Zygmunt J.B. Plater, Dealing with Dumb and Dumber: The Continuing Mission of Citizen Environmentalism, 20 J. Envtl. L. & Litig. 9, 32 (2006).

terms. Corporations thus became the advocates and beneficiaries of today's dominant approach to social policy: neoliberalism. With corporate interests in the center, the drive for profit became the prime directive. In the United States, a mandate to maximize profit for shareholders already had been established under law decades ago.[15] But this memo outlined a relatively concrete plan of action, which set the stage for making everything else in society a "cost" to be reduced—public education, health, disaster management, infrastructure, and more—except public spending for prisons, security, and the military. These are the conditions of neoliberalism.

In 1971, Powell's action plan proceeded from his diagnosis of a systemic problem as seen from the top. It contemplated a starting point for systemic solutions from that perspective, proposed a series of planned actions to implement them, provided resources for them, and specified endpoints. His memo sketches the essentials of any campaign that is well conceived and well executed. In particular, this campaign resulted in the creation of the Heritage Foundation and a rejuvenated American Enterprise Institute, the funding of Federalist Society chapters across the country to influence law students and—over time—judicial choices, and the creation of so-called "public interest law firms" to pursue pro-corporate litigation and policy initiatives.[16] In time, the adjudicative campaign gave corporations the *Citizens United* outcome in 2010, when five justices declared, in the name of the U.S. Constitution, that spending corporate money for political advertising constitutes protected speech.[17]

As *Citizens United* itself shows, this adjudicative campaign was accompanied by equal attention to reasserting control over democracy. In addition to dark-money political action committees to sway elections at all levels of government, this campaign included the establishment in 1973 of the American Legislative Exchange Council (ALEC), a "bill mill" for stealthily spreading rightwing legislation. Corporate lawyers have composed and promoted numerous "model" statutes couched in public interest terms that actually are tailored to corporate agendas. Corporations and their agents, including the institutions they create for this purpose, then use all their power and wealth to push for state-by-state adoption. Slowly but steadily, these organizations steer adjudication and democracy towards self-serving results. These organizations, and others mentioned in the excerpt below, exemplify how elites organize continually to stay on top always.

---

[15] See *Dodge v. Ford Motor Co.*, 170 N.W. 668, 680 (Mich. 1919) (establishing the primacy of shareholder wealth maximization in corporate decision-making).

[16] Plater, Dealing with Dumb, 32.

[17] *Citizens United v. FEC*, 558 U.S. 310 (2010) (invalidating federal campaign reform law that prevented corporations and unions from funding political advertising; arising in the context of a documentary critical of presidential candidate Hillary Clinton, and accompanying advertisements of the film, funded by the conservative organization Citizens United).

Decades later, the daily news provides the measure of that campaign's success. For instance, when the Powell memo was written in 1971, corporations did not pursue efforts to redraw doctrine through adjudication in methodical terms. Since then, and as recommended then, the Chamber of Commerce annually funds litigation designed to reach the Supreme Court with the aim of changing law to serve corporate interests. Since 2006, the Chamber has prevailed in more than 70% of its Supreme Court cases, compared to 43% and 56% during comparable periods of the Burger and Rehnquist Courts. Moreover, "the five conservative Justices have given the Chamber more than ¾ of their total votes. . . . Justices Alito, Gorsuch, Kennedy, Roberts, and Thomas cumulatively voted for the Chamber's position 86% of the time."[18] Decades of Powell memo-influenced campaigning has minted new doctrines to elevate corporate personhood, undermine procedural safeguards against police and prosecutorial abuses, and restrict collective action rights and remedies available to subordinated groups. The continuing follow-ups to the Powell memo illustrate how elites use issue-focused campaigns, in combination with big corporations and other institution-building projects, to strategically exploit their accumulation of symbolic and material advantages.

The Powell plan depends squarely on collectivized resources and actions based on shared interests and despite existing differences. This elite campaign aims to build the resources and capacity of corporations and their allies to influence law both as adjudication *and* as democracy. But as we will see more fully in Part IV, this campaign also aims to "take out" or disempower all others. Indeed, in the world according to Powell, corporations increasingly have become the only kind of collective not under attack. The Powell memo in effect brought into existence a social and legal order in which corporate profit-making squeezes out other systemic commitments or inconvenient values, including equal justice for all. This social consequence is entirely by design. At the same time, systemic advocacy is designed to match and check these very same moves from below.

In the excerpt below, environmental activist Charlie Cray writes an analysis of the Powell memo for the Greenpeace blog, looking back 40 years after its writing to dissect some of its consequences—social and legal, symbolic and material, micro and macro. Note that the Powell plan includes initiatives, institutions, and programs dedicated to building collective power through organizing elite institutions. That campaign would include changing "hearts and minds"—that is, affecting cultural views and understandings. This attention to mainstream cultural attitudes—and the power to shift them intentionally over time—are crucial to any legal change "sticking" for the long term. As we elaborate below,

---

[18] Brian R. Frazwlle, A Banner Year for Business as the Supreme Court's Conservative Majority is Restored, 2017–2018 Term, Constitutional Accountability Center (July 17, 2018).

systemic advocacy pays very close attention to these same two goals—organizing for collective power and culture shifting.

THE LEWIS POWELL MEMO: CORPORATE BLUEPRINT TO DOMINATE DEMOCRACY

Charlie Cray
Greenpeace Blog (Aug. 23, 2011)[19]

... Forty years ago today, on August 23, 1971, Justice Lewis F. Powell, Jr., an attorney from Richmond, Virginia, drafted a confidential memorandum for the U.S. Chamber of Commerce that describes a strategy for the corporate takeover of the dominant public institutions of American society.

Powell and his friend Eugene Sydnor, then-chairman of the Chamber's education committee, believed the Chamber had to transform itself from a passive business group into a powerful political force capable of taking on what Powell described as a major ongoing "attack on the American free enterprise system."

... [Powell] detailed a series of possible "avenues of action" that the Chamber and the broader business community should take in response to fierce criticism in the media, campus-based protests, and new consumer and environmental laws.

Environmental awareness and pressure on corporate polluters had reached a new peak in the months before the Powell memo was written. In January 1970, President Nixon signed the National Environmental Policy Act, which formally recognized the environment's importance by establishing the White House Council on Environmental Quality. Massive Earth Day events took place all over the country just a few months later and by early July, Nixon signed an executive order that created the Environmental Protection Agency (EPA). Tough new amendments to the Clean Air Act followed in December 1970 and by April 1971, EPA announced the first air pollution standards. ...

The overall tone of Powell's memo reflected a widespread sense of crisis among elites in the business and political communities.... [He decried criticism coming] most alarmingly—from "perfectly respectable elements of society," including leading intellectuals, the media, and politicians.

To meet the challenge, business leaders would have to first recognize the severity of the crisis and begin marshalling their resources to influence prominent institutions of public opinion and political power—especially the universities, the media and the courts. The memo emphasized the importance of education, values, and movement-building. Corporations

---

[19] www.greenpeace.org/usa/the-lewis-powell-memo-corporate-blueprint-to-dominate-democracy/.

had to reshape the political debate, organize speakers' bureaus and keep television programs under "constant surveillance." Most importantly, business needed to recognize that political power must be "assiduously cultivated; and that when necessary, it must be used aggressively...."

Powell emphasized the importance of strengthening institutions like the U.S. Chamber—which represented the interests of the broader business community, and therefore key to creating a united front. While individual corporations could represent their interests more aggressively, the responsibility of conducting an enduring campaign would necessarily fall upon the Chamber and allied foundations.... [I]t was important to create new think tanks, legal foundations, front groups and other organizations. The ability to align such groups into a united front would only come about through "careful long-range planning and implementation, in consistency of action over an indefinite period of years, in the scale of financing available only through joint effort, and in the political power available only through united action and united organizations."

... Powell's Memo is widely credited for having helped catalyze a new business activist movement, with numerous conservative family and corporate foundations (e.g. Coors, Olin, Bradley, Scaife, Koch and others) thereafter creating and sustaining powerful new voices to help push the corporate agenda, including the Business Roundtable (1972), the American Legislative Exchange Council (ALEC-1973), Heritage Foundation (1973), the Cato Institute (1977), the Manhattan Institute (1978), Citizens for a Sound Economy (1984—now Americans for Prosperity), Accuracy in Academe (1985), and others.

Because it signaled the beginning of a major shift in American business culture, political power and law, the Powell memo essentially marks the beginning of the business community's multi-decade collective takeover of the most important institutions of public opinion and democratic decision-making. At the very least, it is the first place where this broad agenda was compiled in one document.

That shift continues today, with corporate influence over policy and politics reaching unprecedented new dimensions. The decades-long drive to rethink legal doctrines and ultimately strike down the edifice of campaign finance laws breaking radical new ground with the Roberts Court's decision in *Citizens United v. The Federal Election Commission* continues apace.

Although many new voices have emerged in the 40 years since it circulated Powell's memo, the U.S. Chamber has expanded its leadership position within the corporate power movement, leading dozens of judicial, legislative and regulatory fights each year. Measured in terms of money spent, the Chamber is by far the most powerful lobby in Washington,

DC. . . . The Chamber sponsors the Institute for Legal Reform, which has spearheaded the campaign for tort "reform," making it more difficult for average people who have been injured, assaulted, or harmed to sue the responsible corporations. Along with well over a dozen legal foundations, the Chamber has also helped shape the powerful "business civil liberties" movement that has been a driving force behind the *Citizens United* decision and other judicial actions that have handcuffed regulators and prevented Congress from putting common-sense checks on corporate power.

Cray describes the overarching plan created by Powell and enacted over decades by many actors, working in coordination. It shows how collective power is built. It shows how sustained coordination of adjudication and democracy can empower some and disempower others. An essential part—and consequence—of that plan has been the undermining of collective legal actions and rights for average people. This has been accomplished by expanding corporate personhood rights while restricting the ability of subordinated individuals to confront corporate abuses *as a group*. Limiting collective legal challenge, rights to organize, and protections against retaliation are central mechanisms of elite dominance. In turn, as we explain more fully in Part III, expanding collective legal activity, organizing the capacity to do more, and protecting activists and advocates from attack are primary aims of systemic advocacy.

These aims are made more pressing by top-down efforts to restrict access to civil litigation—particularly collective or class measures—which already have been restricted through changes to liability rules, pleading, summary judgment, and class certification standards, and mandatory arbitration and related individuation of claims.[20] As civil procedure scholar J. Maria Glover points out, the rules of procedure in adjudication have been stacked, with elites focusing on expanding power over, and reducing access of subordinated groups to, collective processes:

> Lobbied by corporate entities, recent procedural reforms by Congress have tended to restrict access to justice and rule of law [norms] rather than preserve [them]. . . . Together, the result is that both Congress and the federal courts (particularly the U.S. Supreme Court) are reforming procedure in ways that restrict access to justice and diminish rule-of-law norms.
>
> The big winner in this power struggle has been neither the judicial nor the legislative branch, but, instead, corporate entities seeking (often successfully) to limit exposure to liability by restricting access to justice, particularly for low-income

---

[20] J. Maria Glover, "Encroachments and Oppressions": The Corporatization of Procedure and the Decline of Rule of Law, 86 Fordham L. Rev. 2113, 2113 (2018).

individuals, those with low-value claims, or citizens with little political power. This power struggle has provided corporate entities with two bites at the procedural apple. If corporations are the big winner in this struggle, there must be a big loser. The loser has been the rule of law.[21]

Class actions provide an apt and key case in point: originally invented in feudal England by lordly elites to make collection of rents (or evictions) cheaper, quicker, and easier for them as individuals. In this original version, the lord of any manor (as plaintiff) could name all the serfs owing him rent as one defendant "class" (of debtors), suing them collectively in a single action for their individual debts to him. By the mid-twentieth century, the United States codified class actions as a rule of civil procedure, allowing not only privileged individuals (as plaintiffs) to sue bottoms collectively as a defendant class, but also allowing bottoms as a plaintiff class to sue collectively an elite defendant. Although designed chiefly to make legal action for small investors more affordable (by grouping together as a plaintiff class), this equalized rule also opened courthouse doors to many other potential classes as well—including those with consumer, environmental, or identity-based claims.[22] Chief Justice Warren Burger explained in 1980 that:

> The aggregation of individual claims in the context of a classwide suit is an evolutionary response. . . . Where it is not economically feasible to obtain relief [through] a multiplicity of small individual suits for damages, aggrieved persons may be without any effective redress unless they may employ the class-action device. . . . This, of course, is a central concept of Rule 23 [governing class actions].[23]

Exactly for this reason, a top-down "holy war" against class actions was gearing up, just as plaintiff classes injured by mass torts, fraud, and other top-down wrongdoing filed and won class action lawsuits.[24] Within a few decades, affected elites had rewritten the law—narrowing federal class actions by enacting the Class Action Fairness Act in 2005, and benefitting from significant federal court decisions, including some from the business-friendly Supreme Court of the recent past, to make class actions ever-less accessible or affordable specifically for injured bottoms. As legal scholar Robert Klonoff describes:

---

[21] *Id.* at 2114.

[22] See these Stephen C. Yeazell articles: Group Litigation and Social Context: Toward a History of the Class Action, 77 Colum. L. Rev. 866 (1977); From Group Litigation to Class Action, Part I: The Industrialization of Group Litigation, 27 UCLA L. Rev. 514 (1979–80); From Group Litigation to Class Action, Part II: Interest, Class, and Representation, 27 UCLA L, Rev. 1067 (1979–80).

[23] *Deposit Guar. Nat'l Bank v. Roper*, 445 U.S. 326 (1980).

[24] Arthur R. Miller, Of Frankenstein Monsters and Shining Knights: Myth, Reality, and the "Class Action Problem," 92 Harv. L. Rev. 664 (1979).

> The class action device, once considered a "revolutionary" vehicle for achieving mass justice, has fallen into disfavor. Numerous courts have become skeptical about certifying class actions.... Even requirements that defendants rarely disputed in the past, such as "numerosity" and "commonality," are now potential impediments to class certification. Moreover, many courts now require that plaintiffs put forward considerably more evidentiary proof at the class certification stage than ever before.... As a result of these developments, experienced class action defense counsel can frequently identify a number of promising arguments to defeat certification, even in fairly routine cases.
>
> ... Defendants can now secure a federal forum much more frequently [through removal of class action claims brought in state court], and they now have a tool for obtaining immediate appellate review of an order certifying a class. With many more class actions in federal court, and with more class certification decisions being reviewed by appellate courts, federal courts have created new hurdles for plaintiffs seeking class certification.[25]

Thus, in the wake of the broad pro-corporate program outlined by the Powell memo, the efficacy of class actions has been dramatically undermined. At times, the Supreme Court has been at the forefront of the "holy war" against class actions and, in recent years, has drastically limited all forms of collectivization of claims. In *Wal-Mart Stores, Inc. v. Dukes*, 564 U.S. 338 (2011), for example, the Court tightened the rules for showing common "questions of law or fact" as required for certifying a class action. In tandem with *Citizens United*, this 2011 opinion shows how elites organize themselves collectively while opposing and disorganizing actual or potential collectives that might challenge their dominance.

Under corporate influence, the Court elevated the interests of corporations in individualized arbitration claims—allegedly to promote efficiency—over the interests of people. This is true of gains for corporations over people in collective bargaining and consumer claims and over small businesses in commercial litigation. In a series of cases, including *Epic Systems Corp. v. Lewis* (2018), *AT&T Mobility LLC v. Concepcion* (2011), and *American Express Co. v. Italian Colors Restaurant* (2013),[26] the Supreme Court upheld mandatory arbitration agreements that require claimants to waive rights to class or collective action in employment, commercial, and consumer disputes. In doing so, as legal scholar Eric Yamamoto explains, the Court suppressed bottom-up activism

---

[25] Robert Klonoff, The Decline of Class Actions, 90 Wash. U. L. Rev. 729, 731–32 (2013).

[26] See *Epic Systems Corp. v. Lewis*, 138 S. Ct. 1612 (2018); *American Express Co. v. Italian Colors Restaurant*, 133 S. Ct. 2304 (2013); *AT&T Mobility LLC v. Concepcion*, 563 U.S. 333 (2011).

and advocacy by "significantly disadvantaging the claims of those less powerful under the guise of neutral efficiency reforms:"[27]

> *AMEX/Concepcion*'s procedural rulings morphed mandatory arbitration into a do-it-yourself claim suppression guide for large companies. More so, the conservative majority's decisions substantially benefit large businesses by keeping out of the public eye dirty legal laundry sought to be aired by employees, consumers, tenants, small businesses, and discrimination claimants.
>
> Justices Kagan, Ginsburg, and Breyer objected strenuously.... For the dissenting justices, after *AMEX* and *Concepcion*, [individual] pursuit of small-to-modest-value claims against large businesses or institutions is "a fool's errand." And without legal liability and public accountability, those businesses and institutions possess little incentive to stop profitably violating the law.
>
> Critical procedure's rejection of the myth of the inherent neutrality of facially uniform procedures and its attention to context and consequences help unearth *AMEX/Concepcion*'s ideological underpinnings.
>
> ... Those ADR cases are not isolated rulings about more efficient dispute resolution....
>
> Critical procedure reveals the impact of the *AMEX/Concepcion* rulings and the conservative ... constriction of court access and claim development. In the words of Judge Young, in the epigraph, "[o]minously, business has a good chance of opting out of the legal system altogether and misbehaving without reproach." ... For in the end, it is not only about procedure. It is about power and substantive advantage for some over others. It is about injustice—or justice—for people and communities. "Do not be fooled."[28]

Since the Powell memo of the 1970s, elites have used the law to constrain collective action that threatens the status quo. Another ongoing example is the federal Racketeer Influenced and Corrupt Organizations Act (RICO), passed with the explicit aim of criminalizing undesirable market and social actors while protecting those seen as legitimate. Although directed explicitly at "racketeer influenced and corrupt organizations" the open-ended question was which collectivities would be so deemed, by whom, and how. The RICO experience shows that prosecutors can turn it against

---

[27] Eric K. Yamamoto, Critical Procedure: ADR and the Justices' "Second Wave" Constriction of Court Access and Claim Development, 70 SMU L. Rev. 765, 815 (2017).

[28] *Id.* at 814–16.

practically any group they don't like. Criminal law scholar Benjamin Levin highlights how RICO was passed in the same era in which the Powell memo was written. Like the memo, this statute is reacting to the same elite desire to retrench progress and consolidate power in the face of vigorous challenges from civil rights, women's, environmental, and consumer rights movements. RICO purports to draw a clear line between legitimate market actors and actions and illegitimate ones, but, as Levin notes, it has been used for "politically inflicted conspiracy prosecutions." Such prosecutions may have rooted out organized crime and corruption in some unions, for example, but may also have targeted unions and union leaders that threatened to challenge corporate power. RICO thus draws a line between "legitimate" and "illegitimate" that may be "reflective of a belief that the private interests represented by state and federal prosecutors are more desirable than the private interests represented by this set of nonstate [labor or other] collective actors."[29] RICO in this sense represents a partial codification of the Powell memo's world view. As Levin observes:

> [Given its timing with the Powell memo], the passage of a statute that defines "legitimate business" and suggests that it is in the public interest to protect these legitimate actors from external threats and "infiltration" becomes striking.... By targeting groups that challenged the functioning of the marketplace, the Act might be viewed as a delaboring of the culture, a renaturalization of the market, and a discrediting of forces that might challenge the nascent neoliberal orthodoxy. That is, where decades earlier organized labor had been treated as crucial to democracy and the American way of life, the Act emphasized the antidemocratic and pernicious role that collective actors might have in the structure of American social and economic life.
>
> ... RICO [emerged] ... within a period in which political actors sought to redefine the boundaries of the legitimate (or perhaps formal) market and of legitimate collective action. Located in this particular cultural context, the war on organized crime ... was a politically inflected decision.... Viewing RICO through [this historical lens] should invite ... inquiries into the interests advanced and hindered by prosecutions and normative reexaminations of what sorts of market action should actually be treated as "legitimate" and "corrupt."[30]

As part of the Powell strategy, RICO grants great power for state actors to file criminal RICO suits and for corporations to file civil RICO suits designed to suppress collective action, including protest action. Elites have taken up this cudgel when convenient. Levin offers a concrete example of

---

[29] Benjamin Levin, American Gangsters: RICO, Criminal Syndicates and Conspiracy Law as Market Control, 48 Harv. C.R.-C.L. L. Rev. 105 (2013).

[30] *Id.*

how elites use democracy to enact laws, enforced through adjudication, to incapacitate any challenge to their rule. In another example, Texas-based Energy Transfer Partners, the developer of the Dakota Access oil pipeline, filed a RICO suit in 2017 against environmental groups BankTrack, Greenpeace, and Earth First, as well as against individual activists who protested or supported the anti-pipeline demonstrations. Among those sued was Krystal Two Bulls, an Oglala Lakota and Northern Cheyenne organizer, represented by the Center for Constitutional Rights and EarthRights International. Ms. Two Bulls described the suit as an effort to suppress protest:

> As an Oglala and Northern Cheyenne woman, and a U.S. Army veteran, I am well aware of the impacts that capitalism and militarism have on our country, communities, culture and People. Capitalism and militarism are just continuations of colonization. I think we need to shift our focus from these ridiculous lawsuits, to address the larger issues of capitalism and militarism and how the rights of corporations supersede the rights of the People in this country.[31]

The suit was dismissed in 2019, but such lawsuits tax resources and create enormous stresses regardless of their outcome. Since then, several states have passed laws—at the behest of corporations and their allied lobbying groups—establishing new felony penalties against protestors opposing pipeline or other energy projects. This phenomenon is expanding worldwide, according to advocacy organizations such as U.S.-based Protect the Protest and London-based Article 19, which focus on collective action rights:

> State repression of protests in Brazil is nothing new. . . .
>
> Since 2013, however, this climate of repression has intensified. Incidences of police violence have increased, new kettling tactics [whereby police surround and contain protestors] have been employed, modern crowd control equipment has been acquired, and ever-larger contingents of police officers are being assigned to oversee demonstrations.
>
> To make matters worse, the rise in repression has not been limited to the streets, but is also mirrored in the judiciary, which has begun sentencing demonstrators on the basis of weak accusations, and in the legislature, where there has been an

---

[31] Native American Protester Calls for Dismissal of Vengeful Dakota Access Pipeline Lawsuit, Center for Constitutional Rights (Jan. 28, 2019), https://ccrjustice.org/home/press-center/press-releases/native-american-protester-calls-dismissal-vengeful-dakota-access. See also Maggie Ellinger-Locke, Anti-Protest Legislation is Threatening our Climate, Greenpeace (May 3, 2019), www.greenpeace.org/usa/issues/the-right-to-dissent/.

explosion in the number of bills aimed at restricting the right to protest.[32]

The Powell memo was no mere musing. The followup has been relentless, ruthless, and lavishly funded, as decisions limiting class actions, expanding RICO prosecutions, promoting anti-protest laws, and other examples since the 1970s show. As the Gilens and Page excerpt in Part I detailed, only organized collective action can develop the power to change outcomes—a finding that documents how power determines outcomes. By collectivizing, organized groups build collective power to shape foundational concepts and ground rules that determine outcomes of both democracy and adjudication.

Legal scholar B.S. Chimni next shows how similar patterns play out on the international stage. The public-private "web" of global states and "international institutions" hides private power behind public power in transnational contexts. In practice, this elite project extends into international systems the same Critical Challenge of using law for equal justice.

INTERNATIONAL INSTITUTIONS TODAY: AN IMPERIAL GLOBAL STATE IN THE MAKING
B. S. Chimni
15 Eur. J. Int'l L. 1 (2004)

... Introduction: The Argument

International Institutions (II) have today acquired a significance for third world states and peoples that they never possessed before. A network of economic, social and political IIs has been established or repositioned, at the initiative of the first world, and together they constitute a *nascent global state* whose function is to realize the interests of transnational capital and powerful states in the international system to the disadvantage of third world states and peoples. The evolving global state formation may therefore be described as having an *imperial* character....

... [T]he United Nations (UN) has embraced the neo-liberal agenda and is being geared towards promoting the interests of transnational capital, in particular by increasing the role that the private corporate sector can play within the organization(s). [Additionally], the relationship between the state and the UN is being reconstituted through a

---

[32] Right to Protest, Article 19: Defending Freedom of Expression, Brutal Repression of Protests Continues in Brazil, www.right-to-protest.org/brutal-repression-of-protests-continues-in-brazil/. See also Article 19, The Right to Protest Background Paper (2016), www.article19.org/data/files/medialibrary/38581/Protest-Background-paper-Final-April-2016.pdf; "Protect the Protest" Coalition Launched to Fight Back Against SLAPPs, Center for Constitutional Rights, https://ccrjustice.org/civicrm/mailing/view?reset=1&id=1083.

reconfiguration of the principle of sovereignty and its relationship with the principle of the prohibition of threat or use of force....

... [S]everal IIs that had adopted a critical discourse in the past have been repositioned and normalized. These include the United Nations Conference on Trade and Development (UNCTAD), United Nations Environment Programme (UNEP), and United Nations Educational, Social and Cultural Organization (UNESCO). The US has played a lead role in undermining the independent thinking of these institutions and their association with third world causes. For example, the US walked out of UNESCO in 1984 to protest the organization's growing politicization and anti-Western bias, rampant budgetary mismanagement, and advocacy of policies that undermine freedom of the press and free markets. A particularly divisive issue was UNESCO's advocacy of a "new world information order" (NWIO) to counter an alleged pro-Western bias in global news agencies ...

The US has now agreed to rejoin UNESCO after it "reforms" itself.

... [Simultaneously], a vast range of non-governmental organizations (NGO) have begun to participate in and influence in diverse ways the norm creation and decision-making process within IIs.... While a large number of NGOs bring the critical voice of an emerging "global civil society" to IIs, others such as the International Chambers of Commerce (ICC) or the World Economic Forum (WEF) seek to promote the cause of transnational capital. Even the critical voices often neglect the concerns of the Third World (for example, by attempting to link trade with labour standards in the WTO).

... [Finally], a web of sub-national authorities and cities undergird IIs or the emerging global state and are, along with NGOs, the decentralized instruments of global governance.... Together, these features limit the possibilities of global redistributive justice and the genuine democratization of both inter-state and intra-state relations....

One cannot make sense of these features of IIs without locating them within the larger global social order, in particular the historical and political contexts in which they originate, evolve and function. Such an approach allows the insight that a coalition of powerful social classes and states decides when an II is the appropriate form in which to pursue their interests, as well as its central preoccupations. This understanding ... lifts the veil from ... influence of certain social classes and forces in shaping the policy of states and IIs at different points in history....

The class which exercises the greatest influence in IIs today, and consequently on the emerging global state, is that of the transnational fractions of the national capitalist class in advanced capitalist countries with the now ascendant transnational fractions in the Third World playing the role of junior partners. Together, they constitute *a transnational capitalist class (TCC) which is in the process of congealing and establishing a global state composed of diverse IIs* that help actualize and legitimize its world-view. The TCC "is comprised of the owners of transnational capital, that is, the group that owns the leading worldwide means of production as embodied principally in the transnational corporations and private financial institutions." ... The TCC culture is lived and produced in the First World by a network of high-profile corporate executives, bankers, brokers, financial management experts, media managers, academics and bureaucrats using the most modern means of communications to create a world of ideas that has material force. In the production of this culture the third world counterparts essentially act as "transmission belts and filtering devices for the imposition of the transnational agenda," although admittedly there are third world globalizing firms that also contribute to the original ensemble of practices. The staff of key IIs, such as the World Bank, IMF and WTO, also play a significant role in reproducing TCC culture. They are mostly hired from first world academic institutions and socialized into particular modes of thinking and life style....

... Needless to add, the developments in the world of IIs are not entirely one-sided; in many ways IIs act as a shield for third world states and also empower third world peoples against their own states (for instance, human rights and environmental organizations).... However, the essence of contemporary developments in the field of IIs is the creation of conditions conducive to the spread and growth of global capitalism and not the improved welfare of third world peoples....

The Emergence of a Nascent Global State: Developments

... Proliferating Human Rights Organizations: Implications

In the post-1945 period a range of international human rights organizations (IHRO) have been set up, a large number of which have come into existence in the last two decades. The IHROs include UN bodies (ECOSOC, UNDP, UNHRC, ILO, UNESCO, UNHCR), expert bodies established by UN organs or under particular human rights treaties (Human Rights Committee, Committee on Economic, Social and Cultural Rights, Committee on the Elimination of Racial Discrimination, Committee on the Elimination of Discrimination against Women, Committee against Torture, Committee on the Rights of the Child, and others), and a set of activities authorized by the UN (such as in the mandates of UN peacekeeping forces)....

It would of course be churlish to deny that international human rights law and organizations have in many ways empowered progressive social forces in third world countries. Even authoritarian governments have had to take human rights on board and take cognizance of criticisms made in IHROs from time to time. But "rights cannot be higher than the economic structure of society and its cultural development conditioned thereby."

Furthermore, since IHROs focus more on civil and political rights, as they lack the mandate, resources and political backing to seriously influence outcomes in the realm of economic and social rights, they have had only a minimal impact on the welfare of ordinary peoples in the third world. Indeed, the emphasis on civil and political rights allows the pursuit of the neo-liberal agenda by privileging private rights over collective social and economic rights. . . . Equally significant is the realization that IHROs can help deflect radical movements into more official channels that can be controlled through procedural formalities. . . . The task of IHROs appears to be, in other words, more damage control than the production of welfare states. . . .

Undermining Third World Democracy

Establishing Polyarchy

The relocation of sovereign powers from states to IIs has transformed the meaning of democracy in the Third World. It has emptied it of its content for it has substantially eliminated the possibility of effecting a choice between political parties/actors with different economic and social programmes. Thus, irrespective of which party or coalition is voted into power in general elections today, the economic and social policies that it would pursue would remain the same in their essentials. This *sameness* is a function of international obligations that are enforced by sanctions that hurt. To put it differently, international law and organizations are today institutionalizing polyarchy or formal democracy in third world countries. The possibility of creating a genuinely participatory democracy has been jettisoned by removing the element of choice. Alternative development paths can no longer be voted for. . . .

Undermining Traditional Forms of Resistance

The relocation of sovereign space in IIs has also undermined traditional forms of resistance. Among other things, those affected in the Third World are prevented by sheer physical distance from expressing their doubts *directly* to concerned IIs. Take, for example, the simple fact that the WTO has no address in India. Similarly, it is impossible for Indian farmers to protest, like their French and Belgian counterparts, in front of the WTO offices in Geneva. It is perhaps true that an international public sphere is emerging and that IIs "offer domestic challengers institutional opportunities to transcend their national arena for consultation, collective action, and contestation at an international level." It may be equally true that electronic resistance may slowly replace more traditional forms of protest. But the effectiveness of either the institutional opportunities or electronic resistance is still very much in doubt, given the extremely limited participation of those directly affected by II activities.

Discrediting Alternatives: Legitimizing Hegemony

IIs not only enforce unjust rules but also possess enormous resources to legitimate them. IIs are, given their global membership, uniquely placed to suggest that the interests of the emerging TCC represents the general interests of humankind. The ideological functions of IIs assume many forms. An II actively promotes norms of international behaviour which facilitate the realization of its objectives. It also frames issues for collective debate and recommends specific policy responses. . . . IIs also evaluate the policies of member states from the standpoint of their mandate and concerns. But above all, IIs offer an 'intellectual and moral unity' to a particular vision of world order in the matrix of which their mandate and functions acquire meaning. . . . The neo-liberal orthodoxy that it promotes today is one that furthers the interests of the TCC. . . .

Need for a Complex and New Internationalism

. . . [Systemic] changes cannot be brought about without *a powerful global social movement* that calls for the requisite changes in the rules and structure of IIs. Only the determined struggle of the oppressed and marginal sections of the third world in alliance with their counterparts in the North can get powerful states and TCC to respond to their concerns. . . . [But NGO] potential is considerably overstated as they lack the resources and political roots to organize and mobilize the vast majority of working people, especially in the Third World. . . .

The global dissent movement should, it is perhaps worth emphasizing, strive to establish networks at the level of sub-national authorities and in cities in order to create counter-hegemonic values and spaces . . . to creat[e] critical consciousness in the people who inhabit them. . . . In other words, what is called for is a critical transgovernmental order as opposed to a hegemonic transgovernmental order.

In conclusion, it only remains to be added that adherence to *the practice of non-violence is essential* to ensure that the global social movement is not subverted from within and outside. More significantly, non-violence, as Mahatma Gandhi taught us, is the only way to create and sustain a just world order.

Chimni charts the corporate construction and social effects of a "global state" as a source of elite power and enrichment. This new infrastructure—part of top-down globalization—is devoted to "the spread and growth of global capitalism" rather than to the welfare of people at the bottom of global hierarchies. Reflecting the legacies of colonialism and imperialism, this globalized system deepens the thicket of the Critical Challenge across borders.

NOTES AND QUESTIONS

1. *Declining Life Expectancy and Legal Epidemiology.* The long-term U.S. elite plan has been multilevel, extending across time and across branches of government. Consider for example how healthcare has been affected. Sociologist Jennifer Karas Montez describes a "machinery of injustice and premature death" that has spurred an actual—and continuing—decrease in life expectancy among low-educated U.S. residents since the 1980s.[33] Low-educated white women were the first to see their longevity decline—well before the much-publicized effects of the U.S. opioid crisis among rural whites. Marginalized groups in urban areas—particularly Black women, transgender individuals, and others—also have been disproportionately affected by healthcare policies. Although the "dominant narrative" attributes the decline to "personal responsibility and decisions"—such as decisions about smoking, food choices, or attending college—this is a "false narrative" not backed by scientific evidence.

The roots of this problem, according to Montez, lie in three structural forces—all connected to the roll-out of long-term strategies following the model set out in the Powell memo: the devolution of policymaking authority in healthcare to the states, combined with cutting aid and loosening strings attached to programs such as welfare or Medicaid; the expansion of state preemption bills forbidding local governments from improving standards on issues related to the social determinants of healthcare, such as antismoking, gun control, minimum wage, or paid sick leave ordinances; and the capture of state legislatures by a "troika" of pro-corporate, policy-influencing groups—ALEC, the State Policy Network, and Americans for Prosperity—which have succeeded in influencing judicial appointees as well as legislators. The result is that legislatures passed, and judges upheld, hardline state laws to reduce investments in programs that enhance well-being; to weaken labor, environmental, and other movements; and to prohibit progressive local lawmaking. Law, as made and enforced along lines laid out in the Powell memo, is literally killing people—or at least contributing to their early death:

> [One] hint that changes in state policies may underlie the changes in U.S. life expectancy is suggested by the timeline of activity of policy-influencing organizations. ALEC's initial success in the mid-1980s corresponds with the time that U.S. longevity started to fall behind other high-income countries and when longevity started to diverge across states. A step change in ALEC's success occurred with the 2010 midterm elections, which corresponds to the time that U.S. longevity notably plateaued and departed from other high-income countries. Another hint can be seen by comparing states of highest and lowest ALEC activity. Take Oklahoma and Connecticut. . . . [I]n 1970 life expectancies in these two states were rather average . . . and differed by 1.5 years. Subsequently, OK became one of the most active

---

[33] Jennifer Karas Montez, Policy Polarization and Death in the United States, 92 Temp. L. Rev. 889 (2020).

states in enacting ALEC legislation and by 2014 had fallen to forty-seventh place in terms of life expectancy; CT was among the least active in enacting ALEC legislation and by 2014 had risen to third place.

. . . [A] necessary first step toward identifying effective and bold solutions is a fundamental reorientation of scientific research on the topic that targets the structural factors (e.g., state policies, corporations, policy-influencing organizations) that undergird the problem. . . . [R]esearchers need to ask new and different questions and integrate perspectives from political science and especially legal epidemiology—"the scientific study and deployment of law as a factor in the cause, distribution, and prevention of disease and injury in a population." . . . [T]he United States' health woes have its roots "in corporate boardrooms[,] advertising and lobbying firms, and legislative and judicial chambers."[34]

2. *Roots of Protest Suppression.* Suppression of any protest has always accompanied identity-based subordinations. Consider that as early as the 1600s, West Indies plantation owners obtained laws to ban drumming, which they believed their slaves were using to spread the code for an insurrection against them.[35] Black Codes passed by Southern states after the Civil War included criminal restrictions on the assembly of Blacks, at least without the presence of a white person, as a means of social control. In short, collective action against elite subordinations, and elite suppression of protest, have equally long histories.

3. *Backlash Against Protest, including "Disaster Repression."* Excessive violence by police against victims of color has sparked protest, backlash against protesters, and efforts to repress protest using law. What if someone in the community assaults or kills a police officer in anger—can a peaceful protest organizer (or organization) be held personally liable, criminally or civilly, on the theory that organizing protest against police-initiated violence somehow incited violence toward the police?[36] Relatedly, as later depicted in the film Straight Outta Compton, the FBI sent a letter in 1989 to the record label of the rap group N.W.A. accusing the group of inciting violence against the police through their music such as "Fuck tha Police." Efforts to repress protest through civil litigation, prosecution, and policymaking—adjudication *and* democracy—abound in history and today. Moreover, crises like the coronavirus pandemic offer potent opportunities. States may exercise emergency powers to restrict protest or to shift liability from corporate or government actors to individuals and organizations. The expanded powers result in policies or decisions that may have an impact long after a crisis has ended. The International Center for Not-for-Profit Law (ICNL) identified several ways

---

[34] *Id.* at 913–15.

[35] See Andrea L. Dennis, Black Contemporary Social Movements, Resource Mobilization, and Black Musical Activism, 79 Law & Contemp. Probs. 29 (2016).

[36] See Katie Mettler, "Permanently Disabled" Baton Rouge Officer Sues Black Lives Matter for 2016 Ambush Shooting, Wash. Post (July 10, 2017).

that civil society groups were impeded in reaching, aiding, and mobilizing marginalized communities in early months of the COVID-19 pandemic:

- Making it harder for civil society to reach and assist those affected by the crisis through curfews, stay-at-home orders, and other restrictions on movement that do not exempt civil society organization or individual activists providing aid (Rwanda, Burkina Faso, Belize, Cameroon, United States);

- Restricting access to information and obscuring the nature of the crisis by suspending freedom of information laws, eliminating deadlines for responding to information requests, or erecting other barriers to public information (El Salvador, Georgia);

- Chilling free expression and penalizing dissent by enacting new laws or increasing punishments targeting those the government accuses of spreading "false information," creating "uncertainty," harming "national integrity," or "falsely" criticizing a public official's response to the pandemic (Zimbabwe, Bolivia, Russia, Jordan);

- Banning assemblies or gatherings without exceptions for peaceful protests and without expiration dates, forbidding or erasing public protest art, or targeting activists or organizations from marginalized groups (Mexico, Algeria, Eritrea, Chile);

- Expanding surveillance allegedly to monitor compliance with quarantine orders without limits on police access to information or restrictions on its usage for pandemic response purposes only (China, Russia, Poland, South Korea, Hong Kong, Armenia);

- Expanding executive branch powers at the expense of judicial or legislative branch powers and limiting civil society groups' ability to bring lawsuits against crisis practices or policies (Hungary, Uganda, Russia); or

- Casting governmental responses in national security terms as a "global war" (United States) and expanding military legal authority or deploying military forces, making it easier to defend infringements on rights or limits on organized groups (Egypt, Serbia, Lebanon, Philippines, Singapore).[37]

In the United States, the start of the coronavirus epidemic occurred at almost the same time as expanded #BlackLivesMatter protests around the country.

---

[37] See Top Trends: COVID-19 and Civic Space, International Center for Not-for-Profit Law (July 2020) (describing nine distinct ways in which freedom of assembly rights or activities of civil society groups were restricted by governmental actions taken in the name of COVID-19 public health and safety), www.icnl.org/post/analysis/top-trends-covid-19-and-civic-space. Yet another dimension of techniques against mobilizing are those drawn from technology, such as geofencing technology that may, in the interest of public health during a pandemic, facilitate contact tracing by identifying all individuals within a certain geographic space, but can equally be used by U.S. law enforcement to chill collectivizing by revealing the identities of all protestors in any given space.

Activists and advocates already involved in protecting protest rights and protestors—as well as combatting police violence—anticipated the likely crackdowns and prepared proactive initiatives. The ICNL and other groups documented how they began working immediately to advance reforms to protect the right to gather, to obtain information, and to protest.[38] These include proposed or passed legislation to prohibit the use of chemical irritants by law enforcement, specifically at protests. Many local municipalities adopted Community Control Over Police Surveillance measures that included various transparency requirements on the purchase of surveillance equipment, community oversight boards on their procurement or use, research to evaluate the anticipated impact or reports on their actual impact, or outright bans on the use of facial recognition technology. These examples show not only that repression can take the form of opportunistic top-down uses of public crises to reassert power, but also that advocates and activists can use such times proactively, as windows of opportunity, if they are well-prepared to make incremental, yet strategic, gains in the course of long-term organized struggle.

6.4 ELITES USE NEOLIBERAL IDEOLOGY AS LAW TO MAGNIFY AND CONCENTRATE THE PUBLIC POWER OF PRIVATE WEALTH

Critical race and LatCrit scholar Charles Pouncy observed that:

> All economic events have distributive consequences. The structure and impact of those consequences are determined both by the event and by the economic instruments deployed to maintain, correct, or amplify the event.... [A]s a consequence, corporations, the instrumentalities of capital, are experiencing unprecedented profitability while working and middle classes are experiencing ever expanding hardship [and ever greater economic precarity].[39]

Elites use this entrenched structure of material inequality to magnify their "private" wealth and its public power from generation to generation. They shift onto others the social cost of their ever-greater profit seeking—that is, they "externalize" pollution and degradation to maximize gains for themselves. They reduce wages and manipulate benefits to improve labor "productivity"—to tighten the screws of worker exploitation and inflate profits for themselves. Today, these and similar well-worn elite techniques are continued and refined under the rule of "neoliberalism"—a top-down

---

[38] Reforms Introduced to Protect the Freedom of Assembly, International Center for Not-for-Profit Law (July 2020), www.icnl.org/post/analysis/reforms-introduced-to-protect-the-freedom-of-assembly; Alexander C. Kaufman, States Have Put 54 New Restrictions on Peaceful Protest Since Ferguson (June 5, 2020) (describing, among others, a new Louisiana law imposing a three-year mandatory minimum sentence for protesters who trespass on infrastructure sites, including pipeline developments, during a state of emergency).

[39] Charles R. Pouncy, Recovery from the Recovery: Law and Contemporary Processes of Accumulation by Dispossession, 26 J. of Civ. Rts. and Eco. Dev. 107 (2010).

socioeconomic ideology that intensifies colonial and imperial legacies based on identities, groups, interests, and power.

Neoliberalism uses law as the principal instrument of top-down politics, increasing while denying systemic inequality. Neoliberalism is neither identity neutral nor opposed to regulation—like other proposals reflected in the Powell memorandum, neoliberalism in practice is opposed only to regulations (or identities) that interfere with elite agendas. Neoliberalism relies affirmatively (though sometimes covertly) on identity, power, *and* law to structure markets as unequal playing fields in pursuit of top-down interests locally, nationally, and internationally. Its effects demonstrate that neoliberalism magnifies precarity—a state of affairs in which most of the world lives close to the edge of poverty and unrelenting personal financial insecurity: living, barely, "paycheck to paycheck."

In addition to entrenching privileged tops locally and globally, neoliberalism purposefully fragments the rest of society. Pierre Bourdieu, sociologist, anthropologist, and philosopher, notes that neoliberal images of "a pure and perfect market" disguise political goals against any collective structures that could impede their imperative of maximum self-enrichment.[40] These structures include public agents—like the nation-state—that regulate "private" capital, as well as private collectives or institutions, like unions, universities, and cooperatives that protect or promote alternatives to neoliberal Darwinism. As law, neoliberalism reflects the politics and priorities of Powell's 1971 memo.

In the now-transnational universe, investors and their interests reign supreme by law. Government and laws exist and function merely or mainly to protect an elite's property, enforce contracts, guard wealth, keep workers under control, and subdue any dissent perceived as an actual threat to elite interests. To do so, governments organize and regulate "free" markets. Using private-public power, elites have made their corporations primary in law and society.

Neoliberal law redistributes wealth from the middle and the bottom to the top by (1) deregulating corporations, (2) privatizing public functions, (3) cutting taxes *and* increasing subsidies for elites, (4) slashing social services for the masses, and (5) repressing or coopting any opposition—the neoliberal recipe for every social issue. The "elite consensus" embodied now in neoliberal ideology and practice is constantly challenged, however. Law can be—and is—used critically; through deconstruction, critical analyses of law uncover links among identity, injustice, and struggle across multiple contexts, helping inform effective collective action.

To elaborate, Athena Mutua, a ClassCrits scholar—a critical School of legal knowledge—explains some fundamental ideas, policies, and practices

---

[40] Pierre Bourdieu, Utopia of Endless Exploitation: The Essence of Neoliberalism, Le Monde Diplomatique (Dec. 1998), www.mondediplo.com/1998/12/08bourdieu (emphasis in original).

of neoliberalism, which in turn are based on preexisting "neoclassical" economic beliefs. What explains the persistence of contradictions in law and society—such as the myth of a free "private" market in a world where all markets plainly are regulated, if not created, by continuous government action?

FRAMING THE ELITE CONSENSUS, IDEOLOGY AND THEORY & A CLASSCRIT RESPONSE
Athena D. Mutua
44 Sw. L. Rev. 635 (2015)

Neoliberalism is a set of ideas, policies and practices . . . based on the intellectual scaffold of neoclassical economic theory. [I]t comprises a theory, an ideology, and a set of policies and practices.

. . . Neoliberalism, inspired by neoclassical economic theory, has two major policy recommendations and practices; these recommendations and practices include deregulation of the economy and privatization of government functions. But it also includes policies promoting tax cuts (particularly for businesses), "free trade," [and] financial liberalization in the name of liberty, while manifesting a hostility toward unions and social safety net provisions. . . . All this rests on "a belief in the power of 'free markets' to produce optimal social welfare."

. . . [T]hough neoliberalism expresses distrust of the state, [it simultaneously] . . . requires and inures the authoritarian coercive power of the state. That is, state power is needed in order to protect and preserve the rights of "private property, individual liberties, and entrepreneurial freedoms" central to the "free market." . . .

For elites, believing in this theory (and ideology) is very attractive and comforting. According to the theory, elites can benefit society by aggressively pursuing their own interests—they need not consider anybody or anything else. . . . [I]t is unsurprising that elites are unconcerned with the inconsistency posed by the notion of a [government-regulated "free" market]. . . . [I]t is further unsurprising that they are resistant to the idea that the theory and the decisions they make in its name fail to work for anyone other than them. . . .

In fact, corporate profits in the US "hit a 60-year high in 2011, right as the effective corporate tax rate hit a 40-year low. America's largest companies . . . [have not] paid the full corporate tax rate in 45 years, and 26 [mega corporations] have avoided taxation altogether for years [at a time]." . . .

. . . [B]y almost "every major statistical measure," income inequality has increased substantially. In fact, the country has not seen the current level of the gap between the rich and the rest in terms of income and wealth since the 1920s. . . .

Calls for fiscal discipline and restricted state spending, in general, while seemingly benign, . . . [disproportionately] cut investment in people, including spending on the social infrastructure of which social security, and social supports like food assistance and unemployment benefits are a part.

. . . [T]hese are policy driven social arrangements (including globalization itself) established and cemented often through legislation which benefit some (the rich) and not others (the rest) and are not the result of some inevitable, naturally occurring invisible economic hand. The increasing inequality spawned by these implemented policy choices have left in their wake a disappearing middle class, increased poverty, and displaced young people.

. . . [E]lites can say that they are doing just what neoclassical theory suggests: aggressively pursuing their self-interests and putting their businesses in a position to maximize shareholder profit. . . . [A]bandoning the theory . . . might be a first step toward putting the welfare of the entire public at the center of economic activity. . . .

As Mutua notes, neoliberalism's U.S. triumph is attested by the greatest economic inequality since the robber baron days of the 1920s Gilded Age preceding the Great Depression. In this legal and economic environment, multinational corporations have become increasingly central in laws and societies around the world. These corporations bring to bear their multinational power on local targets, overwhelming them by sheer disparity of resources. They influence law and society in deeper ways than their smaller predecessors ever could. And they have done so to promote neoliberalism so that elite domination is not only maintained but intensified in law and society, locally and globally.

Below, legal scholars Nancy Ehrenreich and Beth Lyon demonstrate the point. Examining the "corporatization and globalization of agriculture," they show how elites organize to advance their own interests—over time and using law, just as the Powell memo encouraged. They conclude that elites "use their political and economic power to control trade agreements and international financial institutions in ways that reap benefits for their own economies and businesses while threatening the global eco-system and further impoverishing and exploiting the world's poor and hungry." This system consolidates and exacerbates colonial and imperial legacies worldwide. Ehrenreich and Lyon, deepening points made above by Cray, Yamamoto, Levin, and Chimni, demonstrate how identities, groups, interests, and power help to structure by law the production and consumption of even the most basic foodstuffs.

The Global Politics of Food: A Critical Overview
Nancy Ehrenreich and Beth Lyon
43 U. Miami Inter-Am. L. Rev. 1 (2011)

Like many other arenas of life, . . . [i]nequalities of power and privilege across the globe affect who has access to food and who does not, who controls its production and who is harmed by that production, how consumptive choices are constructed and constrained, and whether eating is seen as a complex, biosocial activity or as nothing more than instrumental bodily maintenance. . . .

. . . The global politics of food . . . reveal the interconnectedness of a vast array of seemingly unrelated systems—systems of international trade, rural development, public health, education, environmental protection, and social meaning-making (among others). Food is a critical concern; agriculture occupies more than half the world's population and nearly one-third of the Earth's land surface, and every member of the human race relies on its product.

. . . [F]ood also demonstrates the cross-hemispheric connections among systems of race, class, and gender subordination—as well as environmental degradation and cruelty to animals. The industrial model of farming that poisons farm workers with pesticides . . . depletes the nutritional value of the fruit they grow, and pollutes the environment during both the growing and the shipping processes. . . . [C]omplex systems that produce and deliver food reflect and reinforce global systems of power and privilege, affecting the most intimate recesses of human life—work, health, child-raising, identity, eating.

Challenging the Dominant View

For ease of discussion here we divide food issues into two different domains—production and consumption. . . . Of course, [the two] interrelate and overlap, and both structural adjustment and "free trade" policies, the handmaidens of corporate agriculture, are central to each. Nevertheless, we will employ this somewhat artificial distinction for ease of organization [and] discussion. . . .

The Production Domain

Since [the mid-1970s], corporations have . . . stretched their operations both vertically and horizontally, to the point that it no longer makes sense to speak of national food systems because the agrifood TNCs [transnational corporations] are so globally integrated in their operations.

Introduction

Agricultural production around the world is increasingly dominated by a small number of large, multinational corporations . . . facilitated by domestic subsidies, international monetary policy, and so-called "free trade" agreements....

Impact of Subsidies, Trade Agreements and Structural Adjustment on Agricultural Sectors of the Global South

Within the United States, the agricultural sector has been subsidized for decades. Originally, that subsidization was justified by the predominance (at that time) of small-scale agriculture, which was thought to be uniquely vulnerable to weather and the market. Although large corporations now dominate food production in the United States the subsidies continue, justified by a political discourse that still invokes the image of the small "family farm." Today ... the central impact of agricultural subsidies has been to benefit the bottom line of large, corporate agricultural interests, allowing them to sell their products below the actual cost of production. At the same time, multi-national accords like the North American Free Trade Agreement (NAFTA), along with structural adjustment programs imposed on countries by the International Monetary Fund, have made the agricultural sectors in poorer countries of the Global South more vulnerable to foreign competition. While trade agreements between rich and poor countries demand that the latter open their markets (including agricultural markets) to foreign products and entities, those agreements often still allow countries of the Global North to maintain their agricultural subsidies—subsidies that Southern countries do not have the resources to match. Combined together, farm subsidies, "free trade" agreements, and international monetary policy have created significant competitive advantages for multinational agri-food companies, causing disastrous effects on the small farmers, economies, and overall food security of Mexico and other countries of the Global South.

The Efficiency Myth

... Both trade policy and international monetary policy ... espous[e] neoclassical economics and formally equal access to international trade. Like most "free market" and formal equality approaches, "free trade" policies all too often exacerbate existing inequalities, harming especially small farmers and other rural poor people.... International monetary policy also favors the rich over the poor. By incentivizing neoliberal economic reforms such as "deregulation, privatization of industry and government services, reduction of government spending, financial liberalization, promotion of foreign investment, and enhanced protection of private property rights," it has weakened social safety nets, reduced subsidies and governmental support for farmers, and exposed local producers to highly subsidized foreign competition.

The interests of corporate agriculture and the conventional neoclassical wisdom regarding trade and economic policy dovetail precisely: both seek, first and foremost, efficiency ... to maximize profits by increasing output while reducing costs . . . [regardless of] domestic economies, food quality, worker safety, and the health of the environment. . . .

[I]n actuality trade and development policies are neither efficient nor fair. . . . [D]iscourses of agricultural efficiency and free trade merely obfuscate a reality of economic domination and exploitation.

The Mexican Example

. . . Mexico is a striking example of how subsidies in wealthy countries can combine with trade agreements and structural adjustment programs to produce extremely harmful power imbalances between Northern and Southern agricultural interests. . . .

. . . [B]y allowing subsidized U.S. agricultural products tariff-free access to Mexican markets, NAFTA exposed local growers of corn and other products to withering competition with international corporate agriculture. Subsidies to U.S. growers increased production, which in turn depressed prices. . . . Many small subsistence farms (formerly the main source of the Mexican corn crop) failed in the face of competition with large, U.S. corn growers who could afford to weather the falling prices by selling their subsidized product below the cost of production. . . . [T]rade liberalization policies combined with NAFTA to trap the country in the status of a net food importing nation. . . . Mexico has been an "enormous laboratory of neoliberal experimentation."

. . . [T]he introduction of patented genetically modified seeds into the international food system . . . significantly increase[s] the costs of growing corn, for farmers must buy the seeds themselves (rather than using some from the previous year's harvest) and then must support the crop with expensive fertilizers and pesticides not required for indigenous varieties. Moreover, . . . modified corn seeds were found in non-GMO Mexican fields. Such contamination of the corn crop creates . . . the risk that [farmers] will be exposed to patent infringement lawsuits for the corn they involuntarily and perhaps unknowingly cultivate. This uncontrolled spread of GMO seeds also raises the prospect of a loss of product diversity, as the seeds contaminate fields of indigenous corn. . . .

. . . The catastrophic effects of this series of events included: farmer unemployment and migration to urban areas (followed, in some cases, by emigration to the United States), loss of biodiversity (Mexico has traditionally produced over 150 varieties of corn), environmental and energy impacts (due to industrial farming techniques and long-distance importing of corn into Mexico from the U.S.), and severe nutritional deficits among Mexico's poor (whose diets have deteriorated now that local corn is unaffordable for them). The decimation of Mexican small corn farming, along with trade rules opening Mexico to foreign investment have, in turn, increased opportunities for large food retailers such as Walmart and fast-food companies such as McDonald's to enter the Mexican market, further weakening the Mexican diet (and threatening small grocers as well).

. . . Rather than supporting the economies of poor countries, U.S. and U.S.-supported trade and development policies are effecting a new form of colonialism that perpetuates, rather than diminishes, Northern corporate and economic hegemony throughout the world. . . . Today, economies of the Global North are appropriating the food crops that have formed the very foundation of the subsistence food systems in Mexico and elsewhere for centuries. And that appropriation is threatening the very existence of indigenous peoples. . . .

A Colonial Legacy?

[This status quo is the] legacy of a long history of colonial interference in indigenous cultivation. Interference with agricultural practices was a common and often contentious element of colonial rule. For example, quinoa, a protein-balanced grain cultivated in the Andean region as long ago as 3000 BC, was considered a sacred plant by the Incans when they confronted the Spanish empire. The Spanish rejected quinoa for both cultural and religious reasons. They preferred to derive their protein from meat and grow familiar European grains, and they also opposed quinoa because of its non-Christian religious associations. . . . The British [similarly] insisted on the monoculture of long-staple cotton, which in short order led to severe field erosion when predictable heavy rains came. . . .

Who Pays the Price: Effects on Agricultural Workers and the Environment

The corporatization of subsistence crops turns the most basic elements of poor nations' diets into products that must be purchased from powerful multinational corporations at inflated prices. At the same time, it forcefully converts subsistence farmers, who must now buy their food with currency, into wage and migrant laborers to be exploited by corporate agriculture in their countries and abroad. In short, rural poor communities and farm workers bear the brunt of their nations' inability to control the economic impacts of corporate agriculture, and women and children bear a disproportionate share of that burden. . . . Moreover, "trade liberalization imposes particular risks on traditional land-based cultures whose collective identities are rooted to their ancestral territories and resources." When indigenous farmers are forced to abandon traditional production and migrate to urban areas, they lose not only their lands but their cultural identity as well. Migration not only transforms them into surplus labor but also accelerates their disappearance as a distinct people. . . .

Environmental damage represents another critical dimension of the politics of food . . . [which] has both long-term implications for global public health and more immediate harmful effects on workers and local populations.

Another environmental cost of multinational, export-oriented agriculture is the energy consumed in the production and distribution of food. Long distance shipping wastes energy and increases harmful pollution.... [L]ong-distance trucking not only consumes petroleum but also produces carbon dioxide, which both contributes to global warming.... [It takes] "about 7.3 units of (primarily) fossil energy to produce one unit of food energy in the U.S. food system."

Much of the damage caused by the corporatization and globalization of agriculture has been invisible, in part because it disproportionately affects subordinated countries and communities. Other invisible victims of corporate agriculture are the animals raised for consumption. Unspeakable cruelty is routinely visited upon those animals, and their fate usually plays a negligible role in agriculture [policymaking]....

Conclusion

... [Food production shows that] industrialized nations (and the multinational corporations that increasingly influence those nations' policies and politics) use their political and economic power to control trade agreements and international financial institutions in ways that reap benefits for their own economies and businesses while threatening the global eco-system and further impoverishing and exploiting the world's poor and hungry.

Nevertheless, small but important pockets of resistance deserve celebration and support. Movements to protect traditional farming practices, such as La Via Campesina, Coalition of Immokalee Workers and Farmworker Justice, have emerged in recent decades as a voice for small farms, farm workers, and other people affected by corporate-dominated food production. Organic farming has also made a mark. Although it forms a relatively small part of U.S. agricultural production, organic farming has expanded rapidly in the United States in the last decade, with a growth rate of 19% in all but one of the last five reported years. The European Union has strongly rejected genetically modified foodstuffs and anti-WTO activism has drawn worldwide attention to the flaws of international trade policies. Poor nations are refusing to accept economic conditions that international financial institutions seek to impose upon them and even the World Bank recently acknowledged that structural adjustment policies used in the past had not always produced the intended results.

The Consumption Domain

Just as the effects of industrial agricultural production fall most heavily on marginalized groups, so the structure and ideology of food consumption have a disparately negative impact on poor, rural populations disproportionately composed of people of color. As food quality declines (due to industrialized production), eating well becomes more and more a matter of class privilege. While poor diet is often attributed to poor personal eating habits, inadequate consumption is better understood as a function of economic status—a product of poverty. . . .

Equality in Consumption: the Importance of Access to Quality Food

Falling Food Quality

. . . [I]t has become clear in recent decades that there is an inverse relationship between the [neoliberal claim to] efficiency of food production and the quality of foods produced.

The impact of this relationship is suggested by the decreases in nutritional value that have accompanied the rise of corporate agriculture. . . . [A] recent study of 43 fruits and vegetables . . . found "their nutrient value has declined in recent decades while farmers have been planting crops designed to improve other traits," especially yield. Of 13 nutrients examined, . . . "the average vegetable found in today's supermarket is anywhere from 5% to 40% lower in minerals than those harvested just 50 years ago." . . . [M]onoculture corporate agriculture is not only producing economic and environmental devastation, but is also decreasing the quality of food.

The Ideology of Consumptive Choice

. . . Healthy eating is often depicted as first-and-foremost about individual decision making and self discipline. Informed and health-conscious consumers will eat well and be healthy, while those who are more ignorant or self-indulgent will fall prey to the expanding North American (and, increasingly, Central and South American) waistline. . . . Poor people in particular are seen as preferring to eat unhealthy foods, needing to change their diets, and less informed about and/or receptive to modern nutritional information. And despite evidence to the contrary, immigrants are assumed to bring unhealthy eating practices with them. . . .

Under this "healthy eating" view, a central way to address poor diets is to improve the dissemination of information so that consumers will make better choices. . . . Although obesity experts have generally turned away from the personal choice paradigm, legislators and policy makers operating under this paradigm continue to focus on increasing consumer information (the food pyramid, caloric labeling) . . . rather than on increasing the affordability of healthy food or reforming food production processes. . . .

Access, not Choice; Subordination, not Self-Indulgence

. . . [A]s in the production domain, there is an alternative way to look at issues of food quality and healthy consumptive practices. Under this [bottom-up] view, food policy is yet another arena of class- and race-based inequality and the rhetoric of consumer choice is an obscurantist discourse that blames the economically disempowered for their subordination. Where traditionalists see ignorance and self-indulgence, a critical food analysis sees violations of civil and human rights.

Under this alternative view, unhealthy eating is primarily a product of inadequate income, not ignorance. And consumption can best be improved not (only) by increasing food quantity and consumer information, but equally (and perhaps more) importantly, by addressing the effects of economic disparities on food consumption—in short, by increasing consumer access to healthy food. From this perspective, the introduction of cheap fast food into foreign markets ... as well as the proliferation of advertising and media programming targeted to children ... obscures power inequalities, casting economic subordination as uninformed, self-destructive behavior.

Law is complicit in the social inequalities that characterize the consumption domain today. In the United States, an inadequate regulatory system has created a two-tiered food regime in which the affluent can buy organic products but the rest are left with inferior foodstuffs. The Food and Drug Administration has inadequately regulated food quality for decades. Not only have contamination scandals become routine (with lettuce, tomatoes, spinach, eggs, and peanuts all having been recalled as dangerous to consumers just within the past nine years), but also food quality itself has been allowed to seriously deteriorate.... [D]angerous growth hormones and antibiotics are routinely delivered in our poultry and meat products; irradiation that risks a wide variety of health effects is used to preserve food shipped long distances; harmful chemicals are routinely applied to foods to increase shelf-life and alter taste and appearance; and these dangers are often found in products marketed specifically to children or supplied by the government to children in school lunches.

Of course, healthier and cleaner products are available in upscale supermarkets around the globe, but at prices out of reach of even the average consumer, much less those on low incomes.... [I]n the United States, governmental subsidy programs make the most harmful foods more accessible (e.g., corn syrup, a harmful sweetener that is omnipresent in the U.S. diet), but do not cover the healthiest foods (such as vegetables, whole grains, and fruits). And underfunding of U.S. schools has forced many of them to allow processed- and fast-food producers to flood school cafeterias with harmful, cheap products....

... Food is not only transforming into a homogeneous, mass-produced commodity, but also threatens to become ... yet another mechanism for racialized and ethnicized control and exploitation of the poor.

Conclusion

... Broad dissemination of alternative, critical perspectives is sorely needed to counteract mainstream discourses ... of free market[s], trickledown economics and choice-based, individual rights....

> [T]o effect change, it is crucial that [we] collaborate and exchange ideas with each other, both about the on-the-ground issues in individual countries and about the ways that critical theory can highlight the power dimensions of current practices and discourses concerning food. . . . Cross-hemispheric food-related systems and practices can best be addressed by cross-hemispheric communication, understanding, and activism. . . .

Ehrenreich and Lyon provide a critical overview of the "global politics of food" as shaped by top-down neoliberal globalization. They show how Global North elites turned Mexico into an "enormous laboratory of neoliberal experimentation." Like Mexico, other vulnerable "markets" show the same ideas, politics, practices, and patterns at work.

Consider another example, also from this hemisphere. Below, sociologist José Atiles Osoria describes how Puerto Rico's elected officials used crises—states of "exception" from supposed normal times—as reasons to impose policies of increasing economic austerity and undemocratic concentration of executive power. These measures do not run contrary to the legacy of undemocratic government and economic inequality laid down by elites in colonial times but are a continuation and intensification of colonial patterns. Puerto Rico is an example of "colonial-neoliberalism," a set of "political, socio-legal, and economic transformations" that have "played a central role in guaranteeing colonial and class interests" continue to be served—and justified by law—to this day. This Orwellian legal framework deprives Puerto Ricans of the self-governance tools needed to solve systemic problems while blaming them politically for not solving those problems due to an alleged collective incapacity for self-governance. In the meantime, facts speak for themselves. Have elites made another neoliberal lab for their collective exploitation, profit, and enjoyment?

> On October 17, 2017, twelve years after the economic and financial crisis began, and less than a month after hurricanes Irma and María struck Puerto Rico (P.R.), Puerto Rican governor Ricardo Rosselló-Nevares sent a bill to the Legislative Assembly entitled "Bill to Create the New Government of Puerto Rico." This bill aimed to allow the governor to restructure the executive branch without consulting the legislative branch. . . . [T]his delegation of power would last ten-years, and it would be implemented . . . [also] to further externalize and privatize services traditionally provided by the local government. On December 2017, . . . the bill became Law 122 of 2017. . . .
>
> . . . [Puerto Rico today represents] colonial-neoliberalism . . . [with] the normalization of exceptional [crisis] measures *as* government policies. . . .

> ... [This] has played a central role in guaranteeing colonial and class interests, and therefore, it constitutes the legal framework for systemic corruption. ...
>
> ... The local government began ... not just to control and criminalize anticolonial, student, environmental, and other social movements, as it has since 1952, when the Commonwealth of P.R. was created, but also to ... defend the economic interests of the ruling class.
>
> ... [I]t is important to point out that Rosselló's administration (as all previous administrations) has been vigorously opposed and resisted, even in the midst of the most adverse, life-threatening circumstances for thousands of Puerto Ricans after the hurricane. ... To this day, grassroot community-based organizations (such as Casa Pueblo and Mutual Aid Project of Mariana) and the civil society at large have been organizing[:] ... where there is power, there is resistance.[41]

Osoria concludes that the current crises of debt, natural disaster, and economic failure are products of power, privilege, and subordination based on group identities, interests, and histories. Organized bottom-up actors can expose the deceptions and learn from the ongoing efforts by organized elites to protect their interests, as Ehrenreich, Lyon, and Osoria note. Such efforts are local, national, and transnational, often drawing on the experiences and collectivized power of communities in diaspora. Consider this perspective from Hedge Clippers, a national campaign to unmask "the dark money schemes and strategies the billionaire elite use to expand their wealth, consolidate power, and obscure accountability for their misdeeds:"

> The [current debt] crisis is driving more Puerto Ricans off the island and onto the mainland, fueling an ongoing "population swap" in which unemployed, young Puerto Ricans leave the island in search of work, while ... wealthy [U.S.] financiers are flocking to the island to take advantage of tax exemptions and cuts on corporate taxes, personal income, and capital gains. ...
>
> ... [I]n order to pay back its creditors, the Puerto Rican government has implemented a severe austerity budget that is creating a humanitarian crisis on the island and threatening Puerto Ricans' access to basic services including healthcare, education, and even electricity. ...

---

[41] José Atiles Osoria, The State of Exception and the Puerto Rican Financial Crisis, 25 Tex. Hisp. J. L. & Pol'y 91 (2019).

> ... [But] there is opposition, including ... a Puerto Rican mother of four who ... liv[ed] in Chicago for 33 years[:] ... "I learned more about Wall Street banks' predatory swaps with the Chicago school district and saw how the banks see our schools and communities as just another way to make a profit.... [T]he exact same thing is happening in Puerto Rico. They want public money going to hedge funds before schools, healthcare, and infrastructure.... When will my children's lives matter? ... 'Don't you have enough?' ... It's one thing to be a businessman. It's another to be a monster. In Chicago and Puerto Rico, people are getting educated and rising up. If we don't fight today, we won't see a tomorrow. We have no choice but to fight."[42]

NOTES AND QUESTIONS

1. *Elite Sandboxes.* These excerpts show only the tip of a historical and systemic iceberg, illustrating how U.S. elites use Puerto Ricans as a neoliberal laboratory for personal or corporate profits, and to local public detriment. Can you think of other former colonies that, like Mexico and Puerto Rico, serve as elite profit-seeking laboratories? If so, do they similarly reflect the long-term work of elites to build corporate and other forms of power designed to protect their interests? Can you identify activists and advocates who are engaged similarly in long-term advocacy campaigns and projects, informed by critical histories and incorporating attention to identities, groups, interests, and power?

6.5 ELITES (STILL) SUPPRESS VOTING TO MANIPULATE DEMOCRACY AND CONTROL OUTCOMES

In the United States and elsewhere, democracy often is depicted as a dynamic and vibrant contestation of ideas pressed by different factions based on beliefs, interests, and other personal and collective goals. In this idealized version, these factions and ideas compete on a "level playing field" to ensure that those who triumph do so legitimately—"on the merits." Elections thus must be deemed "free and fair" before their results can be accepted (under the system's own rules) as legitimate and binding. This reality is why control of voting (and hence lawmaking) is an elite obsession.

Originally, as we saw above in the Franks and Steinfeld excerpts, most of the population was formally excluded from the franchise, with rulemaking on voting rights and laws largely left to the states. In addition, the creation of a new peculiar institution—the Electoral College—made direct election of presidents by popular vote impossible, and was

---

[42] Hedgepapers No. 26, Puerto Rico: Pain and Profit (Mar. 21, 2017), www.hedgeclippers.org/wp-content/uploads/2016/03/HP26.pdf.

intentionally skewed to enable minorities in the South to overcome national majorities. For this alchemical reason, losers of the popular national vote—like George W. Bush and Donald Trump, as recent examples—can be transformed into seemingly "democratic" winners of presidential elections. By design, local and national elites—mostly propertied white men—created a system of minority rule that could claim to make and enforce laws in the name, and with the consent, of "the people." Today, as we saw from the empirical results of Gilens and Page in Part I, U.S. democracy is (still) run year-round by organized elites.

As noted in Chapter 3, law, like other systems, is judged on actual results. In the United States and other former European colonies, as we saw also above, these results repeatedly reenact colonial identity castes, in part by creating rules about property, identity, and the right to vote that tilt the democratic playing field in elites' favor. Organized bottom-up collectives organized and organizing groups—are the only (sometimes) effective counterforce, as explained by Guinier and Torres in their Part I excerpt discussing demosprudence, and as Gilens and Page confirmed empirically only recently. Therefore, the existence, resources, and capacities of organized bottom-up collectives are among elites' biggest fears—what they most seek to preclude and destroy—because of their potential to contest ground rules and foundational concepts. For this same reason, organized bottom-up collectives are foundational to systemic advocacy and equal justice.

Given the system's original design, holding free and fair U.S. elections has been an unrelenting struggle ever since 1787. As we saw above in Franks and Steinfeld, the rules and practices restricting access to democracy and law are among the most important ground rules and foundational concepts, and essential for perpetuation of the Critical Challenge. Given the power and interests behind the sweeping original exclusions based on property and identity, gaining recognition of this formal right as equal, and protecting the ability to exercise it freely, is a fierce, unending struggle. The right to vote has been the subject of more constitutional amendments than any other—four in total—even though the right itself is not mentioned in the original text:

1. In 1870, the fifteenth amendment provided that the right to vote "shall not be denied or abridged" on the basis of "race, color, or previous condition of servitude."

2. In 1920, the nineteenth amendment provided that the right to vote "shall not be denied or abridged" on account of "sex."

3. In 1964, the twenty-fourth amendment provided that the right to vote "shall not be denied or abridged" for "failure to pay any poll tax or other tax."

4. In 1971, the twenty-sixth amendment provided that the right to vote of persons over the age of eighteen "shall not be denied or abridged" due to "age."

Each amendment was the result of struggles against exclusion and aimed to shift the ground rules in potentially transformative terms—to make the playing field more level, little by little and group by group. But successive generations of judges have curtailed their potential, and legislators and other government officials have sought to circumvent them, with support from business elites and the use of state violence, as necessary. Original elites put the system in place, and their successors in interest pursue that same goal, or trick, of minority rule today.

Historically and currently, voter suppression is accomplished by misinformation, intimidation, gerrymandering, and restricted access, put in place by legislators, implemented largely by appointed officials, and defended when necessary by judicial actors. This reality came into full view during the 2000 Presidential election between candidates George Bush and Al Gore, when five Supreme Court judges overruled the Florida Supreme Court. By a single vote, they halted vote counting in Florida over the vocal dissents of their four colleagues. The voting difference in Florida stood at 500-and some votes. It could have gone either way, and with it, the Presidency. Instead, the U.S. Supreme Court decided the election in favor of Republican candidate George Bush. Gore, however, won the popular vote nationwide. The struggle to vote, and to suppress it selectively, has only intensified in the decades since *Bush v. Gore*.[43]

Modern voting rights struggles do not just involve the imposition of tangible obstacles to voting by members of marginalized groups. Voting power is concentrated among elites and their "base" or allies, while simultaneously being diluted among the rest, in several ways that bestow affirmative advantages as well as impose targeted restrictions: for instance, like providing an abundance of voting stations in some areas while depriving other areas of sufficient stations—and then, in addition, installing ample voting booths within the abundant friendly stations while limiting booths within the few stations allowed in suppressed areas. This compounding of official obstruction ensures that more votes are cast more quickly by elite bases and allies than by anyone else, thus converting a minority into a seeming majority. Related reinforcing techniques include other purposeful pragmatic obstacles to further reduce access, such as closing or understaffing polling sites and limiting voting hours or access to vote-by-mail or early voting. After skewing access to in-person and other kinds of voting, longstanding critiques of the U.S. Postal Service most recently have been converted into calls for its defunding to impede the mailing and counting of votes not cast in person. This multifaceted array

---

[43] *Bush v. Gore*, 531 U.S. 98 (2000).

of techniques is facially neutral but surgically designed to target identity groups for voting advantages or impediments. This array combines legal and practical proxies for social identities to create an artificial abundance and scarcity in voting access that, along with similar manipulations of the system, suggests a continuing top-down program to hijack democracy no matter what.

As headlines (still) attest, these attempts include official acts that wrongfully divest individuals of the right to vote, such as voter purges, restrictive voter ID laws, and felony disenfranchisement. Anti-democratic exercises of power are evident here. For example, Florida's constitutional Amendment 4 was adopted in 2018 by an overwhelming voter majority in a popular referendum against the state's felony disenfranchisement laws, mandating automatic restoration of felon voting rights upon completion of sentences, including parole and probation. Immediately after Amendment 4's adoption, the state legislature enacted new restrictions "specifically designed to confuse, complicate, and reduce the number of people eligible to vote under Amendment 4." These restrictions made payment of court fees, penalties, and the like a precondition to voting "in direct contravention of the clear and unambiguous language in Amendment 4 which mandates the automatic restoration of voting rights to those who have completed the terms of their sentence."[44] This example puts on display a "smoking gun" of selective voter suppression here and now.

As we see below, elites and their allies work hard to mobilize public support, mostly among white and middle class voters, for these anti-democratic schemes based on myths of electoral fraud—and facilitated by the racial coding and inflections of the facially neutral proxies they use to help steal elections. More broadly and deeply, these myths aim to distract attention from top-down abuses (like those sketched above and elaborated below), and to propagate unfounded, irrational fears of individual fraudsters trying single-handedly to rig electoral results around the country. Using the codes and proxies of "dog whistle" politics, this propagation converges with top-down creation and manipulation of "fake news" to mislead and inflame the public with ever-bigger untruths. This combination of assaults on popular understanding of and participation in formal democracy has worked, as evidenced by U.S. localities reporting anemic voting rates. Over time, and using time, the normalization of low participation rates contributes further to the rule of a minority dominated by elites seeming to be a "free and fair" democracy.

These contemporary, ongoing attempts reflect the same dynamics of preservation through transformation we examined previously in Chapter

---

[44] Catherine Powell and Camille Gear Rich, The "Welfare Queen" Goes to the Polls: Race-Based Fractures in Gender Politics and Opportunities for Intersectional Coalitions, Geo. L.J. 19th Amend. Special Ed. 105 (2020) (quoting from Southern Poverty Law Center lawsuit against the new restrictions).

4. These attempts adapt outlawed or repudiated techniques to redeploy them in combination with new inventions (both conceptual and logistical) to help preserve the status quo. As we have seen before, and now see also here, voter suppression campaigns use change strategically and time proactively to prevent popular, participatory democracy. This is the complex world that systemic advocates step into and work in.

Below, legal scholar Catherine Powell and sociologist Camille Gear Rich lay out some voter suppression methods and the justifications elites offer for effective disenfranchisement. As with the "welfare queen" stereotype of the 1980s and 90s, this top-down framing manufactures a mythical menace—"the voter-trickster." Both the stereotype of welfare queen and voter-trickster, the authors argue, suggest that Black and brown women use fraud to gain a public benefit or right to which they are not entitled, thereby "stealing" from the mostly white "honest" citizens. Attention is focused on deciding who should or should not get to vote: A former felon? Someone on parole? An immigrant in one visa category or another? A U.S.-born person whose mother was undocumented? But Powell and Rich suggest this line-drawing distracts from a bigger point. As before the franchise was extended to Blacks and women, the U.S. population now includes ever-greater numbers of formally "voiceless" residents. And they ask: Can a robust democracy exist where a significant proportion of the population is excluded from the most basic democratic rights?

THE "WELFARE QUEEN" GOES TO THE POLLS: RACE-BASED FRACTURES IN GENDER POLITICS AND OPPORTUNITIES FOR INTERSECTIONAL COALITIONS

Catherine Powell and Camille Gear Rich
Geo. L.J. 19th Amend. Special Ed. 105 (2020)

... Since 2016, Trump has ... explored the power of the welfare queen construct in electoral politics—specifically, raising public anxiety about voter-tricksters at the polls ... [comprised of] a horde of Black and Brown bodies—most vividly represented as Black and Brown women—deceiving officials at polling sites and stealing various elections. According to this view, these women were not legally entitled to vote, but they attempted to trick voting officials into accepting their ballots and in this way diluted the voting power of "real" Americans....

... [The voter-trickster myth] encouraged Americans to believe that voting rights are a scarce resource that must be rationed; that individual malfeasance is a greater threat to government than institutional fraud efforts; and that America naturally has a large class of nonvoting near citizens that must remain voiceless but effectively managed....

The growth of a class of voiceless governed should disturb us in the extreme. As we celebrate the Fifteenth and Nineteenth Amendments' extension of the franchise to the previously voiceless—women and Blacks—we are watching the emergence of the new voiceless governed.... Our history with slavery and making women second-class citizens provides guidance about the exploitation risks and unfairness these arrangements cause. Debates about managing the voter-trickster distract us from the larger questions about the growth of the nonvoting population: those under criminal justice supervision and those persons trapped in the immigration-review process with increasingly small chances of achieving citizenship. The focus on the trickster account encourages attention to the individual fairness of the rules *used to shut people out of the polity*, rather than the overall effect of creating classes of voiceless people in a so-called democracy....

... Although differently situated, the abolition and suffrage movements embraced a shared conception of rights—which Black women were central in articulating and embodying.... [an intersolidarity human rights vision with three primary elements]: (1) that rights and identities are intersectional, (2) that fundamental rights (such as the right to vote) are inalienable, regardless of the state's formal recognition of such rights, and (3) that certain rights (again, such as the right to vote) are exercised and made particularly meaningful in a social and collective context (as opposed to solely viewed from an individualistic rights perspective)....

[Applying this "intersolidarity" vision in modern times] ... would mean ... challenging voting restrictions that disproportionately fall on minorities ... [to secure] broader, more meaningful enfranchisement of Black and Brown persons and women....

... [F]eminists can lead the charge in building the necessary coalitions....

... The path to coalition politics is brighter than ever. With the right coalitions we can build a world in which women currently demonized as welfare queens find it safe to go to the polls. Equally importantly, these women will see their interests more fairly represented on the ballots they cast in service of democracy.

As Powell and Rich document, voter suppression buttresses the Critical Challenge of using law for equal justice. U.S. democracy has been geared for minority elite control and top-down "management" of other groups since this country's inception. This undemocratic grip on democracy uses public power to hide powerful interests and skew outcomes to favor elites.

NOTES AND QUESTIONS

1. *Dog Whistle Politics.* Put yourself in the role of a politician who supports restrictive immigration policies. What are some of the code words or phrases

you might use with voters to stir up enmity toward a particular immigrant group or groups through your symbolism, without explicitly identifying that targeted identity group(s) along race, ethnicity, or religious lines, among others? What are the advantages to politicians and other officials in using proxies and dog whistles?[45] How might advocates and activists effectively "decode" such dog-whistling to expose and combat its supremacist uses?

6.6 ADVOCATES SUPPORT ORGANIZED GROUPS AS "REPEAT PLAYERS" TO CONTEST BACKGROUND PREMISES, GROUND RULES, AND FOUNDATIONAL CONCEPTS

Countless advocates around the globe carry out the day-to-day work of aiding individuals with family, housing, employment, immigration, government benefits, education, healthcare, and other concerns. This day-to-day lawyering by individuals takes place in a variety of practice sites: in small private law firms, legal services offices, pro bono programs, legal clinics, and community group legal departments. Their insights can become "fuel for political action or reform," according to legal scholar and longtime legal services leader Gary Bellow.[46] Advocates who face daily problems together with clients—even in an individuated way within the limits of traditional advocacy—often recognize that the legal system is not dispensing justice. Advocates on the frontlines see patterns of outcomes that privilege other favored groups and that disfavor clients from communities of color or other subordinated groups. This steady work is essential for short-term amelioration of social misery and as scaffolding for systemic transformation efforts.

Systemic advocates, as a result, must become conscious—critically and self-critically—of their client bases and communities. To do so, as the next excerpt emphasizes, trainees and practitioners must evaluate career options based on "the overall moral tenor of their chosen paths in the law." Legal ethics scholar Susan Carle reflects below on the reward system in law that privileges those who serve elites. The existing professional status and pay hierarchy benefits those who serve corporations; conversely, the system disfavors those who serve "ordinary" individuals and families. She argues that legal ethicists, educators, students, and practitioners should set aside supposedly neutral justifications for traditional status hierarchies within law. Instead, they should aim to work helping "average" people and marginalized groups.

---

[45] See Ian F. Haney López, Dog Whistle Politics: How Coded Racial Appeals Have Reinvented Racism and Wrecked the Middle Class (2015).

[46] Gary Bellow, Steady Work: A Practitioner's Reflections on Political Lawyering, 31 Harv. C.R.-C.L. L. Rev. 297, 300 (1996).

Moreover, as a matter of ethics, this practice recognizes the great honor in representing "less powerful clients' interests against the interests of the more powerful." By flipping the status hierarchy, the small-firm divorce lawyer or housing advocate at a legal services organization would merit equal or greater regard and recognition than the big-firm mergers and acquisitions lawyer, law school professor, or powerful politician. Alumni, faculty, and administrators at law schools would fight for the courtyards and buildings to be named, not for wealthy donors, but for unsung advocates who work year-in, year-out for middle-income and working-class clients. Even though practice and client choices may be constrained for most advocates, consider how careful attention to client bases can change a law practice or a specific systemic advocacy project. The conscious self-awareness of client bases—and of their influence on projects and careers—allows an advocate to critically assess options. Could critical awareness of this kind, if widespread, transform the legal profession over time? How? Or why not?

RE-VALUING LAWYERING FOR MIDDLE-INCOME CLIENTS
Susan D. Carle
70 Fordham L. Rev. 719 (2001)

The classic study of the legal profession's dominant status hierarchy . . . emphasized the division of the bar into two distinct "hemispheres." One of those spheres consisted of lawyers who represented corporations and other large organizations and their top representatives. Lawyers who worked in this sphere had high social prestige. The other sphere consisted of lawyers whose practices primarily involved representing individuals. This sphere had lower prestige. . . . [L]awyers working for higher prestige firms representing large organizations tended to have been recruited from more elite schools, made more money, and generally came from different socioeconomic and ethno-religious backgrounds. They maintained professional and social contacts predominantly within their own professional status group and had greater access to powerful figures in the community.

The dominant status hierarchy in the profession, in other words, privileges work for corporations and de-privileges work for individual clients. This status hierarchy is perpetuated in many ways. One is the frequently invoked claim that "the best" lawyers prefer corporate law work because individual client representation is not as "interesting" as the "sophisticated" work corporate lawyers do. This idea is a classic illustration of how prestige hierarchies are socially constructed through the transmission of subtle but powerful messages across professional generations. No neutral standard of judgment compels the conclusion that corporate law is intrinsically more "interesting" than other fields. To a lawyer who has been trained to appreciate the complexity of her role, there are a host of fascinating, complex issues involved in most client representations. Nor is it necessarily true that work for individual clients is by definition not sophisticated or complex from the perspective of procedural or substantive law. Plaintiffs' lawyers are, after all, on the opposite side of the same complex litigation that corporate defense lawyers are handling, in a host of areas including products liability, labor, pension, and employment law. Moreover, plaintiffs' law firms typically staff cases far more thinly than large corporate law firms do, so that plaintiffs' lawyers typically bear greater responsibility, much earlier in their careers, than do their large firm counterparts.

. . . [I]n my view, [educators and advocates should] . . . place more emphasis on the choice of practice setting as an important point [to] promote a vision of ethical law practice that encourages students to make career decisions based on an evaluation of the overall moral tenor of their chosen paths in the law.

. . . [W]e as legal ethics teachers and theorists should urge our students to conceive of their career options as falling on a spectrum, along which the moral honor in representing a particular client base will tend to be inversely related to the social, political, and economic power of those clients. This proposal explains why "the best"—or most ethical and admirable—lawyers would work with unmitigated zealousness for less powerful clients against more powerful ones. There is, according to this model, generally more honor in representing less powerful clients than in representing more powerful ones, especially when representing less powerful clients' interests against the interests of the more powerful. . . .

. . . While it is unrealistic to think that the dominant mentality in the legal profession will change to one in which representing individuals is more prestigious than representing corporations, it seems far more feasible to imagine intervening in the creation of alternative hierarchies that assign prestige to helping real people with real problems and making a real difference in their lives. That hierarchy, I am arguing, should assign value—and hence prestige—to lawyering for middle-income clients.

. . . This approach would help students avoid feeling trapped in an all or nothing world, by illuminating the wide array of possible choices and balances to be struck in finding morally sustainable practice settings. It might also, coincidentally, help to mitigate the apparently growing problems in the provision of high quality legal services to middle-income persons.

Carle posits a provocative reversal of traditional hierarchies within law itself. This reversal, she argues, would promote the formal and repeated verbal commitments of law and lawyers to justice. It would expand access to justice. As Carle indicates, prioritizing advocacy that serves "average" individuals and advances their interest is a key part of piercing the blindfolds and resisting the handcuffs of the legal profession that we will explore more deeply in Part IV. These blindfolds and handcuffs convert the practice of law from a distinct profession designed to safeguard equal justice into an industry serving elite interests much like any other. Prioritizing work on behalf of "average" people represents a significant stepping away from the constraints the legal industry imposes.

But yet another, and equally important step, would be situating advocacy in support of *organized* "average" people. In fact, supporting organized groups with the capacity to contest ground rules and foundational concepts may be the systemically most effective work. This work amounts to helping design and build self-sustaining "repeat players," who can match well enough elite advantages in knowledge, experience, and capacity.

New advocates may have little experience, or a great deal of experience, as members of organized groups of clients drawn from subordinated communities or with other forms of organized group activism. Some students may have been involved in student-led struggles and groups: opposing gun violence after shootings at schools, clubs, concerts, churches, and elsewhere; engaging as Dreamer activists in immigrant rights groups, or as labor rights activists from the United States Students Association or Worker Rights Consortium, sons and daughters of farmworkers active with Student Action with Farmworkers or the Student/Farmworker Alliance; challenging police violence in the wake of the Trayvon Martin shooting or other incidents sparking #BlackLivesMatter and allied groups; working as LGBTQ youth organizers, marijuana reform activists, defenders of ethnic studies, environmental activists concerned about climate change, being active in combatting anti-Islamophobia or anti-Semitism; defending abortion clinics; or resisting the disaster capitalism that has threatened Puerto Rico, New Orleans, and other areas. For others, membership in an activist group is unfamiliar, even alien.

Working with groups is one of the key ways in which systemic advocacy differs from traditional advocacy. As noted earlier, the notion of "group" includes the anti-essentialist, intersectional notion of social identity groups—"Black," "white," "female," "cisgender," "gay," "working class," or other people. For our purposes here, we focus more on intentional collectivities. Intentional groups, in day-to-day life, are the collectivities with which advocates might work or might oppose. These groups can be formally organized or relatively informal and unstructured. They can define themselves in terms of particular social identities—or not.

The most important groups for systemic advocacy are membership or "base" groups. Membership groups may be organized into a formally recognized entity or may be part of an inchoate collective; may operate with a centralized governance structure, decentralized decision making, or some mix; may employ paid staff or may lack professional organizers; may be a single entity or may be structured as a complex, interrelated set of entities; may be self-funded through dues or fees or may rely on governmental or philanthropic sources or entrepreneurial activity; and may operate on a neighborhood, local, regional, national, or transnational scale. Across this broad range, organized action and collective power building remain constants.

"Organizing" is the process for building a group by developing a shared vision, mutual commitments, collective action strategies and resources, and sustainable voice and influence.[47] Community and labor groups, for example, engage individuals in "grassroots organizing: gathering together for collective action, social engagement, and political expression."[48] Grassroots organizing is a mechanism for building group power that is deployed to realign interests in short- and long-term struggles to use law for justice. By definition, organizing is a collective and collectivizing practice that takes place in particular places and times based on the participants and the circumstances. Organizing groups and efforts are rooted in particular contexts and often-deep histories. Ideally, organizing in one generation builds on, departs from, and adds to the organizing efforts of prior generations.

Organizing as a principled and accountable practice builds group power by bringing together individuals based on something shared—whether values, a strategically essential notion of identity, experiences of oppression or exploitation, or friendship and love. Organizing efforts always face opposition, if taking on systemic injustice, and thus entail risks

---

[47] For a range of ideas and practices in support of community and labor organizing, see Myles Horton and Paulo Freire, We Make the Road by Walking (1990); Charles Payne, I've Got the Light of Freedom: The Organizing Tradition and the Mississippi Freedom Struggle (1995); Kim Bobo, Jackie Kendall & Steve Max, Organizing for Social Change, Midwest Academy Manual for Activists 11–13 (2001); Saul Alinsky, Rules for Radicals: A Practical Primer for Realistic Radicals (1971); Edward T. Chambers, Roots for Radicals (2004); Frank Adams and Myles Horton, Unearthing Seeds of Fire: The Idea of Highlander (1975); Marshall Ganz, Why David Sometimes Wins: Leadership, Organization and Strategy in the California Farm Worker Movement (2009); Paulo Freire, Pedagogy of the Oppressed (1970); Daniel Hunter, Building a Movement to End the New Jim Crow: An Organizing Guide (2015); Lee Staples, Roots to Power: A Manual for Grassroots Organizers (2d ed. 2004); Rinku Sen and Kim Klein, Stir It Up: Lessons in Community Organizing and Advocacy (2003); Janice Fine, Worker Centers: Organizing Communities at the Edge of the Dream, 50 N.Y. L. Sch. L. Rev. 417 (2005–2006); Ross Dolloff and Luke Hill, Collaboration with Broad-Based Organizing Projects—The Legal Services Staffer and Organizer Perspectives, Mgmt. Info. Exchange J. 3 (Fall 2000); Julissa Reynoso, The Impact of Identity Politics and Public Sector Reform on Organizing and the Practice of Democracy, 37 Colum. Hum. Rts. L. Rev. 149 (2005).

[48] Barbara L. Bezdek, Alinsky's Prescription: Democracy Alongside Law, 42 John Marshall L. Rev. 723, 728 (2009) (describing and citing the work of Saul Alinsky, a leading organizer in mid-20th century community organizing). See Saul D. Alinsky, Reveille for Radicals 12–14 (1945).

to the activists involved. Motivating individuals to participate in an organizing effort can be difficult because of that risk and because of the time and energy required. Organizing also requires overcoming many divisions based on things not shared—histories, relationships, identities, or relative risks and benefits. But groups that engage in organizing are indispensable for enduring progress.

Organizers are those individuals who help bring groups together and develop strategies and action plans. Organizers may be paid or unpaid, formally trained or acting on instinct, in leadership or staff roles. Organizers are key players in advocacy teams, working closely with advocates but often inculcated in professional norms, skills, incentives, and approaches that are quite distinct—that, in fact, present a cross-"professional culture" challenge. Advocates often work with grassroots organizers in the process of organizing groups and recognize that "organizers are professionals whose very self-definition is grounded in strengthening the collective goals of groups of poor people"[49] or other subordinated groups.

However, "groups or coalitions are the protagonists" in most systemic advocacy.[50] This bottom line is important because it contrasts with traditional notions of advocacy that identify a lawyer as the protagonist, pulling "legal levers" in an effort to make social change, while clients play a limited role in action. Organizers and advocates work to support, not dominate, groups.

All systemic advocates grapple—directly or indirectly—with the challenge of law in relation to organizing. "Unless the lawyer recognizes that advocacy with groups cannot proceed without community organizing, there can be no effective empowering advocacy."[51] The craft of organizing the structures and activities of organizing groups is varied and complex. Marshall Ganz, a former United Farm Workers organizer and now scholar in leadership, organizing, and civil society at Harvard University, lays out some basic principles of organizing:

> Organizers identify, recruit and develop leadership; build community around leadership; and build power out of community. Organizers bring people together, challenging them to act on

---

[49] Sameer M. Ashar, Law Clinics and Collective Mobilization, 14 Clinical L. Rev. 355, 402 (2008).

[50] See Jennifer Gordon, The Lawyer is not the Protagonist, 95 Cal. L. Rev. 2133, 2135 (2007).

[51] William P. Quigley, Reflections of Community Organizers: Lawyering for Empowerment of Community Organizations, 21 Ohio N.U. L. Rev. 455, 456 (1994). See also Charles Elsesser, Community Lawyering—the Role of Lawyers in the Social Justice Movement, 14 Loy. J. Pub. Int. L. 375 (2013) (describing the relationship of community lawyering practitioners to organizers and organizing, as well as new skills, attitudes, and knowledge that may be required); Jim Freeman, Supporting Social Movements: A Brief Guide for Lawyers and Law Students, 12 Hastings Race & Poverty L.J. 191, 198–99 (2015) (noting that "most lawyers simply do not understand organizing" and thus may be "functionally useless within grassroots-led advocacy campaigns").

behalf of their shared values and interests. They develop the relationships, motivate the participation, strategize the pathways, and take the action that enable people to gain new appreciation of their values, the resources to which they have access, their interests, and a new capacity to use their resources on behalf of their interests. Organizers work through "dialogues" in relationships, motivation, strategy and action carried out as campaigns.

... Organizers engage people in deliberating about [how] they can turn what they have (resources), into what they need (power) to get what they want (their interests): strategy. Power is the influence our resources can have on the interests of others who hold resources that can influence our interests. Organizing often requires using our resources to mobilize power interdependently *with* others whose interests we share to challenge the power exercised *over us by* others whose interest[s] conflict with our own.

... Organizers ... build strong communities through which people gain new understanding of their interests as well as the power to act on them—communities which are bounded yet inclusive, communal yet diverse, solidaristic yet tolerant. They develop a relationship between a constituency and its leaders based on mutual responsibility and accountability.[52]

Organizers, then, facilitate the structuring of groups and their efforts. But to achieve steady increments of progress toward Critical Justice, organized groups struggle to change the foundational concepts and "rules of the game." As demonstrated earlier by Levinson and Andrias, advocates and activists must contest not only particular outcomes under existing rules, but they also must understand how underlying concepts and rules already are skewed to create advantages and disadvantages that make those particular outcomes likely.

As we will see more fully in Part IV, elites built and keep the legal industry as a system of rules designed to provide them every advantage possible in every conceivable contestation. They become the original repeat players. In response, organized group struggle similarly engages in particular issue contestations while also contesting—to change—the foundational concepts and ground rules themselves. Only by developing themselves as repeat players can advocates and groups alter the odds of every contestation and build power from below to engineer intentional social transformation, bit by bit, over time. As critical legal scholar Marc Galanter explains below, only in this way can the "have nots" challenge the

---

[52] Marshall Ganz, Organizing: People, Power, Change, Week 1: What is Organizing? (Sept. 2006), www.tryingtothrivenotjustsurvive.files.wordpress.com/2014/07/x-organizing-people-power-change-2006.pdf.

systemic upper hand of the "haves" across contemporary contexts. Galanter begins by sketching some key elements of the rule of law as a system.

WHY THE "HAVES" COME OUT AHEAD: SPECULATIONS ON THE LIMITS OF LEGAL CHANGE

Marc Galanter
9 Law & Soc'y Rev. 95 (1974)

... [T]he basic architecture of the legal system creates and limits the possibilities of using the system as a means of redistributive (that is, systemically equalizing) change. Our question, specifically, is, under what conditions can litigation be redistributive[?] ...

For purposes of this analysis, let us think of the legal system as comprised of these elements:

A body of authoritative normative learning—for short, RULES [and]

A set of institutional facilities within which the normative learning is applied to specific cases—for short, COURTS [as well as lawyers and parties to disputes]

... [T]he architecture of the legal system tends to confer interlocking advantages on overlapping groups whom we have called the "haves." To what extent might reforms of the legal system dispel these advantages? Reforms will always be less total than the utopian ones envisioned.... Reformers will have limited resources to deploy and they will always be faced with the necessity of choosing which uses of those resources are most productive of equalizing change. What ... [a]bout strategies and priorities?

Our analysis suggests that change at the level of substantive rules is not likely in itself to be determinative of redistributive outcomes. Rule change is in itself likely to have little effect because the system is so constructed that changes in the rules can be filtered out unless accompanied by changes at other levels. ... Programs of equalizing reform which focus on rule-change can be readily absorbed without any change in power relations. The system has the capacity to change a great deal at the level of rules without corresponding changes in everyday patterns of practice or distribution of tangible advantages. Indeed rule-change may becom[e] a symbolic substitute for redistribution of [base-line or material] advantages.

The low potency of substantive rule-change is especially the case with rule-changes procured from courts. That courts can sometimes be induced to propound rule-changes that legislatures would not make points to the limitations as well as the possibilities of court-produced change. With their relative insulation from retaliation by antagonistic interests, courts may more easily propound new rules which depart from prevailing power relations. But such rules require even greater inputs of other resources to secure effective implementation. And courts have less capacity than other rule-makers to create institutional facilities and re-allocate resources to secure implementation of new rules. Litigation then is unlikely to shape decisively the distribution of power in society. It may serve to secure or solidify symbolic commitments. It is vital tactically in securing temporary advantage or protection, providing leverage for organization and articulation of interests and conferring (or withholding) the mantle of legitimacy. The more divided the other holders of power, the greater the redistributive potential of this symbolic/tactical role.

Our analysis suggests that breaking the interlocked advantages of the "haves" requires attention not only to the level of rules, but also to institutional facilities, legal services and organization of parties. It suggests that litigating and lobbying have to be complemented by interest organizing, provisions of services and invention of new forms of institutional facilities.

The thrust of our analysis is that changes at the level of parties are most likely to generate changes at other levels. If rules are the most abundant resource for reformers, parties capable of pursuing long-range strategies are the rarest. The presence of such parties can generate effective . . . pressure for institutional reforms and favorable rules. This suggests that . . . [r]ule changes which relate directly to the strategic position of the parties by facilitating organization, increasing the supply of legal services . . . and increasing the costs of opponents—for instance . . . class action suits, award of attorneys fees and costs, award of provisional remedies—. . . are the most powerful fulcrum for change. . . .

The contribution of the lawyer to redistributive social change, then, depends upon the organization and culture of the legal profession. . . . [C]ourt-produced substantive rule-change is unlikely in itself to be a determinative element in producing tangible redistribution of benefits. The leverage provided by litigation depends on its strategic combination with inputs at other levels. The question then is whether the organization of the profession permits lawyers to develop and employ skills at these other levels. The more that lawyers view themselves exclusively as courtroom advocates, the less their willingness to undertake new tasks and form enduring alliances with clients and operate in forums other than courts, the less likely they are to serve as agents of redistributive change. . . .

As Galanter points out, the system might change a great deal without changes in everyday distribution of material benefits. Changes on paper may become "a symbolic substitute" for changes on the ground—perhaps another way of framing Siegel's "preservation through transformation." To counter this systemic setup, systemic advocates work to create and support "parties capable of pursuing long-term strategies" that include resetting background premises, foundational concepts, and ground rules to level playing fields. This capacity to reset systemic baselines through the organized actions of repeat players, Galanter concludes, is "the most powerful fulcrum for change" in systemic outcomes.

In the United States and elsewhere, labor unions provide a quintessential example of organized repeat players supported by their advocates that illustrate Galanter's bottom line. During their long history, unions have rewritten ground rules and foundational concepts through both adjudication and legislation. Over this time, as we see more fully in later chapters, organized workers have had to adapt and innovate—sometimes rewriting rules of the game, and other times reframing their own roles within existing frameworks. In an era of top-down attacks that have eroded their memberships and power, unions demonstrate the ongoing need for critical innovation to create and sustain repeat players.

Consider union advocacy, this time involving bankruptcy and corporate reorganizations. As bankruptcy law scholar Andrew Dawson observed:

> Labor unions have shaped corporate reorganization plans by playing the role of activist stakeholder in addition to, or instead of, their traditional role of concession bargaining agent. For example, the . . . pilots' union pushed American Airlines . . . towards a merger with US Airways.
>
> . . . Labor union activism in bankruptcy is not a new phenomenon, but current corporate reorganization practice potentially makes labor participation increasingly an important factor in bankruptcy decision making. . . .
>
> . . . This labor union activism may provide a partial solution to the problems in bankruptcy governance, specifically, the problem of creditor-driven asset fire sales. Labor union activism in bankruptcy is not likely the best solution to bankruptcy's governance problems; however, it has two main virtues. First, because labor unions are generally long-term investors in the corporate employer, labor union activism might provide a counterweight to the powerful creditors that push for quick asset sales in bankruptcy. Second, labor union activism operates within the current market for corporate control in Chapter 11 without the need for legislative changes to the Bankruptcy Code.[53]

Notice in Dawson's passage the innovative reframing of existing rights and rules to promote bottom-up interests and systemic justice. Take in the need for both constancy and flexibility. Take note of the role(s) that time plays

---

[53] Andrew B. Dawson, Labor Activism in Bankruptcy, 89 Am. Bankr. L.J. 97 (2015).

in social struggles. To deepen these key points, consider another example involving other contexts, issues, and actors.

6.7 SEEDING, SPARKING, AND SUPPORTING LONG-TERM COALITIONS: A TENNESSEE CASE STUDY

One of the difficult realities of systemic advocacy is that strong groups—repeat players—don't always exist in the exact place and time and form that they are needed. Sometimes, helping a group to coalesce is part of early work in three-layered problem solving. Within this framework, if no organized group already exists, help to start one. If an advocacy or organizing group exists but doesn't really take on persistent systemic problems affecting the community, then push. If a group does not think about the implications of intersectional identities or the legacies of history when planning to build coalitions, strengthen leadership, or communicate with the world, ask for more reflection on consciousness, power, and culture. Whatever the circumstance, help the group to improve materially the lives of individuals at the bottom by proposing concrete three-layered goals that synergize amelioration and transformation: winning technical solutions, building group power, and shifting consciousness and culture. Keep learning, listening, and building. All of this work is part of "seeding" collective resistance to systemic injustice, as the following "case study" demonstrates.

The excerpts below show how collectivized resistance to collectivized injustice is seeded over time. These excerpts show why it is important to work on aiming to win concrete and more immediate solutions to social problems while also building group power and shifting individual and collective consciousness for longer-term gains—the three layers of systemic advocacy. As you read, note how both legal advocacy and grassroots organizing have been part of this history of seeding resistance. Track how identities, groups, interests, and power are constructed and played out. Think about how knowledge—and leadership—from the bottom is fostered. Notice the element of time.

We start with a brief example from the New York Times, in which that history of seeding resistance is ignored. In April 2018, federal Immigration and Customs Enforcement agents raided a meatpacking plant in Morristown, Tennessee, the boyhood home of Davy Crockett. Many of the mostly-white, native-born town residents stood with the mostly-Latinx, immigrant workers to help them resist deportation—as those immigrants and their families had become good and valued neighbors. The Times article seems shocked by this "coming out of nowhere" response of solidarity. But the community response did not come out of nowhere. Rather, it resulted from decades of work by many different groups to raise consciousness and fight back against the effects of racism, deindustrialization, anti-unionism, neoliberal globalization, and other ills. As the Times reported in the aftermath of the raid that detained roughly 100 Latinx workers, the town's reaction was immediate and anguished:

> Donations of food, clothing and toys for families of the workers streamed in at such volume there was a traffic jam to get into the parking lot of a church. . . . Schoolteachers cried as they tried to comfort students whose parents were suddenly gone. There was standing room only at a prayer vigil that drew about 1,000 people to a school gym. . . .
>
> [M]uch of the town is reeling.[54]

The news story records the consequences of many decades of hard work—years in which dedicated activists and advocates fought to raise awareness about racial, gender, and economic justice issues, to change patterns of thinking steeped in white supremacy and heteropatriarchy, and to challenge the poverty and precarity created as the economy moved into the age of corporate globalization. To illustrate this historical work, historian Laura Westhoff outlines how the Highlander Center, in New Market, Tennessee, roughly thirty miles from Morristown, seeded resistance through anti-racist education and coalitional advocacy:

> The remarkable story of the Citizenship Schools, the founders Esau Jenkins, Septima Clark, and Berniece Robinson, and the Highlander Folk School staff that worked with them dramatically illustrates [grassroots organizing efforts].
>
> In 1954 Jenkins and Clark attended an interracial workshop at Highlander Folk School in the Cumberland Mountains of Tennessee. Myles Horton had opened the adult education center twenty years earlier to support mountain communities and expand interracial labor organizing into the South.
>
> . . . Jenkins became especially motivated to help his black neighbors register to vote. . . . [On] long bus trips, he had begun teaching riders to read.
>
> Jenkins arrived at Highlander with a vision to expand his ad hoc literacy efforts. . . . Horton then expanded upon Jenkins' vision of the Citizenship Schools, emphasizing an opportunity for Highlander staff to train leaders of communities to run their own schools. . . . "Myles wanted to teach others how to change themselves." Developing community leaders, rather than relying

---

[54] Miriam Jordan, ICE Came for a Tennessee Town's Immigrants. The Town Fought Back, N.Y. Times (June 8, 2018).

on a single leader or someone from outside the community, was Horton's vision of democratic change.

... [I]n 1961, the Southern Christian Leadership Conference took over administration of the program, renaming it the Citizenship Education Program and employing Clark and Robinson to offer workshops across the South; at least 50,000 new voters were registered by 1964 as a direct result of their CEP classes.... Such programs helped African Americans win local elections... throughout the South.

The Citizenship Schools are a powerful illustration of the long Civil Rights Movement that help us rethink the ways we teach this history and Black History more generally. Jenkins and Clark's activist careers show the deep roots of the movement, correcting popular ideas that it began with *Brown* or the Montgomery Bus Boycott.... The focus on grassroots leadership development and local organizing efforts of ordinary citizens challenges the narrative of great leaders and reminds students of the intense effort that transformed thousands of lives in ways not always visible in textbooks or histories focused on a national narrative or conventional political change. And Highlander's long history of interracial education and organizing illustrates too, that white allies in the South had a vital role to play.[55]

This work created skilled activists who spread throughout the U.S. South from Highlander's East Tennessee base. Later, new bases of advocacy and activism emerged in large part to address the devastation wrought by economic change as local industries were moved overseas to cheaper sites of labor and resources as part of globalization and, subsequently, as immigrant workers (sometimes from those same countries) began to arrive and faced both exploitation and anti-immigrant nativism. Delving deeper, legal scholar Fran Ansley next writes about this history, together with social justice educator and filmmaker Anne Lewis. The full multimedia presentation is available online, but the excerpt provided here describes elements of the advocacy that helped to seed solidarity and resistance in unlikely spots.

---

[55] Laura Westhoff, Citizenship Schools and the Civil Rights Movement, National Council for History Education, 26 History Matters Archive (Feb. 2014).

Going South, Coming North: Migrant and Union Organizing in Morristown, Tennessee

Fran Ansley and Anne Lewis
Southern Spaces (May 19, 2011)[56]

Introduction

This multimedia essay complements the 2007 Appalshop film *Morristown: in the air and sun*. Written by independent filmmaker Anne Lewis, the director of *Morristown*, and Fran Ansley, a Tennessee law professor who served as principal humanities adviser on the project, this essay presents aspects of the *Morristown* story that we were unable to include in the one-hour documentary: additional context and perspectives for considering factory flight, international labor migration, and the organized demand for economic justice.

Filmed between 1991 and 2006 and based primarily in the mountains of east Tennessee, *Morristown* explores the lived experiences of workers from Tennessee and Mexico who speak about their lives, work, disappointments, and hopes. . . . *Morristown* concludes with a stunning union victory in 2005–2006 among immigrant workers at a large poultry processing plant.

. . . Making *Morristown* took years and involved a long-term process of building trust with workers and worker organizations on both sides of the US-Mexico border. . . .

Going South: A Trip to the *Maquiladoras*

The movement of industrial capital in search of cheaper labor is nothing new for Tennessee or for the US South. East Tennessee has experienced life at both poles of this dynamic. In the 1960s and earlier, labor-intensive industries such as clothing, textiles, auto parts, and consumer electronics moved their plants from northern cities such as Detroit and Chicago to Morristown, Knoxville, and other cities and small towns along the Interstate 40/81 corridors. They moved to escape union contracts, to minimize their duties under state regulation, and to profit from the incentive programs that have always accompanied industrial recruitment in various versions of the "New South."

Beginning in the 1980s, many of those same industries moved further still, across the national boundary line and into the global South. . . .

It was no accident that multinational corporations looking for favorable terms and cheap labor identified Mexico as a favored destination. Launched by the Mexican government in 1964, the Border Industrialization Program (BIP) created the legal infrastructure for a

---

[56] www.southernspaces.org/2011/going-south-coming-north-migration-and-union-organizing-morristown-tennessee.

bilateral state-promoted export-processing zone of factories known as *maquiladoras* (*maquilas* for short). US-based companies were allowed to produce goods or portions of goods in Mexico that were admitted back into the United States without tariffs as long as production took place within one hundred kilometers of the border. . . .

As Tennessee felt the impact, groups scrambled to understand what was happening and searched for ways that workers in the increasingly insecure, globalized economy might best respond. In 1989, a coalition of labor unions, religious groups, and community organizations came together to create the Tennessee Industrial Renewal Network (TIRN). . . .

Particularly disturbed by how easy it was for many Tennessee workers to blame the closings on Mexican workers who were "stealing" their jobs, TIRN leaders began looking for ways to promote a more accurate economic understanding in local communities. Drawing on lessons learned by the Highlander Center about the importance of peer education, TIRN sought direct contact between workers in east Tennessee and workers in Mexico.

TIRN reached out to several border groups that were working to expose and address *maquila* realities: the Border Committee of Women Workers (in Spanish, the Comité Fronterizo de Obreras, or CFO—a grassroots group of women employed in *maquiladoras*); the Border Project of the American Friends Service Committee, a group that partnered with the CFO; and the Coalition for Justice in the Maquiladoras, a network that brought together labor and community activists from the United States and Mexico. TIRN proposed a two-way worker-to-worker exchange between Tennessee and Mexico, and the CFO and its supporting groups agreed to collaborate.

. . . Women from Tennessee saw first-hand the transformed operations of companies well known to them, but now in the *maquiladora* context unfettered by the rules of home. They witnessed the living conditions of people employed in the *maquilas* and living in makeshift shacks without electricity or running water. Workers shed tears, revealed anxieties, and expressed shock and disorientation. . . .

Coming North: The Long Hard Crossing

. . . In 1991, when the earliest footage was shot, most east Tennessee residents were not aware of the growing numbers of Latino immigrants. But some of the women on the trip—the ones from Morristown—did point out that there were "new people" from Mexico showing up back home. Demographic change in Tennessee was soon evident even to casual observers.

The movement of industrial capital from the United States to the *maquilas* and the movement of low-wage workers from Mexico to the United States were intimately related. The impacts of NAFTA and related neo-liberal policies were felt throughout Mexico. Resulting pressures fed northward streams of migration. An estimated two million Mexican farmers and farm workers lost their livelihoods as cheap US agricultural products, especially corn, flooded Mexican markets. . . .

. . . Meanwhile, the wages companies offered were worth even less. It became impossible for many working class Mexican communities to survive. The forces that took jobs away from factory workers in east Tennessee forced Mexican workers across the international border. For several Mexican states, human beings became the major export.

Although these changes increased local opportunities for cross-national coalition building, they also triggered resistance. If feelings had been intense about distant Mexicans taking far away factory jobs, local responses were volatile when new people, marked by differences of race, ethnicity and language, began moving next door in a region which had not experienced significant immigration for generations. Workers returning from later TIRN exchange trips found themselves in arguments with friends and neighbors—not only about corporate responsibility and factory flight, but also about the rights and wrongs of immigration. . . .

Since labor migration was the flip side of plant closings and another aspect of the neo-liberal development model that NAFTA represented, seeking justice for immigrant workers seemed a natural extension of TIRN's work. . . .

Arriving in Morristown: New Kinds of Borders

The US-Mexico *maquiladora* zone that TIRN delegations had once traveled for days to reach now appeared in Tennessee. Native Tennesseans could meet their Mexican counterparts by visiting any local restaurant kitchen or construction site. And yet differences of race, language, and nationality often separated people as profoundly as physical distance or a geo-political boundary.

Immigrants arriving in Tennessee were entering locales where racial history was at work and racial hierarchies were in place. During slavery and Jim Crow, race was a structural feature of labor markets backed by the full force of law. Although the civil rights movement succeeded in discrediting old racist ideologies and breaking down some barriers to equal opportunity, gross disparities between whites and blacks in the labor force persisted and black unemployment remained at levels far beyond that of whites. These patterns worked to naturalize racial subordination.

Undocumented Latinos disrupted and complicated the existing black-white framework. New political and social alignments seemed likely, though exactly who would align with or against whom was hard to say. . . .

Organizing in a Southern Industry: Immigrants Step Up

The Morristown Chamber of Commerce, long proud of its highly successful industrial recruitment program, constructed Morristown's third industrial park with federal and state grants. Soon they began to fill it with companies like Koch Foods, one of the nation's largest poultry producers and processors. Koch had acquired Morristown's older, family-owned poultry business and was now looking to expand.

Koch's facility was sparkling and bright on the outside, but there were major problems inside. According to reports of workers at the plant, the speed of the line was brutal, wages were minimal, worker health and safety were regularly put at risk, and the relationship between workers and their supervisors was disrespectful and degrading. In the face of these conditions, the work force had become predominantly Latino, many of them undocumented. Workers made several attempts to change their conditions, including a targeted strike where all the workers walked off the line and proceeded to the bathroom as a group in protest over the chronic refusal of line supervisors to allow reasonable bathroom breaks. They won verbal concessions whose results were short-lived.

Eventually, a Koch Foods worker contacted a lawyer from Southern Migrant Legal Services in Nashville about the problem of access to bathroom breaks. Other workers stepped forward to point out problems with health and safety practices. They held meetings, documented grievances, and took their concerns to management. When several leaders were fired in retaliation in front of an assembled group, workers reacted with indignation and reached out for support.

In early 2005, after being contacted by workers at the poultry plant, doing preliminary research, and observing workers' energy and resolve, the United Food and Commercial Workers Union (UFCW) launched an organizing drive. The UFCW local that the workers would join was based primarily in grocery stores, a labor force whose work environment and demographics were dramatically different from those of the poultry workers. At a national level the UFCW had substantial membership in meatpacking and poultry plants, and the organization was aware that inclusion of immigrants was crucial to its survival and strength. . . .

Jobs with Justice of East Tennessee (JwJET), an all-volunteer group headquartered in Knoxville, generated civic, church, and labor union support. They convened a Worker's Rights Board that heard testimony about the right to organize and about the failure of US labor law to adequately protect that right. Jim Sessions, co-chair of the chapter, introduced the panel of witnesses:

> The right to organize is a human right and it's a democratic right and it's the law. But the law's not obeyed very much on this matter in this country. That's what we want to talk about tonight. And

we'll hear how difficult, also the aspirations of people who aspire to that democracy in the work place in our area.

... The union campaign at Koch Foods was well organized and highlighted the rights of workers while building understanding among coalition members about immigration, racism, and xenophobia. JwJET involved churches, other unions, and activists throughout east Tennessee including nearby native-born, factory workers who had been part of TIRN.

These support efforts were important, but the workers made the biggest difference in the success of the election drive. Despite threats of firing and deportation, leaders from the factory floor made house calls to recruit fellow workers and gather signed cards. Organizers anticipated employer behavior and explained the election process and US labor law. Morristown workers showed how effectively immigrants could mobilize when their basic trust was earned.

When the NLRB election day finally arrived, organizers were cautiously optimistic, but no one was sure what was going to happen. Fran remembers standing outside the plant with other supporters, waiting for the vote count:

> Standing along the highway that morning, together with our JwJET delegation from Knoxville, there were black, white, and Latino organizers and union members from the UFCW, and a couple of guys from the Nashville local union to which the Morristown chicken plant workers would be attached if the election went for the union. There was a faithful young intern from the Highlander Research and Education Center whose highly skilled interpreting and translating services had been integral to the organizers' efforts and workers' comprehension, involvement, and morale....
>
> The wait seemed interminable, but at last we made out the sound of cheering. Spilling down the hill toward our waiting group came an elated crew of union-designated election watchers. "Ganamos! We won! Ganamos!"
>
> The workers had scored not a mere victory, but a landslide. The margin was 465 to 18.

Looking Back and Ahead

The moment of victory was sweet.... Winning a union election, however, is no guarantee that workers will build a functioning union with workplace strength. A crucial "first contract" must be achieved. US companies, advised by batteries of management-side lawyers, have refined their ability to stall, delay, and undermine the negotiating process to such a degree that winning a first union contract after a successful organizing campaign has often proven an insurmountable hurdle.

> In Morristown, after the pro-union vote, the UFCW and Koch Foods talked for months without reaching agreement. Finally the company declared there was nothing left to discuss and submitted its "last best offer," a poor set of proposals testing union resolve. Unanimously the workers turned down the company's offer. A month later, after further bargaining, they approved a union contract that included eye protection, bathroom breaks, health insurance, and higher wages.
>
> Meanwhile, in the spring of 2006, immigrants all over the country poured into the streets by the hundreds of thousands to protest a virulent [anti-immigrant] bill that had passed the US House of Representatives. . . .
>
> The Tennessee Immigrant and Refugee Rights Coalition, founded in Nashville in 2001, hired its first organizer for east Tennessee in November, 2005. In April 2006, the Coalition organized rallies all over the state for immigration reform. . . .
>
> . . . [W]e remain convinced that labor rights and immigrants' rights are mutually dependent and inextricably intertwined. Campaigns and organizations that integrate both kinds of claims create spaces where workers can learn from each other and identify shared interests. However, serious obstacles to building class solidarity across divides of race and nation remain. Exclusionary whiteness runs deep, as does an exclusionary kind of Americanism. Anti-immigrant backlash is alive and well around the United States, and that backlash can be found among working class people and union members as among other segments of the population. But as *Morristown* documents, there are also working class southerners, both black and white, who can and do respond differently to immigration and to the question of immigrants' rights, workers who express solidarity and see a basis for common ground. Shirley Reinhardt suggested something like this when she spoke with us before the Koch Foods election about what a victory would mean:
>
>> You're saying to all the others from Mexico, they don't have to treat you worse than anybody else. You can organize. . . . Not only are you saying that to the people from Mexico but you're saying that to the people of Hamblen County, too. . . .

As Ansley and Lewis recount, many organizers invested time and energy to build solidarity and group capacity in East Tennessee civil, labor, and immigrant rights battles. The Tennessee Industrial Renewal Network led efforts to educate the public about plant closings and globalization, Southern Migrant Legal Services led legal advocacy against working conditions in the Koch Foods plant, the United Food and Commercial Workers and sister unions in Morristown supported labor organizing, the Jobs with Justice Knoxville chapter led Worker Rights Board and community direct actions, and the Highlander Center remained active in leadership development and education. Similarly, organizers Mónica Hernández and Francisco Argüelles built a new program rooted in the experience of citizenship schools that Highlander Center created to help jump start immigrant rights coalitions in the South:

> Highlander created the Pueblos de Latinoamérica program in the late 1990s to support grassroots Latino immigrant organizations in the South by providing an opportunity to gather and network with each other and break their geographical and psychological isolation....
>
> ... In 2002, Highlander shifted the program's focus to helping build grassroots immigrant organizations locally, while still providing a space to network with other immigrants from the region.... We developed a three tiered plan. First, we organized Know Your Rights workshops as a way to introduce ourselves to communities that knew little or nothing about Highlander. This allowed us to offer something much needed and concrete, and provided us with an opportunity to recruit. As a second tier, we then planned on doing Justice Schools, local political education and "organizing 101" workshops in part modeled after the Citizenship Schools of the 1960s. The third tier was a regional leadership institute that would bring together Justice School participants for a more advanced training process....
>
> At the same time, Highlander was instrumental in establishing the Tennessee Immigrant and Refugee Rights Coalition. As one of the founding organizations, Highlander played a critical role in helping TIRRC to establish its mission, founding values and principles, including prioritizing community organizing and making a commitment to build grassroots immigrant leadership....
>
> ... Democratic leadership works to create *poder popular*: collective or "people's power" based on local, grassroots organizing capable of mobilizing to win concrete victories and to resist and/or transform specific policies, institutions and structures. *Poder popular* is in stark opposition to the power of elites. It means popular organizations with a clear political agenda and the capacity to move through existing structures while having the ultimate goal to change those structures.... Today, given the level of decomposition of democracy in the United States, *poder popular* means restoring democracy at the local, state and federal levels.
>
> ... Shifting the focus from winning specific campaigns, legislation, etc. to obtaining structural, systemic change requires

an intentional political education process that helps us see beyond the immediate or even medium term win and connects our struggle to the struggles of others.[57]

The investment by organizations like Highlander sparked and strengthened the development of a statewide immigrant rights network, including the Tennessee Immigrant and Refugee Rights Coalition (TIRRC). TIRRC subsequently became the center of action after the Morristown raid, building a coalition of organizations to provide legal defense attorneys for individuals and continuing to advocate for local and state policies that better protect immigrants. Below, a TIRRC update from 2018 describes the legal defense work, followed by another 2018 update from the National Immigration Law Center describing Occupational Safety and Health complaints made by workers affected by the raid.

The legal team coordinated by TIRRC went on the offensive, filing claims about workplace health and safety problems at the plant where the raid occurred. These claims echo earlier complaints that sparked the Koch Foods organizing campaign. These complaints allowed workers to argue that ICE should have focused on employer violations and carried out an audit, instead of focusing on sanctioning undocumented employees through a raid. They brought public attention to the willingness of employers and the state to accept the benefits of low-wage labor performed by immigrant workers in unsafe conditions—even as they denounce such workers. In all of this work, a host of organizations collaborated: Catholic Charities of East Tennessee, the National Employment Law Project, Southern Poverty Law Center, Vanderbilt University's Immigrant Rights Clinic, the National Immigrant Rights Center, and others. This work of seeding and growing resistance is collective and continuous, as these excerpts underscore:

TWO MONTHS AFTER THE RAID: AN UPDATE FROM MORRISTOWN TENNESSEE IMMIGRANT AND REFUGEE RIGHTS COALITION[58]

... Already, 35 of the 54 people who were shipped out of state and held in an immigration detention facility have been released on bond and are back home with their families. This is incredible and is a testament to the power of legal services rooted in community organizing.

We've been organizing families and volunteers in Morristown, gathering critical documents and evidence to help attorneys with the

---

[57] Mónica Hernández with Francisco Argüelles, Building Immigrant Leaders in the South: INDELI 2004–06, www.intergroupresources.com/rc/RESOURCE%20CENTER/OWEN%27S%20CATEGORIZATION%20OF%20RC/Copies%20from%20Curricula%20folder/indeli-final-report%20(Highlander%20Center).pdf.

[58] www.tnimmigrant.org/news/2018/6/13/two-months-after-the-raid-an-update-from-morristown.

Southern Poverty Law Center (SPLC) build a robust legal defense for all workers arrested during this raid.

Since the bond hearings have been overwhelmingly successful, we need to raise more money to help families pay their bond. Many families must pay more than $5,000 to free their loved one, an often impossible amount for them to raise when an income-earner in their household has been detained for more than two months.

Whether from the detention center or at home with their families, all of the workers must prepare for the lengthy legal battle to fight their deportation. We're working with [numerous national and local organizations to create] a pro bono infrastructure to ensure all workers have access to high quality legal counsel to fight for their right to remain.

TENNESSEE OSHA SLAMS MEATPACKING PLANT WHERE MASSIVE ICE RAID TOOK PLACE WITH 27 VIOLATIONS AND $41,775 IN PENALTIES

National Immigration Law Center[59]

NASHVILLE—The Tennessee Occupational Safety and Health Administration (TOSHA) has slammed the Southeastern Provision meatpacking plant in [Morristown], Tennessee, with $41,775 in fines and cited the company for 27 violations, 23 of which were categorized as "serious" because of the risk of physical harm or death posed to workers. These violations and investigations came to light after a raid of the plant in April, during which U.S. Immigration and Customs Enforcement (ICE) agents used aggressive, militaristic force to arrest nearly a hundred workers, including at least one U.S. citizen and others with work authorization.

The fine is among the highest levied by TOSHA and indicates the seriousness of the violations found by the state agency and the dangers facing the workers in the plant. The TOSHA investigation found that the company failed to provide even the most basic safety equipment and sanitary facilities, creating an extremely hazardous work environment for plant employees. Employees faced a wide range of injuries due to dangerous levels of noise, exposure to chemicals, faulty equipment, and poor sanitation.

Southeastern Provision has flagrantly violated laws that are intended to protect all workers in this country.

As a group, the excerpts in this section demonstrate a key point in organizing collective actions: solidarity exists when individuals self-

---

[59] www.nilc.org/2018/08/24/tn-osha-penalizes-ice-raided-meatpacking-plant/.

consciously understand that they share interests, values, and humanity with others in different identity groups, even though histories and relative positions of privilege may differ. Solidarity is expressed and expanded through action in which each group is willing to share gains, make sacrifices, and take risks on behalf of the other. As critical race scholar Jerome McCristal Culp, Jr. famously observed: How do we as African-Americans, we as White-Americans, we as Asian-Americans, we as Latino/Latina Americans participate together in struggles that involve people who are not ourselves?[60]

Solidarity worked, for example, in Morristown when LGBTQ people of color activists from Southerners on New Ground (SONG) engaged in "participatory defense" in the wake of the ICE raid:

> For years now, trans activists have raised the alarm over how LGBTQ+ detainees are treated in ICE custody—an issue that persists today. For SONG, as for its sister organizations and other immigrant-rights groups, the recent death of transgender detainee Roxsana Hernández was a rallying cry. After years of broken promises of reform, LGBTQ+ detainees are still up to 97 times more likely than other detainees to be sexually assaulted in ICE custody. . . .
>
> . . . SONG aims to expand the idea of a sanctuary city to protect all residents from criminalization. . . . According to Alan Ramirez, one of SONG's regional organizers based in western North Carolina, this is called "participatory defense." . . . "[W]hen communities show up for each other, to provide transportation, childcare, interpretation, raising funds, and emotional support, it is all of us who share the burden." Beyond even institutional change, standing in solidarity with the most marginalized is SONG's central mission.[61]

These varied efforts can be seen as idiosyncratic, but they actually are part of methodical investments of time by advocates and activists. As we already have seen, preservation through transformation maintains caste over time; as we emphasize here, systemic advocacy similarly invests time to seed and cultivate resistance. Below, Tennessee-based legal scholar Fran Ansley reflects on both personal and professional experiences that build capacity for seeding solidarity and struggle as a part of long-term systemic advocacy.

Note how Ansley identifies work that includes but transcends familiar legal thinking, rules, methods, and practice. Among others, she includes

---

[60] See Jerome M. Culp, Jr., Latinos, Blacks, Others, and the New Legal Narrative, 2 Harv. Latino L. Rev. 479, 481 (1997).

[61] Robin Happel, The Next Generation of Southern Organization, The Nation (Aug. 17, 2018), www.thenation.com/article/the-next-generation-of-southern-organizing/.

working with organized groups as partners; using popular education tools to generate alternative explanatory frames to undermine anti-immigrant, racist, and classist perceptions; and engaging in advocacy with specific, ambitious, technical aims to change "rules of the game." Take note of the expanded skills and roles that Ansley posits as critical for advocates in the world of movement-building and systemic advocacy. As you read, focus on the idea of solidarity as practiced, not simply espoused, especially as a counter to the elite practice of "containment and repression" of social movements.

Doing Policy from Below: Worker Solidarity and the Prospects for Immigration Reform
Frances Ansley
41 Cornell Int'l L.J. 101 (2008)

... I became involved with immigration policy via twin roads that have criss-crossed throughout my life—the intersecting and co-constructing pathways of race and class. ...

Until I was sixteen, I lived in Atlanta and then Columbus, Georgia, during a time when Jim Crow de jure segregation was alive and ruled daily life. ...

Although inspired and emboldened by the [Civil Rights] movement, the difficulties that the movement encountered troubled me. The same social landscape that offered vistas of change likewise demonstrated the entrenched power of racial hierarchy. Witnessing the dynamics of that period, I could see that institutions and mores that the white South supposedly abandoned, often in fact survived, morphed, and reestablished their dominion in new and perverse forms.

In that situation, it seemed evident to me that racism and its power to divide disadvantaged people explained not only the extreme trials that many members of the black community faced but also much of the entrenched power of Southern elites, the retrograde character of state and local policy, the miserliness of the public sector, and the poverty among white people—all of which were obvious features of the region. ...

Therefore, I was ready and eager to respond to the vision of Martin Luther King Jr. when he announced a campaign to build an inter-racial movement of the poor. Further, it made sense to me when the Student Non-violent Coordinating Committee (SNCC), issued its controversial request that white students leave the organization. SNCC told white well-wishers like me that if we wanted to change a region scarred by racial disparity, we should first organize poor and working-class white people; we should go talk to white folks and bring them into alliance with the movement for racial justice. In other words, at least as I heard them, the key messages of the Poor Peoples' Campaign and the marching orders sent out by both Dr.

King and SNCC were that poor whites were the natural and needed allies in a movement for economic justice both in the South and across the nation.

After all, it seemed clear that poor whites had an obvious and demonstrable interest in joining with people of color.... Evidence all around us in the South demonstrated that time and again whenever poor Southerners moved to demand redistribution of the social surplus or a seat at the table of power, they were disarmed and derailed by the racial divide.

... I am convinced that progressive economic change requires building unity among economically disadvantaged people across lines of race....

At any rate, for the past thirty years, I have pursued and reinvented this work from a base in East Tennessee.... It is home to the long-lived Highlander Research and Education Center, a place where grassroots leaders from community organizations, labor unions, and local movements for change have been coming together across racial lines to participate in educational workshops and strategy sessions for over seventy years.... [My law] students and I have collaborated with both Highlander and a range of grassroots and community-based groups that work on issues of economic inequality and insecurity. These days ... it is clear that any hope for advancing cross-race understanding or mobilizing workers across racial lines requires a serious engagement with issues of immigration and the global economy.

I first started to understand the new international dimension of race in the South when I began working with a new labor-community coalition that had formed to combat plant closings and deindustrialization in our state....

... In the mid-1990s, many of the small towns hardest hit by plant closings began to experience an unprecedented wave of immigration from Mexico and Central America. With this trend continuing strongly into the twenty-first century, Tennessee found itself squarely among the group of "new destinations" in the Southeast and elsewhere that attracted new streams of Latina/Latino migrants.... A high proportion of these newcomers were undocumented. Local natives began to notice and react to this new Latino presence.

Their reactions were not then and are not now monolithic; variation exists across and within these communities. Nevertheless, over time, positions have hardened in some quarters, and the political temperature has risen considerably....

At times the atmosphere of crisis and controversy has felt eerily like being transported back to Georgia in the late 1950s and early 1960s, when at least in the white community, arguments about desegregation of the public schools seemed to rage hot and loud on every agitated hand. The similarities are hard to miss. The Klan is back on board, along with newer white supremacist organizations that have found the troubled waters of immigration debate to be good fishing. Many elements echo much of the talk and reproduce much of the climate that prevailed in that other era of massive racial upset and adjustment: the intense feelings of entitlement that many people voice when complaining about immigrants, the firm conviction that their privileges are well-deserved, and the evident sensation of invasion, displacement, and danger. There is another similarity to that earlier time In that a substantial number of those who respond most favorably to the restrictionist crusade and buy most eagerly into a nationalist or even xenophobic mind-set seem to be working class people, in this newer context, both black and white working class people—the very ones who I believe stand to gain the most if they could find ways of making common cause with low-wage immigrants here and with workers in other countries as well. Native-born workers clearly are hurt by a domestic regime that tolerates the creation of a race-marked and vulnerable underclass within our home labor market. They are also hurt by a global regime that guarantees the mobility of capital while restricting the mobility of people, and pits worker against worker and community against community around the world. Such a regime drains the institutions of electoral democracy of their capacity to set ground rules for the conduct of business and the protection of human and labor rights, yet many workers are apparently all too ready to blame "those Mexicans" in their various guises for the economic insecurity that dominates the current scene....

. . . Workers in this country are dangerously divided on questions of race, class, and nationality, and many anti-immigrant groups actively recruit workers into their organizations and campaigns.

. . . Everything I learned from that [the Civil Rights] saga tells me that today once more the need for cross-race—and now cross-nation—solidarity among working people will be acute and pivotal. In an era of globalization, the obstacles to achieving such internationalist and anti-racist solidarity will be enormous. At the same time, however, new global dynamics expose the moral and material logic of such solidarity and suggest its potential power....

This reflection concludes with a few ideas about concrete ways that lawyers, academics, and other professionals interested in immigration reform might contribute toward movement building. Of course, there is a huge need for lawyers who are ready and willing to work with all kinds of groups interested in building bottom-up power for immigrants and other workers.... [Advocates can contribute by] honing many of the traditional skills that any lawyer needs and must deploy: mastering the crazy intricacies of immigrant workers' rights-and-no-rights, strategizing about discovery in the shadow of unpredictable immigration enforcement, zealously defending their vulnerable clients, anticipating legal and other issues, developing creative arguments, and marshalling relevant facts.

... [L]awyers undertaking this work need other skills as well. In particular, they need to be sophisticated and well-informed about theories of social change, methods of organizing, and ways of analyzing power relations in a given community or worksite. They must be able to envision legal rules and claims that can serve a larger collective strategy, strengthen a given organization, or encourage democratic leadership. The literature on ways that law and lawyering can advance (or retard) the process of organizing and movement building reflects a growing body of experience developed and shared by change-minded practitioners.

Lawyers representing low-wage immigrant workers are well-represented among the people developing these experiences and sharing their lessons. They include attorneys who work with federally-funded legal services and independent non-profits, lawyers who work with workers' centers and labor unions, and clinical law teachers and their students involved in innovative projects that stress the importance of building organizations and supporting the development of grassroots movements.

Lawyering is hardly the only type of professional work that can be put in the service of movement building. Professionals, intellectuals, and artists of all kinds can find information and produce materials that help organizations and movements educate their own members about many things, including policy matters. They can also help organizations and movements develop materials that explain and defend their positions to the outside world. In all such activities, they will encounter important issues that they can help to resolve, such as which coalitions and bedfellows the group should pursue, what slogans and vocabularies it should adopt, and how it should frame and define its issues. A person working creatively with an immigrants' rights organization, for instance, would be in a position to support framing the organization's issues in a way that clarified the importance of class-linked demands and policy proposals. Likewise the person could encourage the organization to conduct its business in a way that builds cross-race alliances.

... This kind of work takes time. It is difficult to be patient when the issues seem so urgent and the stakes are so extreme for immigrant families and others.... Nevertheless, I believe that careful and long-term thought and outreach are still very much in order.

The forces at work in the global economy—forces that put hundreds of thousands of people on the road to migration—are far too strong to be controlled by immigration policy alone. Thus, no matter what happens with immigration reform, much will still be unresolved. In any case, complex issues and realities will remain, such as: mass migration and capital flight, stark disparities among differently situated groups of working class people within the global economy, environmental threats like global warming that form a constant backdrop to the rest of the drama about the future of world development, and the stubborn puzzle of how to align democratic political decision-making with the regulation of economic life when so much economic activity today has gone thoroughly global. Proposing viable solutions to these issues is difficult enough in the abstract, let alone doing so in concert with social movements and managing to reach and connect with a critical mass of working class people in the United States and elsewhere.

. . . In concluding this essay, it strikes me that I should concede that a reader might well ask whether my soupy call to movement building is nothing but an argument from desperation. When ejected from all formal channels of influence, where else does a person have to go? Looking to the federal judiciary for immigration reform, for instance, would appear to be delusional in light of the Supreme Court's ugly decision in *Hoffman Plastic Compounds v. NLRB* [denying damages to an undocumented worker illegally fired for his union organizing activities] as well as in other cases. In its turn, Congress has proven itself incapable of taking present action on the issue. . . .

. . . Perhaps the current bleak landscape makes it unusually clear that winning decent political change will require "looking to the bottom." . . .

Even if Congress were less paralyzed, immigration deliberations in that body would produce unacceptable results unless and until a stronger movement of low-wage immigrants and other working people can exert the political and ideological clout to change the terms of the debate. The movement that is needed—one that reaches beyond a class-purged civil rights frame to embrace a broad and combative vision of economic justice—is necessary both to achieve a decent version of immigration reform and to tackle the many other problems that flow from the development model currently dominating the world economy. We know from other popular movements, not least the African American freedom movement in our own country that touched and transformed so many lives, my own included, that seemingly invincible systems can indeed change, once people find each other and a way to stir.

The Morristown example shows how the investment of time can generate resistance and solidarity that seems spontaneous—but is not. Advocates made central contributions to the development of sustained struggle by and with workers and immigrants in East Tennessee. Advocates helped start key community organizations, led worker-to-worker delegations, brought health and safety claims on behalf of immigrants that then sparked a union organizing campaign, provided training, helped coordinate community-based hearings on worker rights violations, helped carry out interviews and develop a film, demonstrated and testified for and against policies, intervened in immigration raids, and represented individuals and groups in both immigration defense and impact litigation, among other things.

Moreover, advocates and activists engaged in bottom-up political education to help build cross-cultural and multigenerational relationships among individuals from varied identity groups—including native-born African American and white workers, undocumented and documented Latinx immigrants, first- or second-generation U.S. citizens, transgender individuals of many ethnicities and origins, and others. These actions not only served tactical purposes of the moment but also as vehicles to frame collective grievances and solutions and to coordinate and motivate collective action and organizing for the long term. This steady work helped "grow" resistance and solidarity even if the seeds were not necessarily planted with specific intent.

Advocates seed resistance and solidarity over time to support (or spark) movements, and law can be a useful tool. More particularly, as we saw above, advocates contribute to movement-building by strengthening the sorts of organized client-groups that can "collectivize" strategies and contest ground rules. As Gilens and Page noted in Part I in relation to democracy and Galanter demonstrated in this chapter in relation to adjudication, only organized groups can influence the rules of the legal decision-making game and adequately protect bottom-up collective action. Experience confirms that organized groups are stronger when they intentionally identify and use "collectivized" legal actions and promote collectivized legal solutions. As we explore more fully in Part IV, advocates must unlearn the legal individualism that permeates legal culture and relearn to think of legal actions and solutions as vehicles for building collective action through collectivities accountable to subordinated groups.

In shaping ground rules, as we noted earlier, advocates pay close attention to protecting spaces and rights of assembly and organizing, public information access, and rights and capacities to mount protests. Advocates focus on enactment and enforcement of rules that determine collective participation in decision making—like "organizing" rights in legal and extralegal actions—as well as on anti-retaliation protections.[62] This focus is particularly challenging because collective rights and remedies increasingly have been under attack in recent decades. Nonetheless, groups and advocates fight to protect *and* expand existing

---

[62] Such retaliation measures might target the individual or the organization. See, for example, Rebecca Smith, Engaging in Direct Action Campaigns Without Getting SLAPP'ed: Take Action Against Wage Theft!, National Employment Law Project (2007) (describing Strategic Lawsuits Against Public Participation—SLAPP—suits against worker centers and other groups as "lawsuits filed to retaliate against communications to government agencies or attempts to influence governmental action" typically involving "claims like defamation, malicious prosecution, interference with contract, business relationship or economic advantage or restraint of trade").

collective mechanisms that build power, organize groups, and fight to change unjust ground rules.

NOTES AND QUESTIONS

1. *Seeding a Movement.* Legal scholar Nina Kohn considers seeding a movement through legal action in an intentional way to foster an elder rights movement. In part, she proposes that lawyers might engage in "naming and framing" legal issues to create a collective identity and identify collective issues and claims:

> [D]espite the fact that ageism is pervasive and older adults suffer from significant discrimination, the United States has yet to experience the emergence of an elder rights movement.... [T]he term "elder rights movement" [refers] to a collective effort through which individuals (including older adults acting on their own behalf) and organizations join together around the common goal of transforming social, political, and legal structures to allow older adults to fully exercise their civil and human rights and liberties....
>
> Lawyers have played an important role in previous civil rights movements by helping raise awareness of rights violations and by instigating litigation aimed at inciting systemic reform.... [T]he legal community can and should play a similar role with regard to elder rights....
>
> The first step to legal mobilization for elder rights would therefore be for the bar, and, especially the elder law bar, to recognize and name the civil rights concerns affecting older adults. By doing so, they can increase the likelihood that they will address these concerns when working with older clients. They can also help legitimize older adults' rights-related grievances and potentially empower older clients to think more broadly and ambitiously about their rights and their role in society. For example, an elder law attorney advising clients regarding planning for long-term care should recognize that the choice of a long-term care provider is not merely a financial decision, but also a decision that can fundamentally alter an individual's life and liberty. Advising clients of such implications will allow clients to plan more appropriately for their own care. It will also help the clients recognize that they have rights, thereby empowering them to take a more active role in structuring their future living situations—potentially through collective action.
>
> This role of naming and framing, which has been critical in other civil rights movements, may be especially important for an elder rights movement.... By framing the issues older adults face in the powerful language of legal rights, the legal community could play a

much-needed role in creating a sense of shared interest and identity that could encourage older adults to mobilize on their own behalf.[63]

Kohn states that "naming and framing" is a threshold step in organizing collective action. Do you think the proposal Kohn articulates could be the basis for movement-building like that carried out over decades in East Tennessee? What additional work might advocates do, using the Morristown history as a model, to seed an elder rights movement? What about for other justice-seeking groups?

2. *Collectivizing Resistance to the Plea Bargain.* Michelle Alexander, author of The New Jim Crow: Mass Incarceration in the Age of Colorblindness (2010), relates the suggestion of an activist black mother whose drug addiction and experience with the criminal justice system followed the death of her young son run over by a police cruiser: "What would happen if we organized thousands, even hundreds of thousands, of people charged with crimes to refuse to play the game, to refuse to plea out? What if they all insisted on their Sixth Amendment right to trial? Couldn't we bring the whole system to a halt just like that?"[64] Is this suggestion for plea bargaining resistance realistic? Unless everyone acted in unison, how would you expect the state (through its prosecutors) to respond to an initial volley of defendants openly refusing to accept or even entertain a plea bargain? As the lawyer for a criminal defendant, how would you advise your client on whether or not to participate in such an organized resistance? How, then, could such a collectivized response occur? Mindful that, as Alexander points out, "nearly 95 percent of [state] cases are pled out of court, with some 96 percent of federal cases processed by plea bargain," how might a systemic advocate confront the criminal justice system through its lifeblood of the plea bargain?

3. *Redefining Collective Legal Action.* Some groups are organizing to challenge daily practices in criminal courtrooms. These actions might not "bring the whole system to a halt," but they certainly put business-as-usual under the microscope of community scrutiny and review. Criminal legal scholar Jocelyn Simonson describes two such activities—courtwatching and participatory defense—and their effects:

> State criminal courtrooms and courthouse hallways are often crowded with defendants, victims, and their families—the people most affected by local criminal justice. However, despite the presence of marginalized populations in the courthouse, these courthouse visitors are denied the ability to participate meaningfully in everyday justice. Judges conduct short, routine court appearances at inaudible volumes and in inscrutable language, masking the important decisions and policies that have led to a particular prosecution, plea, or sentence. The exclusionary dynamics of criminal courtrooms,

---

[63] Nina A. Kohn, The Lawyer's Role in Fostering an Elder Rights Movement, 37 Wm. Mitchell L. Rev. 49 (2010).

[64] Michelle Alexander, Go to Trial: Crash the Justice System, N.Y. Times (Mar. 10, 2012), www.nytimes.com/2012/03/11/opinion/sunday/go-to-trial-crash-the-justice-system.html.

however, shift and bend when organized groups come together to observe and intervene in courtroom proceedings. Courtwatching groups affiliated with larger social movements, for example, gather volunteers to document everyday proceedings in local courts—bond hearings, arraignments, plea bargains—and report to the public the results of their observations. These community groups become self-appointed watchdogs who can present the results of their observations in their own words, on their own terms, and independent of official accounts of policies and trends. Similarly, community groups involved in "participatory defense" join with families, friends, neighbors, and allies of defendants to learn about the facts and procedures of individual cases, perform investigations, and ultimately aim to "change the landscape of power . . . in the criminal justice system."

The tactics of courtwatching and participatory defense can have an effect on the adjudication of everyday, low-level cases. Courtwatching groups help define the proceedings through their presence, reminding courtroom players that each individual case is connected to larger aggregate harms to families and neighborhoods. And, by doing so, these tactics shift power and build agency among individuals previously delegated to subjects, not objects, of the state. This agency, in turn, can lead to robust engagement with legal and constitutional meanings—for example, when courtwatching organizations uncover the relationship between policing policies and misdemeanor adjudications or participatory defense groups push the boundaries of the right to counsel.[65]

How do these examples expand your understanding of collective legal action beyond traditional notions of civil class actions, for example? How might such activities be organized? What would be the role of a public defender, if any? What resources, staffing, capacities, political education, or other shifts in the organization of public defender offices might be required to effectively support or collaborate with community groups carrying out courtwatching or participatory defense? What might be some objections or hurdles? Are there possible advantages to defenders' offices? Can you imagine benefits to defendants beyond those that Simonson identifies?

CHAPTER RECAP

This chapter emphasized the centrality of collective, collaborative action in both top-down systemic injustice *and* for bottom-up systemic advocacy. We saw that elites organize continually to build and exercise collective power—and advocates must do the same to support group struggles for Critical Justice. Repeat players who can contest ground rules and foundational

---

[65] Jocelyn Simonson, Democratizing Criminal Justice Through Contestation and Resistance, 111 Nw. U.L. Rev. 1609, 1617–18 (2017).

concepts are central to this complex work. Among these ground rules and foundational concepts are the top-down fictions of law, contracts, and property that elites deploy to rule and exploit society. The following part emphasizes how advocates put collaborative work at the center of their advocacy through diverse teams and systemic advocacy projects. As we see in the next chapter, team-based work deepens the knowledge and leverages the capacity of every advocate.

Part III

Learning to Work with Diverse Teams on Systemic Projects

■ ■ ■

CHAPTER 7

ROAD TEST: COLLABORATING TO CONNECT EXPERIENCE AND KNOWLEDGE FOR TEAMWORK AND COALITIONS

■ ■ ■

Table of Sections

7.1   Recognizing Failure by Design to Overcome It
7.2   Crafting Analytical Narratives for Advocacy Projects
7.3   Teams and Teamwork Expand the Capacity of Systemic Advocates
7.4   Collaborative Professionalism and Critical Coalitions Empower Advocacy

OPENING THOUGHTS

Individually, we are one drop. Together, we are an ocean.

> —**Ryunosuke Satoro,** Japanese author

Collaboration is a process that involves shared decision making by fellow collaborators; shared decision making allows for the development of ideas that then leads to emergent knowledge rather than to a simple summation of ideas. Collaboration . . . makes maximum use of the experiences and knowledge that each collaborator brings to the joint work. It . . . cherishes differences and recognizes that conflict can be constructive and valuable.

> —**Susan Bryant,** Collaboration in Law Practice: A Satisfying and Productive Process for a Diverse Profession, 17 Vt. L. Rev. 459, 460 (1993)

Dr. King's "four steps of the non-violent campaign" . . . are: "1) collection of the facts to determine whether injustice exists; 2) negotiation; 3) self-purification; and 4) direct action." . . . When working with allies, one can utilize [this] framework to facilitate the identification of areas where reinforcement and collaboration with others will benefit the work of confronting power.

> —**Edwin Lindo, Brenda Williams, and Marc-Tizoc González,** Uncompromising Hunger for Justice: Resistance, Sacrifice, and LatCrit Theory, 16 Seattle J. Soc. Just. 727, 749 (2018)

INTRODUCTION

It has taken more than half a millennium to design, emplace, and normalize today's Critical Challenge of using law for equal justice. This systemic legacy of trickle-down justice and preservation through transformation is more complex and sprawling than any one advocate effectively can tackle alone. Acting on this bottom line, systemic advocacy is proactive and collaborative. Recognizing current needs for ameliorative relief, systemic advocates defend past gains *and* advance them to get ahead of the injustice curve. This forward-leaning transformative approach requires principled and collaborative professionalism from all participants, whether lawyers, organizers, activists, or others.

But to make lasting and meaningful bottom-up progress, advocates must find—or create—an opening, a starting point. Every journey, including your own career and every project you may undertake during it, begins from where you currently stand. Often, therefore, these openings begin with an advocate's own life experience and knowledge, both professional and personal.

Experience that is personal or proximate—affecting those immediately around you—allows advocates to anchor their knowledge of a systemic problem in concrete settings, events, and reflections. This anchoring, however, depends on the advocate's capacity to connect experience to knowledge and action through personal self-reflection. As a practical matter, advocates often may begin this process with analytical narrations. As we saw with Montoya and others in Part II, these justice-inflected narratives—a kind of legal storytelling—have in common their *analytical* purpose: to expose links that maintain systemic injustice based on identity castes and to help sustain organized group struggles for equal justice.

From this kind of starting point, advocates build advocacy projects that depend on collaborations. Remember Hing's account of Yen's work in Part II: start every project with what the people (and you) know, and build on what the people (and you) have—including your knowledge, skills, and integrity. Building bottom-up consciousness, advocates use Yen's twin starting points contextually to figure out and take "next steps" beyond analytical narratives, whether yours or others'.

One common kind of collaboration is teamwork, which frequently involves experts from various fields and different regions, groups, or backgrounds. In this sort of collaboration, legal experts, like all team members, must recognize that their expertise will not always be front and center; everyone must appreciate their part and their limits within the team. Another kind of collaboration is between team members and clients—a core kind of collaboration that becomes much more complex when the clients are themselves a collective—an organization, coalition, or other kind of group. In collaborating with groups, advocates must take extra care to add value to discussions while playing a principled role in the group's decision making.

Advocates also cultivate collaborations in the form of coalitions that bring together groups and individuals into common causes based on shared principles: critical coalitions. Cross-group coalitional collaborations require a high degree of coordination, perhaps being the messiest of all. But they also can be the most systemically effective, perhaps for that very reason. All three kinds of collaboration—intrateam, with client groups, and intergroup coalitions—are integral to systemic advocacy.[1]

In addition, advocates supplement personal or proximate experience (and analysis) with relevant critical knowledge drawn from other sources. Narrative can be a starting point, but even the most powerful narrative, standing alone, cannot disrupt entrenched patterns of systemic injustice. Thus, advocates combine personal or proximate experience with critical knowledge from the Schools and Approaches reviewed in Part I. These "wells" of cumulative critical knowledge are further supplemented with bottom-up research designed to allow advocates to unlearn and relearn problems and solutions, concretely, in a particular context. Bottom-up research, explored more fully in Part V, draws on methods and norms geared to excavating, documenting, and putting to strategic uses the knowledge from subordinated groups. This knowledge-building process for legal problem solving also is inevitably collaborative. Systemic advocates therefore learn to construct teams and coalitions—and ongoing projects that serve as sites of practice—through which critical bottom-up knowledge becomes actionable and accountable to that bottom.

Focusing on these connections and methods, this part presents two "road test" chapters to help you review, clarify, and use the knowledge already presented in the two previous parts. Parts I and II outlined some foundational concepts and tools of systemic advocacy that these back-to-back road tests should help you to grasp as one whole, and to use as practical, actionable knowledge going forward. Before we turn to the stages and mechanics of systemic advocacy in Part V, we road test these fundamentals here.

In this chapter, we continue unlearning top-down values and attitudes of professionalism that rest on individualism, hierarchy, and specialized expertise alone, while relearning problem solving as collaborative professionalism. Collaborative professionalism expands traditional notions of legal professionalism because it situates individual thoughts and actions in a cooperative group setting informed by critical history and attention to the elements of identities, groups, interests, and power. This critical

---

[1] See Ascanio Piomelli, The Democratic Roots of Collaborative Lawyering, 12 Clinical L. Rev. 541 (2006).

practice of bottom-up collaboration can increase communal knowledge, strength, and solidarity.

The most effective, and perhaps most difficult, collaborations entail working with various kinds of people and collectivities across multiple sources of difference to maximize social impact. As William Quigley notes in his Letter to a Law Student Interested in Social Justice, excerpted below in Part VII:

> Social justice advocacy is a team sport. No one does social justice alone. There is nothing more exciting than being a part of a group that is trying to make the world a better place. You realize that participating in the quest for justice and working to change the world is actually what the legal profession should be about. And you realize that in helping change the world, you change yourself.[2]

As Quigley (and many others) have emphasized, collaborative professionalism cultivates collective consciousness that helps avoid the deceptive "blame frames" that law creates and enforces.[3] As a result, advocates change the way they think about the work that will effectively address social problems and client needs. In particular, advocates respond to client "needs" not *solely* by providing a lawyer or legal service, but *also* by challenging systemic designs and patterns.

Elaborating, J.J. Rosenbaum, director of Global Labor Justice, explains that systemic advocates "bring challenges that will change the system, not just win cases or get people the rights they are due—but to get to the deeper issues of why those rights were not accessible"[4] through the normal operations of law. In effect, collaborative professionalism aims for transformation through critical, collectivized approaches to amelioration. To accomplish this aim, systemic advocates *must* work in multiple, dynamic, and overlapping kinds of collaborations:

> [L]awyering is no longer a unidirectional "professional service." Rather, it is a collaborative communicative practice. This practice demands strategic innovation and critical reflection about the forces that condition poor people's subordination, as well as the ways they might resist and even redirect those forces to achieve justice. Through such action and reflection, poor people and their

---

[2] William P. Quigley, Letter to a Law Student Interested in Social Justice, 1 DePaul J. for Soc. Just. 7, 21 (2007).

[3] See Jon D. Hanson and Kathleen Hanson, The Blame Frame: Justifying (Racial) Injustice in America, 41 Harv. C.R.-C.L. L. Rev. 413 (2006) (excerpted in Part IV infra).

[4] See Susan Butler Plum, Skadden Fellows Share the Impact of the Program After 30 Years, www.skaddenfellowships.org/#section-nav-anchor (audio file).

lawyer-allies voice aspirations, identify concrete action strategies, and discover grounds for political unity.[5]

Applying these points, this road test chapter traces how advocates use analytical narratives based on experience to develop projects that combine critical knowledge from the Schools and Approaches with contextual bottom-up knowledge uncovered through critical methods of research and analysis, as Part V further explains. In this chapter, we road test how advocates build collaborations—teams, projects, coalitions—even as they are building contextual, historical, and practical knowledge. This multifaceted work of unlearning and relearning, designed to guide action, necessarily relies on *deep* collaborations with those affected by systemic injustice and their expertise, as well as *broad* collaborations within multidisciplinary teams and diverse coalitions. These complex kinds of bottom-up collaboration allow advocates—and advocacy teams—not just to know more but to achieve more.

We begin with a key point of unlearning and relearning that compels a fundamental shift in thinking about systems and advocacy, and which underscores again the critical importance of dual consciousness in using law for justice. Law, as a system, is designed to fail equal justice, even as it solemnly promises it, and even as it vehemently denies or covers up its failures. But systemic outputs during the past several centuries are plain enough and show otherwise. Effective advocacy must take this deep, hidden, and normalized systemic contradiction—failure by design—into account when analyzing persistent social problems, and when crafting advocacy projects or actions to ameliorate and transform the status quo.

7.1 RECOGNIZING FAILURE BY DESIGN TO OVERCOME IT

Because law fails by design to achieve equal justice, advocates remain constantly aware that the legal system promises one thing while largely—though not completely—doing another. The legal system depends on this perpetual contradiction and constant tension. And advancing justice depends on advocates' capacity to pierce through and work around these systemic contradictions.

Below, environmental justice advocates Luke Cole and Caroline Farrell illustrate both failure by design and advocacy to confront it as they recount struggles against toxic intrusion in U.S. communities of color. As with the pollution in Flint, Michigan described in Part I, environmental hazards in Camden, New Jersey, are rooted in histories of identity-based injustice which surmount any existing legal mechanisms ostensibly protecting communities. The problem is structural, or systemic, injustice:

---

[5] Lucie White, Collaborative Lawyering in the Field? On Mapping Paths from Rhetoric to Practice, 1 Clinical L. Rev. 157, 158–59 (1994).

environmental benefits and material problems are distributed unevenly on the basis of social identities. Cole and Farrell frame this advocacy story as one of "environmental justice" rather than simply anti-pollution efforts. This framing is similar to the community-based definition of reproductive justice that we saw in Part II. Environmental justice must be experienced—understood and lived—by the members of the community, just as reproductive justice only exists when women have control of their own bodies, the ability to make choices regarding childbearing and childrearing, and decent living standards. As Cole and Farrell demonstrate, recognizing failure by design helps advocates sharpen the design and evaluation of their own work to advance environmental justice. In this example, how do advocates work with individuals and groups, how do they root their work in knowledge from the bottom, and how do they collaborate to shape advocacy plans?

STRUCTURAL RACISM, STRUCTURAL POLLUTION AND THE NEED FOR A NEW PARADIGM

Luke W. Cole and Caroline Farrell
20 Wash. U. J.L. & Pol'y 265 (2006)

Any serious attempt to address the issues of poverty, wealth and the working poor would do well to learn from the Environmental Justice movement, a broad-based national social movement that has emerged from the ground up over the past twenty years. The movement operates at the intersection of race, poverty and the environment, and offers hope in an otherwise bleak landscape of environmental and social justice advocacy. The movement offers a new paradigm for community leadership and control. . . .

Waterfront South and the Failure of Environmental Law

Camden, New Jersey, is an economically depressed community across the Delaware River from Philadelphia. Following the collapse of its industrial base, Camden became one of the most blighted areas of the northeastern United States; when its manufacturing jobs disappeared, all that was left were heavily polluted industrial sites and abandoned factories. Camden became the poorest city in the state, and one of the poorest in the nation, with a per capita income of less than $8000 in 2002.

One Camden neighborhood is even more devastated and environmentally degraded than the rest—Waterfront South, a neighborhood of less than a square mile in South Camden between the river and an interstate. Waterfront South contains the South Jersey Port Corporation, which used to be a major shipbuilder, homes, boarded up stores, two federal Superfund sites, thirteen other known contaminated sites, four junkyards, a petroleum coke transfer station, a scrap metal recycling plant, numerous auto body shops, a paint company, a chemical company, three food processing plants, and other heavy industrial use sites. The huge U.S. Gypsum plant abuts the neighborhood to the north.

Despite this concentration of polluting facilities—and the attendant diesel truck traffic they require—decision-makers in Camden County and at the state level continue to target Waterfront South for undesirable land uses. The County chose Waterfront South as the site of a sewage treatment plant that serves thirty-five municipalities, and of an open-air sewage-sludge- composting facility next to the treatment plant. They also chose to put the garbage incinerator for the entire County's trash in Waterfront South, followed by a massive co-generation power plant. The New Jersey Department of Environmental Protection (DEP) granted permits for all of these projects, over local opposition.

. . . As of 2002, Waterfront South contained slightly more than 2000 residents. Almost half of them were children, who are most vulnerable to pollution.

Thus, in 1999, when the St. Lawrence Cement Company (SLC) announced plans to build a huge cement-grinding facility in Waterfront South that would emit an additional one hundred tons of air pollutants each year, local residents said "enough is enough." They mobilized to fight the plant, but their efforts were hampered by several factors. First, because SLC would construct and operate its plant within the boundaries of the South Jersey Port Corporation, a state agency, the plant was exempt from review by local Camden authorities. Thus, those decision makers closest to the residents—their own local elected officials—had no role in the permit approval process.

. . . Local residents secured legal representation, and, with their lawyers, quickly realized that the new plant was "legal" under environmental law. The DEP had taken the necessary procedural steps in permitting the plant and would not be vulnerable to a legal challenge on environmental grounds.

The experience of Waterfront South residents illustrates the failure of environmental law to protect communities like Camden. . . . Under the law, the community's input was heard only after construction of the facility was underway, and the DEP did not alter a single permit provision in response to that input. Clearly, the old paradigm of environmental law did not work for Waterfront South.

Waterfront South and the Failure of Civil Rights Law

There is another piece to the Camden picture: after thirty years of "white flight," the city is home to an almost exclusively African-American and Latino population. Ninety-four percent of Waterfront South's residents are people of color. . . . [N]ationally, the Environmental Justice Movement arose as a community-based response to the well-documented fact that low-income communities and communities of color bear a disproportionate burden of pollution. . . .

Given the overwhelming concentration of polluting facilities permitted by the DEP in Waterfront South, it was not difficult for the community residents' experts to find that the DEP's actions had a disparate impact on the community. The expert's studies found disparate impact not only in Camden, but throughout New Jersey—black people bore more environmental burdens than white people. Professor Michel Gelobter, looking at the distribution of polluting facilities on a statewide basis, found that ZIP codes with higher than the state-wide average of 20.6% non-white residents had more than twice the air polluting facilities (13.7 facilities per ZIP code) than those with a below-average number of non-white residents. Waterfront South had 2.3 times as many polluting facilities as the average New Jersey ZIP code. . . .

The Civil Rights Lawsuit

Facing a cement-grinding facility that was legal under environmental law, residents turned to the statutes ostensibly enacted to protect people of color—civil rights law. Their experience demonstrates the failure of the old paradigm of civil rights law, as well. The community sued SLC and the New Jersey DEP, alleging intentional discrimination under Title VI of the Civil Rights Act of 1964, and discriminatory effect, or disparate impact discrimination, under the Title VI regulations of the U.S. Environmental Protection Agency (EPA).

Title VI was the Congressional response to the Civil Rights movement, and it bars discrimination by any entity that receives funding from the federal government. . . . Unfortunately, since Title VI's passage in 1964, the Supreme Court has systematically eviscerated the statute, stripping the concept of discriminatory impact from Title VI itself and holding in a series of decisions that one must prove intentional discrimination in order to establish a violation of section 601 of the statute. However, actions having an unjustifiable disparate impact could still be redressed through agency regulations promulgated under section 602 of Title VI, and these regulations provided the basis of the Camden residents' suit.

On April 19, 2001, Judge Orlofsky of the federal District Court in Camden issued an injunction against the cement plant prohibiting its operation. He found that there was indeed a disparate impact as prohibited by EPA regulations. The community's experts had demonstrated that blacks in New Jersey were twice as likely to live near a polluting facility than whites. . . .

The community's victory was short-lived. On April 24, 2001, the U.S. Supreme Court decided *Alexander v. Sandoval* (an unrelated case concerning drivers' licenses in Alabama), holding that there is no private right of action to enforce the disparate impact regulations promulgated by federal agencies under section 602 of Title VI. In response, the Third Circuit quickly lifted Judge Orlofsky's injunction, and, citing *Sandoval*, ruled that the Camden plaintiffs could not sue under a disparate impact theory. Although the district court found discriminatory impact as a result of DEP's decisions—factual findings not overturned on appeal—Camden residents were left without judicial recourse. The old question, "What good is a right if you can't enforce it?," demonstrates the failure of the old paradigm of civil rights law for communities like Camden....

EPA's Title VI Administrative Complaint Process

Camden residents also filed an administrative complaint with the EPA under the agency's Title VI regulations. They might appear to have had an easy route to victory with this administrative complaint—after all, a federal judge had already found discriminatory disparate impact in violation of the EPA's own regulations....

... [However, the] newly-appointed EPA administrator, to whom Camden residents appealed, was, in an unfortunate coincidence, former New Jersey Governor Christine Todd Whitman. Thus, the residents asked the very governor whose DEP had approved the SLC permit, and who had attended the ribbon-cutting for the opening of the SLC plant, to now declare her own gubernatorial administration's actions a violation of civil rights. Given this situation, the residents were unlikely to prevail in their administrative complaint, and, to no one's surprise, they did not.

... The seeming futility of expecting a federal agency to follow and enforce its own regulations starkly illustrates the failure of the old civil rights paradigm.

The Lessons of Waterfront South

... We need a new paradigm....

In the "old paradigm," poverty is a result of individual inadequacy—the poor are to blame for their situation.... [The] disparate impact of some environmental hazards might be explained by the fact that people are "coming to the nuisance;" that is, the polluting industry was there first, and poor people and people of color proceeded to move into the neighborhood. Under this formulation, environmental inequity is essentially volitional. It is the choice of poor people and people of color to live near polluting industries. That is just the "free market.

Within this "old paradigm," there are both liberal and conservative camps, just as in the broader poverty debate. The conservatives say, "We should not interfere with the marketplace, let the free market work." Basically, the status quo is acceptable. Christopher Boerner and Thomas Lambert, apologists for the disparate impact, write that people choose to assume the risk to get the "benefit" of lower housing prices. On the other hand, the liberals say, "Let's make sure that if any industry is located where people live, it is following all of its permits, and if new industry wants to come in, that the people who live there are fully involved." Basically, if industry follows the rules, then no remedy is needed. These outcomes are the natural functionings of our economy, and that is that. . . .

The old paradigm, in both its draconian conservative guise and in its concerned liberal mode, ignores the structural nature of both pollution and racism in our society. Relying on the market to redress environmental injustice is unreasonable. . . . The market is not designed to protect people from pollution—indeed, under our market-based system, there is little disincentive to pollute, as pollution is an externality. Instead, we need to look beyond the market and examine the structural nature of pollution and racism in our society.

A Structural Understanding of Pollution And Racism

It is important to recognize that both pollution and racism have structural underpinnings which will inevitably lead to racist outcomes unless affirmatively attacked and prevented.

Pollution is Structural

Pollution is an externality—a cost of a product that is not borne by the producer or the consumer, but by society at large. This means that the producer is making more profit, as the cost of polluting is less than the cost of purifying the waste prior to discharge. In fact, the market economy tends to create more pollution—by externalizing costs, the producer can lower prices, increase the quantity of goods sold, gain more market share, and eventually reap greater profits. Because profit is the ambition of the market economy, then the market by its very nature creates more pollution as an inevitable by-product of its operation. It is only government intervention into the market, in the form of regulation, that controls pollution. And control is the operative word—the Clean Air Act, the Clean Water Act, and other environmental laws do little to eliminate pollution, instead setting up elaborate systems for regulating its discharge. As anyone who has lived next to a polluting plant can tell you, whether or not it is "legal" pollution—that is, whether or not the emissions are within that factory's permitted limits—it still causes disease, illness, and death. . . . Our market system operates to create pollution, and our regulatory system is designed to control it, but it still exists. It is part of the structure of our economy.

Racism is Structural

Racism in this country is also structural, and therefore the simple workings of the marketplace have a racially disproportionate—indeed, a racist—outcome. Facially neutral decisions can lead to the silent violence of toxic racism.

For example, suppose a business owner in 2006 wants to build a new factory that will emit a certain amount of toxic pollution. There are three main criteria the owner will likely evaluate to find a location for the factory: appropriate zoning, access to transportation, and cheap land. Using these "neutral" criteria, the factory will often be sited in a low-income community of color because each of the three criteria have a racial component. None are "neutral" in their history or in their present day application.

Since its inception in the early part of the last century, zoning has been used to regulate land use. It has also been used to regulate where people live—to segregate people. Environmental racism is found at the intersection of those two uses. Economist Yale Rabin has documented the racial—and racist—history of zoning, wherein predominately white decision-making bodies systematically "down-zoned" the classification of stable residential communities of people of color to allow for industrial uses. White decision-makers routinely placed black neighborhoods next to or within industrial areas or in areas where unpleasant land uses such as stockyards were located. While [such] segregation is no longer legal, the land use patterns (and the industrial zoning) created by these decision-makers still controls in many communities across the country. So if a business person [today] seeks to develop an industrial site and looks solely in areas zoned for industrial uses, in many cases that factory is more likely to end up near communities of color than white communities.

Producers want their factories to be located near freeways, making them more accessible.... The decision-making of the 1950s and early 1960s about the placement of our highway system in urban areas was explicitly racial, and racist. "Urban renewal" of that period meant tearing down or running freeways through the "ghettos"—often stable residential African-American communities. Thus, if a business makes a siting decision based on proximity to freeways, it is disproportionately likely to end up in a black community.

Putting aside the impact of heavy industrial zoning (which drives down land values) and proximity to freeways (which drives down residential land values), land values in and of themselves also have a racial component. Sociologists Douglass Massey and Nancy Denton, in their groundbreaking book American Apartheid, documented the willingness of white people to pay a premium in order to avoid living near or among black people. Because of this racism, land in white communities is more expensive than land in black communities. Therefore, decisions based on land values will steer factories and other businesses toward African-American communities.

In relying on the "neutral" criteria of zoning, access to transportation and land values, the non-racist business owner in 2006 is silently and unwittingly guided by society's structural racism into siting a new polluting plant in a manner that has a racially disparate impact. As Mark Rank notes, "American poverty is largely the result of structural . . . failings." This observation has equal application in the environmental context—the inequitable distribution of environmental hazards in this country is the result of structural failings. Until that is recognized, environmental injustice cannot be appropriately remedied.

The New Paradigm: Environmental Justice

The Environmental Justice movement has contributed a series of significant theoretical perspectives to the discourse on how to solve environmental problems . . .: the ideas of communities speaking for themselves, of pollution prevention, and of the precautionary principle.

"We Speak for Ourselves"

One of the central tenets of the Environmental Justice movement is that communities should speak for themselves—that is, when decisions are being made, those affected by the decisions should have a prominent place at the table. As Bill Quigley advises, "a radical revolution of values prizes the perspective of those at the margins." . . .

Pollution Prevention

When the toxic waste industry asked the question, "Where should we put this incinerator if not in your backyard?," environmental justice activists responded with their own paradigm-shifting question: "Why produce the toxic waste in the first place?" . . . Rather than accepting the status quo of pollution, these activists seek to change production practices upstream so that pollution is eliminated. In many cases they have been successful. . . .

The Precautionary Principle

Perhaps the central failure of environmental regulation is that companies are allowed to pollute until that pollution is deemed harmful. Then, after the harm is found, the pollutant is regulated, or regulated more stringently. The onus of proving a chemical harmful is on those seeking to regulate it, which often means that chemicals with a dramatic and long-term impact on society—DDT or chlorofluorocarbons or methyl bromide— take years to remove from the market. Environmental justice activists have pushed to reframe this debate as well, shifting the presumption of harmful pollution from "innocent until proven guilty" to "guilty until proven innocent." The idea, called the precautionary principle, is that companies must demonstrate that a chemical is safe before it can be introduced for widespread use.

These three principles are the foundational underpinnings of a new paradigm—one that directly involves those affected by environmental hazards in decisions about those hazards; one that challenges industry to change its processes to eliminate, rather than merely control, pollution;

and one that forces industry to prove that chemicals are safe before they can be employed, rather than using communities as live testing laboratories for the effects of toxic chemicals. While it is too late for these concepts to help the Camden residents fight the SLC cement-grinding facility, which has operated now for four years, it is not too late for these concepts to prevent the next toxic intrusion into that community, or into yours. All it takes is the determination to shift the paradigm. As Robert Bullard points out:

> Change in the dominant environmental protection paradigm did not come from an effort made by regulatory agencies, the polluting industry, academia or the industry built around risk management. Instead, impetus for the change came from a movement led by a loose alliance of grassroots and national environmental and civil rights leaders who questioned the foundation of the current environmental protection paradigm.

The legalization of highly-concentrated pollution—by "judicial evisceration and executive non-enforcement"—illustrates how failure by design functions on the basis of identities, groups, interests, and power. Even seemingly neutral decision making such as freeway and industrial plant locations are steeped in identity-laden outcomes of the current and past eras. These cumulative outcomes structure communities of color as "naturally" overpolluted. Advocates and activists may engage in legal actions available under environmental or civil rights law, but those options carry low odds of success. And, on their own, they do little to reveal—or change—the underlying structure. The environmental justice paradigm that Cole and Farrell set out gives advocates and activists tools to reveal and reshape communities—recognizing and working around failure by design. Systemic advocates navigate this work-around—intentionally incorporating elements like prioritizing community voices, not just expert opinions; aiming for pollution prevention, not just mitigation; and distributing burdens so chemical safety must be established before its use rather than by its victims after-the-fact. Thus, the excerpt shows how recognizing failure by design helps advocates overcome it.

7.2 CRAFTING ANALYTICAL NARRATIVES FOR ADVOCACY PROJECTS

Systemic problems invariably contain myriad details, and they also invariably involve "big picture" issues. Their collective, persistent nature ensures it. So, then, how does one begin to tackle interconnected problems like "structural pollution" and "structural racism?" Where does one begin, as a practical matter? The general answer, of course, is: it depends on the context—on what the people know, and what the people have—including you, and your talent, commitment, and skill-set. Within this general framework, advocates in most if not all contexts can find multiple points of entry based on various sources of knowledge and experience. One often-used starting point is narration, which covers a range of types both personal and collective. To elaborate, we focus here on crafting analytical narratives designed to activate critical knowledge for advocacy projects capable of overcoming the disguises and distractions of the Critical Challenge. In effect, these varied kinds of narration (and collaborative projects) aim to get at and beyond the confusion caused *at the bottom* by systemic contradictions like failure by design and other fictions or stratagems that, also by design, obfuscate the facts of systemic outputs or deny their significance. This confusion obstructs bottom-up knowledge, consciousness, and organization, thereby perpetuating—by design—systemic injustice.

Although using personal and proximate experience may seem simple, the practice of self-critical reflection that accompanies narrating is complex. Visualize your dream job as an advocate—or your ideal advocacy project. You likely would prioritize social problems of importance in communities you already care about. Reflect on these and similar questions:

> What are the social problems, groups of people, or places that you believe are of importance? Who are you? What are your identities and communities? What injustices have you experienced or seen? What have you seen others experience? What have you not seen or experienced? What are you curious about? What issue areas interest you? With what groups or communities would you love to work? What languages and cultures are familiar or intriguing? What is personally meaningful and intellectually interesting to you?

These questions call on you to engage not only in critical reflection on social issues but also in self-critical reflection on your own relationship to them. Initially, at least, ask yourself: How can I begin to work on a specific systemic problem given my relationship to and knowledge of that problem and affected populations—as well as my ability to expand my knowledge and capacity?

Finding your way often starts with reflecting on your identity-based experiences and those of people around you. Your own identities—race, ethnicity, sexual orientation, gender, class, religion, age, and others—have affected your life experiences, even if unclear at the time. These identities lead to experiences that include instances of disadvantage or subordination, as well as of advantages or privilege. Consider both; they are distinct yet work in tandem. As you work through questions like these, you might feel uncomfortable because you realize that you know less than you had thought or, alternatively, because you experienced much injustice and struggle. Whatever your circumstances, recall that personal and proximate experience is only a starting point. From whichever point an advocate starts, the process—including collaboration—will lead to new questions and further collaborations.

The advocate's priorities as a professional ultimately must focus on the lives and experiences of subordinated group members, not on the advocate's personal or proximate experience. Experiential knowledge based on personal reflection can be a good starting point but never the end point. This process of reflection is an exercise in connecting micro insights of personal life with macro conditions of persistent group inequality to craft actionable insights and knowledge.

In the next excerpt, Indian legal scholar Robert Williams illustrates how critical and self-critical reflection often (although not necessarily) may be expressed initially in an analytical narrative. As you read Williams, recall the previous excerpts by West, Montoya, Ansley, and others to stay mindful that analytical narratives are not self-congratulatory but rather *always* are critical storytelling—geared specifically to group struggle. As you read, consider what sorts of interests would surface if you were to write about your experiences in childhood, school, and work settings. What sorts of ideas or hopes might emerge, and what sorts of wounds or exclusions might be present? How might that reflection guide your decisions as you imagine contributions you would like to make through advocacy? What would your *analytical* narrative help to expose in personal and concrete (or micro) yet social and systemic (or macro) terms? How might this critical self-reflection provide a starting point for *your* ideal (or "dream") advocacy project?

VAMPIRES ANONYMOUS AND CRITICAL RACE PRACTICE
Robert A. Williams, Jr.
95 Mich. L. Rev. 741 (1997)

... Indian people love their storytellers. We are taught at an early age to love, respect, and surrender ourselves to them. Have you ever seen the storyteller dolls made by the Pueblo Indian potters? Grandmother has six or eight kids hanging on her from everywhere, and notice, she doesn't have a book in her arm. That's how Indians hear their stories, and that's where the love of stories comes from: from the love of a good storyteller. Straight from the mouth, unmediated by impenetrable page and opaque ink, straight from the heart. That's why every time I tell a story now, it's an act of love in honor of the memory and wisdom of my elders who first told me my favorite stories.

... My favorite stories are Pembroke stories (as my family called them), stories about where all my Lumbee relatives are from—Pembroke, North Carolina. ...

I've heard really horrible stories my family tells about being a Lumbee Indian in North Carolina, the tripartite system of racial apartheid we lived under for so many years as disenfranchised "persons of color;" the three separate school systems—one for whites, one for Lumbees, and one for "Negroes"—and things like that. That was nothing compared to the stories of racial terrorism I often heard told by my relatives. My grandmother once had to hide under her bed with her children one night when the "KluKluxers" rode their torches and big white horses outside around the house. My Uncle Boyd, my mother's oldest brother, unarmed, was shot to death by a Klansman. Every one of my aunts and uncles has a story about that tragic event in our family history. So too, the time in the late 1950s when the Lumbees made national news by riding the Klan out of Pembroke. I love every single one of those stories, and those who told them to me.

... I was raised in a traditional Indian home, which meant I was raised to think independently and to act for others. ... For me, my upbringing meant that I had to endure probing questions at the family dinner table, asked by my elders, like, "Boy, what have you done for your people today?"

Now, when you are asked that type of question by one of your Lumbee elders, there's a background context you are presumed to understand. Because acting for others is regarded as an individual responsibility in Lumbee culture, each individual is responsible for making sure that he or she acquires the necessary skills and abilities for assuming that responsibility. So, when you, as a young boy, are asked the question, "What have you done for your people, today?" what you are really being asked is, "Have you studied hard today?," "Have you learned something of use that will help your family, that will help other Lumbee people?" "We know you are just a youngster, but do you understand that you are expected to serve others through your hard work and achievements?"

For me, then, going into law teaching was a way of translating such childhood Lumbee lessons into practice. My "inner child" saw being a law professor who taught and researched in the field of Indian law as a nice, efficient way of being a good person in the eyes of my family, my Indian community, and others. And the pay, considering the hours and flexibility, was damn good.

I was quickly abused and damaged, however, soon upon becoming a law professor. What I didn't know upon entering law teaching was that the law professors who ran the law school where I got my first job didn't give a damn about me saving Indians through Indian law. They cared about one thing and one thing only: themselves. You see, as I soon came to learn, I had been hired to make them and their law school look good.

I admit, I was slow on the uptake. After all, I was the beneficiary of affirmative action at their institution, and to their mind, that meant I really didn't belong there. As a senior faculty member told me soon after arriving at the law school, he had argued that I should be hired, despite the fact that my previous publication record was so "weak." Thank you Masked Man.

. . . The faculty thought that by hiring me, a marginally qualified American Indian with a Harvard Law School degree, they would look good. They'd have looked better, as one of them told me, if I had been Black or Hispanic, or if I had "looked more Indian," but this was the early 1980s, and a lot of law professors had come to accept the idea that every law school had to have at least one affirmative action baby, and I was the best they could deliver at the time.

To really make them look good, however, they told me I had to get tenure. The way for me to do that, as I soon came to learn, was to publish three 100-page law review articles with 400 footnotes.

. . . They had to be published in a select group of "Top Ten" law reviews.

. . . The crazy thing is, I bought into it. Don't ask me why. My first article was 99 pages long (close enough, I thought), with 409 footnotes. I felt it was really something. It had to be, because I learned from a senior colleague that the Three Rules of Acquisition followed by Articles Editors at the Top Six or So law reviews were:

Rule 1) Something by Someone.

Rule 2) Nothing by Someone.

Rule 3) Something by No One.

I was No One, as my senior colleagues liked to remind me. . . . As a No One, I was told I had to write "something important" that had not been adequately "digested" in the "literature" if I was going to get published in a Top Six or So law review.

Have you ever tried to say something really important on a topic that has not been adequately digested in the literature? . . .

You know what you end up doing: you choose a topic that no one has written on, at least within your lifetime. Then you spend two years of your life trying to make it interesting, useful, and maybe even original, if only in the sense that scholarly revisionism can be considered "original," instead of just counter-derivative regurgitation.

That's why I chose a ridiculously obscure topic for my first "major" law review article that no one had written on in Indian law for years: the origin of the Doctrine of Discovery. This was the well-established legal doctrine of European international law, which I traced back to the Crusades of the Middle Ages and the Pope in Rome, by which Columbus and all the other colonizers from Christian Europe who followed him claimed the New World, despite the fact that non-Christian Indians were there first. Get this, and I'm not making this up: because the Indians were "barbarians," they had inferior rights to their property once Europeans came along and "discovered" them.

The novelty of my article on the medieval legal background of the Doctrine of Discovery, so I thought, was that I had discovered the racist origins of modern Indian law. Wasn't that something?

Writing about the racist origins of Indian law, however, turned out to be a mistake, a Big Mistake, as I came to learn during this early, deformative part of my legal academic career. I've still not completely ever recovered from it, even now, years later. It's what made me turn into a Vampire.

. . . I was told by the chair of the tenure and status committee that my article "wouldn't count" as part of my "tenure package" because the committee didn't like it very much, and besides it only got into the Southern California Law Review, . . . a Top Fifteen or So law review. . . .

That's when it all started to fall apart for me, my commitments and stuff like that. All those childhood Lumbee lessons about serving the needs of others; hey, I had to get a life. I had to get tenure.

I learned to play this game of "getting" tenure, to the exclusion of everything else in my life. . . .

Like I've said before, I'm not stupid. I'm not just a beneficiary of affirmative action. I'm Indian. I'm pragmatic. Survival's a big thing with tribal people, understand? I adjust to the environment, I adapt to the terrain, I go with the flow. I got with the program. . . .

. . . I wrote my next article on something that had nothing to do with Indians, a nice little piece on discriminatory zoning by New Jersey's suburban governments.

I followed that up with what I called a "cross-dressing" type piece on the federal tax status of Indian tribes. On that one, I was trying to show the Old Farts that when I wrote on Indian topics, I could go both ways at the same time. I could do "traditional," i.e., really boring, scholarship that had lots of cases in the footnotes (I was citing tax court cases for God's esoteric sakes) and still "advocate" for Indians by developing a strong, well-reasoned, objective, neutral, neutered, "policy-oriented" analysis.

I wanted to show them that I could be a Vampire, just like them.

Ever see the movie *Interview with a Vampire*? ... Tom Cruise and Brad Pitt are these really pasty-faced looking vampire guys who go around turning a few carefully-picked innocent victims into other vampires for their own weird, twisted, personal-type reasons. It's just like when you were hired for your first law school teaching job.

... You know what's really sick about this movie? It's hard to feel really sorry for the minority law professors who are recruited into these Vampire Clubs. It's tough seeing their lifeblood sucked out of them, but it's their choice. No one made them choose to spend seven years of their lives writing law review articles that only other Vampires will read. No, what's really sick and sad is the suffering of the innocent victims of the Vampire Law Professors' hiring and tenure process. It deprives the party of humanity and the minority community of the best and the brightest minority individuals, people with tremendous energy, talent, and potential, people who have a chance to make a real impact on the world and to make it a better place for people of all races, colors, and creeds. It takes these well-trained, eager, young minority people and turns them into Vampires. As untenured Minority Vampires, they are cloistered away in offices, libraries, before a word processing screen. They only come out of their law schools to make presentations at brown-bag faculty lunches and other Vampire Clubs. During what should be the best and most productive years of their professional lives, these untenured Minority Vampire Law Professors are turned into something much worse than simply being useless to their community. They eventually become tenured Old Farts themselves.

That is, unless they become critical race theory scholars....

I don't know exactly what made me join Vampires Anonymous. It was really more of a gradual, awakening-from-the-dead type of deal.

Soon after I got my tenure (at a different law school ...), I came to realize that the model of the law professor that I had bought into during the early, cursed, deformative years of my academic career was, much like the socratic teaching method I used to terrorize my students in the classroom, a nineteenth-century relic. ... Man, life was really cool if you were a law professor back then. Your wife took care of the children, your "negro" maid took care of the housecleaning, the "orientals" down at the laundry starched your shirts just right, there were plenty of good seats to be had in fine restaurants without having to compete with the lower classes, your children would one day ride in the front end of all the amazing new modes of public transportation that were then coming on line, "wetbacks" picked your vegetables at wages so ridiculously low that a good watercress salad could be assembled for pennies, and the "Redskins" and "Braves" weren't racially offensive sports team names, they were a savage race of peoples being rounded up off the plains and put in stockades and prison camps, er, er, reservations, by the United States Army.

Your assigned responsibilities in life were rigorous, demanding, and well-understood. Before you could reward yourself with a good meal, fine cigar, shoulder rub from the Mrs., and glass of port wine at the end of a day, you had to fine-tune the workings of capitalism and the Social-Darwinist state by doing doctrinal scholarship about the things which the enlightened, high-minded fellows like yourself who all ran your nineteenth century Victorian world cared about intensely, like the efficiency of the mailbox rule.

Like I said, I knew all this, I didn't need Vampires Anonymous to figure out that the model was warped and twisted and ill-suited to the demands of a postmodern multicultural world where being a Vampire Law Professor is just one of the more antiquated of the many warped and twisted forms of parasitic deviancy plaguing a sick, decaying, and self-absorbed society in general. No, what made me realize that I needed Vampires Anonymous was my inability to do anything about it. I had so totally bought into the model of the Vampire Law Professor that all I could really do well was write critical race theory articles. I wasn't an Old Fart, but slowly, over the years, I had become a full-fledged Vampire anyway, one who had gotten real comfortable with the idea of tenured Vampire life, meaning that all you really had to do was sit on your ass and deconstruct the world with your word processor.

. . . It was after I moved to Arizona that I . . . figured out that I couldn't be a Vampire Law Professor and do Critical Race Practice at the same time.

Being a law professor at a place like Arizona where Indians are calling you up all the time and asking for help was a new experience for me. . . .

What these Arizona Indians really wanted me to do was to get off my critical race theory ass and do some serious Critical Race Practice. They didn't give a damn about the relationship between hegemony and false consciousness. They wanted help for their problems, and I was a resource. That's why they were so tough on me. See, to be a leader in an Indian community means going off the res[ervation] to bring in resources to help the community. That meant that all these people asking me for help were assuming the responsibility of being Indian leaders which meant they could get right in my face and tell me to "act like an Indian" and give something back, rather than take, take, take. . . .

. . . What really made me understand my need for an organization like Vampires Anonymous was when some Arizona Indian I had just said "no" to would say, right to my face or over the phone, "You know, you don't act Indian." That hurt. It brought back memories of my Lumbee elders looking at me over the dinner table and asking me what had I done for my people today. It brought back images of what I had once thought I was going to do as an Indian law professor—think independently, act for others. It made me go get help, because I realized that as long as I was a Vampire Law Professor, I'd never be able to translate my critical race theory into Critical Race Practice and serve the needs of others.

Kicking a Vampire habit of sitting in an office all your life and writing law review articles is not easy. For me, Vampires Anonymous meant that I had to stop writing law review articles for a while and serve the needs of others in my community.

I started out small, with kids, telling inspirational stories and other neat kinds of stuff to third and fourth graders on occasions like Martin Luther King Day and Columbus Day and things like that. I'd just leave my office, turn off my computer terminal, and go tell stories about Dr. King, or the Iroquois Confederacy and the Great Tree of Peace; positive things, stories of solidarity, struggle, and of rights won, denied, and defended. You know, the type of transcommunal stories that need to be shared with others, particularly children of all races, colors, and creeds, in a disconnected multicultural society like ours.

. . . I started doing all sorts of crazy things with my time. . . . I'd always try to incorporate some critical race theory aspect into [most] student assignments; for example, I'd develop a conflict mediation problem around the topic of environmental racism, or I would ask them to do a research paper on what critical race scholars have to say about John Locke on property or law and economics. Teaching is a vital part of translating critical race theory into practice. It's the students, stupid. They're future practitioners who won't have a whole lot of time to read law review articles on critical race theory when they get out into the real world. Better give it to them now, in meaningful doses.

. . . It was at some point in the middle of all this Critical Race Practice I was doing that I took the biggest step of my life. I developed a Critical Race Practice clinic focused on Indian law at the University of Arizona.

I had probably been doing Critical Race Practice in a semi-serious vein for about two or three years when I decided in 1990 to go really big time and begin offering a clinical seminar on what I called "Tribal Law;" or what became known as the Tribal Law Clinic. It was first offered as a two credit course to second and third year law students, and placed them under my supervision doing clinical placements in tribal courts and directed research requested by Arizona Indian tribes and other Indian tribes and indigenous peoples' organizations outside the state. Presently, the Tribal Law Clinic is offered as a year-round, seven credit hour clinical experience to law students and Indian Studies graduate students in a variety of settings and roles. The clinic has sent law students to Nicaragua to assist in a legal needs assessment for the Indian communities of the Atlantic Coast, to Geneva to assist indigenous nongovernmental human rights organizations at the U.N. Human Rights Commission, and to work as judicial clerks on the Navajo, Hopi, Apache, O'dham, and Yaqui Reservations. . . . The basic mission of the program is to provide pro bono legal research and advocacy assistance, law and graduate student internship and clinical placements, and community-based workshops and other forms of training to strengthen tribal self-governance, institution building efforts, and respect for indigenous peoples' human rights. Basically, in other words, we help Indians in as many ways as we can.

All of the clinical work of the program involves students in projects consciously organized around the important themes of critical race theory. For example, projects are selected and carried out by looking "from the bottom up," that is, students are taught and trained to listen seriously to the concerns, priorities, and experiences expressed by the indigenous communities we work with. We make a point of sending them into these communities, even if that means getting them down to Nicaragua or up to the Navajo Reservation.

All of our projects are approached as efforts aimed at decolonizing United States law and international law relating to indigenous peoples' rights. Students are encouraged to try to understand how the legacy of European colonialism and racism are perpetuated in contemporary legal doctrine, to expose that legacy at work in the project they are working on, and to develop strategies which delegitimate it, literally clearing the ground for the testing and development of new legal theories.

All of the clinic's projects unashamedly endorse the discourse of rights, particularly the emerging discourse of indigenous human rights, as an organizing and empowering strategy for indigenous peoples.

Finally, we globalize wherever possible to make linkages with indigenous communities around the world. Transcommunality . . . is a big part of what we do.

. . . Before they ever step into a courtroom, however, [student advocates] understand that their participation in this program is part of an immersion experience in the most important aspects of critical race theory. First, in the classroom seminar component of the program, we globalize and historicize the dimensions of the problem of tribal control over tribal children. They have to understand the nature and the meaning of the historic struggle of indigenous peoples to exercise their cultural sovereignty for the benefit of their children. They learn how tribal courts in the United States function as the front line institutions in articulating a tribal vision of the law as it should be applied to tribal children. They come to understand that when they finally step into that tribal courtroom, they are responsible to the tribal community as an invited participant in an important human rights struggle to reverse the history of ethnocide and genocide that has resulted in tearing away generations of Indian children from Indian homes and culture.

After this classroom component, we train students next to listen seriously to the stories that Indian people tell about this issue. We do what you might call "cultural sensitivity" training, bringing in tribal elders and tribal social workers to talk to them about tribal family values and culture and traditional beliefs and practices about child rearing and what it means from the tribe's perspective to say something is in the best interest of the child. We've even had them sit down and listen to tribal legends and stories that inculcate these values through storytelling.

Only then do we send them out to the reservation to begin investigating the case. Their first job is to go and collect all the relevant stories from everybody connected with the case: the child's story, the parents,' social workers,' probation officers,' relatives,' neighbors,' victims,' whatever. They become story hearing fools. Then they come back to class and tell the rest of us what they've learned and to help figure out the appropriate disposition that reflects what was learned from looking from the bottom up.

I believe that this whole process teaches them how to be effective advocates for indigenous peoples—and other disempowered groups, for that matter—in a multicultural world. They come to understand that their job as Critical Race Practitioners (whether they are yellow, black, red, or white) is to figure out how indigenous peoples' stories matter, and to find ways to make them matter through community institution building.

All of our projects are organized like that, and if a project can't be organized in that way, we don't take it on. For example, we draft a lot of legislative codes for tribal governments, and before we do a probate code, or an appellate procedure code, or a cultural resources protection code, students first learn about the tribe and its relevant traditions and culture and history, spend time on the tribe's reservation talking to the people who are going to have to work with and live with the code, and then come back and figure out what they've got to do as Critical Race Practitioners to draft legislation for that tribal community. Our litigation support activities are organized around the same principles, as are our internship and externship placements and the workshops we put on for tribal communities on issues like environmental justice and child advocacy.

Our students learn many valuable lessons in the Tribal Law Clinic, but first and foremost, they come to understand that Critical Race Practice is mostly about learning to listen to other people's stories and then finding ways to make those stories matter in the legal system. And no one can say that that's not really something!

That's my story about Critical Race Practice and what Vampires Anonymous has done for me. We all create our own private mythologies, I guess. I'm now recovering as a tri-racial isolate Lumbee legal storyteller putting my critical race theory to good use with the best resources that I believe postmodern multicultural legal education has to offer. You know what they are: the reliable group of bright, energetic, multicultural law students who still come to legal education with these wild and crazy ideas about law serving justice and all that; clinical courses that can motivate and teach these students by awarding academic credit for reaching out to serve the legal needs of others; the human, information, and technical resources available within the modern law school.

This type of Critical Race Practice clinical course isn't really that hard to do at all, if you yourself are really motivated. You know the drill. Your elders taught it to you. Get off your butt, go out and make a difference in the world. Or, think independently, act for others. Whatever, you were taught your responsibilities, you know what it is you have to do.

. . . If only [my colleagues] would join Vampires Anonymous. They would come to learn that understanding other people and their stories really does matter in our efforts to achieve justice in our postmodern multicultural world.

Williams reflects critically *and* self-critically on law and society, on self and systems, to narrate from personal and proximate experience his own approach to advocacy. Williams consciously reflects on personal experience and knowledge as a starting point, supplemented by the Schools and Approaches and by connections to the bottom of local communities. He converts critical race theory into "critical race practice." To accomplish this conversion, he uses experience-based narrative to make critical knowledge actionable in the context of his advocacy project: the Indian Law Clinic. By personal example, Williams illustrates the power of analytical narratives to connect experience with larger patterns of collective injustice to expose the sources of systemic injustice, and to empower personal *and* collective actions.

7.3 TEAMS AND TEAMWORK EXPAND THE CAPACITY OF SYSTEMIC ADVOCATES

Teamwork, in the sense of collaborative professionalism, means much more than simply "working and playing well with others" and requires more than the civility and cooperation skills you may have learned in traditional professionalism classes. The purposeful formation of teams and the active management of teamwork make the team a central hub of advocacy, and the base of collaborations that extend beyond the team itself. Systemic advocates learn to build teams that are cross-cultural, cross-class, cross-generational, and cross-disciplinary and that include client-groups as well as professionals from other fields.[6] Advocates must develop competencies to negotiate complex relationships and to create "collective, reflective antisubordination practice."[7]

Teams and teamwork allow advocates to leverage their knowledge and work across ever-larger groups, including diverse coalitions and communities. Teamwork allows advocates to build capacity and enhance impact while managing the inevitable conflicts and other messiness of collective struggle. But teams (and coalitions) must be customized in composition—in terms of identities, expertise, and roles—to function effectively as problem-solving instruments.

A team is "a small number of people with complementary skills, who are committed to a common purpose, set of performance goals, and approach for which they hold themselves mutually accountable."[8] Teams offer practical advantages: many perspectives and multiple skill sets are inputs, and greater shared ownership is an output of teamwork.[9] Well-composed, well-run teams achieve greater impact by drawing on contributions of all members acting in concert:

> Each member of the team has a role to play and something to contribute. Mutual respect ensures that the members appreciate, support and encourage each other to achieve the group's maximum potential. Respect means that team members acknowledge each other's individual backgrounds and experiences, allowing the team to approach its work using the widest spectrum of knowledge and skills available to it.[10]

To be effective, all team members must be accountable to each other, to the team, and to the communities, clients, or causes they serve. Teamwork is relational, but traditional legal training may exacerbate individualism or fail to provide essential teamwork skills: "[M]uch of legal training, with its emphasis on individual work and achievement, is an impediment to

---

[6] See, for example, the Sargent Shriver National Center on Poverty Law, www.povertylaw.org/?gclid=CjwKCAjw47bLBRBkEiwABh-PkQY84GPjqrGx-Zmsr2h_bvFRAynAE0sl6jSxOmHzt Sb9qXatoXzTqRoCXs4QAvD_BwE; Law for Black Lives, www.law4blacklives.org; Social Justice Lawyers, www.facebook.com/pg/socialjusticelawyers/about/?ref=page_internal; the National Lawyers Guild, www.facebook.com/NLGNational/; and Centro de los Derechos del Migrante, https://cdmigrante.org.

[7] Eric Yamamoto, Critical Race Praxis: Race Theory and Political Lawyering Practice in Post-Civil Rights America, 95 Mich. L. Rev. 821, 878 (1997) (noting the resemblance in critical race praxis to the United Church of Christ's See-Judge-Act method).

[8] Jon R. Katzenbach and Douglas K. Smith, The Discipline of Teams, 71 Harvard Bus. Rev. 111, 112 (1993).

[9] See Beth Gilbertsen and Vijit Ramchandani, Developing Effective Teams: Proven Methods for Smoother and More Productive Teamwork 1–2 (Wilder Foundation, Sept. 2003).

[10] Janet Weinstein et al., Teaching Teamwork to Law Students, 63 J. Legal Educ. 36, 49 (2013).

developing effective team players."[11] This can complicate teamwork, even in unconscious ways.

Because collaboration entails the risk, if not the inevitability, of disputes among friends and allies, advocates additionally must learn to negotiate intrateam and intergroup conflicts. Advocacy teams, after all, are part of the social world, and conflicts can reflect the same divisions as exist in larger society. Where historic injuries or notions of "difference" hinder solidarity, advocates help foster mutual learning, understanding, and conciliation. But conflict also is a necessary part of the collaborative process for effective problem solving. In other words, one purpose of teams is to hash out differences of viewpoint and experience—not suppress them. Intrateam disagreement or professional conflict over tactics and strategies is not, per se, something "bad" that must be circumvented or otherwise avoided. But in helping to manage conflict, advocates aim to act in principled, not personalized, terms.[12]

Legal scholar Scott Cummings has studied conflicts that emerge during advocacy. Rather than supplying a simple formula for managing difference and dissent, Cummings suggests advocates might better learn from experience and consider how diversity and disagreement within a collaboration can serve as a creative force for innovation and accountability. In this approach, conflict is a necessary element of growth and empowerment:

> [W]hat we should ultimately care about are the multiple and context specific ways that dissent is aired and respected in social movement environments.... [I]f we ultimately care about lawyers advancing policy claims that actually reflect the interests of the communities they purport to serve, the approach described in both [top-down and bottom-up] cases—so far as they suggest that advocacy embedded in politics deepens community ties—may be a step in the right direction, even though it is imperfect—as everything is. In this sense, I hope that . . . stories [of collaborative struggles] guide the way toward deeper engagement with dissent that advances democratic social change.[13]

Cummings brings a dual consciousness to collectives and conflicts. Every context raises complex questions about collective self governance, planning, and action that are answerable in many different ways. None of the answers are pure, no individual or position exists outside systemic complexity and complicity, and all conflicts implicate identities, groups,

---

[11] Roberta K. Thyfault and Kathryn Fehrman, Interactive Group Learning in the Legal Writing Classroom: An International Primer on Student Collaboration and Cooperation in Large Classrooms, 3 J. Marshall L.J. 135, 149 (2009).

[12] David Luban, Lawyers and Justice: An Ethical Study 319 (1988).

[13] See Scott I. Cummings, How Lawyers Manage Intragroup Dissent, 89 Chi.-Kent L. Rev. 547, 567 (2014).

interests, and power.[14] Answering complex questions itself takes teamwork and time. Collaborative professionalism practices help build repeat players capable of sustaining collective actions. Advocates and groups harness conflicts and mistakes as part of the ongoing process of building solidarity and capacity.

Even without conflict, critical collaborations can be uncomfortable because they are uncertain and nontraditional. Open-ended learning entails living with ambiguity and complexity—personally and professionally. Confusion, frustration, and discomfort can occur, sometimes for extended periods of time. Systemic advocates do not evade such feelings but aim to anticipate and manage team members' uncertainties, just as advocates aim to anticipate and manage conflict to generate more productive collaborations.

Sources of conflict, of course, are not simply or primarily internal. Rather, professionals who critically reject entrenched systemic teachings—which are widely accepted as "the truth"—can be seen as "outsiders" in legal and personal circles. They can be labeled as annoyances, disturbances, or threats or can be criticized as "unprofessionally" unreasonable, demanding, angry, or absurd. If so, you may be considered just background noise to be ignored, drowned out, excluded as a pariah, or silenced. From this mistaken but dominant perspective, critical thinkers may be dismissed as not serious professionals chiefly because they refuse to silently conform.

Many individuals who engage in critical practice and self-critical reflection already may feel, and already may be, in fact, outsiders in systemic terms. Many already do not conform, sometimes vocally. Recognizing this reality means that critical collaborations also are a way forward: a means of connecting with networks of critical scholars, activists, and practitioners that serve as support. Criticality and collaboration create not only the possibility of opposition and conflict, but also the likelihood of growth and solidarity, personally and collectively.

In fact, collaborative professionalism has many rewards, in addition to its risks. An independent path brings a lifetime of rewards. An advocate can engage in meaningful work. She can develop lifelong practices of empowerment from the bottom, along with vibrant relationships with

---

[14] See Paul R. Tremblay, Counseling Community Groups, 17 Clinical L. Rev. 389 (2010) (noting that advice on working with community groups should take into account "some knotty practical questions about the lawyers' professional responsibilities in their work with such groups"); Michael Diamond and Aaron O'Toole, Leader, Followers, and Free Riders: The Community Lawyer's Dilemma When Representing Non-Democratic Client Organizations, 31 Fordham Urb. L.J. 481, 486–87 (2004); Shauna I. Marshall, Mission Impossible?: Ethical Community Lawyering, 7 Clinical L. Rev. 147 (2000); Susan D. Bennett, Little Engines That Could: Community Clients, Their Lawyers, and Training in the Arts of Democracy, 2002 Wis. L. Rev. 469 (2002); Jayashri Srikantiah and Janet Martinez, Applying Negotiations Pedagogy to Clinical Teaching: Tools for Institutional Client Representation in Law School Clinics, 21 Clinical L. Rev. 283 (2014).

clients and colleagues. Indeed, a recent analysis of the legal profession found that, as a group, "prestige" lawyers working in private firms, particularly large firms, felt a lower sense of well-being, reported higher use of alcohol, and were less satisfied with their competence than were lawyers in public service positions. Lawyers dedicated to public service work reported higher levels of well-being despite lower salaries:

> The data contradict beliefs that prestige, income, and other external benefits can adequately compensate a lawyer who does not regularly experience autonomy, integrity, close relationships, and interest and meaning in her work. . . . In particular, the shared understanding of "success" needs to be amended so that talented students and lawyers consistently avoid choices in the pursuit of material success that will undermine their happiness.[15]

These empirical data underscore downsides of traditional lawyering that we explore further in Part IV, starting with formal training and lasting through professional policing of norms and expectations. These include the atomization of problems and remedies and of advocates and clients. To counter the limiting effects of many legal traditions, systemic advocates use difference as an asset, constructing diverse teams in which members evaluate their individual work and collective performance critically and self-critically. This openness increases the team's capacity to produce knowledge, manage conflict, and get the job done.

Effective teams reflect multiple kinds of diversity tailored to the problem at hand; they are designed to overcome failure by design in that context. Team diversities—in demographics, skills, and disciplines—are carefully targeted to ensure the team possesses all necessary areas of expertise. The excerpt below, written by two law professors and two professors of pediatrics, offers guidance on forming and leading interdisciplinary teams. The authors point out characteristics or "requirements" for effective teams, as well as "stages" or phases of effective teamwork. As you read, ask yourself what you would do if charged with forming an advocacy team: What steps would you take to develop your own knowledge and skills? To define the team's goals? To bring together the best mix of members? To use difference as an asset?

---

[15] Lawrence S. Krieger with Kennon M. Sheldon, What Makes Lawyers Happy?: A Data-Driven Prescription to Redefining Professional Success, 83 Geo. Wash. L. Rev. 554, 623–24 (2015).

TEACHING TEAMWORK TO LAW STUDENTS
Janet Weinstein, Linda Morton, Howard Taras & Vivian Reznik
63 J. Legal Educ. 36 (2013)

... Teamwork concepts are infrequently taught in legal education. In addition, law professors unfamiliar with teamwork theory and practice are unlikely to use teams to engage students in learning.

... Our use of the term "teamwork" does not apply to the occasional use of teams in class exercises, or to a "loosely structured coordination between or among students."

... [We adopt this definition:] "A team is a small number of people with complementary skills, who are committed to a common purpose, set of performance goals, and approach for which they hold themselves mutually accountable." ...

The Rationale for Teamwork Instruction

Enhancement of Students' Professional and Interpersonal Skills

Teaching teamwork involves instructing students in critical life skills, including communication, planning and coordination, leadership and cooperation, as well as conflict resolution, problem solving, and creative thinking. In addition to gaining these life skills, students derive other benefits from the experience, including interpersonal satisfaction:

> The benefits of team-building activities have ... been investigated in education. Studies have found that participants who had team-building experiences had significantly higher levels of trust, social support, openness, and satisfaction. The findings from another study indicate that, when participating in a team project, students who had previously participated in team-building activities had better interactions with team members than those who had not.

Small group work promotes higher academic achievement.... [C]ooperative learning also prepares students for public interest work and improves their marketability and career options.

> Cooperative learning equips students with new vision and strategies to perform [complex] legal services, training them to get at the sources of social breakdown and not simply its latest legal symptoms....

Recognition of Need for Teamwork Skills in the Professions

Today, physicians are expected to become part of interdisciplinary health care teams in the clinical setting to ensure quality patient-centered care, as well as in the research enterprise to solve complex questions. "Medical school graduates will be expected to understand how teams function and be capable themselves of functioning as part of a team. They will need to be competent in the knowledge, skills and attitudes of teams and teamwork." . . .

Teamwork appears to be a key factor in business practice. Since the 1990s, there has been an enormous increase in the number of teams used in work organizations. Seventy-nine percent of Fortune 1000 companies reported using self-managing work teams. "Teamwork skills are in high demand in business, and the ability to work in a team has become one of the top five characteristics necessary for applicants to secure a professional position."

An interest in teamwork skills in the legal profession is relatively recent. "Effective teamwork is critical to law firms." . . . However, in our informal discussions with law firm attorneys, we found no evidence of teamwork training.

In fact, much of legal training, with its emphasis on individual work and achievement, is an impediment to developing effective team players. As the awareness of the power of teamwork grows in the legal community, we can expect greater appreciation of the need to teach teamwork skills in law school.

How Graduate Schools Are Incorporating Teamwork Skills

To be successful, teamwork teaching must be explicit. "[R]esearch has shown that merely putting students in groups and telling them to work together does not, in and of itself, promote higher achievement"—a concept that is supported in the legal literature.

The empirical and anecdotal evidence suggests that students working in teams may perform better in representing their clients and may learn more from the clinical experience than do students providing representation alone. At the same time, that evidence suggests that the benefits of pairing will not accrue automatically and that steps must be taken to increase the likelihood that these benefits will be realized.

More and more disciplines, including law, now include specific teaching of teamwork skills. . . . [M]any legal educators invoke the platitudes of collaborative education but far fewer develop methodology for implementation. . . . Particularly in the United States, there is a more general culture of individuality which is difficult to change. . . .

Teaching Teamwork in Our Courses

. . . In developing our team process, we strive to provide the essential elements that allow for the most productive team learning: 1) positive interdependence; 2) individual accountability; 3) appropriate group composition, size, and duration; 4) face-to-face interaction; 5) genuine learning and challenge; 6) explicit attention to collaborative social skills and regular meetings to discuss group process. . . .

... [W]e discuss theories of teamwork, interdisciplinary collaboration and professional values. We also teach communication, listening and conflict resolution skills. We focus on two theoretical frameworks for teaching teamwork process: the characteristics of successful teams and the stages of a team.

Requirements for Effective Teamwork

... Effective teamwork requires that members of the team share particular knowledge, skills, and attitudes. While the literature on teamwork uses a variety of labels to describe these requirements, there is clear agreement that teams require:

Clear Goals

Teams are created to achieve specific goals with certain ending points, which may include a time limit. Every member of the team must understand the team's goals. . . .

Leadership

There is some uncertainty about whether the team leader should be designated externally or selected by the members, whether an agreed upon rotation of leadership is effective, or whether a leader must be designated at all. Most of the literature, however, subscribes to the theory that one leader is the most effective model for teamwork. . . .

Shared Commitment and Participation

It is essential that each member contribute to the team's work, not only by completing individual assignments, but also by joining the team's discussion of its work and process. Likewise, each member must embrace the commitment to the team's goal. This is reinforced by the team charter. . . .

Resentment can build within the team toward individual team members who are seen as not sharing the commitment. We offer suggestions for communication about this issue. . . . [Advocates must] understand that, as a rule, team members never contribute equally. . . . [Otherwise, they] may become frustrated and, if team efforts at remedying the situation are unsuccessful, . . . decide to ignore the issue without confrontation. . . .

Mutual Respect

Each member of the team has a role to play and something to contribute. Mutual respect ensures that the members appreciate, support and encourage each other to achieve the group's maximum potential. Respect means that team members acknowledge each other's individual backgrounds and experiences, allowing the team to approach its work using the widest spectrum of knowledge and skills available to it.

Throughout the [collaboration, all team members should] reflect on their personal strengths and weaknesses, as well as those of their team members.... [Advocates should prepare] written evaluations to ... discuss them with their team.... [Advocates must exercise] self-evaluation skills, as well as how to offer and receive feedback.... [Over time, teams] learn that the team improves when each member is encouraged to reach her full potential, rather than blamed or criticized.

Open Communication

Team members must be open to giving and receiving communication from each other. Teams also must have an agreed method for communicating about their process. Despite ... conflict resolution skills, teams do break down, occasionally....

Collaborative Environment

There is no place for competition within a team, nor can the focus be on individual accomplishment. We also warn of the dangers of "groupthink," in which pressures to collaborate can lead to reticence in challenging the direction of the group.

... [Each team member must] model collaboration....

Ongoing Team Evaluation

Periodic self-evaluation of the team helps to keep the process on track and to correct problems before they become real obstacles. This evaluation process includes the same requirements (i.e., mutual respect, open communication, collaborative environment, etc.) that are required in working toward the team's goals.... [The] willingness to manage difficulties [is preferred] over any pretense that the team is operating smoothly.

Member Competence

[Occasionally,] there may be problems when some team members believe that they must redo or take over the work of a member who is perceived as less than competent. As in real life, not all team members share the same level of competence. On the other hand, the process needs of a team may bring out new competencies among some members. For example, a [member] may come to the team with strong knowledge and skills about teamwork, allowing that [individual] to make a different kind of contribution to the work of the team.

... [E]ach team [should] discuss the positive competencies of its members ... and also discuss how to realize maximum competence from each member, as well as how to deal with frustrations.

External Support and Recognition

A healthy environment for teamwork is one that provides external support for the team and recognition that what the team is doing is valuable to the organization. . . .

Stages in the Team Process

While those who have studied and written about teamwork may use different terminology for the steps in the process, all agree that teams move through different stages and that it is important for members to understand this process. We have found that when team members know in advance that certain stages can be more difficult than others, they tend to more readily accept the difficulties as part of the process, rather than as shortcomings of their members. . . . We have found through our own experience that the most appropriate sequence and terminology is: "forming, norming, storming, reforming and performing." . . .

Forming

In the formation stage of the team, the members must agree on the team's purpose, what outcomes are expected, whether the team has the authority necessary to achieve the outcomes, how the outcomes will be measured, consequences of success and failure, processes for dispute resolution and how the team's work fits into the larger picture of the institution. The team must also clarify the skills and knowledge of each team member and affirm that each team member is committed to the team's work and personally invested in its success. The formation stage is critical to future success and is often rushed as members seek to deal with the immediate task. Because teams tend to jump into the content of the work without working through these necessary process issues, we require a team charter from every group.

Norming

At this stage, the team begins to bond, enhance its commitment, and create a cohesive unit with a team identity. The team moves from a group of individuals with a common goal to a cohesive unit with a character and culture of its own. . . . [T]eams develop their own team names, work on team worksheets together and meet [as necessary]. Focus is on cooperation, support, and conformity. The danger of this stage is that it can lead to "groupthink" or the tendency to ignore differences and to succumb to group pressures for the sake of conformity. Teams must move on to the storming stage to avoid groupthink.

Storming

Once the team gets to work, it is to be expected that conflicts will occur. "Team members are forming opinions about one another, positive and negative, and individuals are still primarily pursuing their personal interests as they vie for positions. Formal and informal leaders emerge, and weaker team members may recede into the woodwork." ... In the storming stage it is important to refocus the team on its goal and to work on communication to dissipate negative feelings about the team process and team members. While the storming stage may be quite uncomfortable, it is a critical part of team development. "Conflict can be useful for achieving cohesion." Having come through this difficult phase, team members are often drawn more closely together with a more determined sense of mission.

Reforming

In this fourth stage of team development, the team goes back to its charter and potentially reforms it. Members successfully resolve their conflicts so they can proceed with the assigned problem and frequently approach one another with renewed respect. In this stage, members work more harmoniously and view themselves less as individuals and more as members of a team. Members clarify their roles and responsibilities as they adopt a renewed focus on their goals.

Performing

In this stage, the team is functioning at its highest level. There is a strong sense of team spirit and solidarity. When disagreements arise, they are handled by the team's previously agreed upon process. At this point team members truly share a vision and support one another, even when difficult challenges arise. . . .

[Conclusion]

. . . The knowledge, skills and attitudes of teamwork, including clear goals, open communication, mutual respect, awareness of process, collaboration and shared commitment are important to any endeavor involving more than one person. . . . [E]ngaging in teamwork in a thoughtful way also enhances self-awareness, which in turn improves both job performance and job satisfaction. . . .

In the excerpt above, Weinstein and her interdisciplinary coauthors focus on the design, assembly, and management of teams generally—whether for a stand-alone advocacy project or as part of a larger entity. They succinctly itemize "requirements" and "stages" of effective teamwork. These requirements and stages can usefully be revisited as you develop your own systemic advocacy project.

NOTES AND QUESTIONS

1. *Reflection Exercise on Teams and Teamwork.* A web-based collaboration tool defines a team charter as a "common understanding of how a team gets its

work done [that] covers the basic questions of why a team exists, what it's designed to accomplish, and how the work will happen." See www.redbooth. com/blog/7-components-of-an-actionable-team-charter; for an additional team charter example see www.smartsheet.com/essential-guide-creating-effective-team-charter.

In the context of systemic advocacy, this agreement or contract might define roles and ensure mutual accountability. Reflect on a past team (or group) experience you had in a school (such as a study group), work, or other setting. Did you agree on a "charter" at the outset or some other stage of the team's work? If not, would that have been helpful? If so, how did the charter affect the team's dynamics? Was your team a success? By what metrics are you judging success or failure? Evaluate your team experience using, from Weinstein et al. above, the relevant requirements for effective teamwork. Were any requirements missing or failed? Did those missing or failed elements affect attainment of the team goals? How might you better ensure fulfillment of those essential elements in your next teamwork?

7.4 COLLABORATIVE PROFESSIONALISM AND CRITICAL COALITIONS EMPOWER ADVOCACY

Teams and teamwork are key to collaborative professionalism. Teams also frequently work with clients who in turn may also be some kind of group—although with varying levels of collective consciousness, capacity, or cohesion. Although the details depend on context, personal and team collaboration with collective clients also is inevitably key to systemic advocacy.

Below, human rights scholars and practitioners Benjamin Hoffman and Marissa Vahlsing reflect on their work with EarthRights International, where they purposefully practiced "implementing the critical lawyering methodologies at key moments in the lawyer-client relationship." They focus on the "mechanics of the advocate-client relationship" important in both domestic and transnational contexts. These mechanics are adapted to address contextual obstacles of law, time, distance, culture, resources, and knowledge. Collaboration is crucial in overcoming each of those obstacles. Consider how the authors' concluding questions might "guide further investigations" to improve collaboration as antisubordination practice in your own work or plans.

Collaborative Lawyering in Transnational Human Rights Advocacy
Benjamin Hoffman and Marissa Vahlsing
21 Clinical L. Rev. 255 (2014)

Introduction

For years, cause lawyers, particularly those working on poverty and environmental justice issues, have cast a critical eye upon the practice of lawyering and the lawyer-client relationship. They have raised questions regarding the role of the lawyer in the clients' struggle and the possibility that the lawyer might prioritize a legalistic vision of justice at the expense of the clients' visions and needs. To address these concerns, cause lawyers have considered the ways in which adopting a particular methodology based upon critical reflection—be it client-centered-, community-, rebellious-, or collaborative lawyering—might empower communities and serve their clients' visions of justice. To date, however, the practice of transnational human rights lawyering—whether it involves human rights advocacy via public campaigns or impact litigation—has been largely divorced from many of the contributions of theorists and practitioners of these critical models of lawyering. . . .

. . . Drawing upon our own experiences as practitioners and the lessons of the critical methodologies, we present a practical and detailed guide for implementing an effective model of "transnational collaborative lawyering." We conclude with a series of questions to guide further refinement of this methodology.

. . . We are human rights and environmental rights lawyers whose work has primarily involved supporting indigenous communities in the Amazon in their struggles against multinational oil companies. Thus, when we use the term "community" in this paper, we are referring to communities as groups of people situated similarly in time, space, geography and culture who are confronted, collectively, by adverse environmental or human rights impacts. The paradigmatic example in our work is the indigenous community that is already situated in its territory with deep ancestral roots to its environment who is affected by the arrival of an oil company on its land. . . . We recognize that this paradigm represents just one of a multitude of possible "communities" that may call upon a lawyer for support. Similarly much of our work has involved litigation against companies in courts in the United States, and thus litigation features prominently in the strategies that we analyze.

Our work has shown us that many obstacles present in transnational human rights advocacy are variants of problems that are present in the domestic context. Consequently, much of the work of applying the critical lawyering methodologies in the human rights context is one of translation.

Where transnational strategies present qualitatively different obstacles, we aim to bring new and creative thinking to overcome those obstacles. . . .

. . . The ideas that follow represent our effort to identify potential strategies available to transnational human rights lawyers to provide a more collaborative form of representation. . . .

Collaborative, Critical, and Community Lawyering: Key Texts and New Possibilities

Common Themes in Critical Lawyering Methodologies

Over the past three decades, cause lawyers, theorists and clinicians have developed a rich body of literature devoted to both problematizing and reimagining the lawyer-client relationship and its potential for empowerment as well as for subjugation. . . .

The literature seeking a more critical, collaborative, and non-hierarchical theory and practice of lawyering converges around at least one clear point: joint empowerment is key. . . .

Whether framed as "third-dimensional" lawyering or "rebellious lawyering" or community lawyering, community or client empowerment is a critical means, and end, of these practices. . . .

As lawyers and advocates, how can we do this in concrete terms? What changes can we make to the practice of lawyering to make it more collaborative, more critical? [Louise] Trubek provides six key steps: (1) encourage participation, (2) personalize the issues, (3) be skeptical of bureaucracy, (4) be unbiased in approach to advocacy arenas, (5) organize with other lawyers and (6) apply feminist and anti-racist analyses.[16] . . .

The Short-Comings of Human Rights Theory

Human rights, human rights advocacy, and human rights "lawyering" have all faced critique . . . Very little of the critique has examined the mechanics of the advocate-client relationship when the advocate acts as a lawyer. . . .

Lawyering in The Transnational Context

Thus far, transnational human right lawyering has followed a significantly different model than the collaborative, critical, and community based lawyer models we outlined above. Lawyers based out of international or regional offices learn of particular rights violations (often in a different country), travel to that region to collect information, and offer the affected communities a limited set of strategies to address their situation based on the particular expertise of that organization—e.g. report-writing, submission of communications to treaty bodies, litigation before international or national courts—and that organization's mission. This is

---

[16] See Louise G. Trubek, Critical Lawyering: Toward a New Public Interest Practice, 1 B.U. Pub. Int. L.J. 49 (1991).

the same model many law school human rights clinics use. This model is in sharp contrast to clinical practice taught and used in domestic poverty law and community lawyering clinics....

Part of the problem stems from the transnational nature of the advocacy. Much of our experience has come from supporting communities that have been affected by violations of international human rights perpetrated by large multinational corporations or by state security forces with the complicity of multinational corporations.... [Transnational] strategies, however, have often been problematic.

For example, consider litigation in U.S. courts under the Alien Tort Statute, 28 U.S.C. § 1350, a strategy that we have often supported. Litigation under the statute is complex, drawn-out over many years, and results hinge on minute issues of civil procedure. In many cases, the principal legal struggle concerns questions of international law and federal jurisdiction.... Briefing and arguing these questions can take years.... This can have the effect of obscuring, rather than highlighting, the wrongs for which they seek recognition and redress.

... [In these instances,] the struggle to vindicate clients' rights and remedy harms more closely resembles a battle between highly-educated and elite lawyers than an effort to empower the community....

Changing Practice and Engagement: Key Moments and Considerations in the Transnational Lawyer-Client Relationship

Toward a Shared Vision of Justice

At the outset, it should be apparent that in order to achieve "collaboration," it is essential that the lawyer and the client work towards a common goal. In this respect, one of the fundamental challenges for human rights lawyers is that the goals of the lawyer or his organization may not directly align with the goals of the client, often a foreign community....

... We believe that identifying and seeking this shared vision of justice, beyond any abstract notion of empowerment, is the principal goal of the collaborative human rights lawyer through the representation—and the end to which the lawyer owes ultimate allegiance. The lawyer looks for collaboration with the community in pursuing a shared goal that is, necessarily, jointly informed by the lawyer's own vision of social change.

... Without an honest and frank understanding of the interests, goals, and backgrounds of both parties, affected communities and lawyers alike could easily be treated as mere pawns in the other's struggle for social change.

Introducing Yourself and Offering Support

Risks of Undermining Community Power

One of the most salient takeaways from the collaborative lawyering literature is the importance of identifying and managing power dynamics embedded in the lawyer-client relationship....

... [T]he lawyer is often limited by his/her organization's mission, source of funds, or even own academic and professional formation. For example, we have bar licenses in the United States, and thus the menu of legal strategies that we can offer to communities, on our own, is limited to litigation in the United States or before international human rights bodies. At times then, in merely expressing our own organizational or professional limitations, we run the risk of exerting some pressure on communities to adopt strategies that may not align precisely with their own vision for how best to affect change.

An example from our own experience here may be helpful. We were working with an indigenous community in the central Peruvian Amazon that was facing persistent oil extraction and contamination on their lands. We had come to talk with them about supporting their struggle against a powerful U.S. oil company, and about the possibility of using litigation in the United States to do so. But the community had a different idea for how best to achieve reparation for the contamination they were confronting. Drawing upon the history of their relations with the oil companies in their territory, and wary of adopting any strategy that could take years to resolve, the leaders proposed instead a plan of peacefully taking over the oil wells, forcing the company to turn off its machinery, and using their own voices and bodies to make their grievances known, with the end of reaching a negotiated solution with the company. They turned to us, and they said: "and you, *doctores*, you will be a part of our legal commission when we take over the wells, right?"

... Of course we wanted to support them ... [b]ut we also knew that we could not do what they had asked of us ... [because] we had key limitations as lawyers from the United States. We would eagerly support the community in its legal strategies on the international level, but we were afraid that we were unable to represent them in any criminal defense cases in Peru should they be arrested when they take the direct action. Our representation simply could not extend that far.

... As soon as we had expressed our limitations, we realized how limited we were in our goal of helping the community shift the balance of power. At the precise moment when the community was considering a strategy of exercising its power, we started stepping away. How could we really expect to accompany the community in vindicating its human and environmental rights if our representation was limited to the contours of our bar licenses?

Power-Respecting Strategies at Initial Meetings

... [A]fter this experience, we suggested to our organization that they hire a Peruvian lawyer, and they did. The lawyer and his or her organization should develop a funding model that allows for flexibility, and does not depend entirely on contingency fee arrangements that necessarily contemplate civil litigation, or funding grants that explicitly limit the type of strategies that the organization can pursue.... When an alternative strategy may be called for, the lawyer might help the community to identify local actors who possess the skill set necessary to provide the needed support. Here, exploring the possibility of collaborative litigation models—in which lawyers from one country assist lawyers in another country—either with human or economic resources, is also an option for lawyers to explore....

One possibility that we have explored is the use of the initial and introductory workshops as a space to share histories (both the community's and the lawyers') through dynamic exercises. This can serve ... to give the lawyers a chance to ... "try to understand" their collective "conception" of the problem. One technique that we used was to work with the community to draw a timeline of events that the members view as critical to the emergence of the problem....

Another key exercise that we have used in the initial strategic discussions with the communities is mapping relevant actors and strategies. The mapping exercise seeks to identify all the actors that influence the situation facing the communities and then to discuss the motivations of each of these actors and the different points of pressure available to affect those actors. Once completed, this map can serve as the basis for identifying particular legal or advocacy strategies that might be adopted, and for understanding how these strategies interact with one another, impacting multiple actors.

In our own experience, we have coupled this mapping exercise with a workshop that we run on "how corporations think," as we tease out the motivations of the company actor. We have found that these workshops provide us with an opportunity to explain how we are well positioned to understand how corporations think and behave ... because corporations are often "creatures" of the legal system we call home. Through these exercises, we exchange conceptualizations and narratives with the community, and in the process, we begin constructing a shared narrative, combining elements from each of our experiences. This narrative directly influences the discussion of appropriate strategies and the ends they might serve....

Developing and Signing The Retainer

... The retainer agreement is a contract that articulates the precise nature of the relationship between the lawyer and the client.... We take the position that the retainer can and should be a collaborative undertaking for the lawyer and clients . . . [and] a basis for establishing a relationship to which each is committed and bound. . . .

As a matter of content, in addition to the traditional terms regarding costs and the power of the attorney to act on behalf of his or her clients, at minimum, the retainer agreement should also address the legal strategy that is contemplated by the relationship, and most importantly, the goals of the community in pursuing that legal strategy. The vast majority of retainer agreements that lawyers prepare in anticipation of litigation presume that the ultimate goal of the representation is monetary compensation. This assumption informs a number of the attorney's steps in the development of the legal strategies, and [a]ffects such essential decisions as whether the lawyer recommends that the client accept a settlement offer. In many circumstances, however, monetary compensation may not be the community's primary goal in pursuing a legal strategy. Indeed, legal strategies could serve a number of goals in pursuit of the community's own understanding of justice for example, environmental remediation, an end to a company's operations in a given area, a public apology, a chance to demand justice in a courtroom—and the lawyer can design specific strategies to serve those different goals. . . .

Special Considerations Involved in Working with a Client Community

Recognizing both Individual and Collective Interests

A special consideration that lawyers must confront when working with communities, rather than individuals, affected by human or environmental rights violations, is how to address the special nature of collective harms. The lawyer-client model dictated by Professional Ethics does not ask, or tell us . . . how to advocate for a remedy to rights violations experienced by collectivities. . . .

We propose that the individual-centric lawyer-client model is itself an outgrowth of the American legal imagination that problematically focuses on personal/individual rights—or rights that attach to the individual client—while ignoring common or collective rights that attach to a community. . . .

The myopia of the American legal system and the limitations of the individualized lawyer-client model become obvious when one considers a common situation in our work: the existence of multiple separate communities affected by oil or mineral extraction in a particular zone. . . . [T]he U.S. legal dictates of statutes of limitations, causation, or injury-in-fact, all of which analyze an individual's potential cause of action, may act to limit the lawyer's ability to work with the communities as collectivities, or even to work with several communities at all. . . .

Even when it might be possible to bring a class action in the above scenario—or to bring a claim on behalf of a community as a juridical entity whose interests the lawyer can serve without passing through individuals as representatives—a whole host of questions arise that throw the individual-centric lawyer-client model into disarray. For example, as lawyers working with "class" communities, we must ask whose "interests" are we supposed to be zealously representing. The answer, of course, is the class's interest. But, whose voice is being heard and channeled into the "interests" of the class? . . . [I]n this context, are we often really referring to the "male community" or the "leaders of the community"? Both are wholly inadequate if we purport to represent collective interests.

In many of the communities with which we have worked, it is most often the men, and the men only, who speak "on behalf of" the community or dialogue with the lawyers. This should cause us to question whose narrative is being captured when we tell a "community's" story in a legal document, and whose narrative goes untold. . . .

To fully and honestly confront this dilemma, transnational lawyers will have to divest themselves of any romanticized notion that communities, especially indigenous communities, are not complex, internally diverse, and contradictory. . . .

Assessing Community Positions and Priorities

The transnational collaborative lawyer must seek to represent the interest of the community as a whole, while recognizing that that interest might be complex and internally contradictory. At various times in the representation, the lawyer will have to gauge the position of the community as an entity distinct from its individual members. . . . [W]hile not uncomplicated, the task is usually manageable, as the lawyers defer to the community's existing decision-making structures. . . . We should treat these structures with significant deference, but that does not mean we should not raise questions about participation or take steps to ensure that all voices are heard.

. . . In the indigenous communities where we have worked, for example, consensus-based community decisions were reached in community-wide assemblies at which no women were present. These observations should cause the lawyer to question whether or not the decisions adequately consider and include the opinions of the marginalized voices.

. . . [T]he lawyer may use creative strategies to assess the opinions of the marginalized voices. For example, while one member of the legal team participates in the all-male assembly, another member of the team may assist the women of the community in the preparation of food for the assembly, and in the process, conduct an informal meeting of those women present to cover the same issues being discussed in the assembly. . . . These types of strategies allow the concerns for bias to be tested, and potentially even addressed, without openly disrupting the existing decision-making structures.... [Sometimes,] the lawyer and the community may need to modify the operative structures as part of an honest negotiation....

Working With Community Leaders To Facilitate Interactions With the Community

... When engaging with the community ... it is important for the lawyer to seek out and build collaborative relationships with key leaders within the community. These leaders will become vital allies in the tasks of translating the lawyer's communications with the community, working to organize the community around key steps, and collecting necessary information from the community to guide the work of the lawyer....

Community Participation in the Implementation of Legal Strategies

... Active community involvement not only serves the goal of building the capacity of the community to actively defend itself, but also has the potential to radically improve the quality of the legal strategy being implemented.... The lawyer should approach community engagement with humility and openness to learn from the community. Empowerment, in this respect, can be multi-directional. Unfortunately, given the transnational nature of the legal strategies implemented in this area of advocacy, community participation is often one of the first things that lawyers sacrifice for its practical difficulties....

It is thus incumbent on the lawyer to conduct workshops and trainings, and convene working groups within the community, to ensure that the community is informed, involved, and committed to the strategy being implemented. This process begins with the lawyer's first visits to the community and continues ... through each step of the developing legal struggle....

Resolving the Legal Strategy

... [T]he lawyer must do significant work from the very beginning of her engagement to discuss the precise goals of the community, the potential final outcomes of any legal strategy, and how that final outcome will impact the community in the future.

The lawyer cannot merely assume that economic compensation paid directly to affected individuals is the only, or even principal, goal. The communities that we have worked with that have decided to litigate have often been interested in receiving some combination of injunctive and monetary relief to help the community as a whole respond to the violation. An important part of the injunctive relief that oil-affected communities in the Amazon often seek is a meaningful remediation of their land and water sources and access to clean water....

Conclusion

This paper was motivated by three broad questions which also guided our examination: How can the lawyer-client engagement be more empowering, more collaborative? How can collaboration get us to a shared vision of justice and a joint strategy for getting there? And how can that vision and strategy get us back to collaboration? . . . [R]ather than end this paper with a series of traditional conclusions, we end with a non-comprehensive series of questions that we continue to grapple with, and which we hope will guide further investigations.

- What methodology can be used by the lawyer to safeguard against coercing a community into the adoption of any particular strategy?
- How should the lawyer address requests for support for strategies with which the lawyer does not agree?
- What options and opportunities are available for financing this type of collaborative lawyering to expand the possibilities for the type of representation provided and to limit the monetary considerations influencing the lawyer's engagement? . . .
- How can the norms of professional ethics be criticized and improved to contemplate the possibility of collaborative lawyer-client relationships in a transnational setting (so that one might appreciate and represent collective interests rather than individual interests)?
- How should the lawyer address the common task of determining the position of "the community," and the possibility of differing views within that community, and the possibility that the community position can shift over time?
- What strategies are available to the lawyer for engaging with community ideas that are wholly anti-democratic and/or anti-egalitarian? When is it appropriate to challenge those ideas? How can those ideas be challenged? . . .
- In the context of settlement negotiations, what strategies can be implemented to ensure that the community maintains control of the terms and process of the negotiation? . . .
- What happens to the lawyer-community relationship after a case is finished or settled? Can or should the lawyer remain involved in community affairs, and in what role?

Based in transnational struggles, this excerpt reminds us that systems and struggles know no borders and are not limited to formal law. Hoffman and Vahlsing show that changes in the "mechanics" of advocacy can be empowering or disempowering. Advocates can adopt specific practices to be more helpful than not, practices that depend on multiple kinds of collaboration.

Coalitions are among the most effective and complicated kinds of collaboration. Advocates navigate the messiness of intergroup histories and contemporary conflicts to help build "critical coalitions" based both on interest *and* on principle. Identifying shared interests is important, but shared values—specifically a shared commitment to antisubordination solidarity—provide deeper and more durable moorings. Putting in place deeper moorings requires deeper navigations of complexities rooted in identities, groups, interests, and power.

The materials below survey complex litigation on behalf of Latina and Thai workers kept in the United States in effective enslavement. In 1995, officials discovered the enslavement of undocumented and primarily female Thai garment workers in a Los Angeles suburb. These immigrant workers were imprisoned through economic necessity—exacerbated by chronic wage theft—and by barbed wire, armed guards, and threats to harm them and their families left behind in Thailand. They were paid below minimum wage and made to work and live in horrific conditions. The Thai workers filed a civil lawsuit against the factory operators and the operators' customers—U.S. clothing manufacturers and retailers such as Mervyn's, Montgomery Ward, B.U.M. Equipment, and others.

In the course of that ultimately successful lawsuit, the lawyers, who included Julie Su, were contacted by Latina workers at a second garment sweatshop operated by the same family that enslaved the Thai workers. The Latina workers similarly suffered wage theft and were entrapped in economic servitude, though not physically enslaved. The lawsuit presented the opportunity for coalition-building, as Su describes:

> The discovery of slave labor in the California garment industry had, I feared, set a new standard for how bad things had to be before people would be outraged. We would no longer be horrified by conditions that are standard throughout the garment industry: overcrowded conditions and dark warehouses, endless hours for subminimum wage, constant harassment, and degrading treatment. The reasoning would be, ironically, "at least they weren't held and forced to work as slaves; at least we don't see barbed wire." The [Thai and Latina] workers united in their civil suit send a clear message to garment manufacturers and retailers: this case is not just about slave labor. You are not only responsible for involuntary servitude; this case is also about the hundreds of thousands of garment workers, primarily Latina, laboring in sweatshops throughout the United States.
>
> The struggle the workers are engaged in challenges us and challenges various elements of our society.... The first is a

> challenge the workers issue to the corporate powers in the garment industry. The lawsuit has the potential to transform the way manufacturers and retailers do business. The workers' lawsuit forces us to view abuses such as these not as isolated incidents, but as structural deficiencies. Unless and until corporations are held accountable for exploitation, abuse of workers will continue and sweatshops will remain a shameful reality—the dirty laundry of the multi-billion dollar fashion industry.
>
> The second challenge is to workers themselves and to their advocates. The workers have had to learn that even in this country, nothing is won without a fight, no power is shifted without struggle, and no one is more powerful to stand up for them than they themselves. They—and I—have learned that mere access to the legal system and to lawyers does not ensure that justice will be served.[17]

The combined worker lawsuit that resulted overcame "undeniable obstacles" to the formation of critical coalition:

> The ... case offered a unique opportunity to build a strong coalition between Asians and Latinos, the two major ethnic groups that have been exploited in the garment industry. There were undeniable obstacles in the process. The structure of the industry itself creates division between groups at the bottom of the pyramid. The Asian and Latina women tend to have little understanding of each other's cultural backgrounds. Oftentimes the operators, who are exploitative and abusive, are Asian, and thus many Latina workers view Asians not just as strangers but as enemies and the source of endless subjugation. [Julie] Su explained: "Asians and Latinos suffer similar exploitation in the underworld of American garment-industry sweatshops. They often labor side by side, where their inability to talk to each other, given their language differences and the daily indignities they suffer, make them shy away from contact, at best, and hate each other, at worst."
>
> Ultimately, they realized that by working together they had far more power to demand corporate accountability, to expect just treatment and to affect change than if they worked separately. Su described a transformative moment in the relationship between the Asian and Latina workers: "A Thai worker says in Thai, 'We are so grateful finally to be free [from enslavement and then U.S. immigration detention] so we can stand alongside you and to

---

[17] Julie A. Su, Making The Invisible Visible: The Garment Industry's Dirty Laundry, 1 J. Gender, Race and Just. 405 (1998).

struggle with you, to make better lives for us all,' and her words are translated from Thai into English, then from English into Spanish. At the moment when comprehension washed over the faces of the Latina workers, a light of understanding went on in their eyes, and they began to nod their heads slowly in agreement, and you could feel the depth of that connection."[18]

In the brief excerpt below, activist practitioner and now U.S. Deputy Secretary of Labor Julie Su and critical legal scholar Eric Yamamoto discuss how critical coalitions that came together in that worker lawsuit—based both on interests *and* on principles—must become an intentional practice going forward, a "praxis" that connects collective action to critical knowledge and vice versa.

CRITICAL COALITIONS: THEORY AND PRAXIS
Julie A. Su and Eric K. Yamamoto
in Crossroads, Directions, and a New Critical Race Theory
(Francisco Valdes, Jerome McCristal Culp & Angela P. Harris eds. 2002)

... The coalition forged between the Asian and Latina workers and their Asian American attorney and advocates ... provides a glimpse of the pitfalls, triumphs, and potentially transformative nature of new, albeit difficult, progressive coalitions. ...

... Over time and with persistence, humility, and patience, the Thai and Latina workers and their lawyer developed a sense for how to be critical coalition members. While fighting corporations and legal and economic systems, the workers and Julie learned to analyze oppressive class, race, and political structures, to deal with individual conflicts among coalition members face-to-face, and to struggle jointly to address deeper group-to-group grievances.

... Critical coalitions are real, fragile, and vibrant. They grow out of strategic community attempts to change the material conditions of peoples' lives, often at great risk to community members. They reflect a refusal to limit coalitions to alliances based solely on short-term common interests or to alliances only among activists and civil-rights lawyers. And they compel rethinking of traditional civil-rights approaches to justice. ...

... Critical coalition work is hard, messy, and time-consuming. It is usually underfunded, particularly in comparison with the financial resources of its conservative adversaries. This creates practical survival pressures. In addition, individuals in coalition may find themselves fighting for something of indirect, or long-term, benefit. Can coalitions be sustained beyond members' immediate self-interest? To answer that question, critical coalitional theory needs to address the concrete

---

[18] Penda D. Hair, Louder than Words: Lawyers, Communities and the Struggle for Justice (2001), https://drive.google.com/file/d/1HHjy0qGs_mEbwSMPzF6306VhPiueFhZs/view.

challenges communities face in approaching progressive alliances: Do we build coalitions even if they do not directly advance our present position, even if they are difficult and force us to face new foes, and even if they cannot ensure successful outcomes? The Thai and Latina workers' experience tells us, yes. We build critical coalitions not only because of the enhanced potential for favorable outcomes, but also because the process of coalition-building itself sometimes changes each of us. It is a process, small and large, of building a community. It may contribute to the end of sweatshops, the dismantling of white racism, and the eradication of sexism and homophobia. Or it may not. The process nevertheless allows us to know and define ourselves, our friends, and in turn, our visions of a just society. . . .

Su and Yamamoto conclude that critical coalitions must be a priority for advocates in the field and for the knowledge-producing agendas of the Schools and Approaches supporting work in the field. These critical coalitions are "hard, messy, and time-consuming" to sustain. Critical coalitions directly engage and work through intergroup grievances, and they combine collective interests with antisubordination values to guide organized action. Critical coalitions frequently are underfunded in comparison to organizations of elites and their agents—and even in comparison to efforts focused only on the siloed provision of atomized individual services. Nonetheless, advocates help make bottom-up coalitions "real" and "vibrant" by building networks of solidarity that increase collective capacities for long-term struggle.

NOTES AND QUESTIONS

1. *Focus on Team Building.* Remember, teams are designed and made—they don't just happen. Hoffman and Vahlsing offer examples of how advocates intentionally build teams and relationships with client-groups that take into account differences, potential conflicts, and roles in decision making. Imagine now that you are drafting a team charter for an advocacy project. How might you anticipate the likelihood of conflict so that the team is prepared to use conflict constructively? How will you note and plan to use affirmatively sources of difference—like social identities, backgrounds, expertise, or other relevant factors? How will you prepare to go through the phases of team formation noted in the Weinstein et al. excerpt to ensure success?

2. *Systemic Advocacy Across Borders.* Hoffman and Vahlsing situate their methodology for collaborative lawyering in the context of supporting indigenous communities in South America in their struggles against multinational oil companies. Recall earlier examples of particular struggles, like the Mahoney excerpt in Part II describing the struggle by Kmart workers in North Carolina to build solidarity among Black and white workers to advance a union struggle or the Hing excerpt, also in Part II, describing

multinational work carried out by James Yen to expand literacy and democratic participation in China, the Philippines, and other countries? In light of these readings, what knowledges, values, skills, and attitudes might you need to serve your clients? What role, if any, might U.S.-trained and licensed lawyers play to contribute to a struggle affecting a Global South community such as those this book has described? How is this similar to or different from the role such lawyers might play in a struggle like that Mahoney describes in Greensboro, North Carolina?

3. *Collaboration Versus Cooptation.* Jesse Newmark, who has worked both as a legal services advocate and a city attorney, encourages advocates to consider acting as "intermediaries" creating collaborative processes for community-based groups and local governments to solve complex social problems. Such collaborative or deliberative processes can serve as mechanisms for creative problem solving that overcome barriers of access. The actors involved, almost by definition, have significantly different interests, power, and organizational cultures. If the process fails to take into account identities, groups, interests, and power or elides differences, the "collaboration" may operate as cooptation rather than true collaboration. As Newmark details:

> [C]ollaborations often require compromise—in our case, for instance, to convince more moderate government partners to participate. Worse, partnerships may perversely result in the cooption of [bottom-up groups], who otherwise act as important independent checks on government. As one article explains: collaborators "form bonds that at least soften, and may completely extinguish, the organizational rivalries that otherwise make them mindful of one another's overreaching;" collaborations thus "co-opt[ ] potential watchdogs by making them part of the team responsible for generating solutions."
> . . .
> . . . [O]fficials may therefore only work or continue to work with groups willing to pander to their interests, maximizing the cooptive pressure. . . . Moreover, aid attorneys may be especially susceptible to such cooption at times, . . . when our work depends on city agencies or staff, such as rent boards, building inspectors, or the police. . . .
>
> . . . [Collaborations may also] "simply replicate, and perhaps even exacerbate" existing inequities. . . . [Under-resourced or] underrepresented groups will therefore "continue to be disadvantaged in the distribution of . . . benefits and burdens in devolved collaborative processes." With a false promise of inclusion and cooperation, collaboration may also more effectively legitimate these inequitable outcomes than would litigation or other openly adversarial action.[19]

---

[19] Jesse Newmark, Legal Aid Affairs: Collaborating with Local Governments on the Side, 21 B.U. Pub. Int. L.J. 195, 310–11 (2012).

Drawing on insights from Weinstein et al., Hoffman and Vahlsing, and Su and Yamamoto, can you imagine how you might intentionally plan for and counter some of the risks of cooptation that may arise when advocates, community groups, and local governments aim to collaborate in problem solving?

4. *The Creative Ferment of Critical Coalitions.* Critical coalitions, as Su and Yamamoto noted, are constructed around both shared interests and a shared commitment to antisubordination values. Critical coalitions may be key in avoiding post-victory losses of momentum that many saw after cases like *Brown* or *Obergefell* or after passage of key civil rights legislation. Critical coalitions are likely to generate constant creative ferment and cross-pollination because they are built *across* multiple sorts of differences and are sustained *over* time, beyond immediate aims. Critical disability rights scholar Kaaryn Gustafson describes how "collective energy" can fade after victories and calls for a greater—and actionable—"collective commitment to equality and inclusion" as an antidote:

> The Americans with Disabilities Act has made a dramatic difference for those of us who live with disabilities. But as often happens with collective wins for civil rights, after the law passed, the activist communities, the positive expressions of disabled identity and the collective energy that grew during the fight for the A.D.A. faded. . . .
>
> The post-A.D.A. experiences of Americans with disabilities (among whom blacks are overrepresented) parallel the experiences of people of color after passage of the Civil Rights Act. For members of both groups, implementation of the federal mandates was begrudgingly slow. . . .
>
> . . . [W]e have more work to do—and much of it requires a collective commitment to equality and inclusion.[20]

How might one start to build a critical coalition in which different groups come together to both identify shared goals and develop shared antisubordination solidarity? The story of the founding of a genderqueer/disability coalition, People in Search of Safe and Accessible Restrooms (PISSAR), might be an example of the sort of enlightened opportunism that can spark ongoing, creative, and critical coalitional advocacy:

> PISSAR was formed at the 2003 University of California Student of Color Conference, held at UC-Santa Barbara. During the lunch break on the second day of the conference, meetings for the disability caucus and the transgender caucus were scheduled in adjacent rooms. When only a few people showed up for both meetings, we decided to hold a joint session. One of the members of the disability caucus mentioned plans to assess bathroom accessibility on the campus, wondering if there was a similar interest in mapping gender-neutral bathrooms.

---

[20] Kaaryn Gustafson, More Work Needs to be Done to Prevent Exclusion of the Disabled, N.Y. Times (July 26, 2015), www.nytimes.com/roomfordebate/2015/07/26/the-americans-with-disabilities-act-25-years-later/more-work-needs-to-be-done-to-prevent-exclusion-of-the-disabled.

Everyone in the room suddenly began talking about the possibilities of a genderqueer/disability coalition, and PISSAR was born.[21]

Above are just a few examples of advocates doing the daily work of bottom-up collaborations and critical coalitions. Do they affect your understanding of systemic solutions to systemic problems? After reading and reflecting on these materials, would you approach problem-solving differently? If so, how and why?

CHAPTER RECAP

This chapter described how analytical narratives based on personal or proximate experience—and informed by a dual consciousness of law and justice—can provide a starting point for systemic advocacy projects that see and confront systemic failure by design. But these starting points must lead to various kinds of collaboration, within advocacy teams, with client groups, and in coalitions. These diverse yet focused teams provide the basic hub for collaborations that empower bottom-up advocacy. Teamwork develops projects that aim at amelioration and transformation of systemic injustice—that is, they develop *systemic* advocacy projects for three-layered goals. Ultimately, teams and organized groups can build critical coalitions based both on interests and principles for maximum social impact. As a next step, the following road test chapter, working as a pair with this one, delves more deeply into the kinds of collective planning and action required for effective systemic projects.

---

[21] Simon Chess, Alison Kafer, Jessi Quizar & Mattie Udora Richardson, Calling All Restroom Revolutionaries 217, in That's Revolting!: Queer Strategies for Resisting Assimilation (Mattilda Sycamore ed. 2008), www.crippingvisualculture.files.wordpress.com/2018/09/chess-simone-alison-kafer-jessi-quizar-and-mattie-udora-richardson-e2809ccalling-all-restroom-revolutionaries e2809d.pdf.

CHAPTER 8

ROAD TEST: DESIGNING A SYSTEMIC ADVOCACY PROJECT AROUND SOCIAL PROBLEMS AND THREE-LAYERED GOALS

■ ■ ■

Table of Sections

8.1 Mapping the Process and Components of Project Development
8.2 Rights Are Important for Resistance but Insufficient for Transformative Projects
8.3 Situating International Human Rights in Local Systemic Advocacy
8.4 Three-Layered Goals Must Be Integral to Project Design
8.5 The Politics of Funding Require Multiple Ways and Means
8.6 Advocates Act Despite Risks of Retaliation, Cooptation, and Tokenism
8.7 Restrategizing Solutions for Transformative Access to Justice Projects
8.8 Environmental Justice, Private Profit, and Climate Change

OPENING THOUGHTS

Fight for the things that you care about. But do it in a way that will lead others to join you.

> —**Justice Ruth Bader Ginsburg**

Poverty, wealth, racism, materialism and militarism cannot be changed by aiming at small revisions or modest reforms. If we are going to transform our world, we need lawyers willing to work with others to dismantle and radically restructure our current legally protected systems.

> —**William P. Quigley**, Revolutionary Lawyering: Addressing the Root Causes of Poverty and Wealth, 20 Wash. U. J.L. & Pol'y 101, 103 (2006)

[We] must couple our analysis with active participation in the creation of communities that can wrestle with what it means to actually enact democracy and fairness.

> —**Denise Pacheco and Veronica Nelly Velez**, Maps, Mapmaking, and Critical Pedagogy: Exploring GIS and Maps as a Teaching Tool for Social Change, 8 Seattle J. Soc. Just. 273, 294 (2009)

INTRODUCTION

As we saw in the preceding roadtest of some foundational concepts for systemic advocacy, collaborative professionalism requires unlearning and relearning the law-justice relationship, as well as the advocate's own relationship to law, justice, clients, and problem solving. This follow-up roadtest takes the next step in helping you to apply what you already know (from Parts I and II) to concrete problems in specific contexts. This next practical step, as this chapter elaborates, is building your ideal (yet pragmatic) job and team.

This roadtest, like the previous one, requires you to reflect critically and concretely about the world, and self-critically about yourself, in the specific context of a possible advocacy project. Every year, in fact, students and practitioners do this work of critical reflection, broad research, and collaborative learning as they prepare new projects and apply for funding or fellowships designed to support this kind of advocacy. We have modeled this exercise on those processes intentionally to introduce you to their realistic expectations within the conceptual framework of systemic advocacy for critical justice. Used over time, this exercise helps advocates develop skills they will use repeatedly in organized struggles for equal justice.

Specifically, this chapter asks you to reflect on the double-edged nature of formal legal rights, and how a dual consciousness about rights may affect advocacy projects and actions. Similarly, it asks you to consider other obstacles, including retaliation, cooptation, and tokenism, as well as material and other concerns related to funding, capacity, and sustainability. This work, as we see below, is serious, involving time and effort that may go beyond what you already think you know.

We conclude this roadtest with a review of advocacy based on these concepts in two systemic contexts. The first, within legal culture itself, examines responses to the "gaps" in access to justice in the United States. The second, spanning the planet, examines responses to climate change and environmental justice. As a pair, these concluding examples should help you to imagine the development of creative collaborations and meaningful advocacy projects in any issue area. In conjunction with the prior roadtest chapter, these materials should help you to consolidate and apply—or to road test—key points of systemic problem solving across a variety of concrete contexts.

8.1 MAPPING THE PROCESS AND COMPONENTS OF PROJECT DEVELOPMENT

Designing a "dream" job as an advocacy project is a practical exercise because the motivations and choices that define your project can shape your pathways throughout your career. Most immediately, for many students and graduates, an advocacy project design could begin the development of a successful fellowship application. Fellowship opportunities change year-to-year, but among the main social justice advocacy fellowships offered are those by groups like the Skadden Foundation, Equal Justice Works, Open Society Foundation, Echoing Green, and others that may be university-based or organization-funded.[1] In each instance, as Mia Sussman of Equal Justice Works notes, the process is very competitive and requires significant preparation.[2] Susan Butler Plum, longtime leader of the Skadden Foundation Fellowship program, succinctly explains why these fellowships are coveted by committed new advocates and their sponsoring organizations: "We're funding people's dream jobs."[3] Dreams, then, are serious business for systemic advocates—as well as their clients, organizations, and funders.

Although each fellowship application asks applicants to describe the legal or social "need" that the proposal addresses, that description is developed only at the end of a demanding process of exploring complex social problems and evaluating systemic advocacy responses. Remember that systemic advocacy is not a (law) hammer in search of a (legal need) nail, as it were—a reactive process that applies existing legal tools uncritically, in atomized instances, and in isolation from other tools of social change. One should not expect to complete such a process quickly. Expect to work at it. Expect to rework it before you consider it complete. And never forget that the best fellowship applicants—and best systemic advocates—critically reflect on (1) the role of law in producing and maintaining systemic injustice, (2) its role in ameliorating the short-term or atomized effects of persistent social problems, and (3) its potential role in transforming the legal system and its systemic outcomes for the longer term.

J.J. Rosenbaum, a former Skadden Fellow, has guided, supported, and sponsored many applicants in the leading fellowship programs. She developed innovative advocacy initiatives both as founding legal director

---

[1] More information is available from Public Service Jobs Directory, www.psjd.org/Postgraduate_Fellowships. Information about preparing applications is provided by most law school public interest or career services programs. See, for example, the Post Graduate Fellowships guide, Vanderbilt University, https://law.vanderbilt.edu/public-interest/pifellowships/index.php. See also Equal Justice Works, www.equaljusticeworks.org; Skadden Foundation Fellowships, www.skaddenfellowships.org; Echoing Green, www.echoinggreen.org; Open Society Foundation, www.opensocietyfoundations.org/; Immigrant Justice Corps, www.justicecorps.org; Justice Catalyst Fellowships, www.justicecatalyst.org/about/. Other fellowships fund law graduates to work with specific advocacy groups: Earthjustice, Southern Poverty Law Center, the AFL-CIO, the Service Employees International Union, and others. Some law schools offer funding for their graduates to carry out post-graduate public interest work, as well.

[2] Julianne Hill, For More Good: Law Firms Find Other Ways to Provide Service to Society, ABA J. (Feb. 2017), www.abajournal.com/magazine/article/law_firm_pro_bono_alternatives (remarks of Mia Sussman, director of Equal Justice Works fellowship program).

[3] Susan Butler Plum, Skadden Fellows Share the Impact of the Program After 30 Years, www.skaddenfellowships.org/#section-nav-anchor (audio file).

at the New Orleans Workers' Center for Racial Justice and as director of Global Labor Justice. She connects the process of critical and self-critical reflection required for developing a fellowship application to the work of confronting the Critical Challenge in practice: "It brings people to the hardest edges of where we need structural change.... It encourages fellows to bring challenges that will change the system."[4] In other words, the application process asks how your work will contribute to progress toward Critical Justice in micro and macro, as well as material, legal, and cultural terms.

Systemic advocacy of the sort Rosenbaum describes includes but is not simply law-based advocacy that aims for "big" impact—like doing class actions versus individual cases—or "novel" activities—like working in traditional ways with new communities. That work is necessary but remains within the system's limits and thus aims chiefly for amelioration as the goal. Systemic advocacy aims for transformative, system-changing impact that is deep and real in people's lives—especially those at the bottom in a given context.

The template for advocacy projects that follows is designed to help you take concrete steps toward applying this knowledge. Importantly, it is based on but adapts the applications used by funders and host organizations. These applications may not explicitly call for advocacy that is both ameliorative and transformative, and these applications may not directly seek proposals modeling collaboration with organized client communities and others. But the work supported by these fellowships should demonstrate both: collaborative professionalism drawing on knowledge from and accountable to the bottom and systemic advocacy that aims to make progress toward Critical Justice. The work you do in completing this template is crucial for two reasons: it acquaints you with the process used by funders and employers, and it trains you to acquire and analyze information you are expected to find and use. It is worthwhile to take time and make the effort, now, to understand and begin the process of designing an advocacy project.

1. Design an Advocacy Project from Critical and Self-Critical Reflections

As a starting point only, reflect on your individual background and experience and how they might inform a possible project—consider, if helpful, a brief analytical narrative:

To start, brainstorm a list of possible social problems or issue areas, communities or groups, activities, and places that might interest you. Critically reflect on your experiences, interests, skills, identities, connections, obstacles, and aspirations. Think self-critically about where

---

[4] Id.

you have gained or might gain initial knowledge and whether or how that knowledge is informed by those directly affected by the problems you contemplate addressing. Begin to define your driving interests, your concerns, your areas of curiosity, your commitments—as well as your fears, doubts, gaps in knowledge, and needs. This initial reflection—done prior to research steps described below—aids you to find a starting point in this process.

Frame and describe a systemic problem connected to your background or experience:

All advocates must unlearn and relearn to engage effectively in systemic problem solving. This includes unlearning the idea that "legal needs" are like pebbles—naturally occurring, individual, small obstacles that one finds, picks up, and sets aside—and voilà the path is cleared. Legal needs are more like a pile of rocks found at the bottom of a hill after a rockslide—individual pieces that were part of a collective whole affected by a structural mass failure that sent the whole sliding down the hill to devastation. Although advocates may have to define discrete legal actions or services to "pick up" the stones that already hit bottom, this ameliorative work is framed deliberately and thoughtfully to address the underlying structural forces—to stop the next rock slide by changing the configuration of identities, groups, interests, and power that create these recurrent patterns. Constructing an advocacy project involves defining what pile of rocks you will focus on and how you will "pick them up," as well as how you will work to also reduce or change the dynamics of structural mass failure.

Some examples follow of how one frames and describes a systemic problem. We start with the Equal Justice Works fellowship application:

> [Y]ou will engage directly with the issues and communities you care about the most. *Where would you like to work? What would you like to accomplish, and for whom?* With questions like these in mind, you can tailor your project to suit your interests, passions, and personal and professional goals. . . .
>
> The project should serve disenfranchised individuals, groups, or issues not adequately represented in our legal system. Projects may include direct representation, legal education, legal training, community organizing, transactional work, policy work, litigation, administrative representation, or a combination of these strategies.
>
> Describe the need and community to be served by your project. A geographic area, particular population, or cause can be "needy" by virtue of the number of people affected, the size and nature of the geographic area, the dearth of legal assistance available to the population, and the timeliness or potential impact of the issue. The key is to paint a picture of the particular problem

in the specific community you wish to serve. For example, general statistics stating that foster youth neglect is a nationwide problem are compelling but may not be enough to sell the merits of a youth advocacy project specifically based in San Francisco. A stronger proposal would describe the particular crisis facing foster youth in San Francisco, use data to support that assertion, and weave in client stories to humanize the potential impact.

From the Soros Justice Fellowships 2019 Advocacy Fellowship application focused on criminal justice reform:

> (Project Explanation): Provide a clear, detailed, and focused explanation of the project, including the change you hope to achieve through your work, the need for the project (where appropriate, you should use statistics, stories, or other types of information to explain the need for the project), a description of the people or communities affected by the issue the project seeks to address, and what you propose to do.
>
> We will consider projects that focus on one or more of our broad criminal justice reform goals. . . . However, we don't have a defined list of topics or issues that we'll consider. Instead, we expect applicants themselves to make the case that their projects have the potential to contribute something valuable to a particular issue or in a particular place. In this way, the fellowships are designed to be flexible and open—a space for projects that build effectively on work that has come before, that explore new and creative ways of doing things, that take risks, that offer new insights and perspectives on what we thought we knew, and that teach us about what we don't know but should.
>
> It's our belief that the fellowships can be a useful platform for supporting people whose work experiments and pushes boundaries, challenges convention, elaborates novel ways of approaching deeply entrenched and intractable problems, anticipates emerging issues, or seizes upon particular opportunities in creative ways; and that if these things are done well, people supported through the fellowships can, over time and in conjunction with others, exert some influence on the broader field of criminal justice reform.
>
> Applicants may employ, either alone or in combination, any number of strategies to achieve the goals and objectives set forth in their projects. These strategies include but are not limited to: impact litigation, public education, strategic communications, policy advocacy, coalition-building, grassroots organizing and mobilization, and policy-driven research and analysis.

> Regardless of the strategy employed, all Advocacy Fellowship projects must, during the term of the fellowship itself, actively seek some measure of reform. We generally define "reform" as a change to a policy or practice, whether formalized by law or not, that has a particular effect on individuals, families, or communities. Reform can promote or create good policies or practices, as well as change or lessen the harmful effects of bad ones. Moreover, reform should involve more than simply achieving a specific result for a specific person; instead, groups of people defined by certain characteristics or circumstances should benefit from achieving a particular change.
>
> We recognize that criminal justice reform issues are exceptionally complex and involve an array of interrelated social, economic, political, and historical dynamics. We therefore encourage applications that demonstrate a clear understanding of the intersection of criminal justice issues with the particular needs of low-income communities; communities of color; immigrants; LGBTQ people; women and children; and those otherwise disproportionately affected by harsh or unfair criminal justice policies.

From the Skadden Fellowship 2019 application:

> Describe briefly your proposed public interest project. Please specify what legal rights you will be enforcing and how you think your project will work.

Relate in specific terms your background, experience, and knowledge of the context—problems, sites, histories, and communities—of the advocacy project; if helpful, work from your analytical narrative:

Most fellowship applications require your reflection and articulation of how the proposed project and the affected community connect to your individual background and experiences. Consider this from the Equal Justice Works fellowship application:

> In developing this section, you should show how you have developed the experience that makes you the right person to carry out the project you propose. Do you have the substantive knowledge necessary to pursue the project goals or can you explain how it will be obtained? Do you have experience with the target community, whether by working on the specific issue or in the geographic or cultural community? Do you have a personal relationship with the community to be served? Equal Justice Works also seeks candidates with a demonstrated commitment to public service—whether before, during, or after law school—or an explanation of the factors that prevented the candidate from

pursuing public service activities (e.g., the candidate supported a family throughout school), as well as an indication that the candidate now has a long-term commitment to the public interest.

And from the Soros Justice Fellowships 2019 Advocacy Fellowship application:

> (Personal Experiences, Skills, and Attributes): Explain how, based on your experiences (personal, professional, academic, etc.), skills and attributes, you are the right person to carry out this particular project, as well as how you see this fellowship project fitting into your personal or professional trajectory or future plans.

This section of the template builds on your earlier reflections about your own knowledge, interests, and commitments and subsequent research. Reflect on the ways in which your personal or professional experiences make you uniquely qualified to serve the identified community and undertake the project. Consider whether you already have substantive knowledge and practical experience needed to pursue project goals and assemble the team. If not, how might you obtain that knowledge? This effort may require you to undertake some preliminary research and perhaps to seek out new experiences, as well.

2. Engage the Systemic Social Problem Using Criticality and the Three-Layered Goals of Systemic Advocacy

Necessarily, much of your thinking on an advocacy project at this stage will be preliminary—to be developed more in learning and applying the tools of systemic advocacy and through working collaboratively with your teammates, client-groups, and others. Remember, this exercise is only a starting point for road testing criticality, three-layered goals, and collaboration in advocacy.

Critical research and analysis:

Think about from where (and how) you might obtain "knowledge from the bottom" and relevant specialized expertise to better understand the problem and determine/measure what possible technical solutions your project might achieve.

First goal of systemic advocacy:

Consider generally how your project might make a relevant ameliorative (technical-legal fix) difference in the current context.

Second goal of systemic advocacy:

Consider generally how your project might be designed to build collective power in and among marginalized groups to sustain organized group struggles and achieve transformative (more disruptive, system-changing) impacts over time.

Third goal of systemic advocacy:

Consider generally how your project might be designed to begin shifting the consciousness of group members *and* mainstream understandings of the issue or problem on which your project is focused to build social and cultural support for broader collective remedies or reforms.

3. Focus on Teams and Collaborative Professionalism

Identify the team and needed areas of expertise:

Reflect on which sorts of specialized expertise might be useful in light of everything you know at this point, including relationships with clients, client-groups, and other groups. Consider whether and how a client retainer/representation agreement, a team charter, or other "contract" might define roles and ensure mutual accountability for progress based on principled work.

Identify possible sponsor organizations and survey advocacy organizations and efforts:

You must find an organizational home or, sometimes, create an organizational home. You do want to learn about and build on exciting work happening in your field but not simply duplicate work already occurring in your host organization or elsewhere. Thus, you first aim is to learn about organizations doing work in your community or in your field; gather all the information you can about existing projects and approaches. In that process, you also can identify who might be a potential sponsor organization or perhaps a guide or partner for your project. Host organizations and partner-groups might provide legal supervision or expertise, team members, administrative or financial support, and connections to individuals in the community. It is imperative you know the work of possible sponsor- or partner-organizations and include them in your planning and decision-making process.

The Skadden Fellowship and most other programs require fellows to be sponsored by a host organization committed to project goals with the capacity to provide adequate legal supervision and guidance. Equal Justice Works, similarly, requires each fellow to work for a host organization, consistent with these guidelines of determining proper fit:

- What work, if any, has the organization done to address your proposed project issue? What related issues has the organization tackled?

- How large is the organization? Does it have the capacity to provide support and supervision for your project?

- What is the organization's mission? Are its values and culture aligned with yours?

- What is the organization's theory or practice of change-making? Does the organization primarily provide legal services, organize and engage members in advocacy or direct action, produce research and reports, or do some mix of those? Does the organization focus primarily on governmental abuses of power or on private/corporate abuses of power, and how will that affect your project?

- How are decisions made within the organization? Who is on the board or governing body, are they appointed or elected, and do they include any individuals from communities affected by the problems you plan to address?

- Does the organization have experience hosting fellowships, mentoring recent graduates, and supporting emerging public interest leaders? What have been the experiences of former fellows in building and sustaining projects with this organization and in learning advocacy skills and strategies? Has the organization committed adequate resources to recent fellowship projects? Have fellows tended to leave before the end of fellowship terms, to leave at the conclusion of fellowships, or to stay with the organization?

Plan for funding and other kinds of material resources:

Identify possible sources of funding for your project. Although fellowship programs generally pay the fellow's salary, additional costs often must be raised by the host organization. For example, costs of litigation, professional development, office space, materials, and other expenses often are borne by the host organization. How is your host organization funded—through donations, grants, fees, or dues? Who are key funders? What resource commitments from the host organization might be important for your project's success? Consider project-specific expenses in addition to generic expenses. Consider personnel costs and benefits for yourself and others, as well as costs for needed services or tools, which may include interpretation, translation, community outreach, or administrative support staff.

Identify coalitions:

Identify existing coalitions that include groups sharing your interests and goals. Are those coalitions or groups well established or new? How would you establish connections to them? What can you learn about their theories or practices of social change and primary goals? What sort of role might an advocacy project play in relation to the groups or coalition? Assess specifically what sorts of differences in goals, decision-making structures, memberships, or other features—like social identities—might exist among these coalitions and groups. Reflect on how you would marshal likely or known differences as a "plus" to enhance your teamwork and advocacy and as part of coalition building?[5]

4. Determine the Nature and Measure of "Progress"

Establish metrics for measuring increments of progress over time:

Because not all "change" is progress, advocates must have a clear sense of the progress they intend to achieve (along the three layers of systemic advocacy goals) in measurable ways over time—and using time. Deciding how to gauge ongoing progress is key to making social change. To prepare for the long haul from the outset, as an advocate you should:

a. Identify the particular metrics of social impact most relevant to your project along all three layers of goals: what concrete changes do you want to achieve?

b. Describe the mechanisms of ongoing assessment for progress and reaction: how can you best measure whether or not you are achieving what you want?

c. Determine and record the baseline from which you are starting: what are the current conditions in relationship to your metrics?

d. Establish practices and mechanisms for monitoring and defending every achievement: how can you at this time improve the odds that every gain will stick for the long run?

Create an action plan with specific timelines and work products:

Consider how to create an action plan. You might use the Equal Justice Works fellowship application for guidance on some necessary elements that require your attention and reflection:

> The project proposal should strike a balance between being distinct and realistic without being too narrow or unremarkable. Consider whether the project will make a real difference in the issue area. *Do the proposed strategies make sense? Do the goals and timetable reflect good judgment and realistic assessment of how the project will be accomplished?* Additionally, keep in mind that strategies must make sense in light of your chosen host organization. For instance, if you propose to file a class action lawsuit on behalf of migrant farmworkers, the proposal should demonstrate that your host organization has the resources to litigate class actions, the experience to provide adequate supervision, and a history of or interest in working on farmworker

---

[5] Structures, values, and roles for building coalitions vary widely, and legal actors often do not learn systemically about options nor develop skills for bottom-up, rather than top-down, project management. For information about challenges faced by individuals prepared primarily for private sector business or law in developing community-based coalitions, see Collective Impact Forum, 10 Lessons Learned from Engaging the Business Community in Collective Impact (July 14, 2015), www.collectiveimpactforum.org/tags/collaboration?page=2.

rights. Finally, your strategies must make sense for the community you propose to serve. Research which strategies have already been employed, and determine which successful models have been used elsewhere.

Note that your action plan is something that you will implement and then evaluate. Importantly, that evaluation will include assessing both "outputs" (i.e., key activities) and outcomes (meaningful advances along three-layered goals).

5. Prepare for the Long Haul—A Critical Marathon

Finally, as a last step for this initial exercise, reflect on how your project may have "legs" and viability beyond the completion of this academic semester, fellowship duration, or other limited term. Consider how you might continue to pursue some or all of the project and its goals, themes, or mission in your future work and career. How should these or similar considerations affect your choices now for project design? How can you maximize the sustainability of your project from the get-go to pursue both amelioration and transformation? How can the work you do today provide scaffolding for the work that should and must come tomorrow? Review your work product so far, and then refine or amplify as necessary.

The above template provides only a beginning to build your capacity for project design and implementation. Of course, designing and constructing a serious advocacy project—much less a dream job and dream team—entails time and conceptual, material, and practical tools. And the specifics will always depend on context.

But we all have to start from somewhere, and usually we must start from where we presently stand and what we presently know. The knowledge of systemic injustice to which you—or other individuals—have access because of your experience and the experience of others around you is necessarily incomplete. This limitation applies to everyone, including those at the bottom with personal knowledge of systemic injustice. To supplement direct sources of reflection and knowledge, we introduce concrete "diagnostic" and "strategic" advocacy tools in Part V. For now, this road test Chapter provides a practical starting point for envisioning an advocacy project—or even a career—in systemic advocacy.

NOTES AND QUESTIONS

1. *Fellowship Exercise.* While the above exercise focused on some key U.S. fellowships, a variety of other fellowships are relevant to a budding systemic advocate. Some connect to specific subject areas, such as environmental justice, or to specific locations and communities domestically or globally. Do some quick research relevant to the systemic problem and affected communities in

which you are most interested. If possible, try to locate an additional fellowship opportunity specific to that problem or community. Do the application prompts and materials for that fellowship mirror the issues presented for reflection above? Are there any different prompts you find worthwhile or particularly challenging? How do these alter the way you might plan and execute a systemic advocacy project?

2. *Jobs, Internships, and Careers in Public Interest Advocacy.* Next, try to locate an organization doing work in your issue or geographic area of interest, and review the organization's job or internship listings. You often can find internship or employment opportunities on the organization's website or at the Public Service Jobs Directory or National Legal Aid & Defender Association website.[6] Consider the job or internship descriptions. What sorts of advocacy projects are described? Do they seem to be systemic advocacy projects, as we have discussed above? Why or why not? How might the exercise above help prepare you in exploring and applying for internships or employment in public interest law or in developing pro bono work? What questions might you want to ask of, or research might you do about, potential employers? What skills might you want to highlight in an application? How might your knowledge of criticality, collaborative professionalism, and bottom-up methods aid you in obtaining or carrying out an internship or job in an existing program?

8.2 RIGHTS ARE IMPORTANT FOR RESISTANCE BUT INSUFFICIENT FOR TRANSFORMATIVE PROJECTS

We have noted that law is necessary but not sufficient to overcome the Critical Challenge of using law *for* equal justice. This systemic duality ensures that formal legal rights, though important, are contested and manipulable concepts. Whether in civil rights, marriage equality, reproductive justice, environmental justice, or transgender identity struggles, formal rights can appear to be one thing on paper yet be quite another in practice. Additionally, the formal recognition of rights enables elites to proclaim "problem solved" and lecture bottom-up groups to "get over it;" although words on paper don't change facts on the ground, they can be used to dissipate the momentum of progress. Formal recognition of legal rights can be but a step toward preservation through transformation.

However, the very notion or recognition of rights simultaneously provides a vocabulary to express resistance and demand justice, as critical race scholar Patricia Williams emphasized from a Black perspective:

> While rights may not be ends in themselves, . . . [t]he vocabulary of rights speaks to an establishment that values the guise of stability, and from whom social change for the better must come (whether it is given, taken or smuggled). . . .

---

[6] See www.psjd.org or www.nlada.org/job-board.

For blacks, therefore, the battle is not deconstructing rights. . . .

For blacks, the prospect of attaining full rights under the law has always been a fiercely motivational, almost religious, source of hope. . . .

. . . [R]ights are to law what conscious commitments are to the psyche. This country's worst historical moments have not been attributable to rights-*assertion*, but to a failure of rights-*commitment*. From this perspective . . . the body of private laws epitomized by contract, including slave contracts, is problematic not only because it endows certain parties with rights, but because it denies the object of contract any rights at all. . . .

. . . The fact is that each time there is a movement to confer rights onto some new "entity," the proposal is bound to sound odd or frightening or laughable. This is partly because until the rightless thing receives its rights, we cannot see it as anything but a *thing* for the use of "us"—those who are holding rights at the time.

. . . To say that blacks never fully believed in rights is true; yet it is also true that blacks believed in them so much and so hard that we gave them life where there was none before.[7]

Like law, rights may be important, or not, depending on context. At their best, rights provide a platform for claims to prevent, limit, and repair systemic injustice. In your project design, formal legal rights may or may not be central to your advocacy.

To elaborate, legal scholar Muneer Ahmad next discusses an extreme context—Guantánamo Bay's detention facility for terrorist suspects, located at a U.S. Navy base in Cuba. In this context, even basic procedural rights do not exist: a "rights-free zone." The ability of clients and advocates to meet and strategize has been drastically curtailed and surveilled. Paralyzing the capacity to defend has led to sham proceedings and outcomes. The incarcerated are shrouded in secrecy while held in "indefinite detention" during a perpetual "war on terror." For these reasons, places like Guantánamo most clearly manifest the dehumanization at the heart of systemic injustice.

As legal scholar Steven Bender notes, dehumanization has a long history in the United States and elsewhere. Notably, this historical record includes:

---

[7] Patricia J. Williams, Alchemical Notes: Reconstructing Ideals from Deconstructed Rights, 22 Harv. C.R.-C.L. L. Rev. 401 (1987).

clues that should have been evident to policymakers and participants in such regrettable practices as slavery, lynching, Jim Crow laws, involuntary sterilizations of the mentally infirm, and land theft from and killings of Native Americans in the origins of the United States. The most common predictive thread running through these abhorrent policies and practices is the perceived lesser humanity of those we victimized, such as blacks, Natives, and the mentally disabled.[8]

The common element seen, as Bender notes and Ahmad amplifies in the excerpt below, is "the subhuman construction of the particular group [and] the adverse legal and societal consequences that accompany the dehumanized image."[9] In a contemporary setting like Guantánamo, what is the role and function of legal rights? What is the purpose of claiming rights?

RESISTING GUANTÁNAMO: RIGHTS AT THE BRINK OF DEHUMANIZATION
Muneer I. Ahmad
103 Nw. U.L. Rev. 1683 (2009)

Introduction

When the Supreme Court issued its decision in *Boumediene v. Bush* in June 2008—the latest of several cases regarding the rights of terrorist suspects held at Guantánamo Bay—it was hailed by progressive commentators and human rights advocates as a landmark in rights jurisprudence. Holding that the Guantánamo prisoners possess a constitutional right to challenge the legality of their detention through the writ of habeas corpus, Justice Kennedy reached for appropriately lofty language, stating, "The laws and Constitution are designed to survive, and remain in force, in extraordinary times. Liberty and security can be reconciled, and in our system, they are reconciled within the framework of the law." Indeed, the extension of a constitutional provision to noncitizen wartime prisoners held outside the United States was breathtaking. This was especially so in the face of six years of government insistence that the prisoners at Guantánamo had no rights whatsoever, and could be held indefinitely, even for life, without charge or meaningful opportunity to contest their treatment or detention. The decision was a rebuke to the Executive's claims of outsized authority, and, the Court told us, a reassertion of the supremacy of law. It was a rights moment. Or so it seemed.

For many of us who have represented prisoners at Guantánamo, the promise of *Boumediene* felt eerily familiar. While commentators, the press, and even some critics argued that the Court's holding that the prisoners

---

[8] Steven W. Bender, Mea Culpa: Lessons on Law and Regret From U.S. History 8–9 (2015).
[9] *Id.* at 9.

could challenge the legality of their detention augured the closure of Guantánamo, few prisoners' advocates were holding their breath. In the 2004 case of *Rasul v. Bush*, the Court similarly had held that the prisoners had a right of habeas corpus, and yet, four years on, when *Boumediene* was decided, not a single prisoner had received a meaningful opportunity to contest his detention. Like *Boumediene*, commentators greeted *Rasul* as a game-changing decision, and optimism spread among advocates and prisoners alike that the decision would bring law, and therefore justice, to the seemingly lawless zone of Guantánamo. *Rasul* seemed an important example of transformative legal practice—that is, a fundamental change in power arrangements, brought about through law—but the Executive managed to frustrate that decision for years. . . .

This Article is about the work that rights do, and the work of the lawyers who assert them on their clients' behalf, particularly in the face of inordinate state violence, as is the case with Guantánamo. I write this story of Guantánamo based on my experiences of nearly three years of representing a prisoner there. While commentators can point to an unbroken record of legal victories in Guantánamo cases at the Supreme Court, the view from the prisoners' perspective is quite different, and throws into question the claim of transformative legal practice that the Court cases might otherwise suggest. This is not to say that the lawyering has itself been a failure. Rather, I argue that instead of expecting rights-based legal contest at and around Guantánamo to produce transformative results, we might better understand it as a form of resistance to dehumanization. Such a reframing of the Guantánamo litigation invites comparison with other forms of resistance, and helps explain both the power and the limitations of legal practice in extreme instances of state violence.

When placed in a human rights frame, Guantánamo is often described in terms of the government's denial of rights to the prisoners, but equally important has been the denial of their humanity. Guantánamo has been a project of dehumanization, in the literal sense; it has sought to expel the prisoners—consistently referred to as "terrorists"—from our shared understanding of what it means to be human, so as to permit, if not necessitate, physical and mental treatment (albeit in the context of interrogation) abhorrent to human beings. This has been accomplished through three forms of erasure of the human: cultural erasure through the creation of a terrorist narrative; legal erasure through formalistic legerdemain; and physical erasure through torture.

. . . Arguing Rights in a Rights-Free Zone: Tactics, Strategies, and Theories

. . . That a language of rights may gain us strategic advantage is helpful, but does not itself tell us why this is the case. Are rights merely a vocabulary for considering and structuring power contests as between individuals and as between individuals and the state, or do they operate at some other level?

1. *Rights as Recognition.*—... [R]ights can only be understood in the context in which they arise. Indeed, it was only through the assertion of rights in Omar [Khadr's] military commission proceedings that I began to understand what role they might play for him.

In one of our first hearings in the military commissions, I filed a motion asking the commission to find that the Chief Prosecutor had committed prosecutorial misconduct. On the eve of the commencement of Omar's commission proceedings, the Department of Defense held a press conference at Guantánamo, at which both the prosecution and the defense were invited to speak. I spoke first, and decried the lack of rules of the commission, the admissibility of evidence obtained through torture as well as cruel, inhuman and degrading treatment, and the fact that the government had chosen to prosecute a child for alleged war crimes. I repeated allegations that Omar had been tortured, and called the commission a "sham."

The Chief Prosecutor spoke after me, and as I sat at the back of the auditorium listening, he referred to Omar as "a murderer" and "a terrorist," and expressed his personal belief that Omar was guilty of the charges against him and that Omar would have preferred to spend the recently passed Muslim holiday of Eid with Osama Bin Laden than at Guantánamo. . . .

The following day, I argued that the Chief Prosecutor had violated his ethical obligations, thereby committing prosecutorial misconduct. In particular, I argued that his comments contravened the rules governing extrajudicial pretrial statements. In its opposition, the prosecution argued that I had opened the door to the offending statements by claiming that Omar had been tortured and that the commission was a sham. . . . My doctrinal analysis had failed to persuade the presiding officer that the rules themselves apply a higher standard to prosecutors because of the power disparity inherent in prosecution. The presiding officer likewise appeared to reject my argument that just as the power to prosecute strengthens the hand of the prosecutor, so does the weight of an indictment often compel the defense to speak publicly, and aggressively, on behalf of his client. I had exhausted the caselaw—which, I believe, stood clearly on our side—to no avail.

The argument had shifted, from the prosecution defending its clearly prejudicial comments about Omar, to me defending the right to assert publicly Omar's credible claims of torture, and by implication, his right not to be tortured. And it was in this moment of exasperation and exhaustion that I came to a deeper understanding of rights and the work that they do.

Abandoning doctrine, I argued the absolute necessity of my being able to speak publicly and without recrimination of Omar's torture, for the simple reason that he was not able to do so himself.... Finally, I blurted, "[H]e hasn't had available to him the opportunity to speak, the opportunity to say anything. He could not even give his name, raise his hand, and say, 'I'm here.' " ... We lost the motion.

Only later did I come to understand that by claiming rights, we were demanding recognition: raising one's hand, not waiting to be called on before answering, "I am here." The government had sought to remove Omar and the other prisoners from the ambit of law, and in doing so, from the world. They chose Guantánamo because it was remote, then cloaked it in darkness, refusing to disclose the names or identities of those there, refusing access to the outside world. Legal erasure enabled physical erasure. In this context, rights were not just notional, they were existential.

Here, we might consider the existential assertion of rights as a form of bearing witness. The statement, "I am here," is an insistence upon Omar's legibility in the world, made not by him, but by a lawyer who by virtue of citizenship, professional identity, and the speaking platform afforded by the state, can testify to the world as he sees it, the reality of Omar's human existence, even in the face of a master narrative of his invisibility. The assertion of rights helped to gain Omar recognition not merely as a jurisdictional subject, but as his own self—"I"—a human being.

... [Hannah Arendt noted that] political citizenship, membership in the polity, was fundamental. She defined citizenship as "the right to have rights," by which she meant that one could not gain the benefit of first-order rights, such as a right against deprivation of life or liberty, if one was not, a priori, deemed a member of the political community. Arendt wrote with regard to statelessness. The extraordinary violence done to Jews during World War II, she argued, was possible only through political dispossession. Once Jews were removed from any national polity, they lost that a priori right to have and claim rights. The consent to Jewish membership in the polity having been revoked, so, too, was the Jews' ability to claim rights that flow from membership in a polity....

We see at Guantánamo the inverse of Arendt's formulation of citizenship: no right to have rights. The legal debate at Guantánamo has almost never been about the content of the prisoners' rights, their contours, or their meaning. Rather, time and again, the fundamental question has been whether the prisoners have the right to have rights.... This demand to be heard is exactly what the Guantánamo habeas litigation has been about since its inception in 2002, and it is what the government has resisted and rejected ever since.

2. *Rights as Resistance.*—Habeas corpus, whose history has been explored exhaustively by others, translates as "show me the body," and

captures the communitarian, corporeal, and testimonial dimensions of not just rights claims, but citizenship. For a judge to order the government to produce a defendant for the purposes of considering the legality of his detention is to recognize the defendant's a priori membership in the community. To require that the defendant himself—his corpus—be produced, and not just reasons for his detention proffered, is to acknowledge the physicality and inescapably human experience of an otherwise abstract liberty interest. And to permit the defendant to not only attend his own hearing, but to speak on his own behalf, is to credit his standing as an actor and agent. Taken together, the communitarian, corporeal, and testimonial bespeak a shared concern: human dignity.

It is this human dignity, the human as distinguished from the merely biological, with which Arendt was fundamentally concerned. For Arendt, rights are indispensable to humanity, a protective membrane poised between the state and the individual. What she saw, and Giorgio Agamben has recently revived, is the idea that a confrontation between the state and the individual unmediated by rights reduces the individual to bare life, or naked life, which is life without humanity. It is this unmediated, unmitigated confrontation that both requires and enables the rendering of the human inhuman, animal, and savage. It is this rights-free confrontation that permits torture—the hand of the state encumbered by no law other than the laws of physics. And it is this unmediated confrontation that permits the transmogrification of a child into a terrorist. For Arendt, to be a citizen is to be human, and to be anything else is merely, and barely, life.

. . . [T]he American legal embodiment of citizenship as rights is Dred Scott. While Scott was suing for his freedom from slavery, the case turned upon his citizenship. The Supreme Court found that Scott was not a "citizen of a State," and therefore, under the jurisdictional limits of Article III of the Constitution, could not bring suit in federal court. Thus, the case removed Scott's right even to be heard, by removing him from the polity. Like the Guantánamo prisoners, he had no right to have rights, and the negation of his political citizenship condemned him to the unmitigated violence of slavery.

The denial of habeas to Omar and the other prisoners similarly placed them outside the communitarian consent that rights require. . . .

Stripped of the mediation of rights, Guantánamo reveals the essential and inescapable violence of law. Politics may dictate who is entitled to mediation and what form it will take, but all are subject to the force of the state that, fundamentally, animates law. The demand for rights is a plea to blunt state force, and not to fundamentally reorganize the structure of power.

With this understanding of rights in mind, I return to the litigation strategy we adopted in Omar's case. By invoking rights, we sought recognition of Omar in a polity of significance. In this way, rights hailed Omar into the community, though his admission would depend upon community consent.

As Arendt's analysis suggests, the demand for recognition is tantamount to a claim to humanity. To be human, to rise above biological existence and to secure political and social life, requires rights. And yet, once more, this bid was subject to political forces. No amount of rights-claiming could overcome a political will to deny the prisoners' humanity.

In light of this, our strategy can be understood in a third way: rights as resistance. By this account, the rights claim sought not to escape the violence of the state, but to make that violence more costly to the state. To continue its brutal regime at Guantánamo, the government first would have to do violence to rights; to lay its hands on Omar again, the state would have to crash through his rights claims. Rather than avoid the state's confrontation with the individual, this strategy seeks to expose it. The onus then shifts from the prisoner trying to establish the existence of rights to the state establishing their nonexistence, from the individual establishing harm done to the state justifying its own violence.

In some respects, this strategy has worked. So long as it could avoid any discussion of Guantánamo, as it long attempted to do, the government could enact violence without political cost. But rights claims force the government into discourse in which the violence of the state is put on display and must be justified. The claim of rights itself may interpose a membrane between the state and the individual even if the right itself ultimately is found not to exist.

Thus, our rights-based strategy could be understood as interposing a protective membrane between Omar and the state. In this way, we wanted to mediate, and moderate, the relationship between the state and Omar, with the hope of ultimately transforming the relationship from one of potentate and biological mass to one more recognizable as warden and prisoner. This was a form of resistance to Omar's mistreatment, which required the state either to stop its violence or to engage in it in the public forum of the court. This approach had some success, as the worst of the mistreatment of Omar and the other prisoners stopped once the government was forced to grapple with it in the daylight of federal court. And yet, Omar's other fundamental material conditions—indefinite detention, and trial before a substandard tribunal—remained the same, just as the fundamentals of Guantánamo have remained largely the same for the hundreds of other prisoners.

... [This] rights-based lawyering has performed an essential role of mounting resistance to the unbridled exercise of state violence, essential not because there is nothing else to be done, but because of the opportunities and potentialities that resistance creates. This is consistent with what Scott Cummings has termed "constrained legalism," for it capitalizes on what law can accomplish, even as it recognizes what law cannot.

. . . Resistance Reconsidered: The Hunger-Striking Prisoner and the Rights-Asserting Lawyer

What is the value of resistance, and what is the benefit of conceiving of rights in a resistance frame? To answer this question, I first examine modes of resistance engaged in directly by the prisoners at Guantánamo—in particular, the hunger strike. . . . I argue that the rights-based litigation in which the lawyers engaged may be nothing more—but importantly, nothing less—than a mode of resistance to state violence.

. . . [The] seemingly sweeping victories of *Rasul* and *Boumediene* coexist with Guantánamo's ongoing operation, suggesting that the litigation, while effective, might be insufficient. . . .

. . . Hunger strikes have been a persistent feature of Guantánamo since shortly after the interrogation and detention center opened. . . .

Sami al-Haj is one of the prisoners who remained on hunger strike. A Sudanese journalist for Al Jazeera, al-Haj was held at Guantánamo for six years, on various and shifting charges of terrorist affiliations. On January 7, 2007, the fifth anniversary of his imprisonment at Guantánamo, al-Haj began his hunger strike, which continued for sixteen months—the significance of which can only be appreciated by examining how the government's forced-feeding regime works upon the prisoner's body. . . .

For al-Haj and others who know that day after day their continued hunger strike will bring only more painful forced feedings, the strikes seem more than just a passive form of resistance. . . . By refusing food and water, al-Haj forced the unmediated confrontation between state power and the individual of which Arendt wrote. After more than a year of forced feeding, he knew that the government possessed the means and the will to keep him from dying. . . . [He] was able to mount resistance, to make the exercise of state violence more costly to the state, to ensure that the cost for his captors' degradation of him was their degradation of themselves. . . .

We can understand the radical hunger strike—radical not in its ideology, but in its peaceful invitation to violence—as a rejection of the rights-based strategy. Rather than making recourse to rights to intercede in the conflict between state and individual, the hunger striker seeks to force the confrontation. He understands that while rights may mediate the conflict to the individual's advantage, the mediation also serves the interests of the state, as it both legitimizes and masks the violence of state action. The hunger striker has made a strategic calculation that the invocation of rights at Guantánamo does more work for the government than it does for the prisoner, for it contributes to the perception that the prisoners are subject to legal process, that Guantánamo is governed by law, while the government's ability to maintain its detention regime is little disturbed. Thus, the hunger striker seeks to expose the inherent violence of the state by forcing upon the government an unmediated confrontation.

. . . As lawyers, we sought to use rights to mediate the confrontation of state power and the individual, but prisoners like Sami al-Haj have chosen to use their bodies to force the unmediated confrontation. We thought that rights might transform the realities of Guantánamo, but to date they have not (though *Boumediene*, and President Obama's [2009 executive order seeking but not achieving closure of Guantánamo], suggest they still may). Al-Haj thought that his protest might force his captors to return to their own humanity, and for more than a year it did not (though ultimately he was released). In this way, the rights-based litigation of the lawyers and the hunger strikes of the prisoners may be more alike than they are dissimilar. Far from being transformative, rights, in this context, might do something more modest: to serve as resistance, a way of not necessarily stopping the violence of the state, but of making it more costly. Rights claims can be understood as a domesticated hunger strike, a rhetorical, abstracted, and comparatively unmessy form of engaging state power. For the government to continue its practices at Guantánamo, it must crash through the protective membrane of rights that we assert, just as it must force the feeding tube down Sami al-Haj's throat. Both strategies possess transformative potential, but each may have to settle for being resistance and nothing more, but also nothing less.

My point is not to argue that the prisoners' hunger strikes have been more effective than the lawyers' rights-based litigation, or vice versa, nor do I seek to romanticize hunger strikes or denigrate rights. Rather, I see both strategies pulling in the same direction, and both arising from the same conceptual and material challenge of confronting the violence of state power. . . .

Ahmad's deconstruction of lawless conditions imposed by law in the U.S. compound at Guantánamo demonstrates why law, including formal rights, is both necessary and insufficient—sometimes, even dangerous—to justice. Advocates appreciate and act on the dual consciousness about law that comes with critical knowledge from the bottom. This perspective is perhaps most important in the most extreme circumstances of dehumanization—torture in a rights-free zone.

8.3 SITUATING INTERNATIONAL HUMAN RIGHTS IN LOCAL SYSTEMIC ADVOCACY

As we saw in the history of *Brown* and civil rights struggle in Part I, and now here in the context of Guantánamo, the U.S. historical experience has left many analysts and advocates skeptical of strategies that focus mostly or exclusively on securing new rights on paper. In response, they seek deeper ways of ensuring that lived conditions at the bottom of the social and economic order improve. These efforts include human rights or norms drawn from international law, as well as others drawn from other sources of law. In particular, human rights can be crucial in areas where domestic civil rights do not even exist. Advocates aim to "bring human rights home" by using them as the basis of justice claims or group struggles that they otherwise may not be able to press at all.

Human rights came into existence as an element of international law and relations in the wake of the World War II experience with genocide and the Holocaust. The Allies waged that war as a democratic battle defending freedom against tyranny based on group identity, as represented by the ideology of Aryan supremacy propagated by the Nazi state. In 1946, after the war, the United Nations commissioned a Human Rights Commission to synthesize the "universal" basic rights of all humans based on shared humanity and experience. Led by Eleanor Roosevelt, this group examined traditions, customs, and laws of societies across the planet and through the ages to catalog those that recurred. The result was the Universal Declaration of Human Rights, adopted by the U.N. General Assembly on December 10, 1948.[10]

The Universal Declaration spells out three "generations" of "interdependent and indivisible" international human rights all governments are supposed to respect. The first generation pertains to "civil and political" individual rights most familiar in western societies, like rights to expression, religion, and association. The second generation pertains to "social and economic" individual rights most familiar in socialist cultures and societies, like rights to work, education, and health. The third generation addresses collective rights still unfamiliar in most legal systems, including rights to live in a peaceful and non-toxic environment.

As adopted by the U.N., human rights are not automatically enforceable—they do not form binding law unless enacted as law by specific countries. Instead of treating them as interdependent and indivisible, many countries pick and choose which rights they enact, if any; even then, they frequently attach "reservations" to those enactments designed to limit the domestic enforceability of human rights and render them as weak as

---

[10] For the Universal Declaration text, see www.un.org/en/universal-declaration-human-rights/. For background on its adoption and substance, see Mary Ann Glendon, A World Made New (2001).

possible. And every country is free to interpret the meaning of human rights domestically. Therefore, as with all rights, judicial sabotage or systemic non-enforcement is an ever-present possibility.

From the outset, human rights were critiqued as projections of western, Judeo-Christian values. One reason for this critique is that many non-western peoples or countries were unrepresented in the U.N. at that time, including many under western colonial rule, and therefore unable to participate in the drafting and ratification process. A second reason is that the first generation of rights is focused on those most familiar and favored in western countries. Both of these factual critiques are accurate as a historical matter and continue to be debated.

Nonetheless, since 1948, groups and advocates have used human rights successfully at times as platforms for justice claims and movements. Human rights, like all formal rights, can help to spark and sustain resistance to injustice. They provide a vocabulary for demanding justice and can help resolve persistent social problems. Or not. Like civil rights, they are important yet insufficient. The contextual question for every advocate is how best to incorporate human rights domestically into a larger, three-layered local strategy for lived justice at the bottom. Sometimes, this inquiry will lead to an emphasis on human rights—especially where no similar domestic rights may be asserted or leveraged. Other times, human rights may play a background role. Like law and rights generally, human rights are a tool that systemic advocates use as needed for three-layered progress.

As with every aspect of advocacy project design, the role of rights—both civil and human—should flow from critical knowledge and contextualized analysis. Recognizing these fundamentals, the authors of the following excerpt, all U.S. based clinicians, center human rights advocacy as a transnational, multifaceted practice. While writing from personal and professional experience, they also sharpen their analyses and actions through applied theory—through the contextual application of critical knowledge from the Schools and Approaches, and from bottom-up knowledge gained through ongoing collaboration, research, and reflection.

REDEFINING HUMAN RIGHTS LAWYERING THROUGH THE LENS OF CRITICAL THEORY: LESSONS FOR PEDAGOGY AND PRACTICE

Caroline Bettinger-Lopez, Davida Finger, Meetali Jain, JoNel Newman, Sarah Paoletti & Deborah M. Weissman
18 Geo. J. on Poverty L. & Pol'y 337 (2011)

Introduction

... [H]uman rights clinics have mushroomed across United States law schools, specializing in work ranging from direct representation of asylum seekers in U.S. courts, to international litigation, to project-based advocacy that includes fact-finding visits and production of reports documenting human rights violations throughout the world.... [T]hose human rights clinics have begun to address human rights within the United States, and not just in places beyond our borders. At the same time, domestic poverty law clinics are increasingly looking to human rights norms in framing some of their advocacy, which often takes the forms of direct legal services, community lawyering, and law reform....

What Constitutes Human Rights Work?

Human rights advocacy takes on many different forms, from litigation in domestic and international tribunals, to foreign policy initiatives aimed at advancing particular rights agendas, to grassroots advocacy campaigns aimed at advancing a particular right, on behalf of an individual, a group, or a community....

Human Rights in the International Realm

... The historical events of the mid-twentieth century provided the momentum and the political will for the creation of the United Nations with a governing Charter that has as its centerpiece the protection and promotion of human rights, formally institutionalizing human rights at the international level. But the geopolitics of the post-World War II era and the Cold War dominated by Western political and cultural ideology led to the construction of a human rights regime focused largely on civil and political rights and directed at despotic regimes and countries that refused to espouse democracy and capitalism as the benchmarks of good governance.... [In the meantime], international non-governmental organizations whose core missions were to uphold and promote the human rights principles ... sought to advance human rights globally, sometimes despite the particular foreign policy objectives of the state....

Human Rights in the Domestic Social Justice Realm

... Following the establishment of the United Nations and the adoption of the Universal Declaration on Human Rights after World War II, advocates presented their first petition to the United Nations challenging the domestic treatment of African-Americans, framing their struggles in light of the global fight for freedom. But concerned with how the U.S. campaign for racial equality would play on the world stage, Eleanor Roosevelt herself urged the leaders of the movement to keep their struggle internal to the United States.... Indeed, civil rights activists were severely condemned as "un-American" and "communist" for linking domestic racial oppression with international human rights.... Until recently, U.S. advocates implicitly acquiesced to governmental positions in terms of human rights agendas and strategies.

... Today, however, domestic poverty and social justice advocates in the United States find themselves at a unique historical moment for ... civil rights in the United States [because] these advocates are incorporating with more frequency international human rights norms, language and strategies into their work within the U.S. borders. This increase stems, in part, from international human rights bodies such as the United Nations Human Rights Committee and the Inter-American Commission on Human Rights providing accessible and credible opportunities for advocates to raise human rights ... violations occurring at home. At the same time, U.S. courts are systematically closing the door on civil rights litigants, both through procedural rulings making it more difficult for plaintiffs to access the courts, as well as through a substantive narrowing of the scope of constitutional rights.

... The methodologies employed by domestic social justice advocates include the traditional "rights-based" enforcement methodologies—appeals to international human rights tribunals ... arguing that U.S. courts must interpret U.S. law consistently with international norms, or at a minimum should address international norms for their persuasive value. ...

Domestic advocates are also including human rights strategies that employ "broader activism such as documentation, organizing and education." In fact, some of the most successful recent examples of domestic human rights advocacy have been led by grassroots coalitions and social movements, rather than by lawyers or established legal advocacy organizations. ...

... At the same time, [Critical Legal Studies (CLS)] and other critical legal theoretical movements, emerged, including, but not limited to, critical race theory (CRT), feminist legal theory (FLT), LatCrit theory, and queer theory, among other outsider conceptual developments. These theoretical movements ... and the various schools of jurisprudence with which they are associated might be said to have a common purpose: a "dedication to transforming legal practices to serve the values of equality and social solidarity." ...

Influence of Critical Theory on Domestic Poverty Lawyering

... Beginning in the late 1970s and continuing through the early 1990s, ... [a]s critical theory considered poverty law methods, poverty lawyers struggled to develop both more effective and collaborative models [of] practice[:] ... who is the "client?;" how should the lawyer navigate among "the often diverse interests of clients and class?;" and, ultimately, to whom or what value system does the lawyer owe allegiance? These concerns are echoed in the ethical dilemmas confronting today's human rights practitioners and clinicians ... with a domestic focus. ...

... In the international human rights context, there are also serious risks of reprisal and harm for lawyers in challenging the state's authority or failures, but the primary risks are borne by the people they serve who have no escape route from the community in conflict. While the grave risks underscore the tremendous transformative potential of involvement with global struggles, the dynamic of risk creates natural tensions in the lawyer's professional engagement in international human rights issues and conflicts. . . .

Finally, lawyers working in an international human rights context must . . . reimagine what is possible. "[L]awyering success is not measured by whether a case is won. It is rather measured by such factors as whether the case widens the public imagination about right and wrong, mobilizes political action behind new social arrangements, or pressures those in power to make concessions." This ideal is one that can carry lawyers forward in strategic work for justice.

Creating Transnational Partnerships

Building on the importance of collaborative lawyering as a model . . . and reflecting on the importance of the partnership between human rights lawyers and grassroots social movements, . . . we understand even more the critical importance of building transnational alliances in our work, and where our work requires domestic, subnational alliances. These transnational and subnational links allow us to remain grounded in local realities, and constrain opportunities to subvert the agenda of those most affected by replacing it with our own agendas as "outsiders," or "foreigners." . . . Thinking and acting transnationally thus is one antidote to a myopic view of human rights.

Transnationalism serves multiple purposes. First, it serves to strengthen and render more effective the overall human rights project by amplifying within an international context human rights concerns that may be seen as isolated domestic or local concerns. . . .

Second, the shared language of human rights allows advocates to converse with each other and expand possibilities for their own advocacy. . . .

. . . Additionally, transnational engagement allows movements struggling for recognition within their own contexts another platform for such recognition, through legitimizing their efforts abroad and then carrying that badge of legitimacy home. . . .

. . . [E]mbracing a collaborative lawyering model also allows us lawyers to work alongside other professionals [to analyze dominant systems and understand their outputs]. The identification of the structural determinants of human rights violations may enable an examination of the sources of other social problems . . . [and] contribute to a better understanding of the relationship between institutional and individual behaviors [in] the production of rights violations.

Looking Ahead Towards a New Critical Approach to Human Rights Advocacy: Building a Discourse of Hope

... We have learned it is important in doing this work to: critically examine the utility of a human rights approach on a case-by-case basis; carefully select cases and projects considering the unique positioning of the clinic; situate human rights work within a broader grassroots social movement; identify the distinct roles of different players in a human rights advocacy strategy; broaden a litigation strategy with non-litigation endeavors; include a focus on economic, social and cultural rights; adopt a client-centered approach that uncovers and embraces authentic client narrative; develop a framework for ethics in human rights practice; build transnational alliances and consider transnational dimensions of work; teach socio-historic determinants to highlight advocacy opportunities; engage students in routine practice of self-reflective lawyering, particularly encouraging explorations of power differentials, strategically attempt to map the goals and benchmarks of a human rights campaign; and, anticipate any unintended consequences of human rights work.

... The effort to improve our approach to human rights is not a call to develop a monolithic response nor does it suggest that improvement comes easily. Rather, it acknowledges that a critical approach to general legal principles embedded in human rights law provides an opportunity for "a shared vision of justice [which] can be forged through dialogue; in which questions of value can be posed, the exercise of power challenged and the cold logic of the market subordinated to broader human needs."

Critical theory that encompasses the complex historical determinants of rights violations creates the potential for ... new modes of practice....

This excerpt lays out the fundamentals of human rights advocacy as a form of systemic advocacy. Notice how the same complexities or dilemmas we have encountered under law generally also surface in international, or transnational, contexts and systems, and how the same bottom-up responses are developed and made actionable. But take in the bottom line: human rights, like other tools of the trade, must be used contextually, in tandem with other tools in the critical toolkit, to supplement national or other sources of law both "at home" and abroad.

NOTES AND QUESTIONS

1. *Rights, Human Rights, and You*. Consider the excerpt above in light of the knowledge you possess from Parts I and II of this book. Now consider your own advocacy project(s) and work: do human rights have any role to play? Why or why not?

2. *Systemic Constraints of Human Rights.* The uneasy relationship between human rights and migration illustrates the shortcomings described above. Legal scholar Raquel Aldana has examined why the two largest migrant receiving countries in the Americas—the United States and Canada—have not ratified the United Nation's International Convention on the Protection of Migrant Workers and Members of Their Families (ICMW):

> The ICMW does at least two things that respond directly to the concerns of receiving nations. First, the treaty does not codify a transnational freedom of movement regime. To the contrary, Article 34 imposes a duty on migrant workers to comply with all laws of the receiving nation, while article 35 explicitly states that none of the rights contained in the ICMW should imply any right of the regularization of irregular [undocumented] workers nor should they prejudice in any way international laws' efforts to control the flow of migration. . . . [Thus] there is no . . . right to enter or remain in the territory of another without the sovereign's consent. . . . Second, the ICMW confines itself to the protection of a subgroup of migrants— migrant workers and their families, not all migrants. Further, family members are narrowly defined to include only legal marriages and dependent children (Article 4). . . . [T]he elderly, unaccompanied minors, and others unable to perform work . . . are unlikely to be protected under the ICMW. Such exclusion makes a great deal of sense to receiving nations, which are principally interested in the migration of desirable workers who will contribute to the economy through their labor, spending, and taxes. . . .
>
> Despite the ICMW's respect for key concerns of receiving nations, almost all of the rights contained in the treaty apply to all migrant workers and their family members, irrespective of [their documented] status. This position in the treaty is a significant departure from the wishes of receiving nations who would have wanted to preserve most rights in the treaty exclusively for regular [documented] workers. . . . These rights include, the . . . prohibition against torture and other cruel, inhuman, or degrading treatment or punishment (Article 10); protection against slavery or forced labor . . . (Article 11); freedom of thought and religion (Article 12); freedom of expression (Article 13) . . . and the right to unionize (Article 26).[11]

Aldana reveals the compromises of human rights enactments to leave intact systems that produce violence for some groups—here undocumented immigrants in borderlands and beyond. Even with its sovereignty to enforce its borders and workplaces left intact, the United States has not ratified the ICMW because it includes first generation rights for all workers, including those without documented migration status. What does that failure mean for

---

[11] Raquel Aldana, The Challenge and Potential for a Universal Human Rights Regime to Manage Migration in the Americas, in Compassionate Migration and Regional Policy in the Americas 113, 115–16 (Steven W. Bender and William F. Arrocha eds. 2017).

the salience of human rights in the hands of advocates representing, as an example, the undocumented Thai garment workers that Su and Yamamoto discussed in Chapter 7? Would ICMW adoption, in contrast, serve as a platform to aid the cause of such oppressed migrants? Without the ICMW, what protections and strategies exist for advocates seeking to establish rights for undocumented migrants as against government or private actors—what lessons might you derive from Ahmad's description of torture in the rights-free zone of Guantánamo?

8.4 THREE-LAYERED GOALS MUST BE INTEGRAL TO PROJECT DESIGN

As noted above, legal needs are not randomly scattered pebbles that can be simply picked up and set aside one-by-one, but piles of stones created by the rockslide of systemic failure. Helping individuals—or groups of individuals—with problems is vitally important but must be complemented by other work that reduces the likelihood or volume of rocks set to fall next. Once the traditional idea of atomized, short-term legal need is unlearned, advocates can relearn critical notions of remedies and solutions. This relearning for systemic problem solving and hence systemic advocacy, as we emphasize here, is focused on three layered goals and the resulting collaborative activities of a systemic project.

Consequently, each of the three layers must be integral to project design. As we detail more fully in Part IV, these expanded goals are: (1) winning technical fixes to discrete social problems, (2) building organized group power for sustainable struggle, and (3) shifting consciousness and culture. These goals are designed to help advocates better account for the role of identities, groups, interests, and power in top-down systems and bottom-up struggles. In designing projects, advocates look for ways to make the three overlapping and synergistic.

The first layer goal looks much like traditional advocacy: the aim is to win ameliorative, often court-centered, legal remedies for individual clients or classes or collections of clients. The second layer—group power-building—requires systemic analysis of group domination and systemic solutions based, usually, on existing collective capacities. The third layer aims to shift cultural or mainstream understandings of "the problem" that, in turn, enable expanded solutions aiming for broader social transformations. To advance along all three layers, advocates and community groups evaluate how to combine adjudicatory strategies with democratic strategies to maximize their combined impacts in a particular context.

In this scheme, groups and advocates coordinate actions to create windows of opportunity to expand on past gains (or, when needed, defend them). This offensive-defensive work depends on the capacity or power of a group to flip the system's script—to use for bottom-up gains the sorts of tools elites use to dominate society: organize, organize, organize. In this process, the work of power-building and culture/consciousness-shifting goes hand in-hand.

Shifting consciousness is a personal yet collective process; individuals reflect in ongoing and solitary ways, of course, but established and internalized understandings of social conditions are challenged and changed only collectively. As group members diagnose problems and strategize actions together, they listen to each others' experiences. They take into account identities, groups, interests, and power in ways that upset the illusions of dominant ideologies. And they create new understandings of social realities and how to improve them in principled and accountable ways. Building group membership and building collective critical consciousness occur as groups struggle and reflect, unlearn and relearn, research and analyze, and then act—together and for the long term. This helps explain the power of analytical narration and collective reflection to "diagnose" problems and "strategize" solutions in antisubordination struggles.

For instance, a group with only 100 members that focuses on domestic violence might ask lawyers to represent members seeking restraining orders. But the group also might mobilize its members to engage in court watching—monitoring how domestic violence victims, whether members or not, are treated in hearings. The group and advocates might help individuals file a lawsuit or draft and advocate for changes in court rules or laws, if it detects a pattern of discrimination or failure. At the same time, the group will actively seek to grow as a part of these activities—asking individuals to join the group during and after each court watching session, generating petitions in support of lawsuits or legislative action (and asking petition signers to join), seeking donations to expand resources, or holding a rally and mobilizing beyond their membership base both to pressure decision makers and to expand group membership. In this way, the group both devises strategies that expose patterns of exclusion or failure and uses those strategies to strengthen the group's base and its capacities—its strength. A shared political analysis of problems and solutions is developed and used to guide these activities, and that process creates an internal group dialogue that shifts, builds, and coalesces consciousness among group members.

Consider, in this vein, the way that domestic violence groups have changed mainstream language—insisting that individuals be identified as "survivors" and not stay forever labeled as "victims." This is a consciousness shift that starts with intragroup dialogue and expands to the broader culture through struggle, often including adjudicative and democratic advocacy strategies. This third layer of goals—the consciousness- and culture-shifting goals—helps to "stimulate" new sources of group consciousness and cultural resources for long-term collective struggle: seeing oneself, one's problems, and possible solutions in a different light often is necessary for then acting collectively to achieve those solutions. Advocates aim to define goals—at least tentatively—along all three layers to achieve change that both ameliorates and transforms clients' realities in a specific context. The notion of "three-layered goals" thus provides a field-ready checklist to apply in varied contexts that draws on both historical and current experience.

As an example, below are excerpts from a fellowship application presented by then-law student Nejla Calvo to work with Legal Services of Greater Miami (LSGMI) to address the problems of low-income residents of mobile home parks. Calvo's application built on work started by Kit Rafferty, a community organizer working with mobile home park residents, and of Evian White de Leon, a housing attorney at LSGMI who identified patterns of problems faced by park residents and, later, Miami Homes for All, a policy group focused on affordable housing and youth homelessness. White de Leon found a pattern that individuals would be evicted based on common themes unrelated to the homeowner's payment of rent. In this context, residents—mobile homeowners—would get eviction notices based on false claims that they were squatters because titles had been withheld or had mistakes, based on false or real claims of municipal code violations without any opportunity to address the violations, or based on the sale of the mobile home park to new owners who sought to shut down the entire park. Because mobile home parks tend to be located in valuable urban core areas in Miami and many other cities, many park owners would rather shut down and sell the land than maintain this affordable housing.

In the case of park shut-down, Florida law offers some compensation to homeowners for the cost of moving their house to another location, or when they abandon the house in the park, but park owners do not have to pay if the homeowner is successfully evicted. The advocate's response could include individual representation to defend against the eviction, supporting the homeowners in forming a homeowners' association, or litigation to assert individual or collective legal rights. As White de Leon notes, "Trailer parks offer reasonable prices for those who don't receive public assistance. . . . When we lose a property like that one, we're also losing homes that are rented at affordable prices and are not being replaced."[12] Fighting evictions one-by-one is vital and difficult—but not guaranteed to stop any individual eviction and even less well-calculated to stop mass evictions.

Mobile homeowners' associations, however, have greater leverage through collective legal and extralegal action. An association legally holds

---

[12] Sarah Moreno and Enrique Flor, They Have Fixed Up Their Homes and Paid Them Off. Now, They May Wind Up on the Street, Miami Herald (Apr. 19, 2018), www.miamiherald.com/news/local/community/miami-dade/hialeah/article209275669.html#storylink=cpy.

important rights and can develop critical organizational capacities: the right of first refusal when parks are put up for sale, the ability to contest park-wide rent increases or negotiate over park closures, and the capacity to address code enforcement sweeps that served to justify mass eviction notices. With a homeowners' association, owner payouts might be raised considerably above the statutory minimum. So, White de Leon and Calvo developed a new advocacy project to help residents organize associations in advance of park closure notices to be better prepared to contest evictions, to affect mobile home park owners' sales decisions, and to put residents in a position to buy and manage the parks collectively.

We offer this example so you can see concretely how one might aim to develop a critical and self-critical notion of legal "need"—and thus a responsive advocacy project that begins to address progress along all three layers of goals. As you read the excerpt below, note how Calvo challenges the notion that providing direct services that aim at only the first layer—defending an eviction already underway—is adequate to address the insecurity affecting a community of very low-income individuals. Note the difference between focusing on pebbles alone and on pebbles as part of rockslide systems—on particularities as part of patterns.

The identities of those who make up this mobile home community represent the intersections of several interlocking hierarchies of privilege and subordination—people of color, predominantly women, many disabled, many vulnerable as very old or very young, mostly immigrant and often limited English speakers, many undocumented. Thus, second-layer goals of group power-building are constructed around their shared community role as residents, but that role, in itself, is tied to vulnerabilities based on identity-based subordination. Third-layer goals of consciousness raising and culture shifting are hinted at in relation to community education and mobilization but are perhaps not as easy to make explicit. Note how Calvo draws on her experiences with advocates from community lawyering, one of the advocacy Approaches that helps root advocacy in knowledge from and accountability to the bottom. Think about how your initial conceptualization of a systemic advocacy project will change as you incorporate goals along all three layers—problem-solving, power-building, and culture/consciousness-shifting. Think also about the kinds of critical coalitions your work can help nurture for the longer run.

Nejla Calvo

Fellowship Application Project Description:

Provide legal advocacy, outreach and education to mobile home park residents and form homeowners associations to protect residents' rights and to improve park conditions throughout Miami-Dade County.

Statement of Need:

This project will serve residents in mobile home parks (MHPs) throughout Miami, where there are 61 MHPs and an estimated 50,000 people living in mobile homes. These residents are mostly Latino immigrants and families—including children, the elderly, and disabled—who tend to live in the same park for generations. MHP residents are extremely poor and particularly vulnerable because they have few housing options available to them and if faced with eviction, they would likely end up homeless.

Miami is facing an affordable housing crisis. Subsidized housing is largely unavailable; the public housing waiting list in Miami-Dade County has 60,000 applicants.... Overall rent levels make most unsubsidized housing unaffordable to many. The official "fair market rent" for a two-bedroom unit in Miami is $1,166/month, which far exceeds the average mobile home household's combined income of $974/month. In comparison, the average lot rent of a mobile home is $433/month. Thus, MHPs have become a key source of affordable unsubsidized housing in Miami.

Generally, MHP residents own their trailer and rent the land from the park owner. The dynamic of owning a home, but not the land, gives rise to a type of modern-day feudalism. Park owners have more power in these relationships because residents cannot afford to move elsewhere, they do not want to leave their communities, and their fragile homes would be destroyed by a move. Park owners often exploit their position of power by improperly increasing lot rent, failing to provide adequate park maintenance, engaging in selective code enforcement, and initiating retaliatory evictions.

MHP residents have little legal recourse as individuals. Only collective groups of residents have legal standing to challenge improper rent increases that result in tenants' inability to pay. Fla. Stat. Ch. 723 allows residents to form Homeowners Associations (HOAs) and engage in collective representation to protect residents' rights.

However, without guidance or direct legal assistance, this law is virtually useless. This project will utilize existing legal protections by empowering MHP residents to form HOAs and fight for their rights. Legal advocacy, education, and organizing are proven effective strategies to protect the residents' rights and improve their living standards, but Legal Services of Greater Miami [LSGMI] does not have the resources to provide these services. This project will meet this acute and unmet need.

Project Goal:

At the end of this project period, at least 10 Miami MHPs will have active and effective HOAs that protect a total of approximately 800 residents' rights to affordable, safe, sanitary and habitable housing.

HOAs provide a formal framework for residents to organize and engage in collective advocacy. For example, HOAs provide residents legal standing to challenge improper rent increases and can help to prevent code violations by educating residents. Residents who cannot afford lot rent due to improper increases, or are evicted due to code violations, will likely end up homeless. This project will prevent homelessness and improve the quality of life for MHP residents.

Project Activities:

- Identify all MHPs in Miami and develop criteria to choose 10 parks that demonstrate the most need and capacity to either form an HOA or strengthen an existing HOA.
- Survey residents in those 10 parks to identify legal problems concerning their MHPs.
- Collaborate with volunteers from the University of Miami School of Law (UM Law) and South Florida Voices for Working Families (SFVFWF) to conduct a survey.
- Represent 30 clients from the 10 MHPs in eviction defense.
- Refer cases to pro bono attorneys recruited by the sponsor organization.
- Assist in formation of HOAs in parks where capacity and need are demonstrated.
- Provide transactional legal support to HOAs, i.e. draft articles of incorporation and bylaws.
- Represent HOAs in mediation.
- File lawsuits against park owners to enforce the HOAs' and residents' rights, if necessary.

Education and Training:

- Conduct community education trainings.
- Collaborate with volunteers from UM Law and SFVFWF to conduct trainings in additional MHPs.
- Provide leadership training and advocacy tools to existing HOAs.
- Provide HOA formation training and support to targeted MHPs.
- Create and distribute MHP Resident Rights Handbook.
- Design and administer MHP survey to the residents of 10 parks.
- Collaborate with UM Law and SFVFWF to conduct the survey and analyze the results.

- Compile the results and stories from MHP residents to include in a public report to use in advocacy efforts championing the necessity of MHPs as a form of affordable housing and advocating for greater protections for residents.
- Support HOAs' advocacy for residents: encourage HOAs to meet regularly to discuss park issues, facilitate meetings with park owners, and spread awareness through local media.

This project does not represent a new practice area for LSGMI, whose attorneys are recognized experts in the legal areas to be addressed by the project, including landlord-tenant law, mobile home park advocacy, and community outreach. However, the project involves a different approach to resolving those legal matters in that the goal is to form and empower HOAs to utilize the special legal protections afforded them under Florida law, and to engage in holistic analysis, advocacy, and litigation on other issues related to MHP residents' rights, and other efforts to ensure replicability.

This project offers the opportunity to adapt the community lawyering model to advocate for MHP residents. The community lawyering model supplements grassroots organizing to support lasting change. By empowering HOAs, MHP residents can fight for their right to affordable, safe, sanitary and habitable housing. No other group provides the full range of services, including rights training, litigation and transactional legal support, and eviction defense to MHP residents in Florida. This project would serve as a model, starting in Miami, which could later be utilized in other parks throughout the state.

There are approximately 850,000 mobile homes in Florida, mainly located in MHPs. Residents throughout the state experience similar mistreatment by park owners due to economic disparity and power dynamics. This project aims to change that power dynamic by creating and distributing a MHP Resident Rights Handbook, with instructions on how to form and empower HOAs, to MHP residents and housing organizations statewide.

Florida Legal Services (FLS) and LSGMI have worked together in a few MHPs to provide limited representation to HOAs and individual residents. However, LSGMI has done this only sporadically and it should be expanded and consolidated to provide a comprehensive response to the needs of this vulnerable population. This project will provide advocacy, outreach, training, and litigation to HOAs to proactively prevent legal problems, rather than react to them after they occur. . . .

This model will be institutionalized at LSGMI to better serve more MHP residents even after the project period. FLS has prior experience representing HOAs in litigation protecting their members' rights to use mobile home facilities and fighting rent increases. During my internship at

FLS, I developed general knowledge and expertise in this area, and will continue to do so.

While at FLS, I formed relationships with MHP residents and community leaders in several parks. I currently volunteer with LSGMI to work on MHP issues and have maintained these relationships.

Vecinos Unidos South Florida Mobile Home Council is a grassroots group of homeowners that unites residents of low-income MHPs. I have met with Council members, including Kit Rafferty and Juanita Alvarez, who are willing to share information and volunteer time to help organize HOAs in individual parks. Ms. Alvarez also serves on the LSGMI Board of Directors.

There are other community organizations available that are able to conduct trainings. For example, Neighborhood Housing Services of South Florida (NHSSF) recently conducted a financial literacy training class for MHP residents hosted at LSGMI. Also, the Miami Coalition for the Homeless actively works to prevent homelessness. I will collaborate with NHSSF and the Miami Coalition for the Homeless to carry out rights and leadership trainings for HOAs.

. . . Volunteers will be recruited to assist in conducting MHP resident surveys, initial client interviews, and know-your-rights trainings tailored to the specific need of individual parks. The program will consist of an interview with potential volunteers; informational packets on community lawyering, low-income housing, and MHP issues; and training sessions on how to conduct surveys, client interviews, and know-your-rights trainings. Each volunteer will accompany me on a field day where we visit MHPs to conduct surveys and speak with residents to identify legal issues concerning their tenancies. This project is expected to be ongoing.

I will collaborate with pro bono attorneys by referring and co-counseling cases and will provide training to those attorneys who want to help, but do not have expertise in MHP issues. I will also recruit pro bono attorneys to conduct corporate governance trainings to HOAs. Furthermore, I will provide referrals to legal aid organizations and immigrants' rights organizations for MHP residents with additional legal needs.

The sample project application represents an actual effort to develop a project following many of the steps outlined above. We see how personal knowledge can provide a starting point, which Calvo supplemented by seeking out experience working on issues and with communities directly affected by the housing issues in which she was interested. She also conducted ongoing study and research, gaining knowledge from the Schools and Approaches, as well as from sociology, economics, history, and other disciplines. The sample above shows how advocates work within the constraints of a given setting to design projects that pursue three-layered goals.

8.5 THE POLITICS OF FUNDING REQUIRE MULTIPLE WAYS AND MEANS

No site of practice—whether for-profit or nonprofit—is exempt from constraints created by the blindfolds, handcuffs, and hierarchies that pervade the legal industry, including the politics of funding. Funding is a predicate for sustainable collective action. No advocate is immune to the need for, and thus the politics of, funding. Every project design must account for funding and sustainability. As elites know, funding can provide advantage. In advocacy, funding generally comes from overlapping sources: attorney's fees, public monies, membership dues, donors, philanthropic grants, or some combination. All come with strings that shape—or misshape—advocacy possibilities.

Large law firms are explicit in adopting professional norms and hierarchies that prioritize service to elites, including financial incentives and monitoring that control legal actors' time down to six-minute increments. Small law firms serve low-to-moderate-income clients in ways that should be more highly valorized, as noted by Susan Carle in Part II, but face the constraints of competition, time, and limited resources. Both large and small for-profit firms rely mostly on fees for their funding and conduct themselves accordingly. Government lawyers also face constraints—not only because their roles may require the administration or enforcement of laws that limit as much as advance justice but also because of changes in political oversight, myriad rules and regulations, and uncertain resources. Institutional norms and practices, personal profits or ambitions, and other considerations may guide lawyers in these varied sites of practice.

Nonprofit sites of practice may claim to be largely free of constraints. But nonprofits face constraints from funders on the type of work they do, like for-profit firms hired by clients for particular work, and on goals, roles, and institutional rules, as with public institutions. Nonprofits are constrained by professional, material, and ideological carrots and sticks, which can blindfold and handcuff day-to-day decision-making; in addition to maximizing resources and minimizing "strings," advocates also must "follow the money" to understand influence and power in that context.[13]

---

[13] Many groups use the "follow the money" mantra literally to name projects focused on tracking money trails, relationships, and influence in a wide array of arenas. For example, the Follow the Money handbook was created by the Center for Responsive Politics on its Open Secrets website, "to produce and disseminate peerless data and analysis on money in politics to inform and engage Americans, champion transparency, and expose disproportionate or undue influence on public policy," www.opensecrets.org/about/. Follow the Money to Justice is a project of the Inclusive

Showcasing the general point, in early 2020, as the coronavirus pandemic and #BlackLivesMatter protests gained worldwide attention, longstanding patterns in philanthropy were exposed as serving to buttress, rather than change, the status quo of power and privilege. As a result, the ever-present nature of inadequate funding and funding constraints have been challenged recently on several fronts, some specific to advocacy work and others relevant to the nonprofit sector as a whole.

Critics have noted that equality-focused work in all nonprofits is dramatically underfunded. Candid (formerly Foundation Center and Guidestar), for example, noted that only 0.6% of major grants to all nonprofits in 2016 addressed racial equity for women of color.[14] Only 0.2% of foundation grants in 2015 went to LGBTQ+ programs, according to The Nonprofit Quarterly.[15] Funding for Native American organizations and causes fell in recent years, with only .23% of philanthropic dollars given to Native-led organizations, although a slight uptick occurred after the beginning of the coronavirus pandemic.[16] Similarly, although Latinx individuals made up 16% of the U.S. population in 2011, only 1% of total foundation funding was directed toward programs to benefit Latinx communities; that proportion has been growing at only a slow pace since then.[17] Only 1.2% of all million-dollar-plus individual donations in 2018

Development International, providing a resource to "help you follow the money to identify and analyze companies, investors and other actors behind [development] projects. It also explains how to collect evidence and develop tailored advocacy strategies to hold these actors accountable and defend land, housing and resource rights," www.followingthemoney.org. The Autistic Self Advocacy Network has produced Follow the Money: The U.S. Budget and You, "a plain language toolkit" that explains key aspects of the federal budget, taxes, the budget process, and means by which advocates and grassroots activists in the autistic community can influence the budget, www.autisticadvocacy.org/policy/toolkits/budget/. Tracking the influence of money on courts also has emerged as a key endeavor. See Alicia Bannon, Cathleen Lisk, and Peter Hardin, Who Pays for Judicial Races, Brennan Center for Justice (2019), www.brennancenter.org/sites/default/files/2019-08/Report_New_Politics_of_Judicial_Elections_1516.pdf; Alicia Bannon, The Rise of Dark Money is a Threat to Judicial Independence, ABA J. (July 5, 2018), www.abajournal.com/news/article/the_rise_of_dark_money_is_a_threat_to_judicial_independence.

[14] Women of Color Pursue Change Strategies with Limited Resources, Candid: Philanthropy News Digest (July 2, 2020) (citing Ms. Foundation for Women and Strength in Numbers Consulting Group that found the total to be even lower at 0.5%), www.philanthropynewsdigest.org/news/women-of-color-pursue-change-strategies-with-limited-resources. See also Rinku Sen and Lori Villarosa, Grantmaking with a Racial Justice Lens: A Practical Guide, Philanthropic Initiative for Racial Equity (2018), www.racialequity.org/grantmaking-with-a-racial-justice-lens/.

[15] John Brothers, Report: LGBT Nonprofits See Increase in Philanthropic Funding, Nonprofit Quarterly (Jan. 6, 2015) (highlights a report from Funders for LGBTQ Issues that shows that LGBTQ causes receive a minuscule amount of overall funding despite a substantial increase in recent years), www.nonprofitquarterly.org/report-lgbt-organizations-see-increase-in-funding/.

[16] We Need to Change How We Think: Perspectives on Philanthropy's Underfunding of Native Communities and Causes, First Nations Development Institute (2018) (explaining that Native people make up 2% of the population and have disproportionate levels of economic need, but receive only .23% of philanthropic grants), www.firstnations.org/publications/we-need-to-change-how-we-think-perspectives-on-philanthropys-underfunding-of-native-communities-and-causes/; Investing in Native Communities, https://nativephilanthropy.candid.org.

[17] Seema Shah, Reina Mukai & Grace McAllister, Foundation Funding for Hispanics/Latinos in the United States and for Latin America, The Foundation Center in collaboration with Hispanics in Philanthropy (2011), www.foundationcenter.issuelab.org/resources/12839/12839.pdf.

was directed toward gender equality, as noted by the Women's Philanthropy Institute.[18]

Many funders, moreover, use a color- or identity-blind framework for understanding social problems and thus fail to fund the strategies and teams needed to effectively address those problems. As noted in a 2020 report by Echoing Green, an advocacy fellowship funder, and the Bridgespan Group, a consulting group advising philanthropists, those funders who endorse color- and identity-blind approaches fundamentally misunderstand social problems. These funders often see material problems—"needs"—as unrelated to social identities—race in particular—and equality concerns; as a result, they do not support leaders, organizations, coalitions, strategies, and solutions rooted in and accountable to marginalized communities.[19]

Instead of strategic and collaborative initiatives, these funders create "strategic silos." They support direct services provided in isolation from—and instead of—sustained, cross-disciplinary and bottom-up collaborations among advocates, clients, organizers, human services providers, and others. The National Committee for Responsive Philanthropy (NCRP) identifies four sorts of program work important in social justice funding: *direct social or legal services* to address immediate, usually individual, needs; *community organizing* to build collective voice; *legal advocacy* to shift policy decisions;[20] and *civic engagement* to increase public participation. Only 12% of recent foundation grants purporting to advance equality supported anything other than direct social and legal services, dramatically limiting multi-strategy collaborations that allow for the coordinated pursuit of ameliorative *and* transformative goals.[21] But investments in strategic collaborations, especially sustained strategic collaborations, pay off—reaping $115 in benefits for every $1 spent, according to NCRP.[22] And they are, as we have seen, the only way to begin to address longstanding patterns of identity-based castes.

See also Latinx Funders, "an ongoing research project documenting the landscape of foundation funding in the Latinx community and track[ing] changes in its scale and priorities," www.latinxfunders.org.

[18] Giving By and For Women, IUPUI Women's Philanthropy Institute 6 (2018), https://scholarworks.iupui.edu/bitstream/handle/1805/15117/giving-by-and-for-women-update180131.pdf.

[19] Cheryl Dorsey, Jeff Bradach, and Peter Kim, Racial Equity and Philanthropy: Disparities in Funding for Leaders of Color Leave Impact on the Table, Echoing Green and The Bridgespan Group 3 (2020).

[20] Lisa Ranghelli, Leveraging Limited Dollars: How Grantmakers Achieve Tangible Results by Funding Policy and Community Engagement 1, The National Committee for Responsive Philanthropy (2012), www.ncrp.org/wp-content/uploads/2016/11/LeveragingLimitedDollars.pdf.

[21] *Id.* at 1.

[22] *Id.* See also Dimple Abichandani, Pandemic Philanthropy: Moving from Relief to Power, Inside Philanthropy (May 7, 2020) (encouraging funders to shift funding to collaborative power-building strategies in order to reimagine and rebuild the social contract after recognizing that the pandemic had disproportionately affected "black communities, immigrant communities, the

These failures—not centering identity-based, equality-focused work and not supporting multi-strategy, bottom-up collaborations—are compounded by the failure to invest in leaders and organizations from marginalized communities. Nonprofit organizations led by Black individuals receive less funding—even on issues related to race—than those led by white individuals, and a lower proportion of funding takes the forms of unrestricted support as opposed to highly-constrained project grants: "Among groups focused on improving life outcomes of black men, revenue at organizations with black leaders was 45 percent lower than at groups led by whites. . . . [T]he unrestricted assets of groups with leaders of color were 91 percent smaller than those with white leaders."[23] Similar reluctance to trust immigrant-led organizations pervades philanthropy, as "senior nonprofit leaders born outside the U.S. were significantly more likely [than U.S.-born leaders] to say that their ability to succeed was hindered by funders that took a 'wait-and-see' approach to providing grant funding following their ascension to leadership."[24]

Decision-making roles are hoarded by the relatively—or extremely—privileged in both funding and other nonprofit organizations. In recent years, for example, only 16% of nonprofit board members are people of color, and virtually none are low-income.[25] Well-educated and well-heeled individuals control most foundations and many other nonprofits at the staff and board levels. In fact, wealth diversity among board members is not even a diversity goal for most foundations and nonprofits. Pablo Eisenberg of the Georgetown Public Policy Institute noted that "foundation boards shouldn't be filled with just wealthy people" and called the track record on class diversity "dismal," lamenting the loss of valuable bottom-up perspectives.[26] The representation of Latinx individuals in foundation leadership was 2.3% in 2013 and 4% in nonprofit staff leadership in 2017, both far lower than their now 17% share of the population.[27] Gender minorities, disabled individuals, and youth often are left out of leadership roles. A study by RespectAbility found that only 11% of organizations

---

disabled, people in prison, and workers who are paid low wages, and amplifying all the inequities that existed before the virus").

[23] Jim Rendon, Nonprofits Led by People of Color Win Less Grant Money with More Strings, The Chronicle of Philanthropy (May 7, 2020) (explaining the findings of Racial Equity and Philanthropy study by Dorsey et al.).

[24] Judy Lubin, Fred Clavel & Elise Goldstein, Talent Justice Report: Investing in Equity in the Nonprofit Workforce, Fund the People and Center for Urban and Racial Equity 7 (2019), www.fundthepeople.org/toolkit/wp-content/uploads/2019/05/Talent-Justice-Report.pdf.

[25] Larry Dansinger, Class Diversity Improves Your Nonprofit Board, Class Action (Sept. 21, 2017), www.classism.org/lessening-class-divide-among-nonprofit-boards-directors/.

[26] Pablo Eisenberg, Foundation Boards Shouldn't Be Filled with Just Wealthy People, The Chronicle of Philanthropy (June 1, 2011), www.philanthropy.com/article/Foundation-Boards-Shouldnt-Be/158285.

[27] Grace Sato and Seema Shah, Latino Leadership: Foundation Boards, The Foundation Center in Collaboration with Hispanics in Philanthropy (2015), www.foundationcenter.issuelab.org/resources/25147/25147.pdf?_ga=2.68133266.2062179539.1596134612-179427252.1596134612.

without diversity and inclusion policies have people with disabilities in staff leadership and only 17% have people with disabilities on boards. Those numbers increase somewhat—going from miserable to poor—when an express diversity policy is in place, with 22% and 26% of organizations including people with disabilities in professional leadership and board representation, respectively.[28]

Funders also replicate societal inequalities in devaluing occupations in which women predominate. Individuals identifying as women make up roughly three-quarters of all nonprofit employees. "That equates to low wages, increased emotional labor, and the highest paying jobs historically going to men, even though they are the minority in the field."[29] Women of color are most deeply affected because they are concentrated in lower-paying jobs and face significant barriers to advancement.[30] Women lawyers, for example, are "more than twice as likely as men to work in the lower-paid public interest fields."[31] Median salaries in public interest law are roughly half those in private practice (although private practice itself follows a bimodal pattern with a large gap between small- and large-firm salaries).[32] African American, Latinx, and Native American attorneys are paid less than Anglo counterparts in public interest settings, as in private firms and government agencies.[33] The "nonprofit discount" in wages and benefits is explained as the trade-off between "doing good" and "doing well," but both occupational segregation and discrimination contribute to devaluing nonprofit work.

Nonprofit managers and funders both play roles in devaluing work and workers: "84% of nonprofit and foundation respondents stated that competitive salaries and benefits are needed for entry-level nonprofit jobs. Yet only 41% of foundations provide funding to grantees for these purposes. Only a slightly higher percentage (46%) of nonprofits reported investing in competitive salaries and benefits."[34] These problems produce barriers to entry for many newer or younger workers and barriers to advancement and economic stability for experienced staff. Increasingly, staff members in legal services, issue advocacy organizations, think tanks, and other

---

[28] Disability in Philanthropy and Nonprofits: A Study on Inclusion and Exclusion of the 1-in-5 People Who Live with a Disability and What You Can Do to Make Things Better, Respectability 2 (2019) (showing that representation on staff and boards increases in organizations with diversity and inclusion policies and even more in organizations that already have people with disabilities in leadership roles), www.respectability.org/inclusive-philanthropy/.

[29] Lubin et al. Talent Justice Report, at 7.

[30] Ofronama Biu, Race to Lead: Women of Color in the Nonprofit Sector, Building Movement Project (2019), www.racetolead.org/women-of-color/.

[31] Legal Professions: The Status of Women and Men, Center for Research on Gender in the Professions, University of California-San Diego (2013) (citing a 2010 article on findings on salaries for public interest attorneys from the National Association for Law Placement, https://crg-stemm.ucsd.edu/_files/articles/GenderinLegalProfessionsCaseStudy.pdf).

[32] Id.

[33] Id.

[34] Lubin et al., Talent Justice Report, at 6.

nonprofits have tried to form unions, but they often face the further indignity of intense employer opposition when they seek to exercise the fundamental right to organize.[35]

Even funders have joined the chorus of critique of these overt failures, although the jury is still out, so to speak, on whether patterns and constraints of funding will change significantly. Darren Walker, president of the Ford Foundation, is one of the philanthropy leaders who have talked about shifting funders, including Ford, away from a color-blind approach and toward a bottom-up approach emphasizing racial equality. Walker explained, "Listening, learning, and lifting up voices who are most proximate and most essential to unlocking solutions is critical to the type of change making that we seek. This requires examining what gets in the way of trust—deeply rooted cultural norms and structures, including racial, gender, ethnic, class, sexual orientation, and disability biases."[36]

These general critiques of funders and funding patterns are mirrored in top-down philanthropy specifically for legal service providers and issue advocacy organizations. Turning to the legal subsector of the nonprofit industry, legal scholars Catherine Albiston and Laura Beth Nielsen analyze public interest law organizations (PILOs) with these concerns in mind. PILOs are "organizations in the voluntary sector whose activities (1) seek to produce significant benefits for those who are external to the organization's participants, and (2) involve at least one adjudicatory strategy."[37] Legal services organizations, a type of PILO, are funded primarily by the Legal Services Corporation (LSC), a federal agency, and state bar associations, largely through interest collected on lawyer trust accounts (IOLTA) funds. Both LSC and IOLTA grants are dedicated to supporting legal services for the poor, and both have been subjects of controversy and change. Legal services organizations also receive support

---

[35] Eli Rosenberg, Workers Are Forming Unions at Nonprofits and Think Tanks. Their Bosses Aren't Always Happy, Wash. Post (Feb. 4, 2020) (describing union organizing campaigns at the Center for Public Policy Priorities, which proceeded without management opposition, as well as unfair labor complaints at the National Center for Transgender Equality and other groups), www.washingtonpost.com/business/2020/02/04/workers-are-forming-unions-nonprofits-thinktanks-their-bosses-arent-always-happy/.

[36] Dorsey et al., Racial Equity and Philanthropy, at 10. Note that Darren Walker and the Ford Foundation also have faced critique for statements and actions that undermine advocacy efforts toward decarceration. See No New Jails NYC: Ford Foundation President, Darren Walker Requests a Meeting (Sept. 27, 2019) (criticizing a statement by Walker calling for "nuance and complexity" as opposed to "extreme opposition" in reference to a struggle to close Rikers Island jail, specifically, and in social justice work, generally), www.medium.com/@nonewjails.ny/no-new-jails-nyc-ford-foundation-president-darren-walker-requests-a-meeting-4042117f29d3; Keeanga Yamahtta Taylor, Five Years Ahead, Do Black Lives Matter?, The Wire (Oct. 6, 2019) (arguing that Walker's position in the Rikers Island fight represents both the Ford Foundation's and other funders' efforts to "redirect or reshape insurgency and disruptions toward more reasonable means" such as aspirational policy platforms that distract from the building of accountable social movements), www.thewire.in/world/five-years-ahead-do-black-lives-matter.

[37] Catherine R. Albiston and Laura Beth Nielsen, Funding the Cause: How Public Interest Law Organizations Fund Their Activities and Why It Matters for Social Change, 39 Law & Soc. Inquiry 62, 71 (2014).

from other sources—philanthropic foundations, individual and corporate donors, membership dues, fees for services, non-LSC government grants, legal fellowship programs, bar foundations, and others. Albiston and Nielsen found that these and similar funding sources create and constrain opportunities:

> There is reason to believe that the funding structures of PILOs affect not only their viability but also their strategies, independence, and susceptibility to political intimidation. For example, political interests that opposed public interest representation successfully championed legislative limits on the legal strategies of federally funded organizations, and these limitations substantially curtailed representation for individuals who rely on public legal assistance. Similarly, PILOs supported by the private bar faced repercussions when they challenged the private bar's clients in court. Thus, funding models affect the independence and strategies of PILOs, as well as their sustainability.[38]

Legal services organizations are limited by funders who place explicit constraints on their activities. Any funding that comes from government sources, as Albiston and Nielsen note, is subject to constraints or outright attack if advocacy efforts are perceived to threaten elite interests. The Tennessee Justice Center (TJC) is a case in point. TJC was founded to be an independent healthcare advocacy group, free of federal funding constraints, after legislative limits were imposed on LSC-funded groups. TJC received much of its money from the Tennessee Bar Association. But TJC's advocacy to protect TennCare, the state's Medicaid program, brought it into conflict with the former healthcare executive serving as governor, Democrat Phil Bredesen, and the corporate interests he championed. The governor sought to cut coverage from 170,000 financially and medically needy people—at the time perhaps "the largest single drop in the ranks of health-insured Americans ever." The governor's office sought first to stall and coopt TJC's work and then, when that failed, tried to cut off TJC's funding:

> [Bredesen showed] rank intolerance for dissent by public health advocates.... [W]e assumed that Bredesen was negotiating public policy in good faith with advocates such as the Tennessee Justice Center, who were actually standing up for the poor and the sick. Yet it was Bredesen's own finance commissioner ... who betrayed the fiction of it all when he wrote "To hell with TJC" in an email to TennCare's director, adding a not-so-veiled threat:

---

[38] *Id.* at 63.

"We need to significantly lower their ability to stop us by draining their resources."[39]

As the TJC example highlights, elites suppress opposition—they aim to "lower" the capacity of adversaries "by draining their resources." Simultaneously, they seek to deny new resources to "starve" them through defunding. This top-down effort to drain *and* to starve organized bottoms includes *all* funding sources.

For instance, funding for groups like TJC received through state bar associations often comes from IOLTA accounts. This funding thus increases and decreases in response to interest rates and economic fluctuations rather than community needs. IOLTA funding has been used to support both LSC-funded groups and their non-LSC-funded counterparts, groups like TJC that aim to fill the gaps left by LSC restrictions. Existing in every state, IOLTA programs "generate funds from interest on lawyers' trust accounts to support legal aid, legal education for the public, and other programs designed to improve the quality of justice."[40] IOLTA funding is based on both the total quantity of funds that lawyers deposit in banks on behalf of clients and on prevailing interest rates. Since 2007, IOLTA funding has fallen dramatically. According to the American Bar Association, "IOLTA income in 2011 plummeted to $93.2 million, a 75 percent free fall from the 2007 peak," resulting in layoffs and program cutbacks across the country.[41] As noted in a 2012 report from the Boston Bar Foundation (BBF), "[i]n a four-year period, the BBF has suffered a loss of more than half of its IOLTA monies, has exhausted its IOLTA reserves, and, therefore, has some very tough choices to make during the next grants cycle."[42] The dramatic fall perhaps represents a fundamental flaw in IOLTA program rules:

> By making IOLTA interest rates dependent on rates set by the Federal Reserve, states have guaranteed that income from IOLTA programs will, at best, be unpredictable. At worst, IOLTA revenues will be depressed during sustained periods of economic difficulty—periods when the need for legal aid funding tends to increase [but interest rates decrease to stimulate economic growth].[43]

---

[39] Bruce Barry, As Governor, Phil Bredesen Got Absurdly High Marks for C-Grade Work, The Nashville Scene (Jan. 6, 2011), www.nashvillescene.com/news/pith-in-the-wind/article/13036842/as-governor-phil-bredesen-got-absurdly-high-marks-for-cgrade-work.

[40] Albiston and Nielsen, Funding the Cause, at 67.

[41] Robert J. Derocher, The IOLTA Crash: Fallout for Foundations, 37 ABA Bar Leader (Sept.–Oct. 2012).

[42] Elizabeth A. Ritvo and Joel B. Sherman, Grantmaking in a Down Economy: Thoughts from the Boston Bar Foundation, Boston B.J. 7, 8 (Winter 2012).

[43] Andrew Arthur, A Good Rule, Poorly Written: How the Financial Crisis Highlighted the Inadequacy of IOLTA Rate Rules, 64 Cath. U. L. Rev. 729, 749 (2015) (arguing that state programs

Similarly, both IOLTA fees and state appropriations from court filing fees declined during the coronavirus epidemic, diminishing legal aid programs' ability to address pressing issues like evictions, domestic violence, healthcare and other consumer debt, unemployment denials, and government relief entitlements.[44] Despite—or because of—the disempowering precarity of this arrangement, the system remains in place. But critiques go even further to expose the systemic nature of handcuffs and blindfolds.

The "nonprofit industrial complex" (NPIC) refers to the development of the nonprofit sector as a part of the neoliberal capitalist economic system discussed in Part II. This sector includes many institutions organized formally as nonprofit entities to combat poverty, inequality, or other social problems. Many, however, may undermine rather than advance challenges to the power and economic agenda of ruling elites—whether intentionally or inadvertently.[45] A groundbreaking—and controversial—book, The Revolution Will Not Be Funded, outlined a fundamental critique:

> The ruling class created the non-profit legal status primarily to establish foundations so they could park their wealth where it was protected from income and estate taxes. The foundations allowed them to retain control over their family wealth. The trade-off they made with government was a legal mandate to distribute a very small percentage of each foundation's income every year for the public good. A vast network of non-profits was set up to receive and distribute this money. . . . Non-profits also control significant amounts of federal and state monies through contracts for the provision of public services such as health care, education, housing, employment training, and jobs. The ruling class, through the non-profit sector, controls billions of dollars of private and government money ostensibly earmarked for the public good, but subject to virtually no public control.[46]

---

can ask banks to pay a higher-than-average interest rate as a condition of offering IOLTA account services, among other proposed changes).

[44] Jack Karp, "Not Our Best Days": The Fiscal Crisis Coming for Legal Aid, Law360 (Apr. 12, 2020) (describing potentially "devastating" effects of cuts on legal aid programs around the country), www.law360.com/articles/1262255; Mark D. Braley, Legal Aid, Facing State Cuts, Remains Crucial During Pandemic, Va. Mercury (Apr. 22, 2020), www.virginiamercury.com/2020/04/22/legal-aid-facing-state-cuts-remains-crucial-during-pandemic/.

[45] Dylan Rodriguez, remarks at The Revolution Will Not Be Funded: Beyond the Non-Profit Industrial Complex Conference (2004) (quoted in Rickke Manzanala and Dean Spade, The Nonprofit Industrial Complex and Trans Resistance, 5 Sexuality Research & Social Pol'y 53, 56 (Mar. 2008)). See also Edgar Villanueva, Decolonizing Wealth: Indigenous Wisdom to Heal Divides and Restore Balance (2018); Rob Reich, Just Giving: Why Philanthropy is Failing Democracy and How It Can Do Better (2018); and Arnand Giridharadas, Winners Take All: The Elite Charade of Changing the World (2018).

[46] Paul Kivel, Social Service or Social Change?, in The Revolution Will Not Be Funded: Beyond the Non-Profit Industrial Complex 129, 137–38 (INCITE! ed. 2007).

The NPIC is funded largely by top-down philanthropy—foundations and individual donors. As with law, philanthropy is not always what it seems or purports to be—if you look at it from the bottom:

> [R]ather than putting more money into the hands of non-profits that address the needs of the marginalized, . . . the white leadership of the progressive philanthropy movement actually protects white wealth and undermines the work of oppressed communities of color.[47]

This critique of social justice funding applies generally to social services, organizing, legal services, and other sorts of activities.

Rickke Manazala and Dean Spade, transgender justice advocates and writers, make the same points about the politics of funding in transgender contexts. They note that, in recent years, trans-focused advocacy programs have expanded within lesbian and gay organizations while independent trans-focused organizations also have emerged, such as the Sylvia Rivera Law Project, Transgender Law Center, National Center for Transgender Equality, and TGI Justice Project.[48] They view projects developing within established gay and lesbian groups as occupying a different space in relation to funders than do independent, bottom-up trans projects. In response, Mananzala and Spade raise self-critical questions for emerging trans groups and trans activists to consider why and how "the most well-resourced organizations in the gay and lesbian rights arena . . . have used structures and tactics that have resulted in neoliberalism's co-optation of lesbian and gay political aims."[49]

Top-down policies have caused governments to largely defund social services, creating a gap that social movement groups have failed to confront effectively. Many groups have tried to fill that gap with conventional philanthropy—as we have just seen, a shift that pulls groups away from advocacy and organizing, and that steers them toward donor preferences rather than community priorities.[50] Simultaneously, many groups have shifted their agendas to focus more on "narrow individual rights . . . rather

---

[47] Tiffany Lethabo King and Ewuare Osayande, The Filth on Philanthropy: Progressive Philanthropy's Agenda to Misdirect Social Justice Movements, in The Revolution Will Not Be Funded: Beyond the Non-Profit Industrial Complex 80–81 (INCITE!, ed. 2007).

[48] Mananzala and Spade, Nonprofit Industrial Complex (outlining a series of important concerns about the NPIC including: the emergence of the nonprofit sector as the location for social justice work has separated survival services from organizing; the nonprofit structure undermines and contains the radical potential of social justice work leading to more policy and service-based work and less organizing; racism, educational privilege, and classism within nonprofits mirrors colonialism because the direction of work is made by elites rather than by people directly affected by the issues; and the emergence of the nonprofit sector has created a cultural shift in social justice activism, including professionalization, corporatization, and competition between groups for scarce resources).

[49] Id. at 54.

[50] Id. at 55–56.

than on collective and community well-being."⁵¹ Using personal experience and critical knowledge, Mananzala and Spade outline a series of concerns about the dependence on funding from wealthy foundations:

> [M]ost tax-exempt giving benefits the nation's wealthiest people by going to institutions and programs such as conservative think tanks and foundations; upper-class cultural institutions including museums, operas, art galleries, and elite schools; and private hospitals. A large amount also goes back into the pockets of the wealthy through trustee fees, where wealthy people are paid hundreds of thousands of dollars to sit on the boards of foundations. Only a tiny portion of the money ends up in social justice organizations and even then, it comes with many strings attached that allow wealthy philanthropists to have a hand in directing the work.⁵²

Based on that same experience and knowledge, Mananzala and Spade show how those "strings" work systematically as wealthy philanthropists channel money to favored groups, and how advocates and activists push back to create space for bottom-up advocacy.

By way of example, the Sylvia Rivera Law Project (SRLP) started with a legal fellowship awarded to a new law graduate (Spade) to provide free legal help to transgender individuals and evolved to become an independent organization. The Project was structured as a collective to provide free legal services for low-income transgender, intersex, and gender non-conforming individuals; to engage in racial justice organizing; and to sustain systemic policy advocacy and direct action. The group raises funds from donors in the group's constituency as well as from individual allies. Grassroots fundraising, however, provided only about 30% of the group's total funding, with the rest from law fellowships, grants, and other donations. Significantly, the group also engaged in discussions with funders who questioned the group's "prioritization of direct services work and reform of institutions centrally affecting low-income people." These funders encouraged the group to adopt "strategies of the most well-funded (so-called successful) gay rights organizations" that tend to frame their work in terms of the needs and experiences of economically- and racially-privileged members of the community and eschew a multi-strategy approach connecting much-needed direct services to advocacy and organizing.⁵³

But, of course, in a complex world, nothing is simply cut-and-dried. As Albiston and Nielsen noted at the outset of this section, funding both creates opportunities and generates constraints. American Studies scholar

---

⁵¹ *Id.* at 56.
⁵² *Id.* at 58.
⁵³ *Id.* at 67.

Erica Kohl-Arenas additionally notes that the relationship of funders to movement work, including organizing and advocacy work, shifts according to context, across time, and in response to active efforts to realign interests and build structures of accountable decision making. To illustrate, she describes the important role that the Max L. Rosenberg Foundation played over time in seeding and sustaining farmworker organizing in California—while also at times setting limits on funding that aligned more closely with the concerns of the wealthy than those of poor farmworkers and their organizations.

Prior to the formation of the United Farm Workers union, the Rosenberg Foundation supported community-based work. That work combined ameliorative aims—to diminish the effects of oppression and poverty in farmworkers' lives—with transformative hopes—to enable farmworker communities to attain greater levels of prosperity, security, and economic independence. This early work, like much frontline work carried out by advocates in direct service roles, often is undervalued.[54]

As Kohl-Arenas notes, the politics of funding are unavoidable, and top-down philanthropy may be limited to support for amelioration only, leaving *systemic* injustice undisturbed. To reach her conclusions, Kohl-Arenas recalls the lessons of interest convergence and divergence, presented in Part I, and applies them to this context:

> The Max L. Rosenberg Foundation . . . contributed to the initial momentum of the historic Farm Worker Movement of the 1960s. The Rosenberg Foundation invested in valley farmworker communities in three waves leading up to the movement. The first wave included Depression era grants, mostly to support the development of community and childcare centers for migrant families and inter-ethnic education programs. The second funding era is characterized by Rosenberg's investments in farmworker "self-help" projects, aimed at assisting farmworkers in building housing and developing leadership at the same time. The third wave is the foundation's support of early movement organizations . . . which organized alongside [Cesar] Chavez and [Dolores] Huerta leading up to the 1965 National Farm Worker Association (NFWA—later named the United Farm Workers of America, UFW) strike.
>
> . . . [T]he central philosophy of Rosenberg's housing grants at this time was "allowing people to decide for themselves what they want to do and helping them learn how to do it." . . .

---

[54] See Rebecca Sharpless, More Than One Lane Wide: Against Hierarchies of Helping in Progressive Legal Advocacy, 19 Clinical L. Rev. 347 (2012) (arguing that the use of law for social justice purposes is undermined and gender-based inequities are furthered when direct service providers are devalued).

[But in a report written] the same year of the first UFW (then NFWA) strike, the 1965 annual report author recognized that while "Almost everybody approves if farmworkers decide to build houses for themselves; not everybody approves if they decide to go on strike." . . .

. . . The convergence of Farm Worker Movement leaders and funders depended on shared understandings of social positions and identities. . . . While my analysis reasserts the importance of resource mobilization in social movements, especially during the fluid and open-ended beginnings, and opens up the possibility of foundations as movement allies (although fleeting and temporary), it does not deny the hard and fast lines foundation boards draw. These lines are most often drawn at the point at which a nascent organizing campaign directly confronts the economic structures upon which philanthropic wealth is created and maintained.[55]

This example serves as a reminder that alternatives to mainstream organizations or platforms are essential for problem-solving innovation and progress generally. This example also illustrates how nonprofit options do not necessarily provide an escape from the pressures of law as an industry sensitive to, and subservient to, power in symbolic material, ideological, and other ways. Whether public or private, this kind of top-down support usually ends when an advocate or group "directly confronts" the economic structures maintaining philanthropic wealth.

NOTES AND QUESTIONS

1. *A New Vision for Philanthropy.* The Ford Foundation (derived from family fortunes of the Ford Motor Company) is an influential private foundation that defines its mission as advancing:

> a vision of social justice—[to create] a world in which all individuals, communities, and peoples work toward the protection and full expression of their human rights; are active participants in the decisions that affect them; share equitably in the knowledge, wealth, and resources of society; and are free to achieve their full potential.[56]

In 2019, Darren Walker, a Black, gay lawyer and former investment banker serving as the foundation's president, suggested that a transformative "shift" was needed:

> We must trust those we fund, and fund them adequately to do what they believe is best, not what we think is best. This means putting ourselves in the shoes of prospective grantees and communities,

---

[55] Erica Kohl-Arenas, Will the Revolution be Funded? Resource Mobilization and the California Farm Worker Movement, 13 Soc. Movement Stud. 482 (2014).

[56] www.fordfoundation.org/about/about-ford/mission/.

treating them like partners rather than contractors, and entrusting organizations with long-term general support funding and project grants that provide adequate overhead. It means acknowledging the power imbalance that often makes our grantees reluctant to engage honestly and authentically.[57]

Taking into account the varied critiques described above that emerged in the wake of the coronavirus pandemic and #BLM protests, what concrete changes would this vision of philanthropy require in order not to perpetuate the very problem ostensibly being redressed? Consider foundation decision making roles and structures, focus areas for grantmaking, siloed versus multiple and coordinated strategies, grant terms and restrictions, and grantee decision making roles and structures. Can top-down philanthropy align with bottom-up interests in social transformation? Do better alternatives exist? How might critical knowledge from the Schools and Approaches be useful in navigating the politics of top-down funding?

2. *The Salience of Political Economy.* In fact, "those funders working for equity and against inequality are getting their butts kicked"[58] if measured by facts on the ground, which show increasing income and wealth inequality, social program cutbacks, increasing job precarity, loss of affordable housing, and accelerating trends of extreme climate change. David Callahan writes in Inside Philanthropy that promoting equity by treating local groups like partners, as the Ford Foundation's Walker suggested above, is insufficient in the face of the accumulated imbalance of power and wealth in society. Callahan charges that foundations fail to confront the "political economy" of equity—as discussed in Part II, the intersection of power and private interests in public decision making that sets the "rules of the game" in economics and democracy:

> *Because equity-minded foundations keep failing to zero in on the all-important sphere of political economy.* Inequality mainly stems from how the U.S. economy works and, critically, the range of public policies and power arrangements that govern economic life. Yet, instead of focusing laser-like on this fundamental reality, funders embrace overly diffuse, often localized strategies that yield few larger systemic gains. They win battles here and there, while losing the war. [In particular, funders fail because of the following key points:]
>
> Few Foundations Focus on Workers' Rights and Labor Policy . . .
>
> > Fiscal Policy Gets Too Little Attention . . .
> >
> > Equity Funders Ignore Wall Street . . . [and]

---

[57] Ruth McCambridge, The Philanthropy We Need: Ford Foundation President Calls for Transformation (Jan. 10, 2019), www.nonprofitquarterly.org/2019/01/10/the-philanthropy-we-need-ford-foundation-president-calls-for-transformation/?utm_source=email&utm_medium=social&utm_campaign=SocialWarfare.

[58] David Callahan, Systemic Failure: Four Reasons Philanthropy Keeps Losing the Battle Against Inequality, Inside Philanthropy, (Jan. 10, 2018), www.insidephilanthropy.com/home/2018/1/10/systemic-failure-four-reasons-philanthropy-keeps-losing-the-battle-against-inequality.

Foundations Support Little Work on Globalization and Automation.[59]

Based on what you know so far, how might advocates navigate and overcome the anti-transformation politics of social justice funders?

3. *Law Firm Philanthropy*. Many law firms contribute significant pro bono hours toward un- or under-served legal needs. In a prominent example, the international law firm Skadden, Arps, Slate, Meagher & Flom LLP, based in New York City, contributed more than one million pro bono hours in the last seven years and created the prestigious Skadden Fellowship Foundation that funds two-year public interest fellowships, with 90 percent of those fellows continuing on to nonprofit sector, public service jobs, or education work. Consider how you would demonstrate empirically or otherwise how those pro bono contributions are constrained by legal industry handcuffs and blindfolds or how they transcend them? If you were entrusted with overseeing a law firm's pro bono program, while at the same time seeking to advance systemic advocacy, how might you structure that program to further the interests of subordinated groups? Who should make key decisions? Are there potential conflicts with elite interests? Should that matter?

4. *Commitment Versus Accountability*. We have noted before that commitment to marginalized communities is not the same as accountability to those communities—in a formal sense. University boards are dominated by wealthy donors. Law firm governance creates accountability to shareholding partners. Law school clinics do not report to or share decision-making authority with boards representing organized community groups or clients. Nonprofit PILO and funder boards include, at most, individuals loosely representative of client communities but not organized constituencies and not making up a majority of the boards. Moreover, individuals are not necessarily prepared to advance strategic decision making about social problems solely because they have experienced those problems as individuals—experience with organized group struggle often is a necessary predicate and preparation. Individuals from client communities who are not representing organized groups also may advance particular interests in ways unaccountable to the community. How might institutional governance in legal education, funding, or practice change to create greater accountability to the interests of marginalized clients or communities? Think creatively and systemically.

8.6 ADVOCATES ACT DESPITE RISKS OF RETALIATION, COOPTATION, AND TOKENISM

Advocates who reject compliance with entenched social hierarchies are engaging in risk-taking professional behavior. When threatened, elites use diverse strategies—as varied as retaliation, cooptation, capture, and tokenism—to maintain the systemic status quo. In response, advocates and activists collaborate to help and protect each other.

---

[59] *Id.*

These systemic risks may require advocates to use the social and intellectual "capital" they accumulate in their professional roles, institutions, relationships, and coalitions to support antisubordination goals. Legal scholar Aya Gruber elaborates on one kind of collaboration to "create coalitions and advance the antisubordination agenda." Her remarks, made in reference to risk-taking by legal academics, could be generalized to refer to the various forms of "capital" advocates accumulate in different sites of practice:

> [This group] is ... empowered in many ways. Some of the women and gays are white. Some of the minorities and gays are men. Some of the people of color are heterosexual. Many of the participants are non-immigrants. Almost all of us are educationally and economically privileged. ... What we all also possess is a measure of academic capital, which, in effect, is our ability to create change through what we teach, what we say, what we do, and what we write. Academic capital, like political or economic capital, is an asset. Because we cannot talk and write about everything, our capital is limited by time, energy, and even inclination. ... [The question is] how we can marshal our own academic capital so as to create coalitions and advance the antisubordination agenda.[60]

Legal workers generally have choices to make and effectuate. Collectively, we bear a major portion of responsibility for the persistence—or not—of the *status quo*. But these choices can be risky and are constrained by the complexity of institutional sites of practice and systemic design. In every context, opposition is constant. This constancy is not surprising—think back to the Powell memorandum, as well as to the notion of preservation through transformation Siegel laid out, both in Part II. Opposition by elites to social progress can take an active form—overt attempts to defeat an endeavor or quash a group, project, or campaign—or a more covert form, such as cooptation.

Cooptation is a process by which "opponents adopt aspects of the *content* of a movement's discourse, while subverting its *intent*."[61] Thus, cooptation may take the form of "specific policy recommendations and programs, robbed of their radical edge and their transformative potential."[62] For example, "diversity" initiatives often are seen as a cooptation of bottom-up antiracism and antisexism initiatives, promoting a tokenistic sprinkling of "different" groups without changing the white

---

[60] Aya Gruber, Navigating Diverse Identities: Building Coalitions Through Redistribution of Academic Capital—An Exercise in Praxis, 35 Seton Hall L. Rev. 1201, 1205–06 (2005).

[61] Mary C. Burke and Mary Bernstein, How the Right Usurped the Queer Agenda: Frame Co-optation in Political Discourse, 29 Sociological Forum 830, 831 (2014).

[62] Angelika Striedinger, How Organizational Research Can Avoid the Pitfalls of a Co-optation Perspective: Analyzing Gender Equality Work in Austrian Universities with Organizational Institutionalism, 19 Int'l Feminist J. of Politics 201, 201 (2017).

supremacist and patriarchal ideologies and practices that pervade and control institutions.[63] "Reform" initiatives can be "superficial and deceptive" if profound change is sacrificed while preserving the status quo.[64]

Cooptation is a constant danger because any struggle for transformative change is a "long haul"—accomplished over time through incremental steps of progress in contexts characterized by uncertainty and complexity. Recall the debates from Part II surrounding marriage equality as a long-term struggle, and Boucai's conclusion:

> The . . . [early gay marriage] cases remind us what the signal gay rights issue of our time once represented, and they reveal what it may come to represent once more[:] . . . new and unanticipated constituencies for sexual freedom, gender dissent, and alternative family forms. Those ideals, no less than equality, constitute the radical heritage of a now-mainstream movement. Let us not forget them.

In contexts ranging from racial justice to gender equality to gay liberation, activists and advocates continue to ask whether or to what extent antisubordination goals were coopted, and how the continuing struggle can forge new ways and means toward transformative change.

Romanticizing alternative forms of action is not the cure to cooptation. Legal action is not unique in its susceptibility; both organizing as an "extralegal" activity and legal action can be equally (even if differently) subject to top-down cooptation. Labor law scholar Orly Lobel notes that critical reflections on law—often based in the critical Schools and advocacy Approaches—have created what might be called a "contemporary critical legal consciousness—a conventional wisdom about the relative inefficacy of law." That insight, Lobel argues, is more useful if recast. Legal action may be insufficient to achieve transformative change alone, but still is necessary for Critical Justice—and the same goes for organizing and other extralegal forms of action.[65] Both organizing and law are essential forms of

---

[63] In the context of legal education, Sahar Aziz points out that despite the concerted advocacy efforts that increased the number of women students, teachers, and administrators in U.S. law schools, women are still concentrated in more precarious legal writing positions and still paid less than male professors. As she argues, "women who have managed to overcome the hurdles imposed by patriarchy to reach official leadership positions are as subject to institutional capture and conflicts of interest as their male counterparts." Moreover, in this and other contexts, "[t]he reasoning that more women and more minorities in power will necessarily produce less sexism and less racism is flawed if the patriarchal systems are left in place." Sahar F. Aziz, Identity Politics is Failing Women in Legal Academia, 69 J. Leg. Ed. (forthcoming 2021).

[64] Alec Karakatsanis, The Punishment Bureaucracy: How to Think About "Criminal Justice Reform," 128 Yale L.J. Forum 848 (Mar. 28, 2019).

[65] Orly Lobel, The Paradox of Extralegal Activism: Critical Legal Consciousness and Transformative Politics, 120 Harv. L. Rev. 937 (2007).

action in the long struggle for transformative change, and both are susceptible to similar dangers of cooptation:

> [Law's] negative effect is generally understood as "legal cooptation"—a process by which the focus on legal reform narrows the causes, deradicalizes the agenda, legitimizes ongoing injustices, and diverts energies away from more effective and transformative alternatives. . . .
>
> . . . [But a] more accurate inquiry into the limits of change should cast doubt on the privileged role of extralegal activism [such as community organizing, as well]. . . .
>
> The focus on action in a separate sphere broadly defined as civil society can be self-defeating precisely because it conceals the many ways in which law continues to play a crucial role in all spheres of life. . . .
>
> . . . [I]t is possible to accept the need to diversify modes of activism and legal categories while using legal reform in ways that are responsive to new realities. . . . A responsive legal architecture has the potential to generate new forms of accountability and social responsibility and to link hard law with "softer" practices and normativities. Reformers can potentially use law to increase the power and access of vulnerable individuals and groups . . . .
>
> . . . Critique has always been and remains not simply an intellectual exercise but a political and moral act. The question we must constantly pose is how critical accounts of social reform models contribute to our ability to produce scholarship and action that will be constructive. . . .
>
> . . . Understanding the limits of legal change reveals the dangers of absolute reliance on one system and the need, in any effort for social reform, to contextualize the discourse. . . . Marginalized . . . groups have often successfully secured their interests through legislative and judicial victories. Rather than experiencing a disabling disenchantment with the legal system, we can learn from both the successes and failures of past models, with the aim of constantly redefining the boundaries of legal reform and making visible law's broad reach.[66]

Whether focused on law, organizing, or both, advocates must design projects to correct tendencies toward cooptation. As Lobel explains, well-intended actions nonetheless can be coopted—whether from above or from the very structuring of advocacy. Preservation through transformation—the process by which elites control legal reform to reassemble preexisting

---

[66] *Id.* at 939, 978, 983, 987–88.

social and economic hierarchies—can amount to cooptation from above. As West noted in Part II, advocates always are acting to defend old victories, including fighting the coopting effects of preservation by transformation. In the end, however, advocates, organizers, and activists take action despite the risks of cooptation. More than that, advocates affirmatively look for opportunities to go on the offense—to push progress onward toward equal justice for *all*.

Amplifying concerns like cooptation, the next excerpt addresses two top-down tactics that can blunt the force of advocacy for equal justice. Much like top-down cooptation, capture and tokenism can reduce transformative goals into ameliorative cosmetics. Each of these tactics undermines law as an instrument of justice and bolsters the resulting Critical Challenge. But advocates face these risks and engage in struggle despite them, using individual and collective reflection based in critical theories of social change to chart their paths forward.

Legal scholar Gerald Torres, a former president of the Association of American Law Schools, makes clear in the excerpt below that change is not progress, that progress requires intentionality, struggle, power, and time, and that individual advancement can easily coopt collective justice. Advocates must think and act with "double" or dual consciousness, going beyond the confines of "possessive individualism" to support organized bottom-up actions. To do so, advocates "must have an insider/outsider strategy in order to confront the ways in which institutional power is deployed to resist change and to transform the transformer." Elaborating this point, Torres explains how principled and accountable actions (both individual and collective) are rooted in critical "theories of social change"— that is, critical conceptions of the necessary personal and group steps to produce social transformation. Knowing, and sticking to, a solid theory of social change can help minimize the odds of preservation though transformation, cooptation, capture, or tokenism.

SYNECDOCHE
Gerald Torres
14 Harv. Latino L. Rev. 263 (2011)

Synecdoche, n. A figure of speech in which a part is substituted for a whole or a whole for a part, as in 50 head of cattle for 50 cows, or the army for a soldier. . . .

Introduction

. . . [The following] question raises a puzzling kind of synecdoche. Namely, to what extent could the present part (an elite status Latina/o) represent and/or influence a future for the whole (greater success for Latina/os who aspired to social mobility and public service)?

[This article] will make three small but related points....

First, one lesson the author has learned in his years of organizing, is that one always has to be cognizant of the problem of capture....

Second is the problem of the tyranny of tokenism....

Third, every person who is trying to change an institution must have an insider/outsider strategy in order to confront the ways in which institutional power is deployed to resist change and to transform the transformer. This is something that is known—or certainly becomes known—through practice by everyone who has tried to move institutions....

Capture

... When people in law schools talk about the problem of capture, they typically refer to the occasion of a regulatory agency that has ceased to act in the public interest (or towards the specific regulatory objectives detailed in their operative statute) and instead acts in the interest of the parties it is supposed to be regulating.... [B]ecause the regulated parties have higher stakes than the public as a whole in the outcome of any particular regulation, they will concentrate resources on influencing the decision-making process of the regulating agency. This focused tactical and strategic effort to intervene in the regulatory process tends to influence the final outcome in a manner that exceeds the expectations contained in the statutory mission....

The insight of those economists and public choice theorists ought to be generalized to participants in every institution.... Psychologists and other specialists suggest that what drives capture is more than mere rent-seeking behavior. The circulation of power throughout institutions creates the channels through which, to the extent possible, those who are more powerful structure the social situations that produce definitions of what is real. At the same time, they frame responses in ways that so vehemently conceal the force of the institutional structure, that even those who are subject to it cannot see it. This was precisely the point of my mother's observation. Jon Hanson describes this process as "deep capture."

... The main point of the discussion of capture and power is that the mere occupation of a leadership role is not sufficient to promote significant institutional change. Unless an internal leadership role is also accompanied by an agenda and a constituency of accountability, as well as an external force for change, it is highly unlikely that the power will be exercised in the interest of those who were formerly excluded from its benefits.... It is fallacious to assume that there is a deep significance to the simultaneous presence of Latina/os in [law school] leadership positions at this time. The significance should be demonstrated. Thus, an appropriate metric should be determined to measure this significance. One way to begin that inquiry is to ask: what were the forces that produced this cohort of Latina/o legal academics such that they would be in a position to occupy the leadership roles they did? The next question would be: what did they do with those opportunities? . . .

. . . The easiest route to conventional success within [formerly homogenous] organizations is . . . to act consistent with the normative vision, [which] is certainly understandable, but . . . is not the path to change. The next section tries to explain why.

The Tyranny of Tokenism

What happens when a relatively homogeneous institution initiates a movement towards greater heterogeneity? Do the steps undertaken reflect a deep commitment to change or to stability? Surface changes may do more to solidify power in the hands of the powerful than the reverse. The process that leads to the inclusion of those who were previously excluded has, in some sense, helped legitimize the norms that had previously been used to exclude. Token changes at the top may obviate the need to pursue more fundamental structural changes. . . .

One of the dominant norms in our culture is the belief in possessive individualism and our reliance on it to explain social failure or success on the basis of the actions of individual persons rather than on the structural constraints (or opportunities) that institutions may present. . . .

Relatively unconstrained social mobility is another important belief that when linked to the idea of personal individual responsibility, conflates the two convictions. . . . If you create opportunities for individuals, then you do not need to question the deep values ingrained in the exclusionary structure of the institutions that are now, at least on their face, open to former outsiders.

By acting in ways that increase the belief in the permeability of the boundaries between dominant and subordinate groups, what is also reinforced is the idea that those who continue to be excluded deserve their fate as much as the now included persons deserve theirs. This is not premised on the presence of a left/right ideological divide in the struggle over integration of our civic and civil institutions. Instead, by endorsing strategies that are premised on individual advancement in order to achieve social goals, civil rights advocates partake in the same metanarrative as the opponents of those efforts: when individuals get ahead, the group triumphs, and the basic democratic structure of American social life prevails. While the individual Latina/o's advancement to a leadership position involves an act of "transcendence" (moving beyond the reach or stain of group identity and stigma), that same "transcendence" is simultaneously used to legitimize the status of those left behind. . . . The merit of the individual is used to establish the demerit of the group as a whole.

The difference may lie in the definition of the group that is benefitting, but the logical structure is identical. That is why, for example, the *Grutter* opinion [539 U.S. 306 (2003)] upholding the University of Michigan's affirmative action plan pivots on the idea of "critical mass." However, while the concept of "critical mass" is a response to "tokenism," the concept of "critical mass" does not include access for the "masses."

What is the meaning of "critical mass" in the context of educational affirmative action? According to Justice O'Connor's opinion in *Grutter*, it meant a number of things while signifying no commitment to a particular percentage of admits (since such a target would come dangerously close to transforming a constitutionally permissible goal into an unconstitutional quota). Among the many things critical mass did mean was that a sufficient number of "underrepresented minority" students would be admitted to prevent the admittees from feeling isolated or feeling as if they had to speak for their entire group whenever they participated in class. Importantly, there also had to be enough "underrepresented minorities" to ensure that non-members receive the educational benefits gained from the presence of the minority class. The multiple meanings of critical mass suggest that the entire process is not really aimed at transforming the institution in ways that challenge any of its fundamental commitments. A critical mass of former outsiders may safeguard the institution from threats of external pressures and also provide the kind of individual access that will produce institutional loyalty from the beneficiaries. All of this makes sense, but it has costs and it should not be confused with more ambitious transformative goals.

One of the costs is that if a program like *Grutter's* is successful, it will serve to disconnect the admitted individual from the previously excluded group. This happens when the program for inclusion is justified by the same or similar norms that had previously justified exclusion. According to social psychologist Stephen Wright, this process discourages the accepted out-group members from employing disruptive actions, which might be consistent with the interests of the excluded out-group members because it would weaken the identity of the "token" with the dominant group.

. . . Individual social mobility refocuses attention on opportunities for exit from the subordinate group rather than on the fundamental unfairness of the existing institutional relationship.

. . . [T]he creation of an exit strategy for one or two former outsiders reframes the problem for those left behind. They no longer challenge their condition as members of a subordinate group but instead fight each other to claw their way into the dominant group. By providing an individual justification for minor changes to the dominant institutions and by using those changes to suggest the basic permeability of the boundaries between the groups, tokenism can be an effective form of managing dissent. . . . By deflecting attention from the institutional sources of disadvantage, the dominant group can reduce "the level of disruptive collective action . . . [thus] preventing real social change."

A Theory of Change

. . . So how does someone who wants to use his/her access to dominant groups resist the problem of capture or the tyranny of tokenism?

Membership in the elite by a member of a formerly excluded group can lead to change only if that person has a systemic agenda that is supported by an external constituency to whom that individual remains accountable. Consider the experience of a black lawyer in Selma, Alabama in the 1960s. J.L. Chestnut, in his memoir of his days in Selma at the beginning of the civil rights movement, noticed that he was witnessing "a transformation from civil rights leaders to politicians, from outside protesters to inside manipulators." The problem arises from overconfidence on the part of insiders as to their ability to "manipulate" the institutions of which they now find themselves a part. So how is the insider/outsider divide negotiated in the interest of subordinate groups? Professor Guinier and the author have suggested one possibility:

> [O]nce an outsider is put in such a position, the key to resisting power—to the extent that it is a zero-sum resource—is to remain "critical." In the words of W.E.B. DuBois, to be critical means one is capable of experiencing double consciousness. It is not impossible to be an insider and an outsider simultaneously. But . . . outsiders who have become insiders . . . need an independent source of power. In other words, if one is an outsider now operating as an insider, unless mechanisms are in place that give other outsiders power, the insider's power will come to depend increasingly on the views of other insiders. This makes it less likely that an insider, acting alone but in good conscience or with good intentions, can simultaneously enlist and resist authority.

Thus, infiltrating hierarchy in order to redistribute power usually will not succeed unless the new insider has an energized or powerful base of outsiders as support. . . .

Accordingly, an insider/outsider theory of change depends on the correlative construction of a constituency of accountability, i.e., a group of people who share a common identity, who are jointly committed to a transformative vision, and who work together to hold their members accountable to that vision. . . .

A successful insider/outsider strategy . . . [demands of the insider] that he or she maintain a legitimate presence in both the dominant group and in whatever outsider or subordinate groups have produced him or her. . . .

A school reform project in Texas reflects a version of this insider/outsider strategy. In *Edgewood Independent School District v. Kirby*, the Texas Supreme Court declared that the state has an obligation under the Texas State Constitution to equalize funding in public schools. The *Edgewood* court noted that "[t]he wealthiest district ha[d] over $14,000,000 of property wealth per student, while the poorest ha[d] approximately $20,000; this disparity reflects a 700 to 1 ratio."

. . . [T]he ultimate legislative fix was able to reduce the disparity ratio from 700:1 to 28:1. Nonetheless, the reform did not resolve the many problems associated with chronic underfunding.

Because school finance reform had largely failed to produce real educational reform, a local organization called Texas LEADS (Local Empowerment for Accessible and Diverse Schools) was born. The guiding principle behind the organization was that poor schools would have to figure out how to achieve academic success without additional funding. . . . Some poor districts across the state had been achieving academic success for their students and LEADS was determined to figure out how they were doing it.

After LEADS conducted surveys and on-the-ground interviews in the respective schools, a local school was chosen. Texas LEADS entered into a partnership with the school. . . .

. . . One of the first steps was to create a public space that the parents "owned"—through which they could engage the school. . . . A team of teachers, parents, and staff was created to direct and oversee the partnership project and to implement state required site-based planning. A parent was hired as an on-site peer parent coordinator who . . . began implementing parent programming. . . . This group of parents became "The Action Team," which could function as an adjunct to the Campus Advisory Council (CAC), the state-mandated, site-based decision-making body that was made up of teachers, parents, community members, and staff. LEADS intended to incorporate the Action Team into the existing structure to become an "inside" project that would not be perceived or treated as a temporary program operated by outsiders. . . .

Texas LEADS also helped build several links with the community. . . . LEADS formed links with local churches and with El Buen Samaritano, a local Episcopal mission that assists poor, Spanish-speaking, working families. All of the services were available in the Parents' Room or through the Parent Liaison. Moreover, . . . the parent liaison provided a focus and a guiding hand for all parent-related activities. . . . Virtually everyone agreed that the creation of the Parent Liaison and the Parents' Room were among the Project's greatest successes.

By changing the culture of the school, the parents came to feel that the school was theirs. Importantly, the cultural changes that allowed the parents to feel this way were the products of the physical changes in the school as well as a transformation of any us-versus-them dynamic that had predated the LEADS Project. The Parents' Room begot better communication among parents and between parents and the school, leading parents to develop peer driven surveys, a newsletter, a phone tree, and a website.

The story of Texas LEADS illustrates several elements of the theory of change being proposed here. Among them is the crucial idea that for change to be possible it is necessary to avoid both capture and premature or wholesale identification with the dominant powers. Nonetheless, agents of change have to both be invested in the institution, as well as in the community that supports or demands the change. Texas LEADS maintained strong ties to the surrounding community; it did not solely rely on the trust and confidence of the school officials. As an agent of change, Texas LEADS invested in the school as an educational institution and worked to maintain the school as a site of refuge and source of support for community members who sought and demanded significant change. . . . It also learned to function with an ongoing inner tension, sometimes making the project an inside force for change while at other times making it an outside force.

. . . None of its successes could have been achieved if the organization had not succeeded in generating a legitimate presence both inside and outside of the dominant institutions. . . .

Conclusion: Latina/o Education and Justice: Leading Voices, Lessons Learned?

. . . Capture: here the hazard is that those who find themselves in a position to use institutional power may find themselves subject to pressure to conform to the norms and values of those who have traditionally benefitted from the conventional use of that institution's authority. . . . It might be the easiest route to conventional success within such organizations; but acting in a way that is always consistent with the normative vision of the dominant institution has its costs, and one of those costs may be the loss of critical perspective.

The hazards associated with what is called the tyranny of tokenism arise from the impact of that process on neutralizing the energy for collective action. This article suggests that collective rather than individual action is necessary to produce institutional or social change, and any process that neutralizes or redirects that energy for substantive change is not likely to be in the larger interest of the subordinate group. . . . [Tokenism] often creates a gulf between members of the dominant and subordinate groups, even if membership in the dominant group is completely contingent. . . . [A] theory of change that does not retain an argument for continued accountability to members of the subordinate group is not an argument for serious social change.

The problem of synecdoche, the part standing in for the whole, suggests that one be cautious when trying to generalize from the presence of former outsiders in positions of leadership in dominant institutions. Although it may seem socially important, in reality, it might not be. Its meaning can only begin to be understood if one asks questions about those contingent insiders, about the dynamics of the institution within which they are functioning, and about one's own theory of change which will, of course, be informed by the goals one sets.

Torres underscores the difference between tokenistic changes designed to be cosmetic and systemic changes that alter operations and outputs. Tokenism lends itself to business as usual—to capture. Increased representation by outsiders within institutions or in leadership positions represents change—meaningful change for individuals. But institutions may endorse such formal or paper reforms to dissipate momentum and to coopt or capture progress toward systemic, transformative justice. To guard against these risks, Torres emphasizes that advocates need to keep their "critical perspective" and maintain a systemic agenda "supported by an external constituency to whom that individual remains accountable." As with all systems, this perspective measures law according to its outputs. Torres describes one example, the Texas LEADS project, of collective action for principled and accountable advocacy.

Finally, many advocates—and their clients and communities, both domestically and around the world—also risk retaliatory violence or state repression as part of that relentless top-down opposition to any social progress. If so, legal and other actors cannot simply count on the protection of law itself:

> Lawyers who practice for social justice, and especially lawyers who confront the powerful, may encounter political and personal risk. Where law itself is weak, constructing the authority of law and secure sites from which to mobilize law may be the lawyer's paramount cause.... The path to becoming a lawyer who will use law for social justice is guided not only by social conditions, political institutions, and resources (including global resources) that enable such a career, but also by experience, reflection, courage, and choice.[67]

Depending on context, multiple kinds of risky constraints are salient to systemic advocates in their development of sites of practice and career

---

[67] Frank W. Munger, Scott L. Cummings & Louise G. Trubek, Mobilizing Law for Justice in Asia: A Comparative Approach, 31 Wis. Int'l L.J. 353, 366 (2013).

choices, ranging from quiet cooptation to raw violence. Every advocate necessarily must take these and other risks into account as they construct and carry out collaborative advocacy projects. Indeed, as we will explore further below, in some contexts the project itself must be designed to protect advocates, activists, organizers, and community members in their organized action.

NOTES AND QUESTIONS

1. *Implications for Your Advocacy Project.* How might you construct a project to avoid cooptation, capture, or tokenism? What are the relevant institutions? One might be the "target" institution—the equivalent of the Texas schools that Texas LEADS aimed to change and in which an insider/outsider strategy was necessary. Think back to the discussion of constraints on advocacy institutions themselves. Is your site of practice also an institution for which you need an insider/outsider strategy? What is needed to push back against constraints from funders or others that aim to limit work to traditional advocacy only? How can you ensure that you have "a systemic agenda that is supported by an external constituency to whom [you remain] accountable?" How can you best build transformative potential into ameliorative steps as part of your long-term work? What is your theory of long-term social change?

8.7 RESTRATEGIZING SOLUTIONS FOR TRANSFORMATIVE ACCESS TO JUSTICE PROJECTS

"Access to justice" (A2J)—or the lack of it—is a persistent social problem within the legal industry. President Jimmy Carter described the problem in 1978, still true today: "No resource of talent and training in our society, not even medical care, is more wastefully or unfairly distributed than legal skills. Ninety percent of our lawyers serve 10 percent of our people. We are overlawyered and underrepresented."[68] Solutions to the A2J problem must both ameliorate and transform legal institutions, actions, and teams and change the operations of law with respect both to access and justice. Here, we look at A2J projects as advocacy projects designed to incorporate—or not—the lessons of the critical Schools and advocacy Approaches to advance three-layered goals.

Mainstream responses are pervaded by formalism: access to justice equals access to a lawyer or a court. This myopic construction distracts from systemic inequality of access and from the undue narrowness of focusing on access to a lawyer only after a problem emerges. A more robust notion would address "access" to rule-setting power underlying cognizable

---

[68] President Jimmy Carter, Remarks at the 100th Anniversary Luncheon of the Los Angeles County Bar Association, in 64 A.B.A. J. 840, 842 (1978).

problems and resource allocations, and it would be mindful that "justice" as a systemic outcome is a lived condition.

Fundamentally, this narrowed notion of A2J is ahistorical and acontextual. The A2J "gap" as generally conceptualized distracts from repeated *systemic* failures of law, both as democracy and adjudication; the notion of "gaps" in itself obscures the reality of patterns and denies the roles identities, groups, interests, and power play in maintaining systemic injustice. The need for amelioration and transformation is denied—that is, for progress that encompasses the three layers of technical fixes, power building, and cultural shifts.

But A2J remains central because the fact of unmet legal needs is undeniable:[69]

- Fewer than 20% of low-income residents are able to get legal help for known civil legal problems.[70]

- Barriers of cost, language, transportation, and other issues make private attorneys inaccessible.[71]

- Administrative complaint processes are not always adequate.[72]

- Legal services organizations lack needed resources and scopes of practice.[73]

- Critical areas of law are particularly scarce in publicly-funded legal services agencies, such as employment law or immigration.[74]

---

[69] Rebecca L. Sandefur et al., Accessing Justice in the Contemporary USA: Findings from the Community Needs and Services Study 3 (2014). The U.N. Committee on the Elimination of Racial Discrimination cited the "disproportionate impact that the lack of a generally recognized right to counsel in civil proceedings has on indigent persons belonging to racial, ethnic and national minorities." Comm. on the Elimination of Racial Discrimination, Concluding Observations—United States of America, ¶ 22, U.N. Doc. CERD/C/USA/CO/6 (May 8, 2008).

[70] See Legal Servs. Corp., Documenting the Justice Gap in America: The Current Unmet Civil Needs of Low-Income Americans 1 (2009), www.lsc.gov/sites/default/files/LSC/pdfs/documenting_the_justice_gap_in_america_2009.pdf.

[71] See Russell Engler, Connecting Self-Representation to Civil Gideon: What Existing Data Reveal About When Counsel is Most Needed, 37 Fordham Urb. L.J. 37 (2010); Christine Jolls, The Role and Functioning of Public-Interest Legal Organizations in the Enforcement of Employment Laws, in Emerging Labor Market Institutions for the Twenty-First Century 144 (Richard B. Freeman, Joni Hersch & Lawrence Mishel eds. 2004).

[72] See, for example, Government Accountability Office, Department of Labor: Wage and Hour Division's Complaint Intake and Investigative Processes Leave Low Wage Workers Vulnerable to Wage Theft, GAO-09-458T (Mar. 25, 2009).

[73] Am. Bar Found., Access Across America: First Report of the Civil Justice Infrastructure Mapping Project v (2011); David Luban, Taking Out the Adversary: The Assault on Progressive Public Interest Lawyers, 91 Cal. L. Rev. 209 (2003).

[74] See Jennifer Hill, Wage Theft: Low-Income Workers and Community Centers, in American Labor Struggles and Law Histories 591 (Kenneth M. Casebeer ed. 2017); Jolls, Role and Functioning of Public-Interest, at 151; Equal Access to Justice: Ensuring Meaningful Access to Counsel in Civil Cases, Including Immigration Proceedings (July 2014), https://web.law.columbia.

Legal scholar Gary Blasi suggests a reconceived A2J better serves subordinated communities:

> [A] reframing of access to justice would encompass not only problems that have ripened into clear legal controversies but also those that might do so with the benefit of legal assistance. It would extend to a right to assistance in overcoming collective action problems and in asserting group claims where doing so is either necessary or efficient. Finally, it would include a right to effective assistance in which effectiveness is measured, at least in part, by the results achieved.[75]

Framing the problem in terms of "unmet needs" itself fails to capture that many critical A2J "needs" are not the result of past failures of law but are needs that *emerge* in the course of seeking justice. Most importantly, these needs might include protection from widespread retaliation against individuals and organizations challenging corporate and governmental abuses, or seeking full participation in democratic decisions—that is, those who act from the bottom to change the design of systemic injustice. For example, when hunger strikers/activists faced immigration-based retaliation, the New Orleans Worker Center for Racial Justice (NOWCRJ) identified the underlying A2J issues:

> [T]hese workers . . . are actively engaged in exposing violations of both domestic and international law. Unfortunately, instead of protecting migrant workers who speak out against unlawful arrests, racial profiling, forced labor, and other human rights abuses, the federal government's response has often been to use the immigration system for retaliation—or to look the other way when state and local actors engage in this activity.[76]

NOWCRJ purposefully reframed who these activists were—from random, unimportant arrestees to defiant human rights defenders. Such projects expand the notion of "legal actor" to include many sorts of non-lawyers, while still drawing on the expertise of lawyers. The "ongoing, intensive day-

---

edu/sites/default/files/microsites/human-rights-institute/files/equal_access_to_justice_-_cerd_shadow_report.pdf.

[75] Gary Blasi, Framing Access to Justice: Beyond Perceived Justice for Individuals, 42 Loy. L. Rev. 913, 914 (2009). See Michelle S. Jacobs, Pro Bono Work and Access to Justice for the Poor: Real Change or Imagined Change?, 48 Fla. L. Rev. 509, 514–15 (1996) (explaining that "gaps" are systemic in criminal law, too); Ricardo J. Bascuas, The American Inquisition: Sentencing After the Federal Guidelines, 45 Wake Forest L. Rev. 1 (2010) (describing "gaps" in outcomes in criminal cases even when defendants have counsel).

[76] Jacinta Gonzalez and Jennifer J. Rosenbaum, Deporting the Evidence: Migrant Workers in the South Expose How U.S. Immigration Enforcement Against Human Rights Defenders Violates the International Covenant on Civil and Political Rights (2013), https://tbinternet.ohchr.org/Treaties/CCPR/Shared%20Documents/USA/INT_CCPR_NGO_USA_15219_E.pdf. After release of this report, several U.S. Congressional supporters signed onto NOWCRJ's POWER Act—Protect Our Workers from Exploitation and Retaliation. The Act aims to strengthen individual anti-retaliation rights and to protect collective action.

to-day collaboration among lawyers, organizers and worker activists"[77] allowed NOWCRJ to highlight obstacles blocking access to domestic legal processes and fora. When corporations retaliate against workers protesting abuses by calling in law enforcement and when immigration officials detain and deport those protestors, all are complicit in denying access to the use of law for justice. By making retaliation a central concern, advocates and activists redraw the lines of A2J engagement.

More broadly, the National Lawyers Guild (NLG) and similar groups also do this work—through election protection that includes monitoring officials and defending voters or protestors. Fighting to make the rules of the game fair is important; equally important is fighting to protect the people and groups engaged in struggle. The risks that they take "for the cause" is what access and justice are built upon. A2J projects grounded in the critical Schools and advocacy Approaches consider who are the relevant legal actors and what are the sites, nature, and risks of legal action—instead of reflexively narrowing the field to lawyers, cases, and courts.

Each proposal to advance A2J frames problems and sets out solutions differently—some rooted in top-down and others in bottom-up perspectives. Below are some examples. First, a 2006 American Bar Association Recommendation proposes that the profession advance the right to counsel to help low-income individuals obtain basic human needs through legal claims. This conventional "gap" story is an individuated yet still unfulfilled proposal with these main goals:

1. Increase funding for legal services to the poor in civil and criminal cases.

2. Communicate the availability of affordable legal services and information to moderate-income persons.

3. Provide effective representation for the full range of legal needs of low and middle income persons.

4. Encourage the development of systems and procedures that make the justice system easier for all persons to understand and use.[78]

Providing more detail, critical legal scholars Deborah Rhode and Scott Cummings offer an array of proposals to improve A2J in *systemic* terms—proposals one might imagine no legal professional could reject but which, in fact, remain unrealized. They point out that the legal profession has not met its basic service responsibilities, and often has opposed initiatives to

---

[77] Brian Glick, Two, Three, Many Rosas! Rebellious Lawyers and Progressive Activist Organizations, 23 Clinical L. Rev. 611, 617–18 (2017).

[78] American Bar Association Task Force on Access to Civil Justice Et Al., Report to the House of Delegates (2006), www.americanbar.org/content/dam/aba/administrative/legal_aid_indigent_defendants/ls_sclaid_resolution_06a112a.authcheckdam.pdf.

ACCESS TO JUSTICE: LOOKING BACK, THINKING AHEAD
Deborah L. Rhode and Scott L. Cummings
30 Geo. J. Legal Ethics 485 (2017)

expand access. These collective, longstanding failures constitute a professional and national "disgrace."

... [O]ver four-fifths of the legal needs of the poor remain unmet, a figure that has not budged over the last three decades. ... The fact that a majority of those who seek help from federally funded civil legal aid programs are turned away due to lack of resources is a national disgrace, and the situation has not been improving. ...

... In 1998, the LSC funded just 3,590 attorneys. By 2015, that number had grown to only 5,000 attorneys. ... Funding for direct legal services comes out to just $5.85 per eligible person per year. In 2016, Americans spent more on Halloween costumes for pets than on LSC grants. ...

... Other developed democracies devote three to ten times more funding to civil legal aid than the United States.

... [The American Bar Association (ABA) and state Bar associations] have often actively fought self-help publications, nonlawyer providers, and mandatory pro bono obligations. ... Only sixteen percent of lawyers give financial support to legal assistance organizations, and only about a third think that the legal community should bear more of the cost of civil legal aid. ...

... [T]he profession needs to do more. ...

In courts that handle housing, bankruptcy, small claims, and family matters, ... [greater non-lawyer assistance] would reduce complexity, take greater advantage of technology, and train judges and staff in aiding unrepresented parties. Pro se clerks, centers, hotlines, and citizen advice programs are part of the solution. ...

Courts should also develop or permit licensing systems that allow qualified nonlawyers to offer personalized assistance on routine matters. ...

... [The organized bar] should be collaborating with the creators of "disruptive technologies" to ensure that quality services reach people who can benefit most ... [including] access to justice "apps" that seek to help individuals of limited means navigate legal proceedings and connect users with free or low-cost lawyers. ...

... [O]nly about a third of the lawyers reported meeting the aspirational standard of the *Model Rules of Professional Conduct*: more than fifty hours of service to persons of limited means (or organizations that support them) per year. . . .

. . . Pro bono work offers many attorneys their only direct contact with what passes for justice among the poor. Giving lawyers some experience with poverty-related problems and public interest causes can lay crucial foundations for change. . . .

. . . [The profession also should address] the critical importance of ongoing support for career paths in public interest law, which serves constituencies lacking a strong political voice. . . . Although law school and federal loan forgiveness programs have helped graduates cope with otherwise crippling student debt burdens, these initiatives have not adequately addressed the other financial challenges for public interest lawyers. . . .

. . . If we are truly committed to equal justice under law, then we must do more to make that commitment a professional priority.

Rhode and Cummings make plain that A2J "gaps" are the systemic norm, which lawyers collectively—as a profession ostensibly committed to equal justice under law—can but don't rectify, refusing to implement even the most modest reforms. In contrast to this top-down norm, legal scholar Gary Blasi outlines a more critical, robust, bottom-up approach to A2J projects. Blasi outlines a model of "affirmative, collaborative, and collective" action accountable to bottoms rather than tops, generating transformative solutions rooted in three-layered progress.

FRAMING ACCESS TO JUSTICE: BEYOND PERCEIVED JUSTICE FOR INDIVIDUALS

Gary Blasi
42 Loy. L.A. L. Rev. 913 (2009)

. . . I write about the framing of "access to justice." The naïve layperson might think these three words convey the possibility of achieving a just result, a result achieved through a fair process, or more likely both. . . . But over the years, . . . access to justice has come to be framed rather narrowly into four components: (1) access of (2) an individual (3) to a lawyer, or some form of assistance purported to be at least a partial substitute, (4) to help deal with a problem or dispute already framed in legal terms. . . . We are so far from realizing such a vision that one hesitates to suggest, as I do here, that the current vision is too narrow. . . . [But reframing] access to justice would encompass not only problems that have ripened into clear legal controversies but also those that might do so with the benefit of legal assistance. It would extend to a right to assistance in overcoming collective action problems and in asserting group claims where doing so is either necessary or efficient. Finally, it would include a right to effective assistance in which effectiveness is measured, at least in part, by the results achieved.

... [I]f we begin with the limited ambition of providing counsel (or purported alternatives) only in individual, well-defined legal disputes, then that is as far as we are likely to get.... There are already powerful forces driving the provision of legal services toward isolated, individual, and limited assistance. Funders, both government and private, often insist on quantitative indications of service delivery that push service delivery models toward providing limited assistance to large numbers of people. There are powerful political and ideological forces that are extremely hostile to the provision of legal assistance that might challenge entrenched injustice on a wider scale....

... [We need] a wider framing of access to justice—for at least some populations and some kinds of problems—that would encompass [an affirmative] right to assistance to (1) claims making, which would include assistance not only with problems that have ripened into clear legal controversies but also with those that might do so with the benefit of legal assistance; (2) organizing and coordination, which would include legal or organizing assistance to overcome collective action problems and to assert group claims, where doing so is either necessary or demonstrably more efficient or effective; and (3) monitoring and enforcement, which would include legal and investigative assistance to monitor and enforce compliance with equitable relief obtained through litigation or organizational or institutional change obtained by other means....

... The equal application of our laws, particularly for the benefit of the poor and powerless, and in relation to their fundamental human needs, should not be left to politics alone—at least not if we expect to remain a nation of laws predicated on more than mere power....

Blasi notes that "some populations and some kinds of problems," in particular, require an expanded framing of A2J—one that takes into account identities, groups, interests, and power. Blake Strode, Executive Director of Arch City Defenders in St. Louis, focuses on the centrality of identity-based castes to A2J projects:

> There is no version of justice that does not begin by first contending with injustice. And there is no honest conversation about injustice that does not recognize the role of identity. Therefore, as we go about discussing *what* justice is, *why* it is so

critical, and *how* we can ensure access to it, let us also spend a moment on *who* gets to have it.[79]

Relatedly, disabilities advocate Viviana Bonilla-López suggests that focusing on identities leads to a deeper analysis of groups, interests, and power. This analysis can spur a shift in A2J sites, approaches, and actions. She notes that traditional behavioral health-legal partnerships may fail to "account for the painful and often traumatic history between people with mental illnesses and the medical profession" and be "incompatible with the mental health recovery movement and with autonomy-focused lawyer-client relationships."[80] Advocates working on disability rights issues, therefore, might decide to adapt hospital-based medical-legal partnerships to partner, instead, with "recovery-centered clubhouses" in clubhouse-legal partnerships. Clubhouse organizations involve individual members with mental health illnesses in managing day-to-day activities and, at times, in advocacy on healthcare issues. This move would represent a site change—from hospital to community group—and a shift to community- and political lawyering-inspired problem solving with clients engaging in legal and extralegal activities. Such clubhouse-legal partnerships root A2J in attention to identities, groups, interests, and power.

Legal scholar Sagit Mor, in fact, suggests that the lack of attention in traditional A2J efforts to identities, groups, interests, and power might be the most notable "gap" of all. Using a critical disability lens, Mor suggests that the disability rights movement offers instructive lessons on access and accessibility that could help advocates shape A2J projects for both amelioration and transformation. Does Mor's analysis, coupled with the preceding excerpts, help you to clarify critical notions of "access" and "justice" that go beyond formal legal procedures or venues?

WITH ACCESS AND JUSTICE FOR ALL
Sagit Mor
39 Cardozo L. Rev. 611 (2017)

... Access has become an increasingly significant concept in struggles for social justice in recent decades, particularly in two contexts: the access to justice movement and the disability rights movement. ...

---

[79] Jennifer Ching, Thomas B. Harvey, Meena Jagannath, Purvi Shah & Blake Strode, A Few Interventions and Offerings from Five Movement Lawyers to the Access to Justice Movement, 87 Fordham L. Rev. Online (2018), https://ir.lawnet.fordham.edu/flro/vol87/iss1/31/.

[80] Viviana Bonilla-López, Beyond Medical Legal Partnerships: Addressing Recovery-Harming Social Conditions through Clubhouse-Legal Partnerships, 43 N.Y.U. Rev. of L. & Soc. Change 429 (2019). For additional thoughts on integrating critical advocacy approaches into medical-legal partnerships, see Dina Shek, Centering Race at the Medical-Legal Partnership in Hawai'i, 10 U. Miami Race & Soc. Just. L. Rev. 109 (2019); Amy Killelea, Collaborative Lawyering Meets Collaborative Doctoring: How a Multidisciplinary Partnership for HIV/AIDS Services Can Improve Outcomes for the Marginalized Sick, 16 Geo. J. on Poverty L. & Pol'y 413 (2010).

... [T]he combination of the "right to access" and "access to justice" reveals a multiplicity of sites where the ideas of the two movements intersect and interact. ...

... [A]ccessibility, in its broad sense, is the foundation for the entire struggle for disability rights; it is the key for participation in the public sphere and for personal decision-making in the private sphere. ...

... A well-developed and conceptualized right to access is also the basis for a fully developed right to access to justice for disabled people and for all [and includes the following]:

Access to the courts: ... The barriers under this category are *entry barriers* since they concern the absolute denial of access to legal instances due to a subdivision of formal, material, or physical barriers. ... In response, several mechanisms have developed that provided partial solutions to these problems: State-sponsored legal aid, small claims courts, group representation, and class actions. ...

Access to law: The discussion on access to law involves a wider range of barriers, which I call *process barriers, which affect the utilization of law*, and may prevent persons from claiming their rights even in the absence of formal barriers. They include an array of structural, social, cultural, and mental barriers that affect the fairness of the legal process and the legal system more broadly as they expose the deeper impact of power relations on the design of the legal system and its accessibility to a wide range of classes and populations. The barriers under this category may include: *spatial barriers* relating mainly to roads of access and the availability of services and public transportation, which are affected by center-periphery disparities; *communication and language barriers* that mainly affect ethnic and national minorities, migrants, and immigrants but also concern the generally inaccessible and alienating nature of the legal language; *informational barriers*, relating to access to information about the law, including the content of substantive legal rules and their application in specific situations, the nature of the legal process, the content of legal procedures, and the availability of legal services; *awareness barriers*, relating mainly to naming and blaming, that is to the ability to conceptualize an offensive experience as a matter of injustice, resulting, for instance, from discrimination, negligence, or sexual assault; other *psychological and cultural barriers* may relate to the level of alienation from, or trust in, the legal system, particularly when socioeconomic marginality intersects with identity-based social exclusion. Moreover, additional *economic barriers* may further and intensify any of the above barriers, making intersectionality an important factor in the analysis, whether it is spatial, informational, or awareness barriers. This wide range of barriers is relevant to the person's capacity to claim his rights, under any realm of law, from welfare benefits to civil wrongs, to constitutional protection. They are located at the intersection between procedural and substantive justice and expose the complexities of naming, blaming, and claiming, even in absence of formal barriers, and their potential impact on the outcome of the legal process and the evolution of law.

Access to justice: The term "access to justice" expands the discussion further.... I call the barriers under this category *outcome barriers* as they concern *biases in the structure and the content of substantive legal rules and of judicial decisions*, even when a lawsuit was filed and a trial was in place. These structural biases extend to the legislative and regulatory arenas, where legal rules are produced and therefore influenced by the presence or absence of political representation of the affected groups and interests, and by the quality of that representation. These barriers may stem from power dynamics in the legal process, including: *power differences between the parties*, such as differences in bargaining power, as the literature on the "haves" versus "have nots" teaches us through the concept of repeated players versus one-shotters; *cognitive and ideological biases* affecting investigative and enforcement agencies as well as judicial discretion in decisions concerning the initiation of a trial or the results of a trial; *unequal access to law and policy-making* affecting the opportunity to shape the structure and content of legal rules in different legislative and regulatory arenas; and biases in the *landscape of legal norms*, which render some claims inferior to others, such as the inherent inferiority of social and group rights, and other claims impossible or extremely difficult to pursue due to inadequate legal language and tools to define them as injustice and to ask for redress....

... Access to justice ... broadens the scope of the discussion from access to courts, which narrowly focuses on entry barriers, and access to law, which examines the role of process barriers in access to legal proceedings, towards outcome barriers that pertain to the design and content of legal norms. It concerns the deepest effects of social power relations on the legal system and its ability to produce just results....

The legal developments in the realm of disability rights ... offer a critical account of access and accessibility that aims at transforming society, rather than reforming the person, through the redesign of social institutions, the removal of structural and environmental barriers, and the inclusion of all affected groups as integral parts of future planning processes. A fully accessible legal system would allow all human beings to fully enjoy all existing legal facilities and services as equals, while minimizing the impact of social power relations and economic inequalities. Consequently, it will more likely produce just results for all.

Mor's analysis illustrates vividly why formal equality is a failure. She shows how identities, groups, interests, and power can inform advocacy projects geared to improving A2J for any group—and thus for all. She also vividly displays how one School of critical knowledge—Disability Legal Studies—catalyzes positive developments. Mor and others in this section make clear that A2J includes meaningful, affirmative participation in the macro-micro design of systems, rules, and institutions—not simply after-the-fact access to a lawyer and a forum.

NOTES AND QUESTIONS

1. *Designing with Risk in Mind.* We noted, when discussing the NOWCRJ example above, that individuals who engage in protest against rights abuses face the risk of retaliation. But members of vulnerable groups face risk in any encounter with legal institutions—making risk a factor in all A2J projects. Justine Olderman and Runa Rajagopal, who work with The Bronx Defenders, a holistic public interest law organization, describe the experience of one parent, Jazmine Headley, when she tried to resolve problems with her city-issued childcare voucher:

> The wait times at the center were long, and all the seats were taken, so Jazmine and her son sat on the floor where they played quietly and waited. When a security guard approached her and told her to get up, Jazmine remained where she was, explaining that there were no seats available. Jazmine's refusal to get up set into motion a series of events: the center's security calling the New York City Police Department (NYPD), law enforcement violently ripping her son from her arms, the NYPD arresting Jazmine, a judge sending her to Rikers Island [prison] for five days, and her separation from her son.
>
> . . . [Jazmine] is young, Black, single, a mother, employed, and someone who relies on financial assistance to survive. . . . [A]ll of these identities and circumstances contributed to the dehumanizing way she was treated . . .
>
> . . . For low-income Black and Brown people, . . . system involvement through any entry point begets more system involvement and irreparably destabilizes their lives.[81]

What does this experience suggest about the relationship between risk and access to any claims process or legal institution? Do traditional approaches to A2J adequately take into account risks?

2. *Consciousness-Raising as A2J Method.* To counter entrenched fears, legal scholar Elizabeth MacDowell suggests advocates engage in specific practices to assess risks of unwanted state interventions, raise consciousness about the risks of interacting with legal institutions, and develop individual and collective A2J safety strategies:

---

[81] Justine Olderman and Runa Rajagopal, A National Movement for Access to Justice Must Be Holistic, 87 Fordham L. Rev. Online (2018), https://ir.lawnet.fordham.edu/flro/vol87/iss1/29/.

A structural analysis that interrogates the role of the coercive state is required to effectively address access to justice in courts frequented by poor people [and could be implemented using steps like the following]:

1. Redesigning Intake to Account for Interrelated Problems

It is important to develop intake forms that assess . . . vulnerability to state intervention. . . .

In each type of case, the intake form would inquire about safety concerns. Broadening inquiries about safety to cases where the client-litigant has not identified domestic violence as a concern, and to non-family cases, embraces the broader concept . . . [that includes] state and community violence, and also the violence of subordination. . . . The goal is to obtain facts necessary to establish a comprehensive and sound basis for counseling client-litigants entering (or considering entering) poor people's courts. . . .

2. Counseling on Impacts, Intersections, and Options

. . . [T]hose counseling client-litigants should . . . [educate] client-litigants about the potential connections between systems and the possible consequences of each course of action. . . .

For example, an applicant for a protective order with minor children should understand the potential economic ramifications of the order, any vulnerability to intervention by a child welfare agency or by the court, and how the order might impact any other related case. . . .

Counseling . . . may also include identifying opportunities for collective action. . . .

3. Educating about Narrative, Rights, and Resistance

Empowering low-income client-litigants . . . includes teaching client-litigants about the language of court, including legal terminology, and also less formal, but no less important, expectations about verbal presentation and etiquette. Educating client-litigants about the language of court also requires exposing underlying ideologies and expectations. . . .

4. Developing Proactive Strategies

. . . A proactive social justice approach also includes reaching out to community members who have not yet sought access to the court, for example, through community-based education programs. . . . However, . . . [if] people are taught about legal rights and obligations without a critique of their utility or absent meaningful assistance with enforcement, then education is simply another aspect of hegemony: making subordination seem more fair because the subordinated were well-informed but failed to take correct action. . . .

> ... **Promoting Accountability**
>
> ... The evaluative criteria for such a project would look different than the criteria for a program that merely provides access to the courts.... [I]t would also examine whether the program's efforts reduce punitive practices, unwanted interventions, and the influence of bias, while increasing judicial compliance with the law. It would also develop methods to examine whether client-litigants are empowered to address the problems that brought them to the program.[82]

What challenges might you face in advocating for implementation of these suggestions? How would you plan to overcome them (while minimizing the risks of preservation through transformation, of cooptation, of capture, of tokenism, or of retaliation)?

3. *Reframing A2J Through Mindfulness Practices Rooted in Bottom-Up Collaborations.* MacDowell, Rhode, Blasi, Olderman, Rajagopal, and others have called for reforming legal education to prepare students—tomorrow's advocates—to critically reimagine A2J. Legal scholar Thalia González asks students to use mindfulness techniques of reflection and self-reflection as part of their formal legal training in a course focused on analyzing A2J programs. These practices draw on the individual experiences of each student but also bring into the classroom (or conference room or court room) knowledge gained by working with (or observing) clients and advocates in public interest law settings.

> [C]ontemplative pedagogy can aid the development of skills necessary to engage in *critical* self-reflection, produce deliberate and shared knowledge, and connect to historical and contemporary realities of power and privilege....
>
> ... Over time, a quiet revolution of mindfulness—as a pedagogy and a practice—has gained significant recognition. But a look at the broader movement reveals a continued emphasis on the individual, with little focus on how such practices can be integrated into ... legal practice.
>
> ... Students have engaged in ... greater self-reflection, developing consciousness of their connections to others, and asking deeper questions about the extent to which lawyering and law itself reinforce the status quo.[83]

Building a critical capacity for mindfulness takes time, commitment, and discipline. But it helps you to increase your control over your own mind and thoughts. Is this benefit important in law practice or systemic advocacy? Does "mindfulness" have a substantial role to play in the practice of collaborative

---

[82] Elizabeth L. MacDowell, Reimagining Access to Justice in the Poor People's Courts, 22 Geo. J. on Poverty L. & Pol'y 473 (2015).

[83] Thalia González, A Quiet Revolution: Mindfulness, Rebellious Lawyering, and Community Practice, 53 Cal. W.L. Rev. 49 (2016).

professionalism? Why or why not? What advocacy Approaches does González invoke as support for these reflection practices as legal method? Does her analysis encourage you to practice self-reflection as part of your advocacy?

8.8 ENVIRONMENTAL JUSTICE, PRIVATE PROFIT, AND CLIMATE CHANGE

Above, we showed differing perspectives on A2J as examples of advocacy project design in which, to greater and lesser extents, the lessons of the critical Schools and advocacy Approaches were incorporated within legal culture itself. Here, we expand that focus to climate change, emphasizing that advocacy projects often must be designed to address systemic problems that are transnational, emergent, or accelerating rapidly. Recalling LoPucki and Matthew from Part II, what kind of systemic problems arise as part of the emerging—and accelerating—climate crisis? What is the role of law in creating or solving problems related to climate change? How might you distinguish *systemic* from individual or idiosyncratic climate-related problems—taking into account identities, groups, interests, and power? How might you develop an advocacy project related to climate change based in critical, historical, and contextual knowledge to make progress along all three layers of goals—technical fixes, power building, and culture shifts? Climate change as an issue area offers a chance to apply lessons about designing advocacy projects that use law for justice—"climate justice."

From a critical and bottom-up perspective, climate justice includes the following commitments:

> Climate Justice means, first of all, removing the causes of global warming and allowing the Earth to continue to nourish our lives and those of all living beings. . . .
>
> Climate Justice in the United States means the solutions adopted to ward off global warming can't fall hardest on low income communities, communities of color, or the workers employed by the fossil fuel industry. Climate Justice means fostering a *just transition* for these constituencies to a healthier and more just environment to work and live in.
>
> Climate Justice means providing assistance to communities threatened or impacted by climate change, such as the communities devastated by [hurricanes, fires, and similar disasters].
>
> Climate Justice means that . . . industrialized nations, which historically and currently are most responsible for global warming, should lead the transformation. . . .

> Climate Justice for developing nations means that international institutions such as the World Bank and World Trade Organization should . . . foster the transformation to sustainable and equitable development based on clean energy technologies.
>
> Ultimately, Climate Justice means holding fossil fuel corporations accountable[,] . . . stripping transnational corporations of the tremendous power they hold over our lives, and in its place building democracy at the local, national and international levels.[84]

Climate justice advocates and activists work in varied contexts and communities but root their work in critical knowledges and antisubordination values. Indigenous Climate Action, a coalition of environmental groups, for example, defines climate justice based on several bottom-up principles: "Indigenous identity is inseparable from the lands and waters;" "Indigenous knowledge systems, respecting natural laws, and using two eyed seeing—merging collective Indigenous knowledges with western science;" and "using a reciprocal and relational approach, in collaborating to build power, and in prioritizing accountability to community."[85]

As with other issue areas, young people have been leaders in the climate justice movement. The 2019 Climate Justice Youth summit, an annual gathering of young people of color, started with a march "highlighting the impact of climate change on Puerto Rico and the Caribbean . . . [and then] examine[d] ways to move us out of an extractive economy to a regenerative one that respects our people, our bodies, our land, and our future."[86] Participants in this summit, like other climate justice advocates and activists, are driven by a sense of urgency; the problems arising from climate change are developing at a faster pace than the ability to operationalize solutions. Legal scholar Mari Matsuda frames the problem as not simply a challenge for technology and adaptation but a question of systemic injustice—dehumanization—and democracy:

> We live now in the most dangerous of times. If one studies the coming climate disruption, clear and present danger does not come close to capturing where we are going, with loss of human life, upheaval, and forced migration on a scale unprecedented in recorded history. That is my emergency; what is yours? . . .

---

[84] Kenny Bruno, Joshua Karlina & China Brotsky, Greenhouse Gangsters vs. Climate Justice, Transnational Resource and Action Center (Nov. 1999), www.iicat.org/wp-content/uploads/2012/03/Greenhouse-Gangsters-vs-Climate-Justice-1999.pdf.

[85] Indigenous Climate Action, Our Values, www.indigenousclimateaction.com/vision-mission-values.

[86] Climate Justice Youth Summit, Climate Justice Alliance (Oct. 3, 2019), www.climatejusticealliance.org/people-hoods-power/climate-justice-youth-summit-poster/.

> ... The clear and present danger of climate chaos will require all hands on deck—all citizens standing free, equal, and mutual—if we are to respond in a way that does not end democracy itself. Fear and scarcity are twin democracy killers. These killers are coming for us, and if social practices of dehumanization prevail, we will fall.[87]

Below are two excerpts that describe climate change as a complex, emergent, and accelerating set of social problems. Neither excerpt focuses on the design of responsive advocacy projects aimed at achieving "climate justice." Both, however, provide background that helps set the stage for innovative project design in context.

Legal scholar Shalanda Baker considers the legal significance of global environmental change under neoliberal regimes. In this emergent Anthropocene age, Baker concludes, "the background rules of development" will have to be restructured and new "business models" created. This restructuring will require reframing of contract and property law. Baker spotlights how existing ground rules of "private" law frustrate solutions for public problems—and shows that sometimes they help worsen the problem over time. Climate change and climate justice epitomize the Critical Challenge in an unprecedented context.

ADAPTIVE LAW IN THE ANTHROPOCENE
Shalanda H. Baker
90 Chi.-Kent L. Rev. 563 (2015)

... We are now firmly rooted in a new epoch scientists have named the Anthropocene, where the activities of humans will most certainly negatively impact the trajectory of Earth and its inhabitants. What the Anthropocene fully holds is uncertain, but there are a few clues. The global ecology is shifting. The oceans are dying. The planet is getting hotter and drier, and its storms increasingly volatile.

... Amidst this changing climate is evidence of a failed approach to economic development in the Global South. Globally, the poor are becoming poorer. Inequality reigns as the global economy shrinks. ... [R]eliance on neoliberal economic development institutions ... will render states in the Global South even more vulnerable and less resilient in the face of climate change. ...

Anthropocene in the Global South

The Anthropocene refers to the current geological epoch characterized by a distinctively human impact on the trajectory of life on Earth. Man's

---

[87] Mari Matsuda, Dissent in a Crowded Theater, 72 SMU L. Rev. 441, 442, 456 (2019).

reliance on fossil fuels for development has charted a perilous climatic path. Squarely in this path are all of us: the vulnerable. . . .

. . . The most recent United Nations Intergovernmental Panel on Climate Change (IPCC) report places communities in the Global South at heightened vulnerability in this anthropogenic era. . . . Developing states, those who bear the least responsibility for the troubles heralded by the Anthropocene, appear poised to suffer the brunt of its harm.

Defining Characteristics

The thread linking poverty, climate change and vulnerability is unmistakable. . . .

. . . [F]rom a geological standpoint, the dawning of the Anthropocene . . . means that, millions of years from now, the layer of sediment indicating this time in our collective history will reflect a distinct epoch marked by a human-driven geological change. This geologic record will provide evidence of mass animal and plant extinctions, ocean acidification and widespread coral reef die-offs, rapid glacial melting, and relentless mining of the earth's surface for combustible fossil fuels.

The crystallization of the Anthropocene . . . [is] a clarion call for change. . . .

Climate Change Mitigation

. . . Since the Industrial Revolution, humans have emitted tons of carbon dioxide into the atmosphere with astounding effects. On one hand, the extraction of fossil fuels from deep within the Earth has allowed widespread prosperity for citizens of the Global North. . . . The benefits of the Industrial Revolution were not equally distributed, however. Although the overall quality of life increased in industrializing countries, wealth generated by the productive activities of the Global North remained concentrated in a few wealthy families.

Moreover, the Industrial Revolution created vast social and environmental externalities. Environmental damage spanned the spectrum as rivers, soils and previously pristine environments. . . . Perhaps the greatest harm . . . was the emission of carbon dioxide into the atmosphere.

. . . An effective [mitigation] system would both penalize those who historically have emitted the greatest amount of carbon dioxide into the atmosphere—industrialized economies—and allow Southern states to pursue economic development activities with minimal impact on the environment.

Risk, Development and the Neoliberal Moment

. . . If carbon emissions remain at current levels, the . . . question is whether the adaptation project simply refers to the physical architecture of survival, or if it means that something more essential, such as the law and institutions of development, must also become adaptive....

...An exploration of the roots of neoliberalism reveals that the same economic, social, and environmental risks that will increase in the Anthropocene are the risks that are left unchecked in a neoliberal frame.

Political Origins of Neoliberal Development

The dawn of neoliberal development is often traced to the Ronald Reagan and Margaret Thatcher era. With neoliberal development, post-colonial states in the Global South, unable to finance their own development projects and laden with debt, turned to the free market to meet their development needs. This move was precipitated partly by need and, arguably, partly by coercion.

...[F]rom the 1950s into the early 1970s, states in the [Global] South were also coalescing around state sovereignty and calling for a greater role within intergovernmental organizations such as the United Nations.

...In the Reagan-Thatcher era, and well into the 1980s and 1990s, states in the Global South ... borrow[ed] heavily from international financial institutions such as the International Monetary Fund and the Bank; the only significant catch being that such states would also be required to implement neoliberal law reforms. Laws protecting private property and contract rights and opening domestic markets were thus implemented on a broad scale throughout the Global South. These reforms ushered in the neoliberal era of development.... [T]hey also doomed the South to a cycle of dependency and unsustainable natural resource exploitation.

Risk Taking

... [N]eoliberal development is straightforward. With open markets and private law, states are primed for market entry by private actors. These actors—corporations and private banks, with substantial technical and political support from institutions like the Bank—enter states in the Global South in the name of development....

...In project finance, sophisticated actors who are expert and repeat players in the field of development—Chevron, Texaco, or BP, for example—create multiple subsidiaries throughout a region that engage in highly risky and highly leveraged projects to garner high returns. Within this [development] frame, these sophisticated players are largely protected from the risks of their activities. They act behind the shield of limited liability and, for additional protection, through a complex web of contracts that effectively ensure that the environmental, social and financial risks of the activity will never impact the actor responsible for its initiation....

Destabilization

... For neoliberalism to hold, the theory must maintain the fiction that markets create their own conditions for success. Looking across the landscape of the Global South, this premise does not seem to hold. . . . In most cases, unrestrained and open market access led to the wholesale pillaging of domestic capacity for production, thus also limiting a state's adaptive capacity. The North American Free Trade Agreement (NAFTA), [is] a classic neoliberal trade agreement. . . .

NAFTA, with its focus on opening Mexico's markets to foster growth, has been blamed for the evisceration of its agricultural industry. Small farmers, once thriving and selling a diverse array of agricultural products, including Mexican cultivated maize, a sacred grain in the country, are impoverished in the post-NAFTA world. Such farmers are pressured into mono-agriculture transactions supported by large, private, agricultural companies and are now so impoverished they are unable to even afford the food they produce. . . . In the Anthropocene, [these market-based approaches] render states more impoverished, incapable of crop and product diversification, and more vulnerable to climate change. . . .

Advancing an Adaptive Development Law Research Agenda

First, we must develop alternatives to limited liability forms and other business models that externalize the risks of their activities. Such activities create vulnerability and undermine principles of resilience. Doing so will require embracing new relational forms that strengthen our collective resiliency, equitably share risks, and provide social benefits. In the Anthropocene, we may no longer accept that the harmful activity of privileged actors will be externalized, damaging our fragile ecosystem and rendering communities more vulnerable.

Second, we must recognize that the contractual framework of development must be flexible to account for dramatic environmental changes. The Anthropocene requires flexible paradigms of law ... expanding rigid principles of contract and treaty law, such as the doctrine of changed circumstances and impossibility, to allow for a changed development environment. . . .

Finally, going forward, we must develop legal paradigms of property that expand the frame of development possibilities. In the United States, private property rights are often viewed as "absolute;" however, the Anthropocene will require reframing of property law to incorporate collective needs. Such reframing might allow for scaling back of market-driven approaches to development and strengthen local capacity for adaptation.

... We are collectively vulnerable at this critical time in human history. Therefore, we all must get to work to create an adaptive development law that strengthens our collective resilience. ...

Baker emphasizes the need to adapt legal regimes, not just buildings, walls, and bridges, to overcome the growing effects of climate change. She explains how adaptive law provides an opportunity—if not an obligation—to adjust foundational concepts and ground rules to reflect changing conditions. But to ensure climate justice in a world of climate change, adaptive law necessarily must reject as law "the primacy of profit over the environment and the common good." This shift is fundamental because "neoliberal development actors have little incentive to serve as stewards of the environment" by leaving "a light footprint." To the contrary, the formal legal mandate of profit maximization creates an incentive for corporations to exploit all resources—human and environmental—as much as possible (and regardless of context).

This rush to quick and maximum profit despite environmental damage requires legal permission for "externalizing" the harms of development. Those who most damage the environment are rewarded financially because that degradation is excluded from the costs of "doing business." With the damages of pollution shifted by law from private elites to the public at large, the underlying profit imperative shields from accountability the routine practice of private interests despoiling the public environment for their own gain. This "private" corporate freedom to exploit just about everything on Earth—knowing that environmental costs of profit-making will legally be left behind for others—necessarily fuels climate change and injustice.

Expanding these points, international environmental law scholar Carmen Gonzalez examines the colonial roots and neoliberal continuation of systemic inequality through the law of trade, commerce, and profit. Like Baker, Gonzalez explains how neoliberalism structures international trade by law to enable corporations from the Global North to exploit for maximum private profit the public resources of vulnerable countries around the world. Global trade, as regulated by law, becomes the vehicle to transfer wealth from the global have-nots to the global haves on a massive, self-perpetuating scale. These one-way transfers involve foundational principles of public law—like sovereignty itself, as explained by Anghie in Part I. Today, sovereignty in the Global South has been overridden by elites in the Global North through one-sided agreements, including treaties, that "seek to provide foreign investors with unfettered access to natural resources by restricting the ability of host states to adopt health and safety, environmental, labor, and human rights standards." These public areas of law include, as Gonzalez explains, international economic, environmental, and criminal law—interlocking sets of transnational ground rules tailored by (and for) colonialism and neoliberalism.

BRIDGING THE NORTH-SOUTH DIVIDE: INTERNATIONAL ENVIRONMENTAL LAW IN THE ANTHROPOCENE
Carmen G. Gonzalez
32 Pace Envtl. L. Rev. 407 (2015)

. . . International environmental law has generally failed to halt or reverse the rapid deterioration of the planet's life support systems. Conflicts between affluent and poor countries (the North-South divide) over environmental priorities, the allocation of responsibility for environmental harm, and the relationship between environmental protection and economic development have generated gridlock in environmental treaty negotiations, as well as inadequate compliance with existing agreements. . . .

International environmental law must directly challenge the relentless drive toward economic expansion and unbridled exploitation of people and nature rather than merely attempt to mitigate its excesses. An essential step toward such a reconceptualization is to examine the ways in which international law has historically engaged with nature and with the peoples of the global South in order to identify the policies and practices that subordinate the South and hasten the destruction of the planet's ecosystems.

The Colonial and Post-Colonial Origins of the North-South Divide

. . . Colonialism universalized European notions of nature as a commodity for human exploitation while creating a global economy that systematically subordinated the global South. For example, post-colonial states in Asia, Africa, and Latin America were integrated into the Northern-dominated world economy as exporters of primary commodities and importers of manufactured products. Because the terms of trade consistently favored manufactured goods over primary products, the nations of the global South were required to export increasing amounts of their output in order to acquire the same amount of manufactured goods . . . thereby reducing Southern export earnings, exacerbating Southern poverty, and reinforcing the North-South economic divide.

The North's control over a large part of the world's resources from the colonial era to the present fueled the North's industrial development and enabled the North to maintain levels of consumption far beyond the limits of its own natural resource base. . . .

The South's economic dependency on export production enabled the North to exploit Southern resources at prices that did not reflect the social and environmental costs of production. Far from producing prosperity, export-led development strategies depleted the South's natural resources, harmed human health, and reinforced social and economic inequality by imposing disparate environmental burdens on the communities targeted for petroleum extraction, mining, and other forms of resource exploitation. . . .

International Economic Law and the North-South Divide

International economic law intensified the North-South divide and exacerbated the commodification and despoliation of nature. Modern investment law, for example, inherited from the colonial era an instrumentalist view of the environment as an object for Northern exploitation, with no corresponding duty to protect the health of local ecosystems, enhance the well-being of local communities, or advance the goals and interests of the host state. Thus, contemporary bilateral investment treaties (BITs) and regional investment agreements seek to provide foreign investors with unfettered access to natural resources by restricting the ability of host states to adopt health and safety, environmental, labor, and human rights standards. If these social and environmental standards impair the economic value of the investment, they may be challenged as indirect expropriations or breaches of fair and equitable treatment standards. . . . [T]hese one-sided agreements generally . . . provide no mechanism for holding corporations accountable for the harms to human health and the environment that their activities cause in the host state. . . .

The export-led economic policies mandated by the IMF [International Monetary Fund] and the World Bank exacerbated poverty and inequality, reinforced the South's environmentally and economically disadvantageous dependence on the export of primary commodities, and enabled Northern transnational corporations to dominate many of the newly privatized economic sectors. . . .

. . . By depriving Southern nations of the tools used by the global North and by certain middle-income Southern states to diversify and industrialize their economies while imposing new requirements to protect the rights of foreign investors and intellectual property holders, international economic law has institutionalized Southern poverty.

Sustainable Development: Part of the Solution or Part of the Problem?

The root cause of the contemporary ecological crisis is an international economic order premised on unlimited economic growth that impoverishes the global South and facilitates the overconsumption of the planet's resources by its more affluent inhabitants. This economic order reinforces the colonial notion that . . . the apex of civilization [is] represented by the global North. It casts development as "the ubiquitous goal of all states and peoples," and equates development with rising material consumption. Pioneered by Europe and the United States, this economic model has been exported to the global South. . . .

. . . Having industrialized by appropriating the South's natural resources and by using more than its fair share of the global commons for waste disposal, the North's per capita ecological footprint continues to significantly outstrip that of the South. . . . [T]he global North owes an ecological debt to the countries and peoples of the global South for "resource plundering, unfair trade, environmental damage and the free occupation of environmental space to deposit waste." Indeed, this ecological debt is at the heart of many North-South conflicts in international environmental law.

. . . Global environmental degradation has been constructed as an externality . . . through multilateral environmental agreements. . . . International environmental law is a field in crisis because the problems it currently confronts are deeply embedded in the existing economic order and cannot be adequately addressed by tinkering on the margins.

The Way Forward

Environmental justice provides a compelling moral framework for the reconceptualization of international environmental law. The primary cause of global environmental degradation is the over-consumption of the planet's finite resources by global elites located primarily in the global North. However, the South and the planet's most vulnerable communities bear a disproportionate share of the pollution and resource depletion caused by this unsustainable economic activity. In response to this inequity, transnational environmental justice movements have emerged in both the North and the South, including grassroots social movements for climate justice, food justice, energy justice, and water justice. Emphasizing intra-generational justice, many of these movements have framed their demands for environmental justice in the language of human rights. Human rights tribunals have concluded that failure to protect the environment can violate a variety of human rights, including the rights to life, health, property, privacy, the collective rights of indigenous peoples to their ancestral lands and resources, and the right to a healthy environment.

The Rights of Nature and Future Generations

. . . Instead of attempting to "civilize" and "develop" the South in accordance with Northern preferences and priorities, . . . [w]here might we seek inspiration for alternatives to the dominant economic paradigm? . . .

Among the principles of traditional legal systems that can be incorporated into contemporary environmental law are the trusteeship rather than ownership of natural resources, the principle of intergenerational rights, and the rights of the nature. For example, in 2008, Ecuador became the first country to adopt a national constitution recognizing the rights of nature based on the principle of *sumac kawsay,* the Kichwa idea of living in harmony with nature—known in Spanish as *el buen vivir,* or living well. In 2012, New Zealand accorded legal personhood to its longest navigable river, the Whanganui, as an important step toward resolving the historic grievances of Maori peoples. That same year, Bolivia adopted the *Framework Law of Mother Earth and Integral Development for Living Well,* which acknowledged the rights of nature. In addition, several constitutions, including those of South Africa, Ecuador, Bolivia, Kenya, Germany, and Norway, have recognized the rights of future generations.

... Reimagining international environmental law through the histories and traditions of other civilizations might enable us to develop alternative philosophies and economic ... for the benefit of subordinated states and peoples, future generations, and the other living creatures with whom we share the planet.

Minding the Justice Gap—Taking Intra-Generational Equity Seriously

... International environmental law can bridge the North-South divide and promote environmental justice by developing creative solutions to seemingly intractable problems that simultaneously benefit marginalized states and peoples, curb environmental degradation, and forge a new path to sustainability. ...

... [T]o meet the challenges of the Anthropocene, international environmental law must break out of its narrow silo and foster long-term solutions to global environmental problems that advance the interests of socially and economically powerless groups while hastening the transition to more sustainable patterns of production and consumption. Food, energy, and water—the basic necessities of life—should be central rather than peripheral to the mission of international environmental law.

Challenging the Global Economic Order

International law's long-standing commitment to commerce is linked, in complex ways, to its inability to address environmental degradation. From the colonial era to the present, international law and its institutions have facilitated the free flow of goods, services, and capital across national borders without taking into account the impact on local ecosystems and livelihoods.

... [T]his quasi-religious belief in the benefits of liberalized trade has produced an international economic order that generally ignores the environmental and social consequences of production and implicitly encourages environmental subsidies. ...

... International environmental law does not exist in a vacuum. In order to develop effective solutions to the environmental crises of the Anthropocene, it is essential to harmonize the disparate stands of international law. International economic law systematically accelerates environmental degradation, subordinates the global South, and consigns environmental issues to the peripheries of legal discourse and policy-making. Without a fundamental restructuring of international economic law, a just and sustainable planet is impossible. . . .

Gonzalez supplements Baker's account by examining international trade and law from the bottom-up perspective of environmental justice. Like Baker, Gonzalez concludes that neoliberalism is part of the climate justice problem—rather than offering its solution. Both agree that only systemic transformation—changes in foundational concepts, ground rules, and social priorities—can match the systemic problems of this dawning age. And both agree that more activist investment and advocacy innovation is needed to effectively confront climate change to advance climate justice.

NOTES AND QUESTIONS

1. *Rewriting the Rules of the Field in the Face of Elite Cooptation.* Many advocates and activists have taken up the call from scholars like Gonzalez and Baker to reimagine and rewrite rules regulating aspects of international trade and "free" markets. Legal clinician Janie Chuang describes the need, for example, for a "new field and regime of global migration law" [GML] to counter the multifaceted neoliberal globalization projects being advanced by elites. She highlights that a new sort of elite—philanthrocapitalists—has emerged to coopt efforts to improve global migration law. These elites have promoted voluntary, corporate-led codes of conduct and auditing agencies funded by and accountable only to philanthrocapitalists themselves. They thus undermine efforts to win mandatory, government-enforced regulations and accountability to worker groups and migrant worker communities of origin. They accomplish this cooptation *in the name of supporting* challenges by subordinated groups to current regulation that benefits corporate elites. Does Chuang's proposal for the creation of GML offer a model for advocacy projects to tackle emergent problems? Does it create opportunities for creative, bottom-up advocacy and organizing? Chuang notes that:

> [T]he lack of international laws and institutions pertaining to labor migration can enable—if not encourage—the exploitation of migrant workers. . . .
>
> . . . GML could play a crucial role in flipping the script, placing migrants' well-being at the center of concern. . . .
>
> . . . Through the lawmaking process, GML . . . might offer a governance structure that could hold dominant actors to account for their actions, it could also carve out a protected role for other, less powerful, actors whose perspectives are too often excluded from the policymaking fora: the workers themselves. Promoting a migrant-

centered perspective, GML recognizes that migrant workers are uniquely positioned to identify the gaps in migration governance that create vulnerability to exploitation throughout the migration process, across countries of origin, transit, and destination.[88]

2. *Advancing Epistemic Justice through Environmental Justice Struggles.* Like Gonzalez above, Latin America scholar Gustavo Rojas-Páez studied environmental advocacy and activism related to the ownership and control of natural resources in Bolivia. In response to this grassroots activism, Bolivian elites mounted a violent response, including incarceration and militarization, aimed both at maintaining colonial hierarchies and suppressing dissent. Rojas-Páez shows that exploitation of nature is based in colonial understandings carried over to structure modern views of nature. In this ideological scheme, "legal theory conceives nature as nothing more than a lifeless, inert object whose existence is dependent upon the needs, desires and greed of human beings." Recall Tsosie in Part 1. How are non-Western, non-elite knowledges devalued in environmental law—even supposedly protective environmental law? What are the consequences, and how do they differ for indigenous communities versus dominant groups? Who is arrested—polluters or members of the polluted community?

> In 2000 the people of Cochabamba protested against a new water law, which granted the control over the city's rural water systems to a subsidiary of the U.S. transnational [Bechtel]. For four months demonstrators demanded a change in the law and protested the extraordinary rise in the water bills they were charged by [Bechtel's] subsidiary in Bolivia. In response . . ., former dictator and Bolivian president of the time—Hugo Benzer—passed a declaration of "state of siege" under which constitutional rights were suspended. . . . [Eventually, Bechtel] withdrew from Bolivia and the water law was revoked. The victory of the social movement which mobilized around *Kucha Pampa (water in indigenous language Quechua)* was a blow to the neoliberal practices on development promoted by both Bolivian ruling classes and the international institutions such as the IMF and the World Bank. . . .
>
> The Bolivian experience of resistance to neoliberal policies . . . reached the realm of law as demonstrated by the Bolivian constitution of 2009, which granted rights to nature *Pacha Mama (Mother Land)*. . . . [T]he recognition of rights to nature challenges the colonial/modern representation of human beings as separated from nature. . . . [T]he collective action which led to the enactment of the Bolivian constitution represents the form of overcoming the epistemicide of approximately 8 million enslaved Bolivian indigenous people who lost their lives during the colonial era. . . .

---

[88] Janie A. Chuang, Using Global Migration Law to Prevent Human Trafficking, 111 AJIL Unbound 147 (2017).

> ... [T]his is a call for a horizontal dialogue among legalities seeking to understand the historical human suffering and injustice of which the universal character of modernity's knowledge production is complicit. After all, as Boaventura de Sousa Santos maintains: "there will be no social justice without epistemic justice."[89]

Reflecting on these materials, how might systemic advocates plan complex actions to advance both *epistemic* justice—respecting knowledge from the bottom that is excluded as not relevant to legal problem solving—and *social* justice—changing patterns of material deprivation and challenging the suppression of collective power and protest?

CHAPTER RECAP

This roadtest chapter focused on projects, practicalities, and three-layered goals to build on the preceding chapter and help advocates design their work as effectively as possible. As a pair, these back-to-back roadtests aim to help you consolidate and apply your understandings of Part I and II. Sometimes, as we saw in this chapter, formal legal rights—civil, human, or otherwise—may be central to the project and sometimes not. Everything depends on context. Inevitably, however, advocates anticipate and work around constraints, sometimes taking calculated risks, perhaps to self and perhaps to the group. Advocates will encounter and have to deal with tension and conflict—within teams and among allies, as well as with adversaries. Conflicts may focus on fundraising and spending in relationship to strategy and impact. Often, they also will involve the dual roles of advocates with "insider" training aligning with "outsider" groups—an insider/outsider tension we encounter throughout this book. To navigate these insider-outsider tensions productively, advocates return to dual consciousness to continually unlearn and relearn the relationship of law to justice; advocates in this way take risks and test constraints. Shifting attention to the roles of legal training and practice in preserving the Critical Challenge within law, the next part considers the framework for advocacy that dominates the "legal industry" in contrast to the three-layered framework of systemic advocacy.

---

[89] Gustavo Rojas-Páez, Whose Nature? Whose Rights? Criminalization of Social Protest in a Globalizing World, 4 Oñati Socio-Legal Series 1 (2014), http://opo.iisj.net/index.php/osls/article/viewFile/349/354.

Part IV

Transcending the Legal Industry to Pursue Three-Layered Goals

• • •

CHAPTER 9

EXPOSING THE VALUES, HANDCUFFS, BLINDFOLDS, AND HIERARCHIES OF LAW AS AN INDUSTRY

■ ■ ■

Table of Sections

9.1 Law as an Industry Pursues Profits over Justice
9.2 Elites Designed Law as an Industry for Group Power and Privilege and to "Take out" Dissent or Competition
9.3 Legal Education Handcuffs the Industry to Instill Top-Down Conformity
9.4 Legal Formalism Blindfolds Analysis Selectively to Obscure Systemic Injustice at Work
9.5 Legal Individualism—a Key Formalism—Atomizes Law to Mismatch Problems and Solutions
9.6 Elites Use Public Power to Hide Private Power in Law and Society
9.7 Legal Ethics Teach and Enforce Industry Handcuffs, Blindfolds, and Hierarchies

OPENING THOUGHTS

[L]awyers have, to a large extent, allowed themselves to become adjuncts of great corporations and have neglected the obligation to use their powers for the protection of the people.

—**Louis D. Brandeis**, The Opportunity in the Law, in Business—A Profession 321 (1914)

Many lawyers spend the first years of practice entirely inside the library, at their computers, or in a back room somewhere. . . . This is all largely a byproduct of formalism, a mode of legal analysis. . . . [I]f you learn to think like a machine, someone is likely to come along and make you work like one.

—**Richard Delgado**, Law's Violence: Derrick Bell's Next Article, 75 U. Pitt. L. Rev. 435, 449 (2014)

[T]hrough traditional pedagogy, law professors contribute to the continued legal consolidation of power and legal knowledge in preservation of the status quo, that is the preservation of euroheteropatriarchal paradigms. . . . Outcrit pedagogy practices should strive to build in the classroom a

democratic space that is emancipatory, creates conditions for learning, and fosters the critical exploration of society.

> —**Sheila I. Vélez Martínez**, Towards an Outcrit Pedagogy of Anti-Subordination in the Classroom, 90 Chi.-Kent L. Rev. 585, 586, 587 (2015).

INTRODUCTION

The previous three parts have presented key points about the Critical Challenge of using law for equal justice and the advocacy that supports organized bottom-up struggles to overcome it. In this chapter, we explore the legal industry itself—a highly regimented culture of training and practice. Here, as we saw in Part II, formal equality reigns and, as we saw in Part III, professional and institutional constraints are material as well as ideological.

This chapter explores how law as a system blindfolds and handcuffs advocacy through (1) formal training, certification, and regulation, (2) pervasive reliance on doctrine for training and in practice, and (3) material incentives and constraints that mold law schools and sites of practice. Lawyers conform to dominant interests because education, practice, and professional identity present mutually-reinforcing rewards and penalties tied to maintaining the status quo. The legal industry itself operates as part of the problem of systemic injustice *and* as a source of potential solutions, adding further complexities to the Critical Challenge.

Law's complicity in injustice persists because of law's systemic design. In this design, profit and power play an ever-growing role in legal education and practice. This increasingly makes the profession an industry that, like any other in a capitalist society, is designed to pursue profit but that, unlike any other, also is charged with the "administration" of equal justice. This intrinsic duality—a profession wrapped in an industry—helps to explain why professional rules of ethics also accommodate the status quo.

The legal industry bridges the lifespan of a career, from admission to and graduation from an accredited school, followed by professional employment, and, over time, "success." The processes of formal training, professional licensing, and permanent regulation—in for-profit and nonprofit institutions—acculturate trainees and practitioners into servitude to multiple forms of hierarchy. This system combines formal handcuffs, ranging from grades and honors to jobs, with informal handcuffing that ranges from inclusion in professional and social circles to the threat of social pariah status—from praise to scorn in "collegial" relations. This mix of carrots and sticks incrementally but unrelentingly inculcates proper attitudes and, over time, sifts out any improper remains. The inculcation process spans micro-macro aspects of legal culture and produces dramatic material inequalities within law and across society. Given the profession's privileged proximity to law, these inequalities cannot help but distort future law and society. Law's handcuffs—from professional cradle to grave—ensure that actors continue to be witting and unwitting handmaidens maintaining society's castes.

The industry also blindfolds analysis and problem solving. This blindfolding begins during legal training. One principal means is the use of doctrine in the form of judicial opinions as primary materials for education. These materials purport to teach not only legal doctrine but also legal reasoning or "how to think like a lawyer." But the centrality of appellate opinions in legal education inculcates legal formalism in trainees. Because formalism instills selective blindfolding of analysis, it likewise constricts solutions to systemic injustice. Formalism is the professional glue that links education to practice to ensure continued elite control of law and society from generation to generation.

Formalism is a "mechanical" approach to legal problem solving that "entails an interpretive method that relies on the text of the relevant law and that excludes or minimizes extra-textual sources of law."[1] Formalism employs fictions and abstractions, including notions of objectivity and neutrality, that selectively obfuscate social realities that law ostensibly is designed to redress. Thus, formalism functions chiefly by applying abstracted or fictionalized concepts, principles, and rules to selectively narrowed sets of facts purportedly using "logical" deduction to decide winners and losers. The actual relevance of politics, economics, history, and other sources of social facts is made extrinsic to analysis and decision making. Legal formalism—which notably includes the perpetual mismatching of problems and solutions through legal individualism—is the long-and still-dominant approach to legal problem solving.

The ideological blindfolds of formalism work in tandem with lifelong handcuffs created by material rewards and penalties of law as a system. These rewards and penalties, like blindfolding itself, are formal and informal, tangible and intangible. The legal industry's material rewards and penalties tie advocates—as trainees and practitioners—to serving the interests of elites or, at least, not disrupting the flows of privilege and subordination in accord with elite interests. These handcuffs are the result both of inducement and coercion.

Advocates use critical analysis to identify structure and skews of the legal industry and approach education, practice, and professionalism with the aim of removing the industry's handcuffs and blindfolds. The first step to removing these disabling burdens is to expose them—to unlearn and relearn the realities of law as a system and how law constricts legal actors' capacity to know, think, and do. Advocates, however, must work ambitiously in the world *as it is*. That means that legal actors cannot avoid

---

[1] Cass R. Sunstein, Must Formalism Be Defended Empirically?, 66 U. Chi. L. Rev. 636, 639 (1999).

entirely this complex status quo but rather negotiate strategically in situations that may involve risk, uncertainty, ambiguity, and conflict.

Doing so requires advocates to recognize that the legal industry, as a self-regulated profession, currently exercises a monopoly over law. The legal industry's "primary" sites or platforms of practice—particularly the purportedly more prestigious sites like law schools and large law firms—are structured to advance elite interests and mute criticism. But even "alternative" sites or platforms of practice—like nongovernmental organizations, governmental agencies, or small firms serving "average" people—are not insulated from handcuffs and blindfolds. Like law itself, such alternative sites represent important but insufficient initiatives to create opportunity for critical innovation.

Advocates recognize that profit and power shadow our work; we all are constrained and complicit. This clear-eyed recognition lays the groundwork for reflection and action to reduce, in context, the industry's handcuffs and blindfolds wherever they block the path toward Critical Justice. The next step, immediately below, is to look more closely at *how* law operates as an industry to secure for elites status, profits, and power.

9.1 LAW AS AN INDUSTRY PURSUES PROFITS OVER JUSTICE

The legal "profession" is a for-profit industry, with owners, workers, customers, and regulators in constant socioeconomic interplay. Law, like other industries, increasingly obeys economic rules of capitalism as widely practiced in the United States today. Yet law claims to be not only a venerable profession but also a unique one: the only one in which practitioners are charged to act as "officers of the court" because they collectively are entrusted with the "administration of justice" under the rule of law. To situate law as an industry, this section presents three excerpts that examine how the profession operates chiefly as a for-profit industry.

The first excerpt, by labor law scholar Marion Crain, reviews how economic interests pushing for "commodification" and "bureaucratization" are pressuring the legal profession to become increasingly like any industry. In the face of these forces, Crain explores how legal workers—including lawyers—may respond *collectively* to counteract this push toward the "proletarianization" of legal work. In practical terms, Crain asks whether legal workers—lawyers and others—will unionize on a mass scale in light of history's lessons.

THE TRANSFORMATION OF THE PROFESSIONAL WORKFORCE

Marion Crain
79 Chi.-Kent L. Rev. 543 (2004)

Is human labor a commodity? The Clayton Antitrust Act of 1914 proclaimed that it is not. Announcing that labor is not a commodity, however, does not make it so. The institution of slavery represented the complete commodification and objectification of human beings and their labor. Other workers appear almost fully commodified—laboring under inhumane and dangerous conditions for minimal wages in poultry processing plants, slaughterhouses, maquiladoras, sweatshops, and recycling operations. Partially commodified workers toil in industrial settings and service industries alike.... Commodification of human beings' labor, it seems, is an inevitable byproduct of advanced capitalism.

Where do professionals fall on this commodification continuum? For professionals, work has historically been a calling that constitutes personal identity and confers a relatively privileged class status, rather than a commodity to be sold on the market.... Professionals' experience of work has been characterized by autonomy and the privilege to self-regulate through peer review and codes of ethics enforced by professional associations. These professional privileges were secured through a social bargain in which expertise acquired through lengthy education and dedicated to public service was exchanged for a market monopoly over the knowledge area in which expertise was asserted. The professions believed that this social bargain immunized them from the influence of capitalism and its pressures to commodify human beings' labor and constrain autonomy in the quest for higher profits. Professionals' monopoly power over knowledge furnished sufficient leverage that legislation or unions to protect against abuses of power by employers seemed superfluous.

The transformation of professional work over the last quarter century suggests, however, that professionals are not immune from the commodification process.... Professionals who once shunned unions as the antithesis of professionalism are now embracing them, seeking protection from the labor laws against the effects of commodification....

... The transformation of the professional class from a self-employed group to salaried employee status renders professionals vulnerable to the traditional strategies by which management has controlled other workers: ideological proletarianization and technical de-skilling....

What Is A Profession? The Social Bargain Conferring Professional Status and Privilege

Modern societies institutionalize the valuable commodity of scientific knowledge through the concept of professionalism. Professions are conceptualized as occupations characterized by a theoretical knowledge base and skills acquired through extended education and extensive training; the key characteristic of a professional is that she applies this knowledge in a nonroutine fashion using independent discretion and judgment, on a case-by-case basis. Professions traditionally claim the right to structure and regulate the education and credentialing systems that entitle members to practice. At its core, then, professionalism entails the right to autonomy at work and the collective right to exert exclusive authority over members' professional integrity (the right of peer review). Authority to self-regulate is founded upon the esoteric character of professional knowledge, which in turn makes it difficult for the public to assess performance or for the government to regulate it. The professions thus maintain an economic monopoly over recruitment, training, and credentialing, a political monopoly over areas of expertise, and an administrative monopoly over determining what standards shall apply to practitioners.

The fundamental basis of professionals' claim to occupational privilege and a market monopoly over specialized areas of expertise is meritocratic. The university and its professional training program legitimate the cultural privilege of professionals. The link between professional status and knowledge is reinforced by hierarchies internal to the professions. The more closely a professionals' work is linked to pure knowledge, divorced from public service, the more status she possesses. . . .

. . . Professional standards are established by the professions, and monopoly power over the market for them is enforced by the state. Competing products are eliminated; licensure, qualifying exams, and a diploma are the tools by which the monopoly is maintained. In effect, the commodity that professional associations market to society is knowledge itself, and knowledge workers are the delivery system for that commodity.

. . . Thus, the professions have historically acted collectively in establishing and asserting a property right in expertise and a concomitant right to control and exploit that property for personal profit. . . . Control over knowledge and technique is the quintessential element that defines, structures and maintains any craft; professionals are no different than other skilled workers in this regard. The difference in their economic status and socially privileged position is one of degree, rather than one of kind.

The Future of Professions in an Advanced Capitalist Information Economy: Is the Social Bargain Still Viable?

. . . Principles of scientific management (or "Taylorism"), originally developed for application to manual labor, were ultimately applied to white-collar work and to the professions through the medium of bureaucratization.

Scientific Management

An important strategic tool in employers' control over manual labor was scientific management, which achieved popularity during the first half of the twentieth century. Scientific management refers to the systematic process of dividing jobs up into discrete components so as to centralize control over the knowledge of the labor process in management and increase profits. Its aim is to wrest from skilled workers control over the knowledge that constitutes the craft....

Scientific management was used very successfully to maximize output in the industrial workplace, particularly among relatively low-skilled workers.... The assembly line was the prototypical example of technological control: production appeared to be regulated by the technology rather than by people.... No worker possessed a complete picture of the product; the conception of work was divided from its execution....

Bureaucratization

If scientific management was the key tool in bringing unskilled workers under the thumb of the industrial machine, bureaucratization was its parallel in the sphere of the skilled worker. In the bureaucratic reorganization of work, management's profit goals are brought to bear on the labor process in such a way that the skilled worker's work is transformed. Ultimately, the worker's control over his craft is undermined....

... Bureaucratization refers to the manipulation of the social organization of work through a pattern of specialization scientifically designed to maximize productivity; in this respect, it closely resembles scientific management.... [B]ureaucratic control ultimately and insidiously molds workers to organizational objectives and ties them to a division of labor conceptualized by management and policed by the application of "neutral" rules and policies....

Bureaucratic control effectively metamorphoses into ideological control over the work objectives and process because only management speaks and interacts directly with the larger society (*i.e.*, patients are clients of the institution, not patients of an individual doctor). Professionals thus lose the ability to forge their own relationships with clients or to define the uses to which their skills are put; management makes those decisions. Of the various modes of control, bureaucratic control is probably the hardest to resist for professionals because it isolates the worker from the community that he or she serves.

Deprofessionalization

Professionals' historical status as self-employed entrepreneurs was instrumental in avoiding commodification of professional work through scientific management or bureaucratization. The shift away from self-employment and increasing dependence of the professions upon large organizations as an institutional base for the exercise of professional authority create the potential for the application of techniques designed to control and restrict professionals' sphere of influence.... Multi-professional worksites such as hospitals, law firms, accounting firms, and architectural firms organized professionals to work in layers. Such multi-professional worksites developed their own internal hierarchies of professions.

For the first time, professionals found themselves vulnerable to the management techniques to which nonprofessional workers had long been subject. Professionals followed the pattern established in the crafts: they lost control first over the ideological direction of their work (the product itself, and the ends to which it is put), and later over the technical aspects of the labor process (how tasks will be carried out and time/pace of work).

Ideological Control

Ideological proletarianization posed a significant threat to professional identity. It stripped professionals of their sense of professional values and purpose, restricting the professions to the realm of technique. The loss of professional autonomy and ideological control is especially grave for a group that has traditionally approached its work as a calling....

In an effort to adapt their expectations to the shifting conditions of their worksites, professionals dissociated themselves from the ideological context of their work, withdrawing from areas in which they lacked voice or power, and investing instead in the areas in which they still enjoyed power (technical expertise).... The professional adapts further by aligning herself with the employing institution and advancing institutional goals and interests rather than those of clients, professional values and ethics, or larger societal interests. At the same time, professionals redefine their personal goals so that they are congruent with institutional goals....

Technical Control

The professions initially defended their professional status by expanding their technical expertise. The retention of technical discretion over the day-to-day attributes of work assisted professionals in maintaining, at least temporarily, many of their professional privileges and status. Ultimately, however, management began to chip away at professionals' technical expertise as well. As in the crafts, technical proletarianization proceeded in two phases: first, workers lost control over their time; later, the work itself was standardized according to a plan devised by management.

Time

Time is a critical measure of the worth of work. Indeed, the basis of the entire occupational hierarchy is that the time of those in subordinate positions is worth less than the time of those in supervisory positions, so that tasks must be delegated for reasons of cost effectiveness. Not surprisingly, then, loss of control over hours of work and pace of work are a significant source of concern among professionals because they signal a loss of status. The core attribute of professional work is that because it requires the exercise of discretion and judgment and cannot be standardized, "it cannot be established from the outside *that a given result should be obtained in a given time.*" . . .

Standardization of Tasks

Bureaucratic organization of work has proven effective in expropriating knowledge from the professions, standardizing what is known, and dividing it among professionals through specialization of function organized in hierarchical fashion. Like the assembly line, the effect of bureaucratization is to press professionals toward specialization in order to produce economies of scale while potentially raising the quality of service. As the professional specializes, he or she becomes a mere technician, sacrificing the freedom of broad scope professional work and losing the ability to establish the objectives of his or her own work. When specialized professionals perform under the direction of management, often coordinating with other professionals in a division of labor specified by management, they relinquish the autonomy and control over the objectives of their work that they once possessed. Thus, professional knowledge increasingly becomes encoded in the structure of the organizations rather than residing with professionals themselves. . . .

Law

Private Law Firms

Law firms once assumed the form of partnerships, characterized by professional values and a familial spirit. The modern market has pressed them toward a large firm business model organized hierarchically. . . . The modern firm is organized vertically by rank and tenure. When confronted by declining profits in the recession of the 1980s and early 1990s, law firms behaved as their [corporate] clients did—they downsized, starting with associates at the bottom of the firm hierarchy. In short, as Second Circuit Judge Irving Kaufman observed, "the largest law firms have acquired the *characteristics of the corporations* they have represented."

The traditional partnership represented "the ultimate cooperative organization, a marriage of equals" and was characterized by equality in management and profit-sharing among the equity partners. By contrast, the large law firm concentrates power and control in a relatively small number of partners who make decisions with little or no input from the other partners in the firm. An executive committee dominated by a select cadre of senior partners typically exercises ideological control over the firm's work, determining content of the firm's work, the firm's growth rate, and performance standards for associates. A managing partner or partners exerts ultimate control. Rules, procedures, annual performance reviews, and bonuses tied to billable hours or positive performance serve as the enforcement tools for maintaining technical control. Associates are provided with every incentive to identify with management, rather than with labor. Conflict with management is muted; constraints on autonomy are perceived as arising from the client.

Inevitably, lawyers sacrifice autonomy to the larger goals of the bureaucratic law firm. By far the most significant tool of technical discipline that large firms exercise over lawyers is the billable hour.... Billable hour requirements have increased dramatically over the past half-century, moving from 1100 hours per year in 1950 to 1900 hours per year in 2000....

Pressure on the billable hour and the significance of quantity of hours worked was intensified by the trend, led by Cravath, Swaine & Moore in the 1980s, to raise salaries of first year associates to unprecedented levels, a move soon followed by other large law firms across the nation. This shift, which [legal scholar Robert] Gordon calls "one of the most antisocial acts of the bar in recent history,"

> devalues public service by widening the gulf ... between starting salaries in private practice and in government and public interest law. It drives impressionable young associates toward consumption patterns and expectations of opulence that will be hard to shake off if they want to change careers. It forces every lawyer in the firm, especially the associates who are its supposed beneficiaries, to pay heavily for it in extra billable hours and, insofar as high incomes for the partners depend upon low partner-associate ratios, in reduced prospects of reaching partnership.

... Some firms are shifting work to contract or staff attorneys, who are paid much less than partner-track associates and bill at a lower rate, or to nonlawyer professionals like paralegals.... All of these strategies are profit-maximizing moves that reflect the use of scientific management or bureaucratization to divide the professional work into its component parts....

Unions for Professionals? Organizing Doctors and Lawyers

... [H]ow likely is it that professionals' outrage over diminishing status will find expression in unionism?

Shifting Tides

At first blush, professionals' traditional strong commitment to an individualist ethos would appear to make them unlikely candidates for a collectivist strategy. Professionals' working conditions were historically organized around an ideology of individualism: individualized work, individualized clients, and individual specialization of function. Nonetheless, professionals have always been joiners, working collectively through professional associations to maintain their market monopoly (through furthering professional education, conducting peer review, and maintaining and refining licensing and certification standards).... Accordingly, when the professional associations began to respond to the tendency of corporate employers to commodify the professions by endorsing unionization and collective bargaining, the stage was set for change....

Lawyers

Lawyers have been far less inclined toward unionization than doctors, despite the presence of a similar trend in the profession toward employee status, bureaucratization and loss of ideological control over work, loss of control over time, standardization of output, and loss of autonomy.... Why are lawyers relatively quiescent in the face of pressures toward commodification?

The ABA historically opposed unionization for attorneys, and specifically banned government lawyers from joining unions. The bar's primary concern was the creation of divided loyalties (between client and union), specifically, the worry that the union-member-attorney would surrender her independent judgment and be required to submit to direction by the union officers and directors even when client interests were compromised. In 1967, the ABA changed course and permitted attorneys to join unions....

With the ABA's imprimatur, unions gained a foothold among government lawyers and lawyers employed in the nonprofit sector. Government lawyers, court-appointed public defenders, and legal aid attorneys began to seek the protections of collective action or union organization. The impetus for organizing has fallen into two categories: demands for better pay, and demands for improvements in working conditions that would facilitate competent performance of the lawyer's role (such as reduction in case loads, office space consistent with maintaining client confidentiality, adequate library resources, computer equipment, access to online legal research tools, and nonlawyer support staff such as law clerks and paralegals). Both of these sorts of demands involve a defense of professional identity. The first is directed toward defending class status and professional prestige, while the second category demands are necessary for lawyers to fulfill the social bargain as competent professionals. Legal services attorneys have been willing to strike to press their demands.

Private law firms have been the least likely crucibles for unionism. Nonetheless, in April 2003, sixteen lawyers at Parker Stanbury in Phoenix, Arizona voted unanimously to join Teamsters Local 104.... Union substitutes seem even more promising as vehicles for attorney representation and voice. One such vehicle emerged on the Internet in 1998: www.greedyassociates.com. Although the name of the organization and its website connotes only monetary concerns, the website has proved to be a lightning rod for discussion of a variety of issues, many of which reveal a perception that professional identity is under siege at a broader level. . . .[2]

In short, collective protest does exist in the private for-profit sector, albeit in nontraditional forms. In addition to participation on websites, many young attorneys have expressed their dissatisfaction through exit from the profession. Others have stayed in the profession but endured health problems and clinical depression, or adopted dysfunctional coping methods such as substance abuse. An entire genre of books dedicated to assisting lawyers in finding meaning in life has grown up in the last two decades. . . .

Reconceptualizing Unionism: Unions for Individualists

With this positive evidence of willingness to engage in collective action to defend professional identity, why haven't professionals forged a stronger alliance with traditional unions? While some professionals have been willing to do so, many have resisted. The most significant basis for this reluctance to make common cause with traditional unions is a fundamental unwillingness to sacrifice class privilege by allying with workers beneath them in the occupational and social hierarchy. This is often expressed as a profound commitment to an ethos of individual achievement and merit.

The Role of Class Privilege

Privilege and status play a vital role in the construction of professional identity. Professionals' distance from the working class is a significant common bond among professionals. . . . [R]ather than allying itself with the working class to advance common interests, the professional class has sought to differentiate itself from the working class, endeavoring to retain privileges not available to nonprofessionals so as to maintain its status. . . . Because unions are associated exclusively with the working class, resort to unionization would symbolize a loss in status. Ultimately, professional status has become "an ideological consolation used by employers to accommodate professional workers' needs for status privileges, or a negotiating device used by professionals themselves to justify wages and privileges that differ from those of other workers."[3] Thus, alliances between

---

[2] Discussions of lawyers, concerns about professional identity and standards, and unionization have appeared regularly in a variety of blogs and websites. E.g., Law Firm Associates Should Unionize, Prawfsblawg (Feb. 28, 2008), www.prawfsblawg.blogs.com/prawfsblawg/2008/02/law-firm-associ.html.—Eds.

[3] Professionals as New Workers, in Professionals as Workers: Mental Labor in Advanced Capitalism 15–16 (Charles Derber ed. 1982); see also Marion Crain, Colorblind Unionism, 49 UCLA L. Rev. 1313, 1320–22 (2002) (arguing that a similar commitment to white privilege stopped white workers from allying with black workers throughout much of the labor movement); Marion C. Burke, Lessons from Labor Feminists: Using Collective Action to Improve Conditions for

professionals and non-professional workers may threaten professional identity.

More insidiously, professionals' concern with status and privilege also blocks alliances *among professionals*, at least in the form of unionization. Capitalist ideology traditionally links job entitlement to individual performance, ensuring that individuals assume both the credit and the blame for their positions in the employment hierarchy[,] ... [an assumption] attributable to a "pervasive and often unfounded faith in the American Dream of individual opportunity and occupational mobility." ...

Unions for Generation X?

... Nevertheless, evidence is mounting that Generation X workers are favorably disposed toward unions as a vehicle for voice in the workplace. In a recent AFL-CIO study ... [a]mong Generation X, 58 percent said they would join a union if given the opportunity. ...

Reconceptualizing Unionism

... Clearly, unions must reconceptualize themselves if they are to take advantage of these opportunities. ... Despite the widespread perception that unions are for blue-collar workers, architects, engineers, chemists, teachers, journalists, air line pilots, and musicians all formed unions in the New Deal pro-union atmosphere of the 1930s and 1940s. The AFL-CIO reports that 50 percent of union members in 2000 were white-collar employees, and many of those are professionals (primarily government employees, teachers and professors, nurses, physicians, social workers, and psychologists). Professionals are now the largest contingent of union members in any occupational category—greater than 22 percent in 2000. ...

Conclusion: Musings About Workers, Professional Identity, and Organizing

When professional status is challenged at its core, as it has been throughout the 1980s and 1990s by managerial cost cutting strategies and bureaucratization, professionals feel their work becoming commodified and their identity questioned. Perhaps it should not surprise us that such a challenge has led to organizing, even among groups not previously believed to be strongly disposed toward union organizing. ...

Where their investment in professional training and status is so significant, and especially where the deprofessionalization of an occupation is industry-wide, professionals are likely to prefer voice (unionization) over exit. Professionals have become more receptive to collective strategies that offer the hope of reprofessionalization on an occupation-wide level.

Women Lawyers, 26 Am. U. J. Gender Soc. Pol'y & L. 559 (2017) (reviewing top-down and bottom-up efforts at workplace reform and concluding that bottom-up collective strategies may work best for addressing gender bias in the legal industry).—Eds.

Organizing issues for professional employees and white-collar employees thus revolve primarily around dignity and professional autonomy rather than around purely economic issues. . . .

Professional organizing is an expression of outrage at the breach of the social contract between professionals and society, which professionals believed would shield them from commodification. . . . If unions can reconceptualize themselves to provide some of the best features of professional associations (skills training, support for professional achievements and goals at an individual level) while retaining the leverage of collective action and organization, professionals may embrace them. If unions build it, perhaps professionals will come.

Crain reviews "deprofessionalization" in law as part of larger economic pushes for ever-greater profits. Lawyers increasingly have lost ideological and technical control over their work, especially in large institutions, so that the profession is more and more an industry that, like any other, places profit above all.[4] In the face of this loss of control over the nature, purposes, and organization of their work, many lawyers are focusing on becoming technical specialists and "withdrawing from areas in which they lacked voice or power." The adaptation of lawyers in large firms, government services, and even many nonprofits or legal services programs includes aligning with the employer to advance "institutional goals and interests rather than those of clients, professional values and ethics, or larger societal interests." This brings into question the elevation of profit over justice. How does that affect the idea that law is an honorable "profession"? What concerns does that raise about how the legal system will "administer" justice in the future? Will legal workers organize in unions or other collectives? The following excerpt provides an example of bottom-up action in response to these developments.

Legal workers of all sorts—not just lawyers—face the consequences of the commodification of labor and the accelerating conversion of law into an industry like any other. In the following excerpt, legal activist Tyler Kasperek Somes recounts and deconstructs the organized resistance of legal services workers to these conditions during a strike by the Legal Services Staff Association (LSSA) in 2013 against their employer, Legal Services NYC (LSNYC). Somes illustrates how collectivized struggles take place through repeated rounds of contestation involving both legal and extralegal action, underscoring the importance for systemic justice of

---

[4] This phenomenon within law is transnational, driven in part by larger agendas of corporate globalization discussed more fully in Part VI. See Joanne Bagust, The Legal Profession and the Business of Law, 35 Syd. L. Rev. 27, 29 (2013) (describing how "many of Australia's elite corporate lawyers are at risk of being reduced to mere functionaries, proletarianized in a process of capitulation to the power of their clients and to the productive forces of 'big business' ").

The Legal Services NYC Strike: Neoliberalism, Austerity and Resistance

Tyler Kasperek Somes
71 Nat'l Law. Guild Rev. 8 (2014)

... The strike at Legal Services NYC shows that the people working in these agencies are already capable of successful movement-building. It suggests an alternative approach to civil legal services, one where representation is only the beginning of a relationship that leads into issue-based community organizing and strategic campaigning for progressive reform.

Neoliberalism as a Political Project

"Hey Joe, Hey Joe! Your corporate greed has got to go!" chanted hundreds of strikers and their allies as they established picket lines at the entrances of One JP Morgan Chase Plaza ...

Chase Plaza is ... home to Milbank, Tweed, Hadley and McCloy, a corporate law firm where the chairman of the Legal Services board of directors, Joseph Genova, is one of the equity partners. Milbank frequently represents the financial houses, including JP Morgan Chase.... Mr. Genova might seem an unlikely figure to lead the nation's largest provider of civil legal services to low-income individuals, but such is the state of today's non-profit legal services sector.

In the half century since the foundation of the federally funded Civil Legal Services [CLS], the United States Congress has imposed a series of reforms that fundamentally reshaped the program.

... [Before the reforms, d]uring its early years, the CLS program contributed meaningfully to the political empowerment of poor and working class people, but its very success made it a target of neoliberal policymakers intent on neutralizing its effectiveness.

Civil Legal Services and the Welfare Rights Movement

... Congress [funded] a nationwide CLS program in the Economic Opportunity Act Amendments of 1966 as a part of the War on Poverty. In a one-year period, over 300 agencies received $42 million in funding, leading to the creation of over 800 community law offices and over 2,000 lawyers for the poor....

... CLS providers pursuing "law reform" (broad legal challenges to specific practices or systems) would receive priority funding over those emphasizing individual casework. CLS attorneys were markedly successful in this endeavor: they brought 164 cases before the Supreme Court in eight years, of which they won seventy four. . . .

In addition to courtroom victories, CLS attorneys made strategic and operational contributions to campaigns of mass mobilization. Among the best examples is Mobilization for Youth's (MFY) alliance with the welfare rights movement in New York City. . . .

Funded by initial grants from the Kennedy Administration and various foundations, MFY was a precursor to the storefront Community Action Agencies (CAAs) that were established by the hundreds during the War on Poverty. MFY operated offices in several Manhattan neighborhoods where residents could receive direct services like legal assistance and registration for welfare. In addition, MFY conducted aggressive community organizing campaigns that included rent strikes against negligent slum owners, education boycotts against school segregation and demonstrations at constructions sites demanding jobs for people of color.

While working as researchers at MFY, in 1966 Frances Fox Piven and Richard Cloward co-wrote an essay entitled *The Weight of the Poor: A Strategy to End Poverty*, in which they proposed an anti-poverty campaign "based on the fact that a vast discrepancy exists between the [welfare] benefits to which people are entitled and the sums which they actually receive." By organizing people onto the welfare rolls *en masse*, they expected to create a "bureaucratic disruption in welfare agencies and fiscal disruption in local and state governments," which would be resolved with reforms favorable to the poor, such as a guaranteed minimum income.

Mobilization for Youth tested this "crisis theory" with a campaign to flood the Department of Social Services with applications for winter clothing grants, an item provided for under the welfare code but rarely requested by welfare recipients. They hired a community organizer to recruit clients and establish the Lower East Side's Committee of Welfare Families, one of many local welfare rights groups emerging around the city. When grant applications were denied by the city, MFY's Legal Unit would request fair hearing with the Department, the mere request of which was usually sufficient to obtain the clothing allowance. In the end, two-thirds of the committee members received grants, which the organizers considered a resounding success. . . .

The Rise of Neoliberalism: The Case of Legal Services

President Richard Nixon's appointment of Donald Rumsfeld as Director of the OEO in 1969 could symbolically mark the beginning of the neoliberal era, during which White House administrations of both parties supported reducing the government's role in the economy. During this period, which continues today by all appearances, neoliberal policymakers have moved to sharply curtail the political agency of poor and working people and substituted "discipline" for "relief" as the public policy mechanism functioning to regulate social discontent.

Following its peak in the late sixties, the welfare rights movement suffered a series of setbacks as conservative politicians invoked the racialized discourse of "welfare queens" to increase their percentage of the white vote and win elections, both nationally and in New York City. Once in office, these policymakers introduced "welfare-to-work" reforms, transforming redistributive subsidies for people in poverty into a disciplinary mechanism that pushed them onto the lowest rung of the labor market. . . .

After their participation in the welfare rights movement and other causes, MFY staffers came under an intense investigation by the New York Police Department and New York City Council. City Council President Paul Screvane withheld MFY's funding pending the outcome of his inquiry and issued a report that criticized the MFY for fomenting racial discord by, among other things, organizing for the March on Washington. In 1968, MFY's legal department formed a new organization, MFY Legal Services, Inc., which focused exclusively on strategic litigation and individual casework. Today, this is the only branch of the historical MFY remaining. MFY's community organizing efforts ground to a halt when foundations withdrew their funding and Congress eliminated the . . . Community Action Program.

The local response to MFY's campaigns in New York presaged the neoliberal reaction to the CLS program nationwide. In 1974, the Ford Administration moved the program into the Legal Services Corporation (LSC), a new executive agency governed by a board of directors drawn from the partnership ranks of major law firms. . . .

Neoliberal policymakers have transformed the character and purpose of the American CLS program. . . . Today, the Legal Services Corporation polices the activities of its own funding recipients to enforce conformity with regulations designed to inhibit them from achieving that same large-scale reform. . . .

Austerity and Authority

. . . In the 2013 contract negotiations at Legal Services NYC, management presented dramatic deficit projections as the rationale for demanding concessions from union negotiators on wages, retirement contributions and healthcare coverage. Among other cutbacks, these changes would have interrupted physical therapy and mental health treatments midstream for a number of union members. They would have removed fertility procedures as an affordable treatment option; imposing a heteronormative condition on gay, lesbian, transgender and gender non-confirming couples which had not existed previously.

As in all unionized workplaces, the employer faced an obligation to bargain for these demands, rather than impose them unilaterally. . . .

Management's demands were predicated on a "fiscal crisis" resulting from the reallocation of LSC appropriations away from New York City. . . .

The union's negotiating team immediately contested these projections. They pointed out that even using management's estimates, LSNYC could expect a working capital surplus of nearly $7 million at the end of 2014. . . .

With the economic rationale for concessions deconstructed the authoritarian impulse behind management's demands became clearly visible. . . .

The Legal Services NYC Strike

During the contract negotiations, the LSSA bargaining team met with LSNYC management in the Times Square office of Seyfarth Shaw, an infamous union-busting law firm retained by LSNYC to advise them on the bargaining process. . . . [T]he Board of Directors signaled its readiness to use aggressive anti-union tactics typically employed only by for-profit corporations.

Fortunately for the union membership, rank and file activists initiated a campaign of education, mobilization and escalation several months before the strike. . . .

Over the winter, activists from different neighborhood offices convened the Activism Committee. The Committee charted a course of escalating actions that would peak in the spring ahead of a possible strike vote. . . . [Small actions] helped build a culture of resistance, in which people felt increasingly comfortable in their ability to confront authority and to express their perspective on the negotiations.

Street demonstrations were also a crucial part of the pre-strike mobilization. The union organized a traditional rally outside a Board meeting, a *cacerolazo* [where protesters bang pots and pans] inside a Board meeting, a day of lunchtime pickets and even a one-day strike. Each protest built on the previous one by escalating the level of subversion of the normal workplaces roles and routines . . .

By capturing each of these actions on camera, the union was able to produce an impressive amount of independent media. The union was able to build an audience and solidarity network in advance of the strike by promoting these actions on Facebook and Twitter. . . .

On May 1, as May Day demonstrations continued throughout Manhattan, the two bargaining teams met in the glass-walled office space of Seyfarth Shaw. . . . Two weeks later, the union voted to strike by an overwhelming 88 percent [and shifted activities to the Milbank site].

The decision to shift citywide protests to the Milbank office reflected an understanding of the power dynamics at play within Legal Services NYC's management. . . .

By observing board meetings, the union learned that the vast majority of board members were disengaged from their responsibilities and likely to defer to a small group of decision-makers. Thus, the union developed a "corporate campaign" that attempted to engage absent board members and disincentivize the decision makers from prolonging the strike. . . .

On May 30, the *New York Law Journal* ran a front-page article covering the protests outside of Milbank Tweed, doubtlessly embarrassing the firm. . . . The Research Committee pulled the e-mail addresses of Milbank's New York partners and sent them updates on the strike, prompting Mr. Genova to write an office-wide defense of his conduct, which subsequently leaked out of the firm.

Finally, the union identified the recurring corporate clients of Milbank Tweed. The Research Committee collected the contact information of attorneys in their General Counsel's office and sent letters asking them to question Milbank about the strike. The Milbank partners in charge of those relationships were copied in on these communications, creating additional pressure within the firm on Mr. Genova.

At the height of the strike, the board of directors retaliated against the union by terminating the strikers' healthcare without sending individual notices to the employees. . . . In one instance, a member's spouse was denied a chemotherapy treatment in the middle of a hospital visit. . . .

Although the board of directors held formal decision-making authority with respect to negotiations, the various organizations that provide funding to Legal Services NYC could offer significant leverage by threatening to withhold that money. The City Council budget approval process provided the most immediate opportunity to do this, so the union members began regular lobbying on the steps of City Hall. . . .

. . . [M]anagement finally relented. From their pre-strike position, management dropped demands for reduced retirement contributions, increases to healthcare deductibles, increases to healthcare coinsurance and cutbacks across a variety of specific provisions of the healthcare plan. The union secured zero layoffs through the term of the contract and strict ratios in layoffs between management and bargaining unit positions in the events of significant layoffs.

Conclusion: Beyond Services

Civil legal services providers are potentially very well positioned to build power with progressive social movements, as the community members who approach them for representation could also receive political education and integration into campaigns of collective action. Who would be better positioned to organize homeowners against foreclosure practices, for example, than the legal services attorneys and housing counselors to whom they turn for assistance by the thousands?

Most CLS providers have abandoned the goal of organizing for power and are instead focused on resolving as many individual cases as possible, perhaps with an occasional attempt at "impact litigation." This approach has come under sustained criticism for providing only survival-level services to a fraction of the populations in need, enabling the long-term diminution of social services, reproducing oppressive social relationships, siphoning potentially radical challenges into reformist initiatives and failing to challenge the structural systems that perpetuate poverty.... [T]hese service providers comprise a "non-profit industrial complex" that addresses expectations of professional progressives more than the needs of their clients.

... Ultimately, only repealing the prohibitions on community organizing and other activities will enable [CLS providers] to fully join the progressive movement. They can begin building a movement culture by taking small steps, such as referring clients with closed cases to strategic organizing campaigns in relevant practice areas....

Somes provides a concrete example of law as an industry increasingly like any other—the process of deprofessionalization that Crain reviewed above. The lawyers, paralegals, and others working in legal services programs enter with a commitment to helping individuals and combatting injustice. But Congressional restrictions—often reinforced rather than resisted at the level of local legal services management, Board leadership, state Bar foundations, or Bar associations—divide individual services from collective struggle. The top-down result is the devaluation of legal workers who provide most individual services—specifically, those who disproportionately are women, many linked by class, race, ethnicity, and personal histories to the communities they serve. Additionally, these potential sites of holistic social struggle are reduced to atomized centers that separate working class women or women of color from broader struggles. This elite-driven process illustrates industry handcuffs, blindfolds, and hierarchies.

However, legal workers—including lawyers—can organize to protect themselves from top-down exploitation. Legal workers are well positioned to develop a dual consciousness of law and justice and to use legal instruments of advocacy. With collective resources, they can employ extralegal means such as direct actions, media campaigns, tailored interventions to pressure specific decision makers or influencers, and public education. With the experience of workplace struggles like that described by Somes, legal workers become better prepared to tackle sectoral and societal issues. For example, legal workers can act collectively to change their organizations' boards to end the domination of wealthy individuals, fight back against Congressional or other funder restrictions, and expand alliances with community groups to oppose neoliberal austerity measures, using the historic legal services-welfare rights alliance as a model.

Legal scholars Willmai Rivera-Perez and Juan Garcia-Ellin next examine the effects of these same industry trends on law school as professional training. The same dynamics seen above in practice settings also are squeezing "justice" out of legal education, perhaps even more than in earlier times. As with Crain and Somes, this excerpt shows how top-down profit-seeking frequently overcomes all else within law, while blindfolding the public to this reality. The disconnect between law and justice can be measured in material and symbolic metrics. Taken together, these three excerpts suggest that the legal profession increasingly functions as an industry that acts by choice—by design—to maximize profits regardless of the special public role that law and lawyers purportedly play in advancing "equal justice under law."

FLEXIBLE ACCUMULATION: CHANGES IN THE LEGAL PROFESSION AND THEIR EFFECTS IN LEGAL EDUCATION

Willmai Rivera-Perez and Juan C. Garcia-Ellin
49 Rev. Jur. U. Inter. P.R. 629 (2015)

Introduction

... That legal education is in a crisis seems to be a cyclical topic that reappears whenever there is an economic crisis.... After reports of lawyers being fired from big firms, legal education became, once again, the culprit....

Crisis in the Legal Profession

In 2008, media outlets started reporting about a crisis in the legal profession. First, news regarding the firing of hundreds of lawyers from the largest law firms was reported. Then there [was] news reporting that large percentages of law school graduates could not find jobs requiring bar passage. Finally, reports came indicating the high number of law school graduates who are drowning in debt because of the high costs of attendance....

As a response to the perceived lack of jobs, many reasons have been presented to explain the "crisis." The most popular of these are: 1- law school graduates are not "practice-ready," that is, they do not take courses that help with the day-to-day minutiae of legal work; 2- law school is too expensive, primarily because tenured academic-type professors make too much money; and 3- the federal government hands out too much money in student loans with the result of tricking students, particularly those attending non-elite law schools, into incurring debt that they have no chance in being able to repay.

The solutions presented to solve these "problems" that are causing the "crisis" have all been directed at reforming legal education. Some of the more popular solutions are: 1- increasing the number of clinical or lawyering skills courses; 2- eliminating tenure for law professors and substituting them for practicing attorneys to teach in an adjunct basis; 3- changing the JD from a 3-year to a 2-year course of study; and 4- reducing the number of law schools and limiting the availability of student loans. These solutions are supposed to be directed at making law graduates more practice-ready, reducing the expenses of law schools so that they can lower tuition and to shrink the pool of applicants for law positions so as to decrease the percentage of unemployed lawyers.

When the data is examined closely, there is a clash between the statistics and the [alleged] causes.... It is a contradiction that the largest law firms are generating record profits and at the same time hiring a lower number of attorneys. With this increase in capital accumulation, what is the crisis really about?

Changes in the Regime of Accumulation

To better understand the changes in the legal profession, we must first understand the changes in the global economic system.... What we have experienced are changes in the regime of accumulation within capitalism. Simply put, the global economic system is still one in which capital accumulation is the main objective but the social organization and social regulation of that objective [have] changed since the advent of the industrial revolution.

After the Great Depression in the USA, the legal framework of the New Deal adopted much of the ideas brought forward by Milton Keynes regarding government regulation and control of the economy. This way the country transitioned from a *laissez faire* to a Fordist mode of regulation of industrial capitalism. The main characteristics of Fordism are: mass production of goods in which costs were reduced through economies of scale; large amounts of workers needed to be both producers and consumers of goods; and an extensive regulatory scheme (heavily influenced by Keynesian theory) in which the government would regulate the production and consumption process as well as the relationships between employers and employees....

The entire Fordist regime was predicated on mass production and mass consumption of goods.... Within the Fordist regime, full time work and benefits were needed to guarantee a large amount of consumers with economic power.... At the same time, to lower the costs even more, ... a higher level of standardization was achieved to the production process as well as to the product design. . . .

During the 1970s and after the oil crisis, Fordism began to change into what now is called Post-Fordism or Neo-Fordism. These changes are now also encompassed within the term of "flexible accumulation." As the term suggests, this new regime is organized under the premise of more flexibility in the production of goods (and services) that would improve the capital accumulation process. . . .

The Legal Profession as an Economic Activity

. . . [I]t can be fairly easy to forget that the law profession is an economic activity. Similar to any other economic activity, it is influenced by the changes in the regime of capital accumulation.

. . . [S]imilar to many other economic activities during Fordism, the largest law offices in the USA and the UK began utilizing practices associated with more industrial economic endeavors . . . [by attempting] to standardize as much as possible the offering of services that are supposed to be an individualized activity.

Large law firms provide a service: legal representation and counseling. Throughout the Fordist years the organization of law firms had some elements of standardization and tasks were internally organized so as to make their performance more effective. For example, many firms were divided in divisions or departments depending on the topic of the cases they would [handle], such as Civil, Corporate, Contracts, Mergers, Criminal, etc. Also, the less experienced attorneys were tasked with the less specialized work, such as writing motions or reading case files, while more experienced attorneys would do the more specialized work like writing legal briefs and conducting trials or oral argument[s]. . . . Finally, all tasks were performed by employees of the firm within the firm headquarters, under the supervision of the partners.

Until very recently, these large law firms with hundreds of lawyers have worked in a very similar structure. With the recent economic crisis, corporate clients have been attempting to reduce their legal fees as a way to reduce costs and therefore increase their profits. As part of the need to reduce costs large law firms have adopted the practices that other types of businesses had [fallen] into with the goal of flexibilizing their process of capital accumulation. . . .

. . . In simple terms the law firms began to fire employees, reduce benefits, alter working arrangements, and decrease prices. . . .

. . . Now law firms are outsourcing all sorts of tasks. Through the use of technology, law firms are outsourcing non-legal tasks to non-legal firms. Tasks such as answering services or client billing have been outsourced not only to an entirely different firm but in some cases they have been offshored to an entirely different country. Some non-specialized or basic legal tasks, such as organizing and archiving of case files, have been outsourced to non-legal firms. Some of this work would have been performed by junior associates, and now is being performed by non-attorneys off-site.

The most significant tasks that have been outsourced, and in many cases offshored, have been some specialized legal tasks. The most common type, of course, is the sub-contracting of a highly specialized attorney or firm to handle a specific aspect or topic of one case. Yet, there are other law-related tasks that are performed by "legal services" firms. There are firms that specialize in the review, management and analysis of documents for large-scale litigation....

The most controversial of these outsourcing practices is the subcontracting of Legal Process Outsourcing firms (LPOs). These are firms that perform legal tasks for a law firm but the actual task [is] performed in another country. This offshoring of legal work has been questioned due to possible ethical violations but the ABA has expressed itself as having no objection to this type of outsourcing as long as the attorney-client privilege is preserved. Firms like *Pangea3*, *CPA Global* and *Integreon* are some of the better known LPOs, and most of their work is performed in India. Some of the tasks these firms perform are legal research, contract management, intellectual property and even e-discovery. Similar to other types of businesses, law firms can benefit themselves through the exploitation of the spatial unevenness of global capitalism. With the offshoring of legal work, costs are being reduced and therefore capital accumulation expands....

Effects on Legal Education

... How is this reduction in hiring by large law firms causing a problem for law schools? The answer is not that complicated. For decades, many law schools would partially base their prestige in the amount of graduates who could find employment in large law firms and therefore receive a large salary. This view of prestige was supported by some of the ranking systems of law schools in the United States. The possibility (or reality for some law schools) of their graduates finding jobs in these large law firms was used as a way to justify constant increases in law school tuition and expenses. The argument goes that the increasing tuition was an investment that would guarantee the student with a good paying job at a large law firm.

... [W]ith the restructuring of the regime of accumulation and the outsourcing and offshoring of legal work, there are fewer positions available for recent graduates at large law firms.... If the problem is that those students graduating from law school are not finding jobs, how do the proposed solutions attack that problem?

The short answer to the question is that they do not. The proposed solutions to the crisis in legal education do not address the supposed problem.... [W]hat is happening is that large law firms have fewer positions to fill due to the economic restructur[ing] So, it is not that law graduates cannot find jobs but that one possible place of work is less available.

Second, one of the solutions proposed is to change the curriculum so that graduates are more "practice ready." Once again, this proposal does not help with the supposed problem of law graduates not finding jobs. With this solution, law firms are switching the burden to the recent graduates by telling them that they do not possess the necessary skills when in fact, that has nothing to do with this proposal.... After all there are fewer positions to fill and the graduates improving their resumes will not increase the amount of positions available. On the other hand, this solution is just another strategy through which law firms flexibilize their accumulation of capital. If the law schools cave in and change their curricula to satisfy, even more, the needs of the large law firms, then these firms will save time and capital that would otherwise be needed to train the new employees....

Third, another solution proposed is that the law [school] is reduced from three to two years. This proposal is supposed to reduce the amount of money students spend on tuition and therefore reduce the graduates' student-loan debt. Whereas we agree in general terms that student debt should be reduced, this proposal does not necessarily address the supposed problem.... [A] reduction in years may mean that law graduates will not necessarily be better candidates for the job market.

Fourth, the proposals for reducing tuition and eliminating tenure for full time professors, which is geared to decrease costs and therefore lower tuition even more, are not unique to law schools.... [T]he constant reduction in government spending in education, particularly to public universities, is the biggest cause of increasing tuitions. This, of course, is part of the post-Fordist discourse of limiting education to satisfy the needs of the market....

Fifth, the proposals to limit the number of non-elite law schools and to reduce the availability of student loans are problematic on two fronts. On one hand they are based on the premise that the law school graduates who are not getting jobs in large law firms are those who attended non-elite schools. On the other hand, the subtext is that because of the "lack of jobs" it is not fair to let someone incur a debt that he/she will not be able to repay.... [T]herefore, only those people who can afford to pay for it should be the only ones attending law schools. These two proposals' only consequence will be the closing of opportunities for those who cannot afford to attend an elite law school, therefore leaving only the privileged classes with the chance to obtain a legal education and to shape legal doctrine in the future.

Conclusion

... [W]hen analyzing legal education, we should be aware of the socioeconomic changes in the legal profession before accepting proposals that do not address the actual problems that law graduates confront.

Finally, there is no "lack of jobs" for lawyers. A simple internet search will point us to the increasing needs of legal services, particularly representation in criminal matters, by the less privileged, immigrants, and those living away from large urban areas. We should be looking into finding ways to have the continued flow of law school graduates help to fulfill the needs of such a large segment of the population. An increase in clinical courses directed at providing criminal and civil representation to underprivileged and working-class clients would help, as would an increase in subsidies, or forgiveness of student debt, to those willing to provide pro-bono work for indigents. ... [A]n increase in public spending on education, to help with a reduction in tuition costs, should be on the table, and should be included as part of the strategies being pursued towards making the legal profession more accessible to those who are more vulnerable to injustice. During this era in which capital accumulation has become more flexible ... we should not fall into the trap of contributing to that cause and focus on continuing to be aware of what are the real challenges within legal practice today and work towards more social justice, not less.

Rivera-Perez and Garcia-Ellin examine the legal industry—firms and schools—as an economic activity adopting the same techniques as others to flexibilize, and thus maximize, profit making. This top-down push exploits all resources, including human ones, to further concentrate wealth. "Success" in this unrelenting drive for ever-greater profits is measured exclusively in economic gains to elite institutions. The process necessarily drains resources from other endeavors of the system or society: the more that productivity is pocketed by the few, the less it can be put to work for public purposes. At the same time, law becomes less concerned with justice. As a trio, the above excerpts help legal and other "professional" workers better unlearn and relearn the systemic contexts of their industry—across dimensions of training, practice, organization, funding, and social impact.

NOTES AND QUESTIONS

1. *Technology's Promise and Peril.* The legal industry is changing dramatically because of the advent of legal technology to augment and in some instances replace the lawyer. Of course, technology of the last century such as the desktop computer helped eliminate lower-paid administrative positions in law firms and elsewhere, as business professionals increasingly created their own legal documents rather than rely on the old model of staff transcribing

text from dictaphones. But the record $1 billion invested in 2018 in legal technology signaled that investors aim to fundamentally disrupt the work of lawyers, particularly that of lower-level associates, through artificial intelligence and machine-learning.[5] Large law firms themselves are seeking a piece of this burgeoning market, as they form subsidiaries to develop legal technology and sell products directly to clients.[6] If law firms shift their attention and resources more toward developing legal technology for sale to clients, rather than engaging in traditional lawyer-client relationships, what impact would that have on the tension between law as a profession and as a for-profit industry? How might that shift—as law firms become technology innovators—affect the potential for collective resistance strategies that Crain discusses?[7]

9.2 ELITES DESIGNED LAW AS AN INDUSTRY FOR GROUP POWER AND PRIVILEGE AND TO "TAKE OUT" DISSENT OR COMPETITION

Elites have designed and enforced law consistent with their own self- and group-interest; we already know this feature as failure by design. Below we see it in action in excerpts that, first, show how elites build up law as an infrastructure to protect and preserve their interests, while simultaneously taking out adversaries by depriving them of the same resources and capacities. This "double-whammy" secures for elites an advantage in every contest even before it begins. The final excerpt documents how elites originated, consolidated, and institutionalized the current system for self-advantage—using social identities to organize and maintain the profession based on social and economic castes.

We start by examining "wealth management," which encompasses the lawyer practice specialty of trust and estate planning. Economic sociologist Brooke Harrington examines how the legal and financial specialties that make up wealth management operate "in the deepest part of capitalism"[8] to preserve wealth intergenerationally through, and sometimes despite, law. Professionals in wealth management use the tools of law, law

---

[5] https://blog.lawgeex.com/legaltech-hits-1-billion-investment-as-lawyers-embrace-automation.

[6] www.lawsitesblog.com/2019/05/wilson-sonsinis-tech-subsidiary-sixfifty-releases-first-product-for-calif-privacy-compliance.html (discussing the compliance "app" developed by the law firm's technology subsidiary as well as the potential for developing technological advances for access to justice purposes).

[7] For discussion of organizing and resistance within the tech industry, see Rick Paulas, A New Kind of Labor Movement in Silicon Valley, Atlantic (Sept. 4, 2018), www.theatlantic.com/technology/archive/2018/09/tech-labor-movement/567808/ (discussing that most organizing of white-collar tech workers has centered around single-issue campaigns rather than through forming unions); Kate Conger and Noam Scheiber, Employee Activism is Alive in Tech. It Stops Short of Organizing Unions, N.Y. Times (July 8, 2019), www.nytimes.com/2019/07/08/technology/tech-companies-union-organizing.html.

[8] Brooke Harrington, Capital Without Borders: Wealth Managers and the One Percent 232 (2016).

avoidance, and the power to influence law to the advantage of elites. The public power of private law—contracts, trusts, property—serve as "golden handcuffs" tied to elite interests. Wealth managers' work is "somewhat like that of architects, in that they design complex, multifunction structures . . . composed of linked organizational entities, such as trusts, corporations, and foundations," which use legally-binding documents to aid wealthy families to avoid taxes and regulation, maintain control of businesses and assets, plan for succession, and invest:

> From their origins in medieval England, the practices on which wealth management is based have served two related ends: the protection of family fortunes and the reproduction of elites. . . .
>
> . . . In effect these professionals detach assets from the states that wish to tax and regulate them, creating a form of capital that is, like its owners, "transnational" and "hypermobile." By "artificially manipulating paper trails of money across borders" wealth managers are creating not just asset-holding and tax-avoidance structures but a new body of transnational institutions, which are expanding outside of any democratic process of checks and balances. . . .
>
> Much of what wealth managers do as part of their day-to-day practice occurs in [this] "ethical gray area"—a realm of activity that *is* formally legal but socially illegitimate. This includes not only tax avoidance but also the use of trusts, offshore corporations, and other tools to [protect wealth]. . . .
>
> A recent review of world economic and political history, covering thousands of years across Europe, Africa, and the Americas, suggests that the biggest danger of wealth inequality is not economic but rather capture by elites of the political system. . . .
>
> . . . [The most] structurally significant event [is the] inter-generational transmission of wealth. By turning one generation's surplus (created perhaps through tax avoidance and special investment opportunities) into a dynastic fortune, wealth managers contribute to the hardening of class divisions over time. Using trusts, offshore firms, and foundations, professionals can ensure that inequality endures and grows in a way that becomes difficult to reverse short of revolution. . . .
>
> Anyone can be an outlaw, but it is a special privilege to defeat the spirit of the laws without violating them formally. For the price of employing a wealth manager, some elites can achieve this

condition, and also enjoy the benefits of laws written specifically with their interests in mind.[9]

Critical legal scholar Allison Anna Tait builds on this notion below, showing how legal rules and services facilitate by design the ever-greater concentration of wealth. Wealth management professionals, including lawyers, have created a regime of "wealth exceptionalism" that exacerbates economic inequality and political capture by elites.

THE LAW OF HIGH-WEALTH EXCEPTIONALISM

Allison Anna Tait
71 Ala. L. Rev. 981 (2020)

... [H]iding in plain sight, the wealth-management profession has been encouraging high-wealth families to imagine themselves as separate, exceptional entities for decades ... [creating a regime of "high wealth exceptionalism."]

... [I]t is the constellation of laws governing wealth management and transfer that operationalizes this exceptionalism. These wealth rules exempt high-wealth families from a number of financial regulations that limit other families and allow high-wealth families to craft their own rules, set their own rewards and penalties, and engage in self-government in certain areas of wealth management. ...

High-wealth exceptionalism not only intensifies old harms but also creates new ones within the larger polity. In a practical mode, high-wealth-family exceptionalism has the potential to inflict financial harms on ordinary-wealth and lower-wealth families by increasing systemic risk in financial markets, shifting tax burdens from high-wealth to lower-wealth families, and widening the wealth gap. In a political and theoretical mode, high-wealth-family exceptionalism facilitates the growth of a plutarchic and patrimonial system of government in which power is based on family wealth and privilege flows in a circuit between a small number of already exceptionally resourced families. ...

... [In response,] I suggest tax-based solutions—and the estate tax in particular—for redistributing wealth and addressing the problems that come with wealth inequality. In the theoretical domain, I suggest mapping the family constitution onto the national constitution, in an expansive sense, to recover constitutional arguments against economic inequality and the consolidation of power through wealth.

The law of high-wealth exceptionalism—dedicated to high-wealth family sovereignty and the preservation of family wealth—cannot and should not be the law that obliquely governs our larger state.

---

[9] *Id.*

The Inscription of Family Governance...

Forming a Perfect Family Union

Every high-wealth family should write a constitution. That's what wealth managers say....

... Wealth advisors therefore recommend that families begin by gathering the group of family members that will agree and submit to representative family government: *the people*....

... [F]amily constitutions [are the family's private regulatory structure and] tend to create internal forms of both family and corporate law. In the "family law" vein, a family constitution might dictate certain protocols for family members who are planning marriage, such as the execution of prenuptial agreements. Similarly, family constitutions might provide a reliable framework for wealth transfer upon the death of family members.

In the "corporate law" vein, the family constitution can also set forth the rules about the employment of family members and remuneration for family members. Family legislators can decide upon salaries for those who work in the business ... [and] address questions about allowances, distributions, and other forms of subsidy for family members....

Finally, to help resolve conflict when family rules are broken, advisors recommend establishing a judicial branch or "Council of Elders" in addition to the "legislative branch" (the assembly of all the family members)....

The family constitution, then, creates a universe of order ... "designed with the sole purpose of making those particular families wealthier over time."...

High-wealth families are encouraged to think of themselves as "different" and "special"—which may also lead to these high-wealth clients considering themselves to be "above nationality and laws."...

Securing the Wealth of Families

Like family constitutions, which inscribe the exceptionalism and sovereignty of high-wealth families into a governance document, legal rules governing family-wealth management etch high-wealth-family exceptionalism into law.... [There are] three legal frameworks—trust, investment, and charitable-giving law—that are of signal importance to high-wealth families.... [A]s interlocking pieces of a complicated financial strategy, these wealth-management vehicles form the overarching architecture of wealth preservation.

In Families We Trust

... Private trust companies—state-chartered entities designed to provide private financial services to members of a family and often run with the help of the family—are both a time-honored mechanism for facilitating family-wealth preservation as well as legally sanctioned entities exempt from most state regulation. . . . And now, as in the past, these trusts are geared toward serving the ultrarich. Wealth advisors all agree that a family should have at the very least $60 million in assets—but more likely $100 million—for a private trust to make financial sense.

In every state a high-wealth family can create a "lightly regulated" private trust company . . . [and] some states permit the formation of unregulated private trust companies. . . .

One of the biggest draws of unregulated trusts is that they offer unparalleled financial privacy for families through exemptions from state reporting requirements about their holdings, transactions, or investments. . . . [E]xposure of sensitive financial information to outsiders is minimal. . . .

Escape from fiduciary and investment rules in trust law is another draw of the unregulated trust company. Families with private trust companies are free to invest in more idiosyncratic ways than they would otherwise be, no longer beholden to either state trust law regulation or the policies and procedures of any financial institution. . . .

Investing in Family

With roots in the Rockefeller tradition of family financial management, the family office is a multipurpose and flexible vehicle. . . .

. . . [T]he family office is widely used by high-wealth families because family offices for investment receives specialized legal treatment in the form of an exemption from the definition of "investment adviser" under the Dodd-Frank Act of 2010. . . .

. . . The most relevant part of this exemption—that is to say, the one most advertised by wealth managers and appreciated by high-wealth families—is the basic exemption from SEC registration. Registration would require public disclosure about family operations, office staffing, the amount of assets under management, and the office's trading history. . . .

. . . Families can assert a high degree of control over the types of investments that the office makes and can choose to invest in ways that traditional investment firms might not. For example, a family office might want to invest in the ventures of individual family members or friends, providing start-up loans or other funding. . . .

Because of all these advantages, "[f]amily offices . . . are now a must-have accessory for the American super-rich." . . .

Charity Begins at Home

. . . Family foundations, although charitable in nature, have historically been created not just to enable philanthropy but also for the express purpose of protecting and increasing family wealth . . . [and thus often were viewed] with "deep suspicion." . . .[10]

Over time, family foundations have come to be accepted as a standard wealth-planning tool and now are very common for high-wealth families, particularly because they further the twin goals of wealth preservation and philanthropic activity. These goals may seem inconsistent, but the family foundation weaves them seamlessly together by requiring only a minimal annual distribution, by allowing the foundation to fund administrative activities performed by family members, and—most importantly—by enabling high-wealth families to avoid wealth-transfer taxation. . . .

A family will typically create a foundation with one large endowed gift (and then operate on income from that endowment). Immediately upon making the gift, the donor receives tax benefits in the form of a charitable-gift deduction. . . .

Compounding the financial benefit of tax exemption, family foundations do not have to direct more than a minimal amount of the foundation corpus to charitable giving[:] . . . 5% of their assets annually. . . . One strategy is for the foundation to make a payout in the form of a gift to a family-controlled, donor-advised fund. This qualifies as an acceptable distribution and yet the money still stays in the family's control, on reserve until the family chooses to make a distribution from the donor-advised fund. Furthermore, annual distributions may fund certain administrative costs, such as family members receiving reasonable compensation for any work they do on the foundation's behalf, including board service. . . . The foundation can therefore serve not only as a source of tax benefit for family members but also as a source of employment, enrichment, and even income. . . .

The Measurement of Family Power

. . . The lives and fortunes of high-wealth families are deeply connected to those of other families in the larger state . . . "sometimes to the detriment of state power itself, as well as to the rights and well-being of the states' residents and citizens." . . .

The Financial Harms of Exceptionalism . . .

Shadow Banking and Systemic Risk

Governmental or agency failure to monitor the activity, lending, and trading of certain financial entities poses a decided risk because the lack of systemic, coordinated oversight results in less opportunity to see emerging

---

[10] Labor activists and others had suspicion not only of the foundations but also of charitable efforts funded by wealthy donors and foundations since their inception. Harris "Mother" Jones, an early union organizer, is quoted as saying, "Tear down every charitable institution in the country and build on its ruins a temple of justice." Elliott J. Gorn, Mother Jones: The Most Dangerous Woman in America 99 (2001).—Eds.

and possibly troubling patterns at work. One of the most currently discussed areas of unregulated activity is "shadow banking." . . .

High-wealth family assets—those governed by the family constitution and invested through family institutions—form an integral part of the shadow economy. Here's how: the family constitution establishes a family office as the investment arm of the family. The family office is then charged with investing the family's assets, including those parked in the family foundation (for tax avoidance) as well as those tucked away in the family's private trust company (for asset protection). . . . [W]hen these offices lend money, it flows through informal channels not necessarily regulated by the conventional banking system.

Family-office lending, consequently, constitutes "shadow" banking. . . .

Exempt from a high degree of regulation, family-wealth management has the potential to produce negative results for the larger population by causing market instability and creating negative market events. . . .

Financial Secrecy and Tax Burdens

Another problem stemming from the financial exceptionalism of high-wealth families is the resultant financial privacy and opacity. . . . Keeping earnings, transactions, and even ownership out of sight from both the public and regulatory authorities creates optimal conditions for tax avoidance and evasion. . . .

Endowed with a sense of existing apart from the state, high-wealth families view these tax avoidance structures as a right and entitlement, often reframing taxation as governmental overreach rather than a responsibility of citizenship. . . .

. . . [F]inancial-secrecy rules that enable tax avoidance for high-wealth families have negative impacts on lower wealth families. First and foremost, tax avoidance and evasion erode the tax base, depriving the federal government of tax revenue. . . .

. . . [A]t both federal and state levels, revenue that should be available to be spent on the public good is not, and there is less money for public schools, transportation, parks and assistance programs. . . . Furthermore, the burden of paying for the public goods that continue to operate shifts to ordinary-wealth families . . ., [who] assume a greater share of the tax burden. . . .

The Creation of Wealth Inequality

Economic conditions in the United States have become increasingly characterized by economic inequality over the last several decades. The rising phenomenon of wealth inequality in the United States is such that, from 1983–2016, the top 1% "saw their average wealth . . . rise by . . . over 15 million dollars or by 150 percent . . ., while the middle quintile showed

no change and the average wealth of the poorest 40 percent fell by $15,800."
. . .

. . . The law of high-wealth exceptionalism ensures that "[i]nequality's pervasive and pernicious effects are therefore a feedback loop reinforcing the concentration of economic and political power in the hands of the very few at the expense of the great many."

The Return of Patrimonial Plutarchy

In addition to the material costs of exempting high-wealth families from the larger regulatory structure, such exemptions also present political costs to the democratic state. . . .

The Patrimonial Exercise of Political Power

Political scientists have consistently defined plutocracy, with minor variations since Aristotle, as a system of governmental rule by the rich and oligarchy as rule by the few. Plutarchy, then, is rule by the rich few. . . .

A more specific form of plutocracy is patrimonialism, which is also rule by the rich but organized around the family. . . . Patrimonialism . . . is a set of rules written by high-wealth families to favor high-wealth families and the preservation of their wealth. . . .

The key notion in this framework, however, is not just that high-wealth families are able to consolidate their economic power but also that they are able to translate this economic power into political power, writing wealth laws to their liking. That is to say: "For the rich, wealth begets power." . . .

A direct and immediately relevant example of the political power of modern plutarchs is the story of how the lobbying efforts made by a group of high-wealth families, their lawyers, and hired lobbyists resulted in the family-office exemption from the investment-adviser rules. To obtain the desired legislative exemption, as previously mentioned, a number of high-wealth families formed the "Private Investor Coalition, which spent hundreds of thousands of dollars to lobby to keep family offices out of the legislation, according to their lobbying disclosures." Based, then, on their preexisting ability to hire lobbyists and access the halls of political power, high-wealth families obtained a regulatory exemption that facilitates further wealth accumulation and preservation.

. . . Trust law, perhaps more than any set of wealth rules, has been radically refashioned in a number of states to benefit high-wealth clients as a result of lobbying done by trust companies. . . . Recently, for example, Ohio enacted a Family Trust Company Act, authorizing both licensed and unlicensed trust companies for high-wealth families, and the legislation was coauthored by a member of [law firm] BakerHostetler's private wealth team.

... The [policymaking] process appears democratic as these families and their advisors "blend smoothly into the complex give and take of pluralist politics." Nevertheless, "their character, focus, and effect is different: it is to advance the basic material interests of the wealthy." ...

... [T]hese conditions compromise the health of the democratic state. ...

The Problem of "Gilded Giving"

Compounding the problems of plutarchic power that high-wealth families wield in the political arena ... is the problem of "gilded giving," or plutarchic philanthropy. ... [H]igh-wealth philanthropy not only allows certain families too much power in setting national agendas but also substitutes the wealth and power of these families for that of the state in inappropriate ways. ...

... [F]amily foundations are increasingly directing their charitable dollars to public policy institutes, wielding their economic power to shape policy debates. ... This phenomenon, dubbed "philanthro-policy-making," signals that family foundations, because of the size of their gifts, are often able not only to set public agendas by shaping the funding landscape but also to "seek and obtain an outsize influence on public policy."

If family members have strong ideological views favoring family-wealth preservation, for instance, the family foundation can fund policy research at institutions like the American Enterprise Institute, a conservative think tank that defends policies such as a lower tax on capital gains or the loophole on carried interest. In this way, giving to policy institutes can complement the lobbying efforts of a high-wealth family in obtaining specific regulatory results. ...

... These megadonations directed at influencing public policy are reshaping the relationship between private actors and government, creating a democratic deficit in the process. ...

... [And, finally, as] John Stuart Mill remarked in 1848, these gifts do not change the political and economic structures that created offending inequalities in society because "philanthropists ... nibble at the consequences of unjust power, instead of redressing the injustice itself." ...

The Amendment of Family Privilege ...

Inheriting the Family Fortune

One way to address the economic harms, including wealth inequality, produced by high-wealth-family power is through increased regulation. Responding to the problem of nonregulation or light regulation, one set of solutions would be designed to increase regulatory oversight and decrease financial secrecy. This kind of solution would respond directly to the legal privileges that high-wealth families have created for themselves—by retracting them. . . . [This, however,] would be difficult because of the vast network of trust, tax, and investment rules in play, coupled with the low likelihood of collective action.

A more overarching solution to address the profound problems associated with wealth inequality comes in the form of a reimagined and refortified estate tax. The estate tax—currently as well as historically—has often been singled out as the strongest tool available for enabling wealth redistribution and equalizing opportunity. . . .

Today, concerns about inheritance and inequality remain. . . . [T]he estate-tax exemption—recently raised to $11 million per individual—gives high-wealth families great leeway, especially given that a married couple has a $22 million exemption as well as portability at its disposal. Because of this exemption threshold, few estates are actually taxed. . . .

Perhaps even more importantly, just because an individual possesses an estate significant enough to be taxed, this does not necessarily correlate with tax revenue because of the coterie of estate planning techniques available to avoid wealth-transfer taxation. . . . As one wealth manager explains: "As I always tell people, the estate tax in our country is a voluntary tax—you only pay if you don't plan."

. . . [S]ome progressive politicians have very recently pivoted to the idea of wealth taxation as a response to the current state of heightened wealth inequality. Elizabeth Warren, during her presidential campaign, announced an interest in instituting an annual wealth tax on those families with assets of $50 million or more. . . .

. . . Building on this idea of taxing wealth, some politicians are also turning toward annual wealth taxes—in addition to the estate tax—to help solve the problem. . . .

Reframing Citizenship Rights

Addressing the problem of high-wealth exceptionalism from a more theoretical angle, a productive approach to restoring a more democratic and less patrimonial vision of wealth and power is to revitalize the notion of economic citizenship, squarely grounded in constitutional values. . . .

A democratic state is often defined by its extension of suffrage to citizens, and democratic citizenship has long been framed in terms of the right to engage in the political act of voting. Citizenship can, however, also be defined more broadly . . . to include three elements: civil, political, and social. . . . These rights [have been conceived as] the right to economic opportunity, full participation not just in the workplace but also in the cultural realm, and access to all of the diverse institutions that comprise the social order. . . .

... The possession of [economic] citizenship privileges is signified not only by access to gainful employment and paths to advancement but also by equal treatment in areas like access to financial planning opportunities, tax treatment, and modes of wealth transfer. ...

The law of high-wealth exceptionalism undermines equality of economic citizenship by disproportionately supplying economic opportunity and legal privilege to high-wealth families. High-wealth exceptionalism also fosters unequal economic citizenship when the wealth inequality it intensifies keeps wages low, inhibits saving and wealth accumulation for those not in the top stratum of wealth, and reduces the access of ordinary-wealth families to home ownership, education, and stable employment. ...

... Rules that nurture exceptionalism and financial privilege should also be read against the U.S. Constitution, which contains the political promise "to promote opportunity, avoid oligarchy, and build a robust middle class." Reading an explicitly economic dimension into the Constitution, as a growing number of scholars encourage, the problematic nature of high-wealth exceptionalism becomes even more glaring. ...

... [T]he promise of equal citizenship can be renewed by reconstructing a robust understanding of economic citizenship and repositioning economic concerns within the constitutional ambit.

Conclusion

... The law of high-wealth exceptionalism currently serves a few select families—and serves them very well. Wealth law should not, however, exist to facilitate the creation of private islands of wealth for privileged families. Instead, family-wealth law should pave paths and build bridges to prosperity for all families.

Tait lays out how "the law of high-wealth exceptionalism" favors elites. After creating family constitutions to align family activities with wealth accumulation goals, elites use three legal frameworks—trust, investment, and charitable-giving law—as "interlocking pieces of a complicated financial strategy." The structure ensures wealth consolidation through mutually-reinforcing uses of economic and political power. Low- and ordinary-wealth families, frequently of color, suffer reduced public resources, increased relative tax burdens, and increased systemic risks. Advocates and activists might disrupt this machinery, Tait suggests, by changing tax laws to redistribute wealth and marshalling constitutional arguments against economic inequality.

We see in the next excerpt that elites simultaneously are determined to deny that same capacity to act through organized collectivities to anyone they deem an adversary. Instead, adversaries, dissenters, and nonconformists are to be "taken out." As David Luban, a scholar of law and philosophy, notes in the excerpt, elites engineer and re-engineer law and its ground rules not only to build up—but also to tear down—the system according to their (shifting) sense of self-interest. Their intentional elimination of opposition or dissent—to "take out" the other side's lawyer in the context of an adversarial system—"robs the adversary system of its strongest claim to legitimacy." Although this reality is inescapable, systemic advocates must anticipate its complexities to get ahead of its curves.

TAKING OUT THE ADVERSARY: THE ASSAULT ON PROGRESSIVE PUBLIC-INTEREST LAWYERS
David Luban
91 Cal. L. Rev. 209 (2003)

Introduction

... Political partisans do not care about impartial justice. They care about rewarding their friends and defeating their enemies, and that means ensuring that their enemies receive as little money as possible, including money to pay for legal advocacy. Advocacy, after all, might be used to turn the tables. In the last few years, a disturbing pattern of legal attacks on public-interest lawyers has emerged, targeting every one of the principal sources of support for progressive public-interest law: the Legal Services Corporation ("LSC"), state Interest on Lawyers Trust Account ("IOLTA") programs, law school clinics, and civil rights attorney's fees. The attacks seek to win political disputes not by offering better arguments, but by defunding or otherwise hobbling the advocates who make the arguments for the other side.... [Like] dirty politics, this Essay argues that taking out your adversary's lawyers is dirty law.

To understand the issues properly, some background on what is sometimes called the "access to justice" problem in the United States is helpful. Law is a $100 billion per year industry. Of that $100 billion, however, less than $1 billion is dedicated to delivering legal services to low-income Americans. Put in terms of people rather than dollars, there is about one lawyer for every 240 nonpoor Americans, but only one lawyer for every 9,000 Americans whose low income would qualify them for legal aid.... In very real effect, low-income Americans are denied access to justice. The reason is simple: one lawyer per 9,000 clients ... [means that] that 95% of low-income people's legal needs remain unaddressed.

... I argue that "taking out the adversary"—targeting advocates for the other side rather than arguing against them on the merits—robs the adversary system of its strongest claim to legitimacy....

Audi Alteram Partem and the Adversary System

... Even critics of the adversary system concede the importance [of allowing the opponent a chance to be heard in good faith]. However, focusing exclusively on this virtue idealizes the system too much. The problem is that the adversary system also gives parties incentives to keep bad facts and opposing viewpoints out of the system. Try at all costs to keep dangerous evidence out of hostile hands. If you cannot do that, try to have it excluded from trial. And, if that fails, force the other side to use up their money and throw in their cards. . . .

. . . [E]qually important, is the adversarial attempt to exclude voices rather than information from the process. For example, in a typical Strategic Lawsuit Against Public Participation ("SLAPP suit"),[11] citizens protesting corporate policies or actions get sued by a corporation for defamation or tortious interference with business. An activist who testifies against a real estate developer at a zoning-board hearing, or complains about incompetent teachers to the school board, or collects signatures for a petition, may find herself hit with a SLAPP suit. Even though 80% of SLAPP suits are dismissed before trial, the aim is not legal victory but intimidation. Defendants facing ruinous legal bills and the risk of substantial personal liability agree to cease protest activities in return for having the SLAPP suit dropped. . . .

These examples illustrate [that when] judges and legislatures create doctrines that enable well-funded parties to take out the other side's lawyer, they undermine basic fairness and turn the adversary system into a system of procedural injustice.

Silencing Doctrines

My specific topic, then, is the deliberate attempt to keep progressive voices out of the legal system by taking away their lawyers. . . . Their effort cannot succeed, however, without legal weapons. These I call "silencing doctrines." Silencing doctrines include statutes, rules, and judicial decisions that allow opponents to attack the funding or restrict the activity of their adversaries' advocates.

In recent years, a pattern of silencing doctrines has begun to emerge challenging—to greater or lesser extent—virtually every principal source

---

[11] See George W. Pring and Penelope Canan, SLAPPS: Getting Sued for Speaking Out (1996) (describing the emergence of lawsuits aimed at suppressing public participation and coining the term "SLAPP" suits). SLAPP suits are not just a U.S.-based phenomenon and are not directed just at social justice organizing and advocacy groups. Journalists, as well as human rights activists and advocates, are prime targets worldwide. See Sofia Verza, SLAPP: The Background of Strategic Lawsuits Against Public Participation, Resource Centre: European Centre for Press & Media Freedom (July 12, 2018) (explaining that "one core characteristic of this kind of actions is the disparity of power and resources," describing both civil and criminal claims brought against Maltese investigative reporters, and outlining efforts to develop European anti-SLAPP legislation), https://globalfreedomofexpression.columbia.edu/publications/slapps-5-ws-background-strategic-lawsuits-public-participation/—Eds.

of support for low-income public-interest lawyering. . . . Of course it would be just as wrong if the doctrines came from the Left to silence the Right. . . . [T]he criticism concerns procedural injustice, regardless of its political orientation.

The 1996 Legal Services Corporation Restrictions

The single biggest source of funding for poor people's lawyers is the Legal Services Corporation, with a fiscal year 2001 budget of $330 million ($310 million for client representation). . . . The pathetic numbers—one underpaid legal-services lawyer per 10,000 poor people—have not prevented decades of political assaults on the program, including the outright lie that poor people have no trouble finding a free lawyer.

Restrictions on the use of LSC funding have always existed. From the beginning of the program, Congress prohibited LSC recipients from using their federal funds on volatile political issues like abortion, school desegregation, and the military draft. . . . LSC lawyers could still advocate on these issues provided they did not use federal funds to do so. . . . So long as there were other funds and other advocates available, the restrictions were tolerable, and only minimally offended the [advocacy principle of allowing opponents to be heard in good faith].

In 1996, however, Congress enacted restrictions on legal-services lawyers that went much further. Not only do they prohibit LSC recipients from taking on certain issues, but they also forbid them from representing entire classes of clients. These include whole classes of [immigrants], many of whom are legal. The new regulations likewise prohibit the representation of all incarcerated people, including those not convicted of a crime, and those whose cases have nothing to do with why they are in jail, as, for example, in parental-rights lawsuits. The restrictions also prevent LSC attorneys from using specific procedural devices or arguments. They cannot attempt to influence rulemaking or lawmaking, participate in class actions, request attorney's fees under applicable statutes, challenge any welfare reform, or defend anyone charged with a drug offense in a public-housing eviction proceeding. . . .

Perhaps the most devastating regulation, however, is Congress's prohibition on LSC recipients using their nonfederal funds for these prohibited activities. This requirement had a drastic effect. A legal-aid office could no longer accept an LSC grant if it did any prohibited legal work. This provision forced legal-services providers to split into separate organizations with separate offices, one receiving federal funds and abiding by the restrictions, the other maintaining its freedom of action at the cost of its LSC grant. . . . The result was bifurcated organizations substantially weaker than the initial organization. Some organizations had to purchase duplicate computer systems and hire duplicate staff. Some locales could afford only a restricted office, so that clients with the "wrong" cases were forced to travel hundreds of miles to find counsel or, more realistically, do without. . . .

These restrictions are silencing doctrines. Some of them—for example, the ban on attorney's-fees cases, or the ban on class actions—straightforwardly make the activities of progressive public-interest lawyers more expensive. Some of them silence the lawyers less directly by steering them away from otherwise-worthwhile cases that threaten their funding. Furthermore, the overarching requirement that nonfederal funds cannot be used for proscribed activities makes representation of the poor more difficult for legal-services lawyers by forcing them to bifurcate and weaken their organizations, thereby interrupting communications and increasing overhead.

Disappointingly, neither the Bar nor the legal-services establishment offered any organized protest when the 1996 restrictions were enacted—unlike a similar assault in 1981, when law school deans and the organized bar united in protest against efforts to abolish the LSC. The reason was pure fear that Congress, in the heady days of Newt Gingrich's revolution and the Contract With America, would simply abolish the LSC. Even attempts to challenge the restrictions in court were discouraged by many people in the legal-services community. The ABA Ethics Committee's response was entirely typical: instead of writing a formal opinion insisting that the restrictions violate the ideals of the legal profession, it chose instead to write an opinion insisting that a legal-services grant recipient could practice law ethically by abandoning clients to keep its funding intact. The advice is undoubtedly accurate: declining cases is a sure-fire way to stay out of trouble. Nevertheless, the LSC restrictions undercut the legal profession's ideals because they instruct legal-services lawyers not to represent certain classes of clients, regardless of whether they have meritorious or important claims. . . .

. . . *Law School Clinics and the Battle of New Orleans*

[As of the early 2000s], 182 American law schools offer clinics in more than 130 different subject areas, staffed by more than 1,400 clinical instructors. Counting salaries, fringe benefits, and overhead, law schools annually invest perhaps $280 million in clinical education. In return, clinics provide millions of hours each year of unpaid student legal work.

It should be noted that very little clinical work is "cause" lawyering, that is, lawyering "directed at altering some aspect of the social, economic, and political status quo." Civil and criminal litigation clinics form the backbone of clinical education in the United States, and they typically provide one-client-at-a-time, more-or-less routine, direct client representation. Clinical education also includes street-law programs, entrepreneurial clinics with business clients, and externships. . . .

Although relatively infrequently, law school clinics have indeed been subjected to political attacks and silencing doctrines.

The principal lightning rod has been environmental-law clinics, which sometimes take anti-development stances that put them at odds with business interests. In the 1980s, under pressure from the timber industry, the University of Oregon School of Law's environmental-law clinic came under siege, and eventually had to leave the law school. Environmental-law clinics in the University of West Virginia College of Law and University of Wyoming College of Law have also been attacked by politicians and business interests. . . .

The most notorious effort to silence an environmental-law clinic involves Tulane Law School, a private law school in New Orleans. After the Tulane environmental clinic successfully stopped a polyvinylchloride factory from locating in a low-income Black residential neighborhood, angry business groups complained to the Louisiana Supreme Court. In response, the court amended its student-practice rule, Rule XX, to make it harder for students to represent environmental groups. . . .

. . . The heart of the Fifth Circuit's [justification for upholding Rule XX] is that the Louisiana Supreme Court has no obligation to permit unlicensed law students to represent any clients at all. . . . The court explained that, since the Louisiana court was under no obligation to permit any student to practice law, Rule XX suppressed no right because there was no baseline right to suppress. In effect, the Fifth Circuit told the clinic students that they should be grateful that the Louisiana justices let them into court at all.

This argument about baselines is willfully blind to the real baseline—the reality created by custom and history. Law school clinics are not simply a sop thrown to law students, an incidental afterthought in the legal landscape. For thirty years clinics have been an accepted, routine part of that landscape. They are valued everywhere for the services they provide and the training they offer; and it would be difficult to deny that providing legal services and teaching lawyers their craft are central goals of legal institutions. This thirty-year history should set the baseline, not the court's formal power to eliminate clinics by decree.

. . . To my knowledge, only two arguments are ever offered to justify the state-sanctioned professional monopoly [on the practice of law]: restricting the practice of law to trained, barred lawyers is supposed to protect consumers from incompetent representation and unethical representation.

However, no one was complaining about the competence or the ethics of the student lawyers at Tulane or any other Louisiana law school. The complaint was that they represented the wrong causes. The state supreme court had been lobbied by three powerful business associations to clamp down on the law students. The justices were up for re-election. The federal district judge thought this was irrelevant: dismissing the clinicians' lawsuit, he wrote, "in Louisiana, where state judges are elected, one cannot claim complete surprise when political pressure somehow manifests itself within the judiciary." No doubt; but such complacent cynicism seems wholly out of place in a legal opinion about whether a politically motivated rule is viewpoint discrimination. Of course it is viewpoint discrimination, ... the Louisiana Supreme Court was muscled to stop environmental challenges to business.

... [A]ccording to Tulane clinic's director Adam Babich, Rule XX has not prevented the clinic from continuing its work.[12] That is not the point, however. If the attacks failed, they were near misses, and eventually some will succeed. Indeed, they may already have succeeded in one of their aims, because clinic directors will undoubtedly hesitate before taking on volatile cases that may provoke dangerous backlash against the clinics or their law schools.... In effect, the assaults on environmental-law clinics function like SLAPP suits, intimidating law school administrators and clinic directors even when they fail.

Conclusion

Silencing doctrines raise the prospect of an adversary system in which one set of adversaries, the progressive public-interest lawyers and the clients they represent, is relentlessly squeezed by political opponents who would rather muzzle them than argue against them. Those who value procedural justice should find silencing doctrines deeply offensive.

... Public-interest law has long been an active front in the larger culture wars that mark American politics. Surely no one should be shocked ... to learn that politics is going on here. But I am not shocked; I am merely disgusted.... When politics impinges on the imperative to hear both sides, the adversary system threatens to dissolve into farce or fraud....

Political attacks require political responses. Obviously, the injustice of silencing doctrines is unlikely to become an electoral issue—the issues are too specialized and too remote. They are issues for the bar, not the voters, to take up.... [T]hese issues are not discrete; they form a dangerous pattern.... It is important for lawyers and bar groups to speak out against the legal-services restrictions ... [and] to support embattled environmental-law clinics, and to work to enact [remedial] legislation.... These should be regarded as matters of fundamental procedural justice, not partisan politics.

Let me add one final thought. The private demon of all progressive public-interest lawyers is a sense of futility. Few lawyers who win so few

---

[12] In 2010, lawmakers defeated an effort by the Louisiana Chemical Association to tie state funding (primarily directed toward a campus hospital and cancer research) to closure of the Tulane clinic.—Eds.

cases and lose so many are immune from the gnawing sense that they are merely wasting their time. It sometimes seems as though their voices accomplish little beyond making a historical record of rejected arguments on behalf of vanquished causes. But they do win sometimes, and even when they fail, the alternative is not making a historical record, so that the very fact that they had a cause disappears without a trace. Without their voices, a kind of smug consensus—a lie, really—is the outcome. And the adversary system becomes little more than a field of lies. Even enemies of progressive public-interest lawyers should want something more than this.

Luban points out that elites advancing silencing doctrines "would rather muzzle [adversaries] than argue against them." These tactics "form a dangerous pattern" in which "the adversary system becomes little more than a field of lies." Luban concludes that law "threatens to dissolve into farce or fraud" enforced by the raw power of ruling elites. Within two decades, the everyday creation of "fake news"—like claims that the COVID-19 pandemic is a "hoax"—had made Luban's bottom line a systemic reality to many.

Some, but not all, of the restrictions imposed on LSC-funded programs have been lifted since 1996.[13] The restructuring imposed by Congressional restrictions, however, permanently eliminated the state and national "service centers" that were a repository of advocacy expertise. Legal services advocates and historians Alan Houseman and Linda Perle offer this summary:

> The network of state and federal support entities formerly funded by LSC has been substantially curtailed . . .

---

[13] Although some of the 1996 restrictions have been lifted, many remain. The Legal Services Corporation Act, 42 U.S.C. 2996 et seq. and 1996 Appropriations Act (Pub. L. 104–134) and subsequent legislation placed the following restrictions on federally-funded legal services corporations and extended some of those restrictions to work performed under any source of funding. The LSA Act prohibits participation in political activities, including voter assistance or registration; lobbying government agencies or legislative bodies, with limited exceptions; criminal cases except those in Indian tribal courts; habeas corpus actions challenging convictions against law enforcement officers or officers of the court; organizing activities, including training for, or encouraging of, labor or political activities; litigation or other proceedings to obtain non-therapeutic abortions or require providers to offer abortion services over moral or religious objections; and any proceedings related to the desegregation of public schools, assisted suicide, or military service. The 1996 restrictions extend the restriction on lobbying to work carried out under any source of funding; prohibit the representation of non-U.S. citizens with a few exceptions; class actions; in-person solicitation of clients; abortion-related litigation of any kind; representation of prisoners; representing clients facing eviction from public housing if the eviction stems from criminal charges for selling or distributing illegal drugs; most welfare reform-related actions; redistricting activities; or any activity influencing the time or manner of activities related to the U.S. census. In 2010, the Consolidated Appropriations Act (Pub. L. 111–117) ended the 1996 restriction on LSC grantees that prohibited claiming, collecting, or retaining attorneys' fees. See LSC Restrictions and Other Funding Sources to determine which activities are prohibited under LSC funds, private funds, and other public funds, www.lsc.gov/lsc-restrictions-and-funding-sources.

> . . . [N]ew legal services delivery systems have begun emerging in many states that include both LSC-funded programs, operating within the constraints of Congressionally imposed restrictions, as well as separate non-LSC-funded legal services providers that operate unencumbered by the LSC restrictions. . . . The non-LSC-funded providers are generally free to seek attorneys' fees, as are LSC grantees since the end of 2009; engage in class actions, welfare reform advocacy, or representation before legislat[ive] and administrative bodies; and provide assistance to aliens and prisoners.[14]

Each year, opponents of legal services for the poor seek to slash funding for the LSC.[15] This effort has not succeeded entirely. But the number of lawyers providing government-funded services to indigent individuals remains abysmally low in relation to need, and the undermining of collective strategies and law-and-organizing collaborations has continued. Attacks on public interest advocacy groups through SLAPP suits and defunding attempts have continued, as have other top-down efforts to close or curtail the activities of law school clinics. Rebecca Smith of the National Employment Law Project notes that SLAPP lawsuits often increase when collective struggles begin to achieve wins, as when workers' centers started using litigation and direct action successfully to recover unpaid wages:

> [E]mployers who scoff at wage and hour laws have developed a certain "respect" for other laws, and some workers' centers have seen themselves and their members sued for alleged "defamation," "interference with business," or even accused of being "debt collectors." The main purpose of these lawsuits is to tie up a workers center's resources for a sufficient length of time that centers are either silenced by fear of litigation or the diversion of resources makes them unable to aggressively pursue organizational goals. These lawsuits have largely failed on the merits. They can be hugely disruptive to the real work of workers centers—requiring staff members to seek outside counsel, answer burdensome written questions, show up in court to testify and make centers fearful of engaging in the highly effective techniques of direct action.[16]

---

[14] Alan Houseman and Linda E. Perle, Securing Equal Justice for All: A Brief History of Civil Legal Assistance in the United States 40, 50–51 (2018) (a history produced under the auspices of The Center for Law and Social Policy, the National Equal Justice Library, and the National Legal Aid & Defender Association).

[15] These efforts continue. See Tim Ryan, Trump Budget Seeks to Cut Off Legal Aid Group, Courthouse News Service (Mar. 18, 2019), www.courthousenews.com/trump-budget-seeks-to-cut-off-legal-aid-group/ (reporting on the third year the Trump administration suggested eliminating the Legal Services Corporation).

[16] Rebecca Smith, Engaging in Direct Action Campaigns Without Getting SLAPP'ed: Take Action Against Wage Theft!, National Employment Law Project I (Dec. 2007), https://globalfreedomofexpression.columbia.edu/publications/slapps-5-ws-background-strategic-lawsuits-

SLAPP suits can become drawn-out, draining legal battles. Plaintiffs and defendants take actions to change the calculus of costs and benefits, like filing anti-SLAPP suits to push back against efforts to stifle public protest. In 2011, for example, the Board of the Olympia Food Co-op was sued by five co-op members after Board members voted to boycott products made in Israel to show support for Palestinian rights. The food co-op had taken similar measures earlier, banning items from its shelves from China to protest human rights abuses in Tibet and from Colorado in reaction to a state policy of legalized discrimination against LGBTQ individuals. Plaintiffs, however, argued that Board members had acted beyond their authority and had breached fiduciary duties by endorsing the boycott, and they asked for monetary damages. The Center for Constitutional Rights (CCR) worked with private attorneys to address the SLAPP suit:

> [In 2012,] CCR and co-counsel won a motion to strike a lawsuit against Board Members of the Olympia Food Co-op after the Board passed a resolution to boycott Israeli products. The court found that the Board members had acted within their duties on an issue of public concern, and that the lawsuit was designed to hamper their free speech rights to engage in a boycott movement of national proportions. The individuals who brought the lawsuit . . . were directed to pay attorney fees and penalties.[17]

The Board members then filed an anti-SLAPP lawsuit, which was stricken in 2015, after which the SLAPP suit was reinstated. On March 9, 2018, after seven years of legal battle, the court granted defendants' motion for summary judgment. The Washington State Court of Appeals affirmed the dismissal in February 2020, after which plaintiffs' motion for reconsideration was denied in April 2020. In all, the case has taken nine years of effort, required extraordinary steadfastness, and cost tremendous resources.[18] As this case shows, elites use time consciously as an integral element of strategy—in this case, to drain energy and resources—and therefore power and capacity—from adversaries.

Beyond SLAPP suits, attacks on law school clinics serving the poor have been ongoing for decades, as organized elites aim to suppress challenges. Robert Kuehn, legal clinician, and Bridget McCormack, former clinician and now judge, note that law school clinics serving the poor have

---

public-participation/. See also Nicole Hallett, From the Picket Line to the Courtroom: A Labor Organizing Privilege to Protect Workers, 39 N.Y.U. Rev. L. & Soc. Change 475 (2015) (explaining that employers "have responded forcefully with comprehensive anti-organizing campaigns, the purpose of which is to impede the success and growth of the worker center movement," with "the abuse of litigation and the discovery process" through SLAPP suits "at the center of these campaigns").

[17] Palestinian Human Rights Advocacy in the U.S., Palestine Solidarity Legal Support and Center for Constitutional Rights (2013), https://ccrjustice.org/files/3Final-Linked_CCR_Palestinian_Human_Rights_bk_small.pdf.

[18] Davis, et al. v. Cox, et al., Center for Constitutional Rights, https://ccrjustice.org/home/what-we-do/our-cases/davis-et-al-v-cox-et-al.

undergone forty years of attacks or other efforts to influence their decision making. Today's top-down attacks are part of this historical pattern:

> Although efforts to influence law clinic decisions about cases and clients have ebbed and flowed over the last forty years and have varied in approach, interference is an ongoing concern. Even clinics that may not handle controversial cases or clients are vulnerable to the ire of an opposing attorney or party with a connection to the law school or influence in the legislature. As the publicized cases of interference in law clinics demonstrate, "[a]ny law school clinic is just one controversial case, one unpopular client, one angry legislator, alumnus or opposing attorney, or one unsupportive dean or university official away from attempts to interfere in its case and client selection."
>
> . . . [C]linic attorneys often react to the specter of interference by self-censoring what they do about potential cases or say in matters of law school governance. The lesser security of position and status of law clinic attorneys within the legal academy compound these concerns, both making clinic attorneys more vulnerable to employment-related sanctions and less able to speak out internally on law school matters.
>
> Countering this interference is the responsibility of the legal profession, [the Association of American Law Schools], and law schools themselves.[19]

Elites use concurrent strategies to maintain an advantage: building up institutions and individuals that provide infrastructure for advantage in group struggles, while taking out adversaries—persons and institutions—that might threaten their interests. Often enough, "well-intentioned" individuals are behind organized efforts to take out elites' adversaries, mainly because they have truly bought into the top-down idea that those who oppose elites, and the systemic inequalities that preserve entrenched hierarchies, are undermining a valid or fair meritocracy. Recognizing that even "reasonable" individuals can be part of legalized injustice underscores why advocates must focus on systems—their designs and outputs—rather than (only) on "good" or "bad" apples. The following excerpt helps illuminate how elites use the system to justify their continuous efforts to demean, weaken, or crush adversaries.

Below, critical legal scholar Daria Roithmayr provides a history of formal legal education and its invention of "merit" as a concept that promotes identity-based hierarchies. Individual merit, it turns out,

---

[19] Robert R. Kuehn and Bridget M. McCormack, Lessons from Forty Years of Interference in Law School Clinics, 24 Geo. J. Leg. Ethics 59, 90 (2011). See also Robert R. Kuehn and Peter A. Joy, An Ethics Critique of Interference in Law School Clinics, 71 Fordham L. Rev. 1971, 1992 (2003).

amounts to the "social value" given by systems to "different" group identities. Roithmayr explains the origins of the status quo that Tait, Luban, and others have detailed above, showing how distorted notions of merit provide cover for persistent inequalities and for elites' intractable opposition to any challenge. Uncritical acceptance of the concept of "merit" and of existing "meritocratic" processes and institutions allows elites to justify their own advantages, others' disadvantages, and whatever actions elites might take to maintain both. Roithmayr also captures the shift from overt to covert uses of identity in law to normalize and reproduce group hierarchies. As you read, imagine how legal training might be different—and better—if not distorted by systemic uses of formalism to manipulate identities, groups, interests, and power.

DECONSTRUCTING THE DISTINCTION BETWEEN BIAS AND MERIT

Daria Roithmayr
85 Cal. L. Rev. 1449 (1997); 10 La Raza L.J. 363 (1998)

... Much has been written about the issue of merit and bias in law school admission standards. For as long as law schools have administered aptitude tests, Latino/a and African-American applicants disproportionately have achieved lower scores than white applicants. Many scholars have argued that such results are due to improper procedures or a cultural bias in the test itself.... Other scholars contend that Blacks and Latinos/as have disproportionately lower LSAT scores and undergraduate GPAs because they lack comparable educational opportunities and suffer from other forms of disadvantage.

Both arguments assume, however, that there is something "out there" called "merit"—the knack for legal reasoning, smarts, or diligence—that at least in theory is race-neutral. Both arguments also assume that people of color have been unfairly prevented from acquiring "merit" because of discrimination. Finally, both sides appear willing to concede that properly validated tests can theoretically measure an applicant's "true" ability to succeed in law school in a race-neutral way.

When one situates law school admission standards in their historical context, it appears that merit criteria deferred to and depended on the race-conscious social bias of the time to define what constituted "social value" in the legal profession.... [A]dmissions standards reflected the subjective preferences of white male lawyer elites. These leaders had acquired social power or "status" within the legal culture of the early twentieth century, in large part because of their race, given that people of color were affirmatively excluded from the profession at the time. Moreover, the leadership's subjective preferences about "social value" substantially reflected if not embodied the profession's desire to exclude Black and immigrant applicants from the practice of law.

The development of law-school admission standards can be traced to a number of related events occurring in the late nineteenth and early twentieth centuries. First, the number of European immigrants and African-Americans entering into the legal profession and law schools increased dramatically. At the same time, large, elite corporate law firms gained prominence on the Eastern seaboard, and created symbiotic relationships with prestigious Eastern law schools, at least in part to create a "safe haven" from the influx of immigrants. In addition, in an effort to prevent both immigrants and African Americans from gaining admission to practice law, the American Bar Association ("ABA") was formed. The ABA was part of a larger movement to eliminate part-time, night-time, and proprietary law schools, which served the rising numbers of immigrants and African Americans who sought to become lawyers. Reinforcing the hierarchy between prestigious law schools and schools that served immigrants and African Americans, Christopher Columbus Langdell and others introduced the case method into elite law schools, which helped to orient legal education toward abstract legal reasoning and away from practical experience. . . .

Prior to 1870, seasoned lawyers trained aspiring practitioners in an apprenticeship program governed by the Inns of Court. Serving as the central institution governing legal practice at the time, the Inns permitted lawyers to select their apprentices, determine the nature and duration of their apprenticeships, and prescribe attainments necessary for bar membership. Lawyers obtained very little formal training in legal theory, and those who did "read the law"—mostly old English treatises—did so under the guidance of a mentor. Some aspiring lawyers attended proprietary law schools, where practicing attorneys taught a few basic forensic skills and hornbook rules from treatises like Blackstone's Commentaries. Both apprenticeship programs and proprietary schools emphasized practical technique.

From 1870 to 1920, record numbers of immigrants from Eastern and Southern Europe flooded into the United States, and many began to seek entry into the legal profession ... as a gateway to economic opportunity. . . . In response to new demand, proprietary law schools sprang up almost overnight in large numbers, predominantly in cities with heavy immigrant populations.

Typically, the immigrant student had far less formal education than his native-born counterpart, and the immigrant's parents were less likely to be professionals. The immigrant practitioner was also much more likely to practice in criminal law, real estate, and non-commercial civil law. Jerold Auerbach describes how the professional elite began to create "selective" institutions, based in large part on the profile of the immigrant practitioner, in order to protect their elite status.

> As mass immigration and urbanization inundated the dominant Anglo-Saxon culture, the fortunate few moved to the safety of selected social institutions—Eastern schools, for example, and careers in business and finance—which could protect, or extend, their power and status.... Big business served as "a new preserve of the older Americans, where their status and influence could continue and flourish."[20]

These big business clients, whose numbers increased exponentially as America underwent industrialization, in turn, created a demand for large corporate law firms along the Eastern seaboard. Given the demographic makeup of big business at the time, firms catered to those clients by limiting entry into the firm to Easterners of "old-American stock," whose fathers were, like the firm's clients, wealthy professionals or businessmen. Quite predictably, symbiotic relationships formed between these corporate firms and the elite law schools.... Law schools were enthusiastic participants in the process, because they were able to reinforce their elite status by serving as a pipeline to funnel associates into the most prestigious firms.

In addition to closing ranks between big firms and prestigious law schools, prominent members of the profession also responded to the influx of immigrants by calling for "reform" on many fronts. Leaders of the profession created reform-minded bar organizations that limited their membership to the most affluent lawyers, all of whom were of old-American stock. After much discussion about the downward direction of the profession, in 1878 a group of elite lawyers created the American Bar Association for the purpose of restricting entry into the profession, and they vowed to "admit no men who would not be worthy members."... [T]he ABA was instrumental in pushing for reforms relating to the "moral character" and academic aptitude of applicants to the bar, both of which could be traced to anti-immigrant and racist sentiment.

... In 1930, the ABA ... passed a resolution against commercially operated schools. The ABA also created the National Conference of Bar Examiners to centralize the standards for bar examinations; whereupon the conference promptly proposed that bar-exam questions be modeled after questions being tested at the "better" university-affiliated law schools. In 1935, capitalizing on the explosion of racist and nativist sentiment in the bar, the ABA moved to limit the number of lawyers in the bar, citing overcrowding and problems with "moral character."

... [T]he call for more restrictive standards coincided with the move by law schools to formalize legal education. In the late nineteenth century, Christopher Columbus Langdell and James Barr Ames introduced the

---

[20] Jerold S. Auerbach, Unequal Justice: Lawyers and Social Change in Modern America 24–28 (1976).

case-law method of legal instruction, first at Harvard and then at a growing number of elite law schools aspiring to become even more exclusive.... Case-law instruction required the student to distill general principles from philosophical reflection and historical analysis of a particular area of the law, and to apply those principles consistent with the legal system's more general objective principles....

The case-law method fulfilled the requirements of modern education: it was scientific, practical, and best of all, Darwinian in approach—it winnowed out large numbers of students, allowing only the "fittest" and the most able (who also happened to be the most affluent and Anglo-Saxon) to survive. The case law method was a point of professional pride for many elite schools, because it differentiated them from second-tier schools....

In addition to winnowing out large numbers of students, the case-law method "selected against" practitioner professors, and "selected for" professional law teachers by making "demands that neither busy practitioners nor retired gentlemen could meet."... By the turn of the century, defenders of the case method had begun to prevail in their "holy war of supremacy" and the remaining practitioner-teachers quickly disappeared.

Race and Social Value in Legal Education

In Unequal Justice, Jerold Auerbach traces the foregoing events—the ascendance of the elite corporate law firm, the spread of the case-law method, and the ensuing call for "standards"—to virulent anti-immigrant sentiment, Anti-Semitism and racism in the legal profession in the early part of this century. Auerbach contends that middle-class, native-born white lawyers called for "standards," both "moral character" and academic, in order to safeguard their professional respectability and status from what they saw as the threat of dilution by the flood of immigrants and African Americans into the profession....

... Former ABA president Elihu Root declared, "I do not want anybody to come to the bar which I honor and revere ... who has not any conception of the moral qualities that underlie our free American institutions; and they are coming, today, by the tens of thousands."

Auerbach describes the anti-Semitic undertone of the "moral character" debate:

> Even before the war Theron Strong [an influential New York lawyer and author who wrote about the legal profession] complained sourly about "the influx of foreigners." Strong was especially troubled by the rising proportion of Jewish lawyers, which was "extraordinary, and almost overwhelming—so much so as to make it appear that their numbers were likely to

predominate, while the introduction of their characteristics and methods has made a deep impression upon the bar."

... Professional leaders also expressed dismay and doubt concerning the academic abilities of their immigrant counterparts. Future Chief Justice Harlan Fiske Stone "referred to 'the influx to the bar of greater numbers of the unfit,' who 'exhibit racial tendencies toward study by memorization' and display 'a mind almost Oriental in its fidelity to the minutiae of the subject without regard to any controlling rule or reason.' " ... In response to this outpouring of Anti-Semitism and nativism, in 1909, the Section of Legal Education of the ABA adopted the requirement that lawyers be American citizens, even though the foreign student was a market force to be reckoned with, having created a great demand for proprietary and night schools.

Efforts to restrict admission to the bar targeted African Americans as well as immigrants. Paul Finkelman has documented turn-of-the-century efforts to keep Blacks from practicing law:

> Starting in the 1890s, white-dominated southern governments began to disenfranchise and segregate blacks as a backlash against the Civil War and the goals of the Reconstruction. As blacks lost their newly acquired rights, black lawyers disappeared from the scene.... [By] 1940, there were just three blacks practicing law in Mississippi, and five in South Carolina.

... In 1912, the ABA unwittingly admitted three Black lawyers. When informed of the error, the organization rapidly passed a resolution rescinding admission.... In discussing the matter, the Association quite openly declared that, from their perspective, the matter posed "a question of keeping pure the Anglo-Saxon race." Eventually, the ABA reached a compromise; it allowed the three black lawyers to keep their memberships, but it imposed a new requirement that all future applicants identify themselves by race.

Of course, racism pervaded legal education during this time period as well. Many law schools, particularly those in the South, formally denied Blacks admission, and most others informally excluded them. As late as 1939, thirty-four of the eighty-eight accredited law schools had formal policies excluding Blacks....

Although the University of Texas Law School formally excluded Latinos by restricting their admission to white students only, law schools did not need to adopt formal exclusionary policies for Chicanos and other Latinos; pre-existing social and economic constraints alone were sufficient to keep them out....

Admissions programs also became selective for the first time in the early 1920s, in conjunction with the demands of the case-law method of instruction....

... [Law schools initiated] the use of aptitude testing.... Through aptitude-testing, elite law schools solved the problem of admitting students who were not proficient [specifically] in case-method analysis.

The use of aptitude testing continued to spread throughout the 1930s and 40s. In the late 1940s, three law schools formed an early version of what is now the Law School Admissions Council ("LSAC") to develop the Law School Aptitude Test ("LSAT"). Despite the already widespread use of aptitude testing among law schools, the first version of the LSAT, developed in 1947, did not draw from previous classroom testing experiences in legal education, but was based instead upon the Pepsi-Cola Scholarship Test and tests developed for the United States Navy.

Not surprisingly given the foregoing historical context, the Navy tests and other aptitude tests of similar character had their own foundation in racist and anti-immigrant sentiment....

The foregoing critical history of law school admissions illustrates the general deconstructivist insight that merit standards necessarily defer to and depend on subjective, socially constructed preferences about what constitutes social value, in this case in the legal profession. More relevantly, it demonstrates that legal professionals and educators constructed preferences for social value, as well as the corresponding law school admissions standards, at a time when the profession affirmatively sought to exclude people based on their race and ethnicity. Far from being colorblind, law school admissions standards were developed in a context of racial and cultural exclusion, where those professional leaders who developed those standards and values had achieved their leadership status in large part because of their race. Far more troublingly, this critical history raises the possibility that law schoo[l] admissions standards may have been developed as part of a broader professional effort to exclude on the basis of race and ethnicity.

Practically speaking, the history of law school admission may help to explain the admissions standards' disproportionate impact on groups that were excluded from the legal profession at the relevant time. Given the origins of aptitude testing, it is less likely to be mere coincidence that contemporary academic selectivity measures continue to exclude certain people of color disproportionately. For as long as the tests have been administered, Blacks and Latinos have performed at levels significantly below those of white applicants....

... [Thus,] merit actually reinscribes the qualities and characteristics of bias. Indeed, merit can be redescribed as a socially acceptable bias for particular qualities and characteristics and values....

Roithmayr shows that social identities were the basis for organizing legal education as it is today. Identities—those that were intended to be included and those intentionally excluded—were the basis for concentrating the power of law in particular identity groups. By employing critical history as a method, Roithmayr explains why and how the legal profession became and remains predominantly white and male, especially at the top.

NOTES AND QUESTIONS

1. *The "Honorable" Profession.* Law students have long been taught in self-promotional terms how the legal industry is an "honorable profession" that stands above the ethics, morals, and interests of the marketplace. As the then-CEO of NBC television put it in speaking at his alma mater's graduation ceremony at the University of Virginia law school in 2002:

> [M]ake no mistake: no profession is more honorable than the law. The defenders of the Constitution, the guardians of our liberty, the advocates of just causes, no matter how unpopular, the protectors of the powerless, the wise counselors of our society—that is the role of America's lawyers. This is what you have trained to become.[21]

In light of the readings above, critically evaluate the pervasive framing of law as an honorable profession rising above the interests of other industries to defend the powerless. Does that framing help justify and preserve the role of law as defender of the status quo? As a graduation speaker following the above speaker, how might you alternatively frame the Critical Challenge of law? How do you think practitioners, professors, and judges in attendance would react?

2. *Status v. Satisfaction.* Recall the study mentioned in Part III comparing the relative dissatisfaction of "prestige" lawyers to the higher levels of well-being among public service lawyers despite their lower salary. Would wider recognition of that difference in satisfaction help free more lawyers now handcuffed by professionalism training and industry incentives? Why or why not? Who then would serve elite interests? If more of the "best" lawyers (traditionally regarded as those from elite schools with the highest grades) were able to find jobs in public service, what do you imagine prestige law firms might do to counteract any such trend? As noted earlier, there is a gap between supply and demand for legal services that limits employment options; up to 80% of the civil legal needs of low- and moderate-income people are estimated to be unmet even though an adequate number of lawyers is available to fill that gap.[22] In fact, the United States spends more than other countries to get

---

[21] www.law.virginia.edu/static/uvalawyer/html/alumni/uvalawyer/s03/opinion.htm.

[22] Deborah Rhode, Access to Justice: Connecting Principles to Practice, 17 Geo. J. Legal Ethics, 369 (2004); The Justice Gap: Measuring the Unmet Civil Legal Needs of Low-income Americans, Legal Services Corporation (June 2017), www.lsc.gov/sites/default/files/images/The JusticeGap-FullReport.pdf; 3 Ways to Meet the "Staggering" Amount of Unmet Legal Needs, YourABA (July 2018) (reporting that legal aid lawyers serve just 1% of the legal needs each year of low-income families and encouraging expanding the field of non-lawyer practitioners authorized

less in the way of legal services, given that an estimated 1.3–1.8% of gross domestic product is spent on legal services.[23] Why do the government and legal industry not invest to better support legal services for low- and moderate-income residents and promote this work as equally or more prestigious as work to serve wealthy clients, as Carle suggested in Part II? How might the satisfaction study factor into your own career choices, and what changes in legal education or the industry would you advocate to make a broader array of career choices available for all?

3. *Microaggressive Environments and Diversity in Law.* A 2018 study in the United Kingdom found that junior associates at large law firms who "were perceived as different" because of class background suffered routine microaggressions that translated into poorer prospects for career advancement. Junior associates from lower socioeconomic backgrounds were made to feel that they don't "fit" the firm culture because of their accents, diction, school associations, or lack of familiarity with affluent pastimes like "skiing or exotic holidays." Such less-affluent junior associates received higher performance ratings than their peers from more affluent backgrounds but got fewer promotions and were likely to leave the firm more quickly.[24] Firm leaders justified this divergence in professional advancement by assessing the associates from wealthier backgrounds as being more "confident" or "charismatic" or having more "gravitas." These supposed "leadership" qualities proved to be proxies for class, while also overlapping significantly with race, gender, and other identities. The report called out law firm leaders for their complicity in creating or complacency in failing to correct class-based exclusions. But law firms continue to prioritize the appearance and mannerisms associated with affluent, mostly white, mostly male culture, and class is rarely mentioned in discussions of representative "diversity" or the microaggressive environments of legal institutions.[25]

---

to provide services, increasing philanthropic support, and ensuring that access to justice efforts aim at addressing the causes of poverty and economic insecurity, not just the consequences), www.americanbar.org/news/abanews/publications/youraba/2018/july-2018/3-ways-to-meet-the-staggering-amount-of-unmet-legal-needs-/.

[23] Ben Barton, A Comparison Between the American Markets for Medical and Legal Services, 67 Hastings L.J. 1331 (2016) ("We spend more on law as an absolute amount or as a percentage of GDP than any other country. . . . Yet, we barely provide any legal services to the very poor, and American lawyers cost too much for the working poor or even the middle class. . . . Why the mismatch between supply and demand?").

[24] Studies of racial, gender, and ethnic stereotypes in U.S. law firms show similar divergences between performance and assessments, but these studies pay little to no attention to the intersectional nature of class and other identity categories. See Deborah L. Rhode, Leadership in Law, 69 Stan. L. Rev. 1603 (2017) (describing studies finding that the same memo was judged more highly by law firm partners when partners were told it had been written by a white man versus an African American man and that women, particularly women of color, who received more positive comments about their work than men were nevertheless less than half as likely to be recommended as "partner material"). See also Elizabeth B. Cooper, The Appearance of Professionalism, 71 Fla. L. Rev. 1 (2019) (describing "microaggressions and microaggressive environments," often rooted in appearance cues, that create a "skewed lens" negatively affecting outsider law students and new lawyers).

[25] See Allison E. Laffey and Allison Ng, Diversity and Inclusion in the Law: Challenges and Initiatives, ABA (May 2, 2018).

Law firm leaders might say that actions promoting "high class" appearance and behavior are not microaggressions at all—just reasonable steps to encourage "fit" with the firm's institutional culture and view of professionalism. Does this "make sense" to you? Why and how is class injected into professional diversity, leadership, and success—and by whom?

9.3 LEGAL EDUCATION HANDCUFFS THE INDUSTRY TO INSTILL TOP-DOWN CONFORMITY

The studies above of the legal industry—contemporary and historical—examine how elites build up (and take out) institutions for their self-interest. These institutions span legal education and law practice, with implications for society as a whole. This systemic arrangement breeds professional conformity to "traditional" (top-down) biases.

Access to legal training and practice is highly regimented. Persons who are licensed to practice law (with rare exceptions) have to be credentialed by an accredited law school. This mandatory credentialing requires every aspiring lawyer to spend some 1,000 days of intense schooling immersed in legal doctrines. After three years of this immersion, many legal trainees are credentialed as successful, but some are stamped as not. Successful trainees proceed to the next gates and gatekeepers—bar examinations, fitness investigations, a lifetime of fees and dues, oaths of loyalty, and more. It should come as no surprise, then, that trainees declared successful would be among the most interested—and thus avid—defenders of that credentialing system.

Legal education functions as *systemic* training for conformity rather than criticality—even while insisting on its dedication to "critical thinking" in problem solving. Law schools and law practice thus routinely nudge students and practitioners to be uncritical and compliant—to serve elite power not just because they feel they must to get ahead, but because they wholeheartedly endorse the status quo. A founder of the Critical Legal Studies movement, Duncan Kennedy, noted in 1982—a critique still accurate today—that law schools provide "ideological training for willing service in the hierarchies" that still dominate society by force of law (and culture). To do so, law schools combine "a formal curriculum" with "a complicated set of institutional practices" that instill and induce conformity. The process of acculturation—of "training for hierarchy"—is both formal and informal to seamlessly create acceptance: the training "cannot be merely of public as opposed to private life." Law, Kennedy concludes, is "neither apolitical nor meritocratic."

Below, Kennedy describes how law school creates an insular, immersive experience that isolates the trainee from society.[26] Consider

---

[26] Continuing legal education programs after law school are not immune from this tendency to omit critical knowledges and encourage conformity. See, for example, Lorenzo Bowman, Tonette

Kennedy's bottom line: as a system, law is designed to inculcate and reproduce dominant hierarchies, not to promote equal justice. Law, in other words, is not "broken" but rather is designed to reproduce failure. Does your experience with legal training (or practice)—if any—reflect the same bottom line? How so—and how not?

LEGAL EDUCATION AND THE REPRODUCTION OF HIERARCHY

Duncan Kennedy
32 J. Legal Educ. 591 (1982)

... The First Year Experience

A surprisingly large number of law students go to law school with the notion that being a lawyer means something more, something more socially constructive than just doing a highly respectable job. There is the idea of playing the role ... of service through law, carried out with superb technical competence and also with a deep belief that in its essence law is a progressive force, however much it may be distorted by the actual arrangements of capitalism. There is a contrasting, more [critical] notion, that law is a tool of established interests, that it is in essence superstructural, but that it is a tool which a coldly effective professional can sometimes turn against the dominators....

The Ideological Content of Legal Education

One can distinguish in a rough way between two aspects of legal education as a reproducer of hierarchy. Much of what happens is the inculcation through a formal curriculum and the classroom experience of a set of political attitudes toward the economy and society in general, toward law, and toward the possibilities of life in the profession.... Then there is a complicated set of institutional practices that orient students to willing participation in the specialized hierarchial roles of lawyers....

Law students sometimes speak as though they learned nothing in school. In fact, they learn skills, to do a list of simple but important things. They learn to retain large numbers of rules organized into categorical systems (e.g., requisites for contract, rules about breach). They learn "issue spotting," which means identifying the ways in which the rules are ambiguous, in conflict, or have a gap when applied to particular fact situations. They learn elementary case analysis, meaning the art of generating broad holdings for cases, so they will apply beyond their intuitive scope, and narrow holdings for cases so that they won't apply where it at first seemed they would. And they learn a list of balanced, formulaic, pro/con policy arguments that lawyers use in arguing that a

---

Rocco & Elizabeth Peterson, The Exclusion of Race from Mandated Continuing Legal Education Requirements: A Critical Race Theory Analysis, 8 Seattle J. Soc. Just. 229 (2009).

given rule should apply to a situation in spite of a gap, conflict, or ambiguity or that a given case should be extended or narrowed. These are arguments like "the need for certainty" and "the need for flexibility," "the need to promote competition" and the "need to encourage production by letting producers keep the rewards of their labor." . . .

On the other hand, law schools teach these rather rudimentary, essentially instrumental skills in a way that almost completely mystifies them for almost all law students. The mystification has three parts.

First, the schools teach skills through class discussions of cases in which it is asserted that law emerges from a rigorous analytical procedure called "legal reasoning," which is unintelligible to the layman but somehow both explains and validates the great majority of the rules in force in our system. At the same time, the class context and the materials present every legal issue as distinct from every other, as a tub on its own bottom, so to speak, with no hope or even any reason to hope that from law study one might derive an integrating vision of what law is, how it works, or how it might be changed (other than in an incremental, case-by-case, reformist way).

Second, the teaching of skills in the mystified context of legal reasoning about utterly unconnected legal problems means that skills are taught badly, unselfconsciously, to be absorbed by osmosis as one picks up the knack of "thinking like a lawyer." Bad or only randomly good teaching generates and then accentuates real differences and imagined differences in student capabilities. But it does so in such a way that students don't know when they are learning and when they aren't and have no way of improving or even understanding their own learning processes. They experience skills training as the gradual emergence of differences among themselves, as a process of ranking that reflects something that is just "there" inside them.

Third, the schools teach skills in isolation from actual lawyering experience. "Legal reasoning" is sharply distinguished from law practice, and one learns nothing about practice. This procedure disables students from any future role but that of apprentice in a law firm organized in the same manner as a law school, with older lawyers controlling the content and pace of [on-the-job] training in a setting of intense competition and no feedback. . . .

Law schools teach a small number of useful skills. But they teach them only obliquely. It would threaten the professional ideology and the academic pretensions of teachers to make their students as good as they can be at the relatively simple tasks that they will have to perform in practice. But it would also upset the process by which a hierarchical arrangement analogous to that of law-school applicants, law schools, and law firms is established within a given student body. . . .

In communicating class-rank information to each student, law schools convey the implicit corollary that place is individually earned and therefore deserved. The system tells each student that he learned as much as he was capable of learning. If he feels incompetent or that he could have done better, it is his own fault. Opposition is sour grapes. Students internalize this message about themselves and about the world and so prepare themselves for all the hierarchies to follow.

Law schools [then] channel their students into jobs in the hierarchy of the bar according to their own standing in the hierarchy of schools. Students confronted with the choice of what to do after they graduate experience themselves as largely helpless: they have no "real" alternatives to taking a job in one of the conventional firms that hires from their school. . . .

As for any form of work outside the established system—for example, legal services for the poor, and neighborhood law practice—teachers convey to students that, although morally exalted, the work is hopelessly dull and unchallenging and the possibilities of reaching a standard of living appropriate to a lawyer are slim to nonexistent. These messages are just nonsense—the rationalizations of law teachers who long upward, fear status degradation, and above all hate the idea of risk. Legal services practice, for example, is far more intellectually stimulating and demanding, even with a high case load, than most of what corporate lawyers do. It is also more fun. . . .

. . . Law school, as an extension of the educational system as whole, teaches students that they are weak, lazy, incompetent, and insecure. And it also teaches them that if they are willing to accept dependency, large institutions will take care of them almost no matter what. The terms of the bargain are relatively clear. The institution will set limited, cognizable tasks and specify minimum requirements in their performance. The student associate has no other responsibilities than performance of those tasks. . . . In exchange, students renounce any claim to control their work setting or the actual content of what they do and agree to show the appropriate form of deference to those above them and condescension to those below.

By comparison, the alternatives are risky. Law school does not prepare students to run a small law business, to assess realistically the outcome of a complex process involving many different actors, or to enjoy the feeling of independence and moral integrity that comes of creating their own job to serve their own goals. It tries to persuade them that they are barely competent to perform the much more limited roles it allows them and strongly suggests that it is more prudent to kiss the lash than to strike out on your own.

. . . This training is a major factor in the hierarchical life of the bar. It encodes the message of the legitimacy of the whole system into the smallest details of personal style, daily routine, gesture, tone of voice, facial expression, a plethora of little p's and q's for everyone to mind. Partly, these will serve as a language—a way for the young lawyer to convey that he knows what the rules of the game are and intends to play by them. Partly, it is a matter of ritual oaths and affirmations—by adopting the mannerisms one pledges one's troth to inequality. And partly it is a substantive matter of value. Hierarchical behavior will come to express and realize the hierarchical selves of people who were initially only wearers of masks.

. . . In law school, students have to come to grips with implications of their social class, sex, and race in a way that is different from (but not necessarily less important than) the experience of college. People discover that preserving their class status is extremely important to them, so important that no alternative to the best law job they can get seems possible to them. Or they discover that they want to rise or that they are trapped in a way they hadn't anticipated. Students change the way they dress and talk; they change their opinions and even their emotions. . . .

. . . [T]here is [another], more subtle, and less conscious message conveyed in student/teacher relations. Teachers are overwhelmingly white, male, and middle class, and most (by no means all) black and women law teachers give the impression of thorough assimilation to that style or of insecurity and unhappiness. Students who are women or black or working class find out something important about the professional universe from the first day of class: that it is not even nominally pluralist in cultural terms. The teacher sets the tone—a white, male, middle-class tone. Students adapt. . . . [T]he line between adaptation to the intellectual and skills content of legal education and adaptation to the white, male, middle-class cultural style is a fine one, easily lost sight of. . . .

Students, alone in their seats, feel alienated in this atmosphere, but it is unlikely that they will do anything about it in the classroom setting itself, however much they gripe about it with friends. . . .

It is easy enough to see this situation of enforced cultural uniformity as oppressive but somewhat more difficult to see it as training, especially if you are aware of it and hate it. But it is training nonetheless. The students will pick up mannerisms, ways of speaking, gestures, which would be "neutral" if they were not emblematic of membership in the white, middle-class, male universe of the bar. They come to expect that as a lawyer they will live in a world in which essential parts of them are not represented, or are misrepresented, and in which things they don't like will be accepted to the point that it doesn't occur to people that they are even controversial. And they come to expect that there is nothing they can do about it. One develops ways of coping with these expectations—turning off attention or involvement when the conversation strays in certain directions, participating actively while ignoring the offensive elements of the interchange, even reinterpreting as inoffensive things that would otherwise make one boil. These are skills that incapacitate rather than empower, skills that help the student imprison himself in practice....

The final touch that completes the picture of law school as training for professional hierarchy is the placement process. As each firm puts on, with the tacit or enthusiastically overt participation of the schools, a conspicuous display of its relative status within the bar, the bar as a whole affirms and celebrates its hierarchical values and the rewards they bring. This process is most powerful for students who go through the elaborate procedures of firms in about the top half of the profession....

This system allows law firms to get a social sense of applicants, a sense of how they will contribute to the nonlegal image of the firm and to the internal system of deference and affiliation. It allows firms to convey to students the extraordinary opulence of the life they offer, adding the allure of free travel, expense account meals, fancy hotel suites and parties at country clubs to the simple message of big bucks in a paycheck....

By dangling the bait, making clear the rules of the game, and then subjecting almost everyone to intense anxiety about their acceptability, firms structure entry into the profession so as to maximize acceptance of hierarchy. If you feel you've succeeded, you're forever grateful, and you have a vested interest. If you feel you've failed, you blame yourself, when you aren't busy feeling envy. When you get to be the hiring partner, ... it will be hard even to imagine why someone might want to change it.

Insomuch as these hierarchies are generational, they are easier to take than those baldly reflective of race, sex, or class.... Training for subservience is training for domination as well. Nothing could be more natural and, if you've served your time, more fair, than that you as a group should do as you have been done to, for better and for worse. But it doesn't have to be that way....

I have been arguing that legal education causes legal hierarchy. Legal education supports it by analogy, provides it a general legitimating ideology by justifying the rules that underlie it, and provides it a particular ideology by mystifying legal reasoning. Legal education structures the pool of prospective lawyers so that their hierarchical organization seems inevitable and trains them in detail to look and think and act just like all the other lawyers in the system.... [However,] legal education is as much a product of legal hierarchy as a cause of it.... If it is there, it is there because [educators] put it there and reproduce it generation after generation, just as lawyers do.

Students respond in different ways to their slowly emerging consciousness of the hierarchical realities of life in the law. Looking around me, I see students who enter wholeheartedly into the system—for whom the training "takes" in a quite straight-forward way. Others appear, at least, to manage something more complex. They accept the system's presentation of itself as largely neutral, as apolitical, meritocratic, instrumental, a matter of craft. And they also accept the system's promise that if they do their work, "serve their time," and "put in their hours," they are free to think and do and feel anything they want in their "private lives."

... [But] since the law is neither apolitical nor meritocratic nor instrumental nor a matter of craft (at least not exclusively these things), and since training for hierarchy cannot be a matter merely of public as opposed to private life, it is inevitable that [students] do in fact give and take something different than what is suggested by the overt terms of the bargain. ...

Law students, professors, and practitioners do not necessarily knowingly seek to maintain unjust caste systems; this scenario would be too simple. Rather, the status quo self-replicates in chief part because lawyers are taught in seamless ways to presume that the status quo is just, fair, and inevitable. Over time, they become front-line enforcers of the system's outputs. Thus, "professionalism" in law practice also is defined in terms of upholding the status quo. But Kennedy points out that these notions of professionalism are, in fact, "just nonsense." These notions, however, constrain legal actors from using their academic or other capital to build critical coalitions and advance an antisubordination agenda within the legal industry, as Gruber noted earlier in Part III.

Law schools further code conceptions of legal "professionalism" and ethics in class-, race-, and gender-biased ways and teach students to comply. Too often, professionalism is presented as a set of behaviors demonstrating conformity: you must dress in "appropriate" business attire, show up on time, and do precisely and only what the senior partner, judge, or other authority figure orders. Does this description track what you may have learned about professionalism? Or did you have the lucky—but unlikely—experience of learning to challenge class- and gender-based notions of business dress? Were you asked to consider critically whether to follow, stretch, or strategically violate such norms? Lucille Jewel, a legal writing and ClassCrits scholar, critically examines the typical approach to teaching professionalism—an approach that centers on convincing and training students to adopt upper-class mannerisms and behaviors, such as those she describes below:[27]

> 1. *Acquiring Taste and Distinction.* . . . Law students learn to pick up "mannerisms . . . emblematic of membership in the white middle class male universe of the bar." . . .
>
> . . . For instance, through comments by moot court judges, students learn that a woman's legitimacy as an advocate depends on clothing choices that match upper-class ideals of what a professional woman should wear. . . .
>
> 2. *The Language of Distinction.* Law school stresses a measured, unemotional, and grammatically sound form of communication, which correlates to the preferred communication style of the upper-class. . . . [L]aw schools teach students that proper grammar and a formal tone will cause readers to perceive text as legitimate, whereas bad grammar or a strident, emotional tone will cause the reader to view a text and its author with suspicion. . . .
>
> . . . Professional Responsibility courses may offer [a] chance to raise student consciousness of the ways that the legal profession replicates its hierarchical structure. . . . [T]here is no reason not to expose students to the eye-opening historical background behind many of the ABA's canons of professional responsibility, particularly the rules regarding lawyer advertising, direct solicitation, and contingency fees. . . . [T]he cadre of upper-class WASP lawyers who dominated the ABA and local bar associations adopted the first ethics canons in response to a perceived threat to the profession from the influx of ethnic and immigrant attorneys into American cities at the turn of the century. . . .
>
> While students must learn the rules, they should . . . see that many of these rules . . . may have been designed to subordinate lower caste attorneys rather than preventing any kind of palpable harm to the public.[28]

---

[27] Lucille A. Jewel, Bourdieu and American Legal Education: How Law Schools Reproduce Social Stratification and Class Hierarchy, 56 Buff. L. Rev. 1155 (2008).

[28] *Id.* "WASP" is an acronym for "white Anglo-Saxon Protestant." Although the origin of the term is disputed, Fred Shapiro, editor of The Yale Book of Quotations, said that author and anti-Ku Klux Klan activist Stetson Kennedy first used the term in print in The New York Amsterdam News, an African-American newspaper, when he wrote in 1948: "In America, we find the WASPS (White Anglo-Saxon Protestants) ganging up to take their frustrations out on whatever minority group happens to be handy—whether Negro, Catholic, Jewish, Japanese or whatnot." Fred Shapiro, The First WASPs?, N.Y. Times (Mar. 14, 2012), www.nytimes.com/2012/03/18/books/review/the-first-wasp.html.

As Jewel points out, the means by which law schools inculcate and reproduce social and professional hierarchies extend beyond the curricular or the institutional. Even personal appearance, accent, or demeanor are part of this scheme. New generations are thereby trained, thoroughly, to think and behave *obediently*—"like a lawyer"—ironically in the name of thinking *critically*. Those who "learn the law" (and how to "think like a lawyer" and "act professionally") well enough in this cognitively dissonant environment are rewarded. Professional "success" in law creates incentives that encourage lawyers to learn, internalize, and repeatedly re-enact systemic hierarchies.[29] If this deconstruction of professional couture or appearance matters, the next excerpt vividly illustrates how.

In 1994, Lani Guinier, Michelle Fine, Jane Balin, Ann Bartow, and Deborah Lee Stachel, an interdisciplinary group of scholars, provided an empirical snapshot of "how the system does it." By this, they refer to the actual day-by-day, seamless process of law schooling by which women (individually and as a group) learn conformity in a hierarchy that is "hostile, elite, and previously all-male."[30] These scholars carried out research at the University of Pennsylvania School of Law analyzing the makeup of law school classes, the academic performance of students—as recognized by grades, awards, and other markers, and self-reported assessments of experience and success from students. Their data showed that women's experience in law schools differed from men's experience and that the women considered most "successful" tended to be those who most fully and uncritically internalized norms that reflected gender, racial, class, and other hierarchies that Kennedy and Jewel described above. Guinier et al. set out the four principal findings of their study and recommend that law schools should change to diminish gender inequalities—a process that would serve to improve education for all students and realign its structure to better align law with justice. Notice the pervasive roles—both background and foreground, as well as formal and informal—played by identities, groups, interests, and power:

> [We found, first, that] despite identical entry-level credentials, . . . [b]y the end of their first year in law school, men are *three times more likely* than women to be in the top 10%. . . .
>
> Second, we find strong attitudinal differences between women and men in year one, and yet a striking homogenization by year three. . . . A disproportionate number of the women we studied enter law school with commitments to public interest law,

---

[29] See, for example, Pierre Bourdieu, Social Space and Symbolic Power, 7 Soc. Theory 14, 19 (1989); Pierre Bordieu and Loïc J.D. Wacquant, The Purpose of Reflexive Sociology, in An Invitation to Reflexive Sociology 60, 98–99 (1992) (relying on "reflexivity" as a practice that helps professionals see the ways in which they have been trained to defend the status quo).

[30] Lani Guinier, Michelle Fine, Jane Balin, Ann Bartow & Deborah Lee Stachel, Becoming Gentlemen: Women's Experiences at One Ivy League Law School, 143 U. Pa. L. Rev. 1 (1994).

ready to fight for social justice. But their third-year female counterparts leave law school with corporate ambitions and some indications of mental health distress.

Third, many women are alienated by the way the Socratic method is used in large classroom instruction.... Women self-report much lower rates of class participation than do men for all three years of law school.... These women describe a dynamic in which they feel that their voices were "stolen" from them during the first year. Some complain that they can no longer recognize their former selves, which have become submerged inside what one author has called an alienated "social male."...

Even those women who do well academically report a higher degree of alienation from the Law School than their male counterparts, based in part on [the realization that] learning to think like a lawyer means learning to think and act like a man. As one male professor told a first-year class, "to be a good lawyer, behave like a gentleman."

Finally, we document substantial material consequences for those women who exit the Law School after sustaining what they describe as a crisis of identity. These women graduate with less competitive academic credentials, are not represented equally within the Law School's academic and social hierarchies, and are apparently less competitive in securing prestigious and/or desirable jobs after graduation.

... [W]e are inclined to believe that it is law school—not the women—that should change. Indeed, changes to the existing structure of the law school might improve the quality of legal education for all students.[31]

The authors conclude that law schools not only reproduce social stratifications, they "create and legitimate" them. If so, formal legal education functions as a linchpin of entrenched caste systems, and needed changes include formal and informal reforms, including in-classroom practices as well as extracurricular programs. Technical fixes alone, like "diversity" at the top, are too "simple" for transformative results. To be effective, reforms of legal education must improve the institutional conditions that students from subordinated groups, or their advocates, show are oppressive.

Taken together, these excerpts and materials explain how and why legal education functions as a key component of law as a conformist, for-profit industry. This critical, bottom-up exploration of that industry allows

---

[31] *Id.* See also NALP Foundation for Law Career Research and Education and The Center for Women in Law, Women of Color: A Study of Law School Experiences (2020), www.utexas.app.box.com/s/kvn7dezec99khii6ely9cve368q4gj9o.

trainees to unlearn and relearn the ways, means, and ends of formal legal education. Through the daily counter-practices of systemic advocacy, students, graduates, and others can begin to transcend the blindfolds, handcuffs, and hierarchies of this industry.

NOTES AND QUESTIONS

1. *Confronting Conformity.* To confront the effects of conformism, we must first recognize it, and its social omnipresence. For law students, consider both the personal statement you wrote seeking admission to law school and one or more of the cover letters you may have written to prospective legal employers, particularly those engaged in traditional law practice venues such as law firms. Do you cue your conformity to industry values? How? Why? Or not? Compare those letters to your personal statement. Is the latter more idealistic and value-laden? Were you given instruction on how to construct admissions or employment letters that send the "right signals" to law schools, and then to law firms? For non-law students, consider personal statements or similar presentations of yourself for acceptance into schools or for hiring as a worker. Do you recall any of the above in your own experiences? Did you experience any inducement or pressure to conform and be your very best? If so, did it work? More generally, is this how "the world" works? If so, how can advocates overcome, or pierce through, cultures of conformism?

2. *Practice-Readiness.* Kennedy comments above how law schools "teach a small number of useful skills" and "teach them only obliquely." Roithmayr detailed how elite schools oriented legal education more than a century ago "toward abstract legal reasoning and away from practical experience." Yet recall Rivera-Perez and Garcia-Ellin's critique of the current calls to emphasize practice-readiness in modern legal education. Can you reconcile how the move away from, and the current call to turn toward, practice-readiness in legal education serve elite interests?

9.4 LEGAL FORMALISM BLINDFOLDS ANALYSIS SELECTIVELY TO OBSCURE SYSTEMIC INJUSTICE AT WORK

As noted above by Roithmayr, Christopher Columbus Langdell created the so-called "case method," which focuses on Socratic dialogue between law teacher and student framed by legal individualism. This method directs law students to study the minutiae of published opinions of appellate judges and their (assumed) internal logic. But trainee problem solvers—like appellate judges—may be insulated from social realities:

> Langdellian scholars would begin either by stating, in the abstract, a small number of axiomatic principles or by analyzing a series of cases to discover, through inductive reasoning, the necessary axiomatic principles. Those principles then could govern all possible disputes within the relevant field of law. More

specific legal rules and correct resolutions of legal issues could be deduced, through abstract logical reasoning, from the principles. Ultimately, the common law could be logically arranged into a formal and conceptually ordered system.[32]

Formalism thus is a theory and practice in which "legal rules stand separate from other social and political institutions. . . . [O]nce lawmakers produce rules, judges apply them to the facts of a case without regard to social interests and public policy."[33] Formalist approaches to analysis and advocacy teach that power responds (usually) to justice, principle, and persuasion—i.e., that principles control exercises of power and that lawyers thus promote justice by *not* challenging the legal system and its outputs. Formalism's devotion to abstracted legalisms fosters widespread blindfolding to actual social conditions and progress and to the role of power in maintaining systemic injustice. Appellate court doctrine is the fountainhead of this training system and its inculcation of conformity to authority.

Doctrine is presented in the form of judicial opinions that decide disputes. These then function as precedent to be studied carefully because of their binding or persuasive authority. Formalism is inculcated through doctrine-based training into the consciousness of every new legal trainee starting on, if not before, the first day of schooling—well before the student learns the term or its social meaning. Often, students pass through three years of law schooling without ever using (or fully understanding) the term and implications of "formalism," even though they have read and internalized scores of formalisms from countless opinions. Institutionalized formalism is baked into legal education and the industry as a whole.

Those inculcated in this disciplinary framework[34]—legal formalism—necessarily absorb a shared understanding about what they *actually*, as well as what they *should*, think and do. Part of training is to instill a common framework for thinking both about the way the world is, as well as how the world should be. Legal formalism has served this purpose well: first, formalism or "mechanical jurisprudence" purports to describe accurately how problem solving in law, particularly adjudication, *does occur*. Second, formalism promotes fictionalized, abstracted decision making as an "okay" normative theory, signaling how problem solving *should occur*. In theory and as practice, formalism depicts systemic

---

[32] S. M. Feldman, The Transformation of An Academic Discipline, 54 J. Legal Ed. 206 (2004).

[33] Legal formalism, WEX, Cornell Law School Legal Information Institute, www.law.cornell.edu/wex/legal_formalism.

[34] Myra Max Ferree, The Discursive Politics of Feminist Intersectionality, in Framing Intersectionality: Debates on a Multi-faceted Concept in Gender Studies 58 (Helma Lutz, Maria Teresa Herrera Vivar & Linda Supik eds. 2011) (defining frameworks as "institutionalized networks of meaning" and describing how science, law, and other disciplines "privilege certain ways of knowing and direct those who would be productive within them to follow certain practices rather than others").

decision making as unaffected by biases, experiences, or the proverbial "hunches" that guide "discretion" in real life.[35]

Legal formalism as "reasoning" is characterized by the positing of categories designed to appear rooted in nature or logic, which then are deemed to reflect social reality, while using definitions tailored to preferred outcomes. In formalist schemes, "logical" deduction is demanded over inductive or other forms of reasoning. Similarly, sources and uses of "facts" or "evidence" deemed "admissible" in legal proceedings—whether empirical data, narrative stories, analogies, or "authoritative" citations—are selectively narrowed.[36] The cumulative effects of these procedural, evidentiary, or substantive groups rules help explain the detachment of law from reality and from justice.

Moreover, the legal decision-making process itself is assumed to be unaffected by identities, groups, interests, or power. Formalism as reasoning sets up the appearance of autonomous processes and "scientific" outcomes that rely on "objective" standards to yield "neutral" results, confirming the system's claimed utility and legitimacy:

> In law, formalism is connected to the rule of precedent and conservative judging. In legal education, formalism manifests itself in teaching of rules and doctrines at the expense of social implications and policy. It exalts internal values such as consistency over ambiguity, rationality over emotion, rules over social context or competing interests and narratives.[37]

In practice, legal formalism is a disciplinary framework that ties law to elite interests, not neutral reasoning. Consider the opinions of the U.S. Supreme Court in two pairs of cases from the late 20th century and early 21st century. In both pairs, the facts and claims put social identities at the center—but formalism blindfolds the analysis to ignore them. Note how formalist approaches substitute the categories of social life involved in the case with legal categories detached from social experience and the dispute itself, as framed by the parties. As you read, observe how formalism dominates framing *and* outcomes despite dissenting opinions arguing that social realities and context should be taken into account.

Brought by women workers, sex was at the center of the facts and claims in the first pair—*Geduldig v. Ailleo* and *General Electric. v. Gilbert*—involving, respectively, discrimination based on pregnancy or the

---

[35] See Joseph C. Hutcheson Jr., Judgment Intuitive: The Function of the Hunch in Judicial Decision, 14 Cornell L. Rev. 274 (1929) (addressing the role of psychological influences in judicial decision making); Jerome Frank, Law and the Modern Mind (1930).

[36] For a description of the use of stories in traditional and critical legal reasoning, see Linda Edwards, Where Do the Prophets Stand? Hamdi, Myth, and the Master's Tools, 13 Conn. Pub. Int. L.J. 43 (2013).

[37] Jean Stefancic and Richard Delgado, How Lawyers Lose Their Way: A Profession Fails Its Creative Minds xi (2005).

capacity for it. In both cases, a majority of the judges opined that pregnancy-based discrimination was *not* based on sex. Instead, the majority recast the question as one involving a distinction between "pregnant women" and "non pregnant persons"—an abstracted switching of labels designed to sublimate the salience of sex as a social identity even in a case focused factually on pregnancy. In this way, the majority scrambles formally the lines that "count" even though the cases were brought by women who experienced workplace subordination as women. Instead, according to the formalist judges, the cases were not at all about sex because "non pregnant persons" includes "both sexes." Rather than an impermissible difference in treatment of men and women, the pregnancy-based line drawing was formalistically remade into an ordinary, lawful economic transaction. As these cases illustrate, judges can create categories on paper—as formalities—and then act upon these abstractions to recycle identity-based inequalities. Formalism is part of law's failure by design; it is a bulwark of the Critical Challenge preventing the use of law for equal justice.

GEDULDIG V. AIELLO
417 U.S. 484 (1974)

MR. JUSTICE STEWART delivered the opinion of the Court.

. . . The appellees brought this action to challenge the constitutionality of a provision of the California program that, in defining "disability," excludes from coverage certain disabilities resulting from pregnancy. . . .

. . . There is no evidence in the record that the selection of the risks insured by the program worked to discriminate against any definable group or class in terms of the aggregate risk protection derived by that group or class from the program. There is no risk from which men are protected and women are not. Likewise, there is no risk from which women are protected and men are not. . . .

To explain itself further, the majority opinion in *Geduldig* added this extended and revealing footnote:

> . . . The California insurance program does not exclude anyone from benefit eligibility because of gender but merely removes one physical condition—pregnancy—from the list of compensable disabilities. While it is true that only women can become pregnant it does not follow that every legislative classification concerning pregnancy is a sex-based classification. . . . Normal pregnancy is an objectively identifiable physical condition with unique characteristics. Absent a showing that distinctions involving pregnancy are mere pretexts designed to effect an invidious

discrimination against the members of one sex or the other, lawmakers are constitutionally free to include or exclude pregnancy from the coverage of legislation such as this on any reasonable basis, just as with respect to any other physical condition.

The lack of identity between the excluded disability and gender as such under this insurance program becomes clear upon the most cursory analysis. The program divides potential recipients into two groups—pregnant women and nonpregnant persons. While the first group is exclusively female, the second includes members of both sexes. The fiscal and actuarial benefits of the program thus accrue to members of both sexes.

Now consider the dissenting opinion in *Geduldig* of three justices who expose the identity-based inequality denied in the majority's "reasoning" and outcome:

MR. JUSTICE BRENNAN, with whom MR. JUSTICE DOUGLAS and MR. JUSTICE MARSHALL join, dissenting.

. . . California's disability insurance program was enacted to supplement the State's unemployment insurance and workmen's compensation programs by providing benefits to wage earners to cushion the economic effects of income loss and medical expenses resulting from sickness or injury. . . .

. . . [B]y singling out for less favorable treatment a gender-linked disability peculiar to women, the State has created a double standard for disability compensation: a limitation is imposed upon the disabilities for which women workers may recover, while men receive full compensation for all disabilities suffered, including those that affect only or primarily their sex, such as prostatectomies, circumcision, hemophilia, and gout. In effect, one set of rules is applied to females and another to males. Such dissimilar treatment of men and women, on the basis of physical characteristics inextricably linked to one sex, inevitably constitutes sex discrimination.

The same conclusion has been reached by the Equal Employment Opportunity Commission, the federal agency charged with enforcement of Title VII of the Civil Rights Act of 1964, as amended by the Equal Employment Opportunity Act of 1972, which prohibits employment discrimination on the basis of sex. . . .

Geduldig was an equal protection case involving a state worker benefits program. It was followed by *Gilbert*, a Title VII case involving a private employer's benefits plan. As in *Geduldig*, the dissents in *Gilbert* emphasized the fallacies, or selective blindfolding, of legal formalism as applied in both cases.

GENERAL ELECTRIC COMPANY V. GILBERT
429 U.S. 125 (1976)

MR. JUSTICE REHNQUIST delivered the opinion of the Court.

Petitioner, General Electric Co., provides for all of its employees a disability plan which pays weekly nonoccupational sickness and accident benefits. Excluded from the plan's coverage, however, are disabilities arising from pregnancy. Respondents, on behalf of a class of women employees, brought this action seeking, inter alia, a declaration that this exclusion constitutes sex discrimination. . . .

The individual named respondents are present or former hourly paid production employees at General Electric's plant in Salem, Va. Each of these employees was pregnant during 1971 or 1972, while employed by General Electric, and each presented a claim to the company for disability benefits under the Plan to cover the period while absent from work as a result of the pregnancy. These claims were routinely denied on the ground that the Plan did not provide disability-benefit payments for any absence due to pregnancy. . . .

. . . *Geduldig* leaves no doubt that our reason for rejecting appellee's equal protection claim in that case was that the exclusion of pregnancy from coverage under California's disability-benefits plan was not in itself discrimination based on sex. . . .

. . . [Similarly under Title VII,] we have here no question of excluding a disease or disability comparable in all other respects to covered diseases or disabilities and yet confined to the members of one race or sex. Pregnancy is, of course, confined to women, but it is in other ways significantly different from the typical covered disease or disability. The District Court found that it is not a "disease" at all, and is often a voluntarily undertaken and desired condition. We do not therefore infer that the exclusion of pregnancy disability benefits from petitioner's plan is a simple pretext for discriminating against women. . . .

MR. JUSTICE BRENNAN, with whom MR. JUSTICE MARSHALL concurs, dissenting.

The Court holds today that without violating Title VII of the Civil Rights Act of 1964 . . . a private employer may adopt a disability plan that compensates employees for all temporary disabilities except one affecting exclusively women, pregnancy. I respectfully dissent. . . .

The Court . . . views General Electric's plan as representing a gender-free assignment of risks in accordance with normal actuarial techniques.

From this perspective the lone exclusion of pregnancy is not a violation of Title VII insofar as all other disabilities are mutually covered for both sexes....

... [I]n reaching its conclusion that a showing of purposeful discrimination has not been made, the Court simply disregards a history of General Electric practices that have served to undercut the employment opportunities of women who become pregnant while employed. Moreover, the Court studiously ignores the undisturbed conclusion of the District Court that General Electric's "discriminatory attitude" toward women was "a motivating factor in its policy," and that the pregnancy exclusion was "neutral (neither) on its face" nor "in its intent."

Plainly then, the Court's appraisal of General Electric's policy as a neutral process of sorting risks and "not a gender-based discrimination at all," cannot easily be squared with the historical record in this case. The Court, therefore, proceeds to a discussion of purported neutral criteria that suffice to explain the lone exclusion of pregnancy from the program....

Moreover, even the Court's principal argument for the plan's supposed gender neutrality cannot withstand analysis. The central analytical framework relied upon to demonstrate the absence of discrimination is the principle described in *Geduldig*: "There is no risk from which men are protected and women are not ... (and) no risk from which women are protected and men are not." In fostering the impression that it is faced with a mere underinclusive assignment of risks in a gender-neutral fashion that is, all other disabilities are insured irrespective of gender[,] the Court's analysis proves to be simplistic and misleading. For although all mutually contractible risks are covered irrespective of gender, the plan also insures risks such as prostatectomies, vasectomies, and circumcisions that are specific to the reproductive system of men and for which there exist no female counterparts covered by the plan. Again, pregnancy affords the only disability, sex-specific or otherwise, that is excluded from coverage....

Of course, the demonstration of purposeful discrimination is not the only ground for recovery under Title VII. Notwithstanding unexplained and inexplicable implications to the contrary in the majority opinion, this Court ... and every Court of Appeals now have firmly settled that a prima facie violation of Title VII ... also is established by demonstrating that a facially neutral classification has the effect of discriminating against members of a defined class....

... A realistic understanding of conditions found in today's labor environment warrants taking pregnancy into account in fashioning disability policies. Unlike the hypothetical situations conjectured by the Court, contemporary disability programs are not creatures of a social or cultural vacuum devoid of stereotypes and signals concerning the pregnant woman employee.... [T]he company has devised a policy that, but for pregnancy, offers protection for all risks, even those that are "unique to" men or heavily male dominated. In light of this social experience, the history of General Electric's employment practices, the otherwise all-inclusive design of its disability program, and the burdened role of the contemporary working woman, the EEOC's construction of sex discrimination . . . is fully consonant with the ultimate objective of Title VII, "to assure equality of employment opportunities and to eliminate those discriminatory practices and devices which have fostered (sexually) stratified job environments to the disadvantage of (women)." . . .

MR. JUSTICE STEVENS, dissenting.

. . . [T]he constitutional holding in *Geduldig v. Aiello* does not control the question of statutory interpretation presented by this case. And, of course, when it enacted Title VII of the Civil Rights Act of 1964, Congress could not possibly have relied on language which this Court was to use a decade later in the *Geduldig* opinion. We are, therefore, presented with a fresh, and rather simple, question of statutory construction: Does a contract between a company and its employees which treats the risk of absenteeism caused by pregnancy differently from any other kind of absence discriminate against certain individuals because of their sex? . . .

. . . [T]he [company] rule at issue places the risk of absence caused by pregnancy in a class by itself. By definition, such a rule discriminates on account of sex; for it is the capacity to become pregnant which primarily differentiates the female from the male. The analysis is the same whether the rule relates to hiring, promotion, the acceptability of an excuse for absence, or an exclusion from a disability insurance plan. . . .

Both the *Geduldig* and *Gilbert* dissents exposed but did not overcome the fallacies of the formalist majority opinions. The next cases involved claims based, respectively, on ethnicity and indigeneity and put judges to the same test: whether to resort to formalist fictions to manipulate claims based on identity-related facts. The judges again chose formalist manipulation to slant outcomes. In the next opinion, *Hernandez v. New York*, forceful dissents again sounded clear alarms.

HERNANDEZ V. NEW YORK
500 U.S. 352 (1991)

JUSTICE KENNEDY announced the judgment of the Court and delivered an opinion in which THE CHIEF JUSTICE, JUSTICE WHITE and JUSTICE SOUTER join.

Petitioner Dionisio Hernandez asks us to review the New York state courts' rejection of his claim that the prosecutor in his criminal trial exercised peremptory challenges to exclude Latinos from the jury by reason of their ethnicity. If true, the prosecutor's discriminatory use of peremptory strikes would violate the Equal Protection Clause . . .

Petitioner contends that the reasons given by the prosecutor for challenging the two bilingual jurors were not race neutral. . . .

Petitioner argues that Spanish-language ability bears a close relation to ethnicity, and that, as a consequence, it violates the Equal Protection Clause to exercise a peremptory challenge on the ground that a Latino potential juror speaks Spanish. He points to the high correlation between Spanish-language ability and ethnicity in New York, where the case was tried. We need not address that argument here, for the prosecutor did not rely on language ability without more, but explained that the specific responses and the demeanor of the two individuals during *voir dire* caused him to doubt their ability to defer to the official translation of Spanish-language testimony.

The prosecutor here offered a race-neutral basis for these peremptory strikes. As explained by the prosecutor, the challenges rested neither on the intention to exclude Latino or bilingual jurors, nor on stereotypical assumptions about Latinos or bilinguals. The prosecutor's articulated basis for these challenges divided potential jurors into two classes: those whose conduct during *voir dire* would persuade him they might have difficulty in accepting the translator's rendition of Spanish-language testimony and those potential jurors who gave no such reason for doubt. Each category would include both Latinos and non-Latinos. While the prosecutor's criterion might well result in the disproportionate removal of prospective Latino jurors, that disproportionate impact does not turn the prosecutor's actions into a *per se* violation of the Equal Protection Clause. . . .

The trial judge in this case chose to believe the prosecutor's race-neutral explanation for striking the two jurors in question, rejecting petitioner's assertion that the reasons were pretextual. . . .

We discern no clear error in the state trial court's determination that the prosecutor did not discriminate on the basis of the ethnicity of Latino jurors. . . .

JUSTICE O'CONNOR, with whom JUSTICE SCALIA joins, concurring in the judgment. . . .

In this case, the prosecutor's asserted justification for striking certain Hispanic jurors . . . [has] acted like strikes based on race, but they were *not* based on race. No matter how closely tied or significantly correlated to race the explanation for a peremptory strike may be, the strike does not implicate the Equal Protection Clause unless it is based on race. That is the distinction between disproportionate effect, which is not sufficient to constitute an equal protection violation, and intentional discrimination, which is. . . .

JUSTICE STEVENS, with whom JUSTICE MARSHALL joins, dissenting.

. . . In *Batson v. Kentucky*, 476 U.S. 79, 106 S.Ct. 1712, 90 L.Ed.2d 69 (1986), we held that "a 'pattern' of strikes against black jurors included in the particular venire might give rise to an inference of discrimination" sufficient to satisfy the defendant's burden of proving an equal protection violation. "Once the defendant makes a prima facie showing, the burden shifts to the State to come forward with a neutral explanation." . . . [T]he prosecutor's justification must identify "legitimate reasons" that are "related to the particular case to be tried" and sufficiently persuasive to "rebu[t] a defendant's prima facie case." . . .

And, as in any other equal protection challenge to a government classification, a justification that is frivolous or illegitimate should not suffice to rebut the prima facie case.

. . . Even assuming the prosecutor's explanation [for excluding bilingual Latinx people from the jury] was advanced in good faith, the justification proffered was insufficient to dispel the existing inference of racial animus. The prosecutor's explanation was insufficient for three reasons. First, the justification would inevitably result in a disproportionate disqualification of Spanish-speaking venire persons. An explanation that is "race neutral" on its face is nonetheless unacceptable if it is merely a proxy for a discriminatory practice. Second, the prosecutor's concern could easily have been accommodated by less drastic means. As is the practice in many jurisdictions, the jury could have been instructed that the official translation alone is evidence; bilingual jurors could have been instructed to bring to the attention of the judge any disagreements they might have with the translation so that any disputes could be resolved by the court. . . . Third, if the prosecutor's concern was valid and substantiated by the record, it would have supported a challenge for cause. The fact that the prosecutor did not make any such challenge, should disqualify him from advancing the concern as a justification for a peremptory challenge. . . .

The above cases show that formalism is not just a theoretical problem: formalism blindfolds thinking—and thinkers—to prevent systemic analyses and remedies. Consider in this light a Supreme Court case involving indigenous persons and groups in Hawai'i. They sought to maintain a system that ensured only indigenous Hawaiians could vote for trustees administering land held in trust for indigenous peoples and funding of related programs. This case presents the same questions as *Hernandez* and previous cases—whether a specific feature of a specific identity will count in law or not—but generates diametrically different outcomes. In this case, the judges accept the claimant's framing of the litigation around identity. In the previous opinions, the majority rejected the relevance of identity to the group in question. What explains this difference, both in framing and in outcome?

RICE V. CAYETANO
528 U.S. 495 (2000)

JUSTICE KENNEDY delivered the opinion of the Court.

... The District Court granted summary judgment to the State. Surveying the history of the islands and their people, the District Court determined that Congress and the State of Hawaii have recognized a guardian-ward relationship with the native Hawaiians, which the court found analogous to the relationship between the United States and the Indian tribes....

The Court of Appeals affirmed....

We granted certiorari ... and now reverse.

The purpose and command of the Fifteenth Amendment are set forth in language both explicit and comprehensive. The National Government and the States may not violate a fundamental principle: They may not deny or abridge the right to vote on account of race....

The design of the Amendment is to reaffirm the equality of races at the most basic level of the democratic process, the exercise of the voting franchise.... "[B]y the inherent power of the Amendment the word white disappeared" from our voting laws....

Though the commitment was clear, the reality remained far from the promise. Manipulative devices and practices were soon employed to deny the vote to blacks. We have cataloged before the "variety and persistence" of these techniques.... Progress was slow....

... The State maintains this is not a racial category at all but instead a classification limited to those whose ancestors were in Hawaii at a particular time, regardless of their race.... Furthermore, the State argues, the restriction in its operation excludes a person whose traceable ancestors were exclusively Polynesian if none of those ancestors resided in Hawaii in 1778; and, on the other hand, the vote would be granted to a person who could trace, say, one sixty-fourth of his or her ancestry to a Hawaiian inhabitant on the pivotal date.... These factors, it is said, mean the restriction is not a racial classification. We reject this line of argument.

Ancestry can be a proxy for race. It is that proxy here. Even if the residents of Hawaii in 1778 had been of more diverse ethnic backgrounds and cultures, it is far from clear that a voting test favoring their descendants would not be a race-based qualification....

... Simply because a class defined by ancestry does not include all members of the race does not suffice to make the classification race neutral. Here, the State's argument is undermined by its express racial purpose and by its actual effects.

... An inquiry into ancestral lines is not consistent with respect based on the unique personality each of us possesses, a respect the Constitution itself secures in its concern for persons and citizens.

The ancestral inquiry mandated by the State is forbidden by the Fifteenth Amendment for the further reason that the use of racial classifications is corruptive of the whole legal order democratic elections seek to preserve....

Once again, the dissent forcibly pierces the careful formalist blindfolding of the majority opinion:

JUSTICE STEVENS, with whom JUSTICE GINSBURG joins as to Part II, dissenting.

The Court's holding today rests largely on the repetition of glittering generalities that have little, if any, application to the compelling history of the State of Hawaii. When that history is held up against the manifest purpose of the Fourteenth and Fifteenth Amendments, and against two centuries of this Court's federal Indian law, it is clear to me that Hawaii's election scheme should be upheld.

According to the terms of the federal Act by which Hawaii was admitted to the Union, and to the terms of that State's Constitution and laws, the Office of Hawaiian Affairs (OHA) is charged with managing vast acres of land held in trust for the descendants of the Polynesians who occupied the Hawaiian Islands before the 1778 arrival of Captain Cook....

... [T]here is simply no invidious discrimination present in this effort to see that indigenous peoples are compensated for past wrongs, and to preserve a distinct and vibrant culture that is as much a part of this Nation's heritage as any.

Throughout our Nation's history, this Court has recognized both the plenary power of Congress over the affairs of Native Americans and the fiduciary character of the special federal relationship with descendants of those once sovereign peoples....

As our cases have consistently recognized, Congress' plenary power over these peoples has been exercised time and again to implement a federal duty to provide native peoples with special "care and protection." ...

As the history recited by the majority reveals, the grounds for recognizing the existence of federal trust power here are overwhelming. Shortly before its annexation in 1898, the Republic of Hawaii (installed by United States merchants in a revolution facilitated by the United States Government) expropriated some 1.8 million acres of land that it then ceded to the United States. In the Organic Act establishing the Territory of Hawaii, Congress provided that those lands should remain under the control of the territorial government "until otherwise provided for by Congress." . . . Relying on the precedent of previous federal laws granting Indians special rights in public lands, Congress created the Hawaiian Homes Commission to implement its goal of rehabilitating the native people and culture. Hawaii was required to adopt this Act as a condition of statehood in the Hawaii Statehood Admissions Act. . . . And in an effort to secure the Government's duty to the indigenous peoples, § 5 of the Admissions Act conveyed 1.2 million acres of land to the State to be held in trust "for the betterment of the conditions of native Hawaiians" and certain other public purposes. . . .

. . . Among the many and varied laws passed by Congress in carrying out its duty to indigenous peoples, more than 150 today expressly include native Hawaiians as part of the class of Native Americans benefited. . . .

While splendidly acknowledging this history—specifically including the series of agreements and enactments the history reveals—the majority fails to recognize its import. The descendants of the native Hawaiians share with the descendants of the Native Americans on the mainland or in the Aleutian Islands not only a history of subjugation at the hands of colonial forces, but also a purposefully created and specialized "guardian-ward" relationship with the Government of the United States. It follows that legislation targeting the native Hawaiians must be evaluated according to the same understanding of equal protection that this Court has long applied to the Indians on the continental United States: that "special treatment . . . be tied rationally to the fulfillment of Congress' unique obligation" toward the native peoples. . . .

. . . In light of this precedent, it is a painful irony indeed to conclude that native Hawaiians are not entitled to special benefits designed to restore a measure of native self-governance because they currently lack any vestigial native government—a possibility of which history and the actions of this Nation have deprived them. . . .

The foregoing reasons are to me more than sufficient to justify the OHA trust system and trustee election provision under the Fourteenth Amendment.

Although the Fifteenth Amendment tests the OHA scheme by a different measure, it is equally clear to me that the trustee election provision violates neither the letter nor the spirit of that Amendment.

Section 1 of the Fifteenth Amendment provides:

"The right of citizens of the United States to vote shall not be denied or abridged by the United States or by any State on account of race, color, or previous condition of servitude." . . .

As the majority itself must tacitly admit, . . . the terms of the Amendment itself do not here apply. The OHA voter qualification speaks in terms of ancestry and current residence, not of race or color. . . . The ability to vote is a function of the lineal *descent* of a modern-day resident of Hawaii, not the blood-based characteristics of that resident. . . .

The distinction between ancestry and race is more than simply one of plain language. . . .

Ancestry surely can be a proxy for race, or a pretext for invidious racial discrimination. But it is simply neither proxy nor pretext here. All of the persons who are eligible to vote for the trustees of OHA share two qualifications that no other person old enough to vote possesses: They are beneficiaries of the public trust created by the State and administered by OHA, and they have at least one ancestor who was a resident of Hawaii in 1778. A trust whose terms provide that the trustees shall be elected by a class including beneficiaries is hardly a novel concept. . . . The Committee that drafted the voting qualification explained that the trustees here should be elected by the beneficiaries because "people to whom assets belong should have control over them." . . .

. . . The OHA voting qualification . . . *excludes* all full-blooded Polynesians currently residing in Hawaii who are not descended from a 1778 resident of Hawaii. Conversely, unlike many of the old southern voting schemes . . . the OHA scheme excludes no descendant of a 1778 resident because he or she is also part European, Asian, or African as a matter of race. The classification here is thus both too inclusive and not inclusive enough to fall strictly along racial lines.

. . . [Moreover,] it is quite wrong to ignore the relevance of ancestry to claims of an interest in trust property, or to a shared interest in a proud heritage. There would be nothing demeaning in a law that established a trust to manage Monticello and provided that the descendants of Thomas Jefferson should elect the trustees. Such a law would be equally benign, regardless of whether those descendants happened to be members of the same race.

. . . [It is a] permissible assumption in this context that families with "any" ancestor who lived in Hawaii in 1778, and whose ancestors thereafter continued to live in Hawaii, have a claim to compensation and self-determination that others do not. For the multiracial majority of the citizens of the State of Hawaii to recognize that deep reality is not to demean their own interests but to honor those of others.

... In my judgment, the wooden approach adopted by the Court today [is erroneous].

Judges in these cases faced the same issue—the use of "wooden" proxies for group identities. However, they reached decisions in curiously contradictory ways. This difference in framing and outcome prompted a leading mainstream constitutional law casebook to query: "Are *Hernandez* and *Rice* consistent?"[38] If not, why not?

Legal scholars have deconstructed these cases—*Hernandez* and *Rice*—to understand their ongoing implications. Below, Latinx legal scholar Juan Perea critiques *Hernandez*. Next, Native Hawaiian legal scholar Kapua'ala Sproat examines *Rice*. Their analyses show the human costs and judicial techniques of formalism; they highlight the identity-related social realities that legal formalism obscures. They help demonstrate what is at stake when judges manipulate formalism to condone persistent social problems.

HERNANDEZ V. NEW YORK: COURTS, PROSECUTORS, AND THE FEAR OF SPANISH

Juan F. Perea
21 Hofstra L. Rev. 1 (1992)

[J]ustice must satisfy the appearance of justice.[39]

Introduction

... *Hernandez v. New York* considered whether exclusion from a petit jury because of bilingualism and arguably associated traits, traits closely intertwined with Latino national origin, violated the Equal Protection Clause.

... The *Hernandez* opinion reveals that the Court's discourse and its understanding with respect to the ethnic and linguistic differences between Americans are inadequate for the Court to render appropriate decisions when it considers discrimination based on these traits.

Race and Ethnicity in Jury Selection

... *Ethnicity and Jury Selection: A Long History of Bias*

Lawyers for both prosecution and defense have long treated stereotypes and myths about ethnic groups as facts that justify the removal of group members from juries through the use of peremptory challenges. Most lawyers are white and male, with little real knowledge of ethnic groups different from their own. Their reliance on stereotypes is not surprising.

---

[38] Constitutional Law 558 (Geoffrey R. Stone, Louis M. Seidman, Cass R. Sunstein, Mark V. Tushnet & Pamela S. Karlan eds. 8th ed. 2017).

[39] *Offutt v. United States*, 348 U.S. 11, 13 (1954) (Frankfurter, J.).

What is surprising is how recently lawyers were willing publish their, and others', prejudices as guidelines for jury selection.

Some prosecutors have written candidly about their search for jurors who, fairly or otherwise, will vote to convict. One Chief Prosecutor counsels, in a training manual for young prosecutors, "[y]ou are not looking for a fair juror, but rather a strong, biased and sometimes hypocritical individual who believes that Defendants are different from them in kind, rather than degree." This prosecutor gives the following advice: "You are not looking for any member of a minority group which may subject him to oppression—they almost always empathize with the accused. . . . Minority races almost always empathize with the Defendant." . . .

. . . An even more recent statement of the race and national origin jury selection rules appeared in 1986 . . . :

> Stereotypically, people from Mediterranean populations are considered desirable as jurors for the plaintiff. Those of Italian, Spanish, and French descent are thought to empathize more readily with the human and emotional side of a lawsuit. Also, those of Slavic, Irish and Mexican descent, as well as American blacks, are thought to fall into this stereotypical category. Persons of German, Scandinavian, Swedish, Finnish, Dutch, Nordic, Scottish, Asiatic and Russian heritage tend to be stereotypically better for the criminal prosecution. Law and order is highly regarded among these groups.

The advice to attorneys in treatises, handbooks, and practice manuals has been remarkably clear and consistent: Use your peremptories to keep minorities of undesirable racial or national origin groups off your jury if you represent the government. . . .

. . . Although the verbal command of *Batson* was to eliminate consideration of race and ethnicity from the jury selection process, its implementation has been very weak. . . . As Justice Thurgood Marshall wrote, "Any prosecutor can easily assert facially neutral reasons for striking a juror." . . .

Batson-*Style Equal Protection and Latino Ethnicity*

Despite the "race-neutrality" mandated by *Batson* and its progeny, *Batson* has been a resounding disappointment for Latino jurors and the Latino community. It has created a procedural side-show, a promise of equal protection devoid of substantive content. *Batson* and its progeny have created ostensibly fair rules governing the jury selection game (i.e., that no party shall discriminate in jury selection), while the rules are remarkably easy to evade and the nature of the game—discriminatory jury selection—has not changed at all. . . . Even when a court does find that a defendant has made out a prima facie case [of discrimination in jury selection], many trial courts automatically accept the prosecutor's "race-neutral" explanations without critical evaluation. . . .

Many courts . . . apply the *Batson* "race-neutrality" standard in a way that facilitates discrimination based on language and national origin differences. Indeed, it is ironic that courts have found characteristics such as Latino surnames, accents, and bilingualism to be "race-neutral" when the Equal Employment Opportunity Commission and some courts have found discrimination on the basis of these same traits to constitute national origin discrimination in employment under Title VII of the Civil Rights Act of 1964. Discrimination on the basis of language differences often serves as a proxy for discrimination on the basis of national origin. After *Hernandez*, the only Latino jurors not subject to peremptory challenge because of their bilingualism, in cases in which Spanish-language testimony will be offered, are Latinos who are monolingual in English. . . .

The Broad Harms of *Hernandez*

The "Harsh Paradox" of Bilingualism in America: Assimilate and Face Exclusion from the Society of Jurors

. . . [T]he harsh paradox goes like this: A Latino child, raised in a Spanish-speaking family, and born a citizen of the United States, learns Spanish as his first language. In school he learns English, to survive in school and to prepare for the future in his predominantly English-speaking world. He masters English and becomes bilingual. Knowing English, he can participate more fully in society. Living in an area where a substantial proportion of Latinos live, he is called for jury service in a case in which Spanish-language testimony will be offered. Knowing English, he meets the statutory requirements for qualification as a juror. Knowing Spanish, he is likely to be excluded from the jury. . . .

The wrong in this picture is that the prospective Latino juror, having made the effort [through assimilation] to join the mainstream like his fellow citizens, is declared an outsider through state action, by both the prosecutor and the courts. The Court has made clear that the *Batson* right is a right held by the prospective juror "not to be excluded from . . . [a petit jury] . . . on account of his or her race." The Court has recognized the injury of stigma and dishonor suffered by jurors who are peremptorily excluded because of their race. Exactly the same stigma and dishonor are suffered by bilingual jurors who are peremptorily excluded because of a unique characteristic of their ethnicity and their birth.

The Extinction of the Representative Jury: Justice and the Excluded Latino Community

. . . The perception of impartiality and public confidence engendered by citizen participation on juries has important consequences for judges and courts. . . . [J]uries help preserve the credibility and the power of courts.

Jury service also helps educate the jurors and the public about the functioning of the courts. . . .

. . . Juries from which bilingual jurors have been peremptorily excluded cannot be deemed representative of communities in which large numbers of Spanish-speaking and bilingual people live. In an increasingly diverse society in which many parties in a trial may be Spanish-speaking, such as in the *Hernandez* trial, the absence of bilingual Latino jurors, now facilitated by the Court's decision, raises serious questions about whether Latinos will ever be fairly represented on juries and whether Latino litigants can ever receive a trial by a jury of their peers. . . .

Conclusion

. . . *Hernandez* removes from juries the hearing and the understanding of many Spanish-speaking potential Latino jurors. Decisions like *Hernandez*, finding "race-neutrality" when there is none, perpetuate an empty discourse of equal protection.

This empty discourse is not cost-free. It removes from the judicial system one of its pillars of legitimacy, the representative jury. Considering the consequences of not attending to perceptions of fairness and justice . . . the Court should reconsider whether its cramped conception of "race-neutrality" serves the appearance of justice in a nation that, increasingly, looks and sounds different from what the Court thinks.

Perea points out that doctrinal formalist frameworks skew outcomes unjustly. Latinx people who are not fluent in English are excluded or marginalized for that fact. At the same time, Latinx people who are bilingual can be disqualified by this fact. Under this judicial construct, the only Latinx people qualified for juries are those who speak English only—or not Spanish, at least. How can law maintain such a scheme in the name of equal justice? Formalism.

Sproat, in the excerpt below, amplifies our analysis of the mechanisms by which formalism accomplishes these skews. To unlearn and relearn this legal training, notice that formalism ignores history and context to achieve outcomes favoring elites.

WAI THROUGH KĀNĀWAI: WATER FOR HAWAI'I'S STREAMS AND JUSTICE FOR HAWAIIAN COMMUNITIES

Kapua'ala Sproat
95 Marq. L. Rev. 127 (2011)

. . . To earnestly grapple with Indigenous issues in the context of water and beyond, legal analysis cannot focus solely on "traditional" notions of rights because many such notions are grounded in Western concepts of property that are not universally applicable, especially in Hawai'i. There is a need to go beyond the limited application of narrowly drawn legal rules to the selectively shaped facts of cases. The formalist approach to Native Peoples' claims, history shows, legitimized colonialism, the confiscation of land, the destruction of culture, and the destabilization of self-government.

The Limits of Legal Formalism

In the 1800s, legal formalism evolved in an attempt to deem the law a neutral tool that produced justice by mechanistically applying legal rules to cases. Classic legal formalism is a "theory of adjudication according to which (1) the law is rationally determinate, and (2) judging is mechanical. It follows, moreover, from (1), that (3) legal reasoning is autonomous, since the class of legal reasons suffices to justify a unique outcome; no recourse to non-legal reasons is demanded or required."

Formalism, therefore, "holds that the law is an internally consistent and logical body of rules that is independent from the variable forms of its surrounding social institutions." Given these theoretical underpinnings, the "law was objective, unchanging, extrinsic to the social climate, and, above all, different from and superior to politics."

Although the prevailing view for many years—and still embraced by some scholars and many law school curricula—legal formalism's failure to fully consider social and historical context, politics, culture, and a myriad of other social factors impedes both the courts' capacity to render just decisions and the general public's understanding of the law's role in shaping society. Legal formalism also constrains many groups' ability to achieve any semblance of justice. . . .

Formalist analysis . . . can neither explain nor predict how the legal process actually works for Indigenous Peoples. History indicates that legal formalism's narrow lens employs rules (for example, the "intent of the framers") and methods of reasoning (for example, stare decisis) in ways that treat Native Peoples as inferior to Europeans and, therefore, unworthy of self-governance; it also fails to provide either a balanced perspective or a genuine vehicle to address legal and cultural harms.

. . . [Legal formalism] continues to be utilized in contemporary times to perpetuate the status quo while restricting Native Peoples' right to control their destinies. *Rice v. Cayetano* provides a chilling example. In *Rice*, courts wrestled with whether the election of trustees for OHA—a state agency established to combat the lingering effects of colonization on Hawai'i's Indigenous People and to create better conditions for them— could be limited to Maoli.

The lead plaintiff, Freddy Rice, was a White rancher whose ancestors came to Hawai'i in the mid-1800s as Christian missionaries and eventually built a ranching empire on land that had formerly belonged to Native

Hawaiians. Despite having benefitted personally (including accumulating land and other resources) as a direct result of his family's role in colonizing Hawai'i, Rice sued the State of Hawai'i for not allowing him to vote in OHA elections, claiming this restriction contravened the Voting Rights Act of 1965 as well as the Fourteenth and Fifteenth Amendments. Although each of those laws was specifically crafted to protect historically disadvantaged groups, *Rice* turned the laws on their heads, wielding them against a historically disadvantaged group to challenge the group's ability to elect trustees for an agency designed to manage Indigenous resources in partial redress for the devastation imposed by American colonialism.

Judge David Alan Ezra of the District Court for the District of Hawai'i employed contextual analysis to reject Rice's claims and rule in favor of the State of Hawai'i. Judge Ezra examined Hawai'i's history, including Westerners' role in fundamentally altering the Native system of land use and management and eventually overthrowing the sovereign Hawaiian Kingdom. He recognized Maoli as the Indigenous People of Hawai'i whose continuing relationship with the state and federal government was analogous to other Native Peoples. Judge Ezra ruled that OHA's voting requirements were rationally tied to state and congressional trust obligations to Kānaka Maoli. On appeal to the Ninth Circuit, a three-judge panel affirmed.

The United States Supreme Court reversed, relying on formalist analysis. The majority, led by Justice Anthony Kennedy, selectively framed Hawaiian history: it blurred the lines between Indigenous Maoli and Rice's ancestors (American colonists), and it ruled that ancestry was a "proxy for race." Ironically, although the majority invalidated the State's voting process for OHA trustees because the "use of racial classifications is corruptive of the whole legal order democratic elections seek to preserve," it effectively used the rule of law to allow non-natives to once again attempt to direct the management of Indigenous Hawaiian land and other resources, which the establishment of OHA had specifically sought to rectify.

Justice John Paul Stevens' dissent criticized the majority's holding, insisting that it rested "largely on the repetition of glittering generalities that have little, if any, application to the compelling history of the State of Hawaii." The majority failed to acknowledge the effects of annexation, the influx of infectious diseases, and the displacement of Native Hawaiians from their lands, all of which continue to take a toll on Native Hawaiians.

The Supreme Court's majority decision reveals how legal formalists pick and choose their method of analysis, such as applying a certain line of cases to select facts to serve their own purpose. Formalist analysis is often deployed to achieve a desired result, while appearing "neutral" and as if the decision-makers were simply applying the "rule of law." *Rice* demonstrates that legal scholars and practitioners must examine the values and interests that form the lens through which a decision-maker will view and rule on evidence if they hope to rectify historic wrongs. . . .

Sproat cites *Rice* as a "chilling example" of judges manipulating formalism as a tool of dominant groups to sabotage law intended to help subordinated groups. Chemerinsky made a similar point in Part I: After *Brown*, the Supreme Court undermined or eliminated remedies to desegregation—allowing social injustice to reemerge so long as it was accomplished without explicit racial categories. In *Rice*, the Court similarly sabotaged the land trust remedy. The analyses by Perea and Sproat jointly show the continuing influence of formalism as legal reasoning and its consequences for subordinated groups. Nevertheless, formalism remains the dominant perspective presented to students in their legal training.

Displacing formalism, in fact, does and will continue to require intentional and creative effort. Legal writing scholar Teri McMurtry-Chubb suggests that law schools might start by changing first-year legal research, analysis, and writing courses. Students, she argues, would benefit from learning rhetorical theories and strategies that are comparative and critical if they are to see through the formalisms of Western legal education. McMurtry-Chubb offers examples and exercises drawn from Indigenous and Asian Diasporic rhetorics, among others. The materials and exercises she offers depart markedly from conventional "casebook" materials, allowing for a substantive change of perspective, scope, and vocabulary. Can steps like these be starting points toward broader systemic reforms?

STILL WRITING AT THE MASTER'S TABLE: DECOLONIZING RHETORIC IN LEGAL WRITING FOR A "WOKE" LEGAL ACADEMY

Teri McMurtry-Chubb
21 Scholar: St. Mary's L. Rev. & Soc. Just. 255 (2019)

Woke (wok): *An awakening to racial and social injustices*

. . . Each time a court makes a choice to accept some legal arguments over others, some histories over others, it makes a choice about which values it wishes to protect and which it denigrates. Each time a professor teaches a case and the reasoning processes that led to its outcome benignly, the professor fails to "[decenter] and disrupt the implicit and explicit narratives—like Eurocentrism, conflict-resolution through violence, gender stereotypes, and racism—that canonical texts can foster in contemporary classrooms." Formalistic and abstract legal reasoning are situated in the West. Relocating canons of rhetoric outside of the West problematizes the structures by which reasoning takes place by offering oppositional rhetorics as alternatives. . . . Indigenous, African Diasporic, Asian Diasporic, and Latinx rhetorics . . . can be used to create oppositional discourse—discourse that engages "the dominant culture's language, idiom, and rhetoric" while advancing the writer's cultural concerns. . . .

. . . Indigenous rhetorics are characterized by the need for Indigenous peoples to have sovereignty. . . .

Because Asian Diasporic history is an immigrant one (real and mythologized), Asian American rhetoric studies are rooted in the study of language, specifically the fluidity of English as adapted by Asian native English and multiple language speakers for use in a variety of spoken and written contexts. . . . When framed in this manner, language itself, its use and arrangement, becomes the source of argument. Language also becomes epistemic, as it seeks to recreate Asian Diasporic knowledge as Western knowledge by decentering Western knowledge as its source. . . .

The Western canons of rhetoric and their foundation in Western epistemology make meaning of legal reasoning, analytic, and communication processes. They do so even as they assert their neutrality while being dominant and exclusive. Being "woke" to these processes, means that we must actively work to decolonize Western rhetorical practices, the canon and notions of canonicity, throughout the law school curriculum. As the site for knowledge production and the creation of disciplinary norms, legal writing process and practice are the battleground on which the war to decolonize the academy must be fought. . . .

McMurtry-Chubb highlights how industry biases affect analysis and argumentation in training and, ultimately, in practice. She compares indigenous, Asian, and Western conceptions of language that give different social meanings to the same facts or conditions. The dominant Western conception—formalism—asserts "neutrality while being dominant and exclusive." In response, McMurtry-Chubb concludes, research and writing courses can help students to critically understand legal formalism—to become "woke." Such courses can serve as a "battleground" to "decolonize" legal training. In critical terms, decolonization is both a personal and collective enterprise—it is both internal as well as material. As Part VI elaborates, decolonization is an exorcism of the ideologies, cultures, and premises transplanted by colonialism, imperialism, and globalization, and internalized by generations of individuals since then. It is a personal and collective process that entails unlearning and relearning both law and society. In this vein, Jaribu Hill, director of the Mississippi Workers' Center for Human Rights, notes that legal education and scholarship can and should be rededicated to decolonization, encouraging advocates to create "a living, walking, and breathing scholarship that would help the sufferers of some of the most severe human rights abuses develop strategies for change."[40] "Woke" in this way, how might legal writing and practice courses focused on social justice—and legal education and scholarship as a whole—differ from those you may have encountered?

As these excerpts show, formalism provides cover for systemic biases and identity castes. But some formalisms are more destructive than others. We turn next to a systemic formalism that is singularly pervasive and at the center of persistent systemic injustice: legal individualism.

NOTES AND QUESTIONS

1. *Exercise in Exposing Formalism.* Margaret Montoya's narrative, excerpted in Part II, addressed a case—*The People of the State of California v. Chavez*—that she recalled as the first judicial opinion she read as a law student in her Criminal Law course. She lamented the missing facts of the defendant "girl-woman's reality"—the "material realities and cultural context of a poor Latina woman's life," such as the defendant's youth, poverty, and fear over her pregnancy. In the cases excerpted above, you have seen how formalist analysis abstracts away social reality. Consider also a case included in many property law casebooks—*State v. Shack*, 277 A.2d 369 (N.J. 1971). This case involves a farm owner's attempt to exclude a health service provider and a labor lawyer from visiting the migrant workers housed on the farm, using the legal doctrine of trespass that protects property owners from undesirable entrants. As an advocate or a judge, would it matter to you that the farm workers were primarily African Americans from the U.S. South and Puerto Ricans?[41] That they were poor and isolated in the rural workplace? Why or why not?

2. *Unlearning Formalism and Relearning an Expanded Canon of Rhetorics.* After reading the McMurtry-Chubb excerpt above, reflect on what you have learned about canons of rhetoric. Have you learned primarily Western formalistic and abstract legal reasoning? Have you learned African or Asian Diasporic rhetorics, Latinx rhetorics, or Indigenous rhetorics? Why or why not? How could you—through advocacy in school or self-guided study—expand your knowledge of rhetorics that offer tools for decentering the formalism of legal research, analysis, and writing?

3. *Critical Classrooms and Conflict.* McMurtry-Chubb denotes classrooms that critically engage students in deconstructing top-down notions of law and hierarchical methods of teaching as antisubordination "battlegrounds." But who resists the introduction of critical methods and analysis, and why? Oftentimes, it's top-down resistance, but not always. Critical legal research and writing scholar Aníbal Rosario-Lebrón notes that resistance and conflict might come from unexpected sources. He notes that professors may resist the introduction of new pedagogical methods out of fear they may face difficulty

---

[40] Jaribu Hill, In Praise of Hope Lewis—Thank You, 10 N.E. U.L. Rev. 473, 476 (2018).

[41] For additional background and context on *State v. Shack* see Steven W. Bender, From *Sandoval* to Subprime: Excluding Latinos from Property Ownership and Property Casebooks, in Vulnerable Populations and Transformative Law Teaching: A Critical Reader (2011).

establishing the methods as legitimate and maintaining what is seen as appropriate "control" of the classroom, while students may resist the use of such methods because challenges to dominant perspectives may be experienced as too ambiguous to constitute "learning the law." As you read Rosario-Lebrón's description of some critical methods, and the resistance or challenges that arise, consider if you have experienced any of the methods he discusses—horizontal classrooms, a problem-posing method of Socratic dialogue, deconstruction of hegemonic visions of the law, or diversity in materials, skills, and voices? Does the use of such pedagogical methods tend to make you or other students feel empowered, uneasy, or both? Why?

> If we are committed to bringing down those [traditional] hierarchies, we must begin by making sure they do not exist in the classrooms.
>
> A first step to horizontality is introducing ourselves by our first names.... A second step is to address the students by their first names instead of by their last names, as *tradition* dictates....
>
> ... [Classroom] [r]ules should not be an imposition but an agreement....
>
> The problem-posing method engages students and teachers in the process of reflection and action, or praxis. This teaching approach focuses on unveiling reality, rather than hiding it. Students and teachers collectively examine, through inquiry and dialogue, problems related to their positions in the world and engage in generating critical interventions to these problems.
>
> ... Crit-professors should ... challenge also the notion of objectivity ... [and] the idea that Law is in and of itself a good and the solution to every problem....
>
> ... We ask questions about power, privilege, and status quo; attempting to debunk the hegemonic vision of the Law.
>
> ... I am not only talking content-wise (e.g. a curriculum that includes the history and voices of marginalized groups), but also teaching practices that put the students in contact with ostracized communities and help them see their realities....
>
> ... The aim is that students experience first-hand the problems these communities face when they are parties to legal controversies. For instance, ... [I have] students work as interpreters in cases or translators for organizations that work with Latino immigrants, interview attorneys that work with these communities, or prepare materials that address problems of access to justice and make them available to the communities....
>
> ... Students question the self-reflecting strategies, the incorporation of non-traditional materials (e.g. watching movies or reading poems), and even outside assignments such as talking to practicing attorneys and former litigants. They feel their education is

contentless because it does not hinge on the hardcore law, and that they are wasting their time doing these exercises or considering these materials that do not teach one to be an *attorney*....

... *Why are you doing this?* Whereas the first confrontation was about content, this is about authority. Students perceive you as a bad teacher because you allegedly lack control over the classroom. Students question why there are no seats assigned, why you do not *cold-call* on the *lazy students*, or why decisions should be made as a group instead of imposing the teacher's criteria as the norm....

... *Why are you teaching this?* Why are we talking about Crit-scholarship?; why are we considering subjects other than the law?; and how is it useful to understand marginalized voices or read about them? The idea ... [is] that you are not a good professor because you are more concerned about political factors than the law... as opposed to the traditional law professors, who are perceived as agendaless.

... *Why are you even a law professor?* In this front there are many considerations at play, especially if you are a *minority* professor.... If you talk about the struggles of a particular identity it must be because you are angry about your condition and you want to push that political issue into students' lives....

... In order for hegemonic discourses to change, there must be a confrontation.... If I wish to be completely successful ... I should be pursuing further confrontation instead of avoiding it.[42]

Reflecting on the questions preceding the passage above, does Rosario-Lebrón's conclusion surprise you? Is this a moment of unlearning and relearning? Why or why not?

9.5 LEGAL INDIVIDUALISM—A KEY FORMALISM—ATOMIZES LAW TO MISMATCH PROBLEMS AND SOLUTIONS

Although formalisms abound in law, some formalist fictions are more existential to the system than others. Key among these systemic formalisms is legal individualism: the top-down notion that problem solving must be framed around "individual"—or legally individuated—issues, rights, and remedies. In general, legal individualism underpins the architecture of the U.S. legal system both as process ("personal" cases only) and substance ("individual" rights only). This creates a mismatch between remedies (for individuals only) and problems (that are built around group identities). This particular formalism—legal individualism—goes deeper

---

[42] Aníbal Rosario-Lebrón, If These Blackboards Could Talk: The Crit Classroom, A Battlefield, 9 Charleston L. Rev. 305 (2015).

than any one particular doctrine or abstraction and pervades legal training, practice, and culture.

As this section illustrates only partially, this particular formalism is hardwired into the system, affecting all else in law—especially by constraining litigation and adjudication as instruments of systemic justice in the framing of claims, the recognition of standing, and the allowable remedies, for example. Though systemic injuries are communal, the system typically insists on atomizing collectivized injuries into individualized remedies. In this systemic mismatching of injury and remedy, legal individualism hamstrings advocacy consciousness and choices. Advocates must understand this existential formalism, be able to spot its effects, and be ready to counter—or circumvent—it strategically.

Generally, individualism has been a part of law and society since the inception of the United States and undergirds key U.S. foundational myths. Idealized individualism is the crux of the "American Dream" and the "rugged individualism" of U.S. lore. As culture and ideology, individualism shapes the legal and material world to narrow the concepts with which antisubordination advocates and activists must reckon in designing and executing actions. In law specifically, individualism diminishes attention to and advocacy with groups and movements, which helps to preserve the status quo of identity castes.

Consider, in this vein, legal scholar and former national legal director of the ACLU john powell's[43] critical analysis of legal individualism in law and society. In this excerpt, powell unmasks the identity-laden effects of legal individualism, emphasizing how individualism limits collective knowledge and bottom-up collaborations. From a bottom-up perspective, individualism isolates individuals, paradoxically emphasizing difference while demanding sameness: under "the ideology of individuality," as powell reveals, we are all unique individuals—but we also are all one race. Using this critical insight, powell explains how the "language of individuality" (and this paradox) inhibits the coalescence of collective consciousness and action to change systems and their outputs.

---

[43] powell does not follow the dominant U.S. social convention of capitalizing his name, as he believes capitals connote dominance.

DISRUPTING INDIVIDUALISM AND DISTRIBUTIVE REMEDIES WITH INTERSUBJECTIVITY AND EMPOWERMENT: AN APPROACH TO JUSTICE AND DISCOURSE

john a. powell
1 Margins 1 (2001)

... What are the Consequences of the Dominant Ideology of Individualism for Members of Subordinated Groups?

... *The Language of Individuality: Just Who Are Individuals?*

Part of the language of the dominant culture—for us in this society and in this time—is the language of individuality. While I am not suggesting that those of us who are members of subordinate groups are not individuals, it is certainly not true that we are all just individuals. And yet, I believe that the dominant language and ideology of individuality blinds us to the ways in which we are not just individuals.

The ideology of individuality had its origins in the Enlightenment, which came concurrently with the emergence of Colonialism. During this germinative period, the essence of individualism was that Europeans were individuals as opposed to other people who were a "collective." The collectivity of the other served as a rationale and justification for the exploitation of the collective other. In other words, part of the longing to be a member of the dominant group was tied up with being an individual. In that sense, individuality was already racialized. Individuality and membership in the dominant culture meant something in particular in a specific moment related to white Europeans, although it was not clear at that moment that they were white. In fact, they were still in the process of becoming white. The ideology of individualism as opposed to the ideology of collectivity was part of the whiteness process. . . .

Embracing the language of individualism is fraught with dangers. As we think about what it means to be an individual and how the law pulls us into that discourse, the negative effects of insinuating ourselves into the ideology of individuality often blind us. . . . At one time, the discussion of remedying discrimination in employment and education focused on women and people of color deserving to be treated just like everybody else. This begged the question: who is this "everybody else"? . . .

. . . [T]his unreflective desire to be like everyone else is an attempt to reclaim a destroyed social life by reconstructing it in the dominant group's language—the language of individuality.

How Does the Ideology Structure the Relationship Between Dominant and Oppressed Groups?

Distributive Justice vs. Institutional Arrangements

The problem ... we face is a problem of domination and oppression.... [And,] domination, oppression, and exploitation do not occur solely at the individual or interpersonal level, but also at the collective or systemic level. It is apparent that oppression and domination occur at the systemic or collective level when noting that they are often sanctioned by the language, structure, institutions, and practices in a society. Indeed, John Rawls suggested that if we want to know whether a society was just, we should not tarry too long on the individual attitudes people hold in that society. Instead, Rawls calls our attention to the institutional arrangements and structures in those societies....

Individuality: Too High a Price to Pay?

... How does individualism operate on race and gender today? The answer from the individualist camp is that race and gender do not exist. We are all just individuals. Any characteristic that does not reflect that individuality is simply an accident. In other words, any marker of gender, race, or sexuality around which meaning is constructed socially is largely irrelevant.

In a way individuality, even as it purports to take into account our distinctness, [thereby] makes us all the same in fundamental ways. We are all rational, autonomous people and therefore we should all be treated the same.... Thus, individuality becomes a model for assimilation. We are all exactly alike.... But what are the consequences of embracing this stance for subordinated and marginalized groups? ...

As powell points out, individualism in law means assimilation into dominant norms and groups. It means denying that social identities matter, both in law and in society. Paradoxically, legal individualism denies the need for, or the reality of, difference even while insisting that "we" are all unique.

Legal individualism, like formalism in general, is never neutral—by design. Rather, it structures a mismatch between allowable claims and remedies, giving aid and comfort to identity group castes that the equal justice principle expressly repudiates. Coupled with industry handcuffs, selective formalist blindfolding, including individualism, keeps law tethered to the Critical Challenge. As part of its systemic design, law fails justice as intended: "individualism serves to privilege and normalize the dominant groups' preferences. The law has a long history of protecting white people's choices even though they may serve as barriers to the equal participation of blacks in society. Legal decisions that harm the equality interests of blacks are rationalized by the need to protect the neutral ideal of individual liberty."[44]

This formalism likewise pervades economic theory and practice, especially the currently dominant neoliberal framework, thereby reinforcing the disproportionate effects of legal individualism in material micro-macro terms.[45] Legal and economic individualism combine to exaggerate the vulnerabilities of already vulnerable individuals *and* groups.[46] The many myths of individualism—legal, economic, and cultural—belie the very well known fact that individual humans, as a species, are social creatures; if isolated as individuals from other individuals, people wither and die. It truly takes a village, not only for individuals to survive and prosper, but for individuals to organize with others to understand and solve collective injuries. In contexts like workplace democracy or reparations, ideologies of individualism obstruct the collective actions necessary to protect all individuals subject to a common danger or vulnerability.

Individualism, as these materials show, goes beyond legal training focused on doctrine and reasoning. It extends into law practice, structuring the kind of relationship at the core of all advocacy—the one between advocate and client. Legal individualism is a particularly destructive formalism because it permeates law in training *and* as practice. Individualism in law precludes, or dismisses, collective claims for collective remedies to collective problems; instead, it enforces a mismatch between the actual collective problem and the allowed individualized remedies. Over time, individualism and other formalisms have structured the culture of the industry, as well as entrenched societal castes. For these reasons, unlearning and relearning the ideological and social functions of legal individualism, and of formalism generally, are key aspects of systemic advocacy.

9.6 ELITES USE PUBLIC POWER TO HIDE PRIVATE POWER IN LAW AND SOCIETY

As noted above, legal training and practice inculcate formalist explanations of how law operates. Traditional explanations blindfold adherents to social realities and limit the efficacy of advocacy. One key area

---

[44] Christian Sundquist, Critical Praxis, Spirit Healing, and Community Activism: Preserving a Subversive Dialogue on Reparations, 58 N.Y.U. Ann. Surv. Am. L. 659, 661, 677 (2003).

[45] See Part VI for discussion of neoliberalism. See also David Harvey, A Brief History of Neoliberalism 2 (2005).

[46] See Martha Albertson Fineman, Vulnerability and Social Justice, 53 Val. U.L. Rev. 341, 346 (2019) (noting from a "vulnerability theory" perspective that a commitment to "a collective or social assessment of justice has been profoundly undermined in our increasingly individualistic society").

of inquiry is how power affects policymaking. Power, again, means the ability to win desired policy outcomes. Traditional constitutional analysis focuses almost exclusively on power distributions among executive, legislative, or judicial actors or local, state, or federal agencies. Analysts thus focused on the structural "separation of powers" and "checks and balances" fail to account for a basic known fact, documented only recently by Gilens and Page's empirical study of U.S. policy making: despite these "protections," branches of "public" power are systematically manipulated by "private" interests, usually top-down, during the 365 days of every year. Centering public power and its separation in systemic analysis obscures how public power is an instrument, a projection, of private power and interests.

In the excerpt below, constitutional law scholar Daryl Levinson explains why the dominant focus on "checks and balances" among the branches is mistaken: "When the analysis is fully carried through, it reveals that the distribution of power at the structural level seldom bears any systematic relation to the distribution of power at the level of interests." Instead, the focus should be on how power is distributed at the level of interests—the ability of varied "policy-seeking actors" like corporations, community groups, political parties, and others to turn their collective interests into desired policy outcomes. Given Gilens and Page's empirical findings, we know already that at this democratic level, elites dominate policy making, using money and influence to win policies that help them accumulate even more money and influence. Against this backdrop, effective systemic advocacy deconstructs traditional understandings of private-public power to analyze, and act to change, the distribution of power among policy-seeking actors, and thereby to alter systemic outputs and their skewed patterns.

FOREWORD: LOOKING FOR POWER IN PUBLIC LAW
Daryl Levinson
130 Harv. L. Rev. 31 (2016)

... [C]onstitutional law and theory have been looking for power in the wrong places. ...

... The foundational power holders in American democracy are the coalitions of policy-seeking political actors—comprising officials, voters, parties, politicians, interest groups, and other democratic-level actors—that compete for control of these government institutions and direct their decisionmaking. ... [P]arsing power requires "passing it through" government institutions to the underlying democratic [groups and their] interests. Because structural constitutional analysis seldom takes this second step, its analysis of power is not only dubious in accuracy but also superstructural in import. When the analysis is fully carried through, it reveals that the distribution of power at the structural level seldom bears any systematic relation to the distribution of power at the level of interests.

The disconnect between the power of institutions and the power of interests calls into question constitutional law's preoccupation with balancing or diffusing power at the level of branches and units of government. . . . [C]oncerns about diffusing and equalizing power might be better directed toward the democratic rather than the structural level. While constitutional structure is at best a blunt instrument for distributing power among political interests and social groups, . . . other areas of constitutional and public law have more directly, albeit sporadically, taken up that task. The law of democracy . . . [is important, as are] any number of regulatory regimes that affect the distribution of money, mobilization, and other resources that can be leveraged into political influence. . . .

. . . From Institutions to [Groups and] Interests

. . . The central organizing principle of the structural constitution is that power should be divided, diffused, or balanced to prevent the "accumulation of all powers . . ." and hence "tyranny." . . .

But *whose* hands? It is one thing to ensure that power is divided between the President and Congress, but quite another to ensure that power is divided between Democrats and Republicans, the rich and the poor, or racial or religious majorities and minorities. . . . Diffusing or balancing power at the level of government structures and institutions predicts nothing about the consequences for the distribution of power at the level of these groups. . . .

1. Separation of Powers Minus Mixed Government.—A time-honored strategy of constitutional design is to balance the power of competing social and political interests in the structure of government. This is the theory of mixed government. . . .

. . . Professor Lani Guinier has advocated a system of cumulative voting that would empower minority groups to vote strategically to elect some of their candidates of choice, who would then enact or block legislation of critical importance to their constituency.[47] . . . [Others are concerned] that economic elites have managed to capture *all* of the branches of government. . . . A possible solution might be to return to the original model of mixed government, redesigning one of the chambers of Congress to represent the interests of the nonwealthy. . . .

2. Federalism Minus Communities of Interest.—Together with the separation of powers, constitutional federalism is conceived as a mechanism for diffusing and balancing power. . . .

---

[47] See Lani Guinier, The Tyranny of the Majority 107–08 (1994).

First, and most straightforwardly, federalism allows groups to *exit* the policymaking domain of the national state and govern themselves independently. . . .

But federalism-as-exit can work to protect only those minorities that can be grouped into subsidiary territorial governance units . . . [such as] existing state boundaries. . . .

. . . [But] politically salient interests have ceased to align with state boundaries. . . .

. . . Switching metaphors from "exit" to "voice," federalism can empower groups not to flee the national government but to influence its decisionmaking by mobilizing through state governments. . . .

But which minorities, exactly, are empowered by federalism-as-voice? . . . [I]t is hard to make any reliable predictions. . . . [Heather] Gerken highlights the possibility of a "progressive federalism" that would empower groups like racial minorities, proponents of gay rights, and environmentalists. As Gerken recognizes, however, decentralized governance might also amplify the voices of opponents of transgender bathroom choice in North Carolina, anti-immigration forces in Arizona, and anti-abortion activists in Texas—or for that matter *any* group that happens to constitute a local majority. . . .

. . . *Electoral Power*

. . . "[D]emocratic institutions should provide citizens with equal procedural opportunities to influence political decisions (or, more briefly, with equal power over outcomes)."

At a minimum, democratic institutions might be designed to prevent one group in society from unfairly dominating another. . . .

. . . One straightforward strategy for [electoral power] is to shift the composition of the electorate by enfranchising one's own supporters or disenfranchising one's opponents. . . .

Electoral districting is another useful device for manipulating the effective voting power of different constituencies. . . .

[But] . . . [c]ourts have tended to focus on enforcing individual rights, marginalizing systemic concerns about how electoral rules and institutions affect the power of political interests and social groups. . . .

. . . The possibility of protecting other groups [beyond racial minorities] or balancing power along other dimensions has barely been explored. . . . [T]he Court has refused to invalidate even the most blatantly partisan gerrymanders. And other salient power imbalances have been ignored altogether—or worse. Campaign spending is arguably the most flagrant . . . But the Court has insisted for decades that political spending is a constitutionally protected form of speech and has definitively rejected "the concept that government may restrict the speech of some elements of our society in order to enhance the relative voice of others." . . .

Even in the context of race, election law jurisprudence has been more concerned with descriptive representation—electing black or Hispanic representatives—than with bolstering the substantive representation of minority group interests. . . .

. . . [G]laring discrepancies between formal political representation and functional policy responsiveness exist not just for African Americans but also for women and the poor. . . . [A] thoroughgoing concern with the distribution of policymaking power is . . . "too ambitious a goal for election law to achieve." . . .

. . . *Resources*

. . . [V]otes are but one type of political resource, and not necessarily the most valuable.

An especially valuable political resource that economic elites, by definition, possess in abundance is wealth. . . .

Those concerned about power imbalances stemming from unequal resources have considered two kinds of regulatory strategies. One is to attempt to block the conversion of resources into power [through campaign finance or lobbying law reforms]. . . . [Another approach is] to *increase* the influence of "countervailing voices" through these channels—leveling up rather than leveling down. That could mean public financing of elections or campaign finance vouchers that would be distributed equally among citizens, or even public subsidies that would enable currently unrepresented groups to gain access to lobbyists. . . .

The difficulty of preventing inequalities of political resources from being converted into inequalities of power suggests a second and more ambitious strategy: equalizing the resources themselves. . . . Deconcentrating political power may require deconcentrating economic power through the redistribution of wealth and opportunity. . . .

The broader lesson is that *every* law and policy that affects the distribution of wealth or the costs of mobilizing collective action at least potentially serves to redistribute political power. . . .

. . . [R]ights can also be a *source* of political power. This is straightforwardly the case for rights that directly protect avenues of participation in democratic politics. . . . But other rights that are not self-consciously designed for the purpose of empowering groups to more effectively participate in the political process may have that effect. Rights of freedom of association and free exercise of religion may be essential in allowing some groups to organize and mobilize. Similar democracy-facilitating arguments have been made in support of rights to education, welfare, and privacy.... The same is true of rights that contribute to social and economic empowerment, for example by protecting access to birth control and abortion for women....

... If the goal is equalizing the political power of disadvantaged groups and interests, the tax system, social welfare policy, antidiscrimination statutes, antitrust enforcement, financial services regulation, and labor law may be every bit as relevant as the law of democracy, and likely much more so than separation of powers.

... [C]onstitutional law and theory would do well to confront these systemic questions about where democratic-level power is and should be located. Constitutional thought might make greater progress by redirecting its focus from the power of government institutions to the power of groups in society—and correspondingly from structural constitutional law to a broader range of legal regimes that serve to redistribute democratic power....

Levinson's analysis highlights the practical nature of power: it determines "who governs." The abstract concerns of constitutional law with separation of powers and other public law concepts are not as central as supposed, while laws that facilitate democratic participation, equalize resources, or enhance bottom-up collectivities and collective action might be critical. As a system, perhaps private power hides behind public power to enforce private interests by law.

Legal scholar Kate Andrias underscores Levinson's argument, encouraging advocates to study how groups are disempowered through "doctrine, legislation, and legal practice." She identifies two key strategies for changing "rules of the game" to equalize power: "reducing legal barriers to collective action, while simultaneously creating new structures for citizens' collective engagement with government." As Guinier and Torres noted when describing demosprudence in Part I, such change opens up "space to those previously excluded or marginalized and enables them to participate more fully in helping to make decisions that affect their lives," in both private and public affairs.

CONFRONTING POWER IN PUBLIC LAW
Kate Andrias
130 Harv. L. Rev. Forum 1 (2016)

... Traditional separation of powers mechanisms, whatever their other virtues, do little to check or balance elites' concentrated power. Given this political economy, I have argued, public law ought to focus more on facilitating the countervailing power of ordinary citizens and their organizations in governance.

... *First*, confronting particular social problems and their human consequences, rather than remaining at a high level of abstraction, can deepen the account of how power functions in public law. *Second*, confronting power's distribution with material detail can help elucidate a path for reform. That path, I will suggest, involves reducing legal barriers to collective action, while simultaneously creating new structures for citizens' collective engagement with government.

... Consider employment and consumer law, and, in particular, the problem of mandatory arbitration clauses in contracts of adhesion.... Consumers, employees, and small businesses are routinely required, as a condition of doing business, to sign contracts that require them to arbitrate, rather than litigate, any claims.... [T]he Supreme Court has required arbitration even when the contracts deny the possibility of collective action or impose other procedural hurdles. In so doing, the Court has tended to obfuscate the striking disparity of power underlying the contracts.... Justice Kagan had this critique in *American Express Co. v. Italian Colors Restaurant*: "Here is the nutshell version of this case.... The monopolist gets to use its monopoly power to insist on a contract effectively depriving its victims of all legal recourse." ...

... [T]here is a critical need for a range of structural, power-shifting reforms to our law, our economy, and our democracy.

... One place to look [for examples] is to historical and contemporary social movements that have opposed, and are opposing, hierarchies of power.

Ongoing low-wage worker campaigns provide one source. Workers seeking higher minimum wages, new scheduling and benefit laws, limits on private domination, and new protection for those long or newly excluded from labor and employment regimes (think restaurant and domestic workers or Uber drivers) are attempting to shift the distribution of power ... [and expand their] ability to act collectively through strikes, protest, and other concerted action while developing new structures for participation in policymaking. ...

Or consider the movement around policing. ... Black Lives Matter ... is an effort of citizens to hold police departments accountable ... [and] to make broader changes to how power is organized in society, including by democratizing community institutions.

... [O]ngoing social movements embrace two interrelated paths: First, they contest doctrine, legislation, and legal practice that disempower organization, reduce availability of collective action as a tool, and enable social and economic domination. Second, they work to build new structures to facilitate countervailing power of civic organizations in government; they seek to remake policymaking bodies to grant workers, consumers, citizens, and residents greater influence in substantive outcomes.

... [L]awyers, policymakers, and legal scholars ought to pursue these two strategies in a wide range of substantive areas and venues ... [with] attention to the actual reality of how power is distributed as well as normative judgments and real struggle about where and by whom power should be held.

As a pair, these excerpts sketch a critically expanded conception of power and its impact on the potential of law for Critical Justice. They show that power is omnipresent within law—both public and private—to control both democracy and adjudication. And they provide an additional example of another key formalism—the private-public distinction—that elites deploy strategically to sustain entrenched patterns of identity castes and systemic injustice.

NOTES AND QUESTIONS

1. *A Transformative Time Machine.* The delegates or "framers" who drafted the U.S. Constitution in 1787 were all white men—business and landowners. Imagine if you, as an aspiring systemic advocate, were one of those delegates. What ideas for government structure might you suggest? Would you support the electoral college as a democratic means of electing the president? The U.S. Senate as a representative body? Relatedly, assume you were a member of the initial U.S. Congress a couple of years later, which crafted the Bill of Rights. That document did not specify many rights—like the right to vote or the right to marry—that today are considered "fundamental." Within the Bill of Rights itself, the Ninth Amendment textually commands that, "The enumeration in the Constitution, of certain rights, shall not be construed to deny or disparage others retained by the people." If the U.S. Constitution therefore protects explicitly some rights that are not specified (or enumerated) in the text, are there any other rights not currently specified in the U.S. Constitution that would help promote Critical Justice? What rights might be needed to help equalize either electoral power or economic resources that translate into influence over policymaking?

2. *Reflection Exercise on Power.* What did you know about power before reading this textbook? Did you think about it? How would you have defined power? Reflect on what you understand now about power and its uses. Imagine the skillset you might need to help shift power toward dismantling systems of caste that prevent Critical Justice.

9.7 LEGAL ETHICS TEACH AND ENFORCE INDUSTRY HANDCUFFS, BLINDFOLDS, AND HIERARCHIES

Legal training is part of a larger industry designed to instill conformity and muffle dissent in ways large and small. The multifaceted inculcation of top-down agendas comes not only from institutions like law schools and firms but also from peers invested in the industry's reward system. This pervasive pressure is how the industry reproduces hierarchy from year to year and generation to generation.

In this scheme, legal ethics are a distinct body of rules that teaches and enforces industry handcuffs and blindfolds. Written both in aspirational and mandatory terms, legal ethics police the actions of lawyers to ensure the industry allows no serious challenge to elite interests. Some provisions of legal ethics codes may be geared to client protection; legal ethics indeed can serve the public good. But as a set, the rules are designed chiefly for elite protection. Any lawyer who strays too far is subject to discipline—penalties, censure, and disbarment.

Legal ethics as a distinct set of rules emerged from the former Confederacy in the wake of the Civil War. At the time, women and people of color were barred from the legal profession. The principal proponent, Thomas Goode Jones, a former confederate soldier, constructed and billed ethics codes as a way to unify the legal profession, North and South, based on shared white and male conceptions of decorum, morality, "gentlemanliness," and civility:

> Jones' vision of North and South unity was predicated on the common experience of whiteness. In recognizing that the Northerners who died shared three fundamental aspects of identity with Southerners—their race, language, and religion—Jones demonstrated that whiteness was the primary vehicle through which he could advocate for the humanization—and ultimately acceptance—of the North. This recognition of race, language, and religion meant that Jones' unification scheme did not include non-whites, immigrants and non-English speakers, or non-Christians. These are the very groups of people who were barred from practicing law in the late 19th and early 20th centuries. . . . To the extent that Jones' code suggests a notion that civility and gentlemanly composure can and must be expected of all individuals sharing in the pursued goal of practicing law, the key in understanding Jones is understanding that Jones' world of civil lawyers only included white men. . . . Not only did he believe that "unworthy members" should be excluded from entrance into the profession; he also believed in a system that could monitor and police members' behavior.[48]

The first such code, drafted by Jones, was adopted by Alabama in 1887. This became the almost verbatim template for other U.S. state codes. Based on these codes, the American Bar Association promulgated the first

---

[48] Pilar Margarita Hernández Escontrías, Setting the Bar: The Sordid Past of Legal Ethics (unpublished manuscript on file with editors).

national code of model rules for legal ethics in 1908, with Jones serving as the principal drafter. Within two years, almost half of the states had incorporated these provisions into their new state ethics canons, most of them word-for-word. Today, legal ethics rules retain the basic blueprint, substance, and function of those early codes, with the judiciary in control of their implementation and enforcement:

> [Today], the judiciary is a central force in both bar committees and in the Courts where disciplined attorneys appear for adjudication of their ethics violation cases....
>
> Courts ... maintain total control at every stage of the attorney life cycle. The suggestion that the judiciary is impartial when it comes to hearing and imposing sanctions assumes that the judiciary has no vested interest in maintaining control over all aspects of the profession....
>
> Ethics in the U.S. is set up under a paradigm of discipline, punishment, and surveillance. Within U.S. law schools, students ... are taught to fear the consequences of ethical violations.... As lawyers, they come to live with these ethical rules daily.[49]

Ethics are an important element in top-down control of the legal industry to reproduce hierarchy. Legal ethics, for example, are used as a tool for blunting legal challenges to the status quo of castes in law and society. Post-*Brown*, for example, Southern elites used legal ethics to attack challenges to segregation and discrimination made by Black advocacy groups like the NAACP: "[P]rosecuting the NAACP for alleged legal ethics violations constituted one of the southern states' most vicious means of assault on the organization."[50]

Often enough, elite lawyers use their influence to *support* public interest law with money or board service, while *resisting or blocking* bottom-up critiques suggesting that the legal profession as a whole serves elite interests and must be changed: "By supporting the work of public interest organizations like the NAACP, elite lawyers from [earlier generations] to our own have been able to portray the bar's public aspirations as reality without having to significantly alter their own practices, which frequently undermine the public framework that advocacy organizations seek to protect."[51] This work is not based in opposition to the

---

[49] *Id.*

[50] See Susan D. Carle, How Should We Theorize Class Interests in Thinking About Professional Regulation: The Early NAACP as a Case Example, 12 Cornell J.L. & Pub. Pol'y 571 (2003). See also Michael Bennett and Cruz Reynoso, California Rural Legal Assistance (CRLA): Survival of a Poverty Law Practice, 1 Chicano L. Rev. 1 (1972) (describing attacks from within and outside the legal profession accusing farmworker advocates of unethical practice as well as critical support from legal allies).

[51] David B. Wilkins, Class Not Race in Legal Ethics: Or Why Hierarchy Makes Strange Bedfellows, 20 L. & Hist. Rev. 147, 151 (2002). For more consideration of the complex interactions of legal ethics, organizations, social identities, or industry roles and constraints in relation to

ameliorative goals of public interest organizations—but in support for them—so long as transformation of hierarchies of power and prestige are not threatened.[52] As Guinier et al. reported in their study of the University of Pennsylvania discussed above, legal ethics help law schools to train *all* students into "becoming (white) gentlemen," who assimilate into the industry as desired. Industry norms inhibit these gentlemen from thinking or acting critically throughout their careers. More covertly, today's codes of legal ethics continue to serve their original systemic purpose.

Below, Purvi Shah, director of Movement Law Lab and cofounder of Law4BlackLives, sets out the current moment's challenge to the legal profession as an industry. Shah notes that "the sordid truth is the vast majority of American lawyers are working to protect the interests of the rich and powerful." She argues that the status quo-reinforcing role of law has roots in "how lawyers are trained, acculturated, and incentivized." And she makes a bold proposal for reflection and change at both organizational and professional levels. Why can't—or how can—advocates create a new, supplemental code of ethics that provides "an ethical north star versus a bare minimum"? As you read, consider what might be included or discarded in such a code. What are the risks? Remember that, from the perspective of subordinated groups, risk is defined not only as the risks of change but also as the risks of no change. What legal industry blindfolds and handcuffs can be unlearned and relearned, reformed and recreated? What unintended consequences might be generated to the detriment of subordinated groups, and how can those be avoided? What effect could such work have on the Critical Challenge of using law for justice?

---

professional identity and values and hierarchies in the legal industry, see Lawyers' Ethics and the Pursuit of Social Justice: A Critical Reader (Susan D. Carle and Robert W. Gordon eds. 2007); William B. Rubenstein, In Communities Begin Responsibilities: Obligations at the Gay Bar, 48 Hastings L.J. 1101 (1997); Beverly I. Moran, Disappearing Act: The Lack of Values Training in Legal Education, 38 S.U. L. Rev. 1 (2010); Jerold S. Auerbach, Unequal Justice: Lawyers and Social Change in Modern America (1976); Richard L. Abel, American Lawyers (1989); Michael Diamond and Aaron O'Toole, Leaders, Followers, and Free Riders: The Community Lawyer's Dilemma when Representing Non-Democratic Client Organizations, 31 Fordham Urb. L.J. 481 (2004); Scott L. Cummings and Alan K. Chen, Public Interest Lawyering (2013).

[52] Another result of elite influence in the construction of legal ethics has been the promotion of rules favoring a pro bono model of public service and disfavoring "a very different, grass roots model, which blended public and private work and accepted legal fees wherever possible, in order to keep these small practices afloat." Carle, How Should We Theorize, at 598. Recent work to resuscitate low bono practices as a grass roots public interest practice model has addressed economic barriers and, to a lesser extent, ethical constraints. See, for example, Luz Herrera, Reflections of a Community Lawyer, 3 Mod. Am. 39 (2007).

REBUILDING THE ETHICAL COMPASS OF LAW
Purvi Shah
47 Hofstra L. Rev. 11 (2018)

The Current Moment...

We live in an incredibly challenging moment in U.S. history. Emboldened by the Trump presidency, a racist, anti-immigrant, anti-poor movement is gaining momentum....

While popular culture has advanced a myth of lawyers as the noble guardians of justice and equality, the sordid truth is the vast majority of American lawyers are working to protect the interests of the rich and powerful. According to a recent American Bar Association study, less than three percent of America's 1.3 million lawyers work on issues of justice and poverty. Another study found that low-income people seek lawyers for only twenty percent of their civil legal problems, and when they do, they are denied assistance eighty-six percent of the time. Millions of poor and marginalized Americans are enduring some of life's hardest challenges—discrimination, eviction, violence, deportation, and exploitation—without any assistance from our profession.

Some would argue that the gap between supply and demand is the result of sticky challenges including antiquated service delivery models, shrinking funding, and failure to use technology in creative ways. And while all of that is true, I think something more insidious is to blame for our profession's failure to meet the needs of the most vulnerable in our society.

The Legal Profession is in Crisis of Conscience

Our profession largely acts as the private army of corporations, the carceral state, and/or the elites who benefit from both. Sadly, more lawyers are working to preserve injustice rather than transform it. Lawyers serving in these roles—such as prosecutors and law firm partners—are exalted in law schools and elsewhere as the epitome of legal excellence without further critique of the systems they perpetuate. This has long been the case. Historically, lawyers have designed, justified, and advanced some of the most perverse and grotesque practices from slavery, Jim Crow segregation, torture, prolonged arbitrary detention, internment, and war. While every period in history has always had a small minority of lawyers who are deeply committed to social justice, as a profession, lawyers have been silent in the face of some of the most egregious justice issues.

This silence continues to the modern day. I spent the last four years building legal support for communities resisting racialized police violence across the country with and through the broader Movement for Black Lives. I traveled to Ferguson just a week following the killing of Mike Brown, after watching the civil and human rights violations unfolding on live television between police and protesters. As a small group of us attempted to recruit lawyers to assist those arrested, what became immediately clear was that *hundreds* of lawyers in the greater St. Louis area *refused* to get involved in what was happening. We saw that phenomenon happen again in Baltimore, in Charlotte, and in Charlottesville. It took months of organizing and agitating lawyers, combined with a shift in the broader popular narrative around police violence to awaken a sluggish legal sector to respond. The response still falls woefully short of the compounding needs of poor and disenfranchised people.

So what is to blame for our profession's failure to acknowledge its responsibility to address the human suffering we are witnessing on a massive scale?

We Can't Reap What We Don't Sow

I believe we can attribute this failure to take moral responsibility in our field in part to how lawyers are trained, acculturated, and incentivized. Questions of justice rarely are the focus of required law school curriculums or classes, leaving lawyers with substantial analytical gaps in understanding the nature of oppression, what causes it, and what transforms it. It is hard to be motivated to tackle a problem you aren't aware of or don't understand. Law students interested in these topics have to actively seek out or be lucky enough to have some elective courses or professors with an interest in opening a discourse around justice.

Second, legal education promotes many false myths about law, which become etched into the minds of lawyers and prevent us from being compelled to take action. For example, we are taught "The Law" in the United States is the benevolent guarantor of a fair and just society. Few law school classrooms or lawyers poke holes in this myth. Lawyers are trained to see courts as self-actualizing engines of justice, leaving no reason for them to be concerned independently with the questions of structural injustice within the law and legal institutions. But history has shown us that law is neither objective nor neutral and that "The Law" has always trailed behind what was just. We must start being honest about the fact that the law is not ethical or moral on its own. We must push it to be so.

A growing sector of lawyers and legal organizations, deeply invested in the questions of justice, have sought to dispel these myths and are using their skills in more proactive and holistic ways. They see their role as that of conscious tacticians—not saviors or bystanders—in support of marginalized people seeking to transform the conditions of their own lives. These lawyers creatively use legal tools to build the power of, make space for, validate, bolster, defend, and protect social movements and the activists and communities within them. . . .

Finally, I think we can trace this crisis of conscience in the legal field to the failures of how lawyers are taught to think about ethics. The Rules of Professional Conduct, which all lawyers must swear to uphold, offer a baseline standard of legal ethics and professional responsibility for American lawyers. Yet these rules speak primarily about what we should *not* do as lawyers—don't steal our clients' money, don't lie, don't commit fraud, don't disrespect the court. The rules are silent, however, on *what* the *affirmative* role for a lawyer is in society, *which* clients we should represent, *which* circumstances demand our ethical participation, and most importantly, *how* we should work for our clients. The rules say nothing about a larger social responsibility of lawyers. How can we expect lawyers to feel compelled to address the questions of injustice when we have created no incentives or responsibility for them to do so? . . .

In order to meet the demands of the current moment, I believe we must awaken the conscience of a much broader sector of the legal profession. We need thousands of lawyers to feel pulled by the questions of injustice. But how can we get there?

Creating a New Ethical North Star

. . . If a broader cross-section of lawyers must be activated to respond to the needs within our communities, then we will have to usher in a new era of leadership, activism, and morality among the legal profession. . . . I believe it is time to write a new code of ethics for lawyers. One that is aspirational and inspirational; an ethical north star versus a bare minimum. This code should be plain and easy to understand and should lay out ten to fifteen simple values to create a new ethical framework on the social responsibility of lawyers. This code should be used to supplement the Rules of Professional Conduct, designed to facilitate conversation, to encourage interrogation of the status quo, and to revive the heart and soul of our profession.

These values should be holistic and disrupt the normative paradigm of professional responsibility. For example, the code could include concepts like "Dignity: honoring the self-determination of our clients;" or "Integrity: an obligation to respond to moments of great injustice;" or "Collectivity: a commitment to use law to aggregate people with similar problems versus atomize them;" or "Collaboration: a commitment to working with other types of change-makers to address oppression."

The code should be a living document that can be tailored to the current moment and incorporate historical lessons of how law and lawyers have advanced oppression. It can be revisited every few years. It should be drafted by the generation of lawyers, who are black and brown and who come from communities that are oppressed. More importantly, it should be drafted alongside our representatives from marginalized client communities, many of whom have the most intimate understanding of the failures of our profession.

This new code could be voluntarily adopted by individuals, organizations, law schools, and law firms. After it gains critical mass, it can create a common framework for analysis and reflection about our ethical successes and failures as a profession. But more than a written document, we have to ensure the code creates a new culture where questions of morality are discussed, wrestled with, and prioritized in the legal profession. To ensure more day-to-day application of these new standards, we will have to be intentional about operationalizing this code of ethics. For example, every law school and legal organization could have a secular ethics chaplain, a person with whom lawyers can discuss questions of morality and meaning in their work. Alternatively, case review and staff evaluations can incorporate this new code of ethics. The possibilities are endless. . . .

Conclusion

Shifting norms around legal ethics has the power to transform how lawyers orient themselves to injustice, but can also serve the purpose of transforming the broader, hegemonic understanding of law in society. Through shifting ourselves, we shift our profession. By shifting our profession, we can shift the broader culture of society. . . .

As Shah notes, legal training and practice conspire, with the stamp of approval of legal ethics, to create a legal industry that serves elite interests in maintaining the status quo of identity-based castes. However, this view—that the industry suffers at this moment from a "crisis of conscience"—is not necessarily widely shared. The legal industry is effective at instilling conformity in thought and action, and in constructing rewards and penalties for compliance. In this scheme, legal ethics play a distinct role in reinforcing industry handcuffs, blindfolds, and hierarchies. As in other areas, the operation of legal ethics is complex; the self-created and enforced ethical standards of the industry sometimes serve the public good by protecting subordinated groups from some forms of exploitation, while primarily masking and maintaining hierarchies of power and prestige that favor elites.

NOTES AND QUESTIONS

1. *From "Zealous Advocacy" to "Effective Representation."* Legal scholars Kristen Carpenter and Eli Wald point out another way that individualism has skewed legal ethics:

> Zealous advocacy reflects the individualistic impulse of the basic model. It assumes an individual client who establishes clear

objectives and seeks to pursue them either in an adversarial fashion in litigation or aggressively across the negotiation table. It further assumes both that clients will be best served by zeal and that lawyers' main role is advocacy vis-à-vis an opposing party.... But zealous advocacy is simply not a broad enough category to encompass the range of needs for all clients, especially group clients.

... [S]ometimes an important aspect of group representation entails not external needs vis-à-vis opposing parties but rather internal needs of building identity and group relations. For such groups, effective representation might require, at times, not narrow zealous advocacy but tentative and mindful facilitation. A group lawyer in these circumstances might better serve her clients by abandoning warm zeal, aggression, and a combative posture and replacing them with what Deborah Cantrell, writing about lawyers and social change, calls "an approach of curiosity," fostering not the naked pursuit of individualistic self-interest but representation in the spirit of building webs of relationships within groups and vis-à-vis others.

With the benefit of Cantrell's insights, one might reimagine the conversation between a tribal nation and its lawyers. Rather than merely advising the client about the Supreme Court's view of Indian rights (and the likelihood of losing most cases), the lawyer might listen carefully to the tribal leaders' description of the interests and goals associated with rights claims, and then advise the client accordingly. As one example, the Onondaga Nation of New York is working with its lawyers to resolve historic land claims, but rather than focus purely on tribal rights, it has identified objectives including the clean-up of local natural resources and restoration of relationships with non-Indian neighbors. At the insistence of tribal leaders, the Onondaga land-claim complaint drafted by attorneys Joe Heath and Curtis Berkey calls for "healing of the land and water . . . with all people who live within the Onondaga original territory." While still pursuing litigation, the Onondaga Nation's lawyers are working on a strategy that includes community meetings, relationship building, and a discussion of shared interests.

... [T]he experience of tribal lawyers compellingly challenges the dominant ideology and the [ethical] Rules, and suggests not only the need to rethink and reimagine some aspects of the regulatory apparatus but also the professional ideology that legitimizes it.[53]

What does "zealous advocacy" mean to you? How does, or should, justice figure into that zealousness? How does law help? Hurt?

---

[53] Kristen A. Carpenter and Eli Wald, Lawyering for Groups: The Case of American Indian Tribal Attorneys, 81 Fordham L. Rev. 3085, 3145, 3147, 3162 (2013).

2. *Therapeutic Approaches to Law and Practice.* Proponents of "therapeutic jurisprudence" have proposed since the 1990s that legal institutions, processes, and outcomes should be redesigned more consciously to promote social and personal healing as part of a holistic remedial framework. Various scholars of this School of legal knowledge based in the United States have shown how both civil and criminal law can be made more humanistic—that is, how to value law's therapeutic potential over "efficiency" and its dehumanizing effects.[54] How might this approach or emphasis help to achieve effective representation toward Critical Justice?

3. *Learning to Think Like a Systemic Advocate.* "Thinking like a lawyer" is often presented as a process of applying formal legal categories to complex fact situations to reach "logical" solutions that produce "fair" outcomes. But those formal categories are already skewed to promote processes and solutions that favor elite interests and reinforce castes, oftentimes covertly. Legal professionals nevertheless need to master the categories and processes of law—they must learn to think and act within the proverbial box even as they work to undermine the uncritical conformism that prevents change in law as a system. Some legal writing and research professors aim to achieve the difficult balance of building analytical and practice skills while also teaching students to deconstruct formal categories, creatively use law, and intentionally take risks in practice. This work sometimes generates resistance from students, colleagues, and administrators. Below, legal writing scholars describe this difficult balancing act:

> [T]he law actually is an alternate reality constructed by an exclusive subsection of society comprised of predominantly wealthy, elite, powerful, White men. For our students to gain entry, therefore, we must indoctrinate them into the way of life in this toxic alternate reality.
>
> We reward students with high grades when they quickly learn to identify the relevant rule of law and the legally relevant facts. We praise those students who can clearly articulate the holding and apply it to a hypothetical with slightly different facts, and we publicly humiliate those who struggle to do so. We create cut-throat competition and isolation amongst them by grading them comparatively and eschewing independent identity in favor of relational status and hierarchical positioning. These practices discourage students from questioning the correctness of the rule of law and reinforce that lawyers are constrained by status and place as dictated by the realities of rigid rules of law, despite absurd outcomes. . . .

---

[54] See, for example, Judging in a Therapeutic Key: Therapeutic Jurisprudence and the Courts (Bruce J. Winick and David B. Wexler eds. 2003); Astrid Birgden, Maximizing Desistance: Adding Therapeutic Jurisprudence and Human Rights to the Mix, 24 Crim. Just. & Behav. 19 (2015); Suzanna Fay-Ramirez, Therapeutic Jurisprudence in Practice: Changes in Family Treatment Court Norms over Time, 40 L. & Soc. Inquiry 205 (2015); Amanda Wilson, Putting Therapeutic Jurisprudence on Edge: A Gendered Engagement, 47 U. B.C. L. Rev. 1185 (2014).

> ... [However, although legal] categories may become entrenched over time, they are never final. This "never final" principle is where teaching, rather than indoctrination, occurs. The paradox is that students who were once reticent to learn how to "think like a lawyer," have quickly become so conditioned to identify and apply the law that they are terribly uncomfortable questioning the law.... The notion that the law *can* be questioned seems radical, foreign, and wrong.
>
> But, if we are to have any hope that the law will ensure justice and equity for all, we must teach law students how to be *in* this world, and yet not *of* this world. We must continue to equip them with the knowledge of doctrine and legal methods so that they can speak the language of lawyers. Once [practicing], however, these lawyers must know how to interrupt the discourse and deconstruct harmful paradigms using a better toolkit than traditional legal rhetoric is capable of providing. In this respect, law schools have not prepared students well for the creative practice of law.[55]

What has been your experience with critical teaching approaches and methods, both in law school and other institutions? What sorts of resistance do you imagine might occur when aspiring lawyers or others are introduced to the notion that law is not just imperfect but fundamentally flawed? Consider the potential for resistance from students, administrators, alumnae, employers, and community members. How can lawyers be trained—and professors supported—to be both "practice ready" and "ready to practice" systemic advocacy? If you are, or have been, a law student, did you consider yourself well prepared "for the creative practice of law?" If so, how—in which ways? If not, why?

CHAPTER RECAP

This chapter surveyed how legal education and practice function as an industry that primarily serves elite interests, not as the interest-neutral, justice-seeking profession that idealized notions portray. In tandem, formalist training and conformist practice handcuff and blindfold legal work and workers to maintain the self-serving status quo established by entrenched elites. To serve justice under these systemic circumstances, advocates work collaboratively to transform both their legal work and its social results. As the following chapter shows, they work from many sites and platforms. They play varied kinds of roles, all of which are limited yet offer windows of opportunity to transcend failure by design. To show alternatives to this status quo, the next chapter elaborates further the contextual, three-layered goals of systemic advocacy, which as Parts I–III

---

[55] Elizabeth Berenguer, Lucy Jewel & Teri A. McMurtry-Chubb, Gut Renovations: Using Critical and Comparative Rhetoric to Remodel How the Law Addresses Privilege and Power, 23 Harv. Lat. L. Rev. 205 (2020).

detailed, are grounded in critical and bottom-up knowledge applied collaboratively. Consider the next chapter to this one in order to compare and contrast more clearly how systemic advocacy differs from the top-down formalism of today's legal industry in practical, conceptual, and other key ways.

CHAPTER 10

ADVANCING AND DEFENDING THREE-LAYERED GOALS IN SYSTEMIC CONTEXTS

■ ■ ■

Table of Sections

10.1 Systemic Advocacy Centers Persistent Social Problems in Complex Contexts
10.2 Three-Layered Goals Are Geared to Three Recurrent Advocacy Scenarios
10.3 Second-Layer Goals Combine Persuasion and Pressure to Build and Exercise Power
10.4 Third-Layer Goals Connect Micro-Macro Facts to Shift Consciousness and Cultures
10.5 Systemic Advocates Combine Traditional and Critical Tools for Three-Layered Progress

---

OPENING THOUGHTS

The need for change bulldozed a road down the center of my mind.

—**Maya Angelou,** I Know Why the Caged Bird Sings (1969)

Legal reforms can only be successful if accompanied by societal change.

—**Adrien Katherine Wing**, Critical Race Feminism and International Human Rights, 28 U. Miami Inter-Am. L. Rev. 337, 349 (1997)

Collaborative relationships among lawyers, community organizations, and clients can empower the latter to be active decision makers and community leaders.

—**Andrea C. Yang,** Re-considering Progressive Lawyering: The Theory and a Growing Practice in Asian Immigrant Communities, 16 Asian Pac. Am. L.J. 100, 107 (2010–11)

In what ways will law be predictably used to defend state and market power against the social? Are there innovative ways in which law can help buttress the power of the social to challenge organized state and market power? Are there ways in which law can further egalitarianism in the social itself?

—**Berta Hernandez-Truyol, Angela P. Harris & Francisco Valdes**, Afterword—Beyond the First Decade: A

Forward-Looking History of LatCrit Theory, Community and Praxis, 26 Chicano-Latino L. Rev. 237 (2006)

INTRODUCTION

Systemic dominance is daunting yet still contested. Even as identity castes were being established from above, groups and their organizers and advocates prevented the system from resting easy. At each step, they resisted, changing the course of history. They contested both foundational concepts and ground rules.

The resulting contestations and complexities are the inheritance of every advocate today. The legal industry simultaneously constrains justice into individualized, ameliorative compartments and collectivizes injustice by identity-based castes. In contrast, systemic advocacy seeks to collectivize justice, to increase bottom-up power, and to shift systems, consciousness, and culture to help bend the arc of change toward equal justice for all. Although in practice the two overlap, this chapter presents some key points that distinguish systemic advocacy from traditional practice in the industry.

We begin with the critical conception of "context" highlighting how advocates use this concept to carve out manageable entry points into larger systems and patterns of group injustice that otherwise might seem overwhelming. Context is a foundational and practical concept. For systemic advocates, context signifies the convergence of identities, groups, interests, and power in a given time and place. From a problem-solving perspective, understanding how these four elements "add up" to injustice in a given setting—micro or macro—is at the center of understanding the context. This unlearning and relearning of context repositions advocates to plan, research, and execute antisubordination projects aligned with three-layered goals.

We also review the three kinds of recurrent "scenarios" advocates face in any given context: whether some kernel of collective organization already exists in that context. If so, the advocacy must be geared to supporting those efforts; if not, the advocacy must initially consider whether, and how, to help originate or increase those kernels of collective consciousness and collaborative action. Contexts, as shown below, are defined both by their particularities—their unique combinations of elements—as well as by their commonalities—the patterns they form despite their unique differences. Systemic contexts thus come in infinite configurations. But practice scenarios come in three recurrent kinds: (1) those that involve only individuals and do not call for collective action; (2) those that involve collective problems with some level of already-organized group struggle for a systemic solution; and (3) those that similarly involve collective problems, but with no group consciousness or organized capacity.

As the excerpts below show, every (unique) context presents at least one of these three (recurrent) practice scenarios.

As we see in this chapter, both contexts and scenarios underscore the relevance of identities, groups, interests, and power, as well as the importance of other insights from critical and bottom-up knowledge. Advocates use a self-critical awareness of contexts *and* scenarios in making every choice or decision, including how to base themselves where they can best advance organized group struggles, emphasizing group capacities to contest systemic ground rules or foundational concepts that perpetuate injustice. This point is key: *a collective capacity to challenge or modify skewed ground rules and foundational concepts, which by design give established elites an advantage in every contest, is integral to three-layered progress.*

To highlight the importance of ground rules and foundational concepts, this chapter examines in more detail both the second layer of group power-building and the third layer of consciousness and culture-shifting—as well as the functional interrelationship between these two layers. The bottom line is that changing laws is never enough; advocates and groups *additionally* must change distributions of power to shift personal and cultural attitudes. Culture shifts start as an intragroup process—the internal work of shifting consciousness within and among members of organized client-groups engaged in both legal and extralegal action—and expand outwards to alter, over time, the social landscape.

This work, as the previous chapters illustrate, requires an expanded scope of research, analysis, and action. As a practical matter, it requires advocates to know and do more—to expand their capacity to make three-layered progress. Systemic analysis and advocacy depend on an expanded base of critical knowledges, values, skills, and attitudes (CKVSAs). This expanded toolkit combines persuasion with pressure through direct, democratic, and judicial actions. It counteracts systemic injustice in micro, everyday aspects of life as well as in macro, institutional routines. Three-layered goals can help advocates transcend partially the blindfolds, handcuffs, and hierarchies of law as an industry.

We say transcend *partially* because constant opposition and suppression, as well as cooptation, are ever-present risks. As Part III outlined, cooptation, capture, tokenism, retaliation, and other risks inure in all actions—legal and extralegal. The complexity of systems and settings provides opportunities for manipulation. Advocates cannot insulate themselves from these risks—there is no magic formula of words, actions, identities, or relationships that can preclude top-down take-overs of bottom-up insurgencies. Only constant vigilance, personal and collective, can guard against these and similar dangers. Recognizing this reality, advocates regularly practice the basic insights from the Schools and

Approaches noted in Part I: critical and self-critical analysis, coupled with principled actions, which are rooted in and accountable to the bottom. Here, we emphasize that these principled and accountable actions must be designed and carried out, in self-conscious and synergistic ways, along all three layers of systemic problem solving.

To do so, this chapter lays out some key aspects of this expanded critical toolkit, including:

- defining contexts for advocacy in terms of histories and legacies of identities, groups, interests, and power;
- focusing on the centrality of planning and advancing antisubordination advocacy in terms of the three-layered goals;
- demonstrating that second-layer group power-building includes concrete and ultimately testable indicia of the group's ability to generate desired decisions from targeted decision makers, chiefly by selecting indicia important in context based on a critical analysis of members' social conditions and organizational capacities;
- explaining that power-building processes must be designed to advance third-layer goals by engaging individuals within groups to generate a shared critical understanding of legal and cultural "blame frames" to shift consciousness among participants and, eventually, more broadly through group legal and extralegal action;
- showing, thus, that the work of group power-building and of consciousness- and culture-shifting are distinct but intertwined; and
- underscoring that the risks of top-down reactions, ranging from cooptation to retaliation are confronted through ongoing critical and self-critical work to identify and correct anything that diverts advocates and activists from challenging the premises or rules of the game that govern both adjudication and democracy, and determine their outputs.

As you read, reflect on the atomized claims, legal fictions, material incentives, and failure by design of the legal industry. Recall also dual consciousness, critical knowledge, and antisubordination values. Based on those reflections, imagine concretely how you might practice advocacy differently in specific contexts or scenarios. How would a self-critical focus on second-layer and third-layer goals affect your approach to first-layer actions that usually are ameliorative and often individualized? How could your advocacy (or project) be made more transformative by taking the missing elements—identities, groups, interests, and power—into account

10.1 SYSTEMIC ADVOCACY CENTERS PERSISTENT SOCIAL PROBLEMS IN COMPLEX CONTEXTS

in your critical *and* practical understanding of complex problems and contexts?

"Context" is a point of focus and venue of work that advocates use to research and design principled, accountable, and effective projects. Specifically, we turn to contexts in systemic terms—that is, systemic contexts. To start, consider a quandary of advocates seeking to ensure that all women have equal justice in relation to decisions about reproduction:

> In early 2009, Nadya Suleman, now known as the "octo-mom," caught international attention for giving birth to live octuplets. Public sentiment quickly turned from awe to scorn when the media disclosed that Suleman had used assisted reproductive technology to become pregnant while unemployed and receiving public assistance. This national media spectacle once again stirred up hostility toward poor women—leading many to call for increased regulation of women's reproductive choices. Several state legislatures have considered legislation to prevent women from accessing fertility treatments if their age, health or financial circumstances are deemed "unsuitable."
>
> At the heart of the octo-mom debate lies a question . . . of public resources—recognizing that a legal right to reproductive services, without support, leaves many women without meaningful choice.[1]

To answer this question, many advocates and activists began to focus on "reproductive justice," developed through critical reflection by and with poor women of color and defined as "the complete physical, mental, spiritual, political, social, and economic well-being of women and girls, based on the full achievement and protection of women's human rights."[2] Reproductive justice generates changes in approach:

> Reproductive justice is rooted in a rich history of organizing among women of color within movements for social justice and women's health. Additionally, reproductive justice is about shifting resources—in addition to extending rights—to those who

---

[1] Sarah London, Reproductive Justice: Developing a Lawyering Model, 13 Berkeley J. Afr.-Am. L. & Pol'y 71, 71 (2011).

[2] Loretta Ross, SisterSong Women of Color Reproductive Health Collective, What is Reproductive Justice, in Berkeley Law Reproductive Justice Briefing Book: A Primer on Reproductive Justice and Social Change, www.law.berkeley.edu/php-programs/courses/fileDL.php?fID=4051 (attributing the definition to the Asian Communities for Reproductive Organization).

lack the information and means to achieve self-determination in reproduction. Reproductive justice activists recognize that "reproductive choice" does not occur in a vacuum, but in the context of all other facets of a woman's life, including barriers that stem from poverty, racism, immigration status, sexual orientation and disability. To achieve reproductive justice, according to movement leaders, oppressed communities must build power through organizing, education and political mobilization.

One mainstream national reproductive rights organization, Law Students for Reproductive Justice (LSRJ), has wholeheartedly adopted the reproductive justice framework, but has encountered difficulty in defining its role.... [At a student gathering,] Aimee Thorne-Thomsen from Expanding the Movement for Empowerment and Reproductive Justice (EMERJ) provided chapter leaders with an overview of the reproductive justice framework.... As a participant in this gathering, I felt energized by this new direction, so I asked a question: "What should law students do?" The speaker paused, shook her head, and quietly responded: "Well . . . I don't know. You will have to figure it out."[3]

Understanding context as a complex intersection of forces is a starting point for figuring "it" out. The context for systemic advocacy defines how a social problem affects specific people in specific, material ways, in a specific place and time, and as a result of specific histories. Context defines where these identities, histories, structures, and laws intersect. Below, legal scholar John Calmore provides a description of inner city communities as a systemic context—"the intersection of race, space, and poverty." Understanding contexts critically brings into focus "the structured aspect of poverty" and other *systemic* conditions.

Calmore emphasizes a form of collaborative professionalism rooted explicitly in antisubordination values. This twin focus on context and antisubordination challenges dominant notions of advocacy, in which problems are handled in atomistic, decontextualized, and largely ahistorical ways. Against this backdrop, systemic advocacy aims to make change along all three layers to counter the embedded persistence of social problems in complex contexts, which as Calmore emphasizes below, must be understood critically as shifting confluences of intersectional identities, groups, interests, and power. Defining a systemic context—and a contextual advocacy project—in these ways allows advocates to delineate a manageable starting point for action while recognizing the inevitability of complexity. Thinking and doing contextually helps advocates to support

---

[3] London, Reproductive Justice, at 72–73.

A CALL TO CONTEXT: THE PROFESSIONAL CHALLENGES OF CAUSE LAWYERING AT THE INTERSECTION OF RACE, SPACE, AND POVERTY

John O. Calmore
67 Fordham L. Rev. 1927 (1999)

Introduction

Traditional legal analysis and advocacy are too often plagued by the tendency to extrapolate issues from their history and the broader social and normative contexts that bear so heavily on them. Seldom will a client's legal problem be just a legal problem. By issuing a call to context, I am directing attention to the inner-city poor's lived experiences, including the interconnection of legal and non-legal issues they confront, the web of experiences within which they live[,] . . . "their anchor in context." This suggests that we cannot view their issues or the features of context as fixed and unchanging. Instead, we must view them as historically evolving, relational, changing in meaning . . . "to be interpreted in terms of time and place."

In considering why we describe law as a "profession," many focus on the practice of law as a "public calling." From this perspective, perhaps, the most profound issue in providing effective legal services to the poor is whether legal advocacy on their behalf can maintain a positive, operational connection between rights and justice. With or without lawyers, for the inner-city poor, justice is hard to find. In the quest for justice, representing the poor has generally attracted "cause lawyers." Broadly speaking, cause lawyering encompasses various law-related activities, from rights assertion to legal counseling, that relies on law-related means to achieve social justice for individuals and subordinated or disadvantaged groups. Whether representing individuals or groups, cause-oriented poverty lawyers often adopt an orientation of antisubordination advocacy. This requires legal advocates, especially attorneys, to cross traditional boundaries where "the practice of law primarily consists of the hermeneutic reproduction of that which already exists." This lawyering, moreover, must confront the difficulties and contradictions that are part of working for social change within and outside of the legal system's conventional framework.

. . . In this line of work, we must appreciate that poverty has multiple dimensions. In terms of time, there is persistent poverty; in terms of space, there is neighborhood poverty; and in terms of behavior, there is underclass poverty. Sometimes, these dimensions coalesce and those in poverty experience both stigmatizing and oppressive constraints. This predicament is worsened by societal imposition of negative racial characteristics as an overlay. In other words, poverty and space become racialized to the detriment of these poor. This marks the intersection of race, space, and poverty.

. . . The intersection of race, space, and poverty necessarily directs our attention to the significance of the neighborhood aspects of poverty and its concentration effects. . . . [Intersection] connotes a dynamic process that extends beyond identity formation. More than that, intersectionality additionally constitutes context: framing the interconnection of issues and the web of experiences that live at and within the intersection of race, space, and poverty. In some instances, the intersection is the primary defining feature of context.

Within this intersection, or context, I focus on high-poverty neighborhoods—that is, those with poverty rates of at least forty percent. I also focus on people who experience the effects of concentrated poverty. Concentrated poverty sharpens our focus in considering the constraints and social isolation that these poor people face. . . .

Almost beyond the purview of legal advocates and policy makers, the existence of neighborhood poverty has grown dramatically since the 1970s. . . .

"One common impression of poor neighborhoods is correct: they are predominantly inhabited by members of minority groups." . . . In 1990, while one in seven blacks—fourteen percent—lived in ghettos or high-poverty neighborhoods, only one percent of all (non-Hispanic) whites lived in neighborhood poverty. Among Latinos, nineteen percent of Puerto Ricans, nine percent of Mexicans, and three percent of Cubans lived in barrios or high-poverty neighborhoods.

. . . In what follows, I examine the nature of cause lawyering as it may be practiced specifically on behalf of the inner-city poor—clients who are, synergistically and simultaneously, racially and economically subordinated within the spatially constrained and the opportunity-denying circumstances of ghetto and barrio life. In light of these features, I argue that effective representation must collaborate with these clients not only to represent them, but also to represent their place and communities as well. . . .

The Challenges and Opportunities of Cause Lawyering

This part introduces the concept of "cause lawyering," comparing it to [traditional] lawyering and explaining how it can benefit inner-city client communities. It examines the meaning of cause lawyering, with its associated attributes and threats to the legal profession. This part then addresses the forces that drive and direct cause lawyering in various contexts.

The Concept of Cause Lawyering in Context

... Cause lawyering presents a profound professional threat to the dominant bar and its forms of legal practice:

> [Cause lawyers] threaten the profession by destabilizing the dominant understanding of lawyering as properly wedded to moral neutrality and technical competence.... Cause lawyering exposes the fact that [law] is contingent and constructed and, in so doing, raises the political question of whose interests the dominant understanding serves. The result is a threat to ongoing professional projects and the political immunity of the legal profession and the legal process.

... This lawyering is not motivated by a desire to defend and protect rights in the abstract. Instead, rights are means to political ends. Far from asserting rights, the false legitimization function of the law is constantly challenged. This is important, because "[t]he law is a major vehicle for the maintenance of existing social and power relations by the consent or acquiescence of the lower and middle classes." As a consequence, left-activists tend to push their professional role and their organizations into areas that are politically and professionally risky, confrontational, and controversial.

... [However, standing alone,] a genuine, good-faith commitment to antisubordination work does not necessarily insulate one.... [T]he [conventional] mode of lawyering is cultivated under the pressing circumstances of practice. Those circumstances include the social and cultural distance between lawyers and clients, the occasional but significant mutual distrust and disrespect between lawyers and clients, the overwhelming crush of client demand, the burn-out of practice, the differing, sometimes contradictory worldviews of lawyers and clients, and lawyers' self-righteous arrogance. Moreover, its cultivation takes place regardless of whether the practice emphasizes individual client cases, group or institutional impact cases, or mobilization advocacy. It takes place whether the lawyer is non-white or white, male or female, gay or straight, or a stranger to the community or a former resident who has now moved on.

The first step for most of us in becoming effective advocates, then, is to break away from the [dominant] idea of lawyering....

Lawyers must know how to work with the client community, not just on its behalf. There must be collaboration with professional and lay allies, including a willingness to be educated by them.... They must continually assess probable interaction between both legal and non-legal approaches to problems. They must adopt a problem-solving orientation.... Finally, this orientation toward advocacy must nurture the appropriate sensibilities and skills that are "compatible with a collective fight for social change."

The Direction of Cause Lawyering in Context

... The community-based notion of cause lawyering not only allows us to situate our clients as a social group, but also compels us to confront their problems as public issues that reflect systemic "contradictions" or "antagonisms" rather than as "personal troubles." This in turn directs us to adopt a mission of social justice that redresses oppression. Thus, social justice furthers liberation and entails establishing freedom from the features of oppression. These features ... are exploitation, marginalization, powerlessness, cultural imperialism, and violence.... Significantly, within the context of inner-city poverty, these multiple forms of oppression often coalesce in synergistically interlocking ways. They constitute the packaged opportunity-denying circumstances that must be redressed....

... [A] ubiquitous feature of oppression is "the double bind—situations in which options are reduced to a very few and all of them expose one to penalty." Over the years of practicing poverty law from Roxbury to Watts, I was continually struck by the apparently optionless world that most of my clients inhabited. I never associated it with oppression, but rather I saw it as a lack of social and monetary capital. I continued to believe in the myth of Horatio Alger [that an individual's hard work would supply upward mobility]. I simply failed to see the predicament of my clients as oppression—as something that was group-based, structured, and systemic. The life of the oppressed "is confined and shaped by forces and barriers which are not accidental or occasional and hence avoidable, but are systematically related to each other in such a way as to catch one between and among them and restrict or penalize motion in any direction." The constraint is analogous to that of living within a cage where ... "all avenues, in every direction, are blocked or booby trapped." Thus, many of the problems my clients brought to me were recurring: another eviction, another welfare cut, another police beating, another inability to pay bills, an endless and miscellaneous list of booby traps. I did not see that they were linked problems that represented a cage-like structure.

When I represented white working-class clients in Hayward, California in the mid-1970s, I did not really appreciate the race-based exacerbation of poverty that distinguished them from my black and Latino clients. At that time, I was not sharp enough to see the intersection between race and class that I came to see much later in the 1980s. I saw my minority clients as being in a similar boat as the white poor. I knew that Appalachian poverty was different from Harlem poverty, but it was still primarily a class experience that was being played out in different locations. It is the feature of racialized poverty, however, that calls attention to group specificity and the fact that oppression is primarily a function of social group association. The compounded oppression of race-class is the qualitative difference between black-brown poverty and white poverty. My white clients certainly experienced the hardships of poverty. But they generally did not experience these hardships as a social group that was oppressed at the intersection of race and poverty. Almost never did they experience them at the tripartite intersection of race, space, and poverty. When we look at oppression, we must look at the specific social group experience and respond accordingly.

We must also pay attention to the structured aspect of poverty. Clearly poor people must take responsibility for their lives and battle the forces that might compel them to engage in dysfunctional behavior. But this responsibility is not enough. . . .

The inner-city poor are oppressed by "the normal ongoing processes of everyday life." When we speak of empowerment and transformation, we should be referring not only to disrupting stark hierarchy and power imbalances, but also to changing the processes of everyday life as lived by those within the client community.

Finally, cause lawyering must develop a critical vocabulary to present race and racism as part of the poverty story. Here, critical race theory can be useful to the practice. It informs us that race and racism are always concepts in formation. Our notion of race and our experience with racism do not represent fixed, static phenomena. Racism is more than the intentional behavior of the occasional bad actor. Racism mutates and multiplies, creating a range of racisms. We must be able to bring up issues of race and racism without the terms always leading to fear, alienation, and off-point debate. There is no such thing as colorblind poverty. We must appreciate that because the inner-city poor are approximately seventy-five percent black and brown, inner-city poverty itself is "raced." One simply cannot seek economic justice and equal treatment for the poor by separating the quest from considerations of the raced aspects of context, history, social organization, institutional arrangements, and culture. . . .

Representing Clients in Poverty And Place

A key aspect of cause lawyering is understanding that individual clients cannot be treated as separate from their racial, geographical, and class identities. Rather, as this part demonstrates, race, class, and "place" often converge to inform both individual client identity and societal perceptions of certain groups.

The Significance of Intersectional Analysis

. . . The issues confronting the inner-city poor point to a series of problems that we can trace to the inter-connected dynamics of racialized poverty, residential segregation, and the long history of racism.... [W]e must have a comprehensive view of the conditions to be redressed....

In looking at the racial and ethnic data regarding neighborhood poverty, I am struck by two things. First, it is really not a significant problem for whites, as only one percent of all non-Hispanic whites live in poor neighborhoods. Second, for this reason, racism may continue to cultivate broad societal neglect and block efforts at grand-scale redress....

... White support for racial justice remained strong as long as moral issues were salient in the civil rights movement—issues associated with addressing such matters as state-sanctioned segregation, political disenfranchisement, and antiblack violence, largely in the South. Support waned, however, when the movement's attention was redirected to the economic aspects of racial inequality.... "As the civil rights movement moved north after 1964 and pressed demands for open housing, busing, and affirmative action, the northern white civil rights constituency began melting away and undermining the political foundations of antipoverty policy."...

The Anchor of Context: Racialized Class-Space

The racialized inner-city poor, particularly African Americans and [Latinx people], experience concentrated poverty in their neighborhoods that is compounded by a spatial and geographic marginalization that deepens their intersectional racist and economic subordination. Within this context of ghetto and barrio poverty, geographic racism operates in a way that manifests ... "the new poverty." In the context of past poverty, the poor suffered from deprivation, constrained opportunity, and exploitation. These marked their economic inequality. A significant segment of today's poor, in contrast, are superfluous not only to the economy, but also to the nation's societal organization....

Traditional ghettos were sites of opportunity through exploitation. The residents were confined by dominant interests not only to facilitate a strong measure of social control but also to channel ghetto activities in a way to further dominant economic interests. The new ghetto of the excluded is very different.... Society is less inclined to use these residents, even under circumstances of exploitation, because "of fear that their activities, not controlled, may endanger the dominant social peace."

This ghetto, moreover, is conceptually different from an enclave. An enclave is also a spatially concentrated area, but one within which "members of a particular population group, self-defined by ethnicity or religion or otherwise, congregate as a means of enhancing their economic, social, political, and/or cultural development." Transcending class, many African-American, Latino, and Asian communities are spatially organized as cultural and/or immigrant enclaves. Many suburbs are also enclaves, but they are racially or economically exclusionary ...[:]

The exclusionary enclave, although not new, plays a new role today, both quantitatively and qualitatively. It differs from other forms of enclaves (although there are shared characteristics) in that its residents, intermediate and insecure in their economic, political, and social relationships to the outside community, wish to "protect" themselves from a perceived danger from below.

... [This] description is particularly helpful in distinguishing the black ghetto today from the ethnic or cultural enclaves of white immigrants.... Hence, understanding why blacks and Latinos have come to occupy their place in society and how they can move on, will call for group-specific, different analyses....

... This reality renders quite problematic remedies that are predicated on the civil rights tenets of colorblindness, individual equality of opportunity, and integration through assimilation....

... [I]t is not enough to direct intervention efforts at what occurs within poor communities. Rather, we must affect inter-spatial relationships.... Through the process of racialization [geographic separation] transforms many urban problems, particularly those associated with living in the city, into black and Latino problems. Indeed, the array of problems associated with city life get reduced to the black and brown poor, so that they become the problem....

This subordinating spatial organization is illustrated in suburban formation, urban renewal and displacement, exclusionary zoning, gentrification, public housing site selection, and environmental inequities. It is illustrated in the spatial hierarchy [of today], consisting of the ghetto of the excluded, the totalizing suburb [of the mainstream], and the luxury citadel [of the rich].

Thus, we must join inner-city client communities in our shared recognition that "all spatialities are political because they are the (covert) medium and (disguised) expression of asymmetrical relations of power." This means that legal advocacy of impact must join in the client community's challenges to that hegemony which is expressed in terms of place, politics, and identity. Failure here is to retreat from the necessary cutting edge of cause lawyering.

... Here, too, we can better appreciate why we cannot come into the picture with canned claims and prayers for relief. We must be open to being used by the client community in ways that they deem appropriate. We can provide technical assistance and advocacy perspective; we can enhance their stories; and we can help them to leverage their positions. We cannot eliminate poverty; we cannot really move very many out of poverty. But we can join the political project by occupying the real-and-imagined worlds on the margin and helping the community to reclaim these spaces as places of radical openness and possibility.

Fighting the "Underclass" Label and Developing Social Capital

A good deal of debate about policy responses to the ghetto poor, barrio poor, and neighborhood poverty itself is distorted because these poor and their poverty are over-inclusively associated with the image of the undeserving poor. These people are deemed to make up the so-called underclass groups—the inner city, the persistently impoverished, the jobless, the uneducated, the criminal, the violent, and welfare underclasses. The designation of underclass is more than a reference to poverty. It incorporates a societal judgment that these poor violate mainstream rules or norms of behavior. These poor are seen as living in a self-perpetuating culture of poverty that causes them to be so alienated and damaged that even if there were improvements in their economic condition and increased access to a viable opportunity structure, they would be unable to take advantage of these changes. The remedial focus is on changing their behavior and values rather than changing their structured inequality. . . .

The underclass label is problematic in various ways. Labels are not mere words. They carry judgmental and normative connotations that can influence societal institutions and individuals to punish those who are stigmatically labeled. . . . [B]ecause "underclass" is a code word that implies that undeserving people are not or should not be in society, those who accept the term in this way justify excluding the poor from the rest of society without expressly admitting it. Moreover, because the term underclass is racialized, it is a convenient way for masking antiblack or anti-Latino sentiments. As a racial code word, it "accommodates contemporary taboos against overt prejudice. . . . Such taboos sometimes paper over—and even repress—racial antagonisms that people do not want to express openly."

. . . [Thus,] "the key conclusion from a public policy perspective is that programs created to alleviate poverty, joblessness, and related forms of social dislocation should place primary focus on changing the social and economic situations, not the cultural traits, of the ghetto underclass." I do not mean to suggest that there is no problematic behavior or dysfunctional values operating within the dynamics of ghetto or barrio life. . . . [But] many manifestations of inner city social dislocations should be analyzed as symptoms of racial-class inequality, not as cultural aberrations, and, therefore, "changes in the economic and social situations of the ghetto underclass will lead to changes in cultural norms and behavior patterns." . . .

Conclusion

. . . Advocacy on behalf of [impoverished, subordinated] people and their places must be activist, bold, innovative, and radically progressive. It must also be site-specific and targeted in responding to the needs and aspirations of the inner-city poor as a distinct social group. In this response, it must proceed in, literally, an organic manner. It must transgress boundaries, including those that mark the professional role, socialization, and responsibility of attorneys. In representing inner-city poor people, universalistic perspectives and orientations are likely to be ineffective. In many cases, neither poor people nor their troubles can be viewed as fungible. In responding to, and working with, our client communities, we must identify which particular poor people and which particular contexts are the subjects, before we can map advocacy strategies.

When race and space are synergistically involved with poverty, race-neutral or color-blind poverty practice is naively wrong-headed. It reflects an approach that is both ahistorical and de-contextual. It badly underestimates the interlocking elements of oppression. In terms of redress sought, it stops us too far short. . . .

To all advocates, I wonder whether we can really "do good" without respecting the client community's voice, vision, and humanity. . . . In responding to the actual conditions of the racialized, inner-city poor, we must direct our quest for the cause of social justice with respectful regard and comprehensive understanding of a world that is foreign to us, even as we practice within it. Practicing law in the community is not a tourist adventure and, therefore, we must eschew the routine of the autonomous, interloping advocate who dreams up cases in the home office and then tests them on the community. That is, we must search for invitation, opportunity, and connection that legitimate our very presence and committed practice. An open mind and a correct sensibility may be more important than the command of technical craft, because often we must learn as we go. We must approach that learning in non-linear, non-laboratory ways. Learning within our client communities will likely respond to these places as "eco-system[s] of knowledge" where learning is "multi-dimensional, often messy and confusing." Only through this approach will advocates effectively become incorporated within the client community.

. . . At the same time, we must recognize that empowerment must extend beyond support . . . and enable the clients to position themselves to reach out and to assume a greater entry into a more just and open society where opportunity can be leveraged in new and different ways.

. . . From within the space of marginality we can come to know a situatedness that is, in part, self-chosen rather than oppressively imposed by external structures. This marginalization does not write off people, but provides a vantage point from which to see and act differently. From that vantage point, one knows different things and one knows in different ways. This perspective and knowledge can propel resistance and construct radical senses of openness and possibility. As bell hooks implores us: "Enter that space. Let us meet there."

Drawing from experience with "cause lawyering" Calmore illustrates how every "context" is more than just a time and place. Rather, in systemic terms, every context is a volatile convergence of identities, groups, interests, and power in a given time and place and in light of relevant histories and legacies. These convergences create needs—not just for amelioration, but also for transformation. Consequently, every systemic context is thick with complexity.

Understanding a systemic context and its complexities from the bottom up provides critical knowledge to develop strategies and plans for three-layered goals. Contexts provide practical and manageable points of entry for systemic advocacy tailored to advancing and defending three-layered progress. This kind of three-layered progress, as we emphasize in this chapter, recognizes that rights—civil rights and human rights—are important for group struggles but not enough for social transformation.

NOTES AND QUESTIONS

1. *Working Within Contexts.* Can you tentatively itemize the factors or circumstances that Calmore says converge to create the intersectional context in which he worked? Review your list carefully to ensure you have accounted for, but not limited yourself to, the four key elements of systemic advocacy we have emphasized: identities, groups, interests, and power. Now, using your own advocacy project or an issue area in which you are interested, compose a description of its context in light of the factors discussed above. Can you also compare this context from another jurisdiction (local, state, national, or international) facing the same social problem with a seemingly similar social and legal system? Consider critically both similarities and differences that surface through comparison. What lessons or insights can you draw to inform advocacy in the two contexts? How might strategies be the same or different across these two contexts?

2. *Understanding Context to Enhance Advocacy Contributions.* Calmore points out several specific contributions that advocates can make to client-groups in struggles for justice: "We can provide technical assistance and advocacy perspective; we can enhance their stories; and we can help them to leverage their positions." Below is an excerpt from a report describing the widespread occurrence of gender-based violence and harassment (GBVH) in the supply chains of multinational garment producers. The report was released in the lead up to tripartite negotiations among representatives of workers, corporations, and governments at the International Labor Organization (ILO) to craft a new convention aimed at preventing GBVH. As you read, identify aspects of the problem in this context—the particular space and place and time of GBVH in global garment production networks in relation to this specific constellation of identities, groups, interests, and power, as well as laws:

[This report] aims to situate new empirical findings on gender based violence in Walmart factories in Bangladesh, Cambodia, and Indonesia within the broader context of global production networks in general and the garment global production network in particular.... Brands like Walmart, headquartered in high income countries, outsource production to supplier firms in developing countries....

... While brands and retailers do not carry out production, they drive sourcing and production patterns overseas....

Women workers employment in garment supply chains are overwhelmingly employed in nonstandard and precarious forms of employment, typified by informal, low-paid and poorly protected work.... In varied, locally specific ways, international capital relies upon gendered ideologies and social relations to recruit and discipline workers, producing segmented labour forces within and between countries....

Women workers reported being targets of explicitly gendered violence, including verbal abuse linked to gender and sexuality, sexual harassment, and threats of retaliation for refusing sexual advances....

Women are disproportionately impacted by patterns of violence with the garment supply chain because they make up the vast majority of garment workers. In Bangladesh, Cambodia, and Indonesia, women workers represent between 80 and 95% of the garment workforce....

Despite their numerical majority within the garment sector, women workers remain within low skill level employment and rarely reach leadership positions in their factories and unions....

Forms of sexual harassment documented in this study include sexual comments and advances, inappropriate touching, pinching and bodily contact initiated by both managers and male co-workers....

Workers reported ongoing verbal abuse and frequent threats and physical violence....

... [L]ack of access to adequate reproductive and maternal health services [also] is a significant issue. As early as 2012, workers organizations in Cambodia began reporting that pregnant women were regularly threatened with dismissal from garment manufacturing jobs.[4]

---

[4] Global Gender Based Violence in the Walmart Garment Supply Chain, Workers Voices from the Global Supply Chain: A Report to the ILO 2018, Asia Floor Wage Alliance, CENTRAL Cambodia, & Global Labor Justice (May 2018), www.globallaborjustice.org/wp-content/uploads/2018/05/GBV-Walmart-25-May-2018.pdf.

Why, in this context, do you think the report was released publicly prior to negotiations for the GBVH convention? Did the understanding of context enable advocates to better provide effective technical assistance or advocacy perspective, enhance worker stories, or help workers leverage their positions?

10.2 THREE-LAYERED GOALS ARE GEARED TO THREE RECURRENT ADVOCACY SCENARIOS

Mapping the context for cause lawyering in the late 20th century United States, Calmore writes as one of many practitioners and scholars who helped to formulate Approaches to systemic advocacy. Systemic injustice and struggles against it, however, know no borders. We thus turn to another example, by legal scholar Lucie White, drawn from advocacy in a "different" systemic context: South Africa late in the 20th century. Note that in this context, even formal equality does not exist; but antisubordination values do. And notice again the centrality of identities, groups, interests, and power to struggle with and through law toward justice.

White deconstructs three advocacy scenarios to outline the relationship among contexts, advocacy, and goals. Employing terms like "dimensions" or "images" and "visions," White's three practice scenarios correspond roughly to the three layers of systemic advocacy goals. These three likely kinds of scenarios are: (1) an individual (or series of individuals) seeking amelioration, (2) an already-organized group that needs support in responding to collective problems, and (3) group or community members who need help to form or strengthen their collective consciousness and strategic understandings of social problems and solutions. The core question that remains constant across scenarios or dimensions is *how best to advance the three layers of goals that add up to social transformation?*

In the first of White's dimensions, the image or vision of lawyering is focused on the pursuit of ameliorative legal assistance for individual clients. These may be individual court-centered remedies or transactional solutions, like assisting with individual entity formation documents or contracts. In this first dimension, lawyers usually are not engaging more broadly the systemic social ills of caste; this reflects both the constraints of traditional legal education and the response-focused priorities of most sites of practice. In this first recurrent scenario—perhaps the most common—lawyering provides essential immediate services to vulnerable populations; systemic advocacy does not reject but rather aims to reinforce and expand the gains of this work.

In the second dimension of advocacy, the image or vision of lawyering expands to include systemic analysis of group domination and *systemic* solutions based on existing and potential collective capacities. Advocacy work here combines adjudicatory strategies with democratic strategies that allow groups and individuals to intervene in decision making, put pressure on targeted decision makers, and ultimately affect decisions through the exercise of collective power.

In the third recurrent advocacy scenario, the image or vision of lawyering expands even further to "stimulate" new sources of group consciousness for long-term collective struggle: lawyers work with individuals not only on remedies to existing problems and with groups on strengthening group capacities to act in both adjudicatory and democratic settings, but also with individuals and groups to catalyze a critical collective self-awareness. Such collective identity and analysis can help those individuals and groups mobilize themselves to sustain groups and coalitions over long periods of time. Client-groups, formed or strengthened through this collective conscious-raising and analysis, can redefine problems and solutions for themselves. They then can inject these redefinitions and cultural resources into broader society through legal and extralegal action.

White's three "dimensions" effectively present three kinds of recurrent practice scenarios that may exist within any given context. The account below, in conjunction with Calmore's above, provides a basic conceptual framework to guide self-aware choices and three-layered practices in any given context. This framework of three recurrent practice scenarios hinges on one threshold, on-the-ground question: does any organized effort already exist in that context to solve the systemic problem you are facing?

Self awareness of your practice scenario is crucial to sound advocacy: as the advocacy project template in Part III shows, project design and execution require knowledge of individuals and groups contextually relevant to solving the problem. Whether or not organized groups already exist is always a threshold question, which can help determine the structure of your advocacy. This question is a threshold consideration in every context precisely because all else follows from its answering.

In the first scenario (or dimension) the solution involves only truly individual remedies that do not require a collective mobilization, and thus tend to focus on first-layer advocacy and goals. In the second scenario (or dimension)—perhaps the ideal one for systemic advocacy—collective consciousness and organized actions already exist, allowing advocates to focus on supporting power-building and culture-shifting work. In the third practice scenario (or dimension)—perhaps the most challenging one for systemic advocacy—no collective consciousness and organized actions to remedy persistent group problems yet exist, requiring advocates to focus at least initially on sparking and spreading consciousness and action. In practice—in context—these recurrent scenarios may overlap, or morph over time. Most importantly, advocates assess every context to work effectively within and across its practice scenarios (or dimensions) simultaneously, as well as for the long run.

Not surprisingly, these three recurrent practice scenarios also reflect the three-layered goals of systemic advocacy that track—but simplify—the notions that Lucie White elaborates below. These layers (and practice scenarios) clearly overlap and, depending on context, may be less or more viable or useful to particular advocates and groups. Second- and third-layer goals can be imagined distinctly but in practice are interrelated: building power allows for culture shifting, and culture shifting builds power. As a template, these dimensions (or scenarios) provide a field-ready checklist for application in varied contexts that draws on both historical and current experience.

White's excerpt presents a compelling picture of advocacy to nurture and support community opposition against the stark practices of legally justified dispossession in South Africa under its apartheid regime. White recounts the story of community-based advocacy in a particular context: work carried out during 1982–85 in a small South African farming town, addressing a mass eviction and group displacement. The work included gathering and analyzing background information on the people, the problem, the history, and the laws. Community members, an organizer, and lawyers worked together to confront a daunting social problem. As White recounts the experience, we can see how the organizers, advocates, and activists operate on each of the three dimensions of struggle, or across the three practice scenarios, that she defines. In this contextual account of identity-based systemic injustice, we can appreciate how both injustice and struggles against it connect the micro and macro with the symbolic and the material. Notice that White, like Calmore, explains the systemic context in complex ways tracking identities, groups, interests, and power in specific locales. She shows how critical, bottom-up understandings of problems, advocacy, and solutions can provide an entry point for advocacy projects within a pre-existing context *and* (at least one) scenario. Note how advocates and organizers work collaboratively with organized communities along all three layers of transformative progress.

TO LEARN AND TEACH: LESSONS FROM DRIEFONTEIN ON LAWYERING AND POWER

Lucie E. White
1988 Wis. L. Rev. 699 (1988)

Introduction

On August 26, 1985, the South African government announced that it would not force the residents—all of them Black—of a small farming community called Driefontein to relocate to resettlement camps in remote rural areas. Rather, the government acceded to the villagers' demands that they be allowed to continue living, farming, and owning land in a region of the country that had been officially designated as the exclusive domain of whites. The reprieve for Driefontein came just a month after the government had placed a large part of the country under a "state of emergency," tantamount to martial law, in an aggressive effort to quell anti-apartheid activism in Black communities. In the context of these emergency regulations and the heightened repression that they signaled, the government's backing down on the Driefontein removal was hard to comprehend. It did not fit within the overall pattern of events in South Africa at the time. What could have compelled the government to give in, at that time, to a few isolated Blacks on an issue as central to the logic of apartheid as Black ownership and occupancy of land? . . .

A Case Study of Change-Oriented Lawyering

The Political Setting

The forced removal of Blacks from "white-designated" areas has been a recurrent practice in South Africa since whites first colonized the region in the mid-seventeenth century. However, since the Nationalist regime came to power in 1948, forced removal has become a central feature of the state's political and economic policy. To understand the significance of removal, it must be located within the broader system of apartheid.

Apartheid was the political platform of the conservative Nationalist Party, which came to power after World War II. The literal meaning of the term in Afrikaans is "separatehood." The apartheid program was grounded in an ideology of Afrikaner nationalism and racial superiority. Under the apartheid order, the government consolidated existing racial laws and added new ones to create a unified system of racial subjugation.

Under apartheid, the South African government classifies the population into four main racial groups: whites, people of mixed race (called "coloureds"), Indians, and Blacks. Blacks are then subdivided into a multitude of ethnic sub-groups. The government reserves a tract of land in a remote rural area for each group. The total land area which is set aside for the Black population is a mere thirteen percent of the total land area of South Africa, even though Blacks comprise over seventy percent of the country's total population. With a few exceptions, these tracts are located in dry, infertile areas, poorly suited for farming or economic development. . . .

The government assigns each Black person in South Africa to a homeland on the basis of their family's dialect and regional background. Under the original scheme of apartheid, each tract was eventually to be granted nominal political "independence." In theory, as each homeland was granted this status, the South African government would withdraw South African citizenship from Blacks assigned to it. According to the official fiction, the people of the homeland would then belong to a Black nation where they would have the opportunity to develop their political and cultural autonomy.

In reality, this "independence" was a sham. Rather than liberating Blacks from white rule, it greatly increased their subordination. Not only did the homeland policy effectively deprive Blacks of their political rights in South Africa, it also rationalized the withdrawal of government benefits and services from Black communities. By isolating much of the Black population in rural slums, the homeland scheme greatly hampered Blacks' efforts to join together to seek their civil and political rights. . . .

The fiction of the independent homelands has an economic, as well as an ideological, function. The homelands were established in the geographic regions that provide the least potential for agricultural or industrial development. . . . Almost all of the jobs available to Blacks in South Africa are in [faraway] white areas. Thus, most employed Blacks work and live in white areas for most of the year. They spend no more than a few weeks per year in their assigned homelands.

. . . [T]he homelands are populated by the surplus labor pool and the unemployable. Wages for Blacks in South Africa are very low. Yet employed Blacks typically share their paychecks with several family members back in the homelands—spouses, children, elders, the disabled, the able-bodied but unemployed. . . .

The arrangement gives several short-term benefits to the dominant white economy. First, Blacks that are lucky enough to find employment in white areas are very vulnerable to the power of their employers. With no political status and, in many cases, no right of occupancy in white areas except by virtue of their jobs, they face a very high risk when they take action to protest low wages or unsafe working conditions. Thus, employers have been able to pay these workers sub-minimal wages—insufficient to provide subsistence to themselves and their families—without fear of significant labor unrest. . . .

Furthermore, the homeland structure isolates the poverty that is the consequence of apartheid. The remote rural tracts where the poverty comes to rest are far removed from the view of whites, who hold exclusive political power. [This isolation serves the] strategic function of protecting the white community from the dangers which such poverty breeds—risks like cholera epidemics and political resistance. The homelands have become huge rural detention camps, where the unemployed and unemployable Black people in South Africa are confined.

. . . For most of South Africa's colonial history, Blacks have not been permitted to acquire title to land in white areas. However, during a short period of time between 1905 and 1913, this restriction was relaxed, and Blacks were allowed to acquire freehold title to land. During this window of time, a number of small Black farming communities were established.... In 1913, the government passed a Land Act which once again prohibited Blacks from acquiring land in white areas. A subsequent statute designated those areas in which Blacks could legally reside. As a result of these laws, the freehold communities that had spring up between 1905 and 1913 became a legal anomaly.

When the Nationalist government established the formal scheme of apartheid in 1948, the Black farming communities became a major problem. First, they were an ideological embarrassment. Under apartheid, Blacks were not to have any civil or political rights in white areas; yet Black farming communities were flourishing throughout these regions. Second, the communities were a security threat, since they provided refuge for Blacks throughout white-controlled rural areas. Finally, these villages occupied some of the most agriculturally and minerally rich lands in South Africa. The government felt pressure from white interests to open up these lands for white settlement.

To create a public image that these communities were a blight that needed to be eradicated, the government began referring to them as "Black spots." By 1960, it began in earnest the project of systematically confiscating these lands and removing their owners and occupants to the "native reserves."...

The South African legal system is such that it was not difficult for the government to implement these policies within the framework of its law. The constitution contains no proclamation of fundamental political rights and provides for no judicial review of statutes. Rather, the legal system is grounded in an extreme legal positivism in which Acts of Parliament cannot be legally questioned so long as they are deemed procedurally regular, regardless of their content or consequences. Parliament enacted statutes to control the most intimate aspects of Black people's lives, including their residence, personal movement, employment, political expression, and sexuality. This web of apartheid statutes stands as one of the most intricate systems ever devised for controlling the details of personal action through a "rule of law."

Forced removal is authorized under South African law in a series of statutes, all of them properly enacted according to the rules of the all-white Parliament....

... As information about the government's overall removal scheme has spread in rural areas and the political cost of forced removal has increased, the government has developed new methods to cut villagers' ties to their homes and to orient them toward the homeland relocation sites. The government will inflame social conflict in the village—between landowners and tenants or squatters, between headmen and ordinary citizens, between women and men. It will give the most powerful villagers concrete incentives to move, thereby isolating the powerless so that they must resist by themselves. The government will also disrupt village life by breaking up community meetings, cutting off community services, banning self-help projects. It may even instigate physical attacks on individuals who appear to be stirring up resistance. One common tactic to "persuade" villagers to relocate is to require them to go to the homelands to claim their unemployment or pension benefits. But perhaps the most effective means of wearing down a community's resistance is simply drawing out the process indefinitely. . . .

For the first twenty years of the Nationalist regime, the government executed removals with silent efficiency. By targeting one community at a time, the government kept the public—both Black and white—from comprehending the scope of its overall plan. . . . [But] the white progressive community has become increasingly active in opposing the government's removal program. This activism has taken several forms. First, a major effort to document and monitor removals was launched. Second, progressive lawyers began offering legal representation to communities under threat of removal. And third, the Black Sash [a white-women-led anti-apartheid resistance] set up regional projects to give organizational assistance to these communities. All of these initiatives brought the pattern of removals to the attention of the press and the international community.

With these developments, communities under threat of removal began to find material and ideological support for resistance. Villagers began to oppose the government's removal plans. They began to hire lawyers, engage organizers, share information, and rebel when the trucks arrived. In some areas, villages even began to coordinate their resistance efforts. The political costs of removals to the government began to rise. Finally, in February 1985, the convergence of legal and political pressures compelled the government to suspend forced removals altogether. . . . In this context, the story of Driefontein's resistance unfolds.

Driefontein Challenges the Government

The Conflict Takes Shape

Driefontein is a farming village of roughly 10,000 residents. It is located in a dry but fertile area of the Eastern Transvaal southeast of Johannesburg. . . .

The village was founded in an act of resistance against white rule. In 1912, just one year before the enactment of the Land Act that forbade Blacks from purchasing land in white areas, Pixley ka Isaka Seme, a founding member of the African National Congress, organized a company called the Native Farmers' Association to purchase land for resale to Blacks who did not have the money to buy land for themselves. This company purchased the farm which is now the village of Driefontein.

... No action was taken against the village until the early 1960s, when the government informed Driefontein's landowners of its intention to remove them. The threatened removal did not become imminent until the late 1970s, when the government stepped up its policy of eliminating "Black spots."

By the early 1980s, a few prosperous residents, acting through the village's Community Council, began to voice opposition to the proposed removal. . . .

. . . [A] letter from the Deputy Minister of Development and Land Affairs gave . . . implausible assurances:

> [T]he removal and relocation of so-called "Black spots," or poorly situated areas, is carried out in accordance with a policy which has as its goal the improvement of the standard of life of all people of South Africa. You will therefore appreciate that it sometimes becomes necessary for people to be encouraged to move for their own ultimate good.

These claims were so patently insulting to even the least politicized villagers that they had the effect of mobilizing more people into the resistance effort.

The letter went on to commit the government to a position that would ultimately give the villagers a strategy for challenging the removal:

> In regard to your reference to forced resettlements I must emphasize that it is certainly not part of declared policy that people should be forced to move and be resettled elsewhere without due consideration of their residential and other rights, nor that they should be exposed to hardship. In your particular case the reason for your resettlement has been discussed with you and your Board on various occasions. It was pointed out to you that the Department of Water Affairs is building a dam which is of national importance, on the Assegaai River and which will on completion towards the end of 1982, inundate some of your properties.

Thus, . . . the government took the position that the Driefontein removal was not part of its ideological agenda of confining the country's Black population within the homelands. It was rather the entirely innocent consequence of the construction of a dam. . . .

. . . On Easter weekend of 1983, an event occurred which dramatically influenced the course of the villagers' resistance. A white policeman shot and killed Saul Mkhize [a village leader] during a community meeting about the removal at the Driefontein school. The official explanation of the killing was that it was in response to a riot. Eyewitnesses contradicted this report, stating that the shooting had been unprovoked. . . .

The event had a profound effect on the villagers. Getting together to protest, in itself, had given them some power. They were already viewed as a threat by the government; it had resorted to violence to defend against them.

The event had further significance as well. First, it led several community leaders to work closely with lawyers to make the government pay for its violence. This negotiation was successful, in spite of the villagers' apparent lack of power, only because they used every possible circumstance to their advantage. . . . Finally, the Black Sash and the anti-removal coalition successfully used Mkhize's murder to focus international attention on Driefontein. The threat of more such publicity would give the community a crucial source of leverage in future maneuvers against the government.

The Lawyer and Organizer Get Involved

Before his murder, Saul Mkhize and other village leaders had contacted a lawyer to help them resist the removal. This was a surprising step for them to take; it was outside of the cultural experience of most of Driefontein's people to look to lawyers for help. . . . But Saul Mkhize was experienced in the politics of white people; he had dealt with lawyers before. In his words, the community's struggle only became "really serious when the lawyers were invited in." His experience had taught him that the community, and not the lawyers, should issue the invitation. Ironically, one of the first legal issues that the lawyers handled for Driefontein was the tort action against the government for Saul Mkhize's death.

. . . Soon after the lawyer started working with the villagers, they recruited a second outsider, a young Afrikaner with organizing credentials and ties to the Transvaal Rural Action Committee and the Black Sash. Perhaps it was out of desperation, but the villagers appeared ready to test out these whites, to see if the actions of these outsiders might dispel the disabling power that their status itself—their race and class privilege and their professional identity—would carry with it.

The situation presented the outsiders with two different challenges. First, the community had few formal legal protections against the removal. If it was to prevail against the government, it had to discover power for itself in the government's political vulnerability. This task would require imagination, rather than routine competence. . . .

The second challenge came from the social geography of the community. A few villagers were very experienced politically. They were clear on their goals and eager to confront the state. The large majority of the population, however, was not yet mobilized. Many of these people did not own land in Driefontein. Most could not read. None were experienced at bargaining with government officials. These people were likely to agree to the removal if the government threatened force or promised them some security at the relocation site.

From their previous experience, the outsiders expected that the government would try to isolate the landowners and long-time political activists from "rank and file" villagers. Once the village had split, the government could make the removal happen without any dramatic deployment of force. Therefore, to defeat the removal, the outsiders had to help mobilize the less well-off villagers and build unity between them and the elite. They made the judgment that those villagers who were silent were expressing fear, rather than informed aloofness. And they made the hard decision to question that silence, rather than to respect it.

Fortunately for the villagers, the lawyer and organizer got on very well together. They shared the same basic outlook toward their work. But they had different skills and different work schedules and soon took up different tasks. The lawyer came to the village every few weeks on an irregular schedule. He spent most of his time with a small group of veteran activists, searching with them for strategies to impede the removal process. These villagers frequently went to Johannesburg to meet with him in his office. His focus was on helping this group learn how to strategize and negotiate. He also helped them plan public meetings that brought other villagers into the strategizing process.

The organizer spent much more time in the village. She came regularly, every couple of weeks for over two years. She began working with Saul Mkhize's widow, Beauty, who had become the de facto leader of the community after his death. Mrs. Mkhize, with several other women, had taken on the task of bringing new villagers into the resistance effort and building unity among the different groups within the community.

The organizer's work went slowly, but over time, she became a close friend of the women she worked with. She also got to know other villagers who were not involved in the resistance. She did this by simply walking the paths, visiting people in their homes, and talking. She was fluent in their languages and seemed to share their sense of humor. In the way she talked to them, she made it plain that she respected them and that she liked their company. Gradually, some grew to like her, and perhaps even to trust her as well, in spite of her Afrikaner accent and fair skin.

Her casual give-and-take style got people thinking and talking about the problem. In their conversations, the villagers asked the organizer a lot of questions, and sometimes ventured their own opinions. After she left, they would keep on talking among themselves, spreading awareness through their different social networks.

Although her work did not yield many tangible results, it felt rewarding to her—not because she recruited new people to a cause, but because her work connected her to many different villagers and changed how she imagined their joint project. From these many days of just talking, she sensed the complex social patterns within the village. . . . [And] her talk with them became more balanced. She spent less time probing for people's concerns or lecturing at them, and more time in give and take, in a mutual project of naming and understanding a very hard problem.

From the organizer, the villagers learned about the laws that authorized removals and how those laws had come to be written. They learned about the international concern for their plight and condemnation of the government's removal policy. They also learned about other villages that were threatened with removal. . . .

At the organizer's suggestion, a group of women contacted some of these other threatened communities and started a support network among them. Journalists and human rights advocates from Europe and the United States visited the village. . . .

As the villagers learned more about the removal, its "legality" under South African law became less of an obstacle to their activism. Their own conversations showed them that they had the collective power to reason about justice. The organizer showed them that most of the world shared their analysis. These two experiences broke whatever force that South African law still had in their minds and let them ground their own search for justice outside of that system.

Thus, the villagers' informal conversations with the organizer and each other about the removal were a first step in the freeing of their own consciousness from domination by the white regime. As they better understood what the government was doing to them and dared to name those actions as unjust, they gained confidence in their own perspectives, their own voices. With that new confidence came the power to imagine new actions that they could take against the removal. As they began to set their own agenda, the organizer did less teaching in the conventional sense; she spent less of her time bringing information to them from the outside. Instead, she spent more time helping them carry out their ideas.

For example, . . . the villagers created two community projects, a health clinic and a legal clinic. Their immediate goal was to replace some of the services that the government had withdrawn since announcing the removal. At the same time, they hoped that by setting up the clinics they would draw others into community life and learn how to work together more effectively. The organizer helped them coordinate their own work and brought in resources from the outside. . . .

. . . Like the health clinic, [the legal clinic] was very modest in its design. A group of about five women formed a coordinating committee. With help from the organizer and TRAC [a South African non-profit], they got a group of Johannesburg lawyers to come to Driefontein on a rotating basis each month and to follow up on the cases they began at the village.

These lawyers did not necessarily know the villagers' language or culture. Each lawyer would come to Driefontein for the clinic only once or twice in a six month period.

Initially, the committee members would walk through the village each month to find out who needed help.... Although the clinic would occasionally take private disputes, the committee gave priority to claims against the government. They did this because they wanted the community to use the clinic experience to learn how to stand up against the state.

Each month the committee would select eighty to a hundred cases for the visiting lawyer to handle. The most common involved the termination of unemployment or pension benefits—which the government promised it would reinstate when villagers moved to homeland resettlement camps—pass-law violations, wrongful arrest or assault by the police, and inadequate medical care in state-run hospitals.

... Each client would explain her problem. Then the whole group—organizer, committee members, and other waiting clients—would discuss the problem with her. They would express sympathy, recall similar cases from the past, and consider the actions that the client might take. It was the volunteer lawyer's presence that brought villagers together on these occasions and focused their attention on their many particular disputes with the government. But because most of the volunteer lawyers could not speak Zulu, they could not really take part in this discussion. This language barrier actually served an essential function; it ensured that villagers would think together about their problems, rather than simply handing them over to a lawyer to be solved.

Eventually the organizer would sum up what people had said. The lawyer would listen and then explain what she might be able to do about the problem within the month. The clients would then discuss the lawyer's proposal and what they could do themselves on the case during the month. Often this was simply to look after the client as best they could while the lawyer tracked down a missing pension check. Sometimes, though, villagers could help in other ways. They might help the client document some essential fact or gather other instances of the same problem for the lawyer to use in arguing the client's case. Those clients who needed to apply for unemployment or pension benefits were then called together in one area. Several literate villagers then helped them fill out the proper applications....

... [The clinic gave] villagers a place to look at their private problems together. Through the clinic, they saw that those individual problems assumed strikingly common patterns, and they were able to take at least some joint actions to respond to them.

While the organizer's work focused on projects for building collective skill and confidence, the lawyer helped villagers figure out maneuvers for fighting the removal. A committee of villagers volunteered to work with the lawyer. They would go to Johannesburg every few weeks to meet with the lawyer to plan strategy. They soon realized that they did not have any plausible statutory arguments for blocking the removal.... Their only option was to negotiate. If they reached an impasse, their best alternative would be violent resistance.

Even though the alternatives were grim, the villagers had some prospects for leveraging power within the negotiation process. Saul Mkhize's death and the subsequent lawsuit were an embarrassment to the government. The press used the incident to focus attention on forced removals and the growing resistance to them. To curtail further damage, the government paid off the Mkhize family's claim. The committee knew that Pretoria would not want any further public attention focused on Driefontein.

... The critics of apartheid, both inside and outside the country, viewed forced removals as perhaps the most offensive policy of the apartheid government. Especially in light of mortality statistics in the homelands, removals were compared to the practices of the Nazi regime. When the Mogopa community was loaded into trucks at gunpoint in June 1983, the world press ... reacted quickly and with outrage. In response to the uproar, the government issued a statement that forced removals for ideological reasons would be suspended.

As early as 1981, the government had tried to minimize adverse publicity over the Driefontein removal by blaming it on the Heyshope Dam. This dam was indeed under construction, but villagers considered it a pretext for what was clearly an ideological removal. Nevertheless, the community's legal committee made a strategic decision to take the dam seriously. They reasoned that if they could pin down how much of their land would be flooded, they could look for replacement land in the Driefontein area. If they found such land, the government—according to its own logic—would have no need to banish them to a homeland. In order to go forward with the removal, the government would have to admit that the dam story had, indeed, disguised another ideological removal. By focusing on the dam, the villagers were bargaining that in the tense international situation, the government would rather give up on the Driefontein removal than make this admission.

With the lawyer's help, the committee learned that a relatively small portion of their land would be flooded by the dam. They then discovered that the government owned some unoccupied land near Driefontein that was about the same size as the portion that would be flooded. Apartheid policy prevented the government from transferring land to Blacks in white areas. Urging an exception to this policy, the villagers proposed that the government give them this land, rather than the proposed resettlement camp at Oshoek, in compensation for the land they would lose. They supported their claim with documentation that the proposed resettlement area was not equivalent in quality to Driefontein and therefore would not be acceptable under the law....

The government was not prepared for Driefontein's proposal. It studied its maps and finally announced that the village's plan would not work because the government land was too small to fully replace the land that would be submerged by the dam. The committee was encouraged by this response because it meant that the government was meeting their proposal on its own terms.... The government's response only dug it deeper into its dam rhetoric, which was where the committee wanted it to get stuck.

With renewed energy, the community went back to its own maps. They discovered, in addition to the government land a large tract of vacant land owned by the Barlow-Rand Corporation. Barlow-Rand is one of the country's largest industrial conglomerates. In response to unrest within the country and political pressure from without, Barlow-Rand and similar firms support reform in the apartheid system. They consider the homeland scheme an evasion of the central political dilemma of the Black franchise. They also regard it as economically irrational, both because it thwarts their demand for skilled Black labor and stable Black consumers in the urban areas and because it is their corporate profits that are financing it.... There was a chance that Barlow-Rand might be willing to do business with the villagers over a small tract of land.

Until this point, the legal committee had taken the lead in the negotiations.... At this moment, however, they turned to the lawyer. Unlike them, he had a place in the white power structure. They asked him to use that connection to their advantage.

The lawyer happened to be an old acquaintance of one of Barlow-Rand's executives. On behalf of the villagers, he called his old friend and asked if Barlow-Rand might make some of its land available to the villagers. After some persuasion, Barlow-Rand agreed to donate the land to them. The villagers went back to the government with their new proposal. In view of the intense political pressure that Pretoria was under as the unrest intensified, the government could not afford to balk on the proposal.... [T]he government, on August 26, 1985, accepted the proposal. In announcing the settlement, the government and Barlow-Rand took equal credit....

In spite of the government's effort to use Driefontein to enhance its own legitimacy, the villagers won important material and symbolic victories. First, they managed to keep their homes and even to gain some new land in a white area. This unprecedented result undermined the scheme of apartheid in a small way. At the same time, the government's power to carry out removals was weakened. In spite of its formal legal authority and military power, the government chose not to proceed with the removal of Driefontein. The political costs had become too high. . . .

The villagers' victory may not have ended the era of forced removals, but the work they did to achieve their reprieve undermined apartheid in another way. . . . When [rural] communities mobilize around a threatened removal, the social and geographic base of the anti-apartheid movement expands.

How the Outsiders Viewed Their Work

I turn now to the lawyer and organizer, with the risk that this focus might distort their role in Driefontein's resistance, giving them a more central place than they are due. . . . What, then, can we learn by looking more closely at how the outsiders worked with them? . . .

The Lawyer

. . . The [Legal Resources Centre] LRC is a public interest law firm with offices in the major cities of South Africa. It was founded on the model of the NAACP Legal Defense and Education Center and similar American public interest law firms. Initially, it was funded primarily by American corporate-linked foundations. As conceived by its founders, it would engage primarily in "law reform" or "test case" litigation. . . . Several of these cases achieved dramatic results. . . . But many of the specific holdings that LRC litigation established have since been nullified, either when Parliament closed a loophole in the law or when administrators continued abusive practices in spite of a court order.

Since joining the LRC, Driefontein's lawyer had worked closely with the Black Sash, serving as a back-up for the organization's Johannesburg advice center. It was through the Black Sash and the Transvaal Rural Action Committee that the lawyer became involved with removal work and the Driefontein community. . . .

Of all his work, the lawyer found removal cases particularly compelling. This was in part because he found the practice of forced removals morally indefensible. But it was also because the absence, in most of those cases, of clear legal rights and remedies put him and his clients on an equal footing, with nothing but shared imagination, determination, and luck to rely on. . . .

The lawyer explained his approach to his practice in his own writings. He viewed his role as helping the client community develop its own political power. . . . As he stated:

> Once a legal issue is presented to lawyers, as "experts" they tend to take it over. They may succeed in solving the client's immediate legal problem, but the client's position of powerlessness is

reinforced when the lawyer simply "takes over." ... Associated with this is the overwhelming power which the lawyer has in his or her relationship with the poor client. ... [I]t is very easy for the lawyer to define and present alternative forms of action so that the client is compelled to the course of action preferred by the lawyer. ... What this means is that the lawyer involved in this form of practice [working with poor communities for social change] has to be unusually sensitive to the client's perceptions of the problem. Another part of the answer is to go some way towards equalizing the relationships by ensuring that the client has more power, which in this instance means knowledge of the processes involved.

He suggested that initiatives like community-or trade union-controlled legal clinics or advice centers can help equalize this power imbalance by increasing the community's control of legal knowledge and skill. The role of the lawyer in such centers is of "professional back-up ... supplementing the work of these offices without in any way supplanting them."

The danger that the lawyer will disable the community can also be countered, in his view, by the lawyer's work style:

If [the relationship between lawyer and client] is handled with sensitivity on both sides the lawyer can fulfill a most important function in empowering community and worker groups. ... Much of the work that the organisational client will require ... is not as dramatic as major public interest litigation, but is of major importance in enabling others to act.

... In addition to the risk presented by the lawyer's personal power is the greater risk that the use of legal strategies will reinforce within the community the hegemony of the oppressor's law. As the lawyer stated the problem:

[T]he fundamental problem [with the attempt to use law as a means of resolving conflict and promoting social justice] is that inherent in this approach is the acceptance as given of a system of law which may itself be the source of the conflict and injustice. The result may be that the lawyer ends up unintentionally promoting the use of the legal system as a means of accommodating the conflict rather than promoting social justice. ... [T]he legal process may obscure the true nature of the dispute and even obstruct its just resolution.

This risk becomes greater if the lawyer routinely presents litigation to the community as its optimal strategy. Litigation may falsely raise in the community the expectation that appeal to "the law" can somehow give it power. Thus, the community may put its energy into litigation instead of into the much more difficult work of organizing itself. Instead of pushing a community into a lawsuit, the lawyer should help his clients understand the limits of litigation and challenge them to develop creative, rather than reactive, litigation strategies.

The risk that legal strategies will increase the community's ideological subjugation, rather than build its power, can only be countered if the lawyer consciously identifies himself with "ground-level organization" within the community.... The lawyer recognized that this goal "runs directly contrary to the whole ethics of professional training ... and is very difficult to do." However, in his view, the lawyer must take on this unconventional work if he genuinely seeks change.

Several themes repeat in his writings and in what he says about his work. One is the doubleness of the law. The lawyer must not encourage the community to respect unjust laws, or to rely on them. Yet he should help clients learn to use the law as a tool and to demand that it express notions of justice. Another theme is the sense of balance that the lawyer must maintain if he is to share his skill and judgment without leading clients to defer to him. Perhaps the fundamental theme in his writings is the quality of sensitivity that the lawyer must learn in order to work effectively with powerless people. He has said that all the thinking on the subject of the lawyer's role leads finally to one conclusion: "that once lawyers have recognized the limitations of their role, and learned to be just a little bit humble, there is a great deal which they can contribute."...

The Organizer

The organizer's approach to her work was similar to the lawyer's. Unlike him, she had not written about her role. But she had read widely about the sociology and history of Black South Africans and about different "schools" of community organizing. She had spent several years working in rural communities and was fluent in several African dialects.

She rejected "manipulative" or "top-down" organizing in which the organizer would determine the role for the community to play....

Driefontein's organizer saw her work, in contrast, as a slow, circular process of mutual education between herself and community members. The process, if it went well, would build a bond of trust between the organizer and the community. Gradually, the community would acquire from the organizer a wider perspective on its situation. At the same time, the community would become more confident of its own ability to analyze, choose its own strategies, make its own alliances, and build its own institutions. If she had been influenced by any method, it was that of Paulo Freire.

She felt a personal anger about the atrocities that the government sought to commit against the people of Driefontein and expressed deep respect for the community's faith and patience. Although confident of her skill as an organizer, she did not claim to have any solutions for Driefontein or for South Africa. She saw her task as helping the community understand and act against the government's subjugation.

These feelings were reflected in her work. She was extremely direct with the villagers about what she thought. She also continually challenged them to express their views. Because her respect for them was clear from her actions and because she had no pretensions of expertise, villagers quickly become comfortable joking with her and taking her on in argument....

The organizer had studied Zulu language and culture, and sought in her work to help the villagers reclaim the knowledge that still remained from that culture. She urged them to judge the government's actions according to their traditional values, rather than its laws. At the same time, though, she was outspoken about what she regarded as the oppressive features of traditional Zulu culture and challenged the women in particular to take the lead in community life.

Her method of empowering clients by helping them reclaim their own cultural identity can be clearly seen in her work with the legal clinic. She saw to it that the clinic was a place where the villagers felt culturally "at home." They did not have to be "good clients" to get help there. They did not have to listen to lawyers tell them "what the law said" about their problems. Rather, in the clinic, they improvised their own ways of acting with the professionals. They drew upon a problem-solving strategy that they used in their everyday lives, a process of "talking it out" with the family and the neighbors until the common sense of a problem became clear.

In helping the community design the clinic, the organizer tried to counter the "expertise" of the lawyers and the mystique of the law. She made certain that the clinic was conducted in the open, with village members consulting together on each case before they turned it over to the lawyer. Through this collaboration, "individual" problems, like pension and unemployment claims, were recast as collective, as political. As they listened to one person after another describe the same problem, the villagers came to see for themselves that the government's treatment of each individual fit into broader patterns which furthered the government's ultimate goal of the removal.

... The organizer's greatest skills were envisioning such projects, figuring out how each project could draw upon the community's indigenous cultural forms, and helping the villagers feel the confidence to express their own cultural knowledge in their action.

Some Reflections on Driefontein, Lawyering, and Social Change

... [Below], I specify three ideal images of change-oriented lawyering, each of them addressing a different mechanism of domination. In the first image, official channels for political expression are assumed to work for everyone. In most instances, the lawyer can work through those traditional channels. Only occasionally must the lawyer take action to unplug an episodic obstruction in them. In the second image, domination means the systematic exclusion of certain interests from traditional channels for political expression. The lawyer devises strategies that will both expose the exclusion process and give voice to the excluded claims. In the third image, the lawyer's focus expands beyond those systematic barriers to include her own clients. Recognizing that the conditions of subordination force people to suppress their own interests and discount their own power, the lawyer seeks to engage her clients in a process that will help them reclaim their power. . . .

Three Visions of How the Lawyer Promotes Change

Much has been written about "public interest," "impact," "progressive," or "social change" lawyering. There is little consensus in this literature, however, about how lawyering might help promote change. Can we identify methods of lawyering that can alter the *processes* of subordination rather than merely minister to the injuries that those processes generate? . . .

The First Image: The Contest of Litigation

The first image of lawyering corresponds to the first dimension of power. In this image, the role of the public interest lawyer is straightforward and familiar. He is charged with designing and winning lawsuits that will further the substantive interests of client groups. The lawyer "translates" client grievances into legal claims. He crafts the lawsuit so that the judicial remedy, if granted, will directly remove, or at least ameliorate, those grievances.

Within this image, the lawyer assumes that client groups perceive their suffering as injuries that can be redressed, and stand willing to share these perceptions with their lawyers. It is not the lawyer's role to question the structure of the law itself, asking whether it sometimes prevents the lawyer from translating his clients' grievances into good legal claims. Nor is it his role to question the judicial system, asking whether it sometimes prevents him from securing remedies that really work.

Rather than raise such questions, the lawyer assumes that the powerful have dominated the courts in the past because they have been the most effective at litigation. They have commanded more resources and wielded them more skillfully. The lawyer aspires to redress that imbalance. By mobilizing massive professional lawyer-power behind his clients' claims, the first-dimensional lawyer seeks to use the courts as a direct mechanism for redressing the injuries of class, race, and gender, and for redistributing power to subordinated groups.

In order to frame claims that could do justice to their clients' injuries, first-dimensional lawyers must often seek very sweeping, very innovative remedies from the courts. They must ask judges and courts to get involved in the funding, design, or management of public institutions. Yet, in litigating these unconventional cases, first-dimensional lawyers play an essentially traditional professional role.

Because the lawyer relies on the *court*, finally, to effect change, he must, first and foremost, be a good litigator. He must be creative at manipulating and extending accepted doctrine. He must assume a personal style that makes him credible to the judge. He must strive to have the other lawyers accept him as a person who plays to win, but whose ultimate loyalty is to the game itself.

In this image, the lawyer's primary foci are the adversary, the judge, and the courtroom. The client must be sufficiently acculturated to that world to be a good witness when facts are at issue. But apart from the moments when facts are contested, the client is in the background.

Public interest litigation has brought about substantial change, and continues to do so. However, in some circumstances where institutional practices are challenged, courts have difficulty fashioning effective remedies. . . .

In addition to these practical limits on the court-ordered remedy as a device for shifting social power, there is a deeper limitation in the litigation-centered approach to public interest lawyering. . . . [The lawyer] places great pressure on subordinate groups to formulate their interests in forms that the law can "process."

In order to get into court, litigants must present their claims as similar to precedent claims that courts have already accepted. In order to get relief, litigants must propose remedies that are coextensive with these confined claims and that can be feasibly administered by the courts. The result of these pressures is the oft-observed risk that litigation will co-opt social mobilization. Through the process of voicing grievances in terms to which courts can respond, social groups risk stunting their own aspiration. Eventually, they may find themselves pleading for permission to conform to the *status quo*.

The Second Image: Law as a Public Conversation

In the second image of lawyering, the lawyer acknowledges that litigation can sometimes work directly to change the allocation of social power. However, she sees these effects as secondary to law's deeper function in stimulating progressive change. In addition to generating remedies that can coerce change, litigation is also public action with political significance.

The law and its practice has cultural meaning; it constitutes a discourse about social justice.

Recall that second-dimension mechanisms work to shape political institutions and public values so that subordinated groups are excluded from asserting their interests in the official channels of political contest. Lawyers can use litigation to challenge these mechanisms of exclusion. Even when it does not succeed, well-crafted litigation can reveal the law systematically working to contain grievances. Litigants, by reformulating legal norms in light of their intuitions and experience, can project visions that expand the range of social options.

... Under the second-dimensional approach, the lawyer is not indifferent to victory in court. If a claim prevails, so much the better. But the measure of the case's success is not who wins. Rather, success is measured by such factors as whether the case widens the public imagination about right and wrong, mobilizes political action behind new social arrangements, or pressures those in power to make concessions. To accomplish these goals, the lawyer must design the case with the audience—the subordinated group and the wider public—in mind.

Within this second dimension, the lawyer must, first and foremost, be able to produce public happenings that "work." ... [T]he audience is not merely on the periphery. It becomes the focus of the lawyer's attention. The client will "win," ultimately, only if the lawyer moves the audience to action.

The lawyer must learn to read public sentiment, framing cases in which the public will readily see injustice and can be led to see that conventional legal remedies do not really right the wrong. Furthermore, the lawyer must be able to coordinate the lawsuit with any direct political action that the litigation might spark. She must support such mobilization when it arises without either diverting its energy into litigation support or confining its own demands to the legally feasible remedies. Thus, she must at the same time be fluent in the law and attuned to the feelings and beliefs of the relevant audiences.

All litigation has both direct and indirect effects. In many cases, the lawyer can seek simultaneously to persuade the judge and to mobilize the public. The two goals—of winning a legal remedy and influencing public consciousness—do not work at cross purposes. On some occasions however, typically in high visibility political trials, lawyer and client may choose to spurn the legal ground rules and sacrifice a favorable outcome precisely in order to make the litigation speak most effectively to public consciousness. It is on these occasions that the contrast between first- and second-dimensional lawyering is most dramatic.

Thus, the second-dimensional approach looks beyond judge-made remedies to group subordination and seeks to expand public consciousness about justice and mobilize direct action for change. Such an approach is needed to counter mechanisms that structure official contests to exclude certain interests. However, for all of the power of second-dimensional lawyering, it also has limits. In the second-dimension, the lawyer assumes that her clients perceive their grievances clearly and stand ready to challenge the responsible parties directly, regardless of the risks. Second-dimensional lawyering cannot respond to subordinated clients who come to them with a more guarded interpretation of their own suffering or a more realistic assessment of their options.

. . . [T]he clients that are most fully subordinated never get the second-dimensional lawyer's attention. These are the people who feel cheated but have no clear sense of who is responsible, people who describe their suffering to outsiders as their lot in life, or people who distrust the "system" and the remedial processes that it offers. Such people will not give the right answers when the well-meaning lawyer innocently asks, "What's wrong?"

The lawyer then has three choices. She can work for more assimilated groups, those who ask for help in terms that lawyers more readily understand. She can set her own priorities for social change, recruiting token clients to stand for the issues that her own political analysis has led her to pursue. Or, finally, she can take on the dangerous project of listening carefully to the answers that at first might seem "non-responsive." She can work with those groups in a joint project of translating felt experience into understandings and actions that can increase their power. This is the project of lawyering on the third dimension.

The Third Image: Lawyering Together Toward Change

If a lawyer wants to stimulate change on the level of consciousness, she has much to learn from the writings of Paulo Freire and the parallel feminist methodology of consciousness raising. Freire's work shows how an active, critical consciousness can re-emerge among oppressed groups as they reflect together about concrete injustices in their immediate world and act to challenge them. He views this liberation of consciousness as fundamentally a pedagogic process. It is an unconventional, non-hierarchical learning practice in which small groups reflect together upon the immediate conditions of their lives. The groups first search their shared reality for feelings about that reality that have previously gone unnamed. They then attempt to re-evaluate these common understandings as problems to be solved. They collectively design actions to respond to these problems and, insofar as possible, to carry them out. They then continue to reflect upon the changed reality, thereby deepening their analysis of domination and their concrete understanding of their own power.

Although the process sounds formidable, it plays out in a straight-forward, immediate way. For example, a group might discuss a simple picture of a peasant family eating corn while the landlord's family feasts on meat and vegetables. In the group's conversation, new feelings begin to emerge. Feelings of hunger, of grief for their children, of anger at the landlord, and of injury—feelings that people may not have sensed at all prior to the conversations—emerge and get confirmed. The group then explores why the landlord has so much to eat and whether landownership must be allocated as it is. At the same time, the group searches for ways to work together to increase its own supply of food.

Through this dialogic process of reflection and action, subordinated communities can, Freire contends, gradually liberate their consciousness from internalized oppression. Their private methods of surviving and resisting their common oppression can be brought to the surface and their lessons shared. Fatalism and passivity can be transformed into a common recognition of the skills that people already possess and into a shared willingness to risk change. The lawyer must learn how to engage with her clients in a conversational process of naming and critiquing their immediate reality. This process, as laborious as it may seem to the result-oriented lawyer, must be the center of a third-dimensional practice of law.

In Freire's model of learning, no one monopolizes the teacher role. Yet the outsider with professional skills does have a distinct role to play in the mutual learning practice. In the third-dimensional image, the lawyer aspires to learn this role. The outsider helps to bring people together, sets a tone in which collective learning can take place, and teaches a practice of critical reflection by leading the group through its first sessions and helping it plan its first actions. In contrast to the conventional professional, however, the outsider—the lawyer working in the third dimension—does not claim to possess privileged knowledge about politics or reality. "Dialogue, as the encounter of men addressed to the common task of learning and acting, is broken if the parties (or one of them) lack humility."

Furthermore, the outsider recognizes that the group can work effectively only to the extent that members develop trust in each other. To promote this trust, the outsider must allow the process to take its own course. As Freire expresses it, the outsider must have "an intense faith" in the human capacity of the group members to "make and remake, to create and re-create, faith in [their] vocation to be more fully human." At the same time, though, she must engage in unrelenting critique, exposing the ways that subordination distorts the human capacities of all the participants and the ways the oppressor's perspective continues to re-emerge in their midst.

In contrast to the norm of "professional distance," the outsider strives to open the norms of her profession to critique by the group. She takes the lead in questioning her own expertise and the values on which it is based and invites other group members to deepen the critique. Rather than manipulating the group to preserve her own authority, she tries to engage the group to displace her as authority, and to relocate the very concept, transformed, in their own process of conversation. This does not mean that she withholds her own judgments. Rather, she tries to speak honestly, as a person with a different experience, and to demand that her views be taken seriously in the group's practice of understanding.

Challenging subordination on the level of consciousness entails educational work in the broadest sense, working with people to engender changes in how all participants view themselves and the world. Freire gives one model for how such work might be done. It is a model that sets very high demands on all of the participants. Ultimately, these demands may prove unrealistic. I do not offer it as a prescription for the method that third-dimensional lawyers must use. Rather, it suggests one possibility for a process and transformed professional role that might make inroads into third-dimensional processes of subordination.

In addition to pedagogy, lawyering in the third dimension also includes strategic work. The lawyer must help the client-group devise concrete actions that challenge the patterns of domination that they identify. This strategizing is also a learning process. Through it, the group learns to interpret their relationship with those in power as an ongoing drama rather than as a static condition. They learn to interpret the particular configurations that the oppressor's power takes on over time and to respond to those changing patterns with pragmatism and creativity. They learn how to design context-specific acts of public resistance, which work, not by overpowering the oppressor, but by revealing the wrongness and vulnerability of its positions to itself and to a wider public.

Thus, third-dimensional lawyering involves helping a group learn how to interpret moments of domination as opportunities for resistance.... Neither the lawyer nor any single individual is positioned to know what actions the group should take at a particular moment. Sound decisions will come only as those who know the landscape and will suffer the risks deliberate together. The role of the lawyer is to help the group learn a *method* of deliberation that will lead to effective and responsible strategic action.

This image of lawyering bears little resemblance to traditional professional practice....

Why should this "third-dimensional" work be thought of as lawyering at all? It certainly can be done without an attorney's license and, indeed, without any legal training at all. Nevertheless, fluency in the law—that is, a deep practical understanding of law as a discourse for articulating norms of justice and an array of rituals for resolving social conflict—will greatly improve a person's flexibility and effectiveness at "third-dimensional" work. An understanding of law as discourse on norms will help him work with the clients to deepen their own consciousness of their injuries and their needs. Knowledge of the law's procedural rituals will give the group access to a central arena for public resistance and challenge. It is also possible, however, that professional identification as a lawyer can narrow one's strategic imagination. Perhaps the best arrangement is for lawyer-outsiders to work side by side with outsiders trained in other fields.

This third-dimensional image of lawyering may seem very remote from our conceptions of lawyering, even lawyering specifically directed toward social change....

Lawyering in Driefontein

... In Driefontein, the villagers' dilemma was not simply that court-ordered remedies would have limited effect and might therefore be *supplemented* by second- and third-dimensional strategies. Rather, legal remedies were simply not available. The forced removal of the villagers was authorized by South African law; the villagers did not have any established legal grounds on which to challenge it. Furthermore, as Blacks, the villagers could not vote. They had no voice in choosing the people who had legislated the removal policy. Thus, Driefontein presents a case in which second- and third-dimensional methods of lawyering were the only approaches available. It therefore gives a rich example of those approaches skillfully deployed.

The lawyer and the organizer took on distinct tasks as the case developed. The lawyer worked primarily with the negotiating committee and the government, devising strategies to block the removal. The organizer worked primarily with villagers, educating them about the removal threat and helping them build independent community institutions. These two efforts were not isolated from one another. Rather, the tasks of the lawyer and the organizer complemented each other in a single advocacy strategy, one that combined second- and third-dimensional approaches. As the villagers gained confidence in themselves and consolidated their community, the problem of implementing the removal became more difficult for the government. It became more likely that the villagers would move only if direct physical force was used. Similarly, as the lawyer and the organizing committee gained information and got concessions from the government, the villagers' motivation to build their community increased. Thus, the two efforts—of negotiation and community work—built upon one another. They were two aspects of a "lawyering" effort, in which no single actor occupied the "lawyer" role.

Based on the three-dimensional typology I have sketched, this effort combined "second" and "third dimensional" strategies. In the second dimension is the villagers' work of developing and using public opinion in support of the resistance. The villagers used public [opinion] for two purposes. First, active villagers used the events generated by the public interest in the removal—the visits of outside journalists, the press clippings, the play that they produced about the removal—as occasions to motivate their neighbors to get involved in the community building activities. Second, public opinion, both within South Africa and throughout the world, was a central source of leverage that the villagers had against the government....

Public opinion—the audience—became a significant source of power to the villagers only because it was cultivated, consciously, through the lawyering effort. The outsiders—the lawyer and the organizer—were indispensable to this effort; they had the connections to the internal and international press, and they knew the psychology of the white world. Yet the villagers themselves gave the accounts that resonated so deeply in the conscience of the "outside" world and even in some parts of the white community inside South Africa.

Although this focus on the public was central to the negotiation strategy, the primary focus of the lawyering effort was on the third dimension.... These activities include the informal conversations between the organizer and the villagers, the development of the health clinic and the legal clinic, and the strategizing work that the lawyer did jointly with the villagers and the negotiating committee. All of these activities helped the villagers understand the full measure of their own power.

The villagers in Driefontein were not victims of "false consciousness;" they never mistook the government's interests for their own. Nevertheless, for many of them life under apartheid had engendered feelings of isolation, hopelessness, and fear. The third dimension of the lawyering effort challenged those feelings. Through those activities, villagers found themselves working together effectively and successfully in their own community and against the government. As a result, the community coalesced and resolved that it would not cooperate in another "voluntary" removal.

Viewing the case as an example of third-dimensional lawyering does not dispel the questions that I have already raised.... [E]ven as we continue to contemplate these hard questions, we can take from the story an expanded sense of what lawyering might be and of how subordinated people might reclaim their own power.

Conclusion

... [T]he story of Driefontein's resistance ... envisions a practice of advocacy in which the participants—clients and lawyers, group members and outsiders—scrutinize themselves, their relationships, their adversary, their culture and institutions, in the interest of a multidimensional process of emancipation.

This practice is centered in incessant critique of the interests and values and ways of being for which the participants—both clients and lawyers—claim to stand. Every moment of conflict with the adversary becomes an occasion for insight into the stubborn processes of domination and the elusive sources of power. Such a practice must seek guidance from the participants' own conversations—their shared deliberations on what they have lived through and how they might now act together—rather than from codes or rules. These conversations will inevitably be grounded in received wisdom, in the norms that structure the very language in which we speak. Yet at the same time, perhaps paradoxically, the group's vision must not be confined by that history.

Such a practice places enormous demands on its participants. Both lawyer and client must accept, indeed invite, repeated challenge from the other; no longer are the lawyer's supposed skills or the client's claimed desires entitled to deference. Even more problematic, however, is the moral risk that attends this practice. The process simultaneously demands committed action and insists that there can be no secure, external grounding for the consequent choices that must be made.

. . . Perhaps the biggest challenge, given our culture's particular myths, is to accept that our choices are inevitably situated and inevitably ambiguous, and that our most powerful theory, in the end, may be our practice of deliberating together on our experience and our action.

White's dimensions point to three recurrent practice scenarios, which roughly correspond to the three-layered goals of systemic advocacy. This attention to contexts, scenarios, *and* layers underscores the importance of tactics and strategies that depend both on collective consciousness and on organizational capacity. Both Calmore and White thus conclude that advocates must connect and collaborate with local persons and groups: to outsmart the system's failure by design, advocates construct effective three-layered actions and solutions for a given context and scenario.

NOTES AND QUESTIONS

1. *Contexts, Scenarios, and Layers.* Calmore presents "context" as a fluid, complex intersection of identities, groups, interests, and power in a particular place and time. In this sense, every context is unique in some ways, even though it also likely shares some commonalities with other, similar contexts. White then presents three recurrent kinds of practice scenarios focused on the existence (or not) of organized groups in a given context. These three scenarios (or dimensions) track the three-layered goals of systemic advocacy, which call for different approaches toward the same goals depending on the context and scenario: to advance and defend three-layered progress, advocates and advocacy must adjust contextually to the differences among these three recurrent kinds of scenarios. In your own words, what is the distinction between context and scenario as used by Calmore and White, respectively? Based on these materials, what is the practical relationship (if any) between

unique contexts, recurrent scenarios, and three-layered goals for systemic advocates?

2. *A Lesson in Preservation and Change.* Formal legal apartheid in South Africa was abolished in the 1990s. Yet economic equality—and health equity, in particular—was never achieved. Rather, as one Black resident described the absence of material gains from the time of apartheid to the present, "I've gone from a shack to a shack."[5] South Africa is suffering "the largest AIDS epidemic in the world—20 percent of all people living with HIV are in South Africa, and 20 percent of new HIV infections occur there, too."[6] This is a legacy both of the racial caste system entrenched through apartheid and the post-apartheid imposition of neoliberal "reforms" by international organizations, like the International Monetary fund, that have limited redistribution of resources and systemic reforms.[7] This legacy raises questions about preservation and transformation similar to those we encountered in the United States throughout Parts I and II.

Yet three-dimensional struggle has continued, changed, and grown, too. Roughly 25 years after White wrote this article, Hassan Ahmad, a practicing attorney from Canada, spent a summer in the Khayelitsha township in Cape Town, South Africa, assisting individuals discriminated against because of their HIV/AIDS status. He worked with the Treatment Action Campaign (TAC), a nonprofit that aims to expand equitable access to quality healthcare and economic stability for those living with HIV/AIDS. TAC has raised legal claims to assist marginalized groups—helping women gain access to medications in hospitals so their newborns would not be infected and pressing for treatment for prison inmates with HIV. These claims used existing legal procedures—"established avenues in attempting to rectify an injustice."

TAC also helped marginalized groups organize to contest systemic barriers to political participation and contestation, such as "explicit legal exclusions, a threat of retaliation, institutional restrictions," or others. For example, TAC organized the Defiance Campaign to pressure decision makers to end "the superiority of private health care in South Africa, which attracts more doctors and public funding to sustain advanced facilities that cater to the wealthy" and supports the "perpetuation of racial and ethnic inequalities remaining from the apartheid era." The third dimension of lawyering emerged because, Ahmad asserts, the HIV epidemic, coming on the heels of apartheid's end, "left the poor majority who rely on the public system [of healthcare] psychologically defeated and apathetic to its position vis-à-vis the private system, which was mainly utilized by the minority white population during

---

[5] Peter S. Goodman, End of Apartheid in South Africa? Not in Economic Terms, N.Y. Times (Oct. 24, 2017), www.nytimes.com/2017/10/24/business/south-africa-economy-apartheid.html.

[6] Sara M. Allinder and Janet Fleischman, The World's Largest HIV Epidemic in Crisis: HIV in South Africa, Center for Strategic and International Studies: Commentary (Apr. 2, 2019), www.csis.org/analysis/worlds-largest-hiv-epidemic-crisis-hiv-south-africa.

[7] Victoria Scrubb, Political Systems and Health Inequity: Connecting the Apartheid Policies to the HIV/AIDS Epidemic in South Africa, J. of Global Health (Apr. 1, 2011), https://journals.library.columbia.edu/index.php/jgh/article/view/4925/3043.

and after apartheid." TAC created discussions and education programs "at a grassroots level about citizens' legal rights and methods in which to mobilize to cause social change [which] has sparked a reflective process, especially within rural townships." Moreover, TAC created a team of Literacy and Treatment Program volunteers, all local residents of Khayelitsha, who lead discussions and workshops on safe sex practices and other topics: "TAC's grassroots strategy has empowered their volunteers to consider their work with a sense of responsibility and ownership. . . . TAC's approach, which allows communities to forge solutions for themselves . . . is promoting sustainable social progress already manifesting in greater mobilization, confidence, entrepreneurship and higher standards of living." More recently, TAC has expanded this work, creating "Ritshidze—a community-led monitoring system developed by organisations representing people living with HIV," including TAC, the Positive Women's Network, and others.[8]

Does TAC's work reflect attention to all three layers of goals? How, if at all, does this work advance micro-macro justice? In your view, does this example show both preservation through transformation, as well as the importance of three-layered advocacy?

3. *Reflecting on Unlearning and Relearning.* Do the White and Calmore excerpts point out anything about law and justice that causes you to rethink— to unlearn and relearn—some of your ideas or understandings on the Critical Challenge of using law for justice? How do these specific points of unlearning-relearning affect your understanding of law practice today? Describe how these insights and thoughts in turn might make a concrete difference in your conception and execution of an advocacy project.

4. *Reflecting on Relevance in Context.* Generally, relevance is defined in law as anything probative on at least one of the issues a legal case or controversy presents; probative means tending to prove or disprove a particular claim about that issue. More simply, legal relevance purports to welcome any information likely to shed light on the problems in controversy. As applied, however, relevance is narrowed by related legal notions that view individualized instances of systemic problems as atomized, or separated from, each other and from their actual systemic context; legal relevance is shaped by individualism. As a result, *legal* relevance excludes much that is of *actual* relevance to systemic justice and advocacy. How are notions of context and "relevance" connected? What do Calmore's points about context and White's layered scenarios add to your understanding? Recognizing that defining relevance is related to defining contexts can help advocates expand and focus the scope of research necessary for three-layered goals, as we will see in Part V.

---

[8] www.tac.org.za/campaigns/ritshidze/.

10.3 SECOND-LAYER GOALS COMBINE PERSUASION AND PRESSURE TO BUILD AND EXERCISE POWER

In Part II, we defined power, for this book's purposes, as the ability to obtain desired outcomes. Organized groups aim to build that sort of power—the power to either persuade or pressure decision makers to deliver the desired decisions. Group power is built through developing internal capacities and qualities—measured in terms of internal growth through membership numbers, financial and other resources, and other gains—and also in terms of capacities, both individual and collective—measured in terms of skills at outreach or speaking to the press or managing phone banks or direct actions at an individual level. Group power or strength also can be measured more generally in terms of group organizing, research, legal/policy, education, communications, fundraising, and mobilization capacities. Measures of growth and capacity building help advocates evaluate the organizational strengths that can be deployed to move external decision makers in specific contexts.

The sorts of growth and capacities that make an organization stronger will vary according to what sort of power is sought by the given group in the given time and place—that is, according to context and scenario. Advocates and activists analyze what the group or coalition members actually would have to do to pressure elite decision makers to deliver desired change—without the need to rely solely on persuading elite institutions to agree. This bottom-line power—or social power—is what the group needs to build up and exercise.

For example, a tenants' organization may have a great lawyer who can sometimes convince a judge to force a landlord to improve conditions. The ability to identify members willing and able to bring claims and to deploy legal capacity to win such claims, at least some of the time, shows some organizational strength meaningful for a group of tenants aiming to shift power within the landlord-tenant relationship. But that sort of win depends on persuading an elite decision maker—a judge. In contrast, organized tenants who withhold rent in a collective action exercise a form of power more direct, potentially more devastating, and more immediately directed by the tenants themselves—a power that pressures or coerces decision makers without need for the support of any elite institution like a court or elected official. This collective action is pressure-based power, directly exercised by the members. Organized groups always aim to develop such autonomous power.

Of course, neither the end nor the path to that end rests only on the power to persuade or only on the power to pressure directly. And many groups will never attain the size or capacities to exercise significant pressure power (which is one reason why coalitions are very important, too). In large part, that is the result of "rules of the game" that make it difficult for "average" people to build and exercise strong organized power. To build a tenants' organization capable of winning a rent strike, for example, a group would have to overcome significant barriers to forming a tenants' union, funding it for action that might include currently-illegal action, protecting it from reprisals against the members individually and the organization collectively, gaining enough members and reach to affect a significant area, and so on. So, in second-layer goal work, advocates must have a clear-eyed analysis of what power means in the context, and they must move incrementally to strengthen the organization to build needed capacities.

At the same time, advocates must resist the temptation to equate *activity* with *power*. All organizational power is based on having the muscles for activity, but not all activity is power building—and some even distracts or weakens organizations. Advocates measure their work, develop collective strategies, and construct their roles to move client-groups closer to the relevant sorts of member-driven power needed, in context, to change material conditions—even when arriving at that power seems impossible.

Steve Jenkins, a practitioner of worker rights advocacy with both community-based groups and unions, outlines two key forms of social power: *pressure* power based on leverage to move decisions and actions, and advocacy power based on the capacity to *persuade* elite institutions like courts or government bodies. Jenkins notes that the analysis of power has to address issues that matter in context—that relate to the nature of the group's members, the problems they face, the sorts of solutions they might desire, and the decision makers they seek to convince or coerce through the group's work:

> [S]ocial struggles are shaped by the social conditions in which they are situated. . . .
>
> Oppressed people can only transcend the limitations imposed by elite decision-makers when they have the power to force the institutions they are confronting to accept their demands. I will refer to this type of power as "social power." Unlike advocacy, which is based on a group's ability to *persuade* elite institutions to take action, social power must be based in some capacity by the group itself to *coerce* the decision-maker to make the changes they seek. For example, workers have the power to disrupt the production of goods and/or services and interfere with profits. The social power of oppressed people can [include] . . . the power of tenants to withhold rent; electoral power; and the power of disruption through riots, mass demonstrations, or civil disobedience. . . .

> Social power is not an immutable quality; it is a process in development....
>
> For the creation of social power, the types of questions that must be asked are: If this group of people was organized, what power would they have against the forces that are shaping their lives? Where does their power come from? How is it developed?... Answering these questions requires a detailed understanding of the objective conditions that are operative in a certain place and time....
>
> Understanding the complex interplay between objective conditions and our own efforts to change them is the key to transforming both our organizations and society as a whole.[9]

In this view, building group power is a process in which organizers, social workers, lawyers, and other professional actors act synergistically depending on context and its practice scenarios—that is, as somewhat interchangeable professionals using the tools of their trade for internal growth and capacity-building as much as for external wins. They plan and measure their actions using indicia of growth and capacities that might include, for example, increasing membership and leadership numbers and skills, strengthening governance and decision making accountable to the bottom, developing strategic capacities in direct action or legal action or research, increasing or diversifying resources, and other measures important in context. Advocates, organizers, and activists collaboratively must use *all* the tools in their respective toolboxes to build, monitor, and exercise bottom-up group power. Jenkins, Calmore, and White all show, in describing different contexts and scenarios, how advocates must combine persuasion with pressure flexibly. These examples put on display the difference between conventional practices of the legal industry and three-layered advocacy geared to particular contexts and scenarios.

In this broadened calculus, the merit of legal action is evaluated on terms different than just whether the case or contract will conclude successfully: Will the group get bigger or gain capacities or otherwise become stronger so it can take on and win more difficult fights? Will the members be more able to directly exercise pressure to achieve desired outcomes? If not, then the legal action—no matter how meritorious in addressing deplorable conditions—might not be selected. From this perspective, the goal is not solely to "help" individual victims of oppression—although that always is valuable—but also to build organized strength that protects collective wellbeing.

Strategic decision-making is therefore not based only or chiefly on who is most "needy" but also on where organizational resources can be invested

---

[9] Steve Jenkins, Organizing, Advocacy, and Member Power: A Critical Reflection, 6 WorkingUSA 56 (2002).

to obtain the greatest power boost. This view—that advocates must take client-group power building into account—may be most stressful and difficult for advocates trained in the traditional model to help vulnerable clients. Organizationally, this power-building focus requires legal services providers to move away from prioritizing assessing and responding to "legal need" as conventionally understood, such as in traditional access to justice contexts, which we reviewed in Part III. Only if legal "need" is recast as an ongoing power "need"—to end power imbalances between elites and subordinated groups—can second-layer goals be conceived with concreteness and acted on with urgency in each context or scenario. This is a critical step—and stretch—required to deepen *systemic* advocacy projects.

The labor movement provides a useful example. Unions measure strength in various ways: the number of dues-paying members; the number of trained stewards capable of handling tasks like mobilization and grievance handling; the rights and benefits won in collective bargaining agreements; the success of new organizing initiatives; and so on. One of the key measures is union density in an industry or market—the percent of workers in a particular industry or market covered by a bargaining unit. Union density has plummeted in recent decades—from 20.1 percent or 17.7 million workers in both U.S. public and private sector jobs in 1983 to 10.5 percent or 14.7 million workers in 2018.[10] With high union density, labor unions could threaten or undertake job actions—sick-ins, slow downs, grievance actions, or strikes—that immediately and significantly affect production and thus generate pressure on employers to meet union members' demands for specific "technical fixes."

But, as density declined, the ability of labor unions to win technical fixes based on the threat to disrupt production diminished. Reduction in strength has reduced union capacity for pressure, producing a variety of different analyses and responses to confront new realities. If a threat of coordinated workplace action or grievances at organized worksites does not affect employers in significant ways because the numbers are small, employers can maintain production. Markets and industries are largely undisturbed by workplace actions, and unions don't have great power. To retool and rebuild power in the face of new external conditions, unions have to rethink what power "looks like" and what capacities are needed to build and exercise power sufficient to affect targeted employers' decision making in evolving contexts.

As labor historian Lane Windham explains, labor is adapting its approaches to power-building because contemporary contexts require adaptation:

---

[10] Union Members—2018, Bureau of Labor Statistics (Jan. 18, 2019), www.bls.gov/news.release/pdf/union2.pdf.

Corporate structures in early twenty-first century workplaces—in what one scholar titles the "fissured workplace"—are increasingly determined by the breakdown of the vertically integrated firm, which means workers often do not have clearly defined employers with whom to negotiate. In today's gig economy, employers have relinquished not only their social welfare role but often the employer-employee relationship itself. . . . The result is that a new breed of worker organizations—"alt-labor" organizations—is struggling to shore up workers' economic security in new ways, such as through workers' centers, new occupational alliances, and public campaigns to raise wages.

The future workers' rights movement will likely blend traditional labor unions and these new alt-labor forms, potentially on a global scale. As the twentieth-century version of industrial capitalism gives way to new forms, working people find themselves in need of a wholesale redefinition of collective bargaining. This institution may become less of a mediator between one employer and its employees, and more of a platform for "bargaining for the collective," serving as a mediator between centers of concentration of global capital (like e-commerce corporations or financial institutions) and entire swaths of working people who labor in similar occupations. As people no longer receive social welfare through employers, the role of the state may grow. Working people may be more likely to "bargain" with capital and the state by pooling power in political and community-based campaigns; they may no longer depend on specific employers for social welfare, but they will need to find new ways to force corporations to fund universal social welfare issues such as through a basic income, access to adequate and affordable healthcare, and reasonable family leave and child care.

. . . [F]uture union members will strike, protest, campaign, and leverage new laws to improve their own working lives, and to ensure broader distribution of the nation's wealth.[11]

Because the general systemic landscape for worker rights activism has changed, the understanding of worker power has shifted and, as a result, the power-building work focused on organizational forms, growth, and capacities needed to achieve that power also shifts. Stephen Lerner, a labor organizer and strategist, suggests three actions for unions to build—or rebuild—their priorities and capacities to achieve power relevant in today's contexts:

---

[11] Lane Windham, Knocking on Labor's Door: Union Organizing in the 1970s and the Roots of a New Economic Divide 190–91 (2017).

We need to broaden the scope of collective bargaining and collective action to focus on the super rich and corporations whose names are rarely on workers' paychecks. They have the power not only over our jobs and pay but also over housing costs, education, and government budgets. Our challenge is to figure out who controls our jobs and communities and to build power to force them to bargain over wages and to stop them from extracting wealth from our communities. To do this, we have to:

- Be willing to break laws to change laws. The CIO [union], the civil rights, gay rights, immigrant rights, and marijuana legalization movements, and most recently Black Lives Matter, have all violated existing laws as part of building deeply committed bases winning victories, and ultimately, better laws.

- Reinvent the strike to disrupt the real corporate decision makers. Striking workers and their allies using creative non-violence can dramatically affect the business operations of the entities that control their wages and work—even if they are not the "legal" employer.

- Re-popularize collective action and bargaining as the ways to confront concentrated economic power. Collective action and bargaining are not just for workers. New York City, Los Angeles, and Chicago do $600 billion a year in business with Wall Street; they can leverage this money to bargain for lower interest rates and to reduce exorbitant fees charged by Wall Street, freeing up resources to fund public services and workers. The students of Corinthian Colleges are already using a debt strike to force negotiations over the $1.3 trillion in student debt.[12]

As these comments suggest, building power is a complex task. Advocates and activists develop an understanding of organizational dynamics and the technical abilities to strengthen an organization in measurable ways. This work takes place within a continuous evaluation that questions and reconceptualizes exactly what kinds and exercises of power are needed in ever-changing systemic contexts.

But building power is only the second layer. The third layer of goals calls upon advocates and activists to shift consciousness within groups and broader culture. This culture-shifting work changes the way people, groups, problems, and solutions are imagined. And this work is critical because power-building without culture-shifting can lead groups to become insular, self-serving, or static. Again, consider the labor movement. At

---

[12] Stephen Lerner, Breaking Laws to Change Laws, 25 New Labor Forum 17, 17–18 (2015).

their best, labor struggles built power and solidarity based on critical, interracial, cross-class, and transnational movements based on antisubordination as a value. At their worst, labor unions operated as clubs of privilege that served the interests of mostly white, Anglo, cisgender, heterosexual-identified men and that actively excluded others—and it was as clubs of privilege that labor unions both failed to confront internal discrimination and absorbed some of the "DNA" of settler colonialism that crushes solidarity.[13] Bill Fletcher Jr., a labor historian and editor of The Global African Worker, notes that the consciousness of union members and leaders is at issue:

> As the trade union movement emerged both prior to and following the Civil War, the acceptance of the racial settler state was part of its DNA. . . .
>
> One can recognize and oppose overt and covert acts of racist discrimination, while at the same time accept many of the assumptions inherent in settlerism.
>
> Take the struggle around the Keystone XL pipeline, or any number of other pipelines. The fact that a union has demonstrated a commitment to organize workers across racial boundaries does not necessarily translate into their holding advanced views on First Nation rights. Thus, unions such as the Laborers International Union of North America could find itself at odds with a broad coalition of environmentalists, landowners, and Native Americans in which tribal rights played a major role.[14]

As U.S. union history attests, the difference between a members-only club and a social movement organization is neither absolute nor easy to define. Yet, there is a distinction between exclusion and collaboration. To advance third-layer goals (discussed next), social movement groups must demonstrate the will *and* ability to connect first- and second-layer work to ongoing reflection and decision-making animated always by antisubordination values.

NOTES AND QUESTIONS

1. *Winning Through Losing.* Jenkins describes the development of social power as a "process in development." In the same article he also notes that

---

[13] Another movement challenge has been addressing gender-based discrimination and sexual harassment. Ana Avendaño, former assistant general counsel at the AFL-CIO and now director of Minga Strategies, noted that "Lots of women have tried to use the collective bargaining process in male-dominated industries and found that when they tried to grieve the conduct of a fellow union member they were labeled as traitors, as betraying the union or solidarity." Michael Cooper, Caught in the Middle of #MeToo: Unions that Represent Accusers and Accused, N.Y. Times (May 17, 2019), www.nytimes.com/2019/05/17/arts/metoo-unions-ballet-ramasar.html.

[14] Bill Fletcher Jr., Race Is About More Than Discrimination: Racial Capitalism, the Settler State, and the Challenges Facing Organized Labor in the United States, Monthly Rev. (July 1, 2020), www.monthlyreview.org/2020/07/01/race-is-about-more-than-discrimination/.

advocacy efforts that involve complex legal actions, such as a federal class action lawsuit, will not be entirely member-led because of the legal expertise and credentials required. Strategically, such actions therefore are likely to have limited effects on some internal capacity-building goals, such as leadership development. But, as Jenkins argues, under some circumstances—contexts and scenarios—lawsuits can be very useful in advancing both internal growth and capacity-building goals, as well as external culture-shifting goals, as they might spark media coverage that increases group membership, albeit balanced against the negatives of modeling deference to lawyers and to judicial forums for social change. How should advocates assess the utility of legal actions? Jenkins suggests the "touchstone" is the same as for extralegal actions: will the action help build group power? Under this approach, the prospects of winning or losing must be assessed, of course—but the likelihood of winning is never the deciding factor for an advocate or client-group when deciding where to invest their time and resources.

Indeed, as Jenkins explains, sometimes losing the case can better galvanize group membership than a victory sapping organizational resources. In Part II, Douglas NeJaime similarly suggested that the relationship among winning, losing, and progress is complex, and that progress can be particularly difficult to measure. From the three-layered perspective of systemic analysis and advocacy, what does Jenkins add to your understanding of "winning through losing"? Still from a three-layered perspective, how do Calmore's and White's discussion of contexts and scenarios affect your notions of winning and/or losing as presented by NeJaime and Jenkins?

10.4 THIRD-LAYER GOALS CONNECT MICRO-MACRO FACTS TO SHIFT CONSCIOUSNESS AND CULTURES

One of the principal challenges posed by three-layered goals for systemic advocacy is how to shift group members' consciousness and mainstream culture to support transformative social change. To meet this micro-macro challenge, advocates must understand how to affect (individual) consciousness and (group) cultures. Using (frequently obscured) fact-based knowledge, advocates disrupt top-down links between identities and castes—that is, they engage in intentional culture making and shifting from below, much as elites do from above—to counter entrenched beliefs or biases, both in law and society. Unlearning and relearning this third-layer work requires critical reflection and coordinated action.

This challenge focuses advocacy directly on the connection between the micro consciousness of individuals in everyday life and the macro conditions that script the consciousness, interactions, and collective actions of those individuals. To use this micro-macro connection consciously as an asset, advocates aim to understand how people perceive and think in ways that motivate action. Below, Jon and Kathleen Hanson, situationist legal and social scholars, examine how "blame frames" structure thinking at micro and macro levels.[15] These blame frames encapsulate (sometimes) hidden biases that distort individual consciousness and public perceptions of social realities. These framings blame "victims" of systemic injustice for their subordination; deconstructing and changing blame frames is essential to culture shifting in third-level advocacy. For example, recall White's description of collective conversations that were the dynamic vehicle for challenging views of the local South African community as powerless, divided, and lacking effective strategies. By unpacking "blame frames" together, they were able to shift consciousness and to strengthen organized group power.

THE BLAME FRAME: JUSTIFYING (RACIAL) INJUSTICE IN AMERICA
Jon D. Hanson & Kathleen Hanson
41 Harv. C.R.-C.L. L. Rev. 413 (2006)

... The adequate record of even the confusions of our forebears may help, not only to clarify those confusions, but to engender a salutary doubt whether we are wholly immune from different but equally great confusions.

—Arthur O. Lovejoy

Introduction

We Americans, this Article argues, have long suffered from "great confusions." On the one hand, we champion the ideals of equality and freedom. . . .

Yet history shows us repeatedly betraying those principles. . . .

More generally, our history reveals a set of disconcerting truths. The first is that every moment of American history evinces vast disparities of wealth, power, and privilege among groups identified by salient characteristics such as race and gender. The second is that, instead of perceiving those inequalities as conflicting with American ideals, groups with power (and often even groups without) have justified and legitimized those disparities with an arsenal of arguments, assumptions, and stereotypes.

The third general truth is that such justifications often fail the test of time. In hindsight, many of the rationalizations of inequality appear flawed, sometimes shamefully so. Because today we recognize the motivations and prejudices prompting our predecessors to rationalize,

---

[15] Jon Hanson is the director of Harvard's Systemic Justice Project. The Project's mission is to serve as "a policy innovation collaboration . . . devoted to understanding common and systemic sources of injustice by analyzing the historical, cultural, political, economic, and psychological context of particular problems." The Systemic Justice Project, Mission, https://systemicjustice.law.harvard.edu/about/mission/.

perpetuate, and even expand existing inequalities, we judge their historical actions harshly—as fundamentally unjust and un-American.

The final general truth hits closer to home. In America today, similarly vast disparities of wealth, power, and privilege persist among groups identified by race, ethnicity, gender, and other salient characteristics. Groups with power and often those without continue to justify those disparities with arguments, assumptions, and stereotypes that depict inequalities as natural or otherwise legitimate, and thus consistent with American ideals. Combining those four truths raises the disconcerting question that motivates this Article: are we, today, so different? . . .

. . . [E]vidence from social psychology and related fields . . . helps explain how people who imagine themselves fair and just routinely blame the victims of inequities and excuse the perpetrators or passive observers through "blame frames." . . .

. . . [O]nly by understanding the sources and effects of blame frames can we ever hope to end oppression and thereby live according to the fundamental values we espouse. . . .

While injustice is difficult to define, it might fairly be described as an undeserved or unfair allocation of privilege and hardship across individuals or groups. Renowned social psychologist Melvin Lerner and his collaborators devoted years to studying how people respond to evidence of injustice. . . .

. . . Lerner's results powerfully illustrate two ways in which individuals cope when witnessing suffering: we stop the injustice, or we justify it by conceiving of the victim as a person who actually "deserves" to suffer. . . . [I]t is not *justice* that we crave so much as the *perception* of justice. . . .

[To reduce the dissonance created by seeing but not stopping injustice, we make two attributional errors.] First, victims are viewed as deserving of their suffering or disadvantage—we "blame the victim." . . . Second, non-victims . . . are perceived as innocent—we "excuse the non-victim." . . .

. . . In a related phenomenon, we often deem "omissions" that produce suffering far less culpable than "acts" that lead to similar suffering. . . .

. . . [Together, this generates] the "ultimate attribution error:" . . . [we believe that] bad people do bad things, good people do good things, and all "people get what they deserve."

. . . [In addition,] John Jost and his collaborators have discovered that a threat to the stability or legitimacy of existing arrangements ("system threat") leads most people—including those disadvantaged by the system—to defend the status quo through legitimizing attributional schemas.

Because we crave a just system, we justify systematic inequality and suffering by vulnerable groups through power-affirming attributions. . . .

. . . [M]otivated attributions—including the ultimate attribution error, the omission bias, and system-justifying attributions—produce a distorting frame that allows us to perceive justice in the face of oppression, coercion, and injustice. This *blame frame* shields us from ugly truths and, in part for that reason, perpetuates them. . . .

. . . [Our] *basic blame frame* has been fleshed out in various incarnations . . . :

> *The God/devil schema ("God frame")*: Under this frame, outcomes reflect not individual choices, but the presence or absence of God's grace/will/plan. . . . When those in power act to advantage their group but harm (or fail to help) others, the God schema excuses such actions as a situationally determined aspect of God's will or plan, beyond the control of the most powerful mortal.
>
> *The evolution/nature/biology schema ("nature frame")*: Under this frame, outcomes are dictated not (only) by the divine, but (also) by certain genes or inherited qualities. This hereditary baggage makes a person "fit" or "unfit." . . . [T]heir place in society reveals their position in nature's hierarchy. And when those in power act to advantage their group, while harming others, those actions are situationally excused as consistent with nature's laws and desirable evolutionary processes.
>
> *The markets/preference-, personality-, or character-based choice schema ("choice frame")*: According to this narrative, outcomes reflect the choices of individuals, which in turn reflect the individualized preferences (or perhaps character) of each person or group. People's behavior, wealth, living conditions, and position in society reveal their preferences, tastes, identities, and ability to make good choices. When those in power act to advantage their own group but harm others, the choice frame excuses those actions as situationally determined by market forces or autonomous individuals' votes or choices—any other outcome would impede or ignore the preferences of people entitled to choose for themselves.

. . . The choice schema has become dominant in today's society. Choice, then, is the new race. And "choicism" is the new racism. . . .

Because choicism can be applied "equally" to all people in a "color-blind" fashion, we do not (consciously) associate our choice fetish with race or racism. By "making sense" of racial injustice without making explicit reference to race, choicism provides the perfect palliative: we bear no conscious animosity toward people of color, and if we make distinctions among people, we do so based on the "content of their character." Far from being unfair or unjust, unequal outcomes are the product of the very feature that makes America great: free choice.

. . . If patent racial prejudice produces inequalities, then there is injustice. Conversely, if our judgments lack such animus or prejudice (if, for example, they seem "color-blind"), and particularly if no one has "acted" to harm anyone, then the resultant inequalities typically are not considered reflective of racial injustice.

. . . Any suggestion that a person, a group, or our system is "racist" is considered a serious attack. To make such a claim falsely or even to suggest it carelessly—that is, to play the "race card"—is itself an egregious injustice. . . . Anyone alleging that unequal outcomes are the consequence of racism therefore takes a profound risk. In sum, the "race card," is typically trumped by the "race-card card."

. . . Blame frames, therefore, help protect inequalities from being recognized as injustices, not simply by blaming the victim and excusing the non-victim, but also by undermining and deterring those who suggest that the inequalities evince injustice. . . .

Although we Americans have long abhorred injustice, we have for centuries lived in apparent indifference to its presence. . . .

. . . Our mistake is . . . in attributing to "character" what should be attributed to the victim's situation and, in turn, to our system and ourselves. In other words, we have allowed ourselves to be deceived by blame frames—that is our *greatest* confusion. . . .

. . . It is time to embrace self-doubt and humility and to examine our knack for self-deception. . . . Perhaps by clarifying our great confusions, we can discover a path to a world that conforms to our greater aspirations.

Individuals acculturated in dominant blame frames often find it hard to imagine a path toward equal justice. These framings blame "victims" of systemic injustice for their subordination. Bottoms are rightly in misery because "it" is their choice. Contemporary "choicism" perpetuates inequalities: "choicism is the new racism" (and sexism, ableism, and other -isms), as the Hansons conclude. But advocates and activists see through these blame frames—whether based on God, nature, or choice—to reconceptualize problems, construct solidarity, and carry out collective strategies.

Advocates aim to construct micro-level conversations to spotlight background or macro assumptions. Such conversations allow new critical understandings of problems, "blame," and solutions to emerge. In the case of immigration advocacy, for example, one might expand the inquiry from immigrants as good or bad individuals to question borders themselves—national and other borders—as well as those of binary categories—like black and white, male and female, public and private. Both borders and binaries are social constructions enforced both by law and by culture. But why are binary categories as they are, and who benefits from existing borders? Remember Matsuda's practice of asking other questions from Part II? In contrast to industry norms and practices, critical methods question dominant notions that seem self-explanatory, helping to deconstruct them as social inventions.

By way of example, Asian American legal scholars Bob Chang and Keith Aoki questioned the givens of dominant approaches to immigration law and policy:

> One challenge for a critical Asian American legal scholarship and for LatCrit discourse is to disable the regressive construction of borders that enables nativistic racism. In doing so, we must approach this work with "a critical awareness of how borders have been (and continue to be) systematically policed and for whose ideological benefit and material profit."
>
> Last year, [federal immigration officials] conducted a sweep through four southern states to round up and deport undocumented agricultural workers. They called it Operation SouthPAW, "PAW" standing for "Protecting American Workers." The round-up took place mostly before and after the harvest was in [but not during the harvest]. There is no question that Operation SouthPAW worked to police our borders, but for whose ideological benefit and whose material profit? And the material profit here is not limited to farmers and agribusiness—all "Americans" benefit and are thus complicit insofar as food prices are kept low. Asian American legal scholarship and LatCrit discourse enable[ ] us to bring incidents, like SouthPAW, to light and provide[ ] a framework for understanding the deeper origins of those practices.
>
> . . . The long and the short of it is that Asian Americans and Latina/os are neither Black nor White. We will not settle down into the Black/White binary. Most important, we are here—and we are not going away.
>
> The project of rescinding borders includes upsetting the boundaries that privilege any simple binary, whether it be the Black/White racial paradigm, male/female, straight/queer. At times, this will be met with resistance. The challenge, then, is . . . to articulate a set of political commitments around which subordinated peoples and persons of goodwill can organize.

> This hard work is taking place at multiple sites. Our communities and coalitions are (and always will be) ... "under construction."[16]

Advocates and activists perhaps may consider our current understandings as natural or clear, as unmovable. But these understandings arise in particular contexts and are, in fact, continually under construction. The recycling of beliefs and practices that violate justice from groups to individuals and back are the cycles that systemic advocacy aims to break to shift cultures. To displace current or dominant understandings of problems and solutions—that is, to shift individual consciousness and group cultures—micro-macro work in support of these third-layer goals must be deeply connected to the second-layer work and processes of group mobilization and power building; in short, it takes power to change consciousness and culture.

A contemporary example of this linkage between the second- and third layers is advocacy to change cultural understandings of childhood in both law and society. Historically, children and childhood have been conceptualized in different ways in different contexts. In response, emerging critiques of dominant views challenge advocates and activists to reflect on how accepted—even hegemonic—notions might reinforce patterns of injustice both culturally and legally. Cheryl Bratt, a clinician and legal practice scholar, asks advocates to question dominant understandings of childhood in a critical, collaborative process of reflection with youth themselves:

> The dominant narrative about how we currently conceptualize the field of children and the law ultimately ... reflects a triangulation with parents and government at the top points of a triangle trading control over children, who are situated at the bottom point. Children's dependency justifies this prevailing setup. Accordingly, as children mature, the triangle starts to shift, until children reach the age of maturity, thereby triggering full-on autonomy rights and all their attendant features.
>
> ... [This "authorities"] doctrine evolved from property theory—where parents (more accurately, fathers) controlled every aspect of a child's life—to the rise of *parens patriae* and the state's claimed duty to specially protect children.... [T]he authorities framework obscures children's interests in the "here and now" because of its laser-focus on children's trajectory from dependency to autonomy. Children, however, lead rich and meaningful lives *as children:* they have relationships, identities, ideas, experiences, opinions, and more that the law should take into account. But

---

[16] Robert S. Chang and Keith Aoki, Centering the Immigrant in the Inter/National Imagination, 85 Cal. L. Rev. 1395, 1446–47, 10 La Raza L.J. 309 (1997).

because our laws treat children "as lesser versions of adult[s]," those interests are eclipsed. . . .

Children across the country are already advocating for our communities to fully respect them as they exist now. . . . [A Portland, Oregon] school board adopted the students' recommendation to form a committee of students and adults to create a nondiscriminatory gender-neutral dress code. . . .

. . . [Y]outh have mobilized to lead a sweeping and unprecedented campaign against gun violence, dubbed #NeverAgain. . . .

This [youth-led] approach thus helps shift society's perceptions about youth in two important ways: through the direct effects of youth's reform efforts that promote their interests, which create the policy reforms; and through the indirect effects of a method that showcases youth as full people with important ideas, interests, and identities advancing their own agendas. It may also in time spur expanded legal rights. As the marriage equality movement evinces, a societal sea change can pave the way to future constitutional reform.[17]

As Bratt illustrates, organized groups of marginalized individuals should make changing mainstream cultural understandings an explicit advocacy. Mainstream cultural understandings limit all of "the people"—those who vote, legislate, adjudicate, or otherwise live in and staff the systems that enforce the status quo. Without moving the minds and hearts of these people, systemic advocates rarely can accomplish transformative progress that spans micro and macro levels of consciousness.

These materials illustrate how advocates design projects for three-layered progress regardless of context and complexity; within that design, advocates aim to intentionally shift individual consciousness within organized groups and to change dominant attitudes about problems, groups, and solutions in mainstream culture. But shifting dominant beliefs instilled systemically in individuals and groups is no easy or quick task. It takes power—including staying power—to shift consciousness and culture; that is, to induce and sustain the micro-macro displacement of entrenched top-down notions with bottom-up knowledge. For this reason, second-layer work is always concomitant to achieving third-layer goals, just as first-layer work should always lay some groundwork for second-layer goals.

---

[17] Cheryl Bratt, Top-Down or from the Ground?: A Practical Perspective on Reforming the Field of Children and the Law, 127 Yale L.J. Forum 917 (2018).

NOTES AND QUESTIONS

1. *The Blame Frame in Micro and Macro Settings.* The Hansons' article (in a part not excerpted above) uses the modern example of the Hurricane Katrina disaster to illustrate the ready tendency (choicism) to blame the victim's individual character or bad decision making, here in not timely evacuating from New Orleans, rather than macro problems of systemic injustice for the "desperately poor and predominantly black" residents who stayed behind. Consider another recent example—the devastation of Hurricane Maria in Puerto Rico in 2017 and the similarly inept government response.[18] Donald Trump described the geography of the Commonwealth of Puerto Rico as "an island surrounded by water, big water, ocean water" and therefore a challenge for federal relief efforts. He rebuffed criticism, tweeting "[t]hey want everything to be done for them when it should be a community effort." Does this rhetoric feed the relevant blame frames? What longstanding stereotype of Puerto Ricans does it invoke as an excuse for the nation's lackluster emergency aid?

In this instance (and others) the blame frame operates across a variety of identities and castes. For example, consider the way in which homeless persons are portrayed and seen (or unseen).[19] Consider also so-called slut-shaming, most always in a gendered direction, that helps justify or remove the sting from the prevailing rape culture.[20] Can you think of other examples of blame framing that intersect with identities and groups? Consider which blame frames may underlie or intersect with your advocacy project. How might you better incorporate second-layer and third-layer goals into your advocacy to forge solidarity and shift prevailing frames of understanding, as well as to strengthen client-groups, and to advance the power building and culture shifting goals of advocacy? Consider specifically how you might help construct conversations and experiences that help targeted group members see beyond these blame frames and develop alternative understandings rooted in experiences of bottom groups.

2. *Deflecting Blame.* The Hansons' article (in a part outside the above excerpt) also describes how we manage to disassociate ourselves from elite-led travesties of history that we now see as wrong. Unsettling discussions of historical injustices perpetrated in the United States against indigenous groups, Black people, Asian immigrants, or others often draw the response: "It wasn't me" or "You can't blame me for what past generations did." In some instances, this represents successors in interest of colonial settlers shifting the

---

[18] See Yxta Maya Murray, "FEMA Has Been a Nightmare:" Epistemic Injustice in Puerto Rico, 55 Willamette L. Rev. 321 (2019) (describing how federal officials blamed Puerto Rican residents and officials for creating logistical "uncertainties" that undermined relief efforts, rather than taking responsibility for failures to seek out, listen to, or learn from information provided by residents).

[19] See Sara K. Rankin, Punishing Homelessness, 22 New Crim. L. Rev. 99 (2019) (criticizing "laws, fueled by the stigma of visible poverty, [that] function to purge chronically homeless people from public space").

[20] See Wendy N. Hess, Slut Shaming in the Workplace: Sexual Rumors & Hostile Work Environment Claims, 40 N.Y.U. Rev. L. & Soc. Change 581 (2016).

mantle of victimhood to themselves. This rhetorical move positions the speaker as one now standing falsely accused of injustices committed by past generations; a less-acknowledged effect is to obscure patterns of unearned advantages that the person may have received and still may be receiving. This positioning aligns with criminal and tort law and legal notions of responsibility, which generally insulate current beneficiaries of past wrongdoing against blame for the crimes and transgressions of others, including their own ancestors, in another time or place. What might you do, as an advocate, to shift the understanding of an individual who offers this seemingly alluring framing (here of the blamelessness of favored groups)? How might you explain the operations of the blame frame that narrow the understanding of injustice and thus allow the unjustly enriched to diminish or evade their social responsibility for the persistence of systemic inequality and injustice?

3. *Rethinking Alliances to Deepen Solidarity.* Such evasions can occur even among members of marginalized groups. Relationships and histories among communities of color or other marginalized groups can be messy and require thoughtful examination. That examination can chart a way forward to "rethink alliances" but also can open the door to new top-down blame frames, as well. Legal scholar Eric Yamamoto describes both the importance and risks of work that aims to shift historical and cultural understandings among subordinated groups about each other:

> Interracial justice, as I conceive it, reflects a commitment to antisubordination among nonwhite racial groups. . . .
>
> Rather than blaming racial groups for failure to assimilate into the American mainstream, as neoconservative theories tend to do, or blaming white-controlled institutions for all racial ills, as do some nationalism/colonialism theories, the interracial justice concept locates racial group agency and responsibility within the tension between continuing group subordination and emerging group power. It posits that amid social structural shifts, racial groups may be, in varying ways, simultaneously privileged and oppressed, empowered and disempowered, uplifting and subordinating. . . .
>
> . . . [One example is] certain Asian American church groups' proposed resolution of apology to and redress for Native Hawaiians. That resolution acknowledged how many Asians "benefitted socially and economically [from] the illegal overthrow" of the sovereign Hawaiian nation while "disregarding the destruction of Native Hawaiian culture and the struggles" of Hawai'i's indigenous people. The resolution's stated goal was reconciliation and justice in light of "a particular dynamic . . . between Native Hawaiians and Asian Americans, rooted in mutual misunderstanding and mistrust," resulting in the use of "stereotypes and caricatures to demean and dehumanize." [There were] . . . many volatile, complex responses to the resolution. . . .

> ... [T]he framework of a theory of inter-group alliances based on the concept of "interracial justice" [is helpful in such difficult discussions]. Interracial justice acknowledges historical white dominance and contemporary white rhetorical, institutional and economic influence while at the same time decentering whiteness as the singular referent for determining racial identities and interracial relations.... [I]nterracial justice entails a hard acknowledgment of the extent to which nonwhite racial groups situationally have oppressed and continue to oppress one another and a commitment to affirmative efforts to redress past and continuing harm....
>
> ... [There are risks, for example from a] movement gaining considerable popular steam [that] blames racial groups for all of their own ills as well as for most of society's economic and racial problems. In this climate, a discussion about interracial justice as a basis for coalition-building, which addresses how racial groups sometimes oppress each other, ... can be misused to overstate the extent of racial group agency ... [or] to absolve whites of responsibility for continuing structural subordination of racial groups and to recast whites as primary "victims" of racism....
>
> ... I have proceeded nonetheless to address racial group agency and interracial group relations because of the significance of those issues to "living together peaceably and working together politically" and because of the relative scholarly silence in the area.[21]

Can you think of other examples in which "living together peaceably and working together politically"—solidarity in critical coalitions—might benefit from healing among members of subordinated groups? In such situations, how might advocates and activists create an environment for the needed difficult discussion and hoped-for shifts in individual consciousness and organizational cultures within or among client-groups? Such shifts require, among other things, thoughtful attention to participation; the courage to speak with openness, vulnerability, persistence, and even hurt or anger; and a reciprocal willingness to listen, respect, and respond. Yamamoto describes a key moment several days into the meeting of the United Church of Christ Conference in which the proposal for an apology and reparations had been made—a moment that opened the door to shift participants' consciousness and the Conference's organizational culture:

> Reverend Kekapa Lee, a Native Hawaiian-Chinese American pastor of a small church on Maui, stood and spoke: ...
>
> > And I have a very heavy, heavy, heavy heart because I don't understand why an apology is such a big thing.... Some of us are hurting and in pain because of this, and we're asking your support and kokua... because there are many things that face our church and

---

[21] Eric K. Yamamoto, Rethinking Alliances: Agency, Responsibility, and Interracial Justice, 3 Asian Pac. Am. L.J. 33 (Fall 1995).

our community as Hawaiians and we want to move on but feel that this apology is so important.

> While Reverend Lee continued, many more Hawaiians rose.... The emotion was palpable. It was only at that moment, I believe, following days of fractious discussion, that most of the non-Hawaiians there (including many White and Asian Americans) grasped the depth of the continuing pain experienced by Hawaiians within their own Conference. It was only then that they appeared to begin to understand how their refusal to acknowledge that present pain and its myriad historical sources erected huge barriers between groups within the Conference, barriers to addressing collectively the "many things that face our church and our community." It was then that many of the earlier disagreements emerged in a new light. The members of the Conference polity then by consensus adopted an amended version of the broader resolution directing the Conference to apologize to Native Hawaiians for the Conference's predecessor's participation in the overthrow of the Hawaiian nation and to begin a discussion about reparations.[22]

This passage emphasizes several important points. It provides a concrete instance of groups creating a tough conversation intentionally, and working through it with specific follow-up commitments—both tangible (reparations) and intangible (apology). This collective and mutual choice created an opening for disrupting top-down blame frames that tie identities to privilege and subordination, for shifting individual consciousness and organizational culture about systemic problems and social conditions, and for deepening solidarity among individuals and groups to work together for justice. Recalling *Brown* itself, Yamamoto's example demonstrates why equal justice depends on both material remedies (in this instance, reparations) *and* on extralegal, even symbolic, remedies (here, apology).

10.5 SYSTEMIC ADVOCATES COMBINE TRADITIONAL AND CRITICAL TOOLS FOR THREE-LAYERED PROGRESS

In contrast to traditional lawyering approaches exemplified by the legal industry, systemic advocates need, and have assembled, an expanded set of critical knowledges, values, skills, and attitudes (CKVSAs) to make and ground three-layered progress over time. In effect, this expanded problem-solving toolkit is designed to help advocates counter the top-down toolkit outlined in Part II that elites deploy to maintain the status quo above all else. These expanded CKVSAs are geared specifically for work with groups and communities as equal members in problem solving, and to focus on amelioration *and* transformation.

---

[22] *Id.* at 73–74.

The point of this comparative review is to become self-aware of the varied critical tools—CKVSAs—from which you must draw to remain effective, principled, and accountable in your advocacy, and to help you appreciate how combining critical and traditional tools can make three-layered advocacy most effective regardless of context or scenario. Much like a good carpenter, plumber, or electrician, advocates must know the tools in their kit, and which to use when, and how—in which combinations or sequences—to fix problems not only with bandaids, but so that the problem is less likely to recur.

As a set, and when applied self-critically, these CKVSAs guard the integrity and efficacy of your work:

1. Social Values and Professional Identity in Ethical Practice:

Root professional identities, ethics, and practices in social justice commitments and antisubordination values in order to cultivate principled, resilient, and resourceful work habits; be proactively self-critical at all times to ensure integrity.

2. Meaningful Progress and Critical Theory in Effective Advocacy:

Understand the dynamics of principled and durable social change and the workings of public interest-social justice sectors within dominant legal cultures both locally and beyond; be conversant in the comparative approaches, critiques, and languages of critical-outsider theory and movement organizing or community lawyering.

3. Fact-Based Analysis and Complex Systems in Collaborative Action:

Break down complexity and unusual assignments/tasks/problems into step-by-step plans grounded in social reality that account for the role of power in varied collaborative problem-solving contexts; be focused on principled results with a materially meaningful social impact for traditionally subordinated communities.

4. Cultural Competencies and Technical Expertise in Multiple Contexts:

Create and manage conversations, relationships, situations, and action plans to move work forward culturally and technically despite complicated or contradictory problem-solving challenges; be prepared to sustain collaboration across multiple sources of difference (professional, technical, demographic) in order to yield results.

As a set, these mutually reinforcing CKVSAs are designed to maximize your advocacy's social impact and necessarily overlap flexibly as needed in daily practice. Although some of these overlapping CKVSAs may be more salient in a given moment or context, all must be fully engaged self-critically, and in usually complex systemic settings. These CKVSAs, as an expanded toolkit, recognize that solutions are never permanent or self-executing; solutions are hard work and, to stick, take more hard work. All solutions necessarily are provisional because there will always be a next round of struggle, as those with an interest in the status quo reassert and reassemble privilege and subordination. And they also are always incremental because the complexity of systems means that no single change can address all dimensions of a problem or anticipate all consequences of change. Advocates thus combine CKVSAs flexibly, interactively, and deliberately—together with critical and *self*-critical uses of traditional tools—to defend and advance Critical Justice.

NOTES AND QUESTIONS

1. *The Systemic Advocate's Toolkit.* It has become popular in legal education to call for graduates to possess a "practice ready" toolkit of knowledges, skills, and aptitudes (KSAs)—ready, that is, to be deployed for traditional advocacy actions and to act in line with industry norms. For the most part, the emphasis has been on knowledges and skills. Do you recall this toolkit metaphor being presented in your education—if so, in which courses and at what stage(s) of your education?

The examples in this section—and throughout the book—paint a somewhat different picture of the toolkit needed for systemic advocacy. The legal and extralegal norms and techniques that produce three-layered diagnoses and strategies are reflected in an expanded toolkit of *critical* knowledges, values, skills, and attitudes. These tools are interdependent, flexible in practice, and designed to be tailored to specific contexts or scenarios. This toolkit incorporates learning that stretches "advocacy" and "legal actors" beyond the limits of traditional practice. Advocates must learn to act in and beyond traditional venues and engage in both atomistic legal actions like cases and contract negotiations and complex actions like campaigns and projects as the next part will detail. Advocates rely on antisubordination values and critically examine legal ethics to see how they facilitate or constrain collaborations with organized groups. Considering all this, compare the toolkit provided by formal training for law practice to the CKVSAs needed for successful systemic advocacy you have seen so far. What does your comparison suggest that advocates must unlearn and relearn about *critical* (in contrast to traditional) knowledges, values, skills, and attitudes for *systemic* problem solving?

CHAPTER RECAP

In this chapter, we surveyed how advocates must recognize and work within specific systemic contexts to advance three-layered goals that connect micro-macro levels of law and life. Despite constant opposition, these bottom-up goals use both persuasion and pressure in principled and accountable ways that measure actions and their results. With an understanding of key concepts like systemic context, practice scenario, and three-layered goals, we now consider Part V, which outlines the mechanics of systemic advocacy as an expanded set of tools for bottom-up research and action. This expansion is designed to help legal trainees, advocates, and activists remove the handcuffs and blindfolds of law as an industry. It outlines the stages, methods, and actions through which advocates diagnose problems contextually and strategize for solutions collaboratively to advance and defend three-layered goals.

Part V

Outlining the Stages of Systemic Advocacy for Critical Justice

. . .

CHAPTER 11

STAGE ONE—DIAGNOSING PROBLEMS IN CONTEXT THROUGH CRITICAL RESEARCH & ANALYSIS TO PREPARE FOR COMPLEX ACTIONS

■ ■ ■

Table of Sections

11.1   Knowledge Always Has a Politics, Which Can Bias Analysis and Action
11.2   Advocates Diagnose Problems and Strategize Solutions in Two Recurring Stages
11.3   Three Bottom-Up Methods of Critical Research for Three-Layered Progress
11.4   Three Norms Help Expand and Deepen the Impact of Critical Research and Analysis
11.5   Four "Mapping" Techniques Help Tailor and Implement Contextual Action Plans

---

OPENING THOUGHTS

No one is going to give you the education you need to overthrow them. Nobody is going to teach you your true history, teach you your true heroes, if they know that that knowledge will help set you free.

> —**Assata Shakur**

Socially engaged research is, finally, an exercise in solidarity. The road is difficult, and we have only our own moral compass and our relationships with our compañeras to guide us.

> —**Andrea Dyrness**, Research for Change versus Research as Change: Lessons from a *Mujerista* Participatory Research Team, 39 Anthro. & Educ. Q. 23, 41 (2008)

Arguably, the most significant impact of critical theory has been the reformation of legal analytical practices through the use of stories. . . . [T]he narrative potential of critical theory lies in its ability to free us to move backward and forward in time, to "re-story" the past and to "re-imagine" the future.

> —**Angela Harris and Leslie Espinoza**, Afterword—Embracing the Tar-Baby: LatCrit Theory and the Sticky

Mess of Race, 85 Cal. L. Rev. 1585, 1630–31 (1997), 10 La Raza L.J. 499, 544–45 (1998)

INTRODUCTION

We began in Part I with the importance of critical knowledge and its three main sources: personal or proximate experience; insights from the Schools and Approaches; and bottom-up knowledge from expanded concepts and practices. Advocates apply this knowledge contextually to diagnose persistent collective problems and to strategize solutions for them, and they support groups developing capacities to act as repeat players in contesting foundational concepts and ground rules. In this process, they consciously avoid the epistemic injustice of top-down systems. This chapter outlines key methods, norms, and related techniques that systemic advocates use to develop the knowledge on which effective advocacy plans and projects can be based.

Most advocacy begins with research and analysis, so this work can be considered "Stage One" of the advocate's work. Typically, advocates aim to use research and analysis to diagnose problems to craft strategies along the three layers of goals. Those strategies are carried out through "complex actions" presented in the next chapter, which can be considered "Stage Two" of systemic advocacy. However, this description of "stages" of work is useful for only basic comprehension of complex work. In practice, the two stages are continuous, overlapping, recurring, and interactive. They do not unfold in a neat or single sequence. Instead, advocates flexibly combine research and analysis with action throughout the entirety of advocacy work. Therefore, we describe the work of systemic advocacy as comprising two overlapping and recurring stages only to organize the presentation of these materials for easier comprehension.

Research and analysis—applied knowledge—are not limited to the start of a project. Advocates continually assess their choices and nimbly adjust to improve their effectiveness. More often than not, initial strategies must be adapted to evolving circumstances—including the responses of adversaries, third parties, or other intervening events. Usually, then, initial diagnoses shape strategy, and the results of strategy inform ongoing diagnosis. These adjustments are sometimes simple tweaks; other times, they require significant overhauls. Advocates remain vigilant and responsive to changing circumstances and the need for changed strategies. This ongoing critical and self-critical reflection helps keep the work principled and accountable.

Recognizing these starting points, we begin by acknowledging that knowledge *always* has a politics. Knowledge is power—or, more precisely, as strategic researcher David Chu reminds—"Knowledge Is Power . . . If

You Know What to Do With It."[1] Because of this structural, systemic reality, knowledge also is always contestable and frequently contested. These dynamics appear in the creation of knowledge itself—what counts as knowledge—as well as in the lines of accountability and principles that guide its uses. Knowledge production and application therefore frequently entail tensions, conflicts, and ambiguity along many fault lines. These tensions and conflicts, as we saw in earlier chapters, include efforts of elites to atomize, suppress, or control knowledge while activists and advocates aim to liberate critical, collective consciousness for antisubordination purposes. This bottom line endures because knowledge in action is indeed power.

We then introduce three key methods—participatory action research, critical empiricism, and analytical narrative—and three norms—inter/counterdisciplinarity, critical comparativism, and social analytics—that are not part of the traditional legal advocacy toolkit. These methods and norms help break the monopoly of formal equality on what counts as legitimate legal research and analysis—and, ultimately, on what counts as relevant facts. In addition, we focus on mapping as a tool for developing a picture of the identities, groups, interests, power, *and relationships* in a given problem solving context. Although advocates can (and do) use many sorts of mapping techniques relevant to particular problems, we review the nature and applications of four commonly used techniques—concept, asset, stakeholder, and power mapping. These methods, norms, and related techniques effectively connect micro sources of knowledge and action with collective reconceptions of macro conditions to clarify persistent social problems.

Remember, this work is necessarily collaborative, using an expanded toolkit for three-layered advocacy. Recall also that this complex work takes place in particular systemic contexts. But, as Calmore explained in Part IV, the context for advocacy is not only a geographic "space" defined in location and time. In addition to the literal meaning, a systemic context also includes the complexities of that place and time as defined critically in terms of identities, groups, interests, and power. Advocates navigate their way through raw information to develop a realistic picture of complicated contexts—the conceptual and actual spaces of social problems. They build capacity offensively to advance progress and defensively to resist rollbacks and avoid being "taken out." This chapter reviews how raw information is excavated, documented, analyzed, and interpreted—and thus converted

---

[1] David Chu, Setting a Research Agenda: Knowledge Is Power . . . If You Know What to Do With It, 12 Labor Res. Rev. 41, 41–42 (1993) (distinguishing between descriptive research and strategic research in a labor context by explaining that "[a]lone, research simply creates a lot of charts and memos. When we look at things strategically, good information should help the union better understand its industry, the employer, the worksite, the workers, the community, and the issues that bind all these elements together. Good strategic research identifies the issues, targets the union's actions, prepares testimony for regulatory hearings, pushes the union's activities onto the agenda of the corporate boardroom, or simply gives the boss a well-earned headache").

into actionable knowledge to diagnose problems and strategize solutions toward Critical Justice. Recalling Part I's mention of Big Lies as top-down knowledge control, we begin with a bottom-up truth about the politics of knowledge (and knowledge production) that all advocates must internalize for critical analysis and organized action.

11.1 KNOWLEDGE ALWAYS HAS A POLITICS, WHICH CAN BIAS ANALYSIS AND ACTION

Critical research generates "new" knowledge, and new knowledge often threatens the premises and myths of the status quo. This new knowledge is born of collaborations that excavate the experience and wisdom of those "at the bottom" of a given problem-solving scenario. The constraining rules of formal equality and the legal industry do not halt knowledge production here:

> Looking to the bottom—adopting the perspective of those who have seen and felt the falsity of the liberal promise—can assist critical scholars in the task of fathoming the phenomenology of law and defining the elements of justice. . . . When notions of right and wrong, justice and injustice, are examined not from an abstract position but from the position of groups who have suffered through history, moral relativism recedes and identifiable normative priorities emerge.[2]

Critical research generates information, but it also can generate tensions as researchers confront thorny issues of principle and accountability to combat top-down methods of repression, which run the gamut from subtle pressures and distortions to outright attacks—physical, economic, reputational, and otherwise. This continual contestation is integral to the politics of knowledge in antisubordination struggles and advocacy.[3]

Continual contestation exists because information is a commodity in a capitalist society. As a result, the politics of knowledge includes confronting the infrastructure elites have built to control information and give themselves an advantage in policy contestations.[4] Exploiting this

---

[2] Mari Matsuda, Looking to the Bottom: Critical Legal Studies and Reparations, 22 Harv. C.R.-C.L. L. Rev. 323, 325 (1987).

[3] This epistemological point has roots in a number of philosophical traditions, going back to Georg Wilhelm Friedrich Hegel's discussion of master-slave relationships in connection with the production of knowledge. See, for example, Georg Wilhelm Friedrich Hegel, Phenomenology of Spirit (A.V. Miller trans. 1977) (1807). See also feminist standpoint theory such as Sandra Harding, The Science Question in Feminism (1986); Sandra Harding, The Feminist Standpoint Theory Reader: Intellectual and Political Controversies (2004); Janet Kourany, The Place of Standpoint Theory in Feminist Science Studies, 24 Hypatia 209 (2009); Susan H. Williams, Legal Education, Feminist Epistemology, and the Socratic Method, 45 Stan. L. Rev. 1571 (1993).

[4] See, for example, Douglas de Castro, The Colonial Aspects of the International Environmental Law—Treaties as Promoters of Continuous Structural Violence, 5 Groningen J. of Int'l L. 168 (2017) (arguing that international environmental law has maintained its colonial and patriarchal construction into the era of climate change, "which results in a body of law that (1)

advantage, elites aim to gain information through surveillance, discovery in lawsuits, hacking, infiltration, and other strategies to weaken equal justice-seeking organizations and discredit individual advocates and activists. These attacks on information and sources are not coincidental; they generally are part of a legal and public relations strategy aiming to maintain elite dominance of law and society. Elites both build up and tear down sources of information, consciousness, and action to discredit critical knowledge as an element of group struggle.

Consider the following example of such politically-motivated attacks. CASA de Maryland, an immigrant rights organization, suffered continuing information attacks, as described in a report by RoadMap Consulting, which aids groups to avoid or weather such attacks:

> If you're standing up for justice, you will face opposition. Grassroots organizers and advocates know this. Those who may lose political influence, money and cultural control are invested in undermining the organizations that expose or challenge them.
>
> Consider this example: For over 10 years, the right had been watching Casa de Maryland, an organization with a long history of providing [legal and other] services to and advocating for the rights of immigrants. Anti-immigrant groups had not only been watching CASA closely, they had collected hundreds of their documents and had even gained access to private online discussion groups. Opponents used this material to launch an aggressive public attack on CASA, falsely claiming that they were registering "illegals" to vote, among other baseless allegations. . . . CASA spent two years responding to these false charges. In the end, CASA weathered the storm, exposed those who were behind the attacks, and came out more credible and effective than ever.
>
> . . . Every day, social justice groups are subject to politically motivated attacks. While such attacks are not new, there has been a definite change in the political climate leading to: increased intensity of corporate spying; the emergence of more aggressive and systematic legal challenges; more frequent government investigations based on spurious complaints; and increases in digital security attacks and incidents of personal harassment.[5]

In addition to outright attacks, elites also use systems to suppress critical knowledge. Systemic advocates and activists face pressures, personal and professional, asking them to "move beyond" their focus on racial

---

increases vulnerability and inequality; (2) does not allocate properly responsibility; (3) promotes super-development of the already developed countries; and (4) imposes externalities only to Global South countries").

[5] Weathering the Storms: Building Social Justice Resilience Against Opposition Attacks (2015), RoadMap Consulting, www.roadmapconsulting.org/resource/weathering-the-storm/.

oppression, gender abuses, and class consciousness. The pressure to engage in analysis "without a progressive politics and without a material component" is relentless; this pressure comes not just from opponents but also sometimes from friends, family, and well-intentioned colleagues.[6] Due to complex relationships (and differences) among the actors and the varied risks and rewards that each actor faces, "internal" tensions and pressures emerge in the very processes of planning, conducting, analyzing, and using research.

Under these circumstances, systemic advocates and activists continually question how bottom-up research can be executed and deployed in principled and accountable ways. In some cases, a researcher-advocate must resolve tensions between the legal-ethical rules prioritizing zealous advocacy for a client and the professional commitment—also encoded in legal ethics but less often highlighted—to serve a broader justice end. Almost always, advocates have to develop self-awareness that allows the advocate to navigate in multicultural, cross-class, and interdisciplinary settings. In addition, advocates and activists are called upon to reflect self-critically on how the excavation of information or sharing of stories serves to advance work on any and each of the three-layered goals. Advocates make difficult choices recognizing that they are, indeed, making choices—choices with consequences for societal bottoms.

Below, critical race scholar Mari Matsuda offers one way to navigate some of the myriad pressures generated by the complex politics of knowledge, illustrating how the Schools themselves are a product of fundamental choices that prioritize bottom-up knowledge creation. Facing the white-over-black paradigm of formal equality, Matsuda rejects zero-sum games that pit bottoms against each other. She underscores that critical analysis—deconstruction—like knowledge creation through fact-finding—also has a politics. We should always beware.

BEYOND, AND NOT BEYOND, BLACK AND WHITE: DECONSTRUCTION HAS A POLITICS

Mari Matsuda
in Crossroads, Directions, and a New Critical Race Theory 393 (Francisco Valdes, Jerome McCristal Culp & Angela P. Harris eds. 2002)

. . . We in CRT made a choice to put race at the center of our analysis for reasons historical, political, and analytical. . . . [I]nitially [that meant] we were talking primarily about African American history and experience. [Because we cannot understand North American and other non-white/non-black communities in U.S. racism unless we understand African American history as American history. Asian Americans (and other non-white

---

[6] Mari Matsuda, Beyond, and Not Beyond, Black and White: Deconstruction Has a Politics, in Crossroads, Directions, and a New Critical Race Theory, 393–98 (Francisco Valdes, Jerome McCristal Culp & Angela P. Harris eds. 2002).

communities in the U.S.) need to know how the fear of a Black planet was real for U.S. planters in many areas of the South where the enslaved far outnumbered the free, and how this fear of Blackness burrowed into the collective unconscious of this nation in uniquely powerful ways.] . . .

When I say "fear of Blackness," I don't mean that this is all we need to understand. . . . We need to see the blood soaking our land from the genocide that strips sovereignty, home, and family from Indian people. We need to see that without U.S. imperial campaigns of westward expansion that intended to go all the way to Asia, we would be speaking Spanish. Without that imperialism, the nations of Hawaii, Guam, Micronesia, Okinawa, and the Philippines—all these places that don't have independence from U.S. military domination today—would have true sovereignty. We need to know how racism in all its variant forms has played out in our history, how inter- and intragroup oppression makes a people-of-color coalition a fantasy in many contemporary parts of the United States, and as we complexify, we have a challenge. . . .

I am an intellectual. Theory is important. I don't want my comments taken as anti-intellectual, anti-theory, or anti-deconstruction in particular. My attack is on destruction that comes without a progressive politics and without a material component. . . .

. . . A sophisticated, nuanced, thick understanding of human life may call for breaking out of categories. . . .

What does this mean for the future of CRT? I see an emerging consensus among the progressive wing of this band that race, gender, class, ethnicity, and sexuality are complex, interlinked and indisputable locations of oppression, and any attempt to erase or dilute one analysis in order to do another is a reactionary move. This makes our work incredibly hard, but . . . without attention to political effects, [the work] ultimately [would] serve interests that are not our own. . . .

Knowledge, its vocabularies, and the institutions of its production help to shape social power and material realities; for this reason, knowledge production has social and material consequences. Matsuda emphasizes how advocacy choices must be informed by "reasons historical, political, and analytical" that include "a material component"—an understanding of the socioeconomics that maintain the violence of systemic injustice across contexts, generations, and reforms. And she underscores this kind of work must connect the experience and insights of different groups because "that is what gives meaning to all we do." She rejects the blindfolds and handcuffs of the legal industry to press for antisubordination solidarity.

Because knowledge production has a politics, researchers have developed "better practices" to ensure that bottom-up research within social justice collaborations is carried out in principled and accountable ways. Psychology researchers Ruth Fassinger and Susan Morrow, for example, outline some of these better practices in social justice-focused research in counseling and psychology, practices relevant also to legal research for systemic advocacy. They suggest these practices help researchers to "understand systematic social inequities that privilege or marginalize particular groups of people and to work toward social change that results in the re-distribution of power and resources:"

> [C]ultural competence, manifested in the ability to navigate a culture different from one's own, is a foundational necessity for all researchers, whether they are members of dominant or marginalized groups themselves. Effective multicultural [professional] skills can help researchers build rapport, encourage self-reflection, and promote respectful interaction with participants. . . . Also emphasized [are] . . . the importance of understanding such details as participants' cultural histories; relevant laws and policies; values, norms, customs, and traditions of participants and their communities; and the sociopolitical climate as viewed from participants' perspectives. The researcher should possess culturally competent communication skills (including language fluency) and demonstrate respect for participants and their cultures; respect is manifested by adopting a non-pathological stance in regard to cultural manifestations and actively working to dismantle cultural stereotypes. . . .
>
> . . . [A] research team that is constituted to maximize diversity can balance strengths and limitations among teammates, provide growth for its members, challenge stereotypical thinking as well as biases and assumptions, and promote critical thinking. Interdisciplinary teams can broaden the scope of understanding of the phenomenon being studied. . . .
>
> . . . It is important . . . to examine and monitor what power these team members hold to determine who gets added to the team, what analytic decisions get made, [and] how funding is distributed. . . . [E]xplicit attention to relative power on the research team and active efforts to equalize power and maintain balance are essential. . . .
>
> At the core of respectful social justice research is . . . ensuring the opportunity for "meaningful participation" by the members of the community under investigation. . . . [Also,] social justice researchers are deliberate about taking their findings back to communities, presenting the research in a form that will be useful to participants and communities, and making the results

available to all community members—not just those who actively participated in the research.[7]

Fassinger and Morrow's reflection on best practices for research teams echoes the discussion of teamwork and collaborative professionalism in Part III. But Fassinger and Morrow highlight a key additional factor: power infuses every aspect of research and analysis and its misuse can distort research results—knowledge. Even when inadvertent, such distortions may weaken advocacy strategies and outcomes.

In the next excerpt, legal scholar Muneer Ahmad focuses on the relationship between client narratives, critical analysis, and legal ethics in the creation of legal knowledge and action. He shows how "knowledge from the bottom" can complicate advocacy choices and help to resolve those complications. He emphasizes that the complexities of real-world "messiness" make "uncovering facts" far from a straightforward process. In particular, he examines tensions that may arise between the ethical obligation of "zealous representation" and the role of client narratives in channeling that zealousness. Such narratives may be homophobic, sexist, racist, or otherwise contrary to professional (or personal) antisubordination commitments. He centers a critical question asking when, if ever, should lawyers strategically deploy racist, sexist, or homophobic narratives that would advance their clients' individual interests? When should they deploy strategies that capitalize on racism, sexism, homophobia, and other social ills to create knowledge—or perceptions and impressions—that can win a case by invoking systemic biases? How should advocates produce and use social knowledge for antisubordination purposes in the immediate moment while also making that moment a foundation for more transformative equal justice? What critical ethics should guide legal choices that may trade a short-term, individual gain for longer-term, collective injustice? How is the construction of critical ethics an exercise of power in knowledge creation and application?

Ahmad concludes that advocates should exercise "independent moral judgment" grounded in antisubordination purpose to balance immediate duties of zealousness to clients with broader duties owed to third parties or communities—the public welfare—or even to the law's commitment to equal justice. Ahmad notes that zealousness is only a means to an end—justice based on "the truth." As a result, he calls upon advocates to take in and frame facts and strategies critically and self critically. Ahmad calls for a critical, antisubordination praxis woven into the ethics and practice of law that lends no aid or comfort to the politics of identity castes.

---

[7] Ruth Fassinger and Susan Morrow, Toward Best Practices in Quantitative, Qualitative, and Mixed-Method Research: A Social Justice Perspective, 5 J. for Soc. Action in Counseling and Psych. 69 (2013).

THE ETHICS OF NARRATIVE
Muneer I. Ahmad
11 Am. U. J. Gender Soc. Pol'y & L. 117 (2002)

... The question presented is: Do the ethical rules permit, or even require, lawyers to strategically deploy racist, sexist or homophobic narratives that will advance their clients' interests? I begin the consideration of this thorny question by examining a specific teaching tool used in our law school and a series of complexities generated by it, and then propose a modest amendment to the ethical rules that would permit lawyers to better balance their commitments to progressive values and to their clients.

In the Criminal Justice Clinic here at the Washington College of Law, we have used a simulation for a number of years to explore a range of issues relating to the nature of the lawyer-client relationship, and, in particular, approaches to client interviewing and counseling, fact investigation, and development of case theory. The simulation requires that the students defend a thirty-two year old man named Randy Gilles, who, after a night of drinking with a friend, is accused of having forced a woman, Deborah Brand, to engage in oral sex with him and his friend in the backseat of a car. What little information the students are provided—a police report, the complaining witness's statement, the charging documents—is, by design, fraught with inconsistencies and contradictions. The students conduct an interview of their simulated client in which the client reports that he and his friend met Brand early in the morning at the hospital, where the friend was having his hand stitched up following a barroom brawl. Brand asked them for a ride home, they agreed, but later changed their minds and dropped her off well short of her home.

Soon after the client interview, the students are asked to theorize about what might have happened by brainstorming possible explanations for what occurred in the early morning hours of the night in question.

The ambiguity of the facts presented in the simulation lends them to a wide range of exculpatory possibilities: Brand had consensual sex but was angry because the two men dropped her off in the middle of nowhere; Brand was high and made the whole thing up; Brand had sex with the friend but not with our client; Brand was on medication that altered her memory.

This set of explanations can be crudely categorized as "crying rape." As one student put it in the course of a simulated interview, Deborah Brand was a "stank ho." These student-generated characterizations provide the basis for a preliminary classroom discussion of gender, and give rise to a series of feminist inquiries: Do women lie about rape? ... What histories, assumptions, and stereotypes underlie such a conclusion?

The students continue to generate additional possible explanations for what happened between Randy Gilles and Deborah Brand, and inevitably, a student suggests that Brand was trading sex for drugs. Of course, the "crack whore" defense, as some students describe this theory, is susceptible to the same feminist critique as the "crying rape" narrative, but it lends itself to additional critical study on race. A careful review of the police report reveals that Deborah Brand is African American. The documents provided to the students fail to specify the race of the defendant, Randy Gilles. Why does this matter?

First—and this should be obvious—it is fundamentally different to identify a black woman as a "crack whore" than it is to so identify a white woman. Just as crack, by itself, tends to conjure an image of an African American, the "crack whore" stereotype has been plied in racial terms. The "crack whore" is in many ways the cousin of the "welfare queen": both are, in the popular imagination, irresponsible, desperate, manipulative, female and black. The "crack whore" defense is thus both gendered and racialized.

Second, if we assume for the moment that Gilles is white, then the defense is not merely of a woman crying rape, but of a black woman crying rape against a white man. When we make a critical inquiry of this narrative ... we uncover a long Jim Crow history of disbelief when black women accuse white men of rape; if we dig deeper still, we see a slave history of slaveowner rape of black women with complete and utter impunity. In short, the feminist objection to the defense is incomplete without an attendant critique of the racialized dimension of the problem, just as the critical race critique is wanting without a consideration of gender. A "crack whore" is not just a crack whore; there is more to it than that.

Let me note that despite the imaginative, and perhaps speculative, nature of the exercise of brainstorming case theories, the students rarely address Deborah Brand's sexual orientation. By positing the "crying rape" defense, they implicitly theorize about Brand's gender (i.e., what kind of woman is she?). By suggesting the "crack whore" defense, they implicitly theorize about Brand's gender and race (i.e., what kind of black woman is she?). But in both instances, sexual orientation is left uninterrogated, which is to say that even the students' tentative inquiries into gender, race, and gender and race, are presumptively heterosexual. This is, I think, a sign of how deeply closeted sexual orientation remains in even the most progressive of lawyering processes: our consideration of poor black women never countenances the possibility that they might not be straight. To theorize on Brand's sexuality is more than a fanciful digression. In a case where the existence of and consent to a heterosexual sexual encounter are fundamental, the sexual orientation of the putative crime victim may be of enormous relevance. While far from conclusive, Brand's sexual orientation may influence a factfinder's determination of her credibility regarding the sexual conduct alleged. For example, a jury may be less willing to believe that Brand had consensual sex with a man if they believe her to be a lesbian. I do not mean to be reductive about sexuality; sexual identity is hardly determinative of sexual conduct, but it is, within the confines of the courtroom, at the very least probative.

This blind spot reminds us of the importance of Mari Matsuda's demand that we ask the "other question." As Professor Matsuda writes: "When I see something that looks racist, I ask, 'Where is the patriarchy in this?' When I see something that looks sexist, I ask, 'Where is the heterosexism in this? When I see something that looks homophobic, I ask, 'Where are the class interests in this?' " In so doing, we are forced "to look for both the obvious and non-obvious relationships of domination, helping us to realize that no form of subordination ever stands alone." Feminist and critical race inquiries are, then, inadequate, and leave the progressive lawyer's project incomplete. A fuller understanding of subordination, and a greater attention to it, demand the embrace and incorporation of sexual orientation into the progressive lawyer's case analysis.

After exploring these various narratives underlying the "crying rape" and "crack whore" defenses—what I term subordinating narratives—I ask my students the following questions: "So what? Is there anything wrong with advancing these defenses? More broadly, is there anything wrong with advancing arguments that, while advantageous to our clients, may reinforce subordinating racist, sexist, or homophobic stereotypes?" . . .

We can begin to understand the tensions this way: the progressive lawyer has an age-old duty of zealous representation on the one hand and a chosen commitment to anti-subordination on the other. The duty of zealous representation provides, as Lord Brougham famously said in 1821, that "to save [a] client by all means and expedients, and at all hazards and costs to other persons, and, amongst them, to himself, is [the lawyer's] first and only duty." That is to say, in the course of representation, a lawyer should do everything that a lawyer is allowed to do so long as it is advantageous to the client. Although articulated by Lord Brougham in the context of criminal defense . . ., as embodied in the rules of ethics—Canon 7 of the Model Code and in the Model Rules, the preamble and the comment to Rule 1.3—the duty of zealous representation applies to lawyers in all types of representation. The commitment to anti-subordination is something I presume on the part of the progressive lawyer, my only concern today.

The tension arises when we consider modes of persuasion and the centrality of narrative. Narrative, or storytelling, is the primary means by which we as lawyers advance our clients' causes. . . . [N]arrative is the "constructed core of the lawyering process." . . . Because narratives are constructed and do not merely exist in the ether, there for us to discover, the choices we make as to what narratives to construct are subject to moral and ethical scrutiny.

One obvious reason to use storytelling in our lawyering is that it is persuasive. In order for a story to be persuasive, it must resonate with the values, beliefs and assumptions of our audience. Our story ought to resonate with stories our audience is already familiar with and to which it already subscribes: the heroic firefighter, the Good Samaritan. Of course, our audience of judges and jurors may well subscribe to far more pernicious stories: the helpless woman victim, the crack whore, the lascivious fag. There is, of course, a strategic call to make as to which narratives our audiences actually believe and those they do not. At the end of the day, though, in order for our narratives to be effective, they must draw upon prevailing norms and beliefs, no matter how problematic they may be.... "Prejudice exists in the community and in the courthouse, and criminal defense lawyers would be foolhardy not to recognize this as a fact of life."

But this is where the tension lies: some thirty years after the end of de jure racial and gender discrimination, our ability to discern discrimination, and structural forms of discrimination in particular, depends largely upon critical insights, such as the recognition that the characterization of Deborah Brand as a crack whore plays upon subtle, deep-seated stereotypes centered around race and gender. The same is true, I would argue, with regard to sexual orientation, for although much of the homophobia expressed today is obvious on its face, so much more exists in more subterranean forms. Moreover, we can learn from the inability of formal racial and gender equality to root out structural forms of race and gender discrimination that the same is likely to be true of sexual orientation, which is to say that even if we were to achieve anti-discrimination laws on the basis of sexual orientation throughout the country, even if we were to achieve heightened scrutiny of discrimination against lesbians and gays, the discrimination would find ways to persist. We rely, then, upon our critical faculties to unearth subterranean subordination.

Critical study is committed to the project of destabilizing prevailing norms, interrogating assumptions, and otherwise muddying what appear to be clear waters. It is in large part through this methodology that our political awareness of, and political opposition to racism, sexism and homophobia emerge. But our legal institutions, and the courtroom in particular, require that we construct narratives that resonate with well-settled norms, values and attitudes. Arguably, the duty of zealous representation requires that we conform our narratives to these prevailing norms as well. Our commitment to anti-subordination is therefore difficult to square with our duty of zeal, given that as lawyers we operate not only in the defined universe of a particular client representation, but in the indeterminate universe of broader society as well. This is the problem of generalized political commitments meeting individual demands.

The tension here is significant. What if we conclude that the "crack whore" defense, or the homophobic panic defense, is the most effective for our clients? What if we believe, as I do, that criminal defense lawyers are, by virtue of their structural position in the criminal justice system, daily engaged in a battle against the subordination of the state against poor people and against people of color? Does that change our analysis about whether subordinating narratives are okay? Does the duty of zealous representation even allow us not to employ such a narrative?

The ethical rules allow us to engage our clients in a discussion of the broader implications of the narratives we construct. Model Rule 2.1 provides: "In representing a client, a lawyer shall exercise independent professional judgment and render candid advice. In rendering advice, a lawyer may refer not only to law but to other considerations such as moral, economic, social and political factors, that may be relevant to the client's situation." Model Code EC 7–9 allows a lawyer to ask his or her client for permission to forego an action that the lawyer views as unjust, even if the action is in the best interest of the client. However, "the decision whether to forego legally available objectives or methods because of non-legal factors is ultimately for the client and not for the lawyer." And Model Rule 1.16(b)(4) states that a lawyer has discretion to withdraw from representation if "the client insists upon taking action that the lawyer considers repugnant or with which the lawyer has a fundamental disagreement."

The ethical rules just discussed concern the potential conflict between a lawyer's duty to his or her client and the lawyer's fidelity to his or her own moral code. But the ethical rules also recognize a tension between a lawyer's duty to his or her client and an obligation owed to third parties. Ethical Consideration 7–10 states: "The duty of a lawyer to represent the client with zeal does not militate against the concurrent obligations to treat with consideration all persons involved in the legal process and to avoid the infliction of needless harm." Thus, the progressive lawyer's commitment to anti-subordination may find recognition in two qualifications on Lord Brougham's absolutist view of the duty of zealous representation: the lawyer's independent moral judgment and the lawyer's professional duty to third parties and to the public. This is necessarily the case, as the lawyer's moral judgments mediate her determination of what duty she owes to third parties.

. . . The prospect of augmenting professional duty to third parties or to the public good, at the expense of the lawyer's commitment to the wishes of the client, is fraught with difficulty and subject to immediate and predictable challenge. . . . And yet, as lawyers we are called upon to exercise our judgment all the time. Daily practice of law offers the best evidence of the ethical rules' failure to provide bright line rules. This is to say that conformity with the ethical rules demands the exercise of individual judgment. . . .

Returning to the clinic's fictional client Randy Gilles, let us imagine that he is African American. We might consider, first by ourselves as his lawyers and then in conversation with him, how he might feel about advancing a narrative that relies upon negative stereotypes of African American women. The presumption is that he wouldn't care. The presumption is that he will act purely out of self-interest. But even if that is the case, how does he define self-interest? Is it not within the realm of possibility that Randy Gilles would view the lending of support to a racial stereotype about African Americans as against self-interest? Even if, as the rules of ethics currently provide, the ultimate decision rests solely with the client, it is, I would argue, the duty of the lawyer to consider the broader implications of the constructed narrative, and to engage the client in a conversation about them. The language of the ethical rules discussed earlier is permissive, and at best hortatory, of the kind of client counseling I envision. I suggest that the rules should make such counseling mandatory.

It is important that we acknowledge and appreciate that as individual, as particularized, and as client-centered as a representation may be, it does not occur in a vacuum. It is true, as my students have said in reaction to the Randy Gilles simulation, that they are not going to be able to wipe away deeply entrenched sexism or racism or homophobia through the choices they make about the narrative to deploy in an individual case. But that truth cannot be determinative of the question at hand, for just as the students' efforts in an individual representation will not eradicate racism, sexism, or homophobia, nor will a client's individual case, by itself, resolve the systemic oppression of poor people by the criminal justice system. Both efforts depend upon our aggregate efforts, and rely upon the notion that our individual actions, no matter how small, are of consequence. They matter. They are subject to moral scrutiny. Even in the smallest of cases, we are as lawyers creatures in an ecosystem that shifts and responds as we do.

. . . We must be honest in our recognition of the lawyer's role and responsibility in shaping [every] judge's judgment, and how it might affect others in the future.

The lawyer-client relationship may be a confidential one, but it is not wholly a private one. We can learn from queer theory the value of transparency, of understanding that the acts of individuals are of consequence to the collective. Is there a tension between zeal to the individual client and commitment to anti-subordination? Of course there is. But our fidelity to ourselves as lawyers depends upon the honest embrace of such tension as a threshold step to its resolution.

Ahmad finds in legal ethics two touchstones to help square traditional practices with antisubordination purpose—"the lawyer's independent moral judgment and the lawyer's professional duty to third parties and to the public." Both allow an expanded notion of collectivized representation within existing client-attorney rules. With this framing in mind, we turn to the mechanics of this work: the two recurring "stages" of systemic advocacy.

NOTES AND QUESTIONS

1. *Diverse Teams.* Fassinger and Morrow suggest challenges that may exist when conducting socially just research if the researcher lacks cultural competency. A researcher, for example, might lack a status characteristic (e.g., Latinx), identification (e.g., LGBT), or skill (e.g., language fluency) of the community experiencing the problem to be studied or the client-group members participating on a research team. How might such a difference in characteristics affect collaborative research? Is the suggestion of Fassinger and Morrow to form a team that is diverse in skills and identities helpful here? Should status characteristics or skills of other constituencies, such as targeted decision makers, be taken into account in forming the team? Challenges also may exist when the researcher shares identities or skills of the affected group. Do these concerns also apply beyond critical research to analysis and advocacy?

2. *Antisubordination as Principle and Practice.* Ahmad refers to antisubordination as an anchor to legal problem solving for justice. As discussed in Part II, antisubordination as a value expresses a commitment to solidarity with anyone or any group subjected to subordination. This notion is thus both a principle and a practice. In some contexts, as Ahmad illustrates, this fundamental "commitment" can create tensions with short-term tactics that manipulate identity biases for the benefit of (usually) an individual client and, perhaps, at the expense of a larger group of individuals. Can advocates ever ethically promote racist, sexist, homophobic, or other biases by using them strategically? How does he propose that advocates engage and negotiate the politics of those tensions? What else would you add?

3. *Grievances and Possibilities.* What Ahmad describes in an atomized criminal defense context has a parallel in macro history. At times, subordinated groups have invoked stereotypes of other groups to distance themselves and perhaps move closer to the goal of "acceptance" into whiteness and its racial supremacy. For example, the Latinx organization League of United Latin American Citizens (LULAC) once followed the practice of marginalizing Blacks. LULAC approved of segregation, arguing that segregation was necessary to obstruct sexual contact between Mexican girls and African Americans. Moreover, LULAC leaders, together with the Latinx veterans group the American G.I. Forum, reached out to President Johnson in 1965 during a time of urban unrest, suggesting that, " 'unlike blacks, Mexican

Americans eschewed civil disobedience and violent confrontation' in favor of loyalty to whiteness."[8] Such appeals ultimately had limited utility for Mexican Americans as a group: "Although the whiteness strategy enabled them to make gains, Mexican Americans found it unsatisfying because, even if they could compel the state to recognize them as *white* some of the time, they could do little to alter the attitudes of white citizens and officials or the racially discriminatory practices which they enforced."[9] This conditional and contextual acceptance into whiteness failed as a strategy to blunt Mexican American marginalization, but it buttressed anti-Black racism and created schisms between Black and Mexican American communities. Can you think of other examples of such a defensive practice at work, between or within groups? What do such strategies mean for the formation of cross-group coalitions today? Recall Mahoney's discussion of solidarity in Part II and Su and Yamamoto's discussion of critical coalitions between Thai and Latinx workers in Part III. How might an advocate begin to help aggrieved persons and groups to work together based both on values and on interests?

4. *Digital Racial Surveillance.* In Oregon, it was discovered in 2015 that a state Department of Justice investigator identified groups and individuals for scrutiny by searching for those using certain Twitter hashtags—specifically the #BlackLivesMatter hashtag. This investigator's task was to identify potential threats to police. Similarly, law enforcement, immigration authorities, and even private groups can obtain data from geofencing technology to "map" the identity of any BLM or other protestors with smart phones at any given place and time, potentially allowing police to target protestors with outstanding warrants or to retaliate in other ways against those in the "mapped" area. Are these examples a legitimate use of digital surveillance or an abuse of (state) power against individuals or groups? Would such surveillance aid in identifying potential threats efficiently? Would it squelch activism that situates law enforcement officials as potential initiators of community violence and aims at broadscale reform?

5. *Surveillance as Norm or Exception.* The FBI operated a surveillance program called COINTELPRO (a name derived from COunter INTELligence PROgram) between 1956 and 1971, well before the notorious post-9/11 surveillance programs that targeted Muslims and others. COINTELPRO focused on U.S.-based organizing and advocacy groups:

> Virtually every organization in the country perceived by intelligence or law enforcement agencies as advocating social change in any manner was targeted. These organizations included all communist or socialist groups; the "New Left" in general, which included anti-war activists, student organizations, environmentalists, feminists and gay rights advocates; all organizations composed primarily of people

---

[8] Daniel M. Rochmes and G.A. Elmer Griffin, The Cactus That Must Not be Mistaken for a Pillow: White Racial Formation Among Latinos, 197, 200 in Racializing Justice, Disenfranchising Lives: The Racism, Criminal Justice, and Law Reader (Manning Marable, Ian Steinberg & Keesha Middlemass eds. 2007).

[9] Brent M.S. Campney, Brown, Black, and White in Texas, Southern Spaces (Mar. 13, 2012).

of color, from African American civil rights and church groups to the Black Panther Party, the American Indian Movement, the Chicano Brown Berets, and advocates of Puerto Rican independence; and "white hate" groups such as the Ku Klux Klan.[10]

The COINTELPRO program's best-known component was surveillance of these groups through illegal means such as intercepting their mail and using wiretaps. But program objectives went well beyond mere spying to neutralizing and destroying these groups: by disseminating false information about them, creating internal dissension in and among the groups, misusing the criminal justice system against them, and even collaborating in physical assaults and assassinations of group members and leaders.[11] Consider, in light of this and other examples, the need for care against surveillance in researching an advocacy project.

The LittleSis organization, whose power mapping tools we discuss later in this chapter, puts it bluntly: "In this age of widespread surveillance, it's important to keep your research safe and secure from the prying eyes of governments and corporations." Systemic advocates know that threats to their work, whether at the research or action stages, come from a variety of sources, both public and private. Eventually your actions might reveal your systemic targets, but it may be best to ensure privacy for as long as possible, particularly during Stage One research and analysis. Organizations with research expertise collaborate with other advocates and activists to address privacy and security concerns. For example, the organization LittleSis offers digital security tips for researchers, which can be found at www.littlesis.org/toolkit/digital_security. For research conducted or shared outside the digital arena, consider what additional safeguards activists and systemic advocates should take to ensure privacy. Keep this imperative in mind as you read about the three methods of critical research later in this chapter.

11.2 ADVOCATES DIAGNOSE PROBLEMS AND STRATEGIZE SOLUTIONS IN TWO RECURRING STAGES

Systemic advocacy incorporates two stages—critical research and analysis (Stage One) and complex advocacy actions (Stage Two)—that function together to create and apply knowledge from the bottom in principled and accountable ways. Although described as stages, this work occurs and recurs in an iterative manner. In general terms, problem solving begins with contextual research and analysis, which then leads to three-layered advocacy strategies; then, as advocates implement strategies, they assess results, adapt their actions accordingly, and continue to press forward.

---

[10] Natsu Taylor Saito, For "Our" Security: Who Is An "American" and What is Protected by Enhanced Law Enforcement and Intelligence Powers, 2 Seattle J. Soc. Just. 23, 37 (2003).

[11] Natsu Taylor Saito, Whose Liberty? Whose Security? The USA PATRIOT Act in the Context of COINTELPRO and the Unlawful Repression of Political Dissent, 81 Or. L. Rev. 1051 (2002).

Through this ongoing process of recurrent, overlapping cycles or stages, advocates create practical strategies to overcome (old and new) elite mechanisms of systemic injustice. In tandem, Stage One research and analysis and Stage Two advocacy actions address persistent social problems to advance three-layered goals. This chart provides a quick overview:

(Recurring, Overlapping) Cycles of Action	
Stage One, Critical Research & Analysis *Traditional preparation teaches one to define a problem in terms of law and to use legal research to identify relevant facts. Systemic advocacy expands research and analysis to ensure that the perspectives of marginalized groups are included, to expose the ways in which elites benefit from the problem, and ensure information needed to advance three-layered goals is provided.*	Methods of Research: –Participatory Action Research –Critical Empiricism –Analytical Narrative Norms of Research: –Inter/Counterdisciplinarity –Critical Comparativism –Social Analytics Mapping Techniques: –Concept Mapping –Community Asset Mapping –Stakeholder Mapping –Power Mapping
Stage Two, Advocacy Actions *Traditional advocacy actions are ameliorative and usually are individual—a case or a contract, for example. These actions become part of complex advocacy actions in systemic advocacy. They are coordinated and combined with other legal and extralegal activities to engage communities, to pressure/persuade elite decision makers, and do whatever is needed to reach three-layered goals.*	Typical Complex Advocacy Actions: –Issue Campaigns –Community Development (CD) Projects Components of Campaigns/CD Projects: –Understanding Group Clients –Framing Problems and Solutions –Building the Action Team –Developing an Action Plan –Anticipating Opposition –Measuring & Monitoring Success –Generating the Right Resources
Goals *Traditional advocacy goals focus on technical outcomes that solve a social problem by using or*	Three-Layered Goals: –Solving social problems –Building collective power within subordinated groups

creating law. Such solutions remain key as first-layer goals in systemic advocacy. But the second layer—building collective power— and third layer—shifting consciousness and cultural understandings—are just as important. The fact that goals are three-layered affects both what solutions are sought and how solutions are won. Progress along all three layers allows for changing the rules of the game to level the playing field for future struggles.	–Shifting consciousness and cultural norms and practices toward Critical Justice

As the chart illustrates, critical research and analysis uses information to diagnose social problems, to design solutions, and to develop strategies to achieve those solutions. This research is not library-bound nor judge- or law-focused. Rather, it is an expansive form of innovative knowledge production that uses micro sources of knowledge for analysis of persistent macro conditions. Critical research and analysis also uses the insights of critical theory (the Schools and Approaches) to evaluate the limits and biases of traditional sources and to incorporate nontraditional sources. Building on lessons of critical history, critical research and analysis combines knowledge drawn from varied disciplines and previous generations with new research, both from the field and from the files. In Stage One, the aim of critical research is to generate knowledge from the bottom *and* to create accountability to that bottom through principled uses of that knowledge in a particular systemic context.

As advocates conduct research and analyze information, they also begin to spot possible courses of action. This fluid process connects diagnosis with strategy. Stage One research and analysis and Stage Two complex actions are cycled in a recurrent fashion. This ongoing process helps advocates modify future plans as they gather new information and make and evaluate incremental outcomes. When diagnosis and strategy are linked in this manner, legal scholar Gary Blasi notes, legal analysis can "address questions of what could or should be done about the problems it documents."[12] Diagnosing and strategizing are accomplished by "facilitating a common search for insights in many forms, such as stories,

---

[12] Gary Blasi, What's a Theory For?: Notes on Reconstructing Poverty Law Scholarship, 48 U. Miami L. Rev. 1063, 1063, 1096–97 (1994).

schemas, analogs, and mental models" in order "not merely to interpret the world, but to change it."[13]

Stage One research and analysis typically informs courses of action at the beginning of most projects, but of course the object of this knowledge production is its application—the action. Initial research and analysis are tailored in each context or scenario to create knowledge that informs and guides complex advocacy actions. In systemic advocacy, actions therefore are at the center of Stage Two. These actions usually are "complex" precisely because they are designed to match and check the complexities of the Critical Challenge in a given systemic context.

Both stages of advocacy additionally depend on varied kinds of collaboration. No one individual or discipline can hope (or be expected) to provide all of the multiple knowledges and skills from all of the needed disciplines, fields, or perspectives. Therefore, collaboration in advocacy inevitably depends on work being carried out collectively. As we have seen in Part III and since, interdisciplinary and cross-cultural problem-solving teams are tailored to diagnosing particular problems and strategizing to advance solutions along all three layers of goals.

When used *diagnostically*, research generates "facts." Those facts are analyzed to evaluate the particular context and history in which the social problem has emerged and persisted in relation to the relevant identities, groups, interests, and power. Initially, diagnosis thereby leads to strategy. When used *strategically*, research identifies specific important actors and allows for plans and actions that disrupt or realign interests to support technical systemic solutions, as well as power-building and culture shifts. Strategic research can clarify how laws shape, promote, *and* obscure interests and thus how advocates might best advance three-layered goals. However, this "background" role of law in shaping consciousness and projects often is so pervasive and entrenched that it is difficult to pinpoint:

> Law hides the prescriptive power of the state so well that sometimes even lawyers and historians fail to see it. Legal rules helped make class-based interracial organizing difficult in labor history. Judges developed doctrines that made it hard for workers to organize and strike and prevented states from giving workers effective protection in joining unions. Courts struck down most attempts by legislators to enact labor-protective regulation. The rules that made interracial work difficult went beyond the direct regulation of labor. Judges also limited or struck down Reconstruction civil rights statutes that should have protected equality. Taken together, these decisions fostered racial division,

---

[13] *Id.*

promoted insecurity among workers, and placed burdens on class-based organizing.[14]

Mindful of this backdrop, Stage One research and analysis contextually outlines the identities, groups, relationships, interests, and power of a range of actors in relation to a problem *as preparation for Stage Two strategy development and execution*. This research extends beyond the doctrinal confines of formal equality and prepares the advocate to engage the social problem in pragmatic yet principled systemic terms. In practice, as pointed out in Parts I and II and since, critical strategies combine legal and extralegal work—jurisprudence and demosprudence—to persuade and pressure varied actors for progress along the three layers of goals.

Traditional legal research techniques may be necessary but, as the following excerpts underscore, not sufficient for systemic diagnosis and strategic action planning. Thus, systemic advocates must master—but also critically assess and move beyond—the accepted commercial methods and sources for research and analysis. As legal scholars Richard Delgado and Jean Stefancic point out, researchers often are "drowning in a sea of facts (perseverating):"

> [I]magine that one's client is an African American woman who has been fired because she came to work one day wearing her hair in braids. Her employer, who likes black men and white women, has fired her for wearing a hair style he associates with black women, who he thinks are defiant and hard to control. . . .
>
> To find out how other Title VII cases have dealt with this question, the lawyer searches for cases containing the terms "discrimination," "African American woman," "hair," and "braids." The search turns up only a handful of cases, none on point, so the lawyer broadens the search. . . .
>
> What the lawyer can easily overlook is that the case calls for a new theory of *intersectional discrimination*. . . . Title VII needs to develop a theory of intersectional discrimination for cases, like this, . . . [that call for] new law to fill in the gap in Title VII coverage. . . .
>
> One possibility that we must entertain is that when searching for a new legal remedy, we should turn our computers off. Lawyers interested in representing clients who (unlike corporations) do not find a ready-made body of developed law in their favor need to spend time with the computer shut down, mulling over what an ideal legal world would look like from the client's perspective. . . .

---

[14] Martha R. Mahoney, What's Left of Solidarity: Reflections on Law, Race, and Labor History, 57 Buff. L. Rev. 1515, 1515–16 (2009).

It requires a conceptual advance that sees old materials in a new light.[15]

Consequently, critical research often includes, but typically is not limited to, traditional research methods. Moreover, critical research questions the sources of knowledge and also incorporates nontraditional techniques to uncover and understand "outsider" sources of knowledge. As the next excerpt shows, the dangers of uncriticality and misinformation confirm the need for a "reconstructed legal research process" that considers both contents and sources of information. A reconstructed approach to research employs traditional sources, while also mining nontraditional sources and relevant disciplines. This approach "unplugs" from routinized thinking and research to reconceive conventional legal concepts, practices, and outcomes *from the perspective of clients and client-groups affected by a problem*. This approach is based on the critical understanding that knowledge, and knowledge production, always are political.

To illustrate concretely, law librarian and scholar Nicholas Stump confronts the structuring of legal knowledge and knowledge production through research. Stump shows how existing categories and methods of traditional legal research are based on a classification scheme that detaches legal research and knowledge production from the role and relevance of identities, groups, interests, and power. These classifications—themselves a top-down exercise in knowledge control—mask and fail to adequately take account of law's indeterminacy, as discussed in Part I. Stump points out the top-down politics of traditional research and analysis, and he also shows how to counteract them by exploring nontraditional sources and taking seriously bottom-up knowledge. In the following excerpt, Stump illustrates a critically "reconstructed" legal research strategy designed to support social justice efforts in Appalachian coal towns that suffer from deep poverty—an example of actionable knowledge production that, he notes, advocates can adapt to other contexts.

FOLLOWING NEW LIGHTS: CRITICAL LEGAL RESEARCH STRATEGIES AS A SPARK FOR LAW REFORM IN APPALACHIA

Nicholas F. Stump
23 Am. U. J. Gender Soc. Pol'y & L. 573 (2014)

... Introduction

... The overarching crux of the modern critical legal research process is that attorneys ought to look beyond the deeply problematic "ready-made body of developed law" and should instead think "outside the box" in

---

[15] Richard Delgado and Jean Stefancic, Why Do We Ask the Same Questions? The Triple Helix Dilemma Revisited, 99 Law Libr. J. 307, 319–20, 328 (2007).

"reinventing, modifying, flipping, and radically transforming legal doctrines and theories imaginatively."

Although a definitive encapsulation of such a process is elusive (due to its multifaceted and necessarily ever-evolving nature), prominent examples of critical legal research strategies to date include the following: a more nuanced use of premier and alternative legal research databases, based in part on a critical deconstruction of database structure and functionality; a newfound practitioner reliance upon theoretical resources as potential touchstones for innovation, as compared to more traditional legal resources in a vacuum; and a rediscovery of the profound importance of "unplugged" brainstorming sessions as a means for achieving genuine legal innovation. Much may be achieved in terms of progressive law reform by utilizing such critical techniques in conjunction with the more traditional legal research process. . . .

. . . *Traditional Legal Research Process*

The paradigmatic print legal research process can be said to proceed in four steps. The first step in a fact-based legal research query is to examine the presented facts and to predict which legal categories likely control those facts, known historically as the search for the *ratio decidendi*, or the law determining the case. In the second step, a researcher formulates key terms based on the pertinent facts paired with the predicted, controlling legal categories. . . . Third, from these starting points, researchers may then modify the scope of the query through alternate keywords, annotations, cross-references, etc. Fourth, the researcher updates found authority via the Shepard's citator service. Locating primary mandatory authority and primary persuasive authority, as required is commonly understood to be the terminal objective of the classic legal research process.

The transition to the online medium has precipitated a variation on the traditional research process. In theory, an online researcher may begin the research process by keyword searching within secondary resources, as available in each database. Through WestlawNext, a researcher even may perform a search within the online West Topic and Key Number system. However, studies indicate that online researchers tend to eschew these techniques, instead initiating the research process by performing keyword searches within targeted primary sources (e.g., a case law sub-database), or else by keyword searching across the entirety of a database's resources simultaneously. Thereafter, online researchers negotiate the results pages (directing attention to case law, especially), before updating found primary authority via online citator services.

Legal Research Process Viewed as Normatively Neutral

Regardless of such variations, the legal research process has historically been viewed and taught as a normatively neutral enterprise. Legal research commonly is understood to be something of a positivistic science, devoid of any political or ideological influences. Tellingly, in such seminal legal research textbooks as *How to Find the Law* and *Fundamentals of Legal Research* (and in the newer generation of such textbooks) authors "present legal research as a search for 'authority' or the 'the law' that determines the result of a particular legal problem." Legal research textbooks then "reflect a tendency to talk about law as preexisting and given[,] . . . something that can be found."

. . . When Arthur Langdell spoke of the library as a laboratory of law, this then was his meaning: that legal research is an objective science wherein correct, binding law is *discovered*.

Critical Legal Research

Critical Legal Research Theory

The very notion of a critical approach to the legal research process is grounded in the decades-old school—or collective movement—known as critical legal theory. As opposed to a discrete framework, contemporary critical legal theory perhaps is best defined as a diverse and inclusive canon of "literature or ideas," including such schools as feminist legal theory, critical race theory, critical race feminism, LatCrit, queer legal theory, disability theory, law and socioeconomics, and critical examinations of environmental law—the theoretical underpinnings of which were influenced by such foundational movements as legal realism, neo-Marxism, post-structuralism, and deconstruction. As a unifying force, modern critical legal theory arguably offers a "radical, left-oriented critique of contemporary law and jurisprudence," based on the normative premise that "social class stratification and hierarchical power distributions, as they exist in our society, are inherently unjust." Critical legal theory tends to have a liberatory agenda; thus, the overarching aim is to pursue "'human emancipation' in circumstances of domination and oppression," and to generally promote democratic and egalitarian principles.

Doctrinal Incoherency and Indeterminacy

The first wave of critical legal theorists introduced a range of interrelated notions that sparked the genesis of critical work on the institution of legal research specifically. The following are principles associated with the pioneering literature of the Critical Legal Studies (CLS) movement per se (active in the 1970s and 1980s).

First, legal doctrine is "incoherent and indeterminate," as opposed to being formalistic, or a science, because any given body of precedent—no matter how comprehensive—is incapable of covering all conceivable fact situations. More specifically, an application of the tenets of deconstruction to legal texts yields the conclusion that all doctrine is open to innumerable interpretations, and that thus no discrete body of precedent can constrain judicial decisions.

Second, legal reasoning largely is a myth. There exists no neutral mode of rationality through which "correct" law is discovered and applied through *stare decisis*. Instead, the enterprise is driven predominantly by political and ideological considerations—which largely reflect the dominant liberal-capitalist worldview.

Third, and finally, all categorizations of law are inherently subjective. Moreover, like the myth of legal reasoning, such categorizations serve the dominant, homogenous interests of society at the expense of subordinated groups. Taken as a whole then, these three principles demonstrate "the need for radical change" in the mold of progressive thought.

In more recent years, such early insights proffered by the CLS movement have been qualified somewhat and refined. . . . Contemporary critical scholars also continue to maintain that "[t]hrough indeterminacy, the legal system allows powerful interests to dominate outcomes, while retaining the appearance of neutrality and autonomy."

As Charles Barkan argues persuasively in the seminal essay *Deconstructing Legal Research*, the foundational insights proffered by the CLS movement in addition to subsequent discourse refinements are innately applicable to—and in fact, are inseparable from—the longstanding institution of the American legal research process. As Barkan elucidates:

> A CLS analysis of legal research might start with the impression that there is something fundamentally wrong with the way modern legal thinking responds to social problems, and that the traditional methods and materials of legal research contribute to that unsatisfactory state of affairs. . . .

The unreconstructed legal research process demands that the attorney discover the discrete precedent controlling a given fact pattern. For an issue of first impression, the researcher must discover the *ratio decidendi*, which the judge then applies formalistically to fill a gap in the common law.

However, critical principles reveal the sometimes impossibility, and indeed very often the preposterousness, of this conception. For the legal researcher, there might be no objective *ratio decidendi* to discover—as indeterminacy dictates that novel fact patterns potentially could be "controlled" by a veritable sea of competing (and often conflicting) precedent. In making such selections, "a wide variety of interpretations, distinctions, and justifications are available," in that judges and researchers are potentially free to choose among a plethora of competing arguments, authorities, and so on. Ultimately then, law indeed is politics by another name, and the notion of neutral, objective doctrine, devoid of the subjective ideological preferences of judges, is mere fantasy, albeit one in service to society's dominant interests. Therefore, "the search for . . . the rule of the case, leads nowhere."

Legal Categories

... Due to the indeterminacy of legal doctrine, categorizations of law are necessarily subjective social constructs—as opposed to objective renderings of doctrinal truth. One might wonder, how *could* a categorization scheme accurately represent legal doctrine, when the critical analysis demonstrates that doctrine is, at least partially, indeterminate? As succinctly stated by Duncan Kennedy, "all such schemes are lies," and in fact the "very existence of historically legitimated doctrinal categories gives the law student, the teacher, and the practitioner a false sense of the orderliness of legal thought," effectively masking law's indeterminacy.

What is more, legal categorization schemes, through their political, historical, and economic underpinnings, reflect the normativity of the societal status quo. Legal categories "are created and perpetuated by society's dominant interests," in that white, patriarchal, heteronormative, ableist, ageist, anthropocentric, atomistic-capitalist, etc. values are reflected—and advanced—through such schemes. Therefore, "[legal] classification systems can also be biased or insensitive because they may reflect Eurocentric or other dominant ideologies and values and ignore other cultures, races, genders, etc.," and "[t]he end result is that standardized categories may ultimately affect a client's justice."

Jill Anne Farmer writes more on this point . . .: "Because meaning is socially constructed, the groups that control the economic and cultural apparatus of a given society largely determine which meanings are considered most important. Moreover, the cultural process is shaped increasingly by fewer transnational corporations," wherein "profit and ideological conformity" are the controlling interests. To be sure, the legal publishing industry exemplifies this phenomenon, as there exists a "unique concentration of publishing in the hands of only a few companies."

Any doctrinal categorization system then is informed by and arguably is a principal player in, our contemporary late capitalist mode. Rather than constituting objective doctrinal truth, legal categories instead embody the subjective values characteristic of the dominant groups, interests, and systems of modern Westernism.

The West Topic and Key Number system, as the seminal legal categorization scheme, is the supreme exemplar of such normative biases. Commentators have agreed universally that West categories evolve slowly: "The topic 'Labor' received a heading in the 1950s, and until [the 1980s] West classified 'Workers' Compensation' under 'Master and Servant' law." Delgado and Stefancic also have identified numerous instances of problematic race- and sex-based categorizations in the West system. Finally, one need only skim the West Topic and Key Number outline, as it currently exists, to discern its conservative ideological bias—e.g., that West has classified numerous same-sex marriage points of law under the topic

"Husband and Wife" is no small irony. Therefore, through such doctrinal categorizations, the West Topic and Key Number system indeed perpetuates "dominant ideologies and values" while subordinating "other cultures, races, genders, etc."

. . . [W]hen attempting to classify novel fact situations, the range of legal-doctrinal possibilities available to the researcher necessarily is constricted by the established boundaries of West's doctrinal categories—when the fact situation instead may call for innovation. As stated elegantly by Delgado and Stefancic: "[C]ategories contained in current indexing systems are like eyeglasses we have worn a long time. They enable us to see better, but lull us into thinking our vision is perfect and that there may not be a still better pair." . . .

Contemporary Critical Research Process

For the contemporary attorney pursuing progressive law reform initiatives, a number of critical strategies are perhaps uniquely suited for our online age. An overview of such strategies is not and could not be definitive. Legal research technologies change daily . . ., and critical research, as an inherently *creative* process, by its very nature resists a formulaic application. However, based on the insights proffered by luminaries within the discourse to date, the following critical strategies may function admirably as *starting points* for the researcher pursuing legal innovation. Most aptly, the strategies below may be characterized as just one potential version of a reconstructed legal research process.

Internalize Critical Insights

A researcher ought to internalize the central, critical analysis of the research process. . . . Such familiarization is imperative, as the researcher must establish a background foundation upon which to contextualize and to thereafter deploy more concrete critical strategies. For example, the critical research project depends upon a willingness to imaginatively de- and reconstruct legal concepts, an endeavor legitimized, in part, by the understanding that refined notions of doctrinal indeterminacy are no longer radical notions—but instead are the increasingly accepted norm. . . .

The researcher must also be fluent in the precise mechanics through which contemporary legal resources perpetuate the societal status quo. One must be aware of the West Topic and Key Number system's continued (and multifaceted) ascendency, problematic search algorithm enhancements, the closed loop effect of brand-based resource cross-referencing, and so on. To be sure, a reformist-minded attorney must understand just *how* legal research databases continue to function as agents of homogenization for research outcomes.

Concept-Based Research

With such a background foundation established, an attorney may then engage in a traditional, concept-based legal research process. Using databases or print legal resources, if available, the researcher should determine how the given fact pattern likely will be characterized within the existing unreconstructed legal landscape (i.e., the classic hunt for the supposed *ratio decidendi*). The researcher should cultivate concept-based legal research methodologies, as opposed to purely fact-based methods, to locate such "controlling" legal categories that will serve as starting points for the critical interrogation of the existing legal framework at issue. . . .

Alternative Legal Resources

When searching online for doctrinal legal content, an attorney may consider using such alternative resources as Fastcase, the Cornell Legal Information Institute, and GPO FDsys. While any online resource is inherently biased, these alternative resources at least are devoid of many of the explicit commercial channeling agents endemic to the premier legal databases. Alternative resources may provide more neutral avenues through which to view the law.

Legal Scholarly and Multidisciplinary Research

After researching the existing doctrinal landscape, a next step may involve mining legal scholarly and related cross- and multidisciplinary resources. As Farmer writes, "often we fail to look outside the system box in which we are conceptually housed." Searching "outside the system box" is an enterprise traditionally reserved for legal theorists alone, and so "practitioners are often insulated from external questions." Thus, practitioners pursuing systemic change ought to go "beyond the usual" legal resources and should "join legal theorists" in using "materials that reflect on social, political, and cultural theory."

For the attorney searching for law reform ideas vis-à-vis scholarly texts within the commercial legal databases, law review articles, as a selected source or sub-database, are the obvious starting places. . . .

To truly "search outside the system box," researchers also may seek out cross-and multidisciplinary materials. Online repositories make available scholarship across all disciplines—not just law; leading repositories include SSRN, Digital Commons, and JSTOR "Register & Read." Google Books, a repository containing millions of scanned books (including academic monographs) also may constitute a useful research resource. An attorney may seek out relevant interdisciplinary materials through local academic libraries.

Unplugging and Brainstorming Sessions

After such resource-gathering methods have been exhausted, an attorney may engage in (more purely) analytical strategies. Perhaps most importantly, the critical researcher should, at this point, consider unplugging....

The endgame of the critical project—"radically transforming legal doctrines"—has remained fundamentally unchanged in the online era. But as doctrinal innovation ultimately depends upon people, not computers, cultivating a *people*-based analytical methodology is essential for genuinely effective law reform. Brainstorming sessions with diverse perspectives at play is a particularly apt strategy for law reform, because progressive movements, by their very nature, are often defined by collaborative discourse.

... [F]ew attorneys successfully "break free from the constraints of preexisting thought" and proffer "effective new approaches." But such thinkers who do often are "individuals whose life experiences have differed markedly from those of their contemporaries. They may be members of marginal groups, or persons who are in other ways separated from the mainstream." Individuals from *all* corners of the legal profession may have much to add to the law reform landscape. So too, may non-lawyer citizens and activists: to be sure, "[i]nvolving the community can assist in effective law reform strategies." For instance, "synergies between activists working for social change and lawyers seeking law reform" may produce the most dynamic sociolegal change, in that "each activity can catalyze and in turn be amplified by the other." Diverse voices then ought to be a vital component of any meaningful law reform undertaking.

Application of Critical Legal Research: Mountaintop Removal Law Reform

... *Mountaintop Removal Law*

The central Appalachian region of the United States, after more than a century of exploitation at the hands of the coal extraction industry, is perhaps a supreme exemplar of the phenomenon known as the resource curse. Alternatively termed the paradox of plenty, the resource curse is "a designation that denotes a pattern of social, political, and economic problems in areas rich in natural resources."

Presumably, such resource-rich regions would boast high standards of living; however, outside economic interests—the coal industry, in this context—"wield[ ] power over the [region] at the expense of its citizens and the natural environment." That the coal industry is perennially aided by captured ruling elites (e.g., state politicians, regulatory officials, etc.), and has gained the widespread support of the very citizens it subjugates most egregiously, are defining characteristics of the Appalachian resource curse.

One might say that, in Appalachia, coal controls all: vast intersections exist "between environmental problems caused by coal operations . . . and the iniquitous social and economic conditions" of the region.

Any efforts then to achieve transformative change in Appalachia necessarily must involve reform to the sociolegal apparatus governing the coal extraction industry: the epicenter of harm. For the last two decades, mountaintop removal mining has emerged as the increasingly dominant surface mining practice in the region, due to (1) amendments to the Clean Air Act, which have incentivized coal burning plants to favor the low-sulfur coal endemic to central Appalachia; and (2) advances in pertinent mining technology, such as the development of massive excavation equipment. As reported by the Congressional Research Service, mountaintop removal mining now has swelled to "an area of approximately 12 million acres located in portions of Kentucky, West Virginia, Virginia, Tennessee, Pennsylvania, and Ohio."

Mountaintop removal also ranks among the most destructive mining techniques yet devised, scouring Appalachian communities and surrounding ecosystems alike. Thus, from a law reform perspective, mountaintop removal jurisprudence is an ideal site from which to pursue reform vis-à-vis critical legal research strategies.

Mining Process

. . . [T]he direct environmental and human health harms of mountaintop removal are legion. Over one thousand miles of crucial, headwater streams have been "directly impacted" and in many instances, completely "obliterated." . . . [M]ountaintop removal mining is linked to increased flash flooding, and the affected waters downstream from valley fills contain elevated levels of such toxic chemicals as selenium, sulfates, aluminum, zinc, and BTEX compounds, all of which are harmful to aquatic life—and to the Appalachian people drinking the water.

Mountaintop removal mining also produces elevated levels of "airborne hazardous dust," and demonstrably causes "increased adult hospitalizations for lung cancer, heart, lung, kidney disease, and chronic pulmonary disorders; and elevated mortality rates." Recent studies also have established a link between mountaintop removal and birth defects in Appalachia. These costs ultimately are not borne by the coal industry, but instead largely fall on Appalachian coal mining communities, thus constituting textbook examples of negative economic externalities.

Regulation Under the CWA and NEPA

An attorney conducting traditional, concept-based legal research on mountaintop removal would discover that a complex schema of federal and state law, much of it statutory and regulatory-based, has been held to govern the mining practice. . . .

. . . [I]n the search for justice, a wide range of law potentially is implicated. . . . In particular, much of the controversial mountain removal litigation to date has focused on federal agency action vis-à-vis provisions of these key federal statutes.

SMCRA [the Surface Mine Control and Reclamation Act], a federal statute that effectively curtailed the worst mining practices in Appalachia (i.e., *before* the emergence of mountaintop removal mining) mandates a cooperative federalism schema for surface mining. Minimum standards are set at the federal level, and the states then promulgate comprehensive plans to meet those standards. . . .

The EPA's role vis-à-vis [Clean Water Act] CWA § 404 [bears] close scrutiny. While Congress delegated the sole power to grant or deny dredge and fill permits to the [U.S. Army Corps of Engineers], CWA § 404 permits must be issued in accordance with the standards promulgated by the EPA, which are known as the § 404(b)(1) guidelines. A public interest review also is required prior to permit issuances. Additionally, the EPA is granted, through CWA § 404(c), the right "to deny or restrict the use of certain areas as fill disposal sites due to environmental concerns." . . .

NEPA [National Environmental Policy Act] requires agencies "proposing major federal actions 'significantly affecting' the human environment [to] complete an Environmental Impact Statement (EIS) before commencing the project." Recent litigation has stemmed from the Corps' failure to prepare an adequate EIS for mountaintop removal operations, as required by the CWA.

Unfortunately, a "history of adverse outcomes for environmental plaintiffs" largely has marked the pursuit of "court enforcement of federal environmental laws" governing mountaintop removal operations. . . . [T]ime and time again, at the appellate level . . . "the higher court has resolved the diverging government interests . . . in favor of Corps decisions that promote energy extraction," even when the "Corps has granted permits in a manner that directly contradicts the statutory and regulatory commands of NEPA and the CWA." . . .

. . . *Critical Research Strategies Applied to Mountaintop Removal Law*

. . . Whatever the shifting legal, economic, and ideological landscape may be, critical legal research strategies will be of service to the reformist-minded attorney. Innovative approaches to law and discourse can be as necessary in good times as in the bad, and as discussed below, halting mountaintop removal is merely a beginning, and not the end, of easing Appalachia's woes. The following section then demonstrates through one illustration how critical approaches to legal research can assist (i.e., can serve as one methodology, among a potential great many) in ultimately achieving such change.

Concept-Based Research

In locating the mountaintop removal primary authority above, a wide range of concept-based legal research strategies may have been used by a researcher. When searching . . . West Topic and Key Number categories, . . . the sub-topic "*Persons* Entitled to Sue or Seek Review" is telling. Already, in terms of redressability, the researcher is told that only "persons" are "entitled" to seek relief. What of non-human animals or harms to the greater environment? As Delgado points out, there exists "discussions of novel theories for nontraditional plaintiffs, such as . . . animals, indeterminate plaintiffs, or inanimate objects." But in internalizing the explicit category of "*Persons* Entitled to Sue"—in accepting this as objective truth, not as an arbitrary classification barrier that merits de- and reconstruction—such is West's power in framing, and thus in constraining, legal thought.

The classification of "Cognizable Interests and Injuries" also [bears] close scrutiny. As a term of art, "cognizable injuries" specifically denotes that "some source of law treats the injury as sufficient to confer on the injured party the right to bring suit." While the term "cognizable" likely carries with it an air of rational objectivity, such judgments are necessarily value-based. . . . The West-deployed term "cognizable" cloaks value judgments in a veneer of neutral rationality, effectively masking the subjective norms of existing standing doctrine.

. . . Additional law review articles (not available on the commercial legal databases) can be found through similar searches on SSRN, the Bepress Law Reviews Commons, HeinOnline, and Google Scholar. Accordingly, the material discussed below is based on such numerous and varied searches.

Environmental Justice

An overarching, particularly useful discourse as found by searching in law journal sub-databases and online law review repositories involves the intersection of environmental law and critical theory. In its first few decades, "environmental law took root as a reformist project that *avoided* the critical concerns of 'race, class, and gender' and the postmodern insights of late twentieth social thinking and practice." However, in more recent years, scholars have begun examining environmental law in the context of "a larger critical theoretical base," an immensely important project as "the exploitation of the environment with which environmental law is concerned props up the unjust modernism with which critical theory is concerned."

. . . Environmental justice is a prominent sub-discourse within the broader critical environmentalist movement. The basic tenets of environmental justice are as follows:

... Overall, the concept is that when living in an industrialized society, there are both benefits and burdens associated with environmental issues, and when environmental injustice occurs, those burdens are disproportionately thrust upon low-income communities and communities of color.

Therefore, environmental justice advocates focus on the unjust societal distributions of environmental harms.

... Post-essentialist projects have included going "beyond treating race as fixed and biological. It also entails expanding environmental justice to recognize that each racial group is differently situated according to its specific socio-economic needs, political power, cultural values, and group goals." ...

The environmental justice movement has gained considerable traction not just within the academy, but also within the actual environmental regulatory framework. Environmental Justice Executive Order (E.O. 12,898), handed down by President Clinton, and reinvigorated by President Obama, "requires administrative agencies to evaluate the socioeconomic and racial characteristics of communities" located in close proximity to "locally undesirable land uses" such as landfills, hazardous waste sites, and other environmental hazards.

... The environmental justice movement then has made substantial inroads in framing the debate—and even in influencing outcomes—on mountaintop removal mining regulation. ...

Feminism and Environmental Justice

The reformist-minded researcher generally may be aware that feminist discourses exist within the broader critical work on environmental law. But when searching for the intersection of feminist thought and mountaintop removal mining, virtually no pertinent results return on the law journal sub-databases in Westlaw and Lexis.

Similarly, the mountaintop removal primary authority discussed above (e.g., the mandated public interest review criteria) eschews a substantive analysis that extends beyond low-income populations in Appalachia. Therefore, the researcher discovers that feminist thought—among other potentially pertinent discourses, such as critical race theory, masculinities theory, or queer legal theory—is absent *altogether* from both primary authority and the scholarly legal literature covering critical reforms for mountaintop removal mining.

As Delgado and Stefancic demonstrate, the requisite elements for new law reform initiatives may "lie somewhere in a database," but putting such elements "together in a novel way must come from a human researcher." In this instance, conducting a broader search for feminism and environmental issues (i.e., beyond the specific context of mountaintop removal mining) yields beneficial results—that can, in turn, be applied to the law governing mountaintop removal. . . .

Many traditional feminist methodologies have been deployed within the environmental justice movement. A central feminist methodology is "unmasking patriarchy" through demonstrating how supposedly neutral laws in fact perpetuate white male supremacy. . . .

In the environmental justice context, unmasked biases include identifying workplace contaminant laws that set minimum acceptable levels as being "safe for male workers, but not female workers." . . .

Other feminist methodologies used within the environmental justice movement include contextual reasoning and consciousness-raising. . . . [These feminist methodologies] involve thrusting "previously unheard 'bottom-up' perspectives" of subordinated groups to the forefront of environmental legislative, judicial, and administrative policymaking in addition to related activist movements. . . .

The crux of ecofeminism then is that all forms of subordination are, in crucial ways, interlinked, stemming from a "shared dynamic of separation, fear, and resentment" characteristic of "capitalist, patriarchal forces." . . . This [feminist approach] yields the conclusion that meaningful environmental law reform requires "a multi-layered analysis of environmental exploitation in the context of many kinds of discrimination." . . .

The researcher now has learned of pertinent legal scholarly discourses regarding potential avenues for feminist-based reform. . . .

. . . In actually locating such materials, the materials [most relevant are] found via searches in such resources as Google Books and Scholar, EbscoHost, JSTOR, SSRN, and others. . . .

Feminist-Based Reforms to Mountaintop Removal Law

With such a complement of primary authority, legal-analytical, and critical cross- and multidisciplinary materials identified, . . . [one can] engage in a tentative analysis in order to showcase the transformative potential of critical research strategies—across diverse areas of Appalachian law. . . .

In the primary authority and legal analytical materials to date, this inequitable sex- and gender-based distribution of societal harms has not been identified as a prominent issue. But regarding primary authority specifically, where might attorneys look to implement such reforms?

For one, the EPA's public interest review requirements for the issuance of mountaintop removal permits as associated with the pre-permit reviews could be targeted as a site for increased incorporation of such insights. . . . In short, the EPA could direct the Corps to analyze the "disproportionately high and adverse human health or environmental effects on low-income, minority[, and *female*] populations." . . .

In terms of contextual reasoning and consciousness-raising in Appalachia, additional strategies may involve ensuring a strong influence of personal experience in mountaintop removal law reform initiatives. Appalachian women long have been at the forefront of grassroots anti-mountaintop removal efforts—but questions remain over whether such "'bottom-up' perspectives" are prominent components of all legal and related socio-institutional sites for change.

Personal experience already plays a role in the public interest review process associated with the EPA's pre-permit directives. E.O. 12,898 "compels agencies to increase opportunities for public participation in federal decision-making, giving potentially impacted people better access to the lawmaking process before major decisions are made." In accordance with this mandate, the EPA has established an Office of Environmental Justice to "oversee the agency's implementation of the order," which involves, among other functions, providing "low-income and minority communities in Appalachia" with an "adequate opportunity to participate in the permitting process." A feminist-based approach might attempt to broaden and deepen the participation of coalfield communities—and to concurrently ensure that a *full* spectrum of voices is heard within the review process.

But how might such contextual reasoning and consciousness-raising approaches be further expanded in mountaintop removal reform efforts? . . . As an example in a different regional context, a California community demanded that a traditional toxic exposure study conducted on its residents be tempered with a "context-based survey" devised through "group discussion" by the residents themselves. In adopting such a methodology, the "community's participation in solving the problem places them on a more equal footing with the outside researchers," and such an active community role may "discourage researchers from viewing them as mere 'victims' or sources of raw data in the future." Similarly, coalfield residents in Appalachia also might adopt a more proactive approach in pertinent public health research—the findings of which surely will impact future mountaintop removal reform efforts. . . .

. . . In considering more transformative strategies, the core tenets of ecofeminism also might assist in radically "imagining new worlds" of mountaintop removal reform—in terms of both ending mountaintop removal mining and in pursuing strategies of post-coal Appalachian societal reconstruction, which, in the end, may be one in the same issue. . . .

. . . [In this way,] "[e]cofeminism can improve environmental law by proposing alternative conceptual frameworks."

... [T]he question becomes: can one imagine a world in which mountaintop removal mining reform encompasses the *common systemic causes* at work in the Appalachian region? What might such reforms entail? ...

Conclusion

For over a century, dedicated grassroots activists, legal reformers, and ordinary citizens have struggled to free central Appalachia from the natural resource extraction industry and its seemingly eternal pact with the region's captured ruling elites. Much good work has been done, but the purpose of this Article is to bring to light a novel set of critical methodologies that may assist in ushering in a new era of change and renewal.

The manner in which our laws and legal discourses are organized, accessed, and analyzed has a vital impact on research outcomes. As outlined in this Article, the research paradigm by which such outcomes are reached is defined wholly by insidious systems of constraint. In examining—and transcending—such systems, and in adopting approaches that maximize creative law reform potential, a great deal may be accomplished by the reformist-minded attorney.

This Article puts forth just one such version of a reconstructed legal research process, and an accompanying illustration of how it might be used to shape new reforms. However, the overarching aim is for activists and reformers to creatively engage with, critique, expand upon, and ultimately *deploy* such critical legal research strategies to effect meaningful change in Appalachia—and beyond.

Stump draws from the Schools and Approaches to deconstruct and reconstruct the methods of critical knowledge production for systemic advocacy—to unlearn and relearn approaches to research. He reveals through this bottom-up focus how the structuring of legal research under the rule of law promotes failure by design. As Stump confirms, producing knowledge—and determining what counts as knowledge—are professional tasks freighted with political significance; how advocates produce knowledge helps determine what kind of knowledge gets produced and used to construct (and reconstruct) social realities.

Stump illustrates quite concretely some of the ways that legal researchers might excavate knowledge differently than taught in law schools—literally carrying out different computer-based searches, using a variety of interdisciplinary databases, and engaging with communities to reimagine the nature of problems and solutions. Systemic advocates employ this kind of "reconstructed legal research process" to support long term group struggles with diagnosis and strategy across many systemic contexts. Because, as Stump shows, "knowledge" itself is a social construction, experiences from the bottom can help to deconstruct and reconstruct current understandings of problems and solutions for three-layered progress.

11.3 THREE BOTTOM-UP METHODS OF CRITICAL RESEARCH FOR THREE-LAYERED PROGRESS

As just noted, critical research and analysis is a creative fact-finding and fact-generating process that always questions its own assumptions or conclusions. Critical research must include, but is not limited to, traditional research methods focused on formal equality or other doctrinal fictions. And critical analysis based on that research must include, but likewise cannot be limited to, conventional concepts, premises, or knowledge.

In particular, as noted previously, critical research for systemic advocacy often incorporates nontraditional practices specifically to uncover and highlight outsider perspectives from "the bottom" of a given social context. This practice not only centers key overlooked knowledge but also promotes antisubordination outcomes and values. This collaborative approach produces actionable knowledge and, as well, cross-difference understanding and solidarity necessary for building, ultimately, collective power.

Below, we review three prime bottom-up tools: (1) participatory action research, (2) critical empiricism, and (3) analytical narrative. These methods link micro data with macro analysis and collective action. They combine various disciplines and sources to incorporate identities, groups, interests, and power in all diagnosis and strategy. And they help advocates ensure that choices and products are principled and accountable in pursuit of technical fixes, power building, and culture shifting. These methods aim to pierce the Critical Challenge.

These methods supplement, not supplant, the methods and skills emphasized by the legal industry and instilled by traditional training. In law school, students primarily learn to analyze facts presented in court opinions based on existing principles of law. Perhaps students learn to "find" facts through client interviews or to identify or generate facts by reviewing documents. Rarely, however, are students asked to think about what sorts of "facts" matter for justice or how to discover multiple perspectives on issues. Rarely are they asked to reflect on the prevailing construction of "relevance" in narrow, individuated, decontextualized terms.

Skeptical attitudes, combined with the use of nonconventional techniques, are important in systemic advocacy. The goal, again, is to understand social problems that persist across generations—even though mainstream thought suggests they already are (being) resolved in abstracted, individualized compartments informed by traditional research and analysis. That traditional approach leaves the question of systemic injustice begging for recognition:

> Existing legal research systems ... tug the researcher toward the familiar, the conventional. The legal researcher quickly discovers pre-existing ideas, arguments, and legal strategies and is rewarded for staying on familiar ground. Striking out on one's own is costly and inefficient. Courts, other scholars, and one's adversary will all frame the problem in common terms; the temptation is almost irresistible. Stepping outside the framework is like abandoning a well-known and well-mapped coast for the uncharted sea. We never realize that we cannot embark on certain types of journeys armed only with conventional maps.[16]

Consequently, as a predicate for three-layered diagnoses and strategies, systemic fact-finding and knowledge creation requires "stepping outside the frameworks" of top-down law. To help advocates take this step, below are three basic critical methods for contextual, bottom-up research, analysis, and action. All three were developed, and are drawn from, many generations of field work in equal justice struggles, both local and global.

A. PARTICIPATORY ACTION RESEARCH

Action research can be described generally as collaborative, critical, and self-critical efforts that practitioners may use to investigate problems and promote solutions. Action research that includes the participation of individuals affected by social problems or client-groups engaged in community organizing is based on a belief that the experiences of subordination and struggle are important to understanding oppression and designing efforts to win solutions. By design, action research connects the micro to the macro.

Importantly, the defining feature of participatory action research (PAR) is that it involves individuals *affected by* social problems or *engaged in* social struggle in "uncovering," documenting, sharing, and sometimes acting on the knowledge. The experience of engagement in social struggle is valued because PAR often concerns what does and doesn't work to move and develop community members, to deepen alliances, and to pressure/persuade decision makers. Relatedly, legal scholar Fran Ansley and

---

[16] Richard Delgado and Jean Stefancic, Why Do We Tell the Same Stories? Law Reform, Critical Librarianship, and the Triple Helix Dilemma, 42 Stan. L. Rev. 207, 222 (1989).

political sociologist John Gaventa observe this method of research is a democracy-enhancing form of fact-finding:

> Those who draw their understanding from experience—from living and engaging in real-world issues—may find their knowledge dismissed as too subjective. Those who struggle with the messy interconnectedness of real-world problems may find their ideas recast into narrow disciplinary terms and esoteric debates in which they cannot participate. Ultimately, a knowledge system that discredits and devalues common, every-day knowledge serves to disempower common people as well. Such a system represents a contradiction for any vision of democracy that values the participation of people themselves in key deliberations and decisions that affect their lives.[17]

As Ansley and Gaventa point out, top-down knowledge often "discredits and devalues common, everyday knowledge." Using PAR and similar methods, systemic advocates turn these tables. They produce, deploy, and disseminate knowledge that otherwise would remain suppressed.

The excerpt below demonstrates PAR at work in a specific systemic context. Legal scholars Emily Houh and Kristin Kalsem sought to understand why, despite new laws and education programs, households of color still disproportionately lack adequate financial services—why they are unbanked or underbanked. Houh and Kalsem partnered with a local community group to carry out focus groups with women from predominantly Black and low-income neighborhoods in Ohio. The scholar-activist research team investigated the use of fringe banking services using four PAR methods—concept mapping, appreciative inquiry, asset mapping, and photo voice. The research team recorded interviews with community members about their uses of fringe banking services. They then produced a zine and community art show sharing stories and information for purposes of grassroots financial literacy education and outreach. In the end, the women activist-researchers created a manual of study results that included reflections on the process.

In the course of the research project, Houh and Kalsem adapted their plan based on new experiences and lessons. They continually used the results of their PAR to further refine their diagnosis of the social problem of inadequate access to useful financial services, and they laid the groundwork through collaborative analysis to develop subsequent advocacy strategies. Can you track the three layers of goals in their project design and outputs?

---

[17] Fran Ansley and John Gaventa, Researching for Democracy and Democratizing Research, 29 Change 46, 46 (Jan.–Feb. 1997).

IT'S CRITICAL: LEGAL PARTICIPATORY ACTION RESEARCH

Emily M.S. Houh and Kristin Kalsem
19 Mich. J. Race & L. 287 (2014)

... I use them [payday lenders] when I don't have money, don't have family to borrow from. I'd borrow from them because I don't like people bein' in my business. ... And then once you're in there you just keep goin' back. They just call your cell phone, they make sure you got a phone where they can get in touch with you.

—LuShonda Gibson . . .

Looking to the bottom—adopting the perspective of those who have seen and felt the falsity of the liberal promise—can assist critical scholars in the task of fathoming the phenomenology of law and defining the elements of justice. . . . When notions of right and wrong, justice and injustice, are examined not from an abstract position but from the position of groups who have suffered through history, moral relativism recedes and identifiable normative priorities emerge.

—Mari J. Matsuda

Introduction

In 1987, in the pages of an elite law journal (albeit one dedicated to issues of civil rights and civil liberties), Mari Matsuda urged critical and progressive law scholars to "look to the bottom" in doing the important work of (re)theorizing what justice and equality should mean under the law. Twenty-five years later, at a field hearing in Birmingham, Alabama on payday lending—a practice that disproportionately impacts low-income communities and communities of color—Richard Cordray, inaugural Director of the Consumer Financial Protection Bureau (CFPB), expressed similar sentiments about "getting out of Washington" and "hearing from people firsthand." We were likewise interested in "hearing from people firsthand" when, in 2010, we began our own study of the impact that "alternative financial services" such as payday lending have on the communities that use them. We held an initial focus group to discuss payday lending with five women who live in the low-income and predominantly Black West End neighborhood of Cincinnati, Ohio. LuShonda Gibson's comments above reflect the complicated relationship between payday lenders and their customers, who, like Ms. Gibson, recognize both the value of the services such institutions provide and the ways in which she and those like her are exploited by them.

Matsuda's Looking to the Bottom was one of several articles that launched the exponential growth of scholarly literature in critical race theory (CRT) and critical race feminism (CRF), and her thesis continues to inform discussion and study of the various forms of [subordinating status regimes based on race, gender, sexuality, and class that create] social, economic, and political inequalities that permeate American life. . . . The proliferation in low-income communities of "alternative financial services" (AFS) providers, such as the payday lenders referenced above, is symbolic of and perhaps causally related to these status-contingent inequalities. As teachers of both commercial law and critical race theory, critical race feminism, and feminist legal theory, we are particularly concerned with such forms of retrenchment. And as critical race/feminist scholars, we believe that critical perspectives must be brought to bear on conventional legal scholarship. . . .

The Low-Down on Fringe Banking and the Unbanked and Underbanked

. . . Data Snapshot: Who Are the "Unbanked" and "Underbanked"?

In early 2009, the FDIC [the Federal Deposit Insurance Corporation that regulates the U.S. financial system] conducted its first national survey of unbanked and underbanked households in order to "address a gap in the availability of comprehensive data on the number of unbanked and underbanked households in the United States." The FDIC collected data from forty-seven thousand participating households on the number of unbanked and underbanked households in the United States, and also those households' "demographic characteristics, and their reasons for being unbanked and underbanked." Unbanked households are defined by the FDIC as those in which no member has either a checking or savings account. Underbanked households are defined as those in which members have a checking or savings account, but rely on alternative financial products—that is, non-bank money orders, rent-to-own agreements (RTOs), payday loans, or pawn shops—at least twice a year or have taken out a [tax refund anticipation loan] at least once in the past five years.

Published in 2009, this first survey found that approximately thirty million or [25.6] percent of U.S. households were either unbanked or underbanked, with 7.7 percent unbanked and 17.9 percent underbanked. Further, it found that unbanked and underbanked households were more concentrated in the South and that the "proportion of unbanked households declines with education and age." The most common reason given by unbanked households for not having a checking or savings accounts was, not surprisingly, "[n]ot having enough money to feel they need an account."

The FDIC's second survey on unbanked and underbanked households, conducted in 2011, yielded comparable though slightly more concerning data. The 2011 FDIC Survey reported 8.2 percent of U.S. households as being unbanked and 20.1 percent as underbanked. . . .

As to the demographic data referenced above, both the 2009 and 2011 surveys found considerable and comparable variations between different racial and ethnic groups, as well as between married and unmarried households. For example, both surveys reported in their key findings that

Blacks, American Indian/Alaskans, and Hispanics are more likely to be both unbanked and underbanked than the general population, whereas Asians and Whites are less likely to be either unbanked or underbanked. The 2009 survey reported that within racial/ethnic groups, "almost 54 percent of black households, 44.5 percent of American Indian/Alaskan households, and 43.3 percent of Hispanic households are either unbanked or underbanked." Similarly, the 2011 survey reported that close to one-half of Black, American Indian/Alaskan, and Hispanic households are unbanked or underbanked, compared to one-quarter of Asian and white households.... Finally, both surveys also found that family households headed by unmarried females or males are considerably more likely than married households to be unbanked or underbanked. Gender was also a significant factor: for example, 19.5 percent in 2009 and 19.1 percent in 2011 of unmarried female-headed family households were unbanked, compared to 14.8 percent in 2009 and 14.3 percent in 2011 of unmarried male-headed households....

[Low- and middle-income (LMI)] households have no financial slack. And the financial system as it is currently organized makes it harder for families to cope. While many LMI households engage in a range of strategies to manage their finances, these strategies can impose heavy economic and noneconomic costs on those households. Restructuring the financial system to better serve them could improve outcomes and social welfare....

Organizational Reform and Advocacy Efforts

... We draw great inspiration and energy from the work being done by so many organizations to address how long-term debt impacts the unbanked and underbanked. But what do we—as critical race/feminist theorists, law teachers, and hopeful legal [participatory action research (PAR)] scholars—have to bring to a table so stacked with expertise? The answer is twofold. First, we bring an explicit and specific intersectional analysis to the existing work, which almost always mentions the continuing and "unexplained" fact of race- and gender-based economic inequality, but almost never tackles how and why race, gender, and economic inequality are (and always have been) so interconnected. Particularly in light of recent (successful) moves by some policymakers, legal advocates, and academics to disaggregate race and gender from class, we think it necessary to counter this trend by more closely interrogating these interconnections. Second, in trying to examine these interconnections, we attempt to heed Mari Matsuda's call to "look to the bottom" by employing PAR approaches....

Participatory Action Research: Putting Theory Into Practice—Really

Practice needs theory and theory needs practice just like fish need clean water.

—Paulo Freire

As its name suggests, PAR is research that concerns itself with action—making a difference, moving toward solutions—but only when those differences and solutions have been agreed upon by the relevant community members.... PAR is "not so much a methodology as an orientation to inquiry," a perspective on research that "seeks to create participative communities of inquiry in which qualities of engagement, curiosity and question posing are brought to bear on significant practical issues."

Differentiating itself from research that involves "subjects" of study who are not participating as coresearchers, PAR requires ongoing reflection and vigilance concerning issues of power and context. In their glossary of key PAR concepts, Fran Baum, Colin MacDougall, and Danielle Smith identify three distinctive aspects of PAR: first, its focus on action; second, its "careful attention to power relationships, advocating for power to be deliberately shared between the researcher and the researched;" and, third, its emphasis on the important connections between information and data and the specific contexts in which they are collected....

Participatory Action Research: A Brief History

Narratives of Origin

Orlando Fals Borda is credited with coining the term Participatory Action Research in the late 1970s. Fals Borda has traced the development of PAR to two distinct "action research" movements, one that was evolving in the Northern Hemisphere and the other in the Southern Hemisphere. In his narrative of PAR's origin, PAR evolved from convergences in these two movements. The first wave took place in the 1970s and was "predominated by the South," while the second wave took place in the 1980s and became more balanced, with greater involvement by northern theorists. Fals Borda describes the third wave, in the 1990s, as tipping the balance to the North, with important studies taking place within the university setting."...

Persons of Early (Participatory) Influence

The social psychologist Kurt Lewin . . . conceptualized action research as a triangle, with training as the first component and research and intervention as the remaining two. In this approach, Lewin saw a way to "both solve practical problems—e.g., problems of racial prejudice—and to discover 'general laws of group life. . . .'" Central to Lewin's action research was a rejection of the positivist perspective that scientific research was objective and value-free....

In the late 1970s and early 1980s, explicit connections were made between the principles of feminism and PAR. As in most fields, this was a time when the mainstream feminist movement was highlighting the dearth of women's voices and the fact that, for the most part, human experience was studied, defined, and explained based upon a male norm....

As with feminism, connections between PAR and CRT are clear. Both are informed by a deep understanding of the political nature of knowledge-production and the impact such production has on the organization of society, as well as a commitment to addressing sociopolitical inequality by challenging conventional modes of research and action. They both embrace characterization as political, overtly acknowledging their social justice agenda. With its focus on localized research and community-based solutions, PAR also shares with CRT the central tenet that history and context matter.

... While in the 1970s and 80s the action research literature did not make much of the connections between PAR, CRT, Black activism, and research, ... progressive Black sociologists developed a liberation approach to research, using it to "dismantle the master's house, and to achieve social justice." The basic tenets underlying this work were "(1) to move beyond traditional methods, by (2) creating knowledge for the sake of economic, political and social change in the Black community, and (3) without forsaking rigorous social investigation." A key shift from traditional research for this movement was to engage the community in the research process and to work with them on identifying problems and solutions....

[However,] PAR can also foster a more sophisticated understanding of various forms of intersections, including the privilege associated with the position of researcher: "Through open dialogues with both our participants and ourselves, we can begin to understand the nature of oppression, domination, and exploitation as they intersect and interrelate with gender, race, class and other forms of advantage and disadvantage." In this way, PAR not only offers opportunities for [coalitional] action; it also deepens the theoretical analysis of CRT and CRF....

... [A]s Freire emphasized, PAR does not involve only intellectual discoveries; it must involve action....

Our Own Project: Fringe Banking and Intersectionality

About a year after the FDIC published the results of its first (2009) survey on the unbanked and underbanked, we became aware of and fascinated with work that was being conducted out of the Action Research Center (ARC) at the University of Cincinnati. The ARC, under the direction of leading light Mary Brydon-Miller, was launched in 2006. Its mission—"to promote social justice and strengthen communities, locally and globally, by advancing research, education, and action through participatory and reflective practices"—is being carried out through various local projects, such as initiatives for "growing healthy girls" in urban Cincinnati and a Ph.D project on the art and stories of victims of sexual abuse. Its mission is further being promoted globally through partnerships; for example, ARC partners with the University of Puerto Rico to recruit and retain students from low-income families. . . .

[W]e partnered with a local community-based action research organization, Harmony Garden. Harmony Garden had done significant "community based participatory research"—or CBPR, as it is referred to in the context of community health research—addressing the health and well-being of women and girls. Harmony Garden had also trained a community research team from the predominantly Black and low-income West End community in Cincinnati.

We held an initial focus group with five members of the Harmony Garden research team in the fall of 2010. For the women in this focus group, lack of notice about loan terms was not the problem. The women who had used payday lenders knew down to the penny the difference between charges at various locations, as well as when and how they would be charged. They did not, however, anticipate how easy it would be to keep borrowing money and how that would result in the rolling over of debt (that is, incurring more debt to pay off existing debt). They also knew payday loan charges, whether they understood them as interest or fees, were very high. But these terms were not the only things that mattered. More important to them were issues such as the length of the lines, who might see them, and transportation.

Our goal at this initial session was not to identify specific problems with payday lending or discuss possible solutions. Instead, we sought to find out what was on the minds of users of fringe banking services by engaging in conversation with a group of stakeholders who were already comfortable speaking within a PAR setting. . . .

[We] worked together with Powershift [a team of low-income individuals participating in a leadership development program] on our TSP [Team Service Project] for the next nine months. . . .

Powershift indicated that they would like to do more initial reading on fringe banking services and PAR. We provided some key articles on both and then planned a PAR training session led by Brydon-Miller of the ARC. In November 2012, Brydon-Miller conducted a two-hour practical workshop entitled "Action Research: Developing Strategies for Positive Change," during which the allies were taught four specific PAR methodologies: concept mapping, appreciative inquiry and asset mapping, fishbone diagrams, and photovoice.

Over the next few months, Powershift allies used these four methods, other methods they read about, and variations they came up with themselves to research the use of fringe banking services, particularly payday lending, primarily in the downtown area of Cincinnati. . . .

The most comprehensive deliverable Powershift produced is a detailed manual setting out the research methods that the allies used, as well as the substantive results of the study. The manual also includes evaluative sections in which the allies share their thoughts and opinions on which aspects of the project worked well and which did not. . . .

Powershift also produced several lengthy recorded interviews with community members who use payday lending and other short-term loan services. Over the course of the few weeks during which these interviews were conducted, several of the Powershift team members themselves disclosed that they had used or were currently users of payday lending services and subsequently agreed to be interviewed for the project. Some of the interviews were so compelling that they inspired some of the more artistically inclined Powershift allies to create yet another type of "deliverable" in the form of a "zine." The authors of the zine, which translated the story of one of the allies into visual form, created a comic book-like background on which they pasted and arranged the interviewee's words and story. . . . Powershift later distributed the zine at a community art show. . . .

Other deliverables that Powershift developed to help with the continuation of this project include a website (on which all of the interviews are posted), a map of the locations of payday lending facilities in the Greater Cincinnati area (showing, not surprisingly, particularly high concentrations in communities of color), and a "visual dropcloth." Powershift took a dropcloth (a large piece of blank canvas) to several parks and outdoor venues and asked people to illustrate, using crayons and markers, their thoughts on and relationships to various topics, including "money" generally and "payday lending" specifically. Powershift also designed several types of flyers and posters to publicize the visual dropcloth project.

Because PAR happens in cycles, with much reflection and adaptation based on what has come before, the next stage of our research will likely draw on much of the community-building work described above. But before doing so . . . we shifted into our own reflection mode . . . about possible community collaborations and outreach. . . .

What PAR Has to Offer Legal Scholarship and Activism

. . . On an individual level, participatory action researchers grapple with disorienting but necessary questions regarding their own positionality and relationships within the community. For example, in our work with Powershift and our ongoing project, we continue to constantly ask ourselves: when engaged in PAR, what is our role when, as is often the case, we are "outsiders" in some respects to the community with which we are partnering? If and when we write up our findings for purposes of publication in an academic journal, how do we do so without exploiting our community partners? What is and is not the role of researcher?

Those who engage in PAR have developed strategies for constructively addressing these difficult issues. Moreover, they continue to explicitly incorporate those strategies into their own reflective research journeys.... [W]e continue to discover how working through these challenges yields deeply rewarding and meaningful benefits and how doing legal PAR has made us better thinkers, listeners, researchers, teachers, and community members....

A first principle of PAR is that research should empower its participants and stakeholders. PAR actively seeks to examine and break down the power differentials that characterize traditional positivist research, that is, between those doing the studying and those "being studied." Drawing on the work of Michel Foucault on power and knowledge, Baum, MacDougall, and Smith explain that "[t]he PAR movement challenges the system of surveillance and knowledge control established through mainstream research. When communities seek control of research agendas, and seek to be active in research, they are establishing themselves as more powerful agents." Moreover, Francisco Vio Grossi, a Chilean action researcher, describes the work of participatory research as "initiating a process of disindoctrination that allows people to detach themselves from the myths imposed on them by the power structure and that have prevented them from seeing their own oppression or from seeing possibilities for breaking free."

Specifically with respect to academic researchers, it is imperative that they constantly reflect upon and interrogate their roles in the project as the project develops.... "This critical examination of issues of identity requires an analysis of the dynamics of power and privilege."

During our weekly meetings with Powershift, for example, the allies knew we were law professors and thus tended (especially in the beginning stages of the project) to interact with us as if they were students in our classroom rather than coresearchers. As referenced above, we often had to restrain ourselves from intervening in group conversations (over a wide range of topics, from how to collect narratives about fringe borrowing to which segments of the community such outreach should be directed toward) as our "teacher" selves. Also, the age difference between the Powershift allies and us required us to think carefully about how to participate and dialogue together. There were times, for example, when we felt strong urges to assert control based on our simply having lived longer and experienced more than most of the team members. Power issues among the allies themselves also arose. Community efforts to make explicit these power dynamics and issues resulted in deeper and more substantive interactions within the group, which, very significantly, helped build trust.

The diverse race, gender, sexuality, and class makeup of our community—the Powershift members, as well as the other community members recruited to the project—required us to remain vigilantly self-aware and sensitive to our own highly privileged status. Neither of us, for example, has ever used payday lenders or other AFS products, making us "outsiders" in a very key way to this community. But we remind ourselves that we are interested in building this community because we want the insiders to have their say on these issues and because we have other types of knowledge and skills that can contribute to ensuring the insiders' voices are heard. At the same time, we remain vigilant about listening well (and always working to improve our listening skills) and being mindful of our power and privilege, which are baseline requirements for making the research democratic, dynamic, and meaningful to all involved.

... *Questions About "Objectivity"*

PAR aims to bring about social change. It is thus overtly political and openly acknowledges that it is "biased in favor of dominated, exploited, poor and otherwise ignored women and men and groups." As Hall explains, PAR "sees no contradiction between goals of collective empowerment and the deepening of social knowledge." In PAR, "researchers are not separate, neutral academics theorizing about others, but coresearchers or collaborators with people working towards social equality."

Already steeped in the study of PAR, we were fairly comfortable with this overtly political stance when we started working with Powershift. We initially speculated—and were indeed hopeful—that the data we would collect would be narrative, specific, and individualized. We were thus unprepared for the resistance some Powershift team members showed, at the outset, toward PAR's anti-positivist approach. Some members of the team had experience, through school or other community work, conducting traditional social science research. Some of them had, for example, helped develop, administer, and analyze both qualitative and quantitative "objective" surveys and their results. This created a certain amount of conflict and frustration about the kinds of questions we wanted to ask people.

It also caused us to ask ourselves why we had not anticipated this resistance, given the dominance of traditional empirical research methods. We were forced to examine what assumptions we had made about each ally's sociopolitical commitments. This constant interrogation of our own lack of objectivity showed us how questions about "objectivity" in PAR are naturally tied to issues of power and, we believe, ultimately moved us toward a more egalitarian PAR process.

... *Letting Go of Outcomes*

One of the biggest challenges we continue to face—given our identities as law teachers, scholars, and lawyers—is how to respond to the following types of questions posed by our faculty colleagues: I understand that you are trying to do something about predatory lending, but what legal problem are you trying to solve or address? What, exactly, are the desired outcomes of this project, and how will you assess and measure them? And—last but not least—what, exactly, does this have to do with law?

Answering these questions in the context of an academic presentation was not easy, not only because they were traditional types of questions about a nontraditional type of research project, but because we ourselves had puzzled through these same questions. Moreover, our most honest answer—that their questions largely missed the point, because doing legal PAR requires relinquishment of a certain degree of power and control over the project and a willingness to let go of anticipated outcomes—is unsettling. . . .

That is, when the research process is reconceptualized as a dynamic, equalizing, and shared process, concerns about outcomes and assessment recede. As we have discovered, the academic researcher is no longer primarily driven by the desire to find results that she can present for assessment and judgment by some "neutral" body (be it academic peers, judges, lawyers, or policymakers). Nor is she driven by the desire to prove an abstract principle or hypothesis through her data. Rather, she is driven primarily by the desire to bring her own expertise and training to the table in hopes of enabling others ". . . to take action to achieve change." . . .

Rather unexpectedly, one of the most challenging aspects of our work with Powershift was determining how to bring race and gender to the center of our collective thinking about the impact of fringe banking on our local communities. . . .

It was not the case that race and gender never surfaced as issues in our work together. Powershift's compositional diversity was a fairly specific one—including ourselves, it comprised four Black women, five White women, one Asian American woman, two White men, no Black men, and no Latinas/os. In retrospect, we likely assumed that our team's intersectional diversity would result in an explicitly intersectional approach to the work from the start. But this was not the case. It was not until several weeks into our work together, after Powershift had recorded and compiled several interviews with stakeholders about their financial lives, that race and gender began to surface in our weekly meetings due to the fact that everyone who told stories about their use of payday lenders and other AFS products, with the exception of one Black male, were women of color. Nor did the stakeholders and allies tend to explicitly discuss race or gender during their recorded conversations about their experiences with fringe borrowing, or in our many team conversations about community. That most of the stakeholders were people of color, and more specifically women of color, was just a fact. . . .

Going forward, we will prioritize bringing intersectional questions about race, gender, class, and sexuality to the fore, and we will work on developing effective ways of doing so. As equal research partners, our specialized knowledge and expertise about critical race/feminism, in addition to our legal expertise on the state of the fringe economy, is what we can give to the community.

Conclusion

To conclude, we circle back to the question: what does law have to do with any of this, that is, with developing a PAR praxis? . . .

The answer is simply that law—our legal expertise—is what we bring to the table. In the context of this project, our knowledge about fringe banking, critical race/feminism, and how the law works in society, is what we, as research partners and community stakeholders ourselves, have to share with our partners.

We fully understand that this answer can be disorienting for lawyers, law students, and legal scholars and teachers who are used to approaching problems from the top-down and—usually because we are asked and hired to do so—by taking control of difficult situations. But for those of us who are interested in the different ways in which law can be used to generate community empowerment and transformation, both big and small, legal PAR provides a tool with which community stakeholders can more carefully examine their situations and more systematically generate their own action agendas. Law is a tool that need not be wielded by lawyers or pro se litigants alone; it is also a tool that can reach beyond the courtroom, legislative session, and classroom. Everyone should have access to law for the purposes of self-empowerment and action, and legal PAR provides a democratic process by which to gain that access.

. . . Legal PAR can help us "be" critical race/feminists in a way that "intimately connects theory and practice in everyday life." Moreover, it can help us develop a "way of being" that always asks what we are giving back and how we are using our legal knowledge to further a bottom-up approach to creating a more just world. . . .

Houh and Kalsem draw from the Schools and Approaches to show how PAR can clarify understanding of social problems and aid in crafting systemic solutions for three-layered progress. They describe combinations of means for collectively analyzing information, including forms of "mapping" detailed later in this chapter. As Houh and Kalsem show, PAR, like the following two research methods, extends beyond library-bound, book-bound, or law-bound traditions of legal research. In contrast to traditional legal research, PAR recognizes that knowledge and its production are laden with politics and power. For that reason, PAR aims to unearth specifically those bottom-up viewpoints usually marginalized or excluded in traditional legal research and analysis.

B. CRITICAL EMPIRICISM

The second tool of Stage One research and analysis is critical empiricism. This method of inquiry raises questions about the assumed neutrality of micro-macro realities, of observations about them, and of categories used to "see" and explain social phenomena.[18] Empirical "facts" reflect systemic social constructions: the top-down categories used to describe those facts already "are at least partly a product of ideologies that have been dominant"[19] since settler colonialism. Critical empiricism brings underlying assumptions rooted in dominant ideologies to the surface; documenting preexisting social realities while also going further—digging into their roots. In other words, empiricism may document how things are, but critical empiricism also explores and explains why.

A classic example of critical empiricism comes from legal scholar Ian Ayres, who examined disparate results in a systemic context where identities are not supposed to matter: car sales in a major U.S. city in the late 20th century. Car sales generally are deemed part of "free" and competitive marketplaces, and capitalism as a system insists that race and sex discrimination cannot occur in "free" competitive markets except where overt racist and sexist attitudes are tolerated. Both assertions, however, are false.

Ayres found that female and African American car buyers paid more, on average, for cars. The traditional explanation offered to lawmakers and the public is that women and Black people don't bargain for cars as well as men and white people. In the excerpt below, Ayres takes on that canard using intersectional identities very carefully. Ayres demonstrates how relatively simple field research that employs *critical* empiricism can generate data that reshapes diagnoses and strategies for effective legal problem solving. Ayres and his team carried out an experiment, documented outcomes, and showed empirically not only that unequal micro outcomes occur routinely, but also *why* those unequal outcomes create a macro pattern. They determined that automobile sales markets routinely manipulate women and people of color to extract higher-than-average prices from them, individually and collectively, to simultaneously bestow "great deals" on white buyers and men. This study aptly illustrates how critical empiricism challenges in this context the politics of dominant legal knowledge, which depicts economic life as free of irrational biases like

---

[18] David M. Trubek and John Esser, "Critical Empiricism" and American Critical Legal Studies: Paradox, Program, or Pandora's Box, 12 German L.J. 115 (2011); William C. Whitford, Critical Empiricism: A Comment on David M. Trubek & John Esser, Gerd Winter & Volkmar Gessner, 12 German L.J. 179 (2011).

[19] Whitford, Critical Empiricism, at 179.

notions of group superiority and inferiority based on social identities. As this excerpt illustrates, critical empiricism creates or analyzes data to reveal facts and causal connections that uncritical empiricism would fail to reveal, to document, or to question.

FAIR DRIVING: GENDER AND RACE DISCRIMINATION IN RETAIL CAR NEGOTIATIONS

Ian Ayres
104 Harv. L. Rev. 817 (1991)

The civil rights laws of the 1960s prohibit race and gender discrimination in the handful of markets—employment, housing, and public accommodations—in which discrimination was perceived to be particularly acute.... Both legislators and commentators, however, have largely ignored the possibility of discrimination in the much broader range of markets left uncovered by civil rights laws.... Of these unprotected markets, the market for new cars is particularly ripe for scrutiny because, for most Americans, new car purchases represent their largest consumer investment after buying a home....

This Article examines whether the process of negotiating for a new car disadvantages women and minorities. More than 180 independent negotiations at ninety dealerships were conducted in the Chicago area to examine how dealerships bargain. Testers of different races and genders entered new car dealerships separately and bargained to buy a new car, using a uniform negotiation strategy. The study tests whether automobile retailers react differently to this uniform strategy when potential buyers differ only by gender or race.

The tests reveal that white males receive significantly better prices than blacks and women. As detailed below, white women had to pay forty percent higher markups than white men; black men had to pay more than twice the markup, and black women had to pay more than three times the markup of white male testers. Moreover, the study reveals that testers of different race and gender are subjected to several forms of nonprice discrimination. Specifically, testers were systematically steered to salespeople of their own race and gender (who then gave them worse deals) and were asked different questions and told about different qualities of the car.

... Although the 1960s civil rights laws do not reach retail car sales, the finding that car retailers bargain differently with different races might give rise to disparate treatment suits under 42 U.S.C. §§ 1981 and 1982, which originated in the 1866 Civil Rights Act. The test results, by focusing on an unexplored manifestation of disparate treatment, push us to define more clearly what constitutes discrimination generally.

Furthermore, the results highlight a gaping hole in our civil rights laws regarding gender discrimination. Although sections 1981 and 1982 prohibit racial discrimination in contracting and the sale of real and personal property, no federal laws bar intentional discrimination on the basis of gender in the sale of most goods or services. The civil rights laws of the 1960s fail to fill this gap, leaving unregulated a legion of markets in which women contract. Put simply, car dealers can legally charge more or refuse to sell to someone *because* she is a woman. . . .

The goal of Congress in passing the Civil Rights Act of 1866 was to guarantee that "a dollar in the hands of a Negro will purchase the same thing as a dollar in the hands of a white man." The standard argument against enacting civil rights laws has been grounded in the conviction that the impersonal forces of market competition will limit race and gender discrimination to the traditionally protected markets, in which there is significant interpersonal contact. Yet the results of this study give lie to such an unquestioning faith in competition: in stark contrast to congressional objectives, this Article indicates that blacks and women simply cannot buy the same car for the same price as can white men using identical bargaining strategies. . . .

Methodology of the Test

To test whether there is disparate treatment by car retailers on the basis of race or gender, pairs of consumers/testers (for example, a white male and a black female) used the same bargaining strategy in negotiating at new car dealerships. A white male tester was included in each pair of testers. The white male results provide a bench-mark against which to measure the disparate treatment of the non-"white male" tester. Three consumer pairs (black female and white male, black male and white male, and white female and white male) conducted approximately 180 tests at ninety Chicago dealerships.

Each tester followed a bargaining script designed to frame the bargaining in purely distributional terms: the only issue to be negotiated was the price. The script instructed the testers to focus quickly on buying a particular car, and testers offered to provide their own financing. The testers elicited an initial price from the dealers and then, after waiting five minutes, the testers responded with an initial counteroffer that equaled an estimate of the dealer's marginal cost. After the tester's initial counteroffer, the salesperson could do one of three things: (1) attempt to accept the tester's offer, (2) refuse to bargain further, or (3) make a lower offer. If the salesperson attempted to accept the tester's offer or refused to bargain further, the test was over (and the tester left the dealership). If the salesperson responded by making a lower offer, the script instructed the tester to wait five minutes and to split the difference. After the tester split the difference, the salesperson again had the same three choices, and the rounds of bargaining continued until the salesperson accepted a tester offer or refused to bargain further. Testers jotted down each offer and counteroffer, as well as options on the car and the sticker price. Upon leaving the dealership, the testers completed a survey recording information about the test.

This design produced results that permit two tests for discrimination. The first, "short test" of discrimination simply compares the dealer's response to the testers' initial question, "How much would I have to pay to buy this car?" The "long test" of discrimination, on the other hand, compares instead the final offers given to testers after the multiple rounds of concessionary bargaining. By focusing on the initial offer, the short test is well controlled because salespeople had little information from which to draw inferences. By focusing on the final offer, the long test isolates more closely the price a real consumer would pay, but it increases the risk that individual differences among the testers influenced the results.

. . . Testers were chosen to satisfy the following criteria for uniformity:

1. *Age:* All testers were twenty-four to twenty-eight years old.

2. *Education:* All testers had three or four years of college education.

3. *Dress:* All testers were dressed similarly during the negotiations. Testers wore casual "yuppie" sportswear: the men wore polo or buttondown shirts, slacks, and loafers; the women wore straight skirts, blouses, minimal make-up, and flats.

4. *Economic Class:* Testers volunteered that they could finance the car themselves.

5. *Occupation:* If asked by a salesperson, each tester said that he or she was a young urban professional (for example, a systems analyst for First Chicago Bank).

6. *Address:* If asked by the salesperson, each tester gave a fake name and an address for an upper-class, Chicago neighborhood (Streeterville).

7. *Attractiveness:* Applicants were subjectively ranked for average attractiveness.

The testers were trained for two days before visiting the dealerships. The training included not only memorizing the tester script, but also participating in mock negotiations designed to help testers gain confidence and learn how to negotiate and answer questions uniformly. The training emphasized uniformity in cadence and inflection of tester response. In addition to spoken uniformity, the study sought to achieve tester uniformity in non-verbal behavior.

The tester script was also designed to promote tester uniformity through silence. The testers volunteered very little information and were trained to feel comfortable with periods of silence. The script anticipated that the sellers would ask questions and gave the testers a long list of contingent responses to questions that might be asked. The study sought to let the salespeople completely control the bargaining process without letting them know they had such control. . . .

Results of the Test

The results from the tester surveys provide a rich database for investigating how salespeople bargain and whether they treat testers of a different race or gender differently. . . . The tests reveal that salespeople asked testers different types of questions and used different tactics in attempting to sell the cars. . . . In particular, the size of final offers is sensitive not only to the race and gender of both the tester and the salesperson, but also to the information revealed by the tester in the course of bargaining.

Price Discrimination

1. Final Offers.—The final offer of each test was the lowest price offered by a dealer after the multiple rounds of bargaining. By comparing these final offers with independent estimates of dealer cost, it was possible to calculate the dealer profit associated with each final offer (final offer minus dealer cost).

Black female testers were asked to pay over three times the markup of white male testers, and black male testers were asked to pay over twice the white male markup. Moreover, race and gender discrimination were synergistic or "superadditive": the discrimination against the black female tester was greater than the combined discrimination against both the white female and the black male tester.

The reliability of these results is buttressed by an analysis of the relative unimportance of individual effects. The average dealer profits on the non-"white male" testers were statistically different from the average profits on the white males at a five percent significance level. The average profits for the three individual white males were, however, not significantly different from each other. This last result lends support to the proposition that the idiosyncratic characteristics of at least the white male testers did not affect the results. . . .

2. Initial Offers.—This study also constructed a test of disparate treatment on the basis of the initial offers sellers made to the testers. As noted above, this "short test" offers more experimental control because the testers asked only a single question.

The average dealer profit on offers made to white female testers was not significantly different from the average profit on offers made to white male testers. Sellers, however, offered both black males and black females significantly higher prices: sellers asked black males to pay almost twice the markups they charged white males, and they asked black females to pay two and one-half times that markup....

Nonprice Discrimination

The study also examined other ways in which sellers may have treated the testers differently. Although these other types of disparate treatment do not directly concern the sales price, they could facilitate price discrimination. Moreover, these comparisons suggest something about the racial and sexual perceptions that determine the behavior of salespeople.

1. Customer Steering.—As designed, the script allowed dealerships to steer testers to different types of salespeople or different types of cars. The script instructed testers to go to the center of the showroom and wait for a salesperson to approach them. The salespeople chose the tester, so that the testers could be steered to salespeople of a particular race or gender.

The salesperson's race and gender was not randomly distributed across testers. Instead, sellers steered testers to persons of their own race and gender: white male sellers were more likely to serve white male testers; white female sellers were more likely to serve white female testers; and black male sellers were more likely to serve black testers....

2. Disparate Questioning.—The testers recorded how often they were asked specific types of questions. Statistical tests were then conducted to evaluate whether sellers asked non-"white male" testers particular questions significantly more or less often than white male testers. These tests indicate the following:

Sellers asked black female testers *more* often about their occupation, about financing, and whether they were married. Sellers asked black female testers *less* often whether they had been to other dealerships and whether they had offers from other dealers.

Sellers asked black male testers *less* often if they would like to test drive the car, whether they had been to other dealerships, and whether they had offers from other dealers.

Sellers asked white female testers *more* often whether they had been to other dealerships. Sellers asked white female testers *less* often what price they would be willing to pay.

These differences may indicate ways that dealers try to sort consumers in order to price discriminate effectively. For example, the fact that salespeople asked black testers less often about whether they had been to other dealerships (or had other offers) may indicate that salespeople do not think that interdealer competition is as much of a threat with black customers as with white customers. Because the price that sellers are willing to offer any customer may be sensitive to that customer's responses, the disparity among who is questioned may facilitate a seller's attempt to price discriminate.

3. *Disparate Sales Tactics.*—The testers also recorded the different tactics that the salespeople used in trying to sell the car.... These tests indicate the following:

Salespeople tried to sell black female testers *more* often on gas mileage, the color of the car, dependability, and comfort, and asked them more often to sign purchase orders [a contract for the car purchase].

Salespeople tried to sell white female testers more often on gas mileage, the color of the car, and dependability.

With black male testers, salespeople *more* often offered the sticker price as the initial offer and forced the tester to elicit an initial offer from the seller. Salespeople asked black male testers to sign a purchase order *less* often.

These tests suggest that salespeople believe women are more concerned with gas mileage, color, and dependability than are men. The tests also indicate that salespeople try to "sucker" black males into buying at the sticker price by offering the sticker price or refusing to make an initial offer until asked.

4. *Cost Revelation.*—The script also elicited information about the dealers' willingness to reveal their marginal cost to consumers. In half of the bargaining sessions, the testers were told to ask the seller (at the end of the test) what the dealer had paid the car manufacturer. Thirty-five per cent of the sellers represented a specific dollar cost in response to the testers' inquiries. These disclosures, however, were not evenly distributed across the tester groups. Disaggregated by tester type, the disclosure rates indicate that salespeople were less willing to disclose cost data to black testers, especially black female testers.

... When the seller did reveal his cost, the represented cost was substantially higher than independent estimates of seller cost for the same models. Thus, although salespeople are more likely to disclose cost figures to white testers, they systematically overstate their costs. The greatest misrepresentations were made to white female testers....

... In the retail car market, the dealer's ultimate goal is to maximize profits by charging each consumer his or her reservation price—the maximum amount the consumer is willing to pay. Under this theory, race and gender serve as proxies to inform sellers about how much individual consumers would be willing to pay for the car....

In the end, ... [n]o single causal theory may be adequate to explain discrimination against both blacks and women. Whatever its causes, however, the discrimination revealed in this study stands squarely in the face of [any] analysis that reject[s] the need for discrimination laws concerning the sale of goods. . . .

Legal Reform

1. Modernizing Civil Rights Laws.—Lawmakers could respond to bargaining discrimination by expanding the current coverage of the civil rights and consumer protection laws. Most important, Congress could amend sections 1981 and 1982 to extend to women (and other protected classes) the right to be free from discrimination in contracting to buy and sell services as well as goods. Modernized versions of sections 1981 and 1982 could also allow plaintiffs to bring disparate impact suits, currently actionable under title VII, which require no showing of intent. . . .

2. Reinvigorating Consumer Protection Laws.—State and federal governments might also attempt to enforce more rigorously consumer protection laws to reduce the type of discrimination revealed in this Article. Indeed, . . . [t]o the extent that consumer protection laws codify common law remedies such as fraud and duress, they may provide a viable alternative to civil rights remedies. Thus, although consumer protection laws have not yet been used to attack racial disparate treatment as a "deceptive" misrepresentation, this history does not preclude more extensive governmental intervention in the future. . . .

3. Structural Reforms.—The expansion of traditional civil rights and consumer protection laws is unlikely to completely eliminate disparate treatment in bargaining based on race or gender. . . .

In light of these conditions, policymakers might consider structural reforms to improve the workings of the market. . . . Simply put, to formulate effective intervention, policymakers must understand why sellers discriminate.

The earlier analysis of competition suggested that high-markup customers (and the ensuing concentration of profits) are a central cause of dealer price discrimination. As a result, if policymakers can find a way to reduce significantly the profits on these sucker sales, the manner in which dealerships conduct the retail sale of *all* cars would become dramatically more competitive. Without the pathological effects of highly concentrated profits, dealers would no longer have an incentive to force consumers to expend real and psychic resources in bargaining.

. . . [P]olicymakers might restrict the amount of price dispersion permissible in the car market. Regulators might, for example, allow dealerships to engage in bargaining, but void sales with markups that are more than twenty percent above the average markup. Unlike direct unconscionability regulation, firms would retain the freedom to set the average markup for any one model as high as the market would bear but would be prohibited from selling similar cars at significantly different prices....

Finally and least intrusively, regulators might reduce the number of sales with disparately high markups by mandating various types of disclosure from dealerships to consumers. Dealerships, for example, might be required to reveal the average price for which each make of car is sold. Knowing that the dealership is attempting to charge $3000 more than the average price would allow high-markup consumers to protect themselves.... The possibility of hoodwinking uninformed buyers into purchasing at a high markup would diminish as the excessive profits would be directly revealed....

Conclusion

The negotiation of contracts occupies a mysterious and somewhat mythical position in the law and in our society. In *The Wealth of Nations,* Adam Smith opined that people have a natural propensity to "truck and barter" over the sale of goods....

Common experience indicates, however, that many people in the United States are averse to bargaining. The frustration that many consumers experience in bargaining for a car is largely attributable to the ludicrously inefficient manner in which cars are marketed. Although Smith and others attach almost mythic qualities to the process of bargaining, this Article has thrown the equity and efficiency of car negotiations into question. The process of retail car negotiations becomes even more problematic when traditionally disadvantaged members of our society effectively pay a bargaining tax whenever they purchase a new car.

Earlier this year, I asked a car dealer during an interview whether the bulk of his profits were concentrated in a few sales. He told me that his dealership made a substantial number of both "sucker" and "non-sucker" sales. He added: "My cousin, however, owns a dealership in a black neighborhood. He doesn't sell nearly as many [cars], but he hits an awful lot of home runs. You know, sometimes it seems like the people that can least afford it have to pay the most." Although it is dangerous to extrapolate from the results of a single study, the amounts of discrimination uncovered, if representative of a larger phenomenon, are truly astounding. A $500 overcharge per car means that blacks annually pay $150 million more for new cars than they would if they were white males....

Ayres brings to the surface information about bias in car sales based in the experiences of car buyers. To do so, he works with a team of researchers that embody different combinations of gender, race, and class—intersections designed to expose patterns of prejudice. Without this critical deployment of identity, the macro patterns of micro privilege and subordination would remain unexplained. Using this method, Ayres creates new knowledge in a way somewhat akin to "asking other questions"—critical empiricism asks the questions that conventional empirical studies sideline.

Recall from this perspective also the empirical realities of democratic decision making documented by Gilens and Page in Part I. Their macro study-of-studies demonstrates that, contrary to prevalent—and dominant—theories of democracy, the voices and votes of the wealthy carry much more weight than those of the non-wealthy, and why. From that study we learn that economic elites orchestrate the daily, year-round workings of democracy in many ways that minimize the relevance of periodic elections—knowledge startling to many precisely because it upsets the "master narrative" of U.S. democracy so thoroughly. It's not so much the votes of every few years that count, but rather the influence—the pervasive, daily omnipresence of elite agents that steer "democratic" processes (and outcomes) regardless of democratic preferences or majoritarian choices. This reframing of knowledge itself changes basic understandings of systems and of possible corrective actions. Like Ayres, Gilens and Page document empirical facts denied by top-down mythologies to pave the way for new solutions.

While keeping the above in mind, consider a final example from another context. In the following quote, feminist legal scholar Donna Coker assesses the utility of empirical research into cross-sex domestic violence. Invoking LatCrit, one critical School of legal knowledge, she examines intersectional knowledge from the bottom of race, gender, ethnicity, and class castes. Coker emphasizes that even "funding of domestic violence research" suffers from lack of critical empirical knowledge. Notice how she, too, emphasizes the material and social dimensions of knowledge production and application:

> LatCrit Theory invites scholarship that centers the experiences of Latinas/os while tying those experiences to the project of social justice for all.... [Thus] every domestic violence intervention strategy should be subjected to a material resources test. This means that in every area of anti-domestic violence law and policy, whether it be determining funding priorities, analyzing appropriate criminal law or arrest policies, developing city ordinances or drafting administrative rules, priority should be given to those laws and policies which improve women's access to material resources. Further, because women's circumstances differ in ways that dramatically affect their access to material resources, the standard for determining the impact on material resources should be the situation of women in the greatest need who are most dramatically affected by inequalities of gender, race, and class. . . .

> ... [Research conclusions] for poor women of color are uncertain, however, because research often fails to examine the particular experiences of women of color and, when race and ethnicity of victims are considered, only the experiences of African American women and white women are studied. ...
>
> Funding for domestic violence research should prioritize research that addresses the needs of poor women, and especially poor women of color. This research must ... address the particular needs of Latinas and other women of color who are frequently ignored by research.[20]

Critical approaches to empiricism ask expansive contextual questions to spotlight systemic patterns that reinforce the subordination of "different" groups in material and symbolic ways. These micro-macro patterns help advocates to better understand the persistence of systemic injustice. Using this method to ask "other" questions focused on identities, groups, interests, and power—and answering them empirically—advocates and activists expand actionable knowledge from the bottom to overcome formal equality, failure by design, and the legal industry's culture of conformance and hierarchy.

C. ANALYTICAL NARRATIVE

Analytical narrative draws upon personal and group experiences to understand the subordinated positions of marginalized groups, as we saw earlier in Parts II and III, and works in tandem with critical empiricism. Analytical narratives can initiate bottom-up legal analyses of problems and solutions by sharing personal experience with injustice while reflecting on the macro context. Analytical narratives can also be historical. They can be biographical as well as autobiographical. They can be factual or fictional. They can combine these various features in infinite ways. But the point of them all is about systemic injustice—how to recognize it and how to combat it. Analytical narratives provide a "case in point" to bare the larger picture of systemic injustice in various contexts, scenarios, and struggles. The following materials amplify our study of analytical narrative specifically as a method for critical research and analysis leading to actionable knowledge.

Legal storytelling is important even in traditional advocacy. Law students often are asked to think about the nature of the "story" in pleadings or judicial opinions and to evaluate the most sympathetic or persuasive account of a given context or scenario. Yet systemic advocacy draws not only on narratives but also on narrative theory: as with the difference between traditional empiricism and critical empiricism, the

---

[20] Donna Coker, Shifting Power for Battered Women: Law, Material Resources and Poor Women of Color, 33 U.C. Davis L. Rev. 1009, 1010, 1012, 1055 (2000).

difference between traditional legal storytelling and critical approaches to narrative is that the latter aims to uncover more than surface facts about an immediate social reality. Critical narrative questions why a set of facts exists in the first place, and this critical method of storytelling creates new themes and story arcs that may be dissonant, not resonant, with dominant biases and frames. As advocacy, critical approaches to narrative aim to interrogate, not to celebrate or accommodate, the systemic violence of the status quo. At their best, analytical narratives answer some of the "other" questions related to identities, groups, interests, and power that systemic rules and industry practices exclude or distort. They capture large realities that may slip between the "cracks" of knowledge produced through PAR or critical empiricism. As a critical method, they "put a face" on formalist abstractions about the daily violence of systemic injustice. Frequently, they relate one concrete example of systemic injustice that shows or explains the larger workings of identity-based caste systems in law and in society.

Legal scholar Mario Barnes, for example, cites the explanation given by his maternal grandmother in explaining why she was charged as a co-conspirator in a 1967 robbery-murder case. According to her, the causes included "being a Negro and having had a past record of forgery and I am still paying for my [past crime]."[21] Barnes' account of his grandmother's analytical narrative sheds a different light on a top-down action that points to an identity-related abuse of power, which in turn is obscured by "official" explanations or systemic cover stories:

> [P]ersonal narratives reveal types of information and knowledge that are neither manifested in the doctrinal representations of their stories nor necessarily reflected in the statistics that present the quantitative picture of black women within the criminal justice system. If nothing else, both the statistics pertaining to the conviction and incarceration rates of African-American women . . . and stories like those of . . . my grandmother remind us that there is a real cost to being marked by difference within society. Telling our versions of our stories is merely a first step in revealing the reach of institutional power and the systemic nature of oppression.[22]

In addition, therefore, critical analytical narratives—sometimes called counterstorytelling—aim to strengthen collective identities and to motivate collective action in ways that contribute to power building and culture shifting.

Sharing experiences is not simply venting but rather can help advocates, activists, and allies expose and understand inequities to

---

[21] Mario Barnes, Black Women's Stories and the Criminal Law: Restating the Power of Narrative, 39 U.C. Davis L. Rev. 941, 943 (2006).

[22] *Id.* at 943, 958.

challenge mainstream visions of abstract justice "protected" by formal equality: "Narrative can and has been used by outsiders to point out various injuries that they have sustained"[23] and mobilize around those shared experiences. Over time, sharing personal stories about collective inequality fosters empathy, sympathy, and solidarity at the bottom of a given context. In this way, relating stories can help to strengthen the capacity of groups for long-term struggle. Daniella Ann Cook and Adrienne D. Dixson, critical race scholars in the field of education, describe the purposes and common forms of such narrative work:

> Counterstorytelling [or analytical narrative] serves many purposes including (1) psychic preservation by not silencing the experiences of the oppressed and thus exposing neglected evidence (counterstorytelling); (2) challenging normative reality through an exchange that overcomes ethnocentrism and the dysconscious conviction of viewing the world one way; (3) listening to the voices of people of color as the basis for understanding how race and racism function; and (4) purposefully attempting to disrupt liberal ideology.... [S]cholars generally use three forms of counterstorytelling: personal stories or narratives, other people's stories or narratives, and composite stories or narratives.[24]

Thus, like PAR and critical empiricism, analytical narratives also attend contextually to the roles that identities, groups, interests, and power play in persistent social problems and in effective solutions to them. This kind of narrative can be, in itself, a collaboration—an empowering kind of collaborative knowledge production; correspondingly, collaboration across difference can be a knowledge-producing, and knowledge-enhancing, activity that allows both the advocate and the advocacy to sharpen in various ways. To encourage progress, critical narration can be a collaborative venture that challenges—or connects to—mainstream visions of justice.[25]

Of course, personal analytical narratives can be (and frequently are) supplemented with historical or other data (empirical, for instance) to deepen the understanding of the concrete stories and social realities they illuminate. As legal scholar Marc-Tizoc González explains, critical ethnic

---

[23] George Martínez, Philosophical Considerations and the Use of Narrative in Law, 30 Rutgers L.J. 683, 687 (1999).

[24] Daniella Ann Cook and Adrienne D. Dixson, Writing Critical Race Theory and Method: A Composite Counterstory on the Experiences of Black Teachers in New Orleans Post-Katrina, 26 Int'l J. of Qualitative Studies in Educ. 1238 (2013).

[25] See Nancy L. Cook, Outside the Tradition: Literature as Legal Scholarship, 63 U. Cin. L. Rev. 95 (1994); Lindsay Huber, Beautifully Powerful: A LatCrit Reflection on Coming to an Epistemological Consciousness and the Power of Testimonio, 18 Am. U. J. Gender Soc. Pol'y & L. 839 (2010); Nancy Levit, Reshaping the Narrative Debate, 34 Seattle U.L. Rev. 751 (2011); Susan Bandes, Empathy, Narrative, and Victim Impact Statements, 63 U. Chi. L. Rev. 361 (1996).

legal histories may use a narrative structure to challenge traditional understandings of facts, law, and outcomes:

> Researching and writing critical ethnic legal histories is one salutary practice to cultivating and renewing an insurgent critical race praxis of interracial justice. Yet, these should not be heroic, nationally bound, or teleological stories. Rather, critical ethnic legal histories braid together the partial histories of counter-memory as a form of race praxis aspiring to interracial justice by interrogating conventional or regnant views of the past and reformulating them from an array of standpoints that are informed by contemporary, cutting-edge scholarship of comparative ethnic studies and critical outsider jurisprudence.[26]

Recall from this perspective the historical facts that Hing weaves into his narrative about Yen's global education movement and that Ansley includes in her description of seeding and supporting coalitional economic and immigrant justice advocacy in Tennessee, both from Part II. Consider, in contrast, typical "facts" presented in judicial opinions deciding key historical cases, including those we read previously. A narrative that incorporates critical history—itself, drawing on narratives from the bottom—provides additional facts that can change radically one's understanding of both history and of those opinions. Analytical narratives may be micro and personal, yet also may include or connect with historical facts and macro legacies.

Critical uses of narrative in law have been subjected to fierce top-down attacks, frequently dismissed as mere anecdotes of victimization.[27] These attacks attempt to undercut both the veracity of particular narratives as well as the reputation of the teller. These attacks on narrative aim to suppress the potential of critical knowledge as actionable knowledge. But, because analytical narrative as a part of critical practice has proved powerful, scholars and practitioners have persisted in using this method since the late 1980s. Think back, for instance, to the reflections of Sonia Sotomayor and Robert Williams from Parts II and III, which jointly lay out what Richard Delgado calls a "plea for narrative"[28] through which outgroups can challenge the status quo. The following excerpt demonstrates the power of narrative in systemic advocacy *and* across disciplines.

---

[26] Marc-Tizoc González, Critical Ethnic Legal Histories: Unearthing the Interracial Justice of Filipino American Agricultural Labor Organizing, 3 UC Irvine L. Rev. 991 (2013).

[27] See, for example, Daniel A. Farber and Suzanna Sherry, Beyond All Reason: The Radical Assault on Truth in American Law 78 (1997).

[28] Richard Delgado, Storytelling for Oppositionists and Others: A Plea for Narrative, 87 Mich. L. Rev. 2411 (1988). See also Tayyab Mahmud, What's Next? Counter-Stories and Theorizing Resistance, 16 Seattle J. for Soc. Just. 607 (2018).

Below, legal scholar Deleso Alford shows how narrative can help develop greater cultural competency to serve women of color with better medical or legal services. She combines history, medicine, and law in this analysis. She includes, excludes, and characterizes facts intentionally in one way or another to show how the writing of history can suppress or expose facts inconvenient to elites. But, with suppressed facts exposed, readers can open new possibilities for action and progress. As you read, visualize how you might employ critical methods of research and analysis in the field as a systemic advocate.

CRITICAL RACE FEMINIST BIOETHICS: TELLING STORIES IN LAW SCHOOL AND MEDICAL SCHOOL IN PURSUIT OF "CULTURAL COMPETENCY"

Deleso Alford
72 Alb. L. Rev. 961 (2009)

. . . This article examines how slavery and the concept of race intersect with gender to construct a distinct notion of science and technology that has been historically marginalized at best. The particular aspect of "science" that I explore is the development of the medical specialty of gynecology in the United States. I specifically look at "technology," historically referred to as Sims's instruments, Sims's gynecological innovations, and Sims's inventions, circa 1845–1849, which are still used today. . . . The focal point of this article is . . . [t]he reproductive and surgical exploitation meted upon three enslaved women, Anarcha, Betsey, and Lucy, among other un-named enslaved Black women, . . . for purposes of extracting reproductive knowledge, surgical inventions, and innovations to benefit all women. . . . I posit that the telling of Anarcha, Betsey, and Lucy's narrative in medical schools will aid current efforts to attain cultural competency.

The bioethics principle of truth-telling is traditionally viewed from the doctor-patient relationship, however, existing racial and ethnic reproductive health care disparities mandate culturally competent training from a critical race feminist perspective that suggest historical truth-telling in medical schools to students through the use of narrative as a modality. I propose in this article, what I refer to as Critical Race Feminist (CRF) Bioethics as a tool which focuses on the realities of women of color. . . .

This article argues that CRF Bioethics enhances the ability of medical practitioners to humanize present interactions with diverse populations based on knowledge of a historically marginalized past narrative involving medical technology, specifically the specialty of gynecology and the advancement of this specialty through the laws of enslavement. . . .

Narrative in Law and Narrative in Medicine

... [T]he use of storytelling and narrative jurisprudence as a teaching modality in law and, most recently, in medicine lays the foundation for giving voice to the historically silenced, existing in the background but never center stage, no matter how integral to the ultimate story.

The evolving discourse on the notion of "applied legal storytelling," "legal archaeology," and the role of narrative in law provides both lawyers and law professors with an opportunity to explore the ultimate goals for telling the story and enhancing the ability of the storyteller "to see law as narrative or storytelling." ... Narratives and stories energize legal theory due to their ability to hear a multiplicity of voices emanating from the storyteller and moving the story listener.

Th[is] ... "other voice" ... can be found in the acknowledgement of a "multiple consciousness" capable of speaking in many voices. ...

... A CRF analysis of medical advancements in gynecology, which embodies the laws of enslavement, is a story worth being told.... This article focuses on telling the story of medical value and gynecological advancement resulting from the reproductive and sexual exploitation of Black women during enslavement as a step toward cultural competency.

Narrative in Medicine

... The Medical Narrative of Gynecology

The title of Dr. J. Marion Sims's memoir, The Story of My Life, written in 1884 and reprinted in 1968, is ... the medical story of the development of the specialty of gynecology that has become a memoir outside of Sims's interior life, yet they are inextricably bound together, primarily due to his notoriety for discovering a cure for "vesico-vaginal fistula, a medical condition involving internal tears in the vaginal wall leading to urinary and sometimes fetal incontinence, most often caused during traumatic childbirth." A glimpse of Sims's interior life can be gleaned from the federal census of 1850 wherein Sims is recorded as the owner of seventeen slaves when he lived in Montgomery, Alabama.

However, the 1968 foreword of Sims's memoir written by Professor and Physician C. Lee Buxton of Yale Medical School provides insight as to the historically-accepted profile of the main character of this medical story:

> Few Americans have made so great an impression on their special world as J. Marion Sims did on American and European medicine in the middle and late years of the nineteenth century. Dynamic, vital, imaginative, sometimes contentious, always filled with dedication to a burning mission, this ever gentlemanly physician, by professional and personal attributes of permanent quality, helped create gynecology as a specialty. ...

... In his own words, Sims tells how he discovered the cure for vesico-vaginal fistula:

> With a palpitating heart and an anxious mind I turned her [Anarcha] on her side, introduced the speculum and there lay the suture apparatus just exactly as I had placed it.... This was in the month of May (1849). In the course of two weeks Lucy and Betsy were both cured by this same means without any sort of disturbance or discomfort. Then I realized the fact that at last my efforts had been blessed with success and that I had made, perhaps, one of the most important discoveries of the age for the relief of suffering humanity.

Sims's "discovery" and the ultimate resolution of his story has led to either a justification of the end result—scientific medical advancement in the area of gynecology, innovative surgical instrumentation and procedures currently used in contemporary gynecology, or a critical analysis of the means—human experimentation of an enslaved group of Black women over four years.

... The reality of whether a "conflict" exists in the medical narrative of gynecology often lies in the telling of the medical story. As Professor and Physician L. Lewis Wall tells it:

> Sims developed his technique for fistula repair by carrying out a series of experimental operations between early 1846 and the summer of 1849 on a group of enslaved African American women with fistulas who had been given to him by their owners for this purpose. In his writings, Sims consistently maintained that he obtained the consent of these women prior to operating on them, that he promised their owners that he would perform no experiment or operation on them that endangered their lives, and also that he would pay for all of their living expenses while they were under his care. Eventually, these women learned to assist Sims in surgery, helping him operate on each other in turn, until he finally succeeded in repairing their injuries. At the time Sims began his therapeutic surgical experiments on these women, ether anesthesia was as yet unknown. After the anesthetic properties of ether were discovered in late 1846, Sims—like many other American and European surgeons of that time—did not embrace it.

A critical examination of the medical story's setting, the nineteenth century slave-holding state of Alabama, ... [shows that] [t]he enslaved Black women's body was forced by the laws of society to produce wealth—material as well as a body of medical knowledge.

... A most glaring area of conflict in the medical story on the development of gynecology lies in the notion that the enslaved Black women's body was Sims's "experimental property not only in the operation stage, but also during the post-operative healing process." Even the necessity of an operation for the condition of vesico-vaginal fistula has been questioned by modern writers. Sims claimed that the surgical operations on the enslaved Black women for vesico-vaginal fistula was "not painful enough to justify the trouble [of anesthetic] and risk attending the administration." As to the operation stage, Sims reconciles "that was before the days of anesthetics, and the poor girl [Lucy], on her knees, bore the operation with great heroism and bravery." However, . . . [w]hite women with vesico-vaginal fistulas who came to Sims in 1849 . . . were unable to withstand the same operation without anesthesia." The difference in treatment speaks volumes to those marginalized both past and present . . . :

> Sims exploited both Black slaves and poor White women to further his surgical career. He purchased slave women in order to operate experimentally on them. Giving them no anesthesia due to their racial "differences" (Blacks purportedly did not feel pain), he addicted them to opiates to regulate their bowel and bladder function. He operated on several of these women 20 or 30 times before obtaining the results he wanted.

The above narration of stories attempts to intentionally center the women subjected to the discovery, in order to hear their voices, although notably silenced in his-story. . . .

The telling of the medical story on the development of the specialty of gynecology calls for an integration of both his-story and "her-story" in order to acknowledge that Anarcha, Betsey, Lucy, and the other unnamed enslaved Black women—albeit legally sanctioned as inanimate chattel property—no doubt humanly suffered each stitch and restitch during numerous surgical operations without the benefit of anesthesia and underwent postoperative administration of opium during their four-year period of what began as a "season of philosophical experiment." . . .

A CRF lens will enhance one's ability to critically examine issues such as medical ethics and cultural awareness when analyzing Sims's postoperative use of opium on Anarcha, Betsey, Lucy, and the other unnamed enslaved Black women. In the telling of the medical story on the development of gynecology in the United States, C. Lee Buxton comments on Sims:

> . . . Whether it was because they were slaves, or whether their state was so miserable that they were willing to undergo any degree of pain and inconvenience, or whether it was simply that they were regularly given laudenum postoperatively to tie up their bowels for as long as three or four weeks, and thus became addicted, is a matter of conjecture; but it is virtually certain that Sims would not have succeeded had they not been available.

... Sims purposefully avoided discussing the race of his initial subjects of experimentation in his writings after moving from the South to the North, as well as in the original illustrations accompanying his articles, wherein he substituted white female patients for the enslaved ones who actually endured his first experiments. The practice of a "southern medicine" during the late antebellum era, which explained Black inferiority by pointing to physiological differences in the races, served as a veil for the continuation of the institution of slavery and southern nationalism.... It should [therefore] be noted that there is a direct relationship between the story and "the listener's world view." For instance, one of the most significant concerns about critically examining Sims's experiments upon enslaved women is Sims's claim that he "agree[ed] to perform no operation without full consent of the patients" when the laws of enslavement usurped the women's personhood and bestowed consent to their owners....

From Bioethics to CRF Bioethics

A notion of medical ethics for people historically deemed as chattel property must begin with acknowledging past complicity between the laws of enslavement and medical advancement. The application of Bioethics to Black people generally, and Black women specifically, is wholly inadequate to address the particular and unique narrative on the development of gynecology in the United States. CRF Bioethics serves ... [to focus on an outsider] perspective in order to serve as a basis for Bioethical decision-making.

Bioethics

Bioethics is traditionally defined as a branch of ethics concerned with issues surrounding health care and the biological sciences.... Bioethics is interdisciplinary and still undergoing refinement....

"Human" Experimentation and "The End" Result

The accepted narrative on the subject of human experimentation and Bioethics generally starts with Nuremberg. The Nuremberg moral from the story is incomplete without an acknowledgement of the fact that:

> [t]he Nazi experiments were not simply a perversion of medical science; they were also an extension of that science[:] ... the arrogance of modern science led some physicians in the Nineteenth Century intentionally to infect healthy, but obviously uninformed and powerless, men, women, and even children with venereal diseases and to administer noxious and sometimes permanently harmful substances to them.

The extension of science and government complicity in race based human experimentation most notably lies in the Tuskegee Syphilis Experiment....

CRF Bioethics

CRF Bioethics would begin to address the need for a [critical, bottom-up] paradigm that acknowledges how the laws of enslavement and the means to medical advancement support the notion of historical truth-telling in order to inform and cultivate culturally competent physicians, particularly in the area of gynecology. . . .

CRF Bioethics will specifically address the often under-discussed "different" experience of Black enslaved women due to the demand for sexual exploitation for purposes of breeding, particularly after 1808, as well as human experimentation for reproductive knowledge.

Narrative Bioethics offers a reference for acknowledging the "lived experiences" of women . . . which almost invariably include the experiences of past women of color's lives—those stories told and untold through the spoken word, but nevertheless passed down from one generation to the next. . . .

. . . It is the relationship between medical and scientific fact and social meaning, and ethics that should guide physicians and scientists. . . . The most evident power differential in a medical setting is from doctor to patient, in the sense of power and control. [More specifically,] Dorothy Roberts argues that "the political dimension of the doctor-patient relationship is more apparent where the patient is a woman of color. Doctors treat these women differently than they treat their white female patients because of racism." . . .

. . . CRF Bioethics . . . would pay particular attention to historical appropriations of reproductive knowledge [taken] from the bodies of the women of color and their particular experiences interfacing with the healthcare system of the past and of the present.

Medical Schools' Pursuit of "Cultural Competency"

. . . [Educators] have a duty to equip [students] with the ability to see, to articulate, to grasp, and to comprehend the position of the patient.

The existing gap in reproductive health care between white women and women of color in general, and Black women, specifically, can begin to be addressed by acknowledging the narrative behind the narrative of three enslaved Black women in tandem with the existing medical narrative of the development of gynecology in the United States as a means of achieving "cultural competency" in medical schools. The nexus between law and medicine is age-old.

. . . [A] CRF Bioethics approach serves as a tool to help medical schools [and other sites of professional training] attain cultural competency goals.

Cultural Competency Goals

... The goal of cultural competency is to provide health care that meets the patient's "social, cultural and linguistic needs." ... "According to this perspective, the high value we as a society place on informed consent, choice of providers, and equity creates an entitlement to cultural competency regardless of its impact on outcomes." The current synergy between the legal and medical academies' movement toward a narrative approach to pedagogy is in need of a vehicle such as CRF Bioethics to adequately address the traditional notion of a genderless, race-less, generic, English-only speaking "patient." ...

The culturally competent training of physicians should begin with historical truth-telling which present an accurate narrative of medical advancements, science, and technology.

... The recognition of a multiplicity of voices, which invariably deconstruct notions of power and acknowledge race and gendered race "stories," presents an opportunity for theory to meet practice—in law schools and in medical schools. ...

Alford's account of medical research demonstrates that many kinds of narrative can be told analytically—from social history to personal biography. The key point uniting them is connecting a personal experience to its systemic or factual context to forge antisubordination insights and choices. Telling a compelling story is therefore not enough; advocates must contextualize it historically and factually, as Alford illustrates above, to bring *systemic* injustice into sharp relief.

But, recalling the politics of knowledge, a telling of history as a sanitized, self-congratulatory rendition of the past also is not enough—and sometimes can reinforce dominant or "master" narratives undergirding identity castes. Situating a narrative historically, factually, or contextually requires a critical approach to history and self-critical alertness to facts and contexts. These methods are tools to dismantle systems of subordination, not ends in themselves.

Linda Bell Edwards, a legal writing and analysis scholar, notes the significance of counterstories for law in particular:

> Human beings are hard-wired to organize the word narratively, with abstract reasoning and deductive processes arising derivatively from the preexisting narrative structure. Myths and master stories operate widely within cultures ... [to support outcomes that] will seem both true and inevitable. ... But we must be ready to tell counter-stories that teach a different set of lessons—lessons about law as a journey toward wholeness and

healing, toward justice and inclusion, toward fulfillment of America's promise for all her children.[29]

To get there, critical analysts refuse to accept the constricting premises and parameters offered by traditional legal research and analysis under the rule of law—like constricting conceptions of "relevance" that reflect and project the disabling insistence on individualism permeating law as culture, practice, process, and substance. Critical analysts demonstrate how three key methods of critical research can be used in interrelated ways to achieve three-layered progress beyond formal equality. Storytelling can and should be part of a PAR project and empirical data can and should be collected using participatory methods. Used together, these methods add context, reinforcement, and critical insights to anecdotal information. Advocates connect the "portraits" of storytelling with the contextual "landscapes" documented by critical empiricism or participatory action research to increase the likelihood that researchers and audiences alike will accept the structural foundation of, and social responsibility for, systemic inequality.

Over time, enhanced critical understandings and consciousness, based on bottom-up methods and knowledge, increase prospects for enduring progress. Critical knowledge can change minds, views, choices, and possibilities in favor of transformative remedies, rather than atomized, abstracted outcomes. To aid this neverending process, next we turn to three critical norms designed to leverage the impact of knowledge obtained through critical methods.

NOTES AND QUESTIONS

1. *Challenges in Storytelling.* Francesca Polletta and Pang Ching Bobby Chen are scholars who researched the framing of narrative and its deployment in policy and other social change campaigns. They note that storytelling has strategic effectiveness because it is a potent tool of persuasion but also carries great risks. When reading their quoted insights below, think about personal stories you have heard or viewed in recent weeks that aimed to win your support for a policy position. Were the stories moving and "resonant," or did they leave you cold? Who was the narrator, and was that person credible and authentic? Did the stories articulate persuasive reasons to support the policy? What, ultimately, was your position?

> For social movement activists, the key question about narrative is this: Are groups challenging the status quo well-served by telling their stories? ... Our answer ... is mixed. Yes, stories are powerfully persuasive rhetorical devices. ...

---

[29] Linda H. Edwards, Where Do the Prophets Stand? Hamdi, Myth, and the Master's Tools, 13 Conn. Pub. Int. L.J. 43, 51, 66 (2013).

But telling stories is also risky, for at least two reasons. One is that people understand stories in terms of stories they have heard before. Stories that stray too far from the familiar risk seeming unbelievable, idiosyncratic, or simply strange. Insofar as activists often have to challenge the ideological commonsense that underpins laws, policies, and practices, however, they *have* to tell new stories. . . . [A]ctivists have found themselves bedeviled by audiences' tendency to assimilate their stories to the familiar, no matter what they actually say.

. . . The other has less to do with narrative's form than with the conventions of its use and evaluation. Modern Americans view stories in diverse, indeed, contradictory ways: as authentic but deceptive, universal but also idiosyncratic, and normatively powerful but also politically unserious. However, these views are patterned: Concerns about the credibility, generalizability, and value of storytelling are more likely to be triggered by some users and in some contexts rather than others. Narrative's power, in other words, is unevenly distributed. In this sense, culture may curb challenge less through the canonical limits on what kinds of stories can be imagined than through the social conventions regarding when and how stories should be told.[30]

2. *Attacks on Critical Storytelling.* Legal scholars who pioneered critical storytelling promptly fell under attack from some of their colleagues who argued that narrative impermissibly and dangerously appeals to emotion rather than reason. Two such scholars notably decried critical storytelling as making atypical examples of discrimination seem typical: "Storytelling is all too likely to function as a way by which like-minded people reassure each other that their shared perceptions of local events are representative of the world at large."[31] Might systemic advocates face similar critique of their use of narrative from judges, other lawyers, or other elite actors? How might systemic advocates respond effectively to explain the importance of critical storytelling? How might advocates plan and use complementary forms of critical research to provide context that reinforces the impact of critical storytelling?

3. *Ethics of Critical Research.* Prompted by a regrettable history of horrific research on humans, such as the U.S.-based Tuskegee Syphilis Study that Alford mentioned in her excerpt and the routine use of prisoners in medical experiments, federal regulations now govern researchers of human subjects at universities and other institutions receiving federal funds. See 45 C.F.R. § 46. These requirements are meant to ensure privacy of subjects and their informed consent to the research, supply special protections to pregnant women,

---

[30] Francesca Polletta and Pang Ching Bobby Chen, Narrative and Social Movements, in The Oxford Handbook of Cultural Sociology 487, 487–88 (Jeffrey C. Alexander et al. eds. 2012).

[31] Daniel A. Farber and Suzanna Sherry, Beyond All Reason: The Radical Assault on Truth in American Law 78 (1997).

children, and prisoners, and govern all research projects that meet three definitional requirements:

1. obtaining data from a living human subject through intervention or interaction with the individual, or identifiable private information, and

2. the project is an intentional and systematic investigation using prevailing methodologies in the discipline, including research development, testing, and evaluation, and

3. the project's ultimate aim is to generate generalizable results expected to contribute to the development of knowledge in the discipline.

Advocates undertaking critical research, whether or not acting in a federally funded institution, should look to these regulations for an ethical compass on informed consent and privacy. But the regulations don't go far enough to govern all research protocols, particularly when dealing with vulnerable groups. Recall that Houh and Kalsem "constantly" asked themselves, "What is and is not the role of researcher?" They found that attending to identities, groups, interests, and power were as key to ethical research as to effective advocacy:

> Intersectionality plays an important role in this regard, as the legal participatory action researcher "must be willing to embrace the hard work of examining how his or her multiple identities shape and inform engagement with community members. This critical examination of issues of identity requires an analysis of the dynamics of power and privilege." . . .
>
> [And] when the research process is reconceptualized as a dynamic, equalizing, and shared process, . . . the academic researcher is no longer primarily driven by the desire to find results that she can present for assessment and judgment by some "neutral" body (be it academic peers, judges, lawyers, or policymakers). Nor is she driven by the desire to prove an abstract principle or hypothesis through her data. Rather, she is driven primarily by the desire to bring her own expertise and training to the table in hopes of enabling others . . . "to examine their situation and to take action to achieve change."[32]

To accomplish this expanded form of consent and engagement, researchers must understand the goals and gain the trust of partner-groups. Recall the care exhibited by Aldana in Part I in her gathering and telling of stories of resistance in a Guatemalan indigenous community:

> I relied on the blessing of Dr. Yuri Melini, Founding Director of the Center for Legal-Environmental and Social Action of Guatemala (CALAS)) to gain the access and trust of the community. The community entrusted me with telling its story so that other

---

[32] Houh and Kalsem, It's Critical, at 335, 340.

movements across the globe could be inspired and learn from the story of La Puya. The community also wanted U.S. lawyers, law students, and the U.S. public to know its plight and understand that its struggle is not just for them but for all of us.

What research safeguards does this suggest for those advocates gathering and telling group (and individual) stories or generating empirical data in participatory ways? How can the researcher minimize physical (or other) threats to the members of partner-groups and communities in a context where resistance to oppression is often met with physical violence—in other words, where activists are routinely "disappeared" and killed or threatened and intimidated?

4. *Grassroots Critical History Research.* Critical research histories of social struggle sometimes offer individuals the chance to contribute individual stories and photos, organizational or personal records, and strategic documents to collective archives or to establish and use such archives. For example, the UCLA Labor Center set up a site (www.labor.ucla.edu/what-we-do/research-tools/campaigns-and-research/justice-for-janitors/) to document the historic Justice for Janitors movement in Los Angeles, including chronicling contributions of research to strategy development and mobilizations. Justice for Janitors was a sentinel labor campaign, known for its reliance on creative storytelling and community-based and corporate research. More recently, the campaign itself has been the focus of innovative research efforts. The site offers short videos describing aspects of the community-based movement, development of the campaign, and personal narratives that helped create momentum and mobilization:

> Educators at UCLA are working together with an L.A. union to remember three memorable weeks of struggle on the streets of L.A. when the city's labor history changed forever. In 1990 members of the Service Employees International Union launched the "Justice for Janitors" campaign. Their red t-shirts came to symbolize the rising of some of the city's lowest-paid employees, workers who were considered "unorganizable" by many labor leaders.
>
> Their strike and public protest capped a campaign begun five years earlier, and transformed the California labor movement, helping to bring livable wages, health benefits and basic labor protections to members of the workforce dominated by poor immigrants. Now a group of researchers and archivists at UCLA's Department of History and the university's Labor Center are calling on the public to help in an effort to preserve the memory of this seminal event for future generations.

This project helps build technical and strategic understanding of an important campaign that spread to many cities and also highlights the contributions of many individuals that otherwise might be unrecorded. How might you plan to engage in grassroots critical history of a group or community in which you have participated?

Critical histories, as the Justice for Janitors archives example shows, and analytical narratives often aim to commemorate experiences of struggle while critically evaluating their strategies, successes, and limits. Scholars and students have also taken this approach in assessing their schools' records in relation to the promise of equal education and justice. A notable illustration of the use of critical history research came during a challenge to the University of Michigan affirmative action programs. In defending its programs, Michigan relied on the benefits of a diverse student body. Fearing that Michigan would not fully air its own dirty laundry, a group of minority students who had applied or intended to apply to Michigan, and pro-affirmative action groups, successfully intervened as defendants:

> The proposed intervenors ... have presented legitimate and reasonable concerns about whether the University will present particular defenses of the contested race-conscious admissions policies. We find persuasive their argument that the University is unlikely to present evidence of past discrimination by the University itself or of the disparate impact of some current admissions criteria [such as legacy applicants], and that these may be important and relevant factors in determining the legality of a race-conscious admissions policy.

Grutter v. Bollinger, 188 F.3d 394 (6th Cir. 1999). As expected, the intervenors painted a compelling picture of past discrimination at the University of Michigan, particularly affecting Black students, although the Supreme Court ultimately did not rely on this history.[33] How would you undertake to compile a racial history of your school? Recall the work of Guinier et al. in Part IV, documenting gender inequalities at the University of Pennsylvania School of Law. For other examples of such critical histories by legal scholars, see Richard Delgado and Jean Stefancic, Home-Grown Racism: Colorado's Historic Embrace—And Denial—Of Equal Opportunity in Higher Education, 70 U. Colo. L. Rev. 703 (1999); Richard Delgado and Jean Stefancic, California's Racial History and Constitutional Rationales for Race-Conscious Decision Making in Higher Education, 47 UCLA L. Rev. 1521 (2000); William C. Kidder, Does the LSAT Mirror or Magnify Racial and Ethnic Differences in Educational Attainment?: A Study of Equally Achieving "Elite" College Students, 89 Cal. L. Rev. 1055 (2001).

5. *A Checklist for Accountable Engagement.* Feminist psychology researchers Anneliese Singh, Kate Richmond, and Theodore Burns, writing about participatory action research in relation to transgender issues and communities, provide a checklist to help researchers ensure their own accountability, as well as participant engagement. The checklist includes advice like "assess one's intersecting identities (e.g., race/ethnicity, gender identity and expression, etc.) as they relate to privilege and oppression and power as a researcher," "determine community needs by working

---

[33] See, for example, Defendant-Intervenors' Response in Opposition to Plaintiffs' Renewed Motion for Summary Judgment in *Gratz v. Bollinger*, 2000 WL 35504965 (E.D. Mich.).

collaboratively with transgender people and communities," "share all aspects of the research process and data with informants and communities (stake holders)—and be sure to ask for feedback and input along the way," "understand historical oppression of transgender people and communities," and "practice humility about one's knowledge and assumptions, apologize as necessary, and make changes to the study based on this learning."[34] Would a simple checklist like this help you as a researcher to make concrete and actionable the insights of critical theory and participatory action research? If so, what advice do you think is particularly important, and what would you add to a checklist for critical legal research? How would you adjust your checklist to take into account particularities of the context? How would you develop a plan, curriculum, assignments, and assessments to assure that this learning does, in fact, take place?

11.4 THREE NORMS HELP EXPAND AND DEEPEN THE IMPACT OF CRITICAL RESEARCH AND ANALYSIS

In addition to three expanded methods, critical research relies on three norms to push researchers to maximize the effectiveness of their inquiries and their findings:

(1) **Counterdisciplinarity** highlights the need to carry research across/through fields of knowledge to thicken understanding of systems and potential interventions;

(2) **Critical Comparativism** requires expanded research across/through global regions or nations to deepen understanding of problems and effective solutions, and

(3) **Social Analytics** incorporates critical uses of big data or emergent data technologies, including social media, to deepen, texture, and leverage the insights of research.

As these three norms suggest, systemic advocates and other researchers expand research and analysis across disciplines of formal knowledge, across cultures, geographies, or societies, and in ways that utilize technologies and their information in tandem. These three norms are designed to make Stage One research and analysis more complete, persuasive, and effective as groundwork for Stage Two complex advocacy actions. Like the methods, these norms are designed to deconstruct legal failure and reconstruct legal knowledge as a tool of equal justice.

---

[34] Anneliese A. Singh, Kate Richmond & Theodore R. Burnes, Feminist Participatory Action Research with Transgender Communities: Fostering the Practice of Ethical and Empowering Research Designs, 14 Int'l J. of Transgenderism 93, 97 (2013).

A. COUNTERDISCIPLINARITY

The first norm, counterdisciplinarity, emphasizes the need for activists to work proactively in transcending the limits of any discipline. This proactive stance goes beyond cross or interdisciplinarity in recognizing that each discipline represents not only a base of knowledge but also a source of constraints that limit the creation and application of such knowledge. Whether in law, medicine, economics, history, or the sciences, the discipline creates and enforces frameworks, methods, and norms that function to police the boundaries of knowledge and its creation—the sources and kinds of information deemed to be legitimate or not. Over time, the discipline serves to guide and (sometimes literally) discipline future research and researchers. Established frameworks may be accepted by many *both* because they produce useful knowledge and because they serve to maintain status quos of inequality. By design, every discipline regulates open-ended investigation and suppresses intellectual insurgency.

A critical counterdisciplinary stance recognizes the value of knowledge produced by or through that discipline—as well as a rebellious response to the constraints imposed by it. This stance recognizes that bottom-up innovation within *every* discipline is necessary to overcome the top-down limitations that dominate, even stagnate, knowledge production for justice. Reconsider, for example, the approach to legal research and knowledge in Stump's excerpt above as illustrating legal counterdisciplinarity in action: this norm drives advocates to investigate new sources freely and to transcend disciplinary frameworks rigorously to reshape familiar concepts. This norm enables researchers to uncover suppressed knowledge that may be necessary to progress—critical knowledge that otherwise would remain elusive and even unimaginable.

B. CRITICAL COMPARATIVISM

The second norm, critical comparativism, calls on advocates to compare problems and solutions across varied geographies or systemic contexts. This norm not only brings to light background assumptions, categories, and patterns that often go unexamined, but also generates options that aid the creative process of research and analysis to craft solutions. Critical comparativism, in tandem with counterdisciplinarity, aids in both diagnosis and strategy. Consider one example. In 2015, Elizabeth Mosley, Cortney Bouse, and Kelli Stidham Hall studied access to safe water, comparing the U.S. city of Detroit and Monrovia, Liberia:

> [I]n Liberia diminished access to safe water is now a contributor to the ongoing Ebola epidemic. . . . [And many] people in Detroit, Michigan, for instance, lack access to basic resources like safe water. Since 2013, Detroit Water and Sewage Department (DWSD) officials have shut off water to over 50,000 residential

households in the city due to failure to pay water bills. . . . Though certainly not as severe as the Monrovian context, in some ways the living conditions in Detroit more closely approximate those of the developing world than economically stable U.S. cities. . . . [W]e explore parallels between the two timely and compelling water, human rights, and reproductive justices crises: systematic water shut-offs in Detroit and diminished access to water and sanitation services during Monrovia's Ebola outbreak. . . . Considering Detroit and Monrovia specifically, we are able to investigate and explain how transnational processes of race, class, and gender are translated into environmental and reproductive injustices.[35]

Like counterdisciplinarity, a critical approach to comparative studies can bring into sharp relief facts, issues, and bottom-up solutions that otherwise might escape attention. Critical comparativism makes visible the patterns and legacies that transcend specific areas or contexts.

Recall, for instance, Boucai in Part II who began with early 1970s same-sex marriage litigation across various geographies after the Stonewall Riots in New York City to show the bottom-up emphasis on "gay liberation" as the goal of this struggle. At the threshold, the struggle rejected marriage as a social good to be pursued; it insisted on the right to not conform, in this instance, to the identity-based biases baked into "marriage" as a state-enforced institution. Boucai then turned to later cases, comparing them to the earlier ones, to point out how the goal of struggle had been reframed as formal "marriage equality." This comparison allowed for exploration of the gay liberation movement's roots in both small towns and urban areas, relatively conservative and relatively progressive jurisdictions. This comparative approach highlighted the distinctions between early aims to undermine traditional marriage as a patriarchal and homophobic institution and late cases that reinforced the institution of marriage but also opened the door for creative, inclusive family law reforms. This critical comparison highlights how struggles can be framed and reframed, for better and for worse, over the course of time—framings and reframings that systemic advocates proactively strive to tailor for justice. This comparison raises critical questions about the dilution, cooptation, or diversion of struggles that start from the bottom, as well as about the innovation, persistence, and resilience of bottom-up struggles that continually reorient themselves toward antisubordination across time and contexts.

These two examples of this critical comparativism norm illustrate how advocates wed examination of particular contexts or scenarios to larger patterns that exist in different, yet similar, areas or contexts—to link the

---

[35] Elizabeth A. Mosley, Cortney K. Bouse & Kelli Stidham Hall, Water, Human Rights, and Reproductive Justice: Implications for Women in Detroit and Monrovia, 8 Environmental Just. 78 (2015).

micro to the macro, the local to the global, the material to the symbolic, and the past to the present and future. Learning from and through comparative research, systemic advocates bring together contextual and historical lessons drawn from the facts and experience of other struggles against injustice. In this way, comparison illuminates problems, their systemic sources, and potentially transformative solutions.

C. SOCIAL ANALYTICS AND SOCIAL MEDIA

Finally, the third norm, social analytics, centers the daunting but important field of using "big data" and new technologies, including evolving uses of social media, to test critical insights and bottom-up information drawn from more idiosyncratic or limited sources of information. As an emergent practice, the use of social analytics may be unfamiliar to many law-trained advocates. But advocates generally may lack training, organizational capacity, and comfort levels to generate, manage, and effectively use social or systemic data. Even in online environments, identities, groups, interests, and power still are channeled to favor elites. And, building on the legacies of earlier generations, the power to create data and to control communications is used to control, monitor, and "divide and conquer" marginalized communities. Nonetheless, bottom-up struggles and advocacy have a long history of embracing and leveraging emerging technologies to flip top-down systemic scripts and expand the impact of their actions.

Once again, the *Brown* experience is instructive, even on this point of research, information, and technology. Research-led choices of action undergirded the civil rights gains of the 1960s. Those activists and advocates organized their direct and legal actions with a keen appreciation for a then-emergent technology—television. Indeed, the decades-long campaign leading up to *Brown* was kicked off with another nod to technology and its potential for transformative advocacy: the NAACP team's first use of grant money from the Garland Fund for this campaign was to purchase a recording camera to capture on film (and use as evidence in trials) the actual conditions of separated black and white facilities. The gross inequalities were so undeniable when presented visually that legal and popular opinions about the "separate but equal" regime began to shift. Today, many reflect on that work with much critical appreciation, which should include appreciation for the key roles technology can play in creating and disseminating bottom-up knowledge. This history extends, more recently, to bottom-up uses of social media, which combined with social analytics, allows both tops and bottoms to use mass information in very specific ways. *Brown*—both the campaign for it and the resistance that followed—make clear why the production *and* dissemination of knowledge with new technologies is integral to social change.

Nearly seven decades after *Brown*, social analytics refers to the work of gathering, analyzing, and interpreting digital interactions, including assessing the relationships created among people, groups, issues, organizations, and ideas. Digital interactions are just interactions that use digital or computerized technologies—and those run the gamut from social media to online games, mobile phones, learning platforms, or any other electronic tool, device, or system that generates, processes, or stores data. Digital interactions are both structured in part by law and part of the production of legal understandings and advocacy actions. Because social media use is widespread, analysis of data generated through and about social media interactions is a key area of focus for advocates. But other sources of data—from cell phone "pings" to data and mapping using Geographic Information Systems (GIS)—can generate deeper understandings of social problems and creative solutions and more sophisticated movement-building tactics and advocacy plans.

Social information technologies create rapidly-morphing forms of "public relations" or "marketing" designed to influence perceptions and attitudes—the social meaning of facts and knowledge—and to affect decisions and actions. At their best, new information technologies can help loosen the grip of elites on control over knowledge—its production and its meaning. Participatory digital technologies might represent a democratization of knowledge, as some have argued or hoped. If so, social analytics might allow activists and advocates to track and intentionally deploy those technologies to advance social struggles. But social media and other digital technologies are created by corporations with the primary goal of generating profit for elites, and they have been manipulated by government and other actors to target dissenters, control dissent, and undermine elections and other democratic activities.

Given these complex realities, threshold questions for systemic advocates include the following: How can organized struggles for equal justice benefit from these technologies, and from the raw, bulk data they can compile and collate, for practical, contextual uses? How can social analytics generate information that helps advocates and activists expose top-down corporate manipulations and government repression? In general, how can social technologies nudge law and society closer to justice? So far, the record is mixed and answers unclear, as communications scholar Lili Levi has noted specifically about social media—"broadly defined to include both social networking (such as Facebook, Google+, LinkedIn, Twitter and MySpace) and blogs"—and similar emergent vehicles like Instagram:

> The Internet and social media are transforming news as we knew it. Journalists now rely on Twitter, crowdsourcing is available through social media, facts and stories are googled, traditional print newspapers have websites and reporter blogs, "open newsrooms" invite community participation in the editorial

process itself, video from citizen journalists is commonly used in mainstream media storytelling, bloggers consider themselves journalists, and media consolidation marries entities like AOL and the *Huffington Post*.[36]

In the United States, it is well known that politicians, corporations, and other groups (or individuals)—ranging from Barack Obama and Donald Trump to Google, Facebook, and Walmart—have used social analytics to guide their use of traditional media, social media, and other communication and persuasion activities. Even in the 1990s, opponents of corporate globalization fought the "Battle of Seattle" during the World Trade Organization (WTO) meeting there, using digital communications and social media to guide the nimble movements of protesters in response to the shifting tactics of police. But recall the example above of Casa de Maryland, which suffered invasive digital surveillance, infiltration of online communications, and retrieval of records that threatened their organization and its members and clients.

Globally, bottom-up insurrections against established elites in the Middle East in 2011, commonly called the "Arab Spring," used social media for organized collective actions like never before:

> One of the clearest manifestations of regional knowledge transfer among civil society actors has been evident in the use of social media. As an example, the April 6th movement in Egypt coordinated broad strategies in deploying Facebook and Twitter with their counterparts in Tunisia, while also learning basic tactics—such as measures to help offset the effects of tear gas. In a recent public address, one of the leaders of the Egyptian Tahrir Square uprising, Ahmed Maher, noted that these transregional civil society connections were neither arbitrary nor accidental. Rather, beginning with a meeting in Beirut, sponsored by the Carnegie Middle East Center, a collection of "illegal political groups" of the region from Tunisia to Egypt to Syria to Kuwait started coordinating with one another in building grassroots civil society movements in each of their respective contexts. Maher noted that alongside media strategies and protest tactics, broader shared vocabularies and repertoires of protest grew out of this coordination. As the chant "ash-shab yurid isqat an-nizam" ("the people want to overthrow the regime") echoed from capital to capital, so too did the jokes and colloquialisms of the uprisings. . . . The chants, humor, and poetry of revolution across the region generated its own form of cultural and linguistic innovation.[37]

---

[36] Lili Levi, Social Media and the Press, 90 N. Car. L. Rev. 1531 (2012).

[37] Asli U. Bali and Aziz Rana, Pax Arabica?: Provisional Sovereignty and Intervention in the Arab Uprisings, 42 Cal. W. Int'l. L.J. 321, 347–48 (2012).

In time, they succeeded in regime change in Egypt and other states (but perhaps not much in making transformative, systemic changes, because the new bosses were much like the old bosses). Since the Arab Spring, youthful activists in Korea, Hong Kong, and elsewhere similarly have used online communications technologies creatively against status quo politicians and their campaigns for power. They had to learn methods of digital security, as well. Corporations have made and governments have purchased new technologies that enable top-down deception and control—from the United States, to Russia, China, and elsewhere. Analysis of online information spread through social media, for example, shows that top-down efforts to manipulate events, perceptions, and outcomes—both internally and globally—have been effective. By 2020, "cookies" were everywhere, along with the data they gather and store to control knowledge, facts, and their social meanings or implications.

By 2020, U.S. residents and others around the world also had made abundantly clear to ruling elites that bottom-up uses of social information technologies now made it possible for "ordinary" individuals to capture visually the daily patterns of systemic violence, with the resulting images "going viral" and sparking collective protests against those individual examples of identity-driven systemic patterns. Social media and related technologies have made household names of otherwise nameless victims of this routinized, targeted violence. The "Say Their Names" project, for example, which has many organizational bases and online sites, aggregates the names and stories of victims of police brutality.[38] As these examples indicate, advocates and activists adopt new technologies and adapt uses of older technologies to ensure their research, analysis, and messaging yield maximum three-layered impact.

Conversely, however, white supremacists and their sympathizers also have shown the world how emergent or evolving technologies, including social media platforms, can be harnessed to shape the continuing struggle over equal justice and social equity for all. Perhaps the crystallizing experience came in the forensics that followed the attempted insurrection in January 2021, which subsequent investigations confirmed had been diligently planned virtually. Its execution, moreover, was coordinated in real time through use of cell phones, websites, walkie-talkies, and other new/old technologies. Whether from top-down or bottom-up, advocates must be prepared to engage the forces of inequality online as well as in the trenches.

The capacity to critically interrogate and use big data—research guided by the norm of social analytics—in combination with social media

---

[38] Say Their Names, www.saytheirnames.io; Say Every Name, www.sayevery.name; DCP Entertainment, Say Their Name podcast, www.prnewswire.com/news-releases/dcp-entertainment-launches-say-their-name-a-podcast-series-memorializing-black-people-who-have-been-assaulted-or-killed-by-police-301111617.html.

is an important tool for systemic advocacy. Advocates sooner or later must integrate sophisticated analytical methods and social information technologies into their work. But this incorporation does not require every advocate to become an expert in these technologies (although that is useful). Rather, it requires that advocates acquire a "working knowledge" of them and their basic jargon. Advocates then can communicate effectively with experts recruited for the advocacy team, as discussed in Part III. In other words, advocates must consider how these (and forthcoming) technologies can support three-layered struggles in a particular context or scenario. Then, they must include in the project team the necessary knowledge, skills, and capacity. This work, like struggle and advocacy in general, is ongoing.

Every day, more examples of this critical norm arise precisely because social analytics can uncover knowledge that, in turn, can determine outcomes. Sometimes groups have to create data—not always "big data," but nonetheless voluminous data that otherwise simply would not, and does not, exist. As the example below indicates, these data-creation efforts may resemble PAR, but they go further—in volume and in detail—and use digital technologies. As the following example further shows, groups conceive and set up databases, websites, and other depositories of actionable knowledge in all kinds of contextualized ways so that they—and allies—can use that information in the future for varied, and sometimes even unforeseen, purposes. Centro de los Derechos del Migrante (CDM) began a research project to create data needed to track migrant labor recruiting violations in Mexico. CDM set up Contratados, a website and app that allows farmworkers to contribute "reviews" evaluating recruitment sites, conditions, and practices. With this data, both workers and advocates may assess the likelihood and patterns of wage theft, discrimination, retaliation, and forced labor:

> [CDM,] a cross-border NGO advised by a worker participation "comité," has tackled labor recruiter trafficking of guest workers in Mexico by developing . . . an innovative website that permits workers to share electronically their evaluations of their treatment by recruiters and employers in U.S. guest worker programs. By pooling this information, the workers help each other to avoid illegal and abusive working conditions.[39]

By generating and storing bottom-up testimonials, statistics, and other forms of information, advocates use technology to create a basis of alternative and expanded "facts" that can challenge dominant versions of

---

[39] Marley S. Weiss, Human Trafficking and Forced Labor: A Primer, 31 ABA J. of Lab. & Empl. L. 1, 27–28 (2015). See also Contratados, Centro de Los Derechos Del Migrante, Inc., https://contratados.org. Bassina Farbenblum and Justine Nolan, The Business of Migrant Worker Recruitment: Who Has the Responsibility and Leverage to Protect Rights?, 52 Tex. Int'l L.J. 1, 36 (2017) (explaining that the Contratados system "allows migrant workers to rate their experience of recruiters or employers online, by voicemail, or by text message").

the status quo. Social or data analytics can help advocates to make visible systemic patterns, both to themselves and to others, which may be "buried in the data" but that also can challenge top-down stories, explanations, or excuses if framed and disseminated for three-layered advocacy.

Of course, the results of innovative bottom-up fact-finding are not easily accepted by elite-identified legal decision makers, but they give advocates the chance to contest both meaning and meaning-making through rules of law and knowledge from other disciplines. As described below by sociologist Francesca Polletta in relation to AIDS-related research and activism, bottom-up uses of analytics can alter popular and professional perceptions of problems and solutions and redefine the systemic significance of basic social, economic, or political facts—and the actionable knowledge to be derived from them:

> [R]ather than only trying to challenge meaning, activists should challenge the social organization of meaning—the standards that define what counts as authoritative meaning.... [AIDS] activists succeeded in gaining formal representation on federal research review committees. Just as important, they also gained recognition for AIDS patients' personal accounts of their illnesses as authoritative knowledge in drug research. Refusing the conventional antinomies of subjective and objective knowledge, reason and emotion, and science and folklore, they sought and won legitimacy for personal experience as a form of authoritative knowledge. In a similar vein, activists might work to gain authority for storytelling in contexts where statistics are called for and to gain authority for statistics where storytelling is expected.[40]

This passage shows how advocates work within and beyond systemic boxes to build knowledge, shift perceptions, and promote solutions, highlighting how self-criticality helps advocates craft diagnoses and strategies by creatively tailoring combinations of research methods and norms. This passage also emphasizes a second crucial point: critical researchers and analysts take a step back to question the very premises and conclusions (oftentimes unstated) behind the status quo, rather than simply accepting industry blindfolds that provide "authority" and legitimacy for things as they are. They question the meaning given by elites to basic facts, and they expose how systems or elites create those meanings to serve their own interests. Advocates actively counter the continual top-down cultivation of acceptance and conformity, which, from cradle to grave, aims to inhibit organized dissent even before it forms.

---

[40] Francesca Polletta, Three Mechanisms by Which Culture Shapes Movement Strategy: Repertoires, Institutional Norms, and Metonymy, in Strategies for Social Change 43, 54 (Gregory M. Maney et al. eds. 2012).

Social or data analytics already is important because top-down uses of big data are more efficient, aggressive, and institutionalized each day.[41] If for no other reason, advocates must embrace this third norm to "keep up"—that is, because elites already are doing the same. But from a bottom-up perspective, this third norm, like the previous two, requires a critical *and* self-critical questioning of knowledge and its construction.

The three norms outlined above—counterdisciplinarity, critical comparativism, and social analytics—are mutually reinforcing means of maximizing the results and impact of bottom-up research based on the three methods outlined previously. As a flexibly used set, these three methods and three norms help advocates expose and transcend formal equality and other industry formalisms that provide a patina of legitimacy for systemic violence. These methods and norms are designed to help all advocates stay nimble and make principled and accountable progress along the three-layered of goals of this work. They are designed to sidestep failure by design and get past the Critical Challenge of using law for justice. As we discuss next, advocates use these methods and norms to "map" both problems and solutions in ever more detailed, specific, contextualized ways.

NOTES AND QUESTIONS

1. *Reflection Exercise.* Reflect on the three methods of critical research detailed above—participatory action research, critical empiricism, and analytical narrative, and the three "norms" when developing research plans—counterdisciplinarity, critical comparativism, and social analytics. If trained formally in law, were you introduced to any of these methods or norms in your research coursework? What about in your other advocacy skills courses? What concepts or tools did you acquire in that coursework for critical research? Compare critical knowledge production to the research methods and systems emphasized and omitted from legal education: what similarities and differences emerge? Why? Do the similarities and/or differences count for anything that matters to equal justice when viewed from the bottom?

11.5 FOUR "MAPPING" TECHNIQUES HELP TAILOR AND IMPLEMENT CONTEXTUAL ACTION PLANS

In addition to the three methods and the three norms of critical research, systemic advocates often use one or more of four mapping techniques outlined below. These techniques help advocates understand relationships and networks key to implementing solutions. With this knowledge, advocates can tailor how to apply pressure and use persuasion to break through the limits of formal equality.

---

[41] See Simone Browne, Dark Matters: On the Surveillance of Blackness (2015); Trina Jones, Shades of Brown: The Law of Skin Color, 49 Duke L.J. 1487 (2000).

Diagnostic research and analysis, focused on comprehension of problems, deepens the understanding of the social problems at issue in context. *Strategic* research and analysis, focused on action, examines broadly how power might be exercised to deliver the decisions necessary to achieve three-layered goals. In this basic scheme, mapping techniques allow advocates to precisely plan their interventions for maximum effect in specific contexts.

As we outline below, advocates often use one diagnostic community-based mapping technique and three strategic community-based mapping techniques: (1) concept or problem mapping, (2) asset mapping, (3) stakeholder mapping, and (4) power mapping. The first mapping technique is considered diagnostic because it helps advocates to understand problems, and the other three are considered strategic because they help advocates craft and implement solutions. Used contextually, these four mapping techniques help advocates to map systemic injustice itself, as well as the most suitable ways and means to combat it. Thus, mapping is integral to advocacy across a variety of settings.

These four maps—of problems, assets, stakeholders, and power—can range from the simple to the very sophisticated. Advocates use them during both stages of work as necessary to discern at a glance how identities, groups, interests, and power intersect to maintain entrenched patterns of collective injustice. These maps are not organized exclusively around the four missing elements of traditional lawyering, but they nevertheless bring into sharp relief how systemic injustice functions in any context based on the interests in play and in relationship to the identity-based groups often at the center of persistent social problems. By mapping a contextual landscape around these kinds of relationships, advocates are better able to account for the commingled operation of identities, groups, interests, and power in that systemic setting.

Using these community-based "mapping" tools flexibly, advocates, activists, and allies profile and assess their strengths *and* weaknesses—as well as those of their adversaries—in any given advocacy scenario. As a technique, mapping incorporates knowledge from the expansive research methods and norms outlined above to help conceptualize and create the needed maps and then to follow them methodically. Mapping techniques position advocates to fashion three-layered progress with more precision and effect.

A. CONCEPT OR PROBLEM MAPPING

The first of these techniques, concept or problem mapping, is focused on framing—or reframing—the advocate's understanding of injustice in collaboration with those who experience it. As such, this technique, similarly to PAR, serves as "a participatory or collaborative technique through which a problem or topical issue is translated and depicted in a visual illustration to facilitate an in-depth and systematic analysis."[42] This visual aspect brings relationships and connections into view. This sort of mapping charts bottom-up input and opens analytical insights that can be the diagnostic basis for subsequent asset, stakeholder, and power maps. Coupled with knowledge from the methods and norms, these techniques crystallize strategy development. Human rights scholar Muthee Thuku, working with Amnesty International, describes how concept mapping made human rights violations systemically visible in rural Kenya:

> Factors that can be mapped in relation to a human rights situation may include:
>
> - Violence (e.g. all types of violence in a community including violence by state agents, criminal violence, domestic violence). . . .
>
> - Human rights violations or abuses (e.g. excessive use of force by the police or militia, forced evictions, a ban on union meetings, pollution of drinking water by an oil company).
>
> - Trends and patterns of human rights violations or abuses (e.g. an increase in the number of arrests of human rights defenders and journalists or an increase in the use of rape by an armed opposition group, as well as positive trends such as an increasing number of women reporting rape to the police in a situation in which police refused to accept such reports previously).
>
> . . . Concept maps are schematic/graphic representations of concepts or ideas produced in such a way that the connections between different aspects of the central concept or idea are drawn out to facilitate analysis.
>
> Importantly in the human rights context, concept mapping allows for active participation of communities or specific groups in the critical analysis of a situation. The fact that concept mapping is a participatory process . . . facilitates learning and understanding, encourages critical thinking and seeks to move communities towards collective action.[43]

Similarly, the advocacy group Save Wiyabi provides an example through its Save Wiyabi Map, one of several projects showing where in the United States and Canada indigenous women have gone missing and locations of solved and unsolved murders of indigenous women.[44] Indigenous

---

[42] Muthee Thuku, Mapping for Human Rights, Amnesty International 1 (2017), www.amnesty.nl/content/uploads/2017/01/mapping_for_human_rights.pdf?x54531.

[43] *Id.* at 1–2.

[44] See Save Wiyabi Project, www.facebook.com/Save.Wiyabi.Project/. See also Missing and Murdered Indigenous Women & Girls, Urban Indian Health Institute (2016), www.uihi.org/wp-

communities use these maps to document and combat the ongoing patterns of gendered and racialized violence as an ongoing legacy of settler colonialism and its identity castes:[45]

> Lauren Chief Elk, a member of the Nakota and Black Feet nations and co-founder of the "Save Wiyabi Project," . . . states, "Violence against Indigenous women is settler colonialism at work, because you destroy tribes by destroying Indigenous women. . . . [Maps help document the] rate of violence, the lack of response, the structure that helps [settler colonialism] continue."[46]

As these examples illustrate, concept or problem maps combine critical knowledge from various sources to document sources and patterns of injustice to begin strategizing solutions tailored to contexts. This work depends on sharing knowledge and thoughts. Like the methods and norms, these four mapping techniques rely on collaborative professionalism.

B. ASSET MAPPING

Building on concept mapping, asset mapping is a practical tool for seeing "power" creatively in communities affected by persistent social problems. Assets—like power and interests—come in many forms; they can be individual and collective, material and intangible, and so forth. Thus, groups map assets by inventorying community resources, such as the skills individuals have learned through their participation in work, faith organizations, or other life experiences, and by assessing the presence of community groups, social service agencies, businesses, faith groups, and others in a geographically- or ethnically-defined community. Over time, asset-mapping tools enable groups to avoid being "exclusively focused on needs, problems, and deficiencies [but rather to be] effectively connected to the resources, or assets, of the local community."[47]

The Southern Poverty Law Center notes that community asset mapping is a method for "unlocking your community's hidden strengths":

> Community asset-mapping rejects the habit of describing communities by listing their problems. Too often, the neighborhoods and communities whose children are involved in

---

content/uploads/2018/11/Missing-and-Murdered-Indigenous-Women-and-Girls-Report.pdf; Annita Luchisi, Violence Against Native Women and Girls, www.annitalucchesi.com/maps; Nicholas Thorne, Missing and Murdered Indigenous Women and Girls and Pipelines, ArcGIS Story Maps (May 7, 2020), https://storymaps.arcgis.com/stories/2e4aa189164a41e282820ac8731be588.

[45] For further discussion of settler colonialism and its relevance to Critical Justice, see Part VI.

[46] Jenna Winton, Rebranding Valentine's Day for Honoring Murdered and Missing Indigenous Women, Cultural Survival (Feb. 19, 2014), www.culturalsurvival.org/news/rebranding-valentines-day-day-honoring-murdered-and-missing-indigenous-women.

[47] John P. Kretzmann et al., Discovering Community Power: A Guide to Mobilizing Local Assets and Your Organization's Capacity (2005), https://community-wealth.org/content/discovering-community-power-guide-mobilizing-local-assets-and-your-organization-s-capacity.

the juvenile justice system are defined solely by their needs. Unemployment, drug abuse, poor and ineffective schools, crime, and poverty are often seen as defining the communities in which many of our children live.

Instead of focusing on the deficits, community asset-mapping focuses on the hidden wealth that exists in all communities. Churches, local businesses, non-profit organizations, voluntary associations and parks are all assets with valuable resources to offer. Retirees, artists, musicians, and ordinary youth and adult residents can contribute their individual gifts and passions.

Many of the resources that exist in low-income communities have gone unnoticed by government and people interested in building communities. Governments and state agencies tend to look upon the residents of low-income neighborhoods as resource consumers. They are people for whom state agencies must provide, not people who can contribute something to their neighbors. These traditional viewpoints offer no space for residents to step up, be proactive, or take control of their communities. . . .

Community asset-mapping flips the traditional perspective on its head. Instead of resource consumers, residents are seen as potential resource producers.[48]

Asset mapping recognizes all bottoms possess strengths—assets—that give them capacity to effectuate change. Individuals and organized groups use all sources of strength already present in subordinated communities. Inversely, asset mapping also can help advocates to realize where communities lack assets—their relative weaknesses—to minimize or work around them. Mapping assets after mapping problems thereby helps advocates to figure out the most efficient courses of organized, coordinated, bottom-up actions for maximum three-layered impact.

C. STAKEHOLDER MAPPING

The third type of mapping important to systemic problem solving focuses on stakeholder analysis, which uses mapping techniques to develop information from and about a broad set of groups or persons with a capacity to—or an interest in—influencing outcomes. This technique includes mapping those affected by a social problem, but also others who may be affected by possible solutions or somehow touched by the advocacy needed to win systemic solutions—in other words, anyone who may have a stake in preserving *or* in changing the status quo within a given systemic context.

---

[48] Southern Poverty Law Center, Unlocking Your Community's Hidden Strengths: A Guidebook to Community Asset Mapping (2012), www.splcenter.org/20121126/unlocking-your-community's-hidden-strengths-guidebook-community-asset-mapping.

The goal here is to map the array of groups and individuals affected by, or with an interest in, the approval or rejection of a proposed social change goal. Advocates then incorporate this knowledge into strategies and action plans.

In general, in addition to determining who is a stakeholder, stakeholder mapping lays out relationships among stakeholders, and their distinct and common characteristics and interests: such as *what* type of actor they are, *how* they are affected by the problem or the change being sought, and *whether* they are likely supporters or opponents. Legal advocates often use stakeholder analysis at the outset of a planning process to understand the landscape of stakes and the relationships of holders. For example, the Ohio Children's Law Center (CLC) focused on stakeholders in starting a juvenile justice project:

> CLC felt it was imperative to begin a dialogue directly with those working in juvenile justice to learn about their needs, current challenges, and priorities for law and policy reform in the juvenile justice arena. Between February and August 2009, focus groups, interviews, and online surveys were utilized to receive input from the judiciary, law enforcement, parents, youth, attorneys, and probation and diversion officers (collectively referred to as stakeholders).[49]

However, like other kinds of research and analysis, stakeholder mapping is not limited to the early phases of a project or its planning. Instead, the results of stakeholder analysis also can be mapped to create a dynamic tool for managing relationships during a long project or campaign, during which personalities, participants, and circumstances can fluctuate mildly as well as wildly. Illustrating this point, legal scholars and clinical program leaders Jayashri Srikantiah and Janet Martinez explain concretely the importance of stakeholder mapping for managing key relationships over the longer-term course of an advocacy project:

> Organizational clients' legal issues are often quite complex, lasting for many years and involving multiple modes of advocacy, high levels of expertise, and many players (both collaborators and adversaries).... Organizational representation involves interactions with a range of individuals and entities outside the organization, including other organizations in the same field, adversaries, decision-makers (including judges), regulatory bodies, and funders. If the organization works in coalition with other nonprofits, it likely has longstanding relationships with community-based groups, legal aid organizations, elected officials,

---

[49] Ohio Juvenile Justice System: Perspectives from the Field—Summary of Stakeholder's Priorities 1 (2010), https://static1.squarespace.com/static/571f750f4c2f858e510aa661/t/57d97d959 f7456a5d86d18ab/1473871258199/Ohios_Juvenile_Justice_Stakeholder_Report.pdf.

law enforcement, and others. Institutional client representation also encompasses interactions with individuals within the organization—the staff, board of directors, executive director, and others. We believe that, to successfully represent an institutional client, students should learn about the various stakeholders within and outside the organization.[50]

Thus, stakeholder mapping—like asset mapping—not only captures a portrait of existing stakes and holders, but also how to manage them dynamically and strategically to win three-layered solutions, over time and using time, in varied problem-solving settings.

Moreover, like other kinds of mapping—and like effective advocacy in general—stakeholder analysis must be tailored to a particular systemic context. In the United Kingdom, for example, academics and advocates concerned with defending LGBTQ individuals from violence have used stakeholder analysis to identify three different types of stakeholders.[51] In this example, the three types include "primary stakeholders" personally invested in the safety of the LGBTQ individuals and groups; "duty-bearing stakeholders" responsible for providing protection services such as judges and courts or international peacekeeping forces; and "key stakeholders," or allies who might be able to pressure the duty-bearing stakeholders if they fail to effectively protect LGBTQ individuals or their defenders. Advocates then chart stakeholders on a protection matrix and specify each stakeholder's aims and interests, among other contextually relevant characteristics. The resulting visual map allows advocates to decide how to apply both persuasion and coercion to motivate diverse stakeholders to use their power, privilege, or influence to achieve the goals of advocacy in that systemic context or advocacy scenario. Mapping stakeholders in relationship to the problems and assets already mapped thus helps groups and their advocates assemble practical, focused, three-layered action plans that also are principled and accountable.

D. POWER MAPPING

Finally, the fourth kind of mapping that we survey here is power mapping, which focuses even more specifically on actual *decision makers*. The key decision makers in any given context or scenario can represent formal authority—the elected leader, the top corporate official—or informal authority—the lobbyist, informal leader, or staff person who guides the decision making of those with formal authority; or someone else who can

---

[50] Jayashri Srikantiah and Janet Martinez, Applying Negotiations Pedagogy to Clinical Teaching: Tools for Institutional Client Representation in Law School Clinics, 21 Clinical L. Rev. 283, 285 (2014).

[51] See Sexuality and Social Justice: A Toolkit, www.spl.ids.ac.uk/printpdf/book/export/html/220.

influence authoritative acts of discretion directly or indirectly.[52] As we saw in the United Kingdom example above, these can include stakeholders—those with the duty or authority to decide and act. Like assets and stakeholders, decision makers and their power take on many forms, and are mapped always in context for three-layered plans and actions.

Consider how labor studies scholar Tom Juravich describes power mapping to strategize creatively a campaign to pressure corporate decision makers. Emmett Boyle was chief executive officer of the Ravenswood Aluminum corporation during an international organizing campaign led by the U.S. Steelworkers International Union.[53] After carrying out analysis to ascertain who "really" determined outcomes, the union discovered that "Boyle was little more than a puppet and that the firm was controlled by Switzerland-based financier Marc Rich."[54] The power map focused on Marc Rich in relationship to Emmett Boyle. This mapping technique allowed advocates to figure out how to motivate Rich to motivate Boyle.

Power mapping, like other kinds of mapping, goes from simple to quite complex. Simple corporate power mapping "involves placing the target firm in the center of a page and then brainstorming any and all connections to top management, board members, customers, community groups, and the like."[55] A more sophisticated model builds on the same principle:

> [First, it] distinguishes what is inside and outside the target employer. It also distinguishes among three different levels: command and control, operations, and outside stakeholders. Finally, rather than just providing a blank slate, [the researchers] made an effort to make an exhaustive list of the basic areas for strategic corporate research.[56]

This list may include basic company information, products, facilities, workforce, financials, history, strategy, management, stockholders/investors, board, lenders, parent company, subsidiaries, competitors, providers of raw materials/supplies/services, transportation and distribution components, procurement systems, utilities, customers/clients, safety and health issues, environmental issues, other regulatory/legal relationships, community connections, and political ties.[57] And this list is illustrative, not exhaustive. Although burdensome, all the

---

[52] For a general description of tactical mapping in a human rights context, see Douglas A. Johnson and Nancy L. Pearson, Tactical Mapping: How Nonprofits Can Identify the Levers of Change, Nonprofit Q. 92 (2009).

[53] Tom Juravich, Beating Global Capital: A Framework and Method for Union Strategic Corporate Research and Campaigns, in Global Unions: Challenging Transnational Capital through Cross-Border Campaigns 16, 35 (Kate Bronfenbrenner ed. 2007).

[54] Id.

[55] Id. at 25.

[56] Id. at 26–27.

[57] Id.

contextually relevant questions are researched and analyzed thoroughly to ensure the solid grounding of diagnoses and strategies.

Advocates may assist this mapping of power relationships with additional strategic research, focusing on legal arrangements or relationships, regulatory requirements or allowances, and any legal aspects of the action plan. But to lend this support, lawyers and law students also, or first, may need to learn broader research skills (like those discussed above) to carry out strategic corporate or other kinds of critical research more ably.[58] If so, then, in a process of reviewing, analyzing, and "reconceptualizing" the raw data, groups and their advocates begin to identify "profit centers, the growth plan, decision makers, and key relationships"[59] most relevant to the needed solutions. In this process, advocates can identify both the strong and weak "links" in elite networks to plan actions and target interventions. This kind of expansive and detailed mapping of power and relationships allows advocates to be very precise in their uses of persuasion and pressure to incentivize (and defend) three-layered gains.

As we noted earlier, power mapping, like other mapping techniques, can go from low-tech—drawing a simple chart in which one axis indicates the level of importance that individuals or entities play in relation to an issue and the other axis represents the level of support for the client's/community's goals—to very high-tech. Illustrating the high-tech end of this range, Little Sis is an online tool that collects information from advocates, organizers, and activists engaged with problems in many regions, and then converts the whole into multilayered maps for the purpose of "visualizing networks of influence"—such as those profiting from policing in Ferguson, Missouri, or those that bind the Federal Communications Commission to telecom corporations, among other examples.[60] LittleSis explains its collaborative research methods to map power in this sophisticated, nuanced, targeted way:

> "Power research" is investigative research that follows the money and connects the dots between key players in the power structure. It is typically practiced by activists, academic researchers, and

---

[58] Among the resources for learning strategic research for social justice purposes are the joint Cornell University-AFL-CIO week-long summer strategic corporate research program, www.sce.cornell.edu/ss/programs.php?v=STRATCORP&s=Overview; the Corporate Research Project of Good Jobs First, www.corp-research.org, which includes the Dirt Diggers Digest blog and research guide, www.corp-research.org/dddresearchguide3; and others. Dirt Diggers Digest, for example, has created the Violation Tracker database, with records of "all environmental, health and safety cases with penalties of $5,000 or more brought since the beginning of 2010 by 13 federal regulatory agencies" and has plans to add additional categories of "bribery, price-fixing, financial offenses, wage & hour infractions," and others.

[59] Juravich, Beating Global Capital, at 32. See also John Ganzi, Frances Seymour, Sandy Buffett & Navroz Dubash, Leverage for the Environment: A Guide to the Private Financial Services Industry (1998) (identifying a sophisticated method of analyzing financial industry pressure points for purposes of environmental advocacy).

[60] www.littlesis.org/oligrapher.

journalists who have an interest in mapping, challenging, and understanding systems of power.

Power research focuses on networks—people, organizations, and their various business, political, and personal relationships. It also recognizes that the power structure is not contained within the institutions and individuals that we're often told have power in a democracy—elected officials, for instance. Instead, we take a broader view, going up the food chain to look at major corporations and billionaires and other organizations and individuals who wield extraordinary amounts of influence and control in our society.

Who benefits? Who wins? Who governs? Who has a reputation for power? These "power indicators" . . . help guide power research in its analysis of where to focus, and who to study. . . .

. . . If you're an activist or organizer, it can help shape your strategy and identify who or what you are really up against or show you how to gain leverage in your fights. Within social movements, it can also assist in political education efforts, helping build collective knowledge and analysis of the power structure so that it can be effectively challenged. Journalists frequently practice power research to expose conflicts of interest and follow the money. It can also help point journalists towards the topics, people, and institutions they need to be reporting on: not the small-time crook, but the billionaire bandit.[61]

Power mapping, like other methods, norms, and techniques reviewed here, is practical in nature. Each, and the whole, help advocates act in principled, accountable *and* effective ways to support long-term organized struggles. These four mapping techniques contribute to distinct aspects of problem solving—and yet each technique builds on the others to overcome the Critical Challenge of law and justice. They employ both simple and sophisticated visual aids to "connect dots" relevant to *systemic* analysis. Rooted in antisubordination values like the critical research methods and norms, these techniques are overlapping and continuous to inform advocacy choices for diagnosis and strategy. The set is designed to help advocates act in tailored, contextualized ways that reflect the systemic relationships involving identities, groups, interests, and power within any given problem-solving setting.

NOTES AND QUESTIONS

1. *Power Mapping Exercise.* Visit www.littlesis.org/toolkit and review the resources there in the context of your advocacy project, if you have one. If not,

---

[61] What's Up, Map the Power: Research for the Resistance, LittleSis, a project of the Public Accountability Initiative, www.littlesis.org/toolkit/what_is_up#what.

identify a social problem or issue in a particular context and a relevant corporate or individual target of interest for the sake of navigating through the power website resources.

Consider the resources in relation to key questions about the target: What is the target's interest in the issue or problem? What is the target's track record or decision-making history on the issue or problem? What benefit does the target gain from continuation of the problem? What does the target stand to lose in the event of change? Who influences the target, organizationally, professionally, or personally?

Consider the resources also in relation to the *network* of decision makers of which this target is a part that is relevant to this issue or problem in this context: When and where are the decisions made you would like to influence? Who, in addition to the target, participates in those decisions? What are their voting or decision making histories, alliances, and blocs? What does each entity or individual gain or stand to lose? Who is most influential in this network, and why?

Reflect on what you learned and how it thickens your fact-finding, your analysis and, ultimately after your review of the next chapter, your Stage Two advocacy actions.[62]

2. *Mapping Higher Education's Financialization.* The Roosevelt Institute has worked with students around the country to investigate what it calls a "state of crisis" in higher education due to its financialization.[63] Financialization refers to the "increase in the size, scope, and power of the financial sector—the people and firms that manage money and underwrite stocks, bonds, derivatives, and other securities—relative to the rest of the economy."[64] Colleges and universities are encouraged to use risky instruments like interest rate swaps and auction rate securities (ARS). Their use results in "increases in overall borrowing by colleges and universities, increases in the cost of interest payments on debt on a per-student basis, and a concentration of endowment assets at a small group of the wealthiest institutions." Together, these shifts make education a contributor to "social and economic inequalities, instead of serving as the equalizer" that education purports to be. For example, a study of American University in Washington, D.C., found shocking school losses:

---

[62] Creating an actual map or chart can help you visualize your results. Instructions for a simple chart are found at Power Mapping, The Change Agency, www.thechangeagency.org or https://gofossilfree.org/uk/wp-content/uploads/sites/3/2015/05/power_mapping.pdf.

[63] Dominic Russel, Carrie Sloan, and Alan Smith, The Financialization of Higher Education: What Swaps Cost Our Schools and Students (June 2016), www.rooseveltinstitute.org/wp-content/uploads/2016/09/RI-Financialization-of-Higher-Education-201609-1.pdf. See also David Callahan, Felicia Wong on Challenging Neoliberalism and Reimagining Capitalism, Blue Tent (Feb. 12, 2021) (describing the Roosevelt Institute's new broad focus on rewriting economic and political ground rules to advance equality), https://bluetent.us/arenas/ideas-academia/felicia-wong-on-challenging-neoliberalism-and-reimagining-ca/.

[64] Russel et al., Financialization of Higher Education.

American University also paired ARS with swaps. When the ARS market froze, American paid $74 million to buy its own bonds back to avoid the high interest rates it had to pay on the market. American's swaps cost the school more than $91 million to date, and American would have to pay more than $76 million (as of 2015) to exit the swaps that are still on the books.[65]

The Roosevelt Institute works with student groups to research and advocate against these risky investments. Because these "complicated deals are generally more lucrative for banks and law firms than traditional borrowing," identifying the decision makers with connections to institutions that benefit from the school's losses is particularly important in this context:

> American is also a good example of the powerful role that bankers often play at colleges and universities. Several members of the finance industry sit on American's board, including high-level people at Goldman Sachs and JPMorgan Chase. Some of these same financial companies are involved in American's swap deals, as bond underwriters and/or swap counterparties. For example, a high-level executive at Bank of America sat on the board during the period that American entered into its two toxic swaps with Bank of America.[66]

In a toolkit for student groups, the Roosevelt Institute identifies power mapping as a necessary precursor to strategic action and suggests the following research-then-advocacy steps:

- Research [the] school's Board of Trustees or other governing bodies to determine who is connected to the finance industry and map out possible conflicts of interest.

- Demand that schools disclose any conflicts of interest, such as bankers on boards of directors or in other positions of influence at the school.

If you were to look critically at the decision makers in administrative or board roles at colleges or universities with which you have been associated, what would you find? How many represent or have links to institutions serving elite interests? How many represent or have links to organizations made up of members of subordinated communities? How would you map possible conflicts of interest? How would that guide your advocacy for institutional change?

3. *Mapping Comparatively.* As a practical exercise, what would you find if you mapped and compared historically black colleges and universities (HBCUs) with Ivy League universities, or public institutions versus private ones, or community colleges and trade schools? What identities, groups, interests, power-related commonalities, variations, or differences can you map? What, if anything, do these maps reveal and document about systemic

---

[65] *Id.* at 18.
[66] *Id.*

inequalities in contemporary schooling? What meaning do you derive from the facts you find?

CHAPTER RECAP

This chapter explained that the first stage of systemic advocacy focuses on diagnosing problems as the basis for crafting strategies and solutions. To develop factual bases for diagnoses and strategies, advocates engage in traditional research but also use expanded methods like participatory action research, critical empiricism, and analytical narratives. They augment the impact of research with norms that emphasize counterdisciplinary knowledge, critically comparative insights, and social and data analytics. In addition, advocates and activists employ mapping techniques to assess concepts and problems, assets, stakeholders, and power. As part of an expanded critical toolkit, these bottom-up methods, norms, and techniques amplify traditional legal research and analysis to better design and carry out complex actions—or systemic advocacy projects—as the following chapter details more fully in presenting Stage Two of this work.

CHAPTER 12

STAGE TWO—BUILDING CAMPAIGNS AND INSTITUTIONS AS COMPLEX ACTIONS FOR THREE-LAYERED PROGRESS

■ ■ ■

Table of Sections

12.1 Complex Actions Combine Pressure and Persuasion in Stage Two of Systemic Advocacy
12.2 Supporting Complex Actions by Organized Groups: Finding Your Role
12.3 Collaboration and Conflict Coexist in Complex Actions

OPENING THOUGHTS

In order for us as poor and oppressed people to become part of a society that is meaningful, the system under which we now exist has to be radically changed. . . . It means facing a system that does not lend itself to your needs and devising means by which you change that system.

—**Ella Baker**

The understanding that a lawyer's role in change is supporting community organizations and other organized groups of people (i.e., worker/tenant associations, immigrant/community coalitions, and unions), who win benefits and shift power through collective action and strategic campaigns, is central to all types of community lawyering.

—**Charles Elsesser,** Community Lawyering—The Role of Lawyers in the Social Justice Movement, 14 Loy. J. Pub. Int. L. 375, 384 (2013)

[T]he Todos Somos Esperanza campaign . . . [demonstrated that:] (1) we cannot leave our work only to stay in theory; it must be put into practice and it must be available to the world of practical politics; (2) a coalitional critical theory must focus on the similarities that define the basis of identity and oppression in various socially progressive movements; (3) there must be a relentless commitment to work for unity across differences[,] and differences must be seen as a source of strength and not conflict; (4) there must be a refusal to see conflict as a necessary threat; it is an opportunity to learn and to work for empowerment rather than disempowerment; and (5) *there must be an acknowledgement that the enemies are both external and internal.*

—Elvia R. Arriola, Staying Empowered by Recognizing Common Grounds . . ., 71 UMKC L. Rev. 447, 458 (2002)

INTRODUCTION

In the previous chapter, we explained how critical research and analysis during Stage One lays the groundwork for complex advocacy actions, the second stage of systemic advocacy. These actions are designed to overcome the collectivized complexities of persistent social problems. To do so, complex actions combine legal and extralegal activities to achieve three-layered progress. These actions use time as a resource to build collective understandings, consciousness, and solidarity necessary to sustained group struggle. These actions also are complex because they aim to redirect—to transform—not only law as a system but also the symbolic and material realities of society. In this chapter, we describe complex actions as a second stage of—and shift in thinking about—typical field work of advocacy for equal justice.

We focus specifically on two complex actions paradigmatic of Stage Two work in systemic advocacy: issue campaigns and community development (CD) projects.[1] Issue campaigns focus on particular problems, local or global, to make a policy and social difference. CD projects likewise can focus on many kinds of institution-building projects to meet community needs or wants. However, most frequently they focus on material needs and progress: that is, economic kinds of community development.[2] Yet, community development projects are not restricted to economic agendas. Instead, both issue campaigns and community development projects can be, and should be, customized to the context and readjusted as circumstances shift. In practice, as Jim Freeman, director of the Grassroots Action Support Team, notes, both campaigns and CD projects call upon lawyers to "enhance and expand upon our training by adopting different approaches to addressing legal or social problems, embracing a broader collection of advocacy strategies and tactics, acquiring new skillsets, and being willing to discard those aspects of our formative legal education that hinder our efforts."[3]

---

[1] Community education programs, which are not discussed at length here, make up another key form of systemic advocacy action. Community education programs have their own techniques and aims but also may be combined with or incorporated into issue campaigns and CD projects. Popular education techniques are particularly important in relation to systemic advocacy community education. See Ingrid V. Eagly, Community Education: Creating a New Vision of Legal Services Practice, 4 Clin. L. Rev. 433 (1998).

[2] This work is often called "community economic development," but we use "community development" to acknowledge that this sort of complex program- or institution-building effort may address non-economic concerns as well.

[3] Jim Freeman, Supporting Social Movements: A Brief Guide for Lawyers and Law Students, 12 Hastings Race & Poverty L.J. 191, 194 (2015).

Sometimes, issue campaigns and CD projects are used independently, and sometimes combined in innovative ways. For instance, a campaign or CD project may involve one or more lawsuits, contract negotiations, or other typical legal activities—but succeeding in the cases, contracts, or other legal actions is not the end. Legal means like litigation and transactions are combined intentionally with extralegal activities, like organizing, education, and direct action, to craft complex actions toward amelioration and transformation—the three-layered goals.

As discussed in Part IV, this three-layered framework is one key distinction between law as an industry and advocacy for systemic justice. Think of these actions as antisubordination praxis—a union of action and theory—that employs jurisprudence and demosprudence in dynamic ways. Applying the knowledge gathered during Stage One, complex actions like issue campaigns and CD projects are the mechanics through which advocates flip dominant scripts and create windows of opportunity for three-layered progress. As advocates help client-groups to build themselves into repeat players that challenge ground rules, they increase progress, capacity, and sustainability.

As in Stage One research and analysis, Stage Two complex actions are planned to advance goals along all three layers—technical problem solving, building group power, and shifting cultural understandings. Together, these two advocacy stages both diagnose *and* strategize to effectively address social problems along these layers. As with the stages, these two kinds of complex actions also are overlapping, recurring, and mutually reinforcing: CD projects can be designed to undertake campaigns, campaigns can be designed to sustain CD projects, and systemic advocates decide in context how best to combine these actions. As with all else, advocates incorporate materiality into these decisions.

Complex actions use both persuasion and pressure (or "leverage") to achieve systemic changes with transformative potential. Advocates focus these actions on targeted decision makers so that the decision makers take actions that the advocacy team seeks. All three layers of advocacy are constructed to advance the needed persuasion and pressure and to lay the groundwork for future rounds of defensive and offensive work. Targets may include traditional elites—corporate decision makers, legal elites, elected officials—or may include others, like members of the community affected by social problems, other stakeholders or allies, or the general public. The expanded critical methods, norms, and techniques of Stage One research and analysis are mirrored in a broader set of methods and tools developed for complex actions. In this way, advocates and activists pursue micro-macro progress that is both ameliorative and transformative over time—and using time.

Finally, and due also to complexity, the role of the advocate in issue campaigns and CD projects may vary. Advocates prepare to play many roles and to operate from varied sites of practice to contribute effectively. Some may work directly for community or labor groups. Others may work for legal services or other nonprofit law firms. Still others may work for private firms playing advisory roles as part of a collaborative team. Others may assist part-time with legal cases or transactional work, either on a fee or pro bono basis. Still others may work representing targets of campaigns or projects—government agencies, politicians, or corporations (and these advocates can greatly influence the nature of dialogue and negotiation). Likewise, some may play the role of elected official or judge, serving directly as a decision maker over some policies and practices. Depending on context, complex actions can involve advocates—both lawyers and non-lawyers—in any or all of these roles, and more.

This multiplicity of roles can bestow on advocates undue influence over group decisions and actions. Both in issue campaigns and in CD projects, advocates must define their role(s) in the creation and administration of governance methods to help ensure collaboration within teams and accountability to client-groups and communities. Advocates use dual consciousness and their expanded critical competencies to help organized groups function ethically and democratically. Though always difficult, advocates must situate their supporting roles in relation to the group and conflicts in clear, agreed upon, and principled ways. In this process, managing tension and conflict is crucial to success. These are the key points addressed in this chapter on Stage Two of systemic advocacy.

12.1 COMPLEX ACTIONS COMBINE PRESSURE AND PERSUASION IN STAGE TWO OF SYSTEMIC ADVOCACY

Advocates, as we have seen, use persuasive tools to convince elites—like judges, for example—to rule in their favor in a lawsuit. Simultaneously and synergistically, advocates in the United States and internationally also write reports, initiate public hearings, or use other tactics to create material pressure, like threatened or actual lost profits, or reputational pressure that affects targeted decision makers. Transnational human rights scholar Jeremy Perelman describes some uses of "naming and shaming" in advocacy:

> [Many advocates] have increasingly stepped out of their traditional comfort zone of state compliance with internationally protected [civil and political rights advocacy] and begun to address the structural human rights dimension of economic

globalization and global poverty . . . [by developing] new pathways in naming and shaming in international human rights advocacy.[4]

Systemic advocacy does not focus solely on the persuasion. The advocacy action[5]—whether an issue campaign or CD project—is a paradigmatic framework for coordinating activities to generate the desired pressure and persuasive effect needed to achieve advocacy goals within a specific systemic context. As sketched generally below, some distinctions do exist between CD projects and issue campaigns:

	Issue Campaign	**Community Development Project**
Focus	Any issue area	Usually economic opportunity and development
Geography	Varies	Usually local
Duration	Usually limited time frame, with fairly definite time frame	Often ongoing, with indefinite time frame
Goals	Change in the policies or practices of targeted decision makers	Creation of institutions or programs to expand opportunity, often focused on jobs, housing, or small businesses

---

[4] Jeremy Perelman, Transnational Human Rights Advocacy, Clinical Collaborations, and the Political Economics of Accountability: Mapping the Middle, 16 Yale Hum. Rts. & Dev. L.J. 89, 103–04 (2013). See also Richard L. Abel, The Globalization of Public Interest Law, 13 UCLA J. Int'l L. & Foreign Aff. 295, 303–04 (2008) (noting that "[l]aws and treaties, however, like individual promises (of sobriety, fidelity, thrift, responsibility) can be used to shame. That is why they are a basic resource of human rights organizations.").

[5] The nature of "actions" through which law may be mobilized to address fundamental inequalities and social problems are varied, and the presentation of campaigns and CD projects here aims only to provide two typical, illustrative, often interrelated, and instructive examples. Note, however, that the form of "law's mobilization" depends on context, and many other activities and frameworks for coordination are being "enacted by lawyers and others on the ground" around the world. See Jeremy Perelman and Lucie E. White, Introduction to Stones of Hope: How African Activists Reclaim Human Rights to Challenge Global Poverty 1, 2 (Lucie E. White and Jeremy Perelman eds. 2011). See also the growing body of literature on legal mobilizations and global public interest law work, including Globalization from Below: Toward a Cosmopolitan Legality (Boaventura de Sousa Santos and César Rodriguez-Garavito eds. 2006); Austin Sarat and Stuart A. Scheingold, State Transformation, Globalization, and the Possibilities of Cause Lawyering in Cause Lawyering and the State in the Global Era (Austin Sarat and Stuart Scheingold eds. 2001); Austin Sarat and Stuart Scheingold, Something to Believe In: Politics, Professionalism, and Cause Lawyering (2004); Caroline Bettinger-Lopez, Davida Finger, Meetali Jain, JoNel Newman, Sarah Paoletti & Deborah M. Weissman, Redefining Human Rights Lawyering through the Lens of Critical Theory, 18 Geo. J. on Poverty L. & Pol'y 337 (2011); Daniel Bonilla, Legal Clinics in the Global North and South: Between Equality and Subordination—An Essay, 16 Yale Hum. Rts. & Dev. L.J. 1 (2013); Okechukwu Oko, The Problems and Challenges of Lawyering in Developing Societies, 35 Rutgers L.J. 569 (2004).

Legal skills	Varies, but often includes litigation and policy advocacy	Varies, but usually includes transactional work

Thus, campaigns usually are finite, whereas CD projects may not have clearly-delineated endings. Being focused on an issue with a clearly stated goal, campaigns envision a culmination or "victory," whereas a CD project that involves an ongoing investment to expand economic opportunity, power, and equity within a particular population may be more bounded by geography than by time. The CD project aims, among other possibilities, to create a new community-oriented institution or program—not always economic—and to manage ongoing community projects or to implement, monitor, and enforce an agreement achieved previously. Sometimes, then, campaigns lead to settlements that produce community institutions or projects, while other times institutions mount campaigns to secure settlements. These complex actions allow advocates to mix and match knowledge and tools flexibly to fit the context and the goals.

Issue Campaigns

Issue campaigns are coordinated activities, both legal and extralegal, to accomplish a change in policy or practice in relation to a persistent social problem. This has been described by a leading activist manual as coordinated activity "waged to win a victory on a particular issue":

> An issue campaign ends in a specific victory. People get something they didn't have before. Someone with power agrees to do something that he or she previously refused to do. Implied in the word "campaign" is a series of connected events over a period of time, each of which builds the strength of the organization and brings it closer to victory. Few organizations are strong enough to win a major demand just by asking. . . . An issue campaign has a beginning, a middle, and an end. It is seldom a one-shot event, nor is it simply a series of events linked by a common theme. It is a method of building power and building organization.[6]

Issue campaigns may be carried out at a local level, across regions and nations, or transnationally. Unions and non-governmental organizations address issues raised by economic globalization "through strategic corporate research and the development of comprehensive strategic campaigns."[7] Issue campaigns can focus on many persistent social problems:

---

[6] Kim Bobo, Jackie Kendall & Steve Max, Organizing for Social Change, Midwest Academy Manual for Activists, 11–13 (2001).

[7] Tom Juravich, Beating Global Capital: A Framework and Method for Union Strategic Corporate Research and Campaigns, in Global Unions: Challenging Transnational Capital through Cross-Border Campaigns 16 (Kate Bronfenbrenner ed. 2007).

[I]n every U.S. state there are ongoing grassroots-led campaigns to address mass incarceration and police accountability, protect public schools from defunding and closure, create living-wage policies, ensure a comprehensive and humane immigration policy, and protect against the deterioration of the social safety net, among many other worthy issues. This recent surge of grassroots energy creates new possibilities for generating positive social change, and lawyers are in a unique position to be able to support, strengthen, and magnify such social movements.[8]

As this capsule overview shows, a campaign is geared to its systemic context and social purpose. Based on critical research and analysis, groups and advocates design campaign activities—seeking always to act in informed, collaborative, principled, accountable, and practical ways.

Community Development (CD) Projects

Community development projects address concerns with social equity and tend to be centered on material progress: economic development, sustainability, and opportunity. CD projects traditionally have tended to focus on local geographies. William Simon, a longtime scholar and clinician focused on community economic development, notes that CD projects tend to share three elements: "(1) efforts to develop housing, jobs, or business opportunities for low income people, (2) in which a leading role is played by nonprofit, nongovernmental organizations (3) that are accountable to residentially defined communities."[9] Frequently, therefore, a CD project aims to set up an institution—a nonprofit, worker cooperative, or other entity—to carry out ongoing efforts that generate housing, jobs, and business opportunities, with project governance designed for accountability to members or communities. This kind of CD project includes familiar sorts—like those assisting clients with developing small businesses, with market-related tactics for economic and political empowerment, or with advocacy for specific instances of economic justice.[10] CD projects also implement and monitor agreements or plans—which frequently are the results of campaigns—and may be set up to be ongoing indefinitely.

In addition, CD projects open avenues for public participation in economic development and other policy decisions likely to affect the group or community. Because of this feature, advocates like Richard Marcantonio and Samuel Tepperman-Gelfant of Public Advocates have focused on how that participation is best structured for collective justice. The structure of community participation must overcome the typical "cramped approach" in which community members' only inputs into policies are, for example, two-

---

[8] Freeman, Supporting Social Movements, at 102.

[9] William Simon, The Community Economic Development Movement, 2002 Wis. L. Rev. 377, 378–79 (2002).

[10] Scott L. Cummings, Community Economic Development as Progressive Politics: Toward a Grassroots Movement for Economic Justice, 54 Stan. L. Rev. 399, 400–09 (2001).

minute comments at public hearings.[11] Rather, Marcantonio and Tepperman-Gelfant explain, processes of full participation require agencies "to identify pivotal intermediate steps [in the process of policy development] that will shape and constrain the ultimate decision; to develop a range of alternatives; to give timely analysis and information[;] . . . to facilitate the translation of public input into decision-making outcomes; and to fund community groups to engage residents."[12]

In this specific process of structuring public participation in policy decisions, issue campaigns and CD projects again combine and intersect contextually. Advocates, for example, may campaign to create openings for bottom-up participation in policy decisions. Then, using the power afforded by these gains or openings, they push further to develop ongoing employment, small business, housing, healthcare, or other programs. These efforts take advantage of (and defend) access and resources won through previous political participation to continue pushing for "accountable development." This approach strives to empower subordinated communities to take ever greater control of local conditions, choices, and prospects.

As in campaigns, critical research and analysis is necessary to develop contextual action plans to create and sustain CD projects. Reflecting this bottom line, a key challenge for CD projects, explored by legal scholar Daniel Shah of Social Impact Law, is the systemic mismatch created when using "localized strategies in inner city neighborhoods to combat the results of structural economic change in metropolitan regions."[13] In other words, CD projects (or campaigns) that focus research, analysis, and action *only* on their immediate context may miss important insights, dangers, or opportunities discernible only from broader horizons.

For example, "Empowerment Zones" are neighborhoods created in poor urban areas to try to remedy the lack of good local jobs, but these zones did not work particularly well to raise residents out of poverty. Why? An early critique of Empowerment Zones by legal scholar Audrey McFarlane determined the strategy failed as a springboard for effective action because the underlying premise was that urban poverty was "internally driven and internally remediable" by those in poor neighborhoods.[14] The immediate context and its history were—and are—relevant to diagnosis and strategy, but solutions need also to address "the legacy of historic programs" that

---

[11] See Richard A. Marcantonio and Samuel P. Tepperman-Gelfant, Seizing the Power of Political Participation, Clearinghouse 2 (describing "an alternative public-engagement model"), https://d3n8a8pro7vhmx.cloudfront.net/climateplan/pages/44/attachments/original/1509077040/Marcantonio_Tepperman-Gelfant_Clearinghouse_Article_Oct_2015.pdf?1509077040.

[12] *Id.*

[13] Daniel Shah, Lawyering for Empowerment: Community Development and Social Change, 6 Clinical L. Rev. 217, 217–18 (1999).

[14] Audrey McFarlane, Race, Space and Place: The Geography of Economic Development, 36 San Diego L. Rev. 295, 339–43 (1999).

generated inner city poverty, "the impact of globalization and technology," and the "present 'lived' urban context of racialized space."[15] Without critically expansive research and analysis, CD projects and campaigns will have limited, perhaps regressive, social impacts.[16]

We turn to an informal checklist of basic points that help prepare advocates for successful campaigns and CD projects. This "action checklist" is neither exhaustive nor mechanically applicable: as with all else, this listing only provides some guideposts that advocates must adapt as necessary. The basic points that follow are practical and conceptual and designed as a set to help advocates and teams perform at their best in any given context.

Action Checklist

To maximize social impact, advocates must design and execute complex actions proficiently. To do so, they must address core components or continual concerns that underpin successful campaigns and CD projects. Although these are not sequential "steps," these concerns or components reflect as much as possible how they unfold in practice; advocates daily cycle through steps or concerns, under fluid circumstances, so that each builds on previous ones. As applied in the field, the listing below functions as an ongoing checklist to support effective advocacy. Each component includes typically recurrent aspects of practice in campaigns and CD projects and emphasizes the broader-than-traditional skills needed for both.

1. Preparing for Success—Becoming and Staying Grounded

Becoming grounded includes (a) using practices of self-awareness and cross-cultural competence to assess your individual relationships and position in that context; (b) assessing institutional constraints and opportunities in relation to the issue campaign or CD project; (c) evaluating risks consciously; and (d) thinking of the long run.

2. Getting Started—Bringing "Clients" and Organizations into Focus

Bringing organizations into focus as "protagonists" of systemic advocacy involves considerations such as (a) understanding the nature, missions, and theories of change of client-groups and coalition partner-groups; (b) clarifying the decision-making structure of client- and partner-groups to

---

[15] Id. at 299. See also Cummings, Community Economic Development (describing the history of market-driven and politically-based CD projects often focused on racially-homogenous neighborhoods).

[16] See Jessica Gordon Nembhard, Principles and Strategies for Reconstruction: Models of African American Community-Based Economic Development, 12 Harv. J. Afr. Am. Pub. Pol'y 39 (2006) (describing wide-ranging aspects of development planning and the continual analysis needed in the Dudley Street Neighborhood Initiative in Boston and cooperative business initiatives in post-Katrina New Orleans).

ensure accountability to the interests of members or constituents; and (c) identifying ethical challenges that might arise.

3. Setting the Terms of Engagement—Targeting Audiences and Framing Messages

This component entails tasks such as (a) understanding frames critically as resources for advocacy in the short- and long-term; (b) selecting campaign or project key frames; (c) developing messages defined to tell the compelling "portrait" stories of individuals and communities affected *and* to explain the critical contextual "landscape" that created and maintained the social problem; (d) understanding and utilizing technological innovations for communications and mobilization; and (e) evaluating the potential for participatory communications methods for the campaign or project.

4. Devising Strategies and Tactics to Execute Complex Action Plans

Advocacy teams are focused on (a) understanding who are the targeted decision makers and assessing available strategies and tactics in a particular context; (b) clarifying planning processes with client- or partner-groups; (c) defining key legal leverage tactics and team roles in the action plan; and (d) creating a calendar of escalating tactics and compression points; all this work will dovetail into your action plan for long-term progress.[17]

5. Building Coalitions and Managing Teams to Organize Collaboration

Effective teamwork requires (a) understanding the difference between "teams" and other "groups;" (b) planning for effective interdisciplinary communication and team development; (c) managing conflict; and (d) developing spaces for interpersonal and intergroup healing.

6. Staying Proactive and Anticipating Opposition

Because opposition is constant, advocacy teams dedicate time to (a) understanding opposition and backlash; (b) anticipating retaliation against individuals; (c) addressing organizational intimidation; and (d) managing ambiguity in "oppositional" and other relationships.

---

[17] Compression points are key moments when a campaign either advances or fails: "Organize all your escalating activities toward a point of compression, where things become so pressurized the crisis erupts internally and the process of change is underway," www.organizingforpower.org/some-key-organizing-concepts/. Compression points can correspond with an external calendar—for example, the meeting at which targeted decision makers are set to vote for or against the proposal that represents the campaign's goal—or can be created by the campaign itself—by increasing the pressure and persuasion tactics to a degree that the target feels it must respond, positively or negatively, to demands. Managing escalation and compression points is an important skill in using time proactively.

7. Monitoring and Enforcing "Wins" to Make "Progress" Stick

Sustaining gains involves (a) evaluating the strategic importance of implementation, enforcement, and monitoring; (b) creating monitoring programs that empower affected communities; and (c) self-critically evaluating and developing advocacy capacity while remembering to use time and timing proactively for three-layered progress.

8. Securing or Rejecting Resources for Collective Autonomy

This ongoing concern depends on (a) self-critically evaluating the nature and sources of funding for advocates, client-groups, and partner-groups; (b) planning for strategic fundraising; and (c) exploring new initiatives in funding accountable to client-communities.

These practical components or concerns are basic guidelines to help advocates act as effectively as possible. As always, advocacy choices will depend on context and goals.

We have surveyed—rapidly—an array of actions, components, and concerns related to Stage Two of systemic advocacy. Though not difficult concepts in the abstract, they can be extraordinarily challenging in application. To illustrate concretely, below are three excerpts. The first, by law and social movements legal scholar Scott Cummings, describes and reflects critically on a campaign to block construction of a big box store in a California community. This excerpt shows how teams and repeat players collaborate in coalitions, shifting their collective diagnoses and strategies as necessary to overcome obstacles. The second, by Carmen Huertas-Noble, founding director of a law school Community & Economic Development Clinic, describes two ongoing CD projects: one a legal clinic to support the work of the other one, which takes the form of a workers' cooperative. A third excerpt, by legal scholar Jennifer Gordon, describes the building of an institution—a worker center—designed to be the site of ongoing campaigns, among other activities, to address workplace abuses and exclusions. This example shows hybrid efforts in institution-building and campaign-generation. The complex actions described in these excerpts have in common their aim to be guided by knowledge from the bottom and to organize and use law for justice. As a set, this trio shows how Stage Two complex actions distinguish systemic advocacy from the norms and limits of the legal industry, as described in Part IV. Each exemplifies critical praxis—applying critical knowledge to real-world problem solving.

LAW IN THE LABOR MOVEMENT'S CHALLENGE TO WAL-MART: A CASE STUDY OF THE INGLEWOOD SITE FIGHT

Scott L. Cummings
95 Cal. L. Rev. 1927 (2007)

Introduction

... Inglewood is ... located inside a freeway-bound rectangle ..., separated by major arterials from Los Angeles International Airport to the west and upscale cities like Beverly Hills and West Hollywood to the north. A historically African American city—a status that has been challenged as of late by the arrival of Latino immigrants—Inglewood ... has retained its working class character, with a median income of just under $35,000 per year. As of 2000, Inglewood had only one major supermarket ... within its nearly ten-square-mile city limits. In this sense, Inglewood was not unique among urban communities, in which ready access to grocery stores and other retail businesses has been a well-documented problem.

Yet it was precisely because Inglewood's profile mirrored that of many other urban communities that Wal-Mart found it an appealing target for its first Southern California "Supercenter." From an economic standpoint, Inglewood presented a favorable opportunity as an inner city in fiscal need of Wal-Mart's tax revenue boost—and one that housed working class residents who could potentially benefit from Wal-Mart's "always low prices." From a political perspective, Inglewood was also an attractive locale for urban retail development. It already possessed a large vacant lot ... that could easily accommodate the Supercenter footprint. And, most critically, Inglewood was not part of the city of Los Angeles, which meant that it operated according to its own rules, outside the control of Los Angeles's labor-friendly City Council. Additionally, the fact that Inglewood had a strong African American political base was an important factor because Wal-Mart's urban development strategy emphasized building ties with African American organizations by providing financial contributions. In short, Wal-Mart officials ... viewed Inglewood as the ideal test case in a larger campaign announced in 2002 to bring forty Supercenters into California.

This is a case study of why Wal-Mart lost its development bid in Inglewood and the role that law—understood broadly as both the tactical deployment of legal advocacy and the codification of legal policy—played in the anti-Wal-Mart campaign. It is, in part, a story about Wal-Mart's hubris and political miscalculation: ... a politically ill-conceived attempt to gain voter approval of its proposed Supercenter through a city initiative that would have completely circumvented the local planning process. Yet Wal-Mart's Inglewood defeat ... was politically consequential precisely because there was a sophisticated team of labor activists and lawyers who used Wal-Mart's disregard of public input to successfully mobilize community opposition to the Supercenter. This Article provides a close account of the labor-backed campaign to stop the development of the Inglewood Supercenter through legislative and legal challenges—a technique known as the "site fight" because of its focus on blocking Wal-Mart at a specific location....

Contemporary Levers of Labor Reform: Contesting Wal-Mart at the Local Level

Local activism plays out on a political and economic stage shaped by larger systemic dynamics.... Inglewood gained widespread attention precisely because it was emblematic of the larger struggle to redefine labor standards in a deunionized domestic economy....

The Terrain of Modern Labor Activism

The story of the Inglewood site fight is part of a larger tale about the declining power of organized labor over the past fifty years as a force for collective worker action. The 1935 passage of the National Labor Relations Act (NLRA) was a crowning accomplishment of the American labor movement, creating a federal structure for facilitating collective bargaining. Yet under the auspices of the NLRA regime, organized labor has seen its economic power diminished and union density in the private sector fall from about 40% in the early 1950s to below 10% at the beginning of this century. Scholars have offered interrelated political and economic explanations for labor's eroded power.

The political account of labor's decline emphasizes how external changes in the regulatory structure of labor relations and internal changes in the management of labor unions have constrained their ability to effectively organize and represent workers in the contemporary marketplace. At the governmental level, the story is one of political backlash against unionism, marked by legislative reforms curtailing the worker-friendly bargaining framework authorized under the original NLRA, lax enforcement of management-side labor abuses, and court decisions narrowing key provisions of labor law in ways that have hampered worker organizing....

The economic account of labor's descent focuses on the macro- and micro-economic reordering that has diminished union power. From a macro-economic perspective, the major shift in the past twenty-five years has been toward greater global economic interdependence, measured in terms of liberalized trade and capital investment regimes, which have weakened the labor movement by reducing the bargaining position of domestically tethered unions vis-à-vis globally mobile capital and promoting regulatory "races to the bottom" in which countries compete for capital investment by lowering labor standards. The well-documented consequences of globalization have included the exportation of labor-intensive (and historically unionized) manufacturing enterprises to low-cost developing countries and the corresponding rise of the domestic service sector, with its heavy reliance on nonunionized immigrant labor. These macro-level challenges to organized labor have been reinforced by changes in the internal organization of firms, which have moved away from internal labor markets with the promise of long-term employment and intra-firm promotion toward more "flexible" employment forms, including part-time employment, contingent work, and subcontracting. . . .

Organizing Against Bentonville: The Limits of Traditional Unionism

As one of the world's largest companies—and fiercest union opponents—Wal-Mart has become a compelling symbol of labor's organizing dilemma. Wal-Mart's sheer scale is staggering: its three hundred billion in annual sales constitutes over 2% of the United States gross national product, which ranks it as one of the most dominant businesses in economic history. It is this market dominance that makes Wal-Mart at once an appealing target for unionization and, at least thus far, an indomitable adversary.

Wal-Mart's economic power is built upon a retail template that combines low prices with high-volume sales. . . .

. . . Contrary to Wal-Mart's claims, labor argues that low prices can coexist with high-wages, pointing to Ford Motor Company as the historical prototype and Costco as the modern exemplar of this combination. For labor, the issue is therefore how to improve Wal-Mart's meager and (because of its size) industry-setting labor standards, which include average annual earnings of just over $17,000 for all hourly workers (below the federal poverty line for a family of four) and health insurance plans that cover less than half of Wal-Mart's employees. Increasing wage and benefit plans would impose its own trade-offs, requiring some combination of lower profits or lower compensation for higher-level corporate employees, assuming prices are held steady. From labor's perspective, then, the struggle against Wal-Mart centers on redistributing corporate resources away from managers and investors, and toward workers.

The historical approach to the issue of corporate distribution has been unionization, spurred by the ideology of industrial democracy and embodied in the NLRA. . . .

[But] the United Food and Commercial Workers (UFCW) union, the major union representing retail and grocery workers, has nonetheless failed to win a single union contract with Wal-Mart, [with] explanations rooted in: (1) the system of federal labor law enforcement; (2) Wal-Mart's flexible organizational structure; (3) Wal-Mart's institutional culture; (4) Wal-Mart's anti-union policies; and (5) the UFCW's organizing model.

. . . Though the basic legislative structure of labor law has remained intact for more than four decades, administrative and judicial decisions have impeded private sector union organizing under the National Labor Relations Board (NLRB) supervised election process by permitting uncertainty and delay, curtailing employee free speech, and failing to provide sufficient legal protection against employer anti-union retaliation....

Another impediment to union organizing stems from Wal-Mart's "flexible" labor practices.... Part-time workers tend to have less attachment to the company and experience greater vulnerability—a combination that undercuts incentives to organize....

Observers also point to the Wal-Mart "culture" as an additional barrier to unionization.... A strain of anti-unionism is a core component of Wal-Mart's culture, promulgated through employee literature and meetings that emphasize the dangers of unions, which Wal-Mart portrays as "victimizing" workers by charging dues and depriving employees of their individual voices in the service of self-interested union goals....

... [Wal-Mart has] implemented aggressively anti-union policies to thwart organizing drives in their early stages.... Managers are charged with identifying and screening out potentially troublesome employees at the application stage and are required to contact a "Union Hotline" at the first sign of union activity. A call to this Hotline dispatches a team from the Home Office to run a targeted store's anti-union campaign, which consists of mandatory meetings with anti-union presentations and propaganda videos....

Moreover, critics have charged Wal-Mart with a tacit policy of intimidating Wal-Mart workers, primarily by firing union activists. Though such terminations are illegal, the traditional remedy of reinstatement with back-pay usually represents a hollow victory since it is typically awarded well after the union election has been held (and lost). Since 1998, the NLRB has issued nearly one hundred complaints against Wal-Mart for unfair labor practices, including employee terminations, surveillance, interrogations, and unlawful promises or benefits to dissuade organizing.... There are currently no Wal-Mart stores in North America under union contract, despite a nearly decade-long organizing effort by the UFCW.

... [P]art of the failure of the UFCW to make organizing gains has also been attributed to its own miscues.... [The union] devotes only 2% of its national budget to Wal-Mart and has been criticized for the absence of a national strategy that taps into support for Wal-Mart workers.... [A]ctivists have expressed skepticism that they could win a traditional organizing campaign against Wal-Mart, even with a large infusion of union resources and a high-level of inter-union coordination, given the company's vast resources and sophisticated anti-union machinery.

Points of Entry: Localism as an Alternative Labor Strategy

... [Unions have supplemented] traditional organizing with alternative strategies to build support for unions beyond the direct membership. This effort is designed to help raise labor standards for nonunionized workers and to extend the base of political support for unions. By demonstrating that they can deliver benefits to a broad range of community members, the unions seek to overcome the negative stereotype of labor as a special interest group and improve long-term prospects for increasing union density....

... [U]nions in major metropolitan areas have sponsored the formation of local labor rights groups, which have mediated between organized labor and other community-and faith-based groups to facilitate strategic action around economic justice issues. One of these groups, the Los Angeles Alliance for a New Economy (LAANE), formed in 1993 by the Hotel Employees and Restaurant Employees (HERE) union, has become nationally known for its innovative labor campaigns.... Similar groups have developed throughout California, including the East Bay Alliance for a Sustainable Economy in Oakland and the Center on Policy Initiatives in San Diego. Together with LAANE, these organizations have formed the Partnership for Working Families to advocate for greater social and economic returns on public investments....

Labor activists have also turned to legal strategies—including litigation and legislative initiatives—as a way to mobilize workers and enhance labor standards outside of the federal collective bargaining framework.... [T]here are signs that contemporary labor activists view legal advocacy as a pragmatic response to the constraints on the traditional union organizing paradigm, supporting litigation to enforce minimum labor requirements, while actively using legal levers embedded in the local development process to promote labor standards....

LAANE also has been a leader in the "accountable development" movement—an effort to impose higher labor and community benefits standards on developers that receive public assistance to produce commercial and housing projects....

LAANE's accountable development work has fed into its current campaign to challenge big-box stores, which present similar concerns about local governments approving business development that produces low-wage jobs. LAANE's Wal-Mart efforts have thus focused on containing big-box retailing through local planning mechanisms. One tactic has been the site fight, which seeks to stop specific development proposals by blocking local land use approval and challenging the environmental soundness of big-box stores. In addition, because the site fight is reactive and resource-intensive, LAANE has also sought to persuade local governments to pass ordinances restricting big-box development ... [or to condition] Wal-Mart's land use approvals on mitigation measures that would include enhanced wage and benefits standards.

Between Law and Politics: The Inglewood Site Fight

Inglewood emerged in 2003 as labor's signature battle against Wal-Mart, led by activists allied with the UFCW and LAANE....

"The No.1 Enemy": The UFCW's Fight Against the Supercenter "Invasion"

The struggle over the Inglewood Supercenter was framed by the larger threat that Wal-Mart posed to the unionized grocery sector in California. In 2003, there were about 250,000 unionized grocery workers in California and national figures indicated that they earned about one and a half times as much as their Wal-Mart counterparts. Labor leaders at the UFCW were therefore alarmed at the possible entrance of Wal-Mart Supercenters into the California market, which brought with it the potential to drive unionized grocers out of business and force those that remained to make wage and benefits cuts to stay competitive....

Inglewood: The Reluctant Test Case

What became a high-profile fight between labor and Wal-Mart began as a quiet land deal done well before the grocery strike commenced. In 2002, as part of its plan to bring Supercenters to Southern California, Wal-Mart (through its development proxy, Rothbart Development Corporation) purchased an option to buy the largest undeveloped plot of land in Inglewood ...

... [T]he Inglewood campaign began modestly, with the UFCW driving early strategy and LAANE, at that point still a relatively small organization, reluctant to invest major resources. Wal-Mart's plan to develop the Inglewood site became known in March 2002, when LAANE researcher Tracy Gray-Barkan, who was monitoring publicly sponsored development projects in Los Angeles in order to target sites for potential community benefits agreements, learned about the land deal through local government contacts. Once Wal-Mart's intentions were clear, the UFCW and LAANE worked to head off Wal-Mart's development bid, organizing a coalition of community leaders and representatives from the Faithful Central Bible Church that met regularly for several months with Inglewood City Council member Judy Dunlap to devise a strategy. The UFCW also met with Inglewood's Mayor Roosevelt Dorn (who under city law also cast one of five votes on the City Council) and City Council member Lorraine Johnson, who had been recently appointed to fill a vacant council seat. Both indicated their opposition to Wal-Mart.

... [T]he coalition ultimately agreed on pushing for an ordinance banning big-box development in Inglewood. The UFCW's [in-house lawyer] John Grant coordinated community testimony in favor of a ban in front of

Inglewood's City Council, while [UFCW's private firm lawyer] Margo Feinberg helped to draft the ordinance, which in its final form barred retail stores larger than 155,000 square feet that sold more than 20,000 non-taxable items, such as food. In October of 2002, the Inglewood City Council—on a 4–1 vote (with Dunlap, the UFCW ally, opposing on procedural grounds)—passed the ordinance as an emergency measure. Wal-Mart immediately condemned the ordinance and moved to initiate a city-wide referendum to repeal it, collecting the required signatures to place the repeal measure on the ballot. In addition, Wal-Mart threatened to sue the city for procedural irregularities associated with the enactment of the ordinance since it was passed on an emergency basis without being drafted by the City Attorney. Facing an expensive lawsuit and potentially embarrassing referendum, the City Council reversed course and repealed the ordinance on its own accord in December. . . .

In response to this loss, the UFCW sought to tip the balance of power on the City Council against Wal-Mart by backing Ralph Franklin to run against the incumbent Johnson in the 2003 Council elections. John Grant coordinated the UFCW's get-out-the-vote drive for Franklin. . . . Franklin's overwhelming victory, coupled with that of anti-Wal-Mart Council member Eloy Morales Jr., gave Wal-Mart foes the upper hand on [the] City Council. . . . LAANE, for its part, increased its organizing activity in Inglewood after the ordinance's repeal, focusing on building support among unionized grocery workers, clergy, community activists, and small business leaders to counter Wal-Mart's quest for development approval.

Wal-Mart's next move, however, came as a surprise. In August of 2003, Wal-Mart, through a front group called the Citizens Committee to Welcome Wal-Mart to Inglewood, began to collect signatures to place an initiative on the local ballot for voter approval of a large-scale commercial development on the Wal-Mart owned site (called "The Home Stretch at Hollywood Park") that would include a Supercenter and a Sam's Club. The seventy-one page initiative—known as Measure 04-A—sought to amend the city's general land use plan and zoning ordinances to create a commercial zone for the project site. . . . If passed, the initiative would mandate the project's exact physical site plan and leaseable space, its sewage and energy requirements, its transportation plan, its signage, and even its landscape design—all without having to go through the typical city land use approval and environmental review process. Further, Measure 04-A included provisions that would nullify any "Competing Initiative" passed with fewer votes than Measure 04-A, and stated that once approved by a majority vote, it would take a two-thirds supermajority to repeal. . . .

The Coalition for a Better Inglewood: Organizing Against Measure 04-A

The Inglewood campaign moved forward on interrelated organizing and legal tracks. LAANE spearheaded the organizing effort to defeat Measure 04-A, expanding its role in Inglewood dramatically in the fall of 2003 when the UFCW was forced to pull out of Inglewood to devote its resources to full-time work on [a major, simultaneous] grocery strike [while maintaining an interest in the Inglewood campaign].... LAANE's major role in the campaign involved forming and supporting the Coalition for a Better Inglewood (CBI), comprised of Inglewood residents and government officials, local UFCW workers, and representatives from a number of organizations, including the progressive faith-based group Clergy and Laity United for Economic Justice (CLUE), the grassroots economic justice group Association of Community Organizations for Reform Now (ACORN), and LAANE itself....

In Wal-Mart, CBI faced an opponent with a savvy, experienced public relations team that had cultivated key community supporters. In its campaign, Wal-Mart touted the job-creation and sales tax-generating potential of the proposed store—projecting $3 to $5 million in new sales tax revenue—and won endorsements from important local politicians like Mayor Dorn, who argued that Measure 04-A was good for Inglewood because it would create two thousand construction and one thousand permanent jobs.... Wal-Mart's public relations campaign targeted black leaders: the company gave $300,000 to the NAACP in 2001 and another $150,000 in 2003, which critics charged contributed to the civil rights organization's "deafening" silence during the campaign. Moreover, Wal-Mart orchestrated a sophisticated political campaign in favor of Measure 04-A, spending $1 million on outreach and mobilization efforts to influence the roughly ten thousand Inglewood voters who would go to the polls.

To counteract Wal-Mart's efforts, CBI pursued a two-prong strategy for winning the election that emphasized public relations and voter turnout. On the public relations side, CBI worked with Los Angeles-based Democratic political consulting firm SG&A to respond to Wal-Mart's attempt to cultivate a pro-community image ... by circulating fact sheets to community members highlighting Wal-Mart's record of labor abuse ... [with messages] adapted for different demographic groups. The ... late-2003 Rodino report [ ] found that the entrance of Wal-Mart Supercenters would injure low-income communities by shuttering existing businesses and driving down wages and benefits.

Yet, as the election approached, CBI's internal polling data revealed that the message about Wal-Mart's community costs was not gaining sufficient traction and the initiative was still favored by two-thirds of voters. Part of CBI's problem was a lack of sufficient funds: LAANE, for example, was able to spend just $20,000 on its grassroots campaign. The timing of the grocery strike resolution in March 2004 proved fortuitous from a financial perspective, raising the stakes of Inglewood for organized labor, which recognized that a loss there would further erode its already badly damaged credibility as a viable force for grocery worker unionism. The Los Angeles County Federation of Labor gave $125,000 to support the final phase of the campaign, and ... provided crucial logistical and organizational resources.

... About one month before the election, CBI [focused its messaging, arguing] the initiative circumvented the standard legal process in a way that smacked of an illegitimate power grab by Wal-Mart. In the final stretch of the campaign, CBI organized its media and community education efforts around that theme, using phone banks, community presentations, and press conferences to urge voters to reject Measure 04-A on the ground it allowed Wal-Mart to circumvent its legal obligations. CBI benefited from the sophisticated outreach efforts of experienced community partners ... [and] was able to gain media attention through radio talk shows and well-placed opinion pieces in major newspapers like the Los Angeles Times. ...

Finally, CBI and its union allies mounted a vigorous get-out-the-vote campaign in the final weeks before the election. ... This effort included intensive door-to-door vote canvassing, precinct walking, and community meetings. Though under-resourced compared to Wal-Mart, CBI was thus able to marshal its limited funds and leverage its substantial community connections to orchestrate a highly visible and multi-faceted electoral campaign that effectively targeted Inglewood's small pool of likely voters.

The Legal Strategy

CBI's organizing strategy was coordinated with a legal campaign that was designed to give it an opportunity to defeat the Wal-Mart initiative in court, while also reinforcing grassroots efforts to beat Wal-Mart at the ballot box. CBI therefore viewed the legal campaign as part of a comprehensive effort to use all available tools to gain a "win"—in this case, measured by thwarting the Supercenter development. The use of legal tactics as part of a "comprehensive campaign" model was consistent with LAANE's general approach, which combined organizing, policy advocacy, research, communications, fundraising, and legal advocacy to build progressive political power.

In Inglewood, the legal prong of the campaign—focused on derailing Measure 04-A in court—underscored the centrality of land use and election law in labor's anti-Wal-Mart movement in California. The opportunity to challenge Wal-Mart at the local level stems from the plenary power of cities to control land use planning for the public welfare, which gives them broad discretion over the process of granting development entitlements and codifying general land use plans. Developers generally must go through a local planning commission to obtain key discretionary land use approvals, such as zoning variances and conditional use permits, which the City Council must then approve. The structure of the entitlements process permits well-organized opposition groups with strong political connections to delay or even deny key approvals based on legitimate land use concerns. . . .

Another key legal lever in the site fight process is embedded in the process of environmental clearance for development projects. In California, this process centers on the California Environmental Quality Act (CEQA), which requires that a public agency, such as a city's planning commission, evaluate the environmental impact of projects before issuing discretionary development approvals or providing public subsidies. If the public agency determines that the project may have a significant environmental impact, an environmental impact report (EIR) must be prepared and circulated for public comment. The final approval of a project may be challenged in court. . . . Though it is not possible to defeat a project on the grounds of a defective EIR, it is possible to cause costly delays and build additional pressure on local officials to vote against a project if the negative environmental impacts appear to be substantial.

Finally, as the Inglewood example highlighted, the legal framework of the voter-sponsored initiative and referendum process is an important site of contestation over Wal-Mart. [California] voters have a constitutionally guaranteed right to place initiatives (proposing new laws) and referenda (accepting or rejecting previously enacted laws) on state and local ballots. . . . [But Measure 04-A] was an initiative put on the ballot by Wal-Mart to gain affirmative and absolute land use approval of its Supercenter plans before the city had approved it. The UFCW and LAANE believed that this distinction made the initiative legally vulnerable and began to assemble a legal team to consider a lawsuit soon after Wal-Mart announced that it would gather signatures to place Measure 04-A on the ballot in the fall of 2003.

UFCW Local 770 and LAANE jointly retained Margo Feinberg to coordinate legal strategy. Feinberg, an expert in neither land use nor election law, contacted Jan Chatten-Brown, an environmental lawyer who she had known for many years through their work on progressive causes. Chatten-Brown was also not an election law expert (and had never challenged an initiative before), but her environmental law and land use background was deemed critical . . . Her firm, Chatten-Brown & Associates, was a small public interest law office in Westwood that she had built around representing citizen groups and environmental organizations. . . .

. . . Chatten-Brown's firm focused on analyzing the legality of the initiative from a constitutional and statutory perspective. Meanwhile, the

UFCW and LAANE assembled a larger team of lawyers to consult on the case. Feinberg was heavily involved in coordinating the team, which included practicing and academic lawyers who were identified for their capacity to contribute relevant expertise and bring legitimacy to the cause. . . .

A key question raised at the outset was whether to file a pre-election challenge to block the initiative or to wait until after the election to sue in the event that Measure 04-A passed. . . .

Nonetheless, the legal team ultimately agreed to pursue a pre-election challenge. . . . An early filing would put Wal-Mart on notice that, even if it won the election, it would face a strong legal challenge that would at the very least tie up the plan in court for some time. Moreover, LAANE viewed the lawsuit as a way of generating additional media visibility and grassroots momentum for its voter mobilization efforts. . . . [This legal work] would amplify its central argument: that Wal-Mart was attempting to place itself "above the law."

Chatten-Brown's firm filed the lawsuit on behalf of CBI and LAANE on December 17, 2003, in Los Angeles Superior Court. The lawsuit was styled as a writ of mandate that sought to either prevent the City from submitting the initiative to the electorate or require the County Clerk to remove it from the ballot. The petition's complaint centered on the fact that the initiative allowed Wal-Mart to circumvent typical land use approvals and avoid CEQA review. . . .

The court's decision came in late February 2004 . . . [holding] that the petitioners had not made a "clear/compelling showing of invalidity" that would warrant interfering with "the people's constitutional right of initiative." The court's resolution of the petition . . . did not come as a surprise to the legal team or LAANE, which generally credited the lawsuit with providing an important stimulus to the grassroots campaign, attracting widespread national media attention that helped with the final organizing push.

Once it was clear that Measure 04-A would appear on the ballot, the previously assembled legal team focused on preparing for a post-election lawsuit to invalidate Measure 04-A if it passed. Specifically, the lawyers worked to prepare the full briefing for both a temporary restraining order to immediately halt implementation of the land use changes called for by the initiative and for the substantive challenge on the merits. . . .

In the end, a post-election lawsuit was rendered moot by the Inglewood voters, who sent Measure 04-A to defeat by a decisive margin (7,049 voting against and 4,575 voting in favor) in the April 6, 2004 special election for the initiative. . . . [The] outcome was Wal-Mart's first ballot-box defeat. . . . [T]he defeat of Measure 04-A complicated Wal-Mart's long-term development plan: with the Inglewood City Council lining up against a

Supercenter development, it would require a pro-Wal-Mart change in personnel on the Council for the possibility of city approval to re-emerge.

From Ballot-Box Victory to Local Policy Reform

The Inglewood victory also had repercussions for the ongoing effort to legally restrict Wal-Mart's ability to enter the Los Angeles city limits. . . .

. . . LAANE began to advocate for an ordinance [in Los Angeles] requiring retailers to submit an "economic impact analysis" demonstrating the absence of adverse economic impacts prior to big-box approval. . . . While infeasible as a general development requirement, the [economic] impact report idea gained traction in connection with discussions about big-box regulation, and after the Inglewood fight came to represent a way out of the political and legal impasse created by an absolute big-box ban. . . . [A] revised ordinance was introduced to the [Los Angeles] City Planning Commission in May 2004.

UFCW lawyer Margo Feinberg took the lead in coordinating with the City Attorney's office to draft the new ordinance. . . . Feinberg testified and prepared other community members to testify at a City Council hearing in order to build a strong public record for the ordinance. She also was involved in briefing the Council on the goals of the ordinance and coordinating with [then-]Council member Garcetti's staff on executing changes. LAANE staff and UFCW counsel John Grant managed the process of educating Council members and coordinating community input. Grant also mobilized new constituencies in support of the ordinance such as affordable housing groups, like the Southern California Association of Nonprofit Housing, and legal aid lawyers. Despite expressing early hostility, Wal-Mart eventually signaled its support once it became clear that the ordinance had the overwhelming support of the City Council. After a roughly three months of negotiations and revisions, Los Angeles passed the nation's first "Superstores Ordinance" requiring an economic impact analysis in August 2004.

The ordinance applies to any "Superstore" . . . that is slated to be located in an Economic Assistance Area. These Areas include federal and state enterprise zones and city redevelopment project areas covering much of Los Angeles's low-income communities. The law makes the development of a Superstore in such an Area contingent on the receipt of a conditional use permit (CUP). . . . In order to receive a CUP, a Superstore developer must submit an "economic impact analysis" to the city's Community Development Department (or Community Redevelopment Agency if the project is within a redevelopment zone) specifying whether the store would "have an adverse impact or economic benefit on grocery or retail shopping centers," . . . [or] create other "materially adverse or positive economic impacts or blight." . . .

Of course, passage of the Los Angeles Superstores Ordinance did not affect the status of developments in Inglewood, which remained an active big-box site after the 2004 ballot initiative. In fact, in early 2005, Wal-Mart formally purchased the sixty-acre site it had previously held on option, and it was widely expected that the company would renew its Supercenter proposal that year.... Subsequently, the UFCW and LAANE went back to Inglewood with a conscious strategy of adapting the Los Angeles Superstores Ordinance to Inglewood in order to provide an additional layer of protection from big-box development. Inglewood City Council member Franklin sponsored the Inglewood ordinance, but while he had the support of the Inglewood City Council, the Mayor and City Attorney opposed the effort. As a result, Franklin circumvented the City Attorney, instead directing the city's planning division to send to the full Council a proposal that tracked the Los Angeles Ordinance. Feinberg, on behalf of the UFCW and LAANE, helped to draft the Inglewood ordinance, which when it passed in July 2006, mirrored its Los Angeles counterpart by requiring big-box developers to pay for an economic impact analysis before building permits could be approved.

The Inglewood Effect: Echoes of Wal-Mart Activism

The adoption of Superstores Ordinances in Los Angeles and Inglewood capped nearly five years of lobbying, organizing, and legal advocacy by the UFCW and LAANE, and constituted legal codification of their campaign to thwart Wal-Mart's entry into metropolitan Los Angeles. When measured against the benchmark of stopping Wal-Mart from penetrating the Los Angeles market, the campaign was by all accounts a resounding success. Wal-Mart has yet to open a Supercenter in Los Angeles or Inglewood, and the cities' ordinances hold the unique distinction of having avoided legal challenge from the retailer.

The aftermath of the Inglewood fight, however, has underscored the elusiveness of Wal-Mart and the complexities of coordinating a labor movement on a city-by-city basis.... Wal-Mart has pursued a two-tiered strategy, focusing on the international market, while continuing to vigorously press development plans in small domestic cities where it can use its superior resources to wear down local resistance. In Inglewood, for instance, Wal-Mart has not conceded the Supercenter fight....

As a tactical matter, Wal-Mart has avoided proposing any new initiatives preempting local planning, which backfired in Inglewood. Instead, it has followed the approach it pursued successfully before Inglewood, focusing on working behind the scenes to secure city approval for Supercenter developments, while referendizing or litigating city big-box bans....

Law in the Anti-Wal-Mart Movement: Lessons from Los Angeles

... [T]he emergence of powerful community-labor coalitions that coordinate to advance economic reform has both relied upon and reshaped legal activism. ...

Multi-Level Legal Advocacy

The classical model of law reform emphasized the creation of universal rules codified at the federal level. This model—symbolized by the civil-rights era campaign of the NAACP LDF, culminating in *Brown v. Board of Education*, and the subsequent enactment of federal civil rights laws—was egalitarian in its application and top-down in its implementation.... A similar dynamic occurred during the New Deal period, when organized labor invoked federal governmental power to facilitate organizing and counteract the economic influence of industrial capital.

The dominant scholarly perspective is critical of top-down, universal law reform on three basic grounds. First, scholars have been generally dubious of the long-term effectiveness of top-down rules, which operate too far from the ground level to be effectively enforced. Second, scholars have objected to the pursuit of rights as a goal of transformative advocacy, arguing that they are too inflexible to allow for the sort of bargaining necessity to resolve complicated social problems and too individualistic to sustain ongoing collective action. Third, scholars have questioned the absolute benefits of laws of universal application, which can obscure local differences and inhibit local experimentation. The Inglewood case study provides a vantage point for examining each of these critiques.

The Location of Law Reform: Bottom-Up

... [L]ocal advocacy has been viewed as one potential response to some of the weaknesses of top-down law reform. This scholarship has offered examples of client empowerment, community economic development, and immigrant worker organizing as grassroots alternatives to traditional public interest litigation. One critique of these approaches has been to note the absence of any strong linkage between local advocacy and transformative political or economic reforms. The Inglewood case study, in contrast, offers an example of local advocacy in the service of broader redistributive goals that is firmly linked to the labor movement's campaign to codify laws that benefit the working poor. In particular, the successful site fight unfolded as part of a larger policy initiative led by the UFCW and LAANE to protect unionized grocery jobs that culminated in the Los Angeles and Inglewood big-box ordinances requiring Wal-Mart to submit an economic impact report to gain Supercenter approval. The site fight strategy thus deployed both legal and organizing techniques to gain passage of local policy reform. In this sense, the Inglewood campaign resonated with the law reform orientation of classical public interest law efforts, but instead of pursuing law reform in a "top-down" fashion through courts, the Inglewood campaign revealed how lawyers deploy legal advocacy as a complement to grassroots activism to enact law reform from the "bottom-up" through local legislative channels.... [T]he Superstores Ordinance may also be understood as responding to some of the criticisms of court-based law reform efforts, in that it erects a structure for regulating big-box stores that can be monitored and enforced by local labor activists close to the action. The ordinance thus requires ongoing mobilization efforts in order to be an effective check on Wal-Mart's development plans, and is thus consistent with labor's broader goal of promoting laws that promise to reinforce organizing.

The Nature of Law Reform: Hard Versus Soft

The Superstores Ordinance can be viewed as an example of "soft" law that instead of imposing strict regulatory standards on Wal-Mart or barring it outright, sets up a framework for assessing economic impacts as a starting point for discussions about how to maximize the benefits of big-box retail while minimizing its costs. As such, the ordinance requires that Wal-Mart opponents gather evidence demonstrating the costs of big-box retail on particular communities and offer proposals to mitigate such costs. This means that community groups will have to monitor proposed developments and provide rigorous empirical documentation of potential impacts. This process is unlikely to completely block a big-box project because the ordinance permits project approval so long as any adverse material impacts are mitigated (though Wal-Mart may opt not to incur the cost of compliance). Nevertheless, the system requires bargaining between Wal-Mart and labor and community stakeholders over the terms of entry.

One outcome of this bargaining could be a community benefits agreement, like the ones LAANE has entered into with publicly subsidized private developers, which would include private contractual provisions mandating specific mitigation efforts by Wal-Mart. For instance, one possible resolution of a community challenge to the sufficiency of a Wal-Mart economic impact analysis on the grounds of a Supercenter's negative impact on labor standards might be a community benefits agreement requiring Wal-Mart to pay living wage and a baseline threshold of health benefits in order to gain city approval. It is also plausible that such requirements would be memorialized in any development agreement between the city and Wal-Mart....

The Application of Law Reform: Strategies of Diffusion

By focusing on enacting Superstores Ordinances in Inglewood and Los Angeles, labor activists were able to calibrate strategy based on local political dynamics and adapt policies to local conditions.... The main issue raised by this bottom-up approach is the capacity to replicate and extend victories without a central means of coordination and given the distinct political dynamics presented by different cities. After Inglewood, a range of formal and informal mechanisms have developed to draw attention to big-box mobilizations across the country and foster greater coordination.

On the legal front, lawyers active in the Inglewood campaign have developed expertise that has positioned them as valuable resources for national groups. . . .

[Among community groups,] LAANE, in particular, has become a key actor in promoting and coordinating anti-Wal-Mart campaigns. . . . The Partnership for Working Families is now supporting big-box activism in [many] cities[,] . . . [helping] to revise expectations about how local governments should use their power to link economic development to social justice.

The unions themselves have been active participants in the strategic diffusion of Wal-Mart reforms . . . offering communities step-by-step guides to resist Wal-Mart developments. . . .

Tactical Pragmatism

. . . [T]he Inglewood case also shows lawyers operating with a significant degree of tactical flexibility in connection with grassroots labor rights campaigns. Indeed, the Inglewood campaign . . . required the lawyers involved to engage in a range of traditional (litigation) and non-traditional (organizing, lobbying, and publicity) advocacy tactics to achieve labor's goals. In this sense, the Inglewood case illustrates legal advocacy that is problem-solving rather than litigation-focused. Litigation still plays an important role in advancing the larger labor campaign, as the legal challenge to Measure 04-A underscored, yet it is deployed as part of a broader repertoire of advocacy techniques that lawyers bring to bear to resolve political and economic disputes. Thus, the Inglewood lawyers used traditional litigation strategies in an attempt to gain concrete "wins" and to spur ongoing mobilization, while also readily incorporating non-traditional techniques to advance policy goals.

Traditional Advocacy in the Service of Mobilization

. . . In the Inglewood campaign, law was deployed as one type of political resource used to advance strategic ends: a legal challenge was undertaken, but only in the context of a broader political strategy in which activists viewed the lawsuit as complementing their get-out-the-vote drive. Litigation was an important part of the overall site fight campaign, but it was used for purposes distinct from the traditional law reform suit, insofar as one important goal was to have a public relations and organizing impact, rather than gain a definitive adjudication of rights. Specifically, the lawsuit was brought to undermine the ordinance's legal legitimacy in the public eye in order to persuade Inglewood voters to oppose Measure 04-A at the ballot box. In this sense, the use of litigation in the Inglewood campaign was politically pragmatic—not viewed as an end in itself, but rather as a way to enhance and supplement movement activity.

. . . While the use of litigation as a spur to mobilization has received a great deal of scholarly attention, there has been less focus on the relationship between law and mobilization outside the litigation context. . . . When mobilizing against big-box development, community groups organize themselves into coalitions to make political demands on local governments to either block Wal-Mart or condition its development on the promise of benefits for low-income communities. To do this, coalitions take advantage of the legal rights to participate in local political decision making, particularly those embedded in the land use and environmental review process, which permit public input in the city process of Supercenter approval. In this process, lawyers assist the coalitions to identify and navigate routes of legal participation, through which they can exercise their rights to advocate against land use and environmental clearance. The leverage afforded by these participation rights is the threat of disruption, which can be actualized by pressuring decision makers to deny public approval or suing to block developments on the basis of faulty public procedures. . . .

Nontraditional Advocacy in the Service of Legal Reform

To the extent that the Wal-Mart campaign centered on reforming city policy to demand higher standards from Wal-Mart, it invoked an alternative set of advocacy skills focused on drafting ordinances, coordinating public relations, and mobilizing grassroots support. Margo Feinberg, in particular, was closely involved in drafting the economic impact ordinance. . . . The UFCW's John Grant also contributed important nontraditional skills, including preparing community members to testify at government hearings and helping to orchestrate the union's get-out-the-vote drive. Madeline Janis, LAANE's director, helped to plan and implement other aspects of the comprehensive campaign, including designing grassroots strategy, fundraising for the legal and organizing efforts, and providing input on the structure of the Superstores Ordinances. . . .

Professional Interdisciplinarity and Interlocking Motivation

. . . Though Inglewood was, at bottom, a labor rights campaign, its focus on leveraging labor reform through local land use planning, coupled with the unique nature of Wal-Mart's invocation of the initiative process, meant that land use and environmental lawyers were enlisted in the service of labor movement objectives. Thus, labor's local strategy drove the UFCW and LAANE to cast their search for legal assistance broadly, blurring the lines between traditional labor law on the one hand, and land use and environmental law on the other—fields that have often been at odds over the trade-off between promoting job-producing development versus preserving the environment. In this sense, Wal-Mart gave labor and environmental activists a way of forging a concrete, if still fragile, alliance....

Multi-Tier Accountability

The multiplicity of roles played by the lawyers on the anti-Wal-Mart legal team combined with the fluid nature of the activist coalition to raise unique issues of accountability—both the lawyers' accountability to the clients and the clients' accountability to the broader community.

Lawyer-Client

... In the Inglewood context, the nature of the client group and the approach of the lawyers diminished these concerns about the disempowering impact of legal expertise on client mobilization. On the client end, LAANE, in particular, was a relatively powerful community organization, drawing political clout and resources from its labor affiliation, and governed by politically savvy and influential leaders.... The strength and coherence of LAANE's leadership structure tended to insulate it from undue influence from outside lawyers; moreover, LAANE ... did not look for [outside] lawyers to undertake organizing functions, which they viewed as appropriately kept within LAANE's purview.... Because LAANE approached the lawyers as empowered political actors, the lawyering itself focused on achieving a political result defined by the coalition rather than on promoting goals envisioned by the lawyers.

For their part, the lawyers who worked on the campaign approached their engagement with LAANE and CBI from a perspective that mitigated concerns about client autonomy. For one, they were generally "private" sector lawyers retained by the clients to achieve a well-specified result. Their role conception, informed by their position in the market, was quite conventional, emphasizing the importance of client-centeredness in representation....

The conventional nature of the lawyer-client relationship nonetheless raised its own accountability questions. Even within the confines of the lawyer-client relationship as constructed by the parties, the potential for conflicts was ripe. First, there were complexities involved in representing both a multi-organizational coalition (CBI) and the lead organizing group (LAANE) within the same case. Group representation raises difficult questions about who speaks for the group, but here those questions were exacerbated to the degree that CBI itself was an amalgam of several groups that operated with a range of organizational formality and endowed with very different resources. Thus, on the one hand, CBI was composed of representatives from LAANE and the UFCW, who brought critical financial and organizational resources; on the other, CBI contained more loosely constituted resident and faith-based groups that lent credibility and authenticity, but did not have the same decision-making clout. This created inherent questions of governance and authority to make decisions on behalf of the entire coalition.... [D]uring the course of the lawsuit, the Chatten-Brown & Associates lawyers coordinated primarily with LAANE representatives ... as the spokespersons for the broader group. This arrangement, in part, proceeded by necessity, with LAANE serving as the nodal point in a broader network.... However, the lack of formal specification of any type of governance structure within the coalition format complicated the lines of client communication....

... The portrait of lawyering that emerged from the Inglewood study was one attuned to movement goals and deferential to client wishes.... As labor attempts to meet [the Wal-Mart] corporate challenge head on, the legal arena will therefore remain a central field of contestation and—as Inglewood underscores—the role of lawyers will continue to be critical to labor's attempt to rebuild its organizational base and reenergize its economic agenda.

Cummings shows vividly how local advocates and groups combined "legal" and "extralegal" levers to pursue three-layered progress in a campaign to establish terms for the multinational corporation's entry into their local community, economy, and labor market. These levers included but went beyond traditional thinking and lawyering; they "required the lawyers involved to engage in a range of traditional (litigation) and non-traditional (organizing, lobbying, and publicity) advocacy." In this complex action, organized community groups, advocates, and allies worked in coalition, building on preexisting CD projects to some extent and using litigation strategically for purposes just as, if not more, important than a technical legal win: reflecting three-layered goals, the organizing strategy was coordinated using a legal campaign to give the client-groups an opportunity to defeat Wal-Mart's initiative in court, "while also reinforcing grassroots efforts to beat Wal-Mart at the ballot box." This work aptly shows how advocates plan, research, and act diligently and reflect critically in real time, adjusting in light of ongoing results and shifting circumstances. This campaign again shows systemic advocacy tethered to collaborations informed by bottom-up knowledge and choices.

In the next excerpt, legal scholar Carmen Huertas-Noble relates and reflects on clinical work to support the development of worker-owned cooperatives. Huertas-Noble established a clinic as an ongoing CD project with the goal of establishing and supporting others—workers forming their own cooperative entities. Both are directed by and accountable to marginalized community groups and individuals; over time, these projects might also undertake campaigns. The persistent social problem addressed is pervasive income inequality that "creates a lack of food security, stable shelter, educational opportunities, access to health services, and meaningful life chances." Against this backdrop, worker cooperatives have become one organized response that serves three-layered purposes; they provide "democratic business structures" as alternatives to the standard legal structuring of economic wealth, which subordinates the interests of all workers and other community stakeholders to the goal and interests of shareholders to maximize wealth.[18]

This excerpt demonstrates again the importance of research and knowledge that go beyond traditional training or practice—chiefly by using critical methods and norms of Stage One research and analysis, which then guide development of Stage Two complex actions. Similarly, Huertas-Noble reviews multidisciplinary team building and other nontraditional skills that are key to success in this work. As you read, consider: how (if at all) do these projects add to, or go beyond, formal equality and the rules or norms of the legal industry? What can you learn from these examples to grow your own capacity and sharpen your own skills for professional collaboration and systemic advocacy?

WORKER-OWNED AND UNIONIZED WORKER-OWNED COOPERATIVES: TWO TOOLS TO ADDRESS INCOME INEQUALITY

Carmen Huertas-Noble
22 Clinical L. Rev. 325 (2016)

Introduction

Income inequality is prevalent throughout the globe. In the United States income inequality has reached extremes not seen since the Great Depression. And similar to what occurred in the labor market during the Great Depression, living-wage jobs today have become scarce and wages have steeply declined, resulting in an increasing number of Americans who are unable to provide for themselves and their families.

. . . [W]age stagnation and middle class erosion, combined with increased corporate power may even threaten our political system. . . .

Despite wide-ranging legal discretion to choose their form of entity and governance structure, the vast majority of businesses choose a governance structure the author will refer to as "traditional corporate governance"—

---

[18] See also Kenneth M. Casebeer, Community Syndicalism for the United States: Democratic Production in Resisting Hegemonic Globalization and Law, 17 Employee Rts. & Emp. Pol'y J. 237 (2013); Priya Baskaran, Introduction to Worker Cooperatives and their Role in the Changing Economy, 24 J. of Affordable Housing 355 (2015); Gowri J. Krishna, Worker Cooperative Creation as Progressive Lawyering? Moving Beyond the One-Person, One-Vote Floor, 34 Berkeley J. Emp. & Lab. L. 65 (2013); Ariana R. Levinson, Union Co-ops and the Revival of Labor Law, 19 Cardozo J. Conflict Resol. 453 (2018); Scott L. Cummings, Developing Cooperatives as a Job Creation Strategy for Low-Income Workers, 25 N.Y.U. Rev. L. & Soc. Change 181, 201 (1999); Sara Tonneson, Stronger Together: Worker Cooperatives as a Community Economic Development Strategy, 20 Geo. J. on Poverty L. & Pol'y 187 (2012); Ariana Levinson, Founding Worker Cooperatives: Social Movement Theory and the Law, 14 Nev. L.J. 322 (2014).

which results in inattention to the interests of most workers, unjust distribution of profits in the form of dividends instead of wages and undemocratic workplaces. Traditional corporate governance operates under the "standard shareholder-oriented model," a model that provides flexibility for corporations to be guided by the principles of maximizing the wealth of shareholders and prioritizing executive compensation. Workers pay for these priorities, almost always in the form of suppressed wages.

Thus, an important strategy for addressing income inequality more effectively would be to re-examine and institute changes to (or departures from) the traditional corporate model. . . . This article argues that worker-owned cooperatives and unionized worker-owned cooperatives are important alternatives to corporate ownership and governance structures that strongly tend to depress workers' wages.

. . . [This article] describes how worker-ownership has operated successfully in practice, providing as two examples Mondragon in Spain and Cooperative Home Care Associates [CHCA] in the United States. . . . [This article also] highlights an initiative taking place in New York City, in which a coalition composed of the author's Community & Economic Development Clinic (CEDC) and community partners secured substantial economic and political support from the New York City government to expand worker-owned cooperatives and union coops in the City and to help address the challenge of bringing worker-owned cooperatives to scale. . . . CEDC [plays an] integral role in training legal advisors to cooperatives, garnering governmental support and funding, disseminating public information on cooperative formations, and coalition-building among worker-owners, technical support organizations, educational institutions, and community-based organizations to combat income inequality and its impacts. . . .

Some Causes and Impacts of Income Inequality

The report by the Commission on Inclusive Prosperity provides an important reminder that income inequality is not just about pay. It is also about how one's pay affects one's standard of living. Income inequality creates a lack of food security, stable shelter, educational opportunities, access to health services, and meaningful life chances. The report explains "[c]ountries with more inequality are also countries with less opportunity for those with low and middle incomes."

. . . Economic inequality, especially in the context of greatly diminished government programs, often has a cascading effect, resulting in a multitude of injustices that ultimately results in inequality of opportunity and loss of social mobility.

While income inequality in the U.S. has reached levels not seen since the Great Depression, corporate profits have climbed to an all eighty-five-year high. At the same time, the real value of wages has stagnated or, in many cases, declined. . . .

It cannot be a coincidence that the current trend of wage stagnation is occurring at a time when union membership is at an historic low. Indeed, commentators have noted the direct correlation between union membership and equitable income distribution in the U.S. When union membership was at its highest, organized labor exercised significant bargaining power, resulting in a more equitable wage distribution, not only within organized industries but also through labor market effects that influenced wage rates throughout the economy. . . .

Structural Ills of the Traditional Corporate Form and Need for More Egalitarian Forms of Business Organization

Although income inequality, low wages, and wage stagnation undoubtedly flow from a complex [web] of interacting causes, it seems apparent that a significant cause is the traditional corporate structure—with its focus on profit maximization—coupled with the absence of an effective labor-centered counterweight to corporate power. In the U.S., state laws authorize the formation of business corporations and establish standards and parameters that corporations must abide by when adopting governance structures. These laws impose guidelines on the type of governance structure a corporation may adopt, but allow corporations a great degree of discretion in determining decision-making power, including how and on whose behalf those powers are exercised. Such governance structures, in turn, influence ownership, control, and corporate culture.

Generally in a corporation, ownership is based on capital investment and comes with two main rights: the right to share in profits (usually proportional to shareholders' capital investment) and the right to participate in governance. As noted earlier, a "traditional corporation" . . . operates under the Standard Shareholder Oriented Model (hereinafter "SSM") . . . characterized by four principal features:

> . . . [First, the] ultimate control over the corporation should rest with the shareholder class; the managers of the corporation should be charged with the obligation to manage the corporation in the interests of its shareholders;
>
> [Second] other corporate constituencies, such as creditors, employees, suppliers, and customers, should have their interests protected by contractual and regulatory means rather than through participation in corporate governance;
>
> [Third] noncontrolling shareholders should receive strong protection from exploitation at the hands of controlling shareholders; and

[Fourth] the market value of the publicly-traded corporation's shares is the principal measure of its shareholders' interests.

The SSM essentially subordinates the interests of all corporate stakeholders who are not shareholders—including workers—to the goal of maximizing shareholder interests. . . . Because providing employment at a living wage is not necessarily a priority for a traditional corporation, the labor necessary to produce the corporation's goods or services and carry on its business is frequently viewed as just another component of the costs that should be reduced to the lowest level the market will bear in order to maximize shareholder interests.

Business corporation laws allow, but do not mandate, such a severe approach to labor relations and wage setting. Corporate officers may, consistent with their fiduciary responsibilities, adopt more equitable and enlightened approaches to employee compensation. And government may, through direct regulation or economic policy, encourage or require such choices. A combination of these factors likely explains the interval between the close of World War II and the mid 1970s known as "The Great Compression"—a period marked by broadly shared prosperity and large reductions in income inequality. Tax, trade and labor policies, high union density and a different corporate ethos all counteracted the severe logic of SSM—and workers experienced a far more equitable income distribution.

Today, unfortunately, the landscape looks quite different. Union membership has plummeted, in part as a result of hostile state and federal policies, government has significantly relaxed regulation of corporations and instituted tax policies that disproportionately favor the wealthy, and trade policies have placed domestic workers in competition with highly exploited, low-paid workers from developing nations across the globe. . . . Simply stated, pay and productivity—which once moved in tandem—are no longer linked; the idea of shared prosperity holds little, if any, sway in the corporate calculus. The SSM has carried the day. . . .

. . . There are, however, a growing number of alternative, democratic business structures that can and do distribute income and wealth in a more sustainable and equitable fashion. . . .

Principles and Practices of Cooperative Enterprises

Worker-owned cooperatives and union coops represent innovative and viable forms of worker-ownership that are based on principles of democratic governance and equitable distribution of income and wealth. In New York City, worker-owned cooperatives are formed under the Business Corporations Statute, Limited Liability Company Statute and the NY Cooperative Statute. Not all states have cooperative statutes. Even where a state may have a cooperative statute, prospective worker-owners, upon advice of counsel, may choose to form under the state's limited liability company law, the choice of most NYC worker-owned cooperatives because of its flexibility, or the business corporation law.... Once the needs of the prospective worker-owned cooperative are known, lawyers can counsel prospective worker-owned cooperatives on the options for entity formation that work best for that particular group.

In a worker-owned cooperative each worker has one share and one vote. Such cooperatives are governed by democratic principles of shared governance.... [O]wnership in a worker-owned cooperative is based primarily on labor and the democratic principle of one person, one vote. In a worker-owned cooperative, worker-owners share governance responsibilities and profits. Profits are typically distributed equitably based on patronage.

Worker-owned cooperatives have a long history, especially in marginalized communities....

Worker-Owned Cooperatives as an Alternative Model to Traditional Corporations

The worker-owned cooperative model offers a meaningful alternative to the traditional corporation that is of particular import in the quest to reduce income inequality. The worker-owned cooperative model makes capital subordinate to labor and puts a premium on labor rights. Ownership is primarily based on labor and not solely on purchasing shares. To help ensure capital remains subordinate to labor, shares are also generally kept affordable. The worker-owned cooperative model also tends to keep jobs locally based and keep profits circulating in the community. In addition to keeping most profits in hosting communities, worker-owned cooperatives are also more likely to be environmentally friendly and more attuned to environmental injustice because worker-owners live in or near the very communities where their businesses are located.

A union coop is a worker-owned cooperative that is unionized.... Cooperatives may unionize in order to acquire clear structures and processes for democratic workplace governance, including handling workplace disputes. They may also join unions in order to take advantage of the unions' resources, in order to improve the cooperatives' sustainability....

At first, unionization of worker-owned cooperatives may seem counter-intuitive, primarily because it is perceived that owners would be bargaining against their own interests. However, that assumption implies that the interests of the various owners are always aligned, which is not the case. Conflicts between worker-owners and their selected management can mirror conflicts in other workplaces and conflicts may also arise among worker-owners in non-management roles. In one rarely occurring but conceivable example, individual worker-owners can lose their membership by a vote of a majority of other worker-owners and thus lose their ownership interest. Being part of a union, in this context, can serve as a trusted added layer of protection for worker-owners, offering worker-owned cooperatives an external option of conflict resolution by an organization that is mission aligned and has expertise in conflict resolution.

Worker-owned cooperatives may also elect to unionize . . . to increase the cooperatives' sustainability. Union coops can leverage many attractive features of union affiliation: for instance, union purchasing power to secure better benefits packages for worker-owners and union political clout to obtain limited training opportunities to enhance the quality of services or products they provide to the membership. Worker owned cooperatives also may unionize in order more fully to integrate into larger economic justice movements. In addition, . . . the structures which unions have formed to achieve solidarity can also help inform/shape the creation of inter-cooperation among cooperatives, which can help worker-owned cooperatives scale up by creating a steady demand and consumer base.

Worker-Owned Cooperatives as Contributors to Economic Justice Movements

. . . This resurging interest in expanding worker-owned cooperatives is occurring at a time when various economic justice movements are coming together in a shared struggle to fight for human dignity and rights of workers. Many view worker ownership as a major way to address income inequality. . . . [A] significant proportion of worker-owned cooperatives are based on the Mondragon Principles. These Principles include payment solidarity, which means "sufficient and fair pay for work as a basic principle of its management." . . .

Critiques of Worker-Owned Cooperatives and the Union Coop Model

There are two main critiques of cooperatives: (1) they do not always reach their transformative potential to create successful democratic workplaces that are an alternative to a capitalist economy (2) they operate at a small scale (partly because they are difficult to capitalize) and scaling up has proven difficult. . . .

Below are two examples that address the critiques. . . .

Successful Examples of Worker-Ownership: Mondragon and CHCA

. . .

The Mondragon Corporation

Mondragon, the world's largest network of worker-owned industrial cooperatives, is the top Basque region industrial group, ranked tenth in Spain with 80,000 personnel, a presence in 70 countries, and winner of the 2013 Financial Times "Boldness in Business" award. Mondragon's more than sixty-year-old mission is to generate wealth for society through business development and job creation under the "one worker, one vote" cooperative framework, where labor is sovereign and capital, while essential, is subordinate to sustainable job creation. . . .

Mondragon was "developed through the spirit and work carried out by José Maria Arizmendiarrieta, a young priest who in 1941 came to Arrasate-Mondragón, which at the time was living through the painful aftermath of the Spanish civil war in the form of poverty." Father Arizmendiarrieta started to address the issues of poverty by first focusing on health needs and on educational training with the idea that it was first necessary to share knowledge before democratizing power. Father Arizmendiarrieta trained Mondragon's first graduates to create Mondragon's first cooperative, Falgor, based on the ten Mondragon principles.

All of Mondragon's cooperative enterprises are driven by the following ten principles:

1. Open Admission: open to all who agree to the cooperative principles regardless of age, ethnicity, political orientation, spiritual practice or gender.

2. Democratic Organization: All workers must be members, with a few exceptions, and the organization is democratically controlled by the workers on the basis of one worker receiving one vote in electing leadership.

3. Sovereignty of Labor: The cooperatives renounce wage labor and give primacy to workers in distribution of surpluses and attempt to extend the cooperative to all members of society.

4. Instrumental Character of Capital: Capital is [a] necessary factor in business and savings, however, return on capital investment or savings is not directly tied to surpluses or losses of the cooperatives.

5. Self-Management: [C]ooperation is the manifestation of individual responsibility and collective effort. Clear information on the organization's operations must be available to members in order to facilitate both the collective effort of participation in management and individual requirements of ongoing skills development for self-management.

6. Pay Solidarity: Internally this means the ratio between highest and lowest paid worker cannot exceed 6 to 1. Externally this means that wages should be comparable to prevailing wages in neighbouring conventional firms.

7. Group Cooperation: Individual cooperatives organized in groups, between groups and between Mondragon and other movements.

8. Social Transformation: Mondragon is an instrument for social transformation.

9. Universal Nature: The co-ops proclaim their solidarity with all who labor for economic democracy, peace, justice, human dignity, and development.

10. Education: "It is fundamentally important to devote sufficient human and economic resources to cooperative education, professional training, and general education of young people for the future."

The Mondragon model addresses the two main critiques of worker-owned cooperatives. Mondragon has put into effect the transformative tenets expressed in the Principles and is not just another business structure that replicates the status quo. Workers participate in democratic decision-making in businesses that are economically successful. The workers themselves earn living wages. Mondragon also maintains a small CEO to worker pay ratio.

By example, Mondragon has met the critique that cooperatives fail to achieve sufficient scale to put their principles into meaningful practice. Mondragon, while starting out small, has successfully scaled through its unique capitalization strategies, including creating its own bank and creating a network of worker-owned cooperatives that serve to implement its principle of inter-cooperation. By creating its own bank, Mondragon cooperatives were/are able to gain access to loans with non-traditional lending criteria, especially in Mondragon's early stages and by creating different types of worker-cooperatives that exist and operate in a network that purchases good and services from among its network, they were able to help increase and stabilize demand for their products and services.

Cooperative Home Care Associates (CHCA)

CHCA, located in the Bronx, is currently the largest unionized worker-owned cooperative in the US and is very successful. The Community Service Society (CSS) formed CHCA in 1985 as a cooperative under the Business Corporation Law. "CHCA has over 1,600 members and revenues of $40 million."

CHCA works in home health care, an industry that is notorious for exploiting its workers both in terms of low pay and poor working conditions. CSS founded CHCA in 1985 ". . . on the premise that if workers owned their own company they could maximize wages and benefits, and if workers were better trained and better treated, they'd offer better care for their clients." CHCA exemplifies a business example that can be started with little capitalization and grow by leveraging union clout and securing government contracts. This health-care cooperative also provides a good example of unionization's contribution to the transformative potential of worker-owned cooperatives. CHCA focused on industry-wide change.

To that end, CHCA worked on several connected tracks. To raise industry standards, not just for CHCA workers but across the field, CHCA started the worker-run Paraprofessional Health care Institute (PHI) that trains agencies across the country while also fighting policy shifts. (PHI was instrumental in the campaign that recently expanded the Fair Labor Standards Act.)

The union played a major part in securing government contracts, thus strengthening CHCA's continued existence, which in turn raised the worker-owners' earnings. [As of 2016], CHCA worker-owners who labor as home health aides earn[ed] approximately $16 an hour with benefits, double the industry standard. CHCA's worker-owners are also guaranteed an average of 36 hours per week—significantly more hours than the 25 to 30 hours that prevail in the industry. Together, guaranteed hours and increased pay promote work-life balance among worker-owners. These increased wage and benefits are made possible, in part, by a relatively equitable income distribution of pay: the CEO earns just 11 times as much as the average worker.

CHCA worker-owners, who are over 90% women, have consistently commented on their improved quality of life. Worker-owners frequently note that participation in CHCA allows them to spend more time with their families and be more present in their children's lives. . . .

Educating Tomorrow's Transactional Lawyers in Establishing Effective Worker-Owned Cooperatives and Unionized Cooperatives

This is a critical moment to develop and support the teaching of integrated legal and business skills around worker-ownership, especially in a social justice context. . . .

. . . CEDC teaches lawyering for worker-owned cooperative models as part of its empowerment-driven CED practice. CEDC teaches law students the basic tenets of worker-ownership and the challenges that worker-owned cooperatives face in their start-up phases (e.g., capitalization and scaling up). Students also learn how to counsel clients on their options for entity formation, as well as on creating governance structures that will ensure meaningful, democratic, participatory decision-making.

CUNY Law's CEDC is also collaborating with Mondragon's North American Delegation and cooperative incubator, Saiolan, to collaboratively develop a worker-owned cooperative curriculum. CEDC is interested in making the Mondragon educational model available in the U.S. to provide opportunities for students to earn certificates in social economy and cooperative development. . . . Students will learn the legal, structural, transactional, and community-building skills and perspectives necessary to support worker-owner models that are economically viable and that effectively meet the challenges often associated with these models. . . .

Student Lawyering Lessons Learned in Legal Work Supporting CEDC's Participation in the Coalition

As one of the founding members of the Coalition, CEDC has, to date, been working with the [NYC Worker Cooperative Coalition] for two years. Through this collaboration, students engage in many traditional lawyering tasks by representing clients in the Coalition that were incubating worker-owned cooperatives. Such tasks include:

- Conducting policy advocacy and formulating and drafting legislation;

- Counseling clients on entity formation options . . . and forming the respective entities; and

- Counseling clients regarding governance structures and drafting governance documents, including counseling on the intersection between client governance documents and . . . collective bargaining agreements.

In counseling the CEDC clients in the coalition on entity formation options and setting up the coalition's governance structures, students also learned how to navigate the intersection of labor law and entity formation options, not often taught in an integrated way in law schools.

In addition to the lawyering task[s] above, students helped with:

- Movement-building and creating the Coalition's own governance structure and committees;

- Providing community education not only for clients but elected officials, e.g. providing testimony to City Council;

- Advocating for and securing funding for the Coalition; and

- Serving as co-strategists in the Coalition internally and externally and facilitating meetings and negotiations among members.

One major lesson was for the students to learn to serve in multiple roles, including strategist in support of broad efforts to advance a cause such as worker-owned cooperatives in ways that benefit specific clients and many others.

Applying the Skills of Integrative and Collaborative Counseling to an Empowerment-Driven CED Practice

Students in CEDC . . . learned and used intentional counseling skills of collaborative and integrative lawyering when counseling their organizational clients that were also part of the coalition in forming worker owned cooperatives.

Collaborative counseling engages the client as a shared decision-maker in every phase of the counseling process and "... requires lawyer and client to collaboratively identify: the decisions that need to be made, the people empowered to make those decisions and the process for engaging decision-makers in making and evaluating those decisions. This includes involving the client in the generation of strategies and the development of options to choose from." In this context, students made sure to amplify the organizational client's voice, including the voices of its members, by including them in every step of the decision making process.

The students also used the integrative counseling approach as part of their coalition work. Integrative counseling requires an advanced appreciation of the multiple roles that a lawyer may play as both member of and lawyer for a coalition. According to Brian Glick and Sheila [Foster], integrative counseling ... integrates the lawyers' work in two necessary interconnected ways:

> [L]awyers—like their clients—need to integrate flexibly and functionally a broad range of practice areas, skills and ... roles. And they need to make sure that all of their work is thoroughly integrated into the overall strategy, program and process of the organization so that their lawyering is closely tied to the organization's efforts to build community capacity and power. ...

... Inclusive Legal Problem Solving Skills, which include robust information gathering, active listening, language reframing, facilitation, problem-solving, and consensus building skills, were also particularly helpful. This was particularly true when the Clinic served as facilitator and consensus builder within the coalition context. ...

Conclusion

Worker-owned cooperatives are countering severe income inequality. ... Today's stark inequality and the growing interest in cooperative business entities ... present a meaningful opportunity to advocate for the expanding and scaling up [of] worker-owned cooperative models. These conditions also invite lawyers to participate in CED empowerment lawyering that can bring about needed systemic change. ...

The preceding excerpt describes how CD projects like worker collaboratives—and legal clinics—can be designed and operated to function as complex, democratic, and sometimes coalitional three-layered actions. As Huertas-Noble shows, CD projects in particular require ongoing—long-term or indefinite—administration to coordinate multiple kinds of collective activities that transcend traditional lawyering. They require a strategy for using time as a resource, and, as with campaigns, CD projects are complex in many ways.

Building on this pair, Jennifer Gordon below describes the formation and early activities of an organization, The Workplace Project (TWP), an immigrant workers center in Long Island, New York. TWP was designed to be a worker rights organization that would both provide legal services and serve as the springboard for workplace justice campaigns. Gordon founded this center, and soon discovered tensions between using law to solve individual problems and advancing collectivized work on broader second- and third-layer goals.[19] Gordon faced simultaneously the challenges of building an organization—with all the issues of governance, funding, staffing, planning, and so on—and building worker-led campaigns within that organization—with the challenges of action planning, team building, coalition work, and other components. As in the Cummings and Huertas-Noble excerpts, Gordon grounds her analysis in research that draws on knowledge from the bottom. Although the context is different, Gordon, like Cummings and Huertas-Noble, demonstrates how advocates combine persuasion and pressure to accomplish three-layered changes that ameliorate as well as transform entrenched, collectivized, identity-based inequalities.

Note, however, that TWP was not designed to help members form or expand small businesses or cooperatives nor to provide trainings or other support in managing an organization; TWP is an example of a community project formed with priorities other than economic development. As designed, TWP helps local workers (mostly non-white) to redress workplace violations that subordinated, exploited, or impoverished them. Much of this work might seem like ordinary legal services, but in designing this first-layer work TWP incorporated strategies that induced individuals from the community to "get involved" for a larger, systemic, collective agenda of progress. These strategies focused on second-layer goals that endeavor to build bottom-up knowledge and power to build group capacities for ever-greater gains. Moreover, these strategies were designed to build a sense of collective consciousness, personal commitment, and the capacity and will for organized action, so that TWP would become operationally—in everyday fact—a *community* development project run in democratic, principled, and accountable terms—as well as a site from which campaigns were developed and carried out.

Gordon shows how CD projects may begin with first-layer legal services—and, at the same time, that not every legal services project is necessarily a complex action—a CD project—that aims both to ameliorate

---

[19] Gordon describes the challenges of her work with The Workplace Project in this excerpted article and, after receiving a MacArthur Grant, in the book, Suburban Sweatshops: The Fight for Immigrant Rights (2009).

and transform. The difference, as the following account shows, is whether first-layer work is designed and executed to overcome legal individualism and go beyond atomized technical fixes. In addition to pursuing amelioration—like helping to redress individual injuries in the short term—TWP was designed intentionally for long-term struggle and transformation by incorporating second- and third-layer goals organically into its daily work.

WE MAKE THE ROAD BY WALKING: IMMIGRANT WORKERS, THE WORKPLACE PROJECT, AND THE STRUGGLE FOR SOCIAL CHANGE

Jennifer Gordon
30 Harv. C.R.-C.L. L. Rev. 407 (1995)

Maria Luisa Paz, an undocumented woman who worked in a factory in her native Colombia, is employed by a commercial laundry, Sparrow Linens, together with 300 other workers from El Salvador, the Dominican Republic, and other Latin American countries. Their work consists of disinfecting, washing, pressing, and folding mounds of hospital linens. Paz's job is to fold the sheets that come off of the presses. Although these damp sheets are scalding hot, she is rarely given anything to protect her hands. After a recent OSHA [federal Occupational Safety and Health Administration] inspection, the company handed out a few pairs of thin, uninsulated gloves. In the room where she works, the temperature hovers at 100 degrees.

After a few weeks at this station, Paz's gloves have holes burned in every finger and her fingers are covered with large watery blisters. Her shirt is splattered with blood from frequent heat-related nosebleeds, and her arms and legs are flecked with white chemical stains from her days in the washrooms. She is not alone in her injuries: in the past three months at Sparrow Linens, a man lost half of a finger in a washer door; another man was severely burned on the chest by chemical-filled water that had boiled over; and a woman fainted on the job from the heat and fumes.

Efrain Sandoval, a farmer from Guatemala, is one of four dishwashers at the Starburst Diner. While he, the other dishwashers, the busboys, and the three prep and salad cooks are all Latino men, the people who fill the higher-paying jobs of head cook and waiter and waitress are all white and U.S. citizens. The dishwashers' schedule is grueling: 11:00 a.m. to 12:30 a.m., seven days a week, with only a half-hour break—uncompensated—in each thirteen-and-a-half-hour shift. For this 91-hour work-week, they are paid $150 in cash and get no share of the tips, leaving them with an hourly salary of $1.65. On top of this, the head cook is endlessly abusive to the workers, shouting obscenities and threats whenever things heat up in the kitchen.

When Sandoval started working for Starburst four years ago, he was undocumented. After applying for political asylum two years ago, he received work authorization from [U.S. immigration authorities]. Upon receiving his authorization, he brought his social security card and work permit to his boss and asked to be put on the books. His boss refused.... [A]fter watching his boss fire other laborers who are authorized to work and hire more undocumented workers, Efrain has little hope that this is an option.

Raul Melendez, a university teacher in his native El Salvador, waits for work on the street corner in Franklin Square, Long Island every morning during the landscaping season, which runs from March through late November. In mid-summer, he arrives by 6:00 a.m. and joins sixty to seventy other Latino men sitting and standing along the curb.... On this day, when the first truck pulls up, "Nick's Lawn and Garden" painted on its side, it is swarmed by twenty workers.... Over the ensuing tumult, the wage negotiation can be heard: the driver starts at $50 for a day's work but quickly goes down to $45 and then $40 when he realizes the demand....

... Melendez—lucky this time—was hired for a few days of work trimming trees and cutting lawns in Great Neck, a wealthy town. His employer, TrimGreen Contractors, never asks whether he is authorized to work. The job with TrimGreen stretches to a week, and then two. Melendez begins to relax into the pace of the work, waiting for his first paycheck and hoping that the job will take him through the summer.

On the Friday of his second week, he is cleaning the grass out of the blades of a jammed mower. Suddenly free of the clog, the blades begin to spin, badly cutting his hand and severing his middle finger above the knuckle. His employer drives him to the hospital and leaves him at the door, promising to return once he parks the truck. He never does. Melendez—still not paid for any of his work, and badly in need of workers' compensation for his injury—does not know the name of the man who employed him, the license plate number of his truck, or the company's address. TrimGreen is not listed in the phone book and has not registered with the Chamber of Commerce.

In the current hostile political climate, with immigrants as the chosen scapegoats for our country's economic and social woes, public opposition to the exploitation of immigrants in the workplace is minimal. As the executive director of the Workplace Project (the Project), an independent workers center in a Latino community on Long Island, New York, I work with people like Maria Luisa Paz, Efrain Sandoval, and Raul Melendez. Together, we are developing an organization of workers to challenge the dynamic of workplace exploitation faced by too many Latino immigrants....

Context: The Transformation of a Sub/Exurban Economy and the Growth of the Underground Economy

Given its reputation as a white, homogeneous bedroom community for commuters to New York City, many people are surprised that Long Island is home to a center for immigrant workers. In fact, many parts of Long Island are racially and socioeconomically diverse. . . .

. . . Increasingly, many of Long Island's over 250 "hamlets" and "villages" are home to large communities of people of color, including Latinos, African Americans, and Asian Americans, many of whom also work on Long Island.

According to the U.S. Census, Long Island's white population declined by four percent between 1980 and 1990. In contrast, the number of Latino residents grew by 78.8% in Nassau County and 49.7% in Suffolk County, making Long Island home to more than 165,000 Latino residents, 6.3% of its total population. . . .

Many Latino immigrants on Long Island are from Central America, particularly El Salvador. The numbers of Salvadorans swelled in the 1980s, as they were pushed to the United States by violent civil wars and pulled by the promise of service and manufacturing jobs. . . . Long Island has become a center for Central Americans in the New York metropolitan area, and is home to more of them than New York City or any other nearby urban area.

During the same period that Long Island's population became multicultural, it shifted rapidly from an economy with a strong manufacturing sector—based primarily on employment by major defense contractors such as the Grumman Corporation—to one based mostly on services. . . . The many Long Island residents who work in New York City create a demand for low-cost workers who can take care of suburban lawns, homes, and children.

In our experience, the vast majority of Latino immigrants on Long Island work in five trades: landscape and small construction contracting; restaurant work; domestic service; building cleaning and maintenance work; and light manufacturing. As with much work done by immigrants around the country, these jobs belong, in varying degrees, to the underground economy. They are "underground" in the sense that they often take place outside the realm of the law. Employers are rarely registered with the appropriate authorities; many of them neither comply with labor laws nor pay taxes to the government; and often, they fail to participate in mandatory insurance programs such as workers' compensation or disability benefits.

Undocumented workers are the employees of choice in this sector and abuses run high. Few workers are unionized, and those that are frequently complain that their unions do nothing for them. Non-unionized workers have neither job security nor health benefits; their wages—when they are paid—are extremely low and their hours are long and irregular. Health and safety laws are violated with impunity, leading to high rates of injury and occupational disease.

Undocumented workers are further disadvantaged when they have only recently arrived in the United States, have rural backgrounds, and/or are illiterate. These factors, in combination with their fear of deportation and the terrifying repression that many immigrant workers have witnessed in their home countries, make it even harder for them to demand that they be treated with respect. As a result, the vast majority of jobs for immigrants in the underground economy are dead ends, rather than stepping stones to the American Dream.

The globalization of the economy in the second half of this century has spurred growth of the underground economy. Strong international competition has caused economic restructuring on a national level, including a massive decline in large-scale manufacturing. The global economy is accompanied by "whipsawing"—when employers reduce wages by playing workers in a geographic area off workers in another area who are willing to work for less—and a rise in smaller enterprises and services, many functioning through extensive subcontracting. The economic factors underlying the growth of the underground economy are reinforced by lax government enforcement of already weak labor laws, the passage of laws such as the employer sanctions provisions of the Immigration Reform and Control Act (IRCA) of 1986, which encourage a two-tier labor system of "legal" and "illegal" workers, the availability of a cheap and often desperate labor pool, and the legitimization of anti-immigrant and racist sentiment in the current political climate. Taken together, these elements provide fertile soil for a mainstay of the underground economy: the small, low-overhead shop or business that makes its profits on the backs of low-paid immigrant workers.

Inadequate Institutional Responses to Exploitation in the Underground Economy: Government, Legal Services, Unions

Government Agencies

Overview

Prior to the passage of IRCA in 1986, immigrants, even those who were undocumented, and U.S. citizens enjoyed the same basic legal protection under labor laws. It is now unclear whether courts will continue to interpret those laws to protect undocumented immigrants.[20] However,

---

[20] In one subsequent example, the Supreme Court minimized the protection of immigrant workers under the National Labor Relations Act by ruling Congress, in passing the IRCA, did not mean to allow undocumented immigrants wrongfully fired for their union organizing any back pay

undocumented workers are still protected by the Fair Labor Standards Act, which includes minimum wage and overtime laws, and they have the right to organize and unionize under the National Labor Relations Act. Undocumented workers can also bring employment discrimination suits if they are mistreated at work on the basis of gender, race, age, national origin, or other status categories in Title VII. Finally, undocumented immigrants have the right to collect workers' compensation if they are injured on the job.

Legislators and judges support these protections for undocumented workers partly because they believe that U.S. citizens would be seriously disadvantaged without them... The benefits of hiring undocumented workers not covered by overtime and minimum wage laws would far outweigh the cost....

Unfortunately, these protections have done little to weaken the existing underground economy. Federal, state, and local governments have no coherent strategy for enforcing the rights of workers who participate in the underground economy, and they lack the political will to create one. Government agencies responsible for enforcing protective labor laws are sorely underfunded....

Finally, several laws... actively promote the creation of an immigrant workforce whose fear of losing its jobs and being deported are easily exploitable. This is no accident. Many in big business view the existence of a cheap, exploitable labor force as an economic necessity. Undoubtedly, this sector would oppose a crackdown on labor violations against immigrant workers.

In reviewing the Project's experience with local offices of government agencies, it is important to note the point just made: national and state governments have failed to enforce labor laws protecting immigrant workers. This overall failure should not be attributed to office-specific factors, such as slow processing or the attitudes of particular investigators, and excused by other factors, such as underfunding or employee burnout. These are merely symptoms of a larger problem....

Legal Services

When government agencies fail to fulfill their obligations, legal services centers are often the first, and sometimes the only, organizations to challenge them. However, this is rarely the case in the area of immigrant workers' rights. The law prohibits the Legal Services Corporation from assisting immigrants who are not in the country legally, and yet not surprisingly, undocumented workers face the most frequent and the most serious problems. Moreover, legal services offices, most funded by the

---

from their former employer. See *Hoffman Plastic Compounds, Inc. v. National Labor Relations Board*, 535 U.S. 137 (2002).—Eds.

federal government, have not made employment law a primary area of focus. While some legal services offices in New York City offer assistance in one or two employment areas, few, if any, have units devoted to enforcement of workplace rights. Nassau and Suffolk Legal Services, the only Legal Services Corporation office on Long Island, does not offer assistance with labor or employment problems. Finally, immigrants who labor in suburban and exurban settings often fall between the cracks of the legal services system. The federal government is reducing its budget for legal services and state and private funds are limited. As a consequence, legal services offices in suburban and new exurban areas either do not exist or lack adequate staff.

Unions

... Unions and immigrant workers have a long and combative history. Although the U.S. labor movement was in many ways built by immigrants, it has often been anti-immigrant in its stated policy. In looking at the reasons why unions have largely failed to adapt to changes in the economy, however, it would be a mistake to focus only on their relations with immigrants.

Analysts, scholars and labor activists concur that unionism in the United States has declined drastically since its peak in the middle of this century. They propose many different explanations for this national downslide, including the decline of manufacturing and the rise of the service sector as the country's principal employer, the internationalization of the economy, and the weakening of the legal right to unionize. In the case of immigrant workers, these factors are exacerbated by language and cultural barriers that most unions have been slow to bridge, widespread subcontracting in jobs held by immigrants, the undocumented status of many immigrant workers, and the exclusion of jobs held largely by immigrants (such as domestic and farm work) from NLRA coverage.

... Unions were at their peak after World War II, having built a strong base through concentrated organizing efforts in the 1930s and 1940s. The social contract between unions and employers, which tied wage increases to profit gains, worked well during this period. ...

Lulled by the sense of security induced by this successful compact, and strongly influenced by the red-baiting McCarthyism of the period, unions gradually gave up their broader social vision and emphasis on organizing, and focused instead on consolidating their economic gains. ... Employers responded to the rise of global competition in the late 1960s by breaking the compact and going on the offensive against workers. ...

... Unlike their predecessors in the early 1900s, unions no longer envision the creation of a broad working-class movement to achieve social justice. Instead, many unions concentrate on collaborating with management, in weak efforts to stem their declining leverage.

As the most recent wave of workers in need of an active labor movement, immigrants are badly hurt by the business unionism approach to labor organizing. . . .

On Long Island, unions with thousands of Latino members frequently write their contracts only in English, and do not employ field personnel or organizers who speak Spanish. . . . Under these circumstances, it is nearly impossible for a worker who does not speak English to file a grievance with her union. . . .

The rise of the underground economy and business unionism, coupled with a lack of government will to create or enforce protective labor laws, contributes to the exploitation of immigrant workers. Independent workers centers, developing around the country, are building a response to the attack on the multicultural working class, caught in a violent transformation of the economy with little institutional protection or organizational base. The following section describes the experiences of the Workplace Project, one such workers center.

The Workplace Project Model

Description

. . . [T]he Workplace Project in 1992 [began] as an organization through which Latino immigrant workers on Long Island could address the myriad problems that they face at their jobs and in their communities. The Project, also known as "Centro de Derechos Laborales," is now one of a small but growing number of workers centers around the country.

Workers centers are community-based membership organizations that organize workers to fight widespread labor exploitation. Workers centers organize at a grassroots level, across trades and industries, in communities of working-class people. In addition to confronting systematic exploitation in the workplace, the centers also focus their attention on the economic, social, and political concerns of their members. These centers are part of an effort to build a new labor movement, to lead the fight against exploitation of immigrants and other working-class people.

Currently, the Project works in the Latino community. For the Project's first two years, we worked exclusively with Central Americans. As the Workplace Project grew, we expanded our work to the entire Latino community. . . .

The Project is located in the center of Hempstead, a poor and working-class town of about 50,000 people—mostly African American and Salvadoran—with a smattering of older white people and immigrants from other countries. Hempstead has one of the largest communities of Latino immigrants on Long Island. . . .

During the first two years of its existence, we thought of the Workplace Project as housing three distinct programs: (1) a legal clinic for immigrants with labor problems; (2) a community outreach and education program on workers' rights; and (3) an organizing project. We have come to realize that this is not how we want the Project to function. Instead, we now see organizing immigrant workers as both our end goal and our core strategy. Our community education programs and legal clinic are part of this organizing effort. Both of these programs are designed to deepen workers' involvement in the Workplace Project and their analysis of the position of immigrants in the United States economy. As a whole, the programs support and train workers as they turn these analyses into strategies for change.

Labor and Community Organizing Program

The Project has two goals for its organizing program. The first is to build an active, grassroots organization that is run democratically by low-income immigrant workers. Because of this, the Project has an all-worker membership from which the board of directors is elected as well as several worker committees. We see this organizational development work as an essential component of our second goal, mobilizing workers for structural change.

As part of the organizational development work, we sponsor a central workers committee, C-POL (the "Committee for Labor Organizing" or "Comité Pro-Organización Laboral" in Spanish). This group was founded in order to promote the education and organization of other workers by workers attending our Workers Course. The C-POL has developed educational events for community members in churches and other gathering places. The members of C-POL also actively participate in the planning and execution of Workplace Project events such as marches, dances, and organizing campaigns. . . .

In general, we have found that men are much more likely than women to participate in our organizing and educational efforts. . . . Because women face significant barriers to participating in organizing work, the Project has decided to create and fund a position for a woman to coordinate organizing, outreach, and education among Latina immigrant women.

We are at the early stages of meeting our second goal, mobilizing workers for significant change. To this end, we have focused largely on bringing together groups of workers to support efforts designed to shift the power between the worker and the employer in individual cases. . . .

The Project has also begun the next stage, an organizing campaign focused on a particular industry. In the spring and summer of 1994, we began organizing with landscaping and small-scale construction day laborers on two of Long Island's street corners, helping them mobilize to demand a higher daily wage and enforce payment of wages earned. When the season began in April, Henriquez [a Project organizer] and C-POL members joined day laborers as they waited to be picked up by landscaping employers. After hours of watching, they began to understand the unwritten rules of each corner and to talk to the men about their working conditions. After several weeks of quiet observation of the daily routine, Henriquez and C-POL members began to work with the men through a united committee structure on each corner to enforce higher wages, better methods of insuring payment for work done, and safer working conditions.

As a result of his constant presence on street corners, Henriquez is able to help the workers mobilize when their livelihood is threatened. . . .

Community Education and Worker Training

The Workplace Project's Community Education and Worker Training Program has two components: outreach in the Latino community to provide information about workers' rights and a Workers Course designed to develop legal knowledge, organizing skills, and leadership ability in its participants.

Community Outreach

The Project uses a variety of techniques to spread the word about rights on the job. To facilitate communication, Project staff, board and committee members, and volunteers regularly make educational presentations to local Latino churches, English as a Second Language classes, and community groups. Often these presentations are designed and implemented entirely by C-POL members with support from Project staff. In addition to descriptions of Workplace Project programs and information about basic workplace rights, these events usually include testimonials from workers who have had experience fighting problems in their workplaces; a brief talk by a lawyer; short plays written and put on by workers to illuminate or humorize a point about the mistreatment of immigrants on the job or about defending one's rights; live music; and a question-and-answer period.

Project staff and volunteers also develop and distribute material in Spanish designed to explain workers' rights. For example, using grant funds given by the American Bar Association, the Project developed a comic book dealing with immigrant workers' rights. This forty-page book, which [was] published in the spring of 1995, describes the travails and triumphs of three immigrants—a domestic worker, a day laborer, and a factory worker—as they fight non-payment of wages, workplace injuries, and sexual harassment. . . .

Finally, the Project makes liberal use of the Spanish-language media. Long Island is home to several Spanish-language newspapers and radio stations, as well as a cable television network that broadcasts in Spanish. . . . [T]he center has cultivated relationships with each of these media outlets. Stories about the Workplace Project's activities and victories, interviews with Project staff, columns treating labor rights issues, and free advertisements for Project activities run frequently in all of these media.

This ongoing campaign to increase immigrant workers' familiarity with their rights has two effects. First, it raises awareness that abuse does not have to be an unavoidable side-effect of a low-paying job. Second, it moves some workers to take action on their own against a problem at work and others to come into the Center to seek advice or support in order to act effectively.

Workers Course

Once workers are drawn to the center through outreach and legal services, they are encouraged to continue learning about their rights through the more intensive Workers Course. The Project's Workers Course is a focal point of the organization and increasingly draws even those workers without any current labor problems into the fold of the organization. The eight-week course, taught in Spanish three to four times each year, provides participants with information not only about legal rights on the job but also about labor and immigration history. The course also helps workers develop their analytical and organizing skills. Its graduates become members of the organization, eligible to serve on the board of directors. It is heavily advertised, both through ads and articles in local newspapers and through fliers designed and distributed by graduates of the previous course.

Weekly topics discussed during the course include a session about immigration and labor history in the United States; sessions presenting specific areas of labor rights, such as wage and hour laws, health and safety rights, and unemployment benefits; and several sessions on organizing techniques. The course emphasizes the development of leadership skills including speaking in front of a group, analyzing and investigating problems, and developing strategies to tackle complex issues. Throughout the course, we use popular education techniques pioneered in Latin America by Paulo Freire and in the United States by Myles Horton. Through these techniques, the participants use their own experiences as a text for analyzing the problems that their communities face.

Unlike the "know your rights" workshops that public-interest and legal-aid law offices often offer to the community and which are designed only to give people basic information about the law and how to use it, the Workers Course is set up to provide group opportunities for reflection that will lead to analysis and action. For example, a traditional "know your rights" workshop on health and safety might begin with a review of common health and safety hazards and be followed by a talk from a lawyer or an OSHA representative about "how to file a claim with OSHA." In contrast, our first class about health and safety rights begins with a videotape called "Uvas No" ("No Grapes"), put out by the United Farm Workers. In graphic detail, the video demonstrates the effects of pesticides on the farmworkers and on their children, who are often stricken with cancers or born without limbs. The movie closes with a call for a boycott against grapes.

The video provides the starting point for a discussion about the dangers to health and safety that immigrant workers on Long Island face. Workers collaborate in drawing a mural of hazards at their workplaces, ranging from sharp blades used on machines where the safety guards have been removed to extended use of unmarked chemicals without gloves or goggles. Each participant then describes her drawing to the group.

Knowing that the law is supposed to protect their health and safety, the workers then discuss the reasons why such hazards are still so prevalent. Often this leads the group to focus on the government's failure to enforce the law, followed by a conversation about the simultaneous need for and perceived expendability of immigrant workers in the U.S. economy. Later, when OSHA representatives are invited to speak, they are met by a classroom full of people who have already begun to analyze the government's complicity in allowing health and safety violations to occur and who respond critically to OSHA's claims about the protections that the law offers.

At the end of the course, participants design an action plan for a health or safety problem that they face using their analysis of their own situation and the skills they have learned through the class. In one session, the class chose the lack of adequate heat in many workplaces as the focus of their action plan. This topic provided an interesting contrast to the traditional "know your rights" approach. Because there is no legal right to heat on the job in New York State—even in winter—the traditional legalistic approach would have proved inadequate for tackling this problem. By contrast, the methods that we used encouraged the class to develop a strategic plan for fighting this serious problem. This plan included a public information campaign, legislative work to change the law, and work slow-downs in response to individual employers' refusals to provide heat.

Students are charged for the course not in money but in time. Each graduate must put at least ten hours of her time back into the organization and the community in order to teach others what she has learned and to involve more workers in the fight for rights at work. . . . The ten hours that each worker puts into one of these committees builds a bridge between the classroom and the organization, bringing each class participant into the Project so that she begins to participate actively in the work of the center. . . .

Analysis of the Workplace Project Model

Conflict Between Provision of Legal Services and Organizing

Dangers of Reliance on Legal Solutions

As I discussed earlier, [our] goal in founding the Workplace Project was to create an organization directed toward long-term struggle by building a base of support among workers who decided, as a result of our programs or their own analyses, to challenge their position in the U.S. labor system. . . .

It soon became obvious that by providing legal services for individual workers, we were undermining our goal of organizing the community. . . . [Our] initial vision of legal services as a draw for our organizing work was a principal reason for this problem. In our eagerness to develop a good reputation in the community, we initially focused on providing effective legal representation, especially for those who had been denied their back wages. Because we promised free legal consultations every Monday, workers came to the clinic expecting to present their problem to a lawyer and to be advised about possible legal solutions and how to pursue them. Given this set-up, they were reluctant to discuss the larger circumstances surrounding their problem, its root causes, and creative ways to solve it. Our ideal Freirian process—beginning with problem identification and ending with collective action—stopped before it got started.

Furthermore, a successful experience with legal services taught the worker nothing more than reliance on legal services. The worker who benefits from the legal action has not learned the skills that she will need to fight back the next time she is exploited; instead, she has learned that she should seek out a lawyer to solve her problems. . . . Once a problem has been defined as part of the legal sphere, people are reluctant to take it back into their own hands.

We were also disturbed to find that the successful provision of legal services in the employment context often co-opts potential leaders. Going to a community labor-rights office such as ours entails risktaking for an immigrant worker, who knows that other workers or her employer could easily become aware of the step that she has taken. Therefore, the workers who bring their workplace problems to our office tend to be the most motivated . . . [and the] best leaders for a future organizing campaign. Once we win their lawsuit and they get their money, these workers often leave the workplace. . . . By "paying off" the bravest and most determined workers with a settlement or an award, the Workplace Project's legal program plays the role of the employer who decapitates an organizing effort by making a deal with its leaders.

Even when we have been successful in brainstorming solutions with the worker or the group, workers often prefer litigation to carrying out these creative strategies involving group action. . . . In the United States, the chances that the worker will lose her job as a result of organizing are high, the protections are low, and the payoff is unpredictable at best. Finding a lawyer to resolve the problem presents the least risk and the biggest possible benefit. If the worker wins her lawsuit, she reaps the reward; if she loses, at least she has not gone out on such a fragile limb. . . .

Provision of Legal Services Is Not a Long-Term Solution

In our experience, lawsuits that are not backed by a strong group of workers often flounder because they are vulnerable to the pitfalls of the legal process. Legal procedure, bankruptcy laws, the slowness of court and administrative proceedings, and even the rules of legal ethics frequently interfere with the effective representation of immigrant workers.

If employers change their policies in response to a complaint or lawsuit, they often do so in a way that is tailored only to avoid legal liability, leaving the core exploitative conditions intact. Even when employers settle a matter with a small group of workers, they frequently require the workers to sign a binding confidentiality agreement. This agreement enables the employer to avoid correcting the underlying problem by preventing other workers from knowing about it. In each of these instances, unless the lawsuit is part of an organizing strategy, there is no muscle behind the workers' legal demands.

An example from the Workplace Project's experience illustrates some of these problems:

> After being turned away by the Department of Labor and turned down by the unions, Efrain Sandoval came into the center to describe his problem with underpayment of wages. Because Sandoval had been at the restaurant for four years, the amount of money owed to him was considerable. We told Sandoval that we would represent him, but that he should try to get as many other workers involved in the lawsuit as possible. After speaking to other busboys and dishwashers, Sandoval came back to report that he was the only worker still interested in going ahead.
>
> I wrote a demand letter to the employer, which resulted in a series of negotiations between the two parties. A settlement was reached, granting Sandoval five thousand dollars in back pay. However, the employer made a confidentiality agreement a prerequisite of any settlement; Sandoval would be bound not to tell any other workers about his arrangement. I was unable to negotiate for a settlement which included the others because of my ethical obligations to Sandoval as an individual client. Although he would have preferred not to sign a confidentiality agreement, he wanted to get his money rather than scrap the settlement because of this demand. Because the employer saw no worker muscle behind his demands, the chances of the employer

backing down were slim. Sandoval, previously the worker most vocal about mistreatment by the employer, took his money and left the restaurant. The remaining busboys and dishwashers continued to be paid at the below-minimum rate.

While some might argue that the Project would be more successful if we focused on impact litigation, our experience with labor law and the underground economy shows otherwise. The center might be able to win a case that would change the law and increase protections of immigrant workers. However, considering that in the underground economy existing labor laws are violated with impunity, a new law would have little, if any, practical effect.

Although the Workplace Project's legal clinic has achieved numerous victories for our individual clients, it leaves the vast majority of workplaces completely untouched. The underground economy is a transitory place. Factories and restaurants open and close with lightning speed, and unscrupulous employers treat losses in court merely as a transaction cost. The only significant improvement will come when immigrant workers mobilize themselves to shift the balance of power so that they can demand real change.

The Uses of Legal Services

Despite the conflict posed by legal services, the Workplace Project is reluctant to give up the legal clinic entirely. First, the clinic has assisted many people individually. . . .

Furthermore, in certain kinds of cases legal services are the swiftest and least costly way to vindicate a worker's rights. Such cases include those where few workers are involved in the dispute or where the employer is invulnerable to low cost public pressure, such as pickets or a media campaign. . . . In addition, because we are the only source of legal services for immigrants with labor problems on all of Long Island, immigrant workers would have no legal recourse if we closed the clinic.

The clinic is also an effective means for bringing workers into the organization. It attracts new immigrants to the Project each week by demonstrating to them that the organization is willing to fight with them and on their behalf and that challenges to employers can succeed. The new cases that workers bring to the Project occasionally serve as a starting point for organizing by mobilizing workers to challenge their own problems. The flow of workers through the clinic also allows us to monitor what is happening in the community and in workplaces around Long Island. Through the clinic, we have accumulated a database of information about over 350 Long Island employers, many of whom are repeat offenders. Without the clinic, it would be very difficult to keep this invaluable information up to date.

Finally, the legal clinic provides financial sustenance to the organization. Through the clinic, the Project charges workers a nominal legal fee. We also receive funds through court-ordered attorneys' fees and grants that we solicit from foundations that sponsor legal services organizations.

Beyond serving our financial needs, the legal program is an excellent way to recruit and incorporate volunteers, who are crucial to our long-term organizing efforts, into the Workplace Project. Our thriving pro-bono and law student internship programs would be much harder, if not impossible, to maintain without the legal clinic and the cases that it generates.

The Legal Clinic as Part of a Strategy for Collective Action and Structural Change

In response to the concerns detailed in the sections above, the Project staff has restructured the legal services program. The "new" clinic's structure is based on two tenets. First, in the context of limited resources, legal assistance should go to workers who want to be active participants in our programs, rather than to those who expect to be the passive recipients of a service. Second, once a worker is committed to fighting for better working conditions, problems must be addressed through a team approach. This approach necessarily involves as many workers from the affected workplace as possible, an organizer, and when necessary, a lawyer or supervised legal advocate.

A worker who comes to the clinic with a problem—for example, a factory worker who has not been paid wages for a month—first meets with a Project organizer. The organizer explains that the Workplace Project is an organization of workers, not a legal services center. The organizer also explains that, although the Workplace Project will readily provide free legal counseling, for actual services the "client" must commit to giving back to the organization. . . .

After the orientation, the worker meets with a counselor. If the problem is a simple question—for example, do I qualify for unemployment benefits or workers' compensation?—the counselor, in consultation with the Project's lawyer, helps the worker find the answer. If the problem is more complex, the counselor, joined by the organizer and often the lawyer, discusses the problem with the worker. Before discussing the rights of the worker, the group talks about general conditions at the workplace, the number of workers involved, and past efforts to improve conditions. The team also explains the relevant law to the worker.

At this point, the worker must decide if she is willing to fight collectively for better working conditions. The Project's staff asks her to return later with other workers who have the same problem. This way, the group can strategize and decide whether and how they want to take action. When groups of workers are involved, a series of meetings may take place.

If at any point it becomes clear that legal services will be a part of the strategy, the worker or workers are asked to sign a contract. Through the contract, the Workplace Project commits to providing legal services on a particular issue. In exchange, in addition to paying our fee, the worker must participate actively in her own case and in the organization. As a condition for receiving legal services, the worker must agree either to join a workers committee, take the workers course, or participate in a campaign or event sponsored by the Project. Workers who do not make this commitment are offered counseling and referrals, but are not given legal representation.

Once a case is taken, the team which now includes the worker(s), an organizer, a counselor and, when necessary, a lawyer, begins work. For a worker with an individual problem—for example, a domestic worker who has not been paid—the first step is usually a confrontation or negotiation with her employer. Accompanied by the organizer, and often by other workers as a sign of support, the worker goes to the employer's home or workplace to demand payment. If this is not successful, the team follows up with a letter. If the worker is still not able to secure the employer's cooperation, the staff initiates a lawsuit and files a complaint with the Department of Labor and other appropriate agencies. For bigger cases, these legal tactics are part of a larger publicity campaign against the employer. This campaign is waged through the press, pickets, leaflets, and other conventional organizing techniques.

It is unclear whether our attempts to restructure the Workplace Project Legal Clinic will prove successful. Certainly, the new structure is open to criticism. Some may charge that . . . we are picking and choosing our clients, working only with those who have the time, interest, and aptitude to become part of a larger struggle. Unquestionably, our contract imposes requirements on the people who come to us for help.

. . . [W]e do not have the resources to represent everyone who comes to our door, [so] it is imperative that we ration our legal services. Rather than make a "value-neutral" rationing decision, our determination of who will receive legal services coincides with our larger goals. . . .

A Practice-Based Theory of Social Change

As the Workplace Project grows from a young, local organization into a broader movement of workers, we are trying to develop a theory of social change that fits the context in which we work. . . .

In this effort, we have some guidance from history and from theoretical writers. Paolo Freire and Myles Horton's ideas offer descriptions of how daily reality can provide a text for the development of a program of action. The history of other social movements, both in the United States and in other countries, has an enormous amount to teach us. However, we face an economic structure that is completely different . . . [and, with] so little time to reflect, it is difficult even to begin to sort through the available material.

Another possible course of guidance can be found in law review articles on "lawyering for social change." Unfortunately, authors largely focus on the dynamics of an individual lawyer-client relationship, and on the role of the lawyer in either empowering or subordinating the client. The articles that focus on larger social movements tend to do so in the context of an analysis and critique of the lawyer's role in those movements, rather than in an attempt to answer the larger question of how social change occurs.

By necessity, we have been working to create our own theory of social change, strategizing with the workers who constitute the Project and with other workers centers around the country. . . .

Our current goal is to make the Workplace Project a strong center for Latino immigrant workers on Long Island. We are working to develop a broad and active membership of workers and a democratic way of making decisions. The project's focus is on worker leadership and organizing, with workers who come to us going through a process of learning about their rights, analyzing their reality and the political reality of the United States, and developing and carrying out strategies to challenge the abuse that they face on the job. The Workplace Project supports them in this process through education, organizing back-up, and legal services.

This statement puts forth our current theory of social change. Organizing is not simply a matter of mobilization. It is a long-term process of analysis leading to action. . . . It must be the conscious development of a worker-led movement for better communities and better lives. . . .

Concretely, the Project focuses on implementing this theory of social change in two areas. First, as I described above, we seek to build a strong, democratic organization, run by workers. We are trying to develop a long-term process through which workers define their goals, take ownership of the center, and develop and carry out strategies to confront both their immediate problems and the structural causes of those problems. . . .

To move from the existence of a sound worker center structure to real worker leadership and democracy takes a lot of work. To develop an organization, we must work with individuals and small groups of workers to build skills, such as speaking in public, writing an agenda, leading a meeting, talking to funders, and setting long-term goals. . . . The task that is hardest to describe but most crucial, is the development of a constantly evolving group analysis of the context in which our organization is operating, with a parallel strategy for change that is linked to and results from this analysis.

A second way in which we are implementing our theory of social change is in the development of a concrete vision of the future structure of a workers' movement.

The men who formed C-POL first met to discuss problems facing landscaping workers in the coming season. However, when the proposal was made that the group be formed as a "landscapers association," it was voted down. Participants, one after another, described their varied work experiences, as landscapers in the landscape season and as factory workers, busboys, or office cleaners in the colder periods of the year. "We are all workers of one kind or another," one man said, "and we face the same problems on all our jobs, and if we exclude everyone but landscapers we'll never get anything done."

Based on the analysis of these workers, C-POL was formed as a general workers' association to support workers in all industries. Combined with the experiences of other workers centers and a sense of the history of cross-industry labor organizing, workers in C-POL led us to develop the blueprint of a structure of united committees.

The long-term plan of the Project is to build individual workplace committees in each industry—one at each restaurant, each street corner, and each cleaning company where workers are interested in organizing. These individual workplace committees would then collaborate on industry-wide committees, which in turn would send representatives to C-POL or another general workers committee that is part of the Workplace Project. We refer to this as a "united committee structure."

Our goal for the united committee structure in the landscaping industry, for example, is to create a committee on each street corner, elected by the men who wait for work there.... [T]he committee would represent that corner on a larger committee of all street corners in charge of decision-making about, for example, the minimum wage to be accepted by day laborers on all Long Island street corners.

A multi-industry united committee structure would allow us to work on strengthening worker organizing in each industry, while we continue to build cross-trade solidarity among workers on issues that affect them all. . . .

Conclusion

We have a long way before we achieve our goal of organizing a broad-based movement of workers from different industries and communities in struggle against the vast array of social, economic, and political injustices that they face. Informed by the history of movements that came before us, armed with some understanding of the workings of our international economy, and bolstered by old ideas about change adapted to current circumstances, the Workplace Project and other workers centers will have to convert our daily experiences into a theory for future action. As we take our first steps, we are still trying to design a road map that will guide us. Nevertheless, we keep on walking.

Gordon makes explicit how The Workplace Project and its activities reflect a critical vision and three-layered praxis that uses, but also goes beyond, atomized legal assistance. Every aspect of the work is designed to provide amelioration that simultaneously provides the scaffolding for transformation. TWP's design and provision of legal (and other) services uses time as both a short- and long-term resource—to provide relief now as quickly and effectively as possible and to build collective consciousness and group power for the longer haul.

Within this dynamic yet deliberate framework, Gordon also emphasizes why and how advocates learn from their ongoing, cumulative experience—relying on "practice based theo[ries] of social change to make steady progress" in varied contexts. In this ongoing work, the lessons drawn from self-critical reflection on practices and consequences (experience) inform evolving notions or calculations for future choices (theory): in this way, groups and advocates discuss, devise, and adjust "theories of social change" to make "steady progress." As Gordon emphasizes, both action and theory help address the Critical Challenge.

Like Cummings and Huertas-Noble, Gordon illustrates how advocates cycle flexibly, strategically, and continually, through the two stages of complex actions. This unlearning-relearning process enables advocates to plan actions. Using dual consciousness about law and justice, future actions are always rooted self-critically in shared knowledge of the past and present. Advocates and groups diagnose *and* re-diagnose problems in light of the effects that their advocacy produces in order to strategize *and* re-strategize solutions.

As one whole, the preceding excerpts show how complex actions for three-layered progress differ from the norms and practices of law as an industry. Each provides glimpses into ongoing ways that advocates and groups combine instruments of law strategically and innovatively in complex actions to exploit law's potential in complex, varied settings. As Gordon puts it, advocates combine "organizing, policy advocacy, research, communications, fundraising, and legal advocacy to build progressive political power" that helps organized (or organizing) groups advance and defend all three layers of goals.

NOTES AND QUESTIONS

1. *Cooperatives and Traditional Corporate Governance Interests.* Under the traditional model of U.S. corporate governance, decision makers (corporate

officers and directors) owe their primary allegiance to maximizing shareholder wealth, which means reducing labor and other costs no matter the human consequences.[21] In accord with traditional corporate law, U.S. corporations thus reward the societal top (which ranges in this context from often-institutional shareholders to corporate leaders), to the detriment of the bottom. Consider the implications of these industry governance handcuffs for wages: in 2011 McDonald's paid its CEO $8.75 million while workers in its headquarters state of Illinois were paid the state's minimum wage of $8.25 an hour, requiring more than one million hours of work to equal that yearly CEO salary. In what is known as the Great Divergence period of increased income inequality, CEO salaries for large U.S. corporations jumped almost 500 percent between 1980 and 1995. Even more dramatic is an Economic Policy Institute comparison between 1978 and 2018, during which CEO compensation rose a whopping 940 percent while U.S. worker wages rose just 12 percent—producing an average 278-to-1 salary ratio in contrast to the 6–1 and 11–1 ratios in the cooperative models Huertas-Noble described.[22] Did CEOs deserve the enormous boost based on company performance (keep in mind profits increased 145 percent in this 40-year period)? For other reasons? Does corporate culture—or culture more generally—play a role in the disparity? At the other end of the income spectrum, why do you think that government minimum wage floors routinely fail to keep pace with inflation and the cost of living (if they ever once provided a living wage)? Surely there are more workers in the corporate trenches than executives, so shouldn't the power of sheer numbers translate to fair policy (in this case, compensation)? How do worker-owned cooperatives change compensation structures and incentives? Where do you think worker-owned cooperatives will get funding for start-up costs (in the case of a restaurant, for example, to fund everything from remodeling a leased space to tables and chairs and décor)? Will capital come from traditional investors who have the alternative of the prevailing corporate governance model? From banks? For significant hurdles of obtaining co-op capital see Eillie Anzilotti, More U.S. Businesses Are Becoming Worker Co-Ops: Here's Why, www.fastcompany.com/40572926/more-u-s-businesses-are-becoming-worker-co-ops-heres-why.

2. *The Decline of Unions and Today's New Responsive Strategies.* Back in the 1950s, one in three U.S. workers in the private sector was unionized. Today fewer than seven percent are. Immigrants of color fare even worse—despite the famous struggles of the United Farm Workers in the 1960s and 1970s—today unions represent only two percent or fewer of California's field workers. Unions traditionally focused on winning higher wages and benefits directly from the employer. But does that strategy make sense in today's financialized economy driven by powerful elite Wall Street investors who pull those corporate employer strings? One proposed strategy is that unions follow the model used recently by advocates and activists for food justice in the Florida

---

[21] For the iconic judicial opinion establishing the primacy of shareholder wealth maximization, see *Dodge v. Ford Motor Co.*, 170 N.W. 668, 680 (Mich. 1919).

[22] Lawrence Mishel and Julia Wolfe, CEO Compensation Has Grown 940% Since 1978: Typical Worker Compensation Has Risen Only 12% During That Time, Economic Policy Institute (Aug. 14, 2019), www.epi.org/publication/ceo-compensation-2018/.

tomato fields to look to the top of the supply chain, in this case to corporate investors.[23] See Saqib Bhatti and Stephen Lerner, Labor Must Take on Capital (Aug. 9, 2016), www.jacobinmag.com/2016/08/unions-labor-hedge-funds-private-equity/ (arguing that financialization of the economy has rendered the decades-long union structure of bargaining with employers obsolete; rather, "unions need to take their demands directly to those who actually have the money and control. They can often be found on Wall Street."). In this approach, advocates and activists strategize how to reach the "real" decision-makers to serve the interests of the bottom. How does the research and analysis skill of power-mapping you saw in the prior chapter aid this strategy?

3. *South Central Farm Co-Op Case Study.* Proximate to the geography of the Inglewood issue campaign that Cummings described is the ongoing struggle over use of a 14-acre parcel in South Central Los Angeles known as South Central Farm. More than 350 predominantly Latinx families once used this area as a cooperative urban farm, with families sharing costs and decision making in the interest of food security. In the 1990s, a nonprofit food bank gained permission from the city to use the vacant site as a community garden—the city acquired the land from a developer through condemnation with the intent to build a trash incinerator. After community opposition scuttled the incinerator, the developer invoked a right to repurchase the land if used for nonpublic purposes and evicted the urban farmers, whose resistance attracted national attention memorialized in the Academy Award nominee documentary, The Garden (2008). At present, the land is slated for industrial development in this urban garment district, but opposition from the farming cooperative delayed development plans for over a decade since the farm was razed. With the lessons from the Cummings and the Huertas-Noble excerpts in mind, what strategies would you expect the farming cooperative to have pursued, assuming its goal is to reclaim what had been the largest collective urban garden in the United States? How do systemic advocates participate in, and the advocacy stages inform, those strategies and tactics? See generally www.southcentralfarmers.com/scfcoop/shop/vendors.php?vendorid=1 (website for the South Central Farmers' Cooperative, a grassroots community economic development project that grew out of the South Central Farm and which currently leases land elsewhere in California that is farmed by the community members).

4. *Are Co-Ops Coopted?* Forming worker-owned co-ops is a community development strategy that has developed steam and attracted interest across industries and from both bottom-up organizing groups like the National

---

[23] For more information on food industry supply chain and similar advocacy programs, see Manoj Dias-Abey, Justice in Our Fields: Can "Alt-Labor" Organizations Improve Migrant Farm Workers' Conditions, 53 Harv. C.R.-C.L. L. Rev. 167 (2018); Greg Asbed and Sean Sellers, The Fair Food Program: Comprehensive, Verifiable, and Sustainable Change for Farmworkers, 16 U. Pa. J. L. & Soc. Change 39 (2013); Stephen Lee, The Food We Eat and the People Who Feed Us, 94 Wash. U.L. Rev. 1249 (2017); Martin H. Malin, Alt Labor? Why We Still Need Traditional Labor, 95 Chi.-Kent L. Rev. 157 (2020); Steph Tai, Food Sustainability in the Age of Complex, Global Supply Chains, 71 Ark. L. Rev. 465 (2018); Claudia Flores, Beyond the Bad Apple—Transforming the American Workplace for Women After #MeToo, 2019 U. Chi. Legal F. 85 (2019).

Domestic Workers Alliance and top-down analysts and funders from big banks and accounting firms. Carmen Molinari, Lexi Owens, and Robert Fontana argue that supporters are drawn to co-ops in large part as an "off-ramp from organizing against the boss" that offers an illusory easier path to economic equality and self-determination. Often, co-ops have formed after union drives failed:

> Take the United Electrical Workers (UE) campaign at Augie's, a small café chain in Southern California. In July of last year, the employer swiftly shuttered all five locations and laid off all workers after the nascent union "went public" to the employer by asking for voluntary recognition. The union then swiftly pivoted to a public shaming and social media campaign attacking the employer; this was quickly followed by a GoFundMe page to help replace wages and raise startup capital for what would become the "Slow Bloom Coffee Cooperative". . . .
>
> . . . [I]nstead of workers going on to organize at other employers in the industry, they now operate a small business. . . .
>
> . . . [But like any other business, market pressures for co-ops mean] downward wage pressure, unpaid overtime, and most other features of wage labor under capitalism. . . .
>
> . . . The power struggle at the heart of capitalism cannot be side-stepped by making the role of "worker" and "owner" coincide in a particular business inside of an economy that is still run for the sake of making profits.[24]

Many unions have turned to supporting co-ops in industries where traditional forms of organizing have failed. Communication Workers of America (CWA) formed a taxi drivers' co-op in Denver in 2009 to organize workers driving licensed taxis. Later, CWA organized Green Taxi, a second worker-owned company, to establish a foothold among gig workers to aid those driving for platform services like Uber, Lyft, or others. Supporters argue that such co-ops represent "alternative economic strategies" that show less "complicity with capital" and help maintain a deep critique of neoliberal capitalism. Mary Hoyer, The Power of Collaboration, Grassroots Economic Organizing (July 9, 2015), https://geo.coop/story/labor-unions-and-worker-co-ops. What do you think? Do co-op strategies represent labor's capitulation to the inequalities of neoliberal capitalism, critical acquiescence in a moment of limited options, or a strategy of deep critique and reinvention of economic relations? How would you, as a systemic advocate, stay aware of differing strategic perspectives so that you can continually construct stronger projects with organizing partners?

---

[24] Carmen Molinari, Lexi Owens, & Robert Fontana, You Can't Win Without a Fight: Why Worker Cooperatives Are a Bad Strategy, Organizing Work (Jan. 29, 2021), https://organizing.work/2021/01/you-cant-win-without-a-fight-why-worker-cooperatives-are-a-bad-strategy/?fbclid=IwAR1GuDwaUWq37SZU2U5xxmMTwa5VndnKMoNQGrqQAWdQo5CVVZL-r7p-q1c.

12.2 SUPPORTING COMPLEX ACTIONS BY ORGANIZED GROUPS: FINDING YOUR ROLE

Issue campaigns and CD projects necessarily are collaborative projects—personal yet collective forms of praxis that blend jurisprudence and demosprudence to go beyond the limits of formal equality and the legal industry. They depend on organized, mobilized, principled, and accountable groups. They are complex actions in part for this reason. Their complexities also require flexible and innovative advocacy. The roles of advocates in complex actions consequently can and do vary greatly.

An advocate may be an elected leader in an organization. A legally-trained advocate may not always play the role of a lawyer per se, but may draw on lawyering skills and knowledge nevertheless. Alternatively, an advocate may be a community group member, sharing concerns, helping shape strategies, and carrying out tasks like other members. An advocate may start as a member and then move into a representation role.[25] For example, "[m]any native lawyers become counsel for their own tribes."[26] Advocates support complex actions in multiple roles, from multiple sites, using multiple kinds of competencies.

In the grand scheme, few advocates work directly with organized groups. The majority of advocates licensed as lawyers—even public interest lawyers—do not do so. Very little funding and few positions allow advocates to work directly with organized groups. So what does it mean that systemic advocates should take organizing and collective power-building into account when most—the overwhelming majority—would have to do that at some distance from actual, organized groups? This imperative simply means that advocates always aim specifically to advance three-layered goals, as best as possible, under the circumstances. As we have seen, sometimes the systemic context will call for relatively traditional approaches, and sometimes not. In both instances, however, advocates devise creative ways of building collective power in groups, serving group interests in accountable ways, and promoting principled progress—change that is ameliorative *and* transformative—over time.[27]

---

[25] Nancy D. Polikoff, Am I My Client? The Role Confusion of a Lawyer-Activist, 31 Harv. C.R.-C.L. L. Rev. 443, 443–48 (1996) (describing some of the experiences and tensions of moving from the role of activist to lawyer within the gay and lesbian rights movement during a period of significant civil disobedience). Because contexts matter, the appearance of lawyer-activist as client takes different forms. For example, Richard Abel noted that Chinese public interest lawyers at times "have had to become their own clients, forced to claim that they embody the public interest" because of state repression of community organizing and of individual activists. Richard L. Abel, The Globalization of Public Interest Law, 13 UCLA J. Int'l L. & Foreign Aff. 295, 299–300 (2008).

[26] See Christine Zuni Cruz, [On the] Road Back In: Community Lawyering in Indigenous Communities, 24 Am. Indian L. Rev. 229, 258 (2000).

[27] Much of the debate about tensions between traditional representation and systemic advocacy has focused on the distinction between individual and group representation in legal service provision. We suggest the key distinction is not individual versus group—but between atomized services viewed in an acontextual unstrategic manner, rather than those wrapped in a

This imperative *does not* mean, therefore, that one form or role is inherently better than another. Regardless of context, multiple sites, roles, and competencies are necessary to Critical Justice. As immigration law scholar and clinician Rebecca Sharpless notes, lawyers therefore must resist continually any attempt to reduce the rich variety of approaches, strategies, relationships, and roles in advocacy to just "one lane." Rather, advocates and groups strive to construct many on-ramps and pathways to move forward collaboratively and creatively:

> The idea that there is a best way of social justice lawyering assumes that the individual lawyer is the relevant unit of analysis. This fallacy of the ideal progressive lawyer leads us to overlook the ways in which collaborative groups of people with different specialties, talents, and temperaments can and do work together to achieve shared and specific social justice goals. Social justice lawyers come in many stripes, bringing different talents and competencies to the table. Like all groups of people, they display multiple intelligences. Appellate attorneys may not be gifted organizer-lawyers and vice versa. Moreover, lawyers and their non-lawyer collaborators use many and varied tools to achieve results. These include but are not limited to: litigating in courts and other tribunals, organizing or working with organizers on a common campaign, press work, research studies, report writing, lobbying and policy work, education campaigns, protests and other direct action, pro se clinics, and messaging through social media. Given this multiplicity, it might be more effective and realistic to ensure that multiple competencies be available within each office or collection of offices, rather than within each individual attorney.[28]

Without any doubt, individuals can contribute to systemic justice from many different sites or "platforms" of work and in many different roles. But, while roles vary greatly, they all require similar critical foundations and capacities for professional collaboration—like those presented throughout this book. In all roles and settings, the aim is advancement (or protection) of three-layered goals in support of organized (or organizing) group struggles for equal justice.

---

deep understanding of context and history so as to advance three-layered goals and change the rules of the game. It is worth noting that much of this debate has played out in clinical law journals in productive ways. For more examples of how advocates and scholars struggle to take into account three-layered goals in advocacy in different contexts and in the face of differing constraints, see Daniel S. Shah, Lawyering for Empowerment: Community Development and Social Change, 6 Clinical L. Rev. 217 (1999); Hina Shah, Notes from the Field: The Role of the Lawyer in Grassroots Policy Advocacy, 21 Clinical L. Rev. 393 (2015); Peggie R. Smith, Organizing the Unorganizable: Private Paid Household Workers and Approaches to Employee Representation, 79 N.C. L. Rev. 45 (2000).

[28] Rebecca Sharpless, More Than One Lane Wide: Against Hierarchies of Helping in Progressive Legal Advocacy, 19 Clinical L. Rev. 347, 400 (2012).

Within this systemic landscape, some advocates *do* work directly with organizing groups, perhaps as in-house counsel, as is typical with labor union lawyers. And as community groups increasingly develop legal departments, these opportunities grow: Make the Road New York, CASA Maryland, and the New Orleans Workers' Center for Racial Justice are examples of community organizing groups with in-house legal programs. Such in-house departments in membership groups deepen collaboration effectively, as legal clinician Brian Glick notes, by "embedding lawyers within the leadership and strategic campaigns of an activist organization."[29] Others work in legal services organizations or law school clinics that prioritize working with groups, like the Community Justice Project in Florida, collaborations among car wash workers organizing in California with legal services groups like Bet Tzedek and others, or the many legal clinics engaged in immigrant rights, environmental, labor, healthcare, economic development, housing, and other struggles.[30] Some advocates provide individual legal services *and* community education through legal services organizations to spark consciousness and solidarity.[31] Others work in traditional firms or in universities, where (usually informal) forms of accountability to communities are balanced against work in service of their employer's interests—serving clients or educating students. Still others work in roles as government officials, business or nonprofit managers, or many other fields, where roles and agendas are set chiefly by managers of the enterprise.[32] In each instance, advocates inevitably play varied roles in transactions, litigation, and negotiations, aiming to use law in the "public interest" to advance bottom-up progress.

Taking these points further, Michael Grinthal reflects below on lawyering roles. He draws on his experiences as an organizer and subsequently a housing attorney with South Brooklyn Legal Services and Mobilization for Justice (formerly MFY Legal Services), as well as an advisory board member with the Housing Rights Initiative. Grinthal

---

[29] See Brian Glick, Two, Three, Many Rosas! Rebellious Lawyers and Progressive Activist Organizations, 23 Clinical L. Rev. 611 (2017) (describing the role, effectiveness, and challenges of in-house legal departments in organizing groups). See also Make the Road New York, www.bettzedek.org; CASA Maryland, www.wearecasa.org; and New Orleans Workers' Center for Racial Justice, www.nowcrj.org.

[30] See, for example, Community Justice Project, www.communityjusticeproject.com; Bet Tzedek, www.bettzedek.org.

[31] For additional examples of individual legal services that serve to seed resistance and support client education and involvement, see Sharpless, More Than One Lane, at 390–91; Sameer M. Ashar, Law Clinics and Collective Mobilization, 14 Clin. L. Rev. 355, 399 (2008); E. Tammy Kim, Lawyers as Resources in Struggles for Social Change, 13 N.Y. City L. Rev. 213 (2009); Jayashri Srikantiah and Jennifer Lee Koh, Teaching Individual Representation Alongside Institutional Advocacy: Pedagogical Implications of a Combined Advocacy Clinic, 16 Clinical L. Rev. 451 (2010).

[32] Douglas NeJaime, Cause Lawyers Inside the State, 81 Fordham L. Rev. 649 (2012); Margo Schlanger, Offices of Goodness: Influence Without Authority in Federal Agencies, 36 Cardozo L. Rev. 53 (2014); Justin Hansford, Cause Judging, 27 Geo. J. Legal Ethics 1 (2014).

describes a variety of roles that lawyers can play to advance social justice while working with organized communities. As he emphasizes, advocacy for justice depends on multiple kinds of collaborations and competencies to build power through organizing. This connection between organization, power, and justice calls for a new problem solving "paradigm"—one of the advocacy Approaches often called "law and organizing." He outlines five practice models, in each of which the lawyer plays multiple, different, roles.

POWER WITH: PRACTICE MODELS FOR
SOCIAL JUSTICE LAWYERING
Michael Grinthal
15 U. Pa. J. L. & Soc. Change 25 (2011)

... [L]awyers who seek to build countervailing power must work with people who are in the process of transforming themselves from atomized and dispersed to organized and powerful. None of the traditional paradigms of group representation are sufficient to structure lawyers' relationships with constituencies in the process of organizing. Instead, practitioners and theorists have begun to develop a new paradigm: the practice of law and organizing.

Organizing: A Definition

Before it is possible to discuss the practice of law and organizing, it is first necessary to introduce the practice of organizing itself. . . .

For the purposes of this paper, I define organizing as the processes by which people build and exercise power by collecting and activating relationships. . . . By "organizing," I mean those processes by which power is created from multiplied relationships—a phenomenon of energy release that civil rights organizer Bob Moses likened to nuclear fusion. . . .

To be successful—to truly be organizing—an organizing effort must meet three criteria, or core values: (1) it must build the power of the group that is organizing, changing the group's relationships to other, already powerful institutions and groups; (2) it must result in sustainable organizational structures that can be applied to future struggles; and (3) it must result in the development of individual participants' capacities to lead and advocate on their own behalf. . . .

Groups of marginalized people struggling to become powerful by organizing cannot afford to give up the resources and value that lawyers bring to the table. Conversely, lawyers who seek sustainable, structural social change must learn to work with groups that are organizing, developing leadership, and gaining power. . . . In the next section, I explore five different concrete models of lawyers working constructively with groups who are still in the process of organizing.

Models

... These [five models] are not intended to be job descriptions. Nor are they competing strategies.... The value of naming them and setting them out is to provide a vocabulary and a set of landmarks to help lawyers (and those about to become lawyers) imagine how to act and, having acted, reflect on what they have done....

Corporate Model

... The lawyer and the group are engaging in the Corporate Model to the extent that the group has developed an organizational process capable of defining group interests and values, and to the extent that the lawyer represents these interests rather than the legal needs of individual group members.

Further, the Corporate Model is characterized by a strong separation of "core" organizational strategies, from which the lawyer is segregated, and legal circumstances which are the conditions and consequences of "incorporation" as an organization.... Much of this work is transactional, though the lawyer may sometimes litigate offensively or defensively to protect and preserve the organization's incorporated status.

For example, Wiley Branton, a noted African-American attorney, native Southerner, and collaborator with Thurgood Marshall, drafted bylaws, incorporated, and administered the Congress of Federated Organizations (COFO) and the Voter Education Project (VEP), the civil rights umbrella organizations created to channel federal funding through a minefield of tax-exemption laws and competing organizations. When COFO's founders were arrested on trumped-up charges by Mississippi police upon leaving their first organizational meeting, Branton advocated for their release....

... [However, this] limited relationship prevents the organization from getting all the value it can from the lawyer. There is no provision in this model for the lawyer to interact with the organization's membership in their daily struggles to continue organizing and exercising power, so if the lawyer has skills and knowledge that could be relevant to that process, it will never be known.... And the lawyer's values and critical eye, developed through personal experience as well as learned from a long tradition of lawyers struggling for social change, are not welcomed. The lawyer is largely a technician....

Clever lawyers with a deep understanding of organizing who are willing to take risks may begin in this model, but move into the Enabling Model, below, as they discover ways to open opportunities for organizing in even the most seemingly technical projects....

Legal M*A*S*H Unit

Organizing often generates legal casualties—leaders arrested for civil disobedience or in retaliation; opponents suing the organization or leaders; leaders or organizers who make mistakes when venturing into unfamiliar institutional territory. In addition, participants in organizing efforts are often already facing legal liabilities such as eviction, benefit termination, and bankruptcy. The M*A*S*H Lawyer in this model handles short-term legal "first aid" . . . [but] does not directly advance the core goals of the organization—his legal claims are not the same as the constituency's principal demands. . . . Nevertheless, the M*A*S*H Model is not to be confused with traditional delivery of legal services to individuals. Crucially, over time, M*A*S*H lawyering is targeted to indirectly support the constituency's organizing capacity by freeing up leaders to address their core goals—it is more of a field hospital than a civilian emergency room. . . .

The M*A*S*H Model makes great use of lawyers' special access to the courtroom. It may also mobilize lawyers' relationships and knowledge of institutions, if the lawyers are repeat players in the fair hearings, housing courts, and criminal courts in which leaders find themselves tangled. Lawyers indigenous to the community where the organizing effort takes place can act as "fixers," eradicating small problems to enable leaders to concentrate on larger issues. Lawyers may also be freer to incorporate some of their values than in the Corporate Model. . . .

On the other hand, this model is more vulnerable to the distractions of legal thinking than is the Corporate Model. The seductive immediate payoff of traditional legal services delivery competes with the long-term power-building of organizing. . . .

Lawyer as Political Enabler

The Enabling Model bears some resemblance to the Corporate Model, in that the lawyer is concerned with group interests and organizational formation. But this model is distinct from the Corporate Model in that it is concerned specifically with the group's interest in continuing to organize and to build power.

The Enabling Lawyer may engage in the full range of lawyering activities, such as litigation, negotiation, advocacy, drafting, and research, but always toward the goal of facilitating or opening spaces for organizing and the exercise of relational power. For example, the lawyer may work to defeat injunctions against organizing or demonstrating; find creative loopholes in existing law into which community leaders can fit their demands; uncover the legal leverage which organizations can use to target their organizing. . . . The Enabling Lawyer will rarely, if ever, style the group's ultimate demands as legal claims. Rather, she will use her practice to enable the group to make its own demands and seek its own victory through political, economic, social or cultural means. . . .

Research and education are among the most frequent activities of the Enabling Lawyer. Jack Minnis, legal researcher for the Student Nonviolent Coordinating Committee (SNCC), was playing this role when he wrote Stokely Carmichael in 1965 to point out that "Alabama Law says it is possible to bring into existence a totally new political party," provided that it choose a visual symbol that does "not resemble in any way" the white rooster of the Alabama Democratic Party (student volunteers . . . chose a black panther).

Because this role is not modeled on a traditional lawyering role, such as corporate counsel or legal aid, its boundaries are less well defined than the boundaries of the Corporate or M*A*S*H Models. . . .

Additionally, with the lawyer taking such a prominent public role, she can easily come to be seen as the spokesperson for the organization[, and] . . . her portrayal of the organization can be frozen into legal reality. . . . Perhaps the most notorious example of this kind of legal-tail-wagging-the-organizational-dog was Martin Luther King's painful turnaround at the foot of the Pettus Bridge during the second aborted Selma-to-Montgomery march. There, lawyers had represented the SCLC's nonviolence to a federal judge as a desire to avoid violence, rather than to expose state violence; as a result, the judge partially lifted an injunction in order to allow activists to march just far enough to avoid provocation, but not far enough to create the kind of moral drama they needed. . . .

On the other hand, the indeterminacy of the Enabling Lawyer's role presents opportunities for the lawyer to activate the full range of her skills, knowledge, access, and relationships. . . . [T]he Enabling Lawyer must learn a great deal about organizing. . . . It will often be useful for the lawyer to bring unwinnable actions in order to advance political goals by attracting public attention or forcing opponents to commit resources and reveal information about themselves. . . . Similarly, [group members] . . . have the opportunity to learn and perform a new role: that of partners in power with the lawyer. . . .

Organizing on the Scaffold of Litigation

This model flips the organizing-lawyering relationship of the first three models on its head. Here, litigation is the principal strategy for achieving the constituency's demands, but litigation is conducted in such a way as to maximize opportunities for organizing in the shadow or margins of the case. I approach this model warily, as its most common form is a weak version in which sympathizers are mobilized to engage in quick, superficial displays in support of lawyer heroes. [Washington D.C.] public interest firms on both the right and left have grown adept at busing in supporters to picket outside the Supreme Court whenever the firms' lawyers are arguing their impact cases inside. These activities give the appearance of an organizing effort, but in fact they fulfill none of the criteria of organizing. They provide little or no learning and development to demonstrators, and they build no relational structures amongst participants, other than the relationships that develop incidentally between demonstrators passing the time with conversation—no more than would be developed at any supermarket with long checkout lines. In addition, they are ephemeral, with demonstrators rarely seeing one another again, let alone continuing to operate a lasting organizational structure that they can apply to other struggles. . . .

. . . Micro-litigation in municipal bread-and-butter forums such as housing, small claims, and family court, with their quick pace and relative informality, provides a surprising number of opportunities for group action and the emergence of individual leaders. . . .

As public spaces, in my experience, these courts do not work well. They are strictly and often abusively regulated according to arcane procedural rules [enforced] by frustrated judges appointed by local elites. But their centrality to community power relations means that litigation there presents opportunities to alter those relations, and that lawyers for low-income people play an important role in the transformation of these public spaces.

My own experiences with organizing on the scaffolding of litigation have taken place in New York City Housing Courts. The state created these courts in the early 1970s, in response to pressure by the tenant movement, to provide a space for the recognition of tenants' rights to repairs and decent living conditions. . . . What is left from the original vision is one Housing Court part (out of ten parts in each borough) where tenants can sue their landlords for the correction of housing code violations. This part (redundantly called the "HP," or "Housing Part,") is a frequent haunt of lawyers from Legal Services or Legal Aid, as well as of the more vocal, angry, informed (or, as the landlords' bar refers to them, "problem") tenants. Importantly, the HP part is the only Housing Court part in which tenants can bring group actions with multiple plaintiffs. . . .

Professional landlords have long ago learned how to ignore or neutralize traditional tenant organizing efforts. They send low-level service employees to take the heat at angry building lobby meetings, while the actual owners remain anonymous behind generic shell corporations. Tenants looking to take the fight to where their landlords live and work end up gathering impotently at one of the notorious mailbox stores where most building owners keep the post office boxes that are their only registered address. . . .

. . . But in the HP part of the Housing Court, as with all civil litigation, landlords can be subpoenaed and forced to appear, or at least to send representatives fully authorized to agree to demands and be held accountable. Often, when a landlord refuses to meet with a nascent tenant organization, and a legal services attorney initiates an HP action on the organization's behalf, the first court appearance becomes, in effect, the meeting that the tenants had originally sought.

In one such instance, I represented a newly-organizing group of tenants from a severely deteriorated building.... Following the usual real estate naming system, the landlord was known only as "[address of building] LLC." The registered address was a post office box.... I had joined in a few of the tenants' early meetings and met with a number of them in their apartments, where they pointed out the leaks, broken door locks, smoking light fixtures, and sagging ceilings that had accumulated over months of the landlord's neglect. The tenants had requested a meeting with the landlord, but been refused: he would meet with any of them individually, but never together.

Facing immediately hazardous conditions in their homes, the tenants asked me to represent them in an HP action. As an attorney, I drafted and filed the papers necessary to start the case and lay foundations for later arguments, and served them on the landlord's post office box. I also filed a subpoena requiring a principal of "[building address] LLC" to appear.... On [the court] date, half a dozen tenants arrived in court with photographs and other evidence from their apartments—Elizabeth M brought a pill jar full of dead bedbugs she had collected from her children's bedroom. The judge ... sent us off to a conference room to talk settlement. Suddenly, the half-dozen tenants were sitting around a long table with their landlord, having the meeting he had refused earlier. They explained their photographs, with ... court staff gathered around the edges of the room to watch. When Elizabeth held up her bedbug jar, the staffers gasped; when the landlord blustered, they laughed at him. When the landlord filibustered, as a group we stood up, threatening to walk away from the table to go see the judge. Knowing he was beaten, the landlord signed a consent agreement—enforceable as an order of the court—to perform all the repairs. More importantly, he also agreed to meet personally with the tenant association every month from then on. If he failed to do so to the tenants' satisfaction, they and he knew that they could drag him back into court for contempt.

This was an organizing victory, not a litigation victory. An organized group confronted their powerful landlord face-to-face, winning concrete demands, including, most importantly, recognition of their tenant association and a commitment to meet and deal with them in person at their building from them on....

But this was more than simply bargaining in the shadow of the law. The HP proceeding created the only public space in which such bargaining was even possible. Its status as a legal forum forced the landlord to the table, while its informality allowed the tenants to take charge once there. . . .

The Scaffolding Model shares an uneasy border with the Enabling Model; both lawyers engage in large-scale litigation and group representation, and both hope to carve a path for organizing to follow. But unlike Enabling Lawyers, Scaffolding Lawyers do not shy away from naming the constituency's central demands among their legal claims. . . .

This model is attractive to many lawyers because it places them in a high-profile, challenging role. It is also popular with movement strategists because of its potential for catalyzing sweeping, trans-local movement activity. Impact victories also tend to have great expressive effect, asserting rights in the best sense of the word—as invitations to those on the margins to be included as "first-class citizens" in the community. But this model also comes the closest to overwhelming the core values of organizing. Issues are cut, timing is chosen, goals are defined, arguments are formed, and plaintiffs' stories are told at the lawyers' discretion. Of course, lawyers may consult with community leaders, but consultations with disorganized constituencies may be costly or impossible, and nothing holds lawyers accountable to any consultations they stoop to undertake. The idea of lawyers taking it upon themselves to be movement-makers clashes with the bottom-up, power-shifting nature of relational organizing. . . . [This model] does not require that the lawyer learns new skills or even operates in an unfamiliar forum, but it does require that she act with mindfulness and discipline. And this may mean conflict with funders, nonprofit boards, and pro bono partners—the litigator's more immediate "constituency." For this reason, the Scaffolding Lawyer is the most vulnerable to diversion both by capture and by self-delusion.

Lawyer as Organizer

This model does not refer to lawyers who quit lawyering altogether and become organizers. In the Lawyer as Organizer Model, lawyers initiate their organizing through the structural context of direct delivery of legal services. The base of the organizing effort is often some subset of the lawyer's client base. Agenda-setting begins when the lawyer notices patterns among the issues that clients bring to her, and the motivation to organize may come from limitations the lawyer encounters in her ability to resolve client issues through legal means alone. Indeed, the growth of attorney-founded Workers' Centers may be evidence that this model is gaining popularity. Increasingly, lawyers are caught in the conflict between the ideals of legal service provision—equal justice and individual rights—and its frustrating reality—pyrrhic victories, resource shortages, and political restrictions attached to funding. Under such pressure and limitations, attorneys may increasingly turn their practice towards organizing.

... The organizing effort can become stunted by the centrality of the lawyer (and perhaps his limited competence as an organizer), so that the lawyer, rather than decreasing the constituency's dependence on him as a lawyer, has only added a further dependence on him as an organizer. The lawyer has "his" group of plaintiffs, which engages in "extra-legal tactics." This is the paradox of the Lawyer as Organizer Model: while at first it appears the most radical enactment of the core values of organizing, in practice it often aggrandizes and foregrounds the lawyer ... [and it] may prevent lawyers from searching for already existing organizing efforts and community leaders, and expanding the resources available to the organizing process.

But what about situations where there is no readily available organizing effort for the lawyer and client to work with? ... Certainly a lack of powerful, democratic organizing amongst marginalized constituencies is more the rule than the exception in most parts of the United States. There indeed the lawyer must begin with what she has—her relationship with her clients—but should work toward differentiating the roles of lawyer and organizer as soon as possible.... The lawyers who began Make the Road by Walking [, a New York workers' center now called Make the Road NY, similar to The Workplace Project described above by Jennifer Gordon] also mitigated their own leadership somewhat by immediately seeking out relationships with community leaders (in particular with the popular local parish priest), rather than basing the organization entirely on their own client networks. From the start, there were always leaders in the organization who were not dependent on the lawyers either for legal services or for their relationships with other leaders. Additionally, Make the Road's staff structure was decentralized from its beginning, so that it was impossible for lawyers to make organization-wide decisions except via a board that also included community leaders. Community members recruited through legal services were directed to a different staff person from the person who had originally recruited them, making the process of transformation from client to leader dependent on the entire organization, rather than on one lawyer. Some of the founding lawyers ceased acting as lawyers entirely, taking on both the title and work of organizers. After seven years of operating as a "collective," staff members decided in 2005 to establish a bounded "legal department" in order to foster accountability and clarity of roles.... [T]heir principal job is to do the things that non-lawyers cannot....

Conclusion

The reality of the legal profession today is that the majority of lawyers work for groups. Legal education, firm organization, rules of ethics, and substantive law are structured to facilitate lawyers' support of the most well-organized, powerful groups in society. The challenge, then, for lawyers with a calling to work for social change, is to create structures that facilitate lawyering with and for un- or partially-organized constituencies. Such constituencies have not yet completely developed the mechanisms by which to hold lawyers accountable and lack formal recognition by the law.... [Nevertheless,] lawyers contribute the greatest value when they work with groups that are in the process of organizing.... The lawyer supports the organizing process, which in turn structures her role and relationships. It is a cycle, rather than a transfer of power, and therefore relational, sustainable, accountable, and powerful.

Grinthal highlights how complex actions depend on collaboration, that legal action is a vital part of complex actions, and why collaborations in law and organizing must have a clear focus: lawyers contribute "the greatest value" when they work with groups in the process of organizing in ways that are "relational, sustainable, accountable, and powerful." As Grinthal's models confirm, complex actions depend on organized groups supported by advocates with multiple competencies who fulfill varied roles.

NOTES AND QUESTIONS

1. *Reflection on Organizing.* Reflect on some example of organizing (defined by Grinthal as the "processes by which people build and exercise power by collecting and activating relationships") that you participated in through your schooling, employment, or community or as part of some other setting or issue. Then think about Grinthal's three criteria for organizing success: "(1) it must build the power of the group that is organizing, changing the group's relationships to other, already powerful institutions and groups; (2) it must result in sustainable organizational structures that can be applied to future struggles; and (3) it must result in the development of individual participants' capacities to lead and advocate on their own behalf." Did the organizing effort you participated in fulfill these criteria or fall short? If so, in what way? What activities, strategies, education, or resources would have better ensured fulfillment of these measures?

12.3 COLLABORATION AND CONFLICT COEXIST IN COMPLEX ACTIONS

Collaboration is essential for complex actions, even if conflict is then inevitable—both internal and external. Systemic advocacy is a team sport—intrinsically, necessarily, for better and for worse. Advocates must accept that tension and conflict are inevitable, within groups and teams and among coalition partners, as well as with opponents. Collaboration therefore *is* hard yet fundamental. Given these conditions—the constant need for cooperation and the constant possibility of conflict—we conclude this chapter with a practical and important reminder: embrace conflict honestly—as a key part of your work as a collaborative professional. Remember, repeat players and their advocates have to face each other again tomorrow.

As we have seen already, systemic advocates may play roles that put them at the center of intragroup tensions. Advocates often are called upon to help fashion internal governance mechanisms to promote principled and accountable decision making. When team members disagree about tactics and strategies—and jostle for power—advocates may be called upon to critically assess their own power and to bring skills to bear to help reach a resolution. The same is true of intergroup conflicts. When coalition partners talk past each other because of cultural differences and long histories of intergroup oppression, advocates may be called upon to facilitate processes that allow for cross-group listening and healing. When members of different coalition groups genuinely believe, and thus repeat stereotypes hurtful to their partners, advocates may be called upon to share research and knowledge that cultivates respect and solidarity. Just as collaboration entails conflict, conflict entails reconciliation; whether in inter- or intragroup settings, the capacity for collaboration requires a capacity for reconciliations that are restorative and constructive.

Legal scholar Eric Yamamoto describes some of the elements of intergroup healing, or reconciliation, that underpin successful collaborations in pursuit of equal justice:

> The first [element of intergroup healing] is the notion that healing, whether by individual or group, entails some combination of acknowledgment of the humanity of the Other and of the sources of conflict (including the historical roots of present conflict), acceptance of appropriate responsibility (often in the form of an apology) and material change (structural alteration of the relationship). The second is the notion that healing of wounds from perceived wrongful acts, while often messy and incomplete, is a foundation for future communal, or at least cooperative, action. The third commonality is that all of these approaches to intergroup healing incorporate legal concepts only indirectly and move beyond formal notions of legal justice. . . . [H]owever, law and notions of legal justice provide a potentially powerful base for constructing merged theoretical and practical, or praxis, approaches to intergroup healing as well as interracial justice.[33]

---

[33] Eric K. Yamamoto, Rethinking Alliances: Agency, Responsibility and Interracial Justice, 3 Asian Pac. Am. L.J. 33, 69 (1995). See also Eric K. Yamamoto, Critical Race Praxis: Race Theory and Political Lawyering Practice in Post-Civil Rights America, 95 Mich. L. Rev. 821 (1997); Eric K. Yamamoto, Conflict and Complicity: Justice Among Communities of Color, 2 Harv. Latino L. Rev. 495 (1997).

Traditional rules of ethics purport to help advocates resolve conflicts. Sometimes, they do. But, as we saw in Part IV, advocates are both aided and constrained by traditional legal ethics because ethical rules were developed to maintain the status quo as much as to promote equal justice. Top-down dictates provide no definitive answer to critical questions about collaboration, conflict, and reconciliation in antisubordination struggles.

For instance, among the key ongoing conflicts in systemic advocacy are debates about "best" strategies for advancing three-layered goals—or whether three-layered goals really make sense. Across the globe, advocates argue about which "need" should take priority in a given context. The basic framing for these debates often pits ameliorative first-layer goals (often addressing existing problems with atomized technical solutions) against the transformative second and third layers of collective power-building and culture-shifting through complex actions. Against this binary backdrop, does helping someone suffering domestic violence get to a safe space serve a greater need than, for instance, helping a survivors' group develop bylaws and prepare an application for federal tax exempt 501(c)(3) status to begin acting as an organized agent of struggle? Is addressing an eviction more important than assisting in forming a mobile park residents' or public housing tenants' association? These questions cannot be answered, really, in terms of the "greatest need"—which metrics would one use, and why? The questions are subjective, and neither of the binary choices are adequate for systemic justice—which always aims to use ameliorative gains to bootstrap transformative progress. But advocates often are not given the conceptual tools to design three-layered projects that advance Critical Justice in both ameliorative *and* transformative ways. So, an earnest debate continues.

Moreover, debates about "need" can become mired in largely unhelpful criteria if not grounded in a clear understanding of a given social reality. As legal scholar Paul Tremblay noted, assessing need *contextually* is a complicated task, in which considerations related to time and other circumstances are calibrated for amelioration and transformation:

> While the powerfully-felt "rescue mission" can often distort resource allocation choices, as the desire to assist those in distress in the present can easily overshadow the longer-term strategies that might effect meaningful change, a principled response to poverty must overcome such distortion. Every public health initiative or program rests on the principle that short-term gains must at times be sacrificed for long-term benefits.... [Transactional legal services supporting business entities serve], in this sense, as a form of public health legal services. As the health care field understands quite well, a vibrant social policy

must include triage-driven urgent care along with initiatives aimed at prevention and health maintenance over the long term.[34]

Clearly, no easy or absolute answers exist for these uncertainties. Because the work is complex and uncertain, conflicts arise about how best to maximize the chances of success, short- and long-term. And because no one has—or can have—all the answers, authentic tension and conflict about how to advance along each layer is unavoidable—yet necessary—for reaching a workable, if always imperfect, plan. The advocate's objective, then, is principled and accountable choices that are effective, flexible, and meaningful to the bottom in context, not abstractly perfect ones. In practice, advocates and client groups debate continually how best to define strategies and measures of success on all three layers of goals in light of accumulating experience, posing self-critical questions like:

- What are the best technical solutions and ways to win them—what's the best plan for the case, for the negotiations, for the campaign, for the community development project?

- How does one engage in advocacy that builds group power and ensures that the group's decision making stays accountable to the members as well as to the interests of a broader set of (current or future) constituents?

- And how does one shift culture and consciousness to deepen the understanding of groups, problems, and solutions as *systemic*—while also giving one's campaign or project a chance to actually win?

These ongoing debates are complicated by the framing of needs, priorities, and choices, as well as by underlying questions about who gets to make these decisions authoritatively and legitimately in any given context. Legal ethics or ethical guidelines from other disciplines and traditions can be a guide—sometimes and to a point. But neither legal nor other professions' ethics nor faith-based rules "immunize" any decision making against all questioning; indeed, as we have seen, sometimes the rules and teachings of top-down sources inhibit principled and accountable choices. No viewpoint or process stands on a proverbial island, untainted by history or by the operations of identities, groups, interests, and power.

To underscore this bottom line, legal scholar Alicia Alvarez next provides an overview of law-and-organizing as a complex set of collaborations fraught with questions like these. She, like Huertas-Noble above, works with membership groups to support the formation of worker cooperatives. Combining critical knowledge from the Schools and Approaches with personal experience, she spells out seven "principles" of

---

[34] Paul R. Tremblay, Transactional Legal Services, Triage, and Access to Justice, 48 Wash. U. J.L. & Pol'y 11, 17–18 (2015).

cooperatives as "part of an international movement" and outlines the three most common forms of cooperatives—consumer, producer, and worker—all designed to share, not concentrate, the benefits of wealth production. As Alvarez emphasizes, collaboration and conflict necessarily coexist in complex actions designed to empower those at the bottom of any systemic context or advocacy scenario. Alvarez concludes that the workers—the clients—can decide for themselves the difficult questions presented by the coexistence of conflict and reconciliation. In a complex world, collective decisions ultimately must be rooted in the bottom.

However, the advocate's role as a collaborative professional is not to stand passively by, tagging along zealously with any or every group choice. Rather, professional collaborations require advocates to serve as an engaged partner with client-groups to challenge, aid, and support them in making choices. The advocate supports the group as an organization by helping to ensure that collective decisions, as much as possible, are democratic and flow from a critical and self-critical process of research, analysis, reflection, and deliberation.

LAWYERS, ORGANIZERS, AND WORKERS: COLLABORATION AND CONFLICT IN WORKER COOPERATIVE DEVELOPMENT

Alicia Alvarez
24 Geo. J. on Poverty L. & Pol'y 353 (2017)

Introduction

Progressive lawyers are working to support the formation of worker cooperatives as a way to create economic alternatives for low-wage workers and the under-resourced communities in which they live....

This Article explores how lawyers work with organizers supporting the development of worker cooperatives. A key question that arises in forming a cooperative is who directs the lawyer's work: the group of workers forming the cooperative or the organizations that may be supporting the workers? How should lawyers respond to the differing interests and the tensions that may arise? The future members have to make important decisions such as who will form part of the cooperative, who will be eligible for membership, what will members receive, and under what circumstances might someone lose his or her membership stake. These decisions have legal and organizing implications. During this process, no bright lines exist between where the organizing ends and the lawyering begins. The lawyers and organizers must negotiate these responsibilities. Even if the relationship is negotiated from the start, the lawyers, workers, and organizers cannot anticipate all the tensions that may arise. How those questions get resolved has implications for the cooperative being formed, the individuals involved in the formation of the cooperative, the relationship between the lawyers and organizers, and the formation of future cooperatives.

Worker ownership can be a "vital element of a broader job creation, community organizing, or community revitalization strategy." ... The question is how we create a more equitable economy—one in which businesses make decisions considering what is good for workers, families, and communities in order to ensure that the economy benefits everyone, as opposed to promoting an economy that merely focuses on the bottom line and economic growth. Cooperatives may be a way to democratize the economy and reduce inequality. Worker cooperatives are also seen as vehicles for political activism and connections to the larger economic justice movement.

In promoting cooperative development, progressive lawyers see an opportunity to support a broader economic justice movement.... [This work can be described] as political lawyering since it is legal work done "in service to both individuals and larger, more collectively oriented goals." Political lawyering seeks "radical extension of democracy, equality and racial justice" and focuses on "deep-seated structural and cultural change." Ultimately, those working to create worker cooperatives are seeking an economy that is more just and democratic. Political lawyering looks beyond the status quo to what ought to be. . . .

Poverty and Inequality in the United States

. . . Despite efforts to eradicate poverty, the United States continues to have a relatively high percentage of its population living in poverty. Since the mid-1960s, between 10 and 15% of the population of the United States has lived in poverty. In 2015, 13.5% of the population lived in poverty. While the poverty rate is a measure of [extreme] deprivation, individuals and families in fact need an income approximately twice the poverty rate to meet basic financial obligations.

Access to a job that pays enough to support oneself or a family continues to be a challenge for many Americans. Working does not guarantee that someone will not be poor. The working poor tend to be disproportionately women, African-Americans, and Latinos. Individuals employed in service occupations are more likely to be among the working poor. Three labor market problems "hinder a worker's ability to earn an income above the poverty threshold: low earnings, periods of unemployment, and involuntary part-time employment." . . .

. . . [Income inequality] has been increasing in the United States over the past several decades. The "trend shows no sign of reversing." . . . High-income earners have seen substantial increases in income, while low-wage and middle-wage workers have seen modest gains in income. Since 1979, the wages of the top 1% have increased by 138% while the wages of the entire bottom 99% of earners have grown only by 15%. Hourly wages for middlewage workers have increased 6% since 1979, while low-wage workers have actually seen a decrease of 5% in their hourly wages.... Additionally, "the highest wage earners are four times more likely than the poorest Americans to receive paid sick days, nearly twice as likely to have paid vacation days, and five times as likely to have access to paid family leave."

These economic problems are compounded by a racial wealth and income gap. In 2011, ... [t]he median White household had over $110,000 in wealth holdings, while the median African-American household had just over $7,000, and the median Latino household had just over $8,000. While 73% of White households own their own home, only 47% of Latino households and 45% of African-American households own their homes. While 34% of Whites had completed a four-year college degree, just 20% of African-Americans and 13% of Latinos had similar educational attainment.

The Potential of Cooperatives

... Cooperatives are one approach to create community wealth and assets. Around the world, cooperatives are seen as an economic development and poverty reduction strategy.... Cooperatives hold out the possibility for "greater income equality, fairer wealth distribution, and a more democratic economic system." ...

What are Cooperatives?

The International Co-operative Alliance (ICA) defines a cooperative as "an autonomous association of persons united voluntarily to meet their common economic, social, and cultural needs and aspirations through a jointly owned and democratically-controlled enterprise." Cooperatives are businesses owned and run by and for their members.... Cooperatives are based on the values of "self-help, ... democracy, ... equity, and solidarity." Members commit to several ethical values including social responsibility and caring for others.

Cooperatives are generally classified into three categories—consumer, producer, and worker. Consumers join together to buy goods or services. In a consumer cooperative, members seek to control the quality of the goods or services and to obtain a reasonable price. Examples of consumer cooperatives are grocery stores, credit unions, child care providers, housing, and utility. In consumer cooperatives, most of the "profit" of the business is distributed to the members, either in the form of a rebate (a patronage dividend based on the amount of products the member buys from the cooperative) or in lower prices. As in other forms of cooperatives, the members may choose not to distribute all the profit, but may instead reinvest it in the business by setting aside reserves. In producer cooperatives, producers of various products purchase supplies and equipment together in order to jointly process or market their goods or services. The cooperative allows the members to reduce the cost of distribution, advertising, and sale of the products, to help produce or enhance a product, or to supply producers. Agricultural cooperatives are the most common producer cooperatives. Workers in a worker cooperative own and manage a particular business. The cooperative form allows democratic economic participation and economic security for the member-owner in the form of income and wealth generation.

Cooperatives share internationally agreed-upon principles first set out in late nineteenth century England. These principles, as stated by the International Co-operative Alliance, include:

1. **Voluntary and Open Membership.** [Cooperatives] are voluntary organi[z]ations, open to all persons able to use their services and willing to accept the responsibilities of membership, without gender, social, racial, political or religious discrimination.

2. **Democratic Member Control.** [Cooperatives] are democratic organi[z]ations controlled by their members, who actively participate in setting their policies and making decisions. [Elected representatives] are accountable to the membership.... [M]embers have equal voting rights (one member, one vote)....

3. **Member Economic Participation.** Members contribute equitably to, and democratically control, the capital of their cooperative. At least part of that capital is usually the common property of the cooperative.... Members allocate surpluses for any or all of the following purposes: developing their cooperative, possibly by setting up reserves ...; benefiting members in proportion to their transactions with the [cooperative]; and supporting other activities approved by the membership.

4. **Autonomy and Independence.** [Cooperatives] are autonomous, self-help organi[z]ations that are controlled by their members. If they enter into agreements with other[s] or raise capital from external sources, they do so on terms that ensure democratic control by their members and maintain their [cooperative] autonomy.

5. **Education, Training and Information.** [Cooperatives] provide education and training for their members, elected representatives, managers, and employees so they can contribute effectively to the development of their [cooperatives]. [Cooperatives] inform the general public—particularly young people and opinion leaders—about the nature and benefits of [cooperation].

6. **[Cooperation] among [Cooperatives].** [Cooperatives] serve their members most effectively and strengthen the

[cooperative] movement by working together through local, national, regional, and international structures.

7. **Concern for Community.** [Cooperatives] work for the sustainable development of their communities. . . .

Cooperatives are part of an international movement. The economic activity of the largest 300 cooperatives in the world equals the ninth largest national economy. . . . People in the United States may come into contact with cooperatives more than they may realize. The United States has nearly 30,000 cooperative businesses, employing nearly one million people, generating over $650 million in revenue and $25 million in wages, and holding more than $3 trillion in assets. Though worker cooperatives are the least common type of cooperative business in the United States, they have the potential to have the greatest impact on their members. Most worker cooperatives in the United States are small businesses, though some employ more than 250 workers and produce more than $10 million in revenues each year. Worker cooperatives, however, remain a small part of the national economy.

The Promise of Greater Economic Democracy and Less Inequality

Worker cooperatives are democratic economic institutions where worker-owners share profits. Workers are the members of the cooperative, not just the employees. In a traditional corporation, a stockholder's voting rights and rights to receive dividends correlate to the amount of his or her investment. Cooperatives, in contrast, distribute profits to members in proportion to work or other factors, such as hours worked. In cooperatives, each member thus has one vote, and all workers are equal when it comes to membership rights. Membership rights are accordingly linked to the act of working. Cooperatives have a limited return on capital. Capital rights are attached to an internal capital account for each member, with the member entitled to distribution at retirement or after a fixed period of time. Workers have different amounts in their capital accounts, depending on their seniority and pay scale. In addition to the individual capital account, cooperatives have "an individuated collective account." Each year, the cooperative's earnings are divided between the individual account and the collective account at a proportion decided by the cooperative. . . .

Cooperatives build greater wealth by distributing year-end surpluses to their worker-owners in the form of patronage dividends. In some cases, cooperatives have produced higher wages and fuller than normal work schedules as compared to other businesses. Cooperatives have the potential to promote economic equality by reducing income and wealth differences between the various workers of the firm. The wealth gap between CEOs and workers is also lower in worker cooperatives than in other business forms. . . .

Generally, cooperatives treat their workers better than other businesses, and provide greater job security to their members. Cooperatives tend to prioritize job preservation.... These policies not only provide greater economic security for the individuals involved, but also result in lower unemployment rates and insulate local economies during economic crises.

Cooperative businesses benefit from a democratic business structure as well.... Studies have found a correlation between employee ownership and higher productivity rates, and improved business performance.... Cooperatives are more resilient than traditional businesses, have higher survival rates, and fare better during economic downturns.... Cooperatives also have the potential to contribute to strong local economies by "rooting businesses in the community."... Because the worker-owners are simultaneously employees, owners, and community members, they are more likely to promote the well-being of employees, the local economy, and the community.

Cooperatives Provide Business Opportunities for Individuals from Under-Resourced Communities

Cooperatives provide opportunities for low-wealth individuals with "few traditional opportunities to create new economic opportunities for themselves and their co-workers and neighbors."...

Entrepreneurship is promoted as a way to move people out of poverty. Entrepreneurship theory, however, cannot and does not serve as a "viable basis for systemic poverty alleviation." Individuals living in poverty are not "in a position to exploit the market the way that entrepreneurship theory demands." In contrast, focusing on the person and what is necessary to make her or him flourish may actually alleviate poverty. Cooperatives provide this link between the focus on the capability of the individual and the promise of poverty alleviation. Cooperatives provide opportunities for people without traditional access to capital to pool their resources in order to create individual and community wealth. At the same time, businesses founded by members of underresourced communities may need additional support in order to survive and thrive. A recent rise in the number of workers of color in cooperatives provides the potential for members of these communities to benefit from the cooperative business structure.

Supporting the Creation of Worker Cooperatives

... Cooperatives tend to emerge in one of four ways—as a response to an economic crisis, out of a shared desire by workers to build a better world, as business conversions, or as start-ups that were incubated.... The incubation or development model has been the most common model for cooperatives working with low-income members.

The United States Has Relatively Few Worker Cooperatives

Several factors may explain the relative lack of cooperatives in the United States. A worker-owned firm faces the pressures of any competitive business enterprise, with the "added risk to worker-owners and with stress to any underlying democratic values." In addition, cooperatives are more difficult to organize than traditional businesses. . . . On a purely economic level, cooperative ownership is seen as having higher costs of decision-making.

Financing is also more difficult for cooperatives. Cooperatives lack equal access to capital markets, and thus, the costs of capital are greater. . . .

Another possible reason for the absence of more worker cooperatives in the United States may be lack of knowledge and support for worker-owned enterprises. Business schools do not teach about cooperatives as a form of business entities. When business owners approach lawyers about creating an entity, business lawyers may not present this to clients as an option or ask the questions that may help decide whether to even present the cooperative as an option. Until recently, economic development programs did not support the development of cooperatives. . . .

Around the country, incubators provide training for future cooperative owners. These technical assistance providers have been helping entrepreneurs acquire the technical and legal assistance to form and grow worker cooperatives. At times, these incubators are stand-alone organizations providing support to cooperative owners. In other instances, the incubation support is done by an arm of a social service or business development organization. Some of these organizations began to provide technical assistance to cooperatives as part of a workforce development strategy. New York City, for example, has several cooperative incubators.

Factors Necessary for Cooperative Success

Experienced cooperative developers cite six success factors in worker cooperative development. First, successful cooperatives need education, training, and information. . . . These programs build trust and foster teamwork. . . .

Second, cooperatives need to be designed for business success. A cooperative needs to pay attention to business processes at the same time that it is investing in human development. . . . Because cooperatives have multiple business and social goals, the cooperative needs to have a "laser-like focus on how they align or detract from each other." . . .

Third, cooperatives need effective long-term support. Some critical services include "training and development of ongoing workplace participation processes; technical assistance not only for business planning but also for operations and marketing; governance support; and management services." It is not uncommon for cooperative development to take five years from feasibility analysis to the conclusion of incubation services. . . .

Fourth, patient capital is critical to the success of cooperatives. Cooperatives need investors willing to look at longer horizons, those investing for longer periods of time, and not merely looking for a quick profit. Cooperatives founded with member financing—shares or loans from members—have been found to have the greatest longevity. . . .

Fifth, successful cooperatives need strong management and social entrepreneurial leadership. Managers with cooperative experience are more likely to be successful since they are more likely to fit culturally with the model. The managers need the relationship-building capacity key to success within the model.

Finally, the cooperative needs good governance. The board needs business, cooperative, and finance experience. That might entail having outside board members who are not cooperative members in a minority of the board seats. . . .

Lawyers Supporting the Work of Developing Worker Cooperatives

. . . *Lawyers and Organizers*

Progressive lawyers have argued about the best ways to create social change. . . .

While the scholars of the "law and organizing" movement focused primarily on lawyers in the role of organizers, several lawyers and scholars have written about lawyers working with and supporting the work of organizers. Much of the work of lawyers working with organizers happens in the context of litigation, such as employment and housing. But lawyers also work with organizers in the area of community economic development, including the work of lawyers providing transactional assistance to community-based organizations. Cooperative development work takes place in this arena.

The Work of the Lawyer in the Development of the Cooperative

The technical assistance lawyers provide is an essential element of a cooperative growth system. The lawyer works with the worker-owners to decide how to structure the cooperative. This effort includes lawyers facilitating worker decisions about the type of entity to create and how to set up operations. Decisions about which type of entity to create involve questions of state corporate law as well as state and federal tax law.

Lawyers not only file the necessary forms to create the entity under state law, but may also draft the governance documents such as bylaws or operating agreements. Lawyers involved in the early stages of the cooperative development may counsel the worker-owners regarding key organizational decisions such as eligibility for membership and expulsion of members. Lawyers also may advise the worker-owners regarding the capital structure, voting procedures, and governance protocols. . . .

Collaboration Between Lawyer and Cooperative Developer

Peter Pitegoff has observed that the "lawyer role is only one part of a community-based, interdisciplinary approach to developing worker cooperatives." The lawyer working in cooperative development must therefore be willing to integrate law with other disciplines. This is particularly true for the lawyer working in low-wage sectors where the business development may require a "high-touch" form of incubation. The lawyer must be willing to work collaboratively with organizers, in addition to accountants and business consultants, to form and grow the cooperative. In writing about collaboration between lawyers, Susan Bryant observes that collaboration has the potential to maximize the experiences and knowledge each person brings to the joint work, allowing for the ideas that surface to lead to "emergent knowledge" rather than a "simple summation" of the ideas of each contributor.[35] . . .

The lawyer and developer working together will have to decide the lines of responsibility. . . . Each brings a unique perspective to the work. The lawyer understands the requirements of the statutes. The lawyer is likely in a better position to anticipate what may go wrong (risk management questions). The organizer is likely in a better position to facilitate conversations regarding the community and participatory decision-making. . . .

As Hilary Abell, a cooperative developer, writes, the relationship between the developer, the worker-owners, and the lawyer should be carefully designed, understood, and agreed to by all parties. Clear expectations about each party's role should be set in advance. Lawyers and developers should "regularly discuss and recalibrate shared goals." . . .

Lawyers and cooperative developers . . . should consider creating a memorandum of understanding. Such an agreement could spell out the responsibilities of each and the expectations for dealing with conflicts. The lawyer and cooperative developer will need to respect the other and understand the other's role and professional requirements.

Lessons for Lawyers Working with Organizers

Scott Cummings and Ingrid Eagly see three primary tensions between law and organizing. First, privileging organizing has the potential to diminish traditional law practice in the attempt to break "the spell of lawyer-driven social change." As Tammy Kim writes in discussing the triangular relationship between lawyers, organizers, and workers, devaluing legal

---

[35] Susan Bryant, Collaboration in Law Practice: A Satisfying and Productive Process for a Diverse Profession, 17 Vt. L. Rev. 459, 460 (1993).

strategies may lead to an "overly optimistic view of extralegal activism." Lawyers bring an important expertise in developing cooperatives. Appreciating that does not have to lead to devaluing the expertise of others. Organizers can respect the knowledge of lawyers at the same time that lawyers respect the expertise of organizers.

Second, Scott Cummings and Ingrid Eagly find that encouraging lawyers to serve as organizers creates role confusion. When working with cooperative developers, the lawyers are more likely to be in the role of lawyers and not be working as organizers. For lawyers one of the benefits of working with organizers is that the roles are more clearly defined. Finally, the possibility of client coercion is not reduced in the law and organizing context. Lawyers are less likely to have undue influence over the worker-owners because the organizers may serve as a counter-balance to the lawyers. As Sameer Ashar has written, it is not clear that organizers are intrinsically any less susceptible to being coercive than lawyers. The lawyer at times may have to assert the professional responsibility rules "to ensure that the workers [are] not subverted by the organizers."[36] . . .

Organizers and lawyers both have important contributions to make to the formation and development of cooperatives. The expertise of one group does not have to be privileged over the other. . . . Cooperative development requires "tripartite lawyering," with workers, lawyers, and organizers working together for a common goal. The separation and possible tension between the lawyer and organizer can serve a position function. This differentiation between the two is more likely to serve the workers because the workers are more likely to express concerns about the lawyering to the organizers, and about the organizing to the lawyers.

Conclusion: The Risk of Forgetting the Worker

Carmen Huertas-Noble has noted the dual goals that are served by cooperative development—creating meaningful jobs for the individual and "promoting collective empowerment by keeping jobs, income and profits in the community, and by serving as a space for community organizing that enables cooperative members to participate in the larger economic justice movement." Cooperative development may be "viewed not as an end in itself, but rather as a starting point for mobilizing community members around issues of economic justice." This mobilization "creates a feeling of belonging and interconnectedness, which in turn produces commitment and cooperation . . . which [may be] the greatest resource at the community's disposition." Cooperatives may create "sites for collective action," providing the organizing structure to mobilize low-income communities and connect "grassroots efforts to the larger economic justice movement." Activists for social change have relied on three questions in

---

[36] Sameer Ashar, Public Interest Lawyers and Resistance Movements, 95 Cal. L. Rev. 1879, 1919 (2007).

evaluating prospective strategies and tactics: "will it educate people . . . will it build the movement . . . [and] will it address the root problem, rather than a symptom?" Cooperatives educate the workers about collective ownership and collective processes. . . .

Cooperatives face challenges at the heart of "their ability to foster collective action for greater economic, political, and social change." . . . Relatively few worker cooperatives exist in the United States, especially those owned by vulnerable workers. Those that exist have relatively few members. Cooperative development, especially among populations of vulnerable workers, is time and resource intensive. It takes a substantial amount of time and resources to recruit and train the initial members, set up the operations, connect the cooperative to business and legal technical assistance, and provide back office support. Finally, it is not always the case that the worker cooperative trainees are primarily focused on creating systemic social and economic change. More likely, the cooperative is a way to obtain work. . . .

Alvarez emphasizes how collaboration and conflict coexist in complex actions, in this instance a community development project focused on economic development—incubating worker cooperatives as part of a larger, transnational movement. She shows how and why these cooperatives are important as a strategy for reducing poverty, especially among subordinated groups, and for enhancing democratic skills and participation, especially by and in communities of color. But she also notes that lawyers, organizers, and worker-owners have distinct roles to play in the "tripartite lawyering" necessary to successfully incubate and manage a worker cooperative. All are part of legal strategy development and decision making, all bring important expertise, and all help ensure that decisions are accountable to the worker-owners seeking to reduce poverty in their communities and income inequality more broadly.

Echoing Lobel from Part III, Alvarez points out that organizers as people and organizing as a form of extralegal activity are as susceptible as lawyers and law to cooptation, and neither are insulated from concerns about client coercion. Nevertheless, the lawyer's role is likely to be bounded in ways different than organizers. One salutary result is that "the separation and possible tension between the lawyer and organizer can serve a position function." The distinctive roles of organizers and lawyers give worker-owners varied sources of information and resources for raising and resolving concerns. Like the earlier excerpts in this chapter, Alvarez's discussion also shows how the local is linked to the global to inform complex actions: in this case, the local incubation of worker cooperatives is linked to the global movement for economic justice. And she demonstrates again that identities, groups, interests, and power infuse every context and *always* are central to complex actions.

To round out this sketch of complex actions, social movement scholars Myra Max Ferree and Silke Roth deepen a critical point about collaboration and conflict that we encountered earlier in the Guinier and Torres excerpt in Part I and the Bellow and West excerpts in Part III: advocates are more effective in collaborative and coalitional work when they use "insider tactics" *critically* to advance "outsider issues" and interests. This insider-outsider dynamic calls for advocates to serve bridge-building roles with a high degree of awareness. Bridge building is hard work that requires a dual consciousness about the professional knowledge and privilege of all team members. In practice, this work poses a perennial question: how to best use the advocate's insider credentialing or skills as outsider assets in any given context:

> Being able to be both insiders and outsiders simultaneously allows for connections among individuals and organizations that can be mobilized in particular cases.... Coalitions are facilitated to the extent that there are bridging organizations or bridge-building individuals who actively keep lines of communication open and see their own interests as overlapping territories.... Bridge building is work, and specific people need to be mobilized in the intersectional spaces to carry out the necessary framing and organizing tasks.
>
> ... Willingness to upset the status quo may also encourage coalition politics.... Avoiding [top-down] co-optation does not necessarily demand renunciation of all "insider" strategies. Instead, ... there are opportunities to raise "outsider issues" with "insider tactics."[37]

Insider-outsider tensions can become sources of conflict or can become opportunities for critical coalitions. Advocates are insiders due to their professional status and, simultaneously, outsiders when they work to "upset the status quo" supported by the legal industry to serve bottom-up interests. These tensions can be perilous if unmanaged or mismanaged. Advocates thus do well to pay attention when these (or similar) tensions begin to arise.

Even with sophisticated understandings of insider-outsider dynamics, with the cultivation of bridge-building skills and attitudes, and with early, proactive management of tensions, conflict still is likely to arise in most collaborations. When it does, remember there is no more one single best way to manage this insider-outsider reality than there is, as Sharpless noted earlier, only one "lane" or "best" role for advocates in making

---

[37] Myra Max Ferree and Silke Roth, Gender, Class, and the Interaction Between Social Movements: A Strike of West Berlin Day Care Workers, 12 Gender & Soc'y 626, 644–45 (1998).

progress. Alvarez points out that advocates can return in difficult situations to a central touchstone: keep working to support bottom-up decision-making that is democratic, principled, accountable, and pragmatic.

As a closing note in these reflections, recall Scott Cummings' account of the early 2000s Wal-Mart (now Walmart) campaign in Inglewood presented earlier in this chapter. Cummings wrote a follow-up reflection about that campaign, discussing how dissent and conflict were managed and offering some guideposts useful to advocates, organizers, and activists.

HOW LAWYERS MANAGE INTRAGROUP DISSENT
Scott L. Cummings
89 Chi.-Kent L. Rev. 547 (2014)

... In this bottom-up context, key features of the campaign were: (1) the presence of organizationally complex clients, allied in a coalition, with relatively stronger and weaker members; (2) the assembly of legal teams based on expertise, but not (necessarily) long-term commitment to an overarching (in this case, anti-Walmart) cause; and (3) the clients' formulation and execution of a discrete policy objective targeted at the local policy arena. As the case study suggests, this structure mitigates the problem of lawyer domination of clients, but potentially aggravates the problem of the more powerful and vocal client constituency (here, organized labor) disproportionately influencing the agenda setting and tactical aspects of the campaign.

On the client end, LAANE [Los Angeles Alliance for a New Economy] was a relatively powerful community organization, drawing political clout and resources from its labor affiliation, and governed by politically savvy and influential leaders. The strength and coherence of LAANE's leadership structure tended to insulate it from undue influence from outside lawyers. Because LAANE approached the lawyers as empowered political actors, the lawyering itself focused on achieving a result defined by the coalition rather than on promoting goals envisioned by the lawyers who represented them.

For their part, the lawyers who worked on the campaign approached their engagement with LAANE and the broader coalition from a perspective that mitigated concerns about client domination. For one, they were generally private sector lawyers retained by the clients to achieve a well-specified result. Their role conception, informed by their position in the market, was quite conventional. David Pettit, the small firm lawyer retained by LAANE to be part of the legal team, ... approached his ongoing relationship with LAANE from a very deferential counseling perspective, talking to its representatives about their short- and long-term objectives and basing his approach in any particular campaign on their articulated goals.

The conventional nature of the lawyer-client relationship, however, raised its own questions about how much dissenting voices were engaged in the campaign. Even within the confines of the lawyer-client relationship as constructed by the parties, the potential for conflicts was ripe. On the one hand, the coalition included representatives from LAANE and the UFCW [grocery workers union], who brought critical financial and organizational resources; on the other, the coalition contained more loosely constituted resident and faith-based groups that lent credibility and authenticity, but did not have the same decision-making clout. This created inherent questions of governance and authority to make decisions on behalf of the entire coalition—made more difficult by the fact that LAANE was also named as a separate party to the litigation and was paying for the legal representation. In one example of how this played out, civil rights groups, including the NAACP and Urban League, broke ranks with labor to support Walmart on the ground that the Inglewood community had for so long been deprived of access to a local grocery store—and the jobs that went with it.

As this suggests, the existence of multiple attorneys representing relatively powerful client groups may have mitigated the potential for client domination, but it also underscored the possible divisions between those clients and the broader "community" represented by the coalition, suggesting how difficult it is for public interest lawyers to be accountable to the community at large, rather than a particular interest group within it. Indeed, an important division revealed in the anti-Walmart campaign was between class- and race-based conceptions of community. In Inglewood, Walmart was able to drive a wedge between the labor-backed CBI [Coalition for a Better Inglewood] and traditional African American groups, like the Urban League and NAACP, which supported the Supercenter development. As a result, coalition lawyers could not claim to represent an entire working-class community of color in its fight against Walmart—but rather simply one faction within it. In this way, the lawyers could be viewed as choosing sides in an intra-community dispute in a similar fashion to the LDF desegregation lawyers criticized by Derrick Bell.

One crucial difference is that in this type of bottom-up campaign, it is the power of non-legal client groups—such as LAANE—that drives the policy choice, rather than the lawyers themselves. But this also highlights the central trade-off of the bottom-up model: As client groups take the lead in shaping and executing the policy objective, the more powerful among them wield disproportionate influence in the process of defining what constitutes the authentic "community" interest. The lawyers then facilitate the groups' exercise of power. In this sense, bottom-up strategies do not avoid accountability problems, but rather transfer the central locus of conflict from the relationship between lawyers and clients to that between clients and the broader communities they purport to represent.

. . . [One takeaway may be that] social change is difficult and complex, and that to achieve it, some dissent must give way, whether to lawyer initiative or community power. What I want to leave you with is the idea that what we should ultimately care about are the multiple and context specific ways that dissent is aired and respected in social movement environments. Lawyers, for reasons of professional role, and litigation, for reasons of technical adjudication, may do a better or worse job in managing dissent, but in judging their effectiveness we should always ask: as compared to what? That is, we should not presume that lawyers will be structurally worse managing dissent than non-lawyer movement leaders.

. . . [I]n both top-down and bottom-up lawyering contexts, whether client interests are served (and whether we should care if they are) depends on factors such as the degree and power of client organizations, whether clients pay fees (and how much), the extent to which multiple clients and client groups are involved (and how they interact), and the nature and scope of the policy reforms at stake. Yet, if we ultimately care about lawyers advancing policy claims that actually reflect the interests of the communities they purport to serve, the approach[es available]—so far as they suggest that advocacy embedded in politics deepens community ties—may be a step in the right direction, even though it is imperfect—as everything is. In this sense, I hope that they are not only stories of the challenges lawyers confront managing dissent in the post-civil rights political context, but also stories that guide the way toward deeper engagement with dissent that advances democratic social change.

Cummings' self-critical reflection distills why systemic advocates must be flexible in managing—and in using productively—tension, conflict, and reconciliation across a variety of roles, sites, and contexts including tensions arising from insider-outsider complexities. In Stage Two of systemic advocacy, this bottom line is true within both issue campaigns and CD projects: this flexibility allows a "deeper engagement with dissent that advances democratic social change" and helps advocates to stay principled and accountable while becoming more effective in practical terms, too.

In addition to flexibility, advocates, organizers, and activists are called upon to attend more deeply, creatively, and critically to the development of relationships and the formal and informal mechanisms of decision making and accountability; this is key to constructing Stage Two actions. Over time, this engagement must be calibrated—and re-calibrated—based on dual consciousness and according to evolving knowledge and circumstance. Rather than mute dissent or difference, complex actions use tension, conflict, and reconciliation affirmatively, critically, and self-critically to advance contextualized three-layered goals.

NOTES AND QUESTIONS

1. *Complex Actions, Governance, and Accountability.* Cummings notes that lawyers making policy claims should ensure this work constitutes "advocacy embedded in politics [that] deepens community ties." To embed complex advocacy actions in such politics implies creating, assessing, and adjusting decision making processes and governance mechanisms that ensure decisions are principled and accountable; these mechanisms aim to "deepen ties" with current and future members, clients, constituencies, allies, and communities to advance goals on all three layers. What have you learned from the examples in these excerpts about informal and formal decision making and governance mechanisms for complex projects and campaigns? How are client interests and broader community voices reflected in institutional governance of law school clinics, worker centers, or worker rights campaigns? Who makes decisions about the overall direction of the project or campaign? Who can be a member, board member, or staff person? What role do funders play in informal and formal decision-making processes and governance mechanisms? Who is left out of decision making, and why? If law school clinics are one sort of CD project, how is their "governance" different from that of a worker center or worker cooperative? Are community and client voices represented in decisions about the work and staffing of a clinic? If not, why not? What do forms of governance and decision making imply for the conflicts of interest or intergroup tensions that are—or are not—productively addressed within projects and campaigns?

2. *The Long Road to Critical Justice.* The postscript to the site fight Cummings described above is that Walmart forum-shopped for favorable city councils and ultimately opened its stores in the Los Angeles region. For example, it opened a supercenter in predominantly black Compton, nearby to Inglewood where the retail giant lost its battle. Local leaders touted the tax revenues and jobs created for Black workers. Was Inglewood short-sighted? What does the resurgence of Walmart in the region and its tactics suggest for systemic advocates and the use of complex actions toward Critical Justice such as issue campaigns? How does that reality complicate any measure of success of such complex actions? Moreover, the Los Angeles superstore ordinance that Cummings described in his excerpt is no longer consistent with Walmart's emerging "Amazonian" business model of opening small outposts where customers can retrieve their online orders. Here, local jobs might be displaced not by a "superstore" footprint, but by technology. How might the lessons from the Cummings and other excerpts address the complexity of these ever-changing elite techniques, which nonetheless follow the capitalist credo of profits before people? Can worker cooperatives ever match or compete with this scale?

3. *Advocacy Innovations and Next Steps.* Walmart is one of the brands targeted in transnational advocacy and organizing aiming to confront gender-

based violence and harassment (GBVH) in the workplace. Using traditional and participatory action research, Global Labor Justice and the Asia Floor Wage Alliance highlighted the widespread harassment and assaults experienced by women workers in global garment supply chains. The International Labour Organization (ILO), which carries out its work primarily through a tripartite consultation process, brings government representatives, worker organizations, and employer organizations together to address issues of concern. In this way, a new ILO Convention to end GBVH was negotiated in 2019, propelled largely by organized garment workers, international advocacy groups, and #MeToo activism.[38]

In historical terms, negotiation of an ILO Convention is just beginning and must be followed by ratification and implementation in countries around the globe.[39] People and entities in those countries play different roles in the global supply chain for garments as customers; workers and companies producing raw materials, transporting goods, or selling garments; or elected or agency officials managing trade agreements, customs, or health and safety regulations. Given this context, how would you identify U.S. stakeholders and decision makers or those elsewhere with an interest in ratifying this Convention—by the United States or by other countries? In addition to government actors and worker organizations, who else might be a stakeholder that could act as an ally and collaborate in a campaign for U.S. and global ratification? Could diasporic communities play a role? Faith groups? Anti-trafficking agencies? Non-governmental organizations focused on reproductive or racial justice? What sorts of conflicts might arise, and how might you anticipate and prepare for them? Reviewing all that you learned in Parts III and IV, what next steps might you plan to advance this work? What research and analysis might you do? How would you start?

CHAPTER RECAP

This chapter explained how Stage Two advocacy is focused on complex actions that engage systemic complexities through campaigns and community development projects. To support group struggles with these actions, advocates work in different roles and from varied sites or platforms. But organizing collective power from the bottom is always part of this work. For this reason, both collaboration and conflict must become sources of strength in every systemic context.

---

[38] International Labour Conference, Convention 190, Convention Concerning the Elimination of Violence and Harassment in the World of Work, (June 21, 2019), www.ilo.org/wcmsp5/groups/public/---ed_norm/---relconf/documents/meetingdocument/wcms_711570.pdf, and Recommendation 206, Recommendation Concerning the Elimination of Violence and Harassment in the World of Work (June 21, 2019), www.ilo.org/wcmsp5/groups/public/---ed_norm/---relconf/documents/meetingdocument/wcms_711575.pdf.

[39] See Ratifications of C190—Violence and Harassment Convention, 2019 (No. 190) listing the ratifying nations, www.ilo.org/dyn/normlex/en/f?p=NORMLEXPUB:11300:0::NO:11300:P11300_INSTRUMENT_ID:3999810:NO.

PART VI

MAPPING THE HISTORICAL ROOTS AND IDEOLOGICAL DESIGN OF LAW AS A SYSTEM

∎ ∎ ∎

CHAPTER 13

SITUATING THE CRITICAL CHALLENGE IN THE "RULE OF LAW" AS SYSTEMIC IDEOLOGY

■ ■ ■

Table of Sections

13.1 Colonial Settlers Came for Conquest, Not as Immigrants, and Created Identity Castes for Racial States
13.2 Racial States in Historical and International Context—an Admiring Perspective
13.3 Imperialism and Globalization Entrenched and Expanded White Supremacy (and Related Identity Ideologies) by Force and Law
13.4 Law-as-Identity Still Creates, Expands, and Perpetuates Colonial Castes and Ideologies

---

OPENING THOUGHTS

No one is born hating another person because of the color of his skin, or his background, or his religion. People must learn to hate.

—**Nelson Mandela**

Remember that politics, colonialism, imperialism and war . . . originate in the human brain.

—**Vilayanur S. Ramachandran,** neuroscientist

[L]egal rules, and therefore legal decisionmakers, are deeply and directly implicated both in economic globalization and in the [unequal] distribution of benefits and costs that globalization creates.

—**Chantal Thomas**, Globalization and the Reproduction of Hierarchy, 33 U.C. Davis L. Rev. 1451, 1454 (2000)

INTRODUCTION

Throughout this book we have examined how identities, groups, interests, and power produce law and its now-entrenched castes. This persistent reality contrasts sharply with the persistent proclamations of fidelity to equal justice under law. To help complete this systemic picture, this chapter examines how the modern U.S. legal system—known as the rule of law—was transplanted from Europe and how it has functioned and expanded as identity-based ideology over time to sustain the Critical Challenge.

As described in earlier parts, the rule of law has used group identities as the principal social means to dispense privilege and to target subordination since colonial settlement. Law has been used to keep tops and bottoms in place despite inevitable and unpredictable change. This core feature is law's "failure by design"—the planned failure to produce equal justice and instead maintain identity-based hierarchies serving elite interests. Understanding how law fails by design is critical to diagnose social problems and to undertake systemic advocacy that ameliorates the effects of that failure and transforms the legal system itself.

We begin this part by situating law as one among many interlocking social systems put into place around the globe through colonial settlement emanating from Europe, as we noted briefly in Part II's sketch of "the rule of law" as a systemic cousin to colonial conquest. Part II also presented the basic tenets of systems analysis, a contemporary discipline designed to help manage social complexity and, for advocates, legal indeterminacy. Perhaps most notably for systemic advocacy, this analysis holds that all human systems—including law—are judged on their actual results—their outputs. Critical history is key to systemic analysis because history supplies the record of systemic outputs from which to assess their purposes in fact, even if contrary to official declarations of good intentions. Knowing the systemic past critically helps explain the present and plan for the future. This chapter sketches the basic history of "the rule of law" as a system, transplanted from its European origins to European colonies worldwide by generations of armed conquest, occupation, and settlement. Through subsequent generations of imperialism and globalization, this original colonial framework produced, and still governs, today's unequal world.

13.1 COLONIAL SETTLERS CAME FOR CONQUEST, NOT AS IMMIGRANTS, AND CREATED IDENTITY CASTES FOR RACIAL STATES

The rule of law was put in place as a system around the world through colonial conquest. This mission of *conquest* contrasts sharply with *immigration*, in which individuals move with the intent of integrating into existing societies, not conquering or destroying them. Colonial settlers came to establish supremacist communities along European lines, not to assimilate to indigenous communities or to live peaceably in mutual co-existence. The myth that the United States is a "nation of immigrants" was created to disguise this history and to suppress or coopt social struggle. Roxanne Dunbar-Ortiz, a historian and activist, notes:

> A nation of immigrants: This is a convenient myth developed as a response to the 1960s movements against colonialism,

neocolonialism, and white supremacy. The ruling class and its brain trust offered multiculturalism, diversity, and affirmative action in response to demands for decolonization, justice, reparations, social equality, an end to imperialism, and the rewriting of history—not to be "inclusive"—but to be accurate. What emerged to replace the liberal melting pot idea and the nationalist triumphal interpretation of the "greatest country on earth and in history" was the "nation of immigrants" story.[1]

European settlers adapted or invented social identities—like "race"—to assert fundamental differences between themselves (the civilized) and others (the heathen) as the grounding for their social and legal systems. These colonial choices "racialized" the persons, groups, systems, and societies involved in that process. Colonial choice to use social identities, focused on supposed racial differences, created the original form of "identity politics"—the use of identities to structure law and society (despite contrary commitments to equal justice). In European colonialism, top-down identity politics were an elite practice to establish, justify, and entrench specific castes. Below, law and society scholar Sally Engle Merry provides an overview of colonialism and the specific yet flexible roles that law played in imposing European conceptions of difference based on social identities and related ideologies of collective superiority and inferiority. By design, the rule of law played on, and enforced with violence, top-down notions of identity, difference, and caste, functioning as the "cutting edge" of colonialism in social, political, and material terms.

LAW AND COLONIALISM
Sally Engle Merry
25 Law & Soc'y Rev. 889 (1991)

Law has been described as the cutting edge of colonialism. It was central to the "civilizing mission" of imperialism, particularly British imperialism of the nineteenth and early twentieth centuries. The introduction of Western law justified and legitimated conquest and control, particularly for the British and Americans. During the nineteenth and early twentieth centuries, British law represented to the colonizers in India and Africa a substantial advance over the "savage" customs of the colonized. Law was conceptualized . . . as "the gift we gave them."

Colonialism is an instance of a more general phenomenon of domination. Events that happened in the past, such as those in the period of colonial conquest and control, can provide insights into processes of domination and resistance in the present. The study of colonialism

---

[1] Roxanne Dunbar-Ortiz, Stop Saying This is a Nation of Immigrants!, Resisting Colonialism, Colours of Resistance Archive, www.coloursofresistance.org/334/stop-saying-this-is-a-nation-of-immigrants-2/.

describes processes of domination at the periphery of the world system. But the way European societies expanded and endeavored to dominate culturally distinct societies indicates much about the nature of European society itself and about the ways it seeks to achieve control over other societies. This review considers the role law played in the establishment of colonial control in the past and at the periphery, but in doing so, it provides insights into processes of domination in the present and in the core.

Colonialism typically involved the large-scale transfer of laws and legal institutions from one society to another, each of which had its own distinct sociocultural organization and legal culture. The result was a dual legal system: one for the colonized peoples and one for the colonizers. Dual legal systems were widespread in colonized parts of Africa, Asia, Latin America, and the Pacific. Postcolonial countries are now grappling with this legacy as they debate how to fashion a unified legal system out of this duality and how to resurrect and implement the remnants of indigenous, precolonial law.

The language of transfer and duality, however, ignores the central feature of colonialism: It was a process in which one society endeavored to rule and to transform another. The courts and police established by colonial powers, arrayed beside the mission, the school, the store, and the local government office, enforced compliance to a new political order and at the same time sought to impose a new culture. Colonial governments often promulgated regulations concerning land and labor, regulations that frequently extended to specifying conditions of marriage and divorce and patterns of dancing, drinking, and entertainment. Thus, law, along with other institutions of the colonial state, transformed conceptions of time, space, property, work, marriage, and the state. The role law played in the colonizing process is an instance of its capacity to reshape culture and consciousness.

. . . [T]he role of law in the colonial process shows that the process was highly varied in place, time, and situation. Patterns developed in one colony were often transferred to another, but the needs for land and labor varied greatly, as did the strategies of rule and the social order of the colonized and their patterns of resistance. The rich, contextualized, historical work in this field resists generalization. Nevertheless, one can discern some common themes. . . .

. . . European law was central to the colonizing process but in a curiously ambiguous way. It served to extract land from precolonial users and to create a wage labor force out of peasant and subsistence producers. Yet, at the same time, it provided a way for these groups to mobilize the ideology of the colonizers to protect lands and to resist some of the more excessive demands of the settlers for land and labor. . . . Thus, the legal arena became a place of contest among the diverse interest groups in colonial society. The contest included struggles between traditional leaders and new educated elites of the colonized population as well as colonial officials, missionaries, and settler populations. It was an unequal contest, however, in which colonial officials and settler populations exerted vastly greater power than colonized groups. The use of law in colonial processes therefore parallels other state efforts to assert control through law. . . .

The Nature of Colonialism

Colonialism has a narrow definition and a broader one, as it is commonly used. In its broader sense, it is a relation between two or more groups of unequal power in which one not only controls and rules the other but also endeavors to impose its cultural order onto the subordinate group(s). In its narrower sense, the term generally refers to the European political, economic, and cultural expansion into Latin America, Africa, Asia, and the Pacific during the last four hundred years. Although similar processes have been going on for thousands of years, it is the recent European expansion, intimately connected with the spread of capitalism and the search for land, labor, and markets, which has shaped the contemporary world. . . . [One can define] colonialism narrowly as "formal political control of a territory and population by a state, usually through some form of specialized administrative apparatus, with an ideology justifying such control." The ideology includes a definition of the dominated population as different and inferior, usually expressed in an idiom of race. Colonialism is a coercive relationship: In most cases, colonial control is initiated by military force and subordinate groups often resist with violence. In its broader meanings, colonialism has been expanded to include any situation in which a distinctive cultural group exists within a larger society or state which controls it. This situation has been labeled internal colonialism and welfare colonialism.

Colonialism, even in its narrow sense, is a highly diverse process, with great variation geographically, historically, and culturally. It encompasses vastly different geographical regions, quite different historical periods, distinctive styles of colonialism among different European nations, and extraordinary diversity in the cultures of the peoples who were colonized. Tropical areas were less likely to develop substantial settler populations than temperate regions. Metropolitan countries varied in their demands for land and labor as they moved from mercantilism to industrial capitalism, while colonies differed in their capacity to supply the requisite land and labor. For example, British imperialism in Central Africa of the late nineteenth and early twentieth century which focused on the development of mines produced very different labor relations and a different colonial society than did the sugar plantation economies of the Spanish and Portuguese emerging in the Caribbean and Brazil in the sixteenth and seventeenth centuries. Nevertheless, there are some common features to the process, particularly in more limited time periods and regions....

... The colonizers themselves often saw their project as a formidable and possibly futile task of cultural reformation. Although most colonizers were motivated by desires for power and wealth, some were humanitarians endeavoring to bring God, progress, and civilization to unappreciative peoples they thought of as fundamentally different from themselves. In late nineteenth-century British thinking, advanced peoples had an obligation to help those less advanced, to provide guidance and instruction and even to rule them. This duty was expressed in a language of trusteeship, colonial development, and modernization. Many British colonizers acted with a sense of the moral superiority of Christianity, belief in progress and civilization, commitment to an idea of white racial supremacy, and faith in the rule of law and individual rights. Nevertheless, there was constant resistance: armed insurrection, evasion, secret worlds of noncompliance....

And, of course, the colonizers did not operate in an open field. There was competition among potential colonial powers attempting to claim sovereignty. Deep divisions split early settlers and missionaries. The former were typically more concerned with transforming a precapitalist peasantry into a disciplined labor force to work on plantations and mines. The latter sometimes became involved with the problems of the native populations, serving as their spokespeople and representatives, even as they taught them that their customs of marriage and religious life were sinful and wrong. On occasion, the missionaries turned to the imperial government to protect "native" peoples from the exploitation of the settlers. Thus, the colonial situation provides a particularly vivid and stark setting in which to consider the ambiguous and contradictory part law plays in situations of domination: exerting control and establishing new forms of discipline but constraining the very forms of power that it makes possible....

Conclusions

... Law often serves as the handmaiden for processes of domination, helping to create new systems of control and regulation. At the same time, it constrains these systems and provides arenas for resistance.

... [I]n the colonial context, Western law contributed in significant ways (both obvious and subtle) to the cultural transformations accompanying colonialism and capitalist expansion. European law instituted and enforced the new relations of labor and land that undergirded the economic enterprises of the colonies. Colonial authorities fostered the transformation of oral and flexible legal systems to written codes and required the construction of bureaucratic courts with formal procedures. These new systems ... often relied on very different forms of knowledge and representation. As courts created by colonial authorities handled cases, they introduced colonized peoples to different ways of determining truth and making decisions. At the same time, they provided performances in which the experiences of colonized peoples were interpreted according to the rules and categories of metropolitan law....

... [T]he process of imposing the new legal system was complex and subject to political wrangling among various interest groups, over which the colonial government officials and local business leaders exerted disproportionate power....

... [Colonial] studies show the importance of looking at local places in terms of their cultural worlds and at changes over time as larger structures exert different pressures and provide different opportunities. Each shows the historical construction of ... Western law [by which] the subordinate group acquired a denigrated identity as "traditional," "backward," "primitive," or racially or culturally inferior. The [histories] generally reveal a contest between colonizers' visions of law and courts and that of the colonized.... Each illustrates that these struggles occur in discursive realms as well as in terms of who controls the power to judge and to punish....

... As previously subjugated members of postcolonial societies become more active in rewriting their history and culture, they are challenging these earlier modes of thinking and focusing more explicitly on power, including the power inherent in systems of meaning. Reframing the questions for the investigation of law in colonial and postcolonial societies in order to acknowledge the dynamics of domination and resistance is essential.... [D]ynamics of power under conditions of cultural difference and domination demand attention to the power of meanings and the ways these meanings become established and transformed....

Colonialism and its needs produced law—in substantive terms and as systemic architecture. Engle Merry's overview of colonialism as a global phenomenon stretching from Asia to the Americas explains also how and why the rule of law became so tightly intertwined with systemic violence. This intertwining ensured failure by design, which over the next several centuries entrenched the Critical Challenge that advocates worldwide face today.

Legal scholar Natsu Taylor Saito next examines how that process of settler colonialism unfolded specifically in the United States—perhaps the best exemplar of a successful "racial state." Racial states are designed to "employ physical force, violence, coercion, manipulation, deceit, cajoling, incentives, law(s), taxes, penalties, surveillance, military force, repressive apparatuses, ideological mechanisms, and media—in short all the means at a state's disposal—ultimately to the ends of racial rule . . . which is to say, to the ends of reproducing the racial order, and so representing for the most part the interest of the racial ruling class."[2] Saito identifies three "strategies" of colonial settlement—elimination, subjugation, and subordination-with-manipulation—that established white supremacy in relation to diverse non-white groups. Saito also notes that U.S. individuals and groups have long invoked international law to support their claims to basic human rights, but international law is afflicted by the same "tensions and contradictions between law's stated purpose and its lived realities." It is a tool, but no panacea.

This account additionally makes clear the many distinctions between settler colonialism as the foundation for a racial state and "immigration" as we know it today. This distinction leads to Saito's conclusion that, akin to other examples we have encountered, "decolonization" is context-specific, and can begin with critical histories and other kinds of analytical narrative—"the stories we live by." But it also must be reflected in constitutional and international law. Practicing these points, Saito takes account of, but aims to go beyond, law's complicity in the occupation of lands now known as the United States of America. As you read Saito's review, rethink Tsosie's discussion of epistemic injustice in Part I.

TALES OF COLOR AND COLONIALISM: RACIAL REALISM AND SETTLER COLONIAL THEORY

Natsu Taylor Saito
10 Fla. A&M U.L. Rev. 1 (2014)

. . . They came to stay. This article explores the implications of this very simple truth. Coming to stay meant occupying the land; in turn, this meant disappearing the peoples indigenous to that land. It meant making the land profitable, which required the importation of labor—voluntary and involuntary—and establishing structures for controlling that labor. It meant settlers who came with a presumption of their own sovereign prerogative. They did not come to join someone else's society; they came to establish a state over which they exercised complete control. This included determining who would be allowed to remain within the boundaries claimed by the settlers, who could enter from without those boundaries, which peoples would be accorded particular civil or political rights, and the extent to which settler privilege would be promoted and protected by the state. These relations were enshrined in the American legal system, which continues to be utilized to ensure that each person remains in his or her "place," literally and figuratively.

Indigenous peoples' lands are still occupied and the racialized hierarchy established by the early Anglo-American settlers persists.

---

[2] David Theo Goldberg, The Racial State 112 (2002).

Amending the Constitution to abolish slavery and provide formal equality changed the discourse within settler society, but did little to disrupt the fundamental premises of the settler state. Racialized injustice continues to shape the lives and limit the potential of each generation of children in this country. There is little, if any, evidence that the United States is postracial or postcolonial. A new narrative will not change these realities. However, understanding the United States as a colonial settler state explains a great deal about the apparently intractable relations of racialized privilege and subordination that characterize life in this country. As a third generation Japanese American, with immediate family members who are Black, White, and American Indian, I am particularly interested in the implications of settler colonial theory for non-Indigenous communities and write in the hope of contributing to an on-going conversation about race that will "free[ ] us to imagine" remedial options framed in the context of decolonization and self-determination. . . .

Racial Realism and Colonial Relations

. . . [The United States is best viewed as an example of "settler colonialism" rather than through] the lens of external or "classic" colonialism, as exemplified by European colonialism in Africa and Asia. . . . While the United States has maintained external colonies, it is first and foremost a settler society. In other words, the early colonists of North America came not simply to exploit its land, labor, or natural resources and then return to their "mother country," but to settle permanently and, as part of that process, to exercise sovereignty over the territories they occupied.

In the past few decades, settler colonial studies has emerged as a (sub)discipline in its own right, providing an immensely useful framework for understanding the complex relations between population subgroups in settler societies such as the United States, Canada, Australia, New Zealand, South Africa and Israel. . . .

Colonial Relations

What? Post-colonialism? Have they left? Bobbi Sykes, Aborigine Activist

Colonialism: An Overview

. . . Colonialism has taken many forms, and has been described in numerous ways. The *Oxford English Dictionary* defines a colony as "[a] settlement in a new country; a body of people who settle in a new locality, forming a community subject to or connected with their parent state."

This captures the benign way early Anglo-American settler colonists are routinely portrayed in mainstream histories. It also erases the fact that " 'forming a community' in a new land necessarily meant *unforming* or reforming [or forcibly relocating] the communities that existed there already, and involved a wide range of practices including trade, plunder, negotiation, warfare, genocide, enslavement and rebellions."

A key element of colonial ideology is its "civilizing mission," . . . [which] has been the rationale for imposing extensive administrative structures intended to eradicate the cultures, languages and histories, as well as the social, economic, legal and political structures and institutions of the colonized. This project is rendered more-or-less permanent by what [Antony] Anghie terms the "dynamic of difference," an "endless process of creating a gap between two cultures, demarcating one as 'universal' and civilized and the other as 'particular' and uncivilized." Colonial domination is justified only to the extent that "civilization" is being promoted and, thus, the colonized must be rendered perpetually inferior.

As European colonialism extended into Africa, Asia and the Americas, "race" emerged as a shifting political and social construct that incorporated the notion of more and less civilized peoples and provided markers of the "difference" relied upon by colonizing powers to justify their ventures. . . .

Thus, colonial powers could claim to be uplifting and civilizing the colonized through assimilationist measures intended to eradicate their identities, while simultaneously invoking allegedly immutable, race-based characteristics to "cap" their political, social or economic rights. . . .

Settler Colonization

. . . The settlers arrive with a presumption of sovereign entitlement, an unshakeable belief in their right to establish a state under their exclusive control. Their primary purpose is to establish a territorial base, for this is what allows them to create and control a society of their own imagining, and to generate the profits that enable them to consolidate and expand their sovereign prerogative.

Viewing the occupied lands as the site of their own reproduction, settlers see Indigenous peoples as obstacles to be overcome. Settlers . . . "are made by conquest, not just by immigration." . . .

As Indigenous peoples have been "disappeared" in various ways, settlers have turned to strategies of replacement, and what they describe as putting their newly appropriated lands and resources to "productive" use.

This requires active recruitment of a critical mass of settlers; development of a unique cultural identity; formation of independent structures of governance and social control, including but not limited to law; and maintenance of military and economic power sufficient to sustain the settlers in these endeavors. Settlers also perceive a need for labor as well as strategies to subordinate and control the labor force. While some migrants are recruited as fellow settlers, most come—voluntarily or involuntarily—to join someone else's society, on someone else's terms. They bring with them no presumption of sovereign prerogative, and this distinguishes such migrants from the settlers as well as from the peoples indigenous to the lands being occupied.

Settler states establish, maintain, and protect their hegemony by exercising virtually complete control over Indigenous peoples, non-Indigenous others, and "deviant" members of the settler class. Settlers presume a prerogative to determine who will be allowed to enter and who may—or must—remain within their claimed boundaries, which peoples will be accorded particular civil or political rights, and the extent to which settler privilege will be promoted and protected by the state. Many of these determinations are enshrined in the settler state's legal system, which is also utilized to ensure that each population subgroup remains in its assigned place, geographically, socially, economically, and politically. For all of these reasons, . . . colonial "invasion is a structure not an event."

Recasting the Narrative

. . . Narratives of origin, identity, and purpose structure social relations, identifying who belongs, their status with respect to others, and how decisions for the collective will be made and enforced. They tell us who we are, where we have come from and where we are going, what we should fear, what we should want and how we should try to get it. Our stories also shape what will be recognized as substantive justice or injustice, and define remedial options in terms of both means and ends, for . . . "[n]o set of legal institutions or prescriptions exists apart from the narratives that locate it and give it meaning."

Settler Origin Stories

Settler origin stories typically begin with their own arrival, rendering invisible the societies being replaced, or recasting them as part of the wilderness tamed by the colonists' "civilizing mission." The American history most of us were taught is such a story, generally starting with a reference to Christopher Columbus and quickly skipping to the Pilgrims and Puritans, and the "pioneers" who settled the West. The dominant narrative of U.S. history portrays the American "founding fathers" as making a decisive break with British colonialism, thus banishing colonial relations to the distant past and leaving no room for assessing the extent to which they may account for institutionalized structures of privilege and subordination. The founders' desire for democratic governance and religious freedom is emphasized, and the selectivity with which various groups were encouraged—or not—to migrate is obfuscated by the mantra that this is a "nation of immigrants."

The American origin story provides a highly sanitized version of the violence employed against, and exploitation of, Indigenous peoples, persons of African descent, and occasionally some immigrant groups, but relegates these actions to a past for which no one is today responsible.

... [The United States is characterized] as not only "the most prosperous, powerful nation on Earth," but also a beacon of freedom and democracy for the rest of the world.... Historic exclusions from political processes, as well as legalized apartheid, are noted as passing phases in the gradual extension of democratic rights to White women and people of color....

The Stories of Others

... [W]hat we perceive as apathy about struggles for equality may be a perfectly reasonable response to a story that negates meaning in our lives. But we need not be limited by the narratives that purport to define us for, ... "[i]f we change the stories we live by, quite possibly we change our lives."

Indigenous perspectives

If we acknowledge this to be a colonial settler state, we cannot ignore the fact that its land base and natural resources—its very existence, as well as its wealth and power—derive from the elimination of Indigenous peoples and the appropriation of their lands. Any narrative that ignores or glosses over this foundational reality serves to reinforce settler hegemony by entrenching the myth that this was, or might as well have been, unoccupied land....

Getting beyond these constraints involves some appreciation of what settler society has sought to erase and replace, i.e., the hundreds of nations of diverse peoples who trace their origins to this continent. It is estimated that, prior to European contact, some fifteen million people lived in what is now identified as the continental United States....

We can see that the settlers' racialized depictions of American Indians as lawless, godless, warlike and wandering "savages," were not merely the result of ignorance or prejudice—their own documentation refutes this—but provided the rationale for their seemingly contradictory claims that the lands occupied were both "vacant" and legitimately obtained by conquest. Because the settlers had no incentive to distinguish civilians from combatants in their quest for land, they waged "total war on a local scale." By 1890, when the federal government officially declared the "frontier" closed, it estimated that fewer than 250,000 Indians remained, residing on less than 3 percent of their original land base. This had been accomplished directly by military force; by purportedly "rogue" settlers who were, in fact, encouraged to occupy Indian lands; and by individuals motivated by the scalp bounties offered by local governments and "civic" organizations throughout the country. Most of the remaining Indigenous peoples had been forcibly removed from their homelands, interned en masse in unlivable conditions, and confined to alien and inhospitable reservations—processes that predictably resulted in the deaths of forty to fifty percent of those removed or interned.

Some of these realities are acknowledged in mainstream history, albeit in highly sanitized fashion, because they contribute to the perception that American Indians can safely be relegated to the past, notwithstanding their consistent resistance and lived assertion of their right to self-determination. This focus on the "vanishing Indian" has preempted acknowledgement of the equally genocidal measures implemented by the federal government following consolidation of its territorial base.... [T]hese have included the individualized allotment of reservation lands; the imposition of identity through "blood quantum" requirements; the banning of Indigenous cultural and spiritual practices; and the forced relocation of about half of all Native children, for some five generations, to boarding schools whose stated mission was to "kill the Indian, save the man" in each student....

The judiciary continues to allow this exercise of unfettered state power. Courts routinely invoke the plenary power doctrine and Chief Justice Marshall's 1831 characterization in *Cherokee Nation v. Georgia* of Indians as "domestic dependent nations." This conclusion, in turn, rests on the explicitly colonial "doctrine of discovery" and its attendant depiction of American Indians as savage or uncivilized....

At this point, American Indians have been forced off some 97% of their homelands. Even so, taking into account only those lands and resources the federal government acknowledges as Indian-owned, American Indians should be, per capita, the richest demographic group in the U.S. but they are, instead, the poorest. The U.S. government has consistently asserted a right to control Indigenous lives, lands, and resources, claiming to be acting as the "guardian" of its Indian "wards." Among other consequences, in 2005 American Indians living on or near reservations had a 49 percent unemployment rate, and 29 percent of those with jobs earned wages below poverty level. On many reservations, especially on the northern Plains, unemployment rates over 80 or even 90 percent are common. American Indian households are five times more likely than the average American household to lack complete plumbing, over three times as likely to be without complete kitchens, and more than twice as likely to be overcrowded. Among other predictable results, Indigenous peoples have the lowest life expectancies, highest infant mortality rates, highest suicide rates, and highest rates of death from exposure and communicable diseases in the United States.

After overseeing almost a decade of litigation over the federal government's mismanagement of individual Indian trust accounts, Federal District Judge Royce Lamberth concluded,

> For those harboring hope that the stories of murder, dispossession, forced marches, assimilationist policy programs, and other incidents of cultural genocide against the Indians are

merely the echoes of a horrible, bigoted government-past that has been sanitized by the good deeds of more recent history, this case serves as an appalling reminder of the evils that result when large numbers of the politically powerless are placed at the mercy of institutions engendered and controlled by a politically powerful few. . . .

Non-Indigenous Others

Standing outside the triumphalist narrative of American history allows us to grasp the significance of the African slave trade and the institution of chattel slavery in terms of the material and cultural losses systematically inflicted upon those who were, through these processes, both externally and internally colonized. It also allows us to examine the extent to which enslaved labor provided the agricultural and industrial base for settler consolidation and expansion. According to historian Howard Zinn, the early Anglo-American colonists were disinclined to agricultural labor, unable to enslave a sufficient number of Indians, and did not have enough indentured servants to meet their perceived needs. The African slave trade appeared to provide the solution, for by 1619 . . . about one million enslaved Africans had already been brought to European colonies in the Western Hemisphere. By 1800 this total had reached ten to fifteen million, the result of a process of warfare, captivity, and transportation that robbed the African continent of perhaps fifty million people.

Africans, of course, came to the Americas with rich histories of their own; they were from hundreds of different Indigenous societies, each with a distinctive culture and religious, political, and legal traditions established over millennia.

Beginning in the mid-1600s, laws were promulgated in the colonies that not only instituted perpetual, hereditary slavery, but also denied all basic political rights to persons of African descent, forbade their ownership of property, prohibited their education, limited their freedom of movement, and proscribed any means of self-defense. . . .

Thus, following the formal abolition of slavery in 1866, slave codes were replaced by "Black codes" intended to accomplish much of the same purposes. These new laws had the added benefit, from the settlers' perspective, of criminalizing much of the Black population for activities such as idleness, vagrancy, or "disrespect" of White people, while fueling a system of convict labor that served essentially the same purposes as chattel slavery, often at a lower cost to the settlers. Following the Fourteenth Amendment's granting (or imposition, depending on one's perspective) of citizenship to African Americans and its guarantee of due process and equal protection under law, racial segregation was legally mandated in many states and upheld by the Supreme Court in the 1896 case of *Plessy v. Ferguson*. And of course, in the wake of the Court's overturning of *Plessy* and Congress's passage of the Civil Rights and Voting Rights Acts of the mid-1960s, we have again seen that while formal structures of law have changed, the grim realities of life in many Black communities have not. . . .

Each community has its own narratives, of course, only a few of which can be mentioned here. . . . [For example, the] characterization of Chicanos as internally colonized and the contemporary realities of life in Mexican American communities are difficult to comprehend without a rudimentary understanding of the Anglo-American settler occupation of Texas that preceded its annexation and the 1848 war of aggression that, together, resulted in the expropriation of the northern half of Mexico.

These lands were "cleared" for settler occupation by vigilante action and by requiring Mexican residents to affirmatively prove their title claims in U.S. courts with documentation that generally did not exist in the Mexican legal system. Continuous attempts have since been made to convert Mexican communities on both sides of the border into a pool of readily available and easily disposable labor, resulting in the ongoing cycles of reliance upon and rejection of undocumented workers. The inability of the settler society to reconcile these realities with its self-perception is reflected in the recent efforts to ban Mexican American history in Arizona high schools on the premise that such courses "promote racial resentment." . . .

Finally, it is difficult to make sense of the complex and often contradictory dynamics affecting migrant communities of color without deconstructing the mantra of America as a "nation of immigrants." It is a myth that not only erases Indigenous peoples, but obscures the ways in which immigration and naturalization policy has been used to provide low-cost labor while simultaneously limiting popular imagery of "real" Americans to persons of exclusively European—preferably northern and western European—descent. Until the late nineteenth century, immigration was not perceived as a threat to settler goals because "the free global movement of labor was essential to economic development in the New World," and all people of color were precluded from U.S. citizenship. Naturalized citizenship had been limited to "free White person[s]" since 1790—a racial prerequisite that remained in place, in some form, until 1952—and people of color did not become citizens by virtue of birth . . . until 1868.

When the Chinese labor that had serviced settler society on the West Coast and built the transcontinental railroad became superfluous, the federal government implemented its first immigration restrictions. As the Supreme Court explained in the *Chinese Exclusion* cases, the settlers' sovereign prerogative gave them absolute authority to control who would be allowed to enter or remain within their claimed territorial boundaries, regardless of otherwise applicable constitutional constraints. By the 1920s, an upsurge in immigration from southern and eastern Europe had triggered a "nativist" backlash that converged with a shift toward reliance on technology rather than continued expansion of the manufacturing workforce. In response, Congress enacted its first comprehensive restrictions on immigration in 1924, imposing an annual limit on the total number of immigrants from outside the Western Hemisphere and allocating that total according to national origin quotas. These quotas, which remained in effect until 1965, excluded all peoples of color and limited European immigration in proportion to the countries of origin of the White population as of 1910.

Narratives incorporating the exclusion or exploitation of those deemed "Other" illustrate not only how the dynamic of difference has been maintained, but also how the settler class began to see itself as White and . . . converted Whiteness into a form of property. . . .

Strategies of Colonization

. . . In order to envision effective remedial measures, we need to understand not only that harm has been and continues to be done, but also how it is being done, for this is what allows us to make structural change. . . .

Strategies of Elimination

. . . Initially, Anglo-American colonists relied primarily on two of these strategies: direct killing and conceptual displacement. The concept of direct killing encompasses the deliberate introduction of disease, i.e., biological warfare; organized military force; and localized violence by the civilian settler population, including that resulting from scalp bounties. Later, less direct methods were utilized, such as the involuntary sterilization of over forty percent of Native women, and the requirement that Indian children attend boarding schools with fifty percent mortality rates.

Conceptual displacement refers to the characterization of Indigenous peoples as "pathologically mobile and 'nomadic,'" i.e., coming from somewhere else and/or nowhere in particular. This is illustrated by Justice Johnson's concurring opinion in *Cherokee Nation v. Georgia*, describing Indian "tribes" as "nothing more than wandering hordes, held together only by ties of blood and habit." . . .

Since the late 1800s, when the Indigenous population had been reduced to a small fraction of the overall polity, American policy has emphasized . . . assimilation. Ultimately, assimilation is futile, because its success is "never dependent on indigenous performance" but, instead, requires absorption by settler society. This does not happen, except in isolated instances, because the maintenance of settler privilege requires unassimilable difference. . . . Assimilationist ideology [thereby] paves the way for vilifying and criminalizing those Indigenous peoples who are either structurally prevented from assimilating or do not wish to do so. The dysfunction that is found in all impoverished, colonized, and traumatized communities is, in this case, attributed to Indians being "drunk," "lazy," "violent," or "incompetent," and is used to justify high rates of incarceration. . . .

Strategies of Subjugation: Afrodescendant Peoples

As settler societies employed strategies of elimination to claim and occupy lands, the predictable result was that the occupied lands could only be made "productive" by importing a large labor force. While it was foreseen that some of these workers would join the settler class, the bulk of this workforce had to be subordinated if the settler class was to maintain its political and economic hegemony. Thus, we begin considering the role of "non-Indigenous Others" from the premise . . . that "two distinct colonial relationships of inequality are involved here: one (the dispossession of Natives) centering on land and the other (the exploitation of immigrants) cent[e]ring on labour." In other words, "the two societies, Red and Black, were of antithetical but complementary value to White society." . . .

The strategies employed by Anglo-American settler society to subordinate enslaved Africans and their descendants—or perceived descendants—have shifted over time. . . .

The slave trade may be history's largest example of involuntary ethnic transfer, forcing Indigenous peoples off of their traditional lands and onto alien terrain. Indigenous African identities—cultural and spiritual practices, languages, histories, family ties, even names—were erased to the best of settler ability in order to facilitate control over enslaved workers, to justify their classification as property, and to enhance the credibility of settler claims to be uplifting the "uncivilized." This involved . . . the portrayal of Afrodescendant peoples as simultaneously from "somewhere else" and "nowhere in particular."

Legally, persons of African descent have been "disappeared" from settler society by denying them legal personhood, excluding them from citizenship, and limiting their agency by minutely regulating all aspects of their lives. Their intended exclusion from settler society was clearly articulated by Chief Justice Taney in his 1856 *Dred Scott* opinion, which bluntly concluded that "a negro whose ancestors were imported into this country, and sold as slaves" was most definitely not "a member of the political community formed and brought into existence by the Constitution of the United States." In fact, Taney went on, even "free negroes" were not part of "this people" and, as far as the founders were concerned, a person of African descent "had no rights which the White man was bound to respect."

The most obvious difference in the treatment of American Indian and Afrodescendant populations arises from the settlers' desire to encourage the reproduction of enslaved persons. . . . [S]ettlers instituted increasingly inclusive racial classification schemes resulting, ultimately, in the "one-drop" rule. Rather than expanding the settler class or allowing for its "dilution," the offspring of Afrodescendant persons were always to be subordinated, if not directly enslaved. In the meantime, of course, the settler class came to identify itself as White, and to define Whiteness with as much exclusivity as possible. The illogical system by which persons continue to be assigned Black or White identities in American society can thus be traced directly to settler interests.

. . . [Later,] other means of constricting rights and maintaining social control were developed to undermine the impact of the abolition of slavery. . . .

Black labor—both enslaved and nominally free—sustained the earliest Anglo-American settler colonies, provided the agricultural base that supported settler expansion, and generated the material base of American industrialization. Over the past three decades, however, manufacturing jobs have been replaced by technology and/or the outsourcing of production, making African American labor increasingly superfluous to settler goals. One result is that strategies of subjugation have shifted from those which increase the settlers' ability to extract wealth from Black labor to those of containment and control. Criminalization, of course, has again been employed to accomplish these purposes. . . .

Strategies of Subordination and Manipulation: "Voluntary" Immigrants

Peoples of color in contemporary American society who are neither indigenous to this land nor the descendants of enslaved Africans migrated to this continent for reasons that encompass the entire spectrum of volition. Given the United States' remarkably successful campaign to depict this as a "land of opportunity" for all, many undoubtedly came voluntarily, believing—accurately or not—in their ability to share in the benefits accrued by the settler class. Many others, however, have migrated under very different circumstances, from Chinese laborers literally kidnapped and forced to migrate; to Filipinos, Puerto Ricans and Pacific Islanders driven from their homelands by U.S. colonial occupation and its economic consequences; to Central American refugees, themselves Indigenous peoples, forced off their lands by U.S.-backed military governments; to those, like Mexican subsistence farmers, no longer able to feed their families as a result of global economic agreements; to refugees generated by U.S. wars, from Southeast Asia to Iraq and Afghanistan.

Some of these peoples have been subjected to the push-pull dynamics of perceived labor needs. In these cases, governmental policies have facilitated the importation of labor from, for example, China and Mexico, when otherwise available labor was inadequate to settler territorial or economic expansion, and implemented exclusionary policies in response to economic downturns. . . .

[Generally, during this process,] [t]he racialization of migrant Others [is] a strategy that has been used to subordinate peoples of color in a way that erases their particular histories and identities, replacing them with artificially constructed identities that are then used to reinforce a multi-layered racial hierarchy. . . . [Similarly, most recently] we have seen Arab Americans and persons from a wide range of countries in the Middle East, North Africa, and South Asia, collapsed into a racialized identity whose predominant feature might be described as "presumed terrorist."

Regardless of the vagaries of the taxonomy, the first and probably most important point is that all of these categories are Not-White. Functionally, this means that persons so classified are presumed not to be eligible for inclusion in the settler class. Simultaneously, however, such migrant Others are deemed Not-Black, giving them an incentive to collaborate in the maintenance of racial hierarchy. . . .

Constitutional Protection and the Dynamic of Difference

[T]he power to acquire territory . . . implies, not only the power to govern such territory, but to prescribe upon what terms the United States will receive its inhabitants, and what their status shall be in what Chief Justice Marshall termed the "American empire." Downes v. Bidwell [182 U.S. 244 (1901)]

. . . If one accepts that the United States is—still—a colonial settler state, it follows that the primary purpose of this state's legal system would be to sustain the territorial claims and the relationships of privilege and subordination that ensure control of political, economic, and social institutions by the settler class. Simultaneously, however, the legal system must shore up the ideological justifications of settler society, framed in terms of extending the "American values" of freedom, democracy, and human rights to the world at large.

Thus, the dynamic of difference characterizes not only racial attitudes and social relations, but the legal system as well. The tensions and contradictions between the law's stated purposes and its lived realities limit its utility while simultaneously providing opportunities to use this dissonance to extend the reach of formally recognized rights. . . .

Plenary Power

The first thing to note about constitutional protections is that the Supreme Court has simply decreed that they do not apply to very broad and significant sectors of the population over whom the United States asserts jurisdiction. Instead, explicitly colonial power may be exercised over American Indian nations, immigrants, and residents of unincorporated territories by the political branches of government, i.e., Congress and the

Executive branch. This is known as the plenary power doctrine, under which the Court has said the federal government can exercise plenary—full or complete, and therefore unchallengeable—authority over these peoples.

... By the 1830s, the Supreme Court had unilaterally declared Indigenous peoples to be "domestic dependent nations" whose relationship to the United States was that of a "ward" to a "guardian."

The doctrine was more formally articulated in 1903, with the Supreme Court's clearly counterfactual statement that "[p]lenary authority over the tribal relations of the Indians has been exercised by Congress from the beginning, and the power has always been deemed a political one, not subject to be controlled by the judicial department of the government."

Using this rationale, the Court upheld the 1887 Allotment Act, which converted collectively held Indian lands into individual allotments and allowed "surplus" land to be transferred to White settlers, despite the fact that the law violated both the due process clause of the Fifth Amendment and the explicit terms of an 1867 treaty. . . .

Similarly, the United States has, since 1898, exercised jurisdiction over "unincorporated territories" without extending constitutional protections to their inhabitants. From 1898 to 1946, the U.S. considered Filipinos "wards" of the United States, "nationals" who owed allegiance to the U.S. but were not entitled to the full benefits of citizenship. In 1901 Justice White declared in *Downes v. Bidwell* that the colony of Puerto Rico "was foreign to the United States in a domestic sense." This description is still accurate after a century of U.S. rule, as Puerto Ricans still have no representation in Congress, only qualified citizenship and no right to determine their own political status. . . .

... The plenary power doctrine continues to be the foundational principle of U.S. immigration law. . . .

Equal protection and due process

The plenary power doctrine thus exempts certain sectors of the population from constitutional protection. For those to whom the Constitution does apply, it is generally presumed that the guarantees of due process and equal protection provided by the Fifth and Fourteenth Amendments can be used to dismantle racial hierarchy. This proposition, however, warrants scrutiny. . . .

The problem with this narrative—like that of the Anglo-American origin story more generally—is that it fails to account for the persistent patterns of exclusion, elimination, and subordination throughout U.S. history, and the reality that racial disparities in wealth, income, housing, education, employment, access to healthcare, and incarceration rates have not diminished significantly since legalized apartheid was abolished. A brief review of key legal decisions implementing constitutional rights and legislation purporting to protect civil rights illustrates how structural inequality has been maintained.

In the *Civil Rights Cases* of 1883, the Supreme Court declared unconstitutional portions of the Civil Rights Act of 1875 prohibiting private owners of public accommodations from discriminating on the basis of race. In the Court's opinion, it was time for former slaves to "cease[ ] to be the special favorite of the laws." As observed by Mario Barnes, Erwin Chemerinsky, and Trina Jones, "Just eighteen years after the end of slavery... the Supreme Court was ready to declare that U.S. society was ostensibly post-racial." Shortly thereafter, in *Plessy v. Ferguson*, it found "separate but equal" accommodations (meaning legally mandated apartheid) to comport with the Fourteenth Amendment's guarantee of equal protection. As succinctly summarized by Justice Powell in the *Bakke* case, for all practical purposes the Equal Protection Clause had been " 'strangled in infancy."

Confronted with the constitutionality of interning U.S. citizens of Japanese descent during World War II, the Supreme Court declared laws restricting civil rights on the basis of race to be "immediately suspect," thus introducing the notion of "strict scrutiny" into American jurisprudence. Despite its claim to be rigidly scrutinizing mass incarceration on the basis of race, the Court upheld the internment, accepting at face value the government's assertion that it was necessary for national security. A decade later, in *Brown v. Board of Education,* the Supreme Court expanded the reach of the Fourteenth Amendment equal protection ... [but] characterized legalized apartheid as aberrational, noting in a companion case to *Brown* that "[c]lassifications based solely upon race must be scrutinized with particular care, *since they are contrary to our traditions* and hence constitutionally suspect." ...

As a result, the principle that law should not be used to exclude or disadvantage people on the basis of race or ethnicity has been transformed into an ahistorical proposition that does not allow for the recognition of any privilege that White people, collectively, have accrued over several centuries of institutionalized racism.... [and] from any collective legal responsibility for its consequences....

The Role of International Law

Since the founding of the United States, international law has been invoked by peoples within its borders to support their claims to basic human rights....

For the most part, these efforts have met with very limited success. This is due, in part, to the nature of the international legal system and, in part, to the United States' history of selectively exempting itself from compliance with international law. Contemporary international law is explicitly Euroderivative in origin and many of its foundational principles emerged from the attempts of colonial powers to regulate relations among themselves as they expropriated the land, labor, and natural resources of peoples they characterized as "uncivilized." . . .

The transformation [since World War II] of external colonial territories into at least nominally independent states has fueled the expansion of a body of international human rights law that affirms the right of all peoples to self-determination, acknowledges Indigenous rights, and prohibits racial discrimination. . . . While the international legal system is not, for the most part, capable of providing effective remedies for the dispossession and subjugation of peoples within settler states, international law can serve at least two important functions.

The first is that, despite being constrained by state power, international law articulates rights and remedies that go beyond those recognized within our constitutional framework. . . . [D]iscrimination, particularly on the basis of race, has been universally proscribed and the need for remedies that address structural racism has been explicitly stated. Indigenous peoples' rights, not only to survival, but also to control over their traditional lands, resources, cultures and identities are acknowledged. . . .

More significantly, international law confirms the legitimacy of struggles that go beyond asking, or pressuring, the state for more rights, or better enforcement of existing rights, to a more liberatory paradigm. It affirms human dignity as the foundational principle of all other human rights. This empowers us to challenge any regime of rights that strips individuals or communities of their dignity, reminding us . . . that as human beings we have inherent rights—and responsibilities—regardless of what we are told by those in power. Perhaps most fundamentally, international law acknowledges the right of *all peoples* to self-determination. . . .

Self-Determination

The decolonization of settler society is not something that will be imposed from above, but something that must be effectuated from below. The right to self-determination articulated in international law "is understood generally, at its core, as encompassing the idea that human beings, individually and as groups, should be in control of their own destiny, and that systems of government should be devised accordingly, and not imposed upon them by alien domination."

. . . The [UN] General Assembly's 1960 Declaration on the Granting of Independence to Colonial Countries and Peoples (Resolution 1514) "[s]olemnly proclaims the necessity of bringing to a speedy and unconditional end colonialism in all its forms and manifestations.". . .

As with any legal principle, the real debate emerges in its application.... [M]uch hinges on "whether the criteria relied upon to clarify the right to self-determination are to be determined in a top-down manner through the mechanisms of statism and geopolitics or by a bottom-up approach that exhibits the vitality and potency of emergent trends favoring the extension of democratic practices and the deepening of human rights."...

The real question [then] is what steps we will take to exercise our right to self-determination. As we consider our options, we must remain aware that in international law both substantive rights and remedial measures are framed and limited by state actors, and states have little incentive to empower internally subordinated groups or peoples they have colonized....

... Imagining the decolonization of any settler state is a daunting task, for we have no readily available models to consult. Decolonization in the classic colonial context has generally meant that the colonizers "go home" as formerly colonized territories are recognized as independent states.... In settler states we are faced with different and even more complicated circumstances because the territory at issue is considered "home" by both colonized and colonizer. What does it mean for all peoples to be self-determining under these conditions?

There are no easy answers or formulaic solutions, for decolonization is always context-specific. It cannot be legislated or decreed from above. True decolonization entails the ability of the formerly colonized to exercise their right to self-determination and, thus, is a process that must be envisioned and implemented from the ground up....

... A first step in moving beyond colonial dynamics of power and privilege is to "change the stories we live by." There are several dimensions to this process. Perhaps most obviously, we can reclaim our histories, refusing to concede to narratives that erase our identities, our lived realities and, often, even our humanity. This can happen at many levels, and can take many forms....

Over time, settlers, relying on the identity-based "dynamic of difference" that both Engle Merry and Saito describe, produced "racial states." These colonizing elites entrenched their collective dominion in and through these racial states, enforced with violence by the rule of law. They also constructed what today is called international law and the "international community." Ruling elites now are the successors in interest to original settlers, and they have continued this process from colonialism to imperialism and into globalization.

In the excerpt below, international law scholar Tayyab Mahmud shows how race and law are twin byproducts of colonialism not just in the United States but throughout the world. As Mahmud explains in considering colonization and racialization in India, "colonial rule was premised upon the exclusion of the colonized from humanity as essential to their exclusion from institutions of political sovereignty." Compare this analysis to the Franks and Steinfeld excerpts in Part II focused on similar exclusions during the U.S. founding. Recall, as you read, Saito's preceding discussion and Anghie's account in Part I of sovereignty as an international legal concept. Can you see how "the system" is being pieced together for top-down enrichment and control, both locally and globally? Can you see the design of intentional justice failures?

COLONIALISM AND MODERN CONSTRUCTIONS OF RACE: A PRELIMINARY INQUIRY
Tayyab Mahmud
53 U. Miami L. Rev. 1219 (1999)

... The Modern Grammar of Racial Difference

Modern Europe sees itself as the product of the Enlightenment, with the attending ideals of reason, freedom, liberty, equality, progress and the rule of law. Modernity of Europe is, however, coterminous with its colonial expansion and imperial rule, marked by conquest, subjugation and genocide. How were these two contradictory strands reconciled? In the answer to this question lie the roots of modern constructions of race that animate many an inter-national regime of legality and illegality.... Europe's colonial encounter is fundamental to the modern constructions of race, which facilitated the establishment and consolidation of this relationship of domination and subordination. This is not to suggest some unidirectional determinism; it is rather that "Europe was made by its imperial projects, as much as colonial encounters were shaped by conflicts within Europe itself." But while mutually constitutive of the colonizer and the colonized, colonialism is a relationship of domination and difference, with race constituted as a primary marker of difference.

... The age of colonial expansion of Europe also saw the consolidation of History—the unilinear, progressive, Eurocentric, teleological history—as the dominant mode of experiencing time and of being. In History, time overcomes space—a process whereby the geographically distant Other is supposed to, in time, become like oneself; Europe's present becomes all Others' future. Embodying the agenda of modernity, History constitutes a closure that destroys or domesticates alterity of the Other. History, as a mode of being, becomes the condition that makes modernity possible, with the nation-state posited as the agency (the subject of History) that will realize modernity. In Hegel's construction, for example, nations attain maturity only when a people are fully conscious of themselves as subjects of History, and it is only such nations which realize freedom. Those outside History, "non-nations," have no claims or rights; nations have the right to destroy non-nations and bring Enlightenment to them. History becomes a master code, the imaginary, that informs the "civilizing mission" of Europe, posited as a world-historical task.... In the name of enlightened civilization, a hierarchy of "advanced" and "backward" races was posited.... History, then, became a record of progress of superior races and, by that standard, the stagnant, backward races had no History; colonialism, as a project of bringing the backward races into the universal History, bridged Enlightenment with modern constructions of race.

While History furnished the basic contours of modern constructions of race, the notion of the rights-bearing individual posited by liberalism added content to these constructs by reconciling liberty with colonialism. Liberalism and colonialism developed alongside each other.... Liberal discourses of rights, inclusion, and equality could be reconciled with colonial policies of exclusion and discrimination by positing essential differences between different types of individuals and subjectivities.

... Those designated as being unable to exercise reason are deemed incapable of consent, and thus, they can be excluded from political constituency and governed without consent....

The modern grammar of racial difference, inaugurated by History and supplemented by liberal exclusions, had four inter-linked premises: (i) that there is an essential difference between Europeans and other races in the world; (ii) that there is a racial hierarchy with the European at the top, followed by Asians, African and aboriginals, in a descending order; (iii) that Europe, being the subject of History, had the right, nay the duty, to govern other races, to impregnate them with reason, progress and the rule of law; and (iv) that the salvation of lesser races rested in subjugation by Europe, to aspire to Europe's present as their future, this being the only path to enter History.

The Rule of Colonial Difference & the Construction of Race

... Colonialism is absolute government, founded, not on consent, but on conquest.... The universalist claims of modernity floundered in the colony; the rule of law yielded to "the rule of difference," a rule whereby, across differently inflected positions within colonial discursive and institutional practices, the colonized are represented as inferior, as radically Other. Race, constituted as the defining signifier of the difference between the colonizer and the native, reconciled Europe's "civilizing mission" with violence of colonialism. Construction of racial difference ensured that in the colony, the promise of modernizing transition from the "rule of force" to the "rule of law" was most pronounced in its breach, and the Enlightenment's developmental march to reason and freedom did not materialize....

Colonial Power/Knowledge and the Legible Colonized Body

The high noon of British rule in India coincided with the zenith of racial theories in Europe. In vogue were assertions like "[r]ace is everything: literature, science, art—in a word, civilization, depends upon it," and that "[a]ll is race; there is no other truth." It was in the context of Europe's colonial expansion that modern disciplines of geography, anthropology, history, and literature developed to make the expanding world intelligible and manageable. "Scientific racism," which dominated European thought, saw itself as based on " 'science,' the body of knowledge rationally derived from empirical observation, then supported the proposition that race was one of the principal determinants of attitudes, endowments, capabilities and inherent tendencies among human beings. Race, thus, seemed to determine the course of human history." The premise was that each person literally embodied his racial and cultural identity, and that bodies were legible. The goal of colonial sciences was to discover the origins and patterns of the behavior of natives. The key to this knowledge was seen in the study of actual physical characteristics. This mapping of culture within physiology perfectly suited the colonizers' drive to erect a framework of categories which allowed them to understand India in terms of a hierarchy of races/castes/tribes/nations which had discernible features and definable limits, and to catalogue material evidence of behavior patterns and political loyalties. The result was the establishment of a framework for the inspection of natives' bodies, thereby bringing to bear the force of [European] knowledge/power upon them. The colonizer was the subject of this knowledge production; the native only the object who furnished the body on which colonial power was to be inscribed. . . .

Racializing the Colonized: Malleable Classifications & Slippage

. . . The problem is compounded by "chronocentrism" or "presentism," namely, the tendency to interpret other historical periods in terms of concepts, values and understandings of the present. Competing and conflicting modern theories of race make for differing ways in which the concept is used in specific contexts. This elasticity lent by the very vagueness of the concept may well have made for its tenacity. Nowhere was this inchoate nature of the modern concept of race more evident than in colonial India, where it was used to describe a variety of religious, caste, tribal, national and ethnic identities. The end product of racial knowledge-production was racial stereotypes that were always unstable, contingent and malleable, always available to be turned on their head, depending upon who was using them and for what purpose.

Inhabitants of India display a kaleidoscopic diversity of physical attributes, combined with an almost endless variety of languages, religious beliefs, cultural practices, historical memories, and social orders spread over a continental geographical expanse. For the double binary of fair/dark and civilized/savage, India presented an enigma because of its intermediate location, both in the scale of civilization . . . and for the variety of complexions lying between the extremes of the scale of physical types defined by race science. This heterogeneity precluded normalization of the colonized through any single analytical model, or any simple binary application of the grammar of racial difference. The master discourse of racial difference, then, could be maintained only by introducing other analytical categories and classification schemes, while reading race into these. The colonial response was to construct categories of caste, tribe, nation and communal/religious groups, to read race into them, and to locate them within the hierarchical order of History. Often categories of race, caste, tribe, nation, language, and religion were conflated and even used interchangeably. The result was a contextual construction of race, remarkable for its contingency, plasticity, and malleability. The structure of this construction involved: (i) slippage of classificatory categories, whereby "race," "caste," "tribe," "stock," and "nation," were used interchangeably; (ii) racialization of the constructs, whereby all these categories were posited as being essentially biological and hereditary, questions of blood and descent; (iii) a two-tier scheme of racial hierarchy, under which while all natives were deemed racially inferior to the colonizers' race, racialized hierarchies were posited among the colonized; and (iv) legitimization of colonialism, whereby colonial rule was seen as diffusing progressive attributes of the colonizers' race in order to save the native from the degradation induced by his own race. . . .

In the colonial construction of race within the framework of the modern grammar of racial difference, one discerns "the general epistemic violence of imperialism. . . ." . . . This violence was then deployed in specific sites of colonial governance and thereby lent itself to the violence of law, both "the founding violence, the one that institutes and positions law . . . and the violence that conserves, the one that maintains, confirms, insures the permanence and enforceability of law." . . .

The Meek Hindu: Cheaper Than a Slave

Colonialism started integrating India into the modern global system of production and accumulation. As part of this process, starting in the eighteenth century, Indian labor was deployed in Europe's other colonies. The varied institutional forms of this deployment included slavery, penal transportation, and indentured labor. Between 1834 and 1937, 30 million Indians left India as part of the global division of labor, and just under 24 million returned. Most of this migration formed part of the "coolie system" that came into existence in the early nineteenth century, under which Asian labor, primarily from India and China, was deployed in Africa, the Caribbean, Southeast Asia and the South Pacific. Part of this migration was indentured labor: 1.5 million Indians went overseas as indentured labor between 1834 and 1920. The abolition of slavery in the European colonies in early 19th century created a labor crisis in plantation colonies by disturbing the critical ratio between abundant land and cheap labor. The perceived need for "a new system of slavery," was met by importing laborers from India whose "cost [was] not one-half that of a slave." The early consensus was that the planters had found in the meek Hindu a ready substitution for the Negro slave he had lost. Besides providing cheap labor, the Indian workers were to be the medium through which planters expected to reassert control and discipline over the emancipated slaves. The unfolding of this stratagem was accompanied by enabling constructions of racialized identities of African and Indian labor.

Racialized disparaging portrayals of African labor became orthodoxy: Africans were portrayed as lazy, unreliable, untruthful, and unable or unwilling to understand or honor a contract. Set off against these portrayals, a racialized identity of Indian labor was posited, using overlapping categories of race, caste, tribe, stock and nation. Indians were extolled for their docility, industriousness, familiarity with agriculture, strong family ties, respect for authority, and respect for the sanctity of contract. These constructions, however, did not last very long. Once Indians were on the plantations and had adopted strategies of self-preservation and resistance, planters' praises were leavened with distaste and dissatisfaction. Indians, they now observed, were avaricious, jealous and less robust, not to mention dishonest, idolatrous, and filthy. As dissatisfaction with Indians spread among the planters, and as they began looking into opportunities to recruit workers from China, the Indians came to be increasingly and unfavorably compared with the Chinese. Now the Chinese were held out as " 'fully alive to the necessity of authority for their regulation and control . . . generally tractable and manageable,' strong, tough, 'not averse to foreigners.' " . . . Both of the contradictory identities of Indian labor were produced in the context of a hierarchical racial division of labor, under which the European planters, African ex-slaves, Indian indentured and Chinese coolies were constituted in relation to each other. Furthermore, the assigned identity attributes were posited as essential, immutable, and fixed products of biological determinism.

The racialized identity formation of Indian indentured labor had a number of implications. . . . The indenture system played a crucial role in forging an Indian identity and the development of Indian nationalism. Labor transported from India became "Indian" in the context of its being sandwiched between European colonizers and the natives. In pre-colonial India, identities coalesced around religious, caste, ethnic, linguistic and regional differences. In the indenture system, heterogeneous labor drawn from India found itself similarly positioned by this regime of colonial economy. Institutional and discursive practices accompanying indenture constituted this heterogeneity as a singularity. Differences were downplayed by the indentured as they forged a collective identity in resistance to a shared experience. Indian identity, thus, became a field of possibility through suppression of internal difference, occasioned by similarities of conditions created by the colonial regime of indentured labor. Not surprisingly, the indenture system furnished the first sustained target for the nationalist movement during its embryonic phase.

This story of Indian indentured labor raises many questions of contemporary relevance. To what extent does the global labor market in the phase of much heralded globalization remain racialized? Can we locate race in legal regimes and normative conventions that juxtapose unbridled mobility of capital with relative immobility of labor? How are inter-racial and inter-ethnic conflicts in the post-colonial societies rooted in colonial strategies of divide and rule? . . .

Race-Nation & Its Discontents

There is a general consensus that modern nationalism is "a doctrine invented in Europe at the beginning of the nineteenth century," and in its global reach, "an importation from Europe clearly branded with the mark of its origin." . . . [The] discourse of race played a central role in myths of national origin. Because nations were identified as naturally occurring groups identifiable by cultural difference, it was logically possible to assert that these symbols of nation were themselves grounded in race, that "blood or race is the basis of nationality, and that it exists externally and carries with it an unchangeable inheritance." . . . In nineteenth century Europe, a virtual blurring of distinctions between race and nation was the result.

In the colonies, the European idea of race-nation often combined with Social Darwinism to deny nationhood and self-determination to the colonized. In colonial India, colonial constructions of the colonized, where categories of race, caste, tribe, nation, and religion were used interchangeably, were deployed to thwart nationalist aspirations. The racial undertones of these constructions were highlighted to show up multiple divisions that were held to deny Indians the status of one people/"volk"/nation, founded upon common "stock," and hence to deny them the political rights that accrue to nations. . . .

Where the colonizer had used the circular discourse of evolutionary Social Darwinism—race, nation, History—to deny Indian nationhood, the nationalist project in its formative phase recuperated the three terms into systematic nationalist doctrines. Where the racialized notions of "India," "Hindu," and "Aryan," were homogenizing and essentializing devices useful for colonial definition of what they ruled, for the nationalists, these became useful to claim a broad domain that their cultural knowledge qualified them to govern. . . .

Conclusion

In the modern world, the universalist promise of freedom and equality has often floundered when confronted with difference—gender, class, sexuality, and race being the salient sites of this confrontation. By uncovering how difference is constituted to reconcile the professed promise with practiced denial of freedom and equality, we may be better positioned to participate in struggles to secure these cherished goals. To the extent that colonialism furnished particular sites for modern constructions of difference, those struggling to achieve freedom and equality will ignore lessons of colonialism at their own peril. . . .

Mahmud's recounting of race and racialization *by law* as integral to colonization illustrates that settler colonialism spanned the world. Colonialism, as he shows, rewrote foundational concepts and the ground rules of societies. He concludes with a bottom line—of ignoring lessons of colonialism at one's peril—that provides a point of departure for systemic advocacy today. To understand and combat entrenched legacies, advocates learn from, rather than ignore, the critical lessons of systemic histories.

In the United States and elsewhere, the colonial constitution, as amended, purports to be the express U.S. social contract. It is, formally. But the simultaneous use of social identities based on the cross-linking of property, race, and sex also created a "racial contract" that in practice overrides the seemingly equal and neutral text of the social contract.[3] Journalist Adam Brewer aptly described this systemic arrangement in a recent report on the disproportionate impact of the COVID-19 pandemic on specific U.S. groups: blue collar workers, impoverished people, and Black and Latinx communities. Even that global pandemic tracks colonial identity castes. Brewer explained that:

> If the social contract is the implicit agreement amoung members of a society to follow the rules—for example, acting lawfully, adhering to the results of elections, and contesting the agreed-upon rules by nonviolent means—then the racial contract is a codicil rendered in invisible ink, one stating that the rules as written do not apply to nonwhite people in the same way. The Declaration of Independence states that all men are created equal; the racial contract limits this to white men with property. The law states murder is illegal; the racial contract says it's fine for white people to chase and murder black people if they have decided that those black people scare them.

---

[3] Charles W. Mills, The Racial Contract (1997).

> . . . As long as it is invisible, members of a society can proceed as though the provisions of the social contract apply equally to everyone. But when an injustice pushes the racial contract into the open, it forces people to choose whether to embrace, contest, or deny its existence. Video evidence of unjustified shootings of black people is so jarring in part because it exposes the terms of the racial contract so vividly. But . . . the racial contract most often operates unnoticed, relying on Americans who have an implicit understanding of who is bound by the rules, and who is exempt from them.[4]

Colonialism thus began the entrenchment process of racial states run on racial (and other identity) contracts that, by design, contravene the rules, norms, and values they purport to uphold. Later, imperialism and globalization continued this process of colonial entrenchment and elite enrichment. The use of the racial contract to violate the social contract systemically results in failure by design and reproduces the Critical Challenge of using law for justice even today.

NOTES AND QUESTIONS

1. *Race as a Social Construction.* Saito described how settlers used the dynamic of difference to construct racial identities for elite ends. Race is a complex subject. Despite the insights gained from Saito, Mahmud, and others in understanding race as a social construction (as opposed to a biological and natural fact), are there are negative sides to that analysis? Is race, when seen properly as a social construction, always used for the ordering of some group or groups in harmful ways? Can race ever be a positive construct without the need to oppress some other group(s)? Among others, recall here the lessons of Chang and Gott in Part II.

2. *Racial Evolution.* After being a key target of the restrictive 1924 National Origins Act, certain European immigrant groups once deemed of inferior racial stock, such as the Irish and Italians, who arrived long after the settlers emplaced the systems seen above, gradually "whitened" over time in the eyes of the U.S. public and policymakers. Critical scholars see this expansion of the "top" as lending additional force to the critical knowledge that race is socially constructed. Recall also the example from Part II of the "conditional inclusion" of Jewish immigrants in notions of whiteness. In the immigration context, Mexican and Central American immigrants today are the face of undocumented and unwanted U.S. immigration. Are these immigrants generally seen and portrayed today as white? If not, do the same opportunities exist for their image as a group to "whiten" over time (like the Irish or Italians) and for them to no longer be seen as posing a threat to U.S. culture and economic prosperity?

---

[4] Adam Brewer, The Coronavirus Was an Emergency Until Trump Found Out Who was Dying, The Atlantic, (May 8, 2020).

3. *Race—and Racialization—Matter.* As Saito notes, narratives taught about U.S. history obscure how race as a social construct was created and used to support settler erasure and subordination of indigenous and non-indigenous "Others." Given that few advocates are exposed to critical histories of racialization about the identity groups to which they belong and other groups, how have advocacy groups taken on the challenge of changing "the stories we live by"? The Shriver Center on Poverty Law provides one example of a decolonization project in action:

> America has a long and sordid history of racism. Despite progress made during the Civil Rights Movement and the enactment of civil rights protections affecting housing, education, and voting rights, we still live in a country in which persistent and deep racial inequality is the rule, not the exception.
>
> One network of advocates is taking on these issues with an innovative set of approaches. Over the last four years, the Shriver Center's Racial Justice Training Institute (RJTI) has equipped over 160 advocates from 26 states and more than 60 organizations to address race equity as an integral and essential part of anti-poverty advocacy. These advocates, now members of the RJTI Network, are using a racial justice lens and other tools and strategies to take on their communities' unique issues and to create systemic change."[5]

What do you think that advocates should study—beyond the traditional course offerings and continuing legal education topics—to understand law as a racialized colonial system?

13.2 RACIAL STATES IN HISTORICAL AND INTERNATIONAL CONTEXT— AN ADMIRING PERSPECTIVE

Joseph Goebbels' Big Lie strategy, first put into action when he was appointed Propaganda Minister of the German Third Reich, is now commonly recognized (and used by elites) as such worldwide. Most likely, he would be very proud, as emulation is said to be the highest form of praise. But, even if not widely known, history also records another instance of very focused emulation (and admiration) linking the U.S. and German systems (at least during the past century or so): specifically, how the leading architects of Nazi race law used state-enforced U.S. white supremacy as a blueprint for state-enforced Aryan supremacy in Germany.[6] Both the United States and the Third Reich tied citizenship status to social identities by law (U.S. Blacks and Jewish people in Nazi

---

[5] Janerick Holmes, How Advocates in the Deep South Are Putting Race Front and Center of Anti-Poverty Advocacy, The Shriver Brief (Nov. 7, 2017), www.theshriverbrief.org/how-advocates-in-the-deep-south-are-putting-race-front-and-center-of-anti-poverty-advocacy-46c761fe5b9f.

[6] These systemic connections are documented extensively in James Q. Whitman, Hitler's American Model (2017), upon which this synopsis is chiefly based.

Germany, plus additional "others" in both places). Both made identity-based citizenship the red line for access to legal, social, and economic privileges ranging from voting to employment. In both, citizenship functioned as a manipulated proxy for identity-based, formally democratic, and sometimes facially neutral minority rule: "It was the American criminalization of racially mixed marriage that was the forerunner to the [German] Blood Law. It was the American conquest of the West that Nazis invoked so often in the murderous campaigns of the 1940s. . . . [W]hen the Nazis set out to build a racist order, they turned to America first" in search of the best legal models.[7]

To many Nazis, their policies were consequently as legitimate as those of their U.S. model; after all, they arose from the same moral framework of legalized group supremacy based on social identities. Plus, as Part II showed with 1927's *Buck v. Bell* decision, the then-new "science" of eugenics provided a pseudo-framework for legalized group violence in both the United States and Nazi Germany. By the early twentieth century—only half a century after the Civil War—the United States had embraced imperialism (and later globalization) to make itself the world's most enduring racial state devoted specifically to perpetual white supremacy. Nazi analysis regarded the 1930s U.S. as the "forefront" in creating "a conscious unity of the white race" globally.[8] From the Nazi perspective, the United States and the Third Reich were the natural twin pillars and pioneers of white, Nordic, or Aryan nationhood that were destined (jointly if possible) to globalize white supremacy. Not coincidentally, "master race" in German is the linguistic cousin to "white supremacy" in English. "Nordic" blood bound the two and their destinies. The bottom line is: "when the leading Nazi jurists assembled in June 1934 to debate how to institutionalize racism in the new Third Reich, they began by asking how the Americans did it."[9]

As a first step, they meticulously and comprehensively compiled, state by state, all U.S. race laws and organized them into a handbook used widely by Nazi officials in charge of race policy. They debated how various American approaches to defining a "Black" or "colored" person could help them decide how to define Jewish people, as well as "mongrels" and other undesirables, like the "feeble-minded." During this years-long process, Nazi scholars, lawyers, judges, and policy-makers openly marveled at U.S. ingenuity in coordinating rules across various fields of national law, like constitutional law and immigration or citizenship rules, to be mutually reinforcing in maintaining white supremacy as national policy. Through these measures, the Nazis concluded, the United States used law to create and enforce a "political construction of race" designed to "depress the

---

[7] *Id.* at 140.
[8] *Id.* at 94.
[9] *Id.* at 113.

political influence of the Negroes to a minimum" while simultaneously privileging whites. The U.S. example proved that expanding *and* "protecting" the border was foundational to preserving racial purity and white supremacy. To Nazi leaders, this system was all the more "astonishing" because the United States oftentimes is cast, and proclaims itself, as the cutting edge of equality and justice.

In the end, the Nazis focused on three areas of U.S. law, *both local and national*: immigration laws, to expel or exclude the disfavored; criminal (or Jim Crow) laws, to prohibit, punish, and hopefully prevent favored and disfavored groups from "mixing;" and citizenship law, to create tiers of legal status that legalized discrimination in everyday life. Adapting state *and* federal elements of U.S. law to their own purposes, the Nazis started using all three areas, as reflected in the Nuremberg Laws of 1935 (on Citizenship, Blood, and Honor)—considered the legal and moral foundations of Hitler's regime. Tellingly, within Nazi circles, the most ardent Nazis were also the most ardent admirers, proponents, and emulators of racist U.S. concepts and techniques.

However, from the official Nazi perspective, the perfection of the racial state remained incomplete on both sides of the Atlantic; to them, either Germany or the United States must and would complete this historical task, preferably as allies. The careful Nazi assessment of the United States as the leading global racial state inadvertently but sharply demonstrates the Critical Challenge of using law for justice in the United States (and elsewhere). The local-global struggle over racial rule continues to this day.

13.3 IMPERIALISM AND GLOBALIZATION ENTRENCHED AND EXPANDED WHITE SUPREMACY (AND RELATED IDENTITY IDEOLOGIES) BY FORCE AND LAW

Colonialism set in place the basic contours of the rule of law as a system in the United States and other colonies around the world. It established new foundational concepts and ground rules. That system both promised a change from the "rule of force," as Mahmud noted, and established—but obscured and justified—group castes based on racial contracts enforced by racial states. Subsequent eras of imperialism and globalization preserved this basic design.

While the dominant colonizing nations of Europe sent settlers forth and riches back, land-owning feudal elites evolved into industrial and capitalist elites. Simultaneously, newly propertied "leading men" of the colonial era firmed up their hold on colonies across the world. They formed local-regional-transnational networks and institutions designed to entrench them and their successors collectively as global elites. Both old and new European elites continued to dominate societies through subsequent and overlapping eras: imperialism and globalization. Nevertheless, none of the inequalities of colonization, imperialism, or globalization was put into place or enforced without ongoing resistance "from below."

In this historical scheme, imperialism generally refers to the adaptation and extension of colonialism. Imperialism achieves control not through settlement so much as through direct or indirect control of territory, resources, and peoples. Imperialism makes extraction of wealth its first priority, rather than occupation of territory. Imperial conquest sometimes involves "puppet" regimes. During imperial conquest, elites intent on enrichment exercised brute force and used formal law to acquire direct control over a land and its people; alternatively, imperial elites used political and economic influence to achieve effective control of other lands, peoples, and resources in territories they did not formally acquire or occupy. Imperialism is thus both an extension and a refinement of colonialism.

The first formal expression of imperialism as U.S. policy may be the Monroe Doctrine of 1823. This doctrine declared a special "sphere of influence" for the United States across the hemisphere but did not contemplate a hemispheric occupation: U.S. President James Monroe declared this entire hemisphere off limits to European intermeddling and proclaimed the Americas "henceforth not to be considered as subjects for future colonization by any European powers."[10] This proclamation was the political expression of Chief Justice John Marshall's judicial protection (in *M'Intosh* among other opinions) of the "American empire." Through proclamation and doctrine, entrenched settler elites in the United States—itself a former European colony—claimed for themselves the colonial prerogatives of European elites.

But even before the Monroe Doctrine, American expansionism had conquered tribal nations, either exterminating or confining indigenous peoples to U.S.-selected "reservations" in unfamiliar, undesireable, unproductive, and remote locations Thus, the hemispheric reach of Monroe's doctrine also served as reinforcement for the concurrent assertion of Manifest Destiny to legitimize U.S. conquest of yet other continental lands and peoples to exploit—mainly the Southwestern regions of the current United States, including Texas, California, New Mexico, and Arizona. Generally, this period of conquest intensified in the mid-to-late 1800s, with unprovoked U.S. wars not only against Mexico in 1846, but also Spain in 1898. In both imperial adventures, U.S. ambitions were to annex, control, and exploit lands spanning the entire globe. As legal scholar Steven Bender explains with regard to the 1846 start of the U.S.-Mexican War in what is now Texas, that conflict was manufactured by encroaching

---

[10] https://www.loc.gov/rr/program/bib/ourdocs/monroe.html.

settler elites to preserve (and expand) the U.S. racial state and its slave-owning economy:

> [P]rotection of the slave economy and culture, and . . . disdain for Mexican ownership and control of the area's natural resources, . . . [best explain] our territorial acquisitions from Mexico by force. In brief, slavery figured into the three main events that transferred control of the Tejas/Texas region to the United States—the Anglo slave-owning immigrants' decision [as settler elites] to forcibly secede from Mexico and form the independent Republic of Texas, the agreement of the United States to annex the Republic as the 28th state, and the U.S. imperative to fix the Texas border at the Rio Grande by military force. . . .
>
> . . . These same views propelled the Manifest Destiny of U.S. territorial and economic expansion [across the rest of Mexico-controlled lands in the Southwest to the Pacific Ocean]. . . . Addressing California's terrain, [a U.S. newspaper] remarked that under Mexican control, the land was "doomed to desolation and a barren waste, instead of the garden of the world" . . . "devoted to the uses [for] which nature and nature's God designed it."[11]

This territorial acquisition took every tool in the elite toolbox—spanning military force, formal government action to annex territory and confer statehood, private violence whether organized (as in the forcible secession by slaveowning settlers), individual (as when gold rush pioneers flooding California forcibly squatted on land still owned by Mexicans and ostensibly protected by the Treaty of Guadalupe Hidalgo that ended the U.S.-Mexican War in 1848), and mob violence (through lynchings and intimidation to enforce the land takeover by squatters). Although military force ended with U.S. control of the region, it took Congress and the courts to oust Mexican landowners one-by-one, and as a group, from the most desirable parcels, accomplished by requiring landowners to "prove" their land title in the U.S. court system—conducted in English and subject to standards that by design meant most owner claims failed. Being land-rich but cash-poor, most Mexican landowners were forced to rely on English-speaking lawyers, who took a healthy part of the land as their fee if successful in confirming title, and then sometimes forcing a judicial partition sale of the entire parcel in which the lawyer with cash reserves could end up the owner.[12]

---

[11] Steven W. Bender, How the West Was Juan: Reimagining the U.S.-Mexico Border (2017).

[12] See Steven W. Bender, Tierra y Libertad: Land, Liberty, and Latino Housing ch. 2 (2010) (detailing the public and private mechanics of land dispossession in the U.S. Southwest, and implicating the Supreme Court that ignored Spanish-Mexican law and custom and awarded to the U.S. government vast acreage in New Mexico owned communally by Spanish-Mexican land grant recipients); Kim David Chanbonpin, How the Border Crossed Us: Filling the Gap between Plume v. Seward and the Dispossession of Mexican Landowners in California after 1848, 52 Clev. St. L. Rev. 297 (2005).

The upshot was that Mexicans were "all but wiped out as a landholding class in the southwestern United States ... [setting] the stage for a new chapter in U.S.-Mexico relations: the exploitation of low-wage, migratory Mexican and Mexican-American labor."[13]

After the U.S. expanded its reach from "sea to shining sea," the Monroe Doctrine asserted imperial prerogatives hemispherically. Imperialism literally created a new global American empire after it took Spain's former colonies (such as Puerto Rico and the Philippines) as war booty. This empire rested on brute force but was couched in legal fictions. These doctrines or proclamations were expanded by subsequent similar assertions of the prerogative to dominate, including the Open Door policy (against China), the Big Stick policy (throughout the hemisphere), and Dollar Diplomacy (globally). In his annual message of 1904, U.S. President Theodore Roosevelt declared, "Chronic wrongdoing, or an impotence which results in a general loosening of the ties of civilized society, may in America, as elsewhere, ultimately require intervention by some civilized nation, and in the Western Hemisphere ... the Monroe Doctrine may force the United States ... to the exercise of an international police power."[14] This "international police power" depended on Roosevelt's "big stick"—raw power, usually military.

During this period of imperial expansion and extraction, U.S. elites were spectacularly successful. Within a few decades—and especially between 1898 and the start of World War I—U.S. imperial adventures rebounded from Hawai'i, Guam, Samoa, China, and the Philippines to Colombia-Panama, Cuba, Haiti, Dominican Republic, Honduras, Nicaragua, and Puerto Rico, among others. U.S. elites sometimes annexed (like Hawai'i), other times created formal colonies (as with the Philippines and Puerto Rico), and yet other times created protectorates (as in Cuba). Through imperialism, "the United States rounded out its boundaries ... [and] took up a share of the 'White Man's burden' wherever it proved profitable to the white man."[15] As shown earlier in Part II, this expansion is what John Marshall had sought to propel through law in the name of the "American empire."

Political scientist Charles Venator Santiago describes how the legal history of Puerto Rico since 1899—its "ambiguous juridico-politico status"—exemplifies law's role in facilitating imperialist economic exploitation and extraction using a "dynamic of difference" rooted in colonial identity castes:

---

[13] Christopher David Ruiz Cameron, One Hundred Fifty Years of Solitude: Reflections on the End of the History Academy's Dominance of Scholarship on the Treaty of Guadalupe Hidalgo, 5 Sw. J.L. & Trade in the Americas 83, 97–98 (1998).

[14] Scott Nearing and Joseph Freeman, Dollar Diplomacy 261–62 (1925).

[15] Rubin Francis Weston, Racism in U.S. Imperialism 6–7 (1972).

> [T]he ... territorial possession was acquired as war booty, subsequently governed with a civil government that normalized a martial ideology, and has since remained in a perpetual state of juridical and political exception. . . .
>
> ... [T]he Supreme Court would begin to institutionalize the anomalies created by [early] ... laws and decrees in a series of decisions generally known as the *Insular Cases* . . . dating from 1901 to 1922.
>
> [According to the Court in *Downes v. Bidwell,* 1901,] Puerto Rico could be treated as a foreign country for constitutional purposes, while simultaneously remaining under the sovereign power of the [United States]. This argument would in turn affirm the juridical logic established by Congress that enabled the treatment of Puerto Rico as a state of exception where the parts of the Constitution need not apply. . . .
>
> ... In other words, under the logic of *Downes*, Congressional plenary powers could claim a legal power that was outside the limits of the Constitution. . . .
>
> ... This logic has permitted the Sovereign to extend or suspend the extension of constitutional rights and protections to Puerto Rico and the U.S. citizens residing in the island. It follows, that Puerto Rico can become foreign for constitutional purposes, yet domestic for political interests whenever it is convenient for the Sovereign[,] ... [creating a] distinct form of imperialism that does not rely on a colonist narrative. . . .
>
> ... More importantly, [then,] the case of Puerto Rico provides a clear example of the anti-democratic policies and practices that continue to define the contours of U.S. politics today.[16]

Venator Santiago shows how imperialism used and adapted the doctrinal architecture engineered by earlier elites for colonialism. Through imperialism, elites both consolidated *and* expanded their reach, power, and dominance. Though not identical, colonialism and imperialism served the same collectivized systemic purposes, both material and symbolic.

During this same time period, domestic white U.S. elites in the north and south were effecting a new post-Civil War reconciliation designed to unleash the industrial revolution and develop a nationalized economy with the coming of the railroads. This period overlaps with, and was enabled by, the ending of Reconstruction after the U.S. Civil War through judicial

---

[16] Charles R. Venator Santiago, From the Insular Cases to Camp X-Ray, 39 Studies in Law, Politics and Society 15 (2006).

rulings like *Plessy v. Ferguson* (upholding racial segregation in public facilities) in the late 1800s:

> The outcome of the election of 1876 was a compromise between the industrial capitalists of the North and the leaders of the South. The North took a "hands off" attitude as far as the South's treatment of the Negro was concerned. The South in return gave local and congressional encouragement and protection to Northern investments ... [and] Congress failed to reduce the representatives of states which deprived large numbers of Negro citizens of the franchise [as provided in the Fourteenth Amendment]. It was in this atmosphere of national unity [among white elites] that imperialism was born.[17]

This exclusionary "national unity," achieved in the later 19th century at the expense of Blacks, continued into the next century. U.S. elites used arguments about racial superiority to bolster their positions for or against specific imperial adventures. During these decades, Jim Crow laws in the South enforced racial segregation and midwived U.S. industrialism and imperialist expansion, and vice versa. Throughout it all, identities, groups, interests, and power were at the center of these historical processes.

As industrialization proceeded, oil became a larger factor in the imperial calculations of Western elites across Europe and the United States. The military-industrial machines of Europe and the United States demanded fuel (and reserves) from Mexico and other parts of the hemisphere and the Middle East. The ramp-up to World War I during this same time also helped to propel globalized imperial ambitions in Europe and the United States:

> By 1914 economic interest had compelled the chief business groups of Europe to establish large foreign holdings in ... Africa, Asia, Australia, and the Americas. Proceeding from the dictum that "the flag follows the investor" ... these large industrial nations organized a military and naval machine large enough to protect the foreign interests of its traders and investors. Between 1870 and the beginning of the World War [in 1914], the building of this military machine constituted the largest single charge on the budget of each of the principal European nations. After its establishment, the military machine was used, first, to play a more or less active role in the internal life of those countries in which the owners of the military machine held important economic interests; and second, to defend the property of the investors against possible attack from any rivals who might be inclined to interfere with their holdings.[18]

---

[17] Weston, Racism in U.S. Imperialism, at 6–7.
[18] Nearing and Freeman, Dollar Diplomacy, at xiv.

Thus, imperialism throughout much of the 19th and early 20th centuries "implies the use of the machinery of government by private interests, mainly capitalist, to secure for themselves economic gains outside their country" and includes "an over-seas economic expression of western civilization."[19] In this global context, the U.S. variant of imperialism was dubbed Gunboat Diplomacy because the U.S. Navy frequently provided "the big stick." The United States exercised its power by sending gunships to anchor outside of world capitals or other key cities and sometimes to fire upon them. This "diplomacy" intimidated local authorities and peoples into submission because local military machines could not withstand the destructive force of U.S. gunships.

The public-private collusions of U.S. imperialism during the 1800s and early 1900s are exemplified by the wholesale "removal" of some tribal nations and the transfer of their lands to white settlers as "private" property. The infamous Trail of Tears is but one example. Since then, customized combinations of "private enterprise" and public/military force also drove U.S. imperialism in hemispheric terms and, increasingly, in global terms. This expansion of imperialism (and its elite toolkit) is exemplified by the corporate-governmental partnership of the U.S. government and the United Fruit Company during the span of a full century, between the 1870s and the 1970s. Their joint interventions in countries ranging from Costa Rica, Honduras, Nicaragua, Guatemala, Colombia, Panama, Cuba, the Dominican Republic, Chile, and others included doing "whatever it takes" to depose legitimate governments and impose obedient "puppet" dictatorships virtually at will. This extended period of private-public imperialism created the very concept and term of a "banana republic"—a place inhabited by inferior yet exotic others but ruled and exploited, of necessity, by foreign white overlords fulfilling their manifest destiny to civilization and God. In this top-down systemic arrangement, government willingly let itself be used as an instrument of ever-greater private profit, while the corporation cheerfully offered to become the instrument (and main beneficiary) of public policy and systemic violence. In the world that elites built during that century, "slave-like" conditions illegal within the United States prevailed with brutal corporate impunity "south of the border." But, as history would show, this imperial partnership would bring that world back to its U.S. home through imported goods.[20] This century-plus partnership between one of the first multi-national corporations and successive U.S. governments is thus a microcosm not only of expanding imperial adventures throughout the continent, hemisphere and beyond; in addition, it captures the larger systemic transition from imperialism to globalization. Not coincidentally, the United

---

[19] *Id.*

[20] See Peter Chapman, Bananas: How the United Fruit Company Shaped the World 197 (2007).

Fruit Company helped to pioneer today's version of private-public globalization in pursuit of elite agendas.[21] The historical experience and legacies of colonialism followed by imperialism thus provide a template for the contemporary ideologies, practices, and consequences of top-down globalization, as we examine more fully below.

In this century, ever-larger and ever-richer corporations are increasingly important in the historical and material process from colonialism to imperialism and globalization. Colonialism certainly involved private capital and incorporations; in fact, like law, corporations and capitalism grew alongside and in tandem with the agendas of colonial, imperial, and global elites.[22] But now, in this current phase called globalization, multinational corporations and their priorities have taken center-stage. This continuing process already has prompted questions about the benefits, need for, or viability of nation-states and governments. Viewed from a corporate perspective, perhaps all that humans really need is a "market-state" to serve corporate priorities. If so, globalization is a culmination of the racial state and its racial contract: it yields a racial state within a market state to preserve the identity-skewed legacies of law through colonialism, imperialism, and globalization. In complex ways, colonialism established the foundations of imperialism, while imperialism in turn provided the scaffolding for globalization.

Within the United States, this top-down morphing of imperialism into globalization included the unraveling of social "accords"—both domestic and international. Even within the inequities of the racial contract these accords, or societal understandings, had established a domestic equilibrium between tops and (some) bottoms based mostly on class—which in turn is a racialized and gendered construct. As critical scholars Francisco Valdes and Sumi Cho explain below, this systemic devolution enabled corporate neoliberal globalization as we know it today.

CRITICAL RACE MATERIALISM: THEORIZING JUSTICE IN THE WAKE OF GLOBAL NEOLIBERALISM

Francisco Valdes and Sumi Cho
43 Conn. L. Rev. 1513 (2011)

... With the understanding that the world-system and its supporting nation-state structure was always already racialized in multiple intersectional ways, it should be no surprise that the most pertinent color

---

[21] Id. at 203–06.

[22] For instance, both the Dutch and the English empires formed monopolistic "trading companies" to maximize profit from colonialism in India and the South Pacific. See Stephen R. Bown, Merchant Kings: When Companies Ruled the World, 1600–1900 (2010); Adam Clulow and Tristan Mostert, The Dutch and English East India Companies: Diplomacy, Trade and Violence in Early Modern Asia (2019); Nick Robins, The Corporation That Changed the World: How the East India Company Shaped the Modern Multinational (2012); William Dalrymple, The Anarchy: The East India Company, Corporate Violence, and the Pillage of an Empire (2019).

lines of the twentieth century hyperpower nation-state were those drawn racially within its boundaries by dominant core elites. Part of the reason the American Century's racial domination was largely understood to exist within the boundaries of the United States has to do with the development of three hegemonic phenomena from the mid-to late-twentieth century: (1) Pax Americana and the rise of global multilateral organizations that consolidated and cloaked the racialized international order; (2) domestic social structures of accumulation and their implicit accords that produced and exacerbated racial and social disparities; and (3) the self-serving "rule of law" that cruelly declared formal (racial and social) equality while simultaneously limiting its reach. . . .

The Global Accord: The Rise of Multilateral Organizations and Pax Americana

In the wake of World War II, the United States adopted an approach to traditional colonization that favored "facial independence" for the colonized of Africa, Asia, and Latin America, or the "Global South," while simultaneously constructing multilateral organizations and "rules of the game" that would foster economic and political dependence, and thereby disadvantage in enduring ways, newly-independent nations (as well as serve to maintain its own colonial interests in the Caribbean and Pacific). As the racially dominant capitalist power, the United States was best poised to benefit from new inter-governmental economic organizations like the International Monetary Fund and the International Bank for Reconstruction and Development (IBRD, which evolved into one of the five organizations in the World Bank Group), the proposed International Trade Organization (ultimately realized in the 1995 formation of the World Trade Organization or WTO), and the General Agreement on Tariffs and Trade (GATT). Indeed, as we explain below, the modern rules of neoliberal globalization always have been skewed in favor of former colonial and imperial nation-states and their identity-inflected elites.

Through these processes, the United States worked closely to develop international economic systems to valorize and promote "free trade" and "free markets" while undermining those articulated goals by maintaining economic and political advantages and preferential treatment through byzantine institutional arrangements and carefully-constructed "rules of the game." This new transnational regime reflected and projected existing racial hierarchies constructed through colonial and imperial historical processes despite their facial neutrality. For example, in constructing the global system of fixed exchange rates, set forth in the IMF and IBRD, the original plan provided for a world currency unit against which all national currencies would be pegged. . . . The U.S. [delegation], however, . . . prevailed in its lobby for a gold-backed dollar standard, or "dollar hegemony," allowing the Euro-American elites of the United States and their allies to underwrite massive trade deficits.

... With its dollar-backed convertible monetary system in place, the United States was able to trade at great profit to obtain raw materials from poor nations. Those profits would in turn be re-invested in industrial infrastructure in those nations to produce new markets. These new markets similarly projected and protected existing identitarian hierarchies.

Racialized U.S. economic and military interests were similarly safeguarded through the development of the North Atlantic Treaty Organization (NATO) and the U.N. Security Council. U.S. dominance in the formation of these security formations combined with U.S. economic advantage in the international economic system provided for the unprecedented role as "global policeman." In its unchallenged role as global policeman, the United States was free to prop up authoritarian regimes friendly to the United States and the cultural or material agendas of its elites, as well as undermine or eliminate democratically-elected regimes unfriendly to the United States. ...

Undergirding this (new) economic and political world order has been the rule of (white) law. International treaty law, inter-governmental organizations, and specialized agencies to the United Nations have comprised the set of global institutions, organizations, and agreements that have constituted "imperial globality." As a result, two legal constructs are at the crux of today's world system: the nation-state and the so-called free market. Both the state and the market are, in fact, products of law; each is created, constructed, operated, limited, modified, and protected by law. And each, in turn, produces much law-directly or otherwise. In fact, as just described, much law is devoted both directly and indirectly to the maintenance and administration of the nation-state, the so-called free market, and the myriad actors that operate within and across each of these.

Yet, the race-and gender-privileged beneficiaries of the accords in the mid-to late-twentieth century were mostly blissfully unaware of the set of global arrangements that teed up the American Century. Rather than understand these global inter-governmental organizations for the self-serving arrangements that they were, post-war Americans chose instead to view their place in the world grandiosely. As Michael Omi and Howard Winant described U.S. mid-century hegemony and its corresponding gestalt in the Epilogue to their classic, Racial Formation in the United States:

The United States apparently had limitless opportunities. ... Americans delighted in their country's unprecedented preeminence; they viewed themselves as the world's saviors.

This convenient blissful ignorance or nonchalance of imperial globality promoted an understanding that U.S. post-war economic prosperity derived not from systemic and racialized global advantage but from "exceptional" productivity and ingenuity at a national and individual level. In other words, the invisibility of imperial globality and international organizations/law to the operation of the U.S. domestic economy allowed a bounded understanding of U.S. post-war economic prosperity as residing purely within the superpower nation-state and the labors of its productive (white, male) citizens.... In fact, that unprecedented prosperity was the result of particular (and untenable) accords at both the international and national levels-accords with implicit consensual agreements enabled by elites to manipulate international economic policy, as well as internal labor groups and civil society....

Pax Americana's conception can be dated to the Yalta Conference in February 1945, at which the two regional post-war superpowers-the United States and Soviet Union-divided the world militarily, economically, and ideologically.... This Pax Americana global accord therefore conferred great economic and military privilege and discretion upon the United States, which quickly ascended to the pinnacle of power among the nation-states of the West. Pax Americana also helped to maintain the internationalized racial stratification accomplished through prior centuries of European colonialization and Euro-American imperialism.

The Domestic Accords: The Capital-Labor Accord and the Capital-Citizen Accord

Just as the global Pax Americana accord facilitated U.S. economic and military dominance in the international arena, two additional accords in the domestic sphere similarly aided the apparently smooth accumulation of capital from the 1940s to the 1970s—an accumulation of course skewed by race, gender, and similar identity categories to help prop up in cultural and material terms the status quo accumulated through centuries of colonial and imperial rule. Radical economists refer to "social structures of accumulation" to describe the "invisible handshake" between capital and labor and capital and civil society. There are two social structures of accumulation put into place in the post-War era that prevailed at least until the oil crisis of 1973—namely, the Capital-Labor Accord and the Capital-Citizen Accord. Like the Pax Americana accord, both of these accords also continued the identity-oriented politics entrenched by colonial and imperial regimes.

For decades already, a key feature of post-War market economy both within and outside of the U.S. had been the extraction of surplus value from the labor of workers. This ambition, however, to extract as much surplus value or "profit" as possible, encapsulates within it a central tension as workers increasingly pinched for profit begin to "push back." Domestically, the formation of labor unions, the demands for improved wages and workplace conditions, and the prospect of strikes and secondary boycotts all posed disruptive threats that could interrupt the rapid and smooth accumulation of capital. Recognizing that outright repression or coercion of labor has historically produced instability and uncertainty in the source of labor and the return on capital, during this period U.S. capitalists sought another approach to avoid such disruption.

Radical economists identify this alternate approach as the "Capital-Labor Accord," put in place from roughly 1945–73, and consider it central to resolving the inherent instability of capital seeking always to extract maximum "surplus value" from workers that would otherwise result in disruptive (to smooth accumulation) labor strife. Within the United States, the Capital-Labor Accord paved the way for rapid economic growth, with benefits redounding to both sides: on the one hand, workers could gain increased wages and enhanced working conditions, the right to collective bargaining and formation of unions, and ultimately, the ability to undertake labor actions or strikes; on the other hand, domestic capital would gain workforce stability and predictability to enable its smooth and steady accumulation of profits.

But to say that the Capital-Labor Accord was mutually beneficial to both parties is only partially correct. The mutual benefit derived from the accord was discernible for the privileged members of each party, but the overall (and racialized/gendered) advantage remained with capital. The rule of law and the nation-state intervened at various turns to ensure capital's upper hand in the form, for instance, of restricting union membership and labor's right to strike. Likewise, the power and violence of law and its facially-neutral rule led to a determination of (il)legality that worked to cripple secondary boycotts and "wildcat strikes" trying to support labor's struggles with capital, and bestowed a unilateral prerogative upon the Executive to declare "national security" threats under the Taft-Hartley Act that authorized the forced termination of strikes and unionized workers.

Capital's upper hand also was reinforced by the power of law through administrative agencies such as the National Labor Relations Board, appointed by the Executive purportedly to enforce labor's legal right to collective bargaining but repeatedly put to dubious, if not antithetical, uses. Equally important, the nation-state was further able to support the privileges of domestic capital through periodic passage of coercive legislation ("back to work" rules, "right to work" legislation) that used law to maintain class and related categories of hierarchy within the traditional bounds of the nation-state. Inevitably, these legal reinforcements of neocolonial capital within the U.S. also had the effect of buttressing the already-entrenched racial and gendered stratification of this society.

Not surprisingly, then, only some workers were able to unionize, with large swaths of "segmented work forces" populated by peoples of color and women falling outside of the invisible handshake. Further, as labor historians . . . have pointed out, "free labor" (with only few exceptions) was culturally understood to mean "white labor." Further, the nation-state and the law allowed and encouraged unionized labor and union rights to develop over and against race, much as was the case with the accumulation of capital. Indeed, social structures of accumulation theorists conceptualized the capital-labor accord as a "limited capital-labor accord" at the outset, in recognition of the majority of workers left out of the accord given the racial and gender exclusions in the segmented workforce. For this reason, the limited Capital-Labor accord in place from the 1940s to the 1970s constrained unregulated capitalism to better manage mainstream class conflict, in part by racializing the reach of the accord's beneficiaries.

In a similar fashion, the Capital-Citizen accord developed to address the need for domestic capital to better manage racial and other social conflict. In the wake of the Great Depression, it became crystal clear that the unregulated market would not provide security or sustenance for the white citizenry of this nation-state during harsh economic downturns producing high unemployment and related kinds of socio-economic dislocation. The Capital-Citizen accord developed over time in the twentieth century, beginning with President Franklin D. Roosevelt's New Deal policies and continuing through the Great Society reforms of the late 1960s and early 1970s, which arrived to provide health and welfare baselines to "catch" the most vulnerable (and usually colored)—the unfettered market's ravages and victims.

Of course, like the conceptualization of "free labor" as "white labor" under the Capital-Labor accord discussed above, the New Deal ended up being a raw deal for racial minorities and women, who were disproportionately excluded from its bounty. For instance, as Ira Katznelson established in When Affirmative Action Was White, the New Deal was shot through with racial compromise to produce a viable congressional majority reliant upon white Southern Democrats who were intent in preserving Jim Crow apartheid. Thus, it would take another set of more particularized domestic accords to work out another invisible handshake to quell widespread racial and civil unrest across U.S. society during this time.

In particular, the Second Reconstruction following the Civil Rights movement of the 1950s and 1960s and Black Power movements of the 1970s brought a more explicit racial valence to the prior "universal" Capital-Citizen accords (that conveniently and disproportionately excluded people of color from equal relief). In order to stave off increasing social turbulence and racial conflict, newly reformed and expanded Capital-Citizen accords provided laws guaranteeing formal equality, such as the Civil Rights Act of 1964, the Voting Rights Act of 1965, the Immigration and Nationality Act of 1965, and executive orders mandating affirmative action in federal contracting. But the raced Capital-Citizen accords likewise retained the upper hand of capital and white elites by restricting access to legal relief through the invention and deployment of legal doctrines that fabricated obstacles to "equal justice under law" where none previously existed, and which necessarily incurred jurisprudential contradictions that subverted the primal claims of law to social and systemic legitimacy, as we discuss in greater detail below.

Structures of Accumulation and the Overarching Role and Rule of Law: Why the State Matters

... For centuries, during the consolidation of the nation-state world system, human "progress" was the express project of national law. The path toward progress, toward civilization, toward modern, rational, enlightened, and just problem solving, lay in the making of new, more, and better law: law by custom, law by codification, law by regulation, law by adjudication, law by reformation and restatement. Over time, law has become ever-more entangled with every other major social institution—with magic before it became religion, with religion before it became culture, with culture before it became nation, with nation before it became market. Law thus became central to the consolidation of personal identities, social groups and larger communities into the modern nation-state, even as it is now central to the consolidation of nation-states into an increasingly globalized international socio-legal system, formally based on liberal democratic values, such as liberty, property, equality, dignity, and self-determination. Law, in short, consistently has been at the core of modernity's constitution.

But this historical process also exploited within and across the emergent nation-states the weaknesses of the human being. Laws repeatedly were crafted to prevent the individual human from fulfilling primal needs without paying a stiff price. So law was constructed to facilitate exploitation of the poor by the rich—of the less able by the more—as an integral element of the formation of nation-states, and even as the emergent ruling elites proclaimed commitments to diametrically opposite values, again like democracy, equality, and autonomy. . . .

From this perspective, we might describe the twentieth century as the time during which humanity perfected its tools and techniques of oppression within the nation-state, and emplaced the conditions for the development of new tools and techniques suited to the imperatives of corporate globalization. . . .

Today this gigantic contradiction means that law oftentimes is used mainly if not merely to launder politics. It is used to launder the dirtiest kinds of self-interested factional politics, often repackaged as identiarian politics, which in turn produce yet more "law"—in its many forms—oftentimes mainly to sustain traditional patterns of stratification and inter-group subordination. . . . Perversely, then, law becomes the tool for implementing expressly repudiated values—like structural, law-based, identity-oriented inequality—and for deflecting formally endorsed social goals, like equal opportunity for all. . . .

Through the centuries, this gigantic contradiction has spurred historical and continuing justice claims seeking to harmonize law's material or cultural effects with society's overtly professed values. Typically, these antisubordination claims invoked the formal commitments to civil/human rights embodied in numerous instruments of law, thereby seeking to close the gap between profession and action. These historical antisubordination struggles, including struggles for racial and gender justice, in effect sought to use law to cure or ameliorate the gigantic contradiction established by law to begin with. . . .

. . . Both factories in the North and plantations in the South of this nation-state relied on the lives and labors of the enslaved, exploited and marginalized. And the public monuments erected to operate and celebrate this new nation-state were likewise built on enslaved or indentured labor, ranging from the nation's Capitol to its aptly named White House. All of this, the nation-state still tells itself . . . was/is done in the name of freedom, liberty and equality—even as it has imposed policies and practices leading it today to imprison more of its people (disproportionately of color) than any other nation-state on Earth. . . .

The Pillars Crack: The Accords' Demise and Global Neoliberalism's Rise

. . . [T]he election of Ronald Reagan as President in 1980 announced an abrupt but definitive end to the Capital-Labor accord, symbolized by his self-righteous breaking of the air traffic controllers' strike in the summer of 1981. Politically, the Capital-Citizen accord began similarly to unravel, as signaled during the 1960s and 1970s by middle-class (mostly white) youth protesting the war in Vietnam, minorities and women protesting racial and gender inequality, and coalitions of all kinds protesting environmental degradation. These social movements helped yield the "Great Society" programs currently under assault from backlashing elites and their agents in Congress, the courts, and civil society as part of the cultural warfare against liberalism, whether in law or society. Thus, the retreat on anti-poverty programs and civil rights begun by Reagan and continued by George H. Bush accelerated in the 1990s, with the evisceration of social welfare policies under Democratic President Bill Clinton. All of this necessarily was deeply and structurally racialized (and gendered), both culturally and materially, even if not acknowledged openly or honestly.

In the midst of this tumult, but building on the post-War campaign to globalize Western power through institutional systems of internationalization, a facially colorblind version of "neoliberalism" emerged to replace the global and domestic accords not only within the U.S.

nation-state but also transnationally. As Arturo Escobar describes this transition:

> The first decade of this transition represented the apogee of financial capitalism, flexible accumulation, free market ideology, the fall of the Berlin Wall, the rise of the network society, and the so-called new world order. While this picture was complicated in the 1990s, neoliberal globalization still held sway. Landmarks such as the North American Free Trade Agreement (NAFTA), the World Trade Organization, Davos, Plan Puebla, and Plan Colombia were indications of the changing but persistent implantation of capitalist globalization.

. . . It is this "persistent implantation of capitalist globalization" . . . that gives rise to the cultural and material continuities between colonialism, imperialism and globalized neoliberalism.

Consequently, by the mid-1980s and the full ascendancy of the Reagan Revolution, the so-called "golden age" of global and domestic accords that had ushered in unprecedented colorblind prosperity for the accords' beneficiaries within the U.S. and racialized world dominance for the United States was decidedly over. "Corporate responsibility" that oriented capital at least partially towards labor and community under the former accords as a restraint on rank profit-seeking was replaced by "shareholder responsibility" that redirected capital's foremost duty to unfettered profit-seeking, and opened the door to increased financialization of neocolonial capitalism to seek increasingly higher profits, both domestically and globally. As in prior eras, ruling elites during these decades again deployed the rule of law—and its legitimated forms of violence—to help assure neoliberalism's rise within and beyond the nation-state. Under and by law, neoliberalism has starved social lifelines, maximized privilege, property and profit, and vindicated human rights mostly for corporations. . . .

Valdes and Cho summarize how the unraveling of the post-World War II system in the United States helped to set the stage for top-down, neoliberal globalization. This dominant approach to systemic globalism pretends to be identity-neutral but systematically reinforces colonial identity castes that were already entrenched during the decades of imperialism.

To elaborate further, international law scholar Chantal Thomas illustrates how colonial identity-based castes are not uprooted—but rather are renewed and reinforced—through corporate globalization. Thomas completes our bottom-up understanding of the historical and ideological continuities that travel across time, space, and group through colonialism, imperialism, and now globalization. Although specifics vary according to context, identities, groups, interests, and power are as central in globalization as in colonialism and imperialism. Does anything seem familiar here? What about differences? How do they matter to justice?

GLOBALIZATION OR GLOBAL SUBORDINATION?: HOW LATCRIT LINKS THE LOCAL TO GLOBAL AND THE GLOBAL TO THE LOCAL: GLOBALIZATION AND THE REPRODUCTION OF HIERARCHY
Chantal Thomas
33 U.C. Davis L. Rev. 1451 (2000)

... This Article demonstrates that legal rules, and therefore legal decisionmakers, are deeply and directly implicated both in economic globalization and in the distribution of benefits and costs that globalization creates. The premises of the argument are straightforward. First, legal rules have facilitated economic globalization. Second, legal rules have helped to construct the socioeconomic hierarchy that is the field on which economic globalization occurs. The lower rungs of this hierarchy are disproportionately occupied by poor urban minorities. Third, economic globalization may exacerbate this hierarchy. If legal rules helped to produce economic globalization, and legal rules helped to produce a socioeconomic hierarchy, and economic globalization exacerbates this hierarchy, then legal rules, and legal decisionmakers, are partially accountable for this result and the harms it imposes on poor urban minorities. . . .

Conditions Preexisting Globalization

Over the last century, a variety of federal, state, and local laws have entrenched social inequality between whites and minority populations in the United States. Such laws have rendered minorities as a whole worse equipped than whites to benefit from the particular gains brought about by globalization. . . .

Suburbanization: "Incidental" Racial and Economic Segregation

"Starting in 1945, one of the Great Migrations of American history took place": this was the migration of the middle classes away from city centers [to suburbs] after World War II. . . .

. . . Whites were disproportionately large participants in the exodus from the city. . . . Left behind were racial minorities comprised of African Americans, many of them relatively recent arrivals into city centers from their own migrations out of the southern United States; and, increasingly over the postwar era, of African, Asian, Caribbean, Latina/o, and Middle Eastern populations resulting from immigration into the United States. Suburbanization thus split the socioeconomic fortunes of middle-class, previously urban whites on the one hand, and poorer, urban minorities on the other. Once created, the rift continued to deepen over the length of the postwar era.

... Throughout the twentieth century, [federal] law and policy encouraged and at times literally subsidized suburbanization—and therefore segregation [through federal income tax deductions for mortgage interest, federal mortgage insurance programs facilitating home loans, and funding of highway systems connecting suburbs to cities]. . . .

Historical conditions produced socioeconomic inequality between whites and racial minorities. Federal law and policy intended to spur economic growth exacerbated these inequalities by placing white middle-class families in suburbs and poor minority families in the inner city. In addition to acting as an unintentional engine of racial segregation, federal law and policy at times facilitated intentional racial segregation by local state and nonstate actors; at other times federal authorities explicitly promoted racial exclusion. Against these formidable structural dynamics, federal antidiscrimination law has proved relatively ineffectual in undoing segregation. . . . [Globalization operates on this already disproportionate legal and social landscape to distribute its gains and adverse impacts unequally.]

Globalization . . .

The Nature of Globalization

Globalization might preliminarily be defined as the increasingly international nature of production and consumption. Although international production and consumption is as old as the nation-state, the new era of globalization differs from previous eras in the scale and complexity of international flows involved. These differences in turn shape the impact of globalization on the composition of the U.S. economy.

Scale. In the past few decades, international flows of both the "current account" (trade in goods and services) and "capital account" (investment and finance) types have multiplied exponentially. In the area of capital flows, cross-border transactions have increased exponentially in the past few decades. . . . "Indirect" investment—the securities markets—grew even more remarkably. . . . Finally, trading in foreign currency has skyrocketed. . . .

Complexity. The trade and finance vectors of globalization described above regularly combine in multiple ways. For example, domestic production might come from a U.S. subsidiary of a foreign company, financed by a syndicate of domestic and foreign banks or private investors. Imported products might come into the United States from a foreign subsidiary that is owned by a U.S. company financed by capital raised on world markets. . . .

This growing complexity in production is so widespread that it accounts for a significant portion of the postwar increase in international trade. As "the volume of world trade has grown, the traditional role of national markets is increasingly eclipsed by an alternative system: trade generated within multinational companies themselves as they export and import among their own . . . subsidiaries." Within the U.S. economy, over forty percent of exports and almost fifty percent of imports are "actually goods that travel not in the open marketplace, but through these intrafirm channels." The IMF Globalization Survey admitted that the "structure of foreign trade has increasingly become intra-industry and intrafirm."

Law and Policy Creating Globalization

Accounts of globalization tend to portray it as autonomous—a self-powered juggernaut whose appearance on the horizon has caught governments off-guard. Yet globalization does not naturally or inevitably result from market-driven developments in technology. Certainly, stunning improvements in market-driven technology over the past few decades have played an undeniable role in driving globalization. . . .

At the same time, however, law and policy have played an important role in spurring globalization forward. International trade agreements have probably been the most important instruments the federal government has used to catalyze globalization. The General Agreement on Tariffs and Trade, established in 1948, provided for six rounds of trade-liberalizing negotiations between 1948 and 1979 that reduced the average level of tariffs imposed by its member states by more than half.

The United States federal government has also lowered barriers to trade in goods and services in bilateral agreements and regional agreements. In the 1990s two highly visible such steps were the North American Free Trade Agreement with Canada and Mexico, and the agreements establishing the hundred-plus member World Trade Organization in 1995. Each event marked far-reaching liberalizing reforms in both trade and investment.

These reduced trade barriers have allowed not only for greater competition in the U.S. by foreign producers, but also for the off shore relocation of production facilities by U.S. manufacturers who seek the production-cost advantages offered elsewhere. . . .

In finance, the federal government created a number of regulatory devices that helped globalize securities markets. Thus, while some of the fuel driving globalization came from technological innovation, a good portion of it also arose from deliberately pursued policies by governmental actors. In the United States, the executive and legislative branches implemented into law a host of liberalizing measures in trade, investment and finance that facilitated the internationalization of the U.S. economy. To point this out is not to compel a conclusion that globalization is desirable or undesirable; it is only to compel the conclusion that globalization cannot be viewed as a natural or inevitable phenomenon. Rather, the dynamics that the term "globalization" encompasses result at least in part from governmental practices, and governmental actors must therefore be held at least partially accountable for their ill effects.

Of course, these liberalizing measures were pursued in the belief that they would generate positive effects. Classical economic philosophy holds that the liberalization of market activity will increase both national and international efficiency. Because efficiency maximizes wealth creation, such policies could also be said to maximize social welfare.

To equate social welfare with aggregate social wealth, however, is to adopt only one of a number of potential measures of social welfare. Even if one ignores measures of welfare not related to wealth, the equation of social welfare with national wealth overlooks distributive concerns. Indeed, efficiency increasing measures such as economic liberalization may exacerbate preexisting distributive inequalities. Classical economic measures of efficiency and welfare are simply "indifferent to the distribution of income and wealth."

In the United States among the groups that bear the brunt of this distributive inequality . . . are racial minorities in the inner city. . . .

Transformations Resulting from Globalization

. . . One of the most visible aspects of globalization is the degree to which geographically diverse economies are participating in types of production that had previously been concentrated in the West. . . . Whether due to western-company relocation or the growth of nonwestern competitors, manufacturing is now much less economically significant in the West and much more significant in medium and low income countries in Asia and Latin America.

At the same time, as noted above, the West is increasingly specializing in services. Among the industrialized world, according to the IMF, "the share of employment in services in the United States is highest, at about seventy-three percent currently." These dynamics reinforce each other: as manufacturing disperses globally, an increasing array of intermediary services becomes necessary to coordinate global production, and the emergence of such service production in turn facilitates further manufacturing dispersal.

This shift from goods to services production has been called "deindustrialization" and it has "coincided with the growing global integration of economies." . . .

Because city centers harbored most traditional manufacturing, "deindustrialization" has affected them most acutely. In the 1970s and 1980s, Philadelphia, Chicago, New York and Detroit respectively lost 64%

(resulting in the elimination of 160,000 jobs), 60 percent (326,000 jobs), 58% (520,000 jobs), and 51% (108,000 jobs) of their manufacturing sectors. This was also true more generally for the "ten largest old metropolitan areas of the Northeast and north central states." . . .

In sum, the economic base of city centers over the last few decades has shifted from manufacturing and associated management to producer services such as finance, telecommunications and lawyering. These changes were not solely driven by technological innovations. Rather, the federal government took deliberate measures liberalizing trade, investment and finance. These steps were taken in furtherance of a classic economic policy approach that predicted that liberalization would increase aggregate national wealth and therefore welfare. The theory . . . does not address the possibility that entrenched socioeconomic forces antagonizing "discrete and insular" groups—such as racial minorities in the inner city—might prevent those groups from benefiting proportionately in the gains of globalization. . . . The costs of globalization may therefore concentrate at this rigidly constructed bottom. . . .

Conclusions

The theory behind globalization is that everyone benefits from increased efficiency resulting from the removal of government constraints on the market. This theory, however, does not attempt to address the impact of these dynamics on existing inequalities within a society. It is possible that globalization will offer opportunities for some members of previously disadvantaged groups. It is simultaneously possible that globalization will generally entrench existing structural inequalities, and that some of these inequalities will be racial in character. Such inequities may become particularly apparent when the economy enters its cyclical downturn. Consequently, although measures that promote globalization "are not racial in character or construction, that they have a racial dimension should not be ignored." . . .

Law and policy have played a role both in shaping these pre-existing inequalities, and in fostering globalization. Adverse effects of globalization on minority communities thus stem in part from conditions created by a complex web of law and policy at the federal, state and local levels. Law and policy makers at all levels bear a responsibility to rectify these conditions, for example, through concerted reforms in housing, education and lending. Without such reform, significant sectors of our society may be left behind in the rush to the end of the rainbow. . . .

The solutions to such deep-rooted structural problems, of course, are not likely to be popular causes among politicians. Advocates for the urban poor must insist, however, on a continuing focus on these difficulties and on real redress for them. Items on this agenda include imperatives that government resources be redistributed and legal processes reshaped to correct the disadvantages in capital formation, infrastructure, and education and other public services that currently operate to reinforce existing hierarchies.

Thomas demonstrates how identity-based legacies continue to be enforced today by corporate globalization that purports to be oblivious to group identities. Through globalization, the shift from overt supremacy to "colorblind" systemic injustice seems to occur "naturally" but is preserved through new and old legal devices—domestic and international—that maintain entrenched castes. These castes are material and symbolic; micro and macro. This excerpt highlights how top-down globalization functions as an adaptation and extension of colonial and imperial subordination—a mechanism of preservation through transformation based on identities, groups, interests, and power, which remain central, even if more hidden, in today's top-down rush to globalize everywhere and everything.

NOTES AND QUESTIONS

1. *Partners in Expansion, Extraction, and Ideology.* As Saito, Venator Santiago, and others detail, U.S. elites provoked war as a strategy for bringing their rule of law to those "in need" of rescue, such as in the Spanish-American War in 1898 by which the United States took Puerto Rico and other "possessions" around the globe. Lurking behind the takings were elite interests in material gain. The conquest of Northern Mexico, for example, was steeped in the ideology of Manifest Destiny and meant to preserve the economic institution of slavery, while the westward taking of the present U.S. Southwest to the California coast was rooted in the desire for control of Western shipping ports for global trade. With the advent of globalization and today's economy driven by multinational corporate elites, preserving elite interests is not always bloody. Consider the example detailed above of "banana republics,"—foreign dictatorships beholden to serving multinational corporate interests voluntarily, with the tactics of the U.S.-based United Fruit Company in Central America illustrating this imperial (now global) kind of public-private partnership. Corporate domination sparked violent conflicts and interventions in far-away regions despite their sovereignty, such as the 1954 U.S.-backed coup against a democratic government in Guatemala, prompted by the urgings (and interests) of the Boston-based elites who controlled the United Fruit Company and who feared collectively the possibility of land and labor reforms under the rule of law in Guatemala.[23]

Providing more context for this long history of public-private partnerships colluding for top-down expansion, enrichment, and hegemony, legal philosophy scholar Stephen Munzer provides a brief history of Guatemala from colonial

---

[23] See Stephen Schlesinger and Stephen Kinzer, Bitter Fruit: The Story of the American Coup in Guatemala (rev. ed. 2005).

through modern times, highlighting the relationships among U.S. corporate interests and government interventions, and their historical and continuing impacts on indigenous peoples. In particular, he describes the building of one World Bank-funded dam project, needed to provide energy for mining and other sorts of corporate-driven "development," that occurred in the midst of—and because of—the U.S.-supported civil war in Guatemala. Across centuries from colonization through contemporary globalization, these impacts include dispossession, exploitation, repression, and extraction—but were met with continuous bottom-up, community-based struggle undertaken at great risk and cost.

> In 1524, Spain invaded and colonized the territory now known as Guatemala.... Since 1847, Guatemala has been an independent country ... [with rulers who] catered to the aristocracy and foreign business interests.... [The government] encouraged foreign investment, crushed labor unions, and favored cash crops rather than sustainable food production for Guatemalans ... "particularly the United Fruit Company."...
>
> ... [After progressive leaders were elected in the 1950s, however,] the C.I.A. began destabilizing the Guatemalan government ... [fomenting a coup that] led to further military governments [supported by the United States] and eventually a fierce civil war in the period from 1962 to 1996.
>
> It was in this strife-torn historical context that the Guatemalan government decided, in 1975, to build hydroelectric dams as a way to avoid the high cost of buying oil ... [including] the Chixoy Dam across the Rio Negro.... The government obtained no consent or input from the approximately 1,500 Maya Achi who lived in the Rio Negro valley; in fact, initial feasibility studies of the area stated that the valley was uninhabited.
>
> ... [After learning of the project,] Maya Achi met and created a "book" that catalogued their land titles in the Rio Negro valley and riverbanks, recorded the government's promises [of resettlement and compensation], rejected those promises as inadequate, and named two of their members to meet with government officials in Guatemala City. On the way to the capital, the two representatives were kidnapped and disappeared along with the "book." ... Maya Achi reiterated they did not want to leave, and violence erupted. Across five massacres, paramilitary squads killed over 400 Maya Achi.... In 1983, during the filling of the reservoir, additional Maya Achi were killed while attempting to flee or resist forcible resettlement....
>
> After the survivors of the Rio Negro massacres spent two or three years hiding from the military in the mountainous areas around Rio Negro, they began to trickle into the resettlement village of Pacux, where many still remain.... [However,] unlike the moist soil near Rio Negro, the land around Pacux lacked irrigation water

> ..., residents lost access to the medicinal plants that once grew along the river, ... [and there was] no room for livestock or open-air community areas....
>
> ... [M]any residents searched for work in the capital, the coast, or even the United States.... [Many got low-paying jobs in *maquiladoras*—] "export-processing, labor intensive plants that produce goods for international capital.... [Others worked in export-oriented agriculture] in coastal palm oil, banana, sugar cane, or watermelon plantations ... "characterized by semi-slave debt peonage work environments and minimal salaries."...
>
> It is impossible to give context to what has befallen Maya Achi without seeing the building of the Chixoy Dam in terms of international economic development and accordingly the role of the World Bank and the legislative and executive branches of the United States government.[24]

This history continues of exploitation, repression, and extraction, backed by domestic and international capital and enforced by governmental and (often corporate-backed) paramilitary violence. But with constant resistance. As the Jubilee Debt Campaign, a non-governmental organization studying international development, noted in 2012:

> The resistance taking place to mines and dams in Guatemala, and the experiments with popular forms of consultation and democracy which have come out of this resistance, is cause for great hope. But Guatemalans have a long way to go to combat the racism, poverty and injustice that confronts them. The world has a duty to stand with Guatemala's people.... This terror arose from a history of exploitation of Guatemala's natural resources by foreign governments, most notably that of the United States.[25]

In this example, how have the interests of U.S.-based elites been served—even without any formal acquisition of territory? What role has law played—including U.S., Guatemala, and international law? Recalling Aldana's excerpt in Part I, what tools of struggle are evident in or relevant to localized resistance against the top-down dictates of corporate neoliberal globalization? Does this brief critical history of colonialism, imperialism, and globalization in a particular place—Guatemala—help you to better understand and answer these questions?

2. *Global Exemplar of a Racial State?* Above we noted that many bottom-up perspectives view the United States as the global exemplar of a racial state. But the United States may be the most successful example of the racial state in world history from a top-down perspective as well. As detailed above, U.S.

---

[24] Stephen R. Munzer, Dam(n) Displacement: Compensation, Resettlement, and Indigeneity, 51 Cornell Int'l L.J. 823 (2019).

[25] Nick Dearden, Generating Terror: The Role of International Financial Institutions in Sustaining Guatemala's Genocidal Regimes, Jubilee Debt Campaign 3–4 (Dec. 2012), www.jubileedebt.org.uk/wp-content/uploads/2012/12/Generating-terror.pdf.

racial ideology, in theory and practice, was deemed so effective by the early twentieth century that, from an admiring perspective, it served intentionally as a blueprint for the Third Reich's race policies.[26] Hitler copied U.S. eugenics policies and ideology, which had been upheld by the Supreme Court in *Buck v. Bell*, while expanding involuntary sterilization from those seen as feebleminded to those with physical disabilities. Moreover, Hitler praised the U.S. approach to restrictive race-based immigration policies (such as the Chinese Exclusion Laws mentioned by Saito above and addressed also in Part I). Hitler wrote in his manifesto, *Mein Kampf* (translated as My Struggle), that the U.S. exclusion from citizenship of "certain defined races . . . [was] a modest start in the direction of . . . the national State"—essentially an explicit single-race state. Finally, Hitler and the Nazi leaders genuinely admired the U.S. conquest and extermination of Native peoples in the interest of group supremacy under the banner of Manifest Destiny, with Hitler himself speaking approvingly of how the United States had "gunned down the millions of Redskins to a few hundred thousand, and now keep[s] the modest remainder under observation in a cage."[27] The United States may indeed be exceptional—exceptionally successfully at designing and maintaining a racial state by a variety of legal and extralegal means. What is your reaction to this example of critical history?

3. *Linking the Local to the Global and to History*. Social problems, like legal systems, sometimes are seen exclusively in domestic terms, but Thomas demonstrates historical and contemporary links between U.S. residential segregation, economic opportunity, and globalization. Students at CUNY Law School, for example, have been asked to identify social problems in which they are interested. The issue could be anything: homelessness, intimate partner violence, food insecurity, pollution, animal cruelty, disability rights, abortion rights and reproductive justice. Having identified the issue, students then receive the following assignment: identify the historical and contemporary transnational links that help define this problem and the implications for advocacy of those links.[28] How might a critical consciousness of transnational systemic links across time and place influence or alter advocacy choices or roles?

4. *The Role of Corporations and "Private" Interests in Identity Castes*. We saw above that corporations specifically, and "private" interests generally, became increasingly important in the transitions from colonialism to imperialism, and globalization. Gilens and Page showed in Part I how U.S. (racialized and gendered) "economic elites" control democracy here. Many now view corporations as the dominant actors in law-making and social life. If so,

---

[26] See James Q. Whitman, Hitler's American Model: The United States and the Making of Nazi Race Law (2017) (also noting the fascination among German intellectuals, before the Nazi rise to power, of the U.S. treatment of Blacks as second-class citizens, and how the U.S., as the world leader on combatting racial mixing through anti-miscegenation laws, influenced the Nazi "Blood Law" banning race mixing, as well as the other Nuremberg laws commonly regarded as the Third Reich's policy framework for the Holocaust).

[27] *Id.* at 9.

[28] This example was provided by Chaumtoli Huq of CUNY School of Law.

advocates must include corporations in their research, analysis, and actions, as described in Part V. Describe a contemporary or historical context in which corporate priorities determined legal outcomes. Can you trace the roles of identities, interests, groups, and power in your example of corporate priorities determining legal outcomes? Can you better understand how formal pairings, or antinomies—like private-public, material-symbolic, or individual-collective—help jointly and severally to obscure systemic injustice and solutions for it?

5. *The U.S. Culture Wars and Top-Down Identity Politics.* We have seen that colonial settlers from Europe were the first organized practitioners of identity politics. Colonialism, imperialism and now globalization have propelled these original elite politics—and its identity castes—across time, place, and group. Within the United States (and elsewhere), the historical systemic progression from imperialism to corporate globalization unraveled the social accords of the status quo to further favor already-privileged and enriched groups. This unraveling paved the way for globalized neoliberalism, and unleashed "culture wars" to roll back the justice gains of nearly a century, spanning from the Great Depression and the New Deal, through various civil rights movements, and up to today's retrogression on racial justice, reproductive justice, trans justice, economic justice, and climate justice.[29] These top-down culture wars (or "Kulturkampf") use three mutually reinforcing "prongs" to demonize, disempower, and dispossess bottom groups put and kept there by and since colonial identity politics: oppressive electoral politics, partisan judicial appointments, and ideological de/funding choices. These prongs represent organized elite actions to block or suppress—even to roll back—equal justice using coordinated, strategic combinations of democracy and adjudication for long term dominance. With this deepened critical history, can you appreciate more fully why antisubordination advocacy must do the same, except better (and with fewer resources)?

13.4 LAW-AS-IDENTITY STILL CREATES, EXPANDS, AND PERPETUATES COLONIAL CASTES AND IDEOLOGIES

Failure by design is not limited to race. Although race has served as a paradigm for identity caste systems since colonial times, this paradigm was modified from earlier, common law concepts designed for group caste systems based on gender. Legal concepts like coverture for married women denied to women as a group the technical legal capacity for social and economic independence from men. Married women were denied such basic rights as the capacity to enter into and enforce contracts, to hold title to

---

[29] See generally LatCrit Symposium, Countering Kulturkampf Politics through Critique and Justice Pedagogy, 50 Vill. L. Rev. 749 (2005), 35 Seton Hall L. Rev. 1155 (2005); see also Francisco Valdes, Culture, "Kulturkampf" and Beyond: The Antidiscrimination Principle under the Jurisprudence of Backlash, in The Blackwell Companion to Law and Society (Austin Sarat ed. 2003).

property not subject to the control of their husband, and to vote, hold office, or serve as jurors. The legal design of white supremacy in European colonies generally followed the legal design of patriarchy in Europe.

Law adjusts the supremacist logic of colonial conquest as needed to construct many bottoms and few tops. Law, as a colonizing system, established a systemic design that today reproduces original tops (wealthy cis white males) consistently while subjugating bottoms flexibly. This combination of consistency (for tops) and flexibility (for bottoms) enables the system to situate other, even "new," groups that were not part of colonial castes based on race.

Below, for example, feminist legal scholar Julie Nice examines the role of sex and patriarchy in this mix of consistency and flexibility. Nice finds a "major area of divergence" between the equal justice commitments and actual outputs of law as a system. She concludes that judges interpreting the Fourteenth Amendment have "defied these commitments by perpetuating gender injustice throughout U.S. history." But, she notes, constitutional law nonetheless remains important to legal feminism, one of the critical Schools, and to progress toward Critical Justice.

THE GENDERED JURISPRUDENCE OF THE FOURTEENTH AMENDMENT

Julie A. Nice
in Research Handbook on Feminist Jurisprudence (Robin West and Cynthia Grant Bowman eds. 2019)

Feminist jurisprudence and the Fourteenth Amendment converge in their foundational commitments to equality and liberty. Yet judicial interpretation of the Fourteenth Amendment has defied these commitments by perpetuating gender injustice throughout US history. Nonetheless, constitutional law remains important to feminism, which relies on the Fourteenth Amendment for its project to reveal and root out gender as a tool of stratification. . . .

From the outset, the original Constitution of 1789 clearly entrenched both racial enslavement and gender injustice by explicitly protecting the institution of slavery and otherwise failing to guarantee equality. . . .

During the long and hard-fought abolitionist and suffragist campaigns aiming to end slavery, reform marital status laws and extend the right to vote to men of color and women, activists framed their demands around their entitlement to full constitutional inclusion. After the Thirteenth Amendment prohibited slavery at the end of the Civil War, the focus shifted to the Fourteenth Amendment to protect equality and liberty. Ratified in 1868, the Fourteenth Amendment declared that all persons born or naturalized in the United States were citizens and prohibited the states from abridging the privileges and immunities of citizens, from depriving them of life, liberty or property without due process of law and from denying the equal protection of the laws. The great irony is that the Fourteenth Amendment occasioned not only the first protection of equality but also the first appearance of the word "male." . . .

. . . For nearly a century, the Court construed the Fourteenth Amendment in ways that effectively obstructed attempts by women to obtain protection from discrimination. In an early and ominous pair of rulings decided on back-to-back days in 1873, the Court severely constrained the scope of the Fourteenth Amendment. It ruled first in the *Slaughter-House Cases* that the privileges or immunities clause did not apply the Bill of Rights to the states, that the equal protection clause applied only to discrimination based on race and that the due process clause did not protect the right to practice one's trade. On the following day, the Court ruled in *Bradwell v. Illinois* that a state could exclude women from practicing law because doing so was not a privilege of citizenship. . . . One year later, in *Minor v. Happersett*, the Court upheld Missouri's denial of the right to vote to women, unequivocally reaffirming the exclusion of women from participation in the political sphere.

. . . Further, although much of the harm of racial and gender subordination occurred within private homes and enterprises, the Court declared in the *Civil Rights Cases* in 1883 that Congress could not use its power to enforce the Fourteenth Amendment to regulate private conduct. By requiring "state action" to invoke the safeguards of the Fourteenth Amendment, the Court ensured that the so-called private sphere was protected from the amendment's reach. Yet it was precisely within this private sphere that married women had little to no agency or leverage to protect themselves due to the common law doctrine of coverture, which denied their legal and economic personhood.

Most women nonetheless worked long hours for no wages inside the home, and many also worked for low wages outside the home. The Supreme Court approved their economic double-bind when it upheld a maximum-hours law for women in *Muller v. Oregon*, based on their weaker "physical structure" and "maternal functions," and yet struck down a minimum-wage law for women in *Adkins v. Children's Hospital*, based on their "emancipation" from "special protection." . . . The Court similarly relied on a protectionist rationale when it ruled in *Hoyt v. Florida* that, because women in 1961 were "still regarded as the center of the home and family life," a state could exempt women from jury service. . . .

Taken together, these and other decisions from the Supreme Court, over nearly a century from 1873 to 1971, rejected constructions of the Fourteenth Amendment that might have protected women from subordination in both public and private spheres. . . .

The Supreme Court did not declare gender discrimination unconstitutional until 1971 when it struck down a gender preference for selecting an estate administrator in *Reed v. Reed*. Representing challenger Sally Reed, Ruth Bader Ginsburg and the American Civil Liberties Union argued that sex, like race, was a suspect classification and therefore should be reviewed with strict judicial scrutiny. In her brief, Ginsburg credited and cited lawyer Pauli Murray for the argument that legal classifications based on sex, like race, violated the equal protection clause. This inclusion of Murray, who had served on President Kennedy's Commission on the Status of Women and co-found[ed] the National Organization for Women (NOW), closely linked Ginsburg's arguments to the claims of both the civil rights and women's movements. Ginsburg emphasized the "significant changes" in society's attitudes toward the role of women . . . [b]ut she insisted that judicial recognition of "a firm constitutional foundation for equal treatment of men and women by the law" was necessary to remove "law-sanctioned obstacles" to equal rights. . . .

Strict scrutiny was never obtained for classifications based on sex. Three years later in *Craig v. Boren*, the Supreme Court settled on the middle tier of intermediate scrutiny as the appropriate level of judicial review for discrimination based on sex, which requires that the government action be substantially related to an important government interest. . . .

. . . [W]hile women have obtained heightened intermediate judicial scrutiny for claims of sex discrimination by the government, the courts frequently have failed to enforce substantive sex equality, with the architecture of constitutional law often to blame. Yet nothing in the Constitution necessitates such conservative interpretations. . . .

Throughout US history, feminists have insisted that the nation meet its dual commitments to equality and liberty for women and minorities. . . . [But while] a firm constitutional foundation for equality and liberty may be necessary, it is not sufficient. Acknowledging this limitation in her path-breaking brief to the Supreme Court, Ruth Bader Ginsburg underscored that "sex-based discrimination will not disintegrate upon this Court's recognition that sex is a suspect classification." As feminist scholar Mary Becker reminded us, "in the end, there is nothing but politics." And so the dialogue [and struggle] continues.

Nice outlines how patriarchy functions by law in tandem with white supremacy to maintain the United States as a racial and gendered state. Legal uses of gender produced and reproduce a dual system of rules and doctrines that keeps (original) tops and (shifting) bottoms in their assigned systemic places. As a case in point, legal scholar John Tehranian next examines "Middle Eastern" as a social identity that was never part of the original design but has since been socially constructed and assigned to particular individuals. Over time, this identity's meaning has morphed, depending especially on perceived elite interests. This top-down process of "selective racialization" creates both positive and negative identity significations. Tehranian, like Nice, situates his analysis in the Schools of legal knowledge—applying and contributing to them.

SELECTIVE RACIALIZATION: MIDDLE-EASTERN AMERICAN IDENTITY AND THE FAUSTIAN PACT WITH WHITENESS

John Tehranian
40 Conn. L. Rev. 1201 (2008)

Introduction

... Within our nation's racial hierarchy, individuals of Middle Eastern descent have found themselves on the dividing line. On one hand, they suffer from the types of discrimination that face minority groups. On the other hand, formally speaking, Middle Easterners are deemed white by law. This dualistic and contested ontology of the Middle Eastern racial condition creates an unusual paradox. Reified as the other, Americans of Middle Eastern descent do not enjoy the benefits of white privilege. Yet, as white under the law, they are denied the fruits of remedial action. Moreover, this tack has grown increasingly untenable as public and private discrimination against Middle Easterners has increased dramatically in recent years....

... For years, the concept of whiteness has mediated the provision of rights, down to the very notion of citizenship. For example, until 1952, federal law provided naturalization rights only to individuals who were white or black, but nothing "in-between." The American legal system was forced to confront the task of defining what or who constituted the white race for the purposes of naturalization when, during the late nineteenth and early twentieth centuries, a wave of new immigration from non-Anglo-Saxon countries arrived on our shores....

It is within this context of racial hierarchy and social organization around a malleable concept of whiteness that the construction of Middle-Eastern racial identity has taken place. The term "Middle East" likely emerged in the 1850s from Britain's India Office. However, the term did not enjoy widespread usage in policy circles until the early twentieth century.... "Middle East" [was used] to refer to a region of growing strategic importance in the emerging conflict pitting Britain and the United States against Germany and Russia ... ranging on a north-south axis, from Turkey to the Arabian Peninsula, and, on an east-west axis, from Iran to Egypt.... Just as race is a function of social construction, not inherent biology, the Middle East was invented from political considerations, not natural geography....

... [I]t was only in the past half century that the term began to refer to peoples of the region. For example, when the federal courts heard the racial prerequisite/naturalization cases in the first half of the twentieth century, they contemplated the whiteness of individuals of Lebanese, Syrian, Turkish, and Armenian descent. . . . Yet, interestingly enough, the courts never once referred to the petitioners as Middle Easterners [until the late 1940s]. . . .

For prior generations, Americans of Middle Eastern descent came closer to matching our constructed notions of whiteness. They were largely Christian; they came from an exotic but friendly, romantic, and halcyon foreign land imagined to contain magic lanterns, genies, flying carpets, and belly dancers; and they served as a chief vessel of the philosophical and cultural heritage of the West. Thus, in previous generations, people of (what we now call) Middle-Eastern descent were, more often than not, blended into the white category. . . .

. . . [More recently,] Middle Easterners have been irretrievably associated with Islam; they appear to hail from a decidedly unfriendly foreign land imagined to contain nothing but terrorists, obstreperous mobs chanting "Death to America," unabashed misogynistic polygamists, and religious fundamentalists. . . . Thus, they are the quintessential Other and the Middle Easterner category, imposed on them by society at large, has become their appellation. . . .

Given the tendency to conflate race with religious affiliation, and Christianity with assimilability, it is not surprising that, at the beginning of the twentieth century, courts declared Armenians, and even some Arabs, white by law and entitled to the privileges of whiteness, including naturalization. However, the composition of the Middle-Eastern American population has undergone a dramatic change in recent years, especially in the public imagination. Contrary to popular perceptions, only twenty-three percent of present-day Arab-Americans are Muslim. However, about sixty percent of Arab immigrants arriving in the United States since 1965 identify themselves as Muslim. The Middle Eastern population of the United States is, therefore, growing less Christian. As a result, it is perceived as considerably less capable of assimilation and, consequently, less white.

As faith in their assimilatory capacity has diminished, Middle Easterners have come to represent enemy aliens . . . [depicted as the] Arab terrorist, and this vision has firmly taken hold of our immigration policies. . . .

The negotiation of the Middle-Eastern identity is mediated by a twofold process that moves both from the top down and from the bottom up. From the top down, society at large engages in a practice that can best be described as selective racialization. From the bottom up, Middle

Easterners, both privileged and damned by their proximity to the white dividing line, engage in persistent (and frequently effective) covering of their ethnic background. These two social forces combine to create a pernicious stereotyping feedback loop that enervates the political strength of the Middle-Eastern community, heightens its invisibility and leaves little effective resistance to the growing assaults against its civil rights.

... [I]n society at large, Middle Easterners are consistently subjected to a process of selective racialization.... Systematically, famous individuals of Middle-Eastern descent are usually perceived as white. Meanwhile, infamous individuals of Middle-Eastern descent are usually categorized as Middle-Eastern. Thus, when Middle-Eastern actors conform to social norms and advance positive values and conduct, their racial identity as the Other recedes to the background as they merge into the great white abyss. By contrast, when Middle-Eastern actors engage in transgressive behavior, their racial identity as the Other immediately becomes a central, defining characteristic of who they are. The result is an endless feedback loop that calcifies popular prejudices....

Our country is filled with individuals of Middle-Eastern descent who have contributed constructively to American society; yet, surprisingly, few of these Americans are actually perceived of as Middle Easterners. Instead, their ethnicity is frequently whitewashed....

The long list of Middle-Eastern Americans includes individuals from virtually every aspect of American life, including athletes, such as tennis player Andre Agassi (Persian/Armenian), Indy 500 champion Bobby Rahal (Lebanese), and NFL quarterbacks Doug Flutie and Jeff George (both Lebanese); entertainers, such as actresses Cher (Armenian) ... and Gabrielle Anwar (half-Persian) ... [and] prominent entrepreneurs such as hoteliers the Maloof family (Lebanese) and Apple CEO Steve Jobs (half-Syrian)....

The process of selective racialization occurs with regularity in the mass media, serving to bolster existing stereotypes....

... The development of a Middle-Eastern racial identity is not, however, an exclusively top down process, contrary to what the selective racialization process might suggest.... Middle Easterners themselves have played a critical role in actively encouraging recognition of their white status through such assimilatory behavior as covering. In the process, Middle Easterners have made a Faustian pact with whiteness ... [that] enabled them to avoid discrimination at an individual level but lessened the ability of the community, as a whole, to systematically fight invidious discrimination and stereotyping in the long term....

The gravitation toward covering is often irresistible, especially when it has such a power to simplify the lives of its purveyors. In the wake of 9/11, Middle Easterners throughout the United States felt under attack and responded with a series of rational covering responses just to survive the wave of hate surging throughout the country. Lebanese and Persian restaurants conspicuously displayed "Proud to be American" signs over their entrances.... A series of hate crimes prompted many Muslim women and Sikh men to remove their head coverings out of fear of being perceived as Middle Eastern....

We also see covering in even the most simple of choices: hair style....

... Over the past two decades, as images of the lavishly bearded Ayatollah Khomeini and Osama bin Laden have flooded the airwaves, the beard, the Middle East and radical Islam have grown inextricably intertwined in the American imagination. In the post-9/11 world, I do not go to the airport without shaving first....

Mexican Americans provide an instructive example of the tension between individual and collective interests, and of short- and long-term consequences....

... In the landmark suit *Hernandez v. Texas*, Pete Hernandez challenged the systematic exclusion of Mexican Americans from juries in Jackson County, Texas. In response, the State of Texas claimed, among other things, that there was no race discrimination occurring since individuals of Mexican descent were not a separate class from whites. The Supreme Court ultimately sided with Hernandez, holding that Mexicans were a distinct race from whites for equal protection purposes, and that the Equal Protection Clause applied to all forms of race discrimination, not just discrimination against blacks. Surprisingly, however, Hernandez faced strong opposition to his position from within the Mexican-American community.... [To many,] the recognition of their whiteness trumped the vindication of their legal and political rights and the preservation of equal protection under the law. This "Faustian [p]act with [w]hiteness" mirrors the extant Middle Easterners' hunger for judicial affirmations of whiteness, even when it inures to the group's long-term detriment....

... [I]n the aggregate, the phenomena of covering and selective racialization have helped to perpetuate negative stereotypes about Middle Easterners while frustrating the development of an effective community response to issues of concern for Middle Eastern Americans....

Both Nice and Tehrenian demonstrate the sprawling nature of identity castes under the rule of law. Even as bottom groups "shift" or expand, the top group stays constant. It is this resilience and entrenchment of identity castes that systemic advocates must outdo.

The following excerpt underscores that group castes and struggles are both local and global by drawing on knowledge from yet another School introduced in Part I—Third World Approaches to International Law (TWAIL). TWAIL scholar Makau Mutua explores below how the contemporary architecture of "the war against terrorism" tracks the symbolic and material architecture of colonialism and its legacies. Like colonialism, imperialism, and globalization, this ongoing "war" serves as a vehicle for top-down agendas of group supremacy. Recall, as you read, the excerpt by Ahmad and the review of human rights in Part III.

TERRORISM AND HUMAN RIGHTS: POWER, CULTURE, AND SUBORDINATION
Makau Mutua
8 Buff. Hum. Rts. L. Rev. 1 (2002)

Introduction

In the aftermath of the September 11 attacks, the United States has led the Western and European worlds towards a stronger consensus that re-emphasizes the centrality of American—and Western—predestination in geopolitics. The September 11 attacks on the United States have become the pretext for the renewal of a world order centered on Eurocentric norms and processes of global governance and domination. Nothing more poignantly captures this reality than the repeated warning by senior American officials: "you are either with us, or you are against us." The "us-and-them" dichotomy has a familiar ring and logic in the history of the West and of international law. That refrain has remained virtually unbroken in the history of the discipline and its practice. In fact, one cannot understand the history of international law without locating it in the colonial project, which gave birth to it. That period, which I call the Age of Europe, denotes a historical and philosophical paradigm; that of European hegemony imposed over the globe, particularly the South, over the last five centuries, culminating in the domination of the Americas, Africa, Asia, and the Pacific. International law is the legal fiction that was deployed to create and justify the Age of Europe.

The September 11 attacks—and the subsequent declaration of the so-called global war on terrorism—provide the fuel for the further consolidation of globalization. States and other international law-making fora, such as the United Nations, have come under intense pressure from the United States and its European allies to subordinate all other interests and questions, no matter how important and urgent, to a new international security-driven order geared toward the elimination of "global terrorism." Since the September 11 attacks have been presented as an assault on Western civilization, it is important to unpack the meaning of the term. Broken down to its bare bones, Western civilization denotes a complex of political, cultural, and economic arrangements which are rooted in liberal theory and philosophy. The current manifestation of that civilization seems to require some form of political democracy and a free-market system at home. The Judeo-Christian cultural and moral values of the West form the core social bases of Western civilization. It is out of these traditions that the current post-1945 universal human rights corpus was constructed.

. . . [This] reassertion of American and European domination of the globe—under the pretext of the global war on terrorism—will have profound and long-lasting implications on human rights. It crushes dissent and virtually eliminates any opportunities for a robust dialogue on the scope of human rights, their cultural relevance, and the strategies for their enforcement. Secondly, and more importantly, the war on terrorism gives the United States the ability to define its preferred human rights, and to exclude and narrow the scope of others. Third, it allows the United States to define the opponents of its version of human rights as enemies or supporters and sympathizers of global terrorism. In this "us-and-them" dialectic, the project for the reconstruction and multi-culturalization of human rights will become increasingly difficult—if not impossible. . . . But there is hope beneath this mountain of despair. . . . Advocates for a truly universal human rights doctrine should seize the moment to underscore these deep and abiding imbalances in power. And there could be a bonus. Although it is highly unlikely, the official guardians of human rights may develop some sympathy for the position of those of [us] who have critiqued the human rights corpus for its cultural and political biases.

. . . [This] global war on terrorism targets non-Western peoples, cultures, and causes, particularly where they diverge from—or resist subordination to—certain Western interests. The war on terrorism is mainly focused on certain Islamic traditions and political projects. . . . In this contest, the West has not been shy to put forward its script of human history. It is a text that emphatically warns that the summit of human civilization can only exist within the perimeters of liberal theory and philosophy. It seems a foregone conclusion: Muslim societies, like all other non-Western societies, must modernize, democratize, liberalize, and adopt open, free market systems. The message is loud and clear. Islamic societies must Westernize or perish.

The great paradox, however, is the inconsistency of the West. Despite this vocal commitment to spreading and defending Western civilization, the West supports and protects despotic and kleptocratic regimes, if they govern societies of vital military, strategic, or economic interests to it. But only as long as such societies do not pursue interests which are inimical to—or threaten—Western capital and security. This is particularly true of the relationship of the West, especially the United States, with oil-rich or strategically important Arab or Muslim states. The West has not been reticent to jettison principle over strategic interest. In other words, even the commitment of the West to liberalism is highly instrumental and strategic: as long as it retains the hegemony of the West over the globe. That is why this paper focuses on the arrogance of power over morality and argues that the war on terrorism represents yet another fiction that the West is now constructing to strengthen its cultural and political domination of the international legal order, including human rights.

Eurocentrism and International Law

The effects of the September 11 attacks on the United States on human rights and the international legal regimes are best understood as a historical continuum. The unilateral actions taken by the United States under the veil of an allied coalition expose international law as a system of "insider" groups and dominant global interests.... This global white European supremacy over non-European peoples is premised on the notion of Europe as the center of the universe, Christianity as the fountain of civilization, the innateness of capitalist economics, and political imperialism as a necessity....

Thus international law orders the world into the European and the non-European, and gives primacy to the former. This is done by creating the notion of the hierarchy of cultures and peoples. The fundamental principles of international law evidence this inflexible view of the discipline. Sovereignty and statehood are defined in such a way as to exclude or subordinate non-European societies. Membership in international society is a prerogative of American and European powers, which alone decide who—and on what terms—belongs to this international society and can benefit from the privileges of international law. Nowhere has this been more evident than in Afghanistan where the United States has arrogated to itself the right to dismantle the state, and to recreate it....

The Cultural and Political Biases of Human Rights

The international law of human rights, arguably the most benign of all the areas of international law, seeks the universalization of European cultural, philosophical, and political norms and social structures. It is largely a culturally specific doctrine, which is expressed in the idiom of the same culture. The human rights corpus is driven—normatively and descriptively—by what I have called the savage-victim-savior metaphor, in which human rights is a grand narrative of an epochal contest that pits savages against victims and saviors. In this script of human rights, democracy and western liberalism are internationalized to redeem savage non-Western cultures from themselves, and to alleviate the suffering of victims, who are generally non-western and non-European. The images of the savage Taliban, the Afghan victims mired in pre-modernity, and the American saviors put the metaphor in sharp relief.

In the human rights idiom, North America and the European West—acting generally under the guise of the United Nations and other multilateral agencies—are the saviors of hapless victims whose salvation lies only in the transformation of their savage cultures through the imposition of human rights. The human rights corpus is presented as a settled normative edifice, as a glimpse of an eternal, inflexible truth. As a result, attempts to question or reformulate a truly universal regime of rights, one that reflects the complexity and the diversity of all cultures, have generally been viewed with indifference or hostility by the official guardians of human rights.

This refusal to create a culturally complex and diverse human rights corpus is all the more perplexing because the view that the human rights doctrine is an ideology with deep roots in liberalism and democratic forms of government is beyond question.... Understood from this position, human rights are an ideology with a specific cultural and ethnographic fingerprint.... The advocacy of human rights across cultural borders is then an attempt to displace the local non-Western culture with the "universal" culture of human rights. Human rights therefore become the universal culture. It is in this sense that the "other" culture, that which is non-European, is the savage in the human rights corpus and its discourse.

The Savage and the Terrorist as the "Other"

In the pre-September 11 world—if that date is now a point of departure—the accepted wisdom in the West was that human rights composed the genius of the good society....

After the Cold War, the US and the West emerged victorious, and without a credible or formidable foe. Russia was in shambles, and its former clients in East/Central Europe and elsewhere had rushed into the arms of the West. China was perceived as having the potential for mischief but its zest to join the American-led global market would curtail its rivalry with the West....

In the past decade, particularly after the end of the Cold War, the United States started to define the phenomenon now called Islamic fundamentalism as a threat to American and Western interests. But the United States felt that those threats were largely confined to the Middle East and North Africa, and were directed against Israel and the pro-American regimes in the region. Americans have taken the September 11 attacks as evidence that "extremist political Islam" is a real threat to the country's internal security, and not just its clients abroad. As a consequence, the United States is now leading a conceptual struggle to redefine, revise, and amplify the meaning of the savage in the consciousness of Western civilization....

... In more blatant language—language that may have been politically incorrect before September 11—American officials have openly declared the current crisis a struggle between good and evil, a contest pitting civilization against the forces of darkness. It is not lost on anyone as to who and what is described by this evil. Its cultural content is a stew of anti-American politics utilizing Islam as its scaffolding. But it is presented by American officials and the press in the United States as an Islamic and Arab fanatical hatred for the West for being free, liberal, and peace-loving. For how, the press repeatedly asks, can one explain the suicidal voyage of nineteen young Arab men with promising personal futures? Completely demonic and inexplicable fanaticism, the press answers.

There is no [self-critical] introspection on why apparently "normal" individuals would carry out such attacks. There is no real desire to locate this "evil" in American policies in the Middle East, North Africa, and the Muslim world. And, of course, there is no discussion of whether those policies ought to be re-examined or revised. Instead, Arabs and Muslims—the natives of the current crisis—are presented as a dangerous if unmalleable lot. The only way to effectively address this threat, the United States has concluded, is to militarily vanquish states that consciously support the networks of attackers or those that harbor or pursue policies that imperil American and Western political and economic interests. The military defeat of those societies would then be followed by political reconstruction in which "moderate Islam" would rule or in which a more liberal, pro-Western political state would be installed. Afghanistan is the test case.... The United Nations, other multi-lateral agencies, and the most influential European states are co-authors in varying degrees of this project.

It bears saying that the history of international law—including its post-1945 expression through the United Nations—is largely about ordering the lives of non-European native peoples. The purpose of such ordering is to create a world in which American and European interests are not threatened or injured by political and cultural paradigms that may be inconsistent with those interests. That is why the "othering" process is absolutely essential if Western hegemony is to be maintained. Although that process is arduous and usually only produces an elite that has no depth in its own society, the West regards that as the first and necessary step towards the recovery or reclamation of primitive, backward, and pre-modern societies....

It is important to note that the native savage has always been racialized in human rights discourse and international law.... [I]n Western discourse, the native has also been depicted as dangerous, particularly when he has challenged European authority in the anti-colonial movement. The Mau Mau of Kenya, for example, who took up arms against British colonialists were regarded as particularly dangerous. This is where the native savage morphs into a terrorist, primarily because he pursues his political objectives by deploying armed force as an instrument of the struggle. Both the Mau Mau and the Algerian FLN were regarded as terrorists, as was Nelson Mandela's African National Congress. The post-

September 11 crisis returns the world to the image of the native savage as a terrorist. . . .

The Effects of War on Terror on Human Rights

Since September 11, the United States has enacted and promulgated laws, policies, and measures that have a profound effect on civil liberties in the United States. Some of the measures, such as the executive order to establish military tribunals to try individuals designated as terrorists, have been deemed to violate both American constitutional and international human rights standards. Outside the United States, the Bush administration has prosecuted its war on terror without regard to both general international law and international human humanitarian law. In other words, the United States views its perceived security interests as a trump against both domestic and international law. No rule of law is sacred in the prosecution of the war against terror.

. . . Such disregard of human rights, which the United States has forcefully championed before, and for which it has used force against other states, underscores the arrogance of power over morality and international law. . . .

The American encroachment on civil liberties has already led other states to assert security as a pretext for denying human rights. The vague and broad assertions of national security interests and sovereignty provide the perfect excuse for states bent on crushing dissent. In Zimbabwe, for example, President Robert Mugabe has liberally labeled his political opponents terrorists, and has employed harsh police and security measures to muzzle, persecute, and destroy them. Israeli authorities have escalated their military attacks and assassinations of Palestinians in the Occupied Territories, all in the name of the war against terrorism. Repressive states have found new legitimacy by joining the American-led coalition against terrorism.

The war against terrorism allows states and powerful interests to redefine the legitimacy of any struggle, and cast it, if they wish, in an unfavorable light, and therefore justify the most extreme measures against it. Any cause or struggle—and the Palestinian case is a classic example—can be delegitimized because it is presented as detrimental to the interests of American client states in the Middle East. The broad and vague use of the term "terrorist" and their sympathizers has had a chilling effect on legitimate debate and differences on serious issues both in the academe and in popular public and political discourses. . . . Legitimate dissent is being deliberately conflated with sedition and disloyalty to the state. This stifles academic inquiry and compromises the intellectual integrity of the academe.

. . . [A]ttempts to argue for alternative cultural and political norms are now suspect. Ideologies, theories, and analyses that contradict the central tenets of liberalism may be seen as fuel for those intent on attacking the West. Questions, for example, on the excessive individualism espoused by the human rights corpus or the ravages brought about by globalization are treated as attacks on the West. Insistence on the importance of economic, social and cultural rights is being viewed as a rejection of free enterprise. There simply is less room for the proponents of cultural pluralism in the construction of the human rights corpus to pursue the project of reconstruction.

But paradoxically, the American double-talk on human rights could open the window for a discussion on the universality of human rights, their cultural bases, and the terms of their enforcement. If—as is now the case—the state that regards itself as the home of fundamental human rights can so easily abridge them, what is to prevent cultural pluralists from re-opening debate on the cultural legitimacy of human rights? The view that human rights are culturally-specific, and that they are bound by history and politics—that they are not in content eternal and non-negotiable—calls for the conclusion that the corpus is experimental, a work in progress. As such, the text of human rights ought to be re-opened for re-examination and reformulation to reflect the diversity and vitality of other cultures beyond the Atlantic communities.

An Agenda for Thought and Action

Nothing in the recent past has posed a greater challenge to human rights than the war on terrorism. . . .

The human rights movement must abandon the savage-savior-victim metaphor if there is going to be real hope in a genuine international discourse on rights. . . .

Ultimately, a new theory of internationalism and human rights, one that responds to diverse cultures, must confront the inequities of the international order. In this respect, human rights must break from the historical continuum—expressed in the metaphor of human rights—that keeps intact the hierarchical relationships between European and non-European populations. . . .

. . . [T]he contradictions between commitments to sovereign equality, stunning political and economic imbalances, and paternalistic humanitarianism cannot be definitively resolved logically, doctrinally, or institutionally; rather, they must be confronted in ongoing struggle in all legal, political, economic, and cultural arenas. . . .

Human rights thinkers and organizations must step back from paternalism and create a new basis for calculating human dignity, and identifying ways and societal structures through which such dignity could be protected or enhanced. Such an approach would not assume—ab initio—that a particular cultural practice or norm was offensive to human rights.

It would respect cultural pluralism as a basis for finding common universality on some issues. Such an approach would first excavate the social meaning and purposes of cultural practices and norms—as well as their effects—and then investigate the conflicting positions in that society. Rather than demonizing and finger-pointing, under the tutelage of outsiders, the contending positions would be carefully examined and compared to find ways of either modifying or discarding the norm or practice without denigrating its practitioners. It is clear now that the zealotry of current approaches leaves no room for considered intra-cultural dialogue and introspection.

No single culture is original, pure, complete, or superior to others. . . . Human rights can play a big role in changing the unjust international order, and particularly the imbalances between the West and the Third World. But it will not do so unless Western thinkers and advocates end their domination and grip on how human rights are defined and enforced. Nor should the war on terrorism be used as an excuse to exclude the contributions of non-European intellectuals and societies to a more universal human rights corpus.

Tehranian and Mutua underscore the centrality of second- and third-layer goals in antisubordination struggles: advocates not only must accomplish the difficult task of reforming unjust laws—which requires group power—but they also must use this power to shift mainstream cultural perceptions of systems, bottoms, and justice. These goals, laid out in Part IV, depend on the capacity of those at the bottom to develop collective consciousness and organized group capacity for long-term struggles that contest foundational concepts and ground rules, using methods and strategies described in Part V.

Expanding on these points, legal scholar Trina Jones considers how tops have stayed largely on the top in terms of employment and income over time, while those on the bottom have shifted—but resisted through self-organization and challenges to the ideologies and institutions of subordination. Jones notes that systemic injustice is a "complex and evolving tapestry" that must be engaged with an understanding of and strategies to address both what has changed from colonial times and what has stayed stubbornly in place:

> [R]ace and class have interacted to produce and perpetuate socioeconomic hierarchy in this country. White workers, slaves, and immigrants of color were all, at various points, stymied in their quest for the American Dream. Yet their histories reveal that class functions differently depending upon a person's race and that race operates differently depending upon a person's class. . . . [E]ssential are affirmative measures to open previously

closed employment arenas and to ensure that questions of disadvantage and privilege, and of discrimination and merit, are kept in the forefront of policy debates. . . . Importantly, as the United States moves into the future, Americans must continue to look to the past, for history reveals that inequality is a complex and evolving tapestry. Its constitutive threads—racism, sexism, classism, xenophobia, homophobia, religious intolerance—have been seamlessly woven together. To unravel one, we must unravel them all.[30]

Tehranian and Mutua, like Jones, reaffirm a key lesson of experience with long-term struggles against systemic injustice: progress depends more on "layered" goals than on winning formal declarations of more legal rights. Progress toward Critical Justice requires both amelioration and transformation, which in turn depend jointly on targeted changes of law and long-term shifts of power and culture.

NOTES AND QUESTIONS

1. *Supremacy by Another Name.* As the tactics and targets of elite domination evolve over the years, so too does the terminology used to describe the architects and adherents of subordinating systems and their ideologies. For example, Richard Spencer, president of a white nationalist think tank and an advocate of a "peaceful ethnic cleansing," coined the term Alt-Right to replace white nationalist (or white supremacist). Spencer said, "I like the term Alt-Right. It has an openness to it. And immediately understandable. We're coming from a new perspective." What do you "understand" Alt-Right to connote? What about the label of a white nationalist? How do Alt-Right or white nationalist adherents and rallies differ, if at all, from members and practices of the Ku Klux Klan hate group? See generally Matt Thompson, The Hoods Are Off (Aug. 12, 2017), www.theatlantic.com/national/archive/2017/08/the-hoods-are-off/536694/.

2. *Resistance.* The much-publicized Alt-Right rallies of 2017 sparked a discussion of whether identity politics—the political alliance among identity-group members, particularly along race lines—are to blame for the recent rise in (overt) white supremacy. Relatedly, a New York Times op-ed in the wake of the deadly Charlottesville "Unite the Right" rally of 2017 suggested the "social justice warrior alt-left and the white supremacist alt-right [are] two sides of the same coin." Erick-Woods Erickson, What Trump Got Wrong on Charlottesville, N.Y. Times (Aug. 13, 2017). But these views incorrectly assess the origin of the resistance strategy of identity politics, at least as deployed by communities of color and other subordinated groups. As a Washington Post op-ed noted, these views have it backwards. The recent white supremacy rallies may be a response to the identity politics of organizing among minority groups,

---

[30] Trina Jones, Race, Economic Class, and Employment Opportunity, 72 Law & Contemp. Probs. 57, 87 (2009).

but minority identity politics were, in fact, a *prior* response and resistance strategy adopted by bottom groups to confront white supremacy. Moreover:

> [Identity politics] are a response to life in a country that built itself on the theory that "all men are created equal" but a reality where the opposite was true. And they're a response not just to the outright racism that survives on websites such as Stormfront and at Confederate flag rallies but also to the stubborn structural barriers that still hold back people with darker skin.

Molly Roberts, Stop Blaming White Supremacy on "Identity Politics," Wash. Post (Aug. 14, 2017). Roberts also suggests that whites as a group (not just the Alt-Right) have an identity politics, too—it's just called "politics." From your understanding of democracy, do you agree? What do you think accounts for the rise—as shown by such rallies—in white identity politics?

CHAPTER RECAP

This chapter explained that law is both an instrument and a product of colonialism, imperialism, and globalization. As a result, law "fails by design"—it regularly trumps principle with power. This entrenched status quo depends on "private" law as much as on "public" violence. In addition, the legal entrenchment of colonial castes rests on identity ideologies of collectivized superiority and inferiority. Law as ideology systematically converts identities into inequality. The next chapter in this part delves more deeply into these points, showing how identity and law interplay with groups and interests as top-down ideology to inhibit Critical Justice.

CHAPTER 14

ROAD TEST: DISMANTLING "IDEOLOGICAL ILLUSIONS OF EQUALITY" TO RESIST HEGEMONY

■ ■ ■

Table of Sections

14.1 Social Ills—like Sexism, Racism, and Homophobia—Prop up "Ideological Illusions of Equality" to Justify Persistent Group Inequalities
14.2 Over Time, Internalized Ideologies Shape People, Choices, and Castes
14.3 The Social Hegemony of Identity-as-Ideology Kills Bottoms

OPENING THOUGHTS

Ideally, what should be said to every child, repeatedly, throughout his or her school life is something like this: "You are in the process of being indoctrinated. . . . You are being taught by people who have been able to accommodate themselves to a regime of thought laid down by their predecessors. It is a self-perpetuating system. Those of you who are more robust and individual than others will be encouraged to leave and find ways of educating yourself—educating your own judgements. Those that stay must remember, always, and all the time, that they are being moulded and patterned to fit into the narrow and particular needs of this particular society.

—**Doris Lessing,** The Golden Notebook

[H]egemony is a process of assimilation, education, and adaptation consistent with the achievement of dominant group goals. In particular, hegemony ensures a "correspondence" between individual acts and admissions, and between individual conduct and necessary group ends.

—**Anthony V. Alfieri,** The Antinomies of Poverty Law and a Theory of Dialogic Empowerment, 16 N.Y.U. Rev. L. & Soc. Change 659, 678 (1988)

Given that LatCrit theorizing is about anti-subordination, the spaces in which we conduct our work should facilitate our interrogation of relations, examination of institutions, excavation of histories, exposition of contradictions, flaunting of convention, and dissection of hegemony to understand the intricacies of power with its continual reproduction and reconsolidation.

—**Margaret E. Montoya**, Religious Rituals and LatCrit Theorizing, 19 Chicana/o-Latina/o L. Rev. 417, 420 (1998)

INTRODUCTION

In the last chapter, we examined in more detail how law is a system with a history and with a design, which centuries of systemic outputs confirm. As the "cutting edge" of colonialism and all that has followed in its persistent wake, law has played a central, constitutive role, including producing, modifying, justifying, and continuing identity-based castes. In this chapter, we similarly delve more deeply into law as identity ideology. We examine more fully how law, identity, and ideology function culturally and systemically to create hegemonies—pervasive, entrenched, normalized realities that appear unmovable and virtually unassailable.

Day by day and decade by decade, law generates streams of decisions and ripple effects that reinforce already-entrenched patterns of group stratification based on social identities. Over time, supremacist imperatives adapt to ensnare identity groups that were not part of the original colonial castes, subjecting them to the same top-down calculations, legacies, and patterns of entrenched paradigms like white over Black, male over female, rich over poor, and so on. Law's conflation with identity and ideology creates identity-inflected rules of property, contract, commerce, immigration, and citizenship. Law as identity ideology both promises and denies equal justice—and then denies the denial.

Mindful of the many top-down denials and other disguises, distractions, or deflections that prop up systemic "illusions of equality," we dive deeper into the interconnections between identity ideologies (societal -isms and phobias) as social *ills* that cause social *problems*. From a critical perspective, formal equality, as outlined in Part I, functions as one of these top-down ideological illusions: on paper, everyone is equal as an individual but, in fact, every person lives within and in between the material and cultural realities of interlocking identity castes. The social problem we examined there—unequal education—is tethered securely to at least one social ill—white-over-Black racism. In this law-as-ideology scheme, as noted in Parts I and IV, formal rights are important for struggle and resistance but insufficient for enduring, transformative progress.

We therefore start by centering the critical connections between persistent social problems and systemic social ills. Put simply, "social ills" are the identity-related "isms," like racism, sexism, anti-Semitism, classism, and so forth, and "phobias" such as homophobia, Islamophobia, xenophobia, and transphobia. These isms and phobias are collective ills because they spread ideologies that breed social problems.

These isms and phobias not only feed systemic injustice but also obstruct solutions because they shape consciousness and culture connecting micro-macro, as well as cultural-material, realities for both subordinated bottoms and privileged tops. At the micro level, for example, isms and phobias show up, often unquestioned, in conversations:

> [R]aced and gendered power hierarchies are constructed and reinforced through normalizing everyday practices such as jokes, storytelling, generalizations or even so-called compliments. In and of themselves, these practices can be said to be "innocent," "insignificant" or "just for fun." However, when they are continually reiterated, they become culturally normalized and end up functioning as systematic discrimination against minorities, which reinforce majority privilege.[1]

Thus, using law to "fix" problems—the lack of affordable housing, pollution, the opioid epidemic, domestic violence, wage theft—must take into account complex, myriad, unobvious ways that social ills *always* shape social problems. These ideological connections point advocates in search of effective solutions toward the three-layered goals of systemic advocacy. Spotting identity-based isms, phobias, and other social ills in relationship to social problems is integral to designing systemic justice in any context.

If completely successful, law as ideology is a tool in the top-down struggle for hegemony—for unquestioned, voluntary compliance with elite systems and their identity castes. Hegemonies, as noted throughout this book, are built incrementally by ruling elites to dominate other social groups not only materially but also through beliefs—ideologies and biases—in perpetuity. The beliefs embedded in supremacist identity ideologies are accepted culturally as "common sense," even by many individuals among subordinated groups, especially when embodied and enforced for centuries as law. Hegemony, for elites, means achieving cognitive, material, and emotional loyalty from those whom you already rule. Elites aspire to become hegemonic to put their collective dominance beyond any serious challenge, in large part by enlisting those it subordinates in their own subordination.

Ideology and hegemony thus work hand in hand: ideology supports elite drives for hegemony. Hegemony relies on ideology, as well as on violence. Consequently, counter-hegemonic work with groups necessarily is designed to deconstruct dominant myths and create new critical consciousness and cultural resources. To counteract elite ideologies and

---

[1] Philomena Essed and Sara Louise Muhr, Entitlement Racism and Its Intersections: An Interview with Philomena Essed, Social Justice Scholar, 18 Ephemera: Theory and Politics in Organization 183 (2018) (focusing on "everyday racism" and how day-to-day conversations and actions can not only reinforce castes but create a sense of "entitlement racism" on the part of members of dominant groups), www.ephemerajournal.org/sites/default/files/pdfs/contribution/18-1essedmuhr.pdf.

their promotion of hegemony, advocates and activists intentionally construct critical and self-critical conversations, research, and analysis that cultivate awareness and knowledge of histories, systems, and contexts—and test and refine that awareness and knowledge through the work of collaborative teams and actions. Relevant means and methods include issue framing, direct actions, and messaging that includes those affected by social problems and engaged in social struggle, as well as those with legal, economic, or other expertise. Presaging NeJaime's call for "multidimensional" advocacy from Part II, legal scholar Fran Ansley below describes the sort of conversations and issue frames that advocates might need to generate to spur local challenges to globalized inequalities:

> Arguably all actors interested in gaining or maintaining political power—from outsider democratic challengers to well-defended authoritarian rulers—can enhance their power if they are able to articulate an ideological frame that makes sense of their actions, justifies their policies, and legitimizes their claims to authority. In the case of social movements, however, success at framing the issues is particularly crucial because they must be able to move people voluntarily into sometimes risky action, and, ordinarily, they must recruit these volunteers without recourse to the structures, incentives, and general momentum available to those with access to existing political channels. Social movements thus have no alternative but to develop compelling frames that attract and energize members. . . .
>
> . . . [Advocates and activists] must devote substantial time and resources to enabling and supporting horizontal, person-to-person interaction between ordinary members of their movements and people who are in other physical or social locations in the global economy. Such interactions . . . will function as an important incubator for the new images, metaphors, and shared understandings that [advocates and activists] are going to need if they want to help construct more inclusive and more globally conscious frames that resonate with larger publics.[2]

Systemic advocacy's expanded focus on building power from below is linked to the goal of shifting activists' and advocates' own consciousness *and* that of mainstream cultures and groups. This work entails—and uses—time, planning, and organization. Just as elites have used time to pursue hegemony, advocates use time and creativity to counteract that legacy. Social transformation puts a premium on the development of tools, capacities, and resources to serve subordinated groups engaged in organized struggles *for the long haul*. Advocates support organized groups

---

[2] Fran Ansley, Inclusive Boundaries and Other (Im)possible Paths Toward Community Development in a Global World, 150 U. Pa. L. Rev. 353, 358, 407–08 (2001).

to help spark and nurture continual collective struggles from below so that elites remain frustrated in their ambitions for complete hegemony—internalized, unchallenged control of law and society. This road test chapter explores and expands on these points.

14.1 SOCIAL ILLS—LIKE SEXISM, RACISM, AND HOMOPHOBIA—PROP UP "IDEOLOGICAL ILLUSIONS OF EQUALITY" TO JUSTIFY PERSISTENT GROUP INEQUALITIES

As a system, law intentionally and systematically creates "ideological illusions of equality" that convince many of its justice through conscious and unconscious processes. These illusions can blindfold analysis and distort advocacy. In the following excerpt, critical legal scholar Charles Lawrence names and explores these illusions, examining specifically formal equality—the "equal opportunity" promulgated by judicial doctrines focused on the Equal Protection Clause of the Fourteenth Amendment—the most litigated constitutional provision in U.S. history. Lawrence challenges advocates to consider whether today's resulting rules and systems (in the United States) are designed for equal justice—or are (still) designed for "just us"—that is, for colonial elites and their successors in interest. Lawrence shows that ideologies not only hide and justify the legal system's outputs, they help create them. Exposing law's ideological illusions is an active, vital, and justice-seeking endeavor. As you read, consider whether "justice" is an ideological illusion for a system designed to benefit just (some of) "us."

"JUSTICE" OR "JUST US": RACISM AND THE ROLE OF IDEOLOGY
Charles R. Lawrence III
35 Stan. L. Rev. 831 (1983)

An anecdote, related only half in jest on a black ghetto street corner, tells of a local philosopher who journeyed to the courthouse and jail in search of justice and, sure enough, found "just us." The raconteur's commentary on the criminal justice system's disproportionate victimization of his black brothers and sisters is easily transposed to a tale of black children's search for justice in America's public schools. Today, ... decades after the Supreme Court first declared that state-coerced school segregation unconstitutionally deprived blacks of equal educational opportunity, racially segregated schools remain the norm. "Just us" is still far more easily found than "justice." ...

Ideology as an Unconscious Defense Mechanism

When individuals are confronted with the fact that their impulses, wishes, or actual behavior conflict with what they have been taught is morally acceptable behavior, they will often attempt to resolve that conflict by use of an unconscious defense mechanism in the personality structure. This defense mechanism protects the individual from the pain of conscious confrontations with a self that he does not wish to acknowledge. By various techniques, the individual justifies, rationalizes, or even denies the existence of a reality that makes him uncomfortable.

It would be a dangerous oversimplification to argue that theories which were developed to explain individual behavior can be applied without modification to interpret societal or political behavior. But the study of group behavior, whether in anthropology, sociology, political science, or history, is in part the study of the collective behavior of individuals. Each discipline posits that the whole is greater than the sum of its parts, but analysis of the parts is nonetheless significant to understanding the whole.

At the societal level, ideology assumes the role of the defense mechanism in the individual psyche. Elite whites justify, deny, and legitimate the existing racial order by representing reality in ideal terms. This enables them to continue practices that they would otherwise condemn and in which their own complicity would be painful to admit.

Ideology can be thought of in a number of ways. It has most often been thought of as a consciously wielded weapon, an intellectual tool that is used by a group to enhance its own political power. This view sees ideology as the result of rational calculation by those who will gain by the institutionalization of a particular view of reality. Students of ideology have named this view the "interest" theory.

Another view of ideology, a view which shares my skepticism of conspiracy theories, is that ideology is a symptom, a defense mechanism against the anxiety felt by those who hold power through means and with motives they cannot comfortably acknowledge. This "strain" theory explains ideology as a response to the strains created by an individual's or a group's social role or position: Ideology "provides a 'symbolic outlet' for emotional disturbances generated by social disequilibrium." . . .

The ideology of equal opportunity has evolved through the collective efforts of academics writing articles, politicians making speeches, and lawyers arguing and judges deciding cases. These individuals tend to identify with the socioeconomic order in which they hold privileged positions while at the same time feeling the tension between the harsh realities of that order and their ideal images of themselves within that order. They would like to think of themselves as fair individuals who, by virtue of their hard work and superior talent, hold positions of influence in a just society. The natural response of the privileged individual confronted with this tension between the real and the ideal is to resolve it by legitimizing the existing structure to himself. This self-mystification manifests itself in his legal arguments, judicial opinions, or theoretical discussions, which in turn become part of a [systemic] defense mechanism that extends beyond the individual.

Modern Equal Protection Doctrine

The legal system—along with academia and the church—has been a principal vehicle for the development and transmission of ideological thought. The history of the ideology of American race relations illustrates the central role which these institutions have played in creating and disseminating images that justify this country's treatment of blacks while at the same time concealing and distorting its reality.

Slavery was justified through a Christian ideology that saw Africans as nonhumans, heathens, or the descendants of Ham. Enslavement was explained both as just punishment (i.e., "the sins of the father shall be visited . . .") and as the means of salvation for an infidel race that did not know God. . . .

Today, racial injustice finds its justification not in the commands of God or Nature but in the law. Although the equal protection clause gives us a legal command to treat all persons equally, the Court has created a set of ideological images that condition our societal conception of equality. For example, the law tells us that (1) even when blacks are obviously being treated differently because of their race they are not really being wrongfully discriminated against or denied equal opportunity so long as the discrimination is not intentional; (2) even when there is evidence of intentional race-based discrimination, no one has been constitutionally injured unless the discriminators used the government as their instrument of discrimination; and (3) all individuals must be viewed as similarly situated, i.e., they all begin the competition at the same starting line, and therefore must be treated the same. Thus, without proof of specific, government-sponsored, racially motivated discrimination, any injury that might bring blacks to the competition with an obvious disadvantage does not legally exist and may not be taken into account.

These principles create an illusion of equal treatment which takes the place of reality. The law requires that we treat blacks and whites equally. We are a law-abiding country, and the courts tell us that in the vast majority of instances the law is obeyed. Thus, if we are treating blacks and whites equally, and blacks continue to be disproportionately represented at the bottom of the socioeconomic ladder, it must either be because they are failing to avail themselves of the opportunities available to them or because they are not capable of availing themselves of those opportunities. This ideological illusion replaces the reality of continued racial exclusion.

The ideology of equal opportunity tells us that the barriers of segregation and discrimination have been removed: If blacks continue to fail it must be because they are inferior.

The idea that modern equal protection law is part of an ideology that serves the needs of a particular group—elite whites—has been an important theme in the writing of [critical legal scholars in the closing decades of the 20th century] . . . asking questions like "What shared values are asserted [in or by the judges in equality doctrine]?" "Whose values are they?" "In whose interests do they exist as values?" and "What do they presuppose?". . .

[These critical legal scholars identified] an ideological struggle between the perpetrators of discrimination and the victims of discrimination, with each group having conflicting views of society and expectations of the law. The victims, [like] blacks, view the *Brown* decision as an official declaration that racial discrimination had become illegal (and immoral). And the meaning of such a declaration "must include an expectation that there will be, when the task is completed, some significant change in the conditions of life that one associates with the past practices of discrimination—segregated schools, lack of jobs, the worst jobs, lack of political power." The perpetrators, on the other hand, having declared discrimination illegal in *Brown*, have redefined discrimination through a formalistic set of rules so that not everything that looks like discrimination is discrimination. The perpetrator perspective first drastically narrows the legal concept of discrimination and then, despite the continuing presence of the conditions formerly associated with discrimination, proclaims the disease cured, or at least almost cured.

[Critical legal scholars have already exposed how] . . . modern antidiscrimination doctrine has adopted the perpetrator perspective, which allows it to serve as an important ideological tool for societal elites. But although this explains how the perpetrator perspective legitimizes the discriminatory interests of societal elites, it does not tell us how the perspective comes about. Unless there is a conspiracy of lawyers, judges, and legal scholars who act with an awareness of the ideological image they create and of its relationship to the preservation of their position of relative advantage . . . the "strain" theory of ideology helps us complete the picture.

Lawyers, judges, and legal scholars adopt the perpetrator perspective not only because it operates in their material interests but also because it serves their [conscious and unconscious] emotional needs. . . .

Two components of equal protection doctrine—the "state action" requirement and the intent requirement—illustrate the ideology's delusional properties. . . . [Below, I briefly] explore how these rules of law promote illusory ideological images that foster racism and examine why the illusionist and the audience alike so often perceive these images to be the neutral and objective truth.

State action

By restricting the application of the fourteenth amendment to discrimination in which the government is implicated, the state action rule immunizes private discriminators from constitutional scrutiny. While the origin of this rule is textual, countervailing constitutional values of privacy or freedom of non-association have been used to justify the rule's exculpation of private racism. Thus, it is argued that a white family's decision to send its children to private school or to move to a racially exclusive suburb should be accorded respect in spite of the fourteenth amendment's requirement of nondiscrimination because these decisions are part of the right to individual and familial autonomy. In this way, the state action rule's rather arbitrary limit on the scope of the antidiscrimination principle is transformed into a right to privacy, which is presented as the constitutional embodiment of an affirmative, neutral, and universally shared value. A new and positive image emerges, an image which has been abstracted from its original context.

In the abstract, the right to make decisions such as how we will educate our children or with whom we will associate is indeed a value shared by all. But when we view this privacy value in the abstract, we fail to perceive how it operates in the real world. We do not ask ourselves, for example, whether it is a value to which all have equal access. We do not inquire about who can send their children to private school or move to an exclusive suburb. The privacy value, when presented as an ideal image, seems an appropriate limitation on even so important a value as racial justice because we are led to believe that it is a value in which we all hold an equal stake. This is the essence of ideological imagery.

But how does the image come to be? Why do legal [observers], even theorists with a firm commitment to remedying racism, seem to buy the privacy illusion as well as sell it?

As an answer, I suggest that the natural reaction of the legal scholar confronted by the horrible specter of American racial inequality is to disassociate himself from its cause, to say "I am not involved in this inhumanity." For him to merely argue that the text of the Constitution permits private racism is not enough: He is still morally implicated. He must create a neutral image that makes him a helpless and innocent bystander. But this illusion must do more than fool others. To avoid the anxiety of guilt and the fear of condemnation he must also delude himself. This self-mystification occurs on an unconscious level and results in selective perception. This is what [critical legal scholars] refer to when not[ing] that [legal actors] do not seem to hear the victim's voice.

Discriminatory intent

The intent requirement is a second example of how equal protection doctrine promotes an ideological imagery that fosters racism. This rule ensures that no constitutional violation will be found unless the victims of government actions that have racially discriminatory effects prove that the government acted with racially discriminatory animus in creating those conditions.

As with the state action rule, the intent requirement begins as a negative limitation on the application of antidiscrimination law. It immunizes from constitutional scrutiny actions that common sense and experience tell us are discriminatory—actions that result in the maintenance of discriminatory conditions. By denying the existence of discrimination, it makes a remedy unavailable and serves the interests of those who would otherwise bear the burden of the societal dislocation necessitated by that remedy. But the intent requirement is too transparent to serve ideology's delusional purpose. Often, it is obvious that there is actual intent even when legal intent cannot be proved. But, more importantly, the absence of intent is simply not, in itself, a sufficient moral justification for continuing practices that perpetuate racial injustice. Again, legal theorists have surmounted this hurdle by substituting a positive value for the negative. They equate the absence of discriminatory intent with racial neutrality. Thus, the intent requirement is removed from the context of racially discriminatory impact, and the ideal image of "color blindness" or "individual merit" is presented in its place.

This ideological illusion is achieved as follows: (1) If there is no racially motivated intent, then there is no racial discrimination; (2) if there is no racial discrimination, then black and white individuals are similarly situated, i.e., neither is burdened by his race, and so must be treated similarly, i.e., as individuals who are judged solely on the basis of merit; and (3) if this similar treatment results in a condition that burdens blacks more than it does whites, it is nevertheless proper because it pursues the honorable and universally shared values of color blindness and individual merit. Unspoken and more insidious is another step: (4) If blacks continue to fail under similar treatment, it must be because they are somehow inferior.

Again we return to the question of why legal scholars are so susceptible to the equal protection doctrine's ideological sleight-of-hand (or mind) that they believe the magic even when they are the magicians. The answer lies in the scholar's need to avoid responsibility for wrongdoing and the ideology's ability to transform the wrongdoing into virtue. For example, in the context of minority admissions or faculty hiring the implication of racism comes perilously close to home because the implicated institutions are ones in which the legal theorist is directly responsible for policy. When faced with de facto segregation in his own law school, the answer "I did not intend the crime" does not relieve his anxiety. But the ideological images of equal protection theory change him from villain to hero, from criminal to crime-fighter. He opposes racism whether it is directed at blacks or whites. He is the champion of the individual and the individual's right to be judged on his or her own merits. Images with this kind of power of transformation cannot help but seduce. . . .

The Hidden Element of Social Class

[U.S. history makes us] familiar with the more obvious uses of race-baiting as a diversionary tactic—getting poor and working class whites to view their disadvantaged position more favorably by using racism to remind them that they do not occupy the lowest rung on the ladder and, to the extent discontent remains, encouraging them to see blacks as the source of their poor condition. The ideology of equal opportunity uses race more subtly. Instead of simply using blacks as a symbolic whipping boy, it uses race to achieve the old magician's ploy of misdirection in order to disguise and legitimate class oppression. By transforming the negative reality of de facto race discrimination into the positive image of color-blind meritocracy, equal protection law's intent requirement also transforms evaluative devices with clear class biases into unbiased measures of individual merit.

Again, the case of minority admissions to law schools illustrates how this ideological artifice works. The Law School Admission Test indicates an applicant's socioeconomic status far better than it indicates anything else. One might expect that lower class whites would recognize that this type of test excludes them, as well as blacks, from access to the profession and that they would thus join blacks in challenging the test. But "reverse discrimination" claims . . . make it appear that the central issue [for whites, even poor whites,] is race. Poor whites almost uniformly sided with the opponents of special admissions in the [civil rights] debate because they were given a dual ideological message: They were told that preferential programs for minorities excluded them from [prestigious] profession[s] and that "regular" admissions were a fair measure of individual worth. Because the audience focuses on the hand changing racial discrimination into racial neutrality, an illusion which whites are eager to believe, it never sees the simultaneous illusion which transforms an instrument that measures the cultural and educational experiences of children from upper-middle and upper class families into an instrument that measures merit.

Applying strain theory to the illusion that hides class discrimination behind the imagery of color-blind meritocracy provides additional insight into the origins of the ideology of equal opportunity. Legal theorists, advocates, and judges have succeeded within the traditional systems of determining who shall attain influence and power. The transformation of discrimination into meritocracy not only puts them on the side of the angels on the question of race, it also affirmatively justifies their position of privilege vis-a-vis other whites by attributing their success to superior talent and hard work....

Conclusion

... [Equality jurisprudence validates and normalizes] the illusions that make racial justice seem at odds with the interests of the majority of white Americans, and it thus simultaneously promotes the interests of racism and classism....

[Moreover,] [t]he ideology of equal opportunity has done its work even among those of us who believe we have maintained our commitment to the creation of a more egalitarian society. Until we can recognize the fact that we have often unconsciously created and accepted the ideological illusions of equality in order to serve our own emotional and material interests, we will continue to side with the perpetrators of discrimination. The victims will continue to perceive accurately that our goals are [designed for] "just us."

The illusion of equality that Lawrence examines is powerful because the legal system has an existential need to disguise its role in ongoing inequalities, as we saw in Parts II and VI. Social problems exist in contexts infused by identity blindfolding with the top-down "isms" and "phobias" of systemic inequality. Advocates and activists unlearn these fallacies and relearn how identities can be used both to disguise social problems and mobilize subordinated communities. In this way, social problems can be made more obvious, more contentious, and more redressable.

To explain further, legal scholars Richard Delgado and Jean Stefancic demonstrate in the excerpt below how even a cherished legal myth can be unpacked and reconsidered in relation to social ills. The specific question is whether ever-more "free" speech can overcome deeply ingrained social ills, grounded in identities, that control both law and society. The authors' answer is a flat no—a response that challenges traditional teachings about the rule of law, its formal "rights," and identity-blind freedoms. They show that even the most celebrated individual rights can be turned into instruments of unjust power—through which both group domination and collective struggle are simultaneously funneled.

Embedded in First Amendment jurisprudence on the regulation of free speech is the premise that protecting a "marketplace" of ideas for public debate is fundamental to fair and open decision making. This premise assumes both a fair and open marketplace and a society free of widely-embedded isms and phobias. In this top-down view, therefore, the proper democratic response to an unjust condition is, simply, for all of society to debate every question until the truth emerges victoriously. In law, the adversary system epitomizes this fiction. However, the assumed "level playing field" that accompanies this marketplace metaphor is socially false. Rather, in any given context, the risks that individuals face when exercising supposedly free speech are not equal, the resources available to broadcast speech are not equal, and the terms that describe hateful and derogatory sentiments do not apply in equal or neutral ways. These inequalities in turn are protected consistently by the full force of law as a system. By blindfolding itself (and society) to these facts, the formal right to free speech insulates the status quo from any meaningful disruptions. In this way, the system, as law, confines allowed expressions of discontent in skewed ways that might look formally "equal" but are not in fact "equalizing" given the social realities of isms and inequalities. Like "equal opportunity," we see that "free speech" is an ideological illusion.

This status quo thereby serves dominant "private" biases fueled by entrenched power inequalities. Rather than truth-finding or upending inequality, endless rounds of skewed debate can help to normalize and further entrench an unjust status quo. This bottom-up shift in understanding the First Amendment illustrates how systemic advocates deploy unlearning and relearning, in critical and self-critical terms, to counter law—as ideology, or as hegemony.

IMAGES OF THE OUTSIDER IN AMERICAN LAW AND CULTURE: CAN FREE EXPRESSION REMEDY SYSTEMIC SOCIAL ILLS?
Richard Delgado and Jean Stefancic
77 Cornell L. Rev. 1258 (1992)

Introduction

. . . [C]onventional First Amendment doctrine is most helpful in connection with small, clearly bounded disputes. Free speech and debate can help resolve controversies over whether a school disciplinary or local zoning policy is adequate, over whether a new sales tax is likely to increase or decrease net revenues, and over whether one candidate for political office is a better choice than another. Speech is less able, however, to deal with systemic social ills, such as racism or sexism, that are widespread and deeply woven into the fabric of society. Free speech, in short, is least helpful where we need it most. . . .

How Could They? Lessons from the History of Racial Depiction

. . . In every era, then, ethnic imagery comes bearing an enormous amount of social weight. Nevertheless, we sense that we are in control and that things need not be that way. We believe we can use speech, jiujitsu fashion, on behalf of oppressed peoples. We believe that speech can serve as a tool of destabilization. It is virtually a prime tenet of liberal jurisprudence that by talk, dialog, exhortation, and so on, we present each other with passionate, appealing messages that will counter the evil ones of racism and sexism, and thereby advance society to greater levels of fairness and humanity.

Consider, for example, the current debate about campus speech codes. In response to a rising tide of racist incidents, many campuses have enacted, or are considering enacting, student conduct codes that forbid certain types of face-to-face insult. These codes invariably draw fire from free-speech absolutists and many campus administrators on the ground that they would interfere with free speech. Campuses, they argue, ought to be "bastions of free speech." Racism and prejudice are matters of "ignorance and fear," for which the appropriate remedy is more speech. Suppression merely drives racism underground, where it will fester and emerge in even more hateful forms. Speech is the best corrective for error; regulation risks the spectre of censorship and state control. Efforts to regulate pornography, Klan marches, and other types of race-baiting often meet similar responses.

But insights about language and the social construction of reality show that reliance on countervailing speech that will, in theory, wrestle with bad or vicious speech is often misplaced. This is so for two interrelated reasons: First, the account rests on simplistic and erroneous notions of narrativity and change, and second, on a misunderstanding of the relation between the subject, or self, and new narratives.

The First Reason-Time Warp: Why We (Can) Only Condemn the Old Narrative

... [W]e simply do not see many forms of discrimination, bias, and prejudice as wrong at the time. The racism of other times and places does stand out, does strike us as glaringly and appallingly wrong. But this happens only decades or centuries later; we acquiesce in today's version with little realization that it is wrong, that a later generation will ask "How could they?" about *us*. We only condemn the racism of another place (South Africa) or time. But that of our own place and time strikes us, if at all, as unexceptionable, trivial, or well within literary license. ...

This time-warp aspect of racism makes speech an ineffective tool to counter it. Racism is woven into the warp and woof of the way we see and organize the world—it is one of the many preconceptions we bring to experience and use to construct and make sense of our social world. Racism forms part of the dominant narrative, the group of received understandings and basic principles that form the baseline from which we reason.... We interpret new stories in light of the old. Ones that deviate too markedly from our pre-existing stock are dismissed as extreme, coercive, political, and wrong. The only stories about race we are prepared to condemn, then, are the old ones giving voice to the racism of an earlier age, ones that society has already begun to reject. We can condemn Justice Brown for writing as he did in *Plessy v. Ferguson,* but not university administrators who refuse remedies for campus racism, failing to notice the remarkable parallels between the two.

The Second Reason: Our Narratives, Our Selves

... A second and related insight from modern scholarship focuses not on the role of narratives in confining change to manageable proportions, but on the relationship between our selves and those narratives. The reigning First Amendment metaphor—the marketplace of ideas—implies a separation between subjects who do the choosing and the ideas or messages that vie for their attention. Subjects are "in here," the messages "out there." The pre-existing subjects choose the idea that seems most valid and true-somewhat in the manner of a diner deciding what to eat at a buffet.

... [T]his mechanistic view of an autonomous subject choosing among separate, external ideas is simplistic. In an important sense, we *are* our current stock of narratives, and they us. We subscribe to a stock of explanatory scripts, plots, narratives, and understandings that enable us to make sense of—to construct—our social world. Because we then live in that world, it begins to shape and determine *us,* who we are, what we see, how we select, reject, interpret and order subsequent reality.

These observations imply that our ability to escape the confines of our own preconceptions is quite limited.... The notion of ideas competing with each other, with truth and goodness emerging victorious from the competition, has proven seriously deficient when applied to evils, like racism, that are deeply inscribed in the culture. We have constructed the social world so that racism seems normal, part of the status quo, in need of little correction. It is not until much later that what we believed begins to seem incredibly, monstrously wrong. How could we have believed *that?* ...

How the System of Free Expression Sometimes Makes Matters Worse

Speech and free expression are not only poorly adapted to remedy racism, they often make matters worse—far from being stalwart friends, they can impede the cause of racial reform. First, they encourage writers, filmmakers, and other creative people to feel amoral, nonresponsible in what they do. Because there is a marketplace of ideas, the rationalization goes, another film-maker is free to make an antiracist movie that will cancel out any minor stereotyping in the one I am making....

Second, when insurgent groups attempt to use speech as an instrument of reform, courts almost invariably construe First Amendment doctrine against them. As Charles Lawrence pointed out, civil rights activists in the sixties made the greatest strides when they acted in defiance of the First Amendment as then understood. They marched, were arrested and convicted; sat in, were arrested and convicted; distributed leaflets, were arrested and convicted. Many years later, after much gallant lawyering and the expenditure of untold hours of effort, the conviction might be reversed on appeal if the original action had been sufficiently prayerful, mannerly, and not too interlaced with an action component. This history of the civil rights movement does not bear out the usual assumption that the First Amendment is of great value for racial reformers.

Current First Amendment law is similarly skewed. Examination of the many "exceptions" to First Amendment protection discloses that the large majority favor the interests of the powerful. If one says something disparaging of a wealthy and well-regarded individual, one discovers that one's words were not free after all; the wealthy individual has a type of property interest in his or her community image, damage to which is compensable even though words were the sole instrument of the harm. Similarly, if one infringes the copyright or trademark of a well-known writer or industrialist, again it turns out that one's action is punishable. Further, if one disseminates an official secret valuable to a powerful branch of the military or defense contractor, that speech is punishable. If one speaks disrespectfully to a judge, police officer, teacher, military official, or other powerful authority figure, again one discovers that one's words were not free; and so with words used to defraud, form a conspiracy, breach the peace, or untruthful words given under oath during a civil or criminal proceeding.

Yet the suggestion that we create [some] new exception to protect lowly and vulnerable members of our society, such as isolated, young black undergraduates attending dominantly white campuses, is often met with consternation: the First Amendment must be a seamless web; minorities, if they knew their own self-interest, should appreciate this even more than others. This one-sidedness of free-speech doctrine makes the First Amendment much more valuable to the majority than to the minority.

The system of free expression also has a powerful after-the-fact apologetic function. Elite groups use the supposed existence of a marketplace of ideas to justify their own superior position.... Rationalization is easy: our ideas, our culture competed with their more easygoing ones and won. It was a fair fight. Our position must be deserved; the distribution of social goods must be roughly what fairness, merit, and equity call for. It is up to them to change, not us.

A free market of racial depiction resists change for two final reasons. First, the dominant pictures, images, narratives, plots, roles, and stories ascribed to, and constituting the public perception of minorities, are always dominantly negative. Through an unfortunate psychological mechanism, incessant bombardment by images ... inscribe those negative images on the souls and minds of minority persons. Minorities internalize the stories they read, see, and hear every day. Persons of color can easily become demoralized, blame themselves, and not speak up vigorously. The expense of speech also precludes the stigmatized from participating effectively in the marketplace of ideas. They are often poor—indeed, one theory of racism holds that maintenance of economic inequality is its prime function—and hence unlikely to command the means to bring countervailing messages to the eyes and ears of others.

Second, even when minorities do speak they have little credibility. Who would listen to, who would credit, a speaker or writer one associates [through societal stereotyping] with watermelon-eating, buffoonery, menial work, intellectual inadequacy, laziness, lasciviousness, and demanding resources beyond his or her deserved share?

Words, then, can wound. But the fine thing about the current situation is that one gets to enjoy a superior position and feel virtuous at the same time. By supporting the system of free expression no matter what the cost, one is upholding principle. One can belong to impeccably liberal organizations and believe one is doing the right thing, even while taking actions that are demonstrably injurious to the least privileged, most defenseless segments of our society. In time, one's actions will seem wrong and will be condemned as such, but paradigms change slowly. . . .

Racism is not a mistake, not a matter of episodic, irrational behavior carried out by vicious-willed individuals, not a throwback to a long-gone era. It is ritual assertion of supremacy, like animals sneering and posturing to maintain their places in the [group] hierarchy of the colony. It is performed largely unconsciously, just as the animals' behavior is. Racism seems right, customary, and inoffensive to those engaged in it, while bringing psychic and pecuniary advantages. The notion that more speech, more talking, more preaching, and more lecturing can counter this system of oppression is appealing, lofty, romantic—and wrong. . . .

Systemic myths are "appealing, lofty, romantic—and wrong" when insisting that (more) rights will remedy persistent problems. Even though rights are important—if justly enforced—expanding legal rights "on paper" in a world of unequal capacities to exercise or defend them is a systemic strategy that can deepen existing inequalities. To counter this pattern, critical analyses of law, like the excerpts above, help systemic advocates to unlearn and relearn top-down myths.

NOTES AND QUESTIONS

1. *A Note on Terminology.* In Part I, we referred to persistent "social problems" such as poverty, lack of healthcare, inadequate education, violence, tainted food and water, low incomes, and harassment. Other commentators, and occasionally this book, might refer to the target "problems" as systemic problems. In the case of the Delgado and Stefancic excerpt, we hear about

systemic social ills—"isms" and related identity-based social phobias—as prompting systemic injustice. These various terms bring to the foreground the fact that social problems affect people in a patterned way—generally in a *material* way—affecting money, bodies, physical, or economic conditions—and that those patterns are structured or upheld through law. The term "systemic social ills" is a recognition that most social problems are also connected to social groups and therefore rooted in familiar "-isms" like racism, sexism, classism, and ableism, and in familiar phobias. Systemic social ills, then, lurk in most of what we call social problems. Based on your own experience, current headlines, or historical legacies, can you think of specific social problems fueled by social ills and their infection of law as a system?

2. *Vehicles of Ideology.* Lawrence implicates the legal system, along with academia and the church, as principal vehicles to transmit ideological thought. Can you think of other systems or mechanisms for developing, inculcating others into, and implementing ideology in service of today's identity-based castes? Consider both "public" and "private" (and "macro" and "micro") sources or mechanisms for the promulgation and dissemination of supremacist ideologies and the social problems they create and perpetuate across various social and legal contexts.

3. *Regulating Campus Hate Speech.* Campus hate speech codes, even if enacted, tend to fall when challenged on constitutional grounds.[3] Courts have recognized a variety of First Amendment exceptions allowing regulation of speech such as obscenity, which is seen as having such slight social value, while causing so much harm, that it doesn't belong in the marketplace of ideas. Why then won't courts regard hate speech against disfavored social groups as similarly susceptible to government regulation? What would Delgado and Stefancic say is the reason? See also Richard Delgado and David Yen, "The Speech We Hate": First Amendment Totalism, the ACLU, and the Principle of Dialogic Politics, 27 Ariz. St. L.J. 1281, 1298–99 (viewing hate speech as a subordinating weapon used by the empowered to maintain their position against subordinated groups seeking change).

4. *Which Groups Are Essentialized?* Delgado and Stefancic indict stereotyping in media as emboldened and legitimized by the false premise of the marketplace of ideas. Do derogatory, stereotypical depictions work in the same manner for preferred or favored social groups in general as they do for those in subordinated identity groups—the bottom? In other words, is essentialization an elite tool to preserve the status quo of inequality? For example, are white (male) villains (like Timothy McVeigh or Dylann Roof, who hoped to start a race war by killing nine Black church attendees) generally regarded as blueprints for an entire group? Can you see the Hansons' "blame frames" from Part IV at work here—this time in service of protecting the reputation of societal tops? Consider the difference in media treatment between violent acts by those identified as Muslim and those identified as

---

[3] E.g., *Doe v. University of Michigan*, 721 F. Supp. 852 (E.D. Mich. 1989); *UWM Post, Inc. v. Board of Regents*, 774 F. Supp. 1163 (E.D. Wis. 1991).

white, such as most school shooters. In your view, do the media (and law) connect individuals to groups differentially based on race or other social identities? See Jonathan M. Metzl, When the Shooter is White, Wash. Post (Oct. 6, 2017). Can you think of other current examples of this phenomenon, which selectively links individual actions to essentialized group characteristics only for non-white, already-subordinated populations?

14.2 OVER TIME, INTERNALIZED IDEOLOGIES SHAPE PEOPLE, CHOICES, AND CASTES

Law-as-ideology helps to shape consciousness within groups and organizations, as well as throughout society at large. Elites have used law ideologically to create commonly-accepted norms and understandings that justify patterns of domination and subordination. When these ideas are absorbed and those rules are accepted not only by the beneficiaries of the ideologies but also by members of subordinated groups, the result is hegemony. Hegemony thus exists when everybody—the dominant and subordinate alike—cannot pierce the veils and illusions that cloak the system's unequal outcomes. The point of ideological supremacy or hegemony is to preempt the will or capacity to challenge inequality. Failure by design is regarded as normal, right, fair.

Elites aim for hegemony precisely because it puts collective dominance beyond any serious challenge—because hegemonies need to be accepted and protected by those at the bottom, as well as those at the top. Over time, hegemonies link legal concepts to natural or cultural ideas and frames to justify caste systems that incrementally become accepted by most of the people most of the time. The playing fields of democracy and adjudication—as well as economics and culture—are made unlevel but called "fair." The most successful hegemonies enlist the participation of the subordinated in their own continued subordination. Using modern-day U.S. labor law as an apt example, critical labor scholar Karl Klare observed that:

> [C]ollective bargaining law articulates an ideology that aims to legitimate and justify unnecessary and destructive hierarchy and domination in the workplace . . . [and has] evolved an institutional architecture. . . . [C]ollective bargaining law frequently aims to restrain labor unions from serving as vigorous, uninhibited representatives of employee interests. Rather it seeks to place unions in the uncomfortable position of serving as fiduciaries of an imagined societal interest in industrial peace and of serving specific managerial and disciplinary functions. . . . [T]he doctrine of collective bargaining law has been systematically fashioned, particularly at the Supreme Court level, to serve these goals. . . .
>
> In sum, traditional liberal labor law thinking has confronted the enormously complex challenge of inducing organized workers

> to consent to and participate in their own domination in the workplace. . . .
>
> . . . The task of critical labor jurisprudence is to determine how and why even the most progressive state regulation, fought for and won by the victimized and oppressed, may be implemented in a manner that deflects and demoralizes popular participation and, through cooptation of popular struggle, ultimately reinforces the institutional infrastructure of capitalism. The ... "decodification" of legal doctrine [as social ideology] is but a preliminary effort to develop a methodology adequate to this task.
>
> . . . The mission of all critical social thought is to free us from the illusion of the necessity of existing social arrangements. . . . The critique of labor law as ideology . . . [may thus] provide an intimation . . . of freedom.[4]

Law-as-ideology operates to advance, if not quite to perfect, hegemony—a bulwark that can make the Critical Challenge seem impenetrable. In doing so, it interacts with other seemingly legitimate belief systems that also function as ideologies to obscure inequalities. As Tsosie explained in Part I, science, perhaps the most esteemed belief system, can function as an ideology. Science, as she explained, does not simply produce "scientific knowledge" upon which "objective" decisions may be based; science also produces politicized ideological knowledge for decision making that reinforces social castes, often in interaction with law.

In response, advocates and activists resist hegemony by reshaping their understandings of social problems and social identities, as well as by creating new cultural and economic resources at the level of individual consciousness, inter- and intra-group thinking, and mainstream beliefs. Law—as expressed in doctrine and experienced in practice—offers opportunities both for indoctrination and resistance. Historically, "inherent contradictions of legal culture were not only key mechanisms sustaining law's hegemony but simultaneously potential resources for the critique of the legal order."[5] However, individuals have varied experiences based in varied combinations of race, gender, class, and other identities. As a result, "different" persons and groups may absorb these ideologies to different degrees, which affects how they view and act upon hegemonic premises or frameworks of comprehension and decision making.

Feminist legal scholar Nancy Ehrenreich examines below how prevalent legal notions of consent by a pregnant woman to undergo a Caesarian section may not be consensual in fact. As she explains, both

---

[4] Karl E. Klare, Labor Law as Ideology: Toward a New Historiography of Collective Bargaining Law, 4 Indus. Relations L.J. 450, 452–53, 455, 482 (1981).

[5] Pascale Cornut St. Pierre, Investigating Legal Consciousness through the Technical Work of Elite Lawyers: A Case Study in Tax Avoidance, 53 Law & Soc'y Rev. 323, 348 (2019).

"voluntary" and involuntary C-section decisions are infused with the isms and phobias that are hallmarks of law- and science-as-ideology. Like law, "medicine is a hegemonic discourse . . . laden with value choices and beliefs that masquerade as truth, nature, and biological 'fact.'" As you read, reflect back to Minter's analysis in Part I of similar conceptions and their uses for injustice against racial, sexual, and trans persons or groups.

THE COLONIZATION OF THE WOMB
Nancy Ehrenreich
43 Duke L.J. 492 (1993)

. . . In the Cesarean context, conventional analyses have been concerned primarily with whether the woman has freely chosen to birth vaginally and whether there is any justification for overriding that choice. As long as she has formally consented to Cesarean surgery, the case is assumed to be an easy one: her decision should be effectuated. When she has refused, however, the question becomes whether the state can override that choice. Conventional legal analyses thus pose questions such as: 1) Does the right to decide *whether* to procreate necessarily imply a right to decide *how* to procreate?; 2) Does the state's interest in the life and health of [a] full-term fetus outweigh the woman's right to refuse medical treatment?; 3) Does the duty of a parent to rescue a child in danger extend to a mother carrying a full-term fetus? Does it apply even when the rescue involves a risk of death to the mother?

These doctrinal approaches are not unimportant, of course, in that they certainly influence judges' articulated analyses and hence the popular understanding and impact of such cases. . . . [But] this analysis obscures the values and assumptions that underlie judicial outcomes. Moreover, doctrinally-focused inquiries fail to examine the historical antecedents of modern coercive interventions in pregnancy, particularly those directed against outsider women, and fail to explore the effect of race and class factors on the treatment women receive. Finally, in treating the choice to consent to a C-section as an uncontroversial expression of individual autonomy, conventional analyses ignore the extent to which such individual choices are themselves intimately tied to the ideological structures that judicial decisions help to create and sustain. Thus, only by interrogating the ideological components of such decisions, paying particular attention to the impact of race, class, and gender on the results, can we develop a full understanding of how they occur and which segments of society they affect.

. . . [T]he prevailing societal image of medicine as based on neutral, scientific truth obscures the race, class, and gender biases that permeate it. Moreover, that image also reinforces negative stereotypes of outsider women by legitimizing physicians' characterizations of women who refuse C-sections as irresponsible mothers. Disabling the courts from imagining any alternative explanations for such behavior, the legitimacy of medicine contributes to judges' decisions to authorize coercive interventions in labor....

The scientific world view is accepted by scientists and laypeople alike ... because physicians are assumed to be the possessors of objective "expertise" that both courts and consumers believe women should follow this advice and give credence to their identification of particular individuals as good or bad mothers. Hence, the legitimacy of medicine as a scientific discourse obscures the coercive exercise of social power that both consented and court-ordered Cesarean sections represent.

... [M]edicine is a hegemonic discourse ... laden with value choices and beliefs that masquerade as truth, nature, and biological "fact."...

Raising questions about medicine's image as scientific is important to my argument for two reasons. First, as noted above, coercive interventions in the reproductive lives of outsider women are justified not only by the bad girl image of such women but also by the "expert" assessments of medical professionals in their role as "neutral" and "objective" identifiers of bad mothering. Second, challenging the status of medicine is important because, in the area of reproduction, privileged women have been subordinated more by force of habit than by direct and obvious acts of coercion. Although some have certainly been subjected to unwanted surgeries and court-ordered interventions, most privileged women who have undergone such procedures have done so willingly. As previously mentioned, while most forced Cesarean sections are performed on outsider women, a higher proportion of privileged women actually undergo the surgery. Despite the fact that C-sections are notoriously overused in this country, privileged women apparently accede to doctors' orders to have them most of the time.... [T]hese women probably see themselves as good girls and their physicians as neutral experts. Taking seriously their role as selfless nurturers, they probably see obedience to doctors as part of that role and disobedience as evidence that one is a bad mother. Thus, medicine's scientific image simultaneously justifies coercion of outsider women and elicits passive compliance from privileged women.

... [This] power resides not only in the expert's authority to construct reality but also in the complex interactions between groups affected by that reality.... Only by seeing these subtly supportive interconnections between white supremacy, capitalism, and patriarchy can we hope to frame the critiques and forge the coalitions with which to overcome them.

Ehrenreich illustrates how law operates ideologically (as does science) to persuade individuals and groups to accept its logic and thus participate willingly in their own and others' subordination. She also illustrates the ways in which law-as-ideology shapes consciousness—both conformist consciousness and critical consciousness.

Over time, top-down law similarly shapes the social identities of entire groups and effaces their histories and hierarchies. But critical analysis—deconstruction—can re-center identities, groups, interests, and power in the imposition of ideology and hegemony. Below, LatCrit scholar Francisco Valdes relates briefly the history of "Hispanismo" as an ideology that replicates and denies racial hierarchies with both European roots and "new world" complexities and consequences. As Chang and Gott demonstrated in Part II, identities also can be mobilized as assets. Valdes concludes that critical and self-critical reflection enable advocates and activists to develop identity consciousness and knowledge, which can be the basis for collective, coalitional resistance to hegemony.

RACE, ETHNICITY, AND HISPANISMO IN A TRIANGULAR PERSPECTIVE: THE "ESSENTIAL LATINA/O" AND LATCRIT THEORY

Francisco Valdes
48 UCLA L. Rev. 305 (2000)

In recent years—both since and before the emergence of LatCrit theory in 1995—much knowledge and understanding has been excavated about "Latinas/os" and our racialization as a transnational, diasporic, and multiply diverse social group living and working under the Anglo American regimes that are predominant in the United States and beyond. During the past five years in particular, LatCrit, RaceCrit, and other allied scholars—"OutCrits"—have debated the relationship of "race" and "ethnicity" to the construction of Latina/o places, positions, and prospects in American law and society. We have explored the mixture of racism and nativism that afflicts Latinas/os (and other immigrant-identified groups), and elucidated how this combustible admixture props up both white and Anglo supremacy in the United States and beyond.

We have found that sometimes Latinas/os have been decreed, or have sought to be identified, as white—and that sometimes they have not. We have confronted the internal reproduction of white supremacy within and among Latinas/os. We have learned that among Latinas/os, as among other groups, those of the nonwhites who are more pale are structurally and systematically more likely to receive the social and material benefits associated with whiteness. In doing this and more, we also have ascertained that racial formation among Latinas/os is indeed "different" than among African Americans, Asian Americans, and other racialized, nonwhite groups in the United States—though in many ways it is similar as well. . . .

Despite the persistent levels of neglect and marginality endured over time by Latina/o groups, Latinas/os are a pivotal, rapidly growing social group in this country. Inevitably, issues relating to this growth will stretch beyond the familiar and pressing controversies over matters such as immigration and language....

Not coincidentally, therefore, during the past five years "LatCrit theory" has emerged within the legal academy of the United States as one effort to learn more about how law and policy affect this nation's rapidly growing and rapidly changing Latina/o communities, and to then explore how law and policy ought to respond to this knowledge.... Yet, while LatCrit theory both reflects and projects Latina/o growth and its sociolegal implications, this jurisprudential effort seeks to inform our individual and collective reactions to these demographic and political developments with an explicitly antiessentialist and antisubordinationist bent that is both critical and self-critical....

... [A] particular racial ideology among and across Latina/o groups both within and beyond the United States ... known as Hispanismo or Hispanidad, constructs the "essential Latina/o," namely, the "Hispanic" Latina/o. Evoking a real but often exaggerated connection to Spain, and hence to Europe, Hispanismo historically has been and presently is a crucial ingredient in Latina/o racial formation, both under the domestic racial and ethnic regimes of the United States and under the transnational racial and ethnic regimes of Latin America and other "Hispanicized" regions. Whether in Latin American countries or in Latina/o communities within the United States, Hispanismo constructs both whiteness and white supremacy in Hispanicized social settings....

This centering of Hispanismo, in turn, pursues a triangulation of LatCrit analysis and discourse.... Hispanismo's so-called ties link Spain, Latin American societies, and Latina/o communities in the United States for varied historical and contemporary reasons. Triangulation, in effect, is the anti-subordination mirror image of Hispanismo, and thus serves to frame its critical analysis in and through LatCrit theory.

This triangular framing furthermore recognizes that Latinas/os are a cohesive yet multiply diverse and transnational social group whose history and experience is the combined product mostly of Spain, the United States, and Latin America.... In the United States ..., Hispanic refers to people or social phenomena whose neocolonial identity derives, in some socially cognizable way, from Spain. This derivation does not hinge necessarily on biological or innate criteria; like all else racial, Hispanic is a social construction that remains always in progress.... As in other cases, the type of emigrant who left Europe to domesticate the "new" world tended to be among the disempowered or dispossessed, but Spain's imperial needs created opportunities for these Spaniards and their successors to become the new elites of the Hispanicized lands now known as Latin America.

First as conquistadors, and then as a new form of nobility within Spain's American colonies, these emigrant Spaniards acquired racial and ethnic privileges in social, economic, and political arenas. While their relationships with both Spain and the natives were complex and conflicted, the conquistadors and their successors generally served as the agents and surrogates of Spain, employed to dispossess, subordinate, and assimilate the indigenous peoples of this hemisphere. Over time, the successors of the original conquistadors tended to become the landed and relatively wealthy white-identified (even if often racially mixed) gentry of Latinized America. After generations of intermixture, or mestizaje, they became the most Hispanic and structurally privileged type of Latina/o in Spain's former empire.

Thus, Hispanic today describes a particular type of Latina/o—the type that, to some real or imagined degree, is imbued with Spanish heritage, typically but not exclusively in the form of relatives or ancestors said to [hail] from Spain. Because of the enduring legacies of Spain's neocolonial assimilationism throughout the Americas, many Latinas/os today do identify themselves as Hispanic—even if this identification is sometimes exaggerated, more imaginary than real. Today, Spain's Hispanic legacy resides both in Latin America, in the form of cultures and countries, as well as in the United States, in the form of annexed lands, "internal colonies," and most recently, burgeoning immigrant communities. Centuries of Spanish neocolonialism throughout the Americas help to make Hispanic in fact the predominant category of Latina/o identification....

Hispanic is the predominant and paradigmatic—if not hegemonic—Latina/o identity because it has been socially and legally preferred in contexts and relations that are Eurocentric and white supremacist....

In the neocolonial Latina/o racial and ethnic scheme, Hispanic is valuable because it promises, and can yield structurally, the social and material benefits associated with European whiteness in a Eurocentric, white supremacist empire. Formal Hispanic designation thus represents the peak category of racial and ethnic identification in Latina/o societies and communities. Like the Anglo-centric variety, this Hispanic version of European white supremacy has operated as a macrostructure for hierarchical, racialized, and ethnicized relations during and since colonial times, rather than operating only as a way of describing national identity, family heritage, or personal lineage....

Significantly, however, this Eurocentric sense of Spanish or Hispanic white-identified supremacy is not generally or structurally recognized in much of Europe itself, where Spain always has been positioned as inferior in racialized and ethnicized terms compared to the northern—and even whiter—neocolonial powers. Spain's stigmatization by England specifically and by northwestern Europe generally stems from a long and complex history of nation building, national strife, and transcontinental struggle....

Apart from its direct struggles with other colonial powers in Europe, Spain's particular position and history as the battleground between Europe and Africa effectively has cast it as the racially mixed "color line" that separates—or buffers—white northern Europe from the "dark continent" of Africa to the south. Before the "reconquest" and for much of Spain's national history, the Pyrenees mountains along its border with France—rather than Gibraltar's straits—were deemed the border that separated Europe from Africa. And for much of the past millennium, Spain thereby has been unsure of its place along and between the color lines of the old world. Today, Spain still "function[s] as a southern European police over the human mass from the Maghreb and Latin America."...

The neocolonial histories and legacies of Hispanic and Anglo Saxon European powers have erected two parallel systems of white supremacy in the Americas. The Anglo-centric variety reigns in most of North America, and the Hispanic variety reigns in most of the remaining Americas. Both are stridently Eurocentric and privilege their international, ethnocentric version of whiteness; in tandem, they secure the supremacy of European whiteness from the north to the south poles of this hemisphere. But when confronting each other, the two ultimately are oppositional, reflecting long histories of national, transcontinental rivalries....

It is this history and its contemporary ramifications that in part complicate the social "crossover dreams" of Hispanic-identified Latinas/os in the United States today—those Latinas/os who mistakenly believe that Hispanic privileges in Latina/o social contexts will transfer substantially intact to the Anglo-centric race and ethnicity economy of the United States.... Many Latinas/os identify themselves as Indian, black, Asian, and mestiza/o.... Hispanismo... stratifies multiply diverse and diasporic Latina/o groups in racial and ethnic categories structured principally by Spain's version of Eurocentric white supremacy....

[Yet] Spain's Hispanic variety of whiteness goes generally unvalorized in Anglo-centric race and ethnicity contexts, such as in the racial and ethnic economy of the United States.... Hispanic identification purchases relatively modest structural privilege for Latinas/os in the national race and ethnicity economy of this country.... The Anglo-centric attitudes of this country's racial and ethnic politics implicate not only a historical demonization of Spain as inferior and "other," but also a historical denigration of Latin America and Latinas/os developed subsequently by the Anglo American elites of the United States as pretexts for their own claims to a "manifest destiny" of hemispheric imperialism and domination....

As simply culture, Hispanismo can amount to a pernicious disguise of a racist ideology activated unconsciously as well as strategically. Prescriptively, Hispanismo, or Hispanidad, refers to Spain's "aggressive strategy ... to resurrect and spread Hispanic culture, pride, and also hegemony throughout its former colonies." ...

... [I]n 1991 the government of Spain established the Instituto Cervantes for the promotion and teaching of the Spanish language and the dissemination of the Spanish and Hispanic American cultures. With offices on four continents, including two in the United States, in New York City and Chicago, this entity now is "the largest worldwide Spanish teaching organisation" on Earth. It carries out its mission of "promoting" Hispanismo through varied activities, usually funded and directed by Spain, including ... courses that teach Spanish and establishing libraries devoted to Spanish Hispanic culture....

In essentializing Latinas/os as Hispanic and Spanish, Hispanismo invites denial of the demographic, sociopolitical, and material legacies flowing from racialist conquest, slavery, and assimilationism. By definition, the practices and precepts ... celebrate a colonizing culture and its imperial racial and ethnic biases. Spain's aggressive strategy of Hispanismo—both within the United States and globally—therefore is not merely a recognition or commemoration of familial history or national pride.... In promoting Hispanismo uncritically, Spain replays colonial scripts and aggravates post-neocolonial grievances. But Spain's promotion of Hispanismo also affects ... the politics of antiracist coalitions in the United States....

In effect, if not always in practice, uncritical activations of Hispanismo may and do prompt Latinas/os to maneuver toward whiteness personally, socially, and politically as a means of negotiating social status and securing structural privilege. Hispanismo excites Hispanic identification in explicitly racial and ethnic terms precisely because it constitutes the Latina/o variant of white racism, thus providing the preexisting social framework and cultural context for white-oriented identification and stratification among Latinas/os. Hispanismo, at least as cultivated and manipulated by Spain, is a proactive invitation to bask in the neocolonial afterglow of Hispanicized white supremacy—even if the exercise ends up being somewhat, or altogether, socially impossible when attempted in Anglo-centric contexts....

In the Anglo-centric racial and ethnic culture of the United States, Hispanic is ... not (really) white....

In great measure, today's Latina/o communities were spawned during Spain's colonial supremacy, during centuries of conquest throughout the

Americas, and through its physical and cultural assaults on indigenous communities in the new world and elsewhere. Yet, Spain's colonial wane at the same time and place as the ascendancy of United States expansionism gave way to the modern-day hegemony of Anglo-centrism over much Latina/o territory in this hemisphere.

This historical process shifted ideological dominance over many Latinas/os' lives from the Hispanic to the Anglo variants of Eurocentric white supremacy. In different ways, this shift facilitated new forms of neocolonial relations for the continued subordination of Latin America and of Latinas/os in the United States under "different" systems of Eurocentric white supremacy.... Wherever Latinas/os are found, multiply diverse groups live under the hegemonies of Anglo and Hispanic systems of white supremacy despite generations of resistance to both.

To sharpen and continue this resistance, LatCrit, OutCrit, and other allied scholars must become consciously and critically trained on Hispanismo as a form of racial and ethnic politics that, in the end, affirms and buttresses Eurocentric systems of white supremacy....

In this excerpt, Valdes underscores the complexities of law as ideology, including as a transnational phenomenon. These complexities include the internalization of ideology even among the subordinated, which is promoted continually by top-down power. As illustrated by Gilens and Page in Part I, Galanter in Part II, and Levinson in Part IV, law-as-ideology provides concepts—complex explanations—that routinely fail to predict or explain outcomes with any accuracy, whether in democratic policy making or courtroom adjudication. Like the "foundational lies" about which Marshall in Part I and Franks in Part II spoke, law-as-ideology facilitates elite domination in a way that generates buy-in from both dominant and subordinated group members—and creates a complex thicket of myths and misinformation to obstruct critical analysis and action. A foundational aspect of antisubordination work, then, is to diminish the support among subordinated groups for policies and practices that subordinate them by helping clear a path through this thicket. And clearing away the brush is work for a team—work best done in collaboration with client-groups and communities.

Similarly, law-as-ideology situates elites to use tactics and strategies from above that they simultaneously deny to those who attempt struggle from below. As Harrington, Tait, and Luban jointly showed in Part IV, elites simultaneously build up law as an industry for themselves while "taking out" adversaries that challenge their dominance. While conducting all of the above for themselves, elites aim to demonize and destroy any effort to collectivize, organize, or act from below, including denying collective claims and remedies under law. Critical unlearning and relearning upend that process, exposing the hegemonic illusions as a way to identify liberatory possibilities. Because the stakes can be so very high, the drive for hegemony ensures a continual struggle—both from above and from below.

14.3 THE SOCIAL HEGEMONY OF IDENTITY-AS-IDEOLOGY KILLS BOTTOMS

Challenging law-as-ideology requires understanding social problems in relation to social ills in a particular systemic context. But it also—and ultimately—requires developing strategies that disrupt hegemonic understandings and generate new sources of critical consciousness and knowledge. Counter-hegemonic action is risky because ideological illusions protect elites with violence and without scruple.

To illustrate concretely how ideology and hegemony work, legal scholar Angela Harris next analyzes "heteropatriarchy" as a social and legal amalgamation of beliefs and behaviors. She describes how heteropatriarchy was imposed from above and the results, both historically and in contemporary times. Harris outlines the five linked assumptions that underlie this amalgamation, which make this group ideology a *Euro*heteropatriarchy—transplanted globally, like law, through European colonialism and its continuing legacies. Highlighting the stakes involved, Harris documents how "hegemonic masculinity" in the United States is an expression of Euroheteropatriarchy that "kills" in various contemporary social settings. She reframes as "gender-based violence" the social problems undergirded by heteropatriarchy. Gender-based violence is a broader framing than the common notion of "violence against women," that currently dominates social and legal analyses. As Harris explains, the systemic violence of gender kills many cis women but also many others based on varied combinations of gender and other identities. This killing is both literal and metaphorical, underscoring the violent consequences of elite hegemony.

HETEROPATRIARCHY KILLS: CHALLENGING GENDER VIOLENCE IN A PRISON NATION

Angela P. Harris

37 Wash. U. J.L. & Pol'y 13 (2011)

Introduction

In September, 2011, the American Civil Liberties Union (ACLU) National Prison Project and the Southern California ACLU released a report titled "Cruel and Usual Punishment: How a Savage Gang of Deputies Controls LA County Jails." The report describes a jail system completely out of control—rife with corruption, malfeasance, and above all, unchecked violence.

The ACLU alleges that much of the violence is perpetrated by deputies on inmates. One story is illustrative:

> The confrontation began because deputies thought Mr. III had called them "gay." When Mr. III repeatedly denied the accusation, . . . [s]uddenly, [a] deputy grabbed Mr. III's head, slamming his face into the wall. Blood poured down, pooling on the ground. Mr. III passed out.
>
> When Mr. III regained consciousness, one deputy was sitting on his back, punching his face and head. Another was kicking Mr. III's ribs. . . . Mr. III spent two days in the hospital and four days in the jail's medical unit. The deep cut in his forehead took 35 stitches to close.

. . . Call it "toxic," or "destructive," masculinity. Manhood as enacted in these brutal vignettes relies on two negative identities—not being a woman, and not being gay—and violence is the means by which these identities are disavowed. . . . [M]en, individually or in groups, may use violence or the threat of violence as a sword to attack others in the name of their own masculinity, or as a shield to defend themselves against an intolerable threat of being "un-manned." We are familiar with the use of "gender violence" to mean male violence against women. Defense attorneys and scholars have even coined a term—"homosexual panic"—to describe violent attacks by men in a state of emotional overload on men identified as gay or transgender. Less well recognized is the fact that male-on-male violence is also gender violence.

Although destructive masculinity and its prominence in the criminal justice system have seemingly not changed much in the past decade, at least two new developments have taken place. First, scholars and activists committed to ending domestic violence and violence against sexual minorities have become increasingly disenchanted with the criminal justice system, and increasingly aware of its insidious role in the decimation of poor black and brown communities. Meanwhile, racial justice scholars have become increasingly aware of the toll that destructive masculinity takes on those communities. The prospects thus seem better than ever for anti-violence alliances that . . . "acknowledge the race of gender and the gender of race," while similarly acknowledging the importance of sexuality and class. . . .

Masculinities, Gender Violence, and Heteropatriarchy: Toward an Integrated Approach

Theorizing Masculinities: Heteropatriarchy Defined

Understanding gender violence requires us to begin with the familiar claim that identity is a social construction. . . . "One is not born but rather becomes a woman." Drawing on the disciplines of sociology, anthropology, cultural studies, queer theory, feminist theory, and history, masculinities theorists similarly argue that men are not born but made. The genes and genitalia we are born with, they argue, are less important in shaping and expressing our gender identity than are cultural norms.

... In the social world, masculinity is a product both of individual agency and cultural structures. "Men," "women," and people who identify as both, or neither, claim gender identities by the way they dress, walk, and talk. At the same time, they have gender identities ascribed to them under social rules established by institutional practices and cultural beliefs: for example, the rule that people born with penises are always and forever "male."

Scholars often describe this interplay of individual agency and cultural constraint using the metaphor of "performance." Depending on where we find ourselves geographically and socially, a gender performance might be considered secure or suspect—unproblematic and scarcely notable, or outrageous and upsetting. Moreover, even within the same social context there are multiple ways of performing manhood, womanhood, or something else, and multiple ways of demonstrating to others that you claim (or disclaim) a particular gender identity. There is not always social room for changing one's perceived sex, but there is often room for changing the sort of man or woman you want to appear to be. From this perspective masculinities theorists argue that sex/gender is not a thing you have, but a thing you do.

A second important tenet of masculinity theory is that although there are many ways of being a man or a woman, they are not all equally socially valued. "Hegemonic" masculinity is what scholars call the privileged style of masculinity in a given historical moment: the most desirable or most proper way of being a man. Some men have better access to hegemonic masculinity than others, depending on their position in various interconnected hierarchies of privilege and oppression. Nevertheless, hegemonic masculinity functions as an ideal that regulates all men.

Hegemonic masculinity in the contemporary United States emerges from a set of connected beliefs collectively called "heteropatriarchy." Heteropatriarchy includes at least five linked assumptions widely taken for granted in Western culture. First is the assumption that every person is born, and thereafter remains for life, either male or female. Second, one's sex at birth is assumed to determine one's gender; biology therefore controls one's social behavior. (This was the proposition that second-wave feminist theorists rejected when they introduced the distinction between "sex" and "gender.") Third, sex/gender causes males and females to be distinctively and dramatically different along dimensions of appearance, character, behavior, interests, and innate abilities. Indeed, men and women are popularly said to be so different that they are "opposite" sexes.

Fourth, because "opposites attract" and sex differences are complementary, sexual and romantic relationships should occur only between men and women, not between people of the same assigned sex. Moreover, opposite-sex couples are best situated to rear children, because the two sexes have different but complementary capacities and skills, and children need to be exposed to both.

These four linked assumptions constitute the "hetero" of heteropatriarchy. The fifth assumption provides the "patriarchy": though male and female are opposite sexes, they are not quite equal. Masculinity is the privileged sex/gender. In nearly every setting, as feminists have pointed out, masculine characteristics and attributes are considered superior to feminine ones. Little boys are encouraged to distinguish themselves from girls early on, and failure to do so is socially punished. The political and economic order is largely controlled and shaped by men in societies around the globe; and women are everywhere subjected to rape, sexual harassment, forced pregnancy and forced marriage by men. Worldwide, it is better to give birth to a baby boy than a baby girl. . . . [I]n the United States, which prides itself on its commitment to human rights, including women's rights, women lag far behind men on indicators of political and economic power.

Heteropatriarchy and Gender Violence

Heteropatriarchy shapes the two most important rules of hegemonic masculinity: a "real man" is not a woman, and he is not gay. . . . [O]ne of the greatest contributions of feminism has been to show how much one's masculine identity depends on disclaiming femininity—"at best by being 'not a woman,' at worst by excluding, hurting, denigrating, exploiting, or otherwise abusing actual women." In the contemporary United States, distancing oneself from homosexuality is at least as important. Training in not being "gay" (where "gay" is not really about sexual desire but rather denotes a failed or "spoiled" masculine identity), like training in not being female, begins early. For example, researchers studying the social lives of students in middle and high schools have noted that although the kinds of activities that give a boy status and respect vary from school to school, the boys at the bottom of any social totem pole—along with any activities or objects associated with them—will reliably be called "gay" and will be ridiculed and disparaged accordingly.

The need to not be gay, moreover, does not disappear after high school. As literary theorist Eve Sedgwick argues, masculinity is a double bind for men: being a "real man" requires that one secure the love and respect of other men, who hold the ultimate power to affirm one's masculinity. Yet the activities best designed to confer true masculinity—including participation in sport, the military, and mentoring relationships—involve "just the sort of close, emotionally intense, and frequently physical and sexually charged relationships that subject men to the suspicion that they are homosexual."

The result can be, especially for young men unsure of their identities and for older men with few other resources for self-esteem, a profound anxiety.... "[M]en's fear of other men[ ] is the animating condition of the dominant definition of masculinity in America[;] ... the reigning definition of masculinity is a defensive effort to prevent being emasculated." Being judged and found wanting in one's masculinity is a constant possibility for men; they are constantly under the male gaze of judgment.

... James Gilligan, a psychiatrist on the faculty of Harvard Medical School who directed the provision of psychiatric services to Massachusetts prisons and prison mental hospitals for twenty-five years, links the defense of masculinity with violence, through the psychological experience of "shame." ...

Shame, respect, and honor are key words in the production of gender violence. Gilligan notes that in his years doing psychotherapeutic work with violent criminals, "I kept getting the same answer when I asked one man after another why he had assaulted or even killed someone: 'because he disrespected me.' " ...

Gilligan adds that a failed masculine gender performance—as in, for example, the suggestion to a straight-identified man that he is really "gay"—threatens [precisely this kind of violent] shame ...:

> The image or concept of "homosexuality" functions as a kind of universal symbol or equivalent of every form of masculine sexual inadequacy.... [I]t therefore epitomizes every cause of shame; and ... there are few self-images that cause patriarchally conditioned men to feel shame more deeply than the perception (by themselves or others) that they might be "gay." Many men will resort to almost any degree of violence if that is what it takes for them to ward off that perception of themselves.

If Gilligan is correct, then a man hyper-sensitive to shame will likely respond to any denigration of his gender performance with violence. Moreover, violence is connected with heteropatriarchy in another way: violence itself is culturally perceived as masculine. Boys don't cry, but they do fight. Thus, for men acculturated to hegemonic masculinity, engaging in violence is a sword as well as a shield: it is both a way of defending oneself against shame and a way to affirmatively demonstrate one's manhood....

... Tracing gender violence as it moves through different social sites—the street, the home, the prison—makes it clear that heteropatriarchy kills: not only women and sexual minorities, but men, including those who identify as "straight." [Moreover,] the cycle of destructive masculinity makes clear as well that gender violence is a race and poverty issue.

Accordingly, anti-violence theorizing and advocacy must take an integrated approach, understanding the interplay of race, sexuality, class, and gender and taking account of the places where, and the means by which, gender violence is perpetuated. "Violence against women" is not distinct from "violence against sexual minorities." Nor are analyses of the United States as a "prison nation" complete without a reckoning of the toll that gender violence takes on the vulnerable of all sexualities, colors, and genders.

. . . Sometimes the technique that Mari Matsuda named "looking to the bottom" can make such a reframing possible. Thus, even within the "violence against women" frame, scholars have long recognized that women of color tend to be more poorly served by existing institutions and practices, even feminist ones, than white women. But, as we have seen, the move from violence against women to gender violence makes possible an even more comprehensive mapping of the ways in which heteropatriarchy kills. What might initially look like a dilemma—a choice between women's safety or racial justice—turns out to be an instance of interest convergence.

This turn to a gender violence analysis—instead of the "violence against x" analysis—should not be confused with the project of simply making existing programs "diverse" or "inclusive." Advocates for women of color experiencing intimate violence, for example, complain about the effort to "include" them in campaigns framed by and for white women. Instead, the task is to develop anti-violence proposals and projects that are responsive to the experiences of differently situated groups from the very beginning. Efforts to pay attention to the race of gender, the gender of race, and the sexuality and class of each may demand new kinds of conversations with different people at the table. The process may not be an easy one, but the potential is great. . . .

Conclusion

The struggle against gender violence brings us back, again, to the fact that heteropatriarchy kills. The dilemma of anti-violence advocates—that relying on criminal justice to punish the perpetrators of violence against women and sexual minorities in the long run perpetuates more gender violence, directed particularly at the most vulnerable and disenfranchised communities—leads in the end to an even more daunting predicament: a struggle against an ideology so deeply rooted in Western society and culture that it seems ineradicable.

Yet feminist and queer movements have already begun the process of transformation, and in a relatively short time. A gender violence analysis brings us more good news: the fight against heteropatriarchy does not make straight men the enemy. The organizations that have planted themselves at the convergence of the struggles against private and state-sponsored gender violence . . . have goals that can only be considered utopian. Yet their effort to build a social, political, and economic order that would eliminate gender violence and foster genuine security should inspire.

Moreover, the broad vision and ambitious goals of these groups need not put them at odds with more reformist [or ameliorative] projects. . . . [Systemic] justice advocates and gender violence advocates have a common interest in identifying and addressing violence committed under the auspices of the family, the state, and the community. Transformative justice has the potential to link these advocates and critical scholars in alliances that can work on different scales, but with the same horizon of liberation.

Harris shows how law-as-ideology pervades "private" and "public" aspects of human life and kills—both literally and metaphorically—people as well as justice. This ideology certainly kills cis women: "The motivations of men who commit mass shootings are often muddled, complex or unknown. But one common thread that connects many of them—other than access to powerful firearms—is a history of hating women, assaulting wives, girlfriends, and female family members or sharing misogynistic views online, researchers say."[6] However, in school shootings, heteropatriarchal attitudes also, literally, can kill many other kinds of people:

> Many of the recent [school] shootings share a disturbing component: The perpetrators were repeatedly, even relentlessly, accused by "preps and jocks" of being gay. Gay harassment is proposed as a point of departure for understanding the causes of school shootings. When boys who believe on some level that they warrant privilege, are instead harassed, they may feel driven to avenge the "wrong," and re-assert a more dominant, powerful, and victorious masculinity. These circumstances call for a cultural transformation such that "boys will be boys" is no longer used as an alibi for violence.[7]

These examples illustrate how gender and injustice permeate the everyday lives of countless persons and groups. But, as Harris concludes, despite the "daunting predicament" of this hegemonic ideology, organized movements "have already begun the process of transformation." Using three-layered goals, today's (and tomorrow's) systemic advocates are charged with supporting counter-hegemonic movements like these in ways that combine

---

[6] Julie Bosman, Kate Taylor & Tim Arango, A Common Trait Among Mass Killers: Hatred Toward Women, N.Y. Times (Aug. 10, 2019), www.nytimes.com/2019/08/10/us/mass-shootings-misogyny-dayton.html.

[7] Jessie Klein, Sexuality and School Shootings: What Role Does Teasing Play in School Massacres? 51 J. of Homosexuality 39 (2006) (excerpt from article abstract).

democracy with adjudication to pierce through the Critical Challenge and its bulwarks.

NOTES AND QUESTIONS

1. *Reflection Exercise.* If you asked U.S. elites for their opinion on the most dangerous (or harmful) ideology today—whether dangerous is defined in terms of the public safety and welfare, the potential for violence and the harm caused and to which groups, or left undefined, what would you expect in reply? Do you think many would point to white supremacy, heteropatriarchy, or the like? Or is it more likely they would point to something more associated with other countries ("it couldn't happen here") and seen as having been, for the most part, long vanquished by the forces of good—such as fascism or Nazism? If you posed the same question to members of subordinated groups, would you expect their answers to be the same or different? What do you see as the harmful ideology or ideologies of today? Why?

2. *Origins of Subordinating Systems.* The European system of patriarchal sexism, carried across the Atlantic Ocean to the United States with the settlers, predated capitalism and its industrialized class oppression.[8] Homophobia, as it eventually came to be known—or the elevation of heterosexuality and the subordination of homosexuality—came later. For example, an English historian pinpoints the 18th century as the start of heterosexism. Anthony Fletcher, Gender, Sex and Subordination in England, 1500–1800, 83 (1999) ("The distinctions of heterosexuality and homosexuality, though they are so salient for us, did not exist for the 17th century man or woman"). How might the "hetero" in heteropatriarchy have derived from the elevated or privileged status of patriarchy? What broader insights about law as culture and ideology does Harris supply in her dissection of heteropatriarchy and its reproduction of systemic violence? Can you describe an example from your own experience of heteropatriarchy in contemporary action?

CHAPTER RECAP

This chapter has explained how law-as-ideology creates "illusions of equality" that are intentionally hard to pierce or unmask. The ideas in common currency, in both legal doctrine and throughout mainstream culture, are designed to be ineffective tools for seeing through these dominant or hegemonic illusions. Thus, advocates and activists use critical concepts, histories, research, analysis, and everyday actions as tools to unearth the connections between "social ills," social identities, and social problems. Still elites propagate illusions and try to silence, deny, or suppress critical alternatives to them. They endeavor for a totalizing social

---

[8] Joe R. Feagin and Kimberley Ducey, Elite White Men Ruling: Who, What, When, Where, and How 10 (2017).

and legal hegemony—the discrediting of all ideas, sources, and institutions that expose systemic illusions of equality. Using critical knowledge from the bottom innovatively and proactively, generations of activists and advocates have prevented this totalizing aim. Today and tomorrow, systemic advocates build on that progress in the face of intensifying elite domination through corporate globalization. As you find and embark on your own path, the following and concluding part provides a final case study in, and forward-looking points of emphasis on, both the Critical Challenge and Critical Justice.

PART VII

CLOSING REFLECTIONS ON CRITICAL JUSTICE AND SYSTEMIC ADVOCACY

...

CHAPTER 15

RUNNING THE CRITICAL JUSTICE MARATHON—*BROWN*, FORMAL EQUALITY, AND BEYOND IN PUBLIC EDUCATION

■ ■ ■

Table of Sections

15.1 Unpacking Persistent Educational Inequality and Material Injustice
15.2 Upholding by Law the Systemic Linkage of Property to Identity for Unequal Education
15.3 Designing Student Debt in Higher Education as New Professional Handcuffs
15.4 Countering Systemic Violence in the Structuring of Public Education Today
15.5 Cross-Cultural Comparisons—and Their Limits

OPENING THOUGHTS

We have made progress in everything yet nothing has changed.

—**Derrick Bell**

Suppose the United States was a superpower in environmental policy. Suppose the United States was a superpower in treating people equally. See, that's the kind of superpower I'd like to have.

—**former President Jimmy Carter**

[T]he present becomes history, so we must learn from that history to be more than our histories.

—**Margaret Montoya with Angela Harris**, "Who is a LatCrit?," Jerome Culp and Angela Harris Provide Answers and Ways of Being, 16 Seattle J. for Soc. Just. 701, 706 (2018)

[Every] Zapatista's [duty] is this: to plant the seed and guard its growth. . . . [T]his is the difference between the Zapatistas and [most of] the rest of humanity: where everyone sees an apple, the Zapatista sees a seed.

—**Subcomandante Insurgente Marcos**, Conversations with Durito: Stories of Zapatistas and Neoliberalism (2005)

INTRODUCTION

We have seen repeatedly how modern rule of law legal systems incorporate and foster entrenched hierarchies based on group identity while promising equal justice. One result is the ongoing Critical Challenge, which asks advocates and others to use law in a way that acknowledges, uses, disrupts, shifts, and—perhaps—eliminates this deception and improves the lived realities of subordinated group members. Legal action toward equality in education or other settings thus holds both "promise and perils."[1] Using law means using a system designed both to promote and to prevent equal justice.[2] Its efficacy for principled, accountable, and effective problem solving is impeded *by design*—and advocacy to advance equal justice is constructed to match and overcome law's failure by design.

As we already have observed, social change strategies, legal and extralegal, all have limits—carrying risks of cooptation, uncertainty, and ineffectiveness—whether the strategy involves organizing, research, teaching, writing, lawsuits, voting, lobbying, negotiations, or any other sort of social change work. Building the organized power of subordinated groups is vital, but neither organizing as a method, or groups as agents, are free from risks of cooptation and effects of indeterminacy. All "forms of social action . . . potentially have cooptive as well as transformative effects."[3] Thus, the Critical Challenge, while focused on the promises and perils of using law for social change, has a corollary—the promises and perils of *not* using law for social change.

Using law means using lawyers trained to represent elite interests as well as to promote equal justice. Using law means working through legal institutions and practice settings constructed to rebuff non-elite clients, groups, and communities. And using law means using a system that is indeterminate—highly susceptible to power and manipulation. To navigate systemic complexities, advocates must develop and use both a critical *and* a dual consciousness about law, systems, injustice, and solutions. This chapter revisits the post-*Brown* experience to deepen these and similar key points covered throughout this book.

Recall Derrick Bell's article in Part I, written in 1976 and reflecting back on the creative advocacy that led to *Brown v. Board of Education* and

---

[1] Orly Lobel, The Paradox of Extralegal Activism: Critical Legal Consciousness and Transformative Politics, 120 Harv. L. Rev. 937, 942 (2007). See also Scott Cummings, Critical Legal Consciousness in Action, 120 Harv. L. Rev. F. 62 (2007). "Critical legal consciousness" developed in theory and action in multiple sites, and lawyers are not the only ones facing the predicament of the Critical Challenge in using the tools of a trade for social change—organizers and others face similar challenges. See, for example, Scott L. Cummings, Rethinking Foundational Critiques of Lawyers in Social Movements, 85 Fordham L. Rev. 1987 (2017).

[2] Much has been written about the pros and cons of using law in service of equal justice. For example, see Austin Sarat and Stuart Scheingold, What Cause Lawyers Do For, and To, Social Movements: An Introduction, in Cause Lawyers and Social Movements 1 (Austin Sarat and Stuart A. Scheingold eds. 2006).

[3] Lobel, The Paradox of Extralegal Activism, at 940.

ongoing school desegregation efforts.[4] Bell expressed concern about the ways in which hallmark legal victories were followed by slow, partial, or ineffective implementation. Implementation-focused advocacy, in fact, seemed to diminish movement energy, rather than enabling activists to reach new heights of power and action. Schools desegregated far more slowly than expected. *Brown*—and the organizing work surrounding this much-celebrated litigation—were faulted for failing to ensure implementation or to anticipate massive "white flight" from public schools. As Bell noted, even where integration occurred, the result was not necessarily improved education for Black students.[5] Moreover, schools resegregated in waves since then. Recent U.S. news reports indicate that "new" segregation is flourishing:

> Poor, black and Hispanic children are becoming increasingly isolated from their white, affluent peers in the nation's public schools, according to new federal data that the number of high-poverty schools serving primarily black and brown students more than doubled between 2001 and 2014.[6]

Given the formal legal distinction between public and private, litigation victories focused on public schools could not reach "private" decision making and interests. So, the problems of unequal education, including segregated classrooms and schools, although held illegal in 1954, continue to flourish. Displaying the dynamics of preservation through transformation, identity castes in public schooling have changed over time but reemerged with the same hierarchical ordering of groups and unequal distribution of material outcomes.

Nearly seventy years after *Brown*, the system channels opportunity and rewards to those it already has marked for success, while miring in frustration and failure those it has marked as subordinate. The channeling includes intra-school tracking—educating top-end groups with a college preparatory curriculum for high-wage, high-status, high-power careers, while bottom-end groups are given vocational training narrowly focused on readiness for low-wage jobs, and steered away from higher education.[7] This

---

[4] For additional reflections on civil rights legal action and desegregation campaigns, see Mark V. Tushnet, The NAACP's Legal Strategy Against Segregated Education, 1925–1950 (1987); Tomiko Brown-Nagin, Courage to Dissent: Atlanta and the Long History of the Civil Rights Movement (2011); Gerald N. Rosenberg, The Hollow Hope: Can Courts Bring About Social Change? (1991); Michael J. Klarman, Brown, Racial Change, and the Civil Rights Movement, 80 Va. L. Rev. 7 (1994).

[5] Derrick Bell, Jr., Serving Two Masters: Integration Ideals and Client Interests in School Desegregation Litigation, 85 Yale L.J. 470 (1976).

[6] Emma Brown, On the Anniversary of Brown v. Board, New Evidence that U.S. Schools Are Resegregating, Wash. Post (May 17, 2016), www.washingtonpost.com/news/education/wp/2016/05/17/on-the-anniversary-of-brown-v-board-new-evidence-that-u-s-schools-are-resegregating/.

[7] The Community Coalition, an organizing group in South Los Angeles, discovered that many schools there emphasized vocational training—for example, one high school offered nine cosmetology classes and only four chemistry classes. Students routinely either dropped out or found themselves ill-equipped for college. The Coalition pursued a campaign to increase access to

reconsolidation of old castes through new instruments also includes "privatizing" public schooling through charter schools, producing new mostly-white private schools subsidized by public funding, leaving the remaining public school systems anemic and mostly non-white.[8]

During these nearly seventy years, generations have asked, self-critically, whether *Brown* has been coopted since 1954. Is *Brown* an example of preservation through transformation? Has it been captured? Turned tokenistic? From a bottom-up perspective, did law displace the prospects of transformation with amelioration only?

To reconsider the same or similar questions which remain at the crux of the Critical Challenge introduced in Part I, this chapter offers another, updated, look at the persistent social problem of inequality and re-segregation in schools despite decades of formal equality—both top-down reactions to hollow *Brown's* core and bottom-up community campaigns or projects designed to defend and advance *Brown's* gains. In helping to close our study of systemic advocacy, this penultimate chapter provides a case study, of sorts, to which you can apply the key concepts introduced in this text: identities, groups, interests, power, and systems, along with the critical responses and innovations of organizing and advocacy in pursuit of three-layered goals.

15.1 UNPACKING PERSISTENT EDUCATIONAL INEQUALITY AND MATERIAL INJUSTICE

Writing on *Brown's* 50th anniversary, critical race scholars Bob Chang and Jerome Culp brought to light the continuing systemic construction of privilege and subordination under formal equality. They link six systems—housing, education, family, health care, employment, and criminal justice—as mutually-reinforcing fields of law and life that ensure

---

college preparatory courses. See Seema Shah, Kavitha Mediratta, and Sara McAlister, Securing a College Prep Curriculum for All Students (June 2009), https://www.issuelab.org/resources/7663/7663.pdf?download=true&_gl=1*1tltym4*_ga=MTY0NzUxMTQ4Ny4xNjEzODc5NTg4*_ga_5W8PXYYGBX*MTYxMzg3OTU4OC4xLjAuMTYxMzg3OTU4OC4w&_ga=2.216810198.1740707460.1613879588-1647511487.1613879588 (showing how youth-infused organizing was the most critical aspect of a broad advocacy campaign aimed to better serve poor Latinx and Black students). Ultimately, the Coalition formed a citywide grassroots organization, Communities for Educational Equity, which resulted in the school board mandating college preparatory courses for all students, an increase in school district accountability to community constituencies, and the election of new political leadership from the ranks of the community organizers. But a lack of vocational education also can reinforce inequalities in some contexts. Career and technical education can expand opportunity, if directed toward skills and credentials that lead to higher-wage careers. See Fact Sheet, How to Promote Gender Equity in Career and Technical Education: A Primer for Schools, National Women's Law Center (2007), www.nwlc.org/sites/default/files/pdfs/Final%20CTE%20Fact%20Sheet.pdf; Ryan Smith, Advancing Racial Equity In Career and Technical Education, Center for American Progress (Aug. 28, 2019), www.americanprogress.org/issues/education-k-12/news/2019/08/28/473876/advancing-racial-equity-career-technical-education-enrollment/.

[8] See Nick Hanauer, Better Schools Won't Fix America, The Atlantic (July 2019) (describing the efforts of wealthy elites to "fix" schools through privatization and to blame public schools and families in working-class communities for economic inequality and social polarization).

persistent inequality, both public and private, micro and macro, and material and cultural. Recalling Bell, Chemerinsky, Crenshaw and others from Part I, ask yourself as you continue to read and reflect: has the Critical Challenge of using law for justice in public education increased or decreased since 1954? How about since the excerpt's date of 2004?

BUSINESS AS USUAL? *BROWN* AND THE CONTINUING CONUNDRUM OF RACE IN AMERICA
Robert S. Chang and Jerome M. Culp, Jr.
2004 U. Ill. L. Rev. 1181 (2004)

Introduction

Every ten years or so, there are various conferences and symposia that revisit *Brown v. Board of Education*. While these discussions are important, we wonder if the conversations taking place during this fiftieth anniversary are much different from those that took place during the fortieth. In this article, we try to understand why these discussions might be the same. . . .

Stuck in a Moment

During a moment of optimism thirteen years ago, one of us declared an "African American Moment," a time "when different and blacker voices will speak new words and remake old legal doctrines." Two years later, the other of us followed suit and declared a similar "Asian American Moment." These declarations came during the emergence of critical race theory in the legal academy. While different voices did, indeed, speak new words and challenge old doctrines, the hope reflected in these declarations seems naïve in light of the entrenched racial inequality that we protested. Instead of a period of racial advancement, we have found ourselves stuck in a different kind of moment, characterized by what we call the inequality cycle.

The inequality cycle is our description for racial inequality that is entrenched through systems or social institutions that operate to maintain or further inequality. In measuring racial inequality, we use wealth, rather than income, as its primary indicator. The number of such interlocking systems or social institutions that play a role in the inequality cycle is quite large, but we will touch on six: education, housing, family, health care, employment, and criminal justice.

Wealth as a Measure of Racial Inequality

First, we examine a snapshot of racial wealth inequality using 1993 and 2000 data comparing non-Hispanic white (white), black, and Hispanic households. . . . Black wealth . . . remained fairly steady near ten percent of white wealth, while Hispanic wealth appeared to increase slightly from approximately ten percent in 1993 to twelve percent of white wealth in

2000, although this marginal increase is not statistically significant. This seems to indicate that when comparing 1993 to 2000, black and Hispanic households, in the aggregate, are not catching up to white households. . . . [And] the poorest black and Hispanic households have lost ground. . . .

. . . Thus, the picture at *Brown's* fiftieth anniversary does not look much different than it did at its fortieth.

The Inequality Cycle

. . . Our beginning hypothesis is that wealth begets wealth. It operates as a cycle through its intergenerational effects, which include the direct transmission of wealth and the indirect transmission of wealth through opportunities that are associated with or fostered by wealth.

In the same way that we focused on household wealth in the previous section, we will focus on the household as the primary unit of consideration in this section. We do so because children grow up in a household, and the household in which the children grow up fosters or constrains their opportunities.

System 1: Education. The educational attainment of parents has a strong effect on the educational achievement of their children. Educational attainment is the result of what one does with the opportunities that are available. Past (and we would argue present) generations of children have had their opportunities circumscribed because of race. As one commentator notes:

> Black children reared in families without economic or educational resources are unlikely, as adults, to have gained the kind of skills, knowledge, and aspirations that many white children will have gained from the day-to-day experience of being raised by an educated or economically privileged family. This relative lack of experiential knowledge or understanding among black people in one generation will affect the beliefs and aspirations of the next. Our continuing failure to eradicate this race effect means that a primary vehicle for breaking the inequality cycle, education, will not meaningfully change the status quo.

System 2: Housing. Where one lives has a strong impact on both employment and educational opportunities. Residential segregation eviscerated the hope that *Brown* would result in integration, one goal of which was to lessen the prejudice in the hearts and minds of children through their interaction with those of different races. With the fight over bussing, and the Supreme Court ruling against interdistrict remedies, whites who had successfully fled to new school districts in the suburbs were not subject to desegregation orders. The result—underfunded inner city schools that were largely minority, and suburban schools that were largely white—was a situation beyond the scope of legal redress as accepted by the Court.

When the racial wealth effect based on discrimination in housing is considered, a clearer picture of why there is such a large disparity in the wealth of the average white household as compared with black and Latina/o households emerges....

First, the government, until 1950, encouraged the use of racially restrictive covenants in the home loans that it underwrote through the FHA and VA loan insurance programs. Second, the loans underwritten by the FHA and VA went primarily to whites. Third, the Federal Home Owners' Loan Corporation used maps that coded neighborhoods on the basis of race to determine their creditworthiness. The result was that between 1934 and 1962, the FHA and VA programs made possible the purchase of $120 billion of residential real estate. Less than two percent went to nonwhite families. The effect of these discriminatory policies was magnified because private banks used these racial maps that largely determined creditworthiness.

If we take into account property appreciation and intergenerational wealth transfers, then we begin to better understand the wealth disparities discussed above. If we add to this the connection between segregated neighborhoods and educational opportunities, we can see more clearly how our failure to address the racial disparities that exist with regard to housing and its effect on wealth will result in the persistence of racial disparities. Again, the cycle. Inequality begets inequality.

System 3: Family. Thus far, we have talked about some of the ways that wealth begets wealth and is transmitted intergenerationally, directly and indirectly. We should remember, though, that the family is the primary site for this transmission. Also, the family is not a race-neutral institution: racial-sexual policing operated directly through the legal form of antimiscegenation laws, through the extralegal form of lynch law, and indirectly through the segregation of neighborhoods, schools, and workplaces. The result was that as of 1987, ninety-nine percent of married white Americans were married to other white Americans. Although the rate of interracial marriages has risen, families are still very monoracial. Insofar as wealth is concentrated in white households and families, racial minorities have not been able to access this wealth through intermarriage. This has an ongoing impact on wealth disparities between the races.

We are nearing the end of a twenty-five-year period during which the baby boom generation has inherited approximately seven trillion dollars from the previous generation. At the same time, "the average black family headed by a person over the age of sixty-five has no net financial assets to pass down to its children." It is not just that nothing is going to be transmitted to the next generation in black families—the older generation often is not in a position to be self-sufficient. Many of them are drawing resources from their adult children.... We see then how the family, the primary site of wealth accumulation and intergenerational transmission, perpetuates racial wealth and opportunity gaps.

System 4: Health Care. Health care presents another example of the comparative value of black and white lives.... [A] recent study reported in the New England Journal of Medicine shows that race alone has a strong effect on the decisions doctors make. In the study, videotapes were made of a patient interview with a white and black person with identical scripts and identical medical information. Several hundred doctors were asked to view the videotapes and prescribe follow-up treatments. There was a marked disparity in the level and quality of follow-up care based on the race of the patient, with the white patient being recommended for better and more costly procedures than the black patient.

To the extent that health care is less accessible to certain populations, this will have long-standing direct and intergenerational effects. Prenatal and postnatal care and nutrition have a direct effect on brain development and health through one's lifetime. Racial disparities in health care have a tremendous effect on one's opportunities with regard to education and employment, which then includes a strong intergenerational effect.

System 5: Employment. Discrimination in employment limits one's ability to acquire wealth, affects what neighborhoods one can reside in and limits one's access to health care and one's ability to accumulate the kinds of human and social capital that can be transmitted intergenerationally to the next generation. Thus, racial discrimination in one generation transmits itself to the next.

System 6: Criminal Justice. To the extent that there is racial discrimination in the criminal justice system, this too has intergenerational effects. Involvement in the criminal justice system has the immediate effect of taking the person out of the work force during the time of incarceration, and it affects one's prospects for future employment. Inability or difficulty in acquiring gainful employment prevents or limits one from acquiring wealth and affects where one can afford to live, which correlates strongly with the quality of education available for the next generation. Discrimination in the criminal justice system has a compounding effect.

Failure to understand how these systems or institutions operate will lead to partial or ineffective remedies. The result is that the racial disparities documented above will likely persist and continue to plague future generations.

Civil Rights Myopias

Sometimes, an individual or a group faced with discrimination responds reflexively in an attempt to address the immediate harm(s) without sufficient regard for the broader systems of oppression that may be in place. We call this problem "civil rights myopia." We examine three examples of civil rights myopias and the lessons they teach for those formulating civil rights strategies.

"We're Not Black": A Lesson from Gong Lum v. Rice

Sometimes, an oppressed individual or group may seek a remedy that might solve their immediate problem, but which may leave intact the broader system of oppression. The case of *Gong Lum v. Rice* is instructive in this regard. The case is sometimes described in Asian American history texts as an early challenge by a Chinese immigrant father on behalf of his American-born daughter against segregated public education, taken all the way to the Supreme Court. It is also sometimes celebrated as an early example of how Chinese immigrants did not merely acquiesce to discrimination directed against them. The fact that the case arose in Mississippi in the 1920s merely adds to the case's mystique.

. . . At the time, the Mississippi Constitution provided that "separate schools shall be maintained for children of the white and colored races." The challenge to the state of Mississippi was how to deal with the Chinese within the state's black or white racial paradigm.

[Nine-year-old] Martha Lum's "lawyers knew better than to argue that Chinese were White." Instead, they argued that as a person "of pure Chinese origin and descent," she is not "colored," and in the absence of a public school for those of Chinese ancestry, she should be permitted to attend the white public school. This argument succeeded in the trial court . . . [but the] Mississippi Supreme Court . . . classified Martha Lum as colored and left her with the choice of attending the colored public schools of her district or attending a private school. The U.S. Supreme Court later affirmed the state court's decision.

. . . If successful, [the lawsuit] would have resulted in expanded opportunities for children of Chinese ancestry, but it still would have left Negro children with inferior segregated schooling. . . .

As if this litigation strategy was not problematic enough, the Chinese community in Mississippi responded to the *Gong Lum* decision by trying to assimilate as much as possible into the white community, "ceas[ing] all social contact with Blacks and ostraciz[ing] individual Chinese who continued to maintain social relations, including marriages, with Blacks."

This decision by the Chinese living in Mississippi is criticized as gaining at the expense of blacks and negating any possibility for a coalition between blacks and Chinese, essentially "thwarting all hope of substantive racial equality for both groups." Thus, the Chinese, while gaining some racial privilege, participated in their own subordination by promoting a racial order where they remained racially oppressed. By choosing this course, the Chinese forgot what brought them to Mississippi in the first place. In fact, Chinese workers were imported to the South during Reconstruction to replace black workers as part of a strategy to racially stratify the labor force in order to deepen the exploitation of all workers.

This example shows that a binary racial system having two levels of stratification may not be as efficient as a racial system with more levels of stratification. Of course, stratification does not take place only along racial lines, but it also includes class, gender, sexual orientation, and immigration and citizenship status. Consequently, a myopic civil rights vision may improve the conditions for the immediate individual or group. It may, however, result in little overall change and may in fact consolidate or deepen the overall system of oppression that continues to oppress that individual or group along with others.

"We're White, Too": Early LULAC Litigation Strategy

Unlike the attempt to secure a gain for Martha Lum and other Chinese American children by distancing the Chinese from blacks, early LULAC [League of United Latin American Citizens] litigation strategy went further by claiming an explicit white racial identity. This legal strategy took advantage of an 1897 decision which held that a Mexican immigrant claimant was legally white within the purview of the naturalization laws and, therefore, eligible for U.S. citizenship. The decision was premised on the operation of the Treaty of Guadalupe Hidalgo, which provided citizenship for persons of Mexican ancestry, and the naturalization laws, which limited naturalization to free white persons and persons of African nativity or descent. . . . Perhaps most importantly, this litigation strategy, similar to the Gong Lum strategy, did not dismantle the overlying system of racial subordination and, in fact, reinforced it through the active participation and collusion of (some) Mexican Americans in the system of racial subordination. This strategy also foreclosed the possibility of coalition between Mexican Americans and blacks to challenge the overarching system.

Thus far, we have discussed two similar civil rights myopias: *Gong Lum*, which might be characterized as "don't apply Jim Crow to us because Jim Crow applies to blacks, and we're not black," and the early LULAC strategy, which might be characterized as "don't apply Jim Crow to us because Jim Crow applies to blacks and we're white." We turn now to the third civil rights myopia—the dilution claim.

"There's Not Enough to Go Around": African American Resistance to Civil Rights Claims by the Gay/Lesbian/Bisexual Community

... [Some individuals fear that addressing homophobia has] "eclipsed or diminished attention to the importance of racism altogether."

While we are cognizant of the dangers of analogizing between different forms of oppression and understand that, at some level, resources are finite, we find repugnant the notion that adding gay/lesbian/bisexual claims to the civil rights agenda will somehow dilute, or make more difficult, the efforts of traditional minorities to gain justice. We call this homophobia or heterosexism masquerading as a pragmatic claim. One fallacy is the presumption that there is an African American community that is distinct and separate from the gay/lesbian/bisexual community. They are, and have always been, overlapping communities. Another problem is that the dilution claim does not understand that different systems of oppression—racism, sexism, heterosexism, nativism, classism, ableism—are not separate and, in fact, operate in ways that reinforce one another. . . .

A Prescription of Sorts

When addressing oppression, it is always necessary to ask the "other groups" question. In suggesting this prescription, we borrow from feminist legal scholars who ask "[t]he woman question." They ask "about the gender implications of a social practice or rule: have women been left out of consideration? If so, in what way; how might that omission be corrected? What difference would it make to do so?" This strikes us as a remarkably sensible thing to do.

Conclusion

. . . All this leads ultimately to the question of what kind of nation we aspire to be. We can be a nation that tries to honor the best sentiments found in the Constitution. The way to honor those sentiments is to give them meaning, to provide for meaningful relief when we violate those sentiments. But as a nation, we are much better at making lofty statements about liberty and opportunity than we are at creating the material conditions necessary to effectuate liberty and opportunity for communities, families, and individuals who have been denied liberty and opportunity. Perhaps that is one way to understand *Brown I* and *Brown II*. *Brown I* stands for the lofty principle, *Brown II*, for the failure to effectuate it. The result, as we've demonstrated, is a cycle where inequality is perpetuated. Fifty years after *Brown*, . . . if the past is any indication, we predict that *Brown's* promise will remain unfulfilled on its hundredth anniversary. One difference, though, is that we will be the ones who are being judged by the next generations. We would like to leave behind a different legacy. . . .

As Chang and Culp demonstrate, systemic injustice ensured that neither social, nor economic, nor educational equality would result from *Brown*. Rather, inequality increased. In the years since their article, the material conditions of identity-based inequalities worsened further. For instance, a 2016 Congressional Budget Office report found wealth distribution was more unequal in 2013 than in 1989.[9] The top one-tenth of one percent of the wealthiest U.S. households owns as much wealth as the bottom 90 percent of U.S. households.[10]

In this pyramid, women still face wage inequality—those who worked full-time in 2015 earned only 80 cents for every dollar a man earned, and the pay gap was worse for women of color.[11] Black, Native American, and Latinx families are disproportionately poor, suffering nearly three times the rate of white poverty, and one-third of U.S. female-headed single-parent households live in poverty. As Chang and Culp show, micro-macro inequalities in income and wealth translate to (and in turn are caused by) inequalities entrenched by law among identity-correlated neighborhoods, schools, and employment opportunities.

NOTES AND QUESTIONS

1. *Parameters of Whiteness.* As *Brown* found, and as was commonly known, segregated public schools were unequal in quality along racial lines despite the contradictory promise of separate but equal—and not only on white-over-Black frameworks. For example, Mexican American students attending a segregated school in the Orange County, California, city of Westminster were educated in "a terrible little shack." Their recess and lunch yard was separated from an adjoining cow pasture by an electrified fence, so that Mexican students eating lunch got "all the flies from the cow pasture."[12] Southern California schools, and schools throughout the Southwest, routinely segregated Mexicans from white children. California's statutory separation of Native and Asian children from whites further reveals that the systemic design behind school segregation was not just meant to separate Black (and Latinx) youth from white children, but all groups lower than whites in the racial caste hierarchy, as the excerpt by Chang and Culp illustrates for Chinese students.

Nonetheless, some Latinx people can "pass" for white, at least based on physical appearance, and have argued on that basis for their legal whiteness and its privileges, as the Martinez excerpt in Part I illustrates. Recall also that

---

[9] CBO Report: Rich Get Richer, Poor Get Poorer, (Aug. 18, 2016), https://www.sanders.senate.gov/press-releases/cbo-report-rich-get-richer-poor-get-poorer/.

[10] Mapping economic inequality on a global stage is even more compelling—with regard to income disparities, for instance, making just $32,400 U.S. dollars annually places you in the top one percent of worldwide income, https://www.bizjournals.com/bizjournals/how-to/marketing/2017/01/you-may-be-surprised-to-learn-youre-a-1-percenter.html, although to reach the global one percent for net worth—wealth—requires the considerably greater amount of $770,000.

[11] American Association of University Women, The Simple Truth about the Gender Pay Gap, www.aauw.org/research/the-simple-truth-about-the-gender-pay-gap/.

[12] Mendez v. Westminster: For All the Children/Para Todos los Niños (2003 documentary).

some European immigrant groups once seen as non-white are now considered white. Is the goal of racial equality furthered by counting more people as white—or not counting at all? Recalling Obasogie, Wildman & Armstrong, and other Part II excerpts, is racial equality likely to be furthered by so-called colorblind or "post-racial" fictions that deny, disguise, or deflect persistent patterns of documented systemic outputs? How might a critical understanding of this history help you and other advocates to better support organized bottom-up struggles to advance equality for all systemically subordinated groups?

2. *Preservation Through Transformation.* Chang and Culp discuss several systems that impact everyday life along identity-lines, cautioning that advocates must understand how they operate or their efforts will lead to partial or ineffective remedies. The interconnection of systems to preserve caste is another dimension a systemic advocate must consider. For example, clinician and racial justice law scholar Deborah Archer connects local zero-tolerance ordinances—requiring or encouraging landlords to exclude or evict tenants with criminal history—to racial inequality in the criminal justice system, perpetuating racial segregation in neighborhoods:

> Racial segregation continues to be a problem not simply of history, but of current design. . . .
>
> Crime-free ordinances [as a condition of rental housing] are an emerging and increasingly effective tool of exclusionary localism. . . .
>
> . . . [T]he assumption of Black dangerousness stubbornly remains a central part of America's cultural view and a relentless narrative that drives debate and policy ranging from criminal justice reform to education. Crime-free ordinances fit squarely into this historical narrative. So it should be no surprise that laws ostensibly motivated by the desire to keep certain communities "safe" would act as a fence against racial integration. Racial discrimination and racial disparities in the criminal legal system are undeniable. By using contact with the criminal legal system as a tool for exclusion, documented racial biases in policing and the criminal legal system are imported into the private housing market, furthering systemic racial exclusion and residential segregation.[13]

What is the role of housing in the inequality cycle that Chang and Culp discuss? How do the adequacy and location of housing connect to educational (in)equality? Keep the above in mind as you consider the next section.

---

[13] Deborah N. Archer, The New Housing Segregation: The Jim Crow Effects of Crime-Free Housing Ordinances, 118 Mich. L. Rev. 173, 178–79 (2019).

15.2 UPHOLDING BY LAW THE SYSTEMIC LINKAGE OF PROPERTY TO IDENTITY FOR UNEQUAL EDUCATION

The inequalities that Chang and Culp implicate in the persistence of unequal education follow a systemic code, or pattern, that harkens back to colonial designs and castes. Entire groups were excluded by law from property and contract rights based on their social identities. The same groups were excluded from the polity itself—disqualified from voting and participating in lawmaking through democracy or adjudication. We have seen repeatedly in this book that the top-down linkage of property to identity to law is key to the persistence of general group inequalities, including in the specific context of education. The following Supreme Court excerpt demonstrates this linkage of public-private, micro-macro, and material-symbolic systemic interconnections that flexibly yet surely undergird identity castes in public education as it stands today, much as they did before *Brown*.

The Court's decision in *San Antonio Independent School District v. Rodriguez* shows how elites use democratic policy making and adjudication in tandem—at different levels of local, state, and federal decision making—to enforce the status quo. In this case, the Supreme Court was asked to recognize the intentional systemic linkage of class and other social identities to educational inequality.[14] The Court was asked to declare that this form of collectivized inequality is out of constitutional bounds. The Court rejected these pleas and, instead, asserted that formal equality does not require even an effort to achieve substantial equality. Rather, "the Equal Protection Clause does not require absolute equality or precisely equal advantages." But the question of "absolute equalities" or "precisely equal advantages" was not the issue: the legal issue was the built-in persistence of gross funding inequalities in public education, which were systemically correlated very directly to class and race through private property and public law.

SAN ANTONIO INDEPENDENT SCHOOL DISTRICT V. RODRIGUEZ
411 U.S. 1 (1973)

MR. JUSTICE POWELL delivered the opinion of the Court.

This suit attacking the Texas system of financing public education was initiated by Mexican-American parents whose children attend the

---

[14] For additional background see David Waggoner, The Jurisprudence of White Supremacy: Inter Caetara, Johnson v. M'Intosh and San Antonio Independent School District v. Rodriguez, 44 Sw. L. Rev. 749 (2015) (connecting indigenous conquest to the *San Antonio* case and its consequences for poor Latinx people).

elementary and secondary schools in the Edgewood Independent School District, an urban school district in San Antonio, Texas. They brought a class action on behalf of schoolchildren throughout the State who are members of minority groups or who are poor and reside in school districts having a low property tax base....

... Early in its history, Texas adopted a dual approach to the financing of its schools, relying on mutual participation by the local school districts and the State. As early as 1883, the state constitution was amended to provide for the creation of local school districts empowered to levy ad valorem [real estate] taxes with the consent of local taxpayers for the "erection ... of school buildings" and for the "further maintenance of public free schools." Such local funds as were raised were supplemented by funds distributed to each district from the State's Permanent and Available School Funds....

Until recent times, Texas was a predominantly rural State and its population and property wealth were spread relatively evenly across the State. Sizable differences in the value of assessable property between local school districts became increasingly evident as the State became more industrialized and as rural-to-urban population shifts became more pronounced.... In due time it became apparent to those concerned with financing public education that contributions from the Available School Fund were not sufficient to ameliorate these disparities....

Recognizing the need for increased state funding to help offset disparities in local spending and to meet Texas' changing educational requirements, the state legislature ... establish[ed] the Texas Minimum Foundation School Program. Today, this Program accounts for approximately half of the total educational expenditures in Texas....

The school district in which appellees reside, the Edgewood Independent School District, has been compared throughout this litigation with the Alamo Heights Independent School District. This comparison between the least and most affluent districts in the San Antonio area serves to illustrate the manner in which the dual system of finance operates and to indicate the extent to which substantial disparities exist despite the State's impressive progress in recent years. Edgewood is one of seven public school districts in the metropolitan area. Approximately 22,000 students are enrolled in its 25 elementary and secondary schools ... situated in the core-city sector of San Antonio in a residential neighborhood that has little commercial or industrial property. The residents are predominantly of Mexican-American descent: approximately 90% of the student population is Mexican-American and over 6% is Negro. The average assessed property value per pupil is $5,960—the lowest in the metropolitan area—and the median family income ($4,686) is also the lowest. At an equalized tax rate of $1.05 per $100 of assessed property—

the highest in the metropolitan area—the district contributed $26 to the education of each child for the 1967–1968 school year [amounting to, together with state and federal contributions,] a total of $356 per pupil.

Alamo Heights is the most affluent school district in San Antonio. Its six schools, housing approximately 5,000 students, are situated in a residential community quite unlike the Edgewood District. The school population is predominantly "Anglo," having only 18% Mexican-Americans and less than 1% Negroes. The assessed property value per pupil exceeds $49,000, and the median family income is $8,001. In 1967–1968 the local tax rate of $.85 per $100 of valuation yielded $333 per pupil. . . . Coupled with [state and federal monies] Alamo Heights spent $594 per pupil. . . .

. . . [S]ubstantial interdistrict disparities in school expenditures . . . largely attributable to differences in the amounts of money collected through local property taxation, . . . led the District Court to conclude that Texas' dual system of public school financing violated the Equal Protection Clause. The District Court held that the Texas system discriminates on the basis of wealth in the manner in which education is provided for its people. Finding that wealth is a "suspect" classification and that education is a "fundamental" interest, the District Court held that the Texas system could be sustained only if the State could show that it was premised upon some compelling state interest. . . .

Texas virtually concedes that its historically rooted dual system of financing education could not withstanding the strict judicial scrutiny that this Court has found appropriate in reviewing legislative judgments that interfere with fundamental constitutional rights or that involve suspect classifications. . . . We must decide, first, whether the Texas system of financing public education operates to the disadvantage of some suspect class or impinges upon a fundamental right explicitly or implicitly protected by the Constitution, thereby requiring strict judicial scrutiny. If so, the judgment of the District Court should be affirmed. If not, the Texas scheme must still be examined to determine whether it rationally furthers some legitimate, articulated state purpose and therefore does not constitute an invidious discrimination in violation of the Equal Protection Clause of the Fourteenth Amendment.

. . . The precedents of this Court provide the proper starting point. The individuals, or groups of individuals, who constituted the class discriminated against in our prior cases shared two distinguishing characteristics: because of their impecunity they were completely unable to pay for some desired benefit, and as a consequence, they sustained an absolute deprivation of a meaningful opportunity to enjoy that benefit. . . .

. . . [N]either appellees nor the District Court addressed the fact that, unlike each of the foregoing cases, lack of personal resources has not occasioned an absolute deprivation of the desired benefit. The argument here is not that the children in districts having relatively low assessable property values are receiving no public education; rather, it is that they are receiving a poorer quality education than that available to children in districts having more assessable wealth. Apart from the unsettled and disputed question whether the quality of education may be determined by the amount of money expended for it, a sufficient answer to appellees' argument is that, at least where wealth is involved, the Equal Protection Clause does not require absolute equality or precisely equal advantages. Nor indeed, in view of the infinite variables affecting the educational process, can any system assure equal quality of education except in the most relative sense. Texas asserts that the Minimum Foundation Program provides an "adequate" education for all children in the State. By providing 12 years of free public-school education, and by assuring teachers, books, transportation, and operating funds, the Texas Legislature has endeavored to "guarantee, for the welfare of the state as a whole, that all people shall have at least an adequate program of education. This is what is meant by 'A Minimum Foundation Program of Education.'" The State repeatedly asserted in its briefs in this Court that it has fulfilled this desire and that it now assures "every child in every school district an adequate education." No proof was offered at trial persuasively discrediting or refuting the State's assertion. . . .

We thus conclude that the Texas system does not operate to the peculiar disadvantage of any suspect class. But in recognition of the fact that this Court has never heretofore held that wealth discrimination alone provides an adequate basis for invoking strict scrutiny, appellees have not relied solely on this contention. They also assert that the State's system impermissibly interferes with the exercise of a "fundamental" right and that accordingly the prior decisions of this Court require the application of the strict standard of judicial review. . . . It is this question—whether education is a fundamental right, in the sense that it is among the rights and liberties protected by the Constitution—which has so consumed the attention of courts and commentators in recent years. . . .

In *Brown v. Board of Education*, a unanimous Court recognized that "education is perhaps the most important function of state and local governments." . . .

Nothing this Court holds today in any way detracts from our historic dedication to public education. . . . But the importance of a service performed by the State does not determine whether it must be regarded as fundamental for purposes of examination under the Equal Protection Clause. . . . *Lindsey v. Normet*, 405 U.S. 56, 92 S.Ct. 862, 31 L.Ed.2d 36 (1972), decided only last Term, firmly reiterates that social importance is not the critical determinant for subjecting state legislation to strict scrutiny [and rejects] . . . any constitutional guarantee of access to dwellings of a particular quality. . . .

... [T]he key to discovering whether education is "fundamental" ... lies in assessing whether there is a right to education explicitly or implicitly guaranteed by the Constitution. ... Education, of course, is not among the rights afforded explicit protection under our Federal Constitution. Nor do we find any basis for saying it is implicitly so protected. ...

It should be clear, for the reasons stated above and in accord with the prior decisions of this Court, that this is not a case in which the challenged state action must be subjected to the searching judicial scrutiny reserved for laws that create suspect classifications or impinge upon constitutionally protected rights.

We need not rest our decision, however, solely on the inappropriateness of the strict-scrutiny test. A century of Supreme Court adjudication under the Equal Protection Clause affirmatively supports the application of the traditional standard of review, which requires only that the State's system be shown to bear some rational relationship to legitimate state purposes. This case represents far more than a challenge to the manner in which Texas provides for the education of its children. We have here nothing less than a direct attack on the way in which Texas has chosen to raise and disburse state and local tax revenues. We are asked to condemn the State's judgment in conferring on political subdivisions the power to tax local property to supply revenues for local interests. In so doing, appellees would have the Court intrude in an area in which it has traditionally deferred to state legislatures. ... No scheme of taxation, whether the tax is imposed on property, income, or purchases of goods and services, has yet been devised which is free of all discriminatory impact. In such a complex arena in which no perfect alternatives exist, the Court does well not to impose too rigorous a standard of scrutiny lest all local fiscal schemes become subjects of criticism under the Equal Protection Clause.

In addition to matters of fiscal policy, this case also involves the most persistent and difficult questions of educational policy, another area in which this Court's lack of specialized knowledge and experience counsels against premature interference with the informed judgments made at the state and local levels. ...

The foregoing considerations buttress our conclusion that Texas' system of public school finance is an inappropriate candidate for strict judicial scrutiny. These same considerations are relevant to the determination whether that system, with its conceded imperfections, nevertheless bears some rational relationship to a legitimate state purpose. ...

In its reliance on state as well as local resources, the Texas system is comparable to the systems employed in virtually every other State. ... Moreover, if local taxation for local expenditures were an unconstitutional method of providing for education then it might be an equally impermissible means of providing other necessary services customarily financed largely from local property taxes, including local police and fire protection, public health and hospitals, and public utility facilities of various kinds. . . .

In sum, to the extent that the Texas system of school financing results in unequal expenditures between children who happen to reside in different districts, we cannot say that such disparities are the product of a system that is so irrational as to be invidiously discriminatory. Texas has acknowledged its shortcomings and has persistently endeavored—not without some success—to ameliorate the differences in levels of expenditures without sacrificing the benefits of local participation. The Texas plan is not the result of hurried, ill-conceived legislation. It certainly is not the product of purposeful discrimination against any group or class. On the contrary, it is rooted in decades of experience in Texas and elsewhere, and in major part is the product of responsible studies by qualified people. . . . One also must remember that the system here challenged is not peculiar to Texas or to any other State. In its essential characteristics, the Texas plan for financing public education reflects what many educators for a half century have thought was an enlightened approach to a problem for which there is no perfect solution. We are unwilling to assume for ourselves a level of wisdom superior to that of legislators, scholars, and educational authorities in 50 States, especially where the alternatives proposed are only recently conceived and nowhere yet tested. The constitutional standard under the Equal Protection Clause is whether the challenged state action rationally furthers a legitimate state purpose or interest. . . . We hold that the Texas plan abundantly satisfies this standard.

. . . [C]ertainly innovative thinking as to public education, its methods, and its funding is necessary to assure both a higher level of quality and greater uniformity of opportunity. These matters merit the continued attention of the scholars who already have contributed much by their challenges. But the ultimate solutions must come from the lawmakers and from the democratic pressures of those who elect them.

The U.S. Supreme Court issued this opinion in 1973, on the eve of *Brown's* twentieth anniversary—a celebration of failure by design. By that time, the judges were ready to declare as "rational" a public funding scheme that allocated $356 annually for some students (mostly poor and of color) compared to $594 for others (mostly affluent and white). The facts and holding of this case illustrate concretely how judges "sabotage" equal public education, using the implements of formal equality, while proclaiming fidelity to *Brown's* promise of equal equality. To quote Chang and Culp, opinions like this one portend "that *Brown's* promise will remain unfulfilled on its hundredth anniversary."

NOTES AND QUESTIONS

1. *Equality and Funding.* When the prospects for integrated schools dimmed despite *Brown*, advocates for educational equality shifted their goals toward equality of school funding. Yet *San Antonio* shut that door. Rather, the Court asserted solutions to systemic educational inequality "must come from the lawmakers and from the democratic pressures of those who elect them." What might it take for individuals and groups—through voting and ongoing advocacy and activism—to equalize school funding across districts, or even, through invoking change at the federal level, across state lines? Consider this analysis from the Economic Policy Institute of *Brown's* impact, and imagine what forms and scale of advocacy and activism might be needed to address school inequality now:

> *Brown's* 1954 success in highlighting the nation's racial caste system gave encouragement to a wave of freedom rides to desegregate interstate transportation, to national support for Rosa Parks' determination to desegregate local buses and other public facilities, to lunch counter sit-ins to desegregate restaurants and other public accommodations, to heroic efforts to register African Americans in the Deep South to vote, and to confrontations over admission of African Americans to southern universities. It also spurred civil rights legislation in 1957, 1960, 1964, 1965, and 1968 that, in combination, undid the nation's legal support for race-based status. None of this would have taken place without *Brown*.[15]

Think back to the marriage equality campaign covered in Part II and to the excerpts by NeJaime, Hunter, and others. Advocates and activists confronted a situation in which they were losing the vote on state initiatives at the same time that the Supreme Court was steeped in unfriendly precedent and wary of advancing equality ahead of public opinion. Both state-level democracy and federal adjudication (at least at the Supreme Court level) seemed unlikely to generate the desired decisions. How did advocates and activists use legal and extralegal activities and move among levels to create a strategy to win marriage equality? Can you imagine similar strategizing to advance equality in school funding today? What knowledges, skills, teams, coalitions, resources, goals, and metrics might be most important?

---

[15] Richard Rothstein, Brown v. Board at 60: Why Have We Been So Disappointed? What Have We Learned?, Economic Pol'y Inst. Report (Apr. 17, 2014), www.epi.org/publication/brown-at-60-why-have-we-been-so-disappointed-what-have-we-learned/.

15.3 DESIGNING STUDENT DEBT IN HIGHER EDUCATION AS NEW PROFESSIONAL HANDCUFFS

San Antonio vividly shows how dominant groups can shape material conditions to expand systems of subordination, building on previously-created inequalities. During the past few decades, public education has been defunded to build prisons, militarize police forces, increase state surveillance of everyone, and move public monies to private corporations. This crippling of public education is accompanied by a similar effort to undermine and redirect higher education. Recall that Powell's 1971 memo focused on universities as dangerous locations of vitality, criticality, and freedom, and called on elites to act strategically to reverse that supposed reality. As Crain and others showed in Part IV, decades later the legal industry makes it easier to foment insecurity and precarity among legal workers, including lawyers. All these top-down tools are deployed flexibly to reward conformity and "put a lid" on bottom-up dissent, organization, and power.

Adding to the existing elite tool is the creation of debt that, in this systemic context, diminishes the horizons of kids in public schools as well as young adults in college, whether that debt arises in law school or other education settings. Major debt adds immeasurably to career vulnerability. Debt and vulnerability, moreover, are concentrated in students from traditionally subordinated groups. In response, students and allies have crafted and launched a number of projects designed to loosen the shackles of debt for all students. As you read the excerpt below, consider whether the project it describes is ameliorative or also transformative, and why. Can we think of practical ways to improve or implement transformative tweaks within ameliorative actions or increments? Can we curb the use of educational debt specifically, and perhaps general debt also, as occupational chains or industry handcuffs?

THE LAW AND POLITICAL ECONOMY OF A STUDENT DEBT JUBILEE

Luke Herrine
68 Buff. L. Rev. 281 (2020)

Introduction

A student debt jubilee is an idea whose time is coming. Only a few years ago, talk about canceling student debt was confined to the radical fringes. Today there are two competing bills that would cancel different amounts of student debt bouncing around the Senate. . . .

Part of the reason that student debt cancellation has long been excluded from mainstream policy debates, is that the common wisdom is that student debt is mostly harmless. The logic goes that higher education is a high-yield investment in individual productivity and wage-earning potential, so high-yield that the cost of borrowing to fund this investment is well worth it. . . . Student debt was originally a compromise device to fill in small gaps in public subsidy while avoiding charged political debates. At the beginning of the postwar period, using federal spending to universalize public higher education was not far from enactment. Southern segregationist concerns about federal usurpation of state power, Catholic concerns about undermining parochial education, and a widespread assumption that one could work one's way through college without much of a problem (and that doing so was virtuous) presented the main obstacles. Having the federal government subsidize students rather than institutions avoided some of these obstacles, and having it do so through lending rather than grants avoided others. . . .

. . . Student debt truly began to grow in the 1990s. It was then that for-profit colleges consolidated into big businesses designed to suck in as much federal student aid as possible, that Sallie Mae went private and began to develop innovative techniques for expanding student lending, and that state governments began cutting higher education budgets in earnest. Students, colleges, and policymakers all began to view higher education primarily as an investment in future employability, as "human capital." Student debt came to seem a natural part of the lifecourse.

. . . Although some economists continue to insist that there *is* no student debt crisis, the rapidly growing default rate, the overwhelming evidence of systematic fraud at many for-profit colleges, the increasing evidence of student debt's role in deepening the racial wealth gap, and the undermining of the "skills gap" theory of growing income inequality, among other things, have made that an increasingly untenable position. Organizing by student debtors themselves combined with a dawning realization among politicians that the misery caused by student debt could be harnessed for political gain has pushed the possibility of canceling student debt and restructuring the higher education system so it no longer generates more of it into the mainstream.

. . . [S]tudent debt creates [significant burdens]. . . . Student debt deepens the racial wealth gap as well as the class divide. Student debt has also been shown to increase anxiety and even to worsen health outcomes, while preventing people from making major investments such as buying a house or a car, or getting married or having kids. These effects channel through families and communities, further deepening race and class divides. Even for the relatively well off, taking on debt pushes people into more lucrative but less socially valuable and less individually rewarding work, furthering the ongoing "Meritocracy Trap" by which the highly educated work themselves ragged as facilitators of extraction. . . .

Student debt also has knock-on social and political effects. It changes the way individuals, institutions, and policymakers think about the role of higher education in society—making it appear to all as fundamentally an investment in worker productivity, with a cost to be borne primarily by individuals. The idea of education as a collective good gets erased....

... [There are strong] arguments for canceling student debt.... If done in combination with a program to render public higher education free to all who want to access it, it would contribute to the reconstruction of higher education in a formation more fitting for a democratic society....

The Problems with Student Debt

... Burdens on Individuals and Communities

... Unsurprisingly to any student of stratification, some individuals, families, and communities feel these burdens disproportionately. A growing literature indicates that low-income households and Black and Latino households have more burdensome debts, leading to higher delinquency rates and higher concentrations of the other ills that come along with relatively heavy debt loads. This is in part due to the fact that for-profit colleges, which produce unusually high amounts of indebtedness for unusually low benefits, target "non-traditional students." ... [I]ndebtedness among Black households has increased at higher rates than among White or Hispanic households (to use the crude categories of the census). Morgan and Steinbaum estimate that *70 percent* of Black student debtors who left school in 2004 will default.

These findings jibe with the long line of research showing that families that are struggling economically and who have been subject to systematic racialized dispossession have experienced the burdens of any type of indebtedness disproportionately. They can also be contextualized by findings that racial wealth disparities make it such that "black families whose members study and work hard are still hindered in their efforts to generate the resources necessary for their own security and to ensure the well-being of their children."

Macroeconomic Effects

... [A] society that places massive debts on a growing amount of its population at the beginning of adulthood creates a massive demand-suppression program that suppresses employment, especially among the most vulnerable....

... [T]hose burdened with student debt are more likely to take high-paying jobs that they do not like rather than relatively lower-paying jobs that involve giving back to their communities....

But What About the Benefits of Student Debt?

All of this only presents one side of the ledger. Student loans are not just impositions of burdens, after all. They are used to pay for *educations*. It is a perfectly plausible reading of the history of higher education policy to say that millions and millions of people would not have obtained educations without student debt to help them. . . .

While there is no doubt that one cannot account for the burdens of student debt without accounting for the benefits, there are several reasons to doubt that this is the right way to think about the balancing.

First, for many people it is not even clear that they *are* made better off by exposure to the combination of a college education plus student debt. . . .

Even for people for whom post-college incomes justify the amount of debt taken on in terms of lifetime balance sheets (that is, the lifetime amount of debt payments is less than the lifetime amount of the college premium), the cost may not be worth it. . . .

Second, even were the advantages of a college education to clearly outweigh the burden of debts for all who took on student debt, that fact in itself does not make financing higher education through individual indebtedness good policy. . . .

What is more, a focus on the benefits of student debt to individuals and even to productivity fails to account for the reverberating burdens beyond individuals to families and communities. It fails to account for the collective loss—the reduction in goods and services, the increase in unemployment—that results from the dampening of aggregate demand. It fails to account for the diversion of people from socially valuable but low-paying work (teaching, social work, artmaking) into extractive but high-paying work (flash trading, private equity firm-flipping, engineering fracking equipment). A full accounting of the costs and benefits of student debt cannot be reduced to comparison of the aggregate of individual's loan payments over a lifetime compared with the aggregate of their incomes above what they might have expected to earn without a college degree. . . .

Distortions of Higher Education

Student debt has also contributed to the restructuring of higher education. The more higher education is funded by debt, the more transactional the relationship between students and college becomes. . . .

. . . Why would we care whether our fellow Americans have knowledge of, say, the basics of climate science or the history of racialized domination in the United States if this knowledge does not produce returns on the labor market? Why would we care if colleges decide who to hire and fire based on desire to meet job-focused student demand and to adjunctify the college workforce, undermining investment in research and academic freedom?

Indeed, focusing on a return on investment at the retail level obscures the *social* value of investing in the sorts of skills that are useful for doing particular types of labor. Individual students will make "investment" decisions based on the current state of the labor market, with perhaps some information about what the near future will look like. But the labor market can be subject to rapid changes, and society can suddenly need particular types of skills that were not well remunerated previously. The COVID-19 crisis has made abundantly clear how suddenly skills such as knowledge of infectious disease, ability to produce medical devices, ability to design a fiscal and monetary response to a sudden collapse in supply and demand, and the like become highly valuable while others suddenly collapse in market value. As with other areas of investment, it makes sense to have the state fund long-term investments in knowledge and skills that may not produce immediate returns or even be of obvious use in the short term to ensure that such investments are made rather than leaving it to profit-maximizing individuals to invest in the skills most likely to produce returns over their lifetime based on present information. . . .

A Self-Reproducing Political Economy

Funding through student debt also creates a political dynamic in which . . . running a college becomes more and more like running a business. Administrators have to spend more time with budgets, donors, investors, and lobbyists than with curricula, professors, and students. Mutual dependence on student debt among colleges, financial companies, servicers, guaranty agencies, etc. creates a powerful lobby for the expansion of debt with as little accountability as possible. . . .

. . . Student debt . . . creates the conditions for its own perpetuation, transforming the higher education system and many other aspects of our society along with it.

For many years, the only opponents of increased student debt with any voice in Washington were non-profit advocacy groups without mobilized bases, and thus without much political capital to throw around. In addition to the general difficulty of mobilizing a mass group of people without a common identity, many student debtors have internalized the morality of individual responsibility that comes with the legal obligation to repay and had been preoccupied with taking the sorts of risks—political or otherwise—that might put them out of a job and behind on their payments. Some observers have posited that the increase in student debt contributed to the de-mobilization of college students, both by preoccupying students with worries about bills (forcing them to get jobs when they might have spent that time organizing, adding mental stress and thus reducing the capacity to take creative and risky political action) and by socializing students into the consumerist role discussed above. On this theory, student debt functioned as a form of social control, whether intentionally or not.

In recent years, there have been some signs that more and more student debtors have begun to understand their plight not as an individual responsibility but as a collective failure. As these debtors have started to mobilize, politicians have begun to take notice. For the first time since student debt first became part of federal higher education policy, members of Congress and plausible candidates for President have proposed bills containing structural reform of federal higher education policy that includes cancellation of student debt and policies that would prevent further accumulation by making college broadly affordable. The COVID-19 crisis has only heightened the contradictions and made calls for debt cancellation louder. . . .

Reasons to Cancel Student Debt

Canceling student debt would make individual debtors wealthier and end ongoing extractive or coercive relationships between debtors and their creditors, servicers, or collectors. Both the wealth transfer and the elimination of indebtedness (the same thing in accounting terms, but not in every way) would make debtors' lives—and the lives of the families, friends, and communities on which debtors depend—easier. Since student debts' burdens are skewed along race and class lines, these impacts would disproportionately benefit relatively disadvantaged people—though not the *most* disadvantaged (on average, those who have not attended college are worse off). . . .

. . . [Blanket student debt cancellation would end] a burden on individuals and society that has no good justification. Student debt cancellation makes the most sense as a form of restitution and revitalization. It is best situated in a program that wipes our collective hands clean of a way of financing higher education that places the primary burden on individuals, with racist, anti-egalitarian, and anti-democratic effects. Canceling student debt repudiates the legitimacy of this allocation of burdens. When paired with a plan to de-commodify and democratize higher education, . . . it contributes to rebuilding a higher education system on the principle of collective responsibility for investing in skills, forms of knowledge, and ways of knowing that benefit all of us. . . .

That doing so would *also* make millions of peoples' lives better both directly and indirectly cannot be counted against it. That its distributional consequences would be ambiguous in the short term provides reason to pair it with other reforms to make our society more equal, not a reason not to undertake an otherwise worthy plan. . . .

Conclusion

. . . Many of the most important benefits of student debt cancellation—those pertaining to the structural reform of the political economy of higher education—could not be realized merely through an Executive Branch jubilee. That is because such a jubilee could not be paired with a program to prevent future student debt from accumulating.

So it may be. But debt cancellation now does not preclude more reforms later. Jubilees can create fresh starts in more ways than one.

Herrine's systemic analysis of student debt as a contributing factor to educational inequality illustrates *San Antonio's* flip side: skewed public funding, or defunding, raises existing barriers to educational access by redistributing financial burdens downward. As public education at any level is defunded—or funded selectively and unequally—only the more affluent can afford to educate themselves and their successors. And because personal and collective patterns of affluence and poverty are systemically correlated to identity castes (like race and sex), the top-down manipulation of class hierarchies (as measured by income and/or wealth) recycles collectivized racial and gender inequalities, and vice versa.

NOTES AND QUESTIONS

1. *Seeding Resistance in a System Failing by Design.* One can trace a fairly straight historical line from small-scale student debt to the current nationwide financial crisis. Ronald Reagan played a key role, representing the interests of elite financial institutions while also taking on universities as targets in the "culture wars." As governor of California, Reagan made big cuts in budgets for the California public university system, both "solidify[ing] his legacy as a budget hawk" and "directly drain[ing] the main source of income and professional growth for both his academic and working-class detractors."[16] And he repeated these sorts of cuts at the federal level as president, opening the door to both commodification of education and financialization of colleges and universities—both contributing to expanding student debt.

The U.S. public largely accepted Reagan's rationale—that public education, rather than a public good to be subsidized with public funds, was an individual "investment" whose burden must be borne by students and families. As this rationale became normalized, debt ballooned—but not equally among all groups. The education system—with respect to student debt for higher education—remained accessible to wealthy students, most of whom were white, but open to middle- and low-income students, particularly students of color, only at the cost of assuming ever-greater debt.

To combat debilitating and unequally distributed debt, activists and advocates planted the seeds for organizing and three-layered advocacy: (a) developing the capacity to aid individual students with information and assistance to negotiate debt forbearance or reductions; (b) bringing as many as possible of the 45 million owing student debt into organized action; and (c)

---

[16] Nick Martin, The Radical Possibilities of Not Paying Your Student Loans, New Republic (Feb. 7, 2020).

shifting consciousness so that a range of stakeholders—students, parents, politicians, journalists, and scholars—no longer bought the Reaganesque rationale justifying student debt and undermining public education.

Nick Martin, cofounder of the Debt Collective, a debt-cancellation organization that emerged out of Occupy Wall Street activism, explains how "collectivizing" action has gone hand-in-hand with "politicizing" understandings to aid individual students and to challenge systemic student debt abuses:

> The system had been deeply broken—or actually functioning as Reagan intended—for decades. Yet it is only recently that the astronomical rise in student debt is beginning to be treated by establishment political and media figures as the nationwide financial crisis that it is. . . .
>
> But this new awareness did not just spring into existence, and it wasn't just the Debt Collective building this movement, either. This work has long been sustained by those inside the system, both as students and as professors and administrators. . . . It took years of [critical and] public work by [many] people . . . and organizing by grassroots operations and groups like the Debt Collective, Strike Debt, and the Collective-adjacent Rolling Jubilee to get average Americans to a place where they understood their debt as political.[17]

Given this background, how might a systemic advocate employ the methods, norms, and techniques to organize complex actions against oppressive debt? How would identities, groups, interests, and power affect your analysis and actions in this anti-debt context? How would you define three-layered goals and appropriately contextual metrics of success (or not)?

2. *Paying for the "Privilege" of Education.* Asking the "other" question, a method for interrogating and understanding intersectional identities and systems of subordination, was introduced by Matsuda in Part II:

> When I see something that looks racist, I ask, "Where is the patriarchy in this?" When I see something that looks sexist, I ask, "Where is the heterosexism in this?" When I see something that looks homophobic, I ask, "Where are the class interests in this?" Working in coalition forces us to look for both the obvious and non-obvious relationships of domination, helping us to realize that no form of subordination ever stands alone.

A recent report on student debt offers a useful example of asking the "other" question. As the Herrine excerpt notes, student loans reinforce existing racial wealth gaps and affect working class students—those most likely to need loans—most deeply. It may be less well known that student loans also have a gendered impact. Taken together, the gender, class, and race impacts in student loans make education a particularly important, but risky, prospect for

---

[17] *Id.*

women of color—and call into question the equalizing potential of higher education. The American Association of University Women report, Deeper in Debt: Women and Student Loans,[18] finds that women hold two-thirds of outstanding U.S. student debt, although comprising only slightly more than half of college students. One commentator describes the results:

> [There are] surprising, cruel, racist, and regressive ways that student loans hold people hostage for decades, or sometimes for their whole lives . . . [including that] federal student loans have no statute of limitations. They can follow you forever. The federal government doesn't have to sue you to garnish your wages. . . . Oh, you're a disabled veteran barely scraping by on your VA disability checks? The feds will garnish [public] benefits if you have student loans in default. . . .
>
> . . . [Some reasons for the AAUW report findings] are predictable results of student loans plus patriarchy. Women get paid less money to do the same things despite having the same qualifications, so of course the student loan system will punish them with more interest payments for more years [because lower-paid women take longer to pay off their loans].
>
> . . . Women [also] are more likely than men to enroll in [predatory] for-profit colleges (as are nonwhite students), possibly because these colleges make ads that target women (and nonwhite students) directly. . . .
>
> Those disparities both contribute to and result from the absolutely insane gender/race wealth gaps in the U.S. . . .
>
> . . . [W]omen make less money, have less wealth, and yet pay more interest to the federal government than men for the "privilege" of going to college. Black women, in particular, make *much* less money, have *much* less wealth, and yet pay *much* more interest to the federal government for that "privilege."[19]

Student debt in higher education, like skewed government financing of public education, perpetuates identity castes emplaced by centuries of legal violence stretching more than 500 years, from colonialism to today. If you were to plan a new advocacy project to combat systemic injustice through ballooning student indebtedness, how would you begin? Which "other" questions would you ask in your bottom-up research to build coalitions? How might you use social identities as assets?

---

[18] American Association of University Women, Deeper in Debt: Women and Student Loans (2020), www.aauw.org/app/uploads/2020/03/DeeperinDebt-nsa.pdf.

[19] Sparky Abraham, How Student Debt Is Worsening Gender and Racial Injustice, Current Affairs (June 26, 2018), www.currentaffairs.org/2018/06/how-student-debt-is-worsening-gender-and-racial-injustice.

15.4 COUNTERING SYSTEMIC VIOLENCE IN THE STRUCTURING OF PUBLIC EDUCATION TODAY

Systemic violence, as noted in Part I and throughout the book, is routinized injustice. Systemic violence creates and normalizes inequalities, justifying the crushingly unfair results by "blaming the victims." Systemic violence occurs when the lives of individuals in subordinated groups are "regulated" to ensure unequal outcomes and thus maintain identity-based castes.

Students and educational workers are most directly affected by the systemic violence of educational institutions, but parents, advocates, and other community members also may be hurt, as Herrine notes above and as *Brown* recognized in 1954. Today, these harms include day-to-day microaggressions, denials of rewards and opportunity, experiences of discrimination or physical violence, the grinding costs of seeing and being complicit in ongoing unfairness, and lifelong material limits and deprivations. They also include over-policed schools and extreme forms of regulations and punishment, which begin to resemble prison conditions akin to the legal violence of militarized policing, mass incarceration, and crimmigration outlined in Part I.

Law undergirds these and similar harms across many contexts. In public education as in other contexts, those subordinated fight back—in this instance, students, parents, and their communities. In addition to public school financing and crushing student debts, another key front in today's struggles against educational inequality is the "school-to-prison pipeline"—the moniker given to using school disciplinary processes to move students, particularly low-income students of color, disabled, and LGBTQ youth,[20] onto an escalated disciplinary track that pushes them out of classrooms, into criminal law enforcement settings, and often out of schools and toward incarceration.

Students across the country have led challenges to school-to-prison pipeline policies and have developed and won sophisticated alternative

---

[20] A 2020 report on lost student days due to school suspension found, for secondary education, stark disparities along identity-lines:
- Black students lost 103 days per 100 students enrolled, 82 more days than white students lost due to suspension.
- Hawaiian/Pacific Islander students had the second highest rate, 63 days.
- Native American students lost 54 days per 100 students enrolled.
- Students with disabilities lost 68 days per 100 students enrolled, about twice the rate of those without disabilities.
- On gender lines, Black boys lost 132 days and Black girls 77, the latter seven times the rate of lost instruction by white girls.

Daniel J. Losen and Paul Martinez, Lost Opportunities: How Disparate School Discipline Continues to Drive Differences in the Opportunity to Learn (Oct. 2020, updated Jan. 2021), https://civilrightsproject.ucla.edu/research/k-12-education/school-discipline/lost-opportunities-how-disparate-school-discipline-continues-to-drive-differences-in-the-opportunity-to-learn/Lost-Opportunities-REPORT-v17.pdf.

disciplinary processes, including restorative justice processes designed to promote healing rather than mete punishment. These bottom-up efforts involve a wide range of diagnostic and strategic activities. They entail difficult, collaborative research and analysis and coalitional complex actions. Each faces risks like cooptation, capture, and tokenism. Accounting for identities, groups, interests, and power, students, parents, and their allies collaboratively create advocacy projects from scratch. The following excerpt, by legal scholar Heather Gehlert, provides a contemporary example from Kern County, California.

As you read below about the Kern Education Justice Collaborative, assess it as an advocacy project—its team and decision making processes, its research and analysis methods, its understanding of the social problems to be addressed, its solutions—on all three layers. Pay attention to the action planning, and note how the results of one action help inform decisions about next steps. Notice again the importance of combining contextually the available legal and extralegal tools to persuade and pressure systems to change for the better, and the importance of using time as a resource—for instance, to build strong bonds of coalitional solidarity that can withstand and fight back against identity-based systemic injustice, whether in educational or other contexts.

ENDING THE SCHOOL-TO-PRISON PIPELINE: A CASE STUDY OF COMMUNITY-LED DISCIPLINARY REFORM IN KERN COUNTY

Heather Gehlert[21]

In December 2012, Carmen Ramirez, a student at Arvin High School in Kern County, California, was reassigned to an alternative school 30 miles from her home, after being found with marijuana. The paperwork shared with her father, Mario, to explain the suspension and transfer were in English; however, Mario speaks mostly Spanish and allegedly gave consent without being fully informed.

That same semester, Gabriel Elder, a Latino student at Kern Valley High School, was suspended for "talking back," "engaging in profanity," and other minor offenses. Elder had recently been diagnosed with major depression and was exposed to domestic violence, but his mother's requests to have the school provide counseling and special education services for Elder reportedly were refused.

Two years later, Jerry Reagor, an African American student who was attending Foothill High School in Kern County reported being harassed, threatened, and assaulted by gang members on his way to school. His mother raised the issue with administrators and school police, yet the

---

[21] www.cvmb.org/wp-content/uploads/2020/02/Ending-School-To-Prison-Pipeline-Kern.pdf.

school district allegedly did not take action. Instead, staff claimed that Reagor was the aggressor. KHSD later transferred him to another school, citing Reagor's supposed "gang affiliations."

These are just a few of the many allegations that appear in a 2014 lawsuit that a group of parents, students and advocates brought against the Kern High School District, which, data revealed, was suspending and expelling its students of color at higher rates than its white students. The lawsuit referred to this as "systematic discrimination" and said that it had created a "racially hostile educational environment."

"The science really is clear: The more you send a kid away, the worse they get, not better," said Dr. Jeffrey Sprague, a professor of special education at the University of Oregon who, in the late 1990s, helped pioneer Positive Behavioral Interventions and Supports (PBIS), a proactive approach to behavioral issues, which works to establish socially and emotionally supportive school climates. "For the students most at risk in our communities," he added, "simply sending them away essentially trains them to become prisoners. . . . [I]t's called the school-to-prison pipeline."

In July 2017, advocates succeeded in disrupting that pipeline. After three years of public pressure and mounting legal expenses, Kern High School District settled the lawsuit. Under the terms of the settlement, local schools are required to implement disciplinary reforms aimed at helping kids stay in school, rather than pushing them out.

"We consider it a landmark civil rights victory for Kern County," said Dr. Gerald Cantu, benefits and policy director for the Dolores Huerta Foundation and a member of the Kern Education Justice Collaborative (KEJC), which was instrumental in making the reforms happen. The settlement is also a triumph for health. Getting suspended or expelled can exacerbate hidden forms of trauma, such as hunger or violence, that students may be experiencing at home. "If this trauma isn't treated, it's giving rise to these behavioral issues," Dr. Cantu said. "It's going to pile on additional trauma . . . and it's not going to address the root causes of the behavioral issues."

By contrast, non-punitive approaches to discipline, which the school district must now take, can help treat trauma and improve students' behavior, academic achievement, and likelihood of graduating—a strong indicator of health outcomes later in life. These approaches include restorative practices, which empower students to resolve their own conflicts by bringing offenders and victims together to discuss the harms that occurred and possible solutions.

This is the story of how KEJC—the collaborative that drove the lawsuit forward—developed a vision for simultaneously improving health and social justice in their community and, in David-versus-Goliath fashion, toppled the barriers that stood in their way. KEJC's process speaks to how difficult it can be to address forms of systemic racism in environments like Kern County, California, which is socially and politically conservative. Yet, it also underscores the power of collaboration. Local organizers worked with parents, students, faith leaders, educators, and others and realized a common goal. . . .

A picture of inequality emerges

Kern County is a place of great assets but also great barriers. It is home to a robust farm worker population and has a strong tradition of community organizing. Fittingly, civil rights activist Cesar Chavez, who was a farm worker before becoming a labor icon and cofounding the United Farm Workers union in Kern, is buried in Keene, an unincorporated community in the county located at the southern end of the San Joaquin Valley.

Bakersfield, the county seat, is growing rapidly and becoming more cosmopolitan; however, the outlying rural communities continue to face many challenges, including geographical isolation, low educational attainment, and high rates of unemployment and poverty. . . .

Residents in unincorporated areas lack a voice in decision-making and access to public services, and the county's institutions and leaders are not representative of the population. For example, until recently, only one of the Kern County Board of Supervisors' five districts had a Latino majority, even though the county's overall Latino population exceeds 50 percent. Following a lawsuit and voting rights challenge brought by the Mexican American Legal Defense and Educational Fund, a federal judge has since approved new district boundaries, creating two Latino-majority districts and increasing voters' political power.

A politically and socially conservative area with a tough-on-crime mentality, Kern County also has a legacy of zero tolerance in school discipline. That legacy was reflected in a 2010 report from the U.S. Department of Education Office of Civil Rights, which revealed that Kern County had the highest suspension and expulsion rates in the state. . . .

What's more, the data showed that students of color were the most impacted, with their expulsion rates far out of proportion to their enrollment. . . .

. . . Kern County's African American and Latino students also have disproportionately higher dropout rates and lower graduation rates both of which are linked to negative health outcomes later in life.

Further complicating matters, school leaders do not reflect the area's demographics. Data show that although more than two-thirds of the district's student body is Latino, approximately two-thirds of education staff and three-quarters of administrators are white. And, the Kern High School District Trustees include four white males and only one Latino. After the threat of a lawsuit, the trustees agreed to begin redistricting, and advocates are demanding that they create a second Latino-majority district. . . .

Like many other school districts throughout the nation, Kern County has high rates of bullying . . . and harassment in schools—mostly targeted at Latino and Muslim students. . . .

How KEJC formed

This is the backdrop against which the Kern Education Justice Collaborative operates. . . . The makings of it began in 2010, the year The California Endowment launched Building Healthy Communities (BHC), a 10-year initiative focused on improving health outcomes in 14 of the state's communities that experience significant health inequities. . . .

Still, [community members and groups] faced an immediate challenge: There were no local organizations that had the expertise to look at educational issues. Organizers in Kern County had roots in the labor movement, not education, so they had to "start from scratch," Robles said. Many groups including the Dolores Huerta Foundation, California Rural Legal Assistance, and Greater Bakersfield Legal Assistance, wanted to take on the issue of disproportionate discipline, but they needed help framing the issue and understanding viable solutions. So, they sought the expertise of a BHC South Los Angeles partner, CADRE (Community Asset Development Redefining Education). The L.A.-based community organizing group collaborates with parents and uses a human rights framework to advance education reforms and end the school-to-prison pipeline in the Los Angeles Unified School District and at the state level.

CADRE helped Kern organizers build their capacity, engage local parents and students, and figure out what model to use to address the problem. Local advocates then came together to form the Kern Education Justice Collaborative, which they launched in 2011. . . .

In many ways, the group's formation was well-timed. The same year that KEJC formed, then-U.S. Attorney General Eric Holder and then-U.S. Secretary of Education Arne Duncan launched the Supportive School Discipline Initiative, a collaboration between the Department of Justice and Department of Education that was created to identify and reform schools with overly punitive disciplinary practices. This initiative thrust the school-to-prison pipeline into the national news spotlight, with groups like the American Civil Liberties Union immediately hailing the initiative. . . .

This gave advocates in Kern County and across the country the opportunity to piggyback off of the national conversation to bring attention to local issues.

Building people power and creating a roadmap for change

Although KEJC would later implement a strategic multimedia campaign, they first had to figure out their asks and develop a broad base of allies by building people power through engagement with parents, youth, and other community members.

. . . KEJC members developed a set of recommendations for the Kern High School District. These included applying restorative justice practices to disciplinary procedures; implementing Positive Behavioral Interventions and Supports (PBIS); creating resource centers for parents and ensuring those centers are staffed with people who are culturally competent and bilingual; and changing how dollars are spent so that education funds would not go toward increasing campus police or other security personnel.

KEJC also wanted to track the KHSD's suspension and expulsion rates to keep their data current, so they began requesting additional data from the school district. However, members of the collaborative said that the school district stonewalled them. . . .

For three years, KEJC members urged the school district to address its issues with suspension and expulsion rates. They met with school board members to try to get a commitment to change and a timeline for when policies would be implemented.

Meanwhile, KEJC began to conduct outreach to parents, both to learn about their children's experiences within the school district and to help them better understand their rights and become involved in advocating for change. To recruit them, the collaborative used a combination of door-to-door canvassing, recruitment at events, and social media.

Staff from the Dolores Huerta Foundation, which is heavily involved in KEJC, then started recruiting parents to begin holding house meetings, with each host inviting seven to 10 friends to attend. Once they made enough contacts, they began holding larger community meetings and creating subcommittees for specific purposes, like education and civic engagement. At each of these events, parents and other community members received [training]. . . .

"[We] worked closely with the parents, and we started pushing them," Dr. Cantu said. "The organizer is supposed to be pushing them, . . . encouraging them to become leaders themselves and go to board meetings or council meetings and advocate for various issues."

Leticia Prado, a mother of six who is originally from Mexico and now lives in Weedpatch, is a prime example of one of the area's many parents-turned-advocates. . . .

"At the time, we didn't know much about how systems worked, but little by little, we started learning," Prado said, through a translator. "I narrowed in on the education system because, as a parent, I wanted to know about my children's schools."

... [A]dvocates gained other opportunities in 2013 due to legal changes at the state level. California enacted the Local Control Funding Formula (LCFF), which changed the way the state's schools are financed and gave school districts more authority over how funds are spent. Under the new finance rules, schools must develop Local Control and Accountability Plans (LCAP), which require schools to engage parents and community members in decision-making. Seeing an opportunity, KEJC and parents began advocating for discipline reforms through LCAP.

KEJC member organizations ... held trainings to inform parents about school funding and provide them with questions to ask their districts during the LCAP process. Through the trainings, parents learned about the requirements that California school districts must meet when developing their budget strategies, what the implications are for high-need groups like low-income and English Learners, and opportunities for engagement.

For example, the Dolores Huerta Foundation encourages parents to sit on decision-making bodies like school site councils and school wellness committees. Through participation in these groups, parents are able to provide input on how LCAP dollars should be spent and can help hold their children's district accountable for spending the funds as intended. ...

Still, Prado said that many parents are afraid to speak up because of their immigration status and fear of authorities.

[Prado said, "]You can't imagine how difficult that is for some parents—to fight the fear, to find the time to attend meetings after working in the fields all day, to understand a completely foreign and complicated school funding system. That's the challenge before us."

Prado has embraced that challenge in many ways, including by running for—and, ultimately, being elected to—her local Vineland School Board in 2016. When asked what motivates her to continue working on behalf of her community, Prado was quick to respond: "We live in a rural area that is mostly Hispanic. Many are undocumented and work in the labor camps. I know that we don't have political representation and equality. ... We want and deserve the same quality education for our children that other school districts with more money receive." ...

Applying legal pressure

Knowing that systems-level changes would not come easily, the collaborative had to shift its strategy. Fed up with the district's lack of action, in October 2014, a group of parents, students, and community groups, including the Equal Justice Society and some members of the Kern Education Justice Collaborative, such as California Rural Legal Assistance and the Dolores Huerta Foundation, decided to take legal action. Together, they sued the school district for systematic discrimination and alleged that the district had created a "racially hostile educational environment."

The lawsuit stated that the district's discriminatory policies and practices had the effect of creating a "school-to-prison pipeline." The petitioners also cited the school district's racially disproportionate practice of transferring students of color to alternative schools and noted that although students who are transferred do not end up in prison or jail, they end up in a "school-to-nowhere" pipeline because they are more likely to become unemployed, underemployed, or work in low-paying jobs, which stunts their overall ability to flourish. . . .

After two years of pressure, advocates began seeing some signs of progress: The group succeeded in diverting $2.59 million away from law enforcement and toward school climate. Another $1.18 million in LCAP funding was designated for parent engagement, and eight new parent centers have been created in the district.

Members of the collaborative said these changes occurred only because of pressure from the lawsuit. KEJC member Kevin McNeill noted that the opposition was surprised by the group's persistence: "If you have been entrenched in power and had your way for so long, when people start to push back, it's alarming."

Using LCAP funds, the school district promised to start implementing disciplinary reforms. For example, East Bakersfield High School established a Positive Behavioral Interventions and Supports steering committee, which meets once a month to review data specific to their school and discuss solutions. . . .

A landmark legal victory

. . . In July 2017, nearly three years after the lawsuit was filed, that pressure paid off, and the district settled the lawsuit. Now, changes like those happening at East Bakersfield High School will become standard throughout the district and potentially elsewhere. . . .

The settlement shows that the school district acknowledged its history of African American and Latino students being suspended at higher rates than their white peers. District officials also agreed to create new discipline policies, with guidance from experts on implicit bias, or unconscious stereotypes that influence people's thoughts, decisions, and practices.

"We did this lawsuit so that your voices can be heard, and the district can take action to respond to the concerns that you raise," Cynthia Rice, an attorney with California Rural Legal Assistance, told parents and other residents at a community meeting following the settlement. "The settlement agreement provides a platform for you to do that in a number of ways."

The settlement, which Rice emphasized is comprehensive, focuses on four main areas: community engagement, data collection, mandatory training for school personnel, and sustainability.

First, Rice explained, the district will hold two community forums every year for the next three years. During these gatherings, district leaders will report back to the community on rates of suspensions, expulsions, and student transfers, as well as hiring decisions aimed at increasing diversity so that teachers are more representative of the student population. . . .

A new data system created because of the settlement will also benefit teachers and administrators by allowing them to track discipline data in real time. The system will provide them with information not only on individual students, but also on any patterns so that they are better able to determine whether their policies and practices are affecting one group of students more than another. . . .

Teachers, administrators, and staff, including security officers, will receive comprehensive training on the new data systems. They also will receive education on implicit bias and will be coached on restorative—rather than punitive—approaches to discipline.

Additionally, the settlement will require the district to change disciplinary policies so that there is more engagement with parents. If a student receives disciplinary action, the district will now translate any related documents into the primary language of that student and his or her parent. . . .

Finally, the settlement aims to ensure that this work is sustained over the long term. . . .

. . . [Community] participants were also provided cards with a website that provides additional settlement details and a toll-free number that people can call to raise any ongoing or future issues related to discipline and racial injustice in the district. . . .

The special role of strategic communication

Although legal pressure was critical to advocates' victory in Kern County, a multimedia strategic communications campaign, including social media, billboards, radio and print ads, played a vital role throughout the process.

When the lawsuit against the district began in 2014, the community initially reacted with surprise and confusion. According to Aguilar, many residents did not understand the need for disciplinary reform. Their first response was, "Discipline's important; [students] need it," he said. "It's more of a law-and-order kind of reaction." . . .

To garner support and to help parents, teachers, and other members of the public make sense of what was happening, KEJC made communication a top priority.

"The first step in all of this [was] to educate the community that . . . we're not just talking a couple of weeks of bad decisions. We're talking generations of missteps." . . .

. . . [KEJC] began using a "schools not prisons" framework to garner support. According to Robles, they also asked, "How does Kern change its culture to start seeing young people as an asset, not a deficit? How [do we] put young people first and invest in education?"

With those questions and reflections guiding them, the group framed the issue as a matter of equity and tried to consistently make the connections among health, education, and equity clear. . . .

Additionally, KEJC maintains a Facebook page, which they use to amplify education-related news coverage, share criticism of and praise for school leaders' actions, and highlight opportunities for parents and others in the community to get involved. . . .

. . . "The research tells us that in order for institutions to succeed, teachers need to feel supported, administrators need to feel supported, and that will translate into families and children, of course, most importantly, feeling supported. So, the collaborative nature of this work and everyone coming together and looking in a positive way toward what the future can be for the schools and for the kids is what the research tells us will work. And, so, in some sense, everyone's interests are aligned here." . . .

Next steps and vision for the future

Asked what vision they are striving toward and what dreams they hope to realize for their community 15 or more years down the road, KEJC member Tim Douglas said he wants to see equity in access to a fair, quality education, as well as equity in discipline, opportunities, and outcomes. . . .

Others said they want mental health addressed in a more focused way. . . .

As the district moves forward with implementing the terms of the settlement, KEJC members would like to see the mental health services provided as part of the continuum of discipline practices. . . .

To that end, KEJC is currently advocating, through LCAP funding, for increasing the number of social workers and nurses on school campuses. And youth . . . have recently engaged in the LCAP process and advocated for LGBTQ-friendly policies and cultural competency training for district staff. . . .

As the Kern County experience confirms, state regulation, coercion, and punishment function as top-down exercises of power. Whether in public education or other contemporary contexts, only organized bottom-up action can match and check legalized top-down violence. As noted in Part II and illustrated here, antisubordination solidarity provides a critical alternative to systemic values and their imperatives. And, as we emphasize again in closing this chapter, context remains all important.

NOTES AND QUESTIONS

1. *Antisubordination and Solidarity as Systemic Advocacy Imperatives.* We describe antisubordination and solidarity as alternatives to systemic values and their imperatives, and we offered examples throughout the book of social struggles and systemic advocacy built on those critical values. The goals, form, and outcomes of legal actions can and should change in identifiable ways when guided by these values. One recent example is the change in union bargaining strategies in the education industry to take the form of "Bargaining for the Common Good."

As you read the following call to action, consider what you have learned about negotiations through classes, personal experience, or field work in internships or jobs. In traditional bargaining, who sets priorities and how? Who speaks for the individual or group? What information is relevant, and how is it developed? What teams, coalitions, or other collaborations are key? How is success defined, and from whose perspective(s) is it evaluated? What is the time frame for strategic action? Does the passage below represent a shift toward antisubordination and solidarity as values that guide—even mandate—certain strategies and actions and limit or prohibit others?

> It's time for traditional labor organizations, newer worker organizations, and the broader racial justice movement to link together to bring in a radically new economic and social order.... [A] key strategy to achieve this new reality is ... Bargaining for Common Good. Consider a recent example of organizing at the University of California.
>
> AFSCME 3299 led a transformative campaign that put racial justice front and center.... The campaign had many highlights— including striking six times and threatening a seventh, actions and reports that exposed UC's failed Wall Street gamble on hedge funds which squandered over $1 billion of pension and endowment money in fees, a multi-year legislative campaign culminating in the first ever Constitutional Amendment to ban outsourcing, and a "speakers boycott" that culminated in the [Democratic National Committee] moving its December 2019 debate from UCLA.... AFSCME 3299 for years has invested in relationships with other organizations— whether they be student organizations on campus, other unions, or racial justice groups on the ground....

This particular campaign was grounded in research that found racial and gender disparities in AFSCME members' wage rates, largely due to the concentration of Black and Latinx workers, especially women, in lower-paying titles, and a steady decline in Black employment over the course of two decades. . . . After a 3-year campaign . . ., UC executives finally relented to the Union's core demands, including a general prohibition against outsourcing; additional immigrant rights protections; a commitment to advance hiring and training opportunities for underrepresented communities, including formerly incarcerated workers; no cuts to members' retirement security; and a minimum wage of $20 per hour by 2024. . . .

Local 3299's targeting of Wall Street and other corporations was intentional. . . .

. . . [Bargaining for the Common Good] will require . . . targeting the real decision makers in both the public and private sectors that have a vested interest in keeping racial inequities in place.[22]

15.5 CROSS-CULTURAL COMPARISONS— AND THEIR LIMITS

The rule of law is a modern western invention that spread throughout the world. In each place and time, the rule of law manifests similar debilities but takes specific forms. The Critical Challenge of using law for justice, likewise, is omnipresent but not uniform. Thus, as we have suggested throughout this book, attention must be paid to critical histories, to context, to nuanced and accountable factfinding, and to flexible combinations of legal and extralegal actions. We have also paid attention to struggles and lessons learned across borders. But, as with all methods, these have their limits, too. To test those limits, consider the following pair of excerpts.

First, legal scholar Antoinette Sedillo Lopez invokes the critical Schools to showcase the importance of comparison as method in understanding the subordination of women globally, particularly women of color. As she points out, comparative methods do not assert the absolute superiority of one system over others. Rather, critical comparativism, as noted in Part V, "can illuminate differences based on systemic and cultural diversity" to facilitate contextual understandings of problems and solutions.

---

[22] Maurice BP-Weeks and Liz Perlman, Bargaining for the Common Good as Racial Justice, The Forge: Organizing Strategy and Practice (Mar. 31, 2020), www.forgeorganizing.org/article/bargaining-common-good-racial-justice.

Ethnocentrism and Feminism: Using a Contextual Methodology in International Women's Rights Advocacy and Education

Antoinette Sedillo Lopez
28 So. U.L. Rev. 279 (2001)

In the 1990's, international human rights discourse included a disquieting debate about a perceived clash between universal human rights and respect for culture. Nowhere did this debate play out more vigorously than in the area of women's rights. This debate was troubling. Many women had banded together as part of a global women's movement to invade the international human rights arena. That this movement might be seen as imperialistic concerned many of us who worked on international women's issues.

A global glance at the status of women continues to reveal a universal truth: women, particularly women of color or women of minority racial groups, experience subordination across borders, across cultures and across social groups or classes. . . .

We can use comparative law as a tool to help identify laws that successfully address women's needs and those that do not. Comparative theory does not posit an evaluation of the law determining which law or legal system is "better." Rather, comparative theory can illuminate differences based on systemic and cultural diversity. Understanding these differences can help us understand how best to use law to improve women's lives. . . .

Academics of color are developing international theories that strike a balance between western concepts of universal rights and respect for culture. In addition, they are pointing out the shortcomings of liberal western thought and proposing theories that are more nuanced and sensitive to the needs of marginalized and oppressed individuals. They take a look at the status of women of color from the bottom up. . . .

The first step is to examine and understand the cultural context. Prior to any type of advocacy or education, one should review history, literature, ethnography, interview and personal experiences. In addition, demographic, social and educational data can enhance understanding of the country and culture in which the international [human rights concepts and] documents will be used.

The second step is to understand the legal context. In some countries legal reform is accomplished primarily through legislation; in others, the executive/administrative branch is most responsible. In some, the court system can be an effective mechanism to accomplish legal reform. In some countries, legal reform may have more of an impact on the citizenry's lives than in others. In countries where legal reform is unlikely to affect the citizen's lives, educational programs are likely to more effective so resources should be put there. In most countries both educational and legal reform are necessary to change views about women's roles.

Finally, insights from critical race theory, feminism, cultural studies are helpful in considering how best to pursue an agenda for women [and other subordinated groups]. The main lesson is that the women and minority groups within the culture should define for themselves the reforms that are necessary to improve their lives. Many of the lessons from critical race theory, feminism and cultural studies center around self-determination and education. Further a global critical feminist approach can help identify issues that might otherwise be overlooked.

In using [human rights concepts and documents] to advocate to improve lives, we should not impose our values on others. Rather, we should help to empower them to chart their futures for themselves. International advocacy can help us band together across different political, cultural and racial contexts to identify our common quest for improving the quality of life and seeking justice for all and ensuring that women have the opportunity to thrive and create meaningful lives for themselves.

Sedillo Lopez outlines how critical comparativism can help strengthen analysis and advocacy. But the value of comparativism, like the value of any method, depends on context. With these thoughts in mind, consider an educational equity problem that exists in a different rule of law setting with its own long and complex history.

The Roma people in Europe, its largest minority group, might be considered ethnic whites within U.S. racial castes (like Italians, for instance) but suffer extraordinary discrimination as a transnational minority in Europe. International law scholar Antonia Eliason notes below that Roma schoolchildren face segregation and have yet to experience a *Brown* moment of at least a symbolic declaration of their entitlement to integrated (and equal) education. Eliason describes the widespread problem of unequal access to education across Europe but also some of the challenges of legal action because the Roma, as a group, have great skepticism about state power and coercive interventions in their affairs or communities. Does comparison of racial minorities in the United States and the Roma in Europe illuminate differences and diversities helpful to antisubordination analysis? Taking into account both what you have learned about critical histories in Parts I and V and the methodological suggestions of Sedillo Lopez above, how would you start to research and analyze identities, groups, interests, and power in relation to educational inequities in Europe, or some other specific region? How might you begin researching—the problems, the possible collaborators, and any possible solutions?

WITH NO DELIBERATE SPEED: THE SEGREGATION OF ROMA CHILDREN IN EUROPE

Antonia Eliason
27 Duke J. Comp. & Int'l L. 191 (2017)

Since its formal establishment in 1993, the European Union ("EU") has built a reputation as an upholder of human rights, distancing itself from the racism that nearly destroyed the continent in the 1930s and 40s. In today's Europe, however, racism is in fact still alive and well. In particular, the Roma, Europe's largest minority, continue to face shocking levels of discrimination. . . .

. . . The Roma are Europe's largest minority, with an estimated population between ten and twelve million throughout greater Europe, and over six million in the European Union alone. Around seventy percent of the total European Roma population is concentrated in Central and Southeastern Europe. The Roma population is estimated at roughly ten percent of the total population in Bulgaria, nearly nine percent in Romania, nine percent in Slovakia and seven and one-half percent in Hungary. Accurate population data is difficult to obtain in large part because of reluctance of Roma to self-identify for fear of repercussions; the number of individuals who self-identify as Roma is far lower than official estimates.

Originally from India, the Roma migrated westward to Europe somewhere between 500 and 1000 A.D., reaching Europe around the thirteenth century. From the moment they arrived in Europe, the Roma were viewed with suspicion by native populations. Many Roma were enslaved in what is today's Romania beginning in the thirteenth or fourteenth century and some remained enslaved until the mid-nineteenth century. In many European countries, laws were passed in the fifteenth and sixteenth centuries expelling the Roma; in several countries, Roma were sentenced to death if found.

The Roma were historically nomadic. . . . Today, most are no longer itinerant, although the stereotype of the nomadic wanderer lingers in mainstream consciousness. In understanding their historical position in Europe, scholars have argued that the Roma are best viewed as pariah people. The great sociologist Max Weber famously defined the situation of pariah people as one where "the people in question have totally lost their residential anchorage and hence are completely occupied economically in meeting [the] demands of other settled peoples—the gypsies, for instance, or, in another manner, the Jews of the Middle Ages." . . . [T]he absence of residential anchorage . . . has often left the Roma vulnerable to persecution and reliant on the goodwill of the populations around them . . . [and] contributed to the Roma's general failure to develop effective forms of political organizations. . . .

As a result of their wanderings, the Roma borrowed certain elements from the societies around them while retaining their distinct cultural identity. Among the cultural acquisitions were religious beliefs and language. This has resulted in a European Roma minority that is far from monolithic; the Roma's fragmentation often seems to override their commonalities, making a unified Roma civil rights movement difficult to achieve. For instance, Romani, the Roma language, is only spoken by a minority of Roma in Central Europe, while a majority continues to speak it in Southeastern Europe.

The Roma are a physically visible racial minority throughout much of Europe. In Southeastern Europe, however, linguistic differences rather than differences in skin color most distinguish the Roma from non-Roma. This combination of race and ethnicity requires a nuanced approach to understanding the place of Roma in European society. As Lilla Farkas writes,

> Treating Roma simply as a racial minority on account of their skin colour would deny their historical presence in and ties to Member States, and with this, their protection as an ethnic minority. Conversely, treating them only as an ethnic minority would deny protection on account of their skin colour, which distinguishes them from the majority of ethnic minorities indigenous in Member States and which is a characteristic that may exaggerate the extent of discrimination they suffer.
>
> . . . It is the Roma's racial identity, however, that has most profoundly influenced the level of discrimination they face in Central and Eastern Europe. . . .
>
> . . . Roma's lack of educational achievement in an economic milieu that increasingly requires educational certifications . . . [can result in their being] permanently excluded from the labor market.
>
> . . . The Roma have faced a variety of health problems due to their social exclusion. The average Roma life span is nearly ten years less than the majority populations in Central and Eastern Europe, and the Roma experience higher rates of infant mortality, malnutrition and disease. . . .
>
> The Roma are routinely victims of anti-Roma hate crimes in both Western and Eastern Europe. . . . The Roma have also been the frequent target of police brutality. . . .
>
> . . . Three million Roma children attend schools across the European Union, and many face structural discrimination in form of segregation and institutional discrimination. As a result, many fail to complete primary education and many more fail to complete secondary school. In some regions of Europe, only thirty to forty percent of Roma children regularly attend school, and up to ninety percent of adults are illiterate. Education

is a key predictor of future success and without school integration, Roma children will remain disadvantaged.

Segregation is shockingly widespread and overt. Three main types of school-based segregation have arisen: *intra-school segregation*, where Roma students are taught inferior curricula in separate classes within the same school; *intra-class segregation*, where Roma students are instructed under different curricular standards within the same class as non-Roma students; and *inter-school segregation*, where Roma and non-Roma children attend different schools based on either residential segregation, poorly-designed testing that leads to placement in remedial schools, or the creation of private schools that require tuition or testing for admission to the disadvantage of Roma children. Inter-school segregation is widespread; particularly in Bulgaria where many Roma children attend geographically segregated schools, and in Slovakia and the Czech Republic where Roma children are deemed mentally challenged and sent to remedial schools. . . .

. . . [U]nlike in the United States, where segregation prior to *Brown v. Board of Education* was required by law, segregation in Eastern Europe has resulted from a mix of local official policies (state action) and informal forces, like housing policies ("de facto" segregation). This key difference shapes the remedies and responses available to address segregation.

Segregation of Roma in European schools is a result of intentional policies and passive disregard for the obstacles faced by Roma children. These obstacles include cultural differences, inefficiencies within school systems and discrimination by teachers and fellow students. Roma children who speak Romani at home often face linguistic challenges adapting to schools where instruction is in another language. Roma children may also lack social skills as a result of extreme poverty. In many cases, parents lack the educational skills to support their children's schooling, and children subsequently must leave school at a young age to become economically productive. Many Roma children lack birth certificates for a variety of reasons, including parental illiteracy and unawareness of government requirements, parental mistrust of government registration, and hospitals' unwillingness to assist Roma citizens. Without birth certificates, Roma children cannot register for school. Because preschool is not free in many countries, Roma children whose parents lack the means to pay for preschool enter primary school at a disadvantage compared to their white majority peers. Together, these cultural disadvantages—when coupled with systemic discrimination and an unwillingness on the part of school systems and governments to integrate and provide the resources necessary to improve Roma access to education—have resulted in widespread segregation and low levels of educational achievement for Roma children.

The discrimination by peers and teachers experienced by Roma children contributes to their segregation and lack of academic success; in fact, some Roma families prefer segregated schools as a means of avoiding daily discrimination even where educational quality is significantly inferior. Even in integrated school districts, schools often take an assimilationist approach to educating Roma students, believing that Roma students must abandon their Roma identity and become like the white majority to be successful. This attitude devalues Roma identity and contributes to feelings of inferiority among Roma students. . . .

Eliason demonstrates some subordinating parallels between the Roma in Europe and U.S. African Americans. Similar parallels have been noted by other scholars, as well. As Margareta Matache and Cornel West observe, "[f]rom early on in their histories, Roma and African Americans have crossed similar paths, as white policymakers continued to employ similar tactics to maintain white normativity, social power, and privilege."[23] But, in contrast to the United States, which has exhibited "some level" of acknowledgment of its horrific legacy of slavery, Matache and West point out that Romania and the Orthodox Church have yet even to apologize for their enslavement of Roma people. Does this difference matter? How? What does this difference mean for advocacy choices and actions?

Drawing from their comparative analysis, Matache and West conclude that cross-border movements of people and communications reveal "similar structures of domination and subordination" in different contexts. While respecting contextual or group differences, these similarities should heighten local-global awareness of persistent patterns and help cultivate a sense of bottom-up solidarity. This closing note reminds us that comparison, even if limited, ideally can help chart a path "toward a unified movement against injustice across historical and geographical spheres."[24]

NOTES AND QUESTIONS

1. *Transnational Solidarity*. Matache and West offer aspirations but no concrete plan for building cross-border solidarity. Based on the facts that Eliason lays out above about educational inequities and broader forms of systemic violence affecting Roma families in Europe, and on what you know about U.S. educational struggles, where might you begin to make analytical or systemic connections across the Atlantic? How might you help to cultivate solidarity between Roma students, activists, and advocates in Europe, and

---

[23] Margareta Matache and Cornel West, Roma and African Americans Share a Common Struggle, The Guardian (Feb. 20, 2018), www.theguardian.com/commentisfree/2018/feb/20/roma-african-americans-common-struggle.

[24] *Id.*

U.S.-based students, activists, and advocates from low-income communities of color? How is critical comparativism helpful, or not?

2. *Separate Schools by Antisubordination Design.* Eliason mentions that some Roma families prefer segregated schools, even if inferior, as a "means of avoiding daily discrimination" of their children. In the United States, the establishment by New York in the 1980s of the Harvey Milk school—an exclusively LGBTQ-student school so that its students might escape cultural isolation and physical violence at "straight"-integrated schools—generated claims of "reverse" discrimination against sexual majority students. Questions were raised whether this school was equivalent to racially segregated schools before *Brown*. Similarly, what about separate schools for disabled children? Consider the insights of a legal scholar, applying an antisubordination lens, who concluded that "[t]he concept that 'separate is inherently unequal' has outlived its usefulness in the disability context." Ruth Colker, Antisubordination Above All: A Disability Perspective, 82 Notre Dame L. Rev. 1415 (2007). In your view, are schools designed to prevent bullying and stigmatization of bottom-group students "the same" as schools designed to exclude and stigmatize them? Recall the discussion of antidiscrimination and antisubordination approaches to equality from Part II in thinking through this question.

CHAPTER RECAP

This chapter reviewed the Critical Challenge today in the general context of U.S. public education—the same context set out in Part I using the *Brown* case and related materials, except that debt, economic inequality, and material injustice have grown even greater in recent years. This contemporary case study provides an opportunity to revisit those opening lessons from today's perspective and to apply concepts presented throughout this book. The following and final chapter presents forward-looking reflections on Critical Justice and systemic advocacy.

CHAPTER 16

ROAD TEST: CRAFTING LONG-TERM PATHWAYS TOWARD CRITICAL JUSTICE

■ ■ ■

Table of Sections

16.1 Every Advocate Must Unlearn and Relearn Problem Solving to Craft Their Own Lifelong "Road" to Critical Justice
16.2 Pathways Change Along the Way—So Must Groups, Advocates, and Advocacy
16.3 Deep Critique and Systemic Advocacy for the Long Haul

OPENING THOUGHTS

Do not get lost in a sea of despair. Be hopeful, be optimistic. Our struggle is not the struggle of a day, a week, a month, or a year, it is the struggle of a lifetime.

—**John Lewis** (2018 tweet)

While we must ask, what sustains the long-haul [social justice] lawyer?—we should wonder as well, what sustains the long-haul client?

—**Susan Bennett,** On Long-Haul Lawyering, 25 Fordham Urb. L.J. 771, 778 (1998)

What is next is more of the same. The struggle. But what is next is also something completely different. Because the mechanisms of oppression morph and evolve. And so must we. But we have an advantage, we are in this together. We struggle for communion. . . . We imagine, together. We envision, together. We act, together. And in unity there is strength.

—**Saru M. Matambanadzo, Jorge R. Roig and Sheila I. Vélez Martínez**, Foreword to LatCrit 2017 Symposium: What's Next? Resistance Resilience and Community in the Trump Era, 9 U. Miami Race & Soc. Just. L. Rev. 1, 44 (2019)

INTRODUCTION

Persistent social problems abound. You have seen illustrations of that throughout this book. The scale and numbness of systemic violence can be disorienting—and this is why systemic advocates must stay grounded in thinking and doing for the long haul. Steady ethical work is a constant exertion—from moment to moment challenging, draining, puzzling, disturbing, and endless. But carrying out the work in community with others also is a continuing source of joy and hope.

This critical marathon toward Critical Justice may seem like a daily slog—but over time it's a roller coaster kind of slog—and a way of life. You get up, you breathe, you do the work, you laugh a lot, and you do the best you can. As LatCrit and feminist scholar Elvia Arriola has attested, "Yes, it is hard. Sometimes we have to cry. And then we need to get up and do something. We need to hold each other up and nurture the warrior spirit of love and resistance."[1] Every advocate only can—but must—do their daily best. Looking ahead in this spirit, this final chapter provides some reflections and roadmaps for critical pathways that advocates may consider as they work through the diverse contexts of systemic injustice.

As we began, we end now with a range of reflections on advocacy, law, and justice from diversely situated contemporary advocates, which may aid your own personal and professional planning. We then include an iconic example of advocacy as part of organized struggles for the long haul: the heralded struggles of field laborers in the southwest U.S. to establish and maintain the United Farm Workers union—an account that effectively captures fundamental points covered throughout this book. This example illustrates vividly how groups develop into repeat players capable of contesting foundational concepts and ground rules. Using identities as assets, union organizers and their advocates flipped existing scripts. But their example also shows why advocates continually adjust to defend and advance past gains—why advocates and groups must continually, proactively, and self-critically keep adapting. As López counseled in Part II, changing systems requiring changing ourselves. Transformational change within the legal industry itself is required—a "deep critique" generating sustained action to "contest the shape of current legal practice" through bottom-up collaborations based in antisubordination solidarity.

These materials, as a set, emphasize that advocates must keep justice front and center despite tension, conflict, and change—and doing so requires managing complexity flexibly, yet in principled and accountable terms. In light of all we have covered, how might *you* shape your own personal and professional choices going forward? How might you take concrete steps to open windows of opportunity for systemic advocacy and justice starting now? These forward-looking closing notes should help you arrive at your own answers to these ever-pressing questions.

Systemic advocates, as we see below, carve out their own professional and personal journeys toward ethical work and living based on antisubordination values and solidarity. Over time, advocates develop

---

[1] Elvia Arriola, Remarks Upon Receiving the Critical Pioneer Award at Latina/o Critical Legal Theory Conference (Oct. 2017).

critical knowledges, values, skills, and attitudes. Inevitably, advocates create their own "roads" to Critical Justice. But pathways change along the way, and so must advocates and advocacy.

16.1 EVERY ADVOCATE MUST UNLEARN AND RELEARN PROBLEM SOLVING TO CRAFT THEIR OWN LIFELONG "ROAD" TO CRITICAL JUSTICE

Throughout this book, we have encountered diversely-situated advocates learning big-picture lessons about law and justice from their personal engagement of particular issues in a variety of contexts. These examples illustrate the specificity and the patterns of systemic injustice built on identities, groups, interests, and power. These examples illustrate why and how advocates make their own ways through the complexities of systemic injustice to develop three-layered projects. To do so, advocates unlearn and relearn problem solving in critical and self-critical terms. In the following excerpts, four advocates share their intellectual and experiential knowledge about bottom-up, collaborative advocacy to help you make your own choices.

First, legal scholar, clinician, and indigenous community member Christine Zuni Cruz surveys issues that advocates navigate to chart their own "road" into and within systemic advocacy. She writes as a "native, lawyer, and clinician" about lessons learned from living within and representing your own community, in this instance, a tribal nation. As she shows, no easy answers exist; no answers are preordained. Zuni Cruz, like other advocates here, speaks from the experience of her personal journey through the Critical Challenge. For her, a U.S.-based law school clinic, like those described elsewhere in this book, was designed and run as an advocacy project for the long haul. These clinics support individuals taking significant risks to resist injustice and help organized groups at the bottom to develop as repeat players challenging background premises, foundational concepts, and ground rules.

Like other kinds of advocacy projects, clinics have to navigate the contextual complexities of legal failure by design. In response, clinicians, students, and client-groups work together to plant seeds of resistance and develop strategic campaigns and projects for the long haul. They contend continually with the challenge of ensuring principled and accountable bottom-up decisionmaking in an institutional setting that is—like most in the legal industry—geared primarily to serving elite interests. As you read, recall two other indigenous scholar perspectives we encountered—Tsosie's analysis of systemic injustice as epistemic injustice and Williams' description of legal "vampires" within the industry. Do you see any parallels among these three indigenous perspectives on the Critical Challenge of using law for justice?

[ON THE] ROAD BACK IN: COMMUNITY LAWYERING IN INDIGENOUS COMMUNITIES

Christine Zuni Cruz
5 Clinical L. Rev. 557 (1999); 24 Am. Indian L. Rev. 229 (2000)

... I am a member/citizen of the Pueblo of Isleta, one of the nineteen pueblos and one of the twenty-two tribal nations located in the state of New Mexico. I am also of San Juan Pueblo descent. Since leaving college I have had only one goal, and that has been to return "home" to use my education for "the people": an easy thing to say, but not an easy thing to accomplish. First of all, I had to travel what I like to call the "road back in," not an easy road to find, nor an easy road to travel. It seemed like all the roads leading out of the reservation were paved, many by the federal government, but you had to look long and hard for that road leading back in. The temptation of the "brain drain expressway" overcomes a lot of people, and they find themselves hurtling down that road to big cities and bright lights, some detoured for years, and others never to return. I found that, as you travel that road back in, you find yourself critically appraising and then discarding some of the baggage you acquired when you were outside the community, perhaps because the road back in is a hard road, and you find that a lot of what you acquired is just heavy, useless baggage which is actually impeding your journey. I think that everyone who has gone outside the community, acquired a western education and is eventually effective within their own community, has a similar experience on this "road back in."

As a native person, a practitioner, and an instructor of Indian law, my view of community is profoundly affected by the uniqueness of tribal community and native identity. This includes both the attributes of a community or nation of native peoples and an individual's connection to that community.

The three voices I speak in—native, lawyer, and clinician—provide different perspectives. As native, I speak as a native person living within my native community; as lawyer, I speak from my experience in working within the community; as clinician, I speak combining the above voices, seeking to improve the lawyering done in the name of, on behalf of, for, and with native peoples and native nations. These voices inform my discussion of community and culture. The basis of my ideas stem from my experience of being part of a distinct native community, long served by lawyers and a profession external to the community. My perspective on community comes from my work within my own pueblo, and within other pueblos both as a lawyer and a judge. My perspective on culture is closely related to community, but it is also informed by the work I engaged in over several years to revise the New Mexico Children's code to provide greater cultural protection for native children and youth.

One of the main reasons I entered academia was to concentrate on what I term "insider" law in Indian Law. As a former tribal court judge for several pueblos and as an appellate judge, I saw first hand the conflict between traditional and modern anglo-american principles of law, and the tendency of anglo-american principles to be utilized to the exclusion of native principles not only in the structuring of systems, but also in the development of law. Law schools concentrate on teaching law students "federal Indian Law," or what I term "outsider" law which affects Indians. There is nothing particularly "Indian" about "federal Indian law." Little, if any effort, is spent on the concentrated and exclusive teaching of "insider" law—not only foundational and traditional precepts of indigenous law but also the internal law of tribes. As a consequence, few students are adequately prepared to approach work in indigenous communities, nor are they prepared to deal with the tension between traditional and "modern" (anglo-american) law. Even fewer are prepared to assist clients to appear in traditional courts or to argue traditional law in modern tribal courts. This is not to say that federal Indian law is unimportant. . . . It is only to say that "insider" law is equally critical and foundational to working with native communities. . . .

Of the work that I have engaged in at the community level, success has only been possible due to the strengths of the community itself; the technicalities of the law were only a part of the picture. To see so clearly that the law and the lawyer were secondary, tools in the hands of those represented, helped me to see the role of the lawyer as being side by side the client and sometimes behind the client, and rarely, out in front. Serving as counselor and advisor were as critical as serving as mouthpiece. The lawyering done in private is just as important as the lawyering done in public. These were invaluable lessons not taught in law school. My law school experience was primarily that of learning about individual representation. Group representation was only indirectly addressed by cases involving businesses, corporations or class actions. Federal Indian law cases, while involving tribes as parties, were rarely discussed in terms of the challenges, ethics, or responsibilities of representing a tribe as a client. In practice, I saw that my work as a lawyer in identifying the legal issue, the tribe's legal position, and the law were a part of the representation, but the interaction and the explanation of the legalities to the council, the response of the council, the "big picture" and ultimately the legal approach and argument was most appropriately shaped not by the lawyer, but by the forces that give an Indian nation an identity as separate peoples. These include the viewpoint of the client expressed through the leadership, the consideration of "the people," and the larger context of the legal issue both internal and external to the group. . . . Considering the community impacts and changes the lawyering approach. . . . In representing a tribe, community is always a factor, but it is not necessarily always taken into consideration by the attorney. . . .

The questions that arise from community representation include questions of "who" is the client as well as the obligations of a lawyer to the "community" in such representation. These questions are raised not only to obtain answers, but to point out the difficulties that can emerge in considering answers. The questions are raised to provoke thought about the complexities that go beyond the traditional concepts of lawyering for organizations, corporations and state and federal governments that are implicated in answering any (typically, ethical) question of "group" or "class" representation. The Model Rules of Professional Conduct contain provisions which provide some guidance to attorneys in their representation of "organizations." However, insofar as tribes and other communities or other groups are not corporate organizations, the rules are not directly on point. In representing a community, how does one view obligations to the larger community when dealing with a smaller subset of decisionmakers? As to representation of a tribal nation, former Governor Verna Teller of the Pueblo of Isleta states:

> Tribal attorneys represent the tribe. Although this may seem like a very simple statement to most attorneys representing Indian tribes, it is one which is nonetheless important to make. . . . Tribes generally act through their tribal leaders, appointed or elected, and the governing body of the tribe. Generally, this is the Governor, Chairman, or President and the Tribal Council. Although the attorney receives directives from these duly authorized tribal figures, the attorney represents the tribe as a whole and not just the tribal leaders or tribal governing body. This perhaps more than any other single point is worthy of underscoring. The attorney represents the tribe acting through its duly authorized representatives.

In the words of Chief Oren Lyon, it is clear that to native leaders *who* is represented, when representation of Indian nations is undertaken, is much more far-reaching, when situated in a cultural context, than that typically understood by attorneys.

I was asked . . . one time "Well, how many people do you represent?" That's a liberal question; they like numbers. "Well," I said "All I know is that we're mandated as chiefs to look out for the seventh generation to come. How many people are in those generations? That's who we represent. We're not counting the people who sit here today. We're counting the people who are in the future. 'How many?' You tell me."

What if the community is not or has not been formally recognized as a group? In the context of federal Indian Law, I could be referring to communities which seek federal or state recognition as Indian tribes. However, it is possible that a community might be outside the tribe, such as urban Indians within a city, or even internal to a tribe, such as a smaller community seeking to organize formally as a corporation, or seeking to obtain special recognition within a larger tribal community. It might refer to a group of native people who are or may be potential participants in a class action. In all respects, the questions which arise might include: Are we meeting with, speaking to all the people we should be? Do we know enough about the community to know? Have we considered group and individual ramifications? Has the whole community had an opportunity to consider potential drawbacks? Who is responsible for information dissemination? What if the goal of the representation is not in the "best interest" of the larger community? Who is to say what is in the best interest of the larger community?

. . . So the question becomes "Who is directing?" . . .

[Tribes] have recognized for a long time the importance of having counsel. We ask the question of counsel: "What happens if we do it this way? So, they tell us. "What happens if we do it that way?" And they tell us. . . . [The Council] doesn't ask the lawyer, "What do you think is best?" It directs.

Are our obligations different if we are part of the community or if we are not? Many native lawyers become counsel for their own tribes. What impact does being lawyer as well as part of the client community have?

The community lawyering approach helps in preparing the lawyer to place the community in context and thereby understand and counsel the community in a much more helpful way. The community lawyering approach in representing tribes requires that the lawyer possess background which assists the lawyer in understanding the community, including knowledge regarding the community's history, law, both the external law impacting the community and internal law, written and oral, modern and traditional. The community lawyer must also possess an understanding or a respect of the community's culture, knowledge of the community's land base, both traditional and present-day, have knowledge and respect for the community's protocols and ethics, as well as an awareness of the lawyer's boundaries, whether as an insider or an outsider and a grasp on the political realities of the community.

. . . [In the law school's Southwest Indian Law Clinic it] is important to teach about the differences between native principles and precepts of law and the anglo-american system, for several reasons. One, since we practice in tribal court systems it is important to be aware of these principles and of traditional law. There is a marked difference between traditional native concepts of justice and those of the Anglo-American adversarial system.

Traditional indigenous systems emphasize accountability, truth, restoration, forgiveness and integration of the offender back into the community. The adversarial system emphasizes individual rights, including the right of the accused to remain silent and the placement of the burden of proof on the accusers, punishment and removal of the offender from the community by imprisonment. These differences are taught in the clinic's classroom component to help students understand the differences between the systems as they may impact clients appearing in "modern" tribal, state and federal courts. They also inform our work with tribal code development, which also involves working with concepts of traditional law and methods of dispute resolution, tribal court development, and the use of traditional law in legal arguments before tribal forums. It is important for practitioners who practice in tribal forums to be equally versed in federal Indian law and understand principles of traditional law. Some of the issues raised in the classroom component regarding traditional law include how to use and research traditional law, as well as the responsibility practitioners have to raise it in tribal forums. Furthermore, methods of indigenous dispute resolution are important in the community as alternatives to litigation for our clients. We consequently address indigenous methods of dispute resolution, in addition to other methods of alternative dispute resolution.

Second, it is important to be aware of the impact these concepts can have as a socializing influence on native clients. There is a general tendency of native criminal defendants to plead guilty, so it is important to stress the importance of thoroughly counseling clients as to the exactitude of pleading in criminal cases in the anglo-american adversary system, including the requirement of proof of elements, the state's burden of proof, standard of proof (beyond a reasonable doubt) and the underlying theme (innocent until proven guilty), which all run counter to traditional concepts of law within which native clients may be socialized.... The adversarial system runs counter to indigenous approaches to resolving disputes and places a high value on protecting the individual from the excesses of the state, which is directly counter to the mutually beneficial relationship between the individual and the community....

Challenges

The biggest challenge has been to articulate the salient points encompassed in community lawyering for native peoples. This is a work in progress....

Some of the other challenges . . . not surprisingly, related to the work itself which seeks to raise the level of consciousness of community and culture in lawyering to a scale that neither have previously enjoyed. These include 1.) the dismissal of culture and community from the straightforward and competent practice of law, and everyday work with clients and their cases, except in the most unusual cases, 2.) the skepticism and tension that emphasis on community and culture can produce with respect to the practice of law, especially since law is taught aculturally and with an emphasis on individualism in most law schools, and 3.) student apprehensiveness of the challenges that the awareness of culture and community places on them. For example, a student may believe that the law itself and their own skills, are the only factors in representing clients. . . .

Dismissal, skepticism, tension and apprehensiveness from students arise in part because culture and community have not been incorporated into class discussions of law in other law courses, and partly because they raise issues of self-identity, cognizance of place, insider/outsider status, and cross-cultural competency that either have not been directly confronted by students, and which can be difficult and painful for individuals. Reactions can range from appreciation to disdain, from fresh re/consideration to boredom. Teaching and supervising students to be conscious of culture and community is extremely challenging, not always successful, and therefore in need of constant and consistent review.

Another challenge, which cannot be overemphasized, arises from the fact that issues of culture and community are subtle and can be almost invisible in day to day practice. Ideas which are clear in theory and with use of tailored examples, are not so clearly apparent in practice. . . . If dealing with issues of culture can be said to be more emotionally challenging, then dealing with issues of community influence on individual clients can be said to be more obscure and more easily missed and discarded by students, and therefore harder to teach.

Despite the difficulties, the challenges, and sometimes the lack of appreciation of raising issues of culture and community and their relation to the practice of Indian law, it is well worth the effort when it makes a difference for a student, a client or a community. The practice of Indian law which does not take into consideration culture and community and which does not seriously explore either is colonialistic. In order to move beyond the colonial mentality imbedded in much of Indian law and its practice in general, one has to reconsider not only what is encompassed in the law, but what is not. Considering community and culture expands the notion of what is encompassed in the practice of law, and though hard for the practitioner, is of immense value (as I am convinced from years of practice and feedback) to the native client.

Conclusion

Understanding and respecting differences is important to the practice of law. As native people have entered the legal profession, their influence on the practice of Indian law should be felt. The response of Indian people to their own people in the profession who have the ability to influence the practice of law, not only by native peoples but by others, should not be that contained in [jazz artist] Gil Scott Heron's painfully powerful lyrics, "You're

... my lawyer, yeah, but somehow you forgot about me." Instead it is hoped that they see them traveling that road back in.

Zuni Cruz examines how advocacy on behalf of a particular kind of group—a tribal nation—must take into account community and culture. "In order to move beyond the colonial mentality" of law, "one has to reconsider not only what is encompassed in the law, but what is not." Using the cultural and legal concepts of her native tribe, Zuni Cruz provides one example of advocates grappling with present-day complexities of identity-based castes.

Zuni Cruz offers one account of finding, or making, her "road back in" to organized collective struggles against identity-based systemic injustice, using professional advocacy and legal problem solving. Her account underscores a basic fact: every advocate must find their own way through the complexities of the Critical Challenge. Every advocate must engineer her own life and career over time. Although no easy or fixed answers exist, the experiences of preceding generations provide us with useful critical guideposts for professional pathways.

In this vein, we consider next three "letters" addressed directly to you as advocates from legal scholars experienced in community-based advocacy as well as critical scholarship. Here, they reflect on law, clients, communities, and justice to help those starting a legal career enter the trenches of the legal industry with hearts, minds, and souls alert and open. These letters, as a set, are a practical guide for advocates making their own road to Critical Justice.

Betty Hung is a scholar and a public interest lawyer who has spearheaded many campaigns among low-wage immigrant workers. Her letter recounts her experience as an Asian woman in law school—an "outsider" for whom many of the "truths" taught about equal justice under the legal system did not ring true. Her experience can be the basis for greater empathy with clients, insights into dynamics of injustice, and creative collaborations.

Bill Quigley, a clinical professor and Catholic social justice activist, offers fundamental starting points for systemic advocacy. Among them, he emphasizes basing your practice in the recognition that clients from the bottom bring a wealth of knowledge because of their experiences of injustice. He counsels advocates to cultivate the humility necessary to learn from clients and community members with less privilege than you. Simultaneously, he calls on advocates to learn from critical history—the histories of elites making laws and of activists and advocates struggling for progress.

Dean Spade, a U.S. transgender activist and scholar, suggests that formal legal schooling might not be the best route to making an impact on systemic injustice. Like others, he observes that law students endure an education that indoctrinates them into justifying and defending, rather than piercing and combatting, systemic injustice. Critical knowledge, he shows, is not always best learned from formal legal training.

Notice, as you read them, how these three letters to future advocates distill and emphasize a bottom line: systemic advocates must be self-aware and self-critical about identity-based groups, interests, and power—and the resulting group patterns of persistent privilege and subordination in law and society. They must bring their own experience and legal skills to the work, while continually learning, unlearning, and relearning from their collaborations with teams, clients, and communities—and from the actionable insights of the critical Schools and advocacy Approaches. Only critical knowledge, coupled with self-reflective and self-critical vigilance, can ground your work in principle and in accountability—across complex contexts and for the long haul—in this transgenerational marathon toward Critical Justice for all.

LETTER TO A YOUNG PUBLIC INTEREST ATTORNEY
Betty Hung
1 L. A. Pub. Int. L.J. 319 (2009)

Growing up in a working and middle class suburb of Los Angeles, the daughter of immigrant parents from Taiwan, I was fascinated with the civil rights movement of the 1950s and 1960s. Thurgood Marshall and Martin Luther King, Jr. were my heroes. A voracious reader, I devoured every biography of them I could find at the local library. When other children taunted my siblings and me for speaking Taiwanese, or local politicians called for the passage of English-only ordinances, I drew on the history of African Americans and their courage and perseverance in the struggle against slavery and discrimination. Given the absence of Asian Americans in history books, television, and media, I looked instead to King and other civil rights icons for role models of what people of color can overcome and achieve in the United States. I longed to be part of a community and movement for equal rights and justice and, inspired by such examples, decided that I wanted to be a civil rights lawyer.

Mine was one of the first Asian immigrant families to move into the San Gabriel Valley, a [Southern California] region that experienced a demographic sea change in the 1980s and transformed from a primarily white and American-born Chicano community to one that is predominantly Latino and Asian immigrant. Initially in this context, Asian immigrants—such as my family—were at or near the bottom of the racial hierarchy, due in large part to an inability to speak fluent English and perceptions of our cultural "foreignness." I always felt an unease about the tensions simmering under the surface and, while it infuriated me to hear ethnic slurs against Asians, I also cringed when I heard Asians say racist things about people of other races and ethnicities.... I felt that one thing we all had in common, that cut across race, was that our community of Alhambra and Monterey Park was perceived as "lower class" compared to more affluent neighboring cities like San Marino, South Pasadena, and Arcadia....

When I first entered the doors of "the Yale Law School" in 1994, however, I left my smarts outside. Or at least that is how I felt. It did not matter that I had graduated magna cum laude from Harvard. Suddenly in the midst of a small law school class where every other person seemed to be a Rhodes scholar, related to a federal circuit court judge, or an aspiring politician, I felt tongue-tied, overwhelmed, and lost. I was the first person in my family to go to law school, and growing up, I did not know any lawyers. The language, theory, and practice of the law seemed utterly foreign to me. During classes, I was intimidated by the Socratic method and even more intimidated by how other students, especially male students, seemed unfazed and confident. My progressive politics seemed out of place. I felt like overnight I had become a person who was not intelligent enough and not suited to practicing law because I did not fit the traditional mold of an aggressive, commanding, and savvy lawyer.

During much of law school, I felt voiceless and marginalized. Much literature has been written about how women and people of color experience alienation during law school. It was this literature and the discovery of critical race theory that helped me not just to survive law school, but also to draw upon the dissonances of my experience as a strength that over the years has, I believe, helped me to become a better public interest lawyer. Reading books and articles by Patricia Williams, Richard Delgado and Jean Stefancic, Harlon Dalton, Mari Matsuda, and Robert Chang, I realized that there were structural reasons for why I felt so alienated and that the dissonance I was experiencing was not uncommon. Critical race theory gave me the language and concepts to understand and articulate the truth of what I had experienced since childhood-that sociopolitical and legal institutions, structures, and norms reinforce a status quo where select groups wield power and wealth while many others are disenfranchised. As an "outsider," I learned to analyze and dissect such systems to understand how they perpetuate inequalities, and I learned to think both within and outside these systems in order to survive and to change them to be more just and equitable.

Small acts of resistance helped me in the struggle not just to recapture my voice, but to clarify and strengthen it. For example, during my second year, I snuck into the law school in the middle of the night along with two other members of the Women of Color Collective. We put up a display on the school's free speech wall to illustrate the faculty's lack of diversity, creating an inverted pyramid on the wall displaying the photos of every single Yale Law School professor. The visual of 52 white men and handful of women and people of color created a stir amongst students and faculty and received coverage from the Chronicle of Higher Education.

But it was the law school clinical program where I truly felt at home. Under the mentorship of Professors Jean Koh Peters and Kathleen Sullivan, I learned to apply both my legal intellect and humanity to zealously advocate for the interests of our clients. They taught me to strive to be truly client centered, to honor the innate value and dignity of every client, to incorporate an analysis of the structural inequalities that affected our clients' life circumstances and to recognize the necessity of working as hard as I could in order to be as effective as possible because our clients deserved nothing less. Professors Koh Peters and Sullivan helped me to understand that there is a role for human compassion and empathy in lawyering that strengthens, rather than dilutes, one's effectiveness as an advocate. . . .

While I felt most authentic and fulfilled engaging in social justice issues, I grappled with whether to pursue my lifelong dream of becoming a public interest lawyer after law school or to take a high paying job to help my family. . . . Ultimately, I decided that to be true to myself and to honor my parents' experiences and sacrifices, I needed to pursue the path of becoming a public interest lawyer.

With the help of an echoing green fellowship, I launched my public interest career at the Asian Pacific American Legal Center (APALC). I had a life changing experience working under the mentorship of Julie Su, a true shero who broke new ground as lead counsel in the El Monte Thai and Latino garment worker case, in which the workers obtained a multimillion dollar settlement from some of the nation's largest garment manufacturers and retailers. It was liberating to see someone who did not fit the traditional mold of a lawyer and yet was and is one of the most effective and strategic movement lawyers in the country. Moreover, working with Julie helped me to realize that my experiences of being on the margins as a woman, person of color, and daughter of immigrants from a family that had struggled financially could enable me to be a more empathetic, effective, and creative attorney. It also liberated me to seek nontraditional ways of lawyering to add value to and support the efforts of community members to strive for social justice.

I started a project in which I partnered with Asian high school students who are the children of garment workers. Drawing on their bilingual and bicultural backgrounds, the youth assisted us in developing community education workshops, in which we informed Chinese and Latino garment workers about their legal workplace rights. Not only did the youth help us to reach out to their parents, they also mapped out locations of the garment factories near Chinatown and participated in running the workshops.

Since then, in addition to litigating cases in the areas of workers' rights and home equity fraud, I have also been a community organizer with a school safety campaign led by Cambodian high school girls to eliminate sexual harassment at school, in which the girls won significant educational reforms; worked at a corporate law firm where I initiated several diversity efforts on race, gender, and sexual orientation, including launching a Civil Rights Speaker Series; led a coalition effort to advocate that the Los Angeles City Attorney's Office criminally prosecute predatory employers; obtained a published appellate decision in a domestic worker case; been active in a coalition effort to reauthorize a statewide Car Wash Worker Law to clean up sweatshop working conditions in the car wash industry; and represented the Los Angeles Taxi Workers Alliance in drivers' efforts to stamp out corrupt taxi company practices and achieve decent working conditions. All of these were collaborative efforts with community members and colleagues, in which it was essential to think both within and outside existing systems in order to push for change.

While I do not presume to know what it is like to be in the shoes of my clients, I believe that feeling invisible and voiceless in my life experiences, and in law school specifically, has made me a more effective advocate for social justice. The challenge of trying to fit into an institution and system that historically have not equally valued the perspectives and life experiences of the communities from which I come has given me greater empathy for my clients' hardships and enabled me to understand better how structural forces can act to disempower and impoverish people. I have tried to analyze how existing laws and policies often serve to strip people of their rights and prevent them from speaking out and asserting their humanity. It has pushed me to function with a dual consciousness (with acknowledgements to W.E.B. DuBois) both within and outside the legal system in order to transform it to be more just and equitable.

Most importantly, it has taught me the importance of creating true partnerships with clients, community members, and other advocates to pool together our skills, experiences, talents, and resources in order to challenge institutions and systems that perpetuate inequality. By working harder and more creatively than the forces that we are up against, we can shift power to marginalized communities with the overarching hope that the end result will be a more fair and equal society where we learn to value the humanity of each and every person so that no one is marginalized or voiceless.

Sincerely,

Betty Hung

LETTER TO A LAW STUDENT INTERESTED IN SOCIAL JUSTICE
William P. Quigley
1 DePaul J. for Soc. Just. 7 (2007)

Dear [Law Student]:

I am delighted to learn of your commitment to social justice law. Despite many decades practicing some form or other of social justice advocacy, I too still have much to learn. I hope some of these thoughts will help you; it helped me to write them down. . . .

Social Justice Lawyering Is Counter-Cultural in Law School and in the Legal Profession

"The first thing I lost in law school was the reason that I came." What a simple and powerful indictment of legal education and of our legal profession. It is also a caution to those of us who want to practice social justice lawyering.

Many come to law school because they want in some way to help the elderly, children, people with disabilities, undernourished people around the world, victims of genocide, or victims of racism, economic injustice, religious persecution or gender discrimination.

Unfortunately, the experience of law school and the legal profession often dilute the commitment to social justice lawyering.

The repeated emphasis in law school on the subtleties of substantive law and many layers of procedure, usually discussed in the context of examples from business and traditional litigation, can grind down the idealism with which students first arrived. In fact, research shows that two-thirds of the students who enter law school with intentions of seeking a government or public-interest job do not end up employed in that work.

It pains me to say it, but justice is a counter-cultural value in our legal profession. Because of that, you cannot be afraid to be different than others in law school or the profession—for unless you are, you cannot be a social justice lawyer.

Those who practice social justice law are essentially swimming upstream while others are on their way down. Unless you are serious about your direction and the choices you make and the need for assistance, teamwork and renewal, you will likely grow tired and start floating along and end up going downstream with the rest. We all grow tired at points and lose our direction. The goal is to try to structure our lives and relationships in such a way that we can recognize when we get lost and be ready to try to reorient ourselves and start over.

There are many legal highways available to people whose goal is to make a lot of money as a lawyer—that is a very mainstream, traditional goal and many have gone before to show the way and carefully tend the roads.

For social justice lawyers, the path is more challenging. . . .

Your path has different markers than others. The traditional law school and professional marks of success are not good indicators for social justice advocates. Certainly, you hope for yourself what you hope for others—a good family, a home, good schools, a healthy life and enough to pay off those damn loans. Those are all achievable as a social justice lawyer, but they demand that you be more creative, flexible and patient than those for whom money is the main yardstick.

Our profession certainly pays lip service to justice, and because we are lawyers this is often eloquent lip service, but . . . everyone knows that justice work is not the essence of the legal profession. Our professional essence is money, and the overwhelming majority of legal work consists of facilitating the transfer of money or resources from one group to another. A shamefully large part of our profession in fact consists of the opposite of justice—actually taking from the poor and giving to the rich or justifying some injustice like torture or tobacco or mass relocation or commercial exploitation of the weak by the strong. The actual message from law school and on throughout the entire legal career is that justice work, if done at all, is done in the margins or after the real legal work is done.

But do not despair! Just because social justice lawyering is counter-cultural does not mean it is nonexistent. . . .

Be Willing to Be Uncomfortable

One night, I listened to a group of college students describe how they had spent their break living with poor families in rural Nicaragua. Each student lived with a different family, miles apart from each other, in homes that had no electricity or running water. They ate, slept and worked with their family for a week. I knew these were mostly middle-class, suburban students, so I asked them how they were able to make the transition from their homes in the United States to a week with their host families. One student said, "First, you have to be willing to be uncomfortable."

I think this is the first step of any real educational or transformative experience—a willingness to go beyond your comfort zone and to risk being uncomfortable.

The revolutionary social justice called for by Dr. King is not for the faint of heart—it calls on the courage of your convictions. It takes guts.

Questioning the fairness and justice of our laws and policies is uncomfortable for most because it makes other people uncomfortable.

Many people are perfectly satisfied with the way things are right now. For them, our nation is the best of all possible nations, and our laws are the best of all possible laws, and therefore, it is not right to challenge those in authority. For them, to question the best of all possible nations and its laws is uncalled for, unpatriotic and even un-American. These same criticisms were leveled at Dr. King and continue to be leveled at every other person who openly questions the fairness and justice of current laws and policies.

So, if you are interested in pursuing a life of social justice, be prepared to be uncomfortable—be prepared to press beyond your comfort zone, be prepared to be misunderstood and criticized. . . .

Never Confuse Law and Justice

We must never confuse law and justice. What is legal is often not just. And what is just is often not at all legal.

Consider what was perfectly legal 100 years ago: children as young as six were employed in dangerous industries. Bosses could pay workers whatever they wanted. If injured on the job—no compensation, you went home and need not return when you recovered. Women and African Americans could not vote. Any business could discriminate against anyone else on the basis of gender, race, age, disability or any other reason. Industrialists grew rich by using police and private mercenaries to break up unions, beat and kill strikers and evict families from their homes.

One hundred years ago, lawyers and judges and legislators worked in a very professional manner enforcing laws that we know now were terribly unjust.

What is the difference between 100 years ago and now? History has not yet judged clearly which laws are terribly unjust.

Social justice calls you to keep your eyes and your heart wide open in order to look at the difference between law and justice. For example, look at the unjust distribution of economic wealth and social and political power. It is mostly legally supported, but is actually the most unjust, gross inequality in our country and in our world. You must examine the root causes and look at the legal system that is propping up these injustices.

Critique the Law

Critique of current law is an essential step in advancing justice. Do not be afraid to seriously criticize an unjust or inadequate set of laws or institutions. People will defend them saying they are much better than before, or they are better than those in other places. Perhaps they will make some other justification. No doubt many of our laws today and many of our institutions represent an advance over what was in place in the past; however, that does not mean that all of our laws and institutions are better than what preceded them, nor does it mean that the justice critique should stop.

Critique alone, however, is insufficient for social justice advocates. While you are engaged in critique, you should also search for new, energizing visions of how the law should and might move forward. . . .

All laws are made by those with power. There are not many renters or low-wage workers in Congress or sitting on the bench. The powerless, by definition, are not involved in the lobbying, drafting, deliberating and compromising that are essential parts of all legislation. Our laws, by and large, are what those with power think should apply to those without power. As a student of law, you have been taught how to analyze issues and how to research.

Social justice insists that you first examine these laws and their impacts not only from the perspective of their legislative histories, but also from the perspective of the elderly, the working poor, the child with a learning disability and the single mom raising kids, who are often the targets of these laws.

So how do you learn what the elderly, the working poor or the single moms think about these laws? It is not in the statute, nor the legislative history, nor the appellate decision. That is exactly the point. If you are interested in real social justice, you must seek out the voices of the people whose voices are not heard in the halls of Congress or in the marbled courtrooms.

Keep your focus on who is suffering and ask why. Listen to the voices of the people rarely heard, and you will understand exactly where injustice flourishes.

Second, look for the collateral beneficiaries. Qui bono? Who benefits from each law, and what are their interests? Why do you think that the minimum wage stays stagnant for long periods of time while expenditures on medical assistance soar year after year?

This inquiry is particularly important since the poor and powerless—by definition—rarely have any say in the laws that apply to them.

"Follow the money," they say in police work. That is also good advice in examining legislation. Do not miss the big picture. You probably have a hunch that the rich own the world. Do you know the details of how much they actually own? You are a student of the law, you have learned the tools of investigation—you use these tools to find out. Then ask yourself: if the rich own so much, why are the laws assisting poor, elderly and disabled people, at home and abroad, structured in the way they are?

Third, carefully examine the real history of these laws. Push yourself to learn how these laws came into being. Learning this history will help you understand how change comes about....

As part of your quest to learn the history of law and justice, learn about the heroic personalities involved in the social changes that prompted the changes in legislation....

Once you learn about the sheroes and heroes, push beyond these personalities and learn about the social movements that really pushed for revolutionary change. There is a strong tendency for outsiders to anoint one or more people as THE leaders or mothers or fathers of every social justice struggle. Unfortunately, that suggests that social change occurs only when these one-in-a-million leaders happen to be in the right place at the right time. That is false history....

So, look for real histories about the social movements behind social change and legislation. See how they came about. You will again discover some of the methods used to bring about revolutionary social justice.

Fourth, look at the unstated implications of race, class and gender in each piece of the law. Also look carefully at the way laws interconnect into structures that limit particular groups of people. Race, gender and economic justice issues are present in every single piece of social legislation. They are usually not stated, but they are there....

The critique of law is actually a process of re-education—challenging unstated assumptions about law. This is also a lifelong process. I have been doing this work for more than 30 years and I still regularly make mistakes based on ignorance and lack of understanding. We all have much to learn. Real education is tough work, but it is also quite rewarding.

Critique the Myths About Lawyers and Social Justice

There is a lawyer-led law school and legal profession myth that suggests social justice law and the lawyers practicing it are at the cutting edge of social change. I think history demonstrates it is actually most often the opposite—developments in law follow social change rather than lead to it.

Lawyers who invest time and their creativity to help bring about advances in justice will tell you that it is the most satisfying and the most fulfilling work of their legal careers. But they will also tell you that social justice lawyers never work alone—they are always part of a team that includes mostly non-lawyers.

Take civil rights for example. There is no bigger legal, social justice myth than the idea that lawyers, judges and legislators were the engines that transformed our society and undid the wrongs of segregation. Civil rights lawyers and legislators were certainly a very important part of the struggle for civil rights, but they were a small part of a much bigger struggle. . . .

Law school education, by its reliance on appellate decisions and legislative histories of statutes, understandably overemphasizes the role of the law and lawyers in all legal developments. But you who are interested in participating in the transformation of the world cannot rely on a simplistic overemphasis of the role of the law and lawyers. You must learn the truth.

In fact, the law was then and often is now actually used against those who seek social change. There were far more lawyers, judges and legislators soberly and profitably working to uphold the injustices of segregation than ever challenged it. The same is true of slavery, child labor, union-busting, abuse of the environment, violations of human rights and other injustices.

The courts and the legislatures are but a few of the tools used in the struggle for social justice. Organizing people to advocate for themselves is critically important, as is public outreach, public action and public education. Social justice lawyers need not do these actions directly, but the lawyer must be part of a team of people that are engaged in action and advocacy.

Build Relationships with People and Organizations Challenging Injustice: Solidarity and Community

"If you have come to help me, you are wasting your time. But if you have come because your liberation is bound up with mine, then let us struggle together." [Lilla Watson, indigenous Australian activist]

Social justice advocacy is a team sport. No one does social justice alone. There is nothing more exciting than being a part of a group that is trying to make the world a better place. You realize that participating in the quest for justice and working to change the world is actually what the legal profession should be about. And you realize that in helping change the world, you change yourself.

Solidarity recognizes that this life of advocacy is one of relationships. Not attorney-client relationships, but balanced personal relationships built on mutual respect, mutual support and mutual exchange. Relationships based on solidarity are not ones where one side has the questions and the other the answers. Solidarity means together we search for a more just world, and together we work for a more just world.

Part of solidarity is recognizing the various privileges we bring with us. Malik Rahim, founder of the Common Ground Collective in New Orleans, speaks about privilege often . . .:

> First, you have to understand the unearned privilege you have in this country just by being born in your race or gender or economic situation. You have to learn how you got it. You have to learn how to challenge the systems that maintain that privilege. But while you are with us, we want to train you to use your privilege to help our community.

This is the best summary of the challenge of privilege and solidarity in social justice advocacy I have heard recently. This is a lifelong process for all of us. None of us have arrived. We all have much to learn, and we have to make this a part of our ongoing re-education.

So, how do social justice advocates build relationships of solidarity with people and organizations struggling for justice? These relationships are built the old-fashioned way, one person at a time, one organization at a time, with humility.

Humility is critically important in social justice advocacy. By humility, I mean the recognition that I need others in order to live a full life, and I cannot live the life I want to live by myself. By humility, I mean the understanding that even though I have had a lot of formal education, I have an awful lot to learn. By humility, I mean the understanding that every person in this world has inherent human dignity and incredible life experiences that can help me learn much more about the world and myself.

There is a wise saying, "What you see depends on where you stand." Latin American liberation theologians insist that a preferential option for the poor must be one of the principles involved in the transformation of the world.

Our choices in relationships build our community. If we want to be real social justice advocates, we must invest ourselves and develop relationships in the communities in which we want to learn and work. That sounds simple, but it is not. As law students and lawyers, we are continually pulled into professional and social communities of people whose goals are often based on material prosperity, comfort and insulation from the concerns of working and poor people. If we want to be true social justice advocates, we must swim against that stream and develop relationships with other people and groups.

For example, helping preserve public housing may seem controversial or even idiotic to most of the people at a law school function or the bar convention, yet totally understandable at a small church gathering where most people of the congregation are renters.

Seek out people and organizations trying to stand up for justice. Build relationships with them. Work with them. Eat with them. Recreate with them. Walk with them. Learn from them. If you are humble and patient, over time people will embrace you, and you will embrace them, and together you will be on the road to solidarity and community.

Regularly Reflect

In order to do social justice for life, it is important to engage in regular reflection. For physical and mental health, regular reflection on your life and the quest for justice is absolutely necessary. For some people, this is prayer. For others, it is meditation. For still others, it is yoga or some other method of centering reflection and regeneration.

Most of the people I know who have remained engaged in social justice advocacy over the years have been people who regularly make time to reflect on what they are doing, how they are doing it and what they should be doing differently. Reflection allows the body and mind and spirit to reintegrate. Often, it is in the quiet of reflection that insights have the chance to emerge.

I am convinced that ten hours of work is considerably less effective than nine and a half hours of work and 30 minutes of reflection.

In an active social justice life, there is the tendency to be very active because the cause is so overwhelming. Advocates who do not create time for regular reflection can easily become angry and overwhelmed and bitter at the injustices around and ultimately at anyone who does not share their particular view about the best way to respond. They consider themselves activists, but they may be described as hyper-activists. They have often lost their effectiveness and the respect of others, which just makes them even more angry and more accusatory of everyone who disagrees with them. We all sometimes end up like that. When we do, we need to step back, reflect, recharge and reorder our actions.

Practice, Patience and Flexibility in Order to Prepare for Chaos, Criticism and Failure

One veteran social justice advocate told me once, "If you cannot handle chaos, criticism and failure, you are in the wrong business." The path to justice goes over, around and through chaos, criticism and failure. Only by experiencing and overcoming these obstacles can you realistically be described as a social justice advocate. . . .

If you challenge the status quo, you better expect criticism from the people and organizations that are benefiting from the injustices you are seeking to reverse. Though it is tough to really listen to criticism, our critics often do have some truth in their observations about us or our issues. Sometimes criticism can be an opportunity to learn how to better communicate our advocacy or to think about changes we had not fully considered. Other criticism just hurts your backside, and you just have to learn how to tolerate it and move on.

Successes do occur, and we are all pretty good at handling success. However, failure is also an inevitable part of social justice advocacy. Failure itself cannot derail advocacy, it is the response to failure that is the challenge. Short-term social justice advocates feel the sting of failure and are depressed and hurt that good did not triumph. They become disillusioned and lose faith in the ability of people and organizations to create justice. People doing social justice for life are also hurt and depressed by failure. They spend some time tending to their wounds. But then they get back up, and patiently start again, trying to figure out how to begin again in a more effective manner.

Joy, Hope, Inspiration and Love

In order to live a life of social justice advocacy, it is important to have your eyes and heart wide open to the injustices of the world. But it is equally important that your eyes and heart be wide open to and seek out and absorb the joy, hope, inspiration and love you will discover in those who resist injustice....

Hope is also crucial to this work. Those who want to continue the unjust status quo spend lots of time trying to convince the rest of us that change is impossible. Challenging injustice is hopeless they say. Because the merchants of the status quo are constantly selling us hopelessness and diversions, we must actively seek out hope. When we find the hope, we must drink deeply of its energy and stay connected to that source. When hope is alive, change is possible.

Conclusion

Every good law or case you study was once a dream. Every good law or case you study was dismissed as impossible or impractical for decades before it was enacted. Give your creative thoughts free reign, for it is only in the hearts and dreams of people seeking a better world that true social justice has a chance.

Finally, remember that we cannot give what we do not have. If we do not love ourselves, we will be hard pressed to love others. If we are not just with ourselves, we will find it very difficult to look for justice with others. In order to become and remain a social justice advocate, you must live a healthy life. Take care of yourself as well as others. Invest in yourself as well as in others. No one can build a house of justice on a foundation of injustice. Love yourself and be just to yourself and do the same with others. As you become a social justice advocate, you will experience joy, inspiration and love in abundant measure. I look forward to standing by your side at some point.

Peace,

Bill Quigley

FOR THOSE CONSIDERING LAW SCHOOL

Dean Spade
6 Unbound: Harv. J. Legal Left 111 (2010)

I get several emails every week from people who want to go to law school or are trying to figure out if they want to go to law school. Most are queer or trans activists or people who want to somehow transform the world and end various harmful and horrible dynamics impacting people and communities they are a part of or care about.... In general, these conversations are focused on helping them get past the national narratives we have all been fed that tell us that legal cases are the most effective way to dismantle systems of oppression and change people's lives. If we compare that idea to what is really happening in the world and what social movements are strategizing about, we find a more complicated relationship between law and social movements that raises questions about whether, when and how becoming a lawyer could be a good way to participate in transformative change.

Here are a few things worth thinking about when considering law school:

Most legal work maintains, rather than transforms, systems of maldistribution.

Many people's interest in becoming lawyers is driven by the myth that changing law is the way to change lives. However, there is plenty of evidence that changing laws is not as central or as important to social change as we are made to think. In fact, in the face of large scale social movements demanding change, governments often have created laws that declare equality or neutrality in order to quell dissent and maintain the status quo to the greatest extent possible. Very often, legal change that emerges in these moments heavily compromises the demands of grassroots movements in ways that lead to symbolic victories and possibly a small amount of material change to the least vulnerable of the group who the demands were about, but leave most people the same or worse off. U.S. law is fundamentally structured to establish and uphold settler colonialism, white supremacy and capitalism—the legal system will not dismantle these things. When we look at any radical movement in the U.S. challenging these institutions and conditions, whether it's workers organizing against labor exploitation, women organizing against patriarchy, people of color organizing against white supremacy, people with disabilities organizing against ableism, people organizing against destruction of the earth, queer and trans people organizing against violent gender and sexual norms, or anyone else, we can see that those movements' most transformative demands were/are not met by law, and instead that law changes are usually created to maximize the preservation of the status quo while adding a window-dressing of fairness. Even when we win law change that looks like it is supposed to guarantee the redistribution of some essential thing, that law is often quickly repealed, or it is never enforced, or it is twisted through administrative or judicial interpretation to do the reverse of what movements were seeking.

Lots of legal work that needs to be done to support poor people can be done without a law degree.

For those of us who want to directly help people in our communities entangled in battles with horrible legal systems, the good news is that we can do a lot of that without going to law school. Legal advocacy can be done by non-lawyers—non- lawyers can even represent people in and help people prepare paperwork for many types of hearings related to public benefits, immigration, and other urgent issues. Some of the most radical movements in U.S. history have provided direct help to community members in de-professionalized ways, with people learning how to get through systems or get needs met and then helping and teaching other people so that lots of people can help each other, instead of a situation in which expertise is hoarded by a few privileged people. Getting help from someone else who is directly impacted is a powerful experience that brings people into social movements and lets them see themselves as potential providers of such help to others in their circumstances. Getting help from a privileged person with a professional degree does not have the same effect and often mirrors and reproduces dynamics of subordination. A great deal of the work that poverty lawyers help people with is similar to what social workers do—filling out forms, making calls to get people into housing or medical programs, accompanying people to intimidating meetings, explaining systems, figuring out if the government isn't providing some help that it is supposed to provide. You can do a lot of that without going to law school. . . .

. . . We also have to face the reality that the rules mostly don't benefit targeted people and never have, that when good rules get created they are not followed or enforced, and so to actually change conditions of maldistribution we need mass mobilization and direct action to force deep transformation. . . .

Law school is expensive (in most cases) and it's worth thinking about what impact the debt may have on your future.

Law school is extremely expensive and way less financial aid is available for it than for undergraduate education. Many people graduate with more than $100,000 of debt. . . . Being coopted because of debt is a sad and avoidable fate. It is awful to watch people graduate and rationalize taking any job they can find because of the pressure of their debt and the law school culture that equalizes all career choices. . . .

Law school is a very conservative training and rarely a critical intellectual experience.

Law school is not like liberal arts college. It isn't about writing cool papers full of critical ideas. Many law schools, like academia in general, are perceived as "bastions of liberalism" in the context of our outrageously white supremacist, conservative country, but the intellectual and political environments are so mildly reformist (at best) that they will feel shockingly conservative to anyone who wants to see significant change. The things that interest you about law are not what the classes are about. You don't even get to choose your classes until they have had a full year to isolate you from your communities and passions with an enormous workload and tear down and rebuild your way of thinking. Law school classes are about memorizing obscure rules that are likely to have nothing to do with your daily practice as a lawyer. They are about indoctrinating you into the belief that racist, genocidal legal systems and principles are neutral. They are only somewhat about passing the bar exam, an exam that also tests you on things that have very little relevance to social movement lawyering. . . . The traditional pedagogy of law school relies on humiliating students if they bring in other ways of thinking or knowing about the world. . . . It is true that law school sometimes makes people more concise speakers and writers, but it is certainly not the only way to do that, and there is an equal danger that it makes people into bad communicators. . . .

If you go to law school, it's crucial to go to a school where you will have allies and support and where the learning experiences you want are actually being offered. Don't get caught up in the quest for prestige.

. . . You need a school that offers as many classes as possible that are relevant to dismantling white supremacy, settler colonialism, capitalism and patriarchy. You need a school where student activists are taking the institution as their target and engaging in multi-issue activism, teaching each other along the way. You need a school that values clinical legal education and will give you lots of chances to actually do work supporting poor communities while you are in school. As someone who used to be part of hiring attorneys, I can tell you that I did not value fancy degrees. I valued people who had gotten some experience, people who had developed critical thinking about race, disability, poverty, gender and immigration, and people who had thought critically about the role of lawyers in social movements and learned how to think about privilege. Once you are at school, you need to form your own reading groups and other support spaces to learn what is not taught there, including movement history and the role of lawyers in social movements. And you must continue to engage with social movements, not in a lawyer's role, throughout law school and after. This is essential to keeping perspective on the limited role of legal work, maintaining humility, and finding balance and passion.

What Roles Can Lawyers Play in Social Movements?

The idea that people who want to make change will make the biggest impact by becoming lawyers and bringing precedent-setting lawsuits needs to be reevaluated in the face of what movement history reveals. Once you let go of that idea, you can start to think about what role lawyers should or could have in social movements and evaluate whether you see yourself in those roles. In my view, transformation really happens because of the mobilization of large numbers of people directly affected by harmful and violent systems who make collective demands that exceed the limits of law and then force change through direct action (i.e. breaking the law). It doesn't come from the top—from elites granting change through legislation or courts. The question then becomes what role lawyers can have in that broad, participatory, mass mobilization-focused, bottom-up transformation.

Some important roles lawyers can play in such movements are:

Demystifier of legal systems

Lawyers can serve movements by using specialized knowledge to help demystify systems that are targeting vulnerable people but that are often intentionally opaque. Sometimes lawyers can help movement leaders identify and strategize who the targets of various campaigns could be or where weak points in certain legal systems are. However, this is easily overstated, because people targeted by violent legal systems usually know more about how they actually work and lawyers often only know how they work on paper (and sometimes mistakenly believe that to be how they actually work). Legal training can make people less adept rather than more adept at strategizing for change because we tend to buy into how the system works without even realizing it. Law school teaches people how to stop thinking outside of legal solutions to problems, which mostly means we can only think of ways to slightly tinker with harmful systems, and thereby strengthen, stabilize, and legitimize them. The entire focus of legal education is about working inside the existing legal system. Even the small part of legal education that is about poor peoples' struggles is usually about narrow reforms and courtroom strategies, not about supporting rent strikes or squatting or prison abolition or indigenous land struggles—essentially, not about actually challenging the root causes of maldistribution. . . .

Legal service provider

Lawyers are sometimes helpful for people facing abusive legal systems (immigration enforcement, criminalization, welfare cuts, eviction, environmental injustice). If survival services are part of a larger organizing strategy aimed at systemic transformation—meaning that they connect people to a way of joining with others struggling in similar circumstances and are governed by people from the directly affected group—they can be an important entry-point for people into resistance struggles and an important source of support for people to help them take political leadership on matters that concern them. Unfortunately, that is not what legal services look like for the most part. Most legal service provider jobs where lawyers help people navigate violent legal systems (like criminal defender jobs, welfare advocacy, unemployment benefits advocacy, immigration law) are not part of broader social movement strategy. Many lawyers working in those jobs end up feeling like they are just cogs in the machine. . . .

Most legal services are not currently connected to transformative change strategies, and are not going to be unless we marshal resources for much more of that kind of work—direct community organizing, base building, mobilization. This is something to consider about becoming a lawyer—are those the skills most needed by our movements right now? We definitely do need radical people to be criminal defense attorneys and welfare lawyers and all that, but we also need to be building the skills and strategies for seeking bigger change, and the reality is that the mostly privileged people who go to law school—and the few people from targeted communities who get in—end up doing system-maintaining work. Most law students I meet have never worked with and often have never heard of mass mobilization efforts besides a few historical examples like the Civil Rights Movement, and they tend to have a skewed view of mass movements that centers charismatic individuals and law changes and obscures the roles of mass mobilization, direct action, and armed struggle. Unless you have a really clear idea of how you will navigate these tensions and how your work will be different, going to law school may just co-opt you into narrow reform work. . . .

These letters touch on most if not all of the themes on systemic advocacy and justice recurring throughout this book. These self-critical bottom-up reflections, written expressly to you, provide basic guideposts that all advocates can return to, periodically, to maximize the impact and integrity of any advocacy in any context. These letters provide advocates of today and tomorrow with handy and flexible roadmaps toward Critical Justice over time.

NOTES AND QUESTIONS

1. *Reflection Exercise A.* Reflect on the materials in this book. Consider how you feel—energized, hopeful, overwhelmed, or something else? Are you content with the educational choices, or lack of choice, that led you to this particular classroom and class at this stage of your educational career? Do you wish you had done (or studied) something else, and does that something else connect to meaningful social change that makes the world a better place? Quigley

suggests an advocate for social change must learn to be uncomfortable. Are you uncomfortable with some or all of the material in this book? Did any of the examples and reflections speak to your own experiences or those of your community? Did that put you at ease or cause distress?

On the skill and value of reflection, consider Quigley's suggestion on the benefit of (say) a half hour of reflection as part of every ten hours of work. Does that comport with your own educational time-allocation, including class attendance? Have you found reflection valuable? If so, how are you measuring that value? If not, why?

2. *Reflection Exercise B.* Hung details how as a youth she read and looked to Martin Luther King, Jr. as a role model "for equal rights and justice" who, along with other icons, inspired her to become a lawyer. Find online King's "Letter from Birmingham Jail" written in the 1960s while King was incarcerated for civil disobedience. In that letter, King reflects on the civil rights struggle of U.S. racial groups. Even though it was written more than half a century ago, how does his letter confirm the points emphasized in this book since then? How does his letter add to the letters above? How was King, even back then, combatting systemic social ills that now we understand as systemic injustice? Was he—together with colleagues, allies, and advocates, including both lawyers and other actors—engaging in, and thereby developing, a practice that we now know as systemic advocacy?

16.2 PATHWAYS CHANGE ALONG THE WAY—SO MUST GROUPS, ADVOCATES, AND ADVOCACY

All journeys to Critical Justice are hard and uncertain, perhaps forever unfinished. The ways to Critical Justice entail, both personally and collectively, a critical marathon. Using dual consciousness contextually, all advocates moor themselves—flexibly—for this long haul. Navigating failure by design and counteracting preservation through transformation is never ending. So is the need to adapt—in principled, accountable, and impactful ways.

As we have seen throughout, good field-based advocacy reckons with short term (tactical) and longer term (strategic) aspects of systemic advocacy in order to use amelioration for transformation. This daily work uses the ever-shifting present to build assiduously and creatively on the always-contested past toward a necessarily uncertain future. Along the way, advocates monitor, consider, reflect on, and adjust their tactics and strategies to make and defend progress steadily as circumstances change. When circumstances change, so must the pathways of three-layered advocacy. Sometimes, circumstances change radically—in part, perhaps, due to your own success. In those (happy) moments, advocates must pause to reflect about next steps to defend and advance on that success. And the same goes for changes in context or circumstance due to other reasons or sources. Ongoing reflection as professional practice, as we have seen time and again, is serious business.

Illustrating these points vividly, legal scholar Jennifer Gordon recounts below how law, strategy, advocacy, and time played central roles in establishing and sustaining the United Farm Workers as a U.S. labor union. Gordon showcases how organizers, advocates, and client-groups adapted (or not) to time and circumstance to create a strong advocacy program. The labor union developed a program that was deeply collaborative, accountable to farm worker leaders, and focused on meaningful progress. Noting that advocacy is "an act of creating windows of opportunity," Gordon's account tracks defensive and offensive advocacy and shows that adaption and readaptation must be proactive. As you read, consider how notions of winning and losing relate to progress in light of NeJaime's review of sexual minority struggles in Part II and Blasi's and Mor's consideration of meaningful access to justice in Part III. Recall West's mandate for law and lawyers to defend past gains while acting on moments for advancing causes in Part III and cooptive dangers outlined by Lobel and Torres in Part III. Notice also how the advocates and groups work together to navigate changing complexities as circumstances change over time to press forward while defending gains.

LAW, LAWYERS, AND LABOR: THE UNITED FARM WORKERS' LEGAL STRATEGY IN THE 1960S AND 1970S AND THE ROLE OF LAW IN UNION ORGANIZING TODAY

Jennifer Gordon
8 U. Pa. J. Lab. & Emp. L. 1 (2005)

... The United Farm Workers' Use of Law, 1962–1980

... The United Farm Workers [UFW] combined a labor organization for the country's most disenfranchised workers with a mass movement attracting broad support across the continent and beyond. When the UFW was founded in 1962 by Cesar Chavez and fellow Mexican-American community activists in Delano, California, wages on California's large corporate ranches were pitifully low. The UFW's chief opponent was California agribusiness. By the 1960s, agriculture in California had left the small family farm in the dust. From the UFW's birthplace in the southern San Joaquin Valley, large corporate growers whose ranches measured from 10,000 to over 100,000 acres supplied grapes, vegetables, and strawberries to the entire country. Although mechanization was encroaching on work traditionally done by hand, fields were still primarily tilled, planted, and picked by Mexican-Americans, Mexican braceros, migrants from the Philippines as well as other countries, and undocumented immigrants. Wages were pitifully low. Working conditions were inhumane, from the lack of toilets and drinking water in the fields, to the widespread use of "el cortito," the short-handled hoe that required workers to bend at back-breaking angles for hours at a time, to the pesticide residues that hung in the air and clung to leaves, poisoning workers as they labored. When workers protested these abuses, growers had a panoply of tools at their disposal to silence dissent. In the 1950s, from a third to a half of the workers they hired were braceros, whose legal status was conditioned on maintaining their job; uncounted others were illegally present. A quick dismissal or call to the INS could derail many organizing efforts. Where the workers involved were legal permanent residents or citizens, the sheriff or local police could often be relied upon to quell dissent. Farm workers were unprotected by basic national wage and labor laws such as the Fair Labor Standards Act ("FLSA") and the National Labor Relations Act [NLRA], and growers had cultivated political allies to ensure that no new laws were passed.

As decades of sporadically successful strikes had shown, farm workers were not completely without power. But until the UFW, no farm worker organizing effort had been able to create an organization of farm workers with the creativity, persistence, and stability to fight for on-going union representation and win, much less to negotiate multi-faceted contracts and administer them over several seasons.

Chavez knew that a stable worker organization was necessary to overcome the problem of fleeting victories that other organizing efforts had faced, and he was committed to years of base-building before the union launched its first campaign. To draw farm workers into the effort, the UFW offered a range of services and co-operatives, a response both to the breadth of farm workers' needs and to Chavez's philosophy that a union ought to do more for its members than negotiate and administer contracts. Even with broad support, Chavez realized that the battle to win contracts might be long. But as a farm worker himself and a longtime organizer, he also recognized that farm workers had as-yet untapped sources of power. There was a stable Chicano community in some places, and it was in this community (as opposed to, say, among day laborers, as a previous AFL-CIO farm labor organizing campaign had attempted) that UFW built its base. The majority of the workforce was Mexican or Chicano and shared a religious and cultural identity. Drawing on this identity, the UFW's integration of prayer, religious services, and traditional Mexican symbols such as the Virgin of Guadalupe, with Gandhian tactics such as the fast, created a culture and a spirit of determination that kept the Union going despite repeated defeats.

The UFW developed its unique organizing strategy in response to the particular circumstances of farm labor. In the face of the never-ending influx of new workers too mobile and too desperate to be effectively organized to stay out of work for long, traditional union organizing measures such as strikes and pickets were very hard to sustain. A union could not physically stop the flow of labor into the fields for long because the space was so vast and because courts restricted pickets to impossibly small numbers. And, as migrant workers were well aware, if they demanded union representation they could easily be replaced by temporary workers hauled up from Mexico; by undocumented workers, present in growing numbers; and by workers bused in from other parts of the country.

Despite these obstacles, the collective action of farm workers was important to the UFW's strategy. . . .

Given the difficulty of winning contracts for mobile, replaceable farm workers through strikes, the UFW also sought to create a social climate in which the existing treatment of farm workers was seen as unjust. The UFW used that climate to generate moral, economic, and political pressure on growers to recognize the UFW as the legitimate representative of farm workers. To supplement and at times replace field organizing, the Union called on middle-class consumers around the country to boycott non-Union fruits and vegetables. This served as an effective year-round economic weapon that worked in complementary ways with the Union's on-the-ground organizing, particularly between 1965 and 1970 (the first grape boycott) and at various times during the 1970s and 1980s (boycotts of other produce and wine as well as grapes). . . .

The United Farm Workers' Early Legal Strategy

Although the general outline of the UFW's story is well known, the role of lawyers in that story has remained nearly unexplored in published sources. Yet the creative use of law played an important role in the Union's success. At its peak, the UFW legal department had seventeen lawyers and forty-four paralegals, high numbers indeed in the context of a leanly-staffed and financially-struggling movement.

In the Union's first years, it parceled out its legal work to volunteer lawyers and outside counsel. The volunteers, mostly recent law graduates, largely counseled and represented farm workers on individual matters. Chavez also experimented with hiring a staff lawyer whose principal responsibility was to provide members with services. He became overwhelmed by the volume of work and only lasted for a brief period. For more complex legal matters, Chavez turned to outside labor lawyers. But these experiences, too, were frustrating. Farm workers were exempt from the NLRA, but the labor lawyers whom the union consulted were often so mired in its restrictions that they could not respond creatively to the unique possibilities and needs of a farm labor organizing campaign.

Starting in 1966, Chavez began to seek legal support from the newly-founded California Rural Legal Assistance corporation ("CRLA"), one of the first federally-funded legal service organizations. Although CRLA was explicitly prohibited by the terms of its federal funding from representing any union, sympathetic attorneys within CRLA found ways to pursue Chavez's goals through impact litigation. Not unpredictably, this collaboration soon unraveled in the face of tension about goals and strategies. CRLA sought to make decisions about legal tactics that would lead to a victory in court. The Union, on the other hand, often preferred a course of action that was riskier in legal terms but that it judged more likely to advance its long-term organizing goals. But the Union could not be CRLA's client; therefore, it had no official say in the matter. While sporadic collaboration would continue over the years, it was clear by 1967 that CRLA could not consistently provide the UFW with the sort of representation it needed. As Chavez realized, the Union had reached a point where it needed its own sophisticated legal strategist.

For the Union's first general counsel, Chavez chose Jerome "Jerry" Cohen, who had graduated from Boalt Hall and gone to work at CRLA just months earlier.... Over the next thirteen years, Cohen and his staff would break new frontiers in their exploration of how law could protect, open opportunities for, and advance the Union's external organizing goals.

... Chavez worked with Cohen to develop an approach to lawyering that put the achievement of organizing goals above the achievement of legal victories. For example soon after Cohen started work for the UFW a judge took away the Union's right to use bullhorns in an early strike against the Giumarra company. Cohen proudly returned from appellate court with a writ of prohibition blocking the order, but he received a cold response from Chavez, who believed that the best organizing use of the situation would be to use a bullhorn in violation of the judge's order, get thrown in jail, and attract publicity and support for the cause. Through a series of similar encounters, Cohen and Chavez honed their communication. This process was replicated as Cohen brought new attorneys onto the Union's legal staff, each of whom brought his or her own strengths but who also had to be immersed in the culture of UFW legal and organizing strategy before beginning to work effectively as an integral part of it.

Cohen strategized with Chavez not just about the legal aspects of the Union's work but about its overall direction. He and the attorneys he hired led the fight against restrictive farm labor legislation in several states. They negotiated contracts with growers. But most of all, in the UFW's early years, Cohen and his staff litigated. They went to court to defend the Union, its volunteers, and its members. They went to court to establish legal protections for farm worker organizing. And they went to court to spread the word about the UFW and to bring public pressure to bear on opponents in various ways. In each situation, the question was never only "what are our rights here?," but "how can we best turn this legal situation to the Union's organizing advantage?"

Defending the Union

Before long, Cohen hired a few young lawyers to work with him. Much of their daily work involved defending the Union and its members. Like all effective organizing efforts, the UFW generated a strong legal backlash. Pickets were stopped with injunctions, protesters were arrested (sometimes unexpectedly, sometimes en masse after the UFW launched civil disobedience campaigns involving up to thousands of workers at a time), striking workers were evicted from farm labor camps, and the Union was slapped with grower lawsuits intended to slow down its efforts. It was the legal department's responsibility to mount a defense against these onslaughts.

To facilitate this, during the harvest season staff lawyers lived close to the areas where organizing was most active. In major strikes, a law student was assigned to every picket captain to document how strikers were treated and to negotiate with police. Lawyers were on call when organizers needed them to go to the fields because a sheriff had restricted picketing beyond what was delineated in an injunction. A UFW lawyer or paralegal standing by the side of a road bordering the fields, typewriter balanced on the hood of a car, taking affidavits from workers, became a common sight. . . .

Just as lawyers responded to organizers' calls, so organizers turned members out for hearings. Former staff attorney Barbara Rhine recalls,

> [W]hen we went to court . . . we would just pack the courtroom. Boy, were things different if . . . every time the judge had to make a ruling, he was facing an absolutely crowded courtroom, with faces wreathed in wrinkles and hard work, and three languages that had to be spoken, seeing the effect of the way the law works on ordinary people. And we could do that. We could get those people out. . . . But it depended not only on a hotshot legal department, which we certainly had, but also on the hundreds of people on the ground every day.

In the process, many UFW lawyers and law students built strong relationships with the organizers in their area. Rhine describes it as "a . . . partnership . . . a wonderful marriage between what was happening on the ground and in the courts." . . .

Among other aspects of the collaboration, attorneys responded to calls from organizers to free workers from jail or INS [Immigration and Naturalization Services, a predecessor to ICE] detention. They sometimes ended up detained themselves. Attorney Sandy Nathan was jailed in 1975 when he demanded access to a group of workers just arrested by the INS from a Salinas ranch where their votes were crucial in winning an upcoming election. The INS refused, and called the police when he persisted. Two years later, the police arrested Nathan again for insisting on access to twenty-five tomato pickers and a UFW organizer being held in a jail cell. As the door to the cell opened so that an officer could shove him in with the others, the organizer smiled and said to the workers, "See, I told you our lawyer would be here!" On the police report for Nathan's arrest, under the box marked "Weapon," the officer scrawled a single word: "Mouth."

Shaping the Law

As UFW lawyers defended the Union in jail and in court, they also sought to wrest from the Constitution a web of rights—to use bullhorns, to picket, to boycott—that could curtail a judge's leeway to use injunctions to shut down strikes and provide a basic framework for farm worker organizing in the absence of NLRA coverage. The UFW's battle with the injunction echoed that of the labor movement in the days before labor law. In the late nineteenth and early twentieth centuries, judges readily issued injunctions barring or severely limiting strikes and pickets, stymieing union organizing efforts. The passage of the Norris-LaGuardia Act in 1932 had effectively ended this practice under federal law, and the Wagner Act three years later put the final seal on its coffin. But since state law offered ample opportunity to restrict farm labor pickets, and since agricultural workers were exempt from the Wagner Act's protections, the UFW continued to work under a regime of government-by-injunction. . . .

In fighting injunctions, victory in court was often important to Cohen and his staff. Indeed, UFW litigation resulted in a string of important constitutional decisions in California, which . . . guarantee picketers the right to use bullhorns or other amplification to communicate their message to workers in the fields, prohibit the issuance of temporary restraining orders against picketers (or whenever First Amendment rights are implicated) unless all parties have received notice of the hearing, and recognize a First Amendment right for organizers and attorneys to have access to migrant labor camps. These legal victories—as well as the lower-level daily triumphs that delayed eviction by a few days or permitted a picket to continue over a weekend—were concretely useful to the Union's organizers and won the legal department the deep appreciation of leaders such as Dolores Huerta, Gilbert Padilla, and Chavez himself.

Using Legal Strategies Offensively to Build Power

As important as legal victory could be, the Union often had other goals for its lawsuits as well, and it litigated aggressively to achieve them. Cohen refers to much of his work during this period as "legal karate and the law of the jungle," using the law as an offensive weapon to advance the UFW's organizing goals and build power for the Union. The Union threatened and filed lawsuits designed to put collateral pressure on all fronts of its fight: to gain information about particular growers and the industry through discovery, to convince consumers and stores to respect the boycott, to increase the growers' legal bills and weaken their resolve, and to pressure government officials to change their policies and practices.

The UFW recognized that the discovery phase of a lawsuit (in which parties use written interrogatories and oral depositions to gather information from the other side) could uncover otherwise unavailable data about growers, data that could be very useful in planning boycotts and other organizing strategies. Former CRLA lawyer Gary Bellow described one such deposition that he carried out in an early CRLA lawsuit related to a UFW organizing campaign. When a farm worker appeared at the McFarland CRLA office in 1967, angry that he had been fired from the Bernardi grape ranch for his allegiance to the UFW, Bellow brought suit on his behalf alleging that ranch owners' sweetheart contracts with the Teamsters [union] had deprived a UFW member of his rights. Within the framework of the lawsuit, Bellow used depositions as a research tool for the union's ongoing campaign.

> [T]he next thing I did was to take depositions of the Bernardis—"What subsidiaries do you have? What do you own? How much grape do you ship? How many workers do you have that were not members of the union?"—because they were relevant to the law suit. And suddenly the union realized that with a lawyer it could get information that it couldn't get any other way.

The UFW continued to use depositions this way over time. Growers would sue the Union for damages from the boycott, claiming that it had damaged their market. In response, during discovery the UFW would ask relevant questions about the grower's client base and its geographic reach. As Cohen describes it, the Union won either way: either the grower dropped the suit to avoid giving up this valuable data, or it answered, handing the boycott much-needed information.

During some court battles, the UFW sought to influence both public opinion and the legal outcome by using the courthouse as a stage on which to publicize the farm workers' plight. At several critical moments, for example, the union mobilized members to conduct vigils, sing and pray in courthouse corridors as the judge decided a case involving the UFW. As Cohen recalls, in one case in 1968 where Chavez, then on the thirteenth day of a fast, was cited for contempt of a growers' injunction, UFW members came to court by the hundreds.

> [W]orkers all around the building, workers lining every wall of the courthouse.... [T]he workers were singing softly, and they were praying.... We hadn't been having too much luck in that courthouse before, because it's really the growers' courthouse. But I think everybody that morning knew it was our courthouse.

The grower's lawyer asked the judge to remove the farm workers from the courthouse, but the judge refused, saying "If I kick these workers out of this courthouse, that will be just another example of goddamn gringo justice. I can't do it." As Cohen reflects, "Things started to shift there. That had nothing to do with legal argument. That had to do with just raw organizing power." Another approach was to bring farm workers in to tell their stories in court, or to use affidavits to bring farm workers' experiences in the fields and on the picket line into the courtroom. Unlike many of the big political trials of the 1960s and 1970s, the UFW was not trying to disrupt the actual court proceedings or to reveal the legal system as a fraud. The idea was to change the immediate cultural, political, and moral environment in which legal decisions were made. The press played an important role in this strategy, disseminating the Union's message widely and intensifying the pressure on its opponents. . . .

The ALRA [California Agricultural Labor Relations Act]

In December of 1972, as the UFW's grape contracts approached their expiration date, Teamsters president Frank Fitzsimmons appeared at a function for the Farm Bureau Federation (a growers' organization) and exhorted growers to form an alliance with the Teamsters. They listened well. When the UFW contracts expired in 1973, 90% of the grape growers signed agreements with the Teamsters. There were no elections; workers were not consulted in the process. The UFW was left reeling, with no more than 6,500 workers remaining under its representation. It was a dark and bitter time for the Union.

Fast running out of money and desperate to rebuild, the UFW debated whether to seek the passage of a state law that would prevent such raids and create explicit rules for the organization of agricultural workers. The UFW's staff and volunteers had wavered over the years about whether the Union stood to lose or win in seeking to create a law that would govern its conduct. On a practical level, the likelihood of wresting a good law from the California legislature seemed dim for many years. More fundamentally, Chavez and others had observed how legislation had seemed to take the wind out of the sails of the civil rights movement in the South. Certainly wholesale adoption of the NLRA seemed like the wrong solution, given the increasingly evident way that law and the NLRB was coming to shackle the labor unions that it governed. Some leaders further argued that the UFW's freedom from labor legislation was a key to its success, allowing it to operate as a social movement with a wide range of tactics, free of the bureaucracy of the union establishment. But the AFL-CIO was offering a strike fund of $1.6 million to the Union on the condition that it make serious efforts to win an agricultural labor relations law. And in 1974, victory in such an effort began to seem conceivable when Jerry Brown replaced Ronald Reagan as governor of California. The Union decided that its best hope for rebirth was to create an administrative framework that would guarantee the UFW access to farm workers in the fields, bar sweetheart deals between Teamsters and growers, and set legal rules for elections and bargaining that would allow the UFW to recover the contracts it had lost.

Cohen worked with the Union's organizers and lawyers to develop a set of proposals that reflected what they had learned during the UFW's last hard-fought decade about the sort of protections that would facilitate farm labor organizing. Cohen brought these ideas to Chavez, who later recalled that

> Jerry Cohen made a list of all the issues as he saw them. Then he met with the board and with me for many sessions. We went over all the issues. I also met with the field office staffs, the people who had been involved with the strikes, the workers, and we just touched every single base we could. There was tremendous input. So Jerry finally drew up an ideal bill.

One approach might have been to scale down what the Union wanted so it more closely resembled the realm of the possible. Although the Union had sought a minimalist bill the year before, in 1975 Chavez and Cohen did not take that route. Looking at all of the ideas on the table, they decided, "We'll just load up—we'll ask for everything. We'll ask for the whole damn thing." It was not clear how far their political power could take them, but they were unwilling to compromise in advance of discovering the answer.

The initial bill that Jerry Brown introduced, drafted by his Secretary of Agriculture Rose Bird (later Chief Justice of the California Supreme Court), was far from the Union's wish list, indeed so far that the UFW responded with protests around the state. Months of back and forth ensued, as Cohen negotiated with Brown, Bird, and various attorneys. Eventually, Cohen succeeded in convincing Brown to change his bill to reflect most of the UFW's provisions, and the Union gave the measure its full support. . . .

For the growers' part, most put their considerable clout to work to defeat the UFW-supported bill. But some of them, too, had reasons to support it. Growers had already been limited by California courts in the degree to which they could retaliate against union supporters, so they had less to lose than one might think. They wanted an end to the UFW's outlaw tactics and they hoped that a law would prohibit the secondary boycotts [of supermarkets selling grapes] that had worked so effectively for the Union. . . . [Many] thought that an election system was their best bet for avoiding the constant pressure to recognize the UFW under which they had lived for the previous decade.

Farm labor legislation had some other unlikely backers. Supermarket owners, who were tired of the UFW's business-disrupting protests, sought a bill that would ban secondary boycotts and bring customers back to their doors. Some county administrators and sheriffs endorsed the bill, hoping it would free them of the burden of caring for thousands of UFW protesters in their jails as they had the previous summer. The backing of this range of usually conservative forces eventually would make it easier for legislators who might otherwise have opposed the bill to vote in favor of it. . . .

The ALRA as passed offered the UFW a powerful new framework for organizing. . . .

The law began with an unabashed endorsement of the right of farm workers to organize, with a preamble that explicitly stated the Act's goal as "guaranteeing justice for all agricultural workers." . . .

Legal Work in the Wake of the ALRA

. . . In the legal department, a group of lawyers who had prided themselves on their expertise in civil rights law and the battle against injunctions but had little or no experience representing conventional unions suddenly found nothing but a few pages on the calendar between themselves and full-fledged labor law practice. Cohen split the legal department in two, one half to manage ongoing litigation, the other—under the direction of Sandy Nathan—to work on ALRA matters. The department quickly rose to its peak of seventeen lawyers, forty-four paralegals, and a large number of volunteer attorneys playing supporting roles. . . .

To turn a paper law into a real one, the UFW had to work with the new agency created by the ALRA. The ALRB [Agricultural Labor Relations Board] opened its doors on September 2, 1975. On the surface, it looked to be an ideal partner for the UFW. . . .

Matters on the ground, however, proved considerably less simple. Few ALRB staff spoke Spanish, and according to observers at the time—including a fellow board attorney—many treated farm workers with suspicion or outright distaste. The new agency was at once utterly disorganized and instantly bureaucratic. . . .

Meanwhile, growers continued to resist the law with impunity. Three weeks after the ALRB opened for business, Sandy Nathan, the UFW's lead attorney for ALRA matters, commented: "The growers are really lawless at this point. To them it's perfectly permissible to disregard the law and to do everything they can to subvert it. And the board is not recognizing that. . . . They're just looking at it that everybody is a good faith participant." Responding to growers' demands, board staff regularly excluded workers from pre-election conferences; when the board finally responded to UFW pressure to include them, it did so without translation (or with an offer to translate only the "important stuff," leading Sandy Nathan to suggest that they conduct the conference in Spanish and "translate the important stuff into English for the employer"). . . .

[Despite these and other obstacles, more than] 150 elections took place in each of the following two years, with over 9,000 farm workers voting per year. The UFW won 55% of those elections; the Teamsters won 32%. . . .

The benefits for farm workers were immediate: wages rose by 30% to 50%, and many received health and pension benefits for the first time in their lives. At its height two years later, the UFW had over 50,000 members under contract and as many as 50,000 more "affiliated" farm workers. The Union's reputation stretched across the country and indeed the globe.

The Unraveling

The ALRA offered the UFW a remarkable opportunity, and the UFW seized it and held on. And yet within a decade of the ALRA's passage, the UFW was all but dormant, as was the [ALRB]. Many factors contributed to this decline. On all fronts during the 1980s, organizing became more difficult. An influx of undocumented workers increased competition and made raising wages harder. Meanwhile, growers fought back against the advantages the ALRA gave farm workers. They used ALRB appeals to delay decisions on elections, and built support in [the state capital] for their efforts to re-shape the political landscape that had brought the ALRA into being. But the UFW had faced political opposition, intense labor competition, and grower resistance before, and triumphed. Internal changes in the UFW seem to have played the critical role in its inability to respond effectively to this round of challenges.

. . . Managing the large number of workers organized under the new law and administering the contracts the Union had negotiated required more sophisticated administrative systems than the UFW had. But to move in that direction, with an increased focus on contract administration and institutionalization, would have meant acknowledging a shift in the UFW's identity from a social movement to a union, something that Chavez in particular was loath to do.

Matters came to a head when Cohen [and other lawyers] supported a call by organizers and paralegals that they be paid a regular salary, a move away from the "volunteer stipend" system that applied to most field and service staff and toward a more institutionalized system. The lawyers also asked for an increase in their base monthly salary from $600 to $1000. Disagreeing on both fronts, Chavez insisted that the UFW needed to go in the opposite direction, returning to its all-volunteer movement roots. He focused on the lawyers' request. In mid-1978, he proposed to the Executive Board that it begin this process by de-funding the UFW's lawyers and requiring that they participate in the volunteer system like most other staff. The board split along generational lines, with younger members opposed to Chavez's proposal . . . losing to a slim majority of older UFW leaders. Stripped of their income, most of the lawyers left in 1978 and 1979. . . .

At the time of Chavez's death in 1993, the Union had between 5,000 and 10,000 members. In the mid-1990s and early 2000s, the UFW began to regain some vigor [but, despite] some noteworthy legislative victories, the venerable and embattled UFW has not yet managed to regain the public prominence or the level of worker representation it enjoyed in its heyday.

Analysis of a Collaboration

... As the UFW's story so amply illustrates, good lawyers for labor (or for any movement) have one consistent touchstone: the question "what can legal strategies do to help the union win organizing victories"? Although the question is a constant, the answer varies tremendously with context. A labor movement has very different opportunities to use the law to advance its goals depending on the legal, political, economic and social environment in which it operates. Important factors include the laws that explicitly or potentially govern its conduct or its opponents', the courts through which its claims are channeled and the judges before whom they are heard, and the receptivity of politicians and government officials at a range of levels to its cause, among others. At the same time, labor's capacity to take advantage of opportunities to use law to build union power depends on the presence of a particular type of lawyer (and a particular type of union leader) and can be dramatically enhanced by a way of structuring the relationship between law and organizing that puts the power-building question, rather than the more common question of "how can we as lawyers win a legal victory," at center stage.

Legal Strategies in the Jungle

A key contextual change over time in the UFW's story is of course first the lack, and then the emergence, of a governing law. It is important to begin this analysis, however, by challenging the concept of the "law of the jungle," a phrase used frequently by Cohen in discussing the pre-ALRA period and later by AFL-CIO leaders looking back longingly to the time before they became ensnared in the NLRA. "Law of the jungle" implies that at the time in question there is no law at all, that disputes are settled by the brute strength of the powerful and the wiliness of those who might at first glance seem weak. Government, legal rules, and courts all are absent in such an account.

Despite this description, before the UFW was governed by the ALRA it operated in a world where law was very much present, either as a weapon deployed against the Union or as a resource that it came to recognize and of which it took advantage. The state was already an active participant in the struggle between growers and farm workers, and long had been. Employers demanded that the courts issue injunctions against picketers, restrict organizers' access to the fields, and evict striking farm workers from labor camps, all for violations of criminal and property law. They called on the police to enforce those orders. Both were consistently responsive. Growers used immigration policy as a tool of labor market control, obtaining extra workers through the bracero [guest worker] program as long as it lasted and through various other temporary immigration programs after that, and hiring undocumented immigrants as strikebreakers with full confidence that the state would not enforce the law against their presence.

For its part, in the period before the ALRA, the UFW drew on a variety of laws—and on its own capacity to pressure those who made and enforced the law—to build the Union's power. During that time, the UFW won the right to represent workers by generating so much pressure that a grower would agree to a union contract in order to be able to once again harvest and sell its product without interference. The most useful legal work was that which made the greatest contribution to the effort to persuade the grower to give in. Constitutional law, and the very influential example of the then ongoing civil rights movement in using constitutional law to facilitate protest and generate public support, proved critical to the UFW's ability to sustain its strikes, pickets, and marches. . . .

The so-called "law of the jungle" phase, then, was for the UFW not so much about operation in an ungoverned state of nature as it was about maneuvering to achieve the Union's goals through creative use of a wide range of laws, legal fora, and potential state interventions. This sometimes happened directly (as when the constitutional claims were successful in permitting picketing), but more often indirectly, as when depositions gave the union access to information it needed about pickets, or when a legal defeat such as a judge's refusal to mandate release of information about pesticides became a platform for the union to "raise an issue" and tell its story to the public. . . .

The Structure of the Relationship

The UFW's success in integrating law and organizing was not merely the result of creative legal tactics. The internal relationship between the Union's organizing staff and its legal department was very important in facilitating the collaboration, which avoided many of the pitfalls that have plagued similar efforts.

Although it might intuitively seem that the relationship between legal and organizing strategies in an effort to achieve social change should be an easy one—after all, both are important tools in the struggle—it rarely is. Many a would-be collaboration has foundered on the rocks of tension between lawyers and organizers about goals, methods, and leadership, among other issues. A substantial literature lays out the perils. Concern about lawyer domination is a recurring theme. Scholars and activists alike offer a panoply of examples where a lawyer's well-intentioned intervention in an ongoing organizing battle had the effect of de-mobilizing participants, turning the attorney into the "expert" and focusing the group's energy on a court case and its outcome rather than on the need to build power through collective action.

Much of the concern about lawyer domination among scholars and activists arises in settings where the organizing effort is relatively young or weak. In such a situation, there is a heightened danger that a lawyer will be seen as the leader and that legal strategies will overtake collective ones. In this regard, it is important that Cohen came to the UFW five years into its history, after it had already become a broad movement with a clearly defined organizing strategy, a highly visible charismatic leader, and several victories under its belt. In the case of the UFW, the Union's strength and clarity about its goals at the time it first brought Cohen on staff—and Chavez's skill at communicating those goals and in teaching Cohen to be the sort of lawyer who could advance them—proved to be critical elements of the successful collaboration. Cohen was also not on the Union's Executive Committee, he did not and could not organize groups of workers, and he did not seek to limit the Union's tactics or control its approach. Chavez respected Cohen greatly, but there was no question that Chavez was in control of the Union.

Another key element of the UFW's success in merging law and organizing strategies was that legal representation was coordinated and in large measure provided in-house. The UFW had experimented with outside lawyers initially and found them wanting. Likewise, its experience with a staff lawyer whose role was largely to service members had been a frustrating one. Once Cohen joined the Union and began to build a legal department, the UFW's effort to deploy legal strategies to enhance the UFW's organizing power took off. No longer were the UFW's lawyers hemmed in by ideas about labor law steeped in the NLRA and its limitations, by government funding restrictions and by the need to represent individual farm workers to get around those restrictions, by the mission of an advocacy group, or by the limitations on time and resources imposed by pro bono attorney's obligations at an outside firm. They could experiment with the broad range of answers to the department's central charge, to put their legal skills to work "to figure out ways of generating the kind of power that's needed."

Present as they were every day in the Union's small field offices, in the fields and in local courtrooms, these lawyers became repeat players, at once experienced with the local legal context and imbued with the feel and goals of the UFW's ever[y]day work. All of these factors made them more likely to understand what the Union was seeking to achieve and to perceive where emerging opportunities might lie to use legal strategies to realize those aims. Equally important, having an in-house legal department gave the UFW the ability to deploy lawyers very cheaply by contrast with its opponents, who had to pay for [outside] counsel. A UFW staff attorney's annual salary cost roughly the same as two weeks of lawyer time at the rates that the Teamsters and growers had to pay private law firms for representation. While the UFW's opponents' expenses rose with each additional hour their lawyers worked, the Union's costs were both fixed and low. This effect was magnified by the incorporation of large quantities of free outside legal support, from volunteer paralegals and law students to experienced pro bono attorneys.

This in-house work was governed by a clear understanding about what the Union's lawyers were there for: to open the field for organizing and to advance the union's ultimate goal of large-scale farm worker representation. If a lawsuit worked directly or indirectly to build power in these ways, it was brought. If it did not, the Union had no interest. Directed and largely executed by the Union's own full-time lawyers, the UFW's legal strategy skirted much conflict (common in other scenarios where lawyers work to support organizing) about lawyers dictating or dominating or shutting down organizing, and about lawsuits rather than collective action taking center stage. The UFW's legal department built a tremendous amount of power for the Union. Together with strikes and the boycott, it was one of the three legs on which the organizing strategy stood. But the end goal—building a farm workers' movement and union—was always clear, and to that end goal, lawyers were a handmaiden.

... [T]he UFW's legal strategy also took advantage of unique opportunities offered by its time and place. The example of the civil rights movement had a critically important influence on the UFW as a whole; the movement's use of law in tandem with organizing similarly inspired Cohen and other attorneys for the Union. So too was the anti-war movement, with its group of lawyers working to facilitate draft resistance and public protest. The culture in the late 1960s and 1970s was particularly receptive to the emergence of a new social movement and to the call to support boycotts and protests, conveyed through legal cases as well as directly. . . . The routine use of property and criminal law to stymie pickets was low-hanging fruit, subject to constitutional attack. A law governing farm labor organizing had not been written. Growers did not expect, and for a number of years were unprepared for, the high-level representation that farm workers received. None of these aspects of the UFW's context obviate the tremendous creativity, dedication and persistence of Cohen and his legal team. But they will be important to keep in mind when we turn shortly to the question of the very different—in many ways polar opposite—context in which labor lawyers are operating today. . . .

Labor Law, Labor Lawyers, and Unions Today

Today, the universe of lawyers working to advance workers' rights is a broad and dynamic one. . . .

What is most interesting about this work is its move away from the model of labor law practice that reigned for half a century—the technician's command of the NLRA and the NLRB—toward a recognition of the reality that (despite the presence of a governing law that ostensibly seeks to level the playing field between workers and employers) the outcome of labor disputes is once again being argued in the court of public opinion and settled by brute displays of power. Unions, and the attorneys who represent them, have been strategizing to avoid the NLRA's sticky web, seeking out pockets of space in which organizing feels possible again, unconstrained by restrictive legal rules and the molasses-like pace of NLRB and judicial decision-making. That the legal structure has not been repealed, and must still be reckoned with even as unions and their lawyers seek to avoid its grasp, adds another layer of complexity in this work.

Although there are many varieties of organizing in this new land, the core demand they share is that the employer agree to step back from a position of antagonism vis-à-vis the union, retreat from reliance on NLRA rules and NLRB procedures to create delay, and simply allow the workers to make their choice about representation.... [T]he labor movement has ... moved increasingly away from NLRB-supervised elections and toward urging employers to recognize and bargain with a union once a majority of workers sign cards indicating their desire for representation, a process often called "card-check recognition." Where unions do not have sufficient power to win card-check, they often seek a "neutrality" agreement, by which the employer promises to refrain from doing any number of things designed to sway workers away from a vote for the union. These two types of agreements can also be combined.

... To this end, many unions today conduct "corporate" or "comprehensive" campaigns—efforts to generate negative publicity and negative economic consequences for corporations and their board members and/or to work with shareholders to elect corporate boards more sympathetic to their cause—in order to bring an employer to a point where it is willing to accede to an agreement and abide by its terms.

Called on to facilitate card-check campaigns and their comprehensive campaign companions, lawyers have responded in a variety of ways. One has been to litigate and legislate to permit or (ideally) mandate card-check as a route to union recognition. Another has been to use a wide range of legal tactics as leverage in a comprehensive campaign, to bolster union power and batter employer resistance during the course of a card-check effort. And a third has been to use the law as a way to build public support for union organizing as an essential American right....

Some of the most creative legal work today—and that with the greatest parallels to the UFW in its "law of the jungle" days—is being done by lawyers working on comprehensive campaigns. On the theory that employers who violate labor law are likely to be violating other laws as well, lawyers work with organizers and researchers to identify areas where the corporation in question is breaking consumer, zoning, environmental, wage and hour, OSHA and other laws. The lawyers then bring suit or initiate administrative proceedings, both as a way to gain redress for the workers and as leverage against the business. In the context of comprehensive campaigns, lawsuits and public exposés about wage and hour violations, environmental hazards, and dangerous working conditions generate negative publicity that becomes an embarrassment to a company and serves as a goad to sign a recognition agreement. In addition to the role wage suits play in comprehensive campaigns, a few unions . . . have dedicated substantial amounts of legal resources to litigation about wage and hour violations on behalf of non-union workers, with the goal of raising the wage floor in an industry and thus decreasing the disadvantage that unionized contractors face when they face non-union competitors. Such lawsuits also serve as a way for the union to demonstrate to workers its commitment to their well-being and its capacity to deliver concrete benefits. . . .

Comprehensive campaign strategies take unions and their lawyers further out on a limb than many have become used to going. The negative publicity that a union generates against a corporation in the course of such a campaign may become the basis for a defamation lawsuit or a tortious interference with business claim. The threat to move union pension funds out of an investment in a particular corporation might run afoul of ERISA on the grounds that it demonstrates a failure of the duty to maximize shareholder profits. RICO has increasingly been used against unions carrying out comprehensive campaigns on the accusation that labor's alliances with consumers and shareholders constitute blackmail and should subject the union to criminal prosecution. Although these risks are high, unions are nonetheless willing to take them because they are desperate to escape from the NLRA's straightjacket.

A final strategy to which labor lawyers in this group contribute is public education in order to bring the lack of a real right to organize alive for politicians, religious, community leaders, and the public. Formally, labor lawyers have worked with organizers to construct parallel institutions that simultaneously publicize workers' grievances against their employers and unions' grievances against the NLRB. . . .

In a similar vein, labor lawyers have also done extensive work with the media, authored academic reports, and played key roles in efforts to place violations of workers rights to organize within an international human rights framework. . . .

. . . [W]hat lessons are to be learned from it? First, seeking the aid of the state is always a double-edged sword, not only dangerous or only helpful but both simultaneously. The passage of a new law creates new obstacles and new opportunities for players already engaged in an ongoing game. . . .

A union that does not rely on the state-run framework as a substitute for power, but instead uses it to bolster its organizing even as it maintains its capacity to bring pressure to bear outside the framework—much as the UFW did in the first years after the passage of the ALRA—is at least in the short term in a stronger position with the law than without it. And in the face of the temptation to return to the so-called law of the jungle, we would also do well to keep in mind that the absence of a governing law does not guarantee a fertile field for union organizing. Far from it. It just creates a different sort of battlefield on which the same forces war.

Second, we may need to re-configure our understanding of "successful" legislation in relationship to organizing. The world—and particularly the world of work—is a fast-changing place, even as employers' desire to get more from their workers and to pay less remains a constant. Rather than looking for a law that will offer a permanent fix to the problems that unions face, an idea for which there is no better refutation than the ossified NLRA, perhaps it makes more sense to approach law-making as an act of creating "windows of opportunity," as the UFW lawyers put it, windows that will shut (as windows do) but that can be used as periods in which to consolidate power and build a strong base for the next onslaught. Effective legislation and state intervention shift power but they do not eliminate it from the equation. A union that sees a law as more than just a leg up, a modicum of help, will be blindsided by the recurring need to address employers' power head-on....

Third, there is a broad and changing range of possibilities for what lawyers can offer union organizing. Both the UFW story and that of the labor movement more broadly illustrate that if there is only one way to describe what good "lawyers for organizing" do—put law in the service of building the movement's power—there are many, many ways that such a goal can be realized....

The story of the UFW reminds us that law and creative legal strategies can make extremely helpful contributions to building a movement, but that there is no such thing as a static relationship between the two. Organizing to win new laws is followed by organizing to make their promises real. Even where such a cycle is ongoing, passing a new law is no guarantee of a move forward in some inexorable march toward a better world. A law that makes sense in one moment of a movement's history may become an impediment to social change at a later stage. Or the movement may change in a way that renders it unable to take advantage of the law and vulnerable to attack through the very rules and structures it once championed.

Understood in this way, though, the tools that good labor legislation and good labor lawyers offer unions can be powerful indeed. These tools are less like a jack-hammer, more like a pick, moving the process of change-making incrementally along much as the ice-climber stakes out a hold to pull herself up to the next ledge. Falls are inevitable. It is not always clear which way is up. Lawyers and unions need to remain constantly alert to the balance between technical lawyering within the governing framework and opportunities to bring pressure to bear by using other sorts of laws or legal tactics. There is no one point at which victory is declared and the climb is over. As the Talmud [book of Jewish law] says, "Look ahead: You are not expected to complete the task, but neither are you permitted to set it down."

Like the letters and the Zuni Cruz excerpt above, Gordon effectively recaps many takeaways introduced in Part I and addressed throughout this book. Law and organizing must be orchestrated to be mutually reinforcing, and specifically in this context to "put the achievement of organizing goals above the achievement of legal victories" while also looking for opportunities to encode victories into mandatory obligations that bind elites moving forward. This systemic approach to advocacy depends on daily maneuvering in multiple legal forums, both adjudicative and policymaking, to achieve direct and indirect union goals. At times, the union organized to win-by-losing, as "when a legal defeat such as a judge's refusal to mandate release of information about pesticides became a platform for the union to 'raise an issue' and tell its story to the public."

The union's lawyers worked in "cross-disciplinary" teams with organizers, researchers, elected union leaders, and grassroots activists. Their in-house legal roles developed through a mix of intentional planning, ad hoc innovation, and ongoing adjustment; recall Grinthal's outline in Part V of different lawyer roles across varied sites of practice. Legal clinician Brian Glick further explains how advocacy roles help shape the nature and depth of collaboration:

> This [in-house] approach makes lawyers structurally accountable to a collective process and integrates them in a way that enables the lawyers to make a deep contribution to the group's decision-making and activity. It can provide rewarding opportunities for personal and political growth. But it requires an activist organization that has both the financial resources to hire full-time lawyers, and a strong, experienced non-lawyer leadership that cannot be dominated or intimidated by the lawyers.[2]

As Gordon's analysis of the UFW advocacy and organizing program illustrates, and Glick's note reinforces, many settings require activists and advocates to work collaboratively with client-groups, which are complex and diverse. Typically, multiple collaborations provide the only, if not the

---

[2] Brian Glick, Two, Three, Many Rosas! Rebellious Lawyers and Progressive Activist Organizations, 23 Clinical L. Rev. 611, 617 (2017).

surest, way to overcome failure by design. In this multifaceted daily work, collaborative professionals craft long-term pathways toward effective advocacy in support of organized bottom groups, while understanding that, along the way, circumstances will change—and so, therefore, the work must promptly adapt. Can you appreciate how advocates and groups running this critical marathon must keep their focus on "the prize" while adapting and innovating constantly to defend and advance past gains? Keep these closing thoughts and examples with you, to help you carry on through the fluxes of circumstance during the course of an action or career, regardless of context.

NOTES AND QUESTIONS

1. *Structures of Advocacy.* Compare the models of lawyering by the NAACP Legal Defense and Educational Fund that you saw in the Part I *Brown* case study and now the California Rural Legal Assistance organization, on the one hand, and the in-house lawyers of the United Farm Workers (UFW) on the other. In the corporate setting, in-house corporate counsel is a now dominant mode of delivering legal services to business entities. In part, this trend is meant to better control the costs of legal services, but also to inculcate the lawyer within the business culture of the client so that the lawyer better serves its goals. Do you see a similar dynamic present in the UFW lawyering model? Corporate goals (whether short- or long-term) are, with few exceptions, oriented solely toward maximizing profit for the business owners. In contrast, what were the UFW goals, and how did they change?

Louise Trubek, a legal clinician, writes about how models of corporate and community lawyering might and should differ:

> The community lawyering model is sometimes described as doing for poor people and communities what corporate transactional lawyers provide for their business clients. [But a well-founded] critique is that change cannot occur merely by doing for poor communities what corporate lawyers do for the wealthy. To invoke social change, there must be both empowerment and a challenge to the status quo....
>
> ... [A] combination of non-traditional organizational structures, expanded lawyering skills, and intensive collaboration creates practices that encourage client empowerment and promote social transformation.[3]

What should systemic advocacy borrow from traditional corporate lawyering, corporate roles and structures, and more generally the tactics and strategies of elites? In your view, what, in addition to what Trubek suggests, should be different (if anything)?

2. *The Long Arc of Social Justice.* Gordon's account of farm labor organizing efforts is centered in the 1960s–1970s. Arguably, U.S. farm workers caught in

---

[3] Louise G. Trubek, On Long Haul Lawyering, 25 Fordham Urb. L.J. 801, 809–10 (1998).

an increasingly mechanized and globalized economy are worse off today than they were then. Recall the descriptions of agricultural workers' conditions and organizing initiatives presented by Ehrenreich and Lyon in Part II and Kohl-Arenas in Part V. Together with Gordon's account, what do these materials suggest might be new tactics or strategies that farmworkers should use today? What critical knowledges, values, skills, and values thereby become most salient? Why?

16.3 DEEP CRITIQUE AND SYSTEMIC ADVOCACY FOR THE LONG HAUL

The various letters presented above provide good examples of critical and self-critical reflections on the relationship among legal ethics, advocacy strategies, and professional choices. They provide guidelines designed to help keep advocates principled, accountable, and effective for the long haul. None is directly antithetical to traditional codes of conduct, notions of professional identity and responsibility, or conceptions of legal roles and sites of practice. Nevertheless, they depict an approach to advocacy that transcends the confines and priorities of top-down law.

Legal clinician Sameer Ashar provides a final mapping of the legal industry's failure to take into account the missing elements—identities, groups, interests, and power. He shows how "the consistent sidelining of justice within law schools and the lack of underlying theories of lawyering" contributed to "a longstanding existential crisis" in the legal profession. This ongoing crisis is precisely the profession's failure to confront the Critical Challenge of using law to advance equal justice in systemic terms. As a result, law as an industry and lawyers as professionals lack both the ability to offer "deep critique, both of formalistic lawyering roles and of entrenched arrangements of power and resources in society." Ashar maps some of the steps necessary to foster justice-friendly change in law and society:

- Focus on persistent social problems in context—"difficult historically and macro-politically entrenched problems;"

- Use critical histories and theory to guide research and analysis and complex actions because "[h]istory and theory give us the tools to engage in campaigns [and projects], alongside community organizations and political activists, to change institutions of law;" and

- Develop collaborations and critical coalitions based in antisubordination values by developing "community and solidarity against the effects of concentrated wealth and subordination along multiple dimensions of identity, status, and power."

Ashar focuses his analysis on legal education, centering clinical legal education as a fulcrum for change within law schools. But he offers a broader call to action—asking all advocates to be activists within the legal industry itself and to "contest the shape of current legal practice." As you read, consider how this call to antisubordination action affects both the next steps you will take in your professional journey, and how you will undertake them to ensure principled, accountable, and effective three-layered advocacy for the long haul.

DEEP CRITIQUE AND DEMOCRATIC LAWYERING IN CLINICAL PRACTICE

Sameer M. Ashar
104 Cal. L. Rev. 201 (2016)

... This Essay draws on clinical practice to make the case for ... reforms that emphasize justice, connection, and the cogeneration by lawyers and communities of approaches to entrenched social problems.

... [A] longstanding existential crisis ...—the consistent sidelining of justice within law schools and the lack of underlying theories of lawyering—is rarely discussed or confronted. ...

... [This crisis calls for us to] articulate a new set of aspirations for legal education: a vision of law schools that defend community and solidarity against the effects of concentrated wealth and subordination along multiple dimensions of identity, status, and power; [and] a vision of law schools that confront the structural changes in the market for legal services and originate new modalities of legal practice. ... When the profession has lost its moorings under an onslaught of economic forces, law schools have the opportunity, if not the responsibility, to make interventions that emphasize non-market, justice values.

... Visionary reform will build on the core public values of the legal profession and recognize that [systemic advocates] need to be flexible and experimentalist problem solvers, working through complex issues in collaboration with clients and communities. Clinical practice that teaches critical systemic thinking and democratic lawyering has the potential to be an engine of renewal and reform.

... [In the 1990s and 2000s,] a small group of organizations and law school clinics, as well as a few reinvigorated legal services offices, advanced the latest iterations of social change lawyering. Private entities are now more prominent adversaries of public interest lawyers, and diminished government agencies undertake limited intervention on behalf of indigent clients in private ordering. Public interest lawyers practice in a broader range of areas, from foreclosure to education, to workers' rights, to environmental advocacy. The practice is more global as lawyers face multinational employers and financial institutions, represent individuals and organizations with cross-border ties, and use human rights law and forums to fight poverty and marginalization within the United States. Public interest law finds itself in a very different environment, with new adversaries across a range of subject areas. The open question is whether path-dependent legal education, including law school clinics, has kept up with changes in the field. . . .

When law school clinics have attempted to move away from providing individual legal services or describing a more expansive social mission for themselves, commentators within the field have been critical on pedagogical grounds or have expressed discomfort with the possible incongruity with students' political commitments. In addition to the self-generated compunctions regarding the "imposition" of faculty political commitments on students, there are the more obvious external pressures that governments place on clinics to prevent challenges to powerful corporate interests with which they are allied. . . .

Neoliberal assumptions and constructs operate on the broader field of legal education reform as well. "Neoliberalism" is a contested term [with] strong explanatory power[:]

> Neoliberalism . . . [is an economic theory and ideology] in which market-modeled concepts of efficiency and autonomy shape policy, doctrine, and other discourses of legitimacy outside of traditionally "economic" areas. . . . *Neoliberalism, then, takes its meaning from this contest between market imperatives and democratic demands*; it names a suite of arguments, dispositions, presuppositions, ways of framing questions, and even visions of social order that get called on to press against democratic claims in the service of market imperatives.

. . . The economic crisis in U.S. legal education has skewed the reform discourse toward market-based solutions, with little to no attention paid to the profession's justice imperative. . . . Th[e] social power [of lawyers] relies, at least in part, on the idea that lawyers are part of a justice-seeking profession with some commitment to the greater good. The neoliberal reforms further marginalize the public-oriented, justice-seeking elements of legal professional identity and undermine the profession as a whole.

Rather than design backwards from the perspective of economic actors in a portion of the shifting market for legal services, law schools must put large, complex social problems at the center of their curricula. This preserves essential aspects of the legal profession's commitment to seek justice, and teaches transferable approaches to lawyering in a time of foundational change. . . .

. . . To fight to change the systems through which our clients are subordinated is an aspiration that runs across generations. . . . [Critical analysis has shown for some time that] "[s]tructuralist theories may not capture all that exists, but ignoring structure risks missing nearly everything." . . .

This is the field in which we operate, which requires us to develop in ourselves and in our students the capacity of deep critique, of thinking beneath and beyond liberal legalist approaches to social problems. We can develop this capacity only through collaborative work with people, communities, and thinkers at the margins of our social structure. . . . [Through community-based clinical education, our] students gather "local knowledge," . . . about the home communities from which our clients come, as well as how legal regimes bear down on them, even confining them in prisons or prison-like workplaces. We discover that power has reconfigured the land, so that people are dispossessed by law and made vulnerable to fractured systems of neoliberal production. . . . [We] question the efficacy of quasi-adversarial systems in which power is decidedly tilted toward the state or powerful private interests.

However, the clinical standpoint is necessary but not sufficient. History and critical theory denaturalize the worlds our students confront through the practice of poverty law. History and theory give us the tools to engage in campaigns, alongside community organizations and political activists, to change institutions of law. It is immensely difficult to maintain critical consciousness in the trenches of daily warfare with hostile or indifferent interests and with isolated clients. Organizers and other community actors bring consciousness almost necessarily lacking in the circumscribed relationship between lawyers and clients. . . . While critical and interdisciplinary perspectives can be explored in law school classes and seminars, they cannot replicate the experience of an immersive confrontation with an intractable social problem and close work with clients and organizers on that problem.

. . . Democratic lawyering [occurs] when we "regularly work with people and groups involved in struggles for dignity, survival, self-determination, and other basic human needs" and "seek to foster and join collective efforts of low-income and working-class people and people of color to reshape their own lives and communities," "in short, to form and support active *publics*—groups that come together to understand, confront, and attempt to gain some control over the forces and actors shaping their lives."[4] . . .

. . . Collaborators ask [advocates] to employ a range of legal and political advocacy tactics with a range of social justice ends defined in conjunction with them. . . . Practitioners aspire to co-construct legal projects and social justice goals with activated groups of clients[:] "Democratic lawyers collaborate with and nurture grassroots groups in

---

[4] Ascanio Piomelli, The Challenge of Democratic Lawyering, 77 Fordham L. Rev. 1383, 1394 (2009).

which everyday people participate in multiple realms of self-rule or self-government, including tactical and strategic deliberation, public and behind-the-scenes leadership, joint public action, and joint assessment of that action." . . .

. . . [S]ignificant strategic features of the collaborative relationships between lawyers and community groups require that legal teams assess the efficacy of legal action to accomplish goals set by client groups. The slide into legalism is stayed, as students learn to understand client goals and assess legal action as a means toward those goals, alongside a range of other advocacy methods. . . . The open-ended nature of the search for legal mechanisms by which to repair harms identified by communities speaks to the larger pedagogical goal of preparing students to engage . . . difficult historically and macro-politically entrenched problems. The tension between social justice goals and legal means is not inherent. It is a product of the path development of legal practice in which every dispute is characterized and defined as one between individuals or between individuals and the state. The law and organizing and cause lawyering [approaches to social change] contest the shape of current legal practice [as a system]. . . .

In addition to the ability to assess the need for legal action, democratic lawyers learn to collaborate with and nurture partners from the community, mediate complex decision making within organizations and communities, frame social problems, and think carefully about power—how it is created, distributed, used, and lost. . . . Appreciating the plasticity of legal roles preserves motivation and works against individualistic and formalistic assumptions in mainstream professional socialization. Democratic lawyering deepens critique, both of formalistic lawyering roles and of entrenched arrangements of power and resources in society. . . .

. . . "Critique [on its own] does not tell people who they really are and what they ought to do. Instead, . . . critique challenges their understanding of who they are, and it leads them to resist their attachment to their social identities and ideals." . . . Institutionally, law schools have the potential to flourish by resisting extractive, neoliberal approaches and centering social problems as the core content of learning agendas and active publics as collaborative partners. Through this cogenerative work with those at the margins, we can gain the capacity to envision new forms of legal practice, grounded in the profession's justice-seeking, public-good-advancing norms and values.

Ashar calls on advocates and activists to directly confront the Critical Challenge of using law for justice. He illustrates how critical insights and methods help advocates center social problems to construct systemic projects. Like the authors of the letters above, Ashar implicates legal education, ethics, professional identity, financing, roles and collaborations, and sites of practice—the legal industry as a whole—in preserving the status quo of identity-based castes with their concomitant systemic violence. He notes that law and legal action are essential tools of justice-seeking work but insufficient on their own to advance Critical Justice.

Ashar—like the earlier authors—challenges advocates to support organized client-groups through collaborations in advocacy projects and critical coalitions. Work that is "truly collaborative" and rooted in antisubordination solidarity will involve conflicts. But advocates consciously aim to use tensions and conflicts productively. Advocates and activists "engage on issues and argue them out," as legal scholar Eduardo Capulong notes:

> To foster client activism, [advocates] must read prevailing social conditions and strategize with their clients about the political next step, often with an eye toward a long-term goal. But I don't think we necessarily engage in these analyses as consciously, or with as full a picture of the history and dynamics involved or options available, as we could. Often this is because there simply isn't time to engage these questions. Or perhaps not wanting to dominate our clients, we squelch our own political analysis and agenda to allow for organic, indigenous leadership from below. But if we are truly collaborative—and when we feel strongly enough about certain political issues—we engage on issues and argue them out. . . .
>
> . . . Without concrete and comprehensive diagnoses of ultimate political goals, social and economic contexts, and organizing priorities, progressive legal practice will fail to live up to its potential.[5]

Every advocate ultimately must craft their own road and journey toward achieving equal justice for all, engaging in deep critique and addressing conflicts that arise within collaborations honestly and directly. Time and change force everyone to make daily choices. Along the way, we aim to stay purposeful and nimble because systemic injustice remains always in flux, yet also entrenched. The Critical Challenge calls on all advocates to constantly cultivate a dual consciousness about law as justice, to unlearn and relearn systems using knowledge from the bottom, and to remain principled and accountable regardless of the setting or situation of our work.

Having seen and understood how advocates must adapt nimbly and innovatively, we leave you with a brief reminder that takes us back to beginnings: whatever the context or action, start with what the people know, then build on what the people have. As Bill Ong Hing detailed in

---

[5] Eduardo R.C. Capulong, Client Activism in Progressive Lawyering Theory, 16 Clinical L. Rev. 109, 193–94 (2009).

Part II, Yen's simple formula succinctly distills the critical knowledges, values, skills, and attitudes for bottom-up advocacy. If you stay mindful of Yen's irreducible wisdom, it will anchor and carry you through the days and decades of "wins" and "losses" ahead of you. As both Yen and Gordon show by example, cutting-edge advocacy flips the inevitable need to adapt into an opportunity to advance. In this spirit, and borrowing from Bill Quigley's reflection above, we wish you "joy, inspiration and love in abundant measure" in your lifelong journey and work toward Critical Justice.

NOTES AND QUESTIONS

1. *Tying It All Together for Yourself.* Recall your thoughts and perceptions about law and justice before we began these studies. How have they changed, if at all? What is the single most important lesson you learned from this book? What part of the skill set needed for systemic advocacy do you think will need the most work to develop, in your case? Where do you think your own road to systemic advocacy will take you next? Has that road or pathway changed since you began this course?

CHAPTER RECAP

This chapter concluded our study of systemic injustice and systemic advocacy on a forward-looking note, emphasizing key themes introduced earlier. In addition, this chapter presented critical reflections from diversely situated advocates to help *you* make personal and professional decisions grounded in antisubordination values. In making their own "roads" or pathways into systemic advocacy, these advocates show how ever-changing circumstances require advocates to adapt promptly and proactively as well as to stay constant—innovating continually for the long haul in effective, principled, and accountable terms. Over time and using time, advocates preserve and advance prior gains toward transformative, three-layered justice—Critical Justice.

Editors' Closing Reflections

■ ■ ■

We began this study of systemic injustice and advocacy with the Critical Challenge of using law for justice, identifying some key bottom-up tools or sources developed over the generations for this purpose. We repeatedly have seen how actionable knowledge drawn from the critical Schools and advocacy Approaches roots and guides systemic advocacy and its three-layered conceptions of progress. We surveyed how advocates apply anti-essentialist analyses that deconstruct intersectional identities with a dual consciousness of law and society to pursue transformation, incrementally, through amelioration. Sometimes all that's required are small adjustments in thoughts or actions; other times, fundamental reconceptions are necessary. But critical choices are always based on knowledge, and knowledge is based on endless cycles of experience, action, and reflection. Unlearning and relearning are never-ending antisubordination endeavors for this reason, beginning perhaps with identities, groups, interests, and power.

We then paid a fair amount of attention to the top-down playbook developed by settler elites and their successors in interest: using identities as ideologies of superiority and inferiority, collectivizing their own power while "taking out" their adversaries, taking control of foundational concepts and ground rules to skew outcomes, planning ahead and for the very long haul to spin imperialism out of colonialism and globalization out of imperialism. For just about a half millennium, systemic predecessors to today's local-global rulers, as well as today's networks of now-ensconced elites, have used preservation through transformation to coopt, capture, or tokenize social change. All this time, the consolidation of legal injustice as social hegemony has hung in the balance, as it still does now.

Only the persistent, courageous, incredible micro-macro resistance of groups, advocates, organizers, and activists has prevented congealment of systemic injustice and social inequity, both materially and symbolically, within and beyond the United States. Organized, sustained, complex actions have developed as our strongest bottom-up tools to advance and defend justice gains, producing an expanded toolkit of critical knowledges, values, skills, and attitudes that supplements traditional legal problem solving, and which advocates continually refine through research, experience, and self-critical reflection. Working in teams to support groups and promote critical coalitions is the daily bread of systemic advocacy. Working collaboratively in defensive and offensive projects, systemic advocacy connects critical history with contemporary conditions to diagnose problems accurately and to strategize pressure with persuasion maximally. Done self-critically, all of this work fosters democratic structures, respect for difference, and relations of mutual trust. Rather than the Darwinian world of neoliberal education, law, and policy, bottom-up alternatives invite cultures of rigor, cooperation, and affinity.

Earth and humanity are entering a new age together: the Anthropocene, characterized mainly by humanity's exceeding the planet's biophysical limits. This dawning age already is morphing systemic failures into new forms of old problems: widespread, long-lasting droughts, wildfires, extreme weather events, rank and violent bigotry, sinful income inequality, COVID-19 identity skews, more predicted pandemics, entrenched educational inequality, economic sinkholes everywhere, rising abuse of opioids and other pharmaceuticals from coast to coast, trillions annually in increased national debt—and especially military contracts, corporate bailouts, and top-end tax cuts—with the simultaneous impoverishment of the former middle class. Necessarily, the persistent legacies and landscapes of colonialism, imperialism, and globalization are the starting points for a better future, both imagined and actual. Yet, without justice for all, systems cannot guarantee peace and prosperity for any.

It's true: none of us can do everything. Yet most of us can do something. Are you ready? Welcome to our ranks.

INDEX

References are to Pages

ABORTION, 302–313

ACCESS TO JUSTICE, 646–659

ADOPTION, 335–336

ADVOCACY APPROACHES
See Approaches

ADVOCACY PROJECTS, 584–595
    See also Clinics, Worker Cooperatives
Crafting analytical narratives, 543–554
Funding, 620–634
Three-layered goals and, 612–620

AFFIRMATIVE ACTION, 452–453, 641, 933

AFFORDABLE CARE ACT, 205, 310–311

AGRICULTURE, 479–487
Organizing farm workers, 1248–1266

AMELIORATION
Introduced, 159–163

ANALYTICAL NARRATIVES, 364–365, 535, 543–554, 918–929

ANCESTRY
Whether proxy for race, 750–754

ANTHROPOCENE
See Climate Change

ANTIDISCRIMINATION LAW, 108–111, 397–401
See also Antisubordination

ANTIESSENTIALISM, 388–395

ANTISUBORDINATION, 397–401
In criminal defense, 868–871

APPALACHIA, 886–893

APPROACHES
Cause lawyering, 794–801
Chart, 54–55
Rights-based lawyering, 597–604
To advocacy, 54–65, 412–430

ARAB SPRING, 939–940

ARTIFICIAL INTELLIGENCE, 362–363

ASK THE OTHER QUESTION, 371–375, 868, 1198–1199

ASSET MAPPING, 946–947

AUSTRALIA, 8

BIG DATA
See Social Analytics

BIG LIE, 46–47, 1086

BILINGUAL EDUCATION, 116

BLACK LIVES MATTER, 304–305, 377, 475, 774, 779–780

BLACKNESS, 37–40

BLACK POWER, 276

BLAME FRAMES, 841–844, 848–849

BLINDFOLDS AND HANDCUFFS IN LEGAL INDUSTRY
See Legal Industry

BOLIVIA, 669, 671–672

BOTTOM GROUPS
Shifting, 35–42

BOTTOM-UP
See Knowledge from the Bottom

***BROWN V. BOARD* CASE STUDY,** 87–107, 119–120, 1172–1190

CAMDEN, NEW JERSEY
Environmental racism, 536–539

CAMPAIGN
See Issue Campaign

CANADA, 7–8

CAPITALISM
See Neoliberalism

CARCERAL STATE
See Mass Incarceration

CASTE
Defined, 84–85

CHILDREN
Dominant narrative, 846–847
"Illegitimate," 216–220

CHINA, 414–416

CHINESE EXCLUSION LAWS, 209–215, 1069–1070

CITIZENSHIP, 67–76

CIVIL RIGHTS MOVEMENT, 40, 507

CLASS, 405–411
In law firms, 729–730

CLASS ACTIONS, 463–465

CLASSCRIT, 50

CLIENTS
Antisubordination commitment, 868–871
In complex actions, 985–986
In school desegregation litigation, 99–106
In transnational human rights lawyering, 565–574

CLIMATE CHANGE, 659–670

CLINICS
Backlash, 715–717
Clinical legal scholarship, 50
Clinical reform, 1269–1273
Community and economic development clinic, 995–997
Immigrant workers center, 998–1017
South Africa, 814–815
Tribal law clinic, 551–554, 1221–1228

COALITION, 372–374, 383–384, 402–411, 505–526, 533, 574–580, 872–873
Tennessee case study, 505–526

COINTELPRO, 873–874

COLLABORATION
See Collaborative Professionalism

COLLABORATIVE PROFESSIONALISM, 418–420, 533–534, 565–574, 578–579, 635, 1238–1240, 1273
See also Coalition; Teams/Teamwork
In complex actions, 1021–1023

COLLECTIVE ACTION
See Collaborative Professionalism

COLONIALISM
See Settler Colonialism

COLONIAS, 164

COLORBLINDNESS, 352–353, 353–363

COMMERCE, 196–199, 239–240, 480–487
See also Globalization

COMMUNITY DEVELOPMENT PROJECTS, 958–960, 961–962, 963–965
Immigrant workers center, 998–1017

Workers cooperative, 986–998, 1019–1020, 1035–1046

COMPLEX ACTIONS, 958–1052
See also Community Development Projects; Issue Campaigns
Action checklist, 965–967

CONCEPT/PROBLEM MAPPING, 944–946

CONFLICT RESOLUTION, 555–557, 1032–1035, 1048–1050

CONSCIOUSNESS
See Dual Consciousness; Three Layered Goals

CONSTITUTION
Bicentennial, 11–14
Constitutional lies, 430–434
Equality jurisprudence, 1135–1142
First amendment, 1142–1147
"We the People," 11–13, 24, 233–237, 430–434

CONTEXT, 35, 788, 830
In systemic advocacy, 791–802

CONTRACTS
Protection by law, 438, 439–443, 454–455, 774

COOPERATIVES
See Worker Cooperatives

COOPTATION, 635–646

COUNTERDISCIPLINARY, 935

COURTWATCHING
As collective action, 525–526

COVID-19, 202–206, 377, 475, 1084

CRIMINAL JUSTICE
See Mass Incarceration

CRIMMIGRATION
See Immigration

CRITICAL CHALLENGE
Defined, 6

CRITICAL COALITION
See Coalition

CRITICAL COMPARATIVISM, 935–937, 1212–1217

CRITICAL EMPIRICISM
See Empiricism

CRITICAL HISTORY, 206–229, 455–456, 932–933

CRITICAL JUSTICE
Defined, 86, 111

CRITICAL KNOWLEDGES, VALUES, SKILLS, AND ATTITUDES (CKVSAs), 851–853

CRITICAL LEGAL RESEARCH AND WRITING
See Legal Research and Writing; Stage 2 Systemic Advocacy

CRITICAL LEGAL STUDIES, 15–16, 44, 346–347, 881–882

CRITICAL MARATHON, 1219–1220
See also Long Haul Lawyering

CRITICAL RACE THEORY, 45, 46, 65–66, 72, 863

CRITICAL SELF-REFLECTION
See Self-Reflection

CULTURE
See Three Layered Goals

CULTURE WARS, 1113

DECOLONIZATION, 1076–1077, 1086
Of rhetoric, 760–762

DEHUMANIZATION, 596–604

DEMOCRACY/DEMOSPRUDENCE, 22–34, 130–141, 458–463, 489–495, 1184
See also Voting
Flint, Michigan water crisis, 174

DIAGNOSIS AND STRATEGY
See Stage 1 Systemic Advocacy

DISABILITY RIGHTS, 337–339, 363, 375–377, 580, 653–656
Pregnancy discrimination, 742–747

DISCOVERY DOCTRINE, 77–78, 230–233, 547–548

DUAL CONSCIOUSNESS, 71–73, 1047, 1232

EDUCATION
See also Legal Education
Brown v. Board case study, 87–107, 119–120, 1172–1190
Mapping higher education financialization, 953–954
Roma children, 1213–1218
School funding, 96–97, 1184–1190
School reform, 643–644
School to prison pipeline, 1200–1210
Segregation of Chinese, 1179–1180
Segregation of Mexican Americans, 114–117
Student debt, 1191–1199, 1243

ELDER RIGHTS, 524–525

ELECTIONS
See Democracy/Demosprudence; Voting

ELITES, 10, 14, 131–132, 133, 199
Elite toolkit, 426–495
Origins, 427–429
Wealth exceptionalism, 703–711

EMPIRICISM, 908–918

ENGLISH ONLY MOVEMENT, 40–41

ENVIRONMENTAL RIGHTS/JUSTICE, 535–543, 659–672, 889–893

EPISTEMIC INJUSTICE, 76–80

EQUAL JUSTICE
"Under Law," 82

EUROHETEROPATRIARCHY
As ideology, 1159

EUROPE
See also Settler Colonialism
Basis of international law, 47–49, 196–198
Roma children, 1213–1218

FAILURE BY DESIGN, 535–543

FELLOWSHIPS, 584–595, 614–619

FEMINIST LEGAL THEORY, 44
Critical Race Feminist bioethics, 922–928
Feminist Method, 370

FLINT, MICHIGAN, 159–163, 605
As connected to Brown, 173–174

FOOD
See Agriculture

FORMAL LEGAL EQUALITY, 107–113

GARMENT INDUSTRY, 574–577, 802–804, 1052, 1231–1232

GENDER
Disproportionate debt, 1198–1199
Gendered jurisprudence, 1114–1116
In law school, 738–739
Privilege and subordination, 255–264
Violence, 1159–1165

GERMANY, NAZI, 1086–1088

GLOBALIZATION, 1088–1089, 1095–1109

GROUND RULES, 424, 439, 456, 490, 504, 523, 789

GROUPS
See also Organizing
Defined, 83
Shifting bottom groups, 35–42
Working with as lawyer, 825–828, 1021–1032

GUANTÁNAMO BAY, 596–604

GUATEMALA, 165–173, 1109–1111

HATE SPEECH, 1144, 1148

HAWAI'I
Native Hawaiians, 16–18, 19–20, 849–851
Puerto Ricans in, 67–76
Voting for land trustees, 749–754, 757–760

HEALTH, 201–206, 473–474
See also COVID-19
Food and, 485–486
HIV/AIDS, 831–832, 942

HEGEMONY, 1133, 1149–1158

HERMENEUTICAL INJUSTICE, 79–80

HETEROPATRIARCHY, 1159–1165

HISPANISMO
As ideology, 1153–1158

HISTORY
See Critical History

HOUSING, 269–274, 1176–1177
Colonias, 164

HUMAN RIGHTS, 191–195
Concept mapping of, 945
Human rights organizations, 470–471
In advocacy, 565–574, 605–612
Terrorism and, 1121–1128
Women's rights, 1212–1213

IDENTITY
Antiessentialism, 388–395
As assets for organizing, 377–397
As socially constructed, 385–386
Defined, 83
Identity politics, 354
Intersectionality, 388–395
Still matters in law, 229–254

IDEOLOGY
See also Heteropatriarchy
Individualism, 766–767
In legal education, 731–736
Racism and ideology, 1135–1142
Shaping of consciousness, 1149–1150
Vehicles of, 1148

IGIP
Defined, 83–84

IMMIGRATION, 670–671, 845–846, 1085
Chinese exclusion laws, 209–215, 1069–1070
Climate change migration, 662
Constraints on human rights, 611–612
Crimmigration, 149, 152–154
Immigrant workers center, 998–1017
Muslim ban, 249–253
Myth of nation of immigrants, 1056–1057
Solidarity, 401–402
Tennessee case study, 505–526
Tracking migrant labor violations, 941

IMPERIALISM, 1088–1095
See also Hawai'i; Puerto Rico

IMPLICIT BIAS, 275–276

INCOME INEQUALITY, 157, 203, 478–479, 987–997, 1018, 1037–1038

INDETERMINACY, 113–117, 185

INDIA, 1080–1083

INDIGENOUS PEOPLES, 77–80, 230–233, 545–554
See also Hawai'i
Clinics, 551–554, 1221–1228
Concept mapping, 945–946
Settler colonialism and, 1066–1068, 1070–1071

INGLEWOOD, CALIFORNIA
Walmart site fight, 968–986

INHERITANCE
See Trusts and Estates

INSULAR CASES, 69–70, 239–240, 1074, 1092

INTERESTS
Defined, 83
Interest convergence, 118–120, 130, 325

INTERGROUP HEALING
Elements of, 1033

INTERNATIONAL LAW, 47–49, 196–198, 1075–1077
Eurocentrism and, 1123–1125

INTERNMENT, 121–129, 242–243

INTERRACIAL JUSTICE, 849–851

INTERSECTIONALITY, 388–395

IOLTA, 625–628, 712

ISSUE CAMPAIGNS, 958–960, 961–963
Walmart site fight, 968–986, 1048–1050, 1051

JONES ACT, 67

JUDICIARY, 247–248

JURISPRUDENCE, 22, 24
See also Legal Formalism
Equality jurisprudence, 1135–1142

JURORS, 747–749, 754–757

KNOWLEDGE
See also Knowledge from the Bottom
Politics of knowledge, 860–874
Suppression, 860–862

KNOWLEDGE FROM THE BOTTOM, 14–22
Methods to obtain, 894–934

LABOR UNIONS, 504, 508–513, 989, 1018–1019
Farm worker union organizing, 1248–1266
Immigrant workers center, 1004–1005
Power building, 836–838
Shifting culture, 838–839
Union cooperatives, 991–995
Unionizing lawyers, 685–694

LANGUAGE, 40–41
Bilingual education, 116
Jurors, 747–749, 754–757

LATCRIT, 917–918, 1153–1158

LAW
    See also Legal Industry; Rule of Law
As a system, 502–503, 676
Failure by design, 535–543

LEGAL EDUCATION, 58–60, 366–369, 695–700, 721–728, 730–740, 760–762, 780, 1244, 1230–1231
    See also Clinics; Legal Research and Writing
Case study method, 740–741
Critical classroom, 762–764
Women's experience in, 738–739

LEGAL ETHICS, 495–496, 571–572, 737, 775–785, 865–871
Ethics of research, 930–932

LEGAL FORMALISM, 740–764, 765–768

LEGAL INDIVIDUALISM
As formalism, 765–768

LEGAL INDUSTRY, 495–498, 501–503, 634, 678–701, 701–721
See also Legal Ethics

LEGAL REALISM, 42–44, 65

LEGAL RELEVANCE, 44, 832

LEGAL RESEARCH AND WRITING, 760–762, 878–894
Bottom-up methods, 894–934
Critical history research, 932–933
Ethics of research, 930–932
Mapping techniques, 943–955
Norms of critical research and analysis, 934–943

LEGAL SERVICES CORPORATION, 625, 691, 712, 714–715, 718–719, 1003–1004

LEVERAGE
See Power

LGBTQ+ JUSTICE, 220–228, 244–245, 313–314, 314–341, 580, 1166
    See also Same Sex Marriage
Heteropatriarchy and violence, 1159–1165
Homophobia, 373–374

In education, 1218
Privilege and subordination, 262–263
Stakeholder mapping, 949

LONG HAUL LAWYERING, 280–281, 593–594, 636, 1134, 1220–1221, 1247, 1268–1269

LOOKING TO THE BOTTOM
See Knowledge from the Bottom

MANIFEST DESTINY, 1089–1091

MAPPING TECHNIQUES, 943–955

MARRIAGE, 237–239, 314–341, 1113
    See also Same Sex Marriage
Antimiscegenation, 386–388
Domestic violence, 281–290
Marital supremacy, 216–220

MASS INCARCERATION, 143–159

MATERIALITY
Defined, 22, 86

MEXICO, 1089–1091
NAFTA, 482–483

MICROAGGRESSIONS, 264–269, 274–275

MICRO-MACRO, 264–275

MIDDLE EASTERN IDENTITY, 1116–1120

MINING, 165–173, 886–888

MISSISSIPPI FREEDOM DEMOCRATIC PARTY, 25–29

MONROE DOCTRINE, 1089, 1091

MONTGOMERY BUS BOYCOTT, 29–31

MUSLIMS, 378–382
Muslim ban, 249–253

NAFTA, 481–483

NAIL/TWAIL, 45, 47–49, 1120

NEOLIBERALISM, 476–489, 663–665, 670, 1270
    See also Globalization
Role of international institutions, 468–472

NEW ORLEANS WORKER CENTER FOR RACIAL JUSTICE, 7, 648–649

NONPROFIT ORGANIZATIONS
Funding of, 621–625
Legal service providers, 625–628
Nonprofit industrial complex, 628–629
Politics of funding, 629–633

ORGANIZING
See also Labor Unions
Defined and introduced, 499–501
Organizing farm workers, 1248–1266
Practice of law and organizing, 1024–1032
South Africa context, 820–821
Working with organizers, 1036–1046

PARTICIPATORY ACTION RESEARCH, 895–908, 933–934

PAX AMERICANA, 1096–1098

PHILANTHROPY, 621–626, 629–634, 670, 706, 709

PLANNED PARENTHOOD, 304

PLEA BARGAIN, 525

POLICE, 471–476
See also Black Lives Matter; Mass Incarceration

POLITICAL ECONOMY, 207–208, 633, 1195

POLITICAL LAWYERING, 341–342
As an approach, 52–54

POOR PEOPLE'S CAMPAIGN, 410–411

POWELL MEMO, 456–463, 465–468

POWER
Building power, 833–840
Defined, 83–84
In internment experience, 121–129
In policymaking, 132–141
Persuasive power, 834, 959, 960
Power mapping, 949–953
Pressure power, 834, 959, 960
Private-public power, 768–775
White Power, 36–41

POWER MAPPING, 949–953
See also Power

PRAXIS, 576–577
Defined, 55

PREGNANCY
Discrimination, 742–747

PRESERVATION THROUGH TRANSFORMATION, 280, 281–302, 1183
Reproductive liberty, 302–314

PRISONS, 146–150

PRIVATE-PUBLIC DISTINCTION, 271–274, 281, 447, 455–456, 477, 768–775, 1094

PRIVILEGE, 255–264
Of lawyers, 341–342, 452–453

PROGRESS
Metrics of, 328

PROGRESSIVE LAWYERING, 343–348

PROPERTY
Legal constructions of by elites, 434–454
Managing colonized land, 757–760
Whiteness as, 447–454

PROSECUTORS, 158–159

PROTEST
Suppression of, 467–468, 474–476

PUBLIC INTEREST LAWYER
Assault on, 712–721

PUERTO RICO, 239–240, 487–489, 848, 1091–1092
Puerto Ricans in Hawai'i, 67–76

QUEER THEORY, 51, 871

RACIAL STATE, 1061–1062, 1086–1088, 1111–1112

RACKETEER INFLUENCED AND CORRUPT ORGANIZATIONS ACT (RICO), 465–468

REBELLIOUS LAWYERING, 55–56, 64

REFORM
Limits of, 349

RELIGION
Affordable Care Act, 310–311
As blameframe, 843
Catholic religion, 253–254
Jewish identity, 396–397
Microaggressions, 265
Muslims, 249–254, 378–382
Religious liberty, 300–301

REPARATIONS
Internment, 129
Native Hawaiians, 16–22, 851

REPRODUCTIVE JUSTICE, 302–314, 791–792
Exploitation, 922–928, 1150–1152

ROMA CHILDREN
Discrimination of, 1213–1218

RULE OF LAW, 182–183, 189–201, 1056

SAME SEX MARRIAGE, 220–228, 291–293

SCHOOLS OF LEGAL THOUGHT, 42–53
Chart, 50–51

SCHOOL TO PRISON PIPELINE, 1200–1210

SEGREGATION BY LAW, 87–91, 114–116

SELF-REFLECTION, 363–371, 1240
As advocacy project starting point, 586–587

SENTENCING GUIDELINES, 154–155

SETTLER COLONIALISM, 1056–1086, 1088

SLAPP SUITS, 523, 713, 717, 719–720

SLAVERY, 11–13, 37–39, 233–237, 440–442, 449–451, 1068–1069, 1071–1072
In garment industry labor, 574–576
In medical research exploitation, 922–928

SOCIAL ANALYTICS AND SOCIAL MEDIA, 937–943

SOCIAL CONSTRUCTION
See Identity

SOCIAL ILLS, 1135–1149
Defined, 1132–1133

SOCIAL MOVEMENTS, 23–34

SOLIDARITY
See Coalition

SOUTH AFRICA, 806–831

SOVEREIGNTY, 47–49, 1078

SPAIN
Hispanismo as ideology, 1153–1158

STAGE 1 SYSTEMIC ADVOCACY
Diagnosis, 858–955

STAGE 2 SYSTEMIC ADVOCACY
Complex Actions, 958–1052

STAKEHOLDER MAPPING, 947–949

STERILIZATION, 240–242, 306–308

STORYTELLING, 349–350, 364–370, 929–930
See also Analytical Narrative
Counterstorytelling, 117, 928
In criminal defense, 866–871

SUBORDINATION
As distinct from privilege, 255–264

SURVEILLANCE, 873–874

SYNECDOCHE, 638, 645

SYSTEMIC ADVOCACY, 6–9, 175, 784–785, 1233–1241
See also Stage 1 Systemic Advocacy; Stage 2 Systemic Advocacy
Changing systems, changing ourselves, 56–65
CKVSAs of, 851–853
Context in, 788, 791–802, 1245–1246

SYSTEMIC INJUSTICE/VIOLENCE, 6, 76–80, 82, 175–177, 1159–1165
Gender-based violence, 802–804
In education, 1200–1210

SYSTEMIC JUSTICE PROJECT, 6–7

SYSTEMS, 183–189
See also Rule of Law
Law as maintaining, 1242–1243

TEACH FOR AMERICA, 117–118

TEAMS/TEAMWORK, 532–535, 554–565, 1266
See also Collaborative Professionalism

TENNESSEE CASE STUDY, 505–526

TESTIMONIAL INJUSTICE, 78–79

THERAPEUTIC JURISPRUDENCE, 784

THREE LAYERED GOALS, 612–620, 804–832
Building power, 833–840
Shifting culture and consciousness, 840–851

TIME, 112–113, 348–349
See also Long Haul Lawyering

TOKENISM, 638–645

TORTURE, 597–604

TRADE
See Commerce

TRANSGENDER JUSTICE, 294–300, 301, 327, 340–341, 629–630
Participatory action research, 933–934

TRUSTS AND ESTATES, 444–447, 701–711

UNIONS
See Labor Unions

UNLEARNING AND RELEARNING, 182, 280, 352

VIOLENCE
See Systemic Injustice/Violence

VOTING, 67–76, 140–141, 489–495, 770–772
Property and the right to vote, 434–437
Redistricting, 406–409
Voting for land trustees, 749–754, 757–760

WAR ON TERROR, 1121–1128

WATER
Flint, Michigan, 159–163
Mining impacts, 171
Water inequalities, 163–165

WHITE COLLAR CRIME, 156–157

WHITE LAWYERING, 357–361

WHITE SUPREMACY, 110, 1129–1130
As domestic terrorism, 199
White Power, 36–41

WINNING-LOSING
Winning through losing, 329–337

WORKER COOPERATIVES, 986–998, 1019–1020, 1035–1046

WORLD JUSTICE PROJECT, 200–201